lonely planet

England

Oliver Berry, Fionn Davenport, Marc Di Duca, Belinda Dixon,
Damian Harper, Catherine Le Nevez, Lorna Parkes, Greg Ward

Contents

LONDON P54

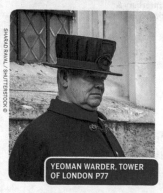

YEOMAN WARDER, TOWER OF LONDON P77

Contents

ON THE ROAD

BAMBURGH CASTLE P623

Contents

SPECIAL FEATURES

Welcome to England

This green and pleasant land, this sceptred isle, this crucible of empire and pioneer of parliamentary democracy: England is eccentric, exhilarating and endlessly intriguing.

Lyrical Landscapes

It might be small, but England packs a lot of scenery into its pint-sized shores: green fields and rumpled hills, chalk cliffs and breezy plains, ancient woods and moody moorland. There are 10 national parks, 34 Areas of Outstanding National Beauty (AONB) and miles of craggy, beach-fringed coastline – 2795 miles, in fact, making England's coast one of Europe's longest, and the only one to have a public coast path the whole way round. Whether you're tramping over the South Downs or wandering above Dover's fabled White Cliffs, England is a never-ending feast for the eyes.

Living History

With a story that stretches back more than 5000 years, England is a place where the past is a constant presence. Ruined castles perch on lonely hilltops. Mysterious menhirs, barrow tombs and stone circles sit in the corner of forgotten fields. Medieval cathedrals, regal palaces and ostentatious stately homes pop up with bewildering regularity. And every English city, town and village has its own tale to tell: a sprawling, historical epic of kings and commoners, industrialists and inventors, dreamers and rebels that's as fascinating as anything Shakespeare, Dickens or JK Rowling could dream up.

Urban Experiences

From York's cobbled streets to Oxford's dreaming spires, from Bristol's Floating Harbour to the Liverpool Docks, England's cities are main attractions. London, of course, is the trump card: a trendsetter, history-maker and game changer for more than a thousand years, encompassing everything from royal residences to world-class museums, landmark theatres and vast urban parks. But there's a varied urban landscape to explore outside London, too: delving into Manchester's pulsing music scene, visiting Newcastle's innovative art galleries, admiring Bath's glittering Georgian architecture or browsing for bargains along Brighton's quirky shopping streets.

Easy Does It

Travel here is a breeze. Granted, it may not be totally effortless, but it's easy compared with many parts of the world. And although the locals may grumble, public transport is very good, and a train ride through the English landscape can be a highlight in itself. But whichever way you get around, in this compact country you're never far from the next town, the next pub, the next restaurant, the next national park or the next impressive castle on your hit list of highlights. The choice is endless.

Why I Love England

By Oliver Berry, Writer

I've travelled all round the world, but England is where I'm from, and I always find myself being drawn back home. I've hiked, biked and road-tripped the nation, from the tip of Cornwall to the coast of Northumberland, and it's the landscapes that make it special: its topography of craggy cliffs, green meadows, rolling hills, rural valleys and wild moors, all stitched together by miles of drystone walls, hedgerows and footpaths. And, wherever you wander, you can always be sure of one thing – a village pub is never too far away. Now that's my kind of country.

For more about our writers, see p704

Above: Clovelly (p312), North Devon

England

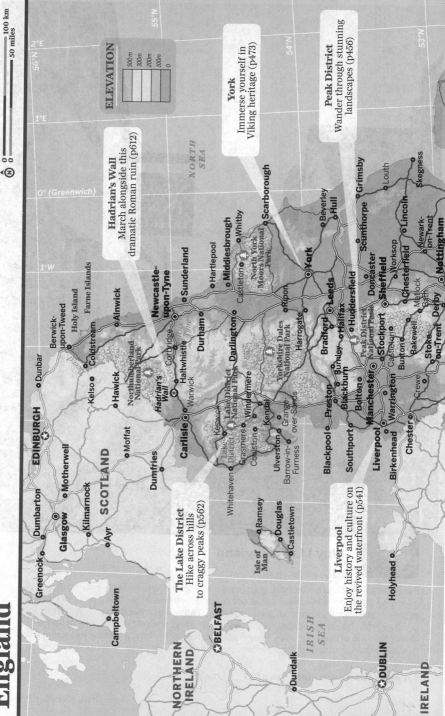

Hadrian's Wall
March alongside this dramatic Roman ruin (p612)

York
Immerse yourself in Viking heritage (p473)

Peak District
Wander through stunning landscapes (p456)

The Lake District
Hike across hills to craggy peaks (p562)

Liverpool
Enjoy history and culture on the revived waterfront (p541)

ELEVATION
500m
300m
200m
100m
0

0   100 km
0   50 miles

NORTH SEA

IRISH SEA

SCOTLAND

NORTHERN IRELAND

IRELAND

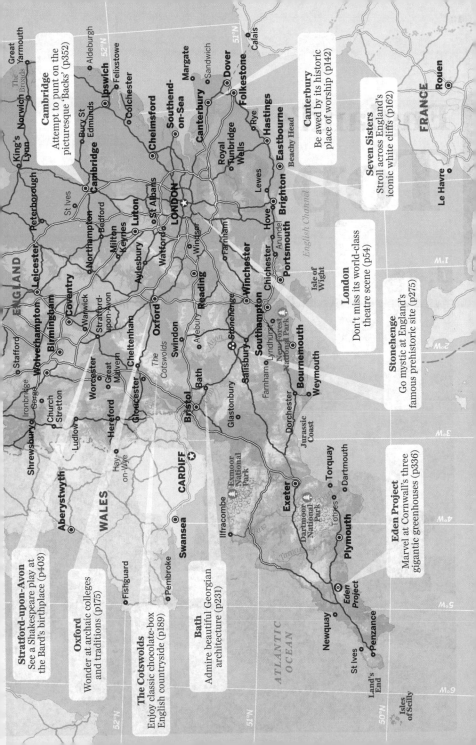

Stratford-upon-Avon
See a Shakespeare play at the Bard's birthplace (p403)

Oxford
Wonder at archaic colleges and traditions (p175)

The Cotswolds
Enjoy classic chocolate-box English countryside (p189)

Bath
Admire beautiful Georgian architecture (p231)

Cambridge
Attempt to punt on the picturesque 'Backs' (p352)

Canterbury
Be awed by its historic place of worship (p142)

Seven Sisters
Stroll across England's iconic white cliffs (p162)

London
Don't miss its world-class theatre scene (p54)

Stonehenge
Go mystic at England's famous prehistoric site (p275)

Eden Project
Marvel at Cornwall's three gigantic greenhouses (p336)

England's
Top 20

1

Stonehenge

1 Mysterious and compelling, Stonehenge (p275) is England's most iconic ancient site. People have been drawn to this myth-laden ring of boulders for more than 5000 years, and we still don't know quite why it was built. Most visitors gaze at the 50-tonne stones from behind the perimeter fence, but with enough planning you can arrange an early-morning or evening tour and gain access to the inner ring itself. In the slanting sunlight, away from the crowds, it's an ethereal place. This is an experience that stays with you.

Oxford

2 A visit to Oxford (p175) is as close as most of us will get to the brilliant minds and august institutions that have made this city famous across the globe. But you'll catch a glimpse of this rarefied world in the cobbled lanes and ancient quads where cycling students and dusty academics roam. The beautiful college buildings, archaic traditions and stunning architecture have changed little over the centuries, coexisting with a lively, modern, working city. Radcliffe Camera (p177)

FUNKYFOOD LONDON - PAUL WILLIAMS / ALAMY STOCK PHOTO ©

CAROL CARPENTER / ALAMY STOCK PHOTO ©

DANIEL_KAY/SHUTTERSTOCK ©

DARREN GROVE/SHUTTERSTOCK ©

The Lake District

3 William Wordsworth and his Romantic friends were the first to champion the charms of the Lake District (p562) and it's not hard to see what stirred them. Already the UK's most popular national park, the Lake District also became a Unesco World Heritage Site in 2017, recognising its long history of hill farming – but for most people it's the chance to hike the hump-backed fells and drink in the gorgeous scenery that keep them returning year after year.

York

4 With its Roman and Viking heritage, ancient city walls and maze of cobbled streets, York (p473) is a living showcase for the highlights of English history. Join one of the city's many walking tours and plunge into the network of snickelways (narrow alleys), each one the focus of a ghost story or historical character. Explore the intricacies of York Minster, the biggest medieval cathedral in all of northern Europe, or admire the exhibits from more recent times at the National Railway Museum, the world's largest collection of historic locomotives. Above right: The Shambles (p477)

Bath

5 In a nation packed with pretty cities, Bath (p231) still stands out as the belle of the ball. Founded by the Romans, who established the spa resort of Aquae Sulis to take advantage of the area's hot springs, Bath hit its stride in the 18th century when the rich industrialist Ralph Allen and architects John Wood the Elder and John Wood the Younger oversaw the city's reinvention as a model of Georgian architecture. Awash with golden stone townhouses, sweeping crescents and Palladian mansions, Bath demands your undivided attention. Top right: Roman Baths (p231)

The Cotswolds

6 The most wonderful thing about the Cotswolds (p189) is that no matter where you go or how lost you get, you'll still end up in an impossibly quaint village of rose-clad cottages and honey-coloured stone. There'll be a charming village green, a pub with sloping floors and fine ales, and a view of the lush green hills. It's easy to leave the crowds behind and find your very own slice of medieval England here – and some of the best boutique hotels in the country. Right: Lower Slaughter (p196)

JNEED / SHUTTERSTOCK ©

Hadrian's Wall

7 Hadrian's Wall (p612) is one of the country's most dramatic Roman ruins, its 2000-year-old procession of abandoned forts, garrisons, towers and milecastles marching across the wild and lonely landscape of northern England. This wall was about defence and control, but this edge-of-empire barrier also symbolised the boundary of civilised order – to the north lay the unruly land of the marauding Celts, while to the south was the Roman world of orderly tax-paying, underfloor heating and bathrooms.

Cambridge

8 One of England's two great historic university cities, Cambridge (p352) highlights include a tour of at least one of the ancient colleges, and time spent marvelling at the intricate vaulting of King's College Chapel. But no trip to Cambridge is complete without an attempt to take a punt (flat-bottomed boat) along the river by the picturesque 'Backs' – the leafy, green lawns behind the city's finest colleges. Polish off the day with a pint in one of the many historic pubs. You'll soon wonder how you could have studied anywhere else.

FRANK BACH / SHUTTERSTOCK ©

DAVID STEELE/SHUTTERSTOCK ©

CHRISDORNEY / SHUTTERSTOCK ©

Peak District

9 Curiously, you won't find many peaks in the Peak District (p456). But you will find blissful miles of tumbling moorland, plunging valleys, eroded gritstone crags, lush farmland and ancient pocket-sized villages. This beautiful landscape attracts a veritable army of outdoor enthusiasts – cyclists, hikers, cavers and rock climbers – on summer weekends, while those seeking more relaxing enjoyment can admire the rural market and famous puddings of Bakewell, the Victorian pavilions of spa-town Buxton, and the architectural drama of Chatsworth House (pictured above left) – the 'Palace of the Peak'.

Stratford-upon-Avon

10 The pretty town of Stratford-upon-Avon (p403) is where William Shakespeare was born and later shuffled off this mortal coil. Today its tight knot of Tudor streets form a living map of Shakespeare's life. Huge crowds of thespians and theatre lovers come to take in a play at the famous theatre. Visit the five historic houses owned by Shakespeare and his relatives, and the schoolroom where he was educated, then take a respectful detour to the old stone church where the Bard was laid to rest.

Top right: Anne Hathaway's Cottage (p405)

Liverpool Museums

11 After a decade of development, the reborn waterfront is once again the heart of Liverpool. The focal point is Albert Dock (p544), a World Heritage Site of iconic and protected buildings, including a batch of top museums: the Merseyside Maritime Museum and the International Slavery Museum ensure the good and bad sides of Liverpool's history are not forgotten, while the Tate Liverpool and the Beatles Story museum celebrate popular culture and the city's most famous musical sons (still). Sculpture of the Beatles by Andy Edwards in Pier Head, Liverpool (p546)

England's Pubs

12 Despite the growth of stylish clubs and designer bars, the traditional neighbourhood or village pub – Ye Olde Trip to Jerusalem (p436; pictured below) is the country's oldest – is still the centre of social life in England, and a visit can be one of the best ways to get under the skin of the nation. A drink may be necessary as well, and ideally that means traditional beer. To outsiders it may be 'warm and flat', but try it and you'll soon learn to savour the complex flavours of the country's many regional varieties.

Canterbury Cathedral

13 Few English cathedrals come close to Canterbury Cathedral (p142), the very fulcrum of the Anglican Church and a place of worship for more than 15 centuries. Its intricate tower dominates the Canterbury city skyline, while at its heart lies a 12th-century crime scene, where Archbishop Thomas Becket was put to the sword after disagreements with the king – an event that launched a million pilgrimages and still pulls in the crowds today. A lone candle mourns the gruesome deed, the pink sandstone before it smoothed by 800 years' worth of devout kneeling.

PAUL PARADDIO / SHUTTERSTOCK ©

CHRISTOPHER FURLONG / GETTY IMAGES ©

JOHN MICHAELS / ALAMY STOCK PHOTO ©

Afternoon Tea

14 Among England's many and varied traditions, afternoon tea is one of the most enticing, and certainly one of the tastiest. Centre of the ritual is the iconic beverage itself – brewed in a pot, ideally silver-plated, and poured carefully into fine bone-china cups and saucers. Depending where you are in the country, this hot drink is served with scones and cream, fruit cake or feather-light cucumber sandwiches. Fancy city hotels and traditional tearooms, such as Bettys (p484; pictured top right) in Harrogate, are among the best places to sample this epicurean delight.

Brighton

15 It's barely an hour's train ride from the capital, but the seaside city of Brighton (p163) has a quirky character that's completely its own. Overlooking the English Channel on England's pebbly south coast, it's a city that's long been known for its oddball, alternative character. The warren of streets known as The Lanes is a good place to soak up the vibe; sprinkled with vegan cafes, espresso bars, huggermugger pubs, record stores and bric-a-brac shops, it's a browser's dream come true. Bottom right: Brighton Pier (p165)

JORDI PRATS / ALAMY STOCK PHOTO ©

KEVIN FOY / ALAMY STOCK PHOTO ©

IOAN PANAITE / SHUTTERSTOCK ©

Seven Sisters Chalk Cliffs

16 Dover's iconic white cliffs grab the most attention, but the colossal chalky walls of the Seven Sisters (p162) are a much more spectacular affair. This 4-mile roller coaster of sheer white rock rollicks along the Sussex shore overlooking the waters of the English Channel, an impressive southern border to the South Downs National Park and most dramatic at the towering headland of Beachy Head. Hikes through the grassy clifftop fields provide wide sea views, breathtaking in every sense.

London's Theatre Scene

17 However you budget your time and money in London, make sure you take in a show. For big names, head for the West End (London's equivalent of Broadway), where famous spots include the National Theatre (p83), the Old Vic, the Shaftesbury and the Theatre Royal at Drury Lane. For new and experimental works, try the Donmar Warehouse (pictured above right) and Royal Court. Either way, you'll see that London's theatre scene easily lives up to its reputation as one of the finest in the world – whatever New Yorkers say.

Tower of London

18 Begun in the 11th century by William the Conqueror, the Tower of London (p77) is Europe's best-preserved medieval fortress and one of Britain's best-known attractions. At almost 1000 years old (more if you count the Roman foundations) it's an enduring landmark of the capital, and over the centuries this sturdy fortress has served the nation as a palace, a prison, an arsenal and a mint. Today it's home to the spectacular crown jewels, the legendary 'Beefeaters' with their distinctive red uniforms, and ravens that are attributed with mythical powers.

Walking in England

19 Call it hiking or rambling – but most often simply walking – England is the perfect place to explore on two feet, thanks to its compact nature and protected network of 'rights of way'. You can stroll the narrow streets and hidden alleyways of the nation's famous historic towns, then head for a patch of open countryside or one of England's network of national parks: the wild tors and heaths of Dartmoor (p304; pictured top) make a fine introduction.

The Eden Project

20 Looking like a cross between a lunar landing station and a James Bond villain's lair, the gigantic hemispherical greenhouses of the Eden Project (p336 pictured bottom) have become a symbol of Cornwall's renaissance. Dreamt up by Tim Smit, and built in an abandoned clay pit near St Austell, Eden's glass-domed 'biomes' recreate major world climate systems in microcosm, from the lush jungles of the Amazon rainforest to the olive trees, citrus groves and colourful flowers of the Mediterranean, South Africa and California.

DRU NORRIS / ALAMY STOCK PHOTO ©

19

KEV WILLIAMS/SHUTTERSTOCK ©

20

Need to Know

For more information, see Survival Guide (p671)

Currency
Pound sterling (£)

Language
English

Visas
Generally not needed for stays of up to six months. Not a member of the Schengen Zone.

Money
ATMs widely available; credit cards widely accepted.

Mobile Phones
The UK uses the GSM 900/1800 network, which covers the rest of Europe, Australia and New Zealand, but isn't compatible with the North American GSM 1900. Most modern mobiles can function on both networks, but check before you leave home.

Time
Greenwich Mean Time (GMT/UTC)

When to Go

Carlisle
GO May–Sep

York
GO May–Sep

Liverpool
GO May–Sep

Norwich
GO May–Sep

London
GO Any time

Exeter
GO Apr–Sep

High Season
(Jun–Aug)

➡ Weather at its best. Accommodation rates high, particularly in August (school holidays).

➡ Roads busy, especially in seaside areas, national parks and popular cities, such as Oxford, Bath and York.

Shoulder
(Easter–May, mid-Sep–Oct)

➡ Crowds reduce. Prices drop.

➡ Weather often good: March to May sun mixes with sudden rain; September and October can feature balmy 'Indian summers'.

Low Season
(Dec–Feb)

➡ Wet and cold is the norm. Snow can fall, especially up north.

➡ Opening hours reduced October to Easter; some places shut for the winter. Big-city sights (especially London's) operate all year.

Useful Websites

BBC (www.bbc.co.uk) News and entertainment.

Enjoy England (www.visit england.com) Official tourism website.

Lonely Planet (www.lonely planet.com/england) Destination information, hotel bookings, traveller forum and more.

National Traveline (www. traveline.info) Great portal site for all public transport around England.

British Arts Festivals (www. artsfestivals.co.uk) Lists festivals – art, literature, dance, folk and more.

Important Numbers

England (and UK) country code	✔44
International access code	✔00
Emergency (police, fire, ambulance, mountain rescue or coastguard)	✔112 or ✔999

Exchange Rates

Australia	A$1	£0.54
Canada	C$1	£0.56
Eurozone	€1	£0.87
Japan	¥100	£0.75
New Zealand	NZ$1	£0.51
USA	US$1	£0.72

For current exchange rates, see www.xe.com.

Daily Costs

Budget: Less than £55

➡ Dorm beds: £15–30

➡ Cheap meals in cafes and pubs: £7–11

➡ Long-distance coach: £15–40 (200 miles)

Midrange: £55–120

➡ Double room in a midrange hotel or B&B: £65–130 (London £100–200)

➡ Main course in a midrange restaurant: £10–20

➡ Long-distance train: £20–80 (200 miles)

Top End: More than £120

➡ Four-star hotel room: from £130 (London from £200)

➡ Three-course meal in a good restaurant: around £40

➡ Car rental per day: from £35

Opening Hours

Opening hours may vary throughout the year, especially in rural areas where many places have shorter hours, or close completely, from October or November to March or April.

Banks 9.30am–4pm or 5pm Monday to Friday; some open 9.30am–1pm Saturday

Pubs & bars noon–11pm Monday to Saturday (some till midnight or 1am Friday and Saturday), 12.30pm–11pm Sunday

Shops 9am–5.30pm or 6pm Monday to Saturday, often 11am–5pm Sunday

Restaurants lunch noon–3pm, dinner 6pm–9pm or 10pm (later in cities)

Arriving in England

Heathrow Airport Heathrow Express train (£27, 15 minutes) is the fastest link to London; Piccadilly line on the London Underground (£6, one hour) is slower but cheaper. Services run from around 5am to midnight. At other times catch the N9 night bus (£1.50, 1¼ hours) or a taxi (£48 to £90).

Gatwick Airport Trains to central London £10 to £20; hourly buses to central London around the clock from £8; taxi £100.

St Pancras International Arrival point for Eurostar trains to/from Europe, with Underground/bus connections across London.

Getting Around

Transport in England can be expensive compared to Continental Europe; bus and rail services are sparse in the more remote parts of the country. For timetables, check out www.traveline.info.

Car Useful for travelling at your own pace, or for visiting regions with minimal public transport. Cars can be hired in every town or city.

Train Relatively expensive, with extensive coverage and frequent departures throughout most of the country.

Bus Cheaper and slower than trains, but useful for more remote regions that aren't serviced by rail.

For much more on **getting around**, see p680

First Time England

For more information, see Survival Guide (p671)

Checklist

➡ Check the validity of your passport.

➡ Check any visa or entry requirements.

➡ Make bookings (sights, accommodation, travel).

➡ Check the airline baggage restrictions.

➡ Put restricted items (eg hair gel, pocket knife) in your check-in baggage.

➡ Inform your credit/debit card company.

➡ Organise travel insurance.

➡ Check mobile (cell) phone compatibility.

What to Pack

➡ UK electrical plug adaptor.

➡ Umbrella – because the rumours about the weather are true.

➡ Waterproof jacket – because sometimes the umbrella is not enough.

➡ Comfortable walking shoes.

➡ A taste for warm beer.

Top Tips for Your Trip

➡ At major London airports, tickets for express trains into central London are usually available in the baggage arrivals hall; this saves queuing or dealing with machines on the station platform.

➡ The best way to get local currency is usually from an ATM, but this term is rarely used in England; the colloquial term 'cash machine' is more common.

➡ If staying more than a few days in London, get an Oyster Card, the travel card the locals use.

➡ Pickpockets and hustlers lurk in the more crowded tourist areas, especially in London. Don't be paranoid, but do be on your guard.

What to Wear

A rain jacket is essential, as is a small backpack to carry it in when the sun comes out. In summer, you'll need sunscreen and an umbrella; you're bound to use both – possibly on the same day.

For sightseeing, comfortable shoes can make or break a trip. If you plan to enjoy Britain's great outdoors, suitable hiking gear is required in higher/wilder areas, but not for casual strolls in the countryside.

Some bars and restaurants have dress codes banning jeans, T-shirts and trainers (sneakers or runners).

Sleeping

Booking your accommodation in advance is recommended, especially in summer, at weekends and on islands (where options are often limited). Book at least two months ahead for July and August.

B&Bs These small, family-run houses generally provide good value. More luxurious versions are similar to a boutique hotel.

Hotels English hotels range from half a dozen rooms above a pub to restored country houses and castles, with a commensurate range of rates.

Hostels There's a good choice of both institutional and independent hostels, many housed in rustic and/or historic buildings.

Money

ATMs (usually called 'cash machines' in England) are common in cities and even small towns. Cash withdrawals from some ATMs may be subject to a small charge, but most are free. If you're not from the UK, your home bank will likely charge you for withdrawing money overseas. Watch out for tampered ATMs; one ruse by scammers is to attach a card-reader or mini-camera.

Bargaining

A bit of mild haggling is acceptable at flea markets and antique shops, but everywhere else you're expected to pay the advertised price.

Tipping

In England you're not obliged to tip if the service or food was unsatisfactory (even if it's been automatically added to your bill as a 'service charge').

Restaurants Around 10% in restaurants and teahouses with table service, 15% at smarter restaurants. Tips may be added to your bill as a 'service charge'. Not compulsory.

Pubs & Bars Not expected if you order drinks (or food) and pay at the bar; usually 10% if you order at the table and your meal is brought to you.

Taxis Usually 10%, or rounded up to the nearest pound, especially in London.

Fish and chips at the Ship Inn (p606), Newcastle-upon-Tyne

Eating

It's wise to book ahead for midrange restaurants, especially at weekends. Top-end restaurants should be booked at least a couple of weeks in advance.

Restaurants England's restaurants range from cheap-and-cheerful to Michelin-starred, and cover every cuisine you can imagine.

Cafes Open during daytime (rarely after 6pm), cafes are good for a casual breakfast or lunch, or simply for a cup of coffee.

Pubs Most of England's pubs serve reasonably priced meals, and many can compete with restaurants on quality.

Etiquette

Manners The English have a reputation for being polite, and good manners are considered important in most situations. When asking directions, 'Excuse me, can you tell me the way to...' is better than 'Hey, where's...'

Queues In England, queuing ('standing in line') is sacrosanct, whether to board a bus, buy tickets at a kiosk or enter the gates of an attraction. Any attempt to 'jump the queue' will result in an outburst of tut-tutting and hard stares – which is about as angry as most locals get in public.

Escalators If you take an escalator (especially at London tube stations) or a moving walkway (eg at an airport) be sure to stand on the right, so folks can pass on the left.

What's New

Crossrail

It's Britain's largest, most complex and costliest engineering project, but after years of work, London's long-awaited new rail line sent its first trains shuttling across the city in 2019. (p55)

The Lake District World Heritage Site

After intensive local lobbying (both for and against), the UK's best-known national park secured World Heritage status in 2017, recognising its unique landscapes and hill-farming culture. (p558)

The England Coast Path

In 2020 a long-held dream to provide walkers with a nonstop walking trail around the coastline of England will be realised – all 2795 miles of it. (p41)

Tate Modern Extension

At long last the Tate Modern can spread its expansive collection into Switch House. The views from the 10th floor are second to none – and free. (p82)

Ashmolean Museum

To mark its 400th birthday, this Oxford museum has a new exhibit celebrating its founder, Elias Ashmole, along with treasures such as the hat worn by the judge at Charles I's trial and a cape belonging to the father of Pocahontas. (p180)

The Endeavour at Whitby

To coincide with the 250th anniversary of Captain Cook's voyage to Australia, a full-size replica of his ship *Endeavour* has docked in Whitby, the Yorkshire town where the original vessel was built. (p494)

Tate St Ives

In 2018 a multimillion pound extension to the Cornish Tate has added new space for contemporary work, as well as a platform for the many famous artists of the St Ives School. (p325)

Being Brunel

A new exhibition at Bristol's SS *Great Britain* explores the life of engineer Isambard Kingdom Brunel, architect of the Great Western Railway and the city's iconic suspension bridge. (p221)

Roman Baths

The city of Bath's 1st-century bathing house now has some 21st-century tech: projections show what it was like to take a dip here 2000 years ago. (p231)

The Swale Trail

A cycle path has been created between the villages of Reeth and Keld in the Yorkshire Dales, snaking beside the River Swale via pubs, tearooms and waterfalls.

Mackie Mayor Market

In disrepair for 30 years, this Manchester market has been restored as a food hall, showcasing producers from across the city and the north of England. (p534)

Hull

Hull's designation as UK City of Culture in 2017 has spurred exciting regeneration, from a new street-food hall to independent boutiques, quirky cafes and maritime attractions. (p518)

For more recommendations and reviews, see lonelyplanet.com/england

If You Like...

Royal England

Buckingham Palace The Queen's official London residence, best known for its royal-waving balcony and the Changing of the Guard. (p67)

Westminster Abbey Where English monarchs are crowned and married – most recently William and Kate. (p62)

Tower of London A castle and royal palace for centuries, now holding the Crown Jewels; 900 years of history in one iconic building. (p77)

Sandringham The monarch's country residence, with a royal memorabilia museum. (p383)

Royal Pavilion Opulent and fantastical palace built for King George IV. (p165)

Althorp House Ancestral home and burial place of Diana, Princess of Wales. (p445)

Osborne House Royal retreat on the Isle of Wight, built for Queen Victoria. (p254)

Castles

Windsor Castle Largest and oldest occupied fortress in the world, and the Queen's weekend retreat. (p213)

Warwick Castle One of the finest castles in England; this well-preserved castle is both impressive and romantic. (p401)

Tintagel Castle Atmospheric clifftop ruin, and the legendary birthplace of King Arthur. (p316)

Bamburgh Castle Spectacularly positioned and largely rebuilt fortress on the Northumberland coast. (p623)

Richmond Castle Among England's oldest castles, with fantastic views from the medieval keep. (p503)

Skipton Castle Little known, but probably the best-preserved medieval castle in the country. (p498)

Museums

British Museum England's largest and most visited museum is also one of the oldest and finest in the world. (p63)

National Railway Museum The epicentre of the nation's obsession with steam engines and railway history. (p475)

Natural History Museum A surefire hit with kids of all ages, with dinosaur skeletons, earthquake simulators and interactive exhibits. (p85)

Museum of Liverpool The city's multilayered past is celebrated at this interactive exploration of cultural and historical milestones. (p545)

Ashmolean Museum England's oldest museum, established in 1683, crammed with Egyptian mummies, rare porcelain and priceless musical instruments. (p180)

Mary Rose Museum Superb modern facility built around the remains of King Henry VIII's 16th-century flagship. (p249)

National Parks

North York Moors National Park Wild and windswept, with whale-back hills stretching all the way to the sea, topped by England's largest expanse of heather. (p488)

Northumberland National Park Arguably the last area of true wilderness left in England, designated a Dark Sky Reserve thanks to its crystal-clear night skies. (p619)

The Lake District A feast of mountains, valleys, views and – of course – lakes; the hilltops that inspired William Wordsworth. (p562)

Yorkshire Dales National Park With scenic valleys, high hills and deep caves, the Dales are designed for hiking, biking and caving. (p497)

Dartmoor Exhilarating wilderness, hidden valleys and southern England's highest hills. (p304)

Peak District OK, so it's the most visited national park in Europe, but all those outdoor enthusiasts can't be wrong. (p456)

Historic Houses

Blenheim Palace Monumental baroque fantasy, Winston Churchill's birthplace and one of England's greatest stately homes. (p188)

Castle Howard An impressive baroque edifice, best known as the setting for TV's *Brideshead Revisited*. (p482)

Audley End One of England's grandest country houses set amid glorious Lancelot 'Capability' Brown landscaped gardens. (p368)

Chatsworth House Quintessential stately home and gardens; a treasure trove of heirlooms and works of art. (p466)

Longleat The first of England's stately homes to be opened to the public, complemented by a safari park on the grounds. (p277)

Wilton House Packed with exquisite art and period furniture; gives a glimpse into the rarefied existence of British aristocracy. (p274)

Cathedrals

St Paul's Cathedral Symbol of London for centuries, and still an essential part of the city's skyline. (p75)

York Minster One of the largest medieval cathedrals in all of Europe, especially renowned for its windows. (p475)

Top: Blue Whale skeleton in Hintze Hall, Natural History Museum (p85)

Bottom: Crooked house in Lavenham (p372)

Canterbury Cathedral Mothership of the Anglican Church, attracting pilgrims and visitors in their thousands. (p142)

Salisbury Cathedral Truly majestic cathedral and an English icon, topped by the tallest spire in England. (p272)

Ely Cathedral Visible for miles across the flatlands of eastern England, and locally dubbed the 'Ship of the Fens'. (p365)

Liverpool Cathedral The largest Anglican cathedral in the world. (p543)

Quaint Villages

Clovelly A picture-postcard fishing village with cute cottages tumbling down a steep cobbled hill to the harbour. (p312)

Bibury Designer William Morris once called it 'the most beautiful village in England', and with its thatched cottages and timeless streets, it's hard to disagree. (p192)

Lacock A favourite for film crews, this Wiltshire village has starred in productions ranging from *Downton Abbey* and *Pride and Prejudice* to *Harry Potter*. (p278)

Lavenham A collection of exquisitely preserved medieval buildings in East Anglia virtually untouched since the 15th century. (p372)

Goathland One of Yorkshire's most attractive villages, complete with village green and traditional steam railway station. (p494)

Hawkshead The picture of a Lakeland village – whitewashed cottages, medieval pubs, village square and all. (p572)

Shopping

Portobello Road Market One of the best-known street markets, surrounded by quirky boutiques and gift stores. (p102)

Leeds' Victorian shopping arcades Elegant passageways of wrought ironwork and stained glass, home to fashion boutiques and quirky independents. (p511)

North Laine The perfect place in Brighton to pick up vegan shoes, Elvis outfits and circus monocycles. (p168)

Ludlow Foodie heaven, where almost everything is organic, artisanal, sustainable or locally sourced. (p430)

Totnes This Devon village is a champion of all things local and sustainable, and its main street is lined with intriguing independent shops. (p297)

Art Galleries

Tate Britain The best-known gallery in London, full to the brim with the finest works. (p69)

Tate Modern London's other Tate focuses on modern art in all its wonderful permutations. (p82)

BALTIC – Centre for Contemporary Art The 'Tate of the North' features work by some of contemporary art's biggest show-stoppers. (p601)

Hepworth Wakefield An award-winning gallery of contemporary sculpture, anchored by a world-class collection of works by local lass Barbara Hepworth. (p509)

Barber Institute of Fine Arts With works by Rubens, Turner and Picasso this provincial gallery is no lightweight. (p391)

Turner Contemporary The south coast's newest art space occupies a purpose-built structure next to the sea. (p148)

Yorkshire Sculpture Park England's biggest outdoor sculpture collection, with key works by artists including Henry Moore and Barbara Hepworth. (p509)

Festivals

Notting Hill Carnival London's Caribbean community shows the city how to party. (p107)

Glastonbury More than 40 years on and still going strong, this is Britain's biggest and best-loved music festival. (p244)

Brighton Festival You know a festival's matured when it grows a fringe; this gathering of all things arts is now firmly placed on the calendar. (p166)

Latitude Festival An eclectic mix of music, literature, dance, drama and comedy, this festival has a stunning location in Southwold. (p375)

Grassington Festival A village in the scenic Yorkshire Dales hosts this amazing two-week cultural extravaganza. (p500)

Reading Festival Venerable rock gathering that traces its roots back to the 1960s. (p215)

Leeds Festival Northern companion to the long-established Reading Festival. (p507)

Coastal Beauty

Holkham Bay Pristine 3-mile beach; the vast expanse of sand gives a real sense of isolation. (p384)

PAUL DANIELS / SHUTTERSTOCKS ©

Ferris wheel and Blackpool Tower (p551), Blackpool

Jurassic Coast Towering rock stacks, sea-carved arches and fossils aplenty, plus some of the best beaches in the country. (p262)

Beachy Head & Seven Sisters Where the South Downs plunge into the sea, these mammoth chalk cliffs provide a dramatic finale. (p162)

Robin Hood's Bay Picturesque fishing village nestled in a nook amid impressive sea-cliff scenery. (p496)

Land's End The cliffs and coves are some of the most dramatic in the country (if you can ignore the theme park). (p330)

Seaside Towns

Brighton London's naughty little seaside sister makes an easy day trip from the capital, with scores of independent shops to explore. (p163)

Blackpool If you're looking for the quintessential English seaside resort – candy floss, deck chairs, pier and all – Blackpool is where you'll find it. (p551)

Whitby A classic northern seaside town with haunted lanes, fossil hunting and arguably England's finest fish and chips. (p492)

Margate Beloved of JMW Turner and Tracy Emin, this once-faded south-coast town is enjoying an exciting artistic renaissance. (p148)

Southwold A genteel seaside town with a lovely sandy beach, a charming pier and rows of colourful beach huts. (p375)

Falmouth Once a hub for nautical traffic between England and the rest of the British Empire, this lively Cornish town is now home to a renowned maritime museum. (p335)

Month by Month

January

After the festivities of Christmas and New Year's Eve, the first few weeks of the year can feel a bit of an anticlimax – never helped by the often bad weather.

✴ The London Parade

A ray of light in the gloom, the New Year's Day Parade in London (to use its official title; www.london parade.co.uk) is one of the biggest events of its kind in the world, featuring marching bands, street performers, classic cars, floats and displays winding their way through the streets.

✴ Chinese New Year

Late January or early February sees London's Chinatown snap, crackle and pop with fireworks, a colourful street parade, lion dances and dim sum aplenty.

February

February is midwinter in England. The country may be scenic under snow and sunshine, but is more likely to be grey and gloomy. Festivals and events to brighten the mood are still thin on the ground.

✴ Jorvik Viking Festival

In chilly mid-February, the ancient Viking capital of York becomes home once again to invaders and horned helmets galore, with the intriguing addition of longship races. (p478)

☆ Six Nations Rugby Championship

This highlight of the rugby calendar (www.rbs6nat ions.com) runs from late January to March, with the England team playing its home matches at London's Twickenham stadium.

March

Spring starts to show itself, with daffodil blooms brightening up the month.

Some people cling to the winter mood, but hotels and inns offer special weekend rates to tempt them out from under their duvets.

✴ Bath Literature Festival

The elegant Georgian streets of Bath fill up with bibliophiles during this major literary event, held from late February to early March.

☆ University Boat Race

An annual race in late March down the River Thames in London between the rowing teams from Cambridge and Oxford Universities – an institution (since 1856) that still enthrals the country. (p107)

April

The weather is looking up, with warmer and drier days bringing out the spring blossoms. Sights and attractions that closed for the low season open up around the middle of the month or at Easter.

☆ Grand National

Half the country has a flutter on the highlight of the

three-day horse race meeting at Aintree: a steeplechase with a testing course and high jumps. First Saturday in April. (p546)

🏃 London Marathon

In early April, superfit athletes cover 26 miles and 385yd in just over two hours. Others dress up in daft costumes and take considerably longer. (p107)

🎭 Stratford Literary Festival

The top event on the cultural calendar in William Shakespeare's home town attracts big hitters from the book world for a week of debates, author events, workshops and humour.

May

With sunny spring days, the calendar fills with more events. Two public holidays (the first and last Mondays of May) mean road traffic is very busy over the adjoining long weekends.

🎭 Padstow May Day

Known locally as 'Obby 'Oss Day, the north Cornish town of Padstow celebrates its ancient pagan spring festival on 1 May, featuring two rival 'osses that swirl through the crowds to the town's maypole. (p320)

☆ FA Cup Final

The highlight of the football season for over a century. Throughout winter, teams from all of England's football divisions have been battling it out in a knock-out tournament, culminating in this heady spectacle at Wembley Stadium – the

home of English football. Held in early May.

🎭 Brighton Festival

The lively three-week arts fest takes over the streets of buzzy south-coast resort Brighton during May. Alongside the mainstream performances there's a festival 'fringe' as well. (p166)

🎭 Chelsea Flower Show

The Royal Horticultural Society flower show in late May is the highlight of the gardener's year. Top garden designers take gold, silver and bronze medals (and TV accolades), while the punters take the plants in the last-day giveaway. (p107)

☆ Glyndebourne

From late May till the end of August, this open-air festival of world-class opera enlivens the pastoral surroundings of Glyndebourne House in East Sussex.

🎭 Cotswold Food & Farming Festival

A celebration of local food and farming (www.thecotswoldfoodandfarmingfestival.com) at the Cotswold Farm Park near Cheltenham, with stalls, displays, activities and demonstrating chefs. Main festival in May; others later in the year.

🏃 Keswick Mountain Festival

A long weekend in late May in the heart of the Lake District is dedicated to celebrating all things outdoor-related, from outdoor activities and celebrity speakers to live music and sporting events.

June

Now it's almost summer. You can tell because June sees the music-festival season kick off properly, while sporting events – from rowing to racing – fill the calendar.

☆ Derby Week

Horse racing, people watching and clothes spotting are on the agenda at this weeklong race meeting (www.epsomderby.co.uk) in Epsom, Surrey, in early June.

🎭 Cotswold Olimpicks

Welly wanging, pole climbing and shin kicking are the key disciplines at this traditional Gloucestershire sports day in early June, held each year since 1612. (p200)

☆ Isle of Wight Festival

Originally held from 1968 to 1970 during the high point of hippie counterculture, this musical extravaganza was resurrected in 2002. Today it attracts top bands, especially from the indie and rock fraternities. Held in mid-June. (p254)

☉ Trooping the Colour

Military bands and bear-skinned grenadiers march down London's Whitehall in this mid-June martial pageant to mark the monarch's birthday. (p107)

☆ Royal Ascot

It's hard to tell which matters more – the fashion or the fillies – at this highlight of the horse-racing

Top: Guy Fawkes Night bonfire (p33)

Bottom: Jorvik Viking Festival participants (p29)

year, held in mid-June at Berkshire's Royal Ascot racetrack. Expect top hats, designer frocks and plenty of frantic betting. (p212)

☆ Wimbledon Lawn Tennis Championships

Correctly titled the All England Club Championship, and the best-known grass-court tennis tournament in the world, Wimbledon attracts all the big names. Held in late June. (p130)

🎪 Glastonbury Festival

England's favourite pop and rock fest held (nearly) every year on a dairy farm in Somerset in late June. Invariably muddy and still a rite of passage for every self-respecting British music fan. (p244)

🎪 Meltdown Festival

In late June, London's Southbank Centre hands over the curatorial reigns to a legend of contemporary music (David Bowie, Morrissey, Patti Smith) to pull together a full program of concerts, talks and films. (p107)

☆ Royal Regatta

In late June or early July, boats of every description take to the water for an upper-crust river regatta at Henley-on-Thames. (p216)

🎪 Broadstairs Dickens Festival

Charles Dickens, one of England's best-known writers, is celebrated at this literary festival in the town where he spent his summers and based many of his novels. (p150)

✨ Pride

The big event on the gay-and-lesbian calendar is a technicolour street parade through London's West End, culminating in a concert in Trafalgar Sq. Late June or early July. (p107)

☆ Aldeburgh Festival

Founded by composer Benjamin Britten in 1948, this exploration of classical music is East Anglia's biggest festival, taking in new, reinterpreted and rediscovered pieces, and extending into the visual arts.

July

This is it: summer, with weekly festivals and county shows. Schools break up at the end of the month, so there's a holiday tingle in the air, dulled only by busy Friday-evening roads.

✨ Great Yorkshire Show

The charming town of Harrogate plays host to one of England's largest county shows. Expect Yorkshire grit, Yorkshire tykes, Yorkshire puddings, Yorkshire beef... (p483)

✨ Latitude Festival

Popular and eclectic festival held near the lovely Suffolk seaside town of Southwold, with top names from the alternative-music scene complemented by theatre, cabaret and literary events. Held in mid-July. (p375)

☆ Cowes Week

The country's biggest yachting spectacular hits the choppy seas around the Isle of Wight in late July. (p254)

✨ Womad

In late July, roots and world music take centre stage at this former Reading-based festival (www.womad.org), now in a country park near Malmesbury in the south Cotswolds.

August

Schools and colleges are closed, parliament is in recess, the sun is shining (hopefully), most people go on holiday for a week or two (some of them abroad), and England is in a holiday mood.

◉ British Fireworks Championships

The biggest fireworks championship in the UK lights up the skies over Plymouth for two nights in mid-August. (p301)

✨ Notting Hill Carnival

A multicultural, Caribbean-style street carnival in late August in London's district of Notting Hill. Steel drums, dancers and outrageous costumes. (p107)

✨ Reading Festival

England's second-oldest music festival. Originally a rock fest, it veers a bit more towards pop these days, but it's still a good bet for big-name bands. Happens in late August. (p215)

✨ Leeds Festival

Leeds' major music festival, and the northern sister of the festival in Reading. The two festivals are held on the same late-August weekend, with the same line-up. If artists play Reading on the Friday, they'll play Leeds on Saturday, and vice versa. (p507)

✨ Manchester Pride

One of England's biggest celebrations of gay, bisexual and transgender life. Happens in late August. (p532)

☆ International Beatleweek

Held in the last week of August, the world's biggest tribute to the Beatles features six days of music, exhibitions, tours and memorabilia sales in Liverpool. (p547)

September

The first week of September feels more like August, but then schools open up again, motorway traffic returns to normal and the summer party's over for another year. Good weather is still a chance.

☆ International Birdman Competition

In the first weekend in September, competitors dressed as batmen, fairies and flying machines compete in an outlandish celebration of self-powered flight (www.birdman.org.uk) at West Sussex' Bognor Regis. The furthest flight takes home a £30,000 prize. So far no one's got near the hallowed 100m goal.

✨ Bestival

Quirky music festival in early September, with a different fancy-dress theme every year. Held at Robin Hill Country Park on the Isle of Wight. (p262)

☆ World Gurning Championships

Gurning is face-pulling, and this has to be one of the weirdest events of the year. Elastic-faced contestants come to Egremont in Cumbria in mid-September every year, contorting their features in a bid to pull the most grotesque expressions. See www.facebook.com/EgremontCrabFairWorldGurningChampionships.

🏃 Great North Run

Britain's biggest marathon is in London, but the Great North Run on Tyneside in September is the biggest half-marathon in the world, with the greatest number of runners of any race over this distance. (p601)

October

October means autumn. Leaves turn golden-brown and, unless there's an 'Indian Summer', the weather begins to get cold. Sights and attractions start to shut down for the low season, and accommodation rates drop.

🍴 Falmouth Oyster Festival

The West Country port of Falmouth hosts this event to mark the start of the traditional oyster-catching ('dredging') season, and to celebrate local food from the sea and farmland of Cornwall. (p336)

☆ Horse of the Year Show

The country's major indoor horse show (www.hoys.co.uk), with dressage, showjumping and other equine activities. Held in early October at the NEC arena near Birmingham.

📚 Cheltenham Literature Festival

Established in 1949, the world's longest-running book-focused festival showcases the biggest names in literature over 10 days in autumn. (p206)

November

Winter's here, and November is dull. The weather's often cold and damp, summer is a distant memory and Christmas seems far away: suitably sombre for Remembrance Day, while Guy Fawkes Night sparks up some fun.

📚 Guy Fawkes Night

Also called Bonfire Night and Fireworks Night (www.bonfirenight.net), 5 November sees fireworks filling the country's skies in commemoration of a failed attempt to blow up parliament in 1605. Effigies of Guy Fawkes, the leader of the Gunpowder Plot, often burn on bonfires.

📚 Flaming Tar Barrels

The unhinged locals of Ottery St Mary carry flaming tar barrels through packed-out streets on 5 November, while paramedics and health-and-safety officials watch on in horror.

👁 Remembrance Day

On 11 November, red poppies are worn and wreaths are laid in towns and cities around the country. The day (www.poppy.org.uk) commemorates military personnel killed and injured in the line of duty, from the world wars to modern conflicts.

☆ World's Biggest Liar Contest

Another whacky event, and it's Cumbria again. Fibbers from all walks of life go head-to-head in a battle of mid-November mendacity at the Bridge Inn in Wasdale. See www.santonbridgeinn.com.

December

Schools break up around mid-December, but most shops and businesses keep going until Christmas Eve. Many towns and cities hold Christmas markets, ideal places for picking up Christmas presents.

📚 Victorian Festival of Christmas

Portsmouth's historic dockyard, home to HMS *Victory* and the Mary Rose Museum, gets a Dickensian makeover for this celebration of Victorian Christmas traditions (www.christmasfestival.co.uk), including street entertainment, carol singing and a Christmas market. First weekend in December or last weekend in November.

📚 New Year Celebrations

On 31 December, fireworks and street parties happen in town squares across the country, lighting up the nation to welcome in the New Year.

Itineraries

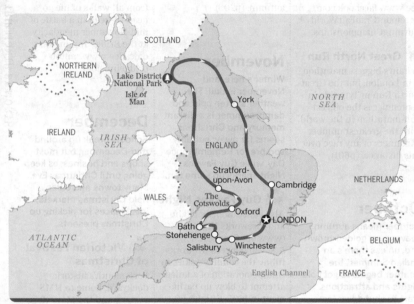

 2 WEEKS **Essential England**

Just over a week is long enough to tick off many of England's highlights. This tour takes in a dozen of the nation's top sights, from London to the Lakes.

Start with a full day in the nation's capital, **London**, simply walking the streets to admire the world-famous sights: Buckingham Palace, Tower Bridge, Trafalgar Sq and more. Then head west for one or both of the grand cathedral cities of **Winchester** and **Salisbury**. Next stop: ancient history – the iconic megaliths of **Stonehenge**.

A short hop northwest leads to the beautiful city of **Bath**, for Roman history and fabulous Georgian architecture. Then cruise across the classic English countryside of the **Cotswolds** to reach that ancient seat of learning, **Oxford**. Not far away is **Stratford-upon-Avon**, for everything Shakespeare.

Next, strike out north for the **Lake District**, one of the country's most scenic areas, then across to **York** for Viking remains and the stunning Minster. End your trip with a visit to **Cambridge**, England's other great university city. Then a final day back in **London**, immersed in galleries, museums, luxury shops, street markets, West End shows or East End cafes – or whatever takes your fancy.

4 WEEKS **The Full Monty**

With a month to spare, you can enjoy a trip taking in all the very best that England offers, without the pressure of a crowded schedule. This circuit covers all the bases.

Kick off in **London,** and spend a couple of days seeing the big-ticket attractions, but make time for exploratory saunters as well – along the south bank of the River Thames, or through the markets of the East End. Next, go down to the sea at the buzzy coastal resort of **Brighton**; then west, via **Portsmouth** for the historic dockyard, to reach the picturesque **New Forest.** Head inland to the grand cathedral cities of **Winchester** and **Salisbury,** and on to England's best-known ancient site, **Stonehenge,** and nearby **Avebury Stone Circle** – bigger than Stonehenge but a more intimate experience.

Onwards into deepest Wessex, via Thomas Hardy's hometown, **Dorchester,** to reach the wild expanse of **Dartmoor National Park.** Then it's time for yet another historic city, **Wells,** with its beautiful cathedral, en route to the Georgian masterpiece of **Bath** and the southwest's big little city, **Bristol.** Next comes the classic English countryside of the **Cotswolds,** with a pause at delightful Stow-on-the-Wold, and maybe Broadway or Chipping Campden, before reaching **Oxford,** England's oldest university city. Not far away is Shakespeare Central at **Stratford-upon-Avon** – plan on seeing a play by the Bard himself. Continue journeying north via the heather-clad moors and tranquil limestone dales of the **Peak District** to reach England's second city, **Manchester,** and cultural crossroads **Liverpool.**

Then it's back to the wilds again with a short hop to the scenic wonders of the **Lake District.** From the sturdy border town of **Carlisle,** follow the ancient Roman landmark of **Hadrian's Wall** all the way to revitalised city **Newcastle-upon-Tyne.** Then it's into the home stretch, south via **Durham** and its world-class cathedral, and then **York** for its Viking remains and stunning minster, to reach England's other great seat of learning, **Cambridge.** From here it's a hop back to **London,** to use up the last few days of your grand tour, taking in highlights such as Trafalgar Sq, the National Gallery, Tate Modern and the Tower of London, all polished off with a stroll across Westminster Bridge as the sun sets over the Houses of Parliament.

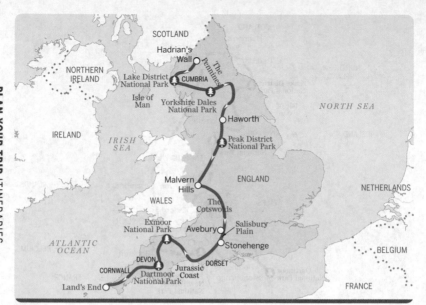

The Wild Side

This is a tour through the best of England's natural landscape, the inspiration for generations of poets, writers and composers. So put on your hiking boots, or have a camera at the ready, as we take a northeast–southwest meander through some of the country's finest national parks and stretches of open countryside.

Start at the spectacular Roman remains of **Hadrian's Wall**, one of England's finest reminders of the classical era, where you can explore the ancient forts and stride beside the ramparts centurion-style. Then continue into Cumbria for the high peaks of the **Lake District National Park**, once the spiritual home of Wordsworth and the Romantic poets, now a mecca for outdoor enthusiasts, with hikes and strolls for all abilities, plus cosy inns and traditional country hotels.

Travelling east from the Lakes carries you across the Pennines – the chain of hills known as the backbone of England – to reach the green hills and valleys of the **Yorkshire Dales National Park**. Nearby are the moors around **Haworth** – inspiration for Emily Brontë's *Wuthering Heights*.

Travel south through the hills and dales of the **Peak District National Park** – stopping off to explore the great park around Chatsworth if time allows – then through central England, via Elgar's beloved **Malvern Hills**, to reach the classic English countryside of the **Cotswolds**. Then continue southwards again to enjoy the epic emptiness of **Salisbury Plain**, home to **Stonehenge** and other archaeological intrigues. Nearby is **Avebury**, England's other great stone circle. A few miles more and you're on Dorset's spectacular fossil-ridden **Jurassic Coast**.

Then head into England's toe, the West Country Peninsula, jutting deep into the Atlantic. Take in the lush farmland of Devon and the heathery hills and sandy coves of **Exmoor National Park**, then it's on to the eerie granite tors of **Dartmoor National Park**, which offers some of the country's most bleakly beautiful views. Next stop: **Cornwall**, for pretty ports, gorse-clad cliffs and sparkling bays. Then finish this bucolic excursion at **Land's End**, where the English mainland finally plunges headlong into the restless ocean.

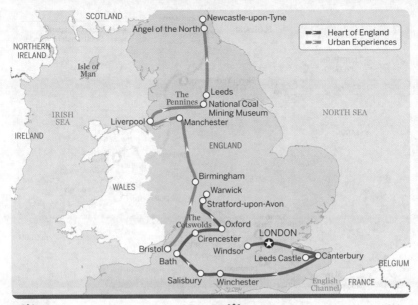

2 WEEKS Heart of England

This journey through the country's heartland takes in the best of 'Olde England', concentrating on castles, cathedrals and picturesque medieval towns and villages.

Start in **London**, with its biggest landmarks: Westminster Abbey, the Tower of London, St Paul's Cathedral and Buckingham Palace. Out of the centre, the gorgeous gardens at Kew, Eton College and **Windsor Castle** are also must-see sights.

Beyond the capital lies old England proper, especially around the market towns of Kent, where **Canterbury Cathedral** and **Leeds Castle** are top sights.

Head to **Winchester**, the ancient capital, which boasts another fine cathedral. Jostling for prominence is nearby **Salisbury**, with its famous cathedral spire dominating the landscape for miles around.

Out west, **Bath** is crammed with Georgian architecture, while the **Cotswolds** conceal a host of pretty towns, such as **Cirencester**, as well as Blenheim Palace. On to picturesque **Oxford** and **Stratford-upon-Avon**, the home of Shakespeare, leaving just enough time to top up on English history at stunning **Warwick Castle**.

8 DAYS Urban Experiences

Outside of London, England's provincial cities provide a vibrant counterpoint to the country's tranquil coast and countryside.

Start in **Bristol**, a thriving regional capital famed for its engineering heritage and lively cultural scene. Then head to **Birmingham** once forlorn but now a byword for successful urban renewal.

Continue north to reach **Manchester**, famous for its music and football team, where architectural highlights include the stunning Imperial War Museum North. Nearby **Liverpool** is reinventing itself as a cultural capital, with the redevelopment most apparent at the historic waterfront, Albert Dock.

Cross the Pennines to reach **Leeds**, the 'Knightsbridge of the North', where rundown factories and abandoned warehouses are now apartments and ritzy boutiques. But don't forget the past: go underground at the **National Coal Mining Museum**.

Further north is **Newcastle-upon-Tyne** and neighbouring Gateshead where heavy industries have given way to art and architecture. Conclude your urban tour with a visit to England's best-known public art, the iconic **Angel of the North**.

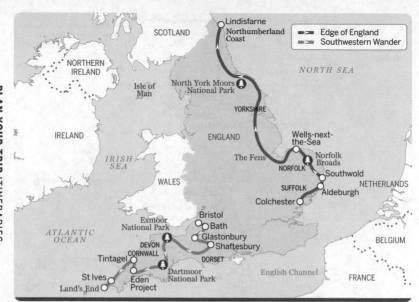

Edge of England

2 WEEKS

If you like the outdoors try this backwater route along England's eastern fringe.

Start in **Colchester**, with its magnificent castle, then visit sleepy **Suffolk**, where quaint villages and market towns such as Sudbury and Lavenham dot the landscape. Along the coast you'll discover wildlife reserves, shingle beaches, fishing ports such as **Aldeburgh,** and the delightfully retro seaside resort of **Southwold**.

Things get even quieter in Norfolk, especially around the misty lakes and windmill-lined rivers of the **Norfolk Broads**. For beach strolls or historic country pubs head for the villages near **Wells-next-the-Sea**.

North of Norfolk lies the eerie, flat landscape of the **Fens**, now a haven for otters and bird life. Then it's north again into Yorkshire to the heather-clad **North York Moors**, where humpbacked hills roll all the way to the coast to drop dramatically into the choppy waters of the North Sea.

Round things off with a stroll between the castles of Bamburgh and Dunstanburgh on the wild **Northumberland Coast**, finishing your tour at the historic island priory of **Lindisfarne**.

Southwestern Wander

2 WEEKS

The southwest of England takes a bit of effort to reach but repays in full with a rich green landscape dotted with hills and moors, surrounded by glittering seas.

Start in the historic university city of **Bristol**, factoring in the M-Shed Museum, a walk around the harbour and a visit to SS *Great Britain*. Detour to beautiful **Bath**, and wander around the Royal Crescent and Roman Baths. Saunter down through Somerset to **Glastonbury** – famous for its annual music festival, ruined abbey and many mystical legends. South leads to Dorset, where highlights include picturesque **Shaftesbury**.

Head west to heathery **Exmoor National Park**, then it's onwards into Devon, where there's a choice of coasts, as well as **Dartmoor National Park**, with the highest and wildest hills in southern England.

Cross into Cornwall to explore the space-age biodomes of the **Eden Project**. Nearby, but in another era entirely, is **Tintagel Castle**, the legendary birthplace of King Arthur. Continue west to visit the galleries of **St Ives**, before concluding your trip at **Land's End**.

Walking near Grasmere (p570), Lake District

Plan Your Trip
The Great Outdoors

What's the best way to slow down, meet the locals and get off the beaten track? Simple: go for a walk or get on a bike. Experiencing the great outdoors is much more rewarding than staring at it through a car window or a camera lens.

Best Outdoors

Best Long-Distance Walks

Coast to Coast, Hadrian's Wall, Cotswold Way, South West Coast Path

Best Areas for Short Walks

Lake District, Yorkshire Dales, Cotswolds, Dartmoor

Best for Coast Walks

Northumberland, Devon & Cornwall, Norfolk & Suffolk, Dorset

Best Time to Go

Summer (June to August) The best time for walking: weather usually warm and hopefully dry; plenty of daylight, too.

Late spring (May) and early autumn (September) The seasons either side of summer can be great for walking: fewer crowds; days often mild and sunny.

Best Maps for Walking

Ordnance Survey (UK's national mapping agency) Explorer series 1:25,000 scale.

Harvey Maps (specially designed for walkers) Superwalker series 1:25,000 scale.

Hiking & Walking

England is covered in a vast network of footpaths, many of which are centuries old, dating from the time when walking was the only way to get from farm to village, from village to town, from town to coast, or valley to valley. Any walk you do today will follow these historic paths. Even England's longest walks simply link up these networks of many shorter paths. You'll also sometimes walk along 'bridleways', originally for horse transport, and old unsurfaced roads called 'byways'.

Nearly all footpaths in England are 'rights of way' – public paths and tracks across private property. Even though most land in England is privately owned, from tiny cultivated areas to vast mountain ranges, a right of way across the land cannot be overruled by the owner. If there is a right of way, you can follow it through fields, woods, pastures, paddocks, even farmhouse yards, as long as you keep to the correct route and do no damage.

Generally speaking, the lower and more cultivated the landscape, the easier the walking, with clear paths and signposts – ideal for beginners. In mountain and moorland areas, if the route is popular there will be a path (although sometimes this is faint), but not many signposts. If the route is rarely trodden, there may be no visible path at all, and absolutely no signposts, so you'll need to know what you're doing – and take a detailed map and compass for navigation.

Best Walking Areas

Although you can walk pretty much anywhere in England, some areas are better than others. Some are suitable for short walks of a couple of hours, others for longer all-day outings.

Dartmoor

In England's southwest, Dartmoor National Park boasts the highest hills for miles around, dotted with weathered granite outcrops known as tors. Much of the landscape is devoid of trees and surprisingly wild. Below the hills, valleys cut into the edges of the moor, perfect for picnics and riverside strolls in summer.

Lake District

England's most popular walking area, the Lake District offers high peaks, endless views, deep valleys and, of course, beautiful lakes. Protected by the Lake District National Park (and often abbreviated to simply 'The Lakes' or 'Lakeland', but never, ever the 'Lakes District'), it is loved by walkers, partly because of the landscape, and partly because of the history; thanks to poet Wordsworth and his Romantic chums, this is where walking for pleasure really began.

Peak District

Despite the name, the Peak District has very few peaks. But there are plenty of hills, valleys and moors, making it a favoured walking area in northern England. Protected as a national park, the landscape falls into two zones: the south is mainly farmland, cut by limestone valleys; in the north are high peaty moors with rocky outcrops, and a more austere character.

Yorkshire

With rolling hills, wild moors, limestone outcrops and green valleys cut by scenic streams, the Yorkshire Dales National Park is another of England's most popular walking areas. Paths are a little gentler and conditions a little less serious than in the Lake District, with the happy addition of some delightful villages nestling in the dales – many with pubs and tearooms providing refreshments for walkers.

Southwest Coast

Cornwall and Devon enjoy the best of the English climate and some of the finest coastal scenery in the country – but the rugged landscape means tough days on the trail. Thanks to those beautiful rivers flowing down steep valleys to the sea, you're forever going up or down. The coastline in neighbouring Dorset – known as the Jurassic Coast thanks to the proliferation of fossils – is less arduous and another great area for seaside walks.

North Downs & South Downs

Between London and the south coast (and within easy reach of both), the North and South Downs are two parallel ranges of broad chalky hills. On the map, the North Downs appear hemmed-in by motorways and conurbations, and while this area can never be described as wilderness, the walking here is often unexpectedly tranquil. The South Downs are higher, and not so cramped by urban expansion, with more options for walks, and a landscape protected by England's newest national park.

Cotswolds

One of the most popular areas for walkers in southern England, the Cotswold Hills offer classic English countryside, where paths meander through neat fields, past pretty villages with cottages of honey-coloured stone. The eastern side of the Cotswolds tends to be a gentler landscape, while the paths undulate more on the western side, especially along the Cotswold Escarpment – although the views are better here.

Exmoor

Just to the north of Dartmoor, and sometimes overshadowed by its larger neighbour, southwest England's other national park is Exmoor. Heather-covered hills cut by deep valleys make it a perfect walking area, edged with the added bonus of a spectacular coastline of cliffs and beaches.

Long Distance Trails

England Coast Path

➡ 2975 miles; www.nationaltrail.co.uk/england-coast-path

When it opens in 2020, this will officially be the longest trail in England – an epic, round-England trek that (even for the fittest walkers) is likely to require the best part of a year to complete.

South West Coast Path

➡ 630 miles; 8-10 weeks; www.southwestcoastpath.com

A roller-coaster romp around England's southwest peninsula, past beaches, bays, shipwrecks, seaside resorts, fishing villages and clifftop castles. Given its length, most walkers do it in sections: the two-week stretch between Padstow and Falmouth around Land's End is most popular.

Hadrian's Wall Path

➡ 84 miles; 7-8 days; www.nationaltrail.co.uk/hadrianswall

A footpath following the world-famous Roman structure across northern England, via forts, castles, ramparts and battlements, and giving the Coast to Coast a run for its money in the popularity stakes.

WEATHER WATCH

While enjoying your walking in England, it's always worth remembering the fickle nature of English weather. The countryside can appear gentle and welcoming, and often is, but sometimes conditions can turn nasty – especially on the higher ground. At any time of year, if you're walking on the hills or open moors, it's vital to be well equipped. You should carry warm and waterproof clothing (even in summer), a map and a compass (that you know how to use), some water, food and high-energy fuel, such as chocolate. If you're really going off the beaten track, leave details of your route with someone.

Cyclist in the Yorkshire Dales National Park (p497)

Pennine Way

➡ 268 miles; 14-21 days; www.nationaltrail. co.uk/pennineway

The granddaddy of them all, an epic trek along the mountainous spine of northern England, via some of the highest, wildest countryside in the country. Even in the summer, the elements can be dire, and many walkers find it an endurance test – but not one without rewards.

Dales Way

➡ 85 miles; 6 days; www.dalesway.org.uk

A nonstrenuous walk through the delightful Yorkshire Dales, via some of the most scenic valleys in northern England, ending at Windermere in the Lake District.

South Downs Way

➡ 100 miles; 7-9 days; www.nationaltrail.co.uk/southdowns

A sweeping hike through southeast England, along an ancient chalky highway from Winchester to the sea, mostly following a line of rolling hills, meaning big skies and wonderful views, plus picture-perfect villages and prehistoric sites.

Coast to Coast

➡ 190 miles; 12-14 days; www.wainwright.org. uk/coasttocoast.html

Also known as Wainwright's Coast to Coast (after the man who devised it), this is not a national trail, but it is England's number-one long-distance route for locals and visitors alike – through three national parks via a spectacular mix of valleys, plains, mountains, dales and moors.

Cycling & Mountain Biking

A bike is the perfect mode of transport for exploring back-road England. Once you escape the busy main highways, a vast network of quiet country lanes winds through fields and peaceful villages, ideal for cycle touring. You can cruise through gently rolling landscapes, taking it easy and stopping for cream teas, or you can thrash all day through hilly areas, revelling in steep ascents and swooping downhill sections. You can cycle from place to place, camping or staying in B&Bs (many of which are

stone walls. Parts of the route trace quiet roads, but most of it is on well-maintained cycle paths. It's not completely flat, but there are just a couple of gentle ascents and plenty of places for a pitstop.

www.sustrans.org.uk Details of Britain's national network of cycling trails.

www.forestry.gov.uk/england-cycling Guide to forest cycling trails in England.

Horse Riding

If you want to explore the hills and moors but walking or cycling is too much of a sweat, seeing the wilder parts of England from horseback is highly recommended. In rural areas and national parks such as Dartmoor and Northumberland, riding centres cater to all levels of proficiency, with ponies for kids and beginners, and horses for the more experienced.

British Horse Society (www.bhs.org.uk) Lists approved riding centres offering day rides or longer holidays on horseback.

Surfing at Sennen (p330), Cornwall

cyclist-friendly), or you can base yourself in one area for a few days and go out on rides in different directions. All you need is a map and a sense of adventure.

Mountain bikers can go further into the wilds on the tracks and bridleways that criss-cross Britain's hills and high moors, or head for the many dedicated mountain-bike trail centres where specially built single-track trails wind through the forests. Options at these centres vary from delightful dirt roads ideal for families to gnarly rock gardens and precipitous drop-offs for hard-core riders, all classified from green to black in ski-resort style.

One paradise for mountain bikers is Swaledale – the quietest and least-visited of the Yorkshire Dales – thanks to the many rough tracks that criss-cross the moors and hillsides around the pretty village of Reeth, 12 miles west of Richmond. In spring 2018 the national park tidied up some of the pre-existing trails to create the Swale Trail: a well-signposted, 12-mile cycleway suitable for novices and families. The picturesque route, between Reeth and Keld, follows the River Swale past abandoned settlements, farms and old dry-

Surfing & Windsurfing

England may not seem an obvious destination for surfing, but conditions are surprisingly good and the large tidal range often means a completely different set of breaks at low and high tides. If you've come from the other side of the world, you'll be delighted to learn that summer water temperatures in southern England are roughly equivalent to winter temperatures

---

WALKING WEBSITES

Ramblers (www.ramblers.org.uk) The country's leading organisation for walkers.

Ordnance Survey (www.ordnance survey.co.uk) The UK's official map-making organisation; buy printed paper maps, or download them to your phone.

National Trail (www.nationaltrail. co.uk) Good resource for planning longer routes.

Top: Canoeing on
Windermere Lake,
Ambleside (p567)

Bottom: Narrowboat in
Stratford-upon-Avon
(p403)

ALTERNATIVE ACTIVITIES

If you're looking for something a bit different to the usual hiking and biking, here are a few more esoteric activities you could try:

SUP Stand-up paddle boarding has become a popular sport, and is a great way to explore England's coasts, estuaries and waterways. Contact www.bsupa.org.uk for details of where you can do it.

Rock climbing England has a long history of rock climbing and mountaineering. The main areas include the Lake District, the Peak District and Yorkshire, plus the sea cliffs of Devon and Cornwall. The UK Climbing website (www.ukclimbing.com) has plenty of useful information.

Coasteering A cross between rock climbing, scrambling and diving, usually followed by a plunge into the sea. Often offered by outdoor activity providers in Devon and Cornwall.

Ghyll scrambling Like coasteering, only along river gorges – it's especially popular in Yorkshire and Cumbria.

Wild swimming Most of Britain's lakes and rivers are open to swimmers, although temperatures can be bracing. Contact www.outdoorswimmingsociety.com.

Orienteering This popular pastime involves navigating your way around a preset course using a map and compass, competing either against the clock or other teams. A variant is geocaching (www.geocaching.com), where you use GPS to find hidden boxes - Dartmoor has loads, but you'll find them in other locations, too.

Archery The heyday of the English longbow is long gone, but archery remains a popular sport. Find a club through www.archerygb.org.

---

in southern Australia (ie you'll still need a wetsuit). At the main spots, it's easy enough to hire boards and wetsuits.

Top of the list are the Atlantic-facing coasts of Cornwall and Devon (Newquay is surf central, with all the trappings from Kombi vans to bleached hair), and there are smaller surf scenes elsewhere, notably Norfolk and Yorkshire in eastern England.

Windsurfing is hugely popular all around the coast. Top areas include Norfolk, Suffolk, Devon and Cornwall, and the Isle of Wight.

www.ukwindsurfing.com Good source of info on windsurfing.

www.surfinggb.com Listings of approved surf schools, courses, competitions and more.

Canoeing & Kayaking

Southwest England's coast, with its sheltered inlets and indented shoreline, is ideal for sea kayaking, while inland lakes and canals across the country are great for Canadian canoeing. Although tame by comparison with alpine torrents, the turbulent spate rivers of the Lake District, Northumberland and Devon offer challenging whitewater kayaking.

Equipment rental and instruction are readily available in major centres such as Cornwall, Devon and the Lake District.

www.gocanoeing.org.uk Lists approved canoeing centres in England.

Sailing & Boating

The south coast of England, with its superb scenery and challenging winds and tides, is one of Europe's most popular yachting areas, while the English canals offer a classic narrow-boating experience. Beginners can take a Royal Yachting Association training course in yachting or dinghy sailing at many sailing schools around the coast. Narrow-boaters only need a quick introductory lesson at the start of their trip.

www.rya.org.uk The Royal Yachting Association's website.

www.canalholidays.com For more info on narrow boats and lessons.

Plan Your Trip
Travel with Children

Britain is ideal for travelling with children because of its compact size, packing a lot of attractions into a small area. So when the kids in the back of the car say, 'Are we there yet?' your answer can often be 'Yes, we are'.

Best Regions for Kids

London
Children's attractions galore – some put a strain on parental purse strings, but many others are free.

Southwest England
Some of the best beaches in England, and fairly reliable holiday weather – though crowded in summer.

Peak District
Former railways that are now traffic-free cycle routes make the Peak District perfect for family outings by bike.

Oxford & the Cotswolds
Oxford has kid-friendly museums plus Harry Potter connections; the Cotswold countryside is ideal for little-leg strolls.

Shropshire
The historic England–Wales borderland has many castles to explore, plus excellent museums for inquisitive minds.

Lake District & Cumbria
This is Outdoor Activity Central: zip wires and mountain bikes for teenagers; boat rides and Beatrix Potter for the youngsters.

England for Kids

Many places of interest cater for kids as much as adults. At the country's historic castles, for example, mum and dad can admire the medieval architecture, while the kids will have great fun striding around the battlements or watching falconry demonstrations. In the same way, many national parks and holiday resorts organise specific activities and events for children. Everything ramps up in the school holidays.

Children's Highlights
Best Hands-on Action

'Please Do Not Touch'? No chance! Here are some places where grubby fingers and enquiring minds are positively welcomed.

Science Museum, London (p89) Seven floors of educational exhibits at the mother of all science museums.

Discovery Museum, Newcastle (p600) Tyneside's rich history on display; highlights include a buzzers-and-bells science maze.

National Railway Museum, York (p475) Clambering into the driver's cab on a steam locomotive, exploring a Royal Mail train, taking part in engineering demonstrations...it's all here.

Action Stations!, Portsmouth (www.action stations.org; Portsmouth Historic Dockyard; adult/child £18/13; ⊙10am-5.30pm Apr-Oct, to 5pm Nov-Mar) Toys with a military spin; your chance to fly a helicopter, control an aircraft carrier, or up-periscope in a submarine.

Enginuity, Ironbridge (p421) Endless interactive displays at the birthplace of the Industrial Revolution.

Best Fresh-Air Fun

If the kids tire of England's castles and museums, you're never far from a place for outdoor activities to blow away the cobwebs.

Conkers, Leicestershire (p451) Play indoors, outdoors or among the trees in the heart of the National Forest.

Puzzlewood, Forest of Dean (p208) A wonderful woodland playground with maze-like paths, weird rock formations and eerie passageways to offer a real sense of discovery.

Whinlatter Forest Park, Cumbria (p579) Highlights include a 'Go Ape' adventure park, excellent mountain-bike trails, plus live video feeds from squirrel-cams.

Bewilderwood, Norfolk (p381) Zip wires, jungle bridges, tree houses, marsh walks, boat trips, mazes and all sorts of old-fashioned outdoor adventure.

North York Moors National Park, Yorkshire (p488) Easy, scenic bike trails at Sutton Bank, hard-core mountain biking at Dalby Forest.

Lyme Regis & the Jurassic Coast, Dorset (p268) Guided tours show you how to find your very own prehistoric fossil.

Tissington Trail, Derbyshire (p458) Cycling this former railway is fun and almost effortless. You can hire kids' bikes, tandems and trailers. Don't forget to hoot in the tunnels!

Best Rainy-Day Distractions

On those inevitable gloomy days, head for the indoor attractions, including the nation's great collection of museums. Alternatively, try outdoor stuff like coasteering in Cornwall or canyoning (check conditions) in the Lake District – always fun, wet or dry.

Cadbury World, Birmingham (p392) Your dentist may cry, but kids love the story of chocolate. And yes, there are free samples.

Eden Project, Cornwall (p336) It may be raining outside, but inside these gigantic semispherical greenhouses, it's forever tropical forest or Mediterranean climate.

Cheddar Gorge Caves, Somerset (p242) Finally nail the difference between stalactites and stalagmites in the West Country's deep caverns.

Underground Passages, Exeter (p289) Explore medieval catacombs – the only system of its kind open to the public in England.

National Media Museum, Bradford (p512) Attractions include a TV studio where you can film yourself, a gallery of 1980s video games (yes, you can play them) and an IMAX cinema.

Honister Slate Mine, Lake District (p583) Explore the dingy depths of a former Lakeland slate mine.

Best Stealth Learning

Secretly exercise their minds while the little darlings think they are 'just' having fun.

We the Curious, Bristol (p224) One of the best interactive science museums in England, covering space, technology and the human brain.

Jorvik Viking Centre, York (p476) An excellent smells-and-all Viking settlement reconstruction.

Natural History Museum, London (p85) Animals everywhere! Highlights include the life-size blue whale and the animatronics dinosaurs.

Thinktank, Birmingham (p391) Every display comes with a button or a lever at this edu-taining science museum.

WEBSITES

Baby Goes 2 (www.babygoes2.com) Advice, tips and encouragement – and a stack of adverts – for families on holiday.

Visit England (www.visitengland. com) Official tourism website for England, with lots of useful info for families.

Mumsnet (www.mumsnet.com) No-nonsense advice on travel and more from a gang of UK mothers.

Lonely Planet (www.lonelyplanet. com/family-travel) Inspirational articles about travelling as a family.

Science Museum (p89), London

National Space Centre, Leicester (p446) Spacesuits, zero-gravity toilets and mini-astronaut training – all guaranteed to fire up little minds.

Kielder Observatory, Northumberland National Park (p618) Attend a stargazing session at this Northumbrian astronomy centre.

National Marine Aquarium, Plymouth (p301) Gaze into the shark tank at the UK's biggest aquarium.

Cotswold Farm Park, The Cotswolds (p197) Watch the cows being milked, feed the lambs and ride pedal tractors.

Shepherding Experience, Ilfracombe (☏01271-870056; www.boroughfarm.co.uk; Borough Farm, near Mortehoe; adult/child £10/5; ⊘Thu evening Jun–mid-Sep) Come by! Away! Lie Down! You'll be herding like a pro in no time.

Best Animal Experiences

England has some superb zoos (London, Bristol and Chester are the standouts) but there are more unusual wildlife experiences on offer, too.

London Wetland Centre, London (p103) Break out the binoculars to spy bitterns, black swans, herons and kingfishers.

Longleat, Wiltshire (p277) Pretend you're driving across the savannah at this Wiltshire country estate, surrounded by rhinos, giraffes, elephants and lions.

Tamar Otter Wildlife Centre, Devon (☏01566-785646; www.tamarotters.co.uk; North Petherwin, near Launceston; adult/child £9/5.50; ⊘10.30am-6pm Apr-Oct) Watch semiwild otters frolic.

Whitby Coastal Cruises, Yorkshire (p494) If you're lucky, you'll spot minke, sei and fin whales off the north coast.

Scilly Seal Snorkelling, St Martin's, Isles of Scilly (p346) Don your fins and swim with playful grey seals off the island of St Martin's.

Planning
When to Go

The best time for families to visit England is pretty much the best time for everyone else – any time from April/May till the end of September. It's worth avoiding August – the heart of school summer holidays – when prices go up and the roads are busy, especially near the coast.

Where to Stay

Some hotels welcome kids (with their parents!) and provide cots, toys and babysitting services, while others maintain an adult atmosphere. Many B&Bs offer 'family suites' – two adjoining bedrooms with one bathroom – and an increasing number of hostels (YHA and independent) have family rooms with four or six beds, some even with private bathroom attached. If you want to stay in one place for a while, renting a holiday cottage is ideal. Camping is very popular with English families, and there are lots of fantastic campsites, but you'll usually need all your own equipment.

Regions at a Glance

London

History
Entertainment
Culture

Historic Streets

London's ancient streets contain many of Britain's most famous and history-steeped landmarks. The echoes of the footfalls of monarchs, poets, whores and saints can still be detected in places such as the Tower of London, Westminster Abbey and St Paul's Cathedral, as well as the pubs and coaching inns that once served Dickens, Shelley, Keats and Byron.

Music, Theatre & Sport

From West End theatres to East End clubs, from Camden's rock venues to Covent Garden's opera house, from tennis at Wimbledon to cricket at Lord's or football at Wembley, London's world-famous venues and arenas offer a perpetual clamour of entertainment.

Museums

While the British Museum is the big crowd-puller, the capital has museums and galleries of every shape and size – including the V&A, Tate Modern and the National Portrait Gallery. Many are free.

p54

Canterbury & Southeast England

Cathedral
History
Food & Drink

Canterbury Cathedral

A major reason to visit southeast England, Canterbury Cathedral is one of the finest in Europe, and one of the most holy places in Christendom. Write your own Canterbury tale as you explore its atmospheric chapels, cloisters and crypts.

Invasion Heritage

The southeast has always been a gateway for arrivals from the Continent, some more welcome than others. Castles and fortresses, the 1066 battlefield and Dover's secret wartime tunnels all tell the region's story of invasion and defence.

The South Coast

Long a favourite spot for English seaside holidays, England's south-coast towns have a faded, genteel grandeur that's all their own. Explore Brighton's eccentric shops, wander Rye's cobbled lanes, visit Margate's new art gallery or feast on Whitstable oysters.

p139

Oxford & the Cotswolds

Architecture
Stately Homes
Villages

University Colleges

Oxford's architecture will never leave you indifferent, whether you gaze across the 'dreaming spires' from the top of Carfax Tower, or explore the medieval streets on foot, or simply admire the fantastic gargoyles on college facades.

Blenheim Palace

Favoured by the rich and powerful for centuries, this region is scattered with some of the finest country houses in England. Top of the pile is the baroque masterpiece of Blenheim Palace, birthplace of Sir Winston Churchill.

Cotswold Villages

Littered with picturesque 'chocolate box' scenes of honey-coloured stone cottages, thatched roofs, neat greens and cobbled lanes, the villages of the Cotswolds provide a charming snapshot of rural England.

p173

Bath & Southwest England

Coastline
History
Activities

Beaches

England's southwest peninsula juts determinedly into the Atlantic, fringed by an almost endless chain of sandy beaches, from the picturesque scenery of Kynance Cove to the rolling surf of Newquay.

Historic Buildings

From Bath's Georgian terraces to grand stately homes, such as Longleat, Tyntesfield and Stourhead, and the medieval castles of St Mawes, Dartmouth and Powderham, the southwest has a fascinating architectural history.

Hiking & Surfing

If you like to take it nice and easy, come to walk the moors or tootle along cycle trails. If you prefer life fast and furious, come to surf the best waves in England or learn to dive or kitesurf.

p217

Cambridge & East Anglia

Architecture
Coastline
Waterways

Historic Churches

From the magnificent cathedrals of Ely, Norwich and Peterborough to Cambridge's King's College Chapel, Trinity's Great Court and the New Court at St John's, East Anglia's architectural splendour is second to none.

Seaside Resorts

With wide sandy beaches, great seafood, delightful old pubs, globally important bird reserves, historic villages still proud of their nautical heritage, and classic seaside resorts including Southwold and Cromer, the coastline of East Anglia is rich and varied.

The Broads

The Norfolk and Suffolk Broads are a tranquil haven of lakes and meandering rivers, and an ideal spot for boating, birdwatching, canoeing, cycling or walking, or just getting back to nature at a leisurely pace.

p348

Birmingham & the Midlands

Activities
Stately Homes
Food & Drink

Hiking & Biking

The Peak District National Park, Cannock Chase, the Shropshire Hills, the Roaches, the Malvern Hills, Offa's Dyke Path, the Tissington Trail and the Pennine Cycleway all make this region great for hiking and biking.

Chatsworth

Grand houses including Haddon Hall, Burghley House and especially Chatsworth – the magnificent home of the Duke and Duchess of Devonshire – promise sprawling landscaped gardens adorned with classical sculptures, grand interiors full of priceless heirlooms and walls dripping with oil paintings.

Curry Capital

Foodies take note: Birmingham is the curry capital of the country (and, increasingly, a magnet for Michelin-starred chefs), while the tiny town of Ludlow is an epicentre of gastronomic exploration.

p387

Yorkshire

Activities
Food & Drink
History

Outdoor Pastimes

With rolling hills, scenic valleys, high moors and a cliff-lined coast, all protected by two of England's best-loved national parks, Yorkshire is a natural adventure playground for hiking, biking, surfing and rock climbing.

Roast Beef & Real Ale

Rich farmland and lush pasture means Yorkshire beef and lamb are much sought-after, while the famous Theakston's and Black Sheep breweries of Masham turn out excellent real ales, best sampled in one of Yorkshire's equally excellent traditional pubs.

Ancient Abbeys

From York's Roman and Viking heritage and the medieval abbeys of Rievaulx, Fountains and Whitby to the industrial archaeology of Leeds, Bradford and Sheffield, Yorkshire allows you to explore several of Britain's most important historical narratives.

p469

Manchester, Liverpool & Northwest England

History
Sport
Seaside Resorts

Museums

The northwest's collection of heritage sites, from the wonderful People's History Museum in Manchester to the International Slavery Museum in Liverpool, is testament to the region's rich history and its ability to keep it alive.

Football

Two cities, Liverpool and Manchester, give the world four famous clubs, including the two most successful in English history. The National Football Museum in Manchester is just another reason for football fans to visit this region.

Seaside Towns

The epitome of the classic English seaside resort just keeps on going, thanks to the rides of the Blackpool Pleasure Beach amusement park, where adrenalin junkies can always find a fix.

p523

The Lake District & Cumbria

Scenery
Activities
Literature

Lakes & Fells

The Lake District National Park is the most mountainous part of England, home to humpbacked hills (known locally as fells) and countless scenic lakes. Some are big and famous – Windermere, Coniston, Ullswater – while others are small, hidden and little known.

Hiking

If anywhere is the heart and soul of walking in England, it's the Lake District. Casual strollers find gentle routes through foothills and valleys, while serious hikers hit the high fells – including Helvellyn, Skiddaw, Blencathra and England's highest mountain, Scafell Pike.

Romantic Writers

The beauty of the Lake District famously moved William Wordsworth to write his ode to 'a host of golden daffodils', and visiting Wordsworth landmarks such as Dove Cottage, Rydal Mount and his childhood home in Cockermouth is one of the region's big draws.

p558

Newcastle & Northeast England

History
Landscapes
Castles

Hadrian's Wall

One of the greatest feats of Roman engineering, this potent symbol of imperial power strides for over 70 miles across the neck of England, from Tyneside to the Solway Firth. You can travel its length, stopping off at forts along the way.

Northumberland National Park

If it's widescreen vistas you're after, the broad moors, stone villages and expansive views of England's most northerly national park never fail to please. As well as landscapes there are starscapes to be enjoyed, in the heart of England's biggest dark-sky park.

Alnwick Castle

Northumberland is dotted with some of Britain's finest castles, including the coastal fortresses of Bamburgh and Dunstanburgh, but Alnwick – setting for the Harry Potter movies – is the most famous.

p596

On the Road

London

📍020 / POP 8.65 MILLION

Best Places to Eat

➡ Hook Camden Town (p117)

➡ Glasshouse (p119)

➡ Ottolenghi (p117)

➡ Ledbury (p119)

➡ Five Fields (p115)

➡ Dinner by Heston Blumenthal (p115)

Best Places to Stay

➡ Qbic (p110)

➡ citizenM Tower of London (p109)

➡ Hoxton Hotel (p110)

➡ Main House (p111)

➡ Hazlitt's (p108)

➡ 40 Winks (p110)

Why Go?

One of the world's most visited cities, London has something for everyone: history, culture, fine food and endless good times. Immersed in history, London's rich seams of eye-opening antiquity are everywhere, with landmarks like the Tower of London, Westminster Abbey and Big Ben. Then there are modern icons like the Shard and the Tate Modern. But London is also a city of ideas and the imagination – whether it's theatrical innovation, contemporary art, music, writing, cutting-edge design or culinary adventure. Throw in charming parks, historic neighbourhoods, leafy suburbs and tranquil riverbanks and you have, quite simply, one of the world's great metropolises.

When to Go

➡ London is a place that you can visit any time of the year. That said, different months and seasons boast different charms.

➡ Spring in the city sees daffodils in bloom and blossom in the trees.

➡ In June, the parks are filled with people, there's Trooping the Colour, summer arts festivals, Field Day in Brockwell Park, other music events, gay pride and Wimbledon.

➡ Although the days are getting shorter, autumn in London is alive with festivals celebrating literature, the arts and culture.

➡ London in December is all about Christmas lights on Oxford and Regent Sts, and perhaps a whisper of snow.

History

London first came into being as a Celtic village near a ford across the River Thames, but the city only really took off after the Roman conquest in AD 43. The invaders enclosed their 'Londinium' in walls that still find refrain in the shape of the City (with a capital 'C') of London today.

By the end of the 3rd century AD, Londinium was home to some 30,000 people. Internal strife and relentless barbarian attacks wore the Romans down, however, and they abandoned Britain in the 5th century, reducing the settlement to a sparsely populated backwater. The Saxons moved in next, their 'Lundenwic' prospering and becoming a large, well-organised town.

As the city grew in importance, it caught the eye of Danish Vikings who launched numerous invasions. In 1016 the Saxons, finally beaten down, were forced to accept the Danish leader Knut (Canute) as King of England, after which London replaced Winchester as capital. In 1042, the throne reverted to the Saxon Edward the Confessor, who built Westminster Abbey.

The Norman Conquest of 1066 saw William the Conqueror march into London, where he was crowned king. He built the White Tower (the core of the Tower of London), negotiated taxes with the merchants, and affirmed the city's right to self-government. From then until the late 15th century, London politics were largely taken up by a three-way power struggle between the monarchy, the Church and city guilds.

An uneasy political compromise was reached between the factions, and the city expanded rapidly in the 16th century under the House of Tudor. In a rerun of the disease that wiped out half of London's population between 1348 and 1350, the Great Plague struck in 1665, and by the time the winter cold arrested the epidemic, 100,000 Londoners had perished.

The cataclysm was followed by further devastation when the Great Fire of 1666 sent the city skywards. One upshot of the conflagration was a blank canvas for master architect Sir Christopher Wren to build his magnificent churches. Despite these setbacks, London continued to grow, and by 1700 it was Europe's largest city, with 600,000 people. An influx of foreign workers brought expansion to the east and south, while those who could afford it headed to the more salubrious environs of the north and west.

Georgian London saw a surge in artistic creativity, with the likes of Dr Johnson, Handel, Gainsborough and Reynolds enriching the city's culture, while architects fashioned an elegant new metropolis. In 1837, 18-year-old Victoria began her epic reign, as London became the fulcrum of the British Empire. The Industrial Revolution saw the building of new docks and railways (including the first underground line in 1863), while the Great Exhibition of 1851 showcased London to the world. During the Victorian era, the city's population mushroomed from just over two million to 6.6 million.

Although London suffered a relatively minor bruising during WWI, it was devastated by the Luftwaffe in WWII, when huge swaths of the centre and East End were flattened and 32,000 people were killed. Ugly housing and low-cost developments followed, but prosperity gradually returned to the city. In the 'Swinging Sixties', London became the capital of cool in fashion and music – a party followed morosely by the austere 1970s.

Since then the city has surfed up and down the waves of global fortunes, hanging on to its position as the world's leading financial centre. In 2000, the modern metropolis won its first mayor of London, an elected role covering the City and all 32 urban boroughs. Boris Johnson was elected in 2008, and retained his post in the 2012 mayoral election. In August 2011, numerous London boroughs were rocked by riots characterised by looting and arson, triggered by the controversial shooting of a man by police in Tottenham.

Both the Olympics and the Queen's Diamond Jubilee concocted a splendid display of pageantry for London in 2012. New overground train lines opened, a cable car was flung across the Thames and a once rundown and polluted area of East London was regenerated for the Olympic Park.

Since the Olympics, the city has changed leadership, with Labour politician Sadiq Khan taking over as mayor from Boris Johnson. Scores of new high-rise buildings have transformed the London skyline. Another key development has been the Crossrail, the capital's largest and costliest construction project, which has added a new east–west train line that promises to ease congestion for commuters. In addition, the Underground's new 24-hour schedule at weekends has been warmly welcomed – but quite what effect Brexit will have on this great city's future remains to be seen.

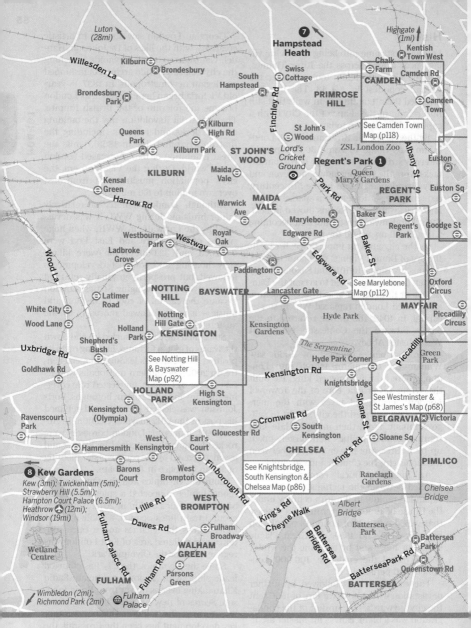

London Highlights

1 Regent's Park (p95)
Watching the world pass by in one of London's loveliest parks.

2 British Museum (p63)
Marvelling at the epoch-spanning collections of the nation's flagship museum.

3 Shakespeare's Globe (p82) Seeing one of the Bard's plays in the theatre for which they were written.

4 Tower of London (p77)
Viewing the dazzling Crown Jewels in this thousand year-old fortress.

5 St Paul's Cathedral (p75)

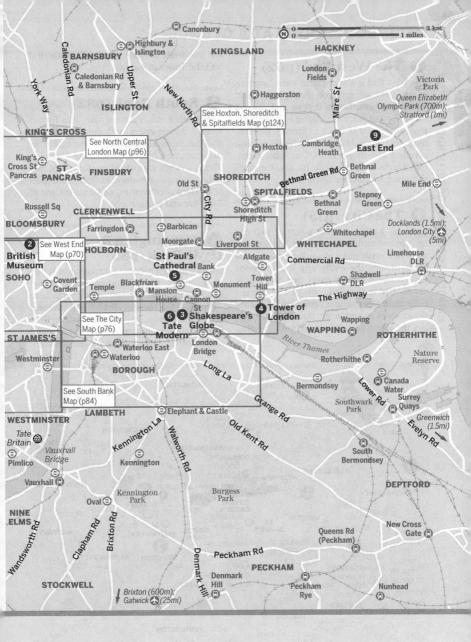

Reaching for the heavens at the top of the dome.

6 Tate Modern (p82) Exploring London's most adventurous and innovative art museum.

7 Hampstead Heath (p97) Wandering the paths and woodlands of North London's loveliest green space.

8 Kew Gardens (p102) Stepping into a miniature rainforest inside the subtropical Palm House.

9 East End (p93) Bar-hopping, artwork-spotting and shopping in the capital's coolest neighbourhoods.

NEIGHBOURHOODS AT A GLANCE

❶ The West End (p62)

The West End is a vague term – any Londoner you meet will give you their own take on which neighbourhoods it does and doesn't include – but what is striking is its variety: from reverentially quiet in literary Bloomsbury and legal Holborn, to bustling with revellers and shoppers 24/7 in Soho, Piccadilly Circus and Oxford St. It's also the city's shopping and theatre district.

❷ The City (p75)

London's historic core is a tale of two cities: packed with office workers during the week and eerily quiet at weekends. For most of its history, the entire city was enclosed here between sturdy walls that were only dismantled in the 18th century. The current millennium has seen a profusion of daring skyscrapers sprout from the City's fringes, but the essential sights have been standing for hundreds of years: St Paul's Cathedral and the Tower of London.

❸ South Bank (p82)

The South Bank is a must-visit area for art lovers, theatre-goers and culture hounds, and has been significantly re-energised by the renowned Tate Modern. Come for iconic Thames views, great food markets, first-rate pubs, dollops of history, striking examples of modern architecture, and a sprinkling of fine bars and restaurants.

❹ Kensington & Hyde Park (p85)

Splendidly well groomed, Kensington is one of London's most handsome neighbourhoods. You'll find three fine museums here – the V&A, the Natural History Museum and the Science Museum – as well as excellent dining and shopping, graceful parklands and elegant streets of grand period architecture.

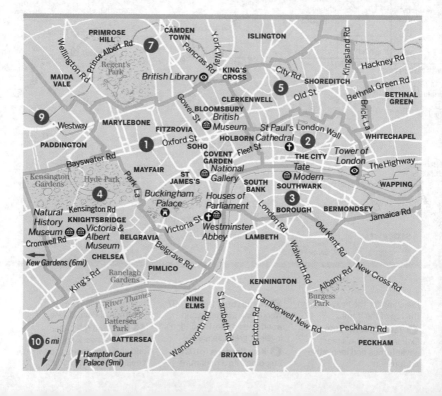

❺ Clerkenwell, Shoreditch & Spitalfields (p93)

These historic city-fringe neighbourhoods contain a few significant sights, mainly around Clerkenwell and Spitalfields, but the area is best known for its nightlife. Shoreditch and Hoxton long ago replaced Soho and Camden as the hippest, most alternative parts of London, and although some of the action has now moved further east, they're still holding their own.

❻ East London (p93)

Anyone with an interest in multicultural London needs to visit the East End. There's standout ethnic cuisine, some interesting museums and galleries, excellent pubs, canal-side eating and drinking, some of London's hippest neighbourhoods, and the vast redeveloped expanse of Queen Elizabeth Olympic Park to explore.

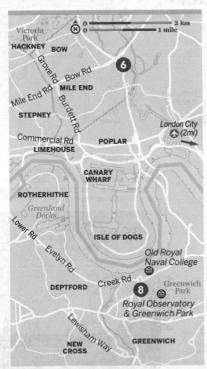

❼ North London (p95)

North London is framed by Camden's famous eponymous market, its unrivalled music scene and excellent pubs. The dynamic area of King's Cross is experiencing a transformation, and is now a destination in its own right and a great place to hang out. There's plenty here for quiet enjoyment, too – from the gorgeous green spaces of Hampstead Heath and Regent's Park to overgrown Victorian cemeteries, such as Highgate and Abbeywood, and canal walks.

❽ Greenwich & South London (p98)

Regal riverside Greenwich complements its village feel with some grand architecture, grassy parkland and riverside pubs. Brixton has the creative edge in its glorious food-and-shop Village, Clapham and Battersea are full of hidden gems, while Dulwich Village is all tranquil, leafy charm.

❾ West London (p102)

Portobello Market, the Design Museum, historic cinemas, niche collections, canal-side charms, superb pubs and clubs, swish parkland and grand mansions, imposing churches, intriguing Victorian bone-yards, diverse shopping and ethnic eats all make Notting Hill and West London an eclectic must-see.

❿ Richmond, Kew & Hampton Court (p102)

To flee London's concrete urban interior and get a look at the city's leafy, riverside complexion – where the crowds thin out, the air is cleaner and the landscapes become increasingly pastoral – make a beeline to Richmond, Kew and Hampton Court. Wander by the river, explore haunted Tudor palaces (Hampton Court), get lost in beautiful Kew Gardens, go deer-spotting in Richmond Park, traipse around Wimbledon Common and down a pint waterside as the sun shimmers on the Thames at sunset.

The River Thames

A FLOATING TOUR

London's history has always been determined by the Thames. The city was founded as a Roman port nearly 2000 years ago and over the centuries since then many of the capital's landmarks have lined the river's banks. A boat trip is a great way to experience the attractions.

There are piers dotted along both banks at regular intervals where you can hop on and hop off the regular services to visit places of interest. The best place to board is Westminster Pier, from where boats head downstream, taking you from the City of Westminster, the seat of government, to the original City of London, now the financial district and dominated by a growing band of skyscrapers. Across the river, the once shabby and neglected South Bank now bristles with as many top attractions as its northern counterpart, including the slender Shard.

In our illustration we've concentrated on the top highlights you'll enjoy from a waterborne

KIEV.VICTOR / SHUTTERSTOCK ©

St Paul's Cathedral
Though there's been a church here since AD 604, the current building rose from the ashes of the 1666 Great Fire and is architect Christopher Wren's masterpiece. Famous for surviving the Blitz intact and for the wedding of Charles and Diana, it's looking as good as new after a major clean-up for its 300th anniversary in 2011.

Blackfriars

Somerset House
This grand neoclassical palace was once one of many aristocratic houses lining the Thames. The huge arches at river level gave direct access to the Thames until the Embankment was built in the 1860s.

3 Temple

Charing Cross

Blackfriars Pier
Blackfriars Bridge

Waterloo Bridge

Victoria Embankment Gardens

National Theatre

Embankment   **Embankment Pier**

OXO Tower

Queen Elizabeth Hall
Southbank Centre

London Eye
Built in 2000 and originally temporary, the Eye instantly became a much-loved landmark. The 30-minute spin takes you 135m above the city from where the views are unsurprisingly amazing.

2

Houses of Parliament
Rebuilt in neo-Gothic style after the old Palace of Westminster burned down in 1834, the most famous part of the British parliament is the clocktower. Generally known as Big Ben, it's named after Benjamin Hall who oversaw its construction.

Westminster Pier

Waterloo Millennium Pier

Westminster

Westminster Bridge

1

VERDOONE / BUDGET TRAVEL ©

vessel. These are, from west to east, the **①Houses of Parliament**, the **②London Eye**, **③Somerset House**, **④St Paul's Cathedral**, the **⑤Tate Modern**, **⑥Shakespeare's Globe**, the **⑦Tower of London** and **⑧Tower Bridge**.

In addition to covering this central section of the Thames, boats can also be taken upstream as far as Kew Gardens and Hampton Court Palace, and downstream as far as Greenwich and the Thames Barrier.

BOAT HOPPING

Thames Clippers hop-on/hop-off services are aimed at commuters but are equally useful for visitors, operating every 15 minutes on a loop from piers at Westminster, Embankment, Waterloo, Blackfriars, Bankside, London Bridge and the Tower. Oyster cardholders get a discount off the boat ticket price.

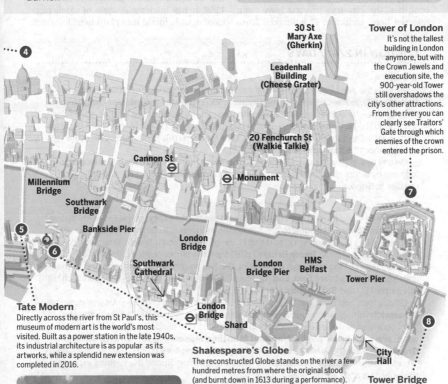

30 St Mary Axe (Gherkin)

Leadenhall Building (Cheese Grater)

20 Fenchurch St (Walkie Talkie)

Cannon St

Monument

Millennium Bridge

Southwark Bridge

Bankside Pier

London Bridge

Southwark Cathedral

London Bridge Pier

HMS Belfast

Tower Pier

London Bridge

Shard

City Hall

Tower of London
It's not the tallest building in London anymore, but with the Crown Jewels and execution site, the 900-year-old Tower still overshadows the city's other attractions. From the river you can clearly see Traitors' Gate through which enemies of the crown entered the prison.

Tate Modern
Directly across the river from St Paul's, this museum of modern art is the world's most visited. Built as a power station in the late 1940s, its industrial architecture is as popular as its artworks, while a splendid new extension was completed in 2016.

Shakespeare's Globe
The reconstructed Globe stands on the river a few hundred metres from where the original stood (and burnt down in 1613 during a performance). The life's work of American actor Sam Wanamaker, the theatre runs a hugely popular season from April to October each year.

Tower Bridge
It might look as old as its namesake neighbour but one of the world's most iconic bridges was only completed in 1894. Not to be confused with London Bridge upstream, this one's famous raising bascules allowed tall ships to dock at the old wharves to the west and are still lifted up to 1000 times a year.

◉ Sights

◉ The West End

★ Westminster Abbey CHURCH

(Map p68; 020-7222 5152; www.westminster
-abbey.org; 20 Dean's Yard, SW1; adult/child £22/9,
cloister & gardens free; ⊙ 9.30am-3.30pm Mon,
Tue, Thu & Fri, to 6pm Wed, to 1.30pm Sat; ⊖ Westminster) A splendid mixture of architectural
styles, Westminster Abbey is considered
the finest example of Early English Gothic
(1190–1300). It's not merely a beautiful place
of worship – the Abbey also serves up the
country's history cold on slabs of stone. For
centuries, the country's greatest have been
interred here, including 17 monarchs from
Henry III (died 1272) to George II (1760).
Never a cathedral (the seat of a bishop),
Westminster Abbey is what is called a 'royal
peculiar', administered by the Crown.

Every monarch since William the Conqueror has been crowned here, with the exception of a couple of unlucky Eds who were
either murdered (Edward V) or abdicated
(Edward VIII) before the magic moment.

At the heart of the Abbey is the beautifully tiled sanctuary (sacrarium), a stage for
coronations, royal weddings and funerals.
George Gilbert Scott designed the ornate
high altar in 1873. In front of the altar is
the Cosmati marble pavement dating to
1268. It has intricate designs of small pieces of marble inlaid into plain marble, which

---

LONDON IN 2/4/7 DAYS

2 Days

Begin with the West End's big-draw sights: **Westminster Abbey**, then **Buckingham Palace** (p67) for the Changing of the Guard. Walk up the Mall to **Trafalgar Square** (p66) for its architectural grandeur and photo-op views of Big Ben down Whitehall, then take a spin round the **National Gallery** (p66). In the afternoon, hop over to the South Bank for a ride on the London Eye and a visit to the **Tate Modern** (p82), followed by an evening performance at **Shakespeare's Globe** (p82).

On day two, spend the day wandering around the marvellous **British Museum** (p63), followed by a spot of shopping around **Covent Garden** and **Oxford St**, and a night on the tiles in **Soho**.

4 Days

On day three, head for London's finance-driven heart in the **City**, home to the sprawling and ancient **Tower of London** (p77). Spend the morning watching the Beefeaters and resident ravens preen and strut, and then marvel at the Crown Jewels. When you're fin-ished, admire the iconic **Tower Bridge** (p78) from the banks of the Thames or through the glass floors of the walkways connecting the two towers. While away the rest of the day exploring the vibrant **East End**, with visits to **Brick Lane** (Map p124; ⊖ Shoreditch High St, Liverpool St) and **Spitalfields Market** (p133).

On day four, hop on a boat from any central London pier and make your way down to **Greenwich** with its world-renowned architecture and links to time, the stars and space. Start your visit at the legendary **Cutty Sark** (p98), a star clipper during the tea-trade years, and have a look into the **National Maritime Museum** (p98). Stroll up through **Greenwich Park** (p99) all the way to the **Royal Observatory** (p99). The views of Canary Wharf, the business district across the river, are stunning. Spend the evening exploring the local bars and bistros.

7 Days

With a few extra days, you'll have time to explore some of London's other neighbour-hoods. On day five, head for **North London**, with a morning at **Camden Market** (p133), a visit to **Highgate Cemetery** (p96) and a walk over **Hampstead Heath** (p97). On day six, explore the famous **Portobello Road Market** (p102) in **Notting Hill**, then spend the rest of the day with chic shopping in **Knightsbridge**, or visiting the museums of **South Kensington**, such as the **Natural History Museum** (p85) and the **Science Museum** (p89). On day seven, head out to **West London**, where you'll discover the delightful green spaces of **Kew Gardens** (p102) and **Richmond Park** (p103), and the grand palace of **Hampton Court** (p103).

predict the end of the world (in AD 19,693!). At the entrance to the lovely Chapel of St John the Baptist is a sublime alabaster Virgin and Child bathed in candlelight.

The most sacred spot in the Abbey, the shrine of St Edward the Confessor, lies behind the main altar; access is restricted to several prayer meetings daily to protect the 13th-century flooring. St Edward was the founder of the Abbey and the original building was consecrated a few weeks before his death. His tomb was slightly altered after the original was destroyed during the Reformation but still contains Edward's remains – the only complete saint's body in Britain. Ninety-minute verger-led tours (£5 plus admission) of the Abbey include a visit to the shrine.

The quire (choir), a space of gold, blue and red Victorian Gothic by Edward Blore, dates back to the mid-19th century. It sits where the original choir for the monks' worship would have been but bears little resemblance to the original. Nowadays, the quire is still used for singing, but its regular occupants are the Westminster Choir – 22 boys and 12 'lay vicars' (men) who sing the daily services and evensong (5pm weekdays, 3pm weekends).

Henry III began work on the new building in 1245 but didn't complete it; the Gothic nave was finished under Richard II in 1388. Henry VII's magnificent Perpendicular Gothic-style Lady Chapel was consecrated in 1519 after 16 years of construction.

At the west end of the nave near the Tomb of the Unknown Warrior, killed in WWI in northern France and laid to rest here in 1920, is St George's Chapel, which contains the rather ordinary-looking Coronation Chair, upon which every monarch since the early 14th century has been crowned (apart from joint-monarchs Mary II and William III, who had their own chairs fashioned for the event).

Apart from the royal graves, keep an eye out for the many famous commoners interred here, especially in Poets' Corner, where you'll find the resting places of Chaucer, Dickens, Hardy, Tennyson, Dr Johnson and Kipling, as well as memorials to the other greats (Shakespeare, Jane Austen, the Brontës etc). Nearby you'll find the graves of Handel and Sir Isaac Newton.

The octagonal Chapter House dates from the 1250s and was where the monks would meet for daily prayer and their job as-signments before Henry VIII's suppression of the monasteries some three centuries later. To the right of the entrance to Chapter House is what is claimed to be the oldest door in Britain – it's been there since the 1050s. Used as a treasury and 'Royal Wardrobe', the cryptlike Pyx Chamber dates from about 1070, though the Altar of St Dunstan within it is even older.

Parts of the Abbey complex are free to visitors. This includes the Cloister and the 900-year-old College Garden (Map p68; ⊘10am-6pm Tue-Thu Apr-Sep, to 4pm Oct-Mar). Adjacent to the abbey is St Margaret's Church (Map p68; ☑020-7654 4840; www.westminster-abbey. org/st-margarets-church; ⊘9.30am-3.30pm Mon-Fri, to 1.30pm Sat, 2-4.30pm Sun), the House of Commons' place of worship since 1614, where windows commemorate churchgoers Caxton and Milton, and Sir Walter Raleigh is buried by the altar.

Completed in 2018, the Queen's Diamond Jubilee Galleries are a new museum and gallery space located in the medieval triforium, the arched gallery above the nave. Among its exhibits are the death masks of generations of royalty, wax effigies representing Charles II and William III (who is on a stool to make him as tall as his wife, Mary II), armour and stained glass. Highlights are the graffiti-inscribed Mary Chair (used for the coronation of Mary II) and the Westminster Retable, England's oldest altarpiece, from the 13th century.

★ British Museum   MUSEUM
(Map p70; ☑020-7323 8299; www.britishmuseum. org; Great Russell St & Montague Pl, WC1; ⊘10am-5.30pm Sat-Thu, to 8.30pm Fri; ⊜Russell Sq, Tottenham Court Rd) FREE The country's largest museum and one of the oldest and finest in the world, this famous museum boasts vast Egyptian, Etruscan, Greek, Roman, European and Middle Eastern galleries, among others. It is frequently London's most-visited attraction, drawing 6.5 million visitors annually.

Don't miss the Rosetta Stone, the key to deciphering Egyptian hieroglyphics, discovered in 1799; the controversial Parthenon Sculptures, taken from the Parthenon in Athens by Lord Elgin (then the British ambassador to the Ottoman Empire); and the large collection of Egyptian mummies.

Other must-see items include the Anglo-Saxon Sutton Hoo burial relics and the Winged Bulls from Khorsabad.

The British Museum

A HALF-DAY TOUR

The British Museum, with almost eight million items in its permanent collection, is so vast and comprehensive that it can be daunting for the first-time visitor. To avoid a frustrating trip – and getting lost on the way to the Egyptian mummies – set out on this half-day exploration, which takes in some of the museum's most important sights. If you want to see and learn more, join a tour or grab an audioguide (£7).

A good starting point is the ❶ **Rosetta Stone**, the key that cracked the code to ancient Egypt's writing system. Nearby treasures from Assyria – an ancient civilisation centred in Mesopotamia between the Tigris and Euphrates Rivers – including the colossal ❷ **Winged Bulls from Khorsabad**, give way to the ❸ **Parthenon Sculptures**, highpoints of classical Greek art that continue to influence us today. Be sure to see both the sculptures and the monumental frieze celebrating the

Winged Bulls from Khorsabad
This awesome pair of alabaster winged bulls with human heads once guarded the entrance to the palace of Assyrian King Sargon II at Khorsabad in Mesopotamia, a cradle of civilisation in present-day Iraq.

Parthenon Sculptures
The Parthenon, a white marble temple dedicated to Athena, was part of a fortified citadel on the Acropolis in Athens. There are dozens of sculptures and friezes with models and interactive displays explaining how they all once fitted together.

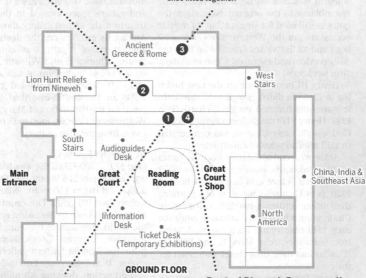

Ancient Greece & Rome ❸

West Stairs

Lion Hunt Reliefs from Nineveh ❷

South Stairs

Audioguides Desk

Main Entrance

Great Court

Reading Room

Great Court Shop

China, India & Southeast Asia

❶ ❹

Information Desk

North America

Ticket Desk (Temporary Exhibitions)

GROUND FLOOR

Rosetta Stone
Written in hieroglyphic, demotic (cursive ancient Egyptian script used for everyday use) and Greek, the 762kg stone contains a decree exempting priests from tax on the first anniversary of young Ptolemy V's coronation.

Bust of Pharaoh Ramesses II
The most impressive sculpture in the Egyptian galleries, this 725kg bust portrays Ramesses the Great, scourge of the Israelites in the Book of Exodus, as great benefactor.

birth of Athena. En route to the West Stairs is a huge **④ Bust of Pharaoh Ramesses II**, just a hint of the large collection of **⑤ Egyptian mummies** upstairs. (The earliest, affectionately called Ginger because of wispy reddish hair, was preserved simply by hot sand.) The Romans introduce visitors to the early Britain galleries via the rich **⑥ Mildenhall Treasure**. The Anglo-Saxon **⑦ Sutton Hoo Ship Burial** and the medieval **⑧ Lewis Chessmen** follow.

EATING OPTIONS

Court Cafe At the northern end of the Great Court; takeaway counters with salads and sandwiches; communal tables.

Gallery Cafe Slightly out of the way off Room 12; quieter; offers hot dishes.

Great Court Restaurant Upstairs overlooking the former Reading Room; sit-down meals.

Lewis Chessmen
The much-loved 78 chess pieces portray faceless pawns, worried-looking queens, bishops with their mitres turned sideways and rooks (or castles) as 'warders', gnawing away at their shields.

ILEANA_BT / SHUTTERSTOCK ©

Egyptian Mummies
Among the rich collection of mummies and funerary objects is 'Ginger', who was buried at the site of Gebelein, in Upper Egypt, almost 5500 years ago, and Katebet, a one-time chantress (ritual performer) at the Amun temple in Karnak.

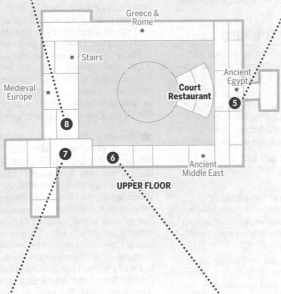

Greece & Rome

Stairs

Medieval Europe

Ancient Egypt

Court Restaurant

⑤

⑧

⑦ **⑥**

Ancient Middle East

UPPER FLOOR

Sutton Hoo Ship Burial
This unique grave of an important (but unidentified) Anglo-Saxon royal has yielded drinking horns, gold buckles and a stunning helmet with face mask.

Mildenhall Treasure
Roman gods such as Neptune and Bacchus share space with early Christian symbols like the *chi-rho* (short for 'Christ') on the find's almost three dozen silver bowls, plates and spoons.

Begun in 1753 with a 'cabinet of curiosities' sold to the nation by royal physician Sir Hans Sloane, the collection mushroomed over the ensuing years partly through acquisitions, bequests and plundering the empire. The grand Enlightenment Gallery was the first section of the redesigned museum to be built in 1823.

The Great Court, restored and augmented by Norman Foster in 2000, has a spectacular glass-and-steel roof, making it one of the most impressive architectural spaces in the capital. In the centre is the Reading Room, with its stunning blue-and-gold domed ceiling made of papier mâché, where Karl Marx researched and wrote *Das Kapital,* and Mahatma Gandhi was a cardholder.

The British Museum's extension, the £135 million World Conservation and Exhibitions Centre in its northwestern corner, opened in 2014, in the same year as the Sainsbury Exhibitions Gallery, which hosts high-profile exhibitions.

The museum is huge, so make a few focused visits if you have time, and consider taking one of the free tours. There are up to 15 free 30- to 40-minute Eye-opener tours of individual galleries each day. The museum also has free 45-minute lunchtime gallery talks (1.15pm Tuesday to Friday), a

1½-hour highlights tour (£14; 11.30am and 2pm Friday, Saturday and Sunday) and free 20-minute spotlight tours on Friday evenings. Audio and family guides (adult/child £7/6) in 10 languages are available from the audio-guide desk in the Great Court.

★ Trafalgar Square   SQUARE
(Map p70; ⊜ Charing Cross) Trafalgar Sq is the true centre of London, where rallies and marches take place, tens of thousands of revellers usher in the New Year and locals congregate for anything from communal open-air cinema and Christmas celebrations to political protests. It is dominated by the 52m-high Nelson's Column and ringed by many splendid buildings, including the National Gallery (p66) and the church of St Martin-in-the-Fields (Map p70; ☑ 020-7766 1100; www.stmartin-in-the-fields.org; ⊗ 8.30am-1pm & 2-6pm Mon, Tue, Thu & Fri, 8.30am-1pm & 2-5pm Wed, 9.30am-6pm Sat, 3.30-5pm Sun).

★ National Gallery   GALLERY
(Map p70; ☑ 020-7747 2885; www.nationalgallery.org.uk; Trafalgar Sq, WC2; ⊗ 10am-6pm Sat-Thu, to 9pm Fri; ⊜ Charing Cross) FREE With some 2300 European masterpieces on display, this is one of the world's great art collections, with seminal works from every important period in the history of art – from the mid-13th to the early 20th century, including masterpieces by Leonardo da Vinci, Michelangelo, Titian, Van Gogh and Renoir.

Many visitors flock to the East Wing (1700–1900), where works by 18th-century British artists such as Gainsborough, Constable and Turner, and seminal Impressionist and post-Impressionist masterpieces by Van Gogh, Renoir and Monet await.

★ Houses of Parliament   HISTORIC BUILDING
(Palace of Westminster; Map p68; www.parliament.uk; Parliament Sq, SW1; ⊜ Westminster) FREE A visit here is a journey to the heart of UK democracy. Officially called the Palace of Westminster, the Houses of Parliament's oldest part is 11th-century Westminster Hall, one of only a few sections that survived a catastrophic fire in 1834. Its roof, added between 1394 and 1401, is the earliest known example of a hammerbeam roof. The rest is mostly a neo-Gothic confection built by Charles Barry and Augustus Pugin over 20 years from 1840. The palace's most famous feature is its clock tower, officially the Elizabeth Tower but better known as Big Ben (Map p68).

ⓘ LONDON TOP TIPS

➡ London is huge – organise your visit by neighbourhood to avoid wasting time (and money) on transport.

➡ An Oyster Card is a cheaper and convenient way to use public transport, but you can also pay by credit or debit card provided it has a contactless function indicated by a wi-fi-like symbol.

➡ Walk – it's cheaper than transport and the best way to discover central London.

➡ For West End performances at bargain prices, opt for standby tickets (which you buy on the day at the venue) or last-minute tickets from the booths on Leicester Sq.

➡ To treat yourself to fine dining without breaking the bank, opt for lunch rather than dinner, or try for pre- or post-theatre dinner deals.

➡ Book online for ticketed attractions to save money and skip queues.

SOHO

London's most bohemian neighbourhood was once pastureland; the name Soho is thought to have evolved from a hunting cry. While the centre of London nightlife has shifted east, and Soho has recently seen landmark clubs and music venues shut down, the neighbourhood definitely comes into its own in the evenings and remains a proud gay district. During the day you'll be charmed by the area's bohemian side and its sheer vitality.

At Soho's northern end, leafy **Soho Sq** (Map p70; ⊜ Tottenham Court Rd, Leicester Sq) is the area's back garden. It was laid out in 1681 and originally called King's Sq; a statue of Charles II stands in its northern half. In the centre is a tiny half-timbered mock-Tudor cottage built as a gardener's shed in the 1870s. The space below it was used as an underground bomb shelter during WWII.

South of the square is **Dean St**, lined with bars and restaurants. No 28 was the home of Karl Marx and his family from 1851 to 1856; they lived here in extreme poverty as Marx researched and wrote *Das Kapital* in the Reading Room of the British Museum.

Old Compton St is the epicentre of Soho's gay village. It's a street loved by all, gay or other, for its great bars, risqué shops and general good vibes.

Seducer and heart-breaker Casanova and opium-addicted writer Thomas de Quincey lived on nearby **Greek St**, while the parallel **Frith St** housed Mozart at No 20 for a year from 1764.

Big Ben is actually the 13.5-tonne bell, named after Benjamin Hall, who was First Commissioner of Works when the tower was completed in 1858.

At the business end, parliament is split into two houses. The green-hued **House of Commons** (Map p68; www.parliament.uk/business/commons; ⊙2.30-10pm Mon & Tue, 11.30am-7.30pm Wed, 10.30am-6.30pm Thu, 9.30am-3pm Fri) is the lower house, where the 650 elected Members of Parliament sit. Traditionally the home of hereditary blue bloods, the scarlet-decorated **House of Lords** (Map p68; www.parliament.uk/business/lords; ⊙2.30-10pm Mon & Tue, 3-10pm Wed, 11am-7.30pm Thu, 10am-close of session Fri), with over 800 members, now has peers appointed through various means. Both houses debate and vote on legislation, which is then presented to the Queen for her Royal Assent (in practice, this is a formality; the last time Royal Assent was denied was in 1708). At the annual State Opening of Parliament, which now takes place in May, the Queen takes her throne in the House of Lords, having arrived in the gold-trimmed Irish State Coach from Buckingham Palace (her crown travels alone with equerries in Queen Alexandra's State Coach).

Visitors are welcome on Saturday year-round and on most weekdays during parliamentary recesses (which includes Easter, summer and Christmas). They can choose either a self-guided audio tour (adult £18.50, one free child with each adult) in one of eight languages lasting about 75 minutes or a much more comprehensive 1½-hour **guided tour** (Map p68; ☑020-7219 4114; www.parliament.uk/visiting/visiting-and-tours; adult/child £28/12) of both chambers, Westminster Hall and other historic buildings conducted by qualified Blue Badge Tourist Guides in a myriad of tongues (adult/child £25.50/11). Afternoon tea (£29) in the Terrace Pavilion overlooking the River Thames is a popular add-on to the tours. Buy tickets from the office in Portcullis House on Victoria Embankment. Tour schedules change with every recess and are occasionally subject to variation or cancellation due to the State Opening of Parliament and other parliamentary business, so check ahead and book. UK residents can approach their MPs to arrange a free tour. The Elizabeth Tower, housing Big Ben, is undergoing conservation works until 2021.

Public access to the Houses of Parliament is via the Cromwell Green Entrance, next to St Stephen's Entrance. If you wish to eat here, the Palace of Westminster's principal dining rooms are open to the public on select dates (see the website for details).

★**Buckingham Palace**　　　　　PALACE
(Map p68; ☑0303 123 7300; www.royalcollection.org.uk/visit/the-state-rooms-buckingham-palace;

Westminster & St James's

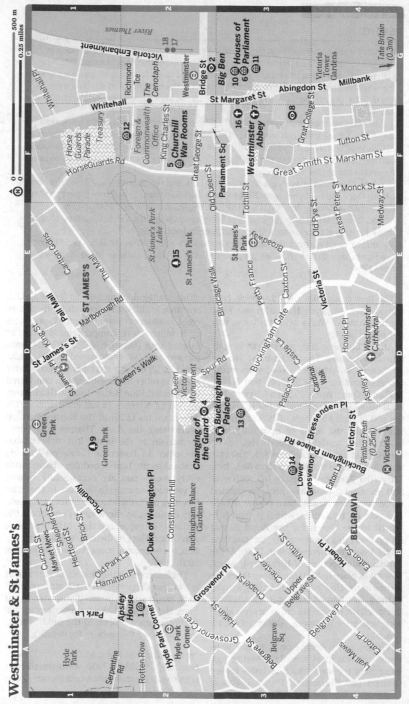

0 500 m
0 0.25 miles

River Thames

Victoria Embankment

18
17

Whitehall Pl

Richmond
Tce
The
Cenotaph

Westminster
Bridge St
2 Big Ben
10 Houses of
6 Parliament
11

Whitehall

Foreign &
Commonwealth
Office
King Charles St
Great George St
St Margaret St

Abingdon St Millbank

Tate Britain
(0.3mi)

Victoria
Tower
Gardens

Treasury

12

5 Churchill
War Rooms

16   7
Westminster
Abbey

8

Great College St

Horse
Guards
Parade
HorseGuards Rd

Old Queen St
Parliament
Sq

Tufton St

Great Smith St Marsham St

Caxton Gdns

St James's Park
Lake

15

St James's Park

Tothill St

Monck St

Great Peter St

ST JAMES'S

The Mall

Marlborough Rd

St James's Park
Birdcage Walk

St James's
Park
Broadway

Petty France

Caxton St

Old Pye St

Medway St

Great Smith St

Victoria St

Westminster
Cathedral

Pall Mall

St James's St

19

St James's Pl

St James's St

Queen's Walk

Queen
Victoria
Monument

Spur Rd

Buckingham Gate

Castle La

Palace St

Howick Pl

Victoria St

Ashley Pl

Green
Park

Green Park

Changing of
the Guard

3   4 Buckingham
Palace

13

Cardinal
Walk

Bressenden Pl

Pimlico Fresh
(0.25mi)

Victoria

Duke of Wellington Pl

Constitution Hill

Buckingham
Palace
Gardens

14

Lower
Grosvenor
Pl

Buckingham Palace Rd

Eaton La

Victoria St

BELGRAVIA

Piccadilly

Curzon St
Market Mews
Shepherd St
Hertford St

Old Park La

Hamilton Pl

Grosvenor Pl

Grosvenor Cres

Halkin St

Chapel St

Wilton St

Upper
Belgrave St

Hobart Pl

Eaton Sq

Apsley
House
1

Hyde Park
Corner

Park La

Hyde
Park

Serpentine
Rd

Rotten Row

Brick St

Belgrave Sq

Chester St

Belgrave Pl

Lyall Mews

Eaton Pl

Westminster & St James's

Buckingham Palace Rd, SW1; adult/child/under 5yr £24/13.50/free; ⊙9.30am-7pm (to 6pm Sep) Jul-Sep only; ⊜Green Park, St James's Park) Built in 1703 for the Duke of Buckingham, Buckingham Palace replaced St James's Palace as the monarch's official London residence in 1837. Queen Elizabeth II divides her time between here, Windsor Castle and, in summer, Balmoral Castle in Scotland. If she's in residence, the square yellow, red and blue Royal Standard is flown; if not, it's the Union Flag. Some 19 lavishly furnished **State Rooms** are open to visitors when Her Royal Highness (HRH) takes her holidays from late July to September.

Hung with artworks by the likes of Rembrandt, Van Dyck, Canaletto, Poussin and Vermeer, the State Rooms are open for self-guided tours that include the **Throne Room**, with his-and-her pink chairs monogrammed 'ER' and 'P'. Access is by timed tickets with admission every 15 minutes (audio guide included) and visits take about two hours.

Admission includes entry to a themed special exhibition (eg royal couture during the Queen's reign, growing up at the palace) in the enormous Ballroom, which changes each summer. It also allows access to part of the palace gardens as you exit, although you must join the three-hour State Rooms & Garden Highlights Tour (adult/child/under five years £33/19.70/free) to see the wisteria-clad Summer House and other famous features, and to get an idea of the garden's full size (16 hectares).

Your ticket to Buckingham Palace is good for a return trip if bought direct from the palace ticket office (ask to have it stamped as you leave). You can even make your ticket purchase a donation and gain free access for a whole year (ask at the ticket office).

At 11am daily in June and July and on Sunday, Monday, Wednesday and Friday, weather permitting, during the rest of the year, the Old Guard (Foot Guards of the Household Regiment) comes off duty to be replaced by the New Guard on the forecourt of Buckingham Palace, an event known as the **Changing of the Guard** (Map p68; http://changing-guard.com). Highly popular, the ceremony lasts about 40 minutes (brace for crowds).

Originally designed by John Nash as a conservatory, the **Queen's Gallery** (Map p68; www.royalcollection.org.uk/visit/the-queens-gallery-buckingham-palace; South Wing, Buckingham Palace, Buckingham Gate, SW1; adult/child £10.30/5.30, incl Royal Mews £19/10; ⊙10am-5.30pm) showcases some of the palace's treasures on a rotating basis, through temporary exhibitions. Enter from Buckingham Gate.

Indulge your Cinderella fantasies while inspecting the exquisite state coaches in the **Royal Mews** (Map p68; www.royalcollection.org.uk/visit/royalmews; adult/child £11/6.40, with Queen's Gallery £19/10; ⊙10am-5pm Apr-Oct, to 4pm Mon-Sat Feb, Mar & Nov; ⊜Victoria), a working stable looking after the royals' immaculately groomed horses and the opulent vehicles they use for getting from A to B. Highlights include the magnificent Gold State Coach of 1762 and the 1911 Glass Coach.

A Royal Day Out (adult/child/under five years £42.30/23.30/free) is a combined ticket including entry to the State Rooms, Queen's Gallery and Royal Mews.

West End

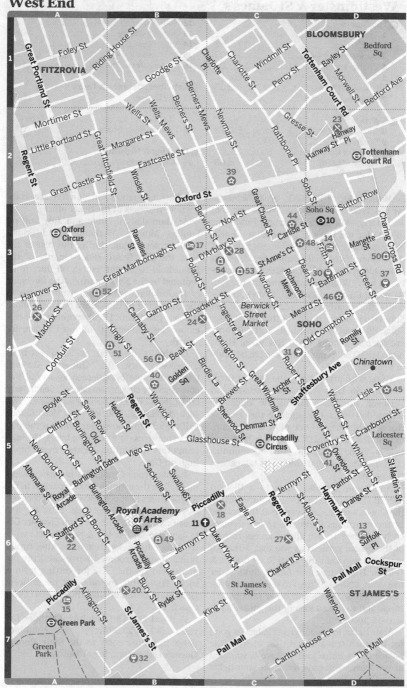

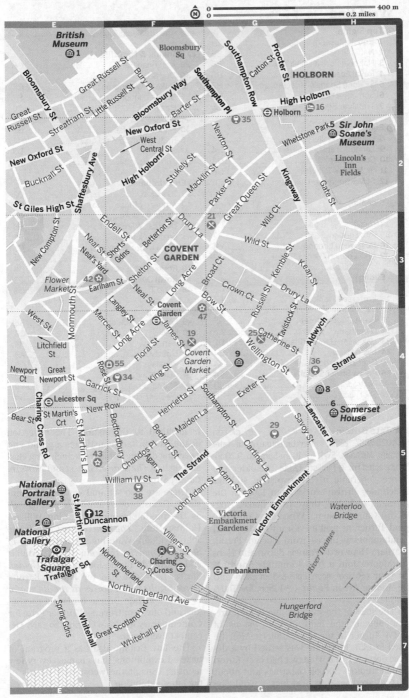

West End

⊙ Top Sights
1	British Museum	E1
2	National Gallery	E6
3	National Portrait Gallery	E5
4	Royal Academy of Arts	B6
5	Sir John Soane's Museum	H2
6	Somerset House	H5
7	Trafalgar Square	E6

⊙ Sights
8	Courtauld Gallery	H4
9	London Transport Museum	G4
10	Soho Square	D3
11	St James's Piccadilly	C6
12	St Martin-in-the-Fields	E6

⊜ Sleeping
13	Haymarket Hotel	D6
14	Hazlitt's	D3
15	Ritz London	A7
16	Rosewood London	H1
17	YHA London Oxford Street	B3

⊗ Eating
18	5th View	C6
19	Battersea Pie Station	F4
20	Cafe Murano	B6
21	Great Queen Street	G3
22	Gymkhana	A6
23	Hakkasan Hanway Place	D2
24	Mildreds	B4
25	Opera Tavern	G4
26	Pollen Street Social	A4
	Portrait	(see 3)
27	Shoryu	C6

28	The Breakfast Club	C3

⊙ Drinking & Nightlife
29	American Bar	G5
30	Dog & Duck	D3
31	Duke of Wellington	C4
32	Dukes London	B7
33	Heaven	F6
34	Lamb & Flag	F4
35	Princess Louise	G2
36	Radio Rooftop Bar	H4
37	Swift	D3
38	Terroirs	F5

⊕ Entertainment
39	100 Club	C2
40	Amused Moose Soho	B4
41	Comedy Store	D5
42	Donmar Warehouse	E3
43	English National Opera	E5
44	Pizza Express Jazz Club	C3
45	Prince Charles Cinema	D4
46	Ronnie Scott's	D3
47	Royal Opera House	F3
48	Soho Theatre	C3

⊜ Shopping
49	Fortnum & Mason	B6
50	Foyles	D3
51	Hamleys	B4
52	Liberty	A3
53	Reckless Records	C3
54	Sister Ray	C3
55	Stanford's	F4
56	We Built This City	B4

★ **Tate Britain** GALLERY
(📞020-7887 8888; www.tate.org.uk/visit/tate-britain; Millbank, SW1; ⊙10am-6pm, to 9.30pm on selected Fri; ⊖Pimlico) FREE The older and more venerable of the two Tate siblings celebrates British works from 1500 to the present, including those from Blake, Hogarth, Gainsborough, Whistler, Constable and Turner, as well as vibrant modern and contemporary pieces from Lucian Freud, Barbara Hepworth, Francis Bacon and Henry Moore. Join a free 45-minute **thematic tour** (⊙11am, noon, 2pm & 3pm daily) and 15-minute **Art in Focus** (⊙1.15pm Tue, Thu & Sat) talks.

The stars of the show at Tate Britain are, undoubtedly, the light infused visions of JMW Turner in the Clore Gallery. After he died in 1851, his estate was settled by a decree declaring that whatever had been found in his studio – 300 oil paintings and about 30,000 sketches and drawings – would be bequeathed to the nation. The collection at the Tate Britain constitutes a grand and sweeping display of his work, including classics such as *The Scarlet Sunset* and *Norham Castle, Sunrise*.

There are also seminal works from Constable, Gainsborough and Reynolds, as well as the pre-Raphaelites, including William Holman Hunt's *The Awakening Conscience,* John William Waterhouse's *The Lady of Shalott, Ophelia* by John Everett Millais and Edward Burne-Jones's *The Golden Stairs*. Look out also for Francis Bacon's *Three Studies for Figures at the Base of a Crucifixion*. Tate Britain hosts the prestigious and often controversial Turner Prize for Contemporary Art from October to early December every year.

The Tate Britain also has a program of ticketed exhibitions that changes every few months; consult the website for details of the latest exhibition.

★ **Wallace Collection** GALLERY
(Map p112; ☑ 020-7563 9500; www.wallace collection.org; Hertford House, Manchester Sq, W1; ⊙ 10am-5pm; ⊜ Bond St) FREE Arguably London's finest smaller gallery, the Wallace Collection is an enthralling glimpse into 18th-century aristocratic life. The sumptuously restored Italianate mansion houses a treasure trove of 17th- and 18th-century paintings, porcelain, artefacts and furniture collected by generations of the same family and bequeathed to the nation by the widow of Sir Richard Wallace (1818–90) on the condition it remain displayed in the same fashion.

★ **Churchill War Rooms** MUSEUM
(Map p68; www.iwm.org.uk/visits/churchill-war-rooms; Clive Steps, King Charles St, SW1; adult/child £21/10.50; ⊙ 9.30am-6pm; ⊜ Westminster) Winston Churchill helped coordinate the Allied resistance against Nazi Germany on a Bakelite telephone from this underground complex during WWII. The **Cabinet War Rooms** remain much as they were when the lights were switched off in 1945, capturing the drama and dogged spirit of the time, while the multimedia **Churchill Museum** affords intriguing insights into the life and times of the resolute, cigar-smoking wartime leader.

★ **National Portrait Gallery** GALLERY
(Map p70; ☑ 020-7321 0055; www.npg.org.uk; St Martin's Pl, WC2; ⊙ 10am-6pm Sat-Wed, to 9pm Thu & Fri; ⊜ Charing Cross, Leicester Sq) FREE What makes the National Portrait Gallery so compelling is its familiarity; in many cases, you'll have heard of the subject (royals, scientists, politicians, celebrities) or the artist (Andy Warhol, Annie Leibovitz, Lucian Freud) but not necessarily recognise the face. Highlights include the famous 'Chandos portrait' of William Shakespeare, the first artwork the gallery acquired (in 1856) and believed to be the only likeness made during the playwright's lifetime, and a touching sketch of novelist Jane Austen by her sister.

★ **Royal Academy of Arts** GALLERY
(Map p70; ☑ 020-7300 8000; www.royalacademy. org.uk; Burlington House, Piccadilly, W1; adult/child from £13.50/free, exhibition prices vary; ⊙ 10am-6pm Sat-Thu, to 10pm Fri; ⊜ Green Park) Britain's oldest society devoted to fine arts was founded in 1768 and moved to Burlington House exactly a century later. The collection contains drawings, paintings, architectural designs, photographs and sculptures by past and present academicians, such as Joshua Reynolds, John Constable, Thomas Gainsborough, JMW Turner, David Hockney and Norman Foster.

No 10 Downing Street HISTORIC BUILDING
(Map p68; www.number10.gov.uk; 10 Downing St, SW1; ⊜ Westminster) The official office of British leaders since 1732, when George II presented No 10 to 'First Lord of the Treasury' Robert Walpole, this has also been the prime minister's London residence since refurbishment in 1902. For such a famous address, No 10 is a small-looking Georgian building on a plain-looking street, hardly warranting comparison with the White House, for example. Yet it is actually three houses joined into one and boasts roughly 100 rooms plus a 2000-sq-metre garden.

★ **Madame Tussauds** MUSEUM
(Map p112; ☑ 0870 400 3000; www.madame-tussauds.com/london; Marylebone Rd, NW1; adult/child 4-15yr £35/30; ⊙ 10am-6pm; ⊜ Baker St) It may be kitschy and pricey, but Madame Tussauds makes for a fun-filled day. There are photo ops with your dream celebrity (be it Daniel Craig, Lady Gaga, Benedict Cumberbatch, Audrey Hepburn or the Beckhams), the Bollywood gathering (sparring studs Hrithik Roshan and Salman Khan) and the Royal Appointment (the Queen, Harry and Meghan, William and Kate). Book online for much cheaper rates and check the website for seasonal opening hours.

★ **Somerset House** HISTORIC BUILDING
(Map p70; ☑ 020-7845 4600; www.somerset house.org.uk; The Strand, WC2; ⊙ galleries 10am-6pm, courtyard 7.30am-11pm, terrace 8am-11pm; ⊜ Temple, Covent Garden) Designed by William Chambers in 1775 for government departments and royal societies – in fact, the world's first office block – Somerset House now contains several fabulous galleries. In the North Wing near the Strand entrance, the **Courtauld Gallery** (Map p70; http://court auld.ac.uk; adult/child £8/free, temporary exhibitions vary; ⊙ 10am-6pm) displays a wealth of 14th- to 20th-century art, including masterpieces by Rubens, Botticelli, Cézanne, Degas, Renoir, Seurat, Manet, Monet, Leger and others. The **Embankment Galleries** in the South Wing are devoted to temporary (mostly photographic, design and fashion) exhibitions; prices and hours vary.

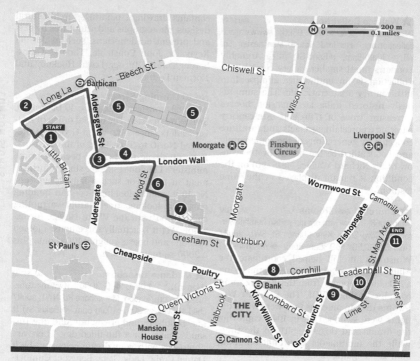

City Walk
A Taste of the City

START ST BARTHOLOMEW-THE-GREAT
END 30 ST MARY AXE (THE GHERKIN)
LENGTH 1.5 MILES; THREE HOURS

The City of London has as much history in its square mile as the rest of London put together, and this walk picks out just a few of its many highlights.

Start by exploring the wonderful 12th-century ❶St Bartholomew-the-Great (p79), whose atmospheric interior has been used frequently as a film set. Head through the Tudor gatehouse and turn right towards the colourful Victorian arches of ❷Smithfield Market, London's last surviving meat market.

Head northeast along Long Lane and take a right at Aldersgate St. Follow the roundabout to the right and nip up the stairs (or take the lift) to the ❸Museum of London (p79). After exploring the museum's excellent free galleries then turn left onto the highwalk and pause to examine the ruins of the ❹Roman city walls and behind them the distinctive towers of the ❺Barbican (p79).

Descend from the highwalk and cross over to Wood St to find the ❻tower of St Alban (1698), all that's left of a Wren-designed church destroyed in WWII bombing in 1940. Turn left into Love Lane and right into Aldermanbury – the impressive 15th-century ❼Guildhall is on your left, behind a modern extension. Crossing its courtyard – note the black outline of the Roman amphitheatre – continue east onto Gresham St, taking a right into Prince's St and emerging onto the busy Bank intersection lined with neoclassical temples to commerce.

From the ❽Royal Exchange, follow Cornhill and take a right down Gracechurch St. Turn left into wonderful ❾Leadenhall Market, roughly where the Roman forum once stood. As you leave the market's far end, ❿Lloyd's of London displays its innards for all to see. Once you turn left onto Lime St, ⓫30 St Mary Axe (p79). Built nearly 900 years after St Bartholomew-the-Great, it's a tangible testimony to the city's ability to constantly reinvent itself.

★ **Sir John Soane's Museum**   MUSEUM
(Map p70; ☏020-7405 2107; www.soane.org; 12 Lincoln's Inn Fields, WC2; ⏲10am-5pm Wed-Sun; ⊖Holborn) **FREE** This little museum is one of the most atmospheric and fascinating in London. The building was the beautiful, bewitching home of architect Sir John Soane (1753–1837), which he left brimming with his vast architectural and archaeological collection, as well as intriguing personal effects and curiosities. The museum represents his exquisite and eccentric tastes, persuasions and proclivities.

London Transport Museum   MUSEUM
(Map p70; ☏020-7379 6344; www.ltmuseum. co.uk; Covent Garden Piazza, WC2; adult/child £17.50/free; ⏲10am-6pm; ⊖Covent Garden) This entertaining and informative museum looks at how London developed as a result of better transport and contains horse-drawn omnibuses, early taxis, underground trains you can drive yourself, a detailed look at Crossrail (a new high-frequency 75-mile rail service linking Reading with Essex), and everything in between, including signage. Start on Level 2 and don't miss the museum shop for imaginative souvenirs, including historical tube posters, 'Mind the Gap' socks and 'Way Out' T-shirts.

Charles Dickens Museum   MUSEUM
(Map p96; ☏020-7405 2127; www.dickensmuseum.com; 48 Doughty St, WC1; adult/child £9/4; ⏲10am-5pm Tue-Sun; ⊖Chancery Lane, Russell Sq) A £3.5 million renovation funded by the Heritage Lottery Fund has made this museum – located in a handsome four-storey house that is the beloved Victorian novelist's sole surviving residence in London – bigger and better than ever. A period kitchen in the basement and a nursery in the attic were added, and the acquisition of 49 Doughty St increased the exhibition space substantially.

St James's Park   PARK
(Map p68; www.royalparks.org.uk/parks/st-jamess-park; The Mall, SW1; ⏲5am-midnight; ⊖St James's Park, Green Park) At just 23 hectares, St James's is the second smallest of the eight royal parks after Green Park (Map p68; www. royalparks.org.uk/parks/green-park; ⏲5am-midnight; ⊖Green Park). But what it lacks in size it makes up for in grooming as it is the most manicured green space in London. It has brilliant views of the London Eye, Westminster, St James's Palace, Carlton Tce and the Horse Guards Parade; the photo-perfect sight of Buckingham Palace from the footbridge spanning the central lake is the best you'll find.

◉ The City

★ **St Paul's Cathedral**   CATHEDRAL
(Map p76; ☏020-7246 8357; www.stpauls.co. uk; St Paul's Churchyard, EC4; adult/child £18/8; ⏲8.30am-4.30pm Mon-Sat; ⊖St Paul's) Towering over diminutive Ludgate Hill in a superb position that's been a place of Christian worship for over 1400 years (and pagan before that), St Paul's is one of London's most magnificent buildings. For Londoners, the vast dome is a symbol of resilience and pride, standing tall for more than 300 years. Viewing Sir Christopher Wren's masterpiece from the inside and climbing to the top for sweeping views of the capital is an exhilarating experience.

The cathedral was designed by Wren after the Great Fire and built between 1675 and 1710; it opened the following year. The site is ancient hallowed ground, with four other cathedrals preceding Wren's English baroque masterpiece here, the first dating from 604.

The world's second-largest cathedral dome is famed for surviving Luftwaffe incendiary bombs in the 'Second Great Fire of London' of December 1940, becoming an icon of London resilience during the Blitz. Outside in the churchyard, north of the church, is a simple and elegant monument to the people of London, honouring the 32,000 Londoners killed.

Inside, rising 68m above the floor, is the dome, supported by eight huge columns. It actually consists of three parts: a plastered brick inner dome, a nonstructural lead outer dome visible on the skyline and a brick cone between them holding it all together. The walkway around its base, accessed via 257 steps from a staircase on the western side of the southern transept, is called the Whispering Gallery, because if you talk close to the wall, your words will carry to the opposite side, 32m away. A further 119 steps brings you to the exterior Stone Gallery, 152 iron steps above which is the Golden Gallery at the very top, with unforgettable views of London.

The crypt has memorials to around 300 of the great and the good, including Wellington and Nelson, whose body lies directly below the dome. But the most poignant is to

The City

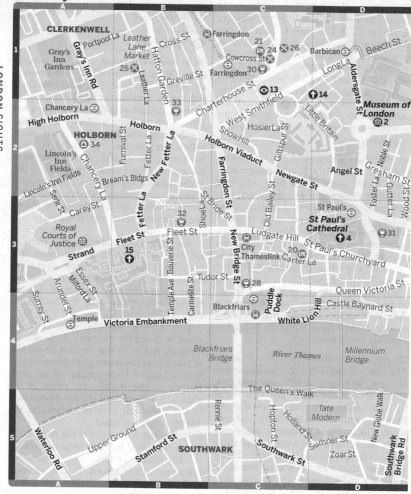

Wren himself. On a simple slab bearing his name, part of a Latin inscription translates as: 'If you seek his memorial, look around you'.

As part of its 300th anniversary celebrations in 2011, St Paul's underwent a £40 million renovation project that gave the church a deep clean. It's not looked this good since they cut the blue ribbon opening the cathedral in 1711.

There's no charge to attend a service. To hear the cathedral choir, attend the 11.30am Sunday Eucharist or Evensong (5pm Monday to Saturday and 3.15pm Sunday), but

check the website as a visiting choir may appear for the latter.

Otherwise, the standard admission price includes a free video- and audio guide. Free 1½-hour guided tours depart four times a day (10am, 11am, 1pm and 2pm); reserve a place at the tour desk, just past the entrance. Around twice a month, 60-minute tours (£8) also visit the astonishing Library, Geometric Staircase and Great Model, and include impressive views down the nave from above the Great West Doors; check the website for dates and hours and book well ahead. Filming and photography is not per-

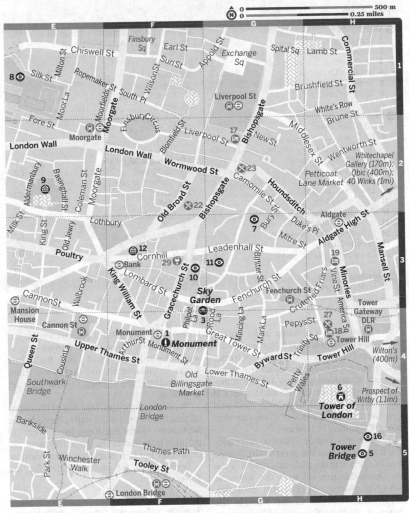

mitted within the cathedral. Book online for cheaper rates.

★ **Tower of London** CASTLE
(Map p76; ☏ 0844 482 7777; www.hrp.org.uk/tower-of-london; Petty Wales, EC3; adult/child £24.80/11.50, audio guide £4/3; ◷ 9am-4.30pm Tue-Sat, from 10am Sun & Mon; ⊖ Tower Hill) The unmissable Tower of London (actually a castle of 22 towers) offers a window into a gruesome and compelling history. A former royal residence, treasury, mint, armoury and zoo, it's perhaps now most remembered as the prison where a king, three queens and

many nobles met their deaths. Come here to see the colourful Yeoman Warders (or Beefeaters), the spectacular Crown Jewels, the soothsaying ravens and armour fit for a *very* large king.

In the 1070s, William the Conqueror started work on the White Tower to replace the stronghold he'd previously built here, in the southeast corner of the Roman walls, shortly after the Norman invasion. By 1285, two walls with towers and a moat were built around it and the defences have barely been altered since.

The City

The most striking building is the central White Tower, with its solid Norman architecture and four turrets. On the entrance floor it houses a collection from the Royal Armouries, including Henry VIII's commodious suit of armour. On the middle floor is St John's Chapel, dating from 1080 and therefore the oldest place of Christian worship still standing in London.

To the north stands Waterloo Barracks, which now contains the spectacular Crown Jewels, including the platinum crown of the late Queen Mother, set with the 106-carat Koh-i-Nûr (Mountain of Light) diamond, and the Imperial State Crown, worn by the Queen at the State Opening of Parliament. Slow-moving travelators shunt wide-eyed visitors past the collection. On the other side of the White Tower is the Bloody Tower, where the 12-year-old Edward V and his little brother Richard were held 'for their own safety' and later murdered, perhaps by their uncle, the future Richard III. Sir Walter Raleigh did a 13-year stretch here too under James I, where he wrote his *Historie of the World*.

In front of the Chapel Royal of St Peter ad Vincula stood Henry VIII's scaffold, where nobles such as Anne Boleyn and Catherine Howard (Henry's second and fifth wives) were beheaded. Look out for the latest in the Tower's long line of famous ravens, which legend says could cause the White Tower to collapse should they leave (their wing feathers are clipped in case they get any ideas).

To get your bearings, take one of the entertaining (and free) guided tours offered by the Beefeaters. Hour-long tours leave every 30 minutes from the bridge near the main entrance; the last tour is an hour before closing.

Book online for cheaper rates for the Tower.

★ **Tower Bridge** BRIDGE
(Map p76; ⊖ Tower Hill) One of London's most recognisable sights, familiar from dozens of movies, Tower Bridge doesn't disappoint in real life. Its neo-Gothic towers and sky-blue suspension struts add extraordinary elegance to what is a supremely functional structure. London was a thriving port in 1894 when it was built as a much-needed crossing point in the east, equipped with a then-revolutionary steam-driven bascule (counter-balance) mechanism that could raise the roadway to make way for oncoming ships in just three minutes.

A lift leads up from the northern tower to the Tower Bridge Exhibition (Map p76;

020-7403 3761; www.towerbridge.org.uk; adult/child £9.80/4.20, incl the Monument £12/5.50; ⊙10am-5.30pm Apr-Sep, 9.30am-5pm Oct-Mar), where the story of building the bridge is recounted. Tower Bridge was designed by architect Horace Jones, who was also responsible for Smithfield and Leadenhall markets, and completed by engineer John Wolfe Barry.

The bridge is still operational, although these days it's electrically powered and rises mainly for pleasure craft. It does so around 1000 times a year and as often as 10 times a day in summer; consult the Exhibition website for times to watch it in action.

★ **Museum of London** MUSEUM
(Map p76; 020-7001 9844; www.museumof london.org.uk; 150 London Wall, EC2; ⊙10am-6pm; ⓔBarbican) FREE As entertaining as it is educational, the Museum of London meanders through the various incarnations of the city, stopping off in Roman Londinium and Saxon Ludenwic before eventually ending up in the 21st-century metropolis. Interesting objects and interactive displays work together to bring each era to life, without ever getting too whiz-bang, making this one of the capital's best museums. Free themed tours take place throughout the day; check the signs by the entrance for times.

★ **Monument** MONUMENT
(Map p76; 020-7403 3761; www.themonument. org.uk; Fish St Hill, EC3; adult/child £5/2.50, incl Tower Bridge Exhibition £12/5.50; ⊙9.30am-5.30pm Apr-Sep, to 5pm Oct-Mar; ⓔMonument) Sir Christopher Wren's 1677 column, known simply as the Monument, is a memorial to the Great Fire of London of 1666, whose impact on London's history cannot be overstated. An immense Doric column made of Portland stone, the Monument is 4.5m wide and 60.6m tall – the exact distance it stands from the bakery in Pudding Lane where the fire is thought to have started.

Note, tickets can only be purchased with cash.

★ **Sky Garden** VIEWPOINT
(Map p76; 020-7337 2344; www.skygarden. london; L35-37, 20 Fenchurch St, EC3; ⊙10am-6pm Mon-Fri, 11am-9pm Sat & Sun; ⓔMonument) FREE The City's sixth-tallest building didn't get off to a good start when it opened in 2014. Officially called 20 Fenchurch St it was quickly dubbed the 'Walkie Talkie' by unimpressed Londoners, and its highly reflective windows melted the bodywork of several cars parked below. However, the opening of this 155m-high, three-storey, public garden in the glass dome at the top has helped win naysayers over. Entry is free, but you'll need to book a slot in advance.

St Bartholomew-the-Great CHURCH
(Map p76; 020-7600 0440; www.greatstbarts. com; West Smithfield, EC1; adult/child £5/3; ⊙8.30am-5pm Mon-Fri, 10.30am-4pm Sat, 8.30am-8pm Sun; ⓔBarbican) Dating to 1123 and adjoining one of London's oldest hospitals, St Bartholomew-the-Great is one of London's most ancient churches. The Norman arches and profound sense of history lend this holy space an ancient calm, while approaching from nearby Smithfield Market through the restored 13th-century half-timbered archway is like walking back in time. The church was originally part of an Augustinian priory, but became the parish church of Smithfield in 1539 when Henry VIII dissolved the monasteries.

Barbican ARCHITECTURE
(Map p76; 020-7638 4141; www.barbican.org. uk; Silk St, EC2; tours adult/child £12.50/10; ⊙9am-11pm Mon-Sat, 11am-11pm Sun; ⓔBarbican) Londoners remain fairly divided about the architectural value of this vast complex built after WWII, but the Barbican remains the City's pre-eminent cultural centre, with the main Barbican Hall, two theatres, a state-of-the-art cinema complex and two well-regarded art galleries: the 3rd-floor **Barbican Art Gallery** (Map p76; www.barbi can.org.uk/artgallery; L3 Barbican Centre; ⊙10am-6pm Sat-Wed, to 9pm Thu & Fri) and the **Curve** (Map p76; L1 Barbican Centre; ⊙11am-8pm) FREE on the ground floor. There's also a large **conservatory** (Map p76; L3 Barbican Centre, Upper Frobisher Cres, EC2; ⊙noon-5pm Sun), filled with tropical plants.

30 St Mary Axe NOTABLE BUILDING
(Map p76; www.30stmaryaxe.info; 30 St Mary Axe, EC3; ⓔAldgate) Nicknamed 'the Gherkin' for its unusual shape, 30 St Mary Axe is the City's most distinctive skyscraper, dominating its skyline despite actually being only the fourth tallest. Built in 2003 by award-winning architect Norman Foster, the Gherkin's futuristic exterior has become an emblem of modern London – as recognisable as Big Ben. The building is closed to the public, though in the past it has opened its doors

Tower of London

TACKLING THE TOWER

Although it's usually less busy in the late afternoon, don't leave your assault on the Tower until too late in the day. You could easily spend hours here and not see it all. Start by getting your bearings on one of the Yeoman Warder (Beefeater) tours; they are included in the cost of admission, entertaining and the easiest way to access the **❶ Chapel Royal of St Peter ad Vincula**, which is where they finish up.

When you leave the chapel, the **❷ Scaffold Site** is directly in front. The building immediately to your left is Waterloo Barracks, where the **❸ Crown Jewels** are housed. These are the absolute highlight of a Tower visit, so keep an eye on the entrance and pick a time to visit when it looks relatively quiet. Once inside, take things at your own pace. Slow-moving travelators shunt you past the dozen or so crowns that are the treasury's centrepieces, but feel free to double-back for a second or even third pass.

Allow plenty of time for the **❹ White Tower**, the core of the whole complex, starting with the exhibition of royal armour. As you continue onto the 1st floor, keep an eye out for **❺ St John's Chapel**.

The famous **❻ ravens** can be seen in the courtyard south of the White Tower. Next, visit the **❼ Bloody Tower** and the torture displays in the dungeon of the Wakefield Tower. Head next through the towers that formed the **❽ Medieval Palace**, then take the **❾ East Wall Walk** to get a feel for the castle's mighty battlements. Spend the rest of your time poking around the many other fascinating nooks and crannies of the Tower complex.

BEAT THE QUEUES

➡ Buy tickets online, avoid weekends and aim to be at the Tower first thing in the morning, when queues are shortest.

➡ An annual Historic Royal Palaces membership allows you to jump the queues and visit the Tower (and four other London palaces) as often as you like.

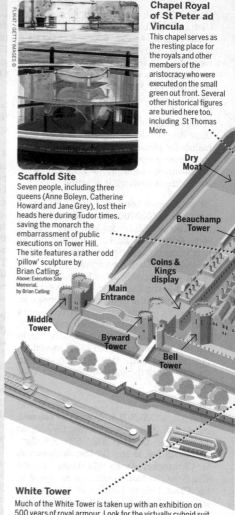

Chapel Royal of St Peter ad Vincula

This chapel serves as the resting place for the royals and other members of the aristocracy who were executed on the small green out front. Several other historical figures are buried here too, including St Thomas More.

FLIK47 / GETTY IMAGES ©

Scaffold Site
Seven people, including three queens (Anne Boleyn, Catherine Howard and Jane Grey), lost their heads here during Tudor times, saving the monarch the embarrassment of public executions on Tower Hill. The site features a rather odd 'pillow' sculpture by Brian Catling.
Above: Execution Site Memorial, by Brian Catling

Dry Moat

Beauchamp Tower

Coins & Kings display

Main Entrance

Middle Tower

Byward Tower

Bell Tower

White Tower

Much of the White Tower is taken up with an exhibition on 500 years of royal armour. Look for the virtually cuboid suit made to match Henry VIII's bloated 49-year-old body, complete with an oversized armoured codpiece to protect, ahem, the crown jewels.

CHRISDORNEY / SHUTTERSTOCK ©

St John's Chapel

The White Tower's unadorned chapel dates from 1080, making it the oldest surviving Christian place of worship in London.

Crown Jewels

When they're not being worn for ceremonies of state, Her Majesty's bling is kept here. Among the 23,578 gems, look out for the 530-carat 1st Star of Africa diamond at the top of the Sovereign's Sceptre with cross, the largest part of what was then the largest diamond ever found.

JOSEPH M. ARSENEAU / SHUTTERSTOCK ©

Flint Tower

Bowyer Tower

Brick Tower

Martin Tower

Royal Fusiliers Museum

Constable Tower

Broad Arrow Tower

Queen's House

Bloody Tower

Roman city wall

Lanthorne Tower

New Armouries

Traitors' Gate & St Thomas's Tower

Wakefield Tower

Salt Tower

Cradle Tower

Well Tower

River Thames

Medieval Palace

This part of the Tower complex was begun around 1220 and was home to England's medieval monarchs. Look for the recreations of the bedchamber of Edward I (1272–1307) in St Thomas's Tower and the throne room of his father, Henry III (1216–72) in the Wakefield Tower.

CRISTIAN SANTINON / SHUTTERSTOCK ©

Ravens

This stretch of green is where the Tower's half-dozen ravens are kept, fed on raw meat and blood-soaked biscuits. According to legend, if the ravens depart the fortress, the Tower will fall.

Wall Walk

Follow the inner ramparts along the Tower's eastern and northern fortifications. Each of the seven towers along the way has themed displays, covering everything from the royal menagerie to the Tower during WWI.

over the Open House London (☎020-7383 2131; www.openhouselondon.org.uk) weekend in September.

👁 South Bank

★ Tate Modern   GALLERY

(Map p84; ☎020-7887 8888; www.tate.org.uk; Bankside, SE1; ⏱10am-6pm Sun-Thu, to 10pm Fri & Sat; 🚹; 🚇Blackfriars, Southwark, London Bridge) FREE One of London's most amazing attractions, this outstanding modern- and contemporary-art gallery is housed in the creatively revamped Bankside Power Station south of the Millennium Bridge. A spellbinding synthesis of modern art and capacious industrial brick design, Tate Modern has been extraordinarily successful in bringing challenging work to the masses, both through its free permanent collection and fee-paying big-name temporary exhibitions. The stunning Switch House extension opened in 2016, increasing the available exhibition space by 60%.

The 4.2 million bricks of the 200m-long former power house (now called Boiler House) is an imposing sight, designed by Swiss architects Herzog and de Meuron, who scooped the prestigious Pritzker Architecture Prize in 2001 for their transformation of the empty power station. Significant achievements include leaving the building's central 99m-high chimney, adding a two-storey glass box onto the roof and employing the cavernous Turbine Hall as a dramatic entrance space. Herzog and de Meuron also designed the new 10-storey extension.

As a supreme collection of modern art, the contents of the museum are, nevertheless, the main draw. At their disposal the Tate Modern curators have works by Georges Braque, Henri Matisse, Piet Mondrian, Andy Warhol, Mark Rothko and Jackson Pollock, as well as pieces by Joseph Beuys, Damien Hirst, Claes Oldenburg and Auguste Rodin.

Tate Modern's permanent collection is arranged by both theme and chronology on levels 2 and 4 of Boiler House and levels 0, 2, 3 and 4 of Switch House. The emphasis in the latter is on art from the 1960s onwards. More than 60,000 works are on constant rotation, so if there's a particular work you would like to see, check the website to see if (and where) it's hanging.

The museum's location is also supreme, made the most of by popular balconies on level 3 of Boiler House and the level 10 viewing gallery in Switch House. The magnificent view is elegantly conveyed by the Millennium Bridge (Map p84; 🚇St Paul's, Blackfriars) directly to St Paul's Cathedral in the City on the far bank of the river.

Free guided highlights tours depart at 11am, noon, 2pm and 3pm daily. Audio guides (in five languages) are available for £4; these contain information about 50 artworks across the gallery and offer suggested tours for adults or children.

To visit the sister museum Tate Britain (p69), hop on the Tate Boat (Map p84; www.tate.org.uk/visit/tate-boat; one-way adult/child £8.30/4.15) from Bankside Pier.

★ Shakespeare's Globe   HISTORIC BUILDING

(Map p84; ☎020-7902 1500; www.shakespeares globe.com; 21 New Globe Walk, SE1; adult/child £17/10; ⏱9.30am-5pm; 🚹; 🚇Blackfriars, London Bridge) Unlike other venues for Shakespearean plays, the new Globe was designed to resemble the original as closely as possible, which means having the arena open to the fickle London skies, leaving the 700 'groundlings' (standing spectators) to weather London's spectacular downpours. Visits to the Globe include tours of the theatre (half hourly) as well as access to the exhibition space, which has fascinating exhibits on Shakespeare and theatre in the 17th century.

★ London Eye   VIEWPOINT

(Map p84; ☎0871 222 4002; www.londoneye.com; adult/child £27/22; ⏱11am-6pm Sep-May, 10am-8.30pm Jun-Aug; 🚇Waterloo, Westminster) Standing 135m high in a fairly flat city, the London Eye affords views 25 miles in every direction, weather permitting. Interactive tablets provide great information (in six languages) about landmarks as they appear in the skyline. Each rotation – or 'flight' – takes a gracefully slow 30 minutes. At peak times (July, August and school holidays) it can feel like you'll spend more time in the queue than in the capsule; book premium fast-track tickets to jump the queue.

Tickets are cheaper if purchased online, especially if you book in advance or combine the London Eye with other attractions. Feeling romantic? Hire a capsule for two (£425), with a bottle of champers (though for health and safety reasons, a 'host' needs to tag along).

The London Eye has also been the focal point of the capital's celebrated and dramatic midnight New Year's Eve fireworks display.

★ **Southbank Centre**　　ARTS CENTRE
(Map p84; ☎020-3879 9555; www.southbank
centre.co.uk; Belvedere Rd, SE1; ⊕; ⊜ Waterloo, Embankment) The flagship venue of the
Southbank Centre, Europe's largest centre
for performing and visual arts, is the Royal Festival Hall. Its gently curved facade
of glass and Portland stone is more hu-
mane than its 1970s brutalist neighbours.
It is one of London's leading music venues
and the epicentre of life on this part of the
South Bank, hosting cafes, restaurants,
shops and bars.

Just north, the austere Queen Elizabeth Hall (p130) is a brutalist icon, the
second-largest concert venue in the centre, hosting chamber orchestras, quartets,
choirs, dance performances and sometimes opera. Underneath its elevated floor
is a graffiti-decorated **skateboarders'
hang-out**.

The opinion-dividing 1968 **Hayward
Gallery** (£14 to £16.50; ⊘ 11am-7pm Mon & Wed,
to 9pm Thu, 11am-7pm Sat & Sun), another brutalist beauty, is a leading contemporary-art
exhibition space.

The QEH recently underwent a 21st-
century facelift, while the Hayward Gallery
reopened after a similar restoration in January 2018.

★ **London Dungeon**　　HISTORIC BUILDING
(Map p84; www.thedungeons.com/london; County Hall, Westminster Bridge Rd, SE1; adult/child
£30/24; ⊘ 10am-4pm Mon-Wed & Fri, 11am-4pm
Thu, 10am-6pm Sat, 10am-5pm Sun; ⊕; ⊜ Waterloo, Westminster) Older kids tend to love the

London Dungeon, as the terrifying queues
during school holidays and weekends test-
ify. It's all spooky music, ghostly boat rides,
macabre hangman's drop-rides, fake blood
and actors dressed up as torturers and
gory criminals (including Jack the Ripper
and Sweeney Todd), with interactive scares
galore.

★ **Southwark Cathedral**　　CHURCH
(Map p84; ☎020-7367 6700; www.cathedral.south
wark.anglican.org; Montague Cl, SE1; ⊘ 8am-
6pm Mon-Fri, 8.30am-6pm Sat & Sun; ⊜ London
Bridge) The earliest surviving parts of this
relatively small cathedral are the retrochoir
at the eastern end, which contains four
chapels and was part of the 13th-century
Priory of St Mary Overie, some ancient ar-
cading by the southwest door and an arch
that dates to the original Norman church.
But most of the cathedral is Victorian. Inside there are monuments galore, including
a Shakespeare memorial. Catch evensong
at 5.30pm on four weekdays a week, 4pm
on Saturdays and 3pm on Sundays.

National Theatre　　THEATRE
(Map p84; ☎020-7452 3000; www.nationalthe
atre.org.uk; South Bank, SE1; ⊕; ⊜ Waterloo) The
nation's flagship theatre complex comprises
three auditoriums for performances. Likened by Prince Charles to a nuclear power
station, the theatre's purpose-designed architecture is considered an icon of the brutalist school. Fantastic **backstage tours**
lasting 1¼ hours (adult/child £9.50/8.25)
are available. Every tour is different but
you're likely to see rehearsals and changes

GETTING HIGH IN LONDON

Not so long ago, getting a good view of London was a near-impossible endeavour. There
was the London Eye (p82), to be sure, but been-there-done-that, yeah? And **Vertigo 42**
(Map p76; ☎020-7877 7703; www.citysociallondon.com; L24, 25 Old Broad St, EC2; mains £26-
38; ⊘ noon-3.30pm & 6-11.30pm Mon-Fri, 5-11.30pm Sat; ⊜ Bank) involved a lot of forward
planning.

Now things are a lot more democratic and, well, the sky's the limit. The 72nd-floor
open-air platform of the Shard (p85) is as high as you'll get in the EU. For nibbles and
views head for the 40th-floor location of Duck & Waffle (p114) or to Madison (p121).
For drinks we love Sky Pod (p121) and the **Radio Rooftop Bar** (Map p70; ☎020-7395
3440; ME London, 10th fl, 336-337 The Strand, WC2; ⊘ noon-1am Mon-Wed, to 2am Thu-Sat,
noon-midnight Sun; ⊜ Temple, Covent Garden). The **5th View** (Map p70; ☎020-7851 2433;
www.5thview.co.uk; 5th fl, Waterstone's Piccadilly, 203-206 Piccadilly, W1; mains from £8.50;
⊘ 9am-9.30pm Mon-Sat, noon-5pm Sun; ⊜ Piccadilly Circus) atop Waterstones bookshop in
Piccadilly is admittedly low on the totem pole but, having taken afternoon tea there, you
can legitimately use the ultimate intellectual's chat-up line: 'I get high on books'.

South Bank

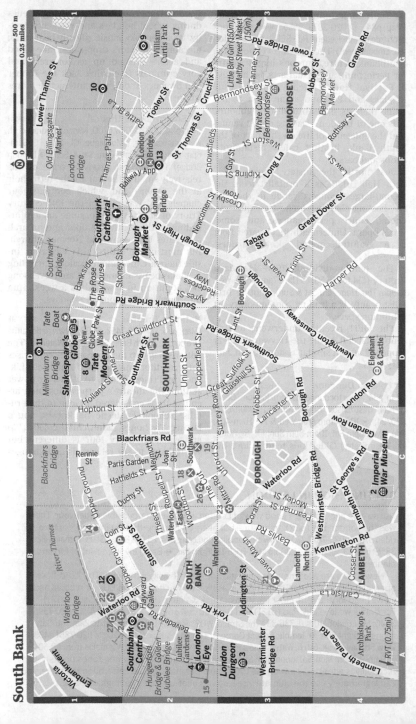

500 m
0.25 miles

River Thames

Victoria Embankment

Waterloo Bridge

Blackfriars Bridge

Jubilee & Golden Bridge & Jubilee Bridge
Hungerford

Jubilee Gardens

22
24
27
Southbank Centre
6
Hayward Gallery
25

London Eye 4
15
London Dungeon 3

Westminster Bridge Rd

York Rd

12
Coin St
Upper Ground
Stamford St
14

SOUTH BANK
Rennie St
Paris Garden
Hatfields St
Duchy St
Theed St
Roupell St
Mepham St
Joan St
18
26
East St
Waterloo
Wootton St
23
The Cut
Waterloo Rd
Lower Marsh
Baylis Rd

Addington St
21

Lambeth North

Carlisle La

LAMBETH
Cosser St
St George's Rd
Kennington Rd
Lambeth Rd
Lambeth Palace Rd

Archbishop's Park

RVT (0.75mi)

Blackfriars Rd
Southwark St
19
The Cut
Whitford St
Coral St
Pearman St
Morley St
Westminster Bridge Rd

BOROUGH
Waterloo Rd
Borough Rd

Surrey Row
Great Suffolk St
Glasshill St
Webber St
Lancaster St
Garden Row
London Rd

2 Imperial War Museum

Millennium Bridge

Tate Boat
5
11
8
Shakespeare's Globe
Tate Modern
Sumner St
New Globe Walk
Globe St
Park St
The Rose Playhouse
Bankside
Hopton St
Holland St

Southwark Bridge

Southwark Cathedral
7

Borough Market 1
Stoney St
Bankside
Southwark Bridge Rd
Great Guildford St
16
Southwark St
SOUTHWARK
Union St
Copperfield St
Ayres St
Redcross Way
Lant St
Southwark Bridge Rd
Borough
Swan St
Trinity St
Tabard St
Trinity St

Newington Causeway
Elephant & Castle
Elephant & Castle

Old Billingsgate Market
Lower Thames St

London Bridge

Thames Path

Battle Br La

10

9
William Curtis Park
17

Tooley St
Railway App
London Bridge
13
London Bridge

St Thomas St
Crucifix La
Snowsfields
Guy St
Kipling St
Crosby Row
Newcomen St

Little Bird Gin (150m);
Maltby Street Market (150m)

Tower Bridge Rd
White Cube Bermondsey
Weston St
Long La
BERMONDSEY
20
Abbey St
Bermondsey St
Tanner St
Bermondsey Market
Rothsay St
Law St
Great Dover St
Harper Rd
Grange Rd

South Bank

of sets or bump into actors in the corridors. There is at least one tour per day, and often more. Consult the website for exact times and make sure you book.

The Shard　　　　　　　　NOTABLE BUILDING
(Map p84; www.theviewfromtheshard.com; 32 London Bridge St, SE1; adult/child £30.95/24.95; ◎10am-10pm; ◉London Bridge) Puncturing the skies above London, the dramatic splinter-like form of the Shard has rapidly become an icon of London. The viewing platforms on floors 69 and 72 are open to the public and the views are, as you'd expect from a 244m vantage point, sweeping, but they come at a hefty price – book online at least a day in advance to make a big saving.

HMS Belfast　　　　　　　　　　　SHIP
(Map p84; www.iwm.org.uk/visits/hms-belfast; Queen's Walk, SE1; adult/child £15.45/7.70; ◎10am-5pm; ◉London Bridge) HMS *Belfast* is a magnet for kids of all ages. This large, light cruiser – launched in 1938 – served in WWII, helping to sink the German battleship *Scharnhorst*, shelling the Normandy coast on D-Day and later participating in the Korean War. Its 6in guns could bombard a target 14 land miles distant. Displays offer a great insight into what life on board was like, in peacetimes and during military engagements.

◎ Kensington & Hyde Park

★**Natural History Museum**　　　MUSEUM
(Map p86; www.nhm.ac.uk; Cromwell Rd, SW7; ◎10am-5.50pm; ◉South Kensington) FREE This colossal and magnificent-looking building is infused with the irrepressible Victorian spirit of collecting, cataloguing and interpreting the natural world. The **Dinosaurs Gallery** (Blue Zone) is a must for children, who gawp at the animatronic T-Rex, fossils and excellent displays. Adults for their part will love the intriguing Treasures exhibition in the **Cadogan Gallery** (Green Zone), which houses a host of unrelated objects each telling its own unique story, from a chunk of moon rock to a dodo skeleton.

Also in the Green Zone, the **Mineral Gallery** is a breathtaking display of architectural perspective leading to the **Vault**, where you'll find the **Aurora Collection** of almost 300 coloured diamonds. In the Orange Zone, the vast **Darwin Centre** focuses on taxonomy, showcasing 28 million insects and six million plants in a giant cocoon; glass windows allow you to watch scientists at work.

At the centre of the museum is **Hintze Hall**, which resembles a cathedral nave – quite fitting, as it was built in a time when the natural sciences were challenging the

Knightsbridge, South Kensington & Chelsea

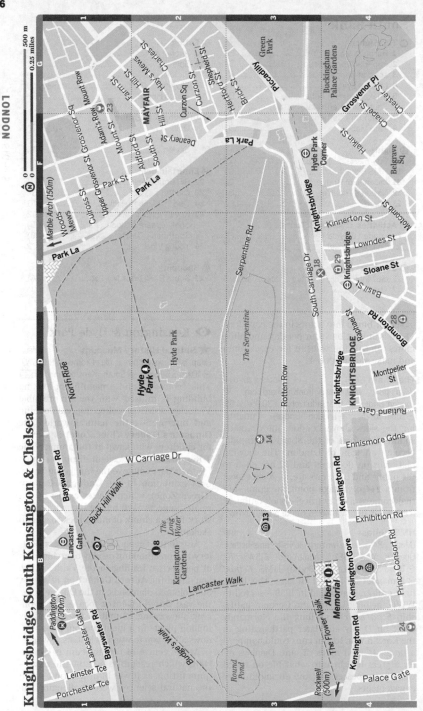

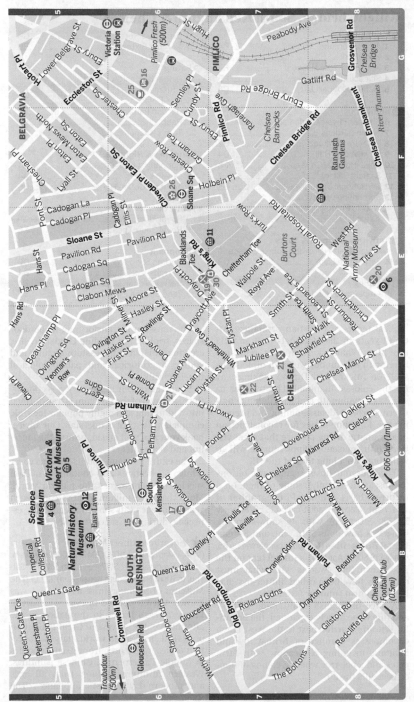

Knightsbridge, South Kensington & Chelsea

biblical tenets of Christian orthodoxy. After 81 years in the Mammals Hall, in 2017 the Blue Whale skeleton was relocated here, with the famous cast of a diplodocus skeleton (nicknamed Dippy) making way for the colossal mammal. The transfer itself was a mammoth and painstaking engineering project, disassembling and preparing the 4.5-tonne bones for reconstruction in a dramatic diving posture that greet visitors to the museum. Dippy himself will go walkabout on a long tour of the UK.

The museum hosts regular exhibitions (admission fees apply), some of them on a recurrent basis. **Wildlife Photographer of the Year** (Map p86; adult/child £13.50/8, family £28-38; ⊙Oct-Sep), with its show-stopping images, is now in its 50th year, and **Sensational Butterflies** (Map p86; per person £5.85, family £19.80; ⊙Apr-Sep), a tunnel tent on the East Lawn that swarms with what must originally have been called 'flutter-bys', has become a firm summer favourite.

A slice of English countryside in SW7 and due to be hugely expanded, the beautiful **Wildlife Garden** next to the West Lawn encompasses a range of British lowland habitats, including a meadow with farm gates and a bee tree where a colony of honey bees fills the air.

The museum is transforming its outdoor spaces, tripling the Wildlife Garden in size, creating a piazza in the eastern grounds and adding a geological and palaeontological timeline walk.

From Halloween to January, a section by the East Lawn of the museum is transformed into a glittering and highly popular **ice rink**, complete with a hot drinks stall. Our advice: book your slot well ahead, browse the museum and skate later.

The entire museum and its gardens cover a huge 5.7 hectares and contain 80 million specimens from across the natural world. More than five million visitors come each year, so queues can sometimes get long, especially during the school holidays.

★**Victoria & Albert Museum**   MUSEUM
(V&A; Map p86; ☑020-7942 2000; www.vam.ac.uk; Cromwell Rd, SW7; ⊙10am-5.45pm Sat-Thu, to 10pm Fri; ⊜South Kensington) FREE The Museum of Manufactures, as the V&A was known when it opened in 1852, was part of Prince Albert's legacy to the nation in the aftermath of the successful Great Exhibition of 1851. It houses the world's largest collection of decorative arts, from Asian ceramics to Middle Eastern rugs, Chinese paintings, Western furniture, fashion from all ages and modern-day domestic appliances. The

(ticketed) temporary exhibitions are another highlight, covering anything from David Bowie retrospectives to designer Alexander McQueen, special materials and trends.

★ **Science Museum** MUSEUM
(Map p86; ☑ 020-7942 4000; www.sciencemuseum.org.uk; Exhibition Rd, SW7; ☺ 10am-6pm; ⊜ South Kensington) FREE With seven floors of interactive and educational exhibits, this scientifically spellbinding museum will mesmerise adults and children alike, covering everything from early technology to space travel. A perennial favourite is **Exploring Space**, a gallery featuring genuine rockets and satellites and a full-size replica of the *Eagle,* the lander that took Neil Armstrong and Buzz Aldrin to the moon in 1969. The **Making the Modern World Gallery** next door is a visual feast of locomotives, planes, cars and other revolutionary inventions.

★ **Hyde Park** PARK
(Map p86; www.royalparks.org.uk/parks/hyde-park; ☺ 5am-midnight; ⊜ Marble Arch, Hyde Park Corner, Queensway) At 145 hectares, Hyde Park is central London's largest open space, expropriated from the Church in 1536 by Henry VIII and turned into a hunting ground and later a venue for duels, executions and horse racing. The 1851 Great Exhibition was held here, and during WWII the park became an enormous potato field. These days, there's boating on the **Serpentine**, summer concerts (Bruce Springsteen, Florence + The Machine, Patti Smith), film nights and other warm-weather events.

★ **Kensington Palace** PALACE
(Map p92; www.hrp.org.uk/kensington-palace; Kensington Gardens, W8; adult/child £15.50/free (when booked online); ☺ 10am-4pm Nov-Feb, to 6pm Mar-Oct; ⊜ High St Kensington) Built in 1605, the palace became the favourite royal residence under William and Mary of Orange in 1689, and remained so until George III became king and moved out. Today, it is still a royal residence, with the likes of the Duke and Duchess of Cambridge (Prince William and his wife Catherine) and the Duke and Duchess of Sussex (Prince Harry and Meghan) living there. A large part of the palace is open to the public, however, including the King's and Queen's State Apartments.

★ **Apsley House** HISTORIC BUILDING
(Map p68; ☑ 020-7499 5676; www.english-heritage.org.uk/visit/places/apsley-house; 149 Picca-

dilly, Hyde Park Corner, W1; adult/child £9.30/5.60, with Wellington Arch £11.20/6.70; ☺ 11am-5pm Wed-Sun Apr-Oct, 10am-4pm Sat & Sun Nov-Mar; ⊜ Hyde Park Corner) This stunning house, containing exhibits about the Duke of Wellington, who defeated Napoleon Bonaparte at Waterloo, was once the first building to appear when entering London from the west and was therefore known as 'No 1 London'. Wellington memorabilia, including the Duke's death mask, fills the basement **gallery**, while an astonishing collection of china and silver, and paintings by Velasquez, Rubens, Van Dyck, Brueghel, Murillo and Goya awaits in the 1st-floor Waterloo Gallery.

Kensington Gardens PARK
(Map p92; ☑ 0300 061 2000; www.royalparks.org.uk/parks/kensington-gardens; ☺ 6am-dusk; ⊜ Queensway, Lancaster Gate) A gorgeous collection of manicured lawns, tree-shaded avenues and basins immediately west of Hyde Park, the picturesque 107-hectare expanse of Kensington Gardens is technically part of Kensington Palace, located in the far west of the gardens.The large **Round Pond** is enjoyable to amble around and also worth a look are the lovely fountains in the **Italian Gardens** (Map p86; Kensington Gardens; ⊜ Lancaster Gate), believed to be a gift from Prince Albert to Queen Victoria; they are now the venue of a handy new cafe.

The **Diana, Princess of Wales Memorial Playground** (Map p92; ⊜ Queensway), in the northwest corner of the gardens, has some pretty ambitious attractions for children. Next to the playground stands the delightful **Elfin Oak** (Map p92), a 900-year-old tree stump carved with elves, gnomes, witches and small creatures. George Frampton's celebrated **Peter Pan statue** (Map p86; ⊜ Lancaster Gate) is close to the lake, while the astonishing **Albert Memorial** (Map p86; ☑ tours 020-8969 0104; tours adult/concession £9/8; ☺ tours 2pm & 3pm 1st Sun of month Mar-Dec; ⊜ Knightsbridge, Gloucester Rd) is in the south of Kensington Gardens, facing the Royal Albert Hall.

Royal Albert Hall HISTORIC BUILDING
(Map p86; ☑ 0845 401 5034, box office 020-7589 8212; www.royalalberthall.com; Kensington Gore, SW7; tours £10.75-16.75; ⊜ South Kensington) Built in 1871, thanks in part to the proceeds of the 1851 Great Exhibition organised by Prince Albert (Queen Victoria's husband), this huge, domed, red-brick amphitheatre,

Victoria & Albert Museum

HALF-DAY HIGHLIGHTS TOUR

The art- and design-packed V&A is vast: we have devised an easy-to-follow tour of the museum highlights to help cover some signature pieces while also allowing you to appreciate some of the grandeur of the museum architecture.

Enter the V&A by the main entrance off Cromwell Rd and immediately turn left to explore the Islamic Middle East Gallery and to discover the sumptuous silk-and-wool **❶ Ardabil Carpet**. Among the pieces from South Asia in the adjacent gallery is the terrifying automated **❷ Tipu's Tiger**. Continue to the outstanding **❸ Fashion Gallery** with its displays of clothing styles through the ages. The magnificent gallery opposite houses the **❹ Raphael Cartoons**, large paintings by Raphael used to weave tapestries for the Vatican. Take the stairs to level 2 and the Britain 1500–1760 Gallery; turn left in

Raphael Cartoons
These seven drawings by Raphael, depicting the acts of St Peter and St Paul, were the full-scale preparatory works for seven tapestries that were woven for the Sistine Chapel in the Vatican.

Fashion Gallery
With clothing from the 18th century to the present day, this circular and chronologically arranged gallery showcases evening wear, undergarments and iconic fashion milestones, such as 1960s dresses designed by Mary Quant.

The Great Bed of Ware
Created during the reign of Queen Elizabeth I, its headboard and bedposts are etched with ancient graffiti; the 16th-century oak Great Bed of Ware is famously name-dropped in Shakespeare's *Twelfth Night*.

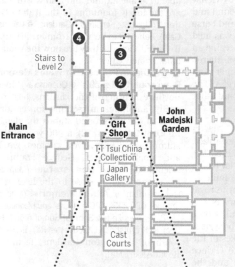

LEVEL 1

LEVEL 2

The Ardabil Carpet
One of the world's most beautiful carpets, the Ardabil was completed in 1540, one of a pair commissioned by Shah Tahmasp, ruler of Iran. The piece is most astonishing for the artistry of the detailing and the subtlety of design.

Tipu's Tiger
This disquieting 18th-century wood-and-metal mechanical automaton depicts a European being savaged by a tiger. When a handle is turned, an organ hidden within the feline mimics the cries of the dying man, whose arm also rises.

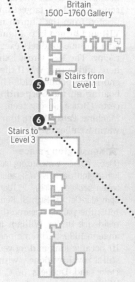

GREG BALFOUR EVANS / ALAMY STOCK PHOTO ©

the gallery to find the **⑤ Great Bed of Ware**, beyond which rests the exquisitely crafted artistry of **⑥ Henry VIII's Writing Box**. Head up the stairs into the Ironwork Gallery on level 3 for the **⑦ Hereford Screen**. Continue through the Ironwork and Sculpture Galleries and through the Leighton Corridor to the glittering **⑧ Jewellery Gallery**. Exit through the Stained Glass gallery, at the end of which you'll find stairs back down to level 1.

TOP TIPS

➡ Museum attendants are always at hand along the route for information.

➡ Photography is allowed in most galleries, except the Jewellery Gallery, the Raphael Cartoons and in exhibitions.

➡ Avoid daytime crowds: visit the V&A in the evening, till 10pm on Fridays.

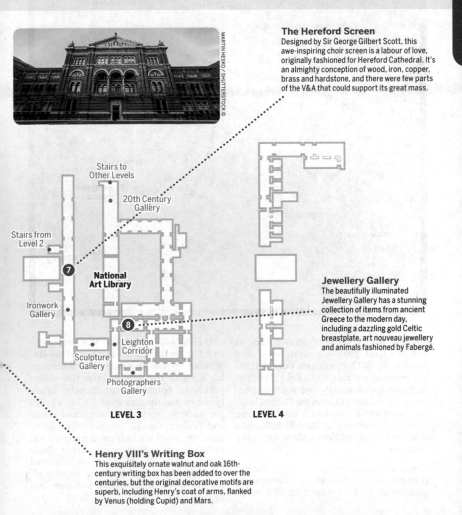

MARTIN HESKO / SHUTTERSTOCK ©

The Hereford Screen
Designed by Sir George Gilbert Scott, this awe-inspiring choir screen is a labour of love, originally fashioned for Hereford Cathedral. It's an almighty conception of wood, iron, copper, brass and hardstone, and there were few parts of the V&A that could support its great mass.

Stairs to Other Levels

20th Century Gallery

Stairs from Level 2

⑦

National Art Library

Ironwork Gallery

⑧

Leighton Corridor

Sculpture Gallery

Photographers Gallery

LEVEL 3

LEVEL 4

Jewellery Gallery
The beautifully illuminated Jewellery Gallery has a stunning collection of items from ancient Greece to the modern day, including a dazzling gold Celtic breastplate, art nouveau jewellery and animals fashioned by Fabergé.

Henry VIII's Writing Box
This exquisitely ornate walnut and oak 16th-century writing box has been added to over the centuries, but the original decorative motifs are superb, including Henry's coat of arms, flanked by Venus (holding Cupid) and Mars.

Notting Hill & Bayswater

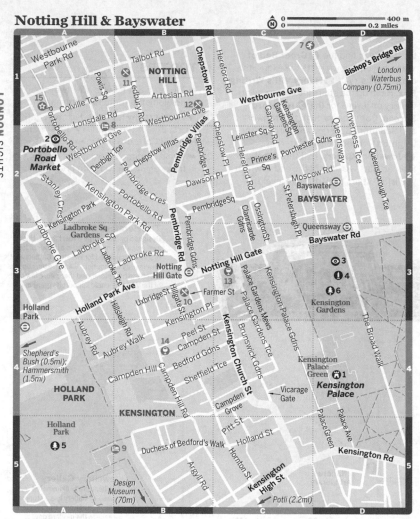

adorned with a frieze of Minton tiles, is Britain's most famous concert venue and home to the BBC's Promenade Concerts (the Proms) every summer. To find out about the hall's intriguing history and royal connections, and to gaze out from the Gallery, book an informative one-hour front-of-house **grand tour** (Map p86; ☑020-7589 8212; adult/child £14/7; ☺hourly 9.30am-4.30pm), operating most days.

Chelsea Physic Garden   GARDENS
(Map p86; ☑020-7352 5646; www.chelseaphysic garden.co.uk; 66 Royal Hospital Rd, SW3; adult/

child £6.10/4.40; ☺11am-5pm Mon, to 6pm Tue-Fri & Sun Apr-Oct, 9.30am-4pm Mon-Fri Nov-Mar; ☻Sloane Sq) You may bump into a wandering duck or two as you enter this walled pocket of botanical enchantment, established by the Apothecaries' Society in 1673 for students working on medicinal plants and healing. One of Europe's oldest of its kind, the small grounds are a compendium of botany, from carnivorous pitcher plants to rich yellow flag irises, a cork oak from Portugal, the largest outdoor fruiting olive tree in the British Isles, rare trees and shrubs.

Notting Hill & Bayswater

Royal Hospital Chelsea MUSEUM
(Map p86; www.chelsea-pensioners.co.uk; Royal Hospital Rd, SW3; ⊙grounds 10am-4.30pm Mon-Sat, Great Hall shuts daily noon-2pm, museum 10am-4pm Mon-Fri; ⊖Sloane Sq) FREE Designed by Christopher Wren, this superb structure was built in 1692 to provide shelter for ex-servicemen. Since the reign of Charles II, it has housed hundreds of war veterans, known as Chelsea Pensioners. They're fondly regarded as national treasures, and cut striking figures in the dark-blue greatcoats (in winter) or scarlet frock coats (in summer) that they wear on ceremonial occasions.

Serpentine Gallery GALLERY
(Map p86; ☑020-7402 6075; www.serpentine galleries.org; Kensington Gardens, W2; ⊙10am-6pm Tue-Sun; ⊖Lancaster Gate, Knightsbridge) FREE This gallery, looking like a 1930s tea-room amid leafy Kensington Gardens, is one of London's most important contemporary-art galleries. Damien Hirst, Andreas Gursky, Louise Bourgeois, Gabriel Orozco, Tomoko Takahashi and Jeff Koons have all exhibited here. A leading architect (who has never built in the UK) is annually commissioned to build a new 'Summer Pavilion' nearby, open from June to October. The galleries run a full program of readings, talks and open-air cinema screenings.

◉ Clerkenwell, Shoreditch & Spitalfields

★**Geffrye Museum** MUSEUM
(Map p124; ☑020-7739 9893; www.geffrye -museum.org.uk; 136 Kingsland Rd, E2; ⊙10am-5pm Tue-Sun; ⊖Hoxton) FREE If you like nosing around other people's homes, you'll love this museum devoted to middle-class domestic interiors. Built in 1714 as a home for poor pensioners, these beautiful ivy-clad brick almshouses have been converted into a series of living rooms dating from 1630 to the present day. The rear garden is also organised by era, mirroring the museum's exploration of domesticity through the centuries. The Geffrye is closed until spring 2020 for major renovations.

★**Dennis Severs' House** MUSEUM
(Map p124; ☑020-7247 4013; www.dennissevers house.co.uk; 18 Folgate St, E1; day/night £10/15; ⊙noon-2pm & 5-9pm Mon, 5-9pm Wed & Fri, noon-4pm Sun; ⊖Liverpool St) This extraordinary Georgian House is set up as if its occupants – a family of Huguenot silk weavers – had just walked out the door. There are half-drunk cups of tea and partially consumed food, lit candles and, in perhaps unnecessary attention to detail, a full chamber pot by the bed. More than a museum, it's an opportunity to meditate on the minutiae of everyday Georgian life through silent exploration.

Old Truman Brewery HISTORIC BUILDING
(Map p124; www.trumanbrewery.com; 91 Brick Lane, E1; ⊖Shoreditch High St) Founded here in the 17th century, Truman's Black Eagle Brewery was, by the 1850s, the largest brewery in the world. Spread over a series of brick buildings and yards straddling both sides of Brick Lane, the complex is now completely given over to edgy markets, pop-up fashion stores, vintage clothes shops, indie record hunters, cafes, bars and live-music venues. Beer may not be brewed here any more, but it certainly is consumed.

◉ East London

★**Whitechapel Gallery** GALLERY
(☑020-7522 7888; www.whitechapelgallery.org; 77-82 Whitechapel High St, E1; ⊙11am-6pm Tue, Wed & Fri-Sun, to 9pm Thu; ⊖Aldgate East) FREE A firm

favourite of art students and the avant-garde cognoscenti, this ground-breaking gallery doesn't have a permanent collection but is devoted to hosting edgy exhibitions of contemporary art. It made its name by staging exhibitions by both established and emerging artists, including the first UK shows by Pablo Picasso, Jackson Pollock, Mark Rothko and Frida Kahlo. The gallery's ambitiously themed shows change every couple of months (check online) and there's often also live music, talks and films on Thursday evenings.

★ **Museum of London Docklands** MUSEUM
(📞020-7001 9844; www.museumoflondon.org.uk/docklands; West India Quay, E14; ⏱10am-6pm; 🚇DLR West India Quay) **FREE** Housed in an 1802 warehouse, this educational museum combines artefacts and multimedia displays to chart the history of the city through its river and docks. The best strategy is to begin on the 3rd floor and work your way down through the ages. Perhaps the most illuminating and certainly the most disturbing gallery is London, Sugar and Slavery, which examines the capital's role in the transatlantic slave trade.

★ **Columbia Road Flower Market** MARKET
(Map p124; www.columbiaroad.info; Columbia Rd, E2; ⏱8am-3pm Sun; 🚇Hoxton) A wonderful explosion of colour and life, this weekly market sells a beautiful array of flowers, pot plants, bulbs, seeds and everything you might need for the garden. It's a lot of fun and the best place to hear proper Cockney barrow-boy banter ('We got flowers cheap enough for ya muvver-in-law's grave' etc). It gets really packed, so go as early as you can, or later on when the vendors sell off the cut flowers cheaply.

★ **Queen Elizabeth Olympic Park** PARK
(www.queenelizabetholympicpark.co.uk; E20; 🚇Stratford) The glittering centrepiece of London's 2012 Olympic Games, this vast 227-hectare expanse includes the main Olympic venues as well as playgrounds, walking and cycling trails, gardens, and a diverse mix of wetland, woodland, meadow and other wildlife habitats as an environmentally fertile legacy for the future. The main focal point is London Stadium (p129), with a Games capacity of 80,000, scaled back to 54,000 seats for its new role as the home ground for West Ham United FC.

LONDON'S LIDOS

The capital's long-running love of outdoor bathing has enjoyed a resurgence in recent years, and its lovely lidos (outdoor pools) are busier than ever. You'll see Londoners taking to the water in pretty much all weathers – even, for the real diehards, the middle of winter.

Serpentine Lido (Map p86; 📞020-7706 3422; Hyde Park, W2; adult/child £4.80/1.80; ⏱10am-6pm daily Jun-Aug, to 6pm Sat & Sun May; 🚇Hyde Park Corner, Knightsbridge) Perhaps the ultimate London pool is inside the Serpentine lake. This fabulous lido is open May to August.

Hampstead Heath Ponds (www.cityoflondon.gov.uk; Hampstead Heath, NW5; adult/child £2/1; 🚇Hampstead Heath) Set in the midst of the gorgeous heath, the brown waters of Hampstead's three bathing ponds (men's, women's and mixed) offer a bracing dip. The water's tested daily, so don't be deterred by the colour.

London Fields Lido (📞020-7254 9038; www.better.org.uk/leisure-centre/london/hackney/london-fields-lido; London Fields West Side, E8; adult/child £4.85/2.85; ⏱6.30am-9pm; 🚇London Fields) Built in the 1930s but abandoned by the '80s, this heated 50m Olympic-size outdoor pool reopened in 2006.

Porchester Spa (Map p92; 📞020-7313 3858; www.porchesterspatreatments.co.uk; Porchester Centre, Queensway, W2; admission £28.90; ⏱10am-10pm; 🚇Bayswater, Royal Oak) Housed in a gorgeous, art deco building, the no-frills Porchester has a 30m swimming pool, a large Finnish-log sauna, two steam rooms, three Turkish hot rooms and a massive plunge pool.

London Aquatics Centre (📞020-8536 3150; www.londonaquaticscentre.org; Carpenters Rd, E20; adult/child from £5.20/3; ⏱6am-10.30pm; 🚇Stratford) Not strictly a lido as it's inside, but Zaha Hadid's award-winning Aquatics Centre, built for the 2012 Olympics, is worth mentioning for its fabulous, undulating architecture.

OFF THE BEATEN TRACK

REGENT'S CANAL

The towpath of the tranquil Regent's Canal (Map p118) makes an excellent shortcut across North London, either on foot or by bike. In full, the ribbon of water runs 9 miles from Little Venice (where it connects with the Grand Union Canal) to the Thames at Limehouse.

You can make do with walking from Little Venice to Camden Town in less than an hour, passing Regent's Park and London Zoo, as well as beautiful villas designed by architect John Nash and redevelopments of old industrial buildings. Allow 25 to 30 minutes between Little Venice and Regent's Park, and 15 to 20 minutes between Regent's Park and Camden Town. There are plenty of well-signed exits along the way.

If you decide to continue on, it's worth stopping at the London Canal Museum (☑ 020-7713 0836; www.canalmuseum.org.uk; 12-13 New Wharf Rd, N1; adult/child £5/2.50; ☺ 10am-4.30pm Tue-Sun & bank holidays; ☻ King's Cross St Pancras) in King's Cross to learn more about the canal's history. Shortly afterwards you'll hit the 878m-long Islington Tunnel and have to take to the roads for a spell. After joining the path again near Colebrooke Row, you can follow the water all the way to the Thames at Limehouse Basin, or divert on to the Hertford Union Canal at Victoria Park and head to Queen Elizabeth Olympic Park.

ArcelorMittal Orbit   TOWER
(☑ 0333 800 8099; www.arcelormittalorbit.com; 3 Thornton St, E20; adult/child £12.50/7.50, with slide £17.50/12.50; ☺ 11am-5pm Mon-Fri, 10am-6pm Sat & Sun; ☻ Stratford) Love it or loathe it, Turner Prize–winner Anish Kapoor's 115m-high, twisted-steel sculpture towers strikingly over the southern end of Queen Elizabeth Olympic Park. In essence it's an artwork, but at the 80m mark it also offers an impressive panorama from its mirrored viewing platform, which is accessed by a lift from the base of the sculpture (the tallest in the UK). A dramatic tunnel slide running down the tower is the world's highest and longest, coiling 178m down to ground level.

Victoria Park   PARK
(www.towerhamlets.gov.uk/victoriapark; Grove Rd, E3; ☺ 7am-dusk; ☻ Hackney Wick) The 'Regent's Park of the East End', this 86-hectare leafy expanse of ornamental lakes, monuments, tennis courts, flower beds and lawns was opened in 1845. It was the first public park in the East End, given the go-ahead after a local MP presented Queen Victoria with a petition of 30,000 signatures. It quickly gained a reputation as the 'People's Park' when many rallies were held here.

Viktor Wynd Museum of Curiosities, Fine Art & Natural History   MUSEUM
(☑ 020-7998 3617; www.thelasttuesdaysociety.org; 11 Mare St, E8; £5; ☺ noon-11pm Wed-Sat, to 10.30pm Sun; ☻ Bethnal Green) Museum? Art project? Cocktail bar? This is not a venue that's easily classifiable. Inspired by Victorian-era cabinets of curiosities (*wunderkabinnet*), Wynd's wilfully eccentric collection includes stuffed birds, pickled genitals, two-headed lambs, shrunken heads, a key to the Garden of Eden, dodo bones, celebrity excrement and a gilded hippo skull that belonged to Pablo Escobar. A self-confessed 'incoherent vision of the world displayed through wonder'; make of it what you will. Or stop by for a cocktail at the bar upstairs.

⊙ North London

Regent's Park   PARK
(Map p112; www.royalparks.org.uk; ☺ 5am-dusk; ☻ Regent's Park, Baker St) The most elaborate and formal of London's many parks, Regent's Park is one of the capital's loveliest green spaces. Among its many attractions are London Zoo, Regent's Canal, an ornamental lake, and sports pitches where locals meet to play football, rugby and volleyball. Queen Mary's Gardens, towards the south of the park, are particularly pretty, especially in June when the roses are in bloom. Performances take place here in an open-air theatre (☑ 0844 826 4242; www.openairtheatre.org; ☺ May-Sep; ☻; ☻ Baker St) during summer.

★ ZSL London Zoo   ZOO
(Map p118; www.zsl.org/zsl-london-zoo; Outer Circle, Regent's Park, NW1; adult/child £29.75/22; ☺ 10am-6pm Apr-Sep, to 5.30pm Mar & Oct, to 4pm Nov-Feb; ☻; ☐ 274) Established in 1828, these 15-hectare zoological gardens are among the oldest in the world. The emphasis nowadays is firmly placed on

North Central London

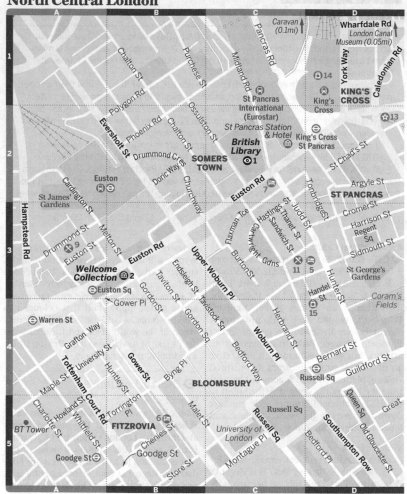

conservation, education and breeding, with fewer animals and bigger enclosures. Highlights include **Land of the Lions, Gorilla Kingdom, Tiger Territory**, the walk-through **In with the Lemurs** and **Butterfly Paradise**. Feeding sessions and talks take place throughout the day. The zoo also organises various experiences, such as Keeper for a Day or sleepovers in the Bug House.

★ **British Library**   LIBRARY
(Map p96; www.bl.uk; 96 Euston Rd, NW1; ☺galleries 9.30am-6pm Mon & Wed-Fri, to 8pm Tue, to 5pm Sat, 11am-5pm Sun; ⊖ King's Cross St Pancras) FREE Consisting of low-slung red-

brick terraces and fronted by a large plaza featuring an oversized statue of Sir Isaac Newton, Colin St John Wilson's British Library building is a love-it-or-hate-it affair (Prince Charles likened it to a secret-police academy). Completed in 1997, it's home to some of the greatest treasures of the written word, including the *Codex Sinaiticus* (the first complete text of the New Testament), Leonardo da Vinci's notebooks and a copy of the Magna Carta (1215).

★ **Highgate Cemetery**   CEMETERY
(www.highgatecemetery.org; Swain's Lane, N6; East Cemetery adult/child £4/free; ☺10am-

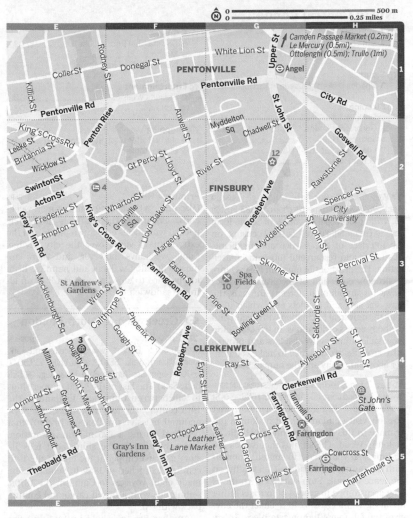

Camden Passage Market (0.2mi);
Le Mercury (0.5mi);
Ottolenghi (0.5mi); Trullo (1mi)

4pm Mon-Fri, 11am-4pm Sat & Sun; ⊖Archway) A Gothic wonderland of shrouded urns, obelisks, broken columns, sleeping angels, Egyptian-style tombs and overgrown graves, Highgate is a Victorian Valhalla spread over 20 wonderfully wild and atmospheric hectares. On the eastern side, you can pay your respects to the graves of Karl Marx and Mary Ann Evans (better known as novelist George Eliot). The real highlight, however, is the overgrown **West Cemetery**, which can only be visited on a **guided tour** (adult/child £12/6; ⊘1.45pm Mon-Fri, every 30min 11am-3pm Sat & Sun Nov-Feb, to 4pm Mar-Oct).

★**Hampstead Heath**   PARK
(www.cityoflondon.gov.uk; ⊖Hampstead Heath, Gospel Oak) Sprawling Hampstead Heath, with its rolling woodlands and meadows, feels a million miles away – despite being approximately four – from the City of London. Covering 320 hectares, most of it woods, hills and meadows, it's home to about 180 bird species, 23 species of butterflies, grass snakes, bats and a rich array of flora. It's a wonderful place for a ramble, especially to the top of **Parliament Hill**, which offers expansive views across the city.

North Central London

◉ Top Sights

1 British Library	C2
2 Wellcome Collection	B3

◉ Sights

3 Charles Dickens Museum	E4

◉ Sleeping

4 Clink78	E2
5 Generator London	D3
6 Jesmond Hotel	B5
7 London St Pancras YHA	C2
8 Zetter Hotel	H4

⊗ Eating

9 Diwana Bhel Poori House	A3
10 Morito	G3
11 North Sea Fish Restaurant	C3

◉ Entertainment

12 Sadler's Wells	G2
13 Scala	D2

◉ Shopping

14 Harry Potter Shop at Platform 9¾	D1
15 Skoob Books	D4

★**Wellcome Collection** MUSEUM
(Map p96; www.wellcomecollection.org; 183 Euston Rd, NW1; ⊙10am-6pm Tue, Wed & Fri-Sun, to 10pm Thu; ⊜Euston Sq, Euston) FREE Focusing on the interface of art, science and medicine, this clever and resourceful museum is fascinating. The heart of the museum is Sir Henry Wellcome's collection of medical curiosities (saws for amputation, forceps through the ages, sex aids and amulets etc), which illustrate the universal fascination with health and the body across civilisations. In the Medicine Now gallery, interactive displays and provocative artworks are designed to make you ponder about humanity and the human body.

Abbey Road Studios HISTORIC BUILDING
(www.abbeyroad.com; 3 Abbey Rd, NW8; ⊜St John's Wood) Beatles aficionados can't possibly visit London without making a pilgrimage to this famous recording studio in St John's Wood. The studios themselves are off-limits, so you'll have to content yourself with examining the decades of fan graffiti on the fence outside. Stop-start local traffic is long accustomed to groups of tourists lining up on the zebra crossing to re-enact the cover of the fab four's 1969 masterpiece *Abbey Road*. In 2010 the crossing was rewarded with Grade II heritage status.

For a strangely engrossing real-time view of the crossing, hit the 'live' tab for the webcam on the studio's website; you can even find your own crossing shot by punching in your time. To reach Abbey Road Studios, take the tube to St John's Wood, cross the road, follow Grove End Rd to its end and turn right. Don't do what some disappointed fans do and head to Abbey Rd Station in West Ham – it's no relation of the true site and miles off course. There are at least 10 Abbey Rds in London, adding to confusion.

Primrose Hill PARK
(Map p118; ⊜Chalk Farm) On summer weekends, Primrose Hill park is absolutely packed with locals enjoying a picnic and the extraordinary views over the city skyline. Come weekdays, however, and there are mostly just dog walkers and nannies. It's a lovely place to enjoy a quiet stroll or an alfresco sandwich.

◉ Greenwich & South London

★**Cutty Sark** MUSEUM
(☏020-8312 6608; www.rmg.co.uk/cuttysark; King William Walk, SE10; adult/child £13.50/7; ⊙10am-5pm Sep-Jun, to 6pm Jul & Aug; ⊠DLR Cutty Sark) The last of the great clipper ships to sail between China and England in the 19th century, the fully restored *Cutty Sark* endured massive fire damage in 2007 that occurred during a £25 million restoration. The exhibition in the ship's hold tells its story as a tea clipper at the end of the 19th century. Launched in 1869 in Scotland, she made eight voyages to China in the 1870s, sailing out with a mixed cargo and coming back with tea.

Another fire took hold in 2014, but fire crews were quick to respond and extinguish the blaze. As you make your way up, there are films, interactive maps and plenty of illustrations and props to get an idea of what life on board was like. Book online for cheaper rates.

★**National Maritime Museum** MUSEUM
(☏020-8312 6565; www.rmg.co.uk/national-maritime-museum; Romney Rd, SE10; ⊙10am-5pm; ⊠DLR Cutty Sark) FREE Narrating the long, briny and eventful history of seafaring Britain, this excellent museum's exhibits are arranged thematically, with highlights in-

cluding *Miss Britain III* (the first boat to top 100mph on open water) from 1933, the 19m-long golden state barge built in 1732 for Frederick, Prince of Wales, the huge ship's propeller and the colourful figureheads installed on the ground floor. Families will love these, as well as the ship simulator and the 'All Hands' children's gallery on the 2nd floor.

Under eights can get to grips with all things nautical in the 'Ahoy!' gallery, also on the ground floor. Adults are likely to prefer the other fantastic (and slightly more serene) galleries. Voyagers: Britons and the Sea on the ground floor is an introduction to the collection and showcases some of the museum's incredible archives. JMW Turner's largest work – controversial for its chronological inaccuracies – the huge 1824 oil painting *The Battle of Trafalgar*, is hung in its namesake gallery on the ground floor.

On the 1st floor, Traders: the East India Company and Asia looks back on Britain's maritime trade with the East in the 19th century, while The Atlantic: Slavery, Trade, Empire explores the triangular trade between Europe, Africa and America from the 1600s to the 1850s.

On the 2nd floor, the award-winning Nelson, Navy, Nation 1688–1815 focuses on the history of the Royal Navy during the conflict-ridden 17th century. It provides an excellent look at the legendary national hero and, through documents and memorabilia, explains his achievements and dazzling celebrity. The coat in which Nelson was fatally wounded during the Battle of Trafalgar takes pride of place.

Opened in 2018, the new Exploration Wing contains four galleries: Pacific Exploration, Polar Worlds, Tudor and Stuart Seafarers and Sea Things, devoted to the theme of exploration and human endeavour.

★ Royal Observatory   HISTORIC BUILDING
(☑ 020-8312 6565; www.rmg.co.uk/royal-observatory; Greenwich Park, Blackheath Ave, SE10; adult/child £10/6.50, incl Cutty Sark £20/11.50; ☉ 10am-5pm Sep-Jun, to 6pm Jul & Aug; ☑ DLR Cutty Sark, DLR Greenwich, Greenwich) Rising south of Queen's House, idyllic Greenwich Park (☑ 0300 061 2380; www.royalparks.org.uk; King George St, SE10; ☉ 6am-around sunset; ☑ DLR Cutty Sark, ☑ Greenwich, Maze Hill) climbs up the hill, affording stunning views of London from the Royal Observatory, which Charles II had built in 1675 to help solve the riddle of longitude. To the north is lovely Flamsteed House and the Meridian Courtyard, where

you can stand with your feet straddling the western and eastern hemispheres; admission is by ticket. The southern half contains the highly informative and free Weller Astronomy Galleries and the Peter Harrison Planetarium (☑ 020-8312 6608; www.rmg.co.uk/whats-on/planetarium-shows; adult/child £8/5.50).

In 1884 Greenwich was designated as the prime meridian of the world, and Greenwich Mean Time (GMT) became the universal measurement of standard time. Becoming a Royal Museums Greenwich Member (from £44 per year) allows you unlimited access to the Royal Observatory, the Peter Harrison Planetarium, the Cutty Sark as well as exhibitions at the National Maritime Museum; see the website for details.

★ Imperial War Museum   MUSEUM
(Map p84; ☑ 020-7416 5000; www.iwm.org.uk; Lambeth Rd, SE1; ☉ 10am-6pm; ☉ Lambeth North) FREE Fronted by a pair of intimidating 15in naval guns, this riveting museum is housed in what was the Bethlehem Royal Hospital, a psychiatric hospital also known as Bedlam. Although the museum's focus is on military action involving British or Commonwealth troops largely during the 20th century, it rolls out the carpet to war in the wider sense. Highlights include the state-of-the-art First World War Galleries and Witnesses to War in the forecourt and atrium above.

Indeed, Witnesses to War is where you'll find everything from a Battle of Britain Spitfire and a towering German V-2 rocket to a Reuters Land Rover damaged by rocket attack in Gaza and a section of the World Trade Center in New York.

On the 1st floor A Family in Wartime poignantly follows WWII through the experiences of the real-life Allpress family of Stockwell. In Secret War on the 2nd floor, there's an intriguing rifle through the work of the Secret Operations Executive (SOE), such as rubber soles resembling feet worn underneath boots to leave 'footprints' on enemy beaches. One of the most challenging sections is the extensive and harrowing Holocaust Exhibition (not recommended for under 14s), the entrance of which is on the 4th floor. Curiosities of War is a jumble sale of fascinating items, such as a makeshift bar used by the Dam Busters crew in 1943, taken from the museum's collection. Other galleries and exhibition spaces are given over to temporary exhibitions (check the website for details).

WILL RODRIGUES / SHUTTERSTOCK ©

1. Yeoman Warders (Beefeaters) at the Tower of London (p77)
2. Windsor Castle (p213) 3. Buckingham Palace (p67)
4. Gardens at Hampton Court Palace (p103)

KIEV VICTOR / SHUTTERSTOCK'S ©

Royal London

Along with Stonehenge and Big Ben, the current monarch, Queen Elizabeth II, is one of the most potent symbols of England. Pretty much anything connected to the country's royal heritage is a guaranteed attraction – especially the capital's fine collection of palaces and castles.

The Tower of London

The Tower of London (p77) has been a feature of the capital's skyline for more than nine centuries, but its foundations date back to Roman times. Over the centuries it's been a royal residence, a treasury, a mint, a prison and an arsenal. Today it's home to the spectacular Crown Jewels, as well as red-coated Beefeaters and ravens attributed with mythical power.

Windsor Castle

Although not actually in London, Windsor Castle (p213) is near enough to visit on a day trip. This is the largest and oldest occupied fortress in the world, an astounding edifice of defensive walls, towers and battlements, used for state occasions and as the Queen's weekend retreat.

Buckingham Palace

Buckingham Palace (p67) has been the monarch's London residence since 1837, and the current Queen divides her time between it, Windsor Castle and Balmoral in Scotland. If she's at home, the 'royal standard' flag flies on the roof. If she's away on her summer holiday, you can take a tour to see inside. Either way, don't miss the famous Changing of the Guard.

Hampton Court Palace

Hampton Court Palace (p103) is England's largest and grandest Tudor structure, used by King Henry VIII as a riverside hideaway. After admiring the grand interior, you can relax in the extensive gardens, but don't get lost in the 300-year-old maze.

Augustus Pugin, famous Gothic Revival architect of the interior of the Houses of Parliament, was once a patient in the psychiatric wards of the former Bethlehem Royal Hospital. The hospital moved in 1930 and the building became home to the Imperial War Museum in 1936.

★ **Old Royal Naval College** HISTORIC BUILDING
(www.ornc.org; 2 Cutty Sark Gardens, SE10; ⊘10am-5pm, grounds 8am-11pm; ⓡDLR Cutty Sark) FREE Sir Christopher Wren's baroque masterpiece in Greenwich and indeed Britain's largest ensemble of baroque architecture, the Old Royal Naval College contains the Neoclassical Chapel and the extraordinary **Painted Hall** (⌨020-8269 4799) FREE. The entire Old Royal Naval College, including the Chapel, the **Visitor Centre** (www.ornc.org/visitor-centre; Pepys Bldg, King William Walk, SE10; ⊘10am-5pm, to 6pm Jun-Sep), and the grounds, can be visited for free. Volunteers lead free 45-minute tours throughout each day from the Visitor Centre.

Queen's House HISTORIC BUILDING
(www.rmg.co.uk/queens-house; Romney Rd, SE10; ⊘10am-5pm; ⓡDLR Cutty Sark) FREE The first Palladian building by architect Inigo Jones after he returned from Italy is as enticing for its form as for its art collection. The house was begun in 1616 for Anne of Denmark, wife of James I, but was not completed until 1638, when it became the home of Charles I and his queen, Henrietta Maria. The beautiful helix-shaped (and reportedly haunted) **Tulip Stairs** form England's first set of centrally unsupported stairs: they constitute a peerless photo op for upward shots.

◉ West London

★ **Portobello Road Market** MARKET
(Map p92; www.portobelloroadmarket.org; Portobello Rd, W10; ⊘8am-6.30pm Mon-Wed, Fri & Sat, to 1pm Thu; ⊜Notting Hill Gate, Ladbroke Grove) Lovely on a warm summer's day, Portobello Road Market is an iconic London attraction with an eclectic mix of street food, fruit and veg, antiques, curios, collectables, vibrant fashion and trinkets. Although the shops along Portobello Rd open daily and the fruit and veg stalls (from Elgin Cres to Talbot Rd) only close on Sunday, the busiest day by far is Saturday, when antique dealers set up shop (from Chepstow Villas to Elgin Cres).

Design Museum MUSEUM
(⌨020-7940 8790; www.designmuseum.org; 224-238 Kensington High St, W8; ⊘10am-6pm, to 8pm 1st Fri of month; ⊜High St Kensington) FREE Relocated in 2016 from its former Thames location to a stunning new £83m home by Holland Park, this slick museum is dedicated to popularising the importance and influence of design in everyday life. With a revolving program of special exhibitions, it's a crucial pitstop for anyone with an eye for modern and contemporary aesthetics. Splendidly housed in the refitted former Commonwealth Institute (which opened in 1962), the lavish interior – all smooth oak and marble – is itself a design triumph.

◉ Richmond, Kew & Hampton Court

★ **Kew Gardens** GARDENS
(Royal Botanic Gardens, Kew; www.kew.org; Kew Rd, TW9; adult/child £17/5; ⊘10am-4.15pm Sep-Mar, closes later Apr-Aug; ⓦKew Pier, ⓡKew Bridge, ⊜Kew Gardens) In 1759 botanists began rummaging around the world for specimens to plant in the 3-hectare Royal Botanic Gardens at Kew. They never stopped collecting, and the gardens, which have bloomed to 121 hectares, provide the most comprehensive botanical collection on earth (including the world's largest collection of orchids). A Unesco World Heritage Site, the gardens can easily devour a day's exploration; for those pressed for time, the **Kew Explorer** (⌨020-8332 5648; www.kew.org/kew-gardens/whats-on/kew-explorer-land-train; adult/child £5/2) hop-on/hop-off road train takes in the main sights.

Don't worry if you don't know your golden slipper orchid from your fengoky or your quiver tree from your alang-alang; a visit to Kew is a journey of discovery for everyone. Highlights include the enormous early Victorian **Palm House**, a hothouse of metal and curved sheets of glass; the impressive **Princess of Wales Conservatory**; the red-brick, 1631 **Kew Palace** (www.hrp.org.uk/kewpalace; with admission to Kew Gardens; ⊘10.30am-5.30pm Apr-Sep), formerly King George III's country retreat; the celebrated **Chinese Pagoda** designed by William Chambers in 1762; the **Temperate House** the world's largest ornamental glasshouse; and the very enjoyable **Rhizotron & Xstrata Treetop Walkway**, where you can survey the tree canopy from 18m up in the air. A lattice fashioned from thousands of pieces of aluminium illuminated with hundreds of LED lights, the 17m-high **Hive** mimics activity within a real beehive. Opened in 2016, the 320m-long **Great Broad Walk Borders** is the longest double herbaceous border in the UK. The idyllic, thatched **Queen Charlotte's Cottage** (⊙11am-4pm Sat & Sun Apr-Sep) in the southwest of the gardens was popular with 'mad' George III and his wife; the beautiful carpets of bluebells around here are a draw in spring. Several long vistas (**Cedar Vista**, **Syon Vista** and **Pagoda Vista**) are channelled by trees from vantage points within Kew Gardens.

Check the website for a full list of activities at Kew, including free one-hour walking tours (daily), photography walks, theatre performances, outside cinema as well as a host of seasonal events and things to do.

Kew Gardens is easily reached by tube, but you might prefer to take a cruise on a riverboat from the Westminster Passenger Services Association (p107), which runs several daily boats from April to October, departing from Westminster Pier.

★**Hampton Court Palace**   PALACE
(www.hrp.org.uk/hamptoncourtpalace; Hampton Court Palace, KT8; adult/child/family £19/10/34; ⊙10am-4.30pm Nov-Mar, to 6pm Apr-Oct; 🚆Hampton Court Palace, 🚇Hampton Court) Built by Cardinal Thomas Wolsey in 1514 but coaxed from him by Henry VIII just before Wolsey (as chancellor) fell from favour, Hampton Court Palace is England's largest and grandest Tudor structure. It was already one of Europe's most sophisticated palaces when, in the 17th century, Christopher Wren designed an extension. The result is a beautiful blend of Tudor and 'restrained baroque' architecture. You could easily spend a day exploring the palace and its 24 hectares of riverside gardens, including a 300-year-old **maze** (adult/child/family £4.20/2.60/12.30; ⊙10am-5.15pm Apr-Oct, to 3.45pm Nov-Mar).

Richmond Park   PARK
(☎0300 061 2200; www.royalparks.org.uk/parks/richmond-park; ⊙7am-dusk; 🚇Richmond) At almost 1000 hectares (the largest urban parkland in Europe), this park offers everything from formal gardens and ancient oaks to unsurpassed views of central London 12 miles away. It's easy to flee the several roads slicing up the rambling wilderness, making the park perfect for a quiet walk or a picnic with the kids, even in summer when Richmond's riverside heaves. Coming from Richmond,

LONDON WETLAND CENTRE

One of Europe's largest inland wetland projects, this 42-hectare **centre** (☎020-8409 4400; www.wwt.org.uk/wetland-centres/london; Queen Elizabeth's Walk, SW13; adult/child/family £12.75/7/35.55; ⊙9.30am-5.30pm Mar-Oct, to 4.30pm Nov-Feb; 🚆Barnes, 🚇Hammersmith) run by the Wildfowl & Wetlands Trust was transformed from four Victorian reservoirs in 2000 and attracts some 140 species of birds, as well as frogs, butterflies, dragonflies and lizards, plus a thriving colony of watervoles. The glass-fronted observatory affords panoramic views over the lakes, while meandering paths and boardwalks lead visitors through the watery habitats of black swans, Bewick's swans, geese, red-crested pochards, sand martins, coots, bitterns, herons and kingfishers.

it's easiest to enter via Richmond Gate or from Petersham Rd.

Strawberry Hill   HISTORIC BUILDING
(☎020-8744 1241; www.strawberryhillhouse.org.uk; 268 Waldegrave Rd, TW1; adult/child £12.50/free; ⊙house 11am-4.30pm Sun-Wed Mar-Oct, noon-4pm Sun-Mon Nov-Feb, garden 10am-5.30pm daily; 🚆Strawberry Hill, 🚇Richmond Station) With its snow-white walls and Gothic turrets, this fantastical and totally restored 18th-century creation in Twickenham is the work of art historian, author and politician Horace Walpole. Studded with elaborate stained glass, the building reaches its astonishing apogee in the gallery, with its magnificent papier-mâché ceiling. For the full magic, join a twilight tour (£20). Last admission to the house is 4pm.

🕿 Tours

★**London Waterbus Company**   CRUISE
(☎020-7482 2550; www.londonwaterbus.com; 32 Camden Lock Pl, NW1; adult/child one-way £9/7.50, return £14/12; ⊙hourly 10am-5pm Apr-Sep, weekends only & less frequent departures other months; 🚇Warwick Ave, Camden Town) This enclosed barge runs enjoyable 50-minute trips on Regent's Canal between Little Venice and Camden Lock, passing by Regent's Park and stopping at London Zoo. There are fewer departures outside high season; check the website for schedules. One-way tickets

Hampton Court Palace

A DAY AT THE PALACE

With so much to explore in the palace and seemingly infinite gardens, it can be tricky knowing where to begin. It helps to understand how the palace has grown over the centuries and how successive royal occupants embellished Hampton Court to suit their purposes and to reflect the style of the time.

As soon as he had his royal hands upon the palace from Cardinal Thomas Wolsey,

Henry VIII began expanding the **①Tudor architecture**, adding the **②Great Hall**, the exquisite **③Chapel Royal**, the opulent Great Watching Chamber and the gigantic **④Tudor kitchens**. By 1540 it had become one of the grandest and most sophisticated palaces in Europe. James I kept things ticking over, while Charles I added a new tennis court and did some serious art-collecting, including pieces that can be seen in the **⑤Cumberland Art Gallery**.

Tudor Kitchens

These vast kitchens were the engine room of the palace, and had a staff of 200 people. Six spit-rack-equipped fireplaces ensured roast meat was always on the menu (to the tune of 8200 sheep and 1240 oxen per year).

⑦ The Maze

Around 150m north of the main building
Created from hornbeam and yew and planted in around 1700, the maze covers a third of an acre within the famous palace gardens. A must-see conclusion to Hampton Court, the maze takes the average visitor about 20 minutes to reach the centre.

Tudor Architecture

Dating to 1515, the palace serves as one of the finest examples of Tudor architecture in the nation. Cardinal Thomas Wolsey was responsible for transforming what was originally a grand medieval manor house into a stunning Tudor palace.

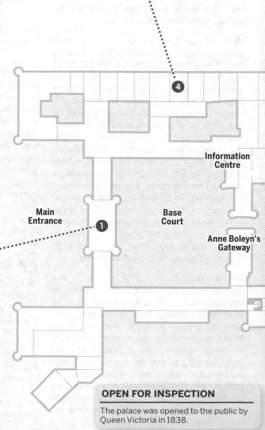

Information Centre

Main Entrance

Base Court

Anne Boleyn's Gateway

OPEN FOR INSPECTION

The palace was opened to the public by Queen Victoria in 1838.

After the Civil War, puritanical Oliver Cromwell warmed to his own regal proclivities, spending weekends in the comfort of the former Queen's bedroom and selling off Charles I's art collection. In the late 17th century, William and Mary employed Sir Christopher Wren for baroque extensions, chiefly the William III Apartments, reached by the **6 King's Staircase**. William III also commissioned the world-famous **7 maze**.

TOP TIPS

➡ Ask one of the red-tunic-garbed warders for anecdotes and information.

➡ Tag along with a themed tour led by costumed historians or do a dusk till dawn sleepover at the palace.

➡ Grab one of the audio tours from the Information Centre.

The Great Hall
This grand dining hall is the defining room of the palace, displaying what is considered England's finest hammer-beam roof, 16th-century Flemish tapestries that depict the story of Abraham, and some exquisite stained-glass windows.

Chapel Royal
The blue-and-gold vaulted ceiling was originally intended for Christ Church, Oxford, but was installed here instead; the 18th-century oak reredos was carved by Grinling Gibbons. Books on display include a 1611 1st edition of the King James Bible, printed by Robert Barker.

The King's Staircase
One of five rooms at the palace painted by Antonio Verrio and a suitably bombastic prelude to the King's Apartments, the overblown King's Staircase adulates William III by elevating him above a cohort of Roman emperors.

Chapel Court Garden

Clock Court

Fountain Court

② ⑤ ⑥ ③

Cumberland Art Gallery
The former Cumberland Suite, designed by William Kent, has been restored to accommodate a choice selection of some of the finest works from the Royal Collection.

(adult/child £27/21), including entry to London Zoo, allowing passengers to disembark within the zoo grounds are available. Buy tickets aboard the narrowboats.

London Bicycle Tour CYCLING
(Map p84; ☎020-7928 6838; www.londonbicycle.com; 1 Gabriel's Wharf, 56 Upper Ground, SE1; tour incl bike from adult/child £24.95/21.95, bike hire per day £20; ☻Southwark, Waterloo) Three-hour tours begin in the South Bank and take in London's highlights on both sides of the river; the classic tour is available in eight languages. A night ride is available. You can also hire traditional or speciality bikes, such as tandems and folding bikes, by the hour or day.

Thames Rockets BOATING
(Map p84; ☎020-7928 8933; www.thamesrockets.com; Boarding Gate 1, London Eye, Waterloo Millennium Pier, Westminster Bridge Rd, SE1; adult/child from £43.50/29.50; ☻10am-6pm; ⛴) Feel like James Bond on this high-speed inflatable boat that flies down the Thames at 30 knots. Tours depart from the London Eye or St Katharine Pier, including the 50-minute Ultimate London Adventure (adult/child £43.50/29.50), the 80-minute Thames Barrier Explorer's Voyage (adult/child £54.50/39.50) or Thames Lates, a 50-minute sunset trip with a cocktail on board (adults only £39.50).

Unseen Tours WALKING
(☎07514 266774; www.sockmobevents.org.uk; tours £12) See London from an entirely different angle on one of these award-winning neighbourhood tours led by the London homeless covering Covent Garden, Camden Town, Brick Lane, Shoreditch and London Bridge. Sixty percent of the tour price goes to the guide.

Big Bus Tours BUS
(☎020-7808 6753; www.bigbustours.com; adult/child £35/18; ☻every 20min 8.30am-6pm Apr-Sep, to 5pm Oct & Mar, to 4.30pm Nov-Feb) Informative commentaries in 12 languages. The ticket includes a free river cruise with City Cruises and three thematic walking tours (royal London, film locations, mysteries). Good online booking discounts available. Onboard wi-fi. The ticket is valid for 24 hours; for an extra £8 (£4 for children), you can upgrade to a 48-hour ticket.

LONDON FOR FREE

Sights It costs nothing to visit the Houses of Parliament (p66) and watch debates. Another institution of public life, the Changing of the Guard (p69), is free to watch. For one weekend in September, Open House London (p82) opens the doors to some 850 buildings for free.

Museums & Galleries The permanent collections of all state-funded museums and galleries are open to the public free of charge. They include the V&A (p88), Tate Modern (p82), British Museum (p63) and National Gallery (p66). The **Saatchi Gallery** (Map p86; www.saatchigallery.com; Duke of York's HQ, King's Rd, SW3; ☻10am-6pm; ☻Sloane Sq) FREE is also free.

Views Why pay good money when some of the finest viewpoints in London are free? Head up to Level 10 of Switch House at Tate Modern (p82) or the Sky Gardens atop the Walkie Talkie (p79).

Concerts A number of churches offer free lunchtime classical music concerts. Try St Martin-in-the-Fields (p66), **St James's Piccadilly** (Map p70; ☎020-7734 4511; www.sjp.org.uk; 197 Piccadilly, W1; ☻8am-8pm; ☻Piccadilly Circus), **Temple Church** (Map p76; ☎020-7353 3470; www.templechurch.com; adult/child £5/3; ☻10am-4pm Mon, Tue, Thu & Fri, 2-4pm Wed, hours & days vary; ☻Temple) and **St Alfege Church** (www.st-alfege.org; Greenwich Church St, SE10; ☻11am-4pm Mon-Fri, 10am-4pm Sat, noon-4pm Sun; ☻Greenwich, DLR Cutty Sark).

Walks Walking around town is possibly the best way to get a sense of the city and its history. Roam through Hampstead Heath (p97) in North London, follow the Thames along the South Bank, or just walk from A to B in the compact West End.

Low-Cost Transport Bike-share your way around through Santander Cycles (p136) – the access fee is £2 for 24 hours; bike hire is then free for the first 30 minutes. Travel as much as you like on London Transport with a one-day Travelcard or an Oyster Card.

City Cruises
BOATING

(Map p68; ☑ 020-7740 0400; www.citycruises. com; adult single/return/day pass from £10.25/14.25/16.88, child £6.50/9.50/10.80; ⊜ Westminster) Ferry service departing every 30 minutes between Westminster, the London Eye, Bankside, Tower and Greenwich piers. A 24-hour Rover Ticket is as cheap as adult/child £10/5 online.

Thames River Boats
BOATING

(Map p68; ☑ 020-7930 2062; www.wpsa. co.uk; Westminster Pier, Victoria Embankment, SW1; Kew adult/child one-way £13/6.50, return £20/10, Hampton Court one-way £17/8.50, return £25/12.50; ☺ 10am-4pm Apr-Oct; ⊜ Westminster) These boats go upriver from Westminster Pier to the Royal Botanic Gardens at Kew (1½ hours, four per day) and on to Hampton Court Palace (another 1½ hours, 11am sailing only), a distance of 22 miles. It's possible to disembark at Richmond, but it depends on the tides; check before you sail.

London Mystery Walks
WALKING

(☑ 07957 388280; www.tourguides.org.uk; £12) Tour Jack the Ripper's old haunts at 7pm on Mondays, Wednesdays, Fridays and Sundays. London chocolate tours (£40) are on Sundays at 12.30pm and gelato tours (£40) are on Fridays at 11am. You must book in advance.

🎪 Festivals & Events

Chinese New Year
CULTURAL

(☺ late Jan/early Feb) Chinese New Year sees Chinatown snap, crackle and pop with fireworks, a colourful street parade and eating aplenty.

The Boat Race
ROWING

(www.theboatrace.org; ☺ late Mar/early Apr) A posh-boy grudge match held annually since 1829 between the rowing crews of Oxford and Cambridge universities. Surging upstream between Putney and Mortlake, the event (which included a female crew boat race for the first time in 2015) draws huge crowds along the river.

Virgin Money London Marathon
SPORTS

(www.virginmoneylondonmarathon.com; ☺ late Apr) Up to half a million spectators watch the whippet-thin champions and bizarrely clad amateurs take to the streets.

Chelsea Flower Show
HORTICULTURE

(☑ 020-3176 5800; www.rhs.org.uk/chelsea; Royal Hospital Chelsea, Royal Hospital Rd, SW3; admission £37-65; ☺ May; ⊜ Sloane Sq) Held at the lovely Royal Hospital Chelsea, this is arguably the world's most renowned horticultural show, attracting green fingers from all four corners of the globe.

Field Day
MUSIC

(www.fielddayfestivals.com; Brockwell Park, SE24; ☺ Jun; ⊜ Hackney Wick) The annual Field Day alternative music festival was held in Victoria Park (p95) from 2007, but in 2018 it moved to Brockwell Park. Performances in recent years have included Run the Jewels, PJ Harvey and James Blake.

Meltdown Festival
MUSIC

(www.southbankcentre.co.uk; ☺ late Jun) The Southbank Centre hands over the curatorial reigns to a legend of contemporary music (Morrissey, Patti Smith, David Byrne) to pull together a full program of concerts, talks and films.

★ Trooping the Colour
PARADE

(www.trooping-the-colour.co.uk; ☺ Jun) Celebrating the Queen's official birthday, this ceremonial procession of troops, marching along the Mall for their sovereign's inspection, is a pageantry overload, featuring 1400 officers and personnel on parade, 200 horses and 400 musicians from 10 bands.

Pride
GAY & LESBIAN

(www.prideinlondon.org; ☺ late Jun/early Jul) The gay community paints the town pink in this annual extravaganza, featuring a smorgasbord of experiences, from talks to live events and culminating in a huge parade across London.

Summer Screen at Somerset House
FILM

(www.somersethouse.org.uk/film; tickets from £20) For a fortnight every summer, Somerset House turns its stunning courtyard into an open-air cinema screening an eclectic mix of film premieres, cult classics and popular requests.

Wireless
MUSIC

(www.wirelessfestival.co.uk; Finsbury Park, N4; ☺ Jul) This popular pop, R&B, grime and hip-hop festival is held over three days in July every year. Recent headliners have included The Weeknd, Nas and Skepta.

Notting Hill Carnival
CARNIVAL

(www.thelondonnottinghillcarnival.com; ☺ Aug) Every year, for three days that include the last weekend of August, Notting Hill echoes to the calypso, ska, reggae and soca sounds of the Notting Hill Carnival. Launched in 1964 by the local Afro-Caribbean community that was keen to celebrate its culture and traditions, it has grown to become Europe's largest street festival (up to two million people) and a highlight of London's calendar.

London Jazz Festival MUSIC
(www.efglondonjazzfestival.org.uk; ⊙Nov) Musicians from around the world swing into town for 10 days of jazz. World influences are well represented, as are more conventional strands.

🛏 Sleeping

🛏 The West End

YHA London Oxford Street HOSTEL £
(Map p70; ☑020-7734 1618; www.yha.org.uk; 14 Noel St, W1; dm £18-36, tw £50-85; @ 🛜; ⊖ Oxford Circus) The most central of London's seven YHA hostels is also one of the most intimate with just 104 beds. The excellent shared facilities include a fuchsia-coloured kitchen and bright, funky lounge. Dormitories have three or four beds, and there are doubles and twins. The in-house shop sells coffee and beer. Free wi-fi in common areas.

Generator London HOSTEL £
(Map p96; ☑020-7388 7666; www.generator hostels.com/london; 37 Tavistock Pl, WC1; dm/r from £9/44; ❄ 🛜; ⊖ Russell Sq) With its industrial lines and funky decor, the huge Generator (it has more than 870 beds) is one of central London's grooviest budget spots. The bar, complete with pool tables, stays open until 3am and there are frequent themed parties. Dorm rooms have between four and 12 beds; backing it up are twins and triples.

Jesmond Hotel B&B ££
(Map p96; ☑020-7636 3199; www.jesmond hotel.org.uk; 63 Gower St, WC1; s £75-95, d £95-125, tr £140-165, q £150-185; @ 🛜; ⊖ Goodge St) The rooms at this popular, 15-room family-run Georgian-era hotel in Bloomsbury are basic but clean and cheerful (four are with shared bathroom): there's a small, pretty garden, and the price tag is very attractive indeed. There's also laundry service and good breakfasts for kicking off your London day. Location is highly central.

★**Haymarket Hotel** HOTEL £££
(Map p70; ☑020-7470 4000; www.firmdalehotels. com/hotels/london/haymarket-hotel; 1 Suffolk Pl,

off Haymarket, SW1; r/ste £335/505; ❄ 🛜 🏊 🏋; ⊖Piccadilly Circus) With the trademark colours and lines of hotelier/designer duo Tim and Kit Kemp, the Haymarket is scrumptious, with hand-painted Gournay wallpaper, signature fuchsia and green designs in the 50 different guest rooms, a sensational 18m pool with mood lighting, an exquisite library lounge with honesty bar, and original artwork throughout.

★**Ritz London** LUXURY HOTEL £££
(Map p70; ☑020-7493 8181; www.theritzlondon. com; 150 Piccadilly, W1; r/ste from £380/850; P ❄ @ 🛜; ⊖ Green Park) What can you say about a hotel that has lent its name to the English lexicon? This 136-room caravanserai has a spectacular position overlooking Green Park and is supposedly the Royal Family's home away from home (it does have a royal warrant from the Prince of Wales and is very close to the palace). All rooms have Louis XVI-style interiors and antique furniture.

★**Rosewood London** HOTEL £££
(Map p70; ☑020-7781 8888; www.rosewoodho tels.com/en/london; 252 High Holborn, WC1; d/ste from £390/702; P ❄ @ 🛜 🏋; ⊖ Holborn) What was once the grand Pearl Assurance building (dating from 1914) now houses the stunning Rosewood hotel, where an artful marriage of period and modern styles thanks to designer Tony Chi can be found in its 262 rooms and 44 suites. British heritage is carefully woven throughout the bar, restaurant, deli, lobby and even the housekeepers' uniforms.

Hazlitt's HISTORIC HOTEL £££
(Map p70; ☑020-7434 1771; www.hazlittshotel. com; 6 Frith St, W1; s/d/ste from £200/230/600; ❄ 🛜; ⊖ Tottenham Court Rd) Built in 1718 and comprising four original Georgian houses, this Soho gem was the one-time home of essayist William Hazlitt (1778–1830). The 30 guest rooms have been furnished with original antiques from the appropriate era and boast a profusion of seductive details, including panelled walls, mahogany four-poster beds, antique desks, Oriental carpets, sumptuous fabrics and fireplaces in every room.

🛏 The City

London St Paul's YHA HOSTEL £
(Map p76; ☑020-7236 4965; www.yha.org.uk; 36 Carter Lane, EC4; dm/tw/d from £14/49/89; @ 🛜; ⊖ St Paul's) Housed in the former boarding

school for St Paul's Cathedral choir boys, this 213-bed hostel has notable period features, including Latin script in a band around the exterior. There's no kitchen, no lift and no en-suite rooms, but there is a comfortable lounge and a licensed cafe.

★ citizenM Tower of London
DESIGN HOTEL ££

(Map p76; ☑ 020-3519 4830; www.citizenm.com; 40 Trinity Sq, EC3; r from £125; ✳@☎; ◉ Tower Hill) Downstairs it looks like a rich hipster's living room, with well-stocked bookshelves, kooky art, Beefeater knick-knacks and lots of work space. Rooms are compact but well-designed, with an iPad to open the curtains, control the TV and adjust the shower lighting. It's worth paying an extra £30 for the extraordinary Tower views, although they're even better from the 7th-floor bar.

Hotel Indigo London – Tower Hill
HOTEL ££

(Map p76; ☑ 020-7265 1014; www.hotelindigo.com; 142 Minories, EC3; r from £166; ✳☎; ◉ Aldgate) This branch of the InterContinental group's boutique-hotel chain offers 46 differently styled rooms, all with four-poster beds and iPod docking stations. Larger-than-life drawings and photos of the neighbourhood won't let you forget where you are.

Andaz Liverpool Street
HOTEL £££

(Map p76; ☑ 020-7961 1234; https://londonliverpoolstreet.andaz.hyatt.com; 40 Liverpool St, EC2; r £295; ✳☎; ◉ Liverpool St) Built as the Great Eastern Hotel in 1884, this is the London flagship for Hyatt's Andaz chain. There's no reception, just black-clad staff who check you in on iPads. Splashes of red add zing to the spacious, elegant rooms, and there are three restaurants, two bars, a pub, a health club and a Masonic temple hidden in the basement.

🛏 South Bank

★ citizenM
BOUTIQUE HOTEL ££

(Map p84; ☑ 020-3519 1680; www.citizenm.com/london-bankside; 20 Lavington St, SE1; r £89-329; ✳@☎; ◉ Southwark) If citizenM had a motto, it would be 'Less fuss, more comfort'. The hotel has done away with things it considers superfluous (room service, reception, heaps of space) and instead has gone all out on mattresses and bedding (heavenly super-king-sized beds), state-of-the-art technology (everything from mood lighting to TV is

controlled through a tablet computer) and superb decor.

The LaLit
BOUTIQUE HOTEL £££

(Map p84; ☑ 020-3765-0000; www.thelalit.com; 181 Tooley St, SE1; r/ste £225/1125; ☎; ◉ London Bridge) Housed in an old Victorian grammar school, and themed on the same, this boutique hotel looks rather unassuming from the outside, but the interior is festooned in Indian decor. The rooms span varying degrees of luxury, from the Cosy Classrooms, with their marble bathrooms, to the LaLit Legacy Suite, with oak panelling, high ceilings and an impressive view of the Shard.

🛏 Kensington & Hyde Park

Lime Tree Hotel
BOUTIQUE HOTEL ££

(Map p86; ☑ 020-7730 8191; www.limetreehotel.co.uk; 135-137 Ebury St, SW1; s incl breakfast £125-165, d & tw £185-215, tr £240; @☎; ◉ Victoria) Family run for over three decades, this beautiful 25-bedroom Georgian town-house hotel is all comfort, British designs and understated elegance. Rooms are individually decorated, many with open fireplaces and sash windows, but some are smaller than others, so enquire. There is a lovely back garden for late-afternoon rays (picnics encouraged on summer evenings). Rates include a hearty full-English breakfast. No lift.

★ Number Sixteen
HOTEL £££

(Map p86; ☑ 020-7589 5232; www.firmdalehotels.com/hotels/london/number-sixteen; 16 Sumner Pl, SW7; s from £192, d £240-396; ✳@☎; ◉ South Kensington) With uplifting splashes of colour, choice art and a sophisticated-but-fun design ethos, Number Sixteen is simply ravishing. There are 41 individually designed rooms, a cosy drawing room and a fully stocked library. And wait till you see the idyllic, long back garden set around a fountain, or sit down for breakfast in the light-filled conservatory. Great amenities for families.

Ampersand Hotel
BOUTIQUE HOTEL £££

(Map p86; ☑ 020-7589 5895; www.ampersandhotel.com; 10 Harrington Rd, SW7; s £170-192, d £216-360; ✳@☎; ◉ South Kensington) It feels light, fresh and bubbly in the Ampersand, where smiling staff wear denims and waistcoats rather than impersonal dark suits. The common rooms are colourful and airy, and the stylish rooms are decorated with wallpaper designs celebrating the nearby arts and sciences of South Kensington's museums.

🛏 Clerkenwell, Shoreditch & Spitalfields

⭐ Hoxton Hotel   HOTEL ££

(Map p124; ☑ 020-7550 1000; www.thehoxton.com; 81 Great Eastern St, EC2; r £69-259; ❋ 🕸; ⊖ Old St) In the heart of hip Shoreditch, this sleek hotel takes the low-cost airline approach to selling its rooms – book long enough ahead and you might pay just £69. The 210 renovated rooms are small but stylish, with flat-screen TVs, desks, fridges with complimentary bottled water and milk, and breakfast (orange juice, granola, yoghurt and banana) in a bag delivered to your door.

⭐ citizenM   DESIGN HOTEL ££

(Map p124; www.citizenm.com; 6 Holywell Lane, EC2A; r from £119; @ 🕸; ⊖ Shoreditch High St) citizenM's winning combination of awesome interior design and a no-nonsense approach to luxury (yes to king-sized beds and high-tech pod rooms; no to pillow chocolates and room service) is right at home in Shoreditch. Room rates are just right, and the convivial lounge/bar/reception downstairs always seems to be on the right side of busy.

⭐ Rookery   HERITAGE HOTEL £££

(Map p76; ☑ 020-7336 0931; www.rookeryhotel.com; 12 Peter's Lane, Cowcross St, EC1; d/ste from £249/650; ❋ 🕸; ⊖ Farringdon) This charming warren of 33 rooms has been built within a row of 18th-century Georgian houses and fitted out with period furniture (including a museum-piece collection of Victorian baths, showers and toilets), original wood panelling shipped over from Ireland and artwork selected personally by the owner. Highlights: the small courtyard garden, and the library with its honesty bar and working fireplace.

Zetter Hotel   BOUTIQUE HOTEL £££

(Map p96; ☑ 020-7324 4444; www.thezetter.com; 86-88 Clerkenwell Rd, EC1; studio £342-558; ❋ 🕸; ⊖ Farringdon) 🌿 The Zetter Hotel is a temple of cool minimalism with an overlay of colourful kitsch on Clerkenwell's main thoroughfare. Built using sustainable materials on the site of a derelict office, its 59 rooms are relatively spacious for the area. The rooftop studios are the real treat, with terraces commanding superb views. There is a hot-drink station on every floor for guest use.

🛏 East London

Qbic   DESIGN HOTEL £

(☑ 020-3021 3300; www.qbichotels.com; 42 Adler St, E1; r from £54; ❋ 🕸; ⊖ Aldgate East) 🌿 There's a modern feel to this snappy hotel, with white tiling, neon signs, and vibrant art and textiles. Rooms are sound-insulated, mattresses excellent and rainforest showers powerful. Prices vary widely depending on when you book, and the cheapest are windowless.

⭐ 40 Winks   B&B ££

(☑ 020-7790 0259; www.40winks.org; 109 Mile End Rd, E1; s/d/ste £120/195/295; 🕸; ⊖ Stepney Green) Short on space but not on style, this 300-year-old townhouse in Stepney Green oozes quirky charm. There are just two bedrooms (a double and a compact single) that share a bathroom – or you can book both as a spacious suite. Owned by a successful designer, the rooms are uniquely and extravagantly decorated with an expert's eye. Book far ahead.

🛏 North London

⭐ Clink78   HOSTEL £

(Map p96; ☑ 020-7183 9400; www.clinkhostels.com/london/clink78; 78 King's Cross Rd, WC1; dm/r incl breakfast from £16/65; @ 🕸; ⊖ King's Cross St Pancras) This fantastic 630-bed hostel is housed in a 19th-century magistrates courthouse where Charles Dickens once worked as a scribe and members of the Clash stood trial in 1978. It features pod beds (including overhead storage space) in four- to 16-bed dormitories. There's a top kitchen with a huge dining area and a busy bar – Clash – in the basement.

London St Pancras YHA   HOSTEL £

(Map p96; ☑ 0345 371 9344; www.yha.org.uk; 79-81 Euston Rd, NW1; dm/r from £16/59; 🕸; ⊖ King's Cross St Pancras) This hostel with 186 beds spread over eight floors has modern, clean dorms sleeping four to six (nearly all with private facilities) and some private rooms. The downside is the noise from busy Euston Rd. There's a small bar and cafe, but no self-catering facilities.

🛏 West London

Safestay Holland Park   HOSTEL £

(Map p92; ☑ 020-3326 8471; www.safestay.co.uk; Holland Walk, W8; dm £20, r from £60; 🕸; ⊖ High St Kensington, Holland Park) This fresh place replaced the long-serving YHA hostel running here since 1958. With a bright and bold colour design, the hostel has four- to eight-bunk dorm rooms, twin-bunk and single-bunk rooms, free wi-fi in the lobby and a fabulous location in the Jacobean east wing of Holland House in Holland Park (Map p92; Ilchester Pl; ⊙ 7.30am-dusk), the only part that survived a Luftwaffe onslaught.

★ **Main House**   HOTEL ££
(Map p92; ☑ 020-7221 9691; www.themainhouse. co.uk; 6 Colville Rd, W11; ste £130-150; ⊛; ⊜ Ladbroke Grove, Notting Hill Gate, Westbourne Park) The four adorable suites at this peach of a Victorian midterrace house on Colville Rd make this a superb choice. Bright and spacious rooms are excellent value and come with vast bathrooms and endless tea and coffee. Cream of the crop is the uppermost suite, occupying the entire top floor. There's no sign, but look for the huge letters 'SIX'. Minimum three-night stay.

Rockwell   BOUTIQUE HOTEL ££
(☑ 020-7244 2000; www.therockwell.com; 181-183 Cromwell Rd, SW5; s £120-125, d £145-180, ste from £200; ❄@⊛; ⊜ Earl's Court) With an understated-cool design ethos and some lovely floor tiling in the entrance, things are muted, dapper and more than a tad minimalist at the 'budget boutique' 40-room Rockwell. Spruce and stylish, the rooms all have showers, the mezzanine suites are peaches and the three rooms looking on to the walled garden (LG1, 2 and 3) are particularly fine.

✗ Eating

✗ The West End

★ **Shoryu**   NOODLES £
(Map p70; www.shoryuramen.com; 9 Regent St, SW1; mains £10-14.50; ⊙ 11.15am-midnight Mon-Sat, to 10.30pm Sun; ⊜ Piccadilly Circus) Compact, well-mannered and central noodle-parlour Shoryu draws in reams of noodle diners to feast at its wooden counters and small tables. It's busy, friendly and efficient, with helpful and informative staff. Fantastic *tonkotsu* (pork-broth ramen) is the name of the game here, sprinkled with nori (dried, pressed seaweed), spring onion, *nitamago* (soft-boiled eggs) and sesame seeds. No bookings.

Battersea Pie Station   BRITISH £
(Map p70; ☑ 020-7240 9566; www.batterseapie station.co.uk; lower ground fl, 28 The Market, Covent Garden, WC2; mains £6.50-9.50; ⊙ 11am-7.30pm Mon-Fri, 10am-7.30pm Sat, 11am-6.30pm Sun; ⊜ Covent Garden) This small, white-tiled cafe is just what Covent Garden needs. It has a terrific choice of pies (baby or big) to satisfy all levels of hunger, from careful nibblers to voracious teens. Meat is all free-range, flavours are classic and rich (lamb and mint; fish; steak and stout; chicken and mushroom; butternut squash and goat's cheese), and each pie comes with a dollop of mashed potatoes.

Mildreds   VEGETARIAN £
(Map p70; ☑ 020-7484 1634; www.mildreds.co.uk; 45 Lexington St, W1; mains £7-12; ⊙ noon-11pm Mon-Sat; ⊛✗; ⊜ Oxford Circus, Piccadilly Circus) Central London's most inventive vegetarian restaurant, Mildreds is crammed at lunchtime so don't be shy about sharing a table in the sky-lit dining room. Expect the likes of Sri Lankan sweet-potato and cashew-nut curry, ricotta and truffle tortellini, Middle Eastern mezze, wonderfully exotic (and filling) salads and delicious stir-fries. There are also vegan and gluten-free options.

Monocle Cafe   CAFE £
(Map p112; ☑ 020-7135 2040; http://cafe.mono cle.com; 18 Chiltern St, W1; mains £5.50-9, snacks £2-5.50; ⊙ 7am-7pm Mon-Wed, to 8pm Thu & Fri, 8am-8pm Sat, to 7pm Sun; ⊛; ⊜ Baker St) A small and cool ground-floor and basement hideout for the Marylebone hipster set, Monocle Cafe (from the eponymous magazine) is a delightful addition to buzzing Chiltern St. It offers eclectic flavours from Swedish pastries to Japanese and Scandinavian breakfasts, Bircher muesli with strawberries or shrimp *katsu* (breaded shrimp) sandwiches.

The Breakfast Club   BREAKFAST £
(Map p70; ☑ 020-7434 2571; www.thebreakfast clubcafes.com; 33 D'Arblay St, W1; mains £5-12.50; ⊙ 7.30am-10pm Mon-Fri, 8am-10pm Sat, 8am-7pm Sun; ⊛; ⊜ Oxford Circus) This fun and friendly original branch of The Breakfast Club chain has been successfully frying up since 2005. Full Monty or All American brekkies are the natural inclination, but chorizo hash browns, pancakes and delights of the El Butty also await (once you reach the front of the queue).

★ **Gymkhana**   INDIAN ££
(Map p70; ☑ 020-3011 5900; www.gymkhana london.com; 42 Albemarle St, W1; mains £10-38, 4-course lunch/dinner £28.50/40; ⊙ noon-2.30pm

Marylebone

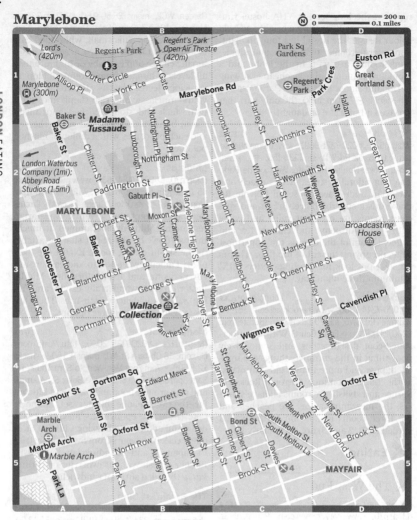

& 5.30-10.15pm Mon-Sat; 🕿 ; ⊖ Green Park) The rather sombre setting is all British Raj – ceiling fans, oak ceiling, period cricket photos and hunting trophies – but the menu is lively, bright and inspiring. For lovers of variety, there is a six-course tasting meat/vegetarian menu (£70/65). The bar is open to 1am.

Cafe Murano   ITALIAN ££
(Map p70; 🕿 020-3371 5559; www.cafemurano. co.uk; 33 St James's St, SW1; mains £18-25, 2-/3-course set meal £19/23; ⊗ noon-3pm & 5.30-11pm Mon-Sat, 11.30am-4pm Sun; ⊖ Green Park) The setting may seem somewhat demure at

this superb and busy restaurant, but with such a sublime northern Italian menu on offer, it sees no need to be flashy and of-the-moment. You get what you come for, and the lobster linguini, pork belly and cod with mussels and samphire are as close to culinary perfection as you'll get.

North Sea Fish Restaurant   FISH & CHIPS ££
(Map p96; 🕿 020-7387 5892; www.northseafish restaurant.co.uk; 7-8 Leigh St, WC1; mains £9.95-24.95; ⊗ noon-2.30pm & 5-10pm Mon-Sat, 5-9.30pm Sun; ⊖ Russell Sq) The North Sea sets out to cook fresh fish and potatoes – a simple

Marylebone

ambition in which it succeeds admirably. Look forward to jumbo-sized plaice or halibut fillets, deep-fried or grilled, and a huge serving of chips. There's takeaway next door with similar hours if you can't face the rather austere dining room and impersonal service.

Opera Tavern   TAPAS **££**
(Map p70; ☑020-7836-3680; www.saltyard group.co.uk/opera-tavern; 23 Catherine St, WC2; Tapas £5-10; ⊙noon-11.30pm Mon-Sat, to 10.30pm Sun; ⊜Covent Garden) Classy but accessible, the Opera Tavern is one of London's best tapas restaurants (no easy feat), and enjoys an unrivalled location just around the corner from Covent Garden's piazza. Regular specials adorn the menu, and the staple Spanish and Italian tapas include a variety of mouth-watering options like roasted sea bass with mussels, and Iberico pork fillet.

Wallace   MODERN EUROPEAN **££**
(Map p112; ☑020-7563 9505; www.wallacecol lection.org/visiting/thewallacerestaurant; Hertford House, Manchester Sq, W1; mains £13.50-22.50; ⊙10am-5pm Sun-Thu, to 11pm Fri & Sat; ⊜Bond St) There are few more idyllically placed restaurants than this spot in the enclosed courtyard of the Wallace Collection (p73). The emphasis is on seasonal French-inspired dishes, with the daily menu offering two- or three-course meals for £22.50/24.50. Afternoon tea is £18.50.

La Fromagerie   CAFE **££**
(Map p112; ☑020-7935 0341; www.lafromagerie. co.uk; 2-6 Moxon St, W1; mains £7-18; ⊙8am-7.30pm Mon-Fri, 9am-7pm Sat, 10am-6pm Sun; ☎; ⊜Baker St) ✐ This deli-cafe has bowls of delectable salads, antipasto, peppers and beans scattered about the long communal table. Huge slabs of bread invite you to tuck in, and all the while the heavenly waft from the cheese room beckons. Cheese boards come in small and large (£9.25 and £16) and breakfast is always a good choice.

Great Queen Street   BRITISH **££**
(Map p70; ☑020-7242 0622; www.greatqueen streetrestaurant.co.uk; 32 Great Queen St, WC2; mains £15.80-19.80; ⊙noon-2.30pm & 5.30-10.30pm Mon-Sat, noon-3.30pm Sun; ⊜Holborn) The menu at one of Covent Garden's best places to eat is seasonal (and changes daily), with an emphasis on quality, hearty dishes and fine ingredients – there are always delicious stews, roasts and simple fish dishes. The atmosphere is lively, with the small **Cellar Bar** (5pm to 11pm Tuesday to Saturday) open for cocktails and drinks. Booking is essential.

★**Portrait**   MODERN EUROPEAN **£££**
(Map p70; ☑020-7312 2490; www.npg.org.uk/ visit/shop-eat-drink.php; 3rd fl, National Portrait Gallery, St Martin's Pl, WC2; mains £19.50-28, 2-/3-course menu £27.95/31.50; ⊙10-11am, 11.45am-3pm & 3.30-4.30pm daily, 6.30-8.30pm Thu-Sat; ☎; ⊜Charing Cross) This stunningly located restaurant above the excellent National Portrait Gallery (p73) comes with dramatic views over Trafalgar Sq and Westminster. It's a fine choice for tantalising food and the chance to relax after a morning or afternoon of picture-gazing at the gallery. The breakfast/brunch (10am to 11am) and afternoon tea (3.30pm to 4.30pm) come highly recommended. Booking is advisable.

★**Claridge's Foyer**
& Reading Room   BRITISH **£££**
(Map p112; ☑020-7107 8886; www.claridges. co.uk; 49-53 Brook St, W1; afternoon tea £60, with champagne £70; ⊙afternoon tea 2.45-5.30pm; ☎; ⊜Bond St) Extend that pinkie finger to partake in afternoon tea within the classic art deco foyer and Reading Room of this landmark hotel, where the gentle clink of fine porcelain and champagne glasses could be a defining memory of your trip to London. The setting is gorgeous and dress is elegant, smart casual (ripped jeans and baseball caps won't get you served).

Pollen Street Social   MODERN EUROPEAN **£££**
(Map p70; ☑020-7290 7600; www.pollenstreet social.com; 8-10 Pollen St, W1; mains £34-38, 3-course lunch £37; ⊙noon-2.30pm & 6-10.30pm

Mon-Sat; ⊜ Oxford Circus) Jason Atherton's cathedral to haute cuisine would be beyond reach of many people not on a hefty expense account, but the excellent-value set lunch (£32/37 for two/three courses) makes it fairly accessible to all. A generous two-hour slot allows ample time to linger over such delights as lime-cured salmon, braised West Country ox cheek and your choice from the dessert bar.

Hakkasan Hanway Place CANTONESE £££
(Map p70; ☑020-7927 7000; www.hakkasan. com; 8 Hanway Pl, W1; mains £12-63.50; ☺noon-3pm & 5.30-11pm Mon-Wed, noon-3pm & 5.30pm-12.30am Thu-Fri, noon-4pm & 5.30pm-12.30am Sat, noon-11.15pm Sun; ☎; ⊜ Tottenham Court Rd) This basement Michelin-starred restaurant – hidden down a back alleyway – successfully combines celebrity status, stunning design, persuasive cocktails and sophisticated Cantonese-style food. The low, nightclub-style lighting makes it a good spot for a date or a night out with friends; the bar serves seriously creative cocktails. Book far in advance or come for lunch (three courses £38, also available from 5.30pm to 6.30pm).

✖ The City

Wine Library BUFFET ££
(Map p76; ☑020-7481 0415; www.winelibrary. co.uk; 43 Trinity Sq, EC3; buffet £18; ☺buffet 11.30am-3.30pm, shop 10am-6pm Mon, to 8pm Tue-Fri; ⊜ Tower Hill) This is a great place for a light but boozy lunch opposite the Tower. Buy a bottle of wine at retail price from the large selection (£9.50 corkage fee) and then head into the vaulted cellar to snack as much as you like from the selection of delicious pâtés, charcuterie, cheeses, bread and salads.

Duck & Waffle MODERN BRITISH ££
(Map p76; ☑020-3640 7310; www.duckandwaffle. com; L40, 110 Bishopsgate, EC2; mains £18-19; ☺24hr; ☎; ⊜ Liverpool St) If you like your views with sustenance round the clock, this is the place for you. Perched atop Heron Tower, it serves a well-waffled breakfast menu, hearty all-day sharing plates (confit duck, roast chicken, miso-glazed rabbit) and round-the-clocktails.

✖ South Bank

★Padella ITALIAN £
(Map p84; www.padella.co; 6 Southwark St, SE1; dishes £4-11.50; ☺noon-3.45pm & 5-10pm Mon-

Sat, noon-3.45pm & 5-9pm Sun; ✐; ⊜ London Bridge) Yet another fantastic addition to the foodie enclave of Borough Market (p133), Padella is a small, energetic bistro specialising in handmade pasta dishes, inspired by the owners' extensive culinary adventures in Italy. The portions are small, which means that, joy of joys, you can (and should!) have more than one dish. Outstanding.

★Watch House CAFE £
(Map p84; www.thewatchhouse.com; 199 Bermondsey St, SE1; mains from £4.95; ☺7am-6pm Mon-Fri, 8am-6pm Sat, 9am-5pm Sun; ✐; ⊜ Borough, London Bridge) ✐ Saying that the Watch House nails the sandwich wouldn't really do justice to this tip-top cafe: the sandwiches really are delicious, and use artisan breads from a local baker. But there is also great coffee, and treats for the sweet-toothed. The small but lovely setting is a renovated 19th-century watch house from where guards looked out for grave robbers in the next-door cemetery.

★Anchor & Hope GASTROPUB ££
(Map p84; www.anchorandhopepub.co.uk; 36 The Cut, SE1; mains £12-20; ☺noon-2.30pm Tue-Sat, 6-10.30pm Mon-Sat, 12.30-3.15pm Sun; ⊜ Southwark) A stalwart of the South Bank food scene, the Anchor & Hope is a quintessential gastropub: elegant but not formal, and utterly delicious (European fare with a British twist). The menu changes daily but think salt-marsh lamb shoulder cooked for seven hours; wild rabbit with anchovies, almonds and rocket; and panna cotta with rhubarb compote.

★Baltic EASTERN EUROPEAN ££
(Map p84; ☑020-7928 1111; www.balticrestaurant. co.uk; 74 Blackfriars Rd, SE1; mains £11.50-22, 2-course lunch menu £17.50; ☺noon-3pm & 5.30-11.15pm Tue-Sat, noon-4.30pm & 5.30-10.30pm Sun, 5.30-11.15pm Mon; ✐; ⊜ Southwark) In a bright and airy, high-ceilinged dining room with glass roof and wooden beams, Baltic is travel on a plate: dill and beetroot, dumplings and blini, pickle and smoke, rich stews and braised meat. From Polish to Georgian, the flavours are authentic and the dishes beautifully presented. The wine and vodka lists are equally diverse.

✖ Kensington & Hyde Park

★Pimlico Fresh CAFE £
(☑020-7932 0030; 86 Wilton Rd, SW1; mains from £4.50; ☺7.30am-7.30pm Mon-Fri, 9am-6pm Sat & Sun; ⊜ Victoria) This friendly two-room cafe

will see you right whether you need breakfast (French toast, bowls of porridge laced with honey or maple syrup), lunch (homemade quiches and soups, 'things' on toast) or just a good old latte and cake.

⭐**Rabbit**   MODERN BRITISH **££**
(Map p86; ☑️020-3750 0172; www.rabbit-restaurant.com; 172 King's Rd, SW3; mains £6-24, set lunch £13.50; ⊘noon-midnight Tue-Sat, noon-6pm Sun, 6-11pm Mon; 🖊️; ⊖Sloane Sq) Three brothers grew up on a farm. One became a farmer, another a butcher, while the third worked in hospitality. So they pooled their skills and came up with Rabbit, a breath of fresh air in upmarket Chelsea. The restaurant rocks the agri-chic (yes) look, and the creative, seasonal Modern British cuisine is fabulous.

⭐**Tom's Kitchen**   MODERN EUROPEAN **££**
(Map p86; ☑️020-7349 0202; www.tomskitchen.co.uk/chelsea; 27 Cale St, SW3; mains £16-28; ⊘8am-2.30pm & 6-10.30pm Mon-Fri, 9.30am-3.30pm & 6-10.30pm Sat, to 9.30pm Sun; 🖊️🖊️; ⊖South Kensington) 🍴 Recipe for success: mix one part relaxed and smiling staff, and one part light and airy decor to two parts divine food and voila: you have Tom's Kitchen. Classics such as grilled steaks, burgers, slow-cooked pork belly and chicken schnitzel are cooked to perfection, while seasonal choices such as the homemade ricotta or pan-fried scallops are sublime.

⭐**Dinner by**
Heston Blumenthal   MODERN BRITISH **£££**
(Map p86; ☑️020-7201 3833; www.dinnerbyheston.com; Mandarin Oriental Hyde Park, 66 Knightsbridge, SW1; 3-course set lunch £45, mains £30-49; ⊘noon-2pm & 6-10.15pm Mon-Fri, noon-2.30pm & 6-10.30pm Sat & Sun; 🖊️; ⊖Knightsbridge) Sumptuously presented Dinner is a gastronomic tour de force, taking diners on a journey through British culinary history (with inventive modern inflections). Dishes carry historical dates to convey context, while the restaurant interior is a design triumph, from the glass-walled kitchen and its overhead clock mechanism to the large windows looking onto the park. Book ahead.

⭐**Gordon Ramsay**   FRENCH **£££**
(Map p86; ☑️020-7352 4441; www.gordonramsayrestaurants.com/restaurant-gordon-ramsay; 68 Royal Hospital Rd, SW3; 3-course lunch/dinner £65/110; ⊘noon-2.30pm & 6.30-11pm Mon-Fri; 🖊️; ⊖Sloane Sq) One of Britain's finest restaurants and London's longest-running with three Michelin stars, this is hallowed turf for those who worship at the altar of the stove. It's true that it's a treat right from the taster to the truffles, but you won't get much time to savour it all. Bookings are made in specific sittings and you dare not linger; book as late as you can to avoid that rushed feeling. The blowout Menu Prestige (£145) is seven courses of perfection.

⭐**Five Fields**   MODERN BRITISH **£££**
(Map p86; ☑️020-7838 1082; www.fivefieldsrestaurant.com; 8-9 Blacklands Tce, SW3; 3-course set meal £85, tasting menu £85; ⊘6.30-10pm Tue-Sat; 🖊️; ⊖Sloane Sq) The inventive British *prix fixe* cuisine, consummate service and enticingly light and inviting decor are hard to resist at this triumphant Chelsea restaurant – now with a Michelin star – but you'll need to plan early and book way up front.

🍴 Clerkenwell, Shoreditch & Spitalfields

⭐**Polpo**   ITALIAN **£**
(Map p76; ☑️020-7250 0034; www.polpo.co.uk; 3 Cowcross St, EC1M; dishes £4-12; ⊘11.30am-11pm Mon-Thu & Sat, to midnight Fri, to 4pm Sun; ⊖Farringdon) Occupying a sunny spot on semi-pedestrianised Cowcross St, this sweet little place serves rustic Venetian-style meatballs, *pizzette* (small pizzas), grilled meat and fish dishes. Portions are larger than your average tapas but a tad smaller than a regular main – the perfect excuse to sample more than one of the exquisite dishes. Exceptional value for money.

Brick Lane Beigel Bake   BAKERY **£**
(Map p124; 159 Brick Lane, E2; bagels £1-4.10; ⊘24hr; ⊖Shoreditch High St) This relic of the Jewish East End still makes a brisk trade serving dirt-cheap homemade bagels (filled with salmon, cream cheese and/or salt beef) to hungry shoppers and late-night boozers. The queues on Sundays are epic.

Prufrock Coffee   CAFE **£**
(Map p76; www.prufrockcoffee.com; 23-25 Leather Lane, EC1N; mains £4-7; ⊘7.30am-6pm Mon-Fri, 10am-5pm Sat & Sun; 🖊️; ⊖Farringdon) Not content with being one of the kings of London's coffee-bean scene (it offers barista training and workshops in 'latte art'), Prufrock also dishes up delicious breakfasts, lunches and cuppa-friendly pastries and snacks. Judging by the number of laptops, plenty of customers treat it as their office.

Boiler House MARKET £
(Map p124; www.boilerhouse-foodhall.co.uk; Old Truman Brewery, 152 Brick Lane, E1; dishes £3-8; ⊘11am-6pm Sat, 10am-5pm Sun; ⊘; ⊜ Liverpool St) More than 30 food stalls selling anything from Argentinian to Vietnamese pitch up in the brewery's impressive old boiler room at the weekend. There is also a bar, and you can sit at the communal tables to tuck in. Come spring and summer, there are dozens more tables in the backyard.

Poppie's FISH & CHIPS ££
(Map p124; www.poppiesfishandchips.co.uk; 6-8 Hanbury St, E1; mains £12.20-16.90; ⊘11am-11pm; ⊜ Liverpool St) This glorious recreation of a 1950s East End chippy comes complete with waitstaff in pinnies and hairnets, and Blitz memorabilia. As well as the usual fishy suspects, it does old-time London staples – jellied eels and mushy peas – plus kid-pleasing, sweet-tooth desserts (sticky toffee pudding or apple pie with ice cream), and there's a wine list. Takeaway is a lot cheaper (£6.50 to £8.50).

St John BRITISH ££
(Map p76; ⊘020-7251 0848; www.stjohngroup. uk.com/spitalfields; 26 St John St, EC1M; mains £14.80-24.90; ⊘noon-3pm & 6-11pm Mon-Fri, 6-11pm Sat, 12.30-4pm Sun; ⊜ Farringdon) Whitewashed brick walls, high ceilings and simple wooden furniture don't make for a cosy dining space but they do keep diners free to concentrate on St John's famous nose-to-tail dishes. Serves are big, hearty and a celebration of England's culinary past. Don't miss the signature roast bone marrow and parsley salad (£8.90).

Morito TAPAS ££
(Map p96; ⊘020-7278 7007; www.morito.co.uk; 32 Exmouth Market, EC1R; dishes £6.50-9.50; ⊘8am-4pm & 5-11pm Mon-Fri, 9am-noon & 5-11pm Sat, 9am-4pm Sun; ⊜; ⊜ Farringdon) This diminutive eatery is a wonderfully authentic take on a Spanish tapas bar and has excellent eats. Seats are at the bar, along the window, or on one of the small tables inside or out. It's relaxed, convivial and often completely crammed; reservations are taken for lunch, but dinner is first come, first served, with couples generally going to the bar.

★ Hawksmoor STEAK £££
(Map p124; ⊘020-7426 4850; www.thehawks moor.com; 157 Commercial St, E1; mains £20-50; ⊘noon-2.30pm & 5-10.30pm Mon-Sat, noon-9pm Sun; ⊜; ⊜ Liverpool St) You could easily miss discreetly signed Hawksmoor, but confirmed carnivores will find it worth seeking out. The dark wood, bare bricks and velvet curtains make for a handsome setting in which to gorge yourself on the best of British beef. The Sunday roasts (£20) are legendary.

✗ East London

★ Towpath CAFE £
(⊘020-7254 7606; rear 42-44 De Beauvoir Cres, N1; mains £7-9.50; ⊘9am-5pm Tue & Wed, to 9.30pm Thu-Sun; ⊜ Haggerston) Occupying four small units on the Regent's Canal towpath, this simple cafe is a super place to sit in the sun and watch the ducks and narrowboats glide by. The coffee and food are excellent, too, with delicious cookies and brownies on the counter and cooked dishes chalked up on the blackboard daily.

★ Corner Room MODERN BRITISH ££
(⊘020-7871 0460; www.townhallhotel.com/food -and-drink/corner_room; Patriot Sq, E2; mains £13-14, 2-/3-course lunch £19/23; ⊘7-10am & noon-4pm Mon-Fri, 7.30-10.30am & noon-2.30pm Sat & Sun, 6-9.45pm Sun-Wed, 6-10.15pm Thu-Sat; ⊜ Bethnal Green) Someone put this baby in the corner, but we're certainly not complaining. Tucked away on the 1st floor of the Town Hall Hotel, this relaxed restaurant serves expertly crafted dishes with complex yet delicate flavours, highlighting the best of British seasonal produce.

Empress MODERN BRITISH ££
(⊘020-8533 5123; www.empresse9.co.uk; 130 Lauriston Rd, E9; mains £13.50-18.50; ⊘6-10.15pm Mon, noon-3.30pm & 6-10.15pm Tue-Sat, 10am-9.30pm Sun; ⊜277) This upmarket pub conversion belts out delicious Modern British cuisine in very pleasant surroundings. On Mondays there's a £10 main-plus-drink supper deal and on weekends it serves an excellent brunch.

✗ North London

★ Chin Chin Labs ICE CREAM £
(Map p118; www.chinchinlabs.com; 49-50 Camden Lock Pl, NW1; ice cream £4-5; ⊘noon-7pm; ⊜ Camden Town) This is food chemistry at its absolute best. Chefs prepare the ice-cream mixture and freeze it on the spot by adding liquid nitrogen. Flavours change regularly and match the seasons (spiced hot cross bun, passionfruit and coconut, for instance).

Sauces and toppings are equally creative. Try the ice-cream sandwich if you can: ice cream wedged inside gorgeous brownies or cookies.

★**Hook Camden Town** FISH & CHIPS £
(Map p118; www.hookrestaurants.com; 65 Parkway, NW1; mains £8-12; ⊙noon-3pm & 5-10pm Mon-Thu, noon-10.30pm Fri & Sat, to 9pm Sun; 🖼; ❺Camden Town) 🍴 In addition to working entirely with sustainable small fisheries and local suppliers, Hook makes all its sauces on-site and wraps its fish in recycled materials, supplying diners with extraordinarily fine-tasting morsels. Totally fresh, the fish arrives in panko breadcrumbs or tempura batter, with seaweed salted chips. Craft beers and fine wines are also on hand.

Diwana Bhel Poori House INDIAN £
(Map p96; ✍020-7387 5556; www.diwanabph. com; 121-123 Drummond St, NW1; mains £5.10-8.95; ⊙noon-11.30pm Mon-Sat, to 10.30pm Sun; 🖋; ❺Euston) One of the best Indian vegetarian restaurants in London, Diwana specialises in Bombay-style *bhel poori* (a tangy, soft and crunchy 'party mix' dish) and *dosas* (filled crispy pancakes made from rice flour). Solo diners should consider a thali (a complete meal consisting of lots of small dishes). The all-you-can-eat lunchtime buffet (£7) is legendary, and there are daily specials (£6.60).

Le Mercury FRENCH £
(✍020-7354 4088; www.lemercury.co.uk; 140a Upper St, N1; mains £10.95; ⊙noon-1am Mon-Sat, to 11pm Sun; ❺Highbury & Islington, Angel) An excellent and wildly popular budget French eatery, Le Mercury seems to have everything you could need in its winning formula: romantic atmosphere with candlelit, petite tables and plants everywhere, combined with superb French food at unbeatable prices. Londoners have long known about this place, so reservations are advised.

KERB Camden Market MARKET £
(Map p118; www.kerbfood.com; Camden Lock Market; mains £6-8; ⊙noon-5pm; 🖋; ❺Camden Town) From Argentinian to Vietnamese, the KERB food-market collective is like an A–Z of world cuisines. Each stall looks more mouth-watering than the next, and there should be enough choice to keep even the fussiest of eaters happy. Eat on the big communal tables or find a spot somewhere along the canal.

★**Ottolenghi** BAKERY, MEDITERRANEAN ££
(✍020-7288 1454; www.ottolenghi.co.uk; 287 Upper St, N1; breakfast £5.90-12.50, mains lunch/dinner from £18.80/11.90; ⊙8am-10.30pm Mon-Sat, 9am-7pm Sun; 🖋; ❺Highbury & Islington) Mountains of meringues tempt you through the door of this deli-restaurant, where a sumptuous array of baked goods and fresh salads greets you. Meals are as light and bright as the brilliantly white interior design, with a strong influence from the eastern Mediterranean.

★**Trullo** ITALIAN ££
(✍020-7226 2733; www.trullorestaurant.com; 300-302 St Paul's Rd, N1; mains £12.50-21; ⊙12.30-2.45pm & 6-10.15pm Mon-Sat, 12.30-3.45pm & 6-9.15pm Sun; ❺Highbury & Islington) Trullo's daily homemade pasta is delicious, but the main attraction here is the charcoal grill, which churns out the likes of succulent Italian-style pork chops, steaks and fish. The extensive and all-Italian wine list is another hit. Service is excellent, although dinner time can get packed; reservations are essential.

Caravan INTERNATIONAL ££
(✍020-7101 7661; www.caravanrestaurants.co.uk; 1 Granary Sq, N1C; mains £7-19; ⊙8am-10.30pm Mon-Fri, 10am-10.30pm Sat, 10am-4pm Sun; 🛜🖋; ❺King's Cross St Pancras) Housed in the lofty Granary Building, Caravan is a vast industrial-chic destination for tasty fusion bites from around the world. You can opt for several small plates to share tapas-style, or stick to main-sized plates. The outdoor seating area on Granary Sq is especially popular on warm days.

Manna VEGETARIAN ££
(✍020-7722 8028; www.mannav.com; 4 Erskine Rd, NW3; mains £8-15; ⊙noon-3pm & 6.30-10pm Tue-Sat, noon-7.30pm Sun; 🖋; ❺Chalk Farm) Tucked away on a side street, this upmarket little place does a brisk trade in inventive vegetarian and vegan cooking. The menu features mouth-watering, beautifully presented dishes incorporating elements of Californian, Mexican and Asian cuisine with nods to the raw-food trend. The cheesecake of the day is always a hit.

✖ Greenwich & South London

Old Brewery MODERN BRITISH ££
(✍020-3437 2222; www.oldbrewerygreenwich. com; Pepys Bldg, Old Royal Naval College, SE10; mains £11.50-25; ⊙10am-11pm Mon-Sat, to 10.30pm Sun; 🛜🖼; 🚆DLR Cutty Sark) Acquired by Young's in 2016 and entirely

Camden Town

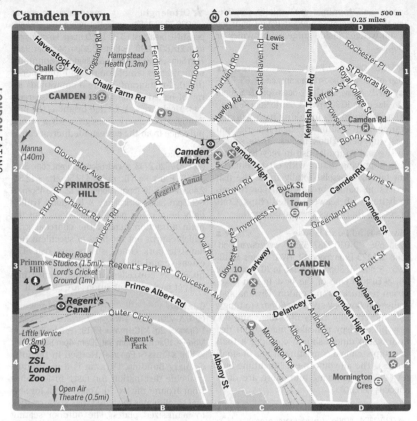

refurbished, this excellent and handsome choice within the grounds of the Old Royal Naval College (p102) is both a ravishing restaurant and a pub, with a heady range of craft beers and cocktails. There's outside seating for sunny days.

✖ West London

★ Potli   INDIAN £

(☎020-8741 4328; www.potli.co.uk; 319-321 King St, W6; weekday 1-/2-course set lunch £7.95/10.95, mains £7.50-15; ⊙noon-2.30pm Mon-Sat, 6-10.15pm Mon-Thu, 5.30-10.30pm Fri & Sat, noon-10pm Sun; 🐟; ⊖Stamford Brook, Ravenscourt Park) With its scattered pieces from Mumbai's Thieves Market, Indian-market-kitchen/bazaar cuisine, homemade pickles and spice mixes, plus an accent on genuine flavour, tantalising Potli deftly captures the aromas of its culinary home. Downstairs there's an open kitchen and service is friendly, but it's the alluring menu – where flavours are teased into a rich and authentic Indian culinary experience – that's the real crowd pleaser.

Taquería MEXICAN **£**
(Map p92; ☑ 020-7229 4734; www.taqueria.co.uk; 139-143 Westbourne Grove; tacos £7.20-10.20; ✆ noon-11pm Mon-Thu, to 11.30pm Fri & Sat, to 10.30pm Sun; ☎; ⊖ Notting Hill Gate) ✎ You won't find fresher or more limp (they're not supposed to be crispy!) tacos anywhere in London because these ones are made on the premises. Starting life as a stall on Portobello Rd and recently refurbished, it's a small casual place with a great vibe, committed to environmental mores: the eggs, chicken and pork are free-range, the meat British, the fish MSC-certified, and the milk and cream organic.

★ **Geales** SEAFOOD **££**
(Map p92; ☑ 020-7727 7528; www.geales.com; 2 Farmer St, W8; 2-course express lunch £9.95, mains £9-33.50; ✆ noon-3pm Tue-Fri, 5.30-11pm Mon-Fri, noon-11pm Sat & Sun; ☎; ⊖ Notting Hill Gate) Frying since 1939 – a bad year for the European restaurant trade – Geales has endured with its quiet location on the corner of Farmer and Uxbridge Sts. The succulent fish in crispy batter is a fine catch, but the fish pie is also worth angling for. Look out for the good-value (two-course, one coffee) express lunch, available from Tuesday to Friday.

★ **Ledbury** FRENCH **£££**
(Map p92; ☑ 020-7792 9090; www.theledbury.com; 127 Ledbury Rd, W11; 4-course set lunch £75, 4-course dinner £120; ✆ noon-2pm Wed-Sun & 6.30-9.45pm daily; ☎; ⊖ Westbourne Park, Royal Oak, Notting Hill Gate) With two Michelin stars and swooningly elegant, Brett Graham's artful French restaurant attracts well-heeled diners in jeans with designer jackets. Dishes such as hand-dived scallops, Chinese water deer, smoked bone marrow, quince and red leaves, or Herdwick lamb with salt-baked turnips, celery cream and wild garlic are triumphs. London gastronomes have the Ledbury on speed dial, so reservations well in advance are crucial.

✖ **Richmond, Kew & Hampton Court**

★ **Glasshouse** MODERN EUROPEAN **££**
(☑ 020-8940 6777; www.glasshouserestaurant.co.uk; 14 Station Pde, TW9; 2-/3-course lunch Mon-Fri £30/35, 1-/2-/3-course dinner £32.50/45/55; ✆ noon-2.30pm & 6.30-10.30pm Tue-Sat, 12.30-4pm Sun; ☎ ⑂; ⊠ Kew Gardens, ⊖ Kew Gardens) A day at Kew Gardens finds a perfect conclusion at this Michelin-starred gastronomic highlight. The glass-fronted exterior envelops a delicately lit, low-key interior, where the focus remains on divinely cooked food. Diners are rewarded with a consistently accomplished menu from chef Berwyn Davies that combines English mainstays with modern European innovation.

🍷 **Drinking & Nightlife**

🍸 **The West End**

★ **Lamb & Flag** PUB
(Map p70; ☑ 020-7497 9504; www.lambandflagcoventgarden.co.uk; 33 Rose St, WC2; ✆ 11am-11pm Mon-Sat, noon-10.30pm Sun; ⊖ Covent Garden) Everybody's favourite pub in central London, pint-sized Lamb & Flag is full of charm and history, and is on the site of a pub that dates from at least 1772. Rain or shine, you'll have to elbow your way to the bar through the merry crowd drinking outside. Inside are brass fittings and creaky wooden floors.

★ **American Bar** COCKTAIL BAR
(Map p70; ☑ 020-7836 4343; www.fairmont.com/savoy-london/dining/americanbar; Savoy, The Strand, WC2; ✆ 11.30am-midnight Mon-Sat, noon-midnight Sun; ⊖ Covent Garden) Home of the Hanky Panky, White Lady and other classic infusions created on-site, the seriously dishy and elegant American Bar is an icon of London, with soft blue and rust art deco lines and live piano music. Cocktails start at £17.50 and peak at a stupefying £5000 (the Original Sazerac, containing Sazerac de Forge cognac from 1857).

★ **Dukes London** COCKTAIL BAR
(Map p68; ☑ 020-7491 4840; www.dukeshotel.com/dukes-bar; Dukes Hotel, 35 St James's Pl, SW1; ✆ 2-11pm Mon-Sat, 4-10.30pm Sun; ☎; ⊖ Green Park) Sip to-die-for martinis like royalty in a gentleman's-club-like ambience at this tucked-away classic bar where white-jacketed masters mix up some awesomely good preparations. Ian Fleming used to frequent the place, perhaps perfecting his 'shaken, not stirred' James Bond maxim. Smokers can ease into the secluded Cognac and Cigar Garden to light up cigars purchased here.

Swift
COCKTAIL BAR

(Map p70; ☑020-7437 7820; www.barswift.com; 12 Old Compton St, W1; ☺3pm-midnight Mon-Sat, to 10.30pm Sun; ☻Leicester Sq, Tottenham Court Rd) Our favourite new place for cocktails, Swift (as in the bird) has a black-and-white, candlelit Upstairs Bar designed for those who want a quick tipple before dinner or the theatre, while the Downstairs Bar (open from 5pm), with its sit-down bar and art deco sofas, is a place to hang out. There's live jazz and blues at the weekend.

Connaught Bar
COCKTAIL BAR

(Map p86; ☑020-7314 3419; www.the-connaught. co.uk/mayfair-bars/connaught-bar; Connaught Hotel, Carlos Pl, W1; ☺11am-1am Mon-Sat, to midnight Sun; ☻Bond St) Drinkers who know their stuff single out the travelling martini trolley for particular praise, but almost everything at this sumptuous bar at the exclusive and very British Connaught Hotel gets the nod: lavish art deco–inspired lines, faultless and cheerful service, and some of the best drinks in town. Cocktails, classic and those given a thoroughly contemporary twist, start at £18.

Princess Louise
PUB

(Map p70; ☑020-7405 8816; http://princesslou isepub.co.uk; 208 High Holborn, WC1; ☺11am-11pm Mon-Fri, noon-11pm Sat, noon-6.45pm Sun; ☻Holborn) The ground-floor saloon of this pub dating from 1872 is spectacularly decorated with a riot of fine tiles, etched mirrors, plasterwork and a stunning central horseshoe bar. The old Victorian wood partitions give drinkers plenty of nooks and alcoves to hide in, and the frosted-glass 'snob screens' add further period allure.

LGBT LONDON

The West End, particularly Soho, is the visible centre of gay and lesbian London, with venues clustered around Old Compton St and its surrounds, but there are gay-friendly venues scattered all over the capital.

Heaven (Map p70; http://heaven-live.co.uk; Villiers St, WC2; ☺11pm-5am Mon, to 4am Thu & Fri, 10.30pm-5am Sat; ☻Embankment, Charing Cross) This perennially popular mixed/gay club under the arches beneath Charing Cross Station is host to excellent live gigs and club nights. Monday's Popcorn (mixed dance party, with an all-welcome door policy) offers one of the best weeknight's clubbing in the capital. The celebrated G-A-Y takes place here on Thursday (G-A-Y Porn Idol), Friday (G-A-Y Camp Attack) and Saturday (plain ol' G-A-Y).

Duke of Wellington (Map p70; ☑020-7439 1274; www.facebook.com/Duke.Of.Welly; 77 Wardour St, W1; ☺noon-midnight Mon-Sat, to 11.30pm Sun; ☻Leicester Sq) This seasoned pub off Old Compton St is often busy but has few pretensions, attracting a more beardy, fun-loving gay crowd, many of whom gather outside in warmer months.

RVT (Royal Vauxhall Tavern; ☑020-7820 1222; www.vauxhalltavern.com; 372 Kennington Lane, SE11; entry £5-25; ☺7pm-midnight Mon-Thu, 9pm-3am Fri, 9pm-2am Sat, 3pm-midnight Sun; ☻Vauxhall) A welcoming gay landmark, the Royal Vauxhall Tavern is the perfect antidote to the gleaming new wave of uppity gay venues now crowding Vauxhall's gay village. Saturday's Duckie, tagged 'London's Authentic Honky Tonk', is the club's signature queer performance night, while Sunday Social is cabaret and dance till midnight and on Monday it's the fun Big Bingo Show!

Two Brewers (☑020-7819 9539; www.the2brewers.com; 114 Clapham High St, SW4; after 10pm £3-8; ☺5pm-2am Sun-Thu, to 4am Fri & Sat; ☏; ☻Clapham Common) Clapham exudes an inner-suburban feel, the High St in particular, but the long-standing Two Brewers endures as one of the best London gay bars outside the gay villages of Soho, Shoreditch and Vauxhall. Here there's a friendly, laid-back, local crowd who come for a quiet drink during the week and some madcap cabaret and dancing at weekends.

Dalston Superstore (☑020-7254 2273; www.dalstonsuperstore.com; 117 Kingsland High St, E8; ☺11.45am-late; ☻Dalston Kingsland) Bar, club or diner? Gay, lesbian or straight? Dalston Superstore is hard to pigeonhole, which we suspect is the point. This two-level industrial space is open all day but really comes into its own after dark when there are club nights in the basement.

Terroirs WINE BAR
(Map p70; ☑ 020-7036 0660; www.terroirswinebar.
com; 5 William IV St, WC2; ☺ noon-11pm Mon-Sat;
☏; ☻ Charing Cross Rd) A fab two-floor spot
for a pre-theatre glass and some expertly
created charcuterie, with informative staff,
tempting and affordable lunch specials
(£10), a lively, convivial atmosphere and a
breathtaking list of organic, natural and bio-
dynamic wines.

Dog & Duck PUB
(Map p70; ☑ 020-7494 0697; www.nicholsons
pubs.co.uk/restaurants/london/thedoganddduck
soholondon; 18 Bateman St, W1; ☺ 11.30am-11pm
Mon-Thu, to 11.30pm Fri, 11am-11.30pm Sat, noon-
10.30pm Sun; ☻ Tottenham Court Rd) With a
fine array of real ales, some stunning Victorian glazed tiling and garrulous crowds
spilling onto the pavement, the Dog &
Duck has attracted a host of famous regulars, including painters John Constable and
pre-Raphaelite Dante Gabrielle Rossetti,
dystopian writer George Orwell and musi-
cian Madonna.

☗ The City

Blackfriar PUB
(Map p76; ☑ 020-7236 5474; www.nicholsons
pubs.co.uk; 174 Queen Victoria St, EC4; ☺ 10am-
11pm Mon-Fri, 9am-11pm Sat, noon-10.30pm Sun;
☻ Blackfriars) Built in 1875 on the site of a
Dominican monastery (hence the name and
the corpulent chap above the door), this
prominent pub was famously saved from
demolition in the 1960s by poet Sir John
Betjeman. The unusual monastic-themed
friezes date from an art nouveau makeover
in 1905. It serves a good selection of ales,
along with speciality sausages and chops.

Ye Olde Cheshire Cheese PUB
(Map p76; ☑ 020-7353 6170; Wine Office Court,
145 Fleet St, EC4; ☺ 11.30am-11pm Mon-Fri, noon-
11pm Sat; ☻ Chancery Lane) Rebuilt in 1667
after the Great Fire, this is one of London's
most famous pubs, accessed via a narrow
alley off Fleet St. Over its long history, Dr
Johnson, Thackeray and Dickens have
all supped in its gloriously gloomy surrounds. The vaulted cellars are thought to
be remnants of a 13th-century Carmelite
monastery.

Sky Pod BAR
(Map p76; ☑ 0333 772 0020; www.skygarden.
london; L35, 20 Fenchurch St, EC3; ☺ 7am-11pm
Mon, to midnight Tue, to 1am Wed-Fri, 8am-1am

Sat, 8am-11pm Sun; ☻ Monument) You'll need a
booking for the Sky Garden (p79) to access
this rooftop bar, and if you'd like a guaranteed table to sit at, you're best to book one
at the same time. The views are extraordinary, although it does get cold up here in
winter. Note, it doesn't admit patrons in
shorts, sportswear, trainers or flip-flops after 5pm.

Counting House PUB
(Map p76; ☑ 020-7283 7123; www.the-counting
-house.com; 50 Cornhill, EC3; ☺ 10am-11pm
Mon-Fri; ☏; ☻ Bank) With its counters and
basement vaults, this award-winning pub
certainly looks and feels comfortable in
the former headquarters of NatWest Bank
(1893), with its domed skylight and elegantly curved central bar. This is a favourite of
City boys and girls, who come for the good
range of real ales and the speciality pies
(from £13.95).

Madison COCKTAIL BAR
(Map p76; ☑ 020-3693 5160; www.madisonlon
don.net; rooftop, 1 New Change, EC4; ☺ 11am-mid-
night Mon-Thu, to 1am Fri & Sat, noon to 9pm Sun;
☻ St Paul's) Perched atop One New Change
with a drop-dead gorgeous view of St Paul's,
Madison offers a large open-air roof terrace
with a restaurant on one side and a cocktail bar on the other; we come for the latter.
Drinkers must be aged over 21; no trainers
or flip-flops admitted, however fashionable.
Expect to queue.

☗ South Bank

★ **Little Bird Gin** COCKTAIL BAR
(www.littlebirdgin.com; Maltby St, SE1; ☺ 5-10pm
Thu & Fri, 10am-10pm Sat, 11am-4pm Sun; ☻ London Bridge) This South London–based distillery opens a pop-up bar in a workshop at
Maltby Street Market (www.maltby.st; dishes
£5-10; ☺ 9am-4pm Sat, 11am-4pm Sun; ☻ Bermondsey) to ply merry punters with devilish-
ly good cocktails (£5 to £7), served in jam
jars or apothecary's glass bottles.

★ **Oblix** BAR
(Map p84; www.oblixrestaurant.com; 32nd fl,
Shard, 31 St Thomas St, SE1; ☺ noon-11pm; ☻ London Bridge) On the 32nd floor of the Shard
(p85), Oblix offers mesmerising vistas of
London. You can come for anything from
a coffee (£3.50) to a cocktail (from £13.50)
and enjoy virtually the same views as the
official viewing galleries of the Shard (but at

a reduced cost and with the added bonus of a drink). Live music every night from 7pm.

★**Scootercaffe** BAR
(Map p84; 132 Lower Marsh, SE1; ⊙8.30am-11pm Mon-Thu, to midnight Fri, 10am-midnight Sat, to 11pm Sun; 🛜; 🚇Waterloo) A well-established fixture on the up-and-coming Lower Marsh road, this funky cafe-bar and former scooter-repair shop with a Piatti scooter in the window serves killer hot chocolates, coffee and decadent cocktails. Unusually, you're allowed to bring in takeaway food. The tiny patio at the back is perfect for soaking up the sun.

Skylon BAR
(Map p84; www.skylon-restaurant.co.uk; Royal Festival Hall, Southbank Centre, Belvedere Rd, SE1; ⊙noon-1am Mon-Sat, to 10.30pm Sun; 🛜; 🚇Waterloo) Ravishing 1950s decor and show-stopping views make Skylon a memorable choice for a drink or meal (Map p84; 📞020-7654 7800; 3-course menu grill/restaurant £25/30; ⊙grill noon-11pm Mon-Sat, to 10.30pm Sun, restaurant noon-2.30pm & 5-10.30pm Mon-Sat, 11.30am-4pm Sun). You'll have to come early to bag one of the tables at the front with plunging views of the river. Drinks-wise, just ask: from superb seasonal cocktails to infusions and a staggering choice of wine and whiskys (plus whiskeys!).

🍷 Kensington & Hyde Park

★**Tomtom Coffee House** CAFE
(Map p86; 📞020-7730 1771; www.tomtom.co.uk; 114 Ebury St, SW1; ⊙8am-5pm Mon-Fri, 9am-6pm Sat & Sun; 🛜; 🚇Victoria) Tomtom has built its reputation on its amazing coffee: not only are the drinks fabulously presented (forget ferns and hearts in your latte, here it's peacocks fanning their tails), but the selection is dizzying: from the usual espresso-based suspects to filter, and a full choice of beans. You can even spice things up with a bonus tot of cognac or whisky (£3).

Queen's Arms PUB
(Map p86; www.thequeensarmskensington.co.uk; 30 Queen's Gate Mews, SW7; ⊙noon-11pm Mon-Sat, to 10.30pm Sun; 🚇Gloucester Rd) Just around the corner from the Royal Albert Hall is this blue-grey-painted godsend. Located in an adorable cobbled-mews setting off bustling Queen's Gate, it beckons with a cosy interior and a right-royal selection of ales – including selections from small, local cask brewers – and ciders on tap. In warm weather, drinkers

stand outside in the mews (only permitted on one side).

🍷 East London

★**Dove Freehouse** PUB
(📞020-7275 7617; www.dovepubs.com; 24-28 Broadway Market, E8; ⊙noon-11pm Sun-Fri, 11am-11pm Sat; 🛜; 🚇London Fields) Alluring at any time, the Dove has a rambling series of rooms and a wide range of Belgian Trappist, wheat and fruit-flavoured beers. Drinkers spill on to the street in warmer weather, or hunker down in the low-lit back room with board games when it's chilly.

★**Netil360** ROOFTOP BAR
(www.netil360.com; 1 Westgate St, E8; ⊙noon-8.30pm Wed & Sun, to 10.30pm Thu-Sat Apr-Nov; 🛜; 🚇London Fields) Perched atop Netil House, this uberhip rooftop cafe-bar offers incredible views over London, with brass telescopes enabling you to get better acquainted with workers in the Gherkin. In between drinks you can knock out a game of croquet on the Astroturf, or perhaps book a hot tub for you and your mates to stew in.

★**Cat & Mutton** PUB
(📞020-7249 6555; www.catandmutton.com; 76 Broadway Market, E8; ⊙noon-11pm Mon, to midnight Tue-Thu, to 1am Fri, 10am-1am Sat, 11.30pm Sun; 🚇London Fields) At this fabulous Georgian pub, Hackney hipsters sup pints under the watchful eyes of hunting trophies, black-and-white photos of old-time boxers and a large portrait of Karl Marx. If it's crammed downstairs, as it often is, head up the spiral staircase to the comfy couches. DJs spin funk, disco and soul on the weekends.

Howling Hops MICROBREWERY
(📞020-3583 8262; www.howlinghops.co.uk; 9a Queen's Yard, White Post Lane, E9; ⊙noon-11pm Sun-Thu, to midnight Fri & Sat; 🚇Hackney Wick) You won't find cans, bottles or barrels in this pleasantly grungy brewery bar, just 10 gleaming tanks containing ales and lagers straight from the source. It shares the old Victorian warehouse with the wonderful-smelling Billy Smokes Barbecue and there's also a counter serving excellent coffee.

Draughts CAFE, BAR
(www.draughtslondon.com; 337 Acton Mews, E8; mains £6-10; ⊙10am-11pm Sun-Fri, to midnight Sat; 🚺; 🚇Haggerston) London's first board-game themed cafe-bar – it has over 600 to

choose from – offers a delightfully geeky way to while away an afternoon. Food, wine and ale are served all day, and there is even a 'game guru' on hand to explain rules and advise which games are best suited to your group's wants. There's a £5 charge if you start playing a game.

Carpenter's Arms PUB
(☏020-7739 6342; www.carpentersarmsfreehouse.com; 73 Cheshire St, E2; ☺4-11.30pm Mon-Wed, noon-11.30pm Thu & Sun, to 12.30am Fri & Sat; ☎; ☺Shoreditch High St) Once owned by infamous gangsters the Kray brothers (who bought it for their old ma to run), this chic yet cosy pub has been beautifully restored and its many wooden surfaces positively gleam. A back room and small yard provide a little more space for the convivial drinkers. There's a huge range of draught and bottled beers and ciders.

Prospect of Whitby PUB
(☏020-7481 1095; www.greenekingpubs.co.uk; 57 Wapping Wall, E1; ☺noon-11pm Mon-Thu, 11am-midnight Fri & Sat, noon-10.30pm Sun; ☎; ☺Wapping) Once known as the Devil's Tavern due to its unsavoury clientele, the Prospect first opened its doors in 1520, although the only part of the original pub remaining is the flagstone floor. Famous patrons have included Charles Dickens and Samuel Pepys. There's a smallish terrace overlooking the Thames, a restaurant upstairs, open fires in winter and a pewter-topped bar.

♉ Clerkenwell, Shoreditch & Spitalfields

★**Worship St Whistling Shop** COCKTAIL BAR
(Map p124; ☏020-7247 0015; www.whistlingshop.com; 63 Worship St, EC2A; ☺5pm-midnight Mon & Tue, to 1am Wed & Thu, to 2am Fri & Sat; ☺Old St) While the name is Victorian slang for a place selling illicit booze, this subterranean drinking den's master mixologists explore the experimental limits of cocktail chemistry and aromatic science, as well as concocting the classics. Many ingredients are made with rotary evaporators in the on-site lab. Also runs cocktail masterclasses.

★**Cargo** BAR, CLUB
(Map p124; www.cargo-london.com; 83 Rivington St, EC2A; ☺noon-1am Mon-Thu, to 3am Fri & Sat, to midnight Sun; ☺Shoreditch High St) Cargo is one of London's most eclectic clubs. Under its brick railway arches you'll find a dance

floor, a bar and an outside terrace adorned with two original Banksy images. The music policy (hip-hop, pop, R&B and club classics) is varied, with plenty of up-and-coming bands also in the line-up. Food is available throughout the day.

★**Ye Olde Mitre** PUB
(Map p76; www.yeoldemitreholborn.co.uk; 1 Ely Ct, EC1N; ☺11am-11pm Mon-Fri; ☎; ☺Farringdon) A delightfully cosy historic pub with an extensive beer selection, tucked away in a backstreet off Hatton Garden, Ye Olde Mitre was built in 1546 for the servants of Ely Palace. There's no music, so rooms echo only with amiable chit-chat. Queen Elizabeth I danced around the cherry tree by the bar, they say.

Fabric CLUB
(Map p76; ☏0207 336 8898; www.fabriclondon.com; 77a Charterhouse St, EC1M; cover £5-25; ☺11pm-7am Fri, to 8am Sat, to 5.30am Sun; ☺Farringdon, Barbican) London's leading club, Fabric's three separate dance floors in a huge converted cold store opposite Smithfield meat market draw impressive queues (buy tickets online). FabricLive (on selected Fridays) rumbles with drum 'n' bass and dubstep, while Fabric (usually on Saturdays but also on selected Fridays) is the club's signature live DJ night. Sunday's WetYourSelf! delivers house, techno and electronica.

XOYO CLUB
(Map p124; www.xoyo.co.uk; 32-37 Cowper St, EC2A; ☺10pm-3am Mon, Tue & Thu, 9.30pm-4am Fri & Sat; ☺Old St) This fantastic Shoreditch warehouse club throws together a pulsing and popular mix of gigs, club nights and art events. Always buzzing, it has a varied line-up of indie bands, hip-hop, electro, dubstep and much in between, and attracts a mix of clubbers, from skinny-jeaned hipsters to more mature hedonists (but no suits).

BrewDog BAR
(Map p124; www.brewdog.com; 51-55 Bethnal Green Rd, E1; ☺noon-midnight Mon-Thu, to 2am Fri, 11am-2am Sat, 11am-midnight Sun; ☎; ☺Shoreditch High St) BrewDog is an ale aficionado's paradise, with 18 different brews on tap, hundreds by the bottle and, to soak it all up, some excellent burgers (including interesting variations such as brisket and soy). Its own crowd-funded eco-brewery is located in Scotland, near Aberdeen, and it stocks other microbrewery beers, too.

Hoxton, Shoreditch & Spitalfields

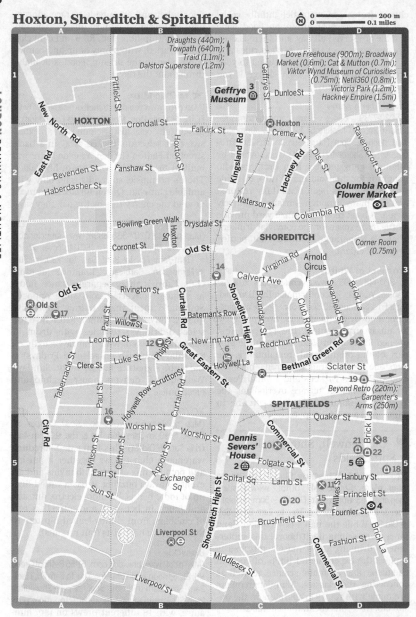

Draughts (440m);
Towpath (640m);
Triad (1.1mi);
Dalston Superstore (1.2mi)

Dove Freehouse (900m); Broadway
Market (0.6mi); Cat & Mutton (0.7mi);
Viktor Wynd Museum of Curiosities
(0.75mi); Netil360 (0.8mi);
Victoria Park (1.2mi);
Hackney Empire (1.5mi)

Geffrye Museum 3

DunloeSt

HOXTON

Crondall St

Falkirk St

Cremer St

Hoxton

Pitfield St

Hoxton St

Kingsland Rd

Hackney Rd

Diss St

Ravenscroft St

Bevenden St

Fanshaw St

Haberdasher St

Waterson St

Columbia Rd

Columbia Road Flower Market 1

Bowling Green Walk

Drysdale St

SHOREDITCH

Coronet St

Hoxton

Old St

Virginia Rd

Arnold Circus

Corner Room
(0.75mi)

Old St

Old St 17

Rivington St

Curtain Rd

14

Calvert Ave

Boundary St

Club Row

Swanfield St

Brick La

7 WillowSt

Leonard St

12 Phipp St

Paul St

Bateman's Row

Great Eastern St

New Inn Yard

6

Redchurch St

13

9

Shoreditch High St

Tabernacle St

Clere St

Luke St

Holywell Row

Scrutton St

Curtain Rd

Holywell La

Bethnal Green Rd

Sclater St

4

19

Beyond Retro (220m);
Carpenter's
Arms (250m)

Paul St

City Rd

16

Worship St

Worship St

SPITALFIELDS

Quaker St

Brick La

Wilson St

Clifton St

Appold St

Dennis Severs' House 2

10

Folgate St

Commercial St

21

8

5

22

18

Earl St

Exchange Sq

Spital Sq

Lamb St

Hanbury St

Sun St

Shoreditch High St

15

11

Princelet St

4

20

Fournier St

Wilkes St

Liverpool St

Brushfield St

Fashion St

Brick La

Liverpool St

Middlesex St

Commercial St

Book Club   BAR
(Map p124; ☏020-7684 8618; www.wearetbc.
com; 100-106 Leonard St, EC2A; ⊙9am-mid-
night Mon-Wed, to 2am Thu & Fri, 10am-2am Sat,
to midnight Sun; ☎; ⊖Old St) A creative vibe
animates this fantastic one-time Victori-

an warehouse. Book Club hosts DJs and
oddball events (life drawing, workshops,
twerking lessons and the Crap Film Club) to
complement the drinking and enthusiastic
ping-pong and pool playing. Food is served

Hoxton, Shoreditch & Spitalfields

⊙ **Top Sights**
1 Columbia Road Flower Market..............D2
2 Dennis Severs' House............................C5
3 Geffrye Museum.......................................C1

⊙ **Sights**
4 Brick Lane D5
5 Old Truman Brewery D5

🛏 **Sleeping**
6 citizenM C4
7 Hoxton Hotel..B3

🍴 **Eating**
8 Boiler House D5
9 Brick Lane Beigel Bake.........................D4
10 Hawksmoor..C5

11 Poppie's D5

🍷 **Drinking & Nightlife**
12 Book Club B4
13 BrewDog D4
14 Cargo..C3
15 Ten Bells D5
16 Worship St Whistling Shop..................A5
17 XOYO A3

🛍 **Shopping**
18 Blitz London D5
19 Brick Lane Market D4
20 Old Spitalfields Market..........................C5
21 Rough Trade East D5
22 Sunday UpMarket....................................D5

throughout the day and there's a scruffy basement bar below.

Ten Bells PUB
(Map p124; www.tenbells.com; 84 Commercial St, E1; ⊙noon-midnight Sun-Wed, to 1am Thu-Sat; 🚇; 🚇Shoreditch High St) This landmark Victorian pub with large windows and beautiful tiles is perfectly positioned for a pint after exploring Spitalfields Market. The most famous of London's Jack the Ripper pubs, it was patronised by his last victim before her grisly end, and possibly by the serial killer himself. Gin menu, pork scratchings and pie of the day offered.

🍷 North London

★**Proud Camden** BAR
(Map p118; www.proudcamden.com; Stables Market, Chalk Farm Rd, NW1; ⊙11am-1.30am Mon-Sat, to midnight Sun; 🚇Chalk Farm) Proud occupies a former horse hospital within Stables Market, with private booths in the old stalls, fantastic artworks on the walls (the main bar acts as a gallery during the day) and a kooky garden terrace complete with a hot tub. It's also one of Camden's best music venues, with live bands and DJs most nights (entry free to £15).

★**Holly Bush** PUB
(www.hollybushhampstead.co.uk; 22 Holly Mount, NW3; ⊙noon-11pm Mon-Sat, to 10.30pm Sun; 🚇🚻🐕; 🚇Hampstead) This beautiful Grade II–listed Georgian pub opens to an antique interior, with open fires in winter. It has a knack for making you stay longer than you planned. Set above Heath St, in a secluded

hilltop location, it's reached via the Holly Bush Steps.

★**Edinboro Castle** PUB
(Map p118; www.edinborocastlepub.co.uk; 57 Mornington Tce, NW1; ⊙noon-11pm Mon-Sat, noon-10.30pm Sun; 🚇; 🚇Camden Town) Large and relaxed Edinboro offers a refined atmosphere, gorgeous furniture perfect for slumping into, a fine bar and a full menu. The highlight, however, is the huge beer garden, complete with warm-weather barbecues and decorated with coloured lights on long summer evenings. Patio heaters come out in winter.

🍷 Greenwich & South London

★**Cutty Sark Tavern** PUB
(📞020-8858 3146; www.cuttysarkse10.co.uk; 4-6 Ballast Quay, SE10; ⊙11.30am-11pm Mon-Sat, noon-10.30pm Sun; 🚇; 🚇DLR Cutty Sark) Housed in a delightful bow-windowed, wood-beamed Georgian building directly on the Thames, the Cutty Sark is one of the few independent pubs left in Greenwich. Half a dozen cask-conditioned ales on tap line the bar, there's an inviting riverside seating area opposite and an upstairs dining room looking out on to glorious views. It's a 10-minute walk from the DLR station.

★**Greenwich Union** PUB
(📞020-8692 6258; www.greenwichunion.com; 56 Royal Hill, SE10; ⊙noon-11pm Mon-Fri, 11.30am-11pm Sat, 11.30am-10.30pm Sun; 🚇; 🚇DLR Greenwich) The award-winning Union plies six or seven Meantime microbrewery beers, including raspberry and wheat varieties, and a

strong list of ales, plus bottled international brews. It's a handsome place, with duffed-up leather armchairs and a welcoming long, narrow aspect leading to a conservatory and beer garden at the rear.

★ **Trafalgar Tavern**   PUB
(☏ 020-8858 2909; www.trafalgartavern.co.uk; 6 Park Row, SE10; ⊙ noon-11pm Mon-Thu, noon-midnight Fri, 10am-midnight Sat, 10am-11pm Sun; ⊠ DLR Cutty Sark) This elegant tavern with big windows overlooking the Thames is steeped in history. Dickens apparently knocked back a few here – and used it as the setting for the wedding breakfast scene in *Our Mutual Friend* – and prime ministers Gladstone and Disraeli used to dine on the pub's celebrated whitebait.

🍷 West London

★ **Troubadour**   BAR
(☏ 020-7341 6333; www.troubadour.co.uk; 263-267 Old Brompton Rd, SW5; ⊙ cafe 9am-12.30am, club 8pm-12.30am or 2am; 🛜; ⊜ Earl's Court) On a comparable spiritual plane to Paris' Shakespeare and Company bookshop, this eccentric, time-warped and convivial boho bar-cafe has been serenading drinkers since 1954. (Deep breath) Adele, Paolo Nutini, Ed Sheeran, Joni Mitchell and (deeper breath) Jimi Hendrix and Bob Dylan have performed here, and there's still live music (folk, blues) and a large, pleasant garden open in summer.

Windsor Castle   PUB
(Map p92; www.thewindsorcastlekensington.co.uk; 114 Campden Hill Rd, W11; ⊙ noon-11pm Mon-Sat, to 10.30pm Sun; 🛜; ⊜ Notting Hill Gate) A classic tavern on the brow of Campden Hill Rd, this place has history, nooks and charm on tap. It's worth the search for its historic compartmentalised interior, roaring fire (in winter), delightful beer garden (in summer) and affable regulars (all seasons). According to legend, the bones of Thomas Paine (author of *Rights of Man*) are in the cellar.

Notting Hill Arts Club   CLUB
(Map p92; www.nottinghillartsclub.com; 21 Notting Hill Gate, W11; ⊙ 6pm-late Mon-Fri, 4pm-late Sat & Sun; 🛜; ⊜ Notting Hill Gate) London simply wouldn't be what it is without places like NHAC. Cultivating the underground-music scene, this small basement club attracts a musically curious and experimental crowd. Dress code: no suits and ties.

🍷 Richmond, Kew & Hampton Court

★ **City Barge**   PUB
(www.metropolitanpubcompany.com/our-pubs/the-city-barge; 27 Strand on the Green, W4; ⊙ noon-11pm Mon-Thu, to midnight Fri, 10am-midnight Sat, 10am-10.30pm Sun; 🛜; ⊜ Gunnersbury) In a line of small riverside cottages facing wooded Oliver's Island (where Cromwell is alleged to have taken refuge), this excellent pub looks straight onto the muddy Thames. Once known as the Navigators Arms, there has been a pub here since the Middle Ages, although the Luftwaffe gave it a dramatic facelift (as has an attractive refurb).

★ **White Cross**   PUB
(☏ 020-8940 6844; www.thewhitecrossrichmond.com; Water Lane, TW9; ⊙ 11am-11pm Mon-Fri, 10am-11pm Sat, 10am-10.30pm Sun; 🛜; ⊜ Richmond) The riverside location and fine food and ales make this bay-windowed pub on the site of a former friary a winner. There are entrances for low and high tides, but when the river is at its highest, Cholmondeley Walk running along the Thames floods and the pub is out of bounds to those not willing to wade. Wellies are provided.

☆ Entertainment

Theatre

Royal Court Theatre   THEATRE
(Map p86; ☏ 020-7565 5000; www.royalcourttheatre.com; Sloane Sq, SW1; tickets £12-38; ⊜ Sloane Sq) Equally renowned for staging innovative new plays and old classics, the Royal Court is among London's most progressive theatres and has continued to foster major writing talent across the UK. There are two auditoriums: the main Jerwood Theatre Downstairs, and the much smaller studio Jerwood Theatre Upstairs. Tickets for Monday performances are £12.

A limited number of restricted-view standing places go on sale one hour before each Jerwood Theatre Downstairs performance for just 10p each. Contact the theatre to check on availability.

★ **Shakespeare's Globe**   THEATRE
(Map p84; ☏ 020-7401 9919; www.shakespearesglobe.com; 21 New Globe Walk, SE1; seats £20-45, standing £5; ⊜ Blackfriars, London Bridge) If you love Shakespeare and the theatre, the Globe (p82) will knock your theatrical socks off. This authentic Shakespearean theatre is a

wooden 'O' without a roof over the central stage area, and although there are covered wooden bench seats in tiers around the stage, many people (there's room for 700) do as 17th-century 'groundlings' did, and stand in front of the stage.

Old Vic THEATRE
(Map p84; ☑ 0844 871 7628; www.oldvictheatre. com; The Cut, SE1; ☺ Waterloo) American actor Kevin Spacey took the theatrical helm of this London theatre in 2003. He was succeeded in April 2015 by Matthew Warchus (who directed *Matilda the Musical* and the film *Pride*), whose aim is to bring eclectic programming to the theatre: expect new writing, as well as dynamic revivals of old works and musicals.

Half the seats of the first five previews of a new production are sold for just £10 each. These PwC £10 Preview Tickets go on sale five weeks before the performance.

Young Vic THEATRE
(Map p84; ☑ 020-7922 2922; www.youngvic.org; 66 The Cut, SE1; ☺ Southwark, Waterloo) This groundbreaking theatre is as much about showcasing and discovering new talent as it is about people discovering theatre. The Young Vic features actors, directors and plays from across the world, many tackling contemporary political and cultural issues, such as the death penalty, racism or corruption, and often blending dance and music with acting.

Donmar Warehouse THEATRE
(Map p70; ☑ 020-3282 3808; www.donmarware house.com; 41 Earlham St, WC2; ☺ Covent Garden) The cosy Donmar Warehouse is London's 'thinking person's theatre'. Josie Rourke, the artistic director until 2019, staged some intriguing and successful productions, including the well-received comedy *My Night with Reg*, George Bernard Shaw's *St Joan* and the political drama *Limehouse* by Steve Waters.

Wilton's THEATRE
(☑ 020-7702 2789; www.wiltons.org.uk; 1 Graces Alley, E1; ☺ bar 5-11pm Mon-Sat; ☺ Tower Hill) A gloriously atmospheric example of a Victorian music hall, Wilton's hosts a variety of shows, from comedy and classical music to theatre and opera. The **Mahogany Bar** is a great way to get a taste of the place if you're not attending a performance.

Hackney Empire THEATRE
(☑ 020-8985 2424; www.hackneyempire.co.uk; 291 Mare St, E8; ☺ Hackney Central) One of London's most beautiful theatres, this renovated Edwardian music hall (1901) offers an extremely diverse range of performances, from hard-edged political theatre to musicals, opera and comedy. It's one of the very best places to catch a pantomime at Christmas.

Live Music

★ Jazz Cafe LIVE MUSIC
(Map p118; ☑ 020-7485 6834; www.thejazzcafe london.com; 5 Parkway, NW1; ☺ live shows from 7pm, club nights 10pm-3am; ☺ Camden Town) The name would have you think jazz is the main staple, but it's only a small slice of what's on offer. The intimate clublike space also serves up funk, hip-hop, R&B, soul and rare groove, with big-name acts regularly dropping in. Saturday club night is soul night, with two live sets from the house band.

★ KOKO LIVE MUSIC
(Map p118; www.koko.uk.com; 1a Camden High St, NW1; ☺ Mornington Cres) Once the legendary Camden Palace, where Charlie Chaplin, the Goons and the Sex Pistols performed, and where Prince played surprise gigs, KOKO is maintaining its reputation as one of London's better gig venues. The theatre has a dance floor and decadent balconies, and attracts an indie crowd. There are live bands most nights and hugely popular club nights on Saturdays.

★ Royal Albert Hall CONCERT VENUE
(Map p86; ☑ 0845 401 5034; www.royalalbert hall.com; Kensington Gore, SW7; ☺ South Kensington) This splendid Victorian concert hall hosts classical music, rock and other performances, but is famously the venue for the BBC-sponsored Proms. Booking is possible, but from mid-July to mid-September Proms punters queue for £5 standing (or 'promenading') tickets that go on sale one hour before curtain-up. Otherwise, the box office and prepaid-ticket collection counter are through door 12 (south side of the hall).

★ 606 Club BLUES, JAZZ
(☑ 020-7352 5953; www.606club.co.uk; 90 Lots Rd, SW10; ☺ 7-11.15pm Sun-Thu, 8pm-12.30am Fri & Sat; ☺ Imperial Wharf) Named after its old address on the King's Rd that cast a spell over jazz lovers London-wide back in the '80s, this fantastic, tucked-away basement jazz club and restaurant gives centre stage to contemporary British-based jazz musicians nightly. The club can only serve alcohol to nonmembers who are dining, and it is highly advisable to book to get a table.

Roundhouse CONCERT VENUE
(Map p118; www.roundhouse.org.uk; Chalk Farm Rd, NW1; ⊖Chalk Farm) Built as a railway repair shed in 1847, this unusual Grade II–listed round building became an arts centre in the 1960s and hosted legendary bands before falling into near-dereliction in 1983. Its 21st-century resurrection as a creative hub has been a great success and it now hosts everything from big-name concerts to dance, circus, stand-up comedy, poetry slams and improvisation.

O2 Arena LIVE MUSIC
(www.theo2.co.uk; Peninsula Sq, SE10; 🛜; ⊖North Greenwich) One of the city's major concert venues, hosting all the biggies – the Rolling Stones, Paul Simon and Sting, One Direction, Ed Sheeran and many others – inside the 20,000-capacity arena. It's also a popular venue for sporting events and you can even climb the roof for ranging views with **Up at the O2** (www.theo2.co.uk/upattheo2; from £30; ⊙hours vary).

Dublin Castle LIVE MUSIC
(Map p118; www.thedublincastle.com; 94 Parkway, NW1; ⊙noon-2am Fri-Sun, 1pm-2am Mon, Wed & Thu, noon-1am Tue; ⊖Camden Town) Live punk or alternative bands play most nights in this comfortingly grungy pub's back room (cover charges are usually £4.50 to £7). DJs take over after the bands on Friday, Saturday and Sunday nights.

★**Scala** LIVE MUSIC
(Map p96; ☑020-7833 2022; www.scala.co.uk; 275 Pentonville Rd, N1; ⊖King's Cross St Pancras) Opened in 1920 as a salubrious golden-age cinema, Scala slipped into porn-movie hell in the 1970s, only to be reborn as a club and live-music venue in the noughties. It's one of the best places in London to catch an intimate gig and is a great dance space too, hosting a diverse range of club nights.

★**Pizza Express Jazz Club** JAZZ
(Map p70; ☑020-7439 4962; www.pizzaexpress live.com/venues/soho-jazz-club; 10 Dean St, W1; tickets £15-40; ⊖Tottenham Court Rd) Pizza Express has been one of the best jazz venues in London since opening in 1969. It may be a strange arrangement, in a basement beneath a branch of the chain restaurant, but it's highly popular. Lots of big names perform here and artists such as Norah Jones, Gregory Porter and the late Amy Winehouse played here in their early days.

Ronnie Scott's JAZZ
(Map p70; ☑020-7439 0747; www.ronniescotts. co.uk; 47 Frith St, W1; ⊙7pm-3am Mon-Sat, 1-4pm & 8pm-midnight Sun; ⊖Leicester Sq, Tottenham Court Rd) Ronnie Scott's jazz club opened in 1965 and became widely known as Britain's best. Support acts are at 7pm, with main gigs at 8.15pm (8pm Sunday) and a second house at 11.15pm Friday and Saturday (check ahead). The more informal Late, Late Show runs from 1am to 3am. Expect to pay from £25; the Late, Late Show and Sunday lunch shows are just £10.

100 Club LIVE MUSIC
(Map p70; ☑020-7636 0933; www.the100club. co.uk; 100 Oxford St, W1; tickets £8-20; ⊙check website for gig times; ⊖Oxford Circus, Tottenham Court Rd) This heritage London venue at the same address since 1942 started off as a jazz club but now leans towards rock. Back in the day it showcased Chris Barber, BB King and the Rolling Stones, and it was at the centre of the punk revolution and the '90s indie scene. It hosts dancing gigs, the occasional big name, where-are-they-now bands and top-league tributes.

Cinemas

BFI Southbank CINEMA
(Map p84; ☑020-7928 3232; www.bfi.org.uk; Belvedere Rd, SE1; tickets £8-12; ⊙10am-11pm; ⊖Waterloo) Tucked almost out of sight under the arches of Waterloo Bridge, the British Film Institute (BFI) contains four cinemas that screen thousands of films each year (many art house); a gallery devoted to the moving image; and a mediatheque, where you watch film and TV highlights from the BFI National Archive.

Electric Cinema CINEMA
(Map p92; ☑020-7908 9696; www.electriccinema. co.uk; 191 Portobello Rd, W11; tickets £8-22.50; ⊖Ladbroke Grove) Having notched up its centenary in 2011, the Electric is one of the UK's oldest cinemas, updated. Avail yourself of the luxurious leather armchairs, sofas, footstools and tables for food and drink in the auditorium, or select one of the six front-row double beds! Tickets are cheapest on Mondays.

Prince Charles Cinema CINEMA
(Map p70; www.princecharlescinema.com; 7 Leicester Pl, WC2; tickets £5-16; ⊖Leicester Sq) Leicester Sq cinema-ticket prices are very high, so wait until the first runs have moved to the Prince Charles, central London's cheapest cinema, where nonmembers pay £5 to

£12 for new releases. Also presents mini-festivals, Q&As with film directors, classics, sleepover movie marathons, and exuberant sing-along screenings of films like *Frozen*, *The Sound of Music* and *Rocky Horror Picture Show* (£16).

Comedy

Comedy Store   COMEDY
(Map p70; ☑ 0844 871 7699; www.thecomedy store.co.uk; 1a Oxendon St, SW1; tickets £11-33.50; ⊖ Piccadilly Circus) This is one of the first (and still one of the best) comedy clubs in London. Wednesday and Sunday night's Comedy Store Players is the most famous improvisation outfit in town, with the wonderful Josie Lawrence, now a veteran of two decades. On Thursdays, Fridays and Saturdays, Best in Stand Up features the best on London's comedy circuit.

Doors at 6.30pm; show kicks off at 8pm. Tickets cost from £11 for King Gong (an open-mic night on the last Monday of the month) to £33.50 (best seats for Best in Stand Up show on Saturdays).

Amused Moose Soho   COMEDY
(Map p70; ☑ box office 020-7287 3727; www.amused moose.com; Sanctum Soho Hotel, 20 Warwick St, W1; ⊖ Piccadilly Circus, Oxford Circus) One of the city's best clubs, the peripatetic Amused Moose (the cinema in the Sanctum Soho Hotel is just one of its hosting venues) is popular with audiences and comedians alike, perhaps helped along by the fact that heckling is 'unacceptable' and all the acts are 'first-date friendly' (ie unlikely to humiliate the front row). Shows are usually at 8.15pm on Saturday.

Soho Theatre   COMEDY
(Map p70; ☑ 020-7478 0100; www.sohotheatre. com; 21 Dean St, W1; tickets £8-25; ⊖ Tottenham Court Rd) The Soho Theatre has developed a superb reputation for showcasing new comedy-writing talent and comedians. It's also hosted some top-notch stand-up or

---

SPORTING LONDON

You may not land tickets to the FA Cup Final at Wembley Stadium or front-row seats for the Wimbledon finals, but there are plenty of ways to enjoy sport in London. You could find yourself watching the Oxford–Cambridge boat race, cheering runners at the London Marathon or hopping on a Santander Cycle – there's lots on offer. Why not check out the impressive facilities in the Queen Elizabeth Olympic Park (p94), which hosts the (former Olympic) London Stadium, the stunning Aquatics Centre and the cutting-edge Velodrome.

Alternatively, take a tour of one of the capital's great sporting stadia:

Lord's (☑ 020-7616 8500; www.lords.org; St John's Wood Rd, NW8; tours adult/child £20/12; ⊙ 4-6 tours daily; ⊖ St John's Wood) The hallowed 'home of cricket', with a fascinating museum.

Wimbledon Lawn Tennis Museum (☑ 020-8946 6131; www.wimbledon.com/museum; Gate 4, Church Rd, SW19; adult/child £13/8, museum & tour £25/15; ⊙ 10am-5pm, last admission 4.30pm; ⊟ Wimbledon, ⊟ Wimbledon, ⊖ Wimbledon, ⊖ Southfields) Chart the history of lawn tennis, and see Centre Court from the 360-degree viewing box.

Wembley Stadium (☑ 0800 169 9933; www.wembleystadium.com; tours adult/child £20/12; ⊖ Wembley Park) The city's landmark national stadium, used for football test matches and mega concerts.

Twickenham Stadium (☑ 020-8892 8877; www.englandrugby.com/twickenham; Rugby Rd, Twickenham, TW1; tours adult/child/family £20/12/50; ⊟ Twickenham, ⊖ Hounslow East) London's famous rugby union stadium, used for international test matches.

London Stadium (☑ 020-8522 6157; www.london-stadium.com; Queen Elizabeth Olympic Park, E20; tours adult/child £19/11; ⊙ tours 10am-4.15pm; ⊟ DLR Pudding Mill Lane) Built as the centrepiece stadium for the 2012 Olympics and now home to West Ham United FC.

Arsenal Emirates Stadium (☑ 020-7619 5000; www.arsenal.com/tours; Hornsey Rd, N5; self-guided tours adult/child £22/14, guided £40; ⊙ 10am-6pm Mon-Sat, to 4pm Sun; ⊖ Holloway Rd) Offers both self-guided tours or tours led by former Arsenal players.

Stamford Bridge (☑ 0871 984 1955; www.chelseafc.com; Stamford Bridge, Fulham Rd, SW6; tours adult/child £22/15; ⊙ museum 9.30am-5pm, tours 10am-3pm; ⊖ Fulham Broadway) Home of Chelsea FC.

sketch-based comedians, including Alexei Sayle and Doctor Brown, plus cabaret. Staff don't always seem to get the joke.

Up the Creek
COMEDY

(www.up-the-creek.com; 302 Creek Rd, SE10; tickets £5-15; ☺7-11pm Thu & Sun, to 2am Fri & Sat; ⑭DLR Cutty Sark) Bizarrely enough, the hecklers can be funnier than the acts at this great club. Mischief, rowdiness and excellent comedy are the norm, with the Blackout open-mic night on Thursdays (www.the-blackout.co.uk; £5) and Sunday specials (www.sundayspecial.co.uk; £7). There's an after-party disco on Fridays and Saturdays. Check full times of acts on the website.

Classical Music

Southbank Centre
CONCERT VENUE

(Map p84; ☎0844 875 0073; www.southbankcentre.co.uk; Belvedere Rd, SE1; ⊜Waterloo) The Southbank Centre comprises several venues – Royal Festival Hall, Queen Elizabeth Hall and Purcell Room – hosting a wide range of performing arts. As well as regular programming, it organises fantastic festivals, including London Wonderground (circus and cabaret), Udderbelly (a festival of comedy in all its guises) and Meltdown (a music event curated by the best and most eclectic names in music).

Royal Festival Hall
CONCERT VENUE

(Map p84; ☎020-7960 4200; www.southbankcentre.co.uk; Southbank Centre, Belvedere Rd, SE1; ⚟; ⊜Waterloo) Royal Festival Hall's amphitheatre seats 2500 and is one of the best places for catching world- and classical-music artists. The sound is fantastic, the programming impeccable and there are frequent free gigs in the wonderfully expansive foyer.

Queen Elizabeth Hall
CONCERT VENUE

(QEH; Map p84; www.southbankcentre.co.uk; Southbank Centre, Belvedere Rd, SE1; ⊜Waterloo) This concert hall hosts music and dance performances on a smaller scale to the nearby Royal Festival Hall, both part of the Southbank Centre. The Hall reopened in April 2018 after its 21st-century facelift.

Sport

Wimbledon Championships
SPECTATOR SPORT

(☎020-8944 1066; www.wimbledon.com; Church Rd, SW19; grounds admission £8-25, tickets £41-190) For a few weeks each June and July, the sporting world's attention is fixed on the quiet southern suburb of Wimbledon, as it has been since 1877. Most show-court tickets for the Wimbledon Championships are allocated

through public ballot, applications for which usually begin in early August of the preceding year and close at the end of December.

Opera & Dance

Sadler's Wells
DANCE

(Map p96; ☎020-7863 8000; www.sadlerswells.com; Rosebery Ave, EC1R; ⊜Angel) A glittering modern venue that was first established in 1683, Sadler's Wells is the most eclectic modern-dance and ballet venue in town, with experimental dance shows of all genres and from all corners of the globe. The Lilian Baylis Studio stages smaller productions.

Royal Opera House
OPERA

(Map p70; ☎020-7304 4000; www.roh.org.uk; Bow St, WC2; tickets £4-270; ⊜Covent Garden) Classic opera in London has a fantastic setting on Covent Garden Piazza and coming here for a night is a sumptuous – if pricey – affair. Although the program has been fluffed up by modern influences, the main attractions are still the opera and classical ballet – all are wonderful productions and feature world-class performers.

English National Opera
OPERA

(ENO; Map p70; ☎020-7845 9300; www.eno.org; St Martin's Lane, WC2; ⊜Leicester Sq) The English National Opera is celebrated for making opera modern and more accessible, as all productions are sung in English. It's based at the impressive London Coliseum, built in 1904 and lovingly restored a century later. The English National Ballet also does regular performances at the Coliseum. Tickets range from £12 to £125.

Barbican Centre
PERFORMING ARTS

(Map p76; ☎020-7638 8891; www.barbican.org.uk; Silk St, EC2; ☺box office 10am-8pm Mon-Sat, 11am-8pm Sun; ⊜Barbican) Home to the London Symphony Orchestra and the BBC Symphony Orchestra, the Barbican (p79) also hosts scores of other concerts, focusing in particular on jazz, folk, world and soul artists. Dance is also performed here, while the cinema screens recent releases as well as film festivals.

🔒 Shopping

🔒 The West End

★ Fortnum & Mason
DEPARTMENT STORE

(Map p70; ☎020-7734 8040; www.fortnumandmason.com; 181 Piccadilly, W1; ☺10am-8pm Mon-Sat, 11.30am-6pm Sun; ⊜Piccadilly Circus) With its classic eau-de-Nil (pale green) colour scheme, 'the Queen's grocery store' established in 1707 refuses to yield to modern times. Its staff – men and women – still wear old-fashioned tailcoats and its glamorous food hall is supplied with hampers, cut marmalade, speciality teas, superior fruitcakes and so forth. Fortnum & Mason remains the quintessential London shopping experience.

Hamleys   TOYS
(Map p70; ✆0371 704 1977; www.hamleys.com; 188-196 Regent St, W1; ⏰10am-9pm Mon-Fri, 9.30am-9pm Sat, noon-6pm Sun; ⊖Oxford Circus) Claiming to be the world's oldest (and some say, the largest) toy store, Hamleys moved to its address on Regent St in 1881. From the basement's Star Wars Collection and ground floor where staff blow bubbles and glide foam boomerangs through the air with practised nonchalance to Lego World and a cafe on the 5th floor, it's a rich layer cake of playthings.

Liberty   DEPARTMENT STORE
(Map p70; ✆020-7734 1234; www.liberty.co.uk; Great Marlborough St, W1; ⏰10am-8pm Mon-Sat, noon-6pm Sun; ⊖Oxford Circus) An irresistible blend of contemporary styles in an old-fashioned mock-Tudor atmosphere (1875), Liberty has a huge cosmetics department and an accessories floor, along with a breathtaking lingerie section, all at sky-high prices. A classic London gift or souvenir is a Liberty fabric print, especially in the form of a scarf.

Foyles   BOOKS
(Map p70; ✆020-7434 1574; www.foyles.co.uk; 107 Charing Cross Rd, WC2; ⏰9.30am-9pm Mon-Sat, 11.30am-6pm Sun; ⊖Tottenham Court Rd) This is London's most legendary bookshop, where you can bet on finding even the most obscure of titles. Once synonymous with chaos, Foyles got its act together and in 2014 moved just down the road into the spacious former home of Central St Martins art school. Thoroughly redesigned, its stunning new home is a joy to explore.

Selfridges   DEPARTMENT STORE
(Map p112; ✆0800 123 400; www.selfridges. com; 400 Oxford St, W1; ⏰9.30am-9pm Mon-Sat, 11.30am-6pm Sun; ⊖Bond St) Selfridges loves innovation – it's famed for its inventive window displays by international artists, gala shows and, above all, its amazing range of products. It's the trendiest of London's one-stop shops, with labels such as Alexander McQueen, Tom Ford, Missoni,

Victoria Beckham and so on; an unparalleled food hall; and Europe's largest cosmetics department.

Stanford's   BOOKS, MAPS
(Map p70; ✆020-7836 1321; www.stanfords. co.uk; 12-14 Long Acre, WC2; ⏰9am-8pm Mon-Sat, 11.30am-6pm Sun; ⊖Leicester Sq, Covent Garden) Trading from this address since 1853, this granddaddy of travel bookshops and seasoned seller of maps, guides, globes and literature is a destination in its own right. Ernest Shackleton, David Livingstone and, more recently, Michael Palin and Brad Pitt have all popped in and shopped here.

Daunt Books   BOOKS
(Map p112; ✆020-7224 2295; www.dauntbooks. co.uk; 83 Marylebone High St, W1; ⏰9am-7.30pm Mon-Sat, 11am-6pm Sun; ⊖Baker St) An original Edwardian bookshop, with oak panels, galleries and gorgeous skylights, Daunt is one of London's loveliest travel bookshops. It has two floors and stocks general fiction and nonfiction titles as well. Helpful, informed staff.

Reckless Records   MUSIC
(Map p70; ✆020-7437 4271; www.reckless.co.uk; 30 Berwick St, W1; ⏰10am-7pm; ⊖Oxford Circus, Tottenham Court Rd) This outfit hasn't really changed in spirit since it first opened its doors in 1984. It still stocks secondhand records and CDs, from punk, soul, dance and independent to mainstream.

Skoob Books   BOOKS
(Map p96; ✆020-7278 8760; www.skoob. com; 66 The Brunswick, off Marchmont St, WC1; ⏰10.30am-8pm Mon-Sat, to 6pm Sun; ⊖Russell Sq) Skoob (you work out the name) has got to be London's largest secondhand bookshop, with some 55,000 titles spread over 2000 sq ft of floor space (plus more than a million further books in a warehouse outside town). If you can't find it here, it probably doesn't exist.

We Built This City   GIFTS & SOUVENIRS
(Map p70; ✆020-3642 9650; www.webuilt-thiscity.com; 56-57 Carnaby St, W1; ⏰10am-7pm Mon-Wed, to 8pm Thu-Sat, 11am-7pm Sun; ⊖Oxford Circus) Taking a commendable stand against Union Jack hats and black-cab key rings, We Built This City is a shop selling London-themed souvenirs that the recipient might actually want. The products are artistic and thoughtful, and celebrate the city's creative side.

Sister Ray　　　　　　　　　MUSIC
(Map p70; ✆ 020-7734 3297; www.sisterray.co.uk; 75 Berwick St, W1; ✆ 10am-8pm Mon-Sat, noon-6pm Sun; ✆ Oxford Circus, Tottenham Court Rd) If you were a fan of the late John Peel on the BBC, this specialist in innovative, experimental and indie music is just right for you. Those of you who have never heard of him will probably also like the shop that 'sells music to the masses'.

The City

London Silver Vaults　　　ARTS & CRAFTS
(Map p76; ✆ 020-7242 3844; www.silvervaults london.com; 53-63 Chancery Lane, WC2; ✆ 9am-5.30pm Mon-Fri, to 1pm Sat; ✆ Chancery Lane) The 30-odd shops that work out of these secure subterranean vaults make up the largest collection of silver under one roof in the world. The different businesses tend to specialise in particular types of silverware – from cutlery sets to picture frames, animal sculptures and lots of jewellery.

Kensington & Hyde Park

★**John Sandoe Books**　　　　BOOKS
(Map p86; ✆ 020-7589 9473; www.johnsandoe. com; 10 Blacklands Tce, SW3; ✆ 9.30am-6.30pm Mon-Sat, 11am-5pm Sun; ✆ Sloane Sq) The perfect antidote to impersonal book superstores, this atmospheric three-storey bookshop in 18th-century premises is a treasure trove of literary gems and hidden surprises. It's been in business for six decades and loyal customers swear by it, while knowledgeable booksellers spill forth with well-read pointers and helpful advice.

Harrods　　　　　DEPARTMENT STORE
(Map p86; ✆ 020-7730 1234; www.harrods.com; 87-135 Brompton Rd, SW1; ✆ 10am-9pm Mon-Sat, 11.30am-6pm Sun; ✆ Knightsbridge) Garish and stylish in equal measure, perennially crowded Harrods is an obligatory stop for visitors, from the cash-strapped to the big spenders. The stock is astonishing, as are many of the price tags. High on kitsch, the 'Egyptian Elevator' resembles something out of an Indiana Jones epic, while the memorial fountain to Dodi and Di (lower ground floor) merely adds surrealism.

Harvey Nichols　　　DEPARTMENT STORE
(Map p86; www.harveynichols.com; 109-125 Knightsbridge, SW1; ✆ 10am-8pm Mon-Sat, 11.30am-6pm Sun; ✆ Knightsbridge) At London's temple of high fashion, you'll find Chloé and Balenciaga bags, the city's best denim range, a massive make-up hall with exclusive lines and great jewellery. The food hall and in-house restaurant, Fifth Floor, are, you guessed it, on the 5th floor. From 11.30am to midday, it's browsing time only.

Conran Shop　　　　　　　　DESIGN
(Map p86; ✆ 020-7589 7401; www.conranshop. co.uk; Michelin House, 81 Fulham Rd, SW3; ✆ 10am-6pm Mon, Tue & Fri, to 7pm Wed & Thu, to 6.30pm Sat, noon-6pm Sun; ✆ South Kensington) The original design store (going strong since 1987), the Conran Shop is a treasure trove of beautiful things – from radios to sunglasses, kitchenware to children's toys and books, bathroom accessories to greeting cards. Browsing bliss. Spare some time to peruse the magnificent art nouveau/deco Michelin House the shop is housed in.

Clerkenwell, Shoreditch & Spitalfields

★**Rough Trade East**　　　　MUSIC
(Map p124; www.roughtrade.com; Old Truman Brewery, 91 Brick Lane, E1; ✆ 9am-9pm Mon-Thu, to 8pm Fri, 10am-8pm Sat, 11am-7pm Sun; ✆ Shoreditch High St) It's no longer directly associated with the legendary record label (home to The Smiths, The Libertines and The Strokes, among many others), but this huge record shop is still the best for music of an indie, soul, electronica and alternative persuasion. In addition to an impressive selection of CDs and vinyl, it also dispenses coffee and stages promotional gigs.

Blitz London　　　　　　　VINTAGE
(Map p124; www.blitzlondon.co.uk; 55-59 Hanbury St, E1; ✆ 11am-7pm; ✆ Liverpool St) One of the capital's best secondhand clothes stores, with more than 20,000 hand-selected items of men's and women's clothing, shoes and accessories spanning four decades since the 1960s. You'll find anything from mainstream brands such as Nike to designer labels like Burberry.

East London

Beyond Retro　　　　　　　VINTAGE
(✆ 020-7729 9001; www.beyondretro.com; 92-100 Stoke Newington Rd, N16; ✆ 10.30am-7pm Mon, Tue & Sat, to 8pm Wed-Fri, 11.30am-6pm Sun; ✆ Dalston Kingsland) A riot of colour, furbelow, frill, feathers and flares, this vast store has every imaginable type of vintage clothing

LOCAL KNOWLEDGE

LONDON'S MARKETS

Perhaps the biggest draw for visitors is the capital's famed markets. A treasure trove of small designers, unique jewellery pieces, original framed photographs and posters, colourful vintage pieces and bric-a-brac, they are the antidote to impersonal, carbon-copy shopping centres.

Camden Market (Map p118; www.camdenmarket.com; Camden High St, NW1; ⊙10am-6pm; ⊜Camden Town, Chalk Farm) London's busiest and best-known market may have stopped being cutting-edge several thousand cheap leather jackets ago, but it remains one of London's most popular attractions. There are three main market areas – Buck Street Market, Camden Lock Market and Stables Market – extending most of the way from Camden Town tube station to Chalk Farm tube station. You'll find a bit of everything: clothes (of varying quality) in profusion, bags, jewellery, arts and crafts, candles, incense and myriad decorative bits and pieces.

Sunday UpMarket (Map p124; www.sundayupmarket.co.uk; Old Truman Brewery, 91 Brick Lane, E1; ⊙11am-6pm Sat, 10am-5pm Sun; ▣Shoreditch High St) Open all weekend, this lively market in the Old Truman Brewery offers a mix of young designers, food stalls in the Boiler House, antiques and bric-a-brac, and a huge range of vintage clothes in the basement across the street.

Old Spitalfields Market (Map p124; www.oldspitalfieldsmarket.com; Commercial St, E1; ⊙10am-5pm Mon-Fri & Sun, 10am-6pm Sat; ⊜Liverpool St) Traders have been hawking their wares here since 1638 and it's still one of London's best markets. Sundays are the biggest and best days, but Thursdays are good for antiques and Fridays for independent fashion. There are plenty of food stalls too.

Borough Market (Map p84; www.boroughmarket.org.uk; 8 Southwark St, SE1; ⊙10am-5pm Wed & Thu, 10am-6pm Fri, 8am-5pm Sat; ⊜London Bridge) Located in this spot since the 13th century (possibly since 1014), 'London's Larder' is always overflowing with food lovers, gastronomes and Londoners in search of dinner inspiration. The full market runs from Wednesday to Saturday, but some traders and takeaway stalls open Mondays and Tuesdays.

Brick Lane Market (Map p124; www.visitbricklane.org; Brick Lane, E1; ⊙10am-5pm Sun; ⊜Shoreditch High St) Spilling out into its surrounding streets, this irrepressibly vibrant market fills a vast area with household goods, bric-a-brac, secondhand clothes, cheap fashion and ethnic food.

Broadway Market (www.broadwaymarket.co.uk; Broadway Market, E8; ⊙9am-5pm Sat; ▣394) There's been a market down this pretty street since the late 19th century. The focus these days is artisan food, arty knick-knacks, books, records and vintage clothing. Stock up on edible treats then head to London Fields for a picnic.

Greenwich Market (www.greenwichmarketlondon.com; College Approach, SE10; ⊙10.30am-5pm; ▣DLR Cutty Sark) This small market has a different theme every day. On Tuesdays, Thursdays and Fridays, you'll find vintage, antiques and collectables. Wednesdays, Fridays and weekends are the best days for artists, indie designers and crafts.

South Bank Book Market (Map p84; Riverside Walk, SE1; ⊙11am-7pm, shorter hours winter; ⊜Waterloo) Prints and secondhand books under the arches of Waterloo Bridge.

for sale, from hats to shoes. There's another branch in **Bethnal Green** (110-112 Cheshire St, E2; ⊙10am-7pm Mon-Wed, Fri & Sat, to 8pm Thu, 11.30am-6pm Sun; ▣Shoreditch High St).

Traid　　　　　　　　　　　　CLOTHING
(☏020-7923 1396; www.traid.org.uk; 106-108 Kingsland High St, E8; ⊙11am-7pm Mon-Sat, to 5pm Sun; ⊜Dalston Kingsland) Banish every preconception you have about charity shops, for Traid is nothing like the ones you've seen before: big and bright, with not a whiff of mothball. The offerings aren't necessarily vintage but rather quality, contemporary secondhand clothes for a fraction of the

usual prices. It also sells its own creations made from offcuts.

🔒 North London

★**Camden Passage Market** ANTIQUES
(www.camdenpassageislington.co.uk; Camden Passage, N1; ⊘8am-6pm Wed & Sat; ⊜Angel) Not to be confused with Camden Market, Camden Passage is a pretty cobbled lane in Islington lined with antique stores, vintage-clothing boutiques and cafes. Scattered along the lane are four separate market areas devoted to antique curios and whatnots. The main market days are Wednesday and Saturday (although the shops are open all week). Stallholders know their stuff, so bargains are rare.

**Harry Potter Shop
at Platform 9¾** GIFTS & SOUVENIRS
(Map p96; www.harrypotterplatform934.com; King's Cross Station, N1; ⊘8am-10pm Mon-Sat, 9am-9pm Sun; ⊜King's Cross St Pancras) With Pottermania refusing to die down and Diagon Alley impossible to find, when your junior witches and wizards are seeking a wand of their own, take the family directly to King's Cross Station. This little wood-panelled store also stocks jumpers sporting the colours of Hogwarts' four houses (Gryffindor having pride of place) and assorted merchandise, including, of course, the books.

ℹ Information

DANGERS & ANNOYANCES
London is a fairly safe city for its size, but exercise common sense.
➡ Several high-profile terrorist attacks have afflicted London in recent years, but the risk to individual visitors is remote. Report anything suspicious to the police by calling 999 (emergency) or 101 (nonemergency).
➡ Keep an eye on your handbag and wallet, especially in bars and nightclubs, and in crowded areas such as the Underground.
➡ Be discreet with your tablet/smartphone – snatching happens.
➡ If you're getting a cab after a night's clubbing, go for a black taxi or a licensed minicab firm.
➡ Victims of rape and sexual abuse can contact the **Rape & Sexual Abuse Support Centre** (☑0808 802 9999; www.rasasc.org.uk; ⊘noon-2.30pm & 7-9.30pm); anyone in emotional distress can contact **Samaritans** (☑toll free 116 123; www.samaritans.org; ⊘24hr).

London's area code	☑020
International access code	☑00
Police, fire or ambulance	☑999
Reverse charge/collect calls	☑155

INTERNET ACCESS
➡ Virtually every hotel in London now provides wi-fi free of charge.
➡ A huge number of cafes, and many restaurants, offer free wi-fi to customers, including major chain cafes. Cultural venues such as the Barbican or the Southbank Centre also have free wi-fi.
➡ Open-air and street wi-fi access is available in areas across London, including Oxford St, Trafalgar Sq, Piccadilly Circus, the City of London and Islington's Upper St. Users have to register but there's no charge.
➡ Most major train stations, airport terminals and even some Underground stations also have wi-fi, but access isn't always free.
➡ See Time Out's Free Wi-fi Map (www.timeout.com/london/things-to-do/where-to-find-free-wi-fi-in-london-9) for more locations.

MEDICAL SERVICES
A number of hospitals have 24-hour accident and emergency departments. However, in an emergency just call an **ambulance** (☑999) and one will normally be dispatched from the hospital nearest to you.

University College London Hospital (☑020-3456 7890; www.uclh.nhs.uk; 235 Euston Rd, NW1; ⊜Warren St, Euston)

Chelsea & Westminster Hospital (☑020-3315 8000; www.chelwest.nhs.uk; 369 Fulham Rd, SW10; ▭14 or 414, ⊜South Kensington, Fulham Broadway)

TOURIST INFORMATION
Visit London (www.visitlondon.com) can fill you in on everything from attractions and events to tours and accommodation. Kiosks are dotted about the city and can also provide maps and brochures; some branches are able to book theatre tickets.

ℹ Getting There & Away

AIR
The city has five airports: Heathrow, which is the largest, to the west; Gatwick to the south; Stansted to the northeast; Luton to the northwest; and London City in the Docklands. For details of London's five main airports, see p680.

BUS

Victoria Coach Station (Map p86; 164 Buckingham Palace Rd, SW1; ⊖Victoria) Long-distance and international buses arrive and depart from Victoria Coach Station, close to the Victoria tube and rail stations.

TRAIN

Main national rail routes are served by a variety of private train-operating companies. Tickets are not cheap, but trains between cities are usually quite punctual. Check National Rail (www.nationalrail.co.uk) for timetables and fares.

Eurostar (www.eurostar.com) High-speed passenger rail service linking London St Pancras International with Paris, Brussels and Lille, with up to 19 daily departures. Fares vary greatly, from £29 one-way standard class to around £245 one-way for a fully flexible business premier ticket (prices based on return journeys). New direct links between London and Amsterdam and Rotterdam commenced in 2018. There are deals on Eurostar Snap (available on Facebook), with best-value fares for those with flexibility around the specific train they travel on.

❶ Getting Around

TO/FROM THE AIRPORTS
Heathrow

The Underground, commonly referred to as 'the tube', is the cheapest way of getting to Heathrow; paper tickets cost one-way £6, Oyster or Contactless peak/off-peak £5.10/3.10. The journey to central London takes one hour and trains depart every three to nine minutes. Leaving from the airport, it runs from just after 5am to 11.45pm (11.28pm Sunday), and heading to the airport it runs from 5.47am to 12.32am (11.38pm Sunday); tube trains run all night Friday and Saturday, with reduced frequency. Buy tickets at the station.

Heathrow Express (www.heathrowexpress. com; one-way/return £27/42; 🖭), every 15 minutes, and **Heathrow Connect** (📞0345 604 1515; www.heathrowconnect.com; adult single/ open return £10.30/20.70), every 30 minutes, trains link Heathrow with Paddington train station. Heathrow Express trains take a mere 15 minutes to reach Paddington. Trains on each service run from around 5am to between 11pm and midnight.

National Express Coaches (www.national express.com; one-way from £6, 35 to 90 minutes, every 30 minutes to one hour) link the Heathrow Central bus station with London Victoria Coach Station. The first bus leaves the Heathrow Central bus station (at Terminals 2 and 3) at 4.20am, with the last departure just after 10pm. The first bus leaves Victoria at 3am, the last at around 12.30am.

At night, the **N9 bus** (£1.50, 1¼ hours, every 20 minutes) connects Heathrow Central bus station (and Heathrow Terminal 5) with central London, terminating at Aldwych.

A metered black cab trip to/from central London will cost between £48 and £90 and take 45 minutes to an hour, depending on traffic and your departure point.

Gatwick

National Rail (www.nationalrail.co.uk) Regular train services to/from London Bridge (30 minutes, every 15 to 30 minutes), London King's Cross (55 minutes, every 15 to 30 minutes) and London Victoria (30 minutes, every 10 to 15 minutes). Fares vary depending on the time of travel and the train company, but allow £10 to £20 for a single.

---

❶ OYSTER CARD

The cheapest way to get around London is with an **Oyster Card**, a smart card on which you store credit as well as Travelcards valid for periods from a day to a year. Oyster Cards are valid across the entire public transport network in London, and fares are lower than standard ones. If you make several journeys in a day, the total is capped at the appropriate Travelcard rate (peak or off-peak).

Oyster Cards can be bought (£5 refundable deposit required) and topped up at any Underground station, travel information centre or shop displaying the Oyster logo. To get your deposit back along with any remaining credit, simply return your Oyster Card at a ticket booth.

All you need to do when entering a station is touch your card on a reader (which has a yellow circle with the image of an Oyster Card on it) and then touch again on your way out. For bus journeys, you only need to touch once upon boarding. Note that some train stations don't have exit turnstiles, so you will need to tap out on the reader before leaving the station; if you forget, you will be hugely overcharged.

Contactless cards (which do not require chip and pin or a signature) are subject to the same Oyster fares, but foreign visitors should bear in mind the cost of card transactions.

Gatwick Express (www.gatwickexpress.com; one-way/return adult £19.90/35.60, child £9.95/17.75) Trains run every 15 minutes from the station near the Gatwick South Terminal to London Victoria. From the airport there are services between 5.51am and 11.20pm. From Victoria they leave between 5am and 10.30pm. The journey takes 30 minutes; book online for the best deals.

National Express (www.nationalexpress.com) Coaches run throughout the day from Gatwick to London Victoria Coach Station (one-way from £8). Services depart hourly around the clock. Journey time is between 80 minutes and two hours, depending on traffic.

EasyBus (www.easybus.co.uk) Runs 13-seater minibuses to Gatwick every 15 to 20 minutes on several routes, including from Earl's Court/ West Brompton and Victoria Coach Station (one-way from £1.95). The service runs round the clock. Journey time averages 75 minutes.

Taxi A metered black-cab trip to/from central London costs around £100 and takes just over an hour. Minicabs are usually cheaper.

Stansted

Stansted Express (☑ 0345 600 7245; www. stanstedexpress.com; one-way/return £17/29) Rail service (45 minutes, every 15 to 30 minutes) links the airport and Liverpool St station. From the airport, the first train leaves at 5.30am, the last at 12.30am. Trains depart Liverpool St station from 3.40am to 11.25pm.

National Express (www.nationalexpress.com) Coaches run around the clock, offering well over 100 services per day.

Airbus A6 (☑ 0871 781 8181; www.national express.com; one-way from £10) Runs to Victoria Coach Station (around one hour to 1½ hours, every 20 minutes) via Marble Arch, Paddington, Baker St and Golders Green. **Airbus A7** (☑ 0871 781 8181; www.nationalexpress. com; one-way from £10) also runs to Victoria Coach Station (around one hour to 1½ hours, every 20 minutes), via Waterloo and Southwark. **Airbus A8** (☑ 0871 781 8181; www. nationalexpress.com; one-way from £6) runs to Liverpool St station (one-way from £6, 60 to 80 minutes, every 30 minutes), via Bethnal Green, Shoreditch High St and Mile End.

Airport Bus Express (www.airportbusexpress. co.uk; one-way from £9-10) Runs every 30 minutes to Victoria Coach Station, Baker St, Liverpool St and Stratford.

EasyBus (www.easybus.co.uk) Runs services to Baker St and Old St tube stations every 15 minutes. The journey (one-way from £4.95) takes one hour from Old St, 1¼ hour from Baker St.

Terravision (www.terravision.eu) Coaches link Stansted to Liverpool St station (one-way from £9, 55 minutes), King's Cross (from £9, 75 minutes) and Victoria Coach Station (from £10, two hours) every 20 to 40 minutes between 6am and 1am. Wi-fi on all buses.

London City

Docklands Light Railway (DLR; www.tfl.gov. uk/dlr) Stops at the London City Airport station (one-way £2.80 to £3.30). Trains depart every eight to 10 minutes from just after 5.30am to 12.15am Monday to Saturday, and 7am to 11.15pm Sunday. The journey to Bank takes just over 20 minutes.

Luton

National Rail (www.nationalrail.co.uk) Runs 24-hour services (one-way from £14, 26 to 50 minutes, departures every six minutes to one hour) from London St Pancras International to Luton Airport Parkway station, from where an airport shuttle bus (one-way/return £2.20/3.50) will take you to the airport in 10 minutes.

Airbus A1 (www.nationalexpress.com; one-way from £5) Runs over 60 times daily to London Victoria Coach Station (one-way from £5), via Portman Sq, Baker St, St John's Wood, Finchley Rd and Golders Green. It takes around 1½ hours.

Green Line Bus 757 (☑ 0344 800 4411; www. greenline.co.uk; one-way/return £10/17) Runs to Luton Airport from London Victoria Coach Station every 30 minutes on a 24-hour service via Marble Arch, Baker St, Finchley Rd and Brent Cross.

BICYCLE

London's cycle-hire scheme is called **Santander Cycles** (☑ 0343 222 6666; www.tfl.gov.uk/ modes/cycling/santander-cycles). The bikes have proved as popular with visitors as with Londoners.

The idea is simple: pick up a bike from one of the 750 docking stations dotted around the capital. Cycle. Drop it off at another docking station.

The access fee is £2 for 24 hours. All you need is a credit or debit card. The first 30 minutes are free; it's then £2 for any additional period of 30 minutes.

You can take as many bikes as you like during your access period (24 hours), leaving five minutes between each trip.

The pricing structure is designed to encourage short journeys rather than longer rentals; for those, go to a hire company. You'll also find that although easy to ride, the bikes only have three gears and are quite heavy. You must be aged 18 to buy access and at least 14 to ride a bike.

CAR

London has a **congestion charge** (☑ 0343 222 2222; www.tfl.gov.uk/roadusers/ congestioncharging) in place to reduce the flow of traffic into its centre.

The congestion-charge zone encompasses Euston and Pentonville Rds to the north, Park Lane to the west, Tower Bridge to the east, and Elephant and Castle and Vauxhall Bridge Rd to the south. As you enter the zone, you will see a large white 'C' in a red circle.

If you enter the zone between 7am and 6pm Monday to Friday (excluding public holidays), you must pay the £11.50 charge (payable in advance or on the day) or £14 on the first charging day after travel to avoid receiving a fine (£160, or £80 if paid within 14 days).

You can pay online or over the phone. For full details visit the website.

PUBLIC TRANSPORT
Boat

Several companies operate along the River Thames; only **Thames Clippers** (www.thames clippers.com; all zones adult/child £9.90/4.95) really offers commuter services, however. It's fast, pleasant and you're almost always guaranteed a seat and a view.

Thames Clipper boats run regular services between Embankment, Waterloo (London Eye), Blackfriars, Bankside (Shakespeare's Globe), London Bridge, Tower Bridge, Canary Wharf, Greenwich, North Greenwich and Woolwich piers from 6.55am to around midnight (from 9.29am weekends).

Thames Clipper River Roamer tickets (adult/child £19/9.50) give freedom to hop on and hop off boats on most routes all day. Book online for good discounts.

You can get a discount of one-third off the standard fare and off the price of River Roamer tickets if you're a pay-as-you-go Oyster Card holder or Travelcard holder (paper ticket or on Oyster Card). Children under five years go free on most boats.

Between April and September, Hampton Court Palace can be reached by boat on the 22-mile route along the Thames from Westminster Pier in central London (via Kew and Richmond). The trip can take up to four hours, depending on the tide. Boats are run by **Westminster Passenger Services Association** (www.wpsa.co.uk; one-way/return adult £17/25, child £8.50/12.50).

The London Waterbus Company (p103) runs canal boats between Camden Lock and Little Venice.

Bus

London's ubiquitous red double-decker buses afford great views of the city, but be aware that the going can be slow, thanks to traffic jams and dozens of commuters getting on and off at every stop.

There are excellent bus maps at every stop detailing all routes and destinations served from that particular area (generally a few bus stops within a two- to three-minute walk, shown on a local map).

Many bus stops have LED displays listing bus arrival times, but downloading a bus app such as London Bus Live Countdown to your smartphone is the most effective way to keep track of when your next bus is due.

Bus services normally operate from 5am to 11.30pm.

Cash cannot be used on London's buses. Instead you must pay with an Oyster Card, Travelcard or a contactless payment card. Bus fares are a flat £1.50, no matter the distance travelled. If you don't have enough credit on your Oyster Card for a £1.50 bus fare, you can make one more bus journey. You must then top up your credit before you can use your Oyster Card again.

Children aged under 11 travel free; 11 to 15 year olds are half price if registered on an accompanying adult's Oyster Card (register at Zone 1 or Heathrow tube stations).

➡ More than 50 night-bus routes (prefixed with the letter 'N') run from around 11.30pm to 5am.

➡ There are also another 60 bus routes operating 24 hours; the frequency decreases between 11pm and 5am.

➡ Oxford Circus, Tottenham Court Rd and Trafalgar Sq are the main hubs for night routes.

➡ Night buses can be infrequent and stop only on request, so remember to ring for your stop.

➡ Don't forget the Night Tube, which runs along five lines for 24 hours on Friday and Saturday, and can either be used as an alternative or in concert with night buses.

Underground, DLR & Overground

The London Underground ('the tube'; 11 colour-coded lines) is part of an integrated-transport system that also includes the Docklands Light Railway (DLR; www.tfl.gov.uk/dlr; a driverless overhead train operating in the eastern part of the city) and Overground network (mostly outside of Zone 1 and sometimes underground). Despite the never-ending upgrades and 'engineering works' requiring weekend closures, it is overall the quickest and easiest way of getting around the city, if not the cheapest.

The first trains operate from around 5.30am Monday to Saturday and 6.45am Sunday. The last trains leave around 12.30am Monday to Saturday and 11.30pm Sunday.

Additionally, selected lines (the Victoria and Jubilee lines, plus most of the Piccadilly, Central and Northern lines) run all night on Friday and Saturday to get revellers home (on what is called the 'Night Tube'), with trains every 10 minutes or so. Fares are off-peak.

During weekend closures, schedules, maps and alternative route suggestions are posted in every station, and staff are at hand to help redirect you.

Some stations, most famously Leicester Sq and Covent Garden, are much closer in reality than they appear on the map.

TAXI
Black Cabs

The black cab is as much a feature of the London cityscape as the red double-decker bus. Licensed black cab drivers have the 'Knowledge', acquired after rigorous training and a series of exams. They are supposed to know 25,000 streets within a 6-mile radius of Charing Cross/ Trafalgar Sq and the 100 most-visited spots of the moment, including clubs and restaurants.

➜ Cabs are available for hire when the yellow sign above the windscreen is lit; just stick your arm out to signal one.

➜ Fares are metered, with the flagfall charge of £2.60 (covering the first 235m during a weekday), rising by increments of 20p for each subsequent 117m.

➜ Fares are more expensive in the evenings and overnight.

➜ You can tip taxi drivers up to 10%, but most Londoners simply round up to the nearest pound.

➜ Apps such as mytaxi (https://uk.mytaxi.com) use your smartphone's GPS to locate the nearest black cab. You only pay the metered fare.

➜ **ComCab** (☎ 020-7908 0271; www.comcab -london.co.uk) operates one of the largest fleets of black cabs in town.

Minicabs

➜ Minicabs, which are licensed, are (usually) cheaper competitors of black cabs.

➜ Unlike black cabs, minicabs cannot legally be hailed on the street; they must be hired by phone or directly from one of the minicab offices (every high street has at least one and most clubs work with a minicab firm to send revellers home safely).

➜ Don't accept unsolicited offers from individuals claiming to be minicab drivers – they are just guys with cars.

➜ Minicabs don't have meters; there's usually a fare set by the dispatcher. Make sure you ask before setting off.

➜ Your hotel or host will be able to recommend a reputable minicab company in the neighbourhood; every Londoner has the number of at least one company. Or phone a large 24-hour operator such as **Addison Lee** (☎ 020-7387 8888; www.addisonlee.com).

➜ Apps such as Uber or Kabbee allow you to book a minicab in double-quick time and can save you money. At the time of writing, Uber had won an appeal to operate in London, but is on 15 months probation.

Canterbury & Southeast England

Best Places to Eat

➡ Royal Victoria Pavilion (p151)

➡ Allotment (p155)

➡ Iydea (p167)

➡ Terre à Terre (p168)

➡ Town House (p171)

Best Places to Stay

➡ Bleak House (p150)

➡ Jeake's House (p158)

➡ No 27 Brighton (p166)

➡ Reading Rooms (p148)

➡ Hotel Una (p167)

Why Go?

Rolling chalk hills, venerable Victorian resorts, fields of hops and grapes sweetening in the sun: welcome to England's southeast, four soothing counties' worth of country houses, fairy-tale castles and the finest food and drink. That fruit-ripening sun shines brightest and longest on the coast, warming a string of seaside towns wedged between formidable chalk cliffs. There's something for everyone here, from the medieval quaintness of Sandwich to the bohemian spirit of hedonistic Brighton and the more genteel grandeur of Eastbourne.

The southeast is also pock-marked with reminders of darker days. The region's position as the front line against Continental invaders has left a wealth of turbulent history, including the 1066 battlefield, Dover Castle's secret war tunnels and scattered Roman ruins.

England's spiritual heart is Canterbury; its cathedral and ancient Unesco-listed attractions are essential viewing for any 21st-century pilgrim.

When to Go

➡ May is a good time to get creative in Brighton at Great Britain's second-largest arts festival.

➡ During June, don your top hat and breeches to revel in frilly Victoriana at the Dickens Festival in Broadstairs.

➡ Any time between May and October is ideal for a hike along the South Downs Way, which runs the length of England's newest national park.

➡ In summer, head to the glorious beaches of Thanet in East Kent for some proper seaside fun.

➡ In late June Eastbourne hosts one of the UK's top tennis tournaments, a Wimbledon warm-up event attracting some of the biggest names in the game.

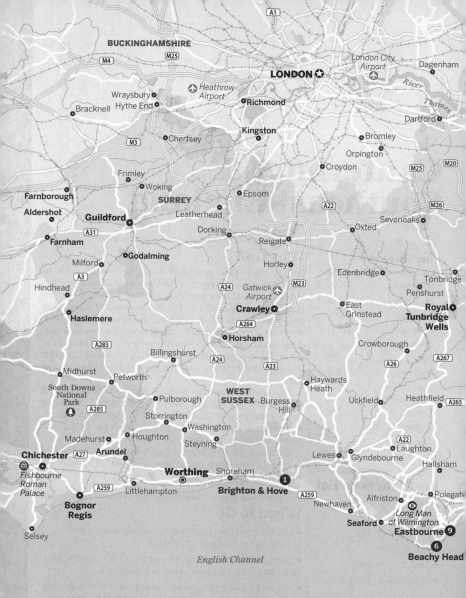

Canterbury & Southeast England Highlights

1 Brighton & Hove (p163) Shopping, tanning and partying in the hedonist capital of the southeast.

2 Canterbury (p142) Making a pilgrimage to one of England's most important religious sites.

3 Dover Castle (p153) Exploring the atmospheric WWII tunnels beneath this sprawling castle.

4 Rye (p156) Wandering the cobbled lanes of one of England's prettiest towns.

5 Leeds Castle (p147) Kicking back at this moated marvel.

NORTH SEA

A127 · Stanford-le-Hope · Canvey Island · **Southend-on-Sea**
Grays · Thurrock · Sheerness
bbsfleet · Tilbury · Gravesend
North fleet · A2 · **Rochester** · Gillingham · Isle of Sheppey · Leysdown-on-Sea · Herne Bay · **Margate** · Isle of Thanet · 7
Ightham · **Chatham** · Sittingbourne · Whitstable · Birchington · Broadstairs
M2 · Seasalter · **Ramsgate**
Faversham · Richborough Roman Fort
Maidstone · Bearsted · **Canterbury** · 2 · Ash · 8 · **Sandwich**
5 · **Leeds Castle** · Chilham · Eastry
M20 · A28 · A2 · Sutton · **Deal**
Stapleburst · **KENT** · Ringwould
Sissinghurst · Ashford · Westcliffe
A21 · **Dover Castle** · 3 · St Margaret's Bay
Tenterden · **Folkestone** · A259 · Capel-le-Ferne · **Dover**
Hawkhurst · Romney Marsh · Hythe · Channel Tunnel
Burwash · Romney Hythe & Dymchurch Railway
A268 · New Romney · St Mary's Bay
EAST SUSSEX · A21 · **Rye** · 4 · Lydd · Lydd-on-Sea
Battle · Strait of Dover
Pevensey Castle · **Bexhill** · A259 · **Hastings**

0 · 20 km
0 · 10 miles
N

6 Beachy Head (p162)
Scrambling up this spectacular headland in snow-white chalk.

7 Margate (p148) Getting down with the hipsters in the art capital of the Southeast.

8 Sandwich (p152) Becoming hopelessly lost in crooked medieval streets.

9 Eastbourne (p161) Strolling the Southeast's most chic seafront to reach the dramatic cliffs of Beachy Head.

🏃 Activities

Cycling

Finding quiet roads for cycle touring takes a little extra perseverance in the southeast of England, but the effort is richly rewarded. Long-distance routes that form part of the National Cycle Network (NCN; www.sustrans.org.uk) include the Downs & Weald Cycle Route (110 miles; NCN Routes 2, 20 and 21) from London to Brighton and on to Hastings, and the Garden of England Cycle Route (172 miles; NCN Routes 1 and 2) from London to Dover and then Hastings.

You'll also find less demanding routes on the NCN website. Meanwhile, there are plenty of uppers and downers to challenge mountain bikers on walking trails, such as the South Downs Way National Trail (100 miles), which takes between two and four days to complete.

Walking

Two long-distance trails meander steadily westward through the region, and there are plenty of shorter ambles to match your schedule, stamina and scenery wish-list.

South Downs Way National Trail (www.nationaltrail.co.uk/south-downs-way) This 100-mile National Trail through England's newest national park is a beautiful roller-coaster walk along prehistoric drove roads between Winchester and Eastbourne.

North Downs Way National Trail (www.nationaltrail.co.uk/north-downs-way) This 153-mile walk begins near Farnham in Surrey, but one of its most beautiful sections runs from near Ashford to Dover; a loop takes in Canterbury near its end.

1066 Country Walk Heads from Pevensey Castle to Rye (32 miles) and serves as a continuation of the South Downs Way.

KENT

Kent isn't described as the garden of England for nothing. Within its sea-lined borders you'll find a fragrant landscape of gentle hills, fertile farmland, cultivated country estates and fruit-laden orchards. It could also be described as the beer garden of England as it produces the world-renowned Kent hops and some of the country's finest ales and wines from its numerous vineyards. At its heart is spellbinding Canterbury, crowned by its enthralling cathedral. You'll also find beautiful coastal stretches dotted with beach towns and villages, from old-school Broadstairs to gentrified Whitstable and the aesthetically challenged port town of Dover.

ℹ️ Getting There & Away

Kent is very well connected to London with two high-speed lines linking the north Kent coast and East Kent to the capital. Connections with East Sussex could be better (there's no Canterbury–Brighton coach for instance), but are still reasonably good. Ferries from Dunkirk and Calais tie up at Dover, Kent's last cross-Channel passenger port and hundreds of cruise ships call in at the town's Western Docks. The Channel Tunnel, which emerges from the chalky ground near Folkestone, is a major gateway to the Continent.

Canterbury

📞 01227 / POP 55,240

Canterbury tops the charts for English cathedral cities and is one of southern England's top attractions. Many consider the World Heritage–listed cathedral that dominates its centre to be one of Europe's finest, and the town's narrow medieval alleyways, riverside gardens and ancient city walls are a joy to explore. But Canterbury isn't just a showpiece for the past – it's a bustling, busy place with an energetic student population and a wide choice of pubs, restaurants and independent shops. Book ahead for the best hotels and eateries: pilgrims may no longer flock here in their thousands, but tourists certainly do.

◉ Sights

★ Canterbury Cathedral   CATHEDRAL
(www.canterbury-cathedral.org; adult/concession/child £12.50/10.50/8.50, tours adult/child £5/4, audio guide £4/3; ⊙9am-5.30pm Mon-Sat, 12.30-2.30pm Sun) A rich repository of more than 1400 years of Christian history, the Church of England's mother ship is a truly extraordinary place with an absorbing history. This Gothic cathedral, the highlight of the city's World Heritage Sites, is southeast England's top tourist attraction as well as a place of worship. It's also the site of English history's most famous murder: Archbishop Thomas Becket was done in here in 1170.

The cathedral is an overwhelming edifice crammed with enthralling stories, arresting architecture and a very real and enduring sense of spirituality – although visitors can't

Canterbury

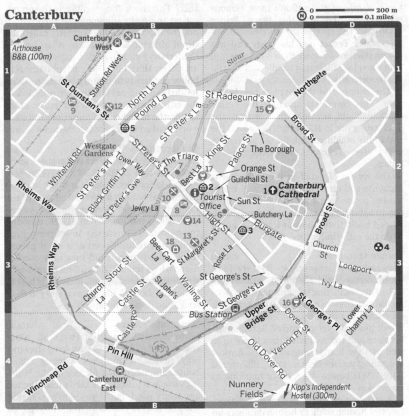

Canterbury

help but pick up on the ominous undertones of violence and bloodshed that whisper from its walls.

This ancient structure is packed with monuments commemorating the nation's battles. Also here are the grave and heraldic tunic of one of the nation's most famous warmongers, Edward the Black Prince (1330–76). The spot in the northwest transept where Becket met his grisly end has drawn pilgrims for more than 800 years and is marked by a flickering candle and a striking modern altar.

The doorway to the crypt is beside the altar. This cavernous space is the cathedral's highlight, the only survivor from the devastating fire in 1174, which destroyed the rest of the building. Look for the amazingly well-preserved carvings among the forest of pillars.

The wealth of detail in the cathedral is immense and unrelenting, so it's well worth joining a one-hour tour (three daily, Monday to Saturday) or taking a 40-minute self-guided audio tour. Allow at least two hours to do the cathedral justice.

Roman Museum
MUSEUM

(www.canterburymuseums.co.uk; Butchery Lane; adult/concession/child £8/6/free; ⊙10am-5pm daily) This fascinating subterranean archaeological site gives an insight into Canterbury's everyday life almost two millennia ago. Visitors can stroll a reconstructed Roman marketplace and rooms, including a kitchen, as well as view Roman mosaic floors. Almost everything you see here was only discovered after WWII bombs did a bit of impromptu excavation.

A standout exhibit is an almost completely intact Roman soldier's helmet dating from Caesar's invasion, dug up near the village of Bridge in 2012. It's the best ever found in the UK.

Beaney House of Art & Knowledge
MUSEUM

(www.canterburymuseums.co.uk; 18 High St; ⊙museum 10am-5pm Tue-Sat, noon-5pm Sun; ♿) FREE This mock-Tudor edifice is the grandest on the main shopping thoroughfare, if not the most authentic. Formerly called the Royal Museum & Art Gallery, it has housed Canterbury's main library, a museum and an art gallery since 1899 – its current name is in honour of the 19th-century benefactor who funded the original building. In addition to the city's main library and the tourist office (p146), the mixed bag of museum exhibits is worth half an hour between the main sights.

St Augustine's Abbey
RUINS

(EH; www.english-heritage.org.uk; Longport; adult/concession/child £6.20/5.60/4.10; ⊙10am-6pm Apr-Sep, to 5pm Oct, to 4pm Sat & Sun Nov-Mar) An integral but often overlooked part of the Canterbury World Heritage Site, St Augustine's Abbey was founded in AD 597, marking the rebirth of Christianity in southern England. Later requisitioned as a royal palace, it fell into disrepair and now only stumpy foundations remain. A small museum and a worthwhile free audio guide do their best to underline the site's importance and put flesh back onto its now-humble bones.

West Gate Towers
MUSEUM

(www.onepoundlane.co.uk; St Peter's St; adult/concession/child £4/3/2; ⊙11am-4pm) The city's only remaining medieval gateway (1380) houses a museum that focuses on the building's use as a prison. The views from the top are pretty good, but if you don't go inside, you can always entertain yourself watching buses, wing mirrors folded back, as they squeeze through the medieval archway.

Tours

Canterbury Historic River Tours
BOATING

(☑07790-534744; www.canterburyrivertours.co.uk; Kings Bridge; adult/child £10.50/9.50; ⊙10am-5pm Mar-Oct) Knowledgeable guides double

---

THE CANTERBURY TALES

If English literature has a father figure, then it is Geoffrey Chaucer (1342–1400). Chaucer was the first English writer to introduce characters – rather than 'types' – into fiction, and he did so to greatest effect in his best-known work, *The Canterbury Tales*.

Written between 1387 and his death, in the hard-to-decipher Middle English of the day, Chaucer's *Tales* is an unfinished series of 24 vivid stories told by a party of pilgrims journeying between London and Canterbury. Chaucer successfully created the illusion that the pilgrims, not Chaucer (though he appears in the tales as himself), are telling the stories, which gave him unprecedented freedom as an author. *The Canterbury Tales* remains one of the pillars of the literary canon. But more than that, it's a collection of rollicking good yarns of adultery, debauchery, crime and edgy romance, and is filled with Chaucer's witty observations about human nature.

up as energetic oarsmen on these fascinating, multi-award-winning River Stour minicruises, which depart from behind the Old Weaver's House.

Canterbury Guided Tours
WALKING
(✆01227-459779; www.canterburyguidedtours.com; adult/concession/child £8/7.50/6; ⊙11am Feb-Oct, plus 2pm Jul-Sep) Walking tours lead by professional blue- and green-badge guides leave from opposite the Canterbury Cathedral entrance. Tickets can be purchased from the tourist office and online.

🛏 Sleeping

Kipp's Independent Hostel
HOSTEL £
(✆01227-786121; www.kipps-hostel.com; 40 Nunnery Fields; dm £12.50-24.50, s £22.50-40, d £40-68; @🛜) Occupying a century-old red-brick town house in a quietish residential area less than a mile from the city centre, these superb backpacker digs enjoy a homely atmosphere, clean (though cramped) dorms, a good kitchen for self-caterers and a large TV lounge.

★ ABode Canterbury
BOUTIQUE HOTEL ££
(✆01227-766266; www.abodecanterbury.co.uk; 30-33 High St; r from £64; 🛜) The 72 rooms at this supercentral hotel, the only boutique hotel in town, are graded from 'comfortable' to 'fabulous' (via 'enviable'), and for the most part live up to their names. They come with features such as handmade beds, chesterfield sofas, tweed cushions and beautiful modern bathrooms. There's a splendid champagne bar, restaurant and tavern, too.

House of Agnes
HOTEL ££
(✆01227-472185; www.houseofagnes.co.uk; 71 St Dunstan's St; r £89-129; 🛜) This rather wonky 13th-century beamed inn, mentioned in Dickens' *David Copperfield,* has eight themed rooms bearing names such as 'Marrakesh' (Moorish), 'Venice' (carnival masks), 'Boston' (light and airy) and 'Canterbury' (antiques and heavy fabrics). If you prefer your room to have straight lines and right angles, there are eight less exciting, but no less comfortable, 'stable' rooms in the garden annexe.

Arthouse B&B
B&B £££
(✆07976-725457; www.arthousebandb.com; 24 London Rd; r from £140; 🅿🛜) A night at Canterbury's most laid-back digs, housed in a 19th-century fire station, is a bit like sleeping over at a really cool art student's pad.

The theme is funky and eclectic, with furniture by local designers and artwork by the instantly likeable artist owners, who have a house-studio out back.

🍴 Eating

Tiny Tim's Tearoom
CAFE £
(www.tinytimstearoom.com; 34 St Margaret's St; mains £6-10; ⊙9.30am-5pm Mon-Sat, 10.30am-5pm Sun) It's no mean feat to be declared 'Kent Tearoom of the Year', but this swish 1930s cafe was awarded the accolade in 2015. It offers hungry shoppers big breakfasts packed with Kentish ingredients, and tiers of cakes, crumpets, cucumber sandwiches and scones plastered in clotted cream. On busy shopping days you are guaranteed to queue for a table.

Refectory Kitchen
BRITISH £
(✆01227-638766; www.refectorykitchen.com; 16 St Dunstan's St; mains around £8; ⊙8am-5pm Mon-Sat, 9am-3pm Sun) This tiny, wood-beamed cafe serves popular, nutrient-packed all-day breakfasts and a short menu of light lunch and dinner mains containing Kentish ingredients as far as possible. The welcome is friendly but things get very busy at mealtimes.

Boho
INTERNATIONAL £
(www.bohocanterbury.co.uk; 27 High St; snacks £5-15; ⊙9am-6pm Mon-Thu, to 9pm Fri & Sat, 10am-5pm Sun) This hip eatery in a prime spot on the main drag is extraordinarily popular and you'll be lucky to get a table on busy shopping days. Cool tunes lilt through the chic retro dining space while chilled diners chow down on humongous burgers, full-monty breakfasts and imaginative, owner-cooked international mains. Boho doesn't do bookings, so be prepared to queue.

★ Goods Shed
MARKET ££
(✆01227-459153; www.thegoodsshed.co.uk; Station Rd West; mains £17.50-20; ⊙market 9am-7pm Tue-Sat, to 4pm Sun, restaurant noon-2.30pm & 6pm-last customer) Aromatic farmers market, food hall and fabulous restaurant rolled into one, this converted warehouse by the Canterbury West train station is a hit with everyone from self-caterers to sit-down gourmets. The chunky wooden tables sit slightly above the market hubbub but in full view of its appetite-whetting stalls. Daily specials exploit the freshest farm goodies the Garden of England offers.

Drinking & Nightlife

Foundry Brewpub MICROBREWERY
(www.thefoundrycanterbury.co.uk; White Horse Lane; ⊙noon-midnight Mon-Thu, til late Fri & Sat, to 11pm Sun) Canterbury's brewpub pumps out award-winning craft beers in the industrial setting of a former foundry where New York's first streetlights were made. It also stocks a wide range of local and national ales and ciders, serves light snacks and meals and is planning its own gin and vodka.

Steinbeck & Shaw CLUB
(www.facebook.com/steinbeckandshaw; 41 St George's Pl; ⊙6pm-2am Mon-Thu, to 3am Fri & Sat) Canterbury's best city-centre nightspot has a supercool, 21st-century interior with urban and retro elements. The weekly program is a mixed bag of rock and house and is as popular with students as with tourists and Kentish trendoids.

Thomas Becket PUB
(www.facebook.com/thethomasbecketpubrestaurant; 21 Best Lane; ⊙10am-midnight Mon-Thu, to 12.30am Fri & Sat, to 11.30pm Sun) A classic English pub with a garden's worth of hops hanging from its timber frame, Thomas Becket attracts many a modern-day pilgrim to its ales. Traditional decor includes copper pots, comfy seating and a fireplace to cosy up to on winter nights. It also serves decent pub grub.

Parrot PUB
(www.parrotcanterbury.co.uk; 1-9 Church Lane; ⊙noon-11pm; 🐾) Built in 1370 on Roman foundations, Canterbury's oldest boozer has a snug, beam-rich, slightly upmarket pub downstairs and a much-lauded dining room upstairs under yet more ageing oak. Many a local ale is pulled in both venues.

Shopping

Chaucer Bookshop BOOKS
(www.chaucer-bookshop.co.uk; 6-7 Beer Cart Lane; ⊙10am-5pm Mon-Sat, 11am-4pm Sun) Antiquarian and used books plus interesting prints and drawings.

Information

Tourist Office (☑01227-862162; www.canterbury.co.uk; 18 High St; ⊙9am-6pm Mon-Wed & Fri, to 8pm Thu, to 5pm Sat, 10am-5pm Sun; 🐾) Located in the Beaney House of Art & Knowledge. Staff can help book accommodation, excursions and theatre tickets.

Getting There & Away

BUS

The city's **bus station** (St George's Lane) is just within the city walls. Canterbury connections:
Dover (£5.70, 34 minutes, three hourly)
London Victoria (National Express; £10, two hours, hourly)
Margate (£5.70, one hour, two hourly)
Ramsgate (£5.70, 45 minutes, hourly)
Sandwich (£4.20, 40 minutes, three hourly)
Whitstable (£5.20, 30 minutes, every 10 minutes)

TRAIN

There are two train stations, Canterbury East for London Victoria and Canterbury West for London's Charing Cross/St Pancras stations. Canterbury connections:
Dover Priory (£8.50, 28 minutes, half-hourly) Runs from Canterbury East train station.
London St Pancras (£38.70, one hour, hourly) High-speed service.
London Victoria/Charing Cross (£32.60, 1¾ hours, two hourly)

Whitstable

☑01227 / POP 32,100

Perhaps it's the oysters harvested since Roman times? Maybe it's the weatherboard houses and shingle beach? Or perhaps it's the pleasingly old-fashioned main street with petite galleries, been-there-forever outfitters and emporia of vintage frillies? Most likely it's for all of these reasons that Whitstable has become a bit of a weekend magnet for metropolitan types looking for refuge from the city hassle. It's also a simple day trip from Canterbury, to which it is linked by regular local bus.

For a week in late July, the town hosts the **Whitstable Oyster Festival** (www.whitstableoysterfestival.co.uk; ⊙late Jul), a seafood, arts and music extravaganza offering a packed schedule of events, from history walks, crab catching and oyster-eating competitions to a beer festival and traditional 'blessing of the waters'.

Sleeping

Whitstable Bay B&B ££
(☑01227-779362; www.whitstablebay.com; 74 Joy Lane; s/d from £65/70; 🅿🐾) This much-lauded B&B is located just a short stroll southwest of High St and offers three very well-appointed and stylishly decorated doubles in a quiet residential area. Continental

LEEDS CASTLE

The immense moated pile of **Leeds Castle** (www.leeds-castle.com; adult/concession/child £24.90/21.90/17.50; ⊙10am-6pm Apr-Sep, to 5pm Oct-Mar; ⛵), just east of Maidstone, is one of the most visited of Britain's fortresses. The formidable, hefty structure balancing on two islands is known as something of a 'ladies castle'. This stems from the fact that in its more than 1000 years of history, it has been home to a who's who of medieval queens, most famously Henry VIII's first wife, Catherine of Aragon.

The castle was transformed from fortress to lavish palace over the centuries, and its last owner, the high-society hostess Lady Baillie, used it as a princely family home and party pad to entertain the likes of Errol Flynn, Douglas Fairbanks and John F Kennedy. The castle's vast estate offers peaceful walks, a duckery, aviary and falconry demonstrations. You'll also find possibly the world's sole dog-collar museum, plenty of kids' attractions and a hedge maze.

Trains run from London Victoria to Bearsted, where you catch a special shuttle coach to the castle.

breakfast is free, but a full English is £6.50 extra.

Hotel Continental
HOTEL **££**

(☎01227-280280; www.hotelcontinental.co.uk; 29 Beach Walk; r from £75; ⛵) The bright and breezy quarters at this elegant seaside art deco building sport light-painted wood cladding, brilliant white beds and sparkling bathrooms. There's a decent restaurant and bar on the premises.

Eating

Samphire
MODERN BRITISH **££**

(☎01227-770075; www.samphirewhitstable.co.uk; 4 High St; mains £13-18; ⊙9am-9.30pm Sun-Thu, 8.30am-10pm Fri & Sat) The shabby-chic jumble of tables and chairs, big-print wallpaper and blackboard menus create the perfect stage for meticulously crafted mains containing East Kent's most flavour-packed ingredients. An interesting side dish is its namesake samphire, an asparagus-like plant that grows on sea-sprayed rocks and cliffs, often found on menus in these parts.

★ Sportsman Pub
BRITISH **£££**

(www.thesportsmanseasalter.co.uk; Faversham Rd, Seasalter; mains around £22; ⊙restaurant noon-2pm & 7-9pm Tue-Sat, 12.30-2.45pm Sun, bar noon-3pm & 6-11pm Tue-Sat, noon-10pm Sun) The anonymous and oddly named village of Seasalter, 4 miles east of Whitstable, would hardly receive a trickle of visitors were it not for the deceivingly ramshackle Sportsman Pub, East Kent's only eatery adorned with a Michelin star. Local ingredients from sea, marsh and woods are crafted by Whitstable-born chef Stephen Harris into tastepacked Kentish creations that have food critics drooling.

Wheelers Oyster Bar
SEAFOOD **£££**

(☎01227-273311; www.wheelersoysterbar.com; 8 High St; mains around £20; ⊙10.30am-9pm Mon & Tue, 10.15am-9pm Thu, 10.15am-9.30pm Fri, 10am-10pm Sat, 11.30am-9pm Sun) Squeeze onto a stool by the bar or into the four-table Victorian dining room of this baby-blue and pink restaurant, then choose from the seasonal menu and enjoy the best seafood in Whitstable. This place knows its stuff, as it's been serving oysters since 1856. Bookings are highly recommended unless you're travelling solo. Cash only.

ⓘ Information

Tourist Office (☎01227-770060; www.canterbury.co.uk; 34 Harbour St; ⊙10am-4pm Mon-Fri, to 5pm Sat, 11am-5pm Sun) Run by the Whitstable Improvement Trust from its shop.

ⓘ Getting There & Away

BUS

Whitstable has connections to Canterbury (£5.20, 30 minutes, every 10 minutes) and London Victoria (£13.70, two hours, daily).

TRAIN

Whitstable has the following connections:
London St Pancras (£28, one hour 20 minutes, hourly)
London Victoria (£22, one hour 20 minutes, hourly)
Margate (£7.20, 20 minutes, twice hourly)
Ramsgate (£9.30, 36 minutes, twice hourly)

WORTH A TRIP

CHATHAM HISTORIC DOCKYARD

On the riverfront in Chatham, this historic dockyard (☑01634-823800; www.thedockyard.co.uk; Dock Rd; adult/concession/child £24/21.50/14; ⊙10am-4pm mid-Feb–Mar & Nov, to 6pm Apr-Oct), a candidate for Unesco heritage status, occupies a third of what was once the Royal Navy's main dock facility. It is possibly the most complete 18th-century dock in the world and has been transformed into a maritime museum examining the Age of Sail. Exhibits include well-restored ships, exhibitions on a variety of shipbuilding themes and a working steam railway.

Margate

☑01843 / POP 49,700

A popular resort for more than two centuries, Margate's late-20th-century slump was long and bleak as British holidaymakers ditched Victorian frump for the carefree *costas* of Spain. But this grand old seaside resort, with fine-sand beaches and artistic associations, has bounced off the bottom. Major cultural regeneration projects – including the spectacular Turner Contemporary art gallery – are slowly reversing the town's fortunes, and on busy days even the odd non-English speaker can be overheard in the hipster cafes and carefully curated junk emporia of the rejuvenated old town.

◉ Sights

★ Turner Contemporary
GALLERY

(www.turnercontemporary.org; Rendezvous; ⊙10am-5pm Tue-Sun) **FREE** This blockbuster contemporary art gallery, bolted together on the site of the seafront guesthouse where master painter JMW Turner used to stay, is one of East Kent's top attractions. Within the strikingly featureless shell the only thing distracting the eye, apart from the artwork on display, is the sea view from the floor-to-ceiling windows. These allow you to appreciate the very thing Turner loved so much about Margate – the sea, sky and refracted light of the north Kent coast.

The gallery attracts top-notch contemporary installations by high-calibre artists such as Tracey Emin (who grew up in Margate)

and Alex Katz. When you're finished with the art, culinary creations await in the cafe and the gift shop is excellent.

Shell Grotto
GROTTO, CAVE

(www.shellgrotto.co.uk; Grotto Hill; adult/concession/child £4/3.50/1.50; ⊙10am-5pm Apr-Oct, 11am-4pm Sat & Sun Nov-Mar) Margate's unique attraction is a mysterious subterranean grotto, discovered in 1835. It's a claustrophobic collection of rooms and passageways embedded with 4.6 million shells arranged in symbol-rich mosaics. It has inspired feverish speculation over the years; some think it a 2000-year-old pagan temple, others an elaborate 19th-century hoax. Either way, it's a one-of-a-kind place worth seeing.

Dreamland
AMUSEMENT PARK

(www.dreamland.co.uk; Marine Tce; entry £5, rides £1.50-5; ⊙10am-6pm, days vary throughout the year; ⊕) Given the kiss of life using lottery and council funds, Margate's famous amusement park has come back to life after many years of lying derelict and stop-start renovation. The main attraction here is the so-called Scenic Railway, a 1920s heritage-listed wooden roller coaster that was rebuilt after an arson attack in 2008. But there are plenty of other period rides and attractions to keep adults and kiddies thrilled, some shipped in from other defunct, 20th-century amusement parks across the country.

🛌 Sleeping

★ Reading Rooms
B&B £££

(☑01843-225166; www.thereadingroomsmargate.co.uk; 31 Hawley Sq; r £170; ␠) Occupying an unmarked 18th-century Georgian town house on a tranquil square just five minutes' walk from the sea, this luxury boutique B&B is as stylish as they come. Generously cut rooms with waxed wooden floors and beautiful French antique reproduction furniture contrast with the 21st-century bathrooms fragrant with luxury cosmetics. Breakfast is served in your room. Bookings essential.

Sands Hotel
BOUTIQUE HOTEL £££

(☑01843-228228; www.sandshotelmargate.co.uk; 16 Marine Dr; r £130-265; ❄␠) This beautifully styled boutique hotel sits right on the Margate seafront. It features an understated sand-hued theme throughout, the southeast's best bathrooms, and a restaurant with spectacular bay views, which around half of the rooms also share. The entrance is hidden under the arches on the seafront next to the hotel's very own summertime ice-cream parlour.

Eating & Drinking

Old Kent Market MARKET £
(www.theoldkentmarket.com; 8 Fort Hill; ⊙9am-8pm; ✐) This resurrected indoor market a few steps from the beach is absolutely crammed with hipster eateries of every kind, from a Singapore street-food stall to a US diner, a pizzeria to an artisan coffee shop. There always seems to be someone stroking some instrument or other and the most striking feature is the red double-decker bus cafe parked in the entrance.

Hantverk & Found SEAFOOD ££
(✐01843-280454; www.hantverk-found.co.uk; 18 King St; mains £7-17; ⊙noon-4pm & 6.30-9.30pm Thu, to 11pm Fri, noon-11pm Sat, noon-4pm Sun) Margate's best seafood cafe plates up mussels, oysters, clams, crab and local fish in imaginative ways, be that in spicy Korean broth, *koji* miso marinated, in cider sauce or on sourdough toast. The dining space is simple, the ingredients Kent-sourced wherever possible and the H&F doubles up as a commissioning gallery with regular changing shows of top-quality art.

The Lifeboat PUB
(1 Market St; ⊙noon-midnight) If you're looking for a pub with real atmosphere, head in the evening to this oh-so hipsterly authentic, wood-rich tavern where there's regular live jazz, craft beers and ciders on tap and a real fire. As every seafarer's drinking den should, it even has sawdust on the floor (adding spit for extra authenticity is probably not allowed).

Information

Tourist Office (✐01843-577637; www.visitthanet.co.uk; Droit House, Stone Pier; ⊙10am-5pm Easter-Oct, 10am-5pm Tue-Sat Nov-Easter) Next to the Turner Contemporary art gallery, the tourist office serves all of Planet Thanet. It hands out *The Isle*, a glossy magazine crammed with Thanet listings published twice a year and a free quarterly newspaper called the *Mercury* containing all the latest happenings.

Getting There & Away

BUS
Departure and arrival points for local buses are Queen St and adjacent Cecil St.
Broadstairs (Thanet Loop Bus; £2.20, 22 minutes, up to every 10 minutes)

Canterbury (£5.70, one hour, two hourly)
London Victoria (National Express; from £8.60, three hours, seven daily)
Ramsgate (Thanet Loop Bus; £2.70, 29 minutes, up to every 10 minutes)

TRAIN
The train station is just a few steps from the beach. There are hourly services to London Victoria (£24.40, one hour 50 minutes) and a high-speed service to London St Pancras (£43, 1½ hours) that runs twice hourly.

Broadstairs

✐01843 / POP 25,000
While its bigger, brasher neighbours seek to revive and regenerate themselves, quaint little Broadstairs quietly gets on with what it's done best for the past 150 years – wowing visitors with its tight sickle of course sand (Viking Bay) and shallow, sun-warmed sea. Charles Dickens certainly thought it an agreeable spot, spending most summers here between 1837 and 1859. The resort now plays the Victorian nostalgia card at every opportunity but this is a minor distraction for the fine-weather crowds that descend from London.

Sights

Dickens House Museum MUSEUM
(www.dickensfellowship.org; 2 Victoria Pde; adult/child £3.75/2.10; ⊙1-4.30pm Easter–mid-Jun & mid-Sep–Oct, 10am-4.30pm mid-Jun–mid-Sep, 1-4.30pm Sat & Sun Nov) This quaint museum

OFF THE BEATEN TRACK

ISLE OF THANET

You won't need a wetsuit or a ferry to reach the Isle of Thanet and its towns of Margate, Ramsgate and Broadstairs: the 2-mile-wide Wantsum Channel, which divides the island from the mainland, silted up in the 16th century, transforming the East Kent landscape forever. In its island days, Thanet was the springboard for several epoch-making episodes in English history. It was here that the Romans kicked off their invasion in the 1st century AD and where St Augustine landed in AD 597 to launch his conversion of the pagans. If global warming forecasts are right, Thanet could once again be an island by the end of the century.

is Broadstairs' top indoor attraction and the former home of Mary Pearson Strong – Dickens' inspiration for the character of Betsey Trotwood in *David Copperfield*. Diverse Dickensiana on display includes letters from the author.

✹ Festivals & Events

Dickens Festival CULTURAL
(www.broadstairsdickensfestival.co.uk; ⊙ mid-Jun) Broadstairs' biggest bash, this annual, week-long festival culminates in a banquet and ball in Victorian fancy dress.

🛏 Sleeping & Eating

⭐ **Bleak House** HISTORIC HOTEL **£££**
(✆ 01843-865338; www.bleakhousebroadstairs.co. uk; Fort Rd; r £135-250, apt £300; 🛜) This former Napoleonic-era fortress overlooking the beach was converted into an opulent Victorian residence just in time for one Charles Dickens to rent it for 22 summers (1837–59). From the lounge bar to the Copperfield suite with its Viking Bay views and five-star bathroom, the whole caboodle oozes unique period character. Building tours run from 11am to 5pm.

⭐ **Wyatt & Jones** BRITISH **££**
(www.wyattandjones.co.uk; 23-27 Harbour St; mains £6-21; ⊙ 8.30am-11pm Wed-Sat, to 5pm Sun) Broadstairs' best gastronomical offering is this contemporary British restaurant just a few steps off the beach. Savour unashamedly local dishes such as Whitstable oysters, local bream, mussels and chips, or a day-launching breakfast in the uncluttered interior of gun-metal blue and scratched timber floors. Then admire your expanding waistline in the retro mirror wall.

❶ Getting There & Away

BUS
Broadstairs connections include the following:
Canterbury (£5.70, 1½ hours, twice hourly)
London Victoria (National Express; from £6, 3¼ hours, seven daily)
Margate (Thanet Loop Bus; £2.20, 22 minutes, up to every 10 minutes)
Ramsgate (Thanet Loop Bus; £1.70, 14 minutes, up to every 10 minutes)

TRAIN
Broadstairs is connected to London Victoria (£36.60, two hours, hourly) and by high-speed service to London St Pancras (£39.30, one hour 20 minutes to two hours, twice hourly).

Ramsgate

✆ 01843 / POP 40,400
The most varied of Thanet's towns, Ramsgate has a friendlier feel than rival Margate and is more vibrant than its quaint little neighbour Broadstairs. A forest of masts whistles serenely in the breeze below the handsomely

---

LOCAL KNOWLEDGE

HOPS & VINES

With booze cruises over to Calais a thing of the past, many Kent and Sussex drinkers have rediscovered their counties' superb home-grown beverages. Both counties produce some of the most delicious ales in the country and the southeast's wines are even out-gunning some traditional Continental vintners.

Kent's **Shepherd Neame Brewery** (✆ 01795-542016; www.shepherdneame.co.uk; 10 Court St, Faversham; tours £14; ⊙ 2pm daily) is Britain's oldest and cooks up aromatic ales brewed from Kent-grown premium hops. Sussex's reply is **Harveys Brewery** (✆ 01273-480209; www.harveys.org.uk; Bridge Wharf), which perfumes Lewes town centre with a hop-laden scent. Book well in advance for tours of either brewery.

Mention 'English wine' not too long ago and you'd likely hear a snort of derision. Not any more. Thanks to warmer temperatures and determined winemakers, English wine, particularly of the sparkling variety, is developing a fan base all of its own.

Award-winning vineyards can be found in both Sussex and Kent, whose chalky soils are likened to France's Champagne region. Many vineyards now offer tours and wine tastings. Some of the most popular are **Biddenden Vineyards** (✆ 01580-291726; www. biddendenvineyards.com; £1 donation to charity; ⊙ 10am-5pm Mon-Sat, from 11am Sun; tours 10am Sat year-round, Wed Jun-Sep), 1.2 miles from Wealden, and **Chapel Down Vinery** (✆ 01580-766111; www.chapeldown.com; Tenterden; tours £15; ⊙ tours daily Mar-Nov), located 2.5 miles south of Tenterden on the B2082.

curved walls of Britain's only royal harbour, and the seafront is surrounded by bars and cosmopolitan street cafes. Just one celebrity chef away from being described as 'up and coming', Ramsgate retains a shabbily undiscovered charm, its sweeping, environmentally sanctioned Blue Flag beaches and some spectacular Victorian architecture making it well worth the visit.

⊙ Sights

Spitfire Memorial Museum MUSEUM
(www.spitfiremuseum.org.uk; Manston Rd; ⊙10am-5pm Apr-Oct, to 4pm Nov-Mar) **FREE** Around 4 miles northwest of Ramsgate's town centre at Manston Airport, this purpose-built museum stores two WWII planes: one a Spitfire, the other a Hurricane. Both look factory-fresh but are surprisingly delicate and so, sadly, there's no clambering on board, though you can now have a go in a rather amateurishly built simulator. Gathered around the planes are myriad flight-associated exhibits, many relating to Manston's role as an airfield during the Battle of Britain where many Spitfires were based.

The museum has a decent cafe with views of the airstrip. Take bus 38 or 11 from King St and ask the driver to drop you off as near as possible.

Ramsgate Maritime Museum MUSEUM
(www.ramsgatemaritimemuseum.org; The Clock House, Royal Harbour; adult/child £2.50/1; ⊙10.30am-5.30pm Tue-Sun Easter-Sep) Interesting but erratically opening museum displaying loot from the more than 600 ships that have been wrecked on the notorious Goodwin Sands off this stretch of coast.

🛏 Sleeping

Glendevon Guesthouse B&B ££
(☎01843-570909; www.glendevonguesthouse.co.uk; 8 Truro Rd; s/d from £52.50/70; ⓟ🤖) 🚭 Run by energetic and knowledgeable hosts, this comfy guesthouse takes the whole ecofriendly thing seriously, with guest recycling facilities, eco-showers and even energy-saving hairdryers. The hallways of this grand Victorian house, a block back from the Ramsgate seafront, are decorated with work by local artists. All rooms have kitchenettes, and breakfast is a convivial affair taken around a communal table.

Royal Harbour Hotel BOUTIQUE HOTEL ££
(☎01843-591514; www.royalharbourhotel.co.uk; 10-12 Nelson Cres; s/d from £79/100; 🤖) Occupying two regency town houses on a glorious sea-

DOWN HOUSE

Charles Darwin's home from 1842 until his death in 1882, **Down House** (www.english-heritage.org.uk; Luxted Rd, Downe; adult/concession/child £11.80/10.60/7.20; ⊙10am-6pm Apr-Sep, to 5pm Oct, Sat & Sun only Nov-Mar) witnessed the development of Darwin's theory of evolution by natural selection. The house and gardens have been restored to look much as they would have in Darwin's time, including Darwin's study, where he undertook much of his reading and writing; the drawing room, where he tried out some of his indoor experiments; and the gardens and greenhouse, where some of his outdoor experiments are recreated.

There are three self-guided trails in the area, where you can follow in the great man's footsteps. Take bus 146 from Bromley North or Bromley South railway station, or service R8 from Orpington.

front crescent, this boutique hotel feels enveloped in warmth and quirkiness – an eclectic collection of books, magazines, games and artwork line the hotel. Rooms range from tiny nautical-esque 'cabins' to country-house style four-poster doubles, most with postcard views over the forest of masts below. All are perfectly appointed with bags of character.

🍴 Eating

★**Royal Victoria Pavilion** PUB FOOD £
(www.jdwetherspoon.com; Harbour Pde; mains £5-11; ⊙8am-midnight Sun-Thu, to 1am Fri & Sat; 🤖) The old pavilion has sat on Ramsgate seafront like an upturned boat since 1904, its grand architecture, based on the Little Theatre at Versailles, a vacant symbol of the British seaside's bygone glory days. However, in 2017 the hall was brought spectacularly back to life by Wetherspoons and is now a place to eat that packs a wow factor.

Bon Appetit FRENCH ££
(www.bonappetitramsgate.com; 4 Westcliff Arcade; mains £8-19; ⊙noon-2.30pm & 6.30pm-late Tue-Sun) The best eatery on Westcliff, this first-rate bistro serves up French-inspired dishes in a simple dining room or with al fresco harbour views. Ingredients on the menu are of the seasonal and locally sourced ilk, with finely crafted mains including delights such as venison sausages and baked camembert.

ℹ Information

Tourist Office (☑ 01843-598750; www.
ramsgatetown.org; Customs House, Harbour
Pde; ⊘10am-4pm) A small, staffed visitor
centre with out-of-hours brochure stands.

ℹ Getting There & Away

BUS

Ramsgate has the following bus connections:
Broadstairs (Thanet Loop Bus; £1.70, up to
every 10 minutes)
London Victoria (National Express; from
£8.60, three hours, six daily)
Margate (Thanet Loop Bus; £2.70, 29 minutes,
up to every 10 minutes)
Sandwich (£3.20, 28 minutes, hourly)

TRAIN

Ramsgate has many services to London Victoria,
London St Pancras and London Charing Cross.
Journey times range from 1¼ to two hours and
ticket prices from £13 to £45. There are also
services to Sandwich (£5.20, 12 minutes, hourly) and Dover (£10, 35 minutes, two hourly).

Sandwich

☑ 01304 / POP 5000

As close as you'll get to a living museum,
Sandwich was once England's fourth city
(after London, Norwich and Ipswich). It's a
fact hard to grasp as you wander its drowsy
medieval lanes, ancient churches, Dutch gables, crooked peg-tiled roofs and overhanging timber-framed houses. Once a port to
rival London, Sandwich began its decline
when the entrance to the harbour silted up
in the 16th century, and this once-vital gateway to and from the Continent spent the
next 400 years retreating into quaint rural
obscurity. Preservation is big here, with huge
local interest in period authenticity. The tiny
100-seat cinema is preserved as an art deco
museum piece and the 1920s garage deals
more in classic cars than modern vehicles.
Within the town's historical core, unlisted
buildings are the exception.

◉ Sights

Sandwich's web of medieval and Elizabethan streets is perfect for ambling through
and getting pleasantly lost (as many do).
Strand St in particular has one of the country's highest concentrations of half-timbered
buildings. Ornate brickwork on some houses
betrays the strong influence of 350 Protestant Flemish refugees (referred to as 'the

Strangers'), who settled in the town in the
16th century at the invitation of Elizabeth I.

Sandwich Quay WATERFRONT
Several attractions line the River Stour. The
cute little flint-chequered Barbican tollgate
was built by Henry VIII and controls traffic
flow over the river's only road bridge. Nearby rises Fishergate, built in 1384 and once
the main entrance to the town, through
which goods from the Continent and beyond once passed. On fair-weather days, hop
aboard the **Sandwich River Bus** (☑ 07958-
376183; www.sandwichrb.co.uk; The Quay; adult/
child 30min trip £7/5, seal spotting £20/14; ⊘every
30-60min 11am-6pm Thu-Sun Apr-Sep) beside the
toll bridge for seal-spotting trips along the
River Stour and in Pegwell Bay.

It's also an interesting way to reach the
Richborough Roman Fort (EH; www.english-
heritage.org.uk; Richborough Rd; adult/concession/
child £6.20/5.20/3.90; ⊘10am-6pm Apr-Sep, to
5pm Wed-Sun Oct, to 4pm Sat & Sun Nov-Mar).

Guildhall Museum MUSEUM
(www.sandwichguildhallmuseum.co.uk; Guildhall;
⊘10am-4pm Wed-Sun) FREE Sandwich's small
but thorough museum is a good place to
start exploring the town. The exhibition
space was fully renovated in 2017 to house
a copy of the Magna Carta, accidentally discovered in Sandwich's archives in 2015. Other exhibitions examine the town's rich past
as a Cinque Port (p158), its role in various
wars, and the gruesome punishments meted
out to felons, fornicators and phoney fishers.

Salutation Gardens GARDENS
(www.the-salutation.com; The Salutation, Knightrid-
er St; £8; ⊘10am-5pm Mar-Oct, to 4.30pm Nov-
Feb) Just along from Fishergate, this set of
exquisite gardens was laid out behind a 1912
mansion by leading early 20th-century garden designers Gertrude Jekyll and Edwin
Lutyens. In the mid-noughties the exquisite site was brought back to life by Dom
and Steph Parker, nationally known as minor celebrities from British TV's *Gogglebox*
show. There's a delightful little tearoom in
the grounds and you can stay with Dom and
Steph in their multimillion-pound mansion.

St Peter's CHURCH
(☑ 01304-617295; www.stpeterschurch-sandwich.
org.uk; King St; tower adult/child £3.50/2.50;
⊘tower noon-4pm Tue-Sun Apr-Sep, to 2pm Oct-
Mar) The oldest church in Sandwich is now
no longer used for worship. It's a real mixture of styles and years: its tower collapsed

in dramatic fashion in 1661 and it was rebuilt with a bulbous cupola by the Flemish 'Strangers'. In 2017 this was made accessible to the public who can now climb the narrow steps for unsurpassed views across the Kent-peg tiled roofs of Sandwich.

Sleeping & Eating

⭐ Bell Hotel
HOTEL £££

(☎01304-613388; www.bellhotelsandwich.co.uk; Sandwich Quay; s/d from £120/130; 🅿🛜) Today the haunt of celebrity golfers, the Bell Hotel has been sitting on the town's quay since Tudor times, though much of the remaining building is from the 19th century. A splendid sweeping staircase leads to luxurious rooms, some with pretty quay views. The Old Dining Room restaurant is one of East Kent's poshest nosh spots.

No Name Shop
DELI, BISTRO ££

(www.nonameshop.co.uk; 1 No Name St; snacks £1.90-6.25, meals £6.95-13.50; ⏰9am-5pm Mon-Sat, 9am-4pm Sun) The far-from-anonymous No Name Shop is a French-owned deli (downstairs) and bistro (upstairs) near the bus stop, a pleasantly aromatic spot for a quick sandwich in Sandwich or an 'oozylicious' croque-monsieur, as well as more sophisticated dishes, followed by a relaxing glass of something Gallic. Popular among locals, some of whom seem to regularly prefer it over their own kitchens.

ℹ Information

Tourist Office (☎01304-613565; www.open-sandwich.co.uk; Guildhall, Cattle Market; ⏰10am-4pm Mon-Sat Apr-Oct) Located in the historic Guildhall.

ℹ Getting There & Away

BUS

Buses go to Ramsgate (£3.20, 21 minutes, hourly), Dover (£4, 45 minutes, two hourly) and Canterbury (£4.20, 40 minutes, three hourly).

TRAIN

Trains run from Dover Priory train station (£7.50, 22 minutes, hourly), Ramsgate (£5.20, 12 minutes, hourly) and London St Pancras (£43, two hours, hourly).

Dover

☎01304 / POP 31,000

One of the Cinque Ports, down-in-the-dumps Dover has certainly seen better days. Its derelict postwar architecture and shabby town centre is a sad introduction to England for travellers arriving on cross-Channel ferries and cruise ships, most of whom pass through quickly. Lucky, then, that the town has a couple of stellar attractions to redeem it. The port's vital strategic position so close to mainland Europe gave rise to a sprawling hilltop castle, which has some 2000 years of history to its credit. The spectacular white cliffs, as much a symbol of English wartime resilience as Winston Churchill or the Battle of Britain, rear in chalky magnificence to the east and west.

◉ Sights

⭐ Dover Castle
CASTLE

(EH; www.english-heritage.org.uk; adult/concession/child £19.40/17.50/12; ⏰10am-6pm Apr-Jul & Sep, 9.30am-6pm Aug, to 5pm Oct, 10am-4pm Sat & Sun Nov-Mar; 🅿) Occupying top spot, literally and figuratively, in Dover's townscape, this most

---

THE WHITE CLIFFS OF DOVER

Immortalised in song, film and literature, the iconic white cliffs of Dover are embedded in the national consciousness, and are a big 'Welcome Home' sign to generations of travellers and soldiers. The cliffs rise to 100m high and extend on either side of Dover, but the best bit is the 6-mile stretch that starts about 2 miles east of town, properly known as the **Langdon Cliffs**, now managed by the National Trust.

From the **Langdon Cliffs tourist office** (☎01304-202756; www.nationaltrust.org.uk; ⏰10am-5pm Mar-Oct, 11am-4pm Nov-Feb), follow the stony path east along the clifftops for a bracing 2-mile walk to the stout Victorian **South Foreland Lighthouse** (NT; www.nationaltrust.org.uk; adult/child £6/3; ⏰guided tours 11am-5.30pm Fri-Mon mid-Mar–Oct). This was the first lighthouse to be powered by electricity and is the site of the first international radio transmissions, in 1898.

A trail runs along the cliffs as far as **St Margaret's Bay**, a popular spot among locals.

At the end of the trail along the cliffs at St Margaret's Bay, bus 81 shuttles back to Dover or onto Deal every hour.

Dover

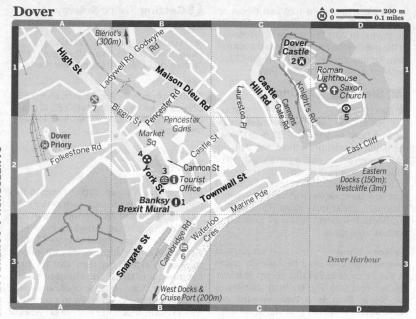

Dover

impressive of castles was built to bolster the country's weakest point at the shortest sea crossing to mainland Europe. The highlights here are the unmissable secret wartime tunnels and the Great Tower, but the huge area it sprawls across has a lot of other interesting sights, so allow at least three hours for your visit, more if you stand to admire the views across the Channel to France.

The site has been in use for as many as 2000 years. On the vast grounds are the remains of a Roman lighthouse (Dover Castle), which dates from AD 50 and may be the oldest standing building in Britain. Beside it lies the restored Saxon Church of St Mary (Dover Castle) in Castro.

The robust 12th-century Great Tower, with walls up to 7m thick, is a medieval warren filled with interactive exhibits and light-and-sound shows that take visitors back to the times of Henry II.

However, the biggest draw of all is the network of secret wartime tunnels. The claustrophobic chalk-hewn passageways were first excavated during the Napoleonic Wars and then expanded to house a command post and hospital in WWII. The highly enjoyable 50-minute guided tour (every 20 minutes, included in the ticket price) tells the story of one of Britain's most famous wartime operations, code-named Dynamo, which was directed from here in 1940 and saw hundreds of thousands of soldiers evacuated from the beaches at Dunkirk. The story is told in a very effective way, with video projected sharply onto the tunnel walls and sounds rumbling through the rock. At one point, the entire passageway is consumed in flames and at others visitors are plunged into complete darkness.

★ Banksy Brexit Mural   PUBLIC ART
(cnr York & Townwall Sts) Despite voting leave, the poor port town of Dover is possibly the

Southeast community set to suffer most post-Brexit. It was perhaps for that reason that Banksy chose a highly visible gable end to create his Brexit mural that appeared overnight one May weekend in 2017. The huge artwork depicts a workman chipping away at one of the yellow stars of the EU flag, cracks splintering off in all directions across the image.

Roman Painted House   RUINS

(www.theromanpaintedhouse.co.uk; New St; adult/child £4/3; ⊙ 10am-5pm Tue-Sun Apr-Sep; P) A crumbling 1960s bunker is the unlikely setting for some of the most extensive, if stunted, Roman wall paintings north of the Alps. Several scenes depict Bacchus (Roman god of wine and revelry), which makes perfect sense as this large villa was built around AD 200 as a *mansio* (hotel) for travellers needing a little lubrication to unwind.

🛏 Sleeping & Eating

Blériot's   GUESTHOUSE £

(☑ 01304-211394; www.bleriotsguesthouse.co.uk; 47 Park Ave; s/d £38/58; P 🛜) Spacious eight-room guesthouse in a quiet residential location but within walking distance of all the sights. Some of the light-filled rooms have original Victorian fireplaces, there's a cosy lounge, and the hosts are the friendliest you'll meet in the southeast. Breakfast is £7 extra.

Dover Marina Hotel   HOTEL ££

(☑ 01304-203633; www.dovermarinahotel.co.uk; Waterloo Cres; s/d from £59/69; 🛜) Just a few steps from Dover's beach, this seafront hotel crams 81 rooms of varying dimensions into a gently curving 1870s edifice. The undulating corridors show the building's age, but there's nothing wonky about the rooms with their trendy ethnic fabrics, big-print wallpaper and contemporary artwork. Half the rooms have unrivalled sea views and 10 boast much-sought-after balconies.

★ Allotment   BRITISH ££

(☑ 01304-214467; www.theallotmentrestaurant. com; 9 High St; mains £5-17; ⊙ noon-9.30pm Tue-Sat) Dover's best dining spot plates up local fish and meat from around Canterbury, seasoned with herbs from the tranquil garden out back, for breakfast, lunch and dinner. Cleanse your palette with a Kentish wine in a relaxed, understated setting as you admire the view of the Maison Dieu (13th-century pilgrims' hospital) directly opposite through the exquisite stained-glass frontage.

ℹ Information

Tourist Office (☑ 01304-201066; www.white cliffscountry.org.uk; Market Sq; ⊙ 9.30am-5pm Mon-Sat year-round, 10am-3pm Sun Apr-Sep) Located in the Dover Museum (www.dovermuseum.co.uk; Market Sq; ⊙ 9.30am-5pm Mon-Sat year-round, 10am-3pm Sun Apr-Sep).

ℹ Getting There & Away

BOAT

Ferries depart for France from the Eastern Docks below the castle. Fares vary according to season and advance purchase. Services seem to be in a constant state of flux with companies rising and falling as often as the Channel's swell.

DFDS (☑ 0871-574 7235; www.dfdsseaways. co.uk) Services to Dunkirk (two hours, every two hours) and Calais (1½ hours, at least hourly).

P&O Ferries (☑ 01304-448888; www.poferries.com) Runs to Calais (1½ hours, every 40 to 60 minutes).

BUS

Dover has bus connections to the following:
Canterbury (£5.70, 34 minutes, three hourly)
London Victoria (Coach 007; from £7.70, 2½ to 3½ hours, every two hours)
Rye (Bus 100; £7.20, 2¼ hours)
Sandwich (£4, 45 minutes, two hourly)

TRAIN

Dover is connected by train to Ramsgate (£10, 35 minutes, two hourly) via Sandwich, Canterbury (£8.50, 27 minutes, two hourly) and London St Pancras, Victoria and Charing Cross (£37-45, one to 2½ hours, up to five hourly).

EAST SUSSEX

Home to rolling countryside, medieval villages and gorgeous coastline, this inspiring corner of England is besieged by weekending Londoners whenever the sun pops out. And it's not hard to see why as you explore the cobbled medieval streets of Rye; wander around historic Battle, where William the Conqueror first engaged the Saxons in 1066; and peer over the edge of the breathtaking Seven Sisters chalk cliffs and Beachy Head near the genteel seaside town of Eastbourne. Brighton, a highlight of any visit, offers some kicking nightlife, offbeat shopping and British seaside fun. Off the beaten track, you can stretch your legs on the South Downs Way, which traverses England's newest national park, the South Downs National Park.

Rye

☏ 01797 / POP 4770

Possibly southeast England's quaintest town, Rye is a little nugget of the past, a medieval settlement that looks like someone hit the pause button on time. Even the most hard-boiled cynic can't fail to be softened by Rye's cobbled lanes, mysterious passageways and crooked half-timbered Tudor buildings. Tales of resident smugglers, ghosts, writers and artists abound.

Rye was once one of the Cinque Ports, occupying a high promontory above the sea. Today the town rises 2 miles from the briny; sheep graze where the Channel's strong tides once swelled.

◎ Sights

Mermaid Street   AREA

Most start their exploration of Rye on famous Mermaid St, a short walk from the Rye Heritage Centre (p159). It bristles with 15th-century timber-framed houses with quirky names such as 'The House with Two Front Doors' and 'The House Opposite'.

Lamb House   HOUSE, MUSEUM

(NT; www.nationaltrust.org.uk; West St; adult/concession £6.80/3.45; ⊙ 11am-5pm Fri-Mon late Mar-Oct) This Georgian town house is a favourite stomping ground for local apparitions, but its most famous resident was American writer Henry James, who lived here from 1898 to 1916, during which time he wrote *The Wings of the Dove*. Until 2017 this was a private house but with the tenants gone, the National Trust has opened up more rooms to the public and created a more hands-on experience. For budding writers there are writing spaces and courses on offer.

Ypres Tower   MUSEUM

(www.ryemuseum.co.uk; Church Sq; adult/concession/child £4/3/free; ⊙ 10.30am-5pm Apr-Oct, to 3.30pm Nov-Mar) Just off Church Sq stands the sandcastle-esque Ypres Tower (pronounced 'wipers'). You can scramble through the 13th-century building to learn about its long history as a fort, prison, mortuary and museum (the last two at overlapping times), and an annexe contains one of the last surviving Victorian women's prisons in the country. From here, there are widescreen views of Rye Bay and even France on very clear days.

Driving Tour
Driving Tour: Dover to Rye

START DOVER EASTERN DOCKS
END RYE
LENGTH 35.5 MILES; AT LEAST FOUR HOURS (WITHOUT DUNGENESS PENINSULA DETOUR)

If you've just rolled off a cross-Channel ferry or have a day away from a cruise ship docked in Dover, instead of heading north to London, why not take this fascinating route along the white cliffs and across the flat marshes of the Kent–Sussex border to discover some of the southeast's hidden corners. Buses 100, 101 and 102 (The Wave) follow this route between Dover, Lydd and Hastings.

Starting at the exit to Dover's frantic ❶ **Eastern Docks**, where all cross-Channel ferries tie up, take the A20 along the seafront. After a few minutes, this dual carriageway begins to climb onto the famous white cliffs west of Dover. Your first stop is just outside town – take the turning for ❷ **Samphire Hoe** nature park, a ledge of parkland created between the white cliffs and the sea using 5 million cu metres of chalk excavated during the construction of the Channel Tunnel. It's a fine spot for a picnic as you watch the 30 local species of butterfly flutter by.

Back on the A20, it's a mere 1.75 miles to the exit for the village of Capel-Le-Ferne (on the B2011). Well signposted at the end of the village is the ❸ **Battle of Britain Memorial**, a striking monument to the pilots who took part in the decisive struggle with the Luftwaffe in the skies above Kent and Sussex. An airman seated at the centre of a huge Spitfire propeller looks out serenely across the Channel and there's a multimedia visitors centre and museum experience to enjoy. Returning to the B2011, a few gear changes will have you on the outskirts of ❹ **Folkestone**. Take a left at the first roundabout then the sixth right onto Dover Rd. This will take you into the centre of this formerly grand old resort, once a favourite stomping ground of royal bon viveur King Edward VII and a forgotten piece of England's seaside past. Take a stroll through the seafront Leas Coastal Park with its sub-

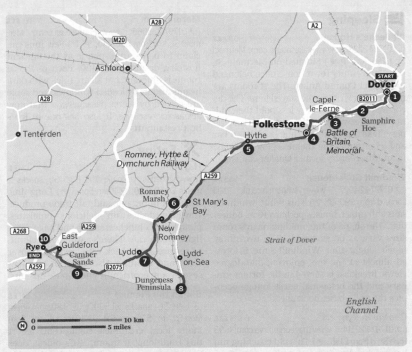

tropical flora, then halt for fish and chips at the old fish market before ambling up through the Creative Quarter, Folkestone's old town, now occupied by artists' studios and craft shops.

Heading out of Folkestone to the west on the A259 Sandgate Rd, you pass through Sandgate with its antique shops and shingle beach. From there it's another 2.5 miles to fascinating little **5 Hythe**. You could spend a full day in this original Cinque Port. Not only is it the eastern terminus of the fascinating narrow-gauge Romney, Hythe and Dymchurch Railway (RH&D Railway), but the Royal Military Canal also flows through the town and there's a quaint high street and beach to explore.

Heading ever west, a series of not-so-attractive shingle resorts such as Dymchurch and St Mary's are strung along the A259, cowering below their huge dykes, which keep the high tides from turning this stretch of the coast into sea bottom. You've now left the white cliffs behind and are entering the **6 Romney Marsh**, a flat, sparsely populated landscape of reed beds and sheep-dotted fields. There's a visitor centre (www.kentwildlifetrust.org.uk) between St Mary's Bay and New Romney (on the A259) for those with time.

Having negotiated New Romney, another of the original five Cinque Ports, just outside the town take the turning to the left onto the B2075, which leads to **7 Lydd**, a quaint former corporate member of the Cinque Ports. From here, detour along the lonely Dungeness Rd, which heads across the flats of the eerie **8 Dungeness Peninsula**, a low shingle spit dominated by a brooding nuclear power station. As well as boasting the southeast's largest seabird colony, it's also the western terminus of the RH&D Railway.

Back in Lydd, stick with the B2075 heading west for 6 miles until you reach Camber. Thought the entire south coast had just shingle beaches? Well, the main attraction here is **9 Camber Sands**, a wide expanse of golden grains and dunes, ideal for picnicking and strolling.

The B2075 winds through shingly, scrubby wetlands until it rejoins the A259 at the hamlet of East Guldeford, where you should turn left towards Rye. Along the roads around here you will see the main source of revenue from the Romney Marsh – thousands of sheep grazing on the verdant flats. The A259 barrels across the marshes, eventually depositing you in **10 Rye**, one of the southeast's quaintest towns.

🛏 Sleeping

★ Jeake's House   HOTEL ££

(✆01797-222828; www.jeakeshouse.com; Mermaid St; r £95-200; [P][≋]) Situated on Mermaid St, this 17th-century town house once belonged to US poet Conrad Aitken. The 11 rooms are named after writers who stayed here. The decor was probably slightly less bold then, minus the beeswaxed antiques and lavish drapery. Take a pew in the snug book-lined bar and, continuing the theme, enjoy breakfast in an 18th-century former Quaker chapel.

Windmill Guesthouse   B&B ££

(✆01797-224027; www.ryewindmill.co.uk; Mill Lane; d from £90; [P][≋]) This white windmill, sails still intact, houses perhaps Rye's oddest digs. The shape of the building means room sizes vary, as do standards. The two-storey much sought-after 'Windmill Suite' is located almost at the top, enjoying 360-degree views. Breakfast is served in the former granary and the octagonal guest lounge occupies the mill's base. Book ahead.

George in Rye   HOTEL £££

(✆01797-222114; www.thegeorgeinrye.com; 98 High St; d from £135; [≋]) This old coaching inn has managed to reinvent itself as a contemporary boutique hotel while staying true to its roots. Downstairs, an old-fashioned wood-panelled lounge is warmed by roaring log fires, while the guest rooms in the main building, created by the set designer from the film *Pride & Prejudice,* are chic and understated.

The highlight of the building is the grand old ballroom, originally built in 1818 as a meeting hall for local farmers.

Mermaid Inn   HOTEL £££

(✆01797-223065; www.mermaidinn.com; Mermaid St; s/d from £90/140; [P][≋]) Few inns can claim to be as atmospheric as this ancient hostelry, dating from 1420. Each of the 31 rooms is different, but all are thick with dark beams and lit by leaded windows, and some are graced by secret passageways that now act as fire escapes. It also has one of Rye's best restaurants.

🍴 Eating

Haydens   CAFE £

(www.haydensinrye.co.uk; 108 High St; snacks & meals £4.50-9.50; ⊗10am-5pm; [≋]) Long-time believers in organic and fair-trade produce, Haydens dishes up delicious omelettes, ploughman's lunches, salads and bagels in a light, breezy cafe. There's a wonderful elevated terrace at the back with great views over town and country. Also runs an excellent seven-room ecofriendly guesthouse upstairs.

Simon the Pieman   CAFE £

(3 Lion St; snacks £1.50-10; ⊗9.30am-4.45pm Mon-Fri, to 5.30pm Sat, 11.30am-4.45pm Sun) Many local cream-tea cognoscenti assert this traditional tearoom, Rye's oldest, does the best scone-cream-jam combo this side of Romney Marsh. Further foes of tooth and waistline tempt from the shop's window, though in the winter you may be lured in by the roaring real fire.

Webbe's at the Fish Cafe   SEAFOOD ££

(www.webbesrestaurants.co.uk; 17 Tower St; mains £13-18; ⊗noon-2pm & 6pm-late) Rye's best fish restaurant is a simple dining room flooded with natural light from large arched win-

---

CINQUE PORTS

Due to their proximity to Europe, southeast England's coastal towns were the frontline against raids and invasion during Anglo-Saxon times. In the absence of a professional army and navy, these ports were frequently called upon to defend themselves, and the kingdom, on land and at sea.

In 1278 King Edward I formalised this ancient arrangement by legally defining the Confederation of Cinque Ports (pronounced 'sink ports'). The five original ports – Sandwich, Dover, Hythe, Romney and Hastings – were awarded numerous perks and privileges in exchange for providing the king with ships and men. At their peak, the ports were considered England's most powerful institution after Crown and Church.

The importance of the ports eventually evaporated when the shifting coastlines silted up several Cinque Port harbours and a professional navy was based at Portsmouth. But still the pomp and ceremony remain. The Lord Warden of the Cinque Ports is a prestigious post now bestowed on faithful servants of the Crown. The Queen Mother was warden until she passed away, succeeded by Admiral Lord Boyce. Previous incumbents include the Duke of Wellington and Sir Winston Churchill.

WORTH A TRIP

BATTLE

'If there'd been no battle, there'd be no Battle', goes the saying in this unassuming village, which grew up around the hillside where invading French duke William of Normandy, aka William the Conqueror, scored a decisive victory over local king Harold in 1066. The epicentre of 1066 country, visitors flock here to see the spot where Harold got it in the eye, with the biggest crowd turning up mid-October to witness the annual re-enactment on the original battlefield.

The aptly named **Battle Abbey** (EH; www.english-heritage.org.uk; High St; adult/concession/child £11.20/10.10/7.80; ⊘10am-6pm Apr-Sep, to 4pm Sat & Sun Oct-Mar) marks the site of the pivotal event, which had an unparalleled impact on the country's subsequent social structure, language and, well, pretty much everything. Four years after, the Normans began constructing an abbey here, a penance ordered by the pope for the loss of life incurred. Only the foundations of the original church remain; the altar's position is supposedly the spot King Harold took an arrow in his eye.

There are train connections to Hastings (£4.30, 15 minutes, twice hourly) and London Charing Cross (£29.40, one hour and 20 minutes, twice hourly).

dows. The menu features local fish such as Rye Bay flounder in cider sauce and Rye cod in beer batter. The restaurant also doubles up as a cookery school and is the venue for the annual Scallop Week in March.

Landgate Bistro BRITISH ££
(☑01797-222829; www.landgatebistro.co.uk; 5-6 Landgate; mains £15-20; ⊘7-11pm Wed-Fri, noon-2.30pm & 6.30-11pm Sat, noon-2.30pm Sun) Escape the medieval excesses of Rye's central eateries to this fresh-feeling bistro, slightly off the tourist trail near the impressive 14th-century Landgate. The focus here is on competently crafted dishes using local lamb and fish. The dining space is understated with tables gathered around an ancient fireplace.

ℹ Information

Rye Heritage Centre (☑01797-226696; www.ryeheritage.co.uk; Strand Quay; ⊘10am-5pm Apr-Oct, shorter hours Nov-Mar) See a town-model audiovisual history for £3.50 and, upstairs, a freaky collection of still-functional penny-in-the-slot novelty machines. Also runs themed walking tours of the town; see the website for details.

ℹ Getting There & Away

BUS
There are hourly buses to Dover (bus 100; £7.20, 2¼ hours) and twice hourly services to Hastings (bus 100/101; £6.40, 40 minutes).

TRAIN
There are hourly trains to Hastings (£5.60, 18 minutes). For London St Pancras (£34.60, 1½ hours, hourly) change in Ashford.

Hastings

☑01424 / POP 98,500

Forever associated with the Norman invasion of 1066 (even though the decisive events took place 6 miles away), Hastings prospered as one of the Cinque Ports and, in its Victorian heyday, was one of Britain's most fashionable resorts. After a period of steady postwar decline, the town is enjoying a mini-renaissance, and these days is an intriguing mix of family seaside resort, working fishing port and arty hang-out.

⊙ Sights

Stade AREA
(Rock-A-Nore Rd) The seafront area known as the Stade (below East Hill) is home to distinctive black clapboard structures known as Net Shops. These were built to store fishing gear back in the 17th century, but some now house fishmongers who sell off the catch of Europe's largest beach-launched fishing fleet, usually hauled up on the shingle behind. All these fishy goings-on keep the Stade very much a working place, with the combined pong of diesel and guts scenting the air.

Hastings Castle RUINS
(www.discoverhastings.co.uk; Castle Hill Rd; adult/concession/child £4.95/4.25/3.95; ⊘10am-4pm Easter-Sep) This fortress was built by William the Conquerer, and an exhibition in the grounds tells the story of the castle and the Battle of Hastings in 1066.

Jerwood Gallery
GALLERY

(www.jerwoodgallery.org; Rock-A-Nore Rd; adult/concession/child £9/6/free; ⊙11am-5pm Tue-Sun) This large, purpose-built exhibition venue at the end of the Stade is used for temporary shows of contemporary British art as well as themed installations from the Jerwood collection. The building has a great cafe with sunny Channel views. The black-tiled building was designed to blend in with the adjacent net shops.

Hastings Museum & Art Gallery
MUSEUM

(www.hmag.org.uk; Johns Place, Bohemia Rd; ⊙10am-5pm Tue-Sat, noon-5pm Sun Apr-Sep, shorter hours Oct-Mar) FREE A short walk west of the train station, this marvellous little museum is housed in a red-brick mansion. Highlights inside include the intricately Moorish Durbar Hall and a section on John Logie Baird, who invented television while recuperating from an illness in Hastings between February 1923 and November 1924.

Hastings Pier
LANDMARK

(www.hastingspier.org.uk; 1-10 White Rock; ⊙10am-9pm daily) FREE Hastings last hit the national news in 2010 when its Victorian pier burnt down. The ballroom at the end, where the likes of The Clash, Sex Pistols, Rolling Stones, The Who, Jimi Hendrix and Pink Floyd once performed, was completely destroyed. Partially funded by the people of Hastings, the pier reopened in 2016 as a multipurpose entertainment space with a fish-and-chip shop, shops and vintage fun-fair rides. See the website for events such as open-air film screenings and concerts.

🛏 Sleeping

The Laindons
B&B ££

(☑01424-437710; www.thelaindons.com; 23 High St; s/d from £110/125; 🕏) Occupying a Georgian grade II–listed former coaching inn, this cosy B&B is just five minutes' amble from the seafront at the quieter end of High St. The five beautifully appointed rooms flood with sea-refracted light from the huge Georgian windows, illuminating the blend of breezy contemporary design and antique furnishings. Owner-cooked breakfasts are taken around a communal table.

★ Swan House
B&B £££

(☑01424-430014; www.swanhousehastings.co.uk; 1 Hill St; s/d from £90/130; @🕏) Inside its 15th-century timbered shell, this place blends contemporary and vintage chic to perfection. The four rooms feature organic toiletries, fresh flowers, hand-painted walls and huge beds. The guest lounge, where pale sofas, painted floorboards and striking modern sculpture rub shoulders with beams and a huge stone fireplace, is a stunner.

🍴 Eating & Drinking

St Mary in the Castle
CAFE £

(www.stmaryinthecastle.co.uk; Pelham Pl; mains £4.50-10; ⊙10am-6pm Sun-Thu, to 10pm Fri & Sat; 🕏) Amid the greasy cafes that line the seafront it's a relief to find this laid-back oasis of decent food offering nutritious titbits such as tofu on toast, halloumi kebabs and a range of tempting specials. The cafe is part of a larger arts centre and gallery, the latter in the crypt of the church above and free to enter.

Hanushka Coffee House
CAFE

(28 George St; ⊙9.30am-6pm) Hastings' best caffeine stop resembles a very well-stocked secondhand bookshop with every inch of wall space packed with browsable titles. The low-lit and tightly packed space in between provokes inter-table interaction, or you can seek sanctuary on the sofas and perches in the window.

ℹ Information

Tourist Office (☑01424-451111; www.visit1066 country.com; Muriel Matters House, Pelham Pl; ⊙9am-5pm Mon-Fri, 10am-3pm Sat & Sun)

ℹ Getting There & Away

BUS

Hastings has the following bus connections:

Battle (£3.20, 28 minutes, hourly)

Eastbourne (Bus 99; £5.20, 75 minutes, three hourly)

London Victoria (National Express; from £7.40, 2¾ hours, daily)

Rye (Bus 100/101; £6.40, 40 minutes, twice hourly)

TRAIN

Hastings has connections with Brighton (£13.90, one hour to 80 minutes, two hourly), via Eastbourne, London Charing Cross (£24.40, two hours, at least hourly), Battle (£4.30, 15 minutes, twice hourly) and Rye (£5.60, 18 minutes, hourly).

ℹ Getting Around

Hastings has two delightful old Victorian funiculars, the East Hill Cliff and West Hill Cliff Railways, useful if you need to get up onto the cliffs and don't fancy the walk. The **East Hill Cliff Railway** (Rock-A-Nore Rd; adult/child return £2.70/1.70; ◷10am-5.30pm Apr-Sep, 11am-4pm Sat & Sun Oct-Mar) funicular ascends from the Stade to Hastings Country Park, while the **West Hill Cliff Railway** (George St; adult/child return £2.70/1.70; ◷10am-5.30pm Mar-Sep, 11am-4pm Oct-Mar) funicular saves visitors' legs when climbing up to Hastings Castle. Otherwise the town can be easily tackled on foot.

Eastbourne

☏01323 / POP 103,000

Despite its semi-official title as 'Britain's sunniest town', Eastbourne has been slow to throw off its unattractive image as death's waiting room by the chilly Channel, all snoozing octogenarians in deckchairs and fusty guesthouses populated by vitamin D–deprived bank-holidaying Scots. But while much of this is still to be found here, since the mid-noughties an influx of students and the arrival of the southeast's largest Portuguese and Polish communities have given the town a sprightlier feel.

Eastbourne's 3.5-mile sweeping, palm-tree-lined seafront is one of the UK's grandest. Add to this a fresh modern art gallery and the South Downs National Park that nudges its western suburbs and Eastbourne certainly makes an enjoyable day trip from London or Brighton. It's also the start and end point for a hike along the 100-mile South Downs Way.

🛏 Sleeping & Eating

Albert & Victoria B&B ££

(☏01323-730948; www.albertandvictoria.com; 19 St Aubyns Rd; s/d from £45/80; 🛜) Book ahead to stay at this delightful Victorian terraced house, whose fragrant rooms, canopied beds, crystal chandeliers and secluded walled garden for summer breakfasts are mere paces from the seafront promenade. The four rooms are named after four of Queen Victoria's offspring.

Half Man! Half Burger! BURGERS £

(www.halfmanhalfburger.com; 43 Grove Rd; burgers around £8; ◷noon-10pm Wed-Sat, to 8pm Sun; 🛜) An island of cool in fusty Eastbourne, HMHB invites you to take a lifejacket-orange seat under bare lightbulbs to enjoy belly-packing burgers containing locally sourced beer, washed on its way with pricey craft beer. The half kid! half burger! £5

menu is a steal and there are several vegie/vegan burgers on the menu.

Lamb Inn PUB FOOD ££

(☏01323-720545; www.thelambeastbourne.co.uk; 36 High St; mains £9-17; ◷11am-11pm Sun-Thu, to midnight Fri & Sat) This ancient Eastbourne institution, less than a mile northwest of the train station in the under-visited Old Town, has been plonking Sussex ales on the bar for eight centuries, and now also serves gourmet British pub grub. A holidaying Charles Dickens left a few smudged napkins here when he stayed across the road. Buses 1, 1A and 13 stop nearby.

🛍 Shopping

★**Camilla's Bookshop** BOOKS

(☏01323-736001; www.camillasbookshop.com; 57 Grove Rd; ◷10am-5pm Mon-Sat) Literally packed to the rafters with over half a million musty volumes, this incredible second-hand-book repository, an interesting amble from the train station, fills three floors of a crumbling Victorian town house. It's the best place to source preloved reading matter on the south coast, if not the entire southeast.

ⓘ Information

Tourist Office (☏01323-415415; www.visiteastbourne.com; Cornfield Rd; ◷9am-5.30pm Mon-Fri, to 5pm Sat, 10am-1pm Sun May-Sep, closed Sun & shorter hours Oct-Apr) Tourist information plus tickets to anything happening in Eastbourne.

ⓘ Getting There & Away

BUS

There are buses to Brighton (bus 12; £4.20, 75 minutes, up to every 10 minutes) and Hastings (bus 99; £5.20, 75 minutes, three hourly).

TRAIN

Twice-hourly trains service Brighton (£11.10, 30 to 40 minutes) and London Victoria (£18.70, 1½ hours).

South Downs National Park

The South Downs National Park (www.southdowns.gov.uk), England's newest, is more than 600 sq miles of rolling chalk downs stretching west from Eastbourne to Winchester, a distance of about 100 miles. The South Downs Way extends its entire length. The park is all about rolling English

CHARTWELL

The home of Sir Winston Churchill from 1924 until his death in 1965, Chartwell (NT; www.nationaltrust.org.uk; Westerham; £14.40; ⏱ 11.30am-5pm Mar-Oct), 6 miles west of Sevenoaks, offers a breathtakingly intimate insight into the life of England's famous cigar-chomping bombast. This 19th-century house and its rambling grounds have been preserved much as Winnie left them, full of books, pictures, maps and personal mementos. Churchill was also a prolific painter and his now extremely valuable daubings are scattered throughout the house and fill the garden studio.

Transport options are limited without a car. Take a taxi from the nearest train station, Edenbridge (4 miles), accessible from London Victoria.

countryside and views down to the coast, a delight at any time of year, though May to October is the best time to come.

⊙ Sights & Activities

Beachy Head LANDMARK
(www.beachyhead.org.uk) The famous cliffs of Beachy Head are the highest point of the chalky rock faces that slice across the rugged coastline at the southern end of the South Downs. It's off the B2103, from the A259 between Eastbourne and Newhaven. From here the stunning Seven Sisters Cliffs undulate their way west. A clifftop path (a branch of the South Downs Way) rides the waves of chalk as far as picturesque Cuckmere Haven.

Beachy Head is a spot of thrilling beauty, the brilliant white chalk rising high into the blue Sussex sky. But on a darker note, it is also known as one of Europe's most frequented suicide spots.

Along the clifftop path, you'll stumble upon the tiny seaside hamlet of Birling Gap. The cafe here is closed due to cliff falls but the secluded beach is still a sun-trap popular with locals and walkers taking a breather.

Pevensey Castle RUINS
(EH; www.english-heritage.org.uk; Castle Rd, Pevensey; adult/concession/child £6.50/5.90/3.90; ⏱ 10am-6pm Apr-Sep, to 5pm Oct, weekends only Nov-Mar) The ruins of William the Conqueror's first stronghold sit 5 miles east of Eastbourne, just off the A259. Regular train ser-

vices between London Victoria and Hastings via Eastbourne stop at Westham, half a mile from Pevensey. Picturesquely dissolving into its own moat, the castle marks the point where William the Conqueror landed in 1066, just two weeks before the Battle of Hastings.

🛏 Sleeping & Eating

★ **Belle Tout Lighthouse** B&B £££
(☎ 01323-423185; www.belletout.co.uk; South Downs Way, Beachy Head; d from £170) Perched precariously close to the edge of the white cliffs, this early 18th-century decommissioned lighthouse somehow manages to contain six rooms, all imaginatively done out and all rather restricted space-wise. But the highlight must be the lantern lounge, a circular guest seating area in the glass top of the building, the perfect place to enjoy a truly memorable Sussex sunset.

Tiger Inn PUB FOOD ££
(The Green, East Dean; mains £6-14; ⏱ noon-10pm; 🐾) Located back from the cliffs, in the village of East Dean, the 15th-century Tiger Inn is one of Sussex' best taverns serving a gastropub menu to walkers and day trippers alike. In summer the action spills out onto the village green. East Dean is served by bus 12.

ℹ Getting There & Away

Bus 12 (up to every 10 minutes) heads through some of the South Downs National Park on the way to Brighton. A great place to alight is Cuckmere Haven from where we can walk back to Eastbourne across the Seven Sisters. Bus 99 (every 20 minutes) runs from Eastbourne to Pevensey.

Lewes

☑ 01273 / POP 17,300
Strung out along an undulating High St flanked by elegant Georgian buildings, a part-ruined castle and a traditional brewery, Lewes (pronounced 'Lewis') is a charmingly affluent hillside town with a turbulent past and fiery traditions. Off the main drag, however, there's a more intimate atmosphere as you descend into twisting narrow streets called twittens – the remainder of the town's original medieval street plan.

One of Lewes' claims to fame is that it straddles the 0 degrees line of longitude. An inconspicuous plaque on Western Rd marks the meridian, though modern measuring methods have actually placed the line around 100m to the east.

Lewes also holds what it claims is the biggest Bonfire Night bash in the world with tens of thousands of people descending on the town on 5 November to watch a carnival, fireworks display and effigies of villains of the day going up in flames.

🛏 Sleeping & Eating

Shelleys HOTEL **£££**
(📞 01273-472361; www.the-shelleys.co.uk; 135-136 High St; r from £130; 🛜) Lewes' top address is a 16th-century manor house full of grand old-fashioned charm. It was once home to the earl of Dorset and was owned by the Shelley family (of Percy Bysshe fame). The stylish, country rooms are the best in Lewes and there's an above standard restaurant overlooking a lovely walled garden.

Riverside FOOD HALL
(www.riverside-lewes.co.uk; Cliffe Bridge; ⊙9am-5pm) Housed in a former garage next to the river, this food hall and market is a fine place for coffee and cakes or a full sit-down brasserie meal in one of several small eateries inside.

Bill's CAFE **££**
(www.bills-website.co.uk; 56 Cliffe High St; mains £10-16; ⊙8am-11pm; 🛜) Part grocers, part delicatessen, part rustic-styled cafe, this insanely popular place envelops customers in its colours and smells then dishes up melt-in-the-mouth tartlets, gourmet pizzas, salads, desserts and other artisanal snacks. Get here early at meal times, and even in-between times, as it's normally chock-a-block.

ℹ Information

Tourist Office (📞 01273-483448; www.lewes.gov.uk; 187 High St; ⊙9.30am-4.30pm Mon-Fri, to 4pm Sat, 10am-2pm Sun Apr-Sep, closed Sun & shorter hours Sat Oct-Mar)

ℹ Getting There & Away

Lewes has the following rail connections:
Brighton (£4.40, 15 minutes, four hourly)
Eastbourne (£8, 20 minutes, four hourly)
London Victoria (£17, one hour to 1½ hours, three hourly)

Brighton & Hove
📞 01273 / POP 260,000

Raves on the beach, Graham Greene novels, mods and rockers in bank-holiday fisticuffs, naughty weekends for Mr and Mrs Smith, the UK's biggest gay scene and the Channel's best clubbing – this coastal city evokes many images for the British. But one thing is certain: with its bohemian, hedonistic vibe, Brighton is where England's seaside experience goes from cold to cool.

Brighton is without doubt Britain's most colourful and outrageous city. Here burlesque meets contemporary design; grotty hostels share thin walls with kinky boutique hotels; microbrewed ales share bar space with 'sex on the beach'; and stags watch drag. The city returned the UK's first Green Party MP, Valentine's Day is celebrated with unusual gusto, and according to the 2001 census, it has the UK's highest Jedi population.

CANTERBURY & SOUTHEAST ENGLAND BRIGHTON & HOVE

THE CHANNEL ISLANDS

Just off the coast of France, Jersey, Guernsey, Sark, Herm and Alderney beckon with exquisite coastlines, shaded lanes and old-world charm. Not quite Britain and not quite France, the islands are proudly independent, self-governing British Crown dependencies that straddle the gap between the two. Their citizens owe their allegiance to Her Majesty, but some still speak local dialects that stem from medieval Norman French.

The warm Gulf of St Malo ensures subtropical plants and an incredible array of birdlife. The Channel Islands enjoy sunnier days and milder winters than the UK, attracting walkers and outdoorsy types for surfing, kayaking, coasteering and diving. Superb local seafood graces the tables of local restaurants in the culture hubs of St Helier (Guernsey) and St Peter Port (Jersey).

Numerous forts and castles dot the coastlines, while poignant museums – some housed in old war tunnels and bunkers – provide an insight into the islanders' fortitude during WWII.

There are daily flights to Guernsey from London Gatwick, as well as from Jersey, Manchester, Birmingham, Southampton, Bristol and London Stansted. Jersey receives daily flights from all major London airports bar Heathrow, as well as from Liverpool, Birmingham, Southampton, Cardiff, Exeter and Guernsey, as well as several flights from Europe.

Brighton & Hove

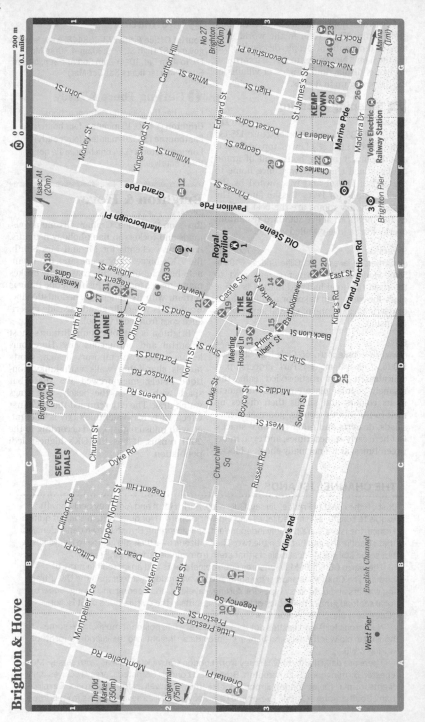

Brighton & Hove

The highlight for the sightseeing visitor is the Royal Pavilion, a 19th-century party palace built by the Prince Regent, who kicked off Brighton's love of the outlandish.

◎ Sights

★ **Royal Pavilion**   PALACE
(☏ 03000 290900; http://brightonmuseums.org.uk/royalpavilion; Royal Pavilion Gardens; adult/concession/child£13/11.50/8; ⊙ 9.30am-5.45pm Apr-Sep, 10am-5.15pm Oct-Mar) The Royal Pavilion is the city's must-see attraction. The glittering party pad and palace of Prince George, later Prince Regent and then King George IV, it's one of the most opulent buildings in England, and certainly the finest example of early 19th-century chinoiserie anywhere in Europe. It's an apt symbol of Brighton's reputation for decadence. An unimpressed Queen Victoria called the Royal Pavilion 'a strange, odd Chinese place', but for visitors to Brighton it's an unmissable chunk of Sussex history.

The entire palace is an eye-popping spectacle, but some interiors stand out even amid the riot of decoration. The dragon-themed banqueting hall must be the most incredible in all of England. More dragons and snakes writhe in the music room, with its ceiling of 26,000 gold scales, and the then-state-of-the-art kitchen must have wowed Georgians with its automatic spits and hot tables. Prince Albert carted away all of the furniture, some of which has been loaned back by the present queen.

Brighton Museum
& Art Gallery   MUSEUM, GALLERY
(https://brightonmuseums.org.uk; Royal Pavilion Gardens; adult/concession/child £5.20/4.20/3; ⊙ 10am-5pm Tue-Sun) Set in the Royal Pavilion's renovated stable block, this museum and art gallery has a glittering collection of 20th-century art and design, including a crimson Salvador Dalí sofa modelled on Mae West's lips. There's also an enthralling gallery of world art, an impressive collection of Egyptian artefacts, and an 'Images of Brighton' multimedia exhibit containing a series of oral histories and a model of the defunct West Pier.

Brighton Pier   LANDMARK
(www.brightonpier.co.uk; Madeira Dr) This grand old Edwardian pier is the place to experience Brighton's tackier side. There are plenty of stomach-churning fairground rides and noisy amusement arcades to keep you entertained, and candy floss and Brighton rock to chomp on while you're doing so. Just west are the sad remains of the West Pier (p166), a skeletal iron hulk that attracts flocks of starlings at sunset.

i360 Tower   TOWER
(☏ 03337-720360; www.britishairwaysi360.com; Lower King's Rd; adult/concession/child £16/13.50/8.25; ⊙ 10am-7.30pm Sun-Thu, to 9.30pm Fri & Sat)

Brighton's newest attraction opened in 2016, at the point the now defunct West Pier used to make landfall. The world's most slender tower is a brutal, 162m-tall column of reinforced steel and concrete rising like a space-age phallus (this is Brighton after all) from the seafront, with a huge, impaled, glass doughnut taking 'passengers' 138m above the city for some gob-smacking vistas of the Sussex coast.

Hove Museum & Art Gallery MUSEUM, GALLERY (https://brightonmuseums.org.uk; 19 New Church Rd; ⊙10am-5pm Mon, Tue & Thu-Sat, 2-5pm Sun) **FREE** Hove can justifiably claim to be the birthplace of British cinema, with the first short film shot here in 1898. You can see it alongside other fascinating films at this attractive Victorian villa. Another highlight is the kids' room, which is full of fairy lights and reverberates to the snores of a wizard and the whir of an underfloor train. It's 2 miles from Churchill Sq; take bus 1, 1A, 6 or 49 from there.

SEA LIFE Brighton AQUARIUM (☑ 01273-604234; www.visitsealife.com/brighton; Marine Pde; £19; ⊙10am-5pm; ⊞) Not just for children, this aquarium is an underground exhibition of nature's fascinating water creatures. Walking around the church-like interior, visitors can get up close to eels, tropical fish and other sealife. For those who are keen, there are opportunities to feed the animals, touch starfish and ride a glass-bottomed boat over a pool of sharks, rays and turtles.

West Pier WATERFRONT (www.westpier.co.uk) The historic West Pier, which closed in 1975, began to collapse into the sea in December 2002 and, having since caught fire twice, is just a dark shadow on the water. It's a sad end for this Victorian marvel, where the likes of Charlie Chaplin and Stan Laurel once performed. Nevertheless it's still quite an arresting, beautiful sight though the only flocks of visitors now are the thousands of starlings who swoop around it in winter.

🧭 Tours

Brighton Food Tours FOOD & DRINK (☑ 07985 230955; www.brightonfoodtours.com; Brighton Unitarian Church, New Rd; per person £40-65; ⊙Fri & Sat) Two enthusiastic local ladies show off the best of Brighton via a trail of tasters and tales. The walking tours highlight

up to 10 small and independent businesses, in keeping with the town's creative vibe. Tour options include Very Independent Brighton, Drink Brighton and Wine Rebellion. Bring comfy shoes and an empty stomach.

🎭 Festivals & Events

Brighton Festival PERFORMING ARTS (☑ 01273-709709; www.brightonfestival.org; ⊙May) After Edinburgh, this is the UK's biggest arts festival. It draws star performers from around the globe for three weeks by the sea.

Brighton Fringe PERFORMING ARTS (www.brightonfringe.org; ⊙May) As with the famous Edinburgh Festival, the Brighton Festival has its fringe, a month of irreverent comedy, art and theatre at numerous venues around the city.

Brighton Pride LGBT (www.brighton-pride.org; ⊙early Aug) The UK's biggest gay bash with a rainbow-hued parade and concerts in Preston Park.

🛏 Sleeping

Kipps Brighton HOSTEL £ (☑ 01273-604182; www.kipps-brighton.com; 76 Grand Pde; dm £15-35, d £42-92; @🖥) The owners of Canterbury's award-winning hostel have created equally commendable budget digs here in Brighton. There's a real cafe vibe around reception, and facilities include a communal kitchen. Free movie, pizza and pub nights are intended to seperate guests from their wi-fi-enabled devices.

Baggies Backpackers HOSTEL £ (☑ 01273-733740; www.baggiesbackpackers.com; 33 Oriental Pl; dm from £16; 🖥) With a warm, familial atmosphere, worn-in charm, attentive service and clean, snug dorms, this long-established hostel is a Brighton institution.There's a cosy basement music and chill-out room, and a TV lounge. The hostel has sister establishments in London and Bournemouth.

★ No 27 Brighton B&B ££ (☑ 01273-694951; www.brighton-bed-and-breakfast. co.uk; 27 Upper Rock Gardens; r £100-160; 🖥) Brighton's top B&B has five sumptuous rooms, perfectly done out with antique flourish. All the fabrics, furniture and decoration have been painstakingly selected to fit an understated theme, based on people related to King George IV. Some rooms have sea views, but the superb decor may have you looking around more than out.

Hotel Pelirocco
HOTEL ££

(📞 01273-327055; www.hotelpelirocco.co.uk; 10 Regency Sq; s/d from £59/89; 📶) One of Brighton's sexiest and nuttiest places to stay, the Pelirocco has become the ultimate venue for a flirty rock-and-roll weekend. Flamboyant rooms, some designed by artists, include the 'Lord Vader's Quarters' paying homage to Star Wars, the 'Modrophenia' room on a mod and pop art theme, and the 'Pretty Vacant' double, a shrine to the Sex Pistols.

Blanch House
BOUTIQUE HOTEL ££

(📞 01273-603504; www.blanchhouse.co.uk; 17 Atlingworth St; r from £110; 📶) Themed rooms are the name of the game at this boutique hotel, but there's nothing tacky about them – swish art deco styling rules in the Legacia Room, while the Snowstorm is a frosty vision in white and tinkling ice. The magnificently stylish fine-dining restaurant is all white leather banquettes and space-age swivel chairs and there's a fine cocktail bar.

Snooze
HOTEL ££

(📞 01273-605797; www.snoozebrighton.com; 25 St George's Tce; s/d from £75/95; 📶) The retro styling at this eccentric Kemptown pad features everything from vintage posters and bright '60s and '70s wallpaper to Bollywood film ads, floral sinks and mad clashes of colour. It's more than just a gimmick – the rooms are comfortable and spotless, and there are great meat-free breakfasts. You'll find it just off St James' St, about 500m east of New Steine.

★ Artist Residence
BOUTIQUE HOTEL £££

(📞 01273-324302; www.artistresidencebrighton. co.uk; 34 Regency Sq; d £120-290; 📶) Eclectic doesn't quite describe the rooms at this wonderful 23-room town-house hotel, set amid the splendour of Regency Sq. As befits the name, every bedroom is a work of funky art with bold wall murals, bespoke and vintage furniture, rough wood cladding and in-room roll-top baths. The Set Restaurant downstairs has a glowing reputation.

★ Hotel Una
BOUTIQUE HOTEL £££

(📞 01273-820464; www.hotel-una.co.uk; 55-56 Regency Sq; s £55-75, d £115-200, all incl breakfast; ✳📶) All of the 19 generous rooms here wow guests with their bold-patterned fabrics, supersized leather sofas, in-room free-standing baths and vegan, veggie or carnivorous breakfast in bed. Some, such as the two-level suite with its own mini-cinema, and the under-pavement chambers with their own spa, are truly show-stopping and not as expensive as you might expect.

Drakes
BOUTIQUE HOTEL £££

(📞 01273-696934; www.drakesofbrighton.com; 43-44 Marine Pde; r £115-300; 🅿✳@📶) This stylishly minimalist boutique hotel oozes understated class. So understated is the entrance, in fact, you could easily miss it. All rooms have similar decor in bold fabrics and European elm panelling, but it's the feature rooms everyone wants – their giant freestanding tubs are set in front of full-length bay windows with widescreen Channel views. The basement restaurant is superb.

✗ Eating

★ Iydea
VEGETARIAN £

(www.iydea.co.uk; 17 Kensington Gardens; mains £5-8; ⊙9.30am-5.30pm; 📶✎) Even by Brighton's high standards, the food at this multi-award-winning vegetarian cafe is a treat. The daily-changing choices of curries, lasagnes, felafel, enchiladas and quiches are full of flavour and can be washed down with a selection of vegan wines, organic ales and homemade lemonades. If you're on the hop, you can get any dish to takeaway in plastic-free packaging.

Wahaca
MEXICAN £

(📞 01273-934763; www.wahaca.co.uk; cnr North St & New Rd; mains £5-12; ⊙noon-11pm Mon-Sat, to 10.30pm Sun; 📶) ✐ The Brighton branch of this national chain is a bright, colourful affair where Mexican street food lands on multihued tables amid eclectic, retro decor. The recipes for the various tacos, tostados and burritos were brought home by the owner after travelling in Mexico, so authenticity is guaranteed. Lots of seats so there's always a free spot.

Choccywoccydoodah
CAFE £

(www.choccywoccydoodah.com; 3 Meeting House Lane; cakes & snacks £2-8; ⊙10am-6pm Mon-Sat, 11am-5pm Sun) Even if you're not hungry or thirsty, this incredible chocolate emporium, painted blood red inside and out, is a must-see. The downstairs is packed with outrageous chocolate creations, fake rococo mirrors, sprays of artificial flowers and tassled lampshades. Head upstairs to the small cafe where every item on sale contains chocolate. Madly popular so be prepared to queue.

DON'T MISS

THE LANES

In the market for a pair of vegan shoes, a gauche portrait of a Lego man or a letter opener in the shape of a ...? Well, whatever item you yearn for, old or new, you'll probably find it in Brighton. Visit Brighton produces a useful *Shopping, Eating and Drinking Guide* that divides the city up into its main areas.

The tightly packed **Lanes** is the most popular shopping district, its every twist and turn jam-packed with jewellers and gift shops, coffee shops and boutiques selling everything from antique firearms to hard-to-find vinyl.

There's another, less-claustrophobic shopping district in **North Laine**, a series of partially pedestrianised thoroughfares north of the Lanes, including Bond, Gardner, Kensington and Sydney Sts, lined with retro-cool boutiques and bohemian cafes.

Infinity Foods Kitchen VEGETARIAN £
(www.infinityfoodskitchen.co.uk; 50 Gardner St; mains £4-9; ⊘9am-5pm Mon-Sat, 10am-4pm Sun; 🛜🖋) The sister establishment of Infinity Foods wholefoods shop (health-food cooperative and Brighton institution) serves a wide variety of vegetarian and organic food, with many vegan and wheat- or gluten-free options including tofu burgers, mezze platters and veggie sausage sandwiches. There's seating upstairs with views of the passing hipster mob and wooden takeaway cutlery to reduce plastic waste.

⭐ **Terre à Terre** VEGETARIAN ££
(☑01273-729051; www.terreaterre.co.uk; 71 East St; mains from £15; ⊘noon-10.30pm Tue-Fri, 11am-11pm Sat, 11am-10pm Sun; 🖋🖺) Take your taste buds around the world without any meat in sight. In this vegetarian restaurant, inventive and flavourful dishes are meticulously plated and the ambience is casual and friendly. For the unconverted, there are nods to nonvegetarian favourites, including battered halloumi and chips, and KFC (Korean Fried Cauliflower). Order the sharing plate for statement elements of the main dishes.

English's of Brighton SEAFOOD ££
(☑01273-327980; www.englishs.co.uk; 29-31 East St; mains £10-30; ⊘noon-10pm) A 75-year-old institution and celebrity haunt, this local seafood paradise dishes up everything from Essex oysters to locally caught lobster and Dover sole. It's converted from fishers' cottages, with shades of the elegant style of the Edwardian era inside, and has alfresco dining on the pedestrian square outside.

Riddle & Finns SEAFOOD ££
(☑01273-721667; www.riddleandfinns.co.uk; 12b Meeting House Lane; mains £14.50-22.50; ⊘noon-10pm Sun-Fri, 11.30am-11pm Sat) Regarded as the town's most refined seafood spot, R&F is light on gimmicky interiors (think white butcher-shop tiles, marble tables and candles) but heavy on taste. With the kitchen open to the street outside, chefs put on a public cooking class with every dish as they prepare your smoked haddock in champagne sauce or some wild sea bass.

Indian Summer INDIAN ££
(☑01273-711001; www.indiansummerbrighton.co.uk; 70 East St; lunch mains £6-14, 2/3 course set dinner menu £28/33; ⊘6-10.30pm Mon-Wed, noon-3pm & 6-10.30pm Thu & Fri, noon-10.30pm Sat, noon-3pm & 6-10pm Sun; 🖋🖺) Brighton's best Indian outfit boasts typical British Indian decor (think high-back, leatherette chairs and modern fittings) and serves a multitude of dishes from across the subcontinent. There's a kids' menu, lots of meat-free choices and rare dishes such as Indian mussels and beef. Regularly voted one of the UK's best Indian restaurants.

Food for Friends VEGETARIAN ££
(☑01273-202310; www.foodforfriends.com; 17-18 Prince Albert St; mains £6-16; ⊘noon-10pm Sun-Thu, to 10.30pm Fri & Sat; 🖋) An ever-inventive choice of vegetarian and vegan food keeps bringing locals back for seconds and thirds at this place to see and be seen – literally, by every passerby through the huge street-side windows. Kept fresh-looking and as popular as it has been since 1981, you should be prepared to wait for a table on busy shopping days.

Gingerman MODERN EUROPEAN ££
(☑01273-326688; www.gingermanrestaurants.com; 21a Norfolk Sq; 2-/3-course menu £17/20; ⊘12.30-2pm & 7-10pm Tue-Sun) Hastings seafood, Sussex beef, Romney Marsh lamb, local sparkling wines and countless other seasonal, local and British treats go into the adroitly flash-fried and slow-cooked dishes served at this snug 32-cover eatery. Reservations are advised. Norfolk Sq is a short walk west along Western Rd from the Churchill Sq shopping centre.

Isaac At
BRITISH £££

(☑ 07765 934740; www.isaac-at.com; 2 Gloucester St; tasting menu £55, set menu £40; ⊙ 6.30-
10.30pm Tue-Fri, 12.30-2.30pm & 6.30-10.30pm
Sat) ◢ Tucked on a street corner is this intimate fine-dining restaurant run by a small
team of culinary talent, all aged under 30.
Every ingredient is locally sourced, including the wines, with food miles for each ingredient noted on the menu. It's probably
the homeliest high-end dining experience
in the area. First-class, fresh and thoughtful
food.

♟ Drinking & Nightlife

Concorde 2
CLUB

(www.concorde2.co.uk; Madeira Dr; ☎) Brighton's best-known and best-loved club is a
disarmingly unpretentious den, where DJ
Fatboy Slim pioneered the Big Beat Boutique and still occasionally graces the decks.
Each month there's a huge variety of club
nights, live bands and concerts by international names.

Patterns
CLUB

(www.patternsbrighton.com; 10 Marine Pde;
⊙ Wed-Sat, hours vary; ☎) Some of the city's
top club nights are held at this ear-numbing
venue. The music is top priority here, attracting big name acts and a young, up-for-it
crowd.

Coalition
BAR

(www.coalitionbrighton.com; 171-181 Kings Rd
Arches; ⊙ 10am-5am Mon-Fri, to 7am Sat; ☎) On
a summer's day, there's nowhere finer to
sit and watch the world go by than at this
popular beach bar, diner and club. All sorts
of events happen here, from comedy to live
music and club nights.

Black Dove
PUB

(www.blackdovebrighton.com; 74 St James's St;
⊙ 4pm-late) Eclectic hang-out with shabby-chic furnishings, huge antique ceiling
fans, a bar stocked with unusual tipples
and a quirky basement snug. Live acoustic
music and local DJs provide the soundtrack
for evening quaffing that spills out onto the
pavements when the mercury is high.

Dorset
PUB

(www.thedorset.co.uk; 28 North Rd; ⊙ 9.30am-mid-
night Sun-Thu, to 1am Fri & Sat; ☎) In fine weather this laid-back Brighton institution throws
open its doors and windows, and tables spill
out onto the pavement. You'll be just as welcome for a morning coffee as for an evening
pint here, and should you not leave between
the two, there's a decent gastropub menu.

☆ Entertainment

Komedia Theatre
COMEDY

(☑ 01273-647100; www.komedia.co.uk; 44-47
Gardner St) The UK's top comedy venue

CANTERBURY & SOUTHEAST ENGLAND BRIGHTON & HOVE

GAY & LESBIAN BRIGHTON

Brighton has the most vibrant LGBT community in the country outside London. Kemptown (aka Camptown) on and off St James's St is where it's all at. The old Brunswick
Town area of Hove is a quieter alternative to the traditionally cruisy (and sometimes
seedy) scene in Kemptown.

For up-to-date information on the LGBT scene in Brighton, check out www.realbright-
on.com, or pick up the free monthly magazine *Gscene* (www.gscene.com) from LGBT
venues.

Brighton Rocks (☑ 01273-600550; www.brightonrocksbar.co.uk; 6 Rock Pl; ⊙ 4-11pm Mon-
Thu, noon-1am Fri & Sat, noon-9pm Sun; ☎) Incongruously located in an alley of garages
and used-car lots, this cocktail bar is firmly established on the Kemptown gay scene,
but welcomes all-comers with Sussex martinis, well-executed plates of food and theme
parties.

Legends Club (www.legendsbrighton.com; 31-34 Marine Pde; ⊙ bar 11am-5am, club 10pm-
5am Wed & Fri-Sun; ☎) Located beneath the Legends Hotel this is arguably the best gay
bar and club in town.

A Bar (☑ 01273-688826; 11-12 Marine Pde; ⊙ noon-2am; ☎) Extremely hip bar and sauna in
the Amsterdam Hotel; its sun terrace is a particular hit.

Queen's Arms (www.theqabrighton.com; 7 George St; ⊙ 5pm-late Mon-Fri, from 2pm Sat &
Sun) And they ain't talking Victoria or Elizabeth! Plenty of camp cabaret and karaoke at
this pub.

attracts the best stand-up acts from the English-speaking world. Book well in advance.

The Old Market
THEATRE

(☑ 01273-201801; www.theoldmarket.com; 11a Upper Market St) TOM has emerged as Hove's top venue for alternative theatre, comedy and live music, all performed in front of small crowds seated cafe-style in an informal space. The stage sees an eclectic mix to say the least with everything from grotesque mime and gay comedy to quirky Shakespeare and local bands on the programme.

Brighton Dome
THEATRE

(☑ 01273-709709; www.brightondome.org; Church St) Once the stables for King George IV's horses, this art deco complex houses three theatre venues within the Royal Pavilion estate. ABBA famously won the 1974 Eurovision Song Contest here. The Dome was under renovation at time of research.

❶ Information

Incredibly, Brighton closed its busy tourist office in 2013, replacing it with 15 information points across the city, mostly racks of brochures in hotels, shops and museums (two of these aren't even in Brighton itself). Contact **Visit Brighton** (☑ 01273-290337; www.visitbrighton.com) for information.

❶ Getting There & Away

BUS

Standard bus connections:

Eastbourne (Bus 12; £4.60, 75 minutes, up to every 10 minutes)

Lewes (Bus 28/29; £3.10, 30 minutes, up to every 10 minutes)

London Victoria (National Express; from £9, 2½ hours, at least every two hours)

TRAIN

London-bound services pass through Gatwick Airport (£8.80, 25 to 35 minutes, up to five hourly).

Arundel (£10.80, 1¼ hours, half-hourly) Change in Barnham.

Chichester (£13.60, 50 minutes, half-hourly)

Eastbourne (£11.10, 30 to 40 minutes, half-hourly)

Hastings (£13.90, one hour to 80 minutes, two hourly)

London St Pancras (£18.10, 1¼ hours, half-hourly)

London Victoria (£26.70, one hour, three-hourly)

Portsmouth (£16, 1½ hours, hourly)

❶ Getting Around

Day bus tickets (£5) are available from the drivers of all Brighton & Hove buses. Alternatively, a £3.70 PlusBus ticket on top of your rail fare gives unlimited bus travel for the day.

The city operates a pricey pay-and-display parking scheme. In the town centre, it costs between £1 and £3.60 per hour for a maximum stay of two hours. Alternatively, there's a Park & Ride 2.5 miles northwest of the centre at Withdean, from where bus 27 (return £5) zips into town.

Cab companies include **Brighton Streamline Taxis** (☑ 01273-202020; www.streamline-taxis.org) and **Brighton & Hove Radio Cabs** (☑ 01273-204060; www.brightontaxis.com) and there's a taxi rank at the junction of East and Market Sts.

WEST SUSSEX

West Sussex offers a welcome respite from fast-paced adventures. The serene hills and valleys of the South Downs ripple across the county, fringed by sheltered coastline. Beautiful Arundel and cultured Chichester make good bases from which to explore the county's winding country lanes and remarkable Roman ruins.

Arundel

☑ 01903 / POP 3500

Arguably the prettiest town in West Sussex, Arundel is clustered around a vast fairy-tale castle, and its hillside streets overflow with antique emporiums, teashops and a host of eateries. While much of the town appears medieval – the whimsical castle has been home to the dukes of Norfolk for centuries – most of it dates back to Victorian times.

◉ Sights

Arundel Castle
CASTLE

(www.arundelcastle.org; adult/concession/child £22/19.50/11; ⊙ 10am-5pm Tue-Sun Easter-Oct) Arundel Castle was first built in the 11th century but all that's left of the early structure are the modest remains of the keep. It was ransacked during the English Civil War, and most of what you see today is the result of reconstruction by the eighth, 11th and 15th dukes of Norfolk between 1718 and 1900. The current Duke still lives in part of the castle, whose highlights include the atmospheric keep, the massive Great Hall and the library.

Arundel Cathedral CATHEDRAL

(www.arundelcathedral.org; London Rd; ⏱9am-6pm Apr-Oct, to dusk Nov-Mar) **FREE** Arundel's ostentatious 19th-century Catholic cathedral is one of the dominating features on the town's impressive skyline. Commissioned by the 15th Duke of Norfolk in 1868, the impressive structure was designed by Joseph Aloysius Hansom (inventor of the Hansom cab) in the French Gothic style, but shows much Victorian economy and restraint. Although small for a cathedral – it holds just 500 worshippers – Hansom's clever layout makes the building seem a lot bigger.

🛏 Sleeping & Eating

Arundel House B&B ££

(☎01903-882136; www.arundelhouseonline.com; 11 High St; d/ste from £90/125; 🛜) The contemporary chambers at this lovely 'restaurant with rooms' may be slightly low-ceilinged, but they're clean-cut and very comfortable, with showers big enough for two. The restaurant downstairs serves some of the best food in Arundel, which, happily, extends to breakfast.

Arden Guest House B&B ££

(☎01903-884184; www.ardenhousearundel.com; 4 Queens Lane; d £99, without bathroom £89; 🅿🛜) For the classic British B&B experience, head to this seven-room guesthouse just over the river from the historical centre. Rooms are kept fresh and tick all the boxes, the hosts are amiable, and the breakfasts are cooked. Only 10% off if you're travelling solo.

★ Town House BRITISH £££

(☎01903-883847; www.thetownhouse.co.uk; 65 High St; set lunch/dinner from £17.50/25.50; ⏱noon-2.30pm & 7-9.30pm Tue-Sat) The only thing that rivals the 16th-century Florentine gilded-walnut ceiling in this compact and very elegant eatery is the sparkling atmosphere and acclaimed British cuisine with a European twist. Dishes such as South Downs venison, south coast cod and roasted partridge are worth a little bit extra – but book ahead. Town House also has well-appointed rooms to let.

❶ Getting There & Away

Arundel has the following train connections:
Brighton (£10.80, 1¼ hours, half-hourly) Change at Barnham or Ford.
Chichester (£4.70, 22 minutes, twice hourly) Change at Ford or Barnham.
London Victoria (£18.70, 1½ hours, twice hourly)

Chichester

📋01243 / POP 26,800

A lively Georgian market town still almost encircled by its medieval town walls, the administrative capital of West Sussex keeps watch over the plains between the South Downs and the sea. Visitors flock to Chichester's splendid cathedral, streets of handsome 18th-century town houses and its famous theatre, and of course to its pedestrianised shopping streets packed with big-name and independent shops. A Roman port garrison in its early days, the town is also a launch pad to other fascinating Roman remains, as well as to Arundel and a popular stretch of coast.

◉ Sights

Chichester Cathedral CATHEDRAL

(www.chichestercathedral.org.uk; West St; ⏱7.15am-7pm, free tours 11.15am & 2.30pm Mon-Sat) This understated cathedral was begun in 1075 and largely rebuilt in the 13th century. The free-standing church tower went up in the 15th century; the spire dates from the 19th century, when its predecessor famously toppled over. Inside, three storeys of beautiful arches sweep upwards and Romanesque carvings are dotted around. Interesting features to track down include a smudgy stained-glass window added by artist Marc Chagall in 1978 and a glassed-over section of Roman mosaic flooring.

CANTERBURY & SOUTHEAST ENGLAND CHICHESTER

FISHBOURNE ROMAN PALACE

Fishbourne (www.sussexpast.co.uk; Roman Way; adult/concession/child £9.50/8.80/4.90; ⏱10am-5pm Mar-Oct, reduced hours & days rest of the year) is the largest-known Roman residence in Britain. The palace lies 1.5 miles west of Chichester, just off the A259 (take bus 700 from outside Chichester Cathedral). Happened upon by labourers in the 1960s, it's thought that this once-luxurious mansion was built around AD 75 for a romanised local king. Housed in a modern pavilion are its foundations, hypocaust and painstakingly relaid mosaics.

The centrepiece is a spectacular floor depicting Cupid riding a dolphin, flanked by sea horses and panthers. There's also a fascinating little museum and replanted Roman gardens.

Pallant House Gallery   GALLERY
(www.pallant.org.uk; 9 North Pallant; adult/child £11/
free; ⊙10am-5pm Tue, Wed, Fri & Sat, to 8pm Thu,
11am-5pm Sun) A Queen Anne mansion built
by a local wine merchant, handsome Pallant
House and a 21st-century wing host this superb gallery. The focus is on mostly British,
20th-century art. Show-stoppers Patrick
Caulfield, Lucian Freud, Graham Sutherland,
Frank Auerbach and Henry Moore are interspersed with international names such as
Emil Filla, Le Corbusier and RB Kitaj. Most
of the older works are in the mansion, while
the newer wing is packed with pop art and
temporary modern and contemporary work.

Chichester City Walls   ARCHITECTURE
(www.chichestercitywalls.org) Chichester's almost complete ring of Roman defensive
walls are around 1.5 miles in length, and
provide a pleasant escape from the retail
bustle they now contain. Pick up a leaflet
and booklet from the tourist office (p172)
and head out along the route, much of which
leads through parkland. Built to defend the
town of Noviomagus Reginorum 1800 years
ago, they are just about the most intact set
of Roman city walls in Britain. Best accessed
from West or East Sts.

Novium Museum   MUSEUM
(www.thenovium.org; Tower St; ⊙10am-5pm
Mon-Sat, to 4pm Sun Apr-Oct, 10am-5pm Mon-Sat
Nov-Mar) FREE Chichester's purpose-built
museum provides a home for the eclectic
collections of the erstwhile District Museum,
as well as some artefacts from Fishbourne
Palace and a huge mosaic from Chilgrove Roman villa. The highlight is the set of Roman
thermae (baths) discovered in the 1970s,
around which this six-million-pound wedge
of architecture was designed.

🛏 Sleeping & Eating

Trents   B&B ££
(☎01243-773714; 50 South St; d from £64; 🛜)
One of very few places to hit the sack in the
thick of the city centre action, the five snazzy
rooms above this trendy bar-restaurant are
understandably popular. Guests heap praise
on the helpful staff and big breakfast.

**Chichester
Harbour Hotel**   BOUTIQUE HOTEL £££
(☎01243-778000; www.chichester-harbour-hotel.
co.uk; North St; s/d from £112/162; 🛜) Big flashes of colour dominate the period rooms at
this Georgian hotel. It's the most enticing
option in town and it also boasts a stylish
restaurant. Book well ahead.

Duke & Rye   AMERICAN £
(www.thedukeandrye.co.uk; 14 West St; mains £4-
14; ⊙11am-11pm Mon-Sat, noon-8pm Sun; 🛜)
Occupying a large deconsecrated church opposite Chichester Cathedral, this temple of
food and ale allows you to refuel and kick
back in an incongruously ecclesiastical setting, dotted with shabby-chic areas of funky
wallpaper, frilly standard lamps and Persian
carpets. The US diner-style menu of burgers
and sundaes is sure to bust your bible belt
and invoke a holy thirst.

❶ Information

Tourist Office (☎01243-775888; www.
visitchichester.org; Tower St; ⊙10am-5pm
Mon-Sat, to 4pm Sun) Located in the Novium
Museum.

❶ Getting There & Away

BUS

Chichester has bus connections to the following:
Brighton (Bus 700; three hours, £5, twice
hourly)
London Victoria (National Express; £23,
three hours 40 minutes, eight daily) Change at
Gatwick Airport.
Portsmouth (Bus 700; £4.70, one hour 10
minutes, twice hourly)

TRAIN

Chichester has train connections to the
following:
Arundel (£4.70, 22 minutes, twice hourly)
Change at Ford or Barnham.
Brighton (£13.60, 50 minutes, half-hourly)
London Victoria (£18.70, 1½ hours, half-
hourly)
Portsmouth (£7.90, 30 to 40 minutes, three
hourly)

Oxford & the Cotswolds

Best Places to Eat

➡ Hind's Head (p216)

➡ Spiced Roots (p185)

➡ Magdalen Arms (p185)

➡ Edamamé (p184)

➡ Le Champignon Sauvage (p207)

➡ Waterside Inn (p216)

Best Places to Stay

➡ Star Cottage (p193)

➡ Barnsley House (p193)

➡ Glove House (p189)

➡ Bradley (p206)

➡ Oxford Coach & Horses (p182)

➡ Wheatsheaf (p196)

Why Go?

Sprinkled with gorgeous villages and medieval towns, the part of England that stretches westwards from London to Wales comes as close to an old-world idyll as you'll ever find. It's a haven of green-cloaked hills, rose-clad cottages, graceful churches and thatched roofs. Add the university city of Oxford to this alluring mix, with its majestic architecture and youthful scene, and it's obvious why the region is a magnet for visitors.

Although the roads are busy in summer, it's easy to escape the tourist trail. The golden-hued Cotswolds work their finest magic when you find your own romantic hideaway. Splendid country houses lie tucked away throughout Buckinghamshire, Bedfordshire and Hertfordshire, while Windsor boasts the world's largest castle. Further west, the Forest of Dean offers the promise of outdoor adventure.

While individual destinations can be seen on easy day trips from London, both Oxford and the Cotswolds deserve several leisurely days.

When to Go

➡ Welcome the dawn with Oxford's Magdalen College Choir, as it sings hymns from atop the college tower to greet May Morning (1 May).

➡ In July, sip champagne and watch the rowers whizzing by at Henley Royal Regatta.

➡ Walking in the Cotswolds is ideal from April to June and in September, when the weather is (mostly) in your favour, without the July and August crowds.

➡ In early October, Cheltenham kicks into bookish action for its famous 10-day Literature Festival.

➡ Mingle with hobnobbing aristocrats in June at the country's greatest annual racing meet, Royal Ascot.

Oxford & the Cotswolds Highlights

❶ **Oxford** (p175) Following in the inspirational footsteps of literary greats as you explore magical colleges.

❷ **The Cotswolds** (p189)

Strolling through perfect gold-tinged Cotswolds villages.

❸ **Windsor** (p212) Catching a glimpse of how royalty relaxes at the Queen's weekend hideaway.

❹ **Blenheim Palace** (p188) Lording it up at one of Britain's greatest stately homes, in Woodstock.

❺ **Stowe Gardens** (p211) Getting lost in a serene world

of spectacular 18th-century landscaped gardens.

❻ **Gloucester Cathedral** (p208) Strolling the elegant cloisters of this exquisite Perpendicular Gothic creation.

❼ **Painswick** (p202) Meandering around a beautiful and unspoilt town.

❽ **The Making of Harry Potter** (p210) Unleashing your inner wizard in Leavesden.

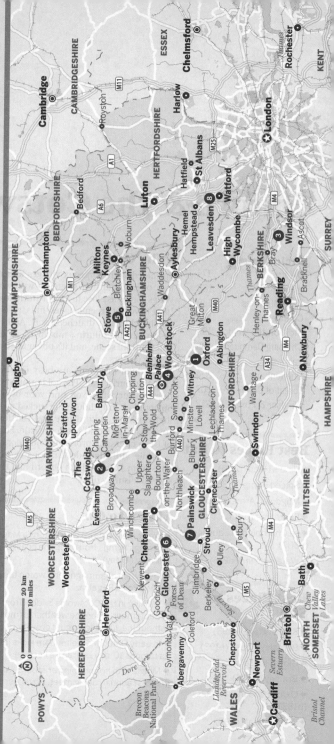

ℹ Getting There & Around

A car will give you the greatest freedom, especially if you want to explore the scattered villages of the Cotswolds.

Local buses, run by various operators, link larger towns to each other and to surrounding villages. For timetables, use the journey planner tool on Traveline (www.traveline.info).

Oxford, Moreton-in-Marsh, Stroud, Cheltenham, Gloucester, Bletchley, Hatfield, St Albans, Henley-on-Thames and Windsor are plugged into the train network; all have services to London, in most cases direct. Other direct trains go as far as Birmingham, Manchester and Newcastle (from Oxford), and Cardiff, Edinburgh and Exeter (from Cheltenham).

OXFORD

📞 01865 / POP 161,300

A gloriously mellow ensemble of golden-hued wonders, Oxford unquestionably ranks among England's most beautiful cities. In fact, as you stroll through its historic and homogenous core, it can be hard to believe you're in modern England at all. Certain specific buildings stand out, like the domed and glowing Radcliffe Camera, and you can admire masterpieces by such great architects as Sir Christopher Wren and Nicholas Hawksmoor. Really, though, the joy of visiting Oxford lies in the sheer cumulative splendour of college after century-old college, each playing its own permutation of Gothic chapels, secluded cloisters, and tranquil quadrangles.

History

Strategically placed at the confluence of the Rivers Cherwell and Thames (called the Isis here, from the Latin Tamesis), Oxford was a key Saxon town, heavily fortified by Alfred the Great during the war against the Danes. It continued to grow under the Normans, who founded its castle in 1071.

By the 11th century, the Augustinian abbey in Oxford had begun training clerics, and when Anglo-Norman clerical scholars were expelled from the Sorbonne in 1167, the abbey began to attract students in droves. The first three colleges – University, Balliol and Merton – were founded in the mid-13th century. Alongside Oxford's growing prosperity grew the enmity between local townspeople and new students ('town and gown'), culminating in the St Scholastica's Day Massacre in 1355, which started as an argument over beer but resulted in 90 deaths. Thereafter, the king ordered that the university be broken up into colleges, each of which developed its own traditions.

The university, largely a religious entity at the time, was rocked in the 16th century by the Reformation; the public trials and burning at the stake of Protestant heretics under Mary I; and by the subsequent hanging, drawing and quartering of Catholics under her successor Elizabeth I. As the Royalist headquarters, Oxford backed the losing side during the Civil War, but flourished after the restoration of the monarchy, with some of its most notable buildings constructed in the late 17th and early 18th centuries.

The arrival of the canal system in 1790 had a profound effect on Oxford. By creating a link with the Midlands' industrial centres, work and trade suddenly expanded beyond the academic core. This was further strengthened by the construction of the railways in the 19th century.

The city's real industrial boom came, however, when William Morris began producing cars here in 1913. With the success of his Bullnose Morris and Morris Minor, his Cowley factory went on to become one of the largest motor plants in the world. Although works have been scaled down since, Minis still run off BMW's Cowley production line today.

◉ Sights

Oxford is a compact little town, with its major sights largely congregated in the centre. Almost all, including the Bodleian Library and the Ashmolean Museum, are connected with the university, while several of the university colleges are themselves prime visitor attractions.

◉ City Centre

★ **Bodleian Library**   LIBRARY
(📞01865-287400; www.bodleian.ox.ac.uk/bodley; Catte St; Divinity School £1, with audio tour £3.50, guided tours £6-14; ⊙9am-5pm Mon-Sat, from 11am Sun) At least five kings, dozens of prime ministers and Nobel laureates, and luminaries such as Oscar Wilde, CS Lewis and JRR Tolkien have studied in Oxford's Bodleian Library, a magnificent survivor from the Middle Ages. Wander into its central 17th-century quad, and you can admire its ancient buildings for free, while it costs just £1 to enter the most impressive of these, the

15th-century Divinity School. To see the rest of the complex, though, you'll have to join a guided tour.

All tours, including the two most popular daily options – the 'mini-tour' (30 minutes, £6) and the 'standard tour' (one hour, £8) – start in the ornate medieval **Divinity School**, the university's earliest teaching room. A superb specimen of English Gothic architecture, it was founded around 1423. Inspect its fan-vaulted ceiling closely, and you'll spot the initials of benefactors, including Thomas Kemp, who features 84 times, who worked on it, as well as three 'Green Men'. In the Harry Potter films, the Divinity School served as the Hogwarts hospital wing.

Every tour also includes on the upper level, which dates from 1488. Visitors are not allowed to enter this magnificently decorated medieval room, or peruse the ancient tomes that it contains, just admire it from the adjoining 17th-century extension. It too featured in the Harry Potter films, as Hogwarts' library.

The standard tours additionally take in two grand chambers at the far end of the Divinity School – **Convocation House**, which hosted the English Parliament three times, once under Charles I and twice under Charles II, and the **Chancellor's Court**, in which Oscar Wilde and Romantic poet Percy Bysshe Shelley went on trial (for debt and promoting atheism, respectively).

Less frequent 'extended tours' cover the same ground while also offering the only public access to the nearby **Radcliffe Camera**, which houses part of the Bodleian's collection. The 'Upstairs, Downstairs' tour (9.15am Wednesday and Saturday, 1½ hours, £14) leads visitors along the underground **Gladstone Link** that connects the main library with the Camera, while the 'Explore the Reading Rooms' tour (11.15am and 1.15pm Sunday, 1½ hours, £14) spends more time in the Camera itself.

Check tour times online or at the information desk; tickets for all tours can be purchased up to two weeks in advance. Note also that a selection of 'Bodleian Treasures' is displayed in the nearby **Weston Library** (www.bodleian.ox.ac.uk/weston; Broad St; ⊙10am-5pm Mon-Sat, from 11am Sun) `FREE`.

★**Christ Church**   COLLEGE
(☎01865-276492; www.chch.ox.ac.uk; St Aldate's; adult/child Jul & Aug £10/9, Sep-Jun £8/7; ⊙10am-5pm Mon-Sat, from 2pm Sun, last admission 4.15pm) With its compelling combination of majestic architecture, literary heritage and double identity as (parts of) Harry Potter's Hogwarts, Christ Church attracts tourists galore. Among Oxford's largest colleges – *the* largest, if you include its bucolic meadow – and proud possessor of its most impressive quad, plus a superb art gallery and even a cathedral, it was founded in 1525 by Cardinal Wolsey. It later became home to Lewis Carroll, whose picnic excursions with the then-dean's daughter gave us *Alice in Wonderland*.

The main entrance to Christ Church, Tom Gate, stands immediately below the imposing 17th-century **Tom Tower**. Sir Christopher Wren, who studied at Christ Church, was responsible for its topmost portions. Pass by at 9.05pm, and you'll hear 101 chimes from its 6-tonne bell, **Great Tom**, to commemorate the curfew inflicted on the college's original students.

All visitors, however, enter further south along St Aldate's, walking through the gardens to reach Meadow Gate (where there may be queues). From there, the self-guided tour route leads to the Renaissance **Great Hall**, the college's jaw-dropping dining room, with its hammer-beam roof and portraits of past scholars including Lewis Carroll and an entire troop of British prime ministers who studied here. It's often closed to visitors at lunchtime, between noon and 2pm.

If the Great Hall looks awfully familiar, that may be because it starred as Hogwarts' dining hall in the Harry Potter films. Although the movie-screen hall was mocked up in the studio, the fan-vaulted staircase via which you enter it appeared in *Harry Potter and the Philosopher's Stone*, as the spot where Professor McGonagall welcomes Harry.

PORT MEADOW

Although archaeologists have identified traces of Bronze and Iron Age settlements bulging from this marshy Thameside meadow, northwest of Jericho, it has remained untouched, never even ploughed, ever since. A treasure trove of rare plants, it's still grazed by cows and horses, but it's also hugely popular with walkers (heading perhaps for The Trout pub) and runners. In winter it gets so waterlogged that hikers have to go round the edge rather than cutting straight across.

The route then crosses one side of **Tom Quad** – Oxford's largest and most impressive quadrangle, overlooked by Tom Tower and with a statue of Mercury adorning its pond – to reach **Christ Church Cathedral** (☑ 01865-276150; www.chch.ox.ac.uk/cathedral; St Aldate's; ☉ 10am-5pm Mon-Sat, from 2pm Sun, last entry 4.15) **FREE**. It stands on the site where the shrine of St Frideswide, Oxford's patron saint, was erected during the 8th century. The cathedral itself was built as the priory church during the 12th century, and became the college chapel when Cardinal Wolsey established what he called Cardinal College in 1525.

Long one of Oxford's wealthiest colleges, Christ Church has amassed an exceptional art collection. Displayed in the small **Christ Church Picture Gallery** (☑ 01865-276172; www.chch.ox.ac.uk/gallery; Oriel Sq; adult/child £4/2; ☉ 10.30am-5pm Mon-Sat, from 2pm Sun Jul-Sep, closed Tue Jun, shorter hours Oct-May, last admission always 45min before closing), added during the 1960s, it includes painting and drawings by Tintoretto, Michelangelo and other Renaissance masters.

Stretching away south and east of the college, and accessible free of charge, **Christ Church Meadow** (www.chch.ox.ac.uk; St Aldate's; ☉ dawn-dusk) **FREE**, a verdant expanse bordered by the Cherwell and Thames (or Isis) rivers, is ideal for a leisurely half-hour walk. Look out for the college's own herd of longhorn cattle.

Bridge of Sighs
BRIDGE
(Hertford Bridge; New College Lane) As you stroll along New College Lane, look up at the steeped Bridge of Sighs linking the two halves of Hertford College. Completed in 1914, it's sometimes erroneously referred to as a copy of the famous bridge in Venice, but it looks much more like that city's Rialto Bridge.

Radcliffe Camera
LIBRARY
(☑ 01865-287400; www.bodleian.ox.ac.uk; Radcliffe Sq; tours £14; ☉ Bodleian tours 9.15am Wed & Sat, 11.15am & 1.15pm Sun) Surely Oxford's most photographed landmark, the sandy-gold Radcliffe Camera is a beautiful, light-filled, circular, columned library. Built between 1737 and 1749 in grand Palladian style, as 'Radcliffe Library', it's topped by Britain's third-largest dome. It's only been a 'camera', which simply means 'room', since 1860, when it lost its independence and became what it remains, a reading room of the Bodleian Library. The only way for nonmembers to see the interior is on an extended 1½-hour tour of the Bodleian (p175).

Balliol College
COLLEGE
(☑ 01865-277777; www.balliol.ox.ac.uk; Broad St; adult/child £3/1; ☉ 10am-5pm, to dusk in winter) Dating its foundation to 'about' 1263, Balliol College claims to be the oldest college in Oxford, though its current buildings are largely 19th-century. Scorch marks on the huge Gothic wooden doors between its inner and outer quadrangles, however, supposedly date from the public burning of three Protestant bishops, including Archbishop of Canterbury Thomas Cranmer, in 1556.

Exeter College
COLLEGE
(☑ 01865-279600; www.exeter.ox.ac.uk; Turl St; ☉ 2-5pm) **FREE** Founded in 1314, Exeter is known for its elaborate 17th-century dining hall, which celebrated its 400th birthday in 2018, and ornate Victorian Gothic chapel, a psychedelic blast of gold mosaic and stained glass that holds a tapestry created by former students William Morris and Edward Burne Jones, *The Adoration of the Magi*. Exeter also inspired former student Philip Pullman to create fictional Jordan College in *His Dark Materials*.

Merton College
COLLEGE
(☑ 01865-276310; www.merton.ox.ac.uk; Merton St; adult/child £3/free; ☉ 2-5pm Mon-Fri, from 10am Sat & Sun) Founded in 1264, peaceful and elegant Merton is one of Oxford's three original colleges. Like the other two, Balliol and University, it considers itself the oldest, arguing that it was the first to adopt collegiate planning, bringing scholars and tutors together into a formal community and providing them with a planned residence. Its distinguishing architectural features

---

TOLKIEN'S RESTING PLACE

Lord of the Rings author JRR Tolkien (1892–1973) is buried with his wife Edith at **Wolvercote Cemetery** (Banbury Rd, Wolvercote; ☉ 7am-8pm Mon-Fri, from 8am Sat & Sun Apr-Sep, to 5pm Oct-Mar) **FREE**, 2.5 miles north of Oxford city centre. Their gravestone bears the names Beren (for him) and Lúthien (for her), referencing the love between a mortal man and an elf maiden who gave up her immortality to be with him.

Oxford

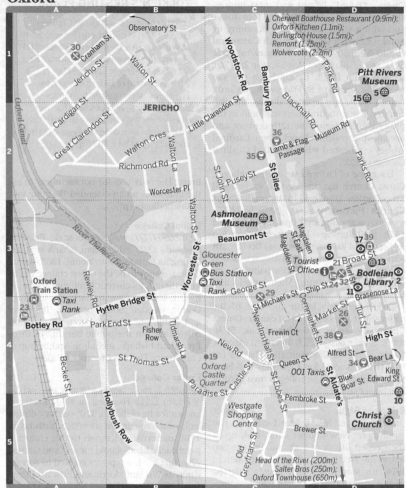

Cherwell Boathouse Restaurant (0.9mi);
Oxford Kitchen (1.1mi);
Burlington House (1.5mi);
Remont (1.75mi);
Wolvercote (2.7mi)

include large gargoyles, whose expressions suggest that they're about to throw up, and the charming, diminutive 14th-century **Mob Quad** – the first college quad.

New College
COLLEGE

(☎ 01865-279500; www.new.ox.ac.uk; Holywell St; adult/child £5/4; ⏰ 11am-5pm Easter-Oct, 2-4pm Nov-Feb) New College isn't really *that* new. Established in 1379 as Oxford's first undergraduate college, it's a glorious Perpendicular Gothic ensemble. Treasures in the chapel include superb medieval stained glass and Sir Jacob Epstein's disturbing 1951 statue of Lazarus, wrapped in his grave shroud; in

term time, visitors can attend the beautiful choral Evensong service (6.15pm nightly). The 15th-century cloisters and evergreen oak featured in *Harry Potter and the Goblet of Fire*, while the dining hall is the oldest in Oxbridge.

Trinity College
COLLEGE

(☎ 01865-279900; www.trinity.ox.ac.uk; Broad St; adult/child £3/2; ⏰ 9.30am-noon & 2pm-dusk) Founded in 1555, this small college boasts a lovely 17th-century garden quad, designed by Sir Christopher Wren. Its exquisite chapel, a masterpiece of English baroque, contains a limewood altar screen adorned with

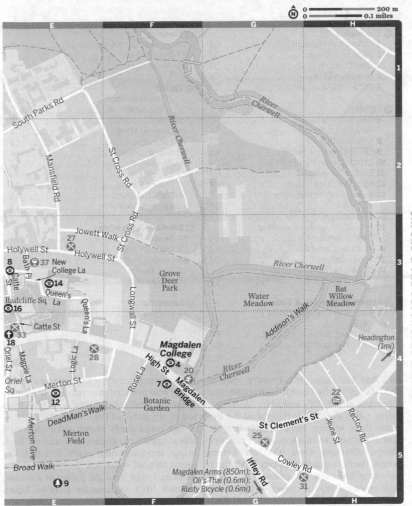

flowers and fruit carved by master craftsman Grinling Gibbons in 1694, and is looking fabulous after recent restoration work. Famous students have included Cardinal Newman, William Pitt the Elder, two other British prime ministers, and the fictional Jay Gatsby, the Great Gatsby himself.

Museum of the
History of Science
MUSEUM

(☎ 01865-277293; www.mhs.ox.ac.uk; Broad St; ⊙noon-5pm Tue-Sun) FREE Students of science will swoon at this fascinating museum, stuffed to the ceilings with awesome astrolabes, astonishing orreries and early electrical apparatus. Housed in the lovely 17th-century building that held the original Ashmolean Museum, it displays everything from cameras that belonged to Lewis Carroll and Lawrence of Arabia to a wireless receiver used by Marconi in 1896 and a blackboard that was covered with equations by Einstein in 1931, when he was invited to give three lectures on relativity.

University Church of
St Mary the Virgin
CHURCH

(☎ 01865-279111; www.university-church.ox.ac. uk; High St; church free, tower £4; ⊙9am-5pm Mon-Sat, from noon Sun Sep-Jun, 9am-6pm daily

Oxford

Jul & Aug) The ornate 14th-century spire of Oxford's university church is arguably the dreamiest of the city's legendary 'dreaming spires'. Otherwise, this is famous as the site where three Anglican bishops, including the first Protestant archbishop of Canterbury, Thomas Cranmer, were tried for heresy in1556, during the reign of Mary I. All three were later burned at the stake on Broad St. Visitors can climb the church's 1280 tower (£4) for excellent views of the adjacent Radcliffe Camera (p177).

◎ Jericho & Science Area

★Ashmolean Museum   MUSEUM

(☑ 01865-278000; www.ashmolean.org; Beaumont St; ☉10am-5pm Tue-Sun, to 8pm last Fri of month) FREE Britain's oldest public museum, Oxford's wonderful Ashmolean Museum is surpassed only by the British Museum in London. It was established in 1683, when Elias Ashmole presented Oxford University with a collection of 'rarities' amassed by the well-travelled John Tradescant, gardener to Charles I. A new exhibition celebrates Ashmole's 400th birthday by displaying original treasures including the hat worn by the judge who presided over the trial of Charles I, and a mantle belonging to 'Chief Powhatan', the father of Pocahontas.

You could easily spend a day exploring this magnificent neoclassical building. Each bright, spacious gallery across its four floors seems to hold some new marvel, be that a dazzling fresco from the palace of Knossos; artwork from Renaissance Italy to Japan, taking in Goya, van Gogh and JMW Turner; or, famously, the Anglo-Saxon Alfred Jewel, a glorious, golden 9th-century gem, thought to have been a sort of bookmark, that was crafted for Alfred the Great. There's a strong connection throughout with Oxford and its heritage, and upstairs there's a beautiful **rooftop restaurant** (☑ 01865-553823; mains £13.50-20; ☉10am-4.30pm Tue, Wed & Sun, to 10pm Thu-Sat; ☜).

★Pitt Rivers Museum   MUSEUM

(☑01865-270927; www.prm.ox.ac.uk; South Parks Rd; ☉noon-4.30pm Mon, from 10am Tue-Sun; ⛟) FREE If exploring an enormous room full of eccentric and unexpected artefacts sounds like your idea of the perfect afternoon, welcome to the amulets-to-zithers extravaganza that is the Pitt Rivers museum. Tucked behind Oxford's natural-history museum (p181), and dimly lit to protect its myriad treasures, it's centred on an anthropological collection amassed by a Victorian general, and revels in exploring how differing cultures have tackled topics like 'Smoking and Stimulants' or 'Treatment of Dead Enemies'.

Oxford University Museum
of Natural History   MUSEUM
(📞 01865-272950; www.oum.ox.ac.uk; Parks Rd; ⏰ 10am-5pm; 🚗) FREE Housed in a glorious Victorian Gothic building, with cast-iron columns, flower-carved capitals and a soaring glass roof, this museum makes a superb showcase for some extraordinary exhibits. Specimens from all over the world include a 150-year-old Japanese spider crab, but it's the dinosaurs that really wow the crowds. As well as a towering T-rex skeleton – the second most complete ever found – you'll see pieces of Megalosaurus, which was in 1677 the first dinosaur ever mentioned in a written text.

👁 Cowley Rd & Southeast Oxford

⭐ **Magdalen College**   COLLEGE
(📞 01865-276000; www.magd.ox.ac.uk; High St; adult/child £6/5; ⏰ 10am-7pm late Jun-late Sep, 1pm-dusk or 6pm late Sep-late Jun) Guarding access to a breathtaking expanse of private lawns, woodlands, river walks and even its own deer park, Magdalen ('mawd-lin'), founded in 1458, is one of Oxford's wealthiest and most beautiful colleges. Beyond its elegant Victorian gateway, you come to its medieval chapel and glorious 15th-century tower. From here, move on to the remarkable 15th-century **cloisters**, where the fantastic grotesques (carved figures) may have inspired CS Lewis' stone statues in *The Chronicles of Narnia*.

🏃 Activities

Magdalen Bridge Boathouse   BOATING
(📞 01865-202643; www.oxfordpunting.co.uk; High St; chauffeured 4-person punts per 30min £32, punt rental per hour £22; ⏰ 9.30am-dusk Feb-Nov) Right beside Magdalen Bridge, this boathouse is the most central location to hire a punt, chauffeured or otherwise. From here you can either head downstream around the Botanic Garden and Christ Church Meadow, or upstream around Magdalen Deer Park. You can also hire rowboats and pedalos.

Salter Bros   BOATING
(📞 01865-243421; www.salterssteamers.co.uk; Folly Bridge; punt/rowboat/motorboat per hour £20/20/45; ⏰ 10am-6pm Easter-Oct) As well as renting punts, rowing boats and motorboats, Salter Bros offers scenic cruises along the Thames, passing college boathouses and busy riverside pubs. Options include the 8-mile, two-hour trip to the historic market town of Abingdon (9.15am and 2.30pm, late May to early September, adult/child £20.80/11.70), and a 2½-hour Alice in Wonderland cruise (£17.50/£10).

👉 Tours

Oxford Official Walking Tours   WALKING
(📞 01865-686441; www.experienceoxfordshire.org; 15-16 Broad St; adult/child from £14/10; ⏰ 10.45am & 1pm, extra tours 11am & 2pm during busy periods; 🚗) Comprehensive two-hour tours of the city and its colleges, plus several themed tours, including one devoted to *Alice in Wonderland* and Harry Potter, another to CS Lewis and JRR Tolkien, and a third to Inspector Morse. Check online for details, or book at the tourist office (p187).

Bill Spectre's Oxford Ghost Trail   WALKING
(📞 07941-041811; www.ghosttrail.org; Oxford Castle; adult/child £10/7; ⏰ 6.30pm Fri & Sat; 🚗) For a theatrical and entertaining voyage through Oxford's uncanny underbelly, plus the occasional magic trick, take a 1¾-hour tour with Victorian undertaker Bill Spectre. No bookings needed, audience participation more than likely.

🛏 Sleeping

Oxford YHA   HOSTEL £
(📞 01865-727275; www.yha.org.uk; 2a Botley Rd; dm/r £26/110; 📶) Set in a purpose-built modern building, behind the station, Oxford's large YHA is a cut above other local hostels, with the feel of a chain hotel – and the prices too, for a private twin or double. The simple, comfortable four- and six-bed en-suite dorms are better value. Abundant facilities include a restaurant, a library, a garden, a laundry, lounges and private lockers.

Tower House   GUESTHOUSE ££
(📞 01865-246828; www.towerhouseoxford.co.uk; 15 Ship St; s £100, d £125, without bathroom £110; 📶) In a peaceful central location, this listed 17th-century town house holds eight good-value double rooms, simple but tastefully decorated. Some share bathrooms (not always on the same floor), while larger

en-suites also have attractive tongue-and-groove panelling. Run in conjunction with the excellent Turl Street Kitchen (p185) next door – slightly higher room rates include breakfast there – it donates profits to a community charity.

University Rooms Oxford

UNIVERSITY ACCOMMODATION ££
(www.universityrooms.com; s £31-79, d £70-125, q from £189; 🛜) During university holidays – Christmas, Easter and summer – and to a lesser extent at other times, visitors can stay in a student room in one of Oxford's hallowed colleges, perhaps looking over the quad, and enjoy breakfast in a grand hall. Functional singles with basic furnishings and shared bathrooms are the most available, but you can also find en-suites, twins and apartments.

Remont

B&B ££
(✉ 01865-311020; www.remont-oxford.co.uk; 367 Banbury Rd, Summertown; d/q £125/180; 🅿 @ 🛜) All modern style, subtle lighting and ultra-colourful furnishings, this boutique guesthouse holds 25 varying rooms decked out in cool neutrals with silky bedspreads, abstract art, vibrant bedheads, writing desks and huge TVs. There's a sunny garden and roomy breakfast hall out back. It's 2.5 miles north of the centre, in an inconspicuous residential setting, but there's good public transport.

Acorn Guest House

B&B ££
(✉ 01865-247998; www.oxford-acorn.co.uk; 260 Iffley Rd; s/d £50/75; 🅿 🛜 🐕) Spread through two adjoining houses, the friendly Acorn offers eight comfortable rooms at very reasonable prices, close to great pubs and restaurants and a short bus ride from the centre. Single rooms and 'budget' doubles share bathrooms; en-suite facilities cost just £5 more. Everything has the feel of a family home, complete with resident labradoodle Annie (visiting dogs welcome).

★ Oxford Coach & Horses

B&B £££
(✉ 01865-200017; www.oxfordcoachandhorses.co.uk; 62 St Clement's St; s/d £125/135; 🅿 🛜) A former 18th-century coaching inn, this fabulous English-Mexican-owned boutique B&B hides behind a fresh powder-blue exterior, just a few metres from the Cowley Rd action. The eight light-filled rooms are cosy, spacious and individually styled in soothing pastels with exposed beams and splashes of turquoise and mauve. The converted

---

🚶 Walking Tour
A Riverside Stroll in Central Oxford

START CHRIST CHURCH
END MAGDALEN COLLEGE
LENGTH 2.5 MILES; TWO HOURS

Few cities can match Oxford for retaining such glorious countryside so close to its centre. Oxford's secret lies in the fact that the riverside meadows just outside the medieval city walls belonged then, and still belong today, to hugely wealthy colleges that have never felt the urge to build on them, let alone sell them. Modern visitors can therefore simply step away from the busy city streets to enjoy an idyllic stroll along delightful rural footpaths.

Start by approaching ❶ **Christ Church** (p176) via the gates on St Aldate's. There's no need to pay for admission. Follow Broad Walk straight ahead for 140m, until the college's visitor entrance is on your left, then turn right onto Poplar Walk. This broad avenue heads directly south, to reach the Thames after 410m. Turning right at the river would bring you to Folly Bridge, spanning the original 'oxen ford' for which Oxford is named, but turn left, downstream, and follow the waterfront footpath known as the Meadow Walk. You'll probably see rowing eights and pleasure boats out on the Thames; looking back the way you've come, you're now separated from Christ Church, a shimmering vision of splendour, by the broad expanse of ❷ **Christ Church Meadow** (p177), where you may see long-horn cattle grazing. After 180m, the path leaves the river, curving beside a cut-off channel that brings you in 360m to the River Cherwell. Once there, keep following the curve, and after another 450m you meet Broad Walk at its eastern end.

Across Merton Field, straight ahead, the long, high wall of ❸ **Merton College** (p177) traces the route of Oxford's medieval city wall. During the Middle Ages, the local Jewish community had to bury their dead outside the walls. Their funerals followed this self-same footpath, which became known as Dead Man's Walk. The trees that tower over it stand within Merton's enclosed Fellows' Garden. JRR Tolkien's rooms overlooked this spot when he

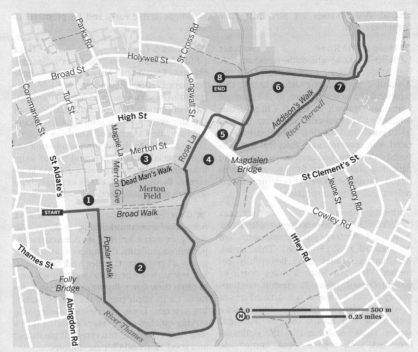

was writing *The Lord of the Rings*; one much-loved tree, now felled, served as the model for the ents of Middle Earth.

Ninety metres north of Broad Walk, fork right along Rose Lane, which leads up to High St along Merton's eastern boundary. The former Jewish cemetery now lies on your right, though for the past four centuries it's served instead as Oxford's ❹ **Botanic Garden**. If you've time, add an extra half-mile to this walk by dropping in to admire its greenhouses of rare plants, and relax in its tranquil spaces.

The visitors' entrance to ❺ **Magdalen College** (p181) is directly across High St from the north end of Rose Lane. To continue your walk, pay for admission and head through the stunning 15th-century cloisters (during the university year, visitors can only enter in the afternoon). Tolkien's contemporary, CS Lewis, lived in Magdalen, and the grotesque carvings here reappeared in his *Chronicles of Narnia*.

Turn right beyond the cloisters, and you're swiftly back on the banks of the Cherwell. Get ready for the absolute highlight of the walk. Magdalen took over these riverside lands almost six centuries ago, and has left them to be enjoyed as open countryside ever since. Cross the footbridge straight ahead of you to reach the ❻ **Water Meadow**, a triangular is-

let in the river. The gloriously bucolic footpath known as Addison's Walk takes just under a mile to loop around its perimeter. At its southern tip, you get a head-on view of punts and rowing boats setting off below Magdalen Bridge. The Water Meadow is one of just a half-dozen places where the snakeshead fritillary still grows; you may spot its purple or white flowers in late April.

Leave the Water Meadow by its northeastern end to enter smaller ❼ **Bat Willow Meadow**, where Mark Wallinger's sculpture *Y*, resembling a two-dimensional tree, was installed amid genuine willows in 2008 to mark Magdalen's 550th anniversary. Immediately south, Angel and Greyhound Meadow was named for two long-vanished coaching inns that pastured their horses here. The secluded Fellows' Garden, across another bridge beyond, was laid out in 1866, and holds an idyllic pond.

When you're ready to re-emerge into city life, retrace your footsteps back to the high street. Spare a glance, though, for the ❽ **Grove Deer Park**, north of the college buildings. If you're here between July and early December, you may have encountered the college's own herd of deer browsing in the riverside meadows; before that, to spare the fritillaries, they're here in the Grove.

ground floor houses an airy, attractive breakfast room.

★ Head of the River
HOTEL £££

(☎ 01865-721600; www.headoftheriveroxford.co.uk; Folly Bridge, St Aldates; r incl breakfast £189; 🛜) A genuine jewel among Oxford hotels, this large and characterful place, at Folly Bridge immediately south of Christ Church, was originally a Thames-side warehouse. Each of its 20 good-sized rooms is individually decorated with contemporary flair, featuring exposed brickwork and/or tongue-and-groove panelling plus modern fittings, while rates include breakfast cooked to order in the (excellent) pub (p186) downstairs.

Burlington House
HOTEL £££

(☎ 01865-513513; www.burlington-hotel-oxford.co.uk; 374 Banbury Rd, Summertown; s/d incl breakfast £102/139; 🅿🛜) This small, well-managed hotel, in a beautifully refreshed Victorian home 2 miles north of central Oxford, offers 12 elegant contemporary rooms - some in a courtyard annex - with patterned wallpaper, immaculate bathrooms and luxury touches. Personal service is as sensational as the delicious breakfast, with organic eggs, homemade bread, yoghurt, granola and fresh juice. Public transport links are good.

Oxford Townhouse
BOUTIQUE HOTEL £££

(☎ 01865-722500; www.theoxfordtownhouse.co.uk; 90 Abingdon Rd; s/d incl breakfast £136/166; 🅿🛜) Fifteen comfortable, subtly chic, minimalist-modern rooms, with white-and-navy striped blankets, varnished-wood desks and blue flourishes, in a gorgeously restyled pair of red-brick Victorian town houses, half a mile south of the centre. Some are quite small for the price, though. Colourful paintings of Oxford adorn the walls, and the breakfasts are classy.

✗ Eating

★ Edamamé
JAPANESE £

(☎ 01865-246916; www.edamame.co.uk; 15 Holywell St; mains £7-10.50; ⏱ 11.30am-2.30pm Wed, 11.30am-2.30pm & 5-8.30pm Thu-Sat, noon-3.30pm Sun; 🍴) No wonder a constant stream of students squeeze in and out of this tiny diner - it's Oxford's top spot for delicious, gracefully simple Japanese cuisine. Changing noodle and curry specials include fragrant chicken miso ramen, tofu stir-fries, or mackerel with soba noodles; it only serves sushi or sashimi on Thursday evenings. No

bookings; arrive early and be prepared to wait.

★ Vaults & Garden
CAFE £

(☎ 01865-279112; www.thevaultsandgarden.com; University Church of St Mary the Virgin, Radcliffe Sq; mains £7-10.50; ⏱ 9am-6pm; 🛜🍴) 🍃 This beautiful lunch venue spreads from the vaulted 14th-century Old Congregation House of the University Church into a garden facing the Radcliffe Camera. Come early, and queue at the counter to choose from wholesome organic specials such as leek and potato soup, tofu massaman curry, or slow-roasted lamb tagine. Breakfast and afternoon tea (those scones!) are equally good.

★ Covered Market
MARKET £

(www.oxford-coveredmarket.co.uk; Market St; ⏱ vary, some close Sun; 🛜🍴♿) A haven for impecunious students, this indoor marketplace holds 20 restaurants, cafes and takeaways. Let anyone loose here, and something's sure to catch their fancy. Brown's no-frills cafe, famous for its apple pies, is the longest-standing veteran. Look out too for Georgina's, serving quiches and burgers upstairs; Burt's superlative Cookies; two excellent pie shops; and good Thai and Chinese options.

Handle Bar
CAFE £

(☎ 01865-251315; www.handlebaroxford.co.uk; Bike Zone, 28-31 St Michael's St; dishes £8-13; ⏱ 8am-6pm Mon & Tue, to 11pm Wed-Fri, from 9am Sat, 10am-5pm Sun; 🛜🍴) Upstairs above a bike shop, this chatty, friendly cafe has bikes galore, including penny-farthings, dangling from its ceiling and white-painted brick walls. A tad more hippy than hipster, it's usually packed with students, professionals and lucky tourists. They're here for luscious, health-focused bites, like spiced avocado-and-feta toast, roasted chicken breast and fresh-fruit smoothie 'pots', plus tasty cakes, teas and coffees.

Grand Café
TEAHOUSE £

(☎ 01865-204463; www.thegrandcafe.co.uk; 84 High St; patisserie items £5-7, mains £9-13; ⏱ 9am-6.30pm Mon-Thu, to 7pm Fri-Sun; ♿) Boasting of being England's first-ever coffee house - though not, unlike its rival opposite, open ever since - the Grand looks very much the part, with its columns and gold leaf. While it serves sandwiches, bagels and a towering afternoon tea (from £18), it's the patisserie counter that's the real attraction: fresh, sweet pastry tarts and feather-light *mille-feuilles* pair brilliantly with tea.

Rusty Bicycle
GASTROPUB £

(📞01865-435298; www.therustybicycle.com; 28 Magdalen Rd; mains £6.50-12; ⏱9am-11pm Sun-Thu, to midnight Fri & Sat; 🐾) This funky neighbourhood pub, tucked off Iffley Rd a mile out of town and brought to you by the people responsible for Jericho's **Rickety Press** (📞01865-424581; www.thericketypress.com; 67 Cranham St; mains £6.50-12; ⏱kitchen noon-2.30pm & 6-9.30pm Mon-Fri, 10am-3pm & 6-9.30pm Sat & Sun), serves top-notch burgers and pizzas, along with excellent local beers.

Café Coco
MEDITERRANEAN £

(📞01865-200232; www.cafecoco.co.uk; 23 Cowley Rd; breakfast £5-9, mains £7.50-15; ⏱10am-midnight Mon-Thu, to 12.30am Fri & Sat, to 10pm Sun; 🐾) Decorated with classic posters, warm yellow walls and chunky mirrors – not to mention the plaster-cast clown – this Cowley Rd veteran is especially popular for brunch. Its global menu ranges from 'healthy' and cooked breakfasts to pizzas, salads, burgers, pastas, mezze platters, Mediterranean mains and zingy fresh juices. Or just swing by for cocktails (happy hour 5pm to 7.30pm).

★ Spiced Roots
CARIBBEAN ££

(📞01865-249888; www.spicedroots.com; 64 Cowley Rd; mains £12-17.50; ⏱6-10pm Tue & Wed, noon-3pm & 6-10pm Thu-Sat, noon-8pm Sun; 🐾) From black rice with pomegranates to oxtail with mac cheese and plantains – and, of course, spicy jerk chicken – everything is just perfection at this flawless new Caribbean restaurant. There are plenty of vegetarian options too, as well as curried fish or goat, while adding a cocktail or two from the thatched rum bar is pretty much irresistible.

★ Turl Street Kitchen
MODERN BRITISH ££

(📞01865-264171; www.turlstreetkitchen.co.uk; 16-17 Turl St; mains £10-16; ⏱8-10am, noon-2.30pm & 6.30-10pm; 🐾) 🍴 Whatever time you drop into this laid-back, not-quite-scruffy, seductively charming all-day bistro, with its fairy lights and faded-wood tables, you can expect to eat well. Fresh local produce is thrown into creative combinations, with the changing menu featuring the likes of roasted beetroot, braised lamb, or, on Sunday, roast beef and Yorkshire pudding. It also serves good cakes and coffee.

★ Magdalen Arms
BRITISH ££

(📞01865-243159; www.magdalenarms.co.uk; 243 Iffley Rd; mains £14-42; ⏱5-11pm Mon, from 10am Tue-Sat, 10am-10.30pm Sun; 🐾🍴) A mile

WORTH A TRIP

LE MANOIR AUX QUAT'SAISONS

Oxford itself has no Michelin-starred restaurants, so local food-lovers make the 9-mile pilgrimage east to this impressive **manor house** (📞01844-278881; www.belmond.com/le-manoir-aux-quat-saisons-oxfordshire; Church Rd, Great Milton; 5-course lunch/7-course dinner £95/190; ⏱6.30-9.30pm Mon, 11.45am-2.15pm & 6.30-9.30pm Tue-Sun), which has two stars of its own. Chef Raymond Blanc has been working his magic here for over 30 years, presenting imaginative and complex dishes that use ingredients from the amazing on-site kitchen garden. Book well ahead and dress smart.

It also has 32 hotel rooms, the cheapest of which costs £625.50 per night.

beyond Magdalen Bridge, this extra-special neighbourhood gastropub has won plaudits from the national press. A friendly, informal spot, it offers indoor and outdoor space for drinkers, and dining tables further back. From vegetarian specials such as broadbean tagliatelle to the fabulous sharing-size steak-and-ale pie – well, it's a stew with a suet-crust lid, really – everything is delicious, with gutsy flavours.

★ Oli's Thai
THAI ££

(📞01865-790223; www.olisthai.com; 38 Magdalen Rd; mains £12-15; ⏱noon-2.30pm & 5-10pm Tue-Fri, noon-3pm Sat) This tiny Thai restaurant is a bit of a trek from town, a mile down Iffley Rd, but it's absolutely worth the effort. The short menu changes frequently, with standouts including turmeric prawns and pork belly with rice. Tables, especially on the sunny terrace, get booked up months in advance, but they usually squeeze in a few walk-ins.

Cherwell Boathouse Restaurant
BRITISH ££

(📞01865-552746; www.cherwellboathouse.co.uk; Bardwell Rd; mains £18-22; ⏱noon-2.30pm & 6-9.30pm; 🐾) With its irresistible riverside setting, 1.5 miles north of central Oxford, the century-old Cherwell Boathouse makes a perfect setting for a lazy lunch or romantic summer evening. Short seasonally changing menus feature British standards like lamb loin with peas or plaice with shrimp sauce, and there are always a couple of vegetarian alternatives.

Oxford Kitchen
MODERN BRITISH £££

(☑ 01865-511149; www.theoxfordkitchen.co.uk; 215 Banbury Rd; set menus £22.50-65; ⊙ noon-2.30pm & 6-9.30pm Tue-Sat) Oxford's not renowned for high-end, cutting-edge cuisine, so if you're crying out for a few foams, mousses, funny-shaped plates and bumpy slates, make haste to Summertown's contemporary Oxford Kitchen. We jest; its Modern British food, served as set menus ranging from £22.50 for a weekday lunch up to the £65 weekend tasting menu, is superb.

🍸 Drinking & Nightlife

★ Turf Tavern
PUB

(☑ 01865-243235; www.turftavern-oxford.co.uk; 4-5 Bath Pl; ⊙ 11am-11pm; 🐾) Squeezed down an alleyway and subdivided into endless nooks and crannies, this medieval rabbit warren dates from around 1381. The definitive Oxford pub, this is where Bill Clinton famously 'did not inhale'; other patrons have included Oscar Wilde, Stephen Hawking and Margaret Thatcher. Home to a fabulous array of real ales and ciders, it's always pretty crowded, but there's outdoor seating, too.

★ The Perch
PUB

(☑ 01865-728891; www.the-perch.co.uk; Binsey Lane, Binsey; ⊙ 10.30am-11pm Mon-Sat, to 10.30pm Sun; 🅿🐾) This thatched and wonderfully rural 800-year-old inn can be reached by road, but it's more enjoyable to walk half an hour upstream along the Thames Path, then follow an enchanting footpath punctuated by floral pergolas. Its huge willow-draped garden is an idyllic spot for a pint or two of Fullers, but summer crowds can mean a long wait for food.

★ Head of the River
PUB

(☑ 01865-721600; www.headoftheriveroxford.co.uk; Folly Bridge, St Aldates; ⊙ 8am-10.30pm Sun-Thu, to 11.30pm Fri & Sat) For a summer-evening riverside drink, central Oxford holds no finer setting than the Thames-facing terrace of this imposing former warehouse – hence the hand-cranked crane, still outside – and later a boatyard. The beer's good, courtesy of Fullers brewery. There's plenty of room indoors – as well as decent food, and a stylish hotel upstairs – but the lure of the river is irresistible.

★ Lamb & Flag
PUB

(12 St Giles; ⊙ noon-11pm Mon-Sat, to 10.30pm Sun; 🐾) This relaxed 17th-century tavern remains one of Oxford's nicest pubs for a sturdy pint or glass of wine. Thomas Hardy wrote (and set) parts of *Jude the Obscure* at these very tables, while CS Lewis and JRR Tolkien shifted their custom here in later years. The food's nothing special, but buying a pint helps fund scholarships at St John's College.

Bear Inn
PUB

(☑ 01865-728164; www.bearoxford.co.uk; 6 Alfred St; ⊙ 11am-11pm Mon-Thu, to midnight Fri & Sat, 11.30am-10.30pm Sun) Oxford's oldest pub – there's been a pub here since 1242 – the creaky old Bear requires almost everyone to stoop while passing from room to room. An ever-expanding collection of ties, framed and fading behind glass, covers walls and ceilings alike. Affiliated with Fuller's brewery, it usually offers interesting guest ales, plus basic pub grub. There's live jazz on Tuesday.

Eagle & Child
PUB

(☑ 01865-302925; www.nicholsonspubs.co.uk/theeagleandchildoxford; 49 St Giles; ⊙ 11am-11pm Mon-Sat, noon-10.30pm Sun) Affectionately nicknamed the 'Bird & Baby', and a favourite haunt of JRR Tolkien, CS Lewis and their fellow Inklings, this quirky, rambling pub dates from 1650. Its narrow wood-panelled rooms still look great, and they're still serving decent real ales, but it's lost its way recently, and owners St John's College have announced an imminent, ominous-sounding makeover.

Varsity Club
COCKTAIL BAR

(☑ 01865-248777; www.tvcoxford.co.uk; 9 High St; ⊙ noon-midnight; 🐾) At this sleekly minimalist rooftop cocktail bar, spectacularly located in the town centre, you can sip fruity cocktails (£7 to £10) while you soak up sensational views across Oxford's dreaming spires. Heaters, blankets and canopies keep things cosy in colder weather, while lounges and dance spaces sprawl across three floors below.

The Trout
PUB

(☑ 01865-510930; www.thetroutoxford.co.uk; 195 Godstow Rd, Wolvercote; ⊙ 11am-11pm Mon-Fri, from 10am Sat, 10am-10.30pm Sun; 🐾) Three miles northwest along the Thames from Oxford – a wonderful walk– this old-world pub has been drawing drinkers for around four centuries, and was popularised by TV detective Inspector Morse. Its expansive riverside terrace is usually packed, and there are peckish ducks patrolling the parapet wall. If you fancy sampling its Modern British cuisine be sure to book way in advance.

🔒 Shopping

★ **Blackwell's** BOOKS
(☑ 01865-792792; www.blackwells.co.uk; 48-51 Broad St; ⊙ 9am-6.30pm Mon & Wed-Sat, from 9.30am Tue, 11am-5pm Sun) The most famous bookshop in the most studenty of cities, Blackwell's is, with its vast range of literature, treatises and guilty pleasures, a book-lover's dream. Be sure to visit the basement Norrington Room, an immense inverted step pyramid, lined with 3 miles of shelves, hailed in the Guinness Book of Records as the largest room selling books in the world.

ℹ Information

Tourist Office (☑ 01865-686430; www.experienceoxfordshire.org; 15-16 Broad St; ⊙ 9am-5.30pm Mon-Sat, 10am-4pm Sun Jul & Aug, 9.30am-5pm Mon-Sat, 10am-4pm Sun Sep-Jun) Covers the whole of Oxfordshire. Sells Oxford guidebooks, makes reservations for local accommodation and walking tours, and sells tickets for events and attractions.

ℹ Getting There & Away

BUS

Oxford's chaotic outdoor **bus station** (Gloucester Green) is in the centre, on Gloucester Green near the corner of Worcester and George Sts. The main bus companies are **Oxford Bus Company** (☑ 01865-785400; www.oxfordbus.co.uk), **Stagecoach** (☑ 01865-772250; www.stagecoachbus.com) and **Swanbrook** (☑ 01452-712386; www.swanbrook.co.uk).

Destinations:

Burford (route 853; £3.80, 45 minutes)
Cambridge (X5; £13.50, 3¾ hours)
Cheltenham (853; £8, 1½ hours)
Chipping Norton (S3; £4.70, one hour)
London Victoria (Oxford Tube/X90; £15, 1¾ hours)
Witney (11/S1/S2/853; £4.20, 40 minutes)
Woodstock (7/S3; £3.20, 30 minutes)

National Express (☑ 0871-7818181; www.nationalexpress.com) coach destinations:

Bath (£11.30, two hours)
Birmingham (£11.10, 2½ hours)
Bristol (£7.10, three hours)
London Victoria (£16, two hours)

CAR & MOTORCYCLE

Driving and parking in central Oxford is a nightmare; consider booking accommodation that offers parking. There are five Park & Ride car parks along the major routes leading into town, all at least 2 miles out. Parking costs £2 to £4 per day, with a total charge of £6.80 if you use the buses that run to/from the centre every 15 to 30 minutes, and take 12 to 25 minutes for the journey.

TRAIN

Oxford's main train station is conveniently located just west of the city centre, roughly 10 minutes' walk from, say, Broad St. Destinations include the following (note that fares vary enormously according to when you travel, when you book, and many other factors):

Birmingham (£19, 1¼ hours)
London Marylebone (£7 to £29, 1¼ hours)
London Paddington (£9.50 to £26.50, 1¼ hours)
Manchester (£38.70, 2¾ hours)
Moreton-in-Marsh (£10.50, 35 minutes)
Newcastle (£73.50, 4½ hours)
Winchester (£18.30, 1¼ hours)

Oxford Parkway station, on Banbury Rd 4 miles north of the centre, has trains to London Marylebone (£7 to £26, one hour). Convenient if you're staying in Summertown, it also has bus links to central Oxford.

ℹ Getting Around

BICYCLE

There's a real cycling culture in Oxford, and it's a popular way to get around the city for students and visitors alike. **Cyclo Analysts** (☑ 01865-424444; www.cycloanalysts.com; 150 Cowley Rd; per day/week from £10/36; ⊙ 9am-6pm Mon-Sat) and **Summertown Cycles** (☑ 01865-316885; www.summertowncycles.co.uk; 200-202 Banbury Rd, Summertown; per day/week £18/35; ⊙ 9am-5.30pm Mon-Sat, 10.30am-4pm Sun) sell, repair and rent out bikes, including hybrids.

BUS

Oxford Bus Company and Stagecoach serve an extensive local network with regular buses on major routes. Single journeys cost up to £2.20 (return £3.70); consider a day pass (£4.20). Pay when you board the bus, either in cash or with a contactless card.

TAXI

There are taxi ranks at the train station and bus station, as well as on St Giles and at Carfax. Alternatively, contact **001 Taxis** (☑ 01865-240000; www.001taxis.com; New Inn Yard, 108

VALE OF THE WHITE HORSE

Lying around 20 miles southwest of Oxford, this verdant valley is home to the historic market town of Wantage, birthplace of Alfred the Great (AD 849–899). Its most interesting attractions, however, are much older even than that. White Horse Hill, 7.5 miles west of Wantage, is decorated with Britain's most ancient chalk figure, the 3000-year-old **Uffington White Horse**, while the nearby hill fort known as **Uffington Castle** dates from 700 BC, and **Wayland's Smithy** is a neolithic long barrow.

The 10m-high, flat-topped mound known as **Dragon Hill** was believed by locals to be the site where St George slew the dragon. Archaeologists prefer to think that it's a natural formation, the summit of which was scraped level during the Iron Age and used for rituals.

St Aldate's) or **Oxford Cars** (☏ 01865-406070; www.oxfordcars.co.uk).

AROUND OXFORD

The Oxfordshire countryside abounds in rustic charm. To the northwest, Witney has a pretty town centre, but the major highlight is magnificent Blenheim Palace, birthplace of Sir Winston Churchill, adjoining attractive Woodstock. Southwest of Oxford, the Vale of the White Horse offers some intriguing prehistoric attractions.

Woodstock

☏ 01993 / POP 2727

Woodstock, 8 miles northwest of Oxford, is a beautiful old town that has long had close links to royalty. Fine stone houses, venerable inns and pubs, and antique shops jostle shoulder to shoulder in its well-heeled centre, but what really draws the crowds here is Blenheim Palace, a majestic baroque extravaganza that was the birthplace of Sir Winston Churchill.

⊙ Sights

★ **Blenheim Palace** PALACE

(☏ 01993-810530; www.blenheimpalace.com; Woodstock; adult/child £26/14.50, park & gardens only £16/7.40; ⊙ palace 10.30am-5.30pm, park & gardens 9am-6.30pm or dusk; P) One of the greatest stately homes in Britain, and a Unesco World Heritage Site, Blenheim Palace is a monumental baroque fantasy, designed by Sir John Vanbrugh and Nicholas Hawksmoor, and built between 1705 and 1722. Queen Anne gave both the land, and the necessary funds, to John Churchill, Duke of Marlborough, as thanks for defeating the French at the 1704 Battle of Blenheim. Sir Winston Churchill was born here in 1874, and Blenheim (blen-num) remains home to the 12th duke.

Inside, beyond majestic oak doors, the palace is stuffed with statues, tapestries, sumptuous furniture, priceless china and giant oil paintings in elaborate gilt frames. Visits start in the **Great Hall**, a soaring space that's adorned with images of the first duke and topped by a 20m-high ceiling. From here, you can either wander through the various grand state rooms independently, or join one of the free 45-minute guided tours, which depart every 30 minutes (except on Sunday, when guides are stationed in all rooms). Highlights include the famous **Blenheim Tapestries**, a set of 10 large wall hangings commemorating the first duke's triumphs; the **State Dining Room**, with its painted walls and trompe l'Iœil ceilings; and the magnificent **Long Library**, overlooked by an elaborate 1738 statue of Queen Anne, where the 56m ceiling was decorated by Nicholas Hawksmoor.

Upstairs, in the **Untold Story**, a phantom chambermaid leads visitors on a half-hour audio-visual tour of tableaux that recreate important scenes from Blenheim's history. Between February and September you can also join additional tours (adult/child £5/4.50) of the Duke's private apartments, the palace bedrooms or the household staff areas.

A separate sequence of rooms downstairs holds the **Churchill Exhibition**, included in the ticket price and dedicated to the life, work, paintings and writings of Winston Churchill. Official history has it that the future prime minister, grandson of the 7th duke and cousin of the 9th, was born by chance at the palace, after his mother went into premature labour. It's widely believed, however, that the tale was concocted to conceal that she was already pregnant when she married his father, seven months earlier. Winston Churchill is buried in the local parish church in Bladon, 1.5 miles south, just outside the grounds.

If the crowds in the house become too oppressive, escape into the vast, lavish **gardens and parklands**, parts of which were landscaped by the great Lancelot 'Capability' Brown. Immediately outside, two large water terraces hold fountains and sphinxes, while a minitrain (50p) takes visitors to the **Pleasure Gardens**, where features include a yew maze, adventure playground, lavender garden and butterfly house.

For quieter and longer strolls, there are glorious walks of up to 4.5 miles, leading past lakes to an arboretum, rose garden, cascade, and Vanbrugh's Grand Bridge. Look out for the Temple of Diana, where Winston Churchill proposed to his future bride, Lady Clementine, on 10 August 1908.

🛏 Sleeping

★ **Glove House** B&B £££

(📞 01993-813475; www.theglovehouse.co.uk; 24 Oxford St; d/ste £170/200; 📶) Luxuriously renovated but proudly displaying evidence of its venerable age, this elegant 400-year-old town house conceals three sumptuous rooms, all with the added bonus of a glorious rear garden. The Charlbury suite has a free-standing copper bathtub in its wonderful lounge-equipped bathroom.

Feathers HOTEL £££

(📞 01993-812291; www.feathers.co.uk; Market St; r incl breakfast £189; 📶) Oozing contemporary chic, this handsome 17th-century town house – previously a sanatorium, a draper's, and a butcher's – offers stylish, comfortable rooms adorned with patterned wallpaper, modern art, fuzzy throws and rich-coloured fabrics. The smart bar downstairs stocks 401 types of gin.

ℹ Getting There & Away

Stagecoach buses (p187) head to/from Oxford (S3; £3.20, 30 minutes), Burford (233; £4.10, 45 minutes), Chipping Norton (S3; £4.10, 20 minutes) and Witney (233; £3.80, 30 minutes). Buses S3 and 233 stop outside Blenheim Palace.

THE COTSWOLDS

Undulating gracefully across six counties, the Cotswolds region is a delightful tangle of golden villages, thatched cottages, evocative churches and honey-coloured mansions. In 1966 it was designated an Area of Outstanding Natural Beauty, surpassed for size in England by the Lake District alone.

No one's sure what the name means, but 'wolds' are rolling hills, while 'cots' might be 'cotes', or sheep pens. Certainly the region owes its wealth, and exquisite architecture, to the medieval wool trade, when 'Cotswold Lion' sheep were prized across Europe. Attentions later turned towards textiles instead, but the Industrial Revolution passed the Cotswolds by. Hailed by William Morris in the 19th century as encapsulating a timeless English rural idyll, it remains both a prime residential area and a treasured tourist destination.

Criss-crossed by long-distance trails including the 102-mile Cotswold Way, these gentle yet dramatic hills are perfect for walking, cycling and horse riding.

🏃 Activities

Cycling

Gentle gradients and wonderfully scenic panoramas make the Cotswolds ideal for cycling. Quiet country lanes and byways crisscross the countryside, and only the steep western escarpment poses a significant challenge to the legs. You can also follow the signposted **Thames Valley Cycle Way** (NCN Routes 4 and 5) between Oxford and Windsor (and on to London).

Companies such as **Cotswold Country Cycles** (📞 01386-438706; www.cotswoldcountrycycles.com; Longlands Farm Cottage; 3 day/2 night tours from £285) organise maps, luggage transfers and B&B stays for a range of self-guided cycling tours.

DON'T MISS

KELMSCOTT MANOR

Nestling near the Thames 20 miles west of Oxford (northwest of Faringdon), **Kelmscott Manor** (📞 01367-252486; www.sal.org.uk/kelmscott-manor; Kelmscott; adult/child £10/5; ⏱ 11am-5pm Wed & Sat Apr-Oct) is a gorgeous garden-fringed Tudor pile that was bought in 1871 by a prestigious pair of artist-poets: Dante Gabriel Rossetti and William Morris, founder of the Arts and Crafts movement. The interior is true to Morris' philosophy that one should own nothing that is neither beautiful nor useful, and displays his personal effects along with fabrics and furniture designed by Morris and his associates.

The Cotswolds

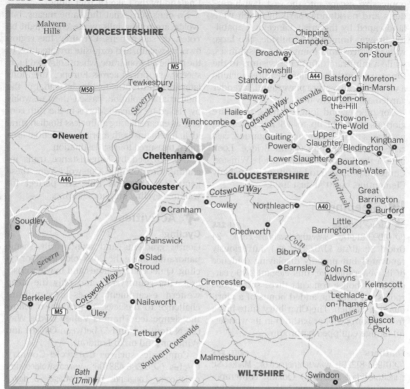

Walking

The 102-mile **Cotswold Way** (www.national trail.co.uk/cotswold-way) gives walkers a wonderful overview of the region. Meandering from Chipping Campden in the northeast to Bath in the southwest, it passes through some lovely countryside, linking ancient sites and tiny villages, with no major climbs or difficult stretches. It's also easily accessible from many points en route, if you fancy tackling a shorter section or a circular walk from your village of choice.

Other long-distance trails that pass through the Cotswolds include the 100-mile **Gloucestershire Way**, which runs from Chepstow to Tewkesbury via Stow-on-the-Wold; the 55-mile **St Kenelm's Way** into Worcestershire; and the 184-mile **Thames Path** (www.nationaltrail.co.uk/thames-path), which tracks from just southwest of Cirencester all the way to London.

Local tourist offices can advise on routes and usually sell walking maps.

Cirencester

☎ 01285 / POP 19,076

Charming Cirencester (siren-sester), the most significant town in the southern Cotswolds, is just 15 miles south of Cheltenham. Amazingly, under the Romans – who knew it as Corinium – Cirencester ranked second only to London in terms of size and importance, but little now survives from that era. The medieval wool trade brought further prosperity, with wealthy merchants funding the construction of a superb church.

Cirencester today is both elegant and affluent, but refreshingly unpretentious. Upmarket boutiques and fashionable delis now line its narrow streets, but its Monday and Friday markets remain at the core of its identity. Beautiful Victorian buildings flank

WARWICKSHIRE

Banbury

M40

Chipping Norton

Great Tew

A44

Wychwood

Woodstock

Swinbrook

Witney

A40

Minster Lovell

Windrush

Thames (Isis)

Oxford

OXFORDSHIRE

Thames (Isis)

Thames Path

A34

Faringdon

Uffington

Ardington

Vale of the White Horse

Wantage

0 — 10 km
0 — 5 miles

the busy central square, while the surrounding streets showcase a harmonious medley of historic architecture.

⊙ Sights

★ Corinium Museum   MUSEUM
(☑ 01285-655611; www.coriniummuseum.org; Park St; adult/child £5.60/2.70; ⊙ 10am-5pm Mon-Sat, 2-5pm Sun Apr-Oct, to 4pm Nov-Mar; 🚼) Most of this wonderful modern museum is, of course, dedicated to Cirencester's Roman past; reconstructed rooms, videos and interactive displays bring the era to life. Among the highlights are some beautiful floor mosaics, unearthed locally and including a 4th-century mosaic depicting the mythical lyre-player Orpheus charming animals, and the 2nd-century 'Jupiter column', a carved capital depicting Bacchus and his drunken mates. There's also an excellent Anglo-Saxon section, plus exhibits on medieval Cirencester and its prosperous wool trade.

St John the Baptist's Church   CHURCH
(☑ 01285-659317; www.cirenparish.co.uk; Market Sq; ⊙ 10am-4pm) One of England's largest parish churches, the cathedral-like St John's boasts an outstanding Perpendicular Gothic tower with flying buttresses (c 1400), plus a majestic three-storey south porch, built as an office in the late 15th century but subsequently used as Cirencester's town hall. Soaring arches, magnificent fan vaulting and a Tudor nave adorn the light-filled interior, where a wall safe holds the Boleyn Cup, made for Anne Boleyn in 1535.

On some Wednesdays and summer Saturdays, it's possible to climb the tower (adult/child £3/1.50).

🛏 Sleeping

YHA Cotswolds   HOSTEL £
(Barrel Store; ☑ 01285-657181; www.yha.org.uk; New Arts Brewery, Brewery Ct; dm/d/q £23/65/75; 🛜) 🅿 This welcome new hostel, in the heart of Cirencester, is the Cotswolds' only YHA. Part of an exciting cultural complex, it's built to the highest environmental standards, with fixtures and furnishings sourced from local artisans. All rooms, from private doubles to two- to four-bunk dorms, have en-suite bathrooms; they're quite minimal, but do have Cotswolds wool blankets.

★ No 12   B&B ££
(☑ 01285-640232; www.no12cirencester.co.uk; 12 Park St; d/ste £130/150; 🅿🛜) This welcoming and very central Georgian town house offers four gloriously unfussy, very private rooms kitted out with a tasteful mix of antiques and modern furnishings. Romantic room 1 has an in-room bath, while the suite has two bathrooms and overlooks the lovely garden, with extra-long beds, piles of feather pillows and splashes of red throughout. The breakfasts are superb.

Kings Head   LUXURY HOTEL ££
(☑ 01285-700900; www.kingshead-hotel.co.uk; 24 Market Pl; d/ste from £119/199; 🛜🐾) A coaching inn since the 14th century, this plush spot facing the church offers slick boudoirs and super-polished service. Exposed beams, red-brick walls and wood panelling pop up between Nespresso machines and Apple TVs. The standard rooms are contemporary and comfy; suite 103, with its in-room copper bath, is a stunner. Enjoy the tucked-away spa, cosy bar and smart **restaurant** (mains £12-27, Sunday lunch £20; ⊙ 7am-10am, noon-2.30pm & 6.30-9.30pm).

✗ Eating

Made by Bob　　　　　MODERN BRITISH ££
(☎01285-641818; www.foodmadebybob.com; Corn Hall, 26 Market Pl; mains £8.50-22.50; ◎7.30am-5pm Mon-Sat, from 10am Sun; ♪) Filling a substantial light-filled space inside a central mall, and focused around an enormous open-plan kitchen, Bob's is part deli, part brasserie, and popular for its casual atmosphere. The breakfast selection is excellent – granola, smashed avocado, full English – while lunch bites include salads, soups, pastas, risottos and charcuterie platters. No bookings.

Jesse's Bistro　　　　MODERN BRITISH £££
(☎01285-641497; www.jessesbistro.co.uk; The Stableyard, 14 Black Jack St; mains £16-28; ◎11.45am-2.45pm Mon, 11.45am-2.45pm & 6.45-9.45pm Tue-Sat, 11.45am-4.45pm Sun) Tucked away in a cobbled yard, Jesse's is a very pleasant little spot, with flagstone floors, wood-beamed ceilings and mosaic tables. Delectable dishes come fresh from the semi-open kitchen and feature seasonal produce such as Cornish fish and Cotswolds meat from the adjacent butcher.

ℹ Information

Tourist Office (☎01285-654180; www.cotswolds.com; Corinium Museum, Park St; ◎10am-5pm Mon-Sat, 2-5pm Sun Apr-Oct, to 4pm Nov-Mar) Doubling as the museum gift store, this helpful office can arrange accommodation, and sells a leaflet detailing a self-guided walk around Cirencester for 50p.

ℹ Getting There & Away

The closest station to Cirencester, at Kemble 4.5 miles south, is connected by train with London Paddington (£28.10, 1¼ hours).

Stagecoach, Pulhams and Cotswold Green serve Cirencester. Most buses stop outside the Corn Hall on Market Pl. Buses run to/from the following:

Cheltenham (route 51; £3.80, 40 minutes)
Gloucester (route 882; £2.80, 50 minutes)

ℹ **COTSWOLDS DISCOVERER**

The **Cotswolds Discoverer**, a great-value one-day pass that gives unlimited travel on bus or train routes throughout the region (adult/child £10/5), can be bought at all UK mainline train stations, and aboard participating buses within the Cotswolds.

Northleach (route 855; £2.90, 20 minutes)
Tetbury (route 882; £2.70, 30 minutes)

National Express (www.nationalexpress.com) coach destinations:
Birmingham (£16, 2½ hours)
London Victoria (£6, 2½ hours)

Bibury

☑ 01285 / POP 627

Memorably described as 'England's most beautiful village' by no less an authority than William Morris, Bibury, 8 miles northeast of Cirencester, epitomises the Cotswolds at its most picturesque. With a cluster of perfect cottages beside the River Coln, and a tangle of narrow streets flanked by attractive stone buildings, small wonder that it's a major halt on large-group Cotswold tours.

◉ Sights

★**Arlington Row**　　　　　STREET
Bibury's most famous attraction, this ravishing row of rustic cottages – as seen in movies like *Stardust* – was originally a 14th-century wool store, before being converted into workers' lodgings. They overlook Rack Isle, a low-lying, marshy area once used to dry cloth and graze cattle, and now a wildlife refuge. Coach parties galore arrive to admire the cottages, and stroll the flower-lined lane alongside. If you'd like to see a photo, look at the inside front cover of a UK passport.

Church of St Mary the Virgin　　CHURCH
(Church Rd; ◎10am-dusk) Bibury's Saxon-built church has been much altered since its original construction, but many 8th-century features are still visible among the 12th-, 13th- and 15th-century additions. It's just off the B4425 in the village centre.

☐ Sleeping

New Inn　　　　　　　PUB ££
(☎01285-750651; www.new-inn.co.uk; Main St, Coln St Aldwyns; r incl breakfast £119-149; P🐕🛜📶) The jasmine-clad 16th-century New Inn, 2.5 miles southeast of Bibury, offers 15 spacious and atmospheric bedrooms divided between the main pub building and a neighbouring cottage. Idiosyncratic contemporary stylings include bold colours, fluffy throws, smart furnishings and the odd free-standing bathtub, while the pub itself, with its exposed beams, is great. Weekend rates soar in summer.

★ **Barnsley House**   LUXURY HOTEL **£££**
(☎01285-740000; www.barnsleyhouse.com; B4425, Barnsley; r incl breakfast from £319; ℗ 🛜 ✻) For pure indulgence and romance, this 1697 country house and its famously beautiful garden take some beating. Each of its 18 rooms is individually styled; some have lavish oriental touches or in-room baths, most are elegantly understated. Facilities include a spa, a pool, a private cinema, the Potager restaurant and the knowingly re-named Village Pub. Guests must be aged 14 or over.

ℹ Getting There & Away

Most drivers approach Bibury along the B4425, which passes through the village centre halfway between Burford (9 miles northeast) and Cirencester (8 miles southwest). Pulhams bus 855 heads to/from Cirencester (£2.40, 15 minutes), Barnsley (£1.70, 5 minutes) and Northleach (£2.40, 20 minutes); there's no Sunday service.

Burford

☎01993 / POP 1410

Gliding down a steep hillside to an ancient (and still single-lane) crossing point on the River Windrush, 20 miles west of Oxford, Burford has hardly changed since its medieval glory days. Locals insist it's a town not a village, having received its charter in 1090, but it's a very small town, and a very picturesque one too, home to an appealing mix of stone cottages, gold-tinged Cotswold town houses, and the odd Elizabethan or Georgian treasure.

Throw in a wonderfully preserved, centuries-old church and an array of delightful hotels and restaurants, and Burford makes an attractive stop. Antique shops, chintzy tearooms and specialist boutiques peddle nostalgia to the many summer visitors, but it's easy to escape the crowds and wander along quiet side streets, seemingly lost in time.

🛏 Sleeping & Eating

★ **Star Cottage**   B&B **££**
(☎01993-822032; www.burfordbedandbreakfast.co.uk; Meadow Lane, Fulbrook; r £110-125, apt £115-140; 🛜) A mile northeast of Burford, this wonderful old Cotswold cottage holds two comfortable and character-filled en-suite rooms done up in tastefully creative blues, whites and greys, with gorgeous quilted curtains. The smaller room holds a grand canopied bed; the larger has a beautiful bathroom; and the back barn hosts a separate four-person apartment. The home-cooked, locally sourced breakfasts are fantastic.

Lamb Inn   PUB **£££**
(☎01993-823155; www.cotswold-inns-hotels.co.uk/the-lamb-inn; Sheep St; s/d incl breakfast from £150/160; ℗ 🛜 ✻) A rambling 15th-century inn, off the main street, where the flagstone floors, exposed beams and creaking stairs are complemented by 17 opulent antique-furnished rooms. A few have four-poster beds, and one even has its own private garden, while modern touches include Nespresso machines and slick bathrooms. Modern British cuisine is served in both the romantic **restaurant** (mains £14-35; ⊙ 7.30-10am, noon-2.30pm & 7-9pm) and the bar.

Swan Inn   PUB **£££**
(☎01993-823339; www.theswanswinbrook.co.uk; Swinbrook; s/d/ste incl breakfast £130/150/250; ℗ 🛜) All soft pastels, country comfort and dashes of colour, the Swan sits beside the River Windrush in tiny Swinbrook, 3 miles east of Burford. Six cosy, elegant rooms in a former barn overlook orchards – the plush top-floor suite is perfect for families – while five delightful rooms in the newer riverside cottage have a more contemporary style. There's an excellent **restaurant** (mains £16-26; ⊙ noon-2pm & 7-9pm; ℗).

Downton Abbey fans: this is the pub where Lady Sybil and Branson planned their elopement.

Huffkins   BAKERY, CAFE **££**
(☎01993-824694; www.huffkins.com; 98 High St; mains £6-15; ⊙ 9am-4.30pm Mon-Fri, to 5pm Sat, 10am-5pm Sun; 🍴) The original outlet of a Cotswolds chain that's been baking and serving delicious scones, cakes and pies since 1890, this lively, friendly cafe is usually packed with locals enjoying quiches, soups, macaroni cheese or burgers. It also offers all-day cooked breakfasts and full-blown afternoon teas. For a quick snack, pick up baked goods in its adjoining deli.

ℹ Information

Tourist Office (☎01993-823558; www.oxfordshirecotswolds.org; 33a High St; ⊙ 9.30am-5pm Mon-Sat, 10am-4pm Sun) Information on local walks.

ℹ Getting There & Away

Stagecoach and Swanbrook buses run to/from Burford. Local buses stop on High or Sheep Sts, but express services stop at the A40 roundabout, five minutes' walk south of the centre. Bus destinations include the following:

Cheltenham (route 853; £4.50, 45 minutes)

Gloucester (route 853; £6, 1¼ hours)

Oxford (route 853; £6.30, 45 minutes to 1¼ hours)

Minster Lovell (route 233/853; £2.30, 15 minutes)

Witney (route 233/853; £3.30, 19 minutes)

Woodstock (route 233; £4.10, 45 minutes)

Northleach

📞 01451 / POP 1838

Oddly under-visited, and refreshingly uncommercialised despite holding some interesting attractions, Northleach, 14 miles southeast of Cheltenham, has been a small market town since 1227. Late-medieval cottages, imposing merchants' stores and half-timbered Tudor houses jostle for position in a wonderful melange of styles around Market Sq and the narrow laneways that lead off it.

⊙ Sights

Chedworth Roman Villa   ARCHAEOLOGICAL SITE
(NT; 📞 01242-890256; www.nationaltrust.org.uk; Yanworth; adult/child £10.50/5.25; ⊙10am-5pm Apr-Oct, to 4pm mid-Feb–Mar & Nov; 🅿) This large and luxurious Roman villa was rediscovered by a gamekeeper in 1864. Though the earliest section dates to around AD 175, it was at its most magnificent around AD 362, equipped with two sets of bathhouses, a water shrine and a dining room with underfloor heating. A fine modern gallery preserves several exquisite mosaics, though yet more, unearthed recently, had to be reburied due to lack of resources.

It's at the far end of a dead-end rural road, 4.5 miles west of Northleach and signposted from the A429.

Mechanical Music Museum   MUSEUM
(📞 01451-860181; www.mechanicalmusic.co.uk; High St; adult/child £8/3.50; ⊙10am-5pm) Join an hour-long tour of this quirky collection of antique music players, and you'll hear some amazing sounds, emerging perhaps from a beautifully handcrafted 18th-century device that cost as much as a London house, or an upright piano eerily 'played' by the invisible fingers of George Gershwin himself.

Church of St Peter & St Paul   CHURCH
(www.northleach.org; Church Walk; ⊙9am-5pm) The grandeur and complexity of this

🚗 Driving Tour
Classic Cotswolds

START BURFORD
END WINCHCOMBE
LENGTH 54 MILES; ONE TO THREE DAYS

Given the Cotswolds' intricate spider's-web of winding country lanes that connect its ancient market towns, time-warped villages and majestic stately homes, it's impossible to cover every highlight in a single day. This tour, though, spans three counties and takes in some of the most picturesque spots in the northern half of the range. You could drive it in a day, but you'll enjoy it more if you stretch it into two or three, with plentiful stop-offs along the way.

Begin in Oxfordshire at the gorgeous hillside market town of ❶ **Burford** (p193), then head 10 miles west on the A40 into Gloucestershire, following signs to classic Cotswolds town ❷ **Northleach** (p194). The Cotswolds Discovery Centre here has excellent displays covering the history, geography, flora and fauna of the Cotswolds Area of Outstanding Natural Beauty (AONB). There's a fine church in town, and a fascinating Roman villa nearby.

From Northleach, spin 7 miles northeast on the A429 to ❸ **Lower Slaughter**, a serene riverside village lined with houses made of that irresistible Cotswolds golden stone. Spare the time if you can to stroll a mile northwest, along the river, to ❹ **Upper Slaughter**, less visited than its sibling but no less attractive, thanks to its idyllic setting between a small ford and the hills. Book ahead, and you can have lunch in an exquisite Jacobean mansion, at Lords of the Manor.

Continue 3 miles north on the A429 to ❺ **Stow-on-the-Wold** (p196), the highest Cotswold village at 244m and a market centre since the 12th century. Explore the market square, then follow the A429 north, along the ruler-straight route of the ancient Roman Fosse Way. After 4.5 miles you'll reach busy ❻ **Moreton-in-Marsh** (p201), known for its weekly Tuesday market and excellent shops.

Next, zip 3 miles west on the A44 to tiny ❼ **Bourton-on-the-Hill**, filled with attractive 17th- and 18th-century cottages. It's famous for two things: the gibbeting cage in which the bodies of dead highwaymen were

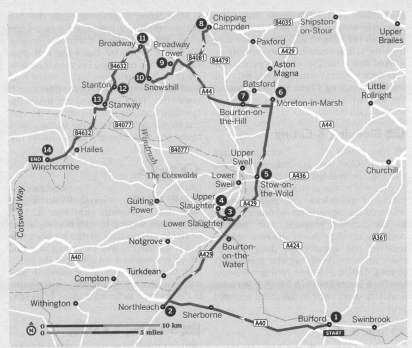

hung in the 19th century, and horse training – there are several stud farms in the vicinity. The Horse & Groom here is a good lunch option.

Head 3 miles west on the A44, then turn right (northeast) onto the B4081 to **8 Chipping Campden** (p198), one of the Cotswold's most bucolic towns. After admiring 15th-century St James' Church and the honey-toned buildings along High St – at least stop for cake and coffee, even if you're not tempted to stay the night – backtrack to the A44. Drive a mile northwest, crossing into the Worcestershire corner of the Cotswolds, and turn off at signposted **9 Broadway Tower** (p200), an 18th-century Gothic folly perched spectacularly atop the escarpment.

Leaving Broadway Tower, continue 1 mile south and turn right (southwest) at the crossing. You'll soon see signs to pretty little **10 Snowshill**, a mile further on and one-time film set for *Bridget Jones's Diary*. If you're visiting in June or July, you'll swing by spectacularly purple fields of flowering lavender. From Snowshill, whizz 2.5 miles north to **11 Broadway** (p199), home to an excellent museum and gallery. After cruising along broad High St, hop on the B4632 southwest towards Cheltenham. After 3 miles, take the left (east) turn-off to **12 Stanton**, a tiny stunner of a village.

Its houses are crafted out of gold-tinged Cotswolds stone. The buildings most likely to catch your eye are Jacobean Stanton Court and St Michael & All Angels' Church, the latter with its fine Perpendicular tower and medieval interior. Stanton Court once belonged to civil architect Sir Philip Stott (1858–1937), who restored many other Stanton houses.

You're sure to see walkers passing through Stanton, heading along the Cotswold Way to **13 Stanway**, a mile south; follow the narrow road that runs parallel to the trail. There's little more to idyllic Stanway than a few thatched-roofed cottages, a church and Stanway House, a magnificent Jacobean manor house concealed behind a triple-gabled gatehouse. Its beautiful baroque water gardens feature Britain's tallest fountain. The private home of the Earls of Wemyss for 500 years, the manor has a delightful, lived-in charm, with much of its original furniture and character intact.

Traverse Stanway, turn right (west) onto the B4077 and then left (southwest) back onto the B4632. After 3.5 miles, you'll reach **14 Winchcombe** (p203), an ancient Anglo-Saxon town and walkers' favourite with good sleeping and eating options, including 5 North St. You'll probably want to stay overnight to explore wonderful Sudeley Castle in the morning.

masterpiece of the Cotswold Perpendicular style testifies to its wool-era wealth. Although the chancel and 30m tower date from the 14th century, it was extensively reworked during the 15th-century wool boom. A modern highlight is the 1964 stained-glass window depicting Christ in Glory, behind the altar, while earlier treasures include an unusual 14th-century font.

Sleeping & Eating

★Wheatsheaf   BOUTIQUE HOTEL ££
(☑ 01451-860244; www.cotswoldswheatsheaf.com; West End; r incl breakfast £123-255; 🅿 🛜 🐾) The 14 different rooms at this former coaching inn, very popular with an exclusive London set, blend atmospheric period touches, such as free-standing bathtubs, with modern comforts including power showers, organic toiletries and country-chic decor. Downstairs, an outrageously popular restaurant (mains £14.50-24; ⊙ 8-10am, noon-3pm & 6-9pm Mon-Thu & Sun, to 10pm Fri & Sat; 🅿 🛜 🐾) adds a contemporary twist to delightful seasonal British dishes.

ℹ Information

Cotswolds Discovery Centre (Escape to the Cotswolds; ☑ 01451-861563; www.cotswolds aonb.org.uk; Fosse Way; ⊙ 9.30am-4pm Thu-Mon; 🅿) The Cotswolds' official visitor centre.

ℹ Getting There & Away

Swanbrook or Pulhams buses head to/from the following destinations:

Burford (route 853; £2.40, 15 minutes)
Cheltenham (route 801/853; £2.90, 45 minutes)
Cirencester (route 855; £2.70; 20 minutes)
Gloucester (route 853; £3.50, one hour)
Moreton-in-Marsh (route 801; £2.40, 40 minutes)
Oxford (route 853; £8, one hour)

The Slaughters

☑ 01451 / POP 400
The picture-postcard villages of Upper and Lower Slaughter, roughly a mile apart and around 3.5 miles southwest of Stow-on-the-Wold, have somehow managed to maintain their unhurried medieval charm, despite receiving a multitude of visitors. Their names have nothing to do with abattoirs; they come from the Old English 'sloughtre', meaning slough or muddy place.

Meandering sleepily through the two villages, the River Eye passes a succession of classic gold-tinged Cotswolds houses. It's Lower Slaughter that's the real gem, with the river canalised between limestone banks to flow just a few inches below road level, and flowery footpaths to either side. If you've time for a stroll, you can follow the Eye from one village to the other – the central stretch is away from the traffic – for a round trip that typically takes around two hours.

⊙ Sights

Old Mill   NOTABLE BUILDING
(☑ 01451-820052; www.oldmill-lowerslaughter. com; Lower Slaughter; adult/child £2.50/1; ⊙ 10am-6pm Mar-Oct, to dusk Nov-Feb) Right on the River Eye, the Old Mill houses a cafe and crafts shop as well as a small museum, where you can find out all about the building's former life as a water-powered flour mill. A watermill is recorded as operating in this location as far back as the Domesday Book (1086).

Sleeping & Eating

Lords of the Manor   HISTORIC HOTEL £££
(☑ 01451-820243; www.lordsofthemanor.com; Upper Slaughter; r incl breakfast £240-465; 🅿 🛜 🐾) Although from the outside this 17th-century mansion appears to embody traditional rural splendour, its spacious, supremely tasteful rooms are surprisingly up to date. Expect fresh white styling, floral-print spreads and exposed beams, along with gorgeous countryside panoramas, superb service and a fantastic Michelin-starred restaurant (3-/7-course dinner £72.50/£90; ⊙ noon-1.30pm Sat & Sun, 6.45-9pm daily; 🅿).

ℹ Getting There & Away

Buses are not permitted in the Slaughters, so unless you're hiking or cycling, a car is your best option. To reach Lower Slaughter, detour half a mile west from the A429, 2.5 miles southwest of Stow-on-the-Wold or 6 miles northeast of Northleach. Upper Slaughter is another mile further west.

Stow-on-the-Wold

☑ 01451 / POP 2035
The highest town in the Cotswolds (244m), Stow-on-the-Wold centres on a large square surrounded by handsome buildings. The high-walled alleyways that lead into it orig-

inally served to funnel sheep into the fair, and it also witnessed a bloody massacre at the end of the English Civil War, when Roundhead soldiers dispatched defeated Royalists in 1646.

Standing on the Roman Fosse Way (now the A429), at the junction of six roads 4.5 miles south of Moreton-in-Marsh, Stow is still an important market town. It's also a major tourist destination, crowded with visitors in summer, and famous for hosting the twice-yearly Stow Horse Fair.

◉ Sights

Cotswold Farm Park   ZOO
(☑ 01451-850307; www.cotswoldfarmpark.co.uk; Guiting Power; adult/child £14/12.50; ☺ 10.30am-5pm mid-Feb–late Dec; P ⽥) ⍋ Owned by TV presenter Adam Henson, Cotswold Farm Park sets out to introduce little ones to the world of farm animals, while also preserving rare breeds, such as Exmoor ponies and Cotswold Lion sheep. There are milking demonstrations, lamb-feeding sessions, an adventure playground, a 2-mile wildlife walk and pedal tractors to ride on. It's 6 miles west of Stow-on-the-Wold, signposted from the B4077 and B4068.

⊨ Sleeping & Eating

Number 9   B&B ££
(☑ 01451-870333; www.number-nine.info; 9 Park St; s £50-60, d £75-85; ☎) Centrally located and wonderfully atmospheric, set in an 18th-century town house that was once a coaching inn, this friendly B&B is all sloping floors, low ceilings and exposed beams. Two of the three comfortable en-suite rooms, styled in white and pastels, are unusually spacious, and there's a homely lounge with a crackling fire downstairs.

King's Head Inn   PUB ££
(☑ 01608-658365; www.thekingsheadinn.net; The Green, Bledington; s/d incl breakfast from £90/100; P ☎) Overlooking a peaceful green 4 miles southeast of Stow, this stylishly revamped 16th-century pub blends old and new to perfection, holding a dozen subtly luxurious, individually styled rooms plus a good **restaurant** (mains £14-25.50; ☺ noon-2pm & 6.30-9pm Mon-Sat, to 9.30pm Fri & Sat, noon-3pm & 6.30-9pm Sun; P ☑) ⍋. The six cosy rooms in the original building burst with old-world character (exposed beams, check-print rugs), while the quieter courtyard rooms offer sumptuous contemporary design.

DAYLESFORD ORGANIC

A country-chic temple to the Cotswolds' organic movement, 4 miles east of Stow, **Daylesford Organic** (☑ 01608-731700; www.daylesford.com; Daylesford; ☺ 8am-8pm Mon-Sat, 10am-4pm Sun) ⍋ was kickstarted 40 years ago, when a family farm turned sustainable. Centring on a gleaming food hall, crammed with Daylesford-brand produce, it also holds an excellent cafe-restaurant serving organic-fuelled treats (£13 to £19), plus an upmarket boutique, rental cottages, and luxury spa.

ℹ Getting There & Away

Pulhams buses serve the following destinations (no Sunday service October to April):
Cheltenham (route 801; £3.20, 1¼ hours)
Moreton-in-Marsh (801; £1.90, 10 minutes)
Northleach (801; £2.30, 30 minutes)

Chipping Norton

☑ 01608 / POP 6300
Chipping Norton ('Chippy') is a handsome but slightly faded hilltop town, home to humdrum banks and businesses but with its market square still boasting stately Georgian buildings and old coaching inns as well as the pillared 19th-century town hall. The pick of the many quiet side streets is Church St, where beyond a row of honey-tinged 17th-century almshouses you'll find a fine wool-era church.

◉ Sights

Rollright Stones   ARCHAEOLOGICAL SITE
(www.rollrightstones.co.uk; off A3400, Great Rollright; suggested donation £1; ☺ 24hr) Linked by a footpath through open fields, the ancient Rollright Stones stand to either side of an unnamed road 4 miles north of Chipping Norton. The most remarkable, the King's Men, consists of the weathered remnants of a stone circle that surrounded a Neolithic ceremonial centre in around 2500BC, while the taller King Stone probably marked a Bronze Age cemetery, a millennium later.

Cotswolds Distillery   DISTILLERY
(☑ 01608-238533; www.cotswoldsdistillery.com; Phillip's Field, Whichford Rd, Stourton; tours with/without tasting £10/6; ☺ tours 11am, 1pm & 3pm,

shop 9am-5pm Mon-Sat, 11am-4pm Sun) 🍴
This ambitious, ecofriendly gin and whisky distillery sits tucked into the northern Cotswolds, 8 miles north of Chipping Norton. Join a tour of the facilities to learn how its delicious Cotswolds-flavoured liquors are produced, then wrap things up with a tasting session. Reservations essential.

🛏 Sleeping & Eating

★ **Falkland Arms**   PUB **££**
(19-21 The Green, Great Tew; s/d incl breakfast £85/90; ⊙ restaurant noon-2.30pm & 6-9pm Mon-Sat, to 8pm Sun; ℗ ♠) For its blissful bucolic setting and historic charm, there's no beating the thatched, 16-century Falkland Arms, in the picture-postcard village of Great Tew, 6 miles east of Chipping Norton. The half-dozen freshly restored and upgraded rooms are great value, the pub downstairs serves fine ales and decent pub grub (mains £13 to £20), and there's lovely walking in every direction.

★ **Wild Thyme**   MODERN BRITISH **££**
(☑ 01608-645060; www.wildthymerestaurant.co.uk; 10 New St; 2-/3-course set menus lunch £20/25, dinner £32/40; ⊙ 7-9pm Tue & Wed, noon-2pm & 7-9pm Thu, noon-2pm & 6.30-9.30pm Fri & Sat) This little 'restaurant with rooms' thrills palates with top-notch creative dishes packed with flavour, such as asparagus and goat's

MINSTER LOVELL

Eighteen miles west of Oxford, set on a gentle slope that leads down to the meandering River Windrush, Minster Lovell is a gorgeous village where a clutch of thatch-roofed stone cottages nestle beside an ancient pub and riverside mill. One of William Morris' favourite spots, this peaceful flower-filled hamlet has changed little since medieval times. The main sight is Minster Lovell Hall (EH; www.english-heritage.org.uk; Old Minster; ⊙ 24hr) FREE, a 15th-century riverside manor house that fell into ruins after being abandoned in 1747. You can pass through the vaulted porch to peek past blackened walls into the roofless great hall, the interior courtyard and the crumbling tower, while the wind whistles eerily through the gaping windows.

cheese risotto or steamed Cornish turbot with Japanese pickles. The desserts – from apple crumble to chocolate fondant – are nothing short of sublime. Hidden upstairs are three brilliantly cosy pastel-painted **rooms** (s £75-85, d £85-100; ♠).

Jaffé & Neale Bookshop Cafe   CAFE
(☑ 01608-641033; www.jaffeandneale.co.uk; 1 Middle Row; ⊙ 9.30am-5.30pm Mon-Fri, 9am-5.30pm Sat, 11am-5pm Sun; ♠) The cosy little cafe in this busy independent bookshop on the main square serves delicious cakes and coffees at tables squeezed between the bookshelves, or in the cosy upstairs reading lounge with sofas.

ℹ Getting There & Away

Stagecoach and/or Pulhams buses head to/from the following destinations:
Oxford (route S3; £4.70, one hour)
Witney (route X9; £4, 45 minutes)
Woodstock (route S3; £4.10, 20 minutes)

Chipping Campden

☑ 01386 / POP 2308

A standout gem, even for an area of such pretty towns, Chipping Campden is a glorious reminder of Cotswolds life in medieval times. While 'Chipping' derives from the Old English 'ceapen', meaning 'market', it owes its conspicuous prosperity to its success in the wool trade. Its gracefully curving main street is flanked by a picturesque array of stone cottages, fine terraced houses, ancient inns and historic homes, most made of that beautiful honey-coloured Cotswolds stone. Westington, southwest of the centre, holds some especially striking thatch-roofed cottages.

As the northeastern end of the Cotswold Way, which rambles 102 miles southwest from here to Bath, Chipping Campden is a popular way station for walkers and cyclists, and welcomes crowds of visitors year-round. Despite its obvious allure, though, it remains surprisingly unspoiled.

◎ Sights

Hidcote   GARDENS
(NT; www.nationaltrust.org.uk/hidcote; Hidcote Bartrim; adult/child £10.90/5.45; ⊙ 10am-6pm Apr-Sep, to 5pm Oct, shorter hours Nov, Dec & mid-Feb–Mar, closed Jan; ℗) Hidcote, 4 miles northeast of Chipping Campden, ranks among the finest Arts and Crafts gardens in Britain. Laid out from 1907 onwards by American

horticulturalist Lawrence Johnston, and acquired by the National Trust in 1948, it consists of a series of outdoor 'rooms' filled with flowers and rare plants from across the globe. There's also a cafe and garden centre.

Grevel House
HISTORIC BUILDING

(High St; ⊘closed to the public) Built around 1380 for the supremely prosperous wool merchant William Grevel, complete with gargoyles and mullioned windows, Grevel House is Chipping Campden's oldest building. It's still a private home, but you can admire its splendid Perpendicular Gothic–style gabled window and sundial from the street.

Court Barn Museum
MUSEUM

(☑01386-841951; www.courtbarn.org.uk; Church St; adult/child £5/free; ⊘10am-5pm Tue-Sun Apr-Sep, to 4pm Oct-Mar) Ever since architect and designer Charles Robert Ashbee (1863–1942) moved his Guild of Handicraft here from east London in 1902, Chipping Campden has been linked with the Arts and Crafts movement. This small but interesting museum displays work by nine luminaries of the movement, which celebrated traditional artisans in an age of industrialisation. Sadly, robberies in 2011 and 2017 removed its prize jewellery collection, but surviving artefacts include sculpture, book-binding and ceramics. It also stages two selling exhibitions each year.

🛏 Sleeping & Eating

Eight Bells Inn
PUB ££

(☑01386-840371; www.eightbellsinn.co.uk; Church St; r incl breakfast £99-143; 🐾) This friendly and atmospheric 14th-century inn offers six bright, modern rooms with iron bedsteads, soothing neutral decor, flowery wallpaper and warm accents. Room 7 – there's no number 4 – with its chunky old-world beams, is especially striking. The cosy pub downstairs serves contemporary country cooking.

★ Badgers Hall
BAKERY £

(☑01386-840839; www.badgershall.com; High St; lunch mains £6-12, afternoon tea per person £6.50-25; ⊘8am-5.30pm Thu-Sat; 🐾) Set in a glorious old mansion facing the market hall, this definitive Cotswold tearoom is renowned for its no-holds-barred afternoon teas, served from 2.30pm onwards. Lunch is also a treat, starring the most wonderful cheese scones you've ever tasted. Guests staying in the cosy B&B rooms upstairs (£140) get to sample its baking all week; nonguests are welcome Thursday to Saturday only.

WORTH A TRIP

BATSFORD ARBORETUM

Created from 1880 onwards by Bertie Mitford (Lord Redesdale), and later briefly home to his famous granddaughters, the Mitford sisters, these exotic 22-hectare **woodlands** (☑01386-701441; www.batsarb.co.uk; Batsford Park; adult/child £7.95/3.30; ⊘9am-5pm Mon-Sat, from 10am Sun; P 🐾) 🐾, 1.5 miles west of Moreton, hold around 1600 species of labelled trees, bamboos and shrubs. Drawn especially from Nepal, China and Japan, many are rare or endangered, or were planted pre-WWI. Highlights include flowering Japanese cherries (at their best in spring), some vast North American redwoods and an enormous davidia, and the strangely churchlike 'cathedral' lime.

A 1.7-mile footpath from Moreton leads direct to the arboretum itself; motorists have to drive a mile north up the approach road from the entrance on the A44.

❶ Information

Tourist Office (☑01386-841206; www. campdenonline.org; Old Police Station, High St; ⊘9.30am-5pm mid-Mar–Oct, 9.30am-1pm Mon-Thu, to 4pm Fri-Sun Nov–mid-Mar) Pick up a town guide (£1.50) for a self-guided walk around Chipping Campden's most significant buildings. Between May and September, the Cotswold Voluntary Wardens run guided tours (suggested donation £3).

❶ Getting There & Away

From Monday to Saturday, Johnsons Excelbus services head to/from Moreton-in-Marsh (route 1/2; £3.90, 50 minutes), Broadway (route 1/2; £2.90, 20 minutes) and Stratford-upon-Avon (route 1/2; £4.40, 50 minutes).

Marchants buses 606 (Monday to Saturday) and 606S (Sunday) run to/from Broadway (£2.90, 20 minutes), Cheltenham (£8.50, one hour 20 minutes), Stratford-upon-Avon (£4.80, 25 minutes) and Winchcombe (£5.60, 35 minutes).

Broadway

☑01386 / POP 2540

The graceful, golden-hued cottages of the quintessentially English village of Broadway, set at the foot of a steep escarpment, now hold antique shops, tearooms and art galleries, interspersed with luxurious hotels. One of the Cotswolds' most popular destinations, just 5 miles west of Chipping Campden, the village attracted the likes of writer-designer William Morris and artist John Singer Sargent during the Victorian era.

The village of Snowshill, 2.5 miles south, may look familiar; a local house starred in the hit film *Bridget Jones's Diary* as Bridget's parents' home.

◉ Sights

Snowshill Manor & Garden HOUSE
(NT; www.nationaltrust.org.uk; Snowshill; adult/child £12.80/6.40; ⊙noon-5pm mid-Mar–Oct, 11am-2.30pm Sat & Sun Nov) Once home to eccentric poet and architect Charles Paget Wade (1883–1956), this wonderful medieval mansion stands just over 2 miles south of Broadway. It now displays Wade's extraordinary collection of crafts and design, ranging from musical instruments to Southeast Asian masks and Japanese samurai armour.

Broadway Tower TOWER
(☑01386-852390; www.broadwaytower.co.uk; Middle Hill; adult/child £5/3, with Cold War Experience £8.50/5; ⊙10am-5pm; Ⓟ) Built in 1798 to resemble an imaginary Saxon fort, this turreted Gothic folly looks down on Broadway from atop the escarpment, 1 mile southeast. William Morris spent a summer here, so exhibitions on its successive levels focus on the

---

SHIN KICKING & CHEESE ROLLING
....

The medieval sport of shin kicking lives on in the extraordinary **Cotswold Olimpicks** (www.olimpickgames.co.uk; Dover's Hill; ⊙late May/early Jun), first celebrated in 1612. One of England's most bizarre and entertaining traditional sports days, it still features many of the original events, such as tug o' war. It's held in Chipping Campden.

Equally odd is the age-old (and surprisingly hazardous) pastime of **cheese-rolling** (www.cheese-rolling. co.uk; Cooper's Hill; admission free; ⊙last May bank holiday). Following a 200-year-old tradition, crowds run, tumble and slide down Cooper's Hill, 4.5 miles northeast of Painswick, pursuing an 8lb round of Double Gloucester cheese. The prize? The cheese itself – and the glory of catching it.

Arts and Crafts movement. The main reason to visit, though, is for the stunning all-round views from its rooftop platform.

Broadway Museum & Art Gallery MUSEUM
(☑01386-859047; www.ashmoleanbroadway. org; Tudor House, 65 High St; adult/child £5/2; ⊙10am-5pm Tue-Sun Feb-Oct, to 4pm Nov & Dec, closed Jan) Set in a magnificent 17th-century coaching inn, Broadway's town museum has close links with Oxford's prestigious Ashmolean Museum (p180). Its fascinating displays of local crafts, art and antiques, and its stimulating temporary exhibitions, draw exclusively on the Ashmolean collection, so the quality is consistently high. Paintings in the sumptuous upstairs galleries include 18th-century works by Joshua Reynolds and Thomas Gainsborough.

🍽 Sleeping & Eating

Crown & Trumpet PUB ££
(☑01386-853202; www.cotswoldholidays.co.uk; 14 Church St; r £60-90; ⊙restaurant 11am-11pm; Ⓟ🛜) This very welcoming, locally loved 17th-century inn holds five good-value retro-furnished en-suite rooms, complete with sloping floors, exposed beams and low ceilings. The downstairs pub is a good bet for real ales, ciders and decent pub grub; it serves a good breakfast (to guests only) for £10 per person. Two-night minimum at weekends.

Russell's HOTEL £££
(☑01386-853555; www.russellsofbroadway.co.uk; The Green, 20 High St; r incl breakfast from £130; ⊙restaurant noon-2.15pm & 6-9.15pm Mon-Sat, noon-2.30pm Sun; Ⓟ🛜🐾) Housed in the former workshop of furniture designer Gordon Russell, this Arts and Crafts–influenced hotel offers seven sizeable rooms, some with exposed beams, four-poster beds and armchairs, and all with contemporary bathrooms and fresh white styling. The modern-British restaurant (mains £15 to £27) serves a good-value three-course menu (£24) for lunch and dinner.

★ Mount Inn PUB FOOD ££
(☑01386-584316; www.themountinn.co.uk; Stanton; mains £13-22; ⊙noon-2pm & 6-9pm Mon-Sat, to 8pm Sun; Ⓟ) Revelling in glorious hilltop views above pretty honey-washed Stanton, just off the Cotswolds Way 3.5 miles southwest of Broadway, this pub is not just idyllically located, it serves great food too: hearty country favourites, prepared with contemporary flair. Menus range over breaded local

St Eadburgha cheese, beer-battered haddock, gammon steaks, mushroom-halloumi burgers and seasonal specials.

ℹ Information

Tourist Office (📞 01386-852937; www.visit-broadway.co.uk; Russell Sq; ⏰10am-5pm Mon-Sat, 11am-3pm Sun Apr-Oct, 10am-4pm Mon-Sat Nov-Mar) Sells maps of local walks.

ℹ Getting There & Away

BUS

Marchants and Johnsons ExcelBus services head to the following destinations:

Cheltenham (route 606/606S; £3.20, 40 minutes)

Chipping Campden (route 1/2/606S; £2.90, 20 minutes)

Moreton-in-Marsh (route 1/2; £3.90, 30 minutes)

Stratford-upon-Avon (route 1/2/24/606S; £4.40, 45 minutes)

Winchcombe (route 606/606S; £3, 30 minutes)

TRAIN

Rail service returned to Broadway in 2018 after a 58-year hiatus, with the reopening of the long-defunct Broadway Station, just under a mile northwest of town. Most days in summer, following an intricate schedule, the volunteer-run Gloucestershire Warwickshire Railway (p204) runs around five excursion trains between Cheltenham racecourse and Broadway, via Winchcombe, for a return fare of £18.

Moreton-in-Marsh

📞 01608 / POP 3820

Graced by an ultrabroad High St that follows the die-straight line of the Roman Fosse Way (now the A429), and is lined with beautiful 17th- and 18th-century buildings, Moreton-in-Marsh is a historic Cotswolds town that's sadly rather marred by the constant heavy traffic that hurtles right through the centre. Take the time to wander around, though – ideally on a Tuesday, when the weekly market bursts into life – and you'll find plenty of tearooms, cafes and pubs, along with intriguing shops. It's 4.5 miles north of Stow-on-the-Wold.

◉ Sights

⭐ Cotswold Falconry Centre   BIRD SANCTUARY
(📞 01386-701043; www.cotswold-falconry.co.uk; Batsford Park; adult/child £10/5; ⏰10.30am-5pm

mid-Feb–mid-Nov; 🅿) Home to over 150 birds of prey (owl, vulture, eagle and, of course, falcon), this exciting spot stages displays of the ancient practice of falconry at 11.30am, 1.30pm and 3pm daily (plus 4.30pm April to October). The birds fly best on windy days. Hands-on experiences (from £40) include a one-hour 'Flying Start' during which visitors get to fly hawks.

Chastleton House   HISTORIC BUILDING
(NT; 📞 01608-674355; www.nationaltrust.org.uk/chastleton-house; Chastleton; adult/child £9.50/5; ⏰1-5pm Wed-Sun Mar-Oct; 🅿) Four miles southeast of Moreton, signposted off the A44 halfway to Chipping Norton, Chastleton is one of England's finest and most complete Jacobean houses. Built between 1607 and 1612 and barely altered since, it's bursting with rare tapestries, family portraits and antique furniture; the Long Gallery is particularly resplendent. Outside, there's a wonderful topiary garden. Free garden tours run most afternoons.

🛏 Sleeping & Eating

White Hart Royal Hotel   HOTEL ££
(📞 01608-650731; www.whitehartroyal.co.uk; High St; s/d £100/110; 🅿🛜) 'Royal' refers to the fact that Charles I stayed in this low-slung honey-coloured inn during the Civil War. He may not have used the iPod docks and flat-screen TVs, but he certainly walked down the atmospheric half-timbered corridors. Standard rooms these days are comfy and well equipped, even if they lack character.

Martha's Coffee House
CAFE £

(📞01608-651999; Gavel Cottage, High St; mains £7-9; ⊘9am-5pm Mon-Sat, to 4pm Sun; 🛜🚻) In an appealing historic cottage on the main road, Martha's is a local mainstay, dependable from the moment it serves the first of its all-day pancake-and-eggs breakfasts to the last of its £7.50-per-person cream teas. Lunchtime sees good-value sandwiches and toasties, but the real highlights are the £4.50 savoury scones, featuring flavours like beetroot and basil.

Horse & Groom
PUB FOOD ££

(📞01386-700413; www.horseandgroom.info; A44, Bourton-on-the-Hill; mains £12-23; ⊘noon-3pm & 6.30-9.30pm Mon-Sat, to 8.30pm Sun; 🅿🛜) 🥘 This laid-back but welcoming pub, in a tiny hamlet 2 miles west of Moreton-in-Marsh, is a firm favourite with well-heeled horsey types who appreciate its extravagant array of gins. As well as serving good food, with a menu that showcases local lamb, beef and fresh produce in general, it also has five swish rooms upstairs (£130 to £170).

❶ Getting There & Away

BUS
Pulhams, Stagecoach and/or Johnsons Excelbus buses head to/from the following:

Broadway (route 1/2; £3.90, 30 minutes)
Cheltenham (route 801; £3.50, 1½ hours)
Chipping Campden (route 1/2; £3.90, 50 minutes)
Northleach (route 801; £2.40, 40 minutes)
Stow-on-the-Wold (route 801; £1.90, 10 minutes)

TRAIN
The station is towards the northern end of town, just off High St. Trains head to/from the following:

Hereford (£19.60, 1¾ hours)
Ledbury (£18.50, 1½ hours)
London Paddington (£14.50, 1½ hours)
Oxford (£10.60, 35 minutes)
Worcester (£13.30, 40 minutes)

Painswick
📞01452 / POP 1736

Among the Cotswolds' most beautiful and unspoiled villages, hilltop Painswick sits 10 miles southwest of Cheltenham. Cars stream through, along its single-lane main road, but other than walkers on the Cotswold Way, few visitors allow themselves the pleasure of wandering its narrow winding streets to admire picture-perfect cottages, handsome stone houses and medieval inns. Keep an eye out for Bisley St, the original main drag, which was superseded by the now ancient-looking New St in medieval times.

Bucolic little Slad, 2 miles south towards Stroud in the Slad Valley, was the much-loved home of writer Laurie Lee (1914–97), who immortalised its beauty in *Cider with Rosie*.

◎ Sights

Painswick Rococo Garden
GARDENS

(📞01452-813204; www.rococogarden.org.uk; off B4073; adult/child £7.50/3.60; ⊘10.30am-5pm mid-Jan–Oct; 🅿🛜) England's only surviving rococo garden, half a mile north of Painswick, was laid out by Benjamin Hyett in the 1740s as a vast 'outdoor room'. Restored to its original glory thanks to a contemporary painting, it's absolutely stunning. Winding paths soften its geometrical precision, leading visitors to scattered Gothic follies that include the eccentric Red House, which has Latin quotes from the Song of Solomon etched into its stained-glass windows. There's also a children's nature trail and maze.

St Mary's Church
CHURCH

(www.beaconbenefice.org.uk/painswick; New St; ⊘9.30am-dusk) Painswick centres on this fine 14th-century, Perpendicular Gothic wool church, surrounded by 18th-century tabletop tombs and clipped yew trees sculpted to resemble giant ice lollies. Legend has it that only 99 trees could ever grow here, as the devil would shrivel the 100th. To celebrate the millennium, they planted one anyway, and – lo and behold! – another one toppled. At the foot of the churchyard there's a rare set of iron stocks.

🛏 Sleeping & Eating

Troy House
B&B ££

(📞01452-812339; www.troyguesthouse.co.uk; Gloucester St; s/d £75/85; 🛜) This great little B&B sleeps guests in four sweet, spacious rooms, two of which occupy a separate rear cottage accessed across an attractive courtyard. They're prettily decked out with soothing cream decor, comfy beds and baskets of toiletries, and the freshly cooked breakfasts are excellent.

★ Painswick
LUXURY HOTEL £££

(📞01452-813688; www.thepainswick.co.uk; Kemps Lane; r/ste from £179/404; ⊘restaurant noon-

2.30pm & 7-9.30pm; P📶) Focused around an imposing 18th-century house somehow squeezed into the heart of the village, and seriously chic within its stern stone walls, the Painswick offers 16 luxurious, individually decorated, pastel-painted rooms, some with four-poster beds, that spread through assorted outbuildings. As well as massage/treatment rooms, there's a futuristic bar, a colour-popping lounge and a good modern restaurant (mains £19 to £28).

Woolpack Inn PUB FOOD ££
(📞01452-813429; www.thewoolpackslad.com; Slad; mains £12-19; ⊙noon-11pm Sun & Mon, to midnight Tue-Thu, to 1am Fri & Sat, food served 6-9pm Mon, noon-3pm & 6-9pm Tue-Sat, noon-4pm Sun; 🎮) This lively little rural pub in Slad, 2 miles south of Painswick, was a favourite watering hole of local author Laurie Lee, whose portrait and books adorn its walls. Perfect for a pint, stocking excellent local beers including Uley Bitter, it also serves a daily-changing menu of classics such as gammon or fish and chips alongside pasta, burgers and curries.

ℹ Information

Tourist Office (📞01452-812278; www.painswicktouristinfo.co.uk; Gravedigger's Hut, St Mary's Church, New St; ⊙10am-4pm Mon-Fri, to 1pm Sat Mar-Oct) Beside the main road, but accessed from within the church grounds.

ℹ Getting There & Away

Stagecoach bus 66 heads to/from Cheltenham (£3.60, 36 minutes) and Stroud (£2.20, 7 minutes).

Winchcombe

📞01242 / POP 5024
Winchcombe, 8 miles northeast of Cheltenham, is very much a living, working town, where butchers, bakers and independent shops line the main streets. Capital of the Anglo-Saxon kingdom of Mercia, it remained a major trading town until the Middle Ages, and was a centre for (illegally) growing tobacco in the 17th century. Reminders of that illustrious past can still be seen in Winchcombe's dramatic stone and half-timbered buildings. Keep an eye out for the picturesque cottages on Vineyard St and Dents Tce. As Winchcombe is on the Cotswold Way and other trails, it's especially popular with walkers.

BERKELEY CASTLE

This superb red-stone castle (📞01453-810303; www.berkeley-castle.com; adult/child £12.50/7; ⊙11am-5pm Sun-Wed Apr-Oct; P♿) has been home to the Berkeleys for nearly 900 years, and little has changed since it was built as a sturdy Norman fortress. Edward II was imprisoned here in 1327 and swiftly died, probably murdered on the orders of his wife and her lover. Highlights include its central 12th-century keep, the King's Gallery, complete with Edward's cell and dungeon, and the spectacular medieval Great Hall, lined with tapestries. Free 45-minute guided tours run every 30 minutes.

◉ Sights

Sudeley Castle CASTLE
(📞01242-604244; www.sudeleycastle.co.uk; adult/child £16.50/7.50; ⊙10am-5pm mid-Mar–Oct; P♿) During its thousand-year history, this magnificent castle has welcomed many a monarch, including Richard III, Henry VIII and Charles I. Half a mile southeast of Winchcombe, it's most famous as the home and final resting place of Catherine Parr (Henry VIII's widow), who lived here with her fourth husband, Thomas Seymour. In fact it's the only private house in England where a queen is buried – Catherine lies in its Perpendicular Gothic St Mary's Church. It also boasts 10 splendid gardens.

Belas Knap Long Barrow ARCHAEOLOGICAL SITE
(EH; www.english-heritage.org.uk; near Charlton Abbots; ⊙dawn-dusk) FREE Dating from around 3000 BC, Belas Knap is one of the country's best-preserved neolithic burial chambers, complete with 'false' portal leading nowhere. The remains of 31 people were found when its four chambers were excavated. At 290m, views across Sudeley Castle and the surrounding countryside are breathtaking. The barrow can be accessed from Winchcombe by a 2½-mile hike south along the Cotswold Way. Alternatively, park on Corndean Lane and take a steep half-mile walk up across fields.

Hailes Abbey RUINS
(EH; www.english-heritage.org.uk; Hailes; adult/child £5.90/3.50; ⊙10am-6pm Jul & Aug, to 5pm Easter-Jun, Sep & Oct; P) Now lying in ruins

3 miles northeast of Winchcombe, this 13th-century Cistercian abbey was once, thanks to a long-running medieval scam, one of England's main pilgrimage centres. The abbey was said – by Geoffrey Chaucer in *The Canterbury Tales*, among others – to possess a vial of Christ's blood. Until that was denounced during the Reformation as containing no more than coloured water, thousands of pilgrims contributed to the abbey's wealth. Free audio guides lead visitors around.

🛏 Sleeping & Eating

Wesley House   B&B **££**
(📞 01242-602366; www.wesleyhouse.co.uk; High St; s £75-85, d £95-110; ⊗ restaurant noon-2pm & 7-9pm Tue-Sat, noon-2pm Sun; 🛜🏠) Methodist founder John Wesley once stayed in this ravishing 15th-century half-timbered town house, which offers five pleasant rooms plus a warm welcome. 'Mumble Meadow', splashed with reds, overlooks the street, while 'Almsbury' has its own terrace gazing out across the countryside. Rates rise on Saturdays. Downstairs. the restaurant serves fabulous modern-British cuisine (mains £16 to £28).

★ 5 North St   MODERN EUROPEAN **£££**
(📞 01242-604566; www.5northstreetrestaurant. co.uk; 5 North St; 2-/3-course lunch £26/32, 3-/7-course dinner £54/74; ⊗ 7-9pm Tue, 12.30-1.30pm & 7-9pm Wed-Sat, 12.30-1.30pm Sun; 🥢) This veteran gourmet restaurant is a treat from start to finish, from its splendid 400-year-old timbered exterior to the elegant, inventive creations you eventually find on your plate. Marcus Ashenford's cooking is rooted in traditional seasonal ingredients, but the odd playful experiment (think duck-egg pasta or malt ice cream) adds that extra magic. Vegetarians can enjoy a separate £40 menu.

ℹ Information

Tourist Office (📞 01242-602925; www.winch combe.co.uk; Town Hall, High St; ⊗10am-4pm daily Apr-Oct, to 3pm Sat & Sun Nov-Mar) Has maps of local walks and runs free guided town tours at 11am and 2.30pm on Sunday, from Easter to October.

ℹ Getting There & Away

BUS

Marchants buses travel to/from Broadway (route 606/606S; £3, 30 minutes) and Chel-

tenham (route 606/606S/W1/W2; £2.70, 20 minutes).

TRAIN

Several days each week in summer, to a convoluted schedule, the **Gloucestershire Warwickshire Railway** (GWR; 📞 01242-621405; www. gwsr.com; day pass adult/child £18/8; ⊗ Mar-Dec; 🚆) runs around five trains that stop at Winchcombe en route between Cheltenham (£5, 25 minutes) and Broadway (£9, 20 minutes).

WESTERN GLOUCESTERSHIRE

West of the Cotswolds, Gloucestershire's greatest asset is the elegant Regency town of Cheltenham, home to tree-lined terraces, upmarket boutiques and a tempting assortment of hotels and restaurants. The county capital, Gloucester, is also worth visiting, to see its magnificent Perpendicular Gothic cathedral, while Berkeley, not far southwest, has a historic Norman castle. Further west, the Forest of Dean is a leafy backwater that's perfect for walking, cycling, kayaking and other adventurous activities.

Cheltenham

📞 01242 / POP 117,500

Cheltenham, on the western edge of the Cotswolds and the region's major town, owes its air of gracious refinement to its heyday as a spa resort during the 18th century. At that time, it rivalled Bath as *the* place for ailing aristocrats to recuperate, and it stills boast many graceful Regency buildings and manicured squares. These days, however, it's better known for its racecourse, where the upper classes still arrive in droves for the mid-March Cheltenham Cup.

Cheltenham's excellent hotel and restaurant offerings make it a much more appealing base than Gloucester (12 miles west), but in the end this mid-tier town is unlikely to be the highlight of your trip.

Central Cheltenham extends around the grand tree-lined Promenade, with the fashionable Montpellier neighbourhood at its southern end.

👁 Sights

The Promenade   STREET
Famed as one of the most beautiful streets in England, this broad, tree-lined boulevard leads down from the high street to Mont-

Cheltenham

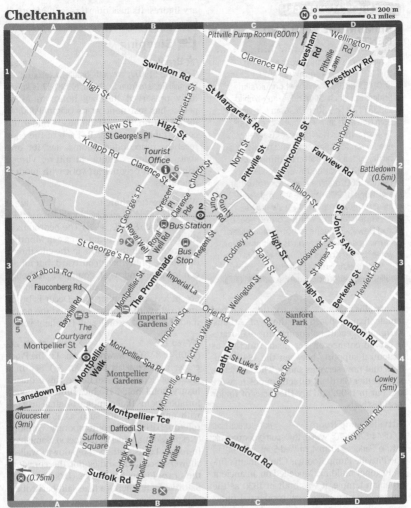

OXFORD & THE COTSWOLDS CHELTENHAM

pellier, and is flanked by imposing period buildings that are now filled with fancy shops. The striking **Municipal Offices**, behind the flower-filled Long Gardens on its western side, were built in 1825 as private residences. A statue in front commemorates Cheltenham-born explorer Edward Wilson (1872–1912), who perished on Captain Scott's ill-fated second expedition to the Antarctic.

Montpellier AREA

As well as plenty of handsome architecture, the village-y Montpellier district hosts a lively assortment of bars, restaurants, hotels, independent shops and boutiques. Along

Cheltenham

OFF THE BEATEN TRACK

SLIMBRIDGE WETLAND CENTRE

A pioneer in wetlands conservation, this 325-hectare **reserve** (WWT; ✆01453-891900; www.wwt.org.uk/slimbridge; Bowditch, Slimbridge; adult/child £13.18/7.72; ◷9.30am-5.30pm Apr-Oct, to 5pm Nov-Mar; [P] ✐, beside the River Severn 5 miles northeast of Berkeley, is a haven for migratory and resident birds. Hides are scattered throughout, and an observation tower affords spectacular 360-degree views for potential sightings of 200-plus feathered species, ranging from visiting swallows, peregrine falcons, white-fronted geese and Bewick's swans to hot-pink resident flamingos. Migratory birds visit in winter, while spring brings plenty of chicks.

Activities include guided walks, otter talks, and self-guided 'canoe safaris' (£7).

Montpellier Walk, 32 caryatids (draped female figures based on those of Athens' Acropolis), each balancing an elaborately carved cornice on her head, function as structural supports between the 1840s edifices that now serve as shops. The attractive Montpellier Gardens, directly opposite, were laid out in 1809, and are the focus of major local festivals.

Pittville Pump Room   NOTABLE BUILDING
(✆0844 576 2210; www.pittvillepumproom.org.uk; Pittville Park; ◷10am-4pm Wed-Sun; ♿) **FREE**
The Pittville Pump Room is Cheltenham's finest Regency building. Modelled on an ancient Athenian temple, it was built in 1830 as the centrepiece of a large new residential quarter a mile north of the town centre. Admire its beautiful columned exterior, then wander into the main auditorium, where, if the pump is currently operating, you can sample the pungent spa waters from the ornate fountain. The lovely surrounding ornamental park is home to a lake, lawns and an aviary.

✫ Festivals

Cheltenham Literature Festival   LITERATURE
(✆01242-850270; www.cheltenhamfestivals.com; ◷early Oct) One of the world's oldest book-focused festivals kicks off over 10 days in autumn, hosting an astounding array of talks, workshops, interviews and debates by 600 top writers, actors, scholars and other literary figures. Its headquarters is in Montpellier Gardens.

🛏 Sleeping

★**Bradley**   B&B ££
(✆01242-519077; www.thebradleyhotel.co.uk; 19 Bayshill Rd; s/d from £110/115; 🛜🖥) This splendidly preserved Regency house in Montpellier has lost none of its original flair in its transition into a fabulous, wonderfully comfortable, luxury B&B. Each of the eight recently redecorated rooms has its own style, blending antique furniture, vintage trinkets and original artwork with modern amenities.

Wyastone Townhouse   B&B ££
(✆01242-245549; www.wyastonehotel.co.uk; Parabola Rd; s/d £85/110; [P]🛜) The bedrooms in this lovely white Victorian house in Montpellier are grander than those in the guesthouse beside the pretty back courtyard, but all are comfortable and well equipped. Although family rooms sleep four guests, it doesn't accept kids aged under four. Decor is bright and fresh, with local artwork, and the homemade breakfasts wonderful. Excellent value.

★**No 131**   BOUTIQUE HOTEL £££
(✆01242-822939; www.no131.com; 131 The Promenade; r incl breakfast £160-230; 🛜) Set in a stunning Georgian town house, this exquisite luxury hotel holds 11 chic, supremely comfortable rooms that combine original artwork with antique touches such as 19th-century roll-top baths and contemporary comforts (Nespresso machines, iPod docks). Some have in-room baths, others step-down walk-in showers. Scented candles dot the corridors, the Crazy Eights bar buzzes (DJs Thursday–Saturday), and there's a luxe, laid-back vibe.

✗ Eating

Boston Tea Party   CAFE £
(✆01242-573935; www.bostonteaparty.co.uk; 45-49 Clarence St; dishes £4.50-11; ◷7am-8pm Mon-Sat, to 7pm Sun; 🛜✐🖥) ✐ A spacious, friendly, vintage-chic cafe, where relaxed decor – all blue faux-leather booths and rough wood tables, fresh flowers and colourful cans – makes the perfect setting for a contemporary British-international menu focused on ethically sourced ingredients. All-day breakfasts and brunches and tasty vegan and gluten-free choices keep it buzzing. Options include halloumi- or spiced-lamb-stuffed flatbreads, grain bowls and Vietnamese Banh-Mi sandwiches.

Tavern   GASTROPUB ££

(📞01242-221212; www.theluckyonion.com/prope
rty/the-tavern; 5 Royal Well Pl; mains £13-30;
⏱noon-3pm & 5.30-10pm Mon-Fri, noon-10.30pm
Sat, to 9.30pm Sun; 🛜🍴) Behind its bare-
bones exterior, this stylish gastropub serves
Modern British food with a punch, amid
exposed brick, bare wooden tables, blue-vel-
vet booths and tile-covered floors. Classy
mains – ricotta dumplings with chanterelle
mushrooms, wild garlic and pine nuts; cod
cheeks with Puy lentils and pancetta – plus
steaks, and pub classics from mac-cheese
to burgers. The warm, welcoming service is
spot on.

⭐ **Le Champignon Sauvage**   FRENCH £££

(📞01242-573449; www.lechampignonsauvage.
co.uk; 24-28 Suffolk Rd; menus £28-70; ⏱12.30-
1.30pm & 7.30-8.45pm Tue-Sat) For over 30
years, chef David Everitt-Matthias has been
thrilling visitors and locals alike in this two-
Michelin-starred Cheltenham favourite. Imaginative flavour combinations in his finely
executed dishes include the likes of lamb
loin with wild garlic pesto, sheep's curd and
anchovy emulsion. We're not alone in thinking it's Gloucestershire's best restaurant. The
set lunch and dinner menus are good value.

Daffodil   BRASSERIE £££

(📞01242-700055; www.thedaffodil.com; 18-20
Suffolk Pde; mains £15-50; ⏱5-11pm Mon, Wed &
Thu, noon-midnight Fri & Sat, noon-7pm Sun; 🛜🍴)
This breathtaking brasserie conjures its retro setting, in a 1920s cinema, into fabulous
art deco glamour, with a delightful daffodil
theme from its tiled floor to the plaster cornicing. Charcoal-grilled offerings range from
halloumi or lobster to calves' liver and, especially, steaks, but it also has veggie options
such as aubergine, coconut and lemongrass
curry and open goat's-cheese ravioli.

ℹ️ Information

Tourist Office (📞01242-387492; www.visit
cheltenham.com; The Wilson, Clarence St;
⏱9.30am-5.15pm Mon-Wed, to 7.45pm Thu, to
5.30pm Fri & Sat, 10.30am-4pm Sun) A desk
inside the Wilson Museum.

ℹ️ Getting There & Away

BUS

Stagecoach, Pulhams, Marchants and Swan-
brook operate local buses from Cheltenham.
Most buses depart from the **bus station** (Royal
Well Rd); some use stops along the Promenade.
Bus destinations include the following:

Broadway (route 606/606S; £3.20, 40
minutes)

Cirencester (51; £3.80, 40 minutes)

Gloucester (10/94; £3.40, 45 minutes)

Oxford (853; £8, 1½ hours)

Stow-on-the-Wold (801; £3.20, 1¼ hours)

Stratford-upon-Avon (606S, Sunday only; £8,
1½ hours)

Stroud (66; £3.80, 45 minutes)

Winchcombe (606/606S; £2.70, 20 minutes)

National Express coach destinations:

Birmingham (£7.40, 1½ hours)

Bristol (£8.10, 1½ hours)

Leeds (£44.20, six hours)

London Victoria (£8, three hours)

Newcastle-upon-Tyne (£42.50, eight hours)

Nottingham (£23.20, 4¼ hours)

TRAIN

Cheltenham Spa train station is a mile west of
the centre. The pleasant 'Honeybourne Line'
footpath leads through parkland to the heart of
town in around 20 minutes, while buses (D/E;
£2) run every 10 minutes. Train connections
include the following:

Bath (£11.90, 1¼ hours)

Bristol (£9.10, 40 minutes)

Cardiff (£19.10, 1½ hours)

Edinburgh (£159.50, six hours)

Exeter (£31.30, 1¾ hours)

Gloucester (£4.80, 10 minutes)

London Paddington (£34.30, two hours)

Forest of Dean

POP 85,400

England's oldest oak forest is a wonderfully
scenic place for outdoor adventures. Designated England's first National Forest Park
in 1938, this 42-sq-mile woodland had previously been a royal hunting ground and a
centre of iron and coal mining. Its mysterious depths supposedly inspired the forests
of JRR Tolkien's Middle Earth, while key
scenes in *Harry Potter & the Deathly Hallows* were filmed here.

There's no 'Dean' in the Forest of Dean –
no one knows what it means – but it also
gives its name to a Gloucestershire district
that includes the towns of Newent and
Coleford, north and west of the forest. To
the northwest, the forest spills over into
Herefordshire, while the River Wye skirts
its western edge, offering glorious views to
canoeists who paddle from the village of
Symonds Yat.

DON'T MISS

GLOUCESTER CATHEDRAL

Gloucester's spectacular **cathedral** (☎ 01452-528095; www.gloucestercathedral.org.uk; 12 College Green; admission free, tours adult/child tower £7/1, crypt £3/1, library £3/1; ☺ 7.30am–6pm) is among the first and finest examples of the English Perpendicular Gothic style.

Inside, the finest features of Norman Romanesque and Gothic design are skilfully combined, with stout columns creating a sense of gracious solidity. The **Cloister**, which featured in the first, second and sixth Harry Potter films, is a real highlight. Completed in 1367, this airy space contains the earliest example of fan vaulting in England and is matched in beauty only by Henry VII's chapel at Westminster Abbey.

From the breathtaking 14th-century wooden **choir stalls**, you'll get a good view of the imposing 22m-high Great East Window. The size of a tennis court, it was the largest in Europe when it was installed in the 1350s, and around 85% of the glass you see today is still original.

Edward II's tomb, originally gilded and bejewelled, stands beneath the window in the northern ambulatory. Behind the altar, the glorious 15th-century **Lady Chapel** was largely destroyed during the Reformation, but following restoration work, completed in 2018, it's looking wonderful once more.

Tours give access to otherwise inaccessible areas including the 15th-century library and its illuminated manuscripts (weekly, 30 minutes); the 69m tower, with its amazing views (three weekly, one hour), and the Norman crypt (daily, 30 minutes).

The Dean Heritage Centre, outside Soudley within the forest's eastern fringe, is a good place to begin exploring.

◎ Sights

★ International Centre for Birds of Prey
BIRD SANCTUARY

(☎ 01531-820286; www.icbp.org; Boulsdon House, Newent; adult/child £11.40/6.30; ☺ 10.30am–5.30pm Feb-Nov; Ⓟ) Watch raptors swoop and dive at this large, long-standing countryside complex, 2 miles southwest of Newent (follow signs). There are three flyings per day (11.30am, 2pm and 4.15pm in summer; 11.30am, 1.30pm and 3.30pm in winter), along with aviaries housing 70 species of owls, falcons, kestrels, eagles, buzzards, hawks, kites and other birds of prey from all over the world. For the hands-on feel, choose from various 'experience days', devoted to specific birds (from £70).

Symonds Yat
VILLAGE

On the northwest edge of the Forest of Dean, squeezed between the River Wye and the towering limestone outcrop known as **Symonds Yat Rock** (Symonds Yat East; ☺ 24hr; Ⓟ) FREE, Symonds Yat is a tiny, endearing tangle of pubs, guesthouses and campsites, with great walks and a couple of canoeing centres. The river splits it into two halves, one in Gloucestershire and one in Herefordshire. They're connected by an ancient hand-hauled ferry (adult/child/bicycle £1.20/60p/60p; dawn to dusk).

Puzzlewood
FOREST, FARM

(☎ 01594-833187; www.puzzlewood.net; Perrygrove Rd, Coleford; adult/child £7/6; ☺ 10am–5pm Apr-Oct, to 3.30pm Wed, Sat & Sun mid-Feb–Mar, Nov & Dec; Ⓟ👪) A pre-Roman open-cast iron mine, overgrown with eerie moss-covered trees, Puzzlewood is a 6-hectare woodland web of paths, weird rock formations, tangled vines, rickety bridges, uneven steps and dark passageways, all seemingly designed to disorientate. Parts of hit TV shows *Doctor Who* and *Merlin*, as well as *Star Wars The Force Awakens*, were shot here. There's a mile of pathways to explore and kids will love the farm animals. Find it a mile south of Coleford on the B4228.

Clearwell Caves
CAVE

(☎ 01594-832535; www.clearwellcaves.com; Clearwell; adult/child £7.50/5.50; ☺ 10am-5pm Apr-Aug, to 4pm mid-Feb–Mar & Sep-Dec; Ⓟ👪) Descend into the damp subterranean world of a 4500-year-old iron and ochre mine, comprising a warren of dimly lit passageways, caverns and pools, and home to several species of bats. 'Deep Level Caving' sessions (adult/child £25/18) take you even further in. From November, the caves are transformed into a hugely popular Christmas grotto. They're signposted off the B4228, a mile south of Coleford.

🏃 Activities

Dean Forest Railway RAIL
(📞01594-845840; www.deanforestrailway.co.uk; Forest Rd, Lydney; day ticket adult/child £13/6; ⊙ Wed, Sat & Sun mid-Mar–Oct; 🚗) Three days a week for most of the year, classic steam engines ply this 4.5-mile line between Lydney and Parkend. Occasionally, though – check online – it operates diesel trains instead. The standard ride is 30 minutes, but special events range from Sunday lunch in 1st-class carriages to 'drive your own steam engine' experiences. Thomas the Tank Engine makes the occasional appearance. Book ahead.

Wyedean Canoe
& Adventure Centre ADVENTURE SPORTS
(📞01600-890238; www.wyedean.co.uk; Symonds Yat East; half-day hire from £30) Hires out canoes and kayaks, and organises white-water trips, archery, high ropes, abseiling, caving, rock climbing and stand-up paddle-boarding (SUP). Hours depend on conditions.

🛏 Sleeping

YHA Wye Valley HOSTEL £
(📞0345 371 9666; www.yha.org.uk; Welsh Bicknor; dm/d/camping/glamping from £13/70/10/45; ⊙ hostel Mar–Oct, glamping May–Sep; 🅿🛜🐕) On the banks of the River Wye, with its own canoe landing platform, this 46-bed hostel in a Victorian former rectory is set within 16 wooded hectares. Glamping bell tents come with a double futon and three single beds, solar lighting and beanbags; premium yurts have a toasty wood burner. There's a self-catering kitchen, a laundry and wi-fi in public areas.

Garth Cottage B&B ££
(📞01600-890364; www.symondsyatbandb.co.uk; Symonds Yat East; s/d £50/85; ⊙ mid-Mar–Oct; 🅿🛜) An exceedingly friendly and efficiently run family-owned B&B, right by the River Wye and alongside the ferry crossing. Comfy, chintzy, spotlessly maintained rooms have floral fabrics, tea and coffee kits and gorgeous river views. Home-cooked breakfasts are excellent. Rates drop for longer stays.

Saracens Head Inn INN ££
(📞01600-890435; www.saracensheadinn.co.uk; Symonds Yat East; s/d incl breakfast £70/90; 🅿🛜) Honey-toned woods, fresh cream decor and understated modern style make this revamped 16th-century riverside inn, overlooking Symond Yat's ferry crossing, a wonderful choice. Eight of its 10 bright, comfortable rooms have river views; the spacious lounge-equipped Upper Boathouse room is especially popular. The downstairs pub-restaurant is excellent.

⭐Tudor Farmhouse BOUTIQUE HOTEL £££
(📞01594-833046; www.tudorfarmhousehotel.co.uk; High St, Clearwell; d/ste incl breakfast from £130/190; 🅿🛜) Sleep in a chic, contemporary world of whites, creams and spiralling Tudor-era staircases, inside a beautifully updated farmhouse. Stylish rooms, most with exposed beams, check-print blankets and Nespresso machines, are scattered through the main house. The spacious 'Roost' suite, with its claw-foot bath, is particularly romantic. More rooms sit in adjacent buildings. There's also an exceptional Modern British restaurant (mains £16-25, 2-/3-course set lunch £25/30; ⊙7am-10pm, noon-5pm & 6.30-9pm; 🅿🛜).

ℹ Information

Dean Heritage Centre (📞01594-822170; www.deanheritagecentre.com; Camp Mill, Soudley; adult/child £8/6; ⊙10am-5pm Apr-Oct, to 4pm Nov-Mar; 🅿🚗) The Forest's heritage museum doubles as its main information office.

ℹ Getting There & Away

BUS
Stagecoach is the main bus company hereabouts, while National Express coaches run to Newent from further afield.

TRAIN
Trains from Gloucester serve Lydney (£8.20, 20 minutes), on the southern side of the forest.

BUCKINGHAMSHIRE, BEDFORDSHIRE & HERTFORDSHIRE

Now poised at the edge of London's commuter belt, these three green-clad counties once served as rural boltholes for the city's rich and titled, especially when the stench and grime of the industrial age was at its peak. The sweeping valleys and forested hills remain scattered with majestic stately homes and splendid gardens, many of which are open to the public.

The 324-sq-mile Chilterns Area of Outstanding Natural Beauty (AONB; www.visitchilterns.co.uk) extends southwest from

Hitchin (Hertfordshire), through Bedfordshire and Buckinghamshire, and into Oxfordshire.

St Albans

☑ 01727 / POP 151,000

As Verulamium, encircled by a 2-mile wall and 26 miles from Londinium (London), St Albans was the third-biggest city in Roman Britain. Its current name derives from Alban, a Christian Roman soldier who was beheaded here around AD 250, becoming the first English martyr. Now a bustling and prosperous market town, just beyond London's north-western fringes, it's home to a huge and historic cathedral, amid a host of crooked Tudor buildings and elegant Georgian town houses.

◉ Sights

★St Albans Cathedral   CATHEDRAL
(☑ 01727-890210; www.stalbanscathedral.org; off High St & Holywell Hill; ☺8.30am-5.45pm, free tours 11.30am & 2.30pm Mon-Fri, 11.30am & 2pm Sat, 2.30pm Sun) FREE Vast out of all proportion to the modern town, St Albans' majestic cathedral was founded as a Benedictine monastery by King Offa of Mercia in AD 793, around a shrine to St Alban, martyred five centuries earlier. It's now a glorious mash-up of Norman Romanesque and Gothic architecture, with rounded arches built using bricks salvaged from Roman Verulamium, and the country's longest medieval nave, adorned with 13th-century murals. A stone reredos screens off the restored tomb of St Alban.

Verulamium Museum   MUSEUM
(☑ 01727-751810; www.stalbansmuseums.org.uk; St Michael's St; adult/child £5/2.50, combined ticket with Roman Theatre £6.50/3.50; ☺10am-5.30pm Mon-Sat, from 2pm Sun) Based in what looks outside like a suburban house, this modern and highly engaging museum celebrates everyday life in Roman Verulamium. Assorted galleries cover themes like death, crafts and trade, with exhibits including farming utensils, armour, coins and pottery. Best of all are the five superb mosaic floors discovered locally, including a beautiful shell-shaped mosaic from AD 130.

🛏 Sleeping & Eating

St Michael's Manor Hotel   HOTEL £££
(☑ 01727-864444; www.stmichaelsmanor.com; Fishpool St; d incl breakfast £155-200; P🐾🛜) In a lovely location, with its own lake, this 500-year-old manor offers 30 opulent rooms hidden down hushed carpeted corridors. Those in the manor itself are unshowy but

---

WORTH A TRIP

THE HOME OF HARRY POTTER

Whether you're a fair-weather fan or a full-on Potterhead, the **Warner Bros Studio Tour: The Making of Harry Potter** (☑ 0345 084 0900; www.wbstudiotour.co.uk; Studio Tour Dr, Leavesden, WD25; adult/child £41/33; ☺8.30am-10pm Jun-Sep, hours vary Oct-May; P♿) is well worth the admittedly hefty admission price. All visitors have to book tickets online, in advance, for a specific time slot, and arrive 20 minutes beforehand; allow three hours or more to do the complex full justice. Visits begin with a short film, before you're ushered through giant doors into the actual set of Hogwarts' enormous Great Hall – just the first of many 'wow' moments.

Beyond that, you can explore the rest of the complex at your own pace. One large hangar contains the most familiar interior sets – Dumbledore's office, the Gryffindor common room, Hagrid's hut – while another holds Platform 9¾, complete with the Hogwarts Express. An outdoor section features the exterior of Privet Dr, the purple triple-decker Knight Bus, Sirius Black's motorbike and a shop selling snacks and (sickly sweet) butterbeer.

Other highlights include the animatronic workshop (say 'Hi' to the Hippogriff) and a stroll down Diagon Alley. All your favourite Harry Potter creatures are on display, from an enormous Aragog to Dobby the House-Elf, as well as props such as Harry's Invisibility Cloak. The most magical treat is saved for last – a shimmering, gasp-inducing 1:24 scale model of Hogwarts, used for exterior shots.

The Studio Tour is 20 miles northwest of London, not far off the M1 and M25 motorways. For drivers, there's a large free car park, plus extensive directions on the website. To come by rail, catch a train from London Euston to Watford Junction (£10.20, 15 minutes), then take the shuttle bus (return £2.50, 10 minutes, cash only).

BLETCHLEY PARK

During WWII, the very existence of **Bletchley Park** (☑ 01908-640404; www.bletchleypark. org.uk; Bletchley; adult/12-17yr £18.25/10.75; ⊘ 9.30am-5pm Mar-Oct, to 4pm Nov-Feb; P) was England's best-kept secret. By breaking German and Japanese codes, as dramatised in the 2014 film *The Imitation Game*, Bletchley's team of almost 8500 scientists and technicians made a huge contribution to winning the war. Up to 20,000 enemy messages were intercepted each day, then decrypted, translated and interpreted. Inside Hut 11A, you can see the Bombe machine itself, crucial to cracking the famous Enigma code; volunteers explain its inner workings.

Entry includes an optional hour-long guided tour of the grounds – dress warm – and a multimedia guide. Both provide a real insight into the complex, frustrating and ultimately rewarding code-breaking process. The machines built here, by pioneers including Alan Turing, are now regarded as major steps in development of programmable computers.

Bletchley is just south of Milton Keynes, off the B4034. Regular trains connect Bletchley station, close to the park, with London Euston (£16, 40 minutes).

comfortable, with historic charm, while the eight more-contemporary 'luxury garden' rooms, named for plants and trees, are sumptuously sleek, with rich colours and patterned wallpaper; two have four-poster beds.

Lussmanns Fish & Grill MODERN BRITISH ££
(☑ 01727-851941; www.lussmanns.com; Waxhouse Gate, off High St; mains £14-28; ⊘ noon-9pm Sun-Tue, to 9.30pm Wed & Thu, to 10.30pm Fri & Sat; ☑) ✔ This bright, modern restaurant, steps from the cathedral, serves a changing, season-focused, ethically sourced menu of creative British dishes with Mediterranean touches, such as pomegranate-infused salad or chicken with pancetta. Good-value set lunches include a glass of wine (two/three courses £13.95/17.50).

ℹ Information

Tourist Office (☑ 01727-864511; www.enjoyst albans.com; Alban Arena, off St Peter's St; ⊘ 10am-4pm Mon-Sat)

ℹ Getting There & Away

Regular trains connect St Albans City, a mile east of the centre, with London King's Cross/ St Pancras (£12.20, 20 minutes) and London Blackfriars (£12.20, 30 minutes).

Stowe

Located 3 miles northwest of the market town of Buckingham, and 14 miles west of Milton Keynes, Stowe has had a manor since before the Norman conquest. While the house itself is now a private school, the ex-

traordinary Georgian gardens that surround it remain intact, and are definitely worth visiting. The most spectacular approach is via the 1.5-mile-long tree-lined Stowe Ave.

◉ Sights

★ **Stowe Gardens** GARDENS
(NT; ☑ 01280-817156; www.nationaltrust.org.uk; New Inn Farm; adult/child £12/6; ⊘ 10am-5pm mid-Feb–Oct, to 4pm Nov–mid-Feb; P) The glorious Stowe Gardens were shaped in the 18th century by Britain's greatest landscape gardeners. Among them was master landscape architect Lancelot 'Capability' Brown, who kickstarted his career here as head gardener from 1741 until 1751. The gardens are famous for the temples and follies commissioned by the superwealthy Richard Temple (1st Viscount Cobham), whose family motto was *Templa Quam Dilecta* (How Delightful are Your Temples). Paths meander past lakes, bridges, fountains and cascades, and through Capability Brown's Grecian Valley.

ℹ Getting There & Away

You'll need a car to get to Stowe House and Gardens, which are well signposted 3 miles northwest of Buckingham.

Woburn

☑ 01525 / POP 933

The peaceful village of Woburn has been nestling blissfully into the Bedfordshire countryside since the 10th century. Despite hosting a couple of big attractions, it's still charmingly sleepy.

◉ Sights

The Woburn Passport (adult/child £32/20.50), which gives access to both Woburn Abbey and Woburn Safari Park, can be used on two separate days between late March and October in the same calendar year.

Woburn Abbey   HOUSE
(☑ 01525-290333; www.woburnabbey.co.uk; Park St; adult/child £17.50/8.50; ☉ house 11am-5pm, gardens 10am-6pm mid-Mar–Oct; ℗) Woburn Abbey, a wonderful country pile within a 1200-hectare deer park, stands on the site of a 12th-century Cistercian abbey that was dissolved by Henry VIII, and awarded to the Earl of Bedford; the current Duke of Bedford still calls it home. Highlights in the opulent house include Queen Victoria's bedroom, beautiful wall hangings, and paintings by Gainsborough, Reynolds and van Dyck, plus no fewer than 24 views of Venice by Canaletto, purchased for the grand sum of £188.

Woburn Safari Park   ZOO
(www.woburnsafari.co.uk; Woburn Park; adult/child £24/17; ☉ 10am-6pm late Mar-Oct) Sprawling across 150 hectares, the country's largest drive-through animal reserve can only be visited in your own car (so long as it's not a convertible!). Animals such as rhinos, tigers, lions, elephants and giraffes – grouped into separate enclosures, for obvious reasons – will approach your car, or, if they're monkeys, climb on top of it. The 'foot safari' area holds sea lions, penguins, meerkats and lemurs.

✖ Eating

★ Paris House   MODERN BRITISH £££
(☑ 01525-290692; www.parishouse.co.uk; Woburn Park, London Rd; lunch £49, dinner £96-115;

⊙ noon-1.30pm & 7-8.30pm Thu, noon-1.30pm & 6.45-9pm Fri & Sat, noon-2pm Sun) On the Woburn Estate, Paris House is a handsome, black-and-white, half-timbered structure to which the 9th duke of Bedford took a shine while visiting the French capital. He shipped it back here, and it now holds Bedfordshire's top fine-dining restaurant, serving exquisite six- to 10-course tasting menus of beautifully presented contemporary cuisine.

❶ Getting There & Away

Woburn is 8 miles southeast of Milton Keynes, 7 miles southeast of Bletchley Park, and 22 miles northwest of St Albans. Woburn itself does not have a train station. You can only visit Woburn Safari Park if you're driving, and no public transport serves Woburn Abbey.

THE THAMES VALLEY

The prosperous valley of the River Thames, west of London, has long served as a country getaway for the English elite, from royalty on down. Within easy reach of the capital, but utterly different in character, its pastoral landscape is peppered with handsome villages and historic houses.

It's Windsor Castle, favoured residence of the Queen, that really draws the crowds here, but Ascot, with its royal race-meet in June, and Henley-on-Thames, with its rowing regatta a month later, both boast their days in the sun. Meanwhile, bizarrely, little Bray has a genuine claim to be the country's gastronomic capital.

Windsor & Eton

☑ 01753 / POP 32,184
Facing each other across the Thames, with the massive bulk of Windsor Castle looming above, the twin riverside towns of Windsor and Eton have a rather surreal atmosphere. Windsor on the south bank sees the daily pomp and ritual of the changing of the guards, while schoolboys dressed in formal tailcoats wander the streets of tiny Eton to the north.

Thanks to its tourist trade, Windsor is filled with expensive boutiques, grand cafes and buzzing restaurants. Eton is far quieter, its single commercial street flanked by antique shops and art galleries. Both are easily accessible on a day trip from London.

ROYAL ASCOT

Don your finest duds and join the glitterati at the biggest racing meet of the year, **Royal Ascot** (☑ 08443-463000; www.ascot.co.uk; Ascot; Windsor Enclosure per day from £37, Queen Anne Enclosure per day from £75; ☉ mid-Jun), going strong since 1711. The royal family, A-list celebrities and other rich and famous folk gather for this five-day festival, 7 miles southwest of Windsor, to show off their Jimmy Choos and place the odd bet. It's essential to book tickets well in advance.

Windsor & Eton

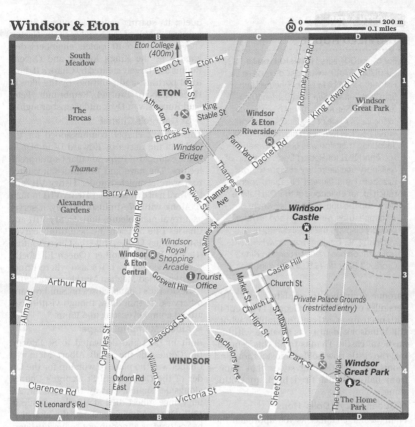

⊙ Sights & Activities

★ **Windsor Castle**   CASTLE
(☎ 03031-237304; www.royalcollection.org.uk; Castle Hill; adult/child £21.20/12.30; ⊗ 9.30am-5.15pm Mar-Oct, 9.45am-4.15pm Nov-Feb, last admission 1hr 15min before closing, all or part of castle subject to occasional closures; ♿; ☐ 702 from London Victoria, ☒ London Waterloo to Windsor & Eton Riverside, ☒ London Paddington to Windsor & Eton Central via Slough) The world's largest and oldest continuously occupied fortress, Windsor Castle is a majestic vision of battlements and towers. Used for state occasions, it's one of the Queen's principal residences; when she's at home, the Royal Standard flies from the Round Tower.

Frequent, free guided tours introduce visitors to the castle precincts, divided into the Lower, Middle and Upper Wards. Free audio tours guide everyone through its lavish State Apartments and beautiful chapels; certain areas may be off limits if in use.

It was William the Conqueror, just five years after his successful invasion of England, who commanded that an earth-and-timber fortress be built beside the Thames. Completed in 1080, it was rebuilt in stone by his great-grandson, Henry II, in 1170. Successive monarchs made their own marks, with Edward III turning Windsor into a Gothic palace and Charles II adding

WORTH A TRIP

HATFIELD HOUSE

For over 400 years **Hatfield House** (☑ 01707-287010; www.hatfield-house.co.uk; Hatfield; adult/child £19/9; ⊘ house 11am-5pm Wed-Sun Apr-Sep, West Garden 10am-5.30pm Tue-Sun Apr-Sep) has been home to the Cecils, one of England's most influential political families. This magnificent Jacobean mansion was built between 1607 and 1611 for Robert Cecil, first earl of Salisbury and secretary of state to both Elizabeth I and James I. Elizabeth spent much of her childhood in the 'Old Palace' here, and the house, which is awash with tapestries, furnishings and armour, proudly displays the Rainbow Portrait, depicting her holding a rainbow. Hatfield train station has trains to London King's Cross/St Pancras (£10.10, 20 minutes).

baroque flourishes to emulate Louis XIV's Versailles outside Paris. George IV swept in with his team of artisans to establish what's still Windsor's identity, as a palace within a medieval castle. Thanks to all this rebuilding, the castle now holds almost a thousand rooms, in architectural styles that range from half-timbered fired brick to Gothic stone.

➤ Queen Mary's Dolls' House

Filling a side chamber as you approach the State Apartments from the North Terrace of the Upper Ward, this astonishing creation is not a toy but a masterpiece of artful miniaturisation. Designed at 1:12 scale by Sir Edwin Lutyens for Queen Mary, and completed in 1924, it displays a phenomenal attention to detail. It's equipped with fully functional plumbing, including flushing toilets, plus electric lights, tiny Crown Jewels, a silver service and wine cellar, and even a fleet of six cars in the garage.

➤ State Apartments

Flanked by armour and weapons, the Grand Staircase sets the tone for the spectacular State Apartments above, dripping in gilt and screaming 'royal' from every painted surface and sparkling chandelier. Presided over by a statue of Queen Victoria, the Grand Vestibule displays artefacts and treasures donated by or captured from the countries of the British Empire, while the Waterloo Chamber celebrates the 1815 victory over Napoleon. St George's Hall beyond still hosts state ban-

quets; its soaring ceiling is covered in the painted shields of the Knights of the Garter.

A succession of 10 opulent chambers, designated as the King's Rooms and Queen's Rooms and largely created by Charles II, hold royal portraits and paintings by the likes of Hans Holbein, Bruegel, Rembrandt, Peter Paul Rubens, van Dyck and Gainsborough.

➤ St George's Chapel

This elegant chapel, commissioned for the Order of the Garter by Edward IV in 1475, is a fine example of Perpendicular Gothic architecture. The nave and beautiful fan-vaulted roof were completed under Henry VII, and the final nail driven under Henry VIII in 1528.

Along with Westminster Abbey, it serves as a royal mausoleum. Both Henry VIII and Charles I lie beneath the beautifully carved 15th-century Quire, while the Queen's father (George VI) and mother (Queen Elizabeth) rest in a side chapel. It's also where Prince Harry married Meghan Markle in May 2018.

St George's Chapel closes on Sundays, and otherwise at 4pm daily, though visitors can attend choral evensong at 5.15pm.

➤ Albert Memorial Chapel

Built in 1240 and dedicated to St Edward the Confessor, the small Albert Memorial Chapel was the place of worship for the Order of the Garter until St George's Chapel, alongside, snatched away that honour. After Prince Albert died at Windsor Castle in 1861, Queen Victoria ordered the chapel to be restored as a monument to her husband, adding a magnificent vaulted roof that incorporates gold mosaic pieces from Venice.

Although the chapel holds a monument to the prince, he's actually buried, with Victoria, in the Royal Mausoleum at Frogmore House in Windsor Great Park. Their youngest son, Prince Leopold (Duke of Albany), is, however, buried here.

➤ Changing of the Guard

A fabulous spectacle, with triumphant tunes from a military band and plenty of foot stamping from smartly attired lads in red uniforms and bearskin caps, the changing of the guard draws crowds to Windsor Castle each day. Weather permitting, it usually takes place at 11am on Tuesdays, Thursdays and Saturdays.

★ **Windsor Great Park** PARK
(☑ 01753-860222; www.windsorgreatpark.co.uk; Windsor; ⊘ dawn-dusk) **FREE** Windsor Great Park stretches south from Windsor Castle almost all the way to Ascot, 7 miles south-

west. Accessed via Park St, it covers just under 8 sq miles and holds a lake, walking tracks, a bridleway, gardens and a deer park where red deer roam free. Its 2.7-mile Long Walk, scene of the royal wedding procession in 2018, leads from King George IV Gate to the 1831 Copper Horse statue (of George III) on Snow Hill, the park's highest point.

Runnymede
HISTORIC SITE

(NT; ☑ 01784-432891; www.nationaltrust.org.uk; Windsor Rd, Old Windsor; parking per hour £1.50; ☺ site dawn-dusk, car park 8.30am-7pm Apr-Sep, to 5pm Oct, Nov, Feb & Mar, to 4pm Dec & Jan; ℗) **FREE** Over 800 years ago, in June 1215, King John met his barons in this unassuming field, 3 miles southeast of Windsor. Together they hammered out an agreement on a basic charter of rights that guaranteed the liberties of the king's subjects, and restricted the monarch's absolute power. The document they signed, the Magna Carta, was the world's first constitution. The field remains much as it was, plus a few modern memorials and two 1929 lodges, designed by Edwin Lutyens.

Eton College
NOTABLE BUILDING

(☑ 01753-370600; www.etoncollege.com; High St, Eton; adult/child £10/free; ☺ tours 2pm & 4pm Fri May-Aug) Eton College is England's most famous public – as in, private and fee-paying – boys' school, and arguably the most enduring symbol of the British class system. High-profile alumni include 19 British prime ministers, countless princes, kings and maharajas, Princes William and Harry, George Orwell, John Maynard Keynes, Bear Grylls and Eddie Redmayne. It can only be visited on guided tours, on summer Fridays, which take in the chapel and the Museum of Eton Life. Book online.

🌏 Tours

French Brothers
BOATING

(☑ 01753-851900; www.frenchbrothers.co.uk; Windsor Promenade, Barry Ave, Windsor; ☺ 10am-5pm mid-Feb–early Dec) Boat trips along the Thames, including cruises around Windsor (adult/child from £9/6) and voyages to/from Runnymede (return adult/child £8.75/5.85).

🍴 Eating & Drinking

Two Brewers
PUB FOOD ££

(☑ 01753-855426; www.twobrewerswindsor.co.uk; 34 Park St, Windsor; mains £14-26; ☺ 11.30am-11pm Mon-Thu, to 11.30pm Fri & Sat, noon-10.30pm Sun) This atmospheric 18th-century inn, at

the gateway to Windsor Great Park, serves tasty, well-prepped food ranging from soups, salads and fishcakes to steaks, cod loin and cheese boards. Sunny benches front the flower-covered exterior; inside are low-beamed ceilings, dim lighting and a roaring winter fire. Dinner isn't served Friday or Saturday, or after 8pm on Sunday.

Gilbey's
MODERN BRITISH £££

(☑ 01753-854921; www.gilbeygroup.com; 82-83 High St, Eton; mains £18-29.50; ☺ 6-10pm Mon, noon-3pm & 6-10pm Tue-Sun; 🐾☑) This bistro-restaurant, not far from the river, is Eton's best dining option. Terracotta tiling, deep-green decor and a sunny courtyard lend the feel of a European cafe, while two-/three-course set menus for both lunch (£15/20) and dinner (£22.50/28.50; not available after 6.45pm Friday and Saturday) offer Modern British favourites including pies and artisan cheeses plus good vegetarian alternatives.

ℹ Information

Tourist Office (☑ 01753-743900; www.windsor.gov.uk; Old Booking Hall, Windsor Royal Shopping Arcade, Thames St, Windsor; ☺ 10am-5pm Apr-Sep, to 4pm Oct-Mar) Tickets for attractions and events, plus guidebooks and walking maps.

ℹ Getting There & Away

BUS

Green Line buses (www.greenline.co.uk) connect Windsor and Eton with London Victoria (route 702/703; £7 to £13, 1½ hours) and Heathrow terminal 5 (route 702/703; £4, 40 minutes). Courtney Buses (www.courtneybuses.com)

READING FESTIVAL

Each August Bank Holiday weekend, up to 87,000 revellers descend on the industrial town of Reading for one of the country's biggest music events, **Reading Festival** (☑ 02070-093001; www.reading festival.com; Reading; tickets day/weekend £76.50/221.40; ☺ late Aug). The three-day extravaganza features world-class artists in all genres, with recent headliners including Kendrick Lamar, Eminem and the Red Hot Chili Peppers. Set up camp for the weekend or just book a day ticket.

Reading has regular trains to/from London Paddington (£20.20, 25 minutes to one hour).

HENLEY-ON-THAMES

The attractive commuter town of Henley, 15 miles northwest of Windsor, is synonymous with its annual rowing tournament, the **Henley Royal Regatta** (www.hrr.co.uk; tickets £25-32, on-site parking £34; ⊙ early Jul). For the rest of the year, it remains a pretty riverside town that's a delight to stroll around, particularly along the Thames.

The excellent **River & Rowing Museum** (🖉 01491-415600; www.rrm.co.uk; Mill Meadows; adult/child £12.50/10; ⊙ 10am-5pm; P ♿) examines why Henley is so crazy for rowing. The airy 1st-floor galleries tell the story of rowing as an Olympic sport, with striking displays that include the early-19th-century Royal Oak, Britain's oldest racing boat. Downstairs, a sweet 3D exhibition pays homage to Kenneth Grahame's *The Wind in the Willows*. The romanticised river that book so lovingly depicts was inspired by the Thames around Henley.

Trains run to/from London Paddington (£16.70, one hour); you have to change at Slough and/or Twyford.

offers services between Windsor and Bray (route 16/16A; £3.30, 30 minutes).

TRAIN

The quickest rail route from London connects London Paddington with Windsor & Eton Central, opposite the castle, but you have to change at Slough (£10.50, 30 to 45 minutes). London Waterloo has slower but direct services to Windsor & Eton Riverside, on Dachet Rd (£10.50, 45 minutes to one hour).

Bray

🖉 01628 / POP 4646

Strangely enough, this tiny village of flint, brick and half-timbered cottages, strung along the Thames 5 miles northwest of Windsor, has a real claim to be considered the gastronomic capital of Britain. Bray is home to two of the four UK restaurants to be awarded the highest possible rating of three stars by foodie bible, the Michelin guide.

There's little more to do here than to dine fabulously.

 Eating

★ **Fat Duck**　　　MODERN BRITISH £££

(🖉 01628-580333; www.thefatduck.co.uk; High St; degustation menu per person £325; ⊙ noon-1.15pm & 7-8.15pm Tue-Sat) Arguably the most famous restaurant in the country, the Fat Duck is the flagship property of whiz-bang chef Heston Blumenthal. A pioneer of 'molecular' cuisine, he transformed it from a rundown pub into a three-starred restaurant that was once voted the best in the world. Reserve four months in advance to enjoy its eye-poppingly priced, journey-themed, seasonally changing set menu.

★ **Waterside Inn**　　　FRENCH £££

(🖉 01628-620691; www.waterside-inn.co.uk; Ferry Rd; mains £55-68, 2-/3-course lunch Wed-Fri £52/63.50; ⊙ noon-2pm & 7-10pm Wed-Sun, closed late Dec–end Jan) From the moment the uniformed valet greets you until the last tray of petit fours is served, this three-Michelin-starred riverfront restaurant is something special. For more than 40 years, chef Alain Roux has worked his magic, constructing exceptional dishes for a small army of staff to serve, in a room overlooking the Thames. It also has rooms (from £275).

★ **Hind's Head**　　　GASTROPUB £££

(🖉 01628-626151; www.hindsheadbray.com; High St; mains £20-40, 5-course tasting menu £62; ⊙ noon-2pm & 6-9pm Mon-Sat, noon-3.30pm Sun; P) Oozing atmosphere, this 15th-century pub offers diners the chance to experience Heston Blumenthal's highly creative cuisine in a relatively affordable, informal setting. The food's less zany than you might expect from his reputation, but still has plenty of whimsical touches. Try the roast cod with mussel-and-saffron broth, or the onion-wrapped brown bread royale with Marmite emulsion.

❶ Getting There & Away

Courtney Buses (www.courtneybus.com) connect Bray with Windsor (route 16/16A; £3.30, 30 minutes).

Bath & Southwest England

Best Places to Eat

➡ Restaurant Nathan Outlaw (p317)

➡ Menu Gordon Jones (p239)

➡ Riverstation (p228)

➡ Black Rat (p248)

➡ Elephant (p294)

➡ Shore (p333)

Best Places to Sleep

➡ Scarlet (p322)

➡ Queensberry (p236)

➡ Hotel du Vin Exeter (p290)

➡ The Pig (p251)

➡ Number 38 (p227)

➡ Artist Residence Penzance (p332)

Why Go?

England's southwest – or the West Country, as it's often known – offers something for everyone: buzzy big cities, iconic monuments, green countryside and golden beaches galore. Stone circles and hilltop castles litter the landscape, while stately homes and serene cathedrals give way to a patchwork of green fields, wild moors, quiet villages and fishing ports. Surrounded by the sea, the region's long history of seafaring lives on in Portsmouth, Plymouth, Dartmouth, Falmouth and the dynamic city of Bristol, while beautiful Bath is a dazzling showpiece of Georgian architecture, and without doubt one of the gems in England's crown.

But it's the pleasures of coast and countryside that draw most people here: whether it's fossil-hunting on the Dorset Coast, hiking on Dartmoor, kayaking the Fowey River or surfing in Cornwall, the southwest is above all a place to enjoy England's outdoors.

When to Go

➡ Cliffs, hillsides and formal gardens burst into fragrance and blooms in April and May, when seasonal attractions also reopen and boat trips start.

➡ Music-festival fever takes hold in June at ultracool Glastonbury and the Isle of Wight.

➡ The peak holiday season and the best weather (in theory) is in July and August.

➡ The end of school summer holidays in September brings cheaper sleep spots, quieter beaches and warmer seas.

➡ Bigger waves draw surfers to Cornwall and north Devon in October; meanwhile Exmoor's deer rut sees huge stags battle for supremacy, and the winter storm-watching season begins.

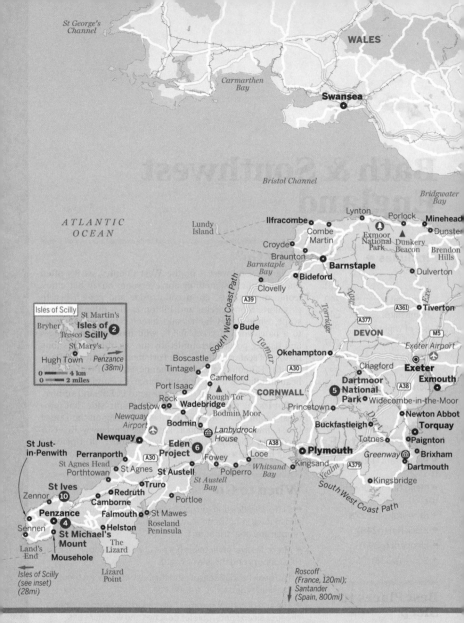

Bath & Southwest England Highlights

1 **Stonehenge** (p275)
Securing a space on a magical
dawn walk inside the ring.

2 **Isles of Scilly** (p343)
Ferry-hopping around the UK's
most idyllic archipelago.

3 **Roman Baths** (p231)
Seeing how the Romans
bathed 2000 years ago.

4 **St Michael's Mount**
(p331) Crossing the causeway
to an island abbey.

5 **Dartmoor National Park**
(p304) Striding the park's
remote, high hills.

6 **Eden Project** (p336)
Marvelling at space-age

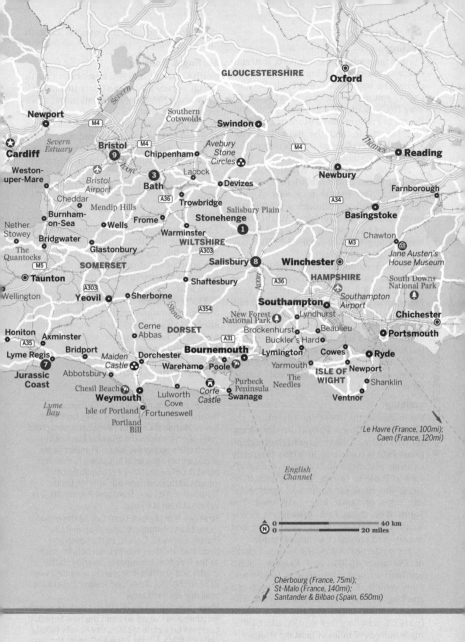

GLOUCESTERSHIRE

Oxford

Newport

Severn

Southern
Cotswolds

Swindon

✪ **Cardiff**

Severn
Estuary

Bristol
9

Chippenham

Avebury
Stone
Circles

M4

● **Reading**

Weston-
uper-Mare

Bristol
Airport

3
Bath

Lacock

Newbury

Farnborough

Cheddar

Mendip Hills

Devizes

A36

Trowbridge

A34

Burnham-
on-Sea

Wells

Frome

Stonehenge

Salisbury Plain

Basingstoke

Chawton

Nether
Stowey

Bridgwater

Warminster

1

M3

Jane Austen's
House Museum

The
Quantocks

Glastonbury

WILTSHIRE

A303

M5

SOMERSET

Salisbury **8**

Winchester

South Downs
National Park

◉ **Taunton**

Yeovil

Shaftesbury

A36

HAMPSHIRE

Wellington

Sherborne

A354

A303

Southampton

Southampton
Airport

Chichester

Honiton

Cerne
Abbas

DORSET

New Forest
National Park

Lyndhurst

Beaulieu

● **Portsmouth**

Axminster

A35

Bridport

Maiden
Castle

Dorchester

A31

Bournemouth

Brockenhurst

Buckler's Hard

Cowes

Ryde

Lyme Regis

7

Abbotsbury

Wareham

Poole

Lymington

Yarmouth

Newport

**Jurassic
Coast**

Chesil Beach

Weymouth

Lulworth
Cove

Corfe
Castle

Swanage

Purbeck
Peninsula

The
Needles

**ISLE OF
WIGHT**

Shanklin

Lyme
Bay

Isle of Portland

Fortuneswell

Ventnor

Portland
Bill

*English
Channel*

*Le Havre (France, 100mi);
Caen (France, 120mi)*

N
0 — 40 km
0 — 20 miles

*Cherbourg (France, 75mi);
St-Malo (France, 140mi);
Santander & Bilbao (Spain, 650mi)*

biomes in a disused Cornish
claypit.

7 **Jurassic Coast** (p262)
Foraging for 200-million-year-
old fossils in the crumbling
cliffs around Lyme Regis.

8 **Salisbury Cathedral**
(p272) Savouring the city's
soaring, serene house of
worship.

9 **SS Great Britain** (p221)
Stepping on the deck of

Brunel's groundbreaking
steamship in Bristol.

10 **Tate St Ives** (p325)
Getting inspired by the artistic
heritage of this Cornish
coastal town.

🏃 Activities

Cycling

Cycling the southwest is a superb, if strenuous, way to experience England's great outdoors. The region's National Cycle Network (NCN) routes include the **West Country Way** (NCN Route 3), a 240-mile jaunt from Bristol to Padstow via Glastonbury, Taunton and Barnstaple, and the 103-mile **Devon Coast to Coast Cycle Route** between Ilfracombe and Plymouth.

The 160-mile, circular **Wiltshire Cycleway** skirts the county's borders. In Hampshire, the New Forest's hundreds of miles of cycle paths snake through a wildlife-rich environment, while the Isle of Wight boasts 62 miles of bike-friendly routes and its very own **cycling festival** (☑ 01983-299314; www.iwcyclefest.com; ☉ late-Aug).

Off-road mountain-biking highlights include the North Wessex Downs, Exmoor National Park and Dartmoor National Park. Many cycle trails trace the routes of old railway lines, including Devon's 11-mile Granite Way between Okehampton and Lydford, and Cornwall's popular 18-mile Camel Trail (p320) linking Padstow with Bodmin Moor.

For more information contact Sustrans (www.sustrans.org.uk) and local tourist offices.

Walking

Often called the 630-mile adventure, the **South West Coast Path** is Britain's longest national walking trail (until the England Coast Path is completed in 2020). It stretches from Minehead in Somerset to Land's End to Poole in Dorset. You can pick it up along the coast for short and spectacular day hikes or tackle longer stretches. The South West Coast Path Association (www.southwestcoastpath.org.uk) has a detailed website and publishes an annual guide.

For wilderness hikes, the national parks of Dartmoor (p304) and Exmoor (p281) are hard to beat. Dartmoor is bigger and more remote; Exmoor's ace in the pack is a cracking 34 miles of precipitous coast. The region's third national park, New Forest (p249), is an altogether gentler affair, offering hundreds of miles of heritage trails.

Other hiking highlights are Exmoor's 51-mile **Coleridge Way** (www.coleridgeway.co.uk), the Isle of Wight and Bodmin Moor, while Wiltshire's 87-mile **Ridgeway National Trail** (www.nationaltrail.co.uk/ridgeway) starts near Avebury and winds through chalk downland and the wooded Chiltern hills.

Surfing & Boating

North Cornwall, and to a lesser extent north Devon, serves up the best surf in England. Party town Newquay is the epicentre; other top spots are Bude in Cornwall and Croyde in Devon. Region-wide surf conditions can be found at www.magicseaweed.com.

For sailing, highlights includes Britain's 2012 Olympic sailing venues at Weymouth and Portland, and the yachting havens of the Isle of Wight, Falmouth, Dartmouth and Poole.

Other Activities

The southwest is prime territory for kitesurfing, windsurfing, diving, sea kayaking, white-water kayaking and wakeboarding. The sport of stand-up paddleboarding (SUP) continues to grow in popularity, especially in calm water spots.

Plenty of firms also offer caving, coasteering, mountainboarding, climbing and kite-buggying. Check out www.visitsouthwest.co.uk for links to the region's counties and activity operators.

ℹ️ Getting Around

BUS

The region's bus network is fairly comprehensive, but becomes patchy away from main towns. **National Express** (www.nationalexpress.com) often provides the quickest bus link between cities and larger towns. **PlusBus** (www.plusbus.info) adds local bus travel to your train ticket (from £2 per day). Participating cities include Bath, Bournemouth, Bristol, Exeter, Plymouth, Salisbury, Truro and Weymouth. Buy tickets at train stations.

First (www.firstgroup.com) One of the region's largest bus companies, operating in Bath, Bristol, Cornwall, Dorset, Portsmouth and Somerset. It offers subregional tickets, such as the Freedom Travelpass, covering Bath, Bristol and northeast Somerset (one day/week £13.50/59). Day Rover and Ranger tickets are available for each area.

More (www.wdbus.co.uk) Useful service across Wiltshire and Dorset and into the New Forest. It operates on a zone system: day tickets (adult/child £8.80/5.70) for Zone ABC cover the largest area and are the best value. An unlimited weekend ticket costs £7.50.

Stagecoach (www.stagecoachbus.com) A key bus provider in Devon, Hampshire and Somerset. Offers a range of Dayrider and weekly Megarider passes covering individual towns (eg

Plymouth and Exeter) as well as wider areas (eg North Devon, South Devon). Most can be purchased within the Stagecoach app.

CAR

The main car-hire firms have offices at the region's airports and main-line train stations; rates reflect those elsewhere in the UK.

TRAIN

Bristol is a main train hub with links including those to London Paddington, Scotland and Birmingham, plus services to Bath, Swindon, Chippenham, Weymouth, Southampton and Portsmouth. Trains from London Waterloo travel to Bournemouth, Salisbury, Southampton, Portsmouth and Weymouth.

Stops on the London Paddington–Penzance service include Exeter, Plymouth, Liskeard, St Austell and Truro. Spur lines run to Barnstaple, Paignton, Gunnislake, Looe, Falmouth, St Ives and Newquay.

Major companies servicing the region include **Great Western Railway** (☑ 0345 7000 125; www.gwr.com), **CrossCountry** (☑ 0844 811 0124; www.crosscountrytrains.co.uk) and **South Western Railway** (www.southwesternrailway. com). All have useful travel apps that allow you to plan journeys and purchase e-tickets that are valid for travel. South Western Railway offers travel between London and the southeast, and to southwest destinations including Bournemouth, Portsmouth, Salisbury, Bristol and Bath, as far west as Exeter.

The **Freedom of the South West Rover** (three days travel in seven days adult/child £102.60/48.20, eight days travel in 15 days £144/72) pass allows unlimited travel in an area west of, and including, Salisbury, Bath, Bristol, Portsmouth and Weymouth.

BRISTOL

POP 454,200

Bristol is on the rise. Derelict docks are becoming leisure venues, heritage attractions ooze imagination and a world-class street-art scene adds colour and spice.

History

Bristol began as a Saxon village and developed into the medieval river port of Brigstow, an important trading centre for cloth and wine. In 1497 'local hero' John Cabot (actually a Genoese sailor called Giovanni Caboto) sailed from Bristol to discover Newfoundland. By the 18th century Bristol's docks were the second largest in the country.

LOCAL KNOWLEDGE

BRISTOL LIDO

Bristol's public **hot tub** (☑ 0117-933 9530; www.lidobristol.com; Oakfield Pl; nonmembers £20; ⊘ nonmembers 1-4pm Mon-Fri) dates back to 1849, and, after falling into disrepair during the early 20th century, this naturally heated, 24m pool has now been restored to its steamy best – with a balmy water temperature of around 24°C. Admission includes three hours' use of the pool, sauna, steam room and outdoor hot tub.

Spa treatments and massage sessions are also available, and there's a good **tapas bar** (9am to 10.30pm) and an acclaimed Mediterranean-themed **restaurant** (noon-3pm and 6pm to 10pm). Priority is given to members; if you want to visit outside the times listed, consider one of their Swim & Eat (£35 to £40) or Spa packages (from £70).

One of their activities was the so called Triangular Trade, in which Africans were enslaved, shipped to New World colonies and bartered for sugar, tobacco, cotton and rum. Much of Bristol's 18th-century splendour – including Clifton's terraces and the Old Vic theatre – were partly financed on the profits. The M Shed museum (p223) takes an honest look at the story, referencing also the local campaigners who fought for abolition.

After being usurped by rival ports, Bristol repositioned itself as an industrial and shipbuilding centre, and in 1840 became the western terminus for the newly built Great Western Railway line from London. It's audacious chief engineer was Isambard Kingdom Brunel, whose Bristol legacy includes the Clifton Suspension Bridge (p225) and SS *Great Britain*.

◉ Sights

★ **Brunel's SS Great Britain** HISTORIC SHIP
(☑ 0117-926 0680; www.ssgreatbritain.org; Great Western Dock, Gas Ferry Rd; adult/child/family £16.50/9.50/45; ⊘ 10am-5.30pm Apr-Oct, to 4.30pm Nov-Mar) This mighty, innovative steamship was designed by engineering genius Isambard Kingdom Brunel in 1843. You get to wander the galley, surgeon's quarters and dining saloon and see a massive replica steam engine at work. Highlights are going below the 'glass sea' on which the ship sits

Bristol

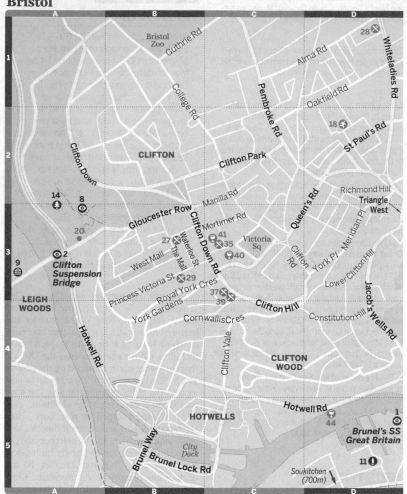

to view the screw propeller and climbing the rigging in **Go Aloft!**. The new **Being Brunel** exhibit has restored the drawing office where Brunel and his team worked to create the vessel.

The SS *Great Britain* was one of the largest and most technologically advanced steamships ever built, measuring 98m from stern to tip. The ship has had a chequered history. Between 1843 and 1886, she served her intended duty as a passenger liner, completing the transatlantic crossing between Bristol and New York in just 14 days. Unfortunately, enormous running costs and

mounting debts led her towards an ignominious fate: she was eventually sold off and subsequently served as a troop vessel, quarantine ship, emigration transport and coal hulk, before finally being scuttled near Port Stanley in the Falklands in the 1930s.

Happily, that wasn't the end. The ship was towed back to Bristol in 1970, and has since undergone an impressive 30-year restoration. It's resulted in a multisensory experience: prepare to stroll the deck, peep into luxury cabins, listen to passengers' stories and catch a whiff of life on board. Those aged 10 and over can also **Go Aloft!** (£10;

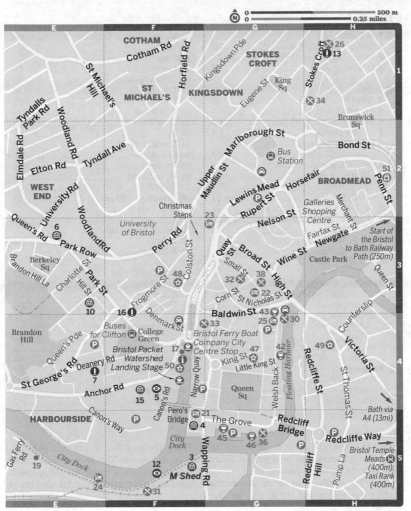

noon to 5pm daily April to October, noon to 3.45pm Saturday and Sunday November to March). This sees you donning a harness and helmet to climb 25m up the rigging and along the yard arm. Tickets for SS *Great Britain* remain valid for a year. Last entry is one hour before closing.

★ M Shed
MUSEUM
(☎ 0117-352 6600; www.bristolmuseums.org.uk; Princes Wharf; ⊙ 10am-5pm Tue-Sun; 📷) FREE Set amid the iconic cranes of Bristol's dockside, this impressive museum is a treasure trove of memorabilia. It's divided into four main sections: People, Place, Life and the vast Working Exhibits outside. They provide an absorbing overview of Bristol's history – from slaves' possessions and Wallace & Gromit figurines to a Banksy artwork and a set of decks once used by Massive Attack.

It's all highly interactive and child-friendly, especially the rides on the steam and electric cranes (tickets £2), steam trains (tickets £2) and tug and fire boats (adult/child £6/4). Another highlight is Banksy's unsettling *Grim Reaper* stencil, which used to sit on the waterline of the party boat *Thekla*. It was removed amid much

Bristol

controversy and can now be found on the 1st floor. The museum also runs guided tours exploring the harbour's history.

There are regular trips on the museum's boats, trains and cranes (£2 to £6); see the website for details.

Matthew   HISTORIC SHIP
(📞0117-927 6868; https://matthew.co.uk; Princes Wharf; ◎10am-4pm Tue-Sun Mar-Oct, Sat & Sun Nov-Feb) FREE The most striking thing about this replica of the vessel in which John Cabot made his landmark voyage from Bristol to Newfoundland in 1497 is its size. At 24m it seems far too small, but it would have carried a crew of around 18. Step aboard to climb below into their quarters, walk the deck and gaze up at the rigging.

Arnolfini   GALLERY
(📞0117-917 2300; www.arnolfini.org.uk; 16 Narrow Quay; ◎11am-6pm Tue-Sun; 🛜) FREE At time of writing, the art galleries here were only open for special events. The ground floor houses the Front Room, a venue for talks, special events and a library of art and design books.

Bristol Aquarium   AQUARIUM
(📞0117-929 8929; www.bristolaquarium.co.uk; Anchor Rd, Harbourside; adult/child/family £15/10/50; ◎10am-4pm Mon-Fri, to 5pm Sat & Sun) The underwater habitats you'll encounter here include a Bay of Rays, Coral Sea, Shark Tank and an Amazon River Zone. The underwater viewing tunnel adds extra appeal. Tickets are 10% cheaper online.

We the Curious   MUSEUM
(📞0117-915 1000; www.wethecurious.org; Anchor Rd; adult/child/family £15/10/40; ◎10am-5pm Mon-Fri, to 6pm Sat & Sun) Bristol's interactive science museum is a playful, hands-on space where 300 'exhibits' fly the flag for curiosity, scientific collaboration and creativity.

Which means you'll be meeting Aardman characters and becoming an animator for the day, discovering cosmic rays, walking through a tornado and exploring subjects ranging from anatomy to flight. There are also performances from the Live Science Team, immersive planetarium shows, and robots. Look out for After Hours – evenings designed for adults that feature games, activities and shows.

Georgian House   HISTORIC BUILDING
(☑ 0117-921 1362; www.bristolmuseums.org.uk; 7 Great George St; ☺ 11am-4pm Sat-Tue Apr-Dec) **FREE** Once the home of the wealthy slave plantation owner and sugar merchant John Pinney, this 18th-century house provides an insight into aristocratic life in Bristol during the Georgian era. It's decorated in period style, with a huge kitchen (complete with cast-iron roasting spit), book-lined library, grand drawing room, and cold-water plunge-pool in the basement.

There's also a small display on Pinney's involvement in the sugar trade and the life of his enslaved valet, Pedro Jones.

Bristol Museum & Art Gallery   MUSEUM
(☑ 0117-922 3571; www.bristolmuseums.org.uk; Queen's Rd; ☺ 10am-5pm Tue-Sun, plus 10am-5pm Mon school & bank holidays; ☎) **FREE** You're in for a few surprises at this classic old Edwardian museum. Look out for the *Paint-Pot Angel* by world-famous street artist Banksy in the entrance hall; a funerary statue with an upturned pink paint pot on her head, she's designed to challenge our expectations of museum exhibits and the value of art. It's also a reminder of the artist's hugely popular 2009 exhibition here. Just above sits the Bristol Boxkite, a prototype propeller-powered biplane, which dangles from the ceiling.

★ **Clifton Suspension Bridge**   BRIDGE
(☑ 0117-974 4664; www.cliftonbridge.org.uk; Suspension Bridge Rd) Clifton's most famous (and photographed) landmark is the 76m-high Clifton Suspension Bridge, which spans the Avon Gorge. It was designed by master engineer Isambard Kingdom Brunel with construction beginning in 1836, although Brunel died before its completion in 1864. It's free to walk or cycle across; car drivers pay a £1 toll.

There's a **visitor centre** (☎) **FREE** near the tower on the western, Leigh Woods side. The bridge **tours** (☺ 3pm Sat & Sun Easter-Oct) **FREE** are excellent.

The Downs   PARK
(🖼 🐾) The grassy parks of Clifton Down and Durdham Down (often referred to as just the Downs) fan out from the Clifton Suspension Bridge and make a fine spot for a picnic. Nearby, the **Clifton Observatory** (☑ 0117-974 1242; www.cliftonobservatory.com; Litfield Rd, Clifton Down; adult/child £2.50/1.50; ☺ 10am-5pm Feb-Oct, to 4pm Nov-Jan) houses a camera obscura and a tunnel leading down to the **Giant's Cave**, a natural cavern that emerges halfway down the cliff with dizzying views across the Avon Gorge.

Bristol Zoo Gardens   ZOO
(☑ 0117-428 5300; www.bristolzoo.org.uk; College Rd; adult/child £22/16; ☺ 9am-5.30pm; ℗) Highlights at the city's award-winning zoo include a family of seven western lowland gorillas (bossed by silverback Jock) and the Seal and Penguin Coast, where African penguins, eider ducks and South American fur seals lounge around. There's also a reptile and bug zone, butterfly forest, lion enclosure, monkey jungle and the **Zooropia** (adult/child £8/7) treetop adventure park. Online tickets are up to a third cheaper. To get here from the city centre, catch bus 8.

🏃 **Activities**

★ **Bristol Street Art Tours**   WALKING
(Where The Wall; ☑ 07748 632663; www.wherethewall.com; adult/child £9/5; ☺ 11am Sat & Sun) There's a plethora of walls dripping with skilfully applied spray paint on show in these two-hour tours that start in the city centre and end in Stokes Croft. Banksy artworks feature strongly but other highlights of the city's great graffiti offering are covered too. Afterwards they run hour-long **Stencil Art Spray Sessions** (£12.50, Saturday and Sunday 1.45pm) where you 'get your hands on the cans', producing artworks to take home.

Bristol Packet   BOATING
(☑ 0117-926 8157; www.bristolpacket.co.uk; Wapping Wharf, Gas Ferry Rd) Bristol Packet's trips include 45-minute cruises around the harbour (adult/child £7/5, six sailings daily April to October, and on winter weekends), and weekly sailings to Beese's Tea Gardens (£14/9, runs April to September). Boats depart from Wapping Wharf near SS *Great Britain,* and the Watershed landing **stage** on the Harbourside.

There are also weekly cruises to the spectacular Avon Gorge from April to September (adult/child £16/14). Cruises to Bath

(£32/24) run once a month from May to September. These two trips depart only from Wapping Wharf.

Bristol Highlights Walk WALKING
(☎0117-968 4638; www.bristolwalks.co.uk; adult/child £6/3; ⊙11am Sat Mar-Sep) Tours the old town, city centre and harbourside, leaving from the tourist office (p230) – there's no need to book. Themed tours exploring Clifton, medieval Bristol and the history of Bristol's slave and wine trades run on request.

Festivals & Events

★Upfest ART
(www.upfest.co.uk; ⊙Jul) Where better for a street art and graffiti festival than the city that brought us Banksy? Europe's largest event of its type sees 300 artists descending on the city to paint live, in front of audiences, at 40 venues. There are music gigs and affordable art sales too.

Bristol Shakespeare Festival THEATRE
(www.bristolshakespeare.org.uk; ⊙Jul) One of Britain's biggest outdoor festivals devoted to the Bard runs throughout July.

International Balloon Fiesta AIR SHOW
(www.bristolballoonfiesta.co.uk; ⊙Aug) More than 100 brightly coloured hot-air balloons, often of mind-boggling shapes, fill the skies at Ashton Court in what is the largest event of its type in Europe. The highlights are the fireworks and Nightglow flights.

Encounters FILM
(www.encounters-festival.org.uk; ⊙Sep) Bristol's largest short-film fest.

Sleeping

★Kyle Blue HOSTEL £
(☎0117-929 0609; www.kylebluebristol.co.uk; Wapping Wharf; dm/s/d £29/52/59; 📶) What a boon for budget travellers: a boutique hostel set on a boat that's moored in easy reach of the central sights. Cabins are compact but supremely comfy, the showers and kitchen gleam and the smart lounge is the ideal spot to watch the river traffic float by.

Bristol YHA HOSTEL £
(☎0345 371 9726; www.yha.org.uk; 14 Narrow Quay; dm £15-35, d £59-90; @📶) Few hostels can boast a position as good as this one,

BANKSY – STREET ARTIST

If there's one Bristolian nearly everyone has heard of, it's Banksy (www.banksy.co.uk) – the guerrilla street artist whose distinctive stencilled style and provocative artworks have earned him worldwide notoriety.

Banksy has tried to remain anonymous but it's believed he was born in 1974 in Yate, 12 miles from Bristol, and honed his artistic skills in a local graffiti outfit. His works take a wry view of 21st-century culture – especially capitalism, consumerism and the cult of celebrity. Among his best-known pieces are the production of spoof banknotes (featuring Princess Diana's head instead of the Queen's), a series of murals on Israel's West Bank barrier (depicting people digging holes under and climbing ladders over the wall) and a painting of a caveman pushing a shopping trolley at the British Museum (which the museum promptly claimed for its permanent collection). His documentary *Exit Through the Gift Shop*, about an LA street artist, was nominated for an Oscar in 2011.

Long despised by the authorities, Banksy's artworks have become a tourist magnet. The **Well Hung Lover** (Frogmore St) depicts an angry husband, a two-timing wife, and a naked man dangling from a window. Nearby the **Castles Stencil** points out 'you don't need planning permission to build castles in the sky'. The startling **Paint-Pot Angel** (think pink paint meets funerary monument) resides in the Bristol Museum & Art Gallery (p225) and is a reminder of the artist's hugely popular 2009 exhibition there. **Mild Mild West** (80 Stokes Croft) features a Molotov cocktail–wielding teddy bear facing three riot police and is thought to be a comment on Bristol's edgy-yet-comfy vibe. A stencil of the **Grim Reaper** rowing a boat, which used to sit on the waterline of the party boat the *Thekla*, is now in the city's M Shed Museum (p223). Hidden away near the SS *Great Britain*, **Girl With A Pierced Eardrum** FREE is the artist's 2014 take on the famous Vermeer portrait.

The tourist office (p230) sells a Banksy info sheet for 50p and can advise on other locations. The excellent Bristol Street Art Tours (p225) take in the main Banksy sites in a walk from the city centre to graffiti-central Stokes Croft.

beside the river in a red-brick warehouse. Facilities include kitchens, a cycle store, a games room and the excellent Grainshed cafe-bar. Weekends and holidays bring the highest prices.

★ **Brooks** B&B ££

(☑ 0117-930 0066; www.brooksguesthousebristol. com; Exchange Ave; d £67-120, tr £90-129, trailers £80-149; 🛜) Welcome to urban glamping – three vintage Airstream trailers sit in a bijou AstroTurf roof garden slap bang in the heart of Bristol. They're predictably tiny (ranging from 16ft to 20ft) but still have sleek seating areas, pocket-sized bathrooms and rooftop views. Guesthouse bedrooms are compact but smart, featuring soft tones and checked throws.

Mercure Bristol Brigstow HOTEL ££

(☑ 0117-929 1030; www.mercure.com; 5 Welsh Back; s £85-125, d £90-210; ❄ 🛜) A harbourside location and attractive modern design make the Mercure a sound, central option. Rooms boast 'floating' beds, curved panel walls and tiny TVs set into bathroom tiles (gimmicky, yes, but fun).

★ **Number 38** B&B £££

(☑ 0117-946 6905; www.number38clifton.com; 38 Upper Belgrave Rd; s £115, d £125-180, ste £220; 🅿 🛜) Set on the edge of the Downs, this up-market B&B is *the* choice for style-conscious travellers. The rooms are huge and contemporary – sombre greys and smooth blues dictate the palette – luxury is provided by waffle bathrobes and designer bath goodies, and sweeping city views unfold from most bedrooms and the roof terrace. The two suites have gleaming, old-fashioned metal baths.

Hotel du Vin HOTEL £££

(☑ 0117-403 2979; www.hotelduvin.com; Narrow Lewins Mead; d £139-164, ste £205-270; 🅿 ❄ 🛜) The Bristol outpost of this luxury hotel brand occupies an old sugar warehouse and mixes heritage chic with smooth minimalism: exposed brick and iron pillars meet futon beds and claw-foot baths. The sumptuous split-level mezzanine suites may see you lose your heart to loft living.

The stylish bistro is great, too.

✕ Eating

★ **Primrose** CAFE £

(☑ 0117-946 6577; www.primrosecafe.co.uk; 1 Boyce's Ave; dishes £6-10; ☺9am-5pm Mon-Sat,

TYNTESFIELD HOUSE

Formerly the home of the Gibbs family, **Tyntesfield** (NT; ☑ 01275-461900; www. nationaltrust.org.uk/tyntesfield; Wraxall; adult/child £15.60/7.80, gardens only £9.60/4.80; ☺ house 11am-5pm Mar-Oct, 11am-3pm Nov-Feb, gardens 10am-5pm year-round) was purchased by the National Trust in 2002. A fairy-tale mansion bristling with pinnacles and turrets, brimful of sweeping staircases and cavernous, antique-filled rooms, the house gives an insight into the lavish lives once enjoyed by England's wealthiest families. Entry is via timed ticket and includes a guided tour. The house is 8 miles southwest of Bristol, off the B3128.

from 9.30am Sun; 🞵) ⏀ The Primrose richly deserves its status as a Clifton institution, thanks to decades of serving towering homemade cakes and imaginative lunches, such as halloumi and courgette burgers, and slow-cooked pheasant. Pavement tables and a secluded roof garden add to the appeal, as do belt-busting brunches that are served impressively late (to 3pm); the eggs Benedict and Belgian waffles are legendary.

Canteen CAFE £

(☑ 0117-923 2017; www.canteenbristol.co.uk; 80 Stokes Croft; mains £5-10; ☺10am-midnight Mon-Thu, to 1am Fri & Sat, to 11pm Sun; 🛜) ⏀ Occupying the ground floor of an old office block, this community-run cafe-bar sums up Bristol's alternative character: it's all about slow food, local suppliers and fair prices, whether you pop in for a breakfast, veggie chilli or sit-down supper. It's not signed on the outside – look out for the hipsters on the terrace and the lettering: Hamilton House.

Pieminister FAST FOOD £

(☑ 0117-942 3322; www.pieminister.co.uk; 24 Stokes Croft; pies £5.50; ☺11.30am-10pm Mon-Fri, 10am-10.30pm Sat, 10am-9.30pm Sun) This Bristol-born chain of pie shops has become a local institution. Choose from Deer Stalker (venison and cured bacon), Heidi (goat's cheese and spinach) and Moo and Blue (yes: beef and Stilton). All are drowned in lashings of gravy (meat-free if you wish).

The main shop is on Stokes Croft; there are also outlets in the city centre in St

Nicholas Market and at **Broad Quay** (📞0117-325 7616; 7 Broad Quay; ⏱11.30am-9.30pm Sun-Thu, 11.30am-11pm Fri & Sat).

St Nicholas Market
MARKET £

(St Nicks Market; www.stnicholasmarketbristol. co.uk; Corn St; ⏱9.30am-5pm Mon-Sat) The city's lively street market has a bevy of food stalls selling everything from Pieminister pies and mezze platters to pulled-pork rolls from barbecue specialists Grillstock. Lines can be long at lunchtime, but it's worth the wait. Look out, too, for the Wednesday farmers market (8am to 2.30pm).

⭐ Riverstation
BRITISH ££

(📞0117-914 4434; www.riverstation.co.uk; The Grove; lunch 2/3 courses £14/17, dinner mains £15-18; ⏱noon-2.30pm & 6-10pm Mon-Sat, noon-3pm Sun) Riverstation's waterside location is hard to beat, with a view over the Floating Harbour, but it's the classical food that truly shines, from confit duck leg with quince and port jus, to pan fried turbot with squid ink sauce.

Cowshed
BRITISH ££

(📞0117-973 3550; www.thecowshedbristol.com; 46 Whiteladies Rd; lunch 2/3-course £12/14, dinner mains £13-28; ⏱8am-11.30am, noon-3pm & 6-10pm Mon-Sat, to 9.30pm Sun) Country food with a modern twist is served at the Cowshed. The focus is on quality, locally sourced meat – aged beef, slow-braised lamb, pork belly, plus the pièce de résistance, 'steak on stone', served sizzling on a hot lava rock. The three-course lunch is excellent value.

Shop 3
BISTRO ££

(📞0117-382 2235; www.shop3bistro.co.uk; 3a Regent St; mains £15-25; ⏱6-11pm Tue-Sat) It's a bit like heading into a French neighbourhood bistro when you step through the door at Shop 3 to encounter the rich aromas of rustic food. The focus is firmly on local and foraged – expect delicate presentation but robust flavours from ingredients such as venison, oxtail, pheasant, artichokes and kale.

Thali Café
INDIAN ££

(📞0117-974 3793; www.thethalicafe.co.uk; 1 Regent St; meals £9-12; ⏱5-10pm Mon-Fri, from noon Sat & Sun) In Thali, something of the makeshift exuberance of Indian street food comes to Clifton's hills. Richly flavoured dishes infused with spices include the eponymous thalis (multicourse meals), showcasing different curry styles. To drink? Perhaps a Jaipur IPA, dry gin with homemade tonic, or cup of chai.

Soukitchen
MIDDLE EASTERN ££

(📞0117-966 6880; www.soukitchen.co.uk; 277 North St; mains £8-14; ⏱5.30-9.30pm Mon & Tue, noon-3pm & 5.30-9.30pm Wed-Fri, 10am-2.30pm & 5.30-9.30pm Sat & Sun,) Middle Eastern market food is the stock-in-trade at this friendly diner in Southville, with characteristic dishes such as borek (filo pies stuffed with meat or vegetables), mix-and-match mezze platters and flame-grilled kebabs. Honest food with heart.

Clifton Sausage
BRITISH ££

(📞0117-973 1192; www.cliftonsausage.co.uk; 7 Portland St; mains £11-17; ⏱noon-4pm & 6-9pm Mon-Sat, 10am-4pm & 6-9pm Sun) One for Brits to go all misty-eyed over: a cool eatery that places the much-beloved sausage on a culinary pedestal. The varieties on offer here include Gloucester pork, Cotswold lamb, and beef and Butcombe ale – all come with a dollop of gourmet mash.

Fishers
SEAFOOD ££

(📞0117-974 7044; www.fishers-restaurant.com; 35 Princess Victoria St; mains £14-25; ⏱5.30-10pm Mon, noon-3pm & 5.30-10pm Tue-Sun) Bristol's top choice for fish dishes rustles up everything from garlicky pan-fried bream with pesto, to succulent grilled whole lobster. The hot shellfish platter (£46 for two people) is memorable. The simple setting, with its whitewashed walls, ship's lanterns and nautical knick-knacks, adds to the maritime vibe.

It also offers a ridiculously good-value set lunch and early-evening menu (two/three courses £9.50/13).

Ox
STEAK ££

(📞0117-922 1001; www.theoxbristol.com; The Basement, 43 Corn St; mains £13-27; ⏱noon-2.30pm Mon-Fri, 5-10.30pm Mon-Sat, noon-4pm Sun) Gorgeous, highly polished wood, glinting brass, low lighting and cool jazz ensure this sleek eatery resembles a posh Pullman dining car that's somehow been bestowed with some Pre-Raphaelite murals. The food is aimed firmly at meat eaters; expect charcuterie platters, gourmet burgers and five choices of steak cut.

Olive Shed
BISTRO ££

(📞0117-929 1960; www.theoliveshed.com; Princes Wharf; tapas £4-8.50, mains £12-19; ⏱noon-10pm Thu-Sat, to 5pm Sun) With tables right beside

Bristol harbour, this rustic eatery is a top spot for a waterfront lunch. It serves tapas and twists on Mediterranean food such as pork with manzanilla glaze, fragrant rosemary cured manchego and spicy courgette, chickpea and cumin kofta.

Glassboat
FRENCH £££

(☑ 0117-332 3971; www.glassboat.co.uk; Welsh Back; lunch 2/3 courses £12/15, dinner mains £20-32; ☉ noon-2.45pm & 5.30-9.45pm Mon-Sat, noon-4.45pm Sun) This converted river barge is an ideal spot for a romantic dinner, with candlelit tables and harbour views through a glass extension. The refined food revolves around French and Italian flavours.

The early-evening set meals (two/three courses £12/15), served between 5.30pm and 6.30pm, are great value.

🍷 Drinking & Nightlife

★ Amoeba
CRAFT BEER

(☑ 0117 946 6461; www.amoebaclifton.co.uk; 10 Kings Rd; ☉ 1pm-1am Fri & Sat, 1pm-midnight Sun, 4pm-midnight Mon-Thu) Sixty-five craft beers, 60 cocktails (£8 to £9) and a hundred-and-something (who's counting?) spirits draw style-conscious drinkers to this chilled-out wine bar, where patrons sit on bench seats smothered in cushions and nibble on platters of charcoal crackers and artisan cheese (£8).

★ Mud Dock
PUB

(☑ 0117-934 9734; www.mud-dock.co.uk; 40 The Grove; ☉ 10am-10pm Tue-Sat, to 4pm Mon & Sun) Mud Dock epitomises the laid-back charm of Bristol's harbourside. In this long attic bikes, fairy lights and a massive metal swordfish hang from the girders. Summer sees drinkers packing the mellow waterside terrace, drinking in craft ales and cracking views.

It's set above a bike shop – head up the metal fire escape around the side to get in. The bar-food menu (mains £10 to £13) isn't massive but the quality is good.

BrewDog Bristol
CRAFT BEER

(☑ 0117-927 9258; www.brewdog.com; 58 Baldwin St; ☉ noon-midnight Sun-Wed, to 1am Thu-Sat) The Bristol outlet of Britain's punk brewery draws both the just-finished work crowd and those who want to linger at the cluster of tables out front. Expect ales such as Elvis Juice, Vagabond Pale, and Nanny State (that'll be 0.5%) on tap. Not sure which to try? Opt for the sampler of three glasses of a third of a pint (£6.70).

Thekla
CLUB

(☑ 0117-929 3301; www.theklabristol.co.uk; The Grove, East Mud Dock; ☉ Thu-Sat 9.30pm-3am or 4am) Bristol's club-boat has nights for all moods: electro-punk, indie, disco and new wave, plus regular live gigs during the week. Check the website for the latest.

Albion
PUB

(www.thealbionclifton.co.uk; Boyce's Ave; ☉ 9am-midnight Mon-Sat, to 11pm Sun) Cliftonites make a beeline for this village local for a post-work pint, drawn by the mini armchairs, log burner, a beer terrace framed by fairy lights and Bath Ales on tap.

Grain Barge
PUB

(☑ 0117-929 9347; www.grainbarge.com; Mardyke Wharf, Hotwell Rd; ☉ noon-11pm Sun-Wed, to 11.30pm Thu-Sat) This lovingly converted 1930s cargo vessel used to transport barley and wheat. Fittingly it's now used by the Bristol Beer Factory to showcase its craft ales. The beer terrace on the barge's roof is a cool spot to watch river traffic drift by.

Apple
BAR

(☑ 0117-925 3500; www.applecider.co.uk; Welsh Back; ☉ noon-midnight Mon-Sat, to 10.30pm Sun summer, 5pm-midnight Mon-Sat winter) Around 40 varieties of cider are served on this converted barge, including raspberry, strawberry and six perries (pear cider). Best enjoyed at a table set on the canalside cobbles.

☆ Entertainment

Watershed
CINEMA

(☑ 0117-927 5100; www.watershed.co.uk; 1 Canon's Rd) Bristol's digital-media centre has a three-screen, art-house cinema. Regular film-related events include talks and the Encounters Festival (p226) in September.

★ Bristol Old Vic
THEATRE

(☑ 0117-987 7877; www.bristololdvic.org.uk; 16 King St) Established in 1766, the much-respected Old Vic is the longest continuously running theatre in the English-speaking world, and has just had a £12.5m revamp. It hosts big touring productions in its historic Georgian auditorium, plus more experimental work in its smaller studio.

Check the website for details of its fabulous backstage and heritage tours (£12).

Fleece
LIVE MUSIC

(☑ 0117-945 0996; www.thefleece.co.uk; 12 St Thomas St; £5-25; ☉ 7.30-11pm Mon-Fri, to 4am Fri & Sat) A lively gig-pub favoured by indie artists. Past performers include Oasis, Muse and Radiohead.

Colston Hall LIVE MUSIC

(☑0117-203 4040; www.colstonhall.org; Colston St) Bristol's historic concert hall now has a gleaming five-floor annexe. Performers include rock, pop, folk and jazz bands, plus classical musicians and big-name comedy acts.

🛍 Shopping

High-street chains cluster around **Cabot Circus** (☑0117-952 9361; www.cabotcircus.com; Glass House; ☺10am-8pm Mon-Sat, 11am-5pm Sun) and Broadmead. The city centre has St Nicholas Market, plus other independent shops dotted around Corn St and Colston St.

Stokes Croft and Gloucester Rd are good for non-chain stores, especially those selling vintage clothing, crafts and secondhand music. Clifton is more upmarket, with high-end designer, homeware and antiques shops.

ℹ Information

Bristol Royal Infirmary (BRI; ☑0117-923 0000; www.uhbristol.nhs.uk; Upper Maudlin St; ☺24hr) Offers 24 hour emergency and urgent care.

Bristol Tourist Office (☑0333 321 0101; www.visitbristol.co.uk; E-Shed, 1 Canons Rd; ☺10am-5pm; 🕾) Offers information and advice, plus free wi-fi, accommodation bookings, and luggage storage (£5 per item).

ℹ Getting There & Away

AIR

Bristol International Airport (☑0371 334 4444; www.bristolairport.co.uk) Bristol's airport is 8 miles southwest of the city. Destinations in the UK and Ireland include Aberdeen, Belfast, Edinburgh, Cork, Glasgow and Newcastle (mainly handled by easyJet). Direct links with cities in mainland Europe include those to Barcelona, Berlin, Milan and Paris.

BUS

Bristol's **bus station** (Marlborough St; ☺ticket office 8am-6pm) is 500m north of the city centre. From there buses shuttle into central areas and fan out around the city. There's a taxi rank (p231) nearby.

National Express (www.nationalexpress.com) coaches include those running direct to:

London (£18, 2½ hours, hourly).
London Heathrow (£30, three hours, two-hourly).
Plymouth (£14, three hours, seven daily).
Bath (£5, 45 minutes, two daily).

TRAIN

DESTINATION	COST (£)	TIME (HR)	FREQUENCY
Birmingham	30	1½	hourly
Edinburgh	90	6½	hourly
Exeter	17	1	half-hourly
Glasgow	90	6½	hourly
London	34	1¾	half-hourly
Penzance	37	5½	hourly
Truro	45	4	hourly

ℹ Getting Around

TO/FROM THE AIRPORT

Bristol Airport Flyer (http://flyer.bristolairport.co.uk) Runs shuttle buses (one-way/return £7/11, 30 minutes, every 10 minutes at peak times) from the bus station and Bristol Temple Meads train station.

Arrow (☑01275-475000; www.arrowprivatehire.co.uk) Bristol Airport's official taxi service. Prices start from around £30 (one-way) from the city centre.

BICYCLE

Bristol Cycle Shack (☑0117-955 1017; www.bristolcycleshack.co.uk; 25 Oxford St; per 24hr from £15; ☺10am-5pm Mon, Tue & Thu-Sat) Hires out bikes from its base near Bristol Temple Meads train station.

Cycle the City (☑07873 387167; www.cyclethecity.org; 1 Harbourside; tours from £18) Rents out bikes and runs cycling tours from the central harbour area.

BOAT

Bristol Ferry Boat Company (☑0117-927 3416; www.bristolferry.com) boats leave roughly hourly from the dock at Cannon's Rd near the tourist office. Its Hotwells service runs west, with stops including Millennium Sq and the SS *Great Britain*, while the Temple Meads service runs east, with stops including Welsh Back, Castle Park (for Cabot Circus) and Temple Meads (for the train station). Fares depend on distance travelled; an all-day pass is adult/child £6.50/5.50.

BUS

Bus journeys in Bristol's city centre cost £1 for up to three stops; longer trips cost £1.50. A BristolRider pass (£4.50) provides unlimited travel.

Bus 8 Runs every 15 minutes from Bristol Temple Meads train station, via College Green in the city centre, to Clifton and on to Bristol Zoo Gardens.

Bus 73/X73 Runs every 20 minutes from Bristol Parkway Station to the centre (£3.50, 30 minutes).

MetroBus The M2 service (www.metrobusbristol.co.uk; single £1.50) provides efficient links between Bristol Temple Meads train station, Long Ashton Park & Ride, the city centre and SS *Great Britain*.

CAR & MOTORCYCLE

Heavy traffic and pricey parking make driving in Bristol a headache.

Park & Ride Buses (☎ 0345-602 0121; www.travelwest.info/park-ride/bristol; peak/off-peak return £4.50/3; ⏱ 6am-9pm Mon-Sat, 9.30am-6pm Sun; 🚲) run approximately every 15 to 20 minutes from Portway, Bath Rd and Long Ashton. Note that overnight parking is not allowed at the Park & Ride car parks.

TAXI

You can usually find a cab at the taxi ranks at the train and bus stations and on **St Augustine's Pde** (Narrow Quay).

To phone for a cab, try **Streamline Taxis** (☎ 0117-926 4001; www.bristolstreamlinetaxis.com) or **1st Call Taxi** (☎ 0117-955 5111; ⏱ 24hr). If you're taking a nonmetered cab, agree on the fare in advance.

BATH

POP 88,850

Bath is one of Britain's most appealing cities. Exquisite Roman and Georgian architecture, hipster hang-outs and swish spas make it hard to resist.

History

Legend has it King Bladud, a Trojan refugee and father of King Lear, founded Bath some 2800 years ago when his pigs were cured of leprosy by a dip in the muddy swamps. The Romans established the town of Aquae Sulis in AD 44 and built the extensive baths complex and a temple to the goddess Sulis-Minerva.

In 944 a monastery was founded on the site of the present abbey, helping Bath's development as an ecclesiastical centre and wool-trading town. But it wasn't until the early 18th century that Ralph Allen and the celebrated dandy Richard 'Beau' Nash made Bath the centre of fashionable society. Allen developed the quarries at Coombe Down, constructed Prior Park and employed the two John Woods (father and son) to create Bath's signature buildings.

During WWII, Bath was hit by the Luftwaffe during the so-called Baedeker raids, which targeted historic cities in an effort to sap British morale. In 1987, Bath became the only city in Britain to be declared a Unesco World Heritage Site in its entirety.

◎ Sights

★ **Roman Baths**   HISTORIC BUILDING
(☎ 01225-477785; www.romanbaths.co.uk; Abbey Churchyard; adult/child/family £17.50/10.25/48; ⏱ 9.30am-5pm Nov-Feb, 9am-5pm Mar–mid-Jun, Sep & Oct, 9am-9pm mid-Jun–Aug) In typically ostentatious style, the Romans built a bathhouse complex above Bath's 46°C (115°F) hot springs. Set alongside a temple dedicated to the healing goddess Sulis-Minerva, the baths now form one of the world's best-preserved ancient Roman spas, and are encircled by 18th- and 19th-century buildings. To dodge the worst of the crowds avoid weekends, and July and August; buy fast-track tickets online to by-pass the queues. Saver tickets covering the Roman Baths and the Fashion Museum cost adult/child/family £22.50/12.25/58.

The heart of the complex is the **Great Bath**, a lead-lined pool filled with steaming, geothermally heated water from the so-called 'Sacred Spring' to a depth of 1.6m. Though now open-air, the bath would originally have been covered by a 45m-high barrel-vaulted roof.

More bathing pools and changing rooms are to the east and west, with excavated sections revealing the **hypocaust system** that heated the bathing rooms. After luxuriating in the baths, Romans would have reinvigorated themselves with a dip in the circular **cold-water pool**.

The **King's Bath** was added sometime during the 12th century around the site of the original Sacred Spring. Every day, 1.5 million litres of hot water still pour into the pool. Beneath the Pump Room are the remains of the **Temple of Sulis-Minerva**.

Digital reconstructions pop up in some sections of the complex, especially in the Temple Courtyard, and the West and East

> ### ⓘ MUSEUM DISCOUNTS
>
> Saver tickets covering the Roman Baths and the Fashion Museum cost adult/child/family £22.50/12.25/58.
>
> There is also a joint ticket (adult/child/family £17/8/40) covering Beckford's Tower, No 1 Royal Crescent, the Museum of Bath Architecture and the Herschel Museum of Astronomy.

Bath

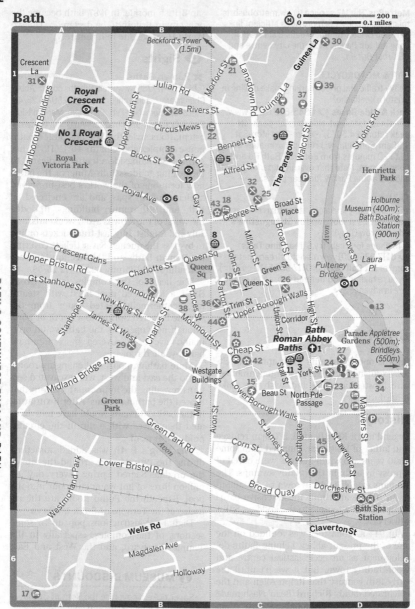

0 200 m
0 0.1 miles

Beckford's Tower (1.5mi)

Crescent La
31

Marlborough Buildings

Royal Crescent 4

No 1 Royal Crescent 2

Royal Victoria Park

Upper Church St

Julian Rd

Morford St

Lansdown Rd

28 Rivers St

Circus Mews
22

Brock St

The Circus
35
12

Bennett St

5
Alfred St

Guinea La
30

Guinea La

21

40
37

39

9

Walcot St

The Paragon

Royal Ave 6

Gay St

Royal Ave

32
25
43 18

George St

Broad St Place

St John's Rd

Henrietta Park

Holburne Museum (400m); Bath Boating Station (900m)

Crescent Gdns

Upper Bristol Rd

Gt Stanhope St

Charlotte St

Monmouth Pl

New King St

7

James St West

Stanhope St

Charles St

29

8

Queen Sq

Queen Sq

33

Princes St

38

Monmouth St

44

John St

Milsom St

Barton St

Trim St

Green St

Queen St
19

26

Upper Borough Walls

Union St

Corridor

Broad St

Pulteney Bridge

10

Laura Pl

Grove St

Avon

13

41
Cheap St
42

15

Westgate Buildings

Milk St

Avon St

St James's Pde

Lower Borough Walls

Bath Roman Baths 1

11 3
York St

Beau St

North Pde Passage

Stall St

High St

Parade Gardens

Bath Abbey

24
27
14
23 16
20

Appletree Brindleys (500m); (550m)

34

Manvers St

Corn St

Southgate

45

St Lawrence St

Midland Bridge Rd

Green Park

Green Park Rd

Avon

Lower Bristol Rd

Westmorland Park

Broad Quay

Dorchester St

Bath Spa Station

Wells Rd

Magdalen Ave

Holloway

Claverton St

17

Baths, which feature projections of bathers. There is also a fascinating **museum** displaying artefacts discovered on the site. Look out for the famous gilded bronze head of Minerva and a striking carved gorgon's head, as well as some of the 12,000-odd Roman coins thrown into the spring as votive offerings to the goddess.

The complex of buildings around the baths was built in stages during the 18th and 19th centuries. John Wood the Elder and the Younger designed the buildings

Bath

◉ Top Sights
1 Bath Abbey..............................D4
2 No 1 Royal Crescent.................A2
3 Roman Baths..........................C4
4 Royal Crescent.......................A1

◉ Sights
5 Bath Assembly Rooms................C2
  Fashion Museum...................(see 5)
6 Georgian Garden.....................B2
7 Herschel Museum of Astronomy.......B3
8 Jane Austen Centre.................C3
9 Museum of Bath Architecture........C2
10 Pulteney Bridge.....................D3
11 Pump Room..........................C4
12 The Circus..........................B2

⊕ Activities, Courses & Tours
  Bath Abbey Tower Tours............(see 1)
13 Bath City Boat Trips................D3
14 Bizarre Bath Comedy Walk...........D4
  Mayor's Guide Tours..............(see 11)
  Pulteney Cruisers................(see 13)
15 Thermae Bath Spa...................C4

⊜ Sleeping
16 Bath Backpackers...................D4
17 Grays Bath..........................A6
18 Halcyon Apartments.................C2
19 Haringtons..........................C3
20 Henry...............................D4
21 Hill House Bath.....................C1
22 Queensberry.........................B2
23 Three Abbey Green...................D4

⊗ Eating
24 Acorn...............................D4
25 Adventure...........................C2
26 Bertinet Bakery.....................C3
27 Café Retro..........................D4
28 Chequers............................B1
29 Farmers Market......................B4
30 Hudson Steakhouse...................D1
31 Marlborough Tavern..................A1
  Pump Room
    Restaurant.......................(see 11)
  Sally Lunn's.....................(see 24)
32 Same Same But Different.............C2
33 Scallop Shell.......................B3
34 Sotto Sotto.........................D4
35 The Circus..........................B2
36 Thoughtful Bread
  Company.............................C3

◉ Drinking & Nightlife
37 Bell................................C1
38 Colonna & Smalls....................B3
39 Corkage.............................D1
40 Star................................C1

◉ Entertainment
41 Komedia.............................C4
42 Little Theatre Cinema...............C4
43 Moles...............................C2
44 Theatre Royal.......................C4

◉ Shopping
45 SouthGate...........................D5

around the Sacred Spring, while the famous **Pump Room** (Stall St; ◷9.30am-5pm) FREE was built by their contemporaries, Thomas Baldwin and John Palmer, in neoclassical style, complete with soaring Ionic and Corinthian columns. The building now houses a **restaurant** (✑01225-444477; snacks £7-9, mains £13-17), where offerings include magnificent afternoon teas (£26, or £35 with champagne). You can also taste free samples of the spring waters, which were believed in Victorian times to have curative properties. If you're lucky, you might even have music provided by the Pump Room's string trio.

Admission to the Roman Baths includes an audio guide, featuring commentary in 12 languages – there's also one especially for children and a guide in sign language. One of the English guides is read by bestselling author Bill Bryson. Free hourly guided tours start at the Great Bath on the hour. The last entry to the complex is an hour before closing.

★ **Bath Abbey** CHURCH
(✑01225-422462; www.bathabbey.org; Abbey Churchyard; suggested donation adult/child £4/2; ◷9.30am-5.30pm Mon, 9am-5.30pm Tue-Fri, to 6pm Sat, 1-2.30pm & 4.30-6pm Sun) Looming above the city centre, Bath's huge abbey church was built between 1499 and 1616, making it the last great medieval church raised in England. Its most striking feature is the west facade, where angels climb up and down stone ladders, commemorating a dream of the founder, Bishop Oliver King.

Tower tours (adult/child £8/4; ◷10am-5pm Apr-Aug, 10am-4pm Sep & Oct, 11am-4pm Nov-Mar, closed Sun) leave on the hour from Monday to Friday, and every half-hour on Saturdays. Tours can only be booked at the Abbey shop, on the day.

Jane Austen Centre MUSEUM
(✑01225-443000; www.janeausten.co.uk; 40 Gay St; adult/child £12/6.20; ◷9.45am-5.30pm Apr-Oct, 10am-4pm Sun-Fri, 9.45am-5.30pm Sat

WORTH A TRIP

PRIOR PARK ESTATE

Partly designed by the landscape architect Lancelot 'Capability' Brown, the grounds of this 18th-century **estate** (NT; ☑ 01225-833977; www.national trust.org.uk; Ralph Allen Dr; adult/child £7.40/3.70; ⊗ 10am-5.30pm daily Feb-Oct, 10am-4pm Sat & Sun Nov-Jan) on Bath's southern fringe feature cascading lakes and a graceful Palladian bridge, one of only four such structures in the world (look out for the period graffiti, some of which dates back to the 1800s).

The park is a mile south of Bath's centre. Bus 2 (every 30 minutes) stops nearby, as does Bath City Sightseeing's 'City Skyline' tour (Bath Bus Company; ☑ 01225-444102; www.bathbuscompany. com; adult/child/family £15/9.50/43; ⊗ 10am-5pm, reduced services Jan-Mar).

Nov-Mar) Bath is known to many as a location in Jane Austen's novels, including *Persuasion* and *Northanger Abbey*. Although Austen lived in Bath for only five years, from 1801 to 1806, she remained a regular visitor and a keen student of the city's social scene. Here, guides in Regency costumes regale you with Austen-esque tales as you tour memorabilia relating to the writer's life in Bath.

Herschel Museum of Astronomy MUSEUM (☑ 01225-446865; www.herschelmuseum.org.uk; 19 New King St; adult/child £6.50/3.20; ⊗ 11am-5pm Jul & Aug, 1-5pm Mon-Fri, 10am-5pm Sat & Sun Mar-Jun & Sep) In 1781 astronomer William Herschel discovered Uranus from the garden of his home, now converted into a museum. Herschel shared the house with his wife Caroline, also an important astronomer. Their home is little changed since the 18th century; an astrolabe in the garden marks the position of the couple's telescope.

★**Royal Crescent** ARCHITECTURE Bath is famous for its glorious Georgian architecture, and it doesn't get any grander than this semicircular terrace of majestic town houses overlooking the green sweep of Royal Victoria Park. Designed by John Wood the Younger (1728–82) and built between 1767 and 1775, the houses appear perfectly symmetrical from the outside, but the owners were allowed to tweak the interiors, so no two houses are quite the same. **No 1 Royal Crescent** (☑ 01225-428126; www.no1royalcres cent.org.uk; adult/child/family £10.30/5.10/25.40; ⊗ 10am-5pm) offers you an intriguing insight into life inside.

A walk east along Brock St from the Royal Crescent leads to **the Circus**, a ring of 33 houses divided into three semicircular terraces. Plaques on the houses commemorate famous residents such as Thomas Gainsborough, Clive of India and David Livingstone. The terrace was designed by John Wood the Elder, but he died in 1754, and the terrace was completed by his son in 1768.

To the south along Gravel Walk is the **Georgian Garden** (☑ 01225-394041; off Royal Ave; ⊗ 9am-7pm) **FREE**, restored to resemble a typical 18th-century town-house garden.

Bath Assembly Rooms HISTORIC BUILDING (NT; ☑ 01225-477786; www.nationaltrust.org.uk; 19 Bennett St; ⊗ 10.30am-6pm Mar-Oct, to 5pm Nov-Feb) **FREE** When they opened in 1771, the city's stately Assembly Rooms were where fashionable Bath socialites gathered to waltz, play cards and listen to the latest chamber music. Today they're unfurnished; rooms that are open to the public include the Great Octagon, tearoom and ballroom – all lit by their original 18th-century chandeliers.

The city's fine Fashion Museum is in the basement.

Fashion Museum MUSEUM (☑ 01225-477789; www.fashionmuseum.co.uk; Assembly Rooms, 19 Bennett St; adult/child £9/7; ⊗ 10.30am-5pm Mar-Oct, to 4pm Nov-Feb) The world-class collections on display in this museum within the basement of the city's Georgian Assembly Rooms include costumes from the 17th to late 20th centuries. Some exhibits change annually; check the website for the latest.

Pulteney Bridge BRIDGE Elegant Pulteney Bridge has been spanning the River Avon since the late 18th century and continues to be a much-loved and much-photographed Bath landmark (the view from Grand Parade, southwest of the bridge, is the best). Browse the shops that line both sides of the bridge or have a rest and a Bath bun in the Bridge Coffee Shop.

Museum of Bath Architecture MUSEUM (☑ 01225-333895; www.museumofbatharchitec ture.org.uk; The Vineyards, The Paragon; adult/child £5.50/2.50; ⊗ 2-5pm Tue-Fri, 10.30am-5pm Sat

& Sun mid-Feb–Nov) The stories behind the building of Bath's most striking structures are explored here, using antique tools, displays on Georgian construction methods and a 1:500 scale model of the city.

Holburne Museum
GALLERY

(☎01225-388569; www.holburne.org; Great Pulteney St; ⊙10am-5pm Mon-Sat, 11am-5pm Sun) **FREE** Sir William Holburne, the 18th-century aristocrat and art fanatic, amassed a huge collection, which now forms the core of the Holburne Museum, in a lavish mansion at the end of Great Pulteney St. The museum houses a roll call of works by artists including Turner, Stubbs, William Hoare and Thomas Gainsborough, as well as 18th-century majolica and porcelain.

American Museum in Britain
MUSEUM

(☎01225-460503; www.americanmuseum.org; Claverton Manor; adult/child £12.50/7; ⊙10am-5pm Tue-Sun late Mar–Oct) Britain's largest collection of American folk art, including First Nations textiles, patchwork quilts and historic maps, is housed in a fine mansion a couple of miles from the city centre. Several rooms have been decorated to resemble a 17th-century Puritan house, an 18th-century tavern and a New Orleans bedroom c 1860. A free shuttle bus (11.40am to 5pm) leaves from Terrace Walk, beside Parade Gardens.

🏃 Activities

Soaking in Bath's thermal waters is a real city highlight, as are guided tours that could see you clambering up to the roof of Bath Abbey or heading out on an acclaimed comedy walk-show.

Pulteney Cruisers (☎01225-863600; www. bathboating.com; Pulteney Bridge; adult/child £9/4; ⊙mid-Mar–Oct) and **Bath City Boat Trips** (☎07980 335185; www.bathcityboattrips. com; Pulteney Sluice Gate; adult/child £11/9) offer cruises up and down the River Avon from the Pulteney Bridge area.

★Thermae Bath Spa
SPA

(☎01225-331234; www.thermaebathspa.com; Hot Bath St; spa £36-40, treatments from £65; ⊙9am-9.30pm, last entry 7pm) Taking a dip in the Roman Baths might be off limits, but you can still sample the city's curative waters at this fantastic modern spa complex, housed in a shell of local stone and plate glass. The showpiece is the open-air rooftop pool, where you can bathe in naturally heated, mineral-rich waters with a backdrop of Bath's cityscape – a don't-miss experience, best enjoyed at dusk.

Bath Boating Station
BOATING

(☎01225-312900; www.bathboating.co.uk; Forester Rd; adult/child per hour £7/3.50, per day £18/9; ⊙10am-5.30pm Wed-Sun Easter-Sep) You can pilot your own vessel down the Avon from this Victorian-era boathouse, which rents out traditional rowing boats, punts, kayaks and Canadian canoes. It's in the suburb of Bathwick, a 20-minute walk northeast from the city centre.

🍳 Tours

★Bizarre Bath Comedy Walk
WALKING

(www.bizarrebath.co.uk; adult/student £10/7; ⊙8pm Apr-Oct) A fabulously daft city tour mixing street theatre and live performance that bills itself as 'hysterical rather than historical'. Leaves nightly from outside the tourist office. There's no need to book.

Mayor's Guide Tours
WALKING

(www.bathguides.org.uk; ⊙10.30am & 2pm Sun-Fri, 10.30am Sat) **FREE** Excellent historical tours provided free by the Mayor's Corp of Honorary Guides; tours cover about 2 miles and are wheelchair accessible. They leave from within the Abbey Churchyard, outside the Pump Room. There are extra tours at 7pm on Tuesdays and Thursdays May to August.

✨ Festivals & Events

Bath has a busy program of festivals. All bookings are handled by Bath Festival.

Bath Festival
CULTURAL

(☎01225-614180; www.bathfestivals.org.uk; ⊙May) A new multi-arts festival that combines the Bath Literature and Bath International Music festivals, combining classical, jazz, world and folk music with fiction, debate, science, history, politics and poetry.

Bath Fringe Festival
THEATRE

(www.bathfringe.co.uk; ⊙mid-May–early Jun) Theatre-focused festival that also includes folk and world music gigs, dance and performance walks.

Great Bath Feast
FOOD & DRINK

(www.greatbathfeast.co.uk; ⊙Sep) A 15-day celebration of Bath's fine-food tradition, featuring tastings, demonstrations and markets and showcasing local producers and chefs.

🛏 Sleeping

Bath has a wide range of hotels and B&Bs, and gets extremely busy in the height of summer when prices peak. Be aware, they also rise by anything from £10 to £60 a room at weekends year-round. Few hotels have on-site parking, although some offer discounted rates at municipal car parks.

Bath YHA   HOSTEL £

(☑ 0345 371 9303; www.yha.org.uk; Bathwick Hill; dm £23, d/q from £49/69; ⊙ check in 3-11pm; P @ 🛜) Split across an Italianate mansion and modern annexes, this impressive hostel is a steep climb (or a short hop on bus U1) from the city. The listed building means the rooms are huge, and some have period features such as cornicing and bay windows.

A revamped reception, cafe-bar and new all-en suite wing opened in April 2018.

Bath Backpackers   HOSTEL £

(☑ 01225-446787; www.hostels.co.uk; 13 Pierrepont St; dm £17-21; 🛜) The showers are scarce, and it's grimy and battered, but this hostel is still on budget travellers' radars for bargain rates, a prime location and a 24-hour 'dungeon' (in truth a sound-proofed basement where you don't have to 'keep the noise down').

⭐ Three Abbey Green   B&B ££

(☑ 01225-428558; www.threeabbeygreen.com; 3 Abbey Green; s £108-144, d £120-200, q £240; 🛜) Rarely in Bath do you get somewhere as central as this Georgian town house with such spacious rooms. Elegant, 18th-century-style furnishings are teamed with swish wet-room bathrooms, while the opulent Lord Nelson suite features a vast four-poster bed. There's a fabulous vibe here – friendly, family-run and proud of it.

Henry   B&B ££

(☑ 01225-424052; www.thehenry.com; 6 Henry St; s £85-105, d £105-150, f £180-210; 🛜) This tall terrace has one of the best positions in Bath, literally steps from the centre. The seven rooms are jazzed up by modern floral motifs, striped cushions and mints on the pillows.

It's a great option for families – one room sleeps up to four, and cots and high chairs can be provided.

Appletree   B&B ££

(☑ 01225-337642; www.appletreebath.com; 7 Pulteney Gardens; r £95-165; P 🛜) Owner, Ling, ran a city-centre hotel for 15 years, and those skills shine throughout this classy B&B. Bedrooms are named after the eponymous fruit.

The best is Royal Gala, which features a sleigh bed and sofa, but even the cheaper rooms are bright and fresh and dotted with Asian art.

Hill House Bath   B&B ££

(☑ 01225-920520; www.hillhousebath.co.uk; 25 Belvedere; r £115-135; P 🛜) When you walk through the door here it almost feels like you're staying with friends. The decor is quietly quirky: moustache-themed cushions, retro pictures and objets d'art abound.

Haringtons   HOTEL ££

(☑ 01225-461728; www.haringtonshotel.co.uk; 8 Queen St; r £135-200; 🛜) Bath's classical trappings aren't to everyone's taste, so things are kept strictly modern at this city-centre crash pad, with vivid colour schemes and clashing wallpapers giving it a fun, young vibe. The location is fantastic, but some rooms are a tad small. Off-site parking costs £11.

⭐ Queensberry   HOTEL £££

(☑ 01225-447928; www.thequeensberry.co.uk; 4 Russell St; r £112-290, ste £250-460; P 🛜) Stylish but unstuffy Queensberry is Bath's best boutique spoil. In these terraced Georgian town houses heritage roots meet snazzy gingham checks, bright upholstery, original fireplaces and free-standing tubs. It's witty (see The Rules on their website), independent (and proud of it), and service is first rate.

Prices almost double on Friday and Saturday night. Valet parking is £7. The hotel's Olive Tree Restaurant is excellent, too.

⭐ Grays Bath   B&B £££

(☑ 01225-403020; www.graysbath.co.uk; 9 Upper Oldfield Park; r £115-245; P 🛜) Boutique treat Grays is a beautiful blend of modern, pared-down design and family treasures, many picked up from the owners' travels. All the rooms are individual: choose from floral, polka dot or maritime stripes. Perhaps the pick is the curving, six-sided room 12 in the attic, with partial city views.

The owners also run Brindleys (☑ 01225-310444; www.brindleysbath.co.uk; 14 Pulteney Gardens; r £115-200; P 🛜), a smaller but equally smart B&B on the east side of town.

Halcyon Apartments   RENTAL HOUSE £££

(☑ 01225-585100; www.thehalcyon.com/apartments; 16 George St; two-person apt £160-240, six-person apt £265; 🛜) The spacious apartments in this Georgian building blend heritage features (sash windows and high ceilings) with modern fixtures and furnishings. Quite the stylish pied-à-terre.

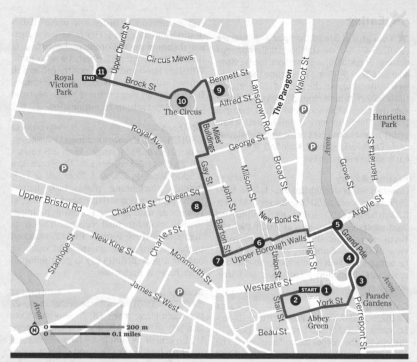

🏃 Walking Tour
Historic Bath

START BATH ABBEY
FINISH ROYAL CRESCENT
LENGTH 1.5 MILES; TWO HOURS

Start this architectural amble at ❶ **Bath Abbey** (p233), the city's iconic ecclesiastical edifice, built on the site of an 8th-century chapel. From the abbey square, head south along Stall St for a view of the 19th-century ❷ **Pump Room** (p233). Turn left onto York St, and follow it east to ❸ **Parade Gardens**, a landscaped Victorian park framed by the River Avon.

From here, the Grand Parade leads north; look out for the building on the corner, ❹ **The Empire**, built as a luxurious hotel in 1901. At the northern end of the Grand Parade is ❺ **Pulteney Bridge**, designed by Robert Adams in 1773, one of only a handful in the world to be lined with shops (the most famous other example is Florence's Ponte Vecchio). West of the bridge, ❻ **Upper Borough Walls** marks the northern extent of medieval Bath; if you look closely, you might spot some sections of the medieval wall that remain.

At Sawclose, you'll see the elaborate facade of Bath's ❼ **Theatre Royal** (p239), which has been staging productions since 1805. From here, follow Barton St on to ❽ **Queen Sq**, the oldest of Bath's Georgian squares, built as a showpiece development between 1728 and 1736 to demonstrate the talents of its architect, John Wood the Elder.

Head north on to Gay St, and right on to George St. Next to Clayton's Kitchen restaurant, an alley leads north, emerging next to the ❾ **Assembly Rooms** (p234), the heart of Georgian Bath's social life. Continue to Bennett St and turn left until you reach ❿ **the Circus** (p234), designed to echo the Colosseum in Rome. The three-tiered pillars exhibit the key styles of classical architecture (Doric, Ionic and Corinthian) and the facades are supposedly studded with masonic symbols.

From here, Brock St leads west to Bath's Georgian glory, the Royal Crescent. Constructed by John Wood the Younger in 1774, the terrace is now Grade I listed, making it as architecturally significant as Buckingham Palace. ⓫ **No 1 Royal Crescent** (p234) is open to the public.

✕ Eating

★ **Thoughtful Bread Company** BAKERY £
(☑ 01225-471747; www.thethoughtfulbreadcompany.com; 19 Barton St; ◷ 8am-5pm Tue-Fri, 8am-4pm Sat & Sun) ✐ Come lunchtime they could well be queuing out the door of this snug artisan bakery, where chunky loaves sit alongside delicate macaroons and salted caramel bombs. They also have a stall at Bath's Saturday **farmers market** (www.greenparkstation.co.uk; Green Park; ◷ 9am-1.30pm Sat) ✐ – come early as they sell out fast.

Bertinet Bakery BAKERY £
(www.bertinet.com/bertinetbakery; 1 New Bond St Pl; baked goods £2.50-5; ◷ 8am-5pm Mon-Fri, 8.30am-5.30pm Sat) The flavourful fillings and light pastry of the pasties at baker Richard Bertinet's take-out shop could change your view of that foodstuff for good. You'll also be tempted by rich quiches, cheese-studded croissants, French-inspired cakes and irresistible pistachio swirls.

Café Retro CAFE £
(☑ 01225-339347; www.caferetro.co.uk; 18 York St; mains £5-10; ◷ 9am-5pm; ☎) A poke in the eye for the corporate coffee chains. The paint job's scruffy, the crockery's ancient and none of the furniture matches, but that's all part of the charm: this is a cafe from the old school, and there are few places better for burgers, croques or cake. Takeaways (in biodegradable containers) are available from Retro-to-Go next door.

Adventure CAFE, BAR £
(☑ 01225-462038; www.adventurecafebar.co.uk; 5 Princes Bldgs, George St; mains £5-10; ◷ 8am-3am Mon-Fri, from 9am Sat & Sun; ☎✐) This cool cafe-bar offers something for everyone at most times of the day: breakfast cappuccino, lunchtime soup and late-night beer and cocktails. There's great outdoor seating at the back.

Sally Lunn's CAFE £
(☑ 01225-461634; www.sallylunns.co.uk; 4 North Pde Passage; mains £6-17, afternoon tea £8-40; ◷ 10am-9pm) Eating a bun at Sally Lunn's is a Bath tradition. It's all about proper English tea here, brewed in bone-china teapots, with finger sandwiches and dainty cakes served by waitresses in frilly aprons.

★ **The Circus** MODERN BRITISH ££
(☑ 01225-466020; www.thecircusrestaurant.co.uk; 34 Brock St; mains lunch £12-15, dinner £16-23; ◷ 10am-midnight Mon-Sat; ✐) Chef Ali Golden has turned this bistro into one of Bath's destination addresses. Her taste is for British dishes with a Continental twist, à la British food writer Elizabeth David: rabbit, Wiltshire lamb and West Country fish are all infused with herby flavours and rich sauces. It occupies an elegant town house near the Circus. Reservations recommended.

★ **Acorn** VEGETARIAN ££
(☑ 01225-446059; www.acornvegetariankitchen.co.uk; 2 North Pde Passage; lunch 2/3 courses £18/23, dinner 2/3 courses £28/37; ◷ noon-3pm & 5.30-9.30pm, to 3.30pm & 10pm Sat; ✐) ✐ Proudly proclaiming 'plants taste better', Bath's premier vegetarian restaurant tempts you inside with aromas reflecting its imaginative, global-themed cuisine. The wine flights (two/three courses £15/22) matched to the set dinner menus are good value; or opt for a pear Bellini (£7) to get the liquid refreshments under way.

Scallop Shell FISH & CHIPS ££
(☑ 01225-420928; www.thescallopshell.co.uk; 22 Monmouth Place; mains £10-15; ◷ noon-9.30pm Mon-Sat) ✐ One of Bath's best fish eateries is also one of its simplest – bags of potatoes piled up beside the door and plain wooden tables. The theme continues with the food – unfussy and unafraid to let the freshness of the ingredients and the quality of the cooking speak for themselves.

Chequers GASTROPUB ££
(☑ 01225-360017; www.thechequersbar.com; 50 Rivers St; mains £14-25; ◷ bar noon-11pm, food noon-2.30pm & 6-9pm) A discerning crowd inhabits Chequers, a Georgian pub that's now morphed into a classy gastropub. Here the menu ranges from well-executed bar-food favourites to relative rarities such as mallard and smoked eel, and partridge with quince.

Sotto Sotto ITALIAN ££
(☑ 01225-330236; www.sottosotto.co.uk; 10 North Pde; mains £11-25; ◷ noon-2pm & 5-10pm) The setting – an artfully lit vaulted brick chamber – is superb, and the food matches it for style. Authentic Italian dishes could include herb-crusted lamb in a rich red wine sauce, and sweet potato gnocchi with fresh sea bass. Top tip: don't forgo the garlicky sautéed spinach side.

Marlborough Tavern GASTROPUB ££
(☑ 01225-423731; www.marlborough-tavern.com; 35 Marlborough Bldgs; mains £13-25; ◷ bar noon-11pm, food noon-2pm & 6-9.30pm) The queen of

Bath's gastropubs has food that's closer to that of a fine-dining restaurant – smoked white bean puree, and crab and ginger salad rather than bog-standard meat-and-two-veg. Chunky wooden tables and racks of wine behind the bar give it an exclusive, classy feel.

Canny diners head here in the early evening to get 25% off the food bill.

★ **Menu Gordon Jones** MODERN BRITISH £££
(☑ 01225-480871; www.menugordonjones.co.uk; 2 Wellsway; 5-course lunch £50, 6-course dinner £55; ☺ 12.30-2pm & 7-9pm Tue-Sat) If you enjoy dining with an element of surprise, then Gordon Jones' restaurant will be right up your culinary boulevard. Menus are dreamt up daily and showcase the chef's taste for experimental ingredients (expect mushroom mousse and Weetabix ice cream) and eye-catching presentation (test tubes and paper bags). It's superb value given the skill on show. Reservations essential.

Hudson Steakhouse STEAK £££
(☑ 01225-332323; www.hudsonsteakhouse.co.uk; 14 London St; mains £19-31; ☺ 5-10.30pm Mon-Sat) Steak, steak and more steak is this acclaimed eatery's raison d'être. Tuck into top-quality cuts from porterhouse to prime fillet, all sourced from a Staffordshire farmers' co-op.

🍷 Drinking & Nightlife

★ **Colonna & Smalls** CAFE
(☑ 07766 808067; www.colonnaandsmalls.co.uk; 6 Chapel Row; ☺ 8am-5.30pm Mon-Fri, from 8.30am Sat, 10am-4pm Sun; 🐾) If you're keen on caffeinated beans, this is a cafe not to miss. A mission to explore coffee means there are three guest espresso varieties and smiley staff happy to share their expertise. They'll even tell you that black filter coffee – yes, filter coffee – is actually the best way to judge high-grade beans.

★ **Star** PUB
(☑ 01225-425072; www.abbeyales.co.uk; 23 The Vineyards, off the Paragon; ☺ noon-2.30pm & 5.30-11pm Mon-Fri, noon-midnight Sat, to 10.30pm Sun) Few pubs are registered relics, but the Star is just that, and it still has many of its 19th-century bar fittings. It's the brewery tap for Bath-based Abbey Ales; some ales are served in traditional jugs, and you can even ask for a pinch of snuff in the 'smaller bar'.

Bell PUB
(www.thebellinnbath.co.uk; 103 Walcot St; ☺ 11.30am-11pm Mon-Thu, to midnight Fri & Sat,

noon-10.30pm Sun; 🐾) Get chatting to Bath's bohemian muso crowd around the real fire at this laid-back locals' favourite. Conversation starters include the table football, bar billiards, backgammon and chess – and live music ranging from acoustic, country and folk to blues.

Same Same But Different CAFE ££
(☑ 01225-466856; www.same-same.co.uk; 7a Prince's Bldgs, Bartlett St; tapas £5, mains £10-12; ☺ 8am-11pm Tue-Fri, 9am-11pm Sat, 10am-5pm Sun, 8am-6pm Mon; 🐾) In this boho hang-out for the town's trendies you can tuck into picante poached eggs for breakfast, gourmet sandwiches for lunch and afternoon cappuccino and cake. Evenings bring creative tapas – think a zesty lime and coriander octopus – best sampled with a glass from the short but strong wine list.

Corkage WINE BAR
(☑ 01225-422577; www.corkagebath.com; 132a Walcot St; ☺ noon-11pm Tue-Sat) There's a distinct air of a French bistro in this intimate, friendly wine bar where the aromas of flavour-packed dishes fill the air and regiments of bottles fill the shelves. It offers scaled-down versions of main courses (£4 to £8) and an extensive international wine list.

☆ Entertainment

Moles LIVE MUSIC
(☑ 01225-437537; www.moles.co.uk; 14 George St; ☺ 5pm-3am Mon-Thu, to 4am Fri & Sat) Bath's main music venue keeps the crowds happy with a musical diet of indie, electro pop, punk, metal, club classics, DJ sets and cheese.

Little Theatre Cinema CINEMA
(☑ 0871 9025735; www.picturehouses.com; St Michael's Pl) Bath's excellent art-house cinema screens fringe films and foreign-language flicks in art deco surrounds.

Theatre Royal THEATRE
(☑ 01225-448844; www.theatreroyal.org.uk; Sawclose) Bath's historic theatre dates back 200 years. Major touring productions go in the main auditorium and smaller shows appear in the Ustinov Studio.

Komedia COMEDY
(☑ 01225-489070; www.komedia.co.uk; 22-23 Westgate St) Renowned comedy venue featuring touring shows and the sell-out Krater Saturday Comedy Club. Also live music, bingo and discos.

🛍 Shopping

Bath's shops are some of the best in the west. The city's main shopping centre is **South-Gate** (www.southgatebath.com; ⊙ shops 9am-6pm Mon-Wed, Fri & Sat, 9am-7pm Thu, 11am-5pm Sun), where you'll find all the major chain stores.

High-quality, independent shops line the narrow lanes just north of Bath Abbey and Pulteney Bridge. Milsom St is good for up-market fashion, while Walcot St has food shops, design stores, vintage-clothing retailers and artisans' workshops.

ⓘ Information

Bath Tourist Office (☎ 01225-614420; www. visitbath.co.uk; 2 Terrace Walk; ⊙ 9.30am-5.30pm Mon-Sat, 10am-4pm Sun, closed Sun Nov-Jan) Offers advice and information. Also runs an accommodation booking service and sells a wide range of local books and maps.

Royal United Hospital (☎ 01225-428331; www.ruh.nhs.uk; Combe Park; ⊙ 24hr) Offers 24 hour emergency and urgent care.

ⓘ Getting There & Away

BUS

Bath's **bus and coach station** (Dorchester St) is near the train station. From there regular local buses fan out into the city, there's also a taxi rank nearby, or order a cab through **Bath Taxis** (☎ 0845 003 5205; www.bath-taxis.co.uk).

National Express (www.nationalexpress.com) coaches include those running direct to:

London (£20, 2½ hours, hourly)
London Heathrow (£25, three hours, two-hourly)
Plymouth (£26, four hours, seven daily)
Bristol (£5, 45 minutes, two daily)

Services to many other destinations change at Bristol.

First Bus (www.firstgroup.com) is the biggest local bus company. Services to:

Bristol (38/39/X39; £6, 50 minutes, four per hour Monday to Saturday, half-hourly on Sunday)
Wells (172/173/174; £6, 1½ hours, two per hour Monday to Saturday, hourly Sunday)

TRAIN

Bath's train station, Bath Spa, is at the south end of Manvers St. Some services connect through Bristol, including many to the southwest and north of England. Direct services include:

Bristol (£8, 15 minutes, half-hourly)
Cardiff Central (£21, one hour, hourly)
London Paddington (from £35, 90 minutes, half-hourly)

Salisbury (£18, one hour, hourly)

There's a taxi rank at Bath Spa station, or call Bath Taxi (p240). Many city buses also leave from the train station.

ⓘ Getting Around

BICYCLE

Bath is hilly. The canal paths along the Kennet and Avon Canal and the 13-mile Bristol & Bath Railway Path (www.bristolbathrailwaypath.org. uk) are great to explore by bike.

Bath Bike Hire (☎ 01225-447276; www. bath-narrowboats.co.uk; Sydney Wharf; adult/ child per day £15/10; ⊙ 9am-5pm) A 10-minute walk from the centre. Handy for the canal and railway paths.

Take Charge Bikes (☎ 01225-789568; www. takechargebikes.co.uk; 1 Victoria Bldgs, Lower Bristol Rd; per day £30; ⊙ 9am-5pm Mon-Fri, to 4pm Sat) Rents electric bikes.

BUS

BathRider (adult/child £4.50/3.50) A multi-operator, all-day ticket covering a 3 mile radius of central Bath. It's valid until 3am the next day. A seven-day ticket costs adult/child £20/15.

Bus U1 Runs from the bus station, via High St and Great Pulteney St, up Bathwick Hill, past the YHA to the university every 20 minutes (£2.50).

Bus 265 Goes to Bathampton (£2.50, 10 minutes, one to two per hour).

CAR & MOTORCYCLE

Bath has serious traffic problems, especially at rush hour. **Park & Ride services** (☎ 01225-394041; return Mon-Fri £3.40, Sat & Sun £3; ⊙ 6.15am-8.30pm Mon-Sat, 9.30am-6pm Sun) operate from Lansdown to the north, Newbridge to the west and Odd Down to the south. It takes about 10 minutes to the centre; buses leave every 10 to 15 minutes.

There's a good, central car park underneath the SouthGate shopping centre (two/eight hours £3.50/11).

SOMERSET

With its pastoral landscape of hedgerows, fields and hummocked hills, sleepy Somerset is the very picture of the rural English countryside, and makes the perfect escape from the bustle of Bath and the hustle of Bristol. Things certainly move at a drowsier pace around these parts – it's a place to wander, ponder and drink in the sights at your own pace.

The cathedral city of Wells is an atmospheric base for exploring the limestone caves and gorges around Cheddar, while the hippie haven of Glastonbury is handy for venturing on to the wetlands of the Somerset Levels and the high hills of the Quantocks.

ℹ Information

➡ The Taunton **tourist office** (☑ 01823-340470; www.visitsomerset.co.uk/taunton; Market House, Fore St; ⊙ 9.30am-4.30pm Mon-Sat) is the best source of information about Somerset as a whole.

➡ Two websites – www.visitsomerset.co.uk and www.visitsouthsomerset.co.uk – are useful sources of information.

ℹ Getting There & Around

➡ The M5 heads south past Bristol to Bridgwater and Taunton, while the A39 leads west across the Quantocks to Exmoor.

➡ Key train services link Bath, Bristol, Bridgwater, Taunton and Weston-super-Mare.

➡ **First** (www.firstgroup.com) is a key local bus operator.

➡ For timetables and general information, contact **Traveline South West** (www.travelinesw.com).

Wells & Around

POP 11,340

In Wells, small is beautiful. This is England's smallest city, and only qualifies for the title thanks to a magnificent medieval cathedral, which sits beside the grand Bishop's Palace – the official residence of the Bishop of Bath and Wells since the 12th century.

Medieval buildings and cobbled streets radiate out from the cathedral green to a marketplace that has been the bustling heart of Wells for some nine centuries (Wednesday and Saturday are market days). Film buffs might also recognise it from the hit British comedy *Hot Fuzz* – the film's final shoot-out was filmed here.

◉ Sights

★ **Wells Cathedral**   CATHEDRAL
(Cathedral Church of St Andrew; ☑ 01749-674483; www.wellscathedral.org.uk; Cathedral Green; requested donation adult/child £6/5; ⊙ 7am-7pm Apr-Sep, to 6pm Oct-Mar) Wells' gargantuan Gothic cathedral sits plumb in the centre of the city, surrounded by one of the largest cathedral closes in England. It was built

in stages between 1180 and 1508, and consequently showcases several Gothic styles. Among its notable features are the **West Front**, decorated with more than 300 carved figures, and the famous **scissor arches** – an ingenious architectural solution to counter the subsidence of the central tower. Don't miss the **High Parts Tour** (adult/child £10/8; ⊙ Mon-Sat May-Oct) that heads up into the roof.

Bishop's Palace   HISTORIC BUILDING
(☑ 01749-988111; www.bishopspalace.org.uk; Market Place; adult/child £8/4; ⊙ 10am-6pm Apr-Oct, to 4pm Nov-Mar) Built for the bishop in the 13th century, this moat-ringed palace is purportedly the oldest inhabited building in England. Inside, the palace's state rooms and ruined great hall are worth a look, but it's the shady gardens that are the real draw. The natural springs after which Wells is named bubble up in the palace's grounds.

Wookey Hole   CAVE
(☑ 01749-672243; www.wookey.co.uk; Wookey Hole; adult/child £19/15; ⊙ 10am-5pm Apr-Oct, to 4pm Nov-Mar) The River Axe has gouged out this network of deep limestone caverns, which are famous for striking stalagmites and stalactites, one of which is the legendary Witch of Wookey Hole who, it's said, was turned to stone by a local priest. Admission to the caves is by guided tour; up on top you'll find 20 beyond-kitsch attractions ranging from animatronic dinosaurs to pirate adventure golf. Wookey Hole is 3 miles northwest of Wells; look out for brown tourist signs on the A371.

🛏 Sleeping

Stoberry House   B&B ££
(☑ 01749-672906;   www.stoberryhouse.co.uk; Stoberry Park; s £85, d £95-158; P Ⓗ) It's hard to know which is more beautiful: the lush, 2.5-hectare garden, or the house that overflows with rich fabrics, plush cushions and boutique flourishes. Expect pod coffee machines, luxury teas, books to browse and the use of a well-stocked pantry. It's all tucked away in a private estate.

Ancient Gate House Hotel   HOTEL ££
(☑ 01749-672029;   www.ancientgatehouse.co.uk; 20 Sadler St; s £95-100, d £115-130; Ⓗ) This old hostelry is partly built right into the cathedral's west gate. Rooms are decorated in regal reds and duck-egg blues. The best of these have four-poster beds and knockout

WORTH A TRIP

CHEDDAR GORGE

Carved out by glacial meltwater during the last ice age, **Cheddar Gorge** (☎01934-742343; www.cheddargorge.co.uk; adult/child £20/15; ⊗10am-5pm) is England's deepest natural canyon, in places towering 138m above the twisting B3135. The gorge is riddled with subterranean caverns with impressive displays of stalactites and stalagmites. The easiest to reach are **Gough's Cave** and **Cox's Cave**; deeper caves can be explored on caving trips with **Rocksport** (☎01934-742343; www.cheddargorge.co.uk/rocksport; adult/child £22/20).

Along with its caves, Cheddar is also famous as the home of the nation's favourite cheese, produced here since the 12th century. At the **Cheddar Gorge Cheese Company** (☎01934-742810; www.cheddargorgecheeseco.co.uk; The Cliffs, Cheddar; adult/child £2/free; ⊗10am-5pm Easter-Oct, winter hours vary), you can watch the cheesemaking process, sample the produce, then buy some whiffy souvenirs at the shop.

Cheddar Gorge is 20 miles northwest of Wells on the A371.

cathedral views through latticed windows; they're £15 extra, and worth it.

Beryl B&B ££
(☎01749-678738; www.beryl-wells.co.uk; Hawkers Lane; s £75-100, d £100-170, tr from £155; P 🤝 🛋) This grand gabled mansion offers a taste of English eccentricity. Every inch of the house is crammed with antique atmosphere, and the rooms boast grandfather clocks, chaise longues and four-posters galore. It's about a mile from Wells.

★ **Babington House** LUXURY HOTEL £££
(☎01373-812266; www.babingtonhouse.co.uk; Babington, near Frome; r £255-380; P 🤝 🛋) It's eye-poppingly pricey, but this lauded design hotel is one of Britain's most luxurious. It's a mash-up of *Homes & Gardens* and *Wallpaper:* heritage beds, antique dressers and period fireplaces meet minimalist furniture, sanded wood floors and retro lamps. There's a cool library, 45-seat private cinema and spa in the old cowshed. It's 14 miles east of Wells.

✖ Eating

Strangers with Coffee CAFE £
(☎07728 047233; 31 St Cuthbert St; cakes £3-5; ⊗7.30am-4pm Tue-Sat) 'Life is too short to drink bad coffee' says the sign – something they've taken to heart here as they work caffeinated magic with some of the best beans in town. There's a tempting selection of cakes to match.

Goodfellows Cafe & Seafood Restaurant CAFE ££
(☎01749-673866; www.goodfellowswells.co.uk; 5 Sadler St; mains £11-24; ⊗10am-3pm daily,

6-9.30pm Wed-Sat) There's a choice of eating options in Goodfellows' three vibrant rooms: the continental cafe menu offers cakes, pastries and light lunches (opt to pay either £11 or £20 for two courses and a drink). Or book for an evening fine-dining experience: £30 gets you three classy courses, while the five-course seafood tasting menu (£50) is an absolute treat.

Square Edge BISTRO ££
(☎01749-671166; www.square-edgecafe.co.uk; 2 Town Hall Bldgs; mains £7-12; ⊗9am-5pm Mon-Sat 10am-4pm Sun) There's an easygoing charm to Square Edge, a retro eatery where 1950s movie posters frame old jukeboxes and vintage radios. Treats range from full-blown cooked breakfasts and American pancakes to tangy salt beef toasties and slow-cooked ribs. The cakes are creative and great.

ⓘ Information

Tourist Office (☎01749-671770; www.wells somerset.com; Wells Museum, 8 Cathedral Green; ⊗10am-5pm Mon-Sat Easter-Oct, to 4pm Nov-Easter)

ⓘ Getting There & Away

The bus station is south of Cuthbert St, on Princes St. Useful services include:

Bath (bus 173; £5.80, 1¼ hours, at least hourly)

Bristol (bus 376; £5.80, 1¼ hours, half-hourly)

Cheddar (bus 126; £4.70, 25 minutes, hourly Monday to Saturday, four on Sunday); continues to Weston-super-Mare (£5.80, 1½ hours)

Glastonbury (bus 376; £3.70, 15 minutes, several hourly)

Glastonbury

POP 8900

Ley lines converge, white witches convene and every shop is filled with the aroma of smouldering joss sticks in good old Glastonbury, the southwest's undisputed capital of alternative culture. Now famous for its musical mudfest of a festival, held on Michael Eavis' farm in nearby Pilton, Glastonbury has a much more ancient past: the town's iconic tor was an important pagan site, and is rumoured by some to be the mythical Isle of Avalon, King Arthur's last resting place. It's also allegedly one of the world's great spiritual nodes, marking the meeting point of many mystical lines of power – if you feel the need to get your chakras realigned, this is definitely the place. Whatever the truth of the various legends swirling round Glastonbury, one thing's for certain – watching the sunrise from the top of the tor is an experience you won't forget in a hurry.

◎ Sights

★ Glastonbury Tor   LANDMARK

(NT; ⊘24hr) **FREE** Topped by the ruined, medieval Chapel of St Michael, the iconic hump of Glastonbury Tor is visible for miles around, and provides Somerset with one of its most unmistakable landmarks. It takes half an hour to walk up from the start of the trail on Well House Lane; the steepest sections are stepped. Between April and September a regular Tor Bus (adult/child £3/1.50) runs every half hour from St Dunstan's car park near Glastonbury Abbey to the trailhead on Well House Lane.

The tor is the focal point for a wealth of local lore. According to Celtic legend, the tor is the home of Arawn or Gwyn ap Nudd, king of the underworld and lord of the faeries. A more famous legend identifies the tor as the mythic Isle of Avalon, where King Arthur was taken after being mortally wounded in battle, and where Britain's 'once and future king' sleeps until his country calls again. Others believe that the tor marks an ancient mystical node where invisible lines of energy, known as ley lines, converge.

It's easy to see why the tor has inspired so many myths. It's a strange presence in an otherwise pan-flat landscape, and in ancient times (when the area around Glastonbury was covered by water for much of the year), the tor would indeed have appeared as an island, wreathed in mists and cut off by rivers, marshes and bogs.

Chalice Well & Gardens   GARDENS

(⊘01458-831154; www.chalicewell.org.uk; Chilkwell St; adult/child £4.30/2.15; ⊘10am-6pm Apr-Oct, to 4.30pm Nov-Mar) Shaded by yew trees and criss-crossed by quiet paths, the Chalice Well & Gardens have been sites of pilgrimage since the days of the Celts. The iron-red waters from the 800-year-old well are rumoured to have healing properties, good for everything from eczema to smelly feet; some legends also identify the well as the hiding place of the Holy Grail.

★ Glastonbury Abbey   RUINS

(⊘01458-832267; www.glastonburyabbey.com; Magdalene St; adult/child £7.50/4.50; ⊘9am-8pm Jun-Aug, to 6pm Mar-May, Sep & Oct, to 4pm Nov-Feb) The scattered ruins of Glastonbury Abbey give little hint that this was once one of England's great seats of ecclesiastical power. It was torn down following Henry VIII's dissolution of the monasteries in 1539, and the last abbot, Richard Whiting, was hung, drawn and quartered on the tor. Today's striking ruins include some of the nave walls, the remains of St Mary's chapel, and the crossing arches, which may have been scissor-shaped like those in Wells Cathedral.

BATH & SOUTHWEST ENGLAND GLASTONBURY

OFF THE BEATEN TRACK

SOMERSET LEVELS

Flat as a pancake, sub-sea-level and criss-crossed with canals (known locally as rhynes), the Somerset Levels are one of England's largest native wetlands. Covering almost 250 sq miles between the Quantock and Mendip Hills, they're brilliant for bird spotters – particularly in October and November, when huge flocks of starlings (properly known as murmurations) descend on the area. Nature reserves have been established at Ham Wall, Shapwick Heath, Sedgemoor and Westhay.

The flat landscape of the Levels also makes it ideal for cycling. Several trails pass through the village of Langport, including the long-distance River Parrett Trail.

Glastonbury

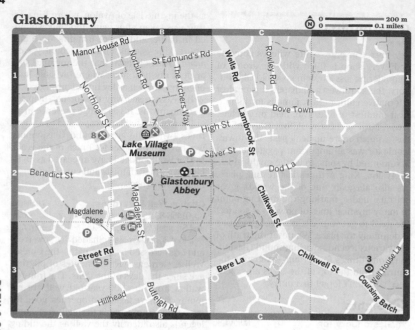

Glastonbury

The grounds also contain a museum, cider orchard and herb garden. According to legend, the abbey's famous holy thorn tree sprang from the staff of Joseph of Arimathea, Jesus' great-uncle, who supposedly visited the abbey following Christ's death. It blooms at Christmas and Easter.

The abbey even has an Arthurian connection. In the 12th century, monks supposedly uncovered a tomb in the abbey grounds inscribed *Hic iacet sepultus inclitus rex arturius in insula avalonia,* or 'Here lies buried the renowned King Arthur in the Isle of Avalon'. Inside the tomb were two entwined skeletons, purportedly those of Arthur and his wife Guinevere. The bones were reburied beneath the altar in 1278, but were lost following the abbey's destruction.

★ **Lake Village Museum**   MUSEUM
(The Tribunal, 9 High St; adult/child £3.50/2; ◷10am-3pm Mon-Sat) The Lake Village Museum displays finds from a prehistoric bog village discovered in nearby Godney. The houses were clustered in about six groups and built from reeds, hazel and willow. It's thought they were occupied by summer traders who lived the rest of the year around Glastonbury Tor.

✫ Festivals & Events

**Glastonbury Festival of
Contemporary Performing Arts**   MUSIC
(www.glastonburyfestivals.co.uk; tickets from £238; ◷Jun or Jul) A majestic (and frequently mud-soaked) extravaganza of music, theatre, dance, cabaret, carnival, spirituality and general all-round weirdness that's been held on farmland in Pilton, just outside Glastonbury, since 1970 (bar the occasional off-year to let the farm recover). Tickets usually go on sale in the autumn, and always sell out within a matter of minutes.

🛏 Sleeping

Street YHA
HOSTEL

(☑ 0345-3719143; www.yha.org.uk; Ivythorn Hill, Street; dm/tr/q £20/65/75; 🅿) A Swiss-chalet style building surrounded by green fields, with friendly staff and a good stock of books in the public rooms. It's set on the outskirts of the village of Street, a few miles south of Glastonbury.

★ Covenstead
B&B ££

(☑ 01458-830278; www.covenstead.co.uk; Magdalene St; s £70, d £80-110; 🅿 🛜) It's as if they've distilled the wacky essence of Glastonbury and poured it all over this weirdly wonderful B&B. The downstairs is a riot of oddities: mock skeletons, witches hats, upcycled antlers and draped python skins. Bedroom themes range from fairy via green man and Gothic to Halloween honeymoon. A tad crazy, yes, but also delightfully done.

Magdalene House
B&B ££

(☑ 01458-830202; www.magdalenehouseglastonbury.co.uk; Magdalene St; s £75-100, d £95-110, f £130-145; 🅿 🛜) Artfully decorated Magdalene used to be a school run by Glastonbury's nuns, and one room still overlooks the abbey grounds. Each of the tall, light rooms is an array of olive, oatmeal and other soft tones, while tasteful knick-knacks give it all a homely feel.

Glastonbury Townhouse
B&B ££

(☑ 01458-831040; www.glastonburytownhouse.co.uk; Street Rd; r £95-130; 🅿 🛜) Nothing too outlandish about this place – just a solid, red-brick, Edwardian town house, with a clutch of quiet rooms, lots of painted furniture and a contemporary vibe. Breakfast, served overlooking the garden, can be vegetarian, vegan, or dairy- or gluten-free.

✖ Eating

Rainbow's End
VEGETARIAN £

(☑ 01458-833896; www.rainbowsendcafe.com; 17b High St; mains £6-9; ⏱ 10am-4pm; ✎) This psychedelic cafe sums up the Glastonbury spirit, with its all-veggie food, potted plants and mix-and-match furniture. Tuck into homity pie or a hot quiche, followed by scrumptious homemade cake. The vegan and gluten-free menu is extensive and there's a small patio out back.

★ Bocabar
BRITISH ££

(☑ 01458-440558; http://glastonbury.bocabar.co.uk; Morland Rd; mains £8-17; ⏱ 9.30am-11pm Tue-Thu, to 1am Fri & Sat, 10am-5pm Sun & Mon) Formerly a sheepskin factory, now a hip hang-out, at cavernous red-brick Bocabar a pan-global menu takes in mezze platters, fish stews, gourmet burgers and adventurous puddings. Live bands play several times a week, the G&T menu boasts 22 types of gin and an industrial-chic vibe adds to the appeal.

It's about 1.5 miles southwest of the town centre along Morland Rd.

Who'd a Thought It Inn
PUB FOOD ££

(☑ 01458-834460; www.whodathoughtit.co.uk; 17 Northload St; mains £12-18; ⏱ noon-9.30pm) In this pleasantly peculiar locals' pub vintage advertising signs sit beside an old red telephone box and an upside-down bike dangles from the ceiling. The food is solid pub fare – sausages, pies and steaks – but there are usually specials chalked above the bar.

ⓘ Information

Tourist Office (☑ 01458-832954; www.glastonburytic.co.uk; Magdalene St; ⏱ 10am-4pm Mon-Sat, 11am-3pm Sun) In the town hall.

ⓘ Getting There & Away

There is no train station in Glastonbury.

Useful bus routes include:

Taunton (bus 29; £5.70, 1½ hours, four to seven daily Monday to Saturday)

Wells (bus 376; £3.70, 15 minutes, several times an hour)

WORTH A TRIP

LORD POULETT ARMS

At Hinton St George's deliciously olde-worlde village pub, the **Lord Poulett Arms** (☑ 01460-73149; www.lordpoulettarms.com; High St, Hinton St George; mains £15-26; ⏱ noon-2pm & 6-9pm; 🅿), the assured food pairs classic ingredients with imaginative additions – here prime meat and fish come with wild garilc pesto, chipotle mayonnaise and horseradish crème fraîche. The building oozes country atmosphere, with beams, roaring fires and stacks of ale barrels behind the bar. Hard to fault.

You can make a night of it by checking into one of their quirky rooms (singles £65, doubles £95). It's roughly 15 miles from Yeovil and Taunton.

WORTH A TRIP

MONTACUTE HOUSE

Built in the 1590s for Sir Edward Phelips, a speaker of the House of Commons, **Montacute** (NT; ☑01935-823289; www.nationaltrust.org.uk; Montacute; adult/child £12/6; ⏲house 11am-4pm Mar-Oct 11am-3pm Nov & Dec noon-3pm Sat & Sun Jan-Mar, gardens 10am-5pm Mar-Oct, 11am-4pm Wed-Sat Nov-Feb) contains some of the finest 16th- and 17th-century interiors in the country. It's plasterwork, chimney pieces and tapestries are renowned, but the highlight is the Long Gallery – the longest such hall in England, it's rich in Elizabethan portraits.

Montacute is 5 miles west of Yeovil off the A3088.

HAMPSHIRE

Hampshire's history is regal and rich. Kings Alfred the Great, Knut and William the Conqueror all based their reigns in its ancient cathedral city of Winchester, whose jumble of historic buildings sits in the centre of undulating chalk downs. The county's coast is awash with heritage, too – in rejuvenated Portsmouth you can clamber aboard the pride of Nelson's navy, HMS *Victory*, and wonder at the *Mary Rose* (Henry VIII's flagship), before wandering wharfs buzzing with restaurants, shops and bars. Hampshire's southwestern corner claims the open heath and woods of the New Forest National Park.

Winchester

POP 116,600

Calm, collegiate Winchester is a mellow must-see. The past still echoes strongly around the flint-flecked walls of this ancient cathedral city. It was the capital of Saxon kings and a power base of bishops, and its statues and sights evoke two of England's mightiest myth makers: Alfred the Great and King Arthur (he of the round table). Winchester's architecture is exquisite, from the handsome Elizabethan and Regency buildings in the narrow streets to the wondrous cathedral at its core, while its river valley location means there are charming waterside trails to explore.

⊙ Sights

★**Winchester Cathedral** CATHEDRAL
(☑01962-857200; www.winchester-cathedral.org.uk; The Close; adult/child £8/free; ⏲9.30am-5pm Mon-Sat, 12.30-3pm Sun) One of southern England's most awe-inspiring buildings, 11th-century Winchester Cathedral boasts a fine Gothic facade, one of the longest medieval naves in Europe (164m), and a fascinating jumble of features from all eras. Other highlights include the intricately carved medieval choir stalls, which sport everything from mythical beasts to a mischievous green man, Jane Austen's grave (near the entrance) and one of the UK's finest illuminated manuscripts. The excellent **Tower and Roof Tours** (tours £6.50; ⏲Wed 2.15pm, Sat 11.30am & 2.15pm Jan-May, Oct & Nov, Mon, Wed & Fri 2.15pm, Sat 11.30am & 2.15pm Jun-Sep) get busy – book well ahead.

As the biggest, brightest and best surviving 12th-century English Bible, the dazzling, four-volume **Winchester Bible** has vivid illuminated pages. It was commissioned in 1160, possibly by the grandson of William the Conqueror. At the time of writing, long-term conservation work meant only one volume of the Bible was on display, in a temporary exhibition in the North Transept (open from 10am to 4pm Monday to Saturday). Check online for the latest.

Today's cathedral sits beside foundations that mark Winchester's original 7th-century minster church. The cathedral was begun in 1070 and completed in 1093, and was subsequently entrusted with the bones of its patron saint, St Swithin (Bishop of Winchester from 852 to 862). He is best known for the proverb stating that if it rains on St Swithin's Day (15 July), it will rain for a further 40 days and 40 nights.

Soggy ground and poor construction spelled disaster for the early church. The original tower collapsed in 1107 and major restructuring continued until the mid-15th century. Look out for the monument at the far end of the building to diver William Walker; he saved the cathedral from collapse by delving repeatedly into its waterlogged underbelly from 1906 to 1912 to bolster rotting wooden foundations with vast quantities of concrete and brick. In the crypt, look out for *Sound II,* an enigmatic life-size depiction of a contemplative man by Anthony Gormley.

The highly informative, one-hour **Cathedral Body Tours** (10am to 3pm Monday to Saturday) and atmospheric **Crypt Tours** (10.30am, 12.30pm and 2.30pm Monday

Winchester

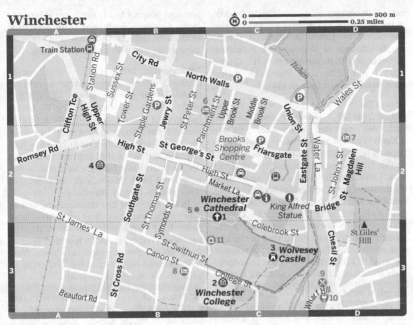

to Saturday) are included in the admission price for Winchester Cathedral.

Choral **evensong** (5.30pm Monday to Saturday, 3.30pm Sunday) is atmospheric; other Sunday services take place at 8am, 9.45am and 11am. Listen out, too, for the magnificent peal of bells at 8.45am and 2.30pm each Sunday.

The cathedral's **tree-fringed lawns** make for tranquil spots to take time out, especially on the quieter south side beyond the cloisters; the permanent secondhand book stall in the **Deanery Porch** (⊙10am-4pm) provides great bargain hunting.

★ **Winchester College**   HISTORIC BUILDING
(☐01962-621209; www.winchestercollege.org; College St; adult/child £8/free; ⊙10.15am & 11.30am Mon-Sat, plus 2.15pm Mon, Wed & Fri-Sun) Winchester College delivers a rare chance to nosey around a prestigious English school. It was set up by William Wykeham, Bishop of Winchester, in 1393, 14 years after he founded Oxford's New College. Hour-long guided tours take in the 14th-century Gothic chapel, complete with wooden vaulted roof, the dining room (called College Hall), and a vast 17th-century open classroom (called School) where exams are still held. A revealing insight into how the other half learns.

Winchester

◉ Top Sights

◉ Sights

✦ Activities, Courses & Tours

⊨ Sleeping

⊗ Eating

⊖ Drinking & Nightlife

⊜ Shopping

★ **Wolvesey Castle**   CASTLE
(EH; ☐0370 333 1181; www.english-heritage. org.uk; College St; ⊙10am-5pm Apr-Oct) **FREE** The fantastical, crumbling remains of

early-12th-century Wolvesey Castle huddle in the protective embrace of the city's walls. Completed by Henry de Blois, it served as the Bishop of Winchester's residence throughout the medieval era, with Queen Mary I and Philip II of Spain celebrating their wedding feast here in 1554.

Round Table & Great Hall   HISTORIC BUILDING
(✆01962-846476; www.hants.gov.uk/greathall; Castle Ave; suggested donation £3; ⏰10am-4.30pm) Winchester's cavernous Great Hall is the only part of 11th-century Winchester Castle that Oliver Cromwell spared from destruction. Crowning the wall like a giant-sized dartboard of green and cream spokes is what centuries of mythology have dubbed King Arthur's Round Table. It's actually a 700-year-old copy, but is fascinating nonetheless. It's thought to have been constructed in the late 13th century and then painted in the reign of Henry VIII (King Arthur's image is unsurprisingly reminiscent of Henry's youthful face).

Hospital of St Cross   HISTORIC BUILDING
(✆01962-878218; www.stcrosshospital.co.uk; St Cross Rd; adult/child £4.50/2.50; ⏰9.30am-5pm Mon-Sat, 1-5pm Sun Apr-Oct, 10.30am-3.30pm Mon-Sat Nov-Mar) Welcome to the oldest charitable institution in the country, founded in 1132 by the grandson of William the Conqueror, Henry de Blois. As well as healing the sick and housing the needy, the hospital was built to care for pilgrims and crusaders en route to the Holy Land. Today, it's roamed by elderly black- and red-gowned brothers, who hand out the Wayfarer's Dole – a crust of bread and horn of ale (now a swig of beer) from the Porter's Gate.

🛏 Sleeping & Eating

St John's Croft   B&B ££
(✆01962-859976; www.st-johns-croft.co.uk; St John's St; s/d/f £55/90/140; 🅿🛜) You may well fall in love with this oh-so-casually stylish, rambling Queen Anne town house, where rattan carpets are teamed with bulging bookcases, and Indian art with shabby-chic antiques. The rooms are vast, the garden is tranquil and breakfast is served beside the Aga in the country-house kitchen.

★**Hannah's**   B&B £££
(✆01962-840623; www.hannahsbedandbreakfast. co.uk; 16a Parchment St; r £155-225; 🛜) The word 'boutique' gets bandied around quite freely but here it really fits. The sumptuous conversion of this old dance hall sees an antique piano and honesty bar frame a wood-burning stove. Gorgeous bedrooms feature exposed brick, lofty ceilings, vast beds, and baths on the mezzanines with views of the stars.

★**Wykeham Arms**   INN £££
(✆01962-853834; www.wykehamarmswinchester. co.uk; 75 Kingsgate St; s/d/ste £85/150/200; 🅿🛜) At 250-odd years old, the Wykeham bursts with history – it used to be a brothel and also put Nelson up for a night (some say the events coincided). Creaking stairs lead to plush bedrooms that manage to be both deeply established but also on-trend; sleigh beds meet jazzy throws, oak dressers sport stylish lights. Simply smashing.

In the eccentric **bar** tankards and school canes hang from the ceiling and worn school desks lend pint-supping an illicit air. The **menu** (served noon to 2.30pm and 6pm to 9pm) covers the bar food standards, from well-executed burgers and fish and chips, to 24oz rib-eye steaks on the bone.

★**Black Rat**   MODERN BRITISH £££
(✆01962-844465; www.theblackrat.co.uk; 88 Chesil St; 3 courses £38-46; ⏰noon-2.15pm & 7-9.15pm) The aromas are irresistible, the food frankly fabulous, the cooking highly technical and the ingredients dare to surprise – expect duck pastrami to be joined by pomegranate, turbot by squid ink, and pigeon breast by pine nuts and scents of Douglas fir. That's why the Black Rat deserves its Michelin star.

🍷 Drinking & Nightlife

Black Boy   PUB
(✆01962-861754; www.theblackboypub.com; 1 Wharf Hill; ⏰noon-11pm Mon-Thu, to midnight Fri & Sat, to 10.30pm Sun) Two open fires, a random array of dented antiques, a clutch of draught ciders and five real ales make this a legendary local. Any time after noon, check to see if it still has any Black Boy Bangers (£2.50) – a sausage in a crispy roll – the fried onions and mustard are optional.

ℹ Information

Tourist Office (✆01962-840500; www.visit winchester.co.uk; Guildhall, High St; ⏰10am-5pm Mon-Sat, plus 11am-4pm Sun May-Sep) Set in Winchester's Victorian Guildhall.

ℹ Getting There & Away

➜ Winchester is 65 miles west of London.
➜ Direct National Express (www.nationalex-press.com) buses depart from the bus station

PORTSMOUTH HISTORIC DOCKYARD

The world-class collection of maritime heritage at **Portsmouth Historic Dockyard** (☑023-9283 9766; www.historicdockyard.co.uk; Victory Gate; All Attractions ticket adult/child/family £35/15/60; ⊘10am-5.30pm Apr-Oct, to 5pm Nov-Mar) demands a day trip.

The blockbuster draw is Henry VIII's favourite flagship, the **Mary Rose** (☑023-9281 2931; www.maryrose.org; adult/child/family £16/8/25; ⊘10am-5.30pm Apr-Oct, to 5pm Nov-Mar), which sank suddenly off Portsmouth while fighting the French in 1545. She was raised from the bottom in 1982, an extraordinary feat of marine archaeology, and a £35-million, boat-shaped museum has been built around her, giving uninterrupted views of the preserved timbers of her massive hull.

Equally impressive is **HMS Victory** (☑023-9283 9766; www.hms-victory.com; adult/child/family £18/13/37; ⊘10am-5.30pm Apr-Oct, to 5pm Nov-Mar), Lord Nelson's flagship at the Battle of Trafalgar (1805) and the site of his famous dying words 'Kiss me, Hardy', after victory over the French had been secured. This remarkable ship is topped by a forest of ropes and masts, and weighted by a swollen belly filled with cannons and paraphernalia for an 850-strong crew.

Other nautical sights include the Victorian **HMS Warrior** (☑023-9283 9766; www.hmswarrior.org; adult/child/family £18/13/37; ⊘10am-5.30pm Apr-Oct, to 5pm Nov-Mar), the WWII-era submarine **HMS Alliance** (☑023-9283 9766; www.submarine-museum.co.uk; Haslar Rd, Gosport; adult/child £13.50/9; ⊘10am-5pm Apr-Oct, 10am-4pm Wed-Sun Nov-Mar) and a wealth of imaginative museums and harbour tours. Visiting more than one exhibit makes the All Attractions ticket, not single issue tickets, the best value (although it now excludes entry to the Mary Rose Museum). There's a 20% discount for buying online.

Portsmouth is 100 miles southwest of London. Direct trains run hourly from London Victoria (£20, two hours) and half-hourly from London Waterloo (£37, 2¼ hours). For the Historic Dockyard, get off at the final stop, Portsmouth Harbour.

Other departures:

Brighton (£16, two hours, hourly)

Chichester (£8, 30 minutes, half-hourly)

Southampton (£10, one hour, half-hourly)

Winchester (£12, one hour, hourly)

for London Victoria every two hours (£16, two hours).

➡ Trains leave half-hourly to hourly for London Waterloo (£25, 1¼ hours) and hourly for Portsmouth (£12, one hour).There are also fast links to the Midlands.

ⓘ Getting Around

Bicycle Bikes can be hired from **Bespoke Biking** (☑07920 776994; www.bespokebiking.com; Brooks Shopping Centre; per half/full day from £15/25; ⊘9.30am-5pm Tue-Sat).

Park & Ride car parks (per day £3) are signed off junctions 10 and 11 of the M3. Services run roughly from 6.30am to 6.30pm, Monday to Saturday.

There are taxi ranks on the High St, and outside the train station and tourist office, or call **Wintax** (☑01962-878727; www.wintaxcars.com).

New Forest

With typical, accidental, English irony the New Forest is anything but new – it was first proclaimed a royal hunting preserve in 1079. It's also not much of a forest, being mostly heathland ('forest' is from the Old French for 'hunting ground'). Designated a national park in 2005, the forest's combined charms make it a joy to explore. Wild ponies mooch around pretty scrubland, deer flicker in the distance and rare birds flit among the foliage. Genteel villages dot the landscape, connected by a web of walking and cycling trails.

🏃 Activities

⭐**New Forest Activities**   ADVENTURE SPORTS (☑01590-612377; www.newforestactivities.co.uk; High St, Beaulieu) Runs a wide range of sessions including canoeing (adult/child per 90 minutes from £25/19), kayaking (per 90 minutes from £20/25) and archery (adult/child per 90 minutes £22/17).

Walking

The forest is gentle, largely level hiking territory. Ordnance Survey (OS) produces a detailed, 1:25,000 Explorer map (New Forest; No OL22, £9); Crimson's *New Forest Short Walks* (£8) features 20 circular day hikes of 2 to 6 miles.

The New Forest Centre in Lyndhurst stocks maps and guides.

Ranger Walks   WALKING
(🖉0300 068 0400; www.forestry.gov.uk/newforestevents; from £6) Forestry Commission–run day walks including those themed around photography, ponies and the unique way the New Forest is managed.

Cycling

➜ The New Forest makes for superb cycling country, with 100 miles of routes linking the main villages and the key railway station at Brockenhurst.

➜ *The New Forest By Bike* map (£4.50) features 12 routes ranging from 8 to 32 miles. The *New Forest Cycling Guide* (£4) features six day-cycle routes of between 4 and 22 miles on a 1:25,000 OS map.

➜ Maps and guides can be bought from an information point in Lyndhurst's New Forest Centre.

➜ To rent bikes, you'll need to pay a deposit (usually £20 to £25) and provide identification.

AA Bike Hire   CYCLING
(🖉02380-283349; www.aabikehirenewforest.co.uk; Fern Glen, Gosport Lane, Lyndhurst; adult/child per day £10/5; ⊙9am-5pm Apr-Oct) Based in Lyndhurst's main car park.

The Woods Cyclery   CYCLING
(New Forest Cycle Hire; 🖉02380-282028; www.thewoodscyclery.co.uk; 56 High St, Lyndhurst; adult/child per day £18/10; ⊙9am-5pm) Also rents out electric bikes and kids' bike seats.

Cyclexperience   CYCLING
(New Forest Cyclehire; 🖉01590-624808; www.newforestcyclehire.co.uk; Train Station, Brockenhurst; adult/child per day £18/9; ⊙9am-5.30pm) Based in a vintage railway carriage – they also deliver bikes across the national park.

Forest Leisure Cycling   CYCLING
(🖉01425-403584; www.forestleisurecycling.co.uk; The Cross, Burley; adult/child per day £18/10; ⊙9am-5pm) Has easy links onto nine cycle routes.

Horse Riding

Arniss Equestrian Centre   HORSE RIDING
(🖉01425-654114; www.arnissequestrian.co.uk; Godshill, Fordingbridge; per hr £30) Caters for all skill levels.

Burley Villa   HORSE RIDING
(Western Riding; 🖉01425-610278; www.burleyvilla.co.uk; Bashley Common Rd, near New Milton; per hour £45) Runs rides using traditional English and also Western saddle styles (per 90 minutes £54).

ℹ Information

Tourist Information (🖉01425-880020; www.thenewforest.co.uk; Main Car Park, Lyndhurst; ⊙10am-5pm Apr-Oct, to 4pm Nov-Mar) This Visitor Information Point is set inside the New Forest Centre, and features leaflets, maps and books.

🛌 Sleeping

The New Forest is a haven for campers. The Forestry Commission (www.campingintheforest.co.uk) runs 10 relatively rural sites.

The official visitor website, www.thenewforest.co.uk, has a database of accommodation options ranging from campsites and holiday parks, via B&Bs and farm stays to hotels.

ℹ Getting There & Around

BUS
➜ National Express (www.nationalexpress.com) buses stop at Ringwood and Southampton.

➜ Bus 6 (hourly Monday to Saturday, five on Sunday) runs from Southampton to Lyndhurst (£4.70, 40 minutes), Brockenhurst (£6.30, 50 minutes) and Lymington (£6.30, 1¼ hours).

➜ Bus X1/X2 runs from Bournemouth to Lymington (£6, 1½ hours, half-hourly Monday to Saturday, four on Sunday)

➜ The **New Forest Tour** (🖉01202-338420; www.thenewforesttour.info; per 1/2/5 days adult £17/22/33, child £9/12/17; ⊙9am-6pm early-Jul to early-Sep) has three connecting routes of hop-on/hop-off buses, stopping at Lyndhurst's main car park, Brockenhurst train station, Lymington, Ringwood, Beaulieu and Exbury.

TRAIN
➜ Two trains an hour run to Brockenhurst from London Waterloo (£25, two hours) via Winches-

ter (£15, 30 minutes) and on to Bournemouth (£8, 20 minutes).

➡ Local trains also shuttle twice an hour between Brockenhurst and Lymington (£4, 11 minutes).

Lyndhurst, Brockenhurst & Around

The quaint country villages of Lyndhurst and Brockenhurst are separated by just 4 miles. Their picturesque accommodation options and superb eateries ensure they're atmospheric bases from which to explore the New Forest.

⊙ Sights

New Forest Centre MUSEUM
(☏ 02380-283444; www.newforestcentre.org.uk; Main Car Park, Lyndhurst; ⊙ 10am-5pm Apr-Oct, to 4pm Nov-Mar) FREE Features a local labourer's cottage (complete with socks drying beside the fire), potato dibbles and a cider press. The minifilm makes for an accessible introduction to the park – listen, too, for recordings of the autumn pony sales, which take place after the annual drifts (round-ups).

Beaulieu HISTORIC BUILDING
(☏ 01590-612345; www.beaulieu.co.uk; adult/child £25/13; ⊙ 10am-6pm Apr-Sep, to 5pm Oct-Mar) Petrolheads, historians and ghost-hunters gravitate to Beaulieu (*bew*-lee) - a vintage car museum, stately home and tourist complex centred on a 13th-century Cistercian monastery. Motor-maniacs will be in raptures at Lord Montague's **National Motor Museum**. Tickets are valid for a year; it's up to £5 cheaper to buy in advance, online. Beaulieu is served by the New Forest Tour.

⛏ Sleeping

★ The Pig BOUTIQUE HOTEL £££
(☏ 0345 225 9494; www.thepighotel.co.uk; Beaulieu Rd, Brockenhurst; r £185-300; [P][☎]) One of the New Forest's classiest hotels remains an utter delight: log baskets, croquet mallets and ranks of guest gumboots give things a country-house air; espresso machines and minilarders lend bedrooms a luxury touch. In fact, all this effortless elegance makes it feel like you've just dropped by a friend's (very stylish) rural retreat.

Daisybank Cottage B&B £££
(☏ 01590-622086; www.bedandbreakfast-newforest.co.uk; Sway Rd, Brockenhurst; s £120-130, d £135-145; [P][☎]) The seven gorgeous themed bedrooms here are mini pamper palaces.

Expect aromatic smellies in gleaming bathrooms, stylish luxurious furnishings and lots of little extras: breakfasts laden with New Forest goodies, handmade chocolates, smartphone docks, DAB radios and range-baked cakes on arrival.

ⓘ Getting There & Away

➡ Bus 6 shuttles between Lyndhurst and Lymington (£4, hourly Monday to Saturday, five on Sunday), via Brockenhurst; so does the New Forest Tour (p250).

➡ Trains run twice an hour between Brockenhurst and Lymington (£3.40, 10 minutes).

Buckler's Hard

For such a tiny place, this picturesque huddle of 18th-century cottages, near the mouth of the River Beaulieu, has a big history. It started in 1722, when a duke of Montague built a port to finance a Caribbean expedition. His dream faltered, but when war with France came, this embryonic village and sheltered gravel waterfront became a secret boatyard where several of Nelson's triumphant Battle of Trafalgar warships were built. In the 20th century it played its part in the preparations for the D-Day landings.

⛏ Sleeping & Eating

★ Master Builder's House HOTEL £££
(☏ 01590-616253; www.hillbrookehotels.co.uk; d £130-175; [P]) In this beautifully restored 18th-century hotel, room styles range from crisp with hints of nauticalia to more stately, with soft lighting, burnished trunks and plush fabrics.

Your dining options range from classy restaurant to family-friendly grub in the cool hotel **bar** (mains £12-24; ⊙ noon-9pm).

Lymington

POP 15,400

Yachting haven, New Forest base and jumping-off point to the Isle of Wight – the appealing Georgian harbour town of Lymington has several strings to its tourism bow. This former smuggler's port offers nautical shops, prime eating and sleeping spots and, in Quay St, an utterly quaint cobbled lane.

⛶ Activities

Puffin Cruises BOATING
(☏ 07850-947618; www.puffincruiseslymington.com; Lymington Quay; from adult/child £8/4;

⏱10am-4pm Apr-Oct) Runs hour-long cruises on the *Puffin Billi* that meander down the winding Lymington River to saltmarshes packed with birds. Smaller swashbucklers love the pirate-themed *Black Puffin* trips that set off to search for lost treasure.

🛏 Sleeping

Auplands
B&B ££

(📞01590-675944; www.auplands.com; 22 Southampton Rd; s £55-65, d £75-85, f from £90; 🅿🛜)
Your genial hosts have been running this B&B for more than 30 years, and it shows in their supremely efficient systems and easy charm. Snug rooms feature pine, bottled water and big plants, while the eateries of Lymington are only a 10-minute stroll away.

★ Mill at Gordleton
BOUTIQUE HOTEL £££

(📞01590-682219; www.themillatgordleton.co.uk; Silver St, Hordle; d £129-149, ste £194-295; 🅿🛜)
Step inside here and know, instantly, you're going to be looked after beautifully. Velvet and gingham dot exquisite rooms (each one comes with a sweet soft toy duck), while the garden is a magical mix of rushing water, fairy lights and modern sculpture. The Mill is 4 miles west of Lymington.

🍴 Eating

Deep Blue
FISH & CHIPS £

(www.deepbluerestaurants.com; 130 High St; mains £9; ⏱noon-2.30pm & 4.30-8.30pm Mon-Fri, noon-9pm Sat, noon-7.30pm Sun) They're often queuing out the door at this classic British chippy, which boasts sustainable fish, freshly cut chips, mushy peas and pickled eggs. Eat in or take away.

Ship
PUB FOOD ££

(📞01590-676903; www.theshiplymington.co.uk; The Quay; mains £11-24; ⏱kitchen noon-10pm Mon-Sat, to 9pm Sun; 🍴) A pub for all seasons: knock back summertime drinks on the waterside terrace; in winter, a toasty log burner gets you warm. Well-judged food ranges from Mediterranean mezze and gooey baked camembert via pizza and koftas to pan-fried venison with port jus.

★ Elderflower
MODERN BRITISH £££

(📞01590-676908; www.elderflowerrestaurant.co.uk; 5 Quay St; mains £24-30, 5/7 courses £55/65; ⏱noon-2.30pm & 6.30-9.30pm Tue-Sat) An Anglo-French feel infuses Elderflower – from the wild nettle and doc leaf velouté to the black treacle cured ham. Innovative puddings are a real treat – where else can you get cigar-smoked chocolate with your chocolate and whisky mousse?

ℹ Getting There & Away

Lymington has two train stations: Lymington Town and Lymington Pier. Isle of Wight ferries connect with Lymington Pier. Trains run to Southampton (£12, 40 minutes), with a change at Brockenhurst, twice an hour.

Wightlink Ferries (📞0333 999 7333; www.wightlink.co.uk) has car and passenger ferries that run hourly to Yarmouth on the Isle of Wight (40 minutes). An adult/child foot-passenger single costs £11/5. Summer-time fares for a car and two passengers start at around £60 for a short-break return.

ISLE OF WIGHT

On the Isle of Wight these days there's something groovy in the air. For decades this slab of rock anchored off Portsmouth was a magnet for family holidays, and it still has seaside kitsch by the bucket and spade. But now the proms and amusement arcades are framed by pockets of pure funkiness. A long-running music festival draws party-goers, just-caught seafood is served in kooky fishers' cafes, and cool camping rules – here sites are dotted with yurts and vintage campervans. Yet still the isle's principal appeal remains: a mild climate, myriad outdoorsy activities and a 25-mile shore lined with beaches, dramatic white cliffs and tranquil sand dunes.

🏃 Activities

Cycling

With 200 miles of cycle routes, the Isle of Wight makes pedal pushers smile. The island's official visitor website (www.visitisleofwight.co.uk) lists suggested trips (complete with maps), ranging from family-friendly tootles along former railway lines, to the 60 mile **Round the Island Cycle Route**. The IW Cycle Fest is held in late-August.

Bike rentals start at around £16/60 per day/week. Many firms deliver and collect on orders over £30.

Walking

This is one of the best spots in southern England for rambling, with 500 miles of well-marked walking paths, including 67 miles of coastal routes. The island's two-week walking festival each May is billed as the UK's largest.

Isle of Wight

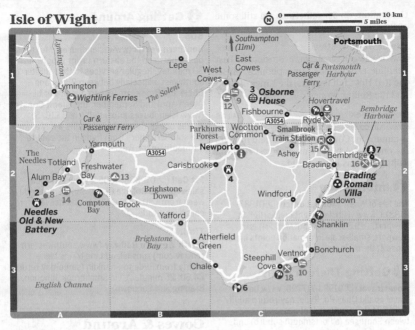

Isle of Wight

Watersports

Watersports are serious business on the Isle of Wight. Cowes is the sailing centre; surfers windsurfers and kitesurfers flock to the southwest, especially around Compton Bay; while powerboats run trips out to the Needles rocks.

Isle of Wight
Adventure Activities ADVENTURE SPORTS
(☏0800 180 4025; www.adventureactivitiesisle ofwight.co.uk; Freshwater) Runs activities ranging from surfing, stand-up paddleboarding and kayaking (per two hours adult/child £40/25) to bushcraft (per person £25) and one-hour climbing and archery taster sessions (adult/child £14/12).

✨ Festivals

The isle's festival tradition kicked off in 1968, when an estimated 200,000 hippies came to see The Doors, The Who, Joni Mitchell and rock icon Jimi Hendrix' last performance.

Generations on, its gatherings are still some of England's top musical events.

Isle of Wight Festival

MUSIC

(www.isleofwightfestival.com; ⊙ mid-Jun) Past headline acts include Stereophonics, Muse, the Red Hot Chili Peppers, the Kings of Leon and the Rolling Stones.

Cowes Week

SAILING

(www.aamcowesweek.co.uk; ⊙ early Aug) Cowes is famous for Cowes Week; first held in 1826, it's one of the biggest and longest-running sailing regattas in the world.

❶ Information

The Isle of Wight's **tourist office** (☑ 01983-813813; www.visitisleofwight.co.uk; High St, Newport; ⊙ 9.30am-3.30pm Mon-Fri) is in Newport; small-scale information points include those at the main ferry ports.

❶ Getting There & Away

Hovertravel (☑ 01983-717700; www.hovertravel.co.uk; Quay Rd, Ryde; day-return adult/child £24/12) Shuttles foot passengers between Southsea (a Portsmouth suburb) and Ryde, half-hourly to hourly.

Red Funnel (☑ 02380-248500; www.redfunnel.co.uk) Runs car-and-passenger ferries between Southampton and East Cowes (same-day return adult/child £17.80/8.90, from £45 with car, 60 minutes, hourly) and high-speed passenger ferries between Southampton and West Cowes (same-day return adult/child £25.60/12.80, 25 minutes, one to two per hour).

Wightlink Ferries (☑ 0333 999 7333; www.wightlink.co.uk) Operates passenger ferries every half-hour from Portsmouth to Ryde (day-return adult/child £20/10, 22 minutes). It also runs hourly car-and-passenger ferries from Portsmouth to Fishbourne (45 minutes) and from Lymington to Yarmouth (40 minutes). For both, an adult/child foot passenger day-return costs £16/8. Car fares start at around £60 for a short-break return.

---

❶ CAR FERRY COSTS

The cost of car ferries to the Isle of Wight can vary enormously. Save by booking ahead, asking about special offers and travelling off-peak (midweek and later in the day). Long stays tend to be cheaper and some deals include admission to island attractions. Booking online can mean paying £20 less.

---

❶ Getting Around

BUS

Southern Vectis (www.islandbuses.info) runs buses between the eastern towns roughly every 30 minutes. Regular services to the remoter southwest, especially between Blackgang Chine and Brook, are less frequent, but between April and September, the **Island Coaster** (www.islandbuses.info; adult/child £10/5) makes one to three return circuits a day along the southern shore from Ryde in the east to Yarmouth, in the west.

CAR

1st Call (☑ 01983-400055; www.1stcallcarsales.com; 15 College Close, Sandown; per day/week from £30/150) Collects and delivers hire cars island-wide.

TRAIN

South Western Railway (www.southwesternrailway.com) runs Island Line trains twice hourly from Ryde to Shanklin (same-day return £4.60, 25 minutes), via Smallbrook Junction, Brading and Sandown.

Cowes & Around

Pack your yachting cap – the hilly Georgian harbour town of Cowes is famous for Cowes Week in early August; first held in 1826, it's one of the biggest and longest-running sailing regattas in the world. Fibreglass playthings and vintage sailing boats line Cowes' waterfronts, which are lopped into East and West Cowes by the picturesque River Medina.

The island's capital, Newport, is 5 miles south.

◉ Sights

★ **Osborne House**

HISTORIC BUILDING

(EH; ☑ 01983-200022; www.english-heritage.org.uk; York Ave, East Cowes; adult/child £17.20/10/30; ⊙ 10am-6pm Apr-Sep, to 5pm Oct, 10am-4pm Sat & Sun Nov-Mar; ℗) Lemon-frosted and Italianate, Osborne House is pure Victorian pomp. Built in the 1840s at the behest of Queen Victoria, the monarch grieved here for many years after her husband's death. Extravagant rooms include the opulent Royal Apartments and Durbar Room; other highlights are horse and carriage rides, the Swiss Cottage – where the royal ankle-biters would play – and the stroll down Rhododendron Walk to Her Majesty's private beach.

Carisbrooke Castle

CASTLE

(EH; ☑ 01983-522107; www.english-heritage.org.uk; Castle Hill, Newport; adult/child £10/6;

⊘10am-6pm Apr-Sep, to 5pm Oct, 10am-4pm Sat & Sun Nov-Mar; P) Charles I was imprisoned here before his execution in 1649. Today you can clamber the sturdy ramparts and play bowls on the very green the doomed monarch used.

🛏 Sleeping

⭐ onefiftycowes   B&B **££**

(📞 07795 296399; www.onefiftycowes.co.uk; 150 Park Rd, West Cowes; s/d £75/105; P 🛜) All the trappings of a luxury hotel, all the individuality of a B&B – at onefiftycowes, wicker chairs sit beside stand-alone sinks; feature fireplaces are stacked with sea-smoothed pebbles. The best room is Solent, where a pair of binoculars is waiting to help you gaze at the partial sea views.

Fountain   HOTEL **££**

(📞 0845 608 6040; www.oldenglishinns.co.uk; High St, West Cowes; s £70-97, d £90-117; 🛜) Georgian-repro style rules at this appealing harbourside inn, where mock-flock wallpaper and old, wooden furniture define comfy rooms; number 21 has slanting ceilings and prime views of the ferry quay. The snug bar and sunny terrace are good places to sample pints and pub-grub classics (mains from £10; food served 11am to 10pm).

Ryde & Around

The nippiest foot-passenger ferries between Wight and Portsmouth alight in Ryde, a workaday but appealing Victorian town rich in the trappings of the British seaside. Next come the cutesy village of Brading, with its fine Roman villa, and photogenic Bembridge Harbour, which is fringed by sandy beaches.

Further south lie the twin resort towns of Sandown and Shanklin, boasting promenades and hordes of families wielding buckets and spades.

◉ Sights

⭐ Brading Roman Villa   RUINS

(📞 01983-406223; www.bradingromanvilla.org.uk; Morton Old Rd, Brading; adult/child £9.50/4.75; ⊘10am-5pm) The exquisitely preserved mosaics here (including a famous cockerel-headed man) make this one of the finest Romano-British sites in the UK. Wooden walkways lead over rubble walls and brightly painted tiles, allowing you to gaze right down onto the ruins below.

St Helens Duver   NATURE RESERVE

(NT; 📞 01983-741020; www.nationaltrust.org.uk; near St Helens; ⊘24hr; P) At this idyllic sand-and-shingle spit bordering the mouth of the River Yar, trails snake past swathes of sea pink, marram grass and rare clovers. It's signed from the village of St Helens, near Bembridge Harbour.

Isle of Wight
Steam Railway   HERITAGE RAILWAY

(📞 01983-882204; www.iwsteamrailway.co.uk; Smallbrook Junction; return adult/child from £13/6.50; ⊘mid-Apr–Sep) Regularly chugs the one-hour journey from Smallbrook Junction to Wootton Common.

🛏 Sleeping

⭐ Vintage Vacations   CAMPSITE **££**

(📞 07802 758113; www.vintagevacations.co.uk; Hazelgrove Farm, Ashey Rd; 2-/4-person caravans per week £620/725; ⊘Apr-Oct; P) The bevy of 1960s Airstream trailers on this farm is vintage chic personified. The gleaming aluminium shells shelter lovingly selected furnishings ranging from cheerful patchwork blankets to vivid tea cosies. Alternatively, opt for a beach-shack retreat, a 1930s scout hut, or the Mission: a late-Victorian tin chapel.

Harbourside   B&B **££**

(📞 01983-339084; www.harbourside-iow.co.uk; Embankment Rd, Bembridge Harbour; d £85-120 ste £120-170; P) How's this for a unique sleep – a boat B&B set right on the waterfront at tranquil Bembridge Harbour. The furnishings are stylish, the fixtures are often salvaged from old ships and the decked seating areas are framed by flowers. At high tides the swans drift right up to the sides.

🍴 Eating

Black Sheep   CAFE **£**

(📞 01983-811006; www.theblacksheepbar.co.uk; 53 Union St, Ryde; snacks £3-6, mains £8-12; ⊘noon-3pm Mon-Fri, 6-9pm Wed-Fri, 10am-5pm Sat, 10am-3pm Sun) Chilled tunes on the music system, piles of newspapers and a palm-dotted terrace draw the locals to this laid-back Ryde venue – as do the regular live music sessions and a menu that spans homemade burgers, smoked salmon and avocado sandwiches, and steaming bowls of mussels.

Best Dressed Crab   SEAFOOD **££**

(📞 01983-874758; www.thebestdressedcrabintown.co.uk; Fisherman's Wharf, Bembridge Harbour;

mains £8-24; ⊙10am-4pm daily Mar-Dec, Sat & Sun Jan & Feb) Welcome to an idyllic spot to munch your lunch. At this bijou cafe tacked on to a pontoon, the day's crab and lobster harvest is turned into supremely tasty sandwiches, salads and soups. Best eaten at one of the tables perched beside the water as local fishing boats unload their catch. It's deservedly popular – book.

Ventnor & Around

The Victorian town of Ventnor slaloms so steeply down the island's southern coast that it feels more like the south of France. The shops in the town's winding streets are worth browsing, the seafront is worth a stroll, and nearby atmospheric Steephill Cove is well worth a detour.

◉ Sights & Activities

St Catherine's Lighthouse   LIGHTHOUSE
(☑01983-730435; www.trinityhouse.co.uk; near Niton; adult/child £5/3; ⊙1-4.30pm Jun-Sep, hours vary Apr & May; 🅿) A crenellated 19th-century navigational aid that marks the island's southernmost point. Tours climb the 90-odd steps up to the lantern room, revealing sweeping sea views.

St Catherine's Oratory   LIGHTHOUSE
(near Niton) FREE Known locally as the Pepperpot, this 34ft, octagonal, 14th-century tower constitutes England's only surviving medieval lighthouse.

🛏 Sleeping & Eating

Harbour View   GUESTHOUSE ££
(St Augustine Villa; ☑01983-852285; www.harbour viewhotel.co.uk; The Esplanade, Ventnor; s £74-90, d £83-99; 🅿🛜) Country-house collectables dot this Italianate Victorian villa, where wing-backed chairs sit in stately bedrooms and rich red fabrics frame superb sea views. They'll have you watching the sun set from your sofa or the waves roll from your four-poster bed. The window-seated Tower Room has light pouring in from three sides.

Hambrough   B&B £££
(☑01983-856333; www.thehambrough.com; Hambrough Rd, Ventnor; d £150-230 ste £190-250; 🛜) What you see from the pick of the rooms at the Hambrough is truly fabulous – the suites have balconies with wraparound sea views, while you can watch the waves from

the bathtub in room 4. The furnishings are smooth and smart, rather than stunning, and comfort comes courtesy of minifridges, underfloor heating and espresso machines.

Ale & Oyster   BISTRO £££
(☑01983-857025; www.thealeandoyster.co.uk; The Esplanade, Ventnor; mains £22-25; ⊙noon-2pm & 6-9pm Wed-Sun) The modern takes on Isle of Wight produce served at this top-notch little bistro have won a loyal following. Refined dishes might include crab parfait, seared scallops, confit duck, or local pigeon breast dotted with mushrooms and blackberries. Best enjoyed at a table overlooking Ventnor Bay.

Steephill Cove

Steephill Cove's tiny, sandy beach is fringed by buildings that range from stone cottages to rickety-looking shacks. Beach finds festoon porches dotted with driftwood furniture and draped with fishing nets; a tiny clapboard lighthouse presides over the scene. It's all studiedly nautical, but still very nice.

🍴 Eating

Crab Shed   CAFE £
(☑01983-855819; www.steephillcove-isleofwight. co.uk; snacks from £5; ⊙noon-3pm Apr-Sep) Lobster pots and fishing boats line the slipway outside a shack that's a riot of sea-smoothed spas, cork floats and faded buoys. Irresistible treats include meaty crab salads, mackerel ciabatta and crumbly crab pasties.

★ Boathouse   SEAFOOD £££
(☑01983-852747; www.steephill-cove.co.uk; mains £20-45; ⊙noon-3pm Thu-Tue late May–early Sep) Arrive early enough, and you'll see Steephill Cove's fishers (Jimmy and Mark) landing your lunch – the sanded wooden tables here are just steps from the sea. It makes a spellbinding spot to sip chilled wine, sample succulent lobster and revel in Wight's new-found driftwood chic. Booking essential.

❶ Getting There & Away

Steephill Cove is 1 mile west of Ventnor and is off-limits to cars. Walk from the nearby Botanical Gardens (parking £5), or hike from the hillside car park 200m west of Ventnor Esplanade, then follow the (sometimes steep) coast path until you arrive.

West Wight

Rural and remote, Wight's westerly corner is where the island really comes into its own. Sheer white cliffs rear from a surging sea as the stunning coastline peels west to Alum Bay and the most famous chunks of chalk in the region: the Needles. These jagged rocks rise, shardlike, out of the sea, like the backbone of a prehistoric sea monster. West Wight is also home to arguably the isle's best beach: sandy, windswept Compton Bay.

◉ Sights & Activities

★ **Needles Old & New Battery**   FORT

(NT; ✆ 01983-754772; www.nationaltrust.org.uk; The Needles; adult/child £6.80/3.40; ⊗ 11am-4pm mid-Mar–Oct) The Victorian fort complex at Wight's western tip is home to two gun emplacements where engrossing displays reveal how the site was established in 1862, served in two world wars and then became a secret Cold War rocket-testing base. Walk to the battery along the cliffs from Alum Bay (1 mile) or hop on the open-top tourist bus (www.islandbuses.info; per 24hr adult/child £10/5; ⊗ 10am-5pm mid-Mar–Oct) that runs twice hourly between battery and bay.

Needles Pleasure Cruises   BOATING

(✆ 01983-761587; www.needlespleasurecruises. co.uk; Alum Bay; adult/child £6/4; ⊗ 10.30am-4.30pm Easter-Oct) Twenty-minute voyages run half-hourly from Alum Bay beach to the towering Needles chalk stacks, providing cracking views of those soaring white cliffs.

🛏 Sleeping

Totland Bay YHA   HOSTEL £

(✆ 0345 260 2191; www.yha.org.uk; Hirst Hill, Totland Bay; dm/d/q £25/62/100; P @ 🛜) Creaking, cheerfully run Victorian house with a maximum of eight beds per room and staff happy to share local info.

★ **Tom's Eco Lodge**   CAMPSITE ££

(✆ 01983-758729; www.tomsecolodge.com; Tapnell Farm, Yarmouth; 4-person pod per 3 nights £300; P 🛜) 🍃 Eco pods, log cabins, safari tents – the full gamut of comfy camping options sit happily on this spacious, sea-view site. They're beautifully decked out with their own showers and loos – some even have wood-fired hot tubs. Additional extras include breakfast hampers (per person £5) and food packs (for four people £40) for your own private BBQ.

DORSET

Holiday hot spot Dorset offers a checklist of charms. Its shoreline is one of Britain's best and boasts the Jurassic Coast – a World Heritage Site flecked with sea-carved bays, crumbly cliffs and beaches loaded with fossilised souvenirs. Swimming, kayaking and hiking here are memorable indeed. Inland, Thomas Hardy's lyrical landscape serves up vast Iron Age hill forts, rude chalk figures, fairy-tale castles and must-see stately homes. Then there are resorts alive with party animals, golden beaches flanked by millionaires' mansions, and sailing waters that have hosted Olympic events. Time then to add Dorset to your holiday list.

ℹ Information

Visit Dorset (www.visit-dorset.com) The county's official tourism website.

Lonely Planet (www.lonelyplanet.com) Destination information, hotel bookings, traveller forum and more.

ℹ Getting There & Around

TRAIN

One train route provides direct services from Bristol, via Bath and Dorchester West, to Weymouth (£20, three hours, at least six daily).

Another direct, hourly service connects London Waterloo with Weymouth (£34, three hours), via Southampton, Bournemouth, Poole and Dorchester South.

BUS

First (www.firstgroup.com/wessex-dorset-south-somerset) runs bus routes linking the main towns. A key route is bus X53 which travels regularly west from Weymouth to Axminster along the shore.

More (www.morebus.co.uk) is the key bus operator in Bournemouth, Poole and surrounding rural areas.

Bournemouth

POP 183,491

If one thing has shaped Bournemouth, it's the beach. This glorious, 7-mile strip of soft sand first drew holidaymakers in the Victorian days. Today the resort attracts both elderly coach parties and youthful stag parties – on Saturday nights fancy-dress is everywhere; angels in L-plates meet men in mankinis. But Bournemouth is more than just a full-on party town. It also boasts some hip hideaways, great restaurants, tempting watersports, and

WORTH A TRIP

KINGSTON LACY

Dorset's must-see stately home, **Kingston Lacy** (NT; ☑ 01202-883402; www.nationaltrust.org.uk; Wimborne Minster; adult/child £13.60/6.80; ☺ house 11am-5pm Mar-Oct, grounds 10am-6pm Mar-Oct, 10am-4pm Nov-Feb; ℗) looks every inch the setting for a period drama. It overflows with rich decor, most famously in the Spanish Room, which is smothered with gold and gilt. Other highlights are the hieroglyphics in the Egyptian Room and the elegant marble staircase and loggia. Artworks include the overwhelming ceiling fresco *The Separation of Night and Day*, by Guido Reni, and paintings by Rubens, Titian and Van Dyck.

Kingston Lacy is 2.5 miles west of Wimborne.

in Boscombe, 2 miles east of the centre, a suburb with a cool urban-surfer vibe.

◉ Sights

Bournemouth Beach   BEACH

Bournemouth's sandy shoreline regularly clocks up seaside awards. It stretches from Southbourne in the far east to Alum Chine in the west – an immense promenade backed by some 3000 deckchairs, ornamental gardens, kids' playgrounds, cafes and 200 beach huts that are available for hire (☑ 01202-451781; www.bournemouthbeachhuts.co.uk; per day/week from £40/115). The resort also has two piers. Around **Bournemouth Pier** you can rent deckchairs (per day £3), windbreaks (£6) and parasols (£6). **Boscombe Pier** is a focus for watersports.

Russell-Cotes   MUSEUM

(☑ 01202-451858; www.russellcotes.com; East Cliff Promenade; adult/child £7.50/4; ☺ 10am-5pm Tue-Sun) Ostentation oozes from almost every inch of this arresting structure – a mash-up of Italianate villa and Scottish baronial pile. It was built at the end of the 1800s for Merton and Annie Russell-Cotes as somewhere to showcase the remarkable range of souvenirs gathered on their world travels.

Alum Chine   GARDENS

(Mountbatten Rd; ☺ 24hr) **FREE** Bournemouth's 1920s heyday is beautifully evoked at a subtropical enclave containing plants from the Canary Islands, New Zealand, Mexico and the Himalayas; their bright-red bracts, silver thistles and purple flowers are set against a glittering sea. It's 1.5 miles west of Bournemouth Pier.

⌕ Sleeping

★ B&B by the Beach   B&B £ £

(☑ 01202-433632; www.bedandbreakfastbythebeach.co.uk; 7 Burtley Rd, Southbourne; s/d £70/110; ℗🖥) Prepare for a winning combo: charming owners and delightful rooms. Themes and colours encompass yachting, deep aquamarine and ruby red. Relaxation comes courtesy of the flower-framed terrace, posh chocs and homemade cake – best sampled with the complimentary glass of wine.

★ Urban Beach   BOUTIQUE HOTEL £ £

(☑ 01202-301509; www.urbanbeach.co.uk; 23 Argyll Rd; s £58-75, d £120-140; ℗@🖥) Still slumber spot of choice for Bournemouth's hip visitors, Urban Beach revels in a 'no-worries' air that sees free loans of wellingtons, umbrellas and DVDs. Soft brown, dark grey and flashes of terracotta define stylish bedrooms, while the decked terrace sees you tucking into upscale bistro fare that's served from morning (8am) till night (10pm).

Mory House   B&B £ £

(☑ 01202-433553; www.moryhouse.co.uk; 31 Grand Ave, Southbourne; s/d/f £90/115/150; ℗🖥) In this serene, pristine B&B, stained glass and an elegant stairwell hint at the house's Edwardian age. Contemporary bedrooms are styled in muted colours; the pick is number 3, where the pint-sized balcony is an ideal spot to nibble on a home-baked cookie.

Amarillo   B&B £ £

(☑ 01202-553884; www.amarillohotel.co.uk; 52 Frances Rd; s £40-45, d £70-90; ℗🖥) Amarillo's smart, stylish bedrooms are great value; expect jazzy wallpaper, snazzy throws and subtle lighting.

There's a three night minimum stay in summer.

✗ Eating

★ Urban Reef   BISTRO £ £

(☑ 01202-443960; www.urbanreef.com; Undercliff Dr, Boscombe; snacks from £5, mains £14-22; ☺ 8am-10pm, winter times vary; 🖥🅿) On sunny weekends a cool crowd queues out the door at Urban Reef. No wonder: a waterfront deck and balcony, punchy coffee, top-notch snacks and quality, sustainable restaurant fare. On stormy days snuggle down beside the log burner and listen to the sound of the sea.

Reef Encounter
BISTRO ££

(☏01202-280656; www.reef-encounter.com; 42 Sea Rd, Boscombe; mains £11-21; ⊙11am-10pm Mon-Fri, 9am-10pm Sat & Sun, shorter hours winter; 🛜) Big squishy sofas, a mellow soundtrack and a sea-view terrace give this chilled-out eatery a surf-bar vibe. Brunch can be healthy (avocado, salmon and egg) or decadent (maple syrup-drenched French toast). Or opt for juicy burgers and roasted veg skewers – perhaps while sipping a cool beer, watching the waves.

West Beach
SEAFOOD ££

(☏01202-587785; www.west-beach.co.uk; Pier Approach; mains £15-40; ⊙9am-9.30pm) The seafood and setting are hard to beat – bag a chair on the decking beside the sand, watch the waves lap Bournemouth Pier and tuck into perfectly cooked, perfectly fresh fish: perhaps turbot with chorizo and capers, or a shellfish platter piled high with oysters, langoustines, cockles and clams.

🍷 Drinking & Nightlife

⭐ **Sixty Million Postcards**
PUB

(www.sixtymillionpostcards.com; 19 Exeter Rd; ⊙noon-midnight Sat-Thu, to 2am Fri) An oasis of hipster grunginess amid pound-a-pint Bournemouth, Sixty Million draws a decidedly beatnik crowd. Worn wooden floors and fringed lampshades set the scene for DJ sets, live bands and retro gaming nights.

ℹ Information

Tourist Office (☏01202-451734; www. bournemouth.co.uk; Pier Approach; ⊙9am-5pm Apr-Oct, to 4pm Nov-Mar) Set right beside Bournemouth Pier.

ℹ Getting There & Around

BUS
Direct National Express (www.nationalexpress. com) buses departing from Bournemouth's coach station include:

Bristol (£18, four hours, daily Monday to Saturday)
London Victoria (£15, three hours, hourly)
Oxford (£15, three hours, three daily)
Southampton (£8, 50 minutes, hourly)
Useful local buses include:
Poole (M1/M2, £2, 35 minutes, every 15 minutes)
Salisbury (X3, £6.50, 1¼ hours, at least hourly)

Morebus Zone A Dayrider (adult/child £4.10/2.60) gives a day's unlimited travel in much of Poole, Bournemouth and neighbouring Christchurch.

TRAIN
Destinations include the following:
Dorchester South (£13, 45 minutes, half-hourly)
London Waterloo (£30, 2½ hours, half-hourly)
Poole (£4, 12 minutes, half-hourly)
Weymouth (£14, one hour, hourly)

Poole
POP 147,645

In the quaint old port of Poole there's a whiff of money in the air: the town borders Sandbanks, a gorgeous beach backed by some of the world's most expensive chunks of real estate. Big bucks aside, Poole also boasts excellent eateries and is the springboard for a raft of watersports and some irresistible boat trips.

◎ Sights & Activities

Brownsea Island
ISLAND

(NT; ☏01202-707744; www.nationaltrust.org.uk; Poole Harbour; adult/child £7.20/3.60; ⊙10am-5pm late Mar–Oct) On this small, wooded island in the middle of Poole Harbour, trails weave through heath and woods, past peacocks, red squirrels, red deer and a wealth of bird life – the water-framed views

---

LAWRENCE OF ARABIA

Clouds Hill (NT; ☏01929-405616; www. nationaltrust.org.uk; King George V Rd, Bovington; adult/child £7/3.50; ⊙11am-5pm Mar-Oct; 🅿), the tiny cottage that was home to TE Lawrence (1888–1935) provides a compelling insight into a complex man. The British soldier became legendary after working with Arab forces in WWI. Look out for Lawrence's evocative desert-campaign photos, his French crusader castle sketches and the desk where he abridged *Seven Pillars of Wisdom*.

The four idiosyncratic rooms include a surprisingly comfortable cork-lined bathroom, an aluminium foil–lined bunk room and a heavily beamed music room. The house is much as Lawrence left it – he died at the age of 46 after a motorbike accident on a nearby road.

on to the Isle of Purbeck are stunning. Free guided walks focus on the wartime island, bird life, smugglers and pirates. Boats, run by **Brownsea Island Ferries** (☎ 01929-462383; www.brownseaislandferries.com; ☺ 10am-5pm late Mar–Oct), leave from Poole Quay (adult/child return £11.50/6.75) and Sandbanks (adult/child return £7/5) at least hourly.

Poole Museum　　　　　　　　MUSEUM
(☎ 01202-262600; www.boroughofpoole.com/mus eums; 4 High St; ☺ 10am-5pm Apr-Oct) FREE The building alone is worth seeing – a beautifully restored 15th-century warehouse. The star exhibit is a 2300-year-old **Iron Age logboat** dredged up from Poole Harbour. At almost 10m long and over 12 tonnes, it's the largest to be found in southern Britain and probably carried 18 people.

Sandbanks　　　　　　　　　　BEACH
A 2-mile, wafer-thin peninsula of land that curls around the expanse of Poole Harbour, Sandbanks is studded with some of the most expensive houses in the world. But the white-sand beaches that border them are free, have some of the best UK water-quality standards and are home to a host of watersports operators.

Brownsea Island Ferries shuttle from Poole to Sandbanks (adult child return £11.50/6.75), as does bus 60 (£3.60, 25 minutes, hourly).

Poole Harbour Watersports　WATER SPORTS
(☎ 01202-700503; www.pooleharbour.co.uk; 284 Sandbanks Rd) Does lessons in stand-up paddleboarding (SUP; per 1½ hours £25), windsurfing (per six hours £78) and kitesurfing (per day £99), plus memorable kayak and SUP tours (per three hours £35 to £40).

🛏 Sleeping

Old Townhouse　　　　　　　B&B ££
(☎ 01202-670950; townhousepoole@btconnect. com; 7 High St; s/d £65/95; 🛜) A delightful air of old England settles cosily over this quayside B&B. It's largely down to the gleaming wood, big burnished brass taps and furnishings that aren't afraid to echo heritage styles. A central setting and tiny patio add to the appeal.

Quayside　　　　　　　　　　B&B ££
(☎ 01202-683733; www.quaysidepoole.co.uk; 9 High St; s/d £55/75; 🛜) Snug rooms in floral prints in the heart of the old harbour.

Merchant House　　　　　　B&B £££
(☎ 01202-661474; www.themerchanthouse.org.uk; 10 Strand St; s £100, d £140-160) Tucked just one street back from the water's edge, tall, redbrick Merchant House is boutiquery at its best. Hefty wood sculptures, wicker rocking chairs and crisp linen ensure it's stylish; the odd teddy bear keeps it cheery, too.

🍴 Eating

Deli on the Quay　　　　　　DELI £
(☎ 01202-660022; www.delionthequay.com; Dolphin Quays; mains from £4.50; ☺ 9am-5pm, to 4pm Nov-Mar) The perfect place to stock up for a beach picnic: crab cakes, old-school potato salad, and gourmet sandwiches – plus corking coffee and gooey chocolate brownies.

Storm　　　　　　　　　　SEAFOOD ££
(☎ 01202-674970; www.stormfish.co.uk; 16 High St; mains £15-21; ☺ 6.30-9pm Mon-Sat) How rare is this? The dish you're eating could well have been caught by the chef! At chilled-out Storm, fisher Pete also rattles the pots 'n' pans, delighting in dishing up intense Goan fish curry, seafood ramen, and a classic Poole Bay Dover Sole *à la meuniére*.

Poole Arms　　　　　　　PUB FOOD ££
(☎ 01202-673450; www.poolearms.co.uk; 19 Poole Quay; mains £12-17; ☺ noon-9pm Sun-Thu, to 9.30pm Fri & Sat) The grub at this ancient pub is strong on locally landed seafood – try the homemade fish pie, local crab or pan-fried herring roe. Order some New Forest beer, then settle down in the snug, wood-lined bar with the locals, or on the terrace overlooking the quay.

★ Guildhall Tavern　　　　FRENCH £££
(☎ 01202-671717; www.guildhalltavern.co.uk; 15 Market St; mains £18-23; ☺ 11.30am-3.30pm & 6-9.30pm Tue-Sat) Poole's top table consistently delights as it combines local ingredients with lashings of French flair. Predictably, fish features strongly – the spicy sautéed squid with samphire is superb; chargrilled sea bass is flambéed with Pernod – but rosemary-scented Dorset lamb also makes carnivores smile. Book.

ℹ Information

Tourist Office (☎ 01202-262600.; www.poole tourism.com; 4 High St; ☺ 10am-5pm Apr-Oct, 10am-4pm Mon-Sat, noon-4pm Sun Nov-Mar) Set inside Poole Museum.

ℹ Getting There & Around

BOAT
Brittany Ferries (☎ 0330 159 7000; www. brittany-ferries.com) sails between Poole and

CORFE CASTLE

The startling, fractured battlements of **Corfe Castle** (NT; ☑ 01929-481294; www.national
trust.org.uk; The Square; adult/child £9.50/4.75; ⏱ 10am-6pm Apr-Sep, to 5pm Mar & Oct, to
4pm Nov-Feb) were once home to Sir John Bankes, Charles I's right-hand man. The Civil
War saw the castle besieged by Cromwellian forces; in 1646 the plucky Lady Bankes
directed a six-week defence and the castle fell only after being betrayed from within. The
Roundheads then gunpowdered Corfe Castle apart; turrets and soaring walls still sheer
off at precarious angles – the splayed-out gatehouse looks like it's just been blown up.

These huge fortifications also lend their name to the attractive village that has grown
up alongside.

Bus 40 shuttles hourly between Poole, Wareham, Corfe Castle and Swanage. The
10-minute trip to Wareham costs £4.

Swanage Steam Railway (☑ 01929-425800; www.swanagerailway.co.uk; adult/child
return £13/8; ⏱ daily Apr-Oct, Sat & Sun Nov, Dec & Mar) stops at Corfe Castle as it journeys
between Swanage and Norden.

Cherbourg in France (4½ hours, one daily). Summer return prices start at around £80 for foot passengers and £335 for a car and two adults.

Sandbanks Ferry makes the four-minute trip from **Sandbanks** (Sandbanks Terminal; ☑ 01929-450203; www.sandbanksferry.co.uk; per pedestrian/car £1/4.50; ⏱ 7am-11pm) to **Studland** (Studland Terminal; ☑ 01929-450203; www.sandbanksferry.co.uk; Ferry Rd; per pedestrian/car £1/4.50; ⏱ 7am-11pm) every 20 minutes. It's a shortcut from Poole to Swanage, Wareham and the Isle of Purbeck, but the summer queues can be a pain.

BUS

A Morebus Zone A Dayrider (adult/child £4.10/2.60) gives a day's unlimited travel in much of Poole and Bournemouth.

Bournemouth (Bus M1/M2, £2, 35 minutes, every 15 minutes)

London Victoria (National Express, £18, 3½ hours, every two hours)

Sandbanks (Bus 60, £3.60, 25 minutes, hourly)

TAXI

Dial-a-Cab (☑ 01202-666822; www.pooletaxis.co.uk)

TRAIN

Bournemouth (£4, 12 minutes, half-hourly)

Dorchester South (£10, 30 minutes, hourly)

London Waterloo (£30, 2¼ hours, half-hourly)

Weymouth (£12, 45 minutes, hourly)

Lulworth Cove & Around

POP 740

In this stretch of southeast Dorset the coast steals the show. For millions of years the elements have been creating an intricate shoreline of curved bays, caves, stacks and weirdly wonderful rock formations – most notably the massive natural arch at Durdle Door.

The charismatic hamlet of Lulworth Cove is a pleasing jumble of thatched cottages and fishing gear, which winds down to a perfect crescent of white cliffs.

◉ Sights & Activities

Lulworth Cove Visitor Centre MUSEUM
(☑ 01929-400587; www.lulworth.com; main car park; ⏱ 10am-5pm Easter-Sep, to 4pm Oct-Easter) Excellent displays outline how geology and erosion have combined to shape the area's remarkable shoreline. Staff can advise about walks, too.

Stair Hole Bay BAY
Stair Hole Bay sits just a few hundred metres west of Lulworth Cove. This diminutive semicircle is almost enclosed by cliffs that feature tiny rock arches – a route in that's popular with kayakers. On the landward side is the delightfully named Lulworth Crumple, where layers of rock form dramatically zigzagging folds.

★ Durdle Door LANDMARK
The poster child of Dorset's Jurassic Coast, this immense, sea-fringed, 150-million-year-old Portland stone arch was created by a combination of massive earth movements and erosion. Today it's framed by shimmering bays; bring a swimsuit and head down the hundreds of steps for an unforgettable dip. You can park at the top of the cliffs (two hours £4, four hours £5), but it's best to hike the coast path from Lulworth Cove (1 mile).

Lulworth Castle
CASTLE

(EH; ☑ 01929-400352; www.lulworth.com; adult/child £6/4; ☉ 10.30am-5pm Sun-Fri Apr-Dec) A confection in creamy, dreamy white, this baronial pile looks more like a French chateau than a traditional English castle. Built in 1608 as a hunting lodge, it's survived extravagant owners, extensive remodelling and a disastrous fire in 1929. It has been extensively restored – check out the reconstructed kitchen and cellars, then climb the tower for sweeping coastal views. It costs £3 to park.

★ Jurassic
Coast Activities
ADVENTURE SPORTS

(☑ 01305-835301; www.jurassiccoastactivities.co.uk; per person £60-70) This unmissable, three-hour paddle offers jaw-dropping views of Dorset's heavily eroded coast. Starting at Lulworth Cove, you glide through Stair Hole's caves and stacks, across Man O'War Bay, then under the stone arch at Durdle Door, stopping for swims and picnics along the way.

🎉 Festivals & Events

Bestival
MUSIC

(www.bestival.net; ☉ Aug) Held in early August, Bestival delights in an eclectic, alternative feel, drawing the likes of the Super Furry Animals, Scissor Sisters, London Grammar and Candi Staton to Dorset's Lulworth Estate.

For more than 10 years, Bestival was held on the Isle of Wight.

🛏 Sleeping

Lulworth YHA
HOSTEL £

(☑ 0345 371 9331; www.yha.org.uk; School Lane, West Lulworth; dm £13-17, q £50-100; ☉ Fri-Sun & school holidays Mar-Oct; P) Hills stretch out alongside, and sheep bleat outside, this cosy, chalet-style, edge-of-the-village hostel.

Durdle Door Holiday Park
CAMPSITE £

(☑ 01929-400200; www.lulworth.com; sites £28-44; ☉ Mar-Oct; P) Attractive, spacious site, just minutes from the creamy cliffs, and 1.5 miles west of the hamlet of Lulworth Cove. Opt for a good old tent, or a four-person wooden pod (£80).

Prices rocket in the school holidays, when there also tends to be a two night minimum stay.

★ Lulworth Cove
INN ££

(☑ 01929-400333; www.lulworth-coveinn.co.uk; Main Rd; d £120-135; P 🐾) One to delight your inner beachcomber. In this veritable vision of driftwood-chic whitewashed floorboards and aquamarine panels frame painted wicker chairs and roll-top baths. Add cracking sea views, a mini roof terrace and top-quality gastropub grub (mains £10 to £16; food served from noon to 9pm) and you have an irresistible inn.

Rudds of Lulworth
B&B £££

(☑ 01929-400552; www.ruddslulworth.co.uk; Main Rd; d £90-185; 🐾 🔆) An idyllic setting, pared-down designs, top-notch linen and pamper-yourself toiletries combine to make this a

---

JURASSIC COAST

The kind of massive, hands-on geology lesson you wish you'd had at school, the Jurassic Coast is England's first natural World Heritage Site, putting it on a par with the Great Barrier Reef and the Grand Canyon. This striking shoreline stretches from Exmouth in East Devon to Swanage in Dorset, encompassing 185 million years of the Earth's history in just 95 miles. It means you can walk, in just a few hours, many millions of years in geological time.

It began when layers of rocks formed, their varying compositions determined by different climates: desertlike conditions gave way to higher then lower sea levels. Massive earth movements then tilted all the rock layers, forcing most of the oldest formations to the west, and the youngest to the east. Next, erosion exposed the different strata.

The differences are very tangible. Devon's rusty-red Triassic rocks are 200–250 million years old. Lyme Regis' fossil-rich, dark-clay Jurassic cliffs are 190 million years old. Pockets of much younger, creamy-coloured Cretaceous rocks (a mere 65–140 million years old) pop up, notably around Lulworth Cove, where erosion has sculpted a stunning display of bays, stacks and rock arches.

The coast's website (www.jurassiccoast.org) is a great information source; also look out locally for the highly readable *Official Guide to the Jurassic Coast* (£4.95), or buy it from the website's online shop.

memorable place to stay – especially if you opt for a room with Lulworth Cove views. Or just lounge beside the pool, which also overlooks that circle of bay.

🍴 Eating & Drinking

Cove Fish   SEAFOOD £
(📞 01929-400807; fish from £5; ⏰ 10am-4pm Tue-Sun Easter-Sep, plus some winter weekends) The seafood piled high in this shed by the path to the beach has been caught by ninth- and 10th-generation fishermen Joe and Levi. Bag some fish for the barbecue, or tuck into Lulworth Cove crab (from £4) or lobster – a meal that's travelled food yards not miles.

Boat Shed   CAFE £
(📞 01929-400810; www.lulworth.com; Main Rd; snacks from £3; ⏰ 9.30am-5pm, winter hours vary) Views don't come much better than from the terrace of this converted fishers' storage shack set right beside Lulworth Cove's glittering circular cove. The food spans fine brunches, Dorset cream teas, mezze platters and – of course – fish.

Castle   PUB
(📞 01929-400311; www.thecastleinn-lulworthcove. co.uk; 8 Main Rd, West Lulworth; ⏰ noon-10pm; 🛜) A picture-perfect, rambling thatched inn with a swish new interior, garden and regularly changing selection of prime Dorset ciders.

ℹ️ Getting There & Away

Bus X54 (two daily, Monday to Saturday, no service winter Sundays) stops at Lulworth Cove en route between Weymouth and Wareham and Poole.

Dorchester & Around

POP 19,143

With Dorchester, you get two towns in one: a real-life, bustling county town and Thomas Hardy's fictional Casterbridge. The Victorian writer was born nearby and his literary locations can still be found among Dorchester's Georgian terraces. Here you can also visit Hardy's former homes and see his original manuscripts. Add cracking archaeological sites and attractive places to eat and sleep and you have an appealing base for a night or two.

⦿ Sights

★ Dorset County Museum   MUSEUM
(📞 01305-262735; www.dorsetcountymuseum.org; High West St; adult/child £6.35/3.50; ⏰ 10am-5pm

Mon-Sat Apr-Oct, to 4pm Nov-Mar) The Thomas Hardy collection here is the world's largest, offering extraordinary insights into his creative process. You can see from text in Hardy's cramped handwriting where he's crossed out one word and substituted another. There's also an atmospheric reconstruction of his study at Max Gate and a letter in which Siegfried Sassoon requests permission to dedicate his first book of poems to Hardy.

Jurassic Coast fossil exhibits include a huge ichthyosaur and 1.8m plesiosaur fore paddle. Bronze and Iron Age finds from Maiden Castle (p263) include a treasure trove of coins and neck rings, while Roman artefacts include 70 gold coins, nail cleaners and (toe-curlingly) ear picks.

Roman Town House   HISTORIC BUILDING
(www.romantownhouse.co.uk; Northern Hay; ⏰ 24hr) FREE The knee-high flint walls and beautifully preserved mosaics here powerfully conjure up the Roman occupation of Dorchester (then Durnovaria). Peek into the summer dining room to see the underfloor heating system (hypocaust), where charcoal-warmed air circulated around pillars to produce a toasty room temperature of 18°C (64°F).

★ Maiden Castle   ARCHAEOLOGICAL SITE
(EH; www.english-heritage.org.uk; Winterborne Monkton; ⏰ dawn-dusk; 🅿️) FREE Occupying a massive slab of horizon on the southern fringes of Dorchester, Maiden Castle is the largest and most complex Iron Age hill fort in Britain. The first defences were built on the site around 500 BC – in its heyday it was densely populated with clusters of roundhouses and a network of roads. The Romans besieged and captured Maiden Castle in AD 43 – an ancient Briton skeleton with a Roman crossbow bolt in the spine was found at the fort.

🛏️ Sleeping

★ Beggars Knap   B&B ££
(📞 07768 690691; www.beggarsknap.co.uk; 2 Weymouth Ave; s £70-80, d £90-115, f from £115; 🅿️🛜) Despite the name, this altogether fabulous, vaguely decadent guesthouse is far from impoverished. Opulent rooms drip with chandeliers and gold brocades; beds draped in fine cottons range from French sleigh to four-poster. You could pay much, much more and get something half as nice.

Westwood   B&B ££
(📞 01305-268018; www.westwoodhouse.co.uk; 29 High West St; s/d/f £80/100/140; 🛜) A

BATH & SOUTHWEST ENGLAND DORCHESTER & AROUND

THOMAS HARDY'S DORCHESTER

Thomas Hardy fans can hunt down the *Mayor of Casterbridge* locations tucked away in modern Dorchester's streets. They include **Lucetta's House**, a grand Georgian affair with ornate doorposts in Trinity St, while in parallel South St, a red-brick, mid-18th-century building (now a bank) is named as the inspiration for the **house of the mayor** himself. The tourist office sells book location guides.

Max Gate (NT; ☏01305-262538; www.nationaltrust.org.uk; Alington Ave; adult/child £7/3.50; ⊙11am-5pm Mar-Oct, 11am-4pm Thu-Sat Nov-Feb; ℗) Hardy was a trained architect and designed this attractive house, where he lived from 1885 until his death in 1928. *Tess of the D'Urbervilles* and *Jude the Obscure* were both written here, and the house contains several pieces of original furniture. It's a mile east of Dorchester, on the A352.

Hardy's Cottage (NT; ☏01305-262366; www.nationaltrust.org.uk; Higher Bockhampton; adult/child £7/3.50; ⊙11am-5pm Mar-Oct, 11am-4pm Thu-Sun Nov-Feb; ℗) This picturesque cob-and-thatch house is the birthplace of Thomas Hardy. It features evocative, sparsely furnished rooms and a lush garden. It's in Higher Bockhampton, 3 miles northeast of Dorchester.

skilled designer's been at work in this 18th-century town house, producing a contemporary-meets-Georgian style: muted greens, brass lamps, subtle checks and minisofas. The modern bathrooms glint, while tiny fridges harbour fresh milk for your tea.

Yalbury Cottage　　　　HOTEL **££**
(☏01305-262382; www.yalburycottage.com; Lower Bockhampton; s/d £85/125; ℗🛜) It's almost your archetypal English cottage: framed by flowers and crowned by moss-studded thatch. Inside fresh, simple, gently rustic bedrooms overlook the garden or fields. Yalbury is in Lower Bockhampton, 3 miles east of Dorchester.

The restaurant (two/three courses £35/40) serves up top-notch takes on British classics in convivial, clublike rooms; bookings are required. Food is served from 6.30pm to 8.30pm Tuesday to Saturday, and between noon and 2pm on Sunday.

✖ Eating

⭐**Taste**　　　　BRASSERIE **££**
(☏01305-257776; www.tastebrasserie.co.uk; Trinity St; mains £9-20; ⊙8.30am-4pm Mon-Fri, 9am-5pm Sat, 10am-4pm Sun) One of Dorchester's best, buzziest brunch and lunch spots has fleets of fans thanks to a buy-local ethos and emphasis on superfresh sustainable ingredients. They crop up in everything from platters, tapas and melts to classy bistro dishes: grilled steak, confit duck, garlicky linguine.

Cow & Apple　　　　BURGERS **££**
(☏01305-266286; www.cowandapple.co.uk; 30 Trinity St; mains £9-15; ⊙9am-8.30pm) Piled high and oozing all the trimmings, the dirty burgers here are decidedly good – spice things up with jalapeños, brie or a seriously sticky BBQ sauce. The cider list – more than 50 types – could take a while to work through.

Sienna　　　　MODERN BRITISH **££**
(☏01305-250022; www.siennadorchester.co.uk; 36 High West St; mains £14.50, 4/6/8 courses £35/55/70; ⊙noon-2pm Wed-Sun & 6.30-9pm Tue-Sat) The menu at sleek Sienna is peppered with rarities; expect to find fermented blackberry, jerk carrot or squid ink artfully arranged on your plate. The desserts are imaginative, too – perhaps try the chocolate pudding with surprising additions of orange and brown bread.

❶ Information

Tourist Office (☏01305-267992; www.visit-dorset.com; Dorchester Library, Charles St; ⊙10am-5.30pm Mon & Thu, to 1pm Wed, to 7pm Tue & Fri, to 4pm Sat)

❶ Getting There & Away

BUS

London Victoria (National Express, £18, four hours, one daily)

Lyme Regis (Bus X51, £4.80, 1¼ hours, hourly Monday to Saturday)

Sherborne (Bus X11, £4.70, 1¼ hours, four to seven daily Monday to Saturday)

Weymouth (Bus 10, £2, 30 minutes, half-hourly)

TRAIN

Dorchester has two train stations.

Trains leave Dorchester West for Bath and Bristol (£20, two to 2½ hours, at least six daily).

Services from Dorchester South, running at least hourly, include the following:

Bournemouth (£13, 45 minutes)
London Waterloo (£34, 2¾ hours)
Southampton (£26, 1½ hours)
Weymouth (£5, 10 minutes)

Weymouth

POP 52,168

At just over 225 years old, Weymouth is a grand dame of a resort with a couple of tricks up her faded sleeve. Candy-striped kiosks and deckchairs line a golden, 3-mile beach; chuck in cockles and chippies and prepare to promenade down seaside memory lane. But Weymouth is about more than just that sandy shore; the town boasts a historic harbour, some superb seafood restaurants and easy access to the watersports centres of the neighbouring Isle of Portland.

⊙ Sights & Activities

Weymouth Beach   BEACH
The nostalgia-inducing offerings along Weymouth's fine sandy shore could see you marvelling at highly skilled sand sculptors, renting a deckchair or pedalo, descending a helter-skelter, trampoline-bouncing, watching Punch & Judy shows, or taking a donkey ride.

Nothe Fort   FORT
(☑ 01305-766626; www.nothefort.org.uk; Barrack Rd; adult/child £8/2; ⊙ 10.30am-5.30pm Apr-Oct) Weymouth's photogenic 19th-century defences are studded with cannons, searchlights and 30cm coastal guns. Exhibits detail Dorset's Roman invasion, a Victorian soldier's drill and Weymouth in WWII.

Sea Life   AQUARIUM
(☑ 01305-761070; www.visitsealife.com; Lodmoor Country Park; adult/child £23/19; ⊙ 10am-5pm Apr-Oct, to 4pm Nov-Mar; ℗) Highlights include sharks, penguins and seahorses, and talks and feeding demonstrations are held throughout the day. Tickets fall to £14 for adults and £11 for children if bought online, in advance.

Coastline Cruises   BOATING
(☑ 01305-785000; www.coastlinecruises.com; Trinity Rd; adult/child return £10/6; ⊙ Apr-Oct) Coastline runs the Portland Ferry, a wind-blown 90-minute sailing from Weymouth's historic fortifications, across vast Portland Harbour and on to Portland itself. Boats leave from Weymouth Harbour's west side three to four times daily from April to October.

⊨ Sleeping

★ Roundhouse   B&B ££
(☑ 07825 788020; www.roundhouse-weymouth.com; 1 The Esplanade; d £105-125; 🛜) The decor here is as gently eccentric as the owner –

BATH & SOUTHWEST ENGLAND WEYMOUTH

WORTH A TRIP

THE CERNE GIANT

Nude, full frontal and notoriously well endowed, the **Cerne Giant** (NT; www.nationaltrust.org.uk; Cerne Abbas; ⊙ 24hr; ℗) FREE chalk figure, on the hillside above the village of Cerne Abbas, is revealed in all his glory – and he's in a state of excitement that wouldn't be allowed in most magazines. The giant is around 60m high and 51m wide and his age remains a mystery; some claim he's Roman but the first historical reference comes in 1694, when three shillings were set aside for his repair. These days a car park provides grandstand views.

The Victorians found it all deeply embarrassing and allowed grass to grow over his most outstanding feature. Today the hill is grazed by sheep and cattle, though only the sheep are allowed to do their nibbling over the giant – the cows would do too much damage to his lines.

Down in the village, the **New Inn** (☑ 01300-341274; www.thenewinncerneabbas.co.uk; 14 Long St; d £100-140, ste £150-180; ℗🛜) – which is actually more than 400 years old – makes a quaint place to stay.

Dorchester is 8 miles south. Bus X11 (four to six daily Monday to Saturday) goes to Dorchester (£2.80, 30 minutes) and Sherborne (£3.20, 30 minutes).

vivid interiors combine sky blue, purple and shocking pink with fluffy cushions and snazzy modern art. But the best bit is the views; you can see both the beach out front and the harbour behind from all bedrooms.

Old Harbour View B&B ££
(☎01305-774633; www.oldharbourviewweymouth.co.uk; 12 Trinity Rd; s/d £80/98; P 🛜) In this pristine Georgian terrace you get boating themes in the fresh, white bedrooms, and boats right outside the front door. One room overlooks the busy quay, the other faces the back.

B+B B&B ££
(☎01305-761190; www.bb-weymouth.com; 68 The Esplanade; s £60-80, d £80-90; P 🛜) B+B delivers simple, streamlined rooms – some with sea views – and a first-floor lounge overlooking the bay that's stocked with guest laptop, daily newspapers, coffee and cookies. Nonnight-owls: note some of the front facing rooms can be noisy at night.

✖ Eating

Marlboro FISH & CHIPS £
(www.marlbororestaurant.co.uk; 46 St Thomas St; mains £7-13; ⊙11.30am-9.45pm) 🖉 A sustainable slant and a 40-year history help lift this traditional chippy, just metres from Weymouth's quay, above its rivals – mackerel features among the long list of super-fresh fish. Take it away and duck the seagulls or get munching in the bay-windowed, licensed cafe (open till 8pm).

★ Crustacean SEAFOOD ££
(☎01305-777222; www.crustaceanrestaurant.co.uk; 59 St Mary St; mains £12-29; ⊙noon-9pm Sun-Thu, to 9.30pm Fri & Sat) At Crustacean, you'll find an imaginative head chef with Sri Lankan heritage and a passion for French cuisine. Get cracking on a whole lobster, slurp some oysters, lunch on mussels laced with lemongrass, dine on pan-fried sea bass with a creamy saffron sauce. Or yield to temptation and go for the excellent-value three-course set menu (£25). Book.

Manbos BISTRO ££
(☎01305-839839; www.manbosbistro.com; 46 St Mary St; ⊙noon-2.30pm & 6-9pm Tue-Sat, 6-9pm Mon) No wonder the locals love Manbos: a cosy atmosphere, great service, good prices and flavoursome, homemade bistro dishes packed with local produce. Pasta and seafood are a speciality, expect fish chowder, steaming bowls of mussels and a zesty prawn pesto linguine.

ℹ Information

Weymouth's tourist information point has maps and brochures and is set inside the **Harbour Office** (www.visit-dorset.com; 13 Custom House Quay; ⊙7.30am-8pm).

ℹ Getting There & Away

BUS
An open-top bus 501 runs to Portland Bill, Isle of Portland, from late July to August (£2.40, 45 minutes, seven daily). Four buses also run there on Saturday and Sunday from April to late July and in September.

The Jurassic Coaster (bus X53, four daily to hourly, no service winter Sundays) travels west from Weymouth to Axminster (2½ hours), via Abbotsbury (35 minutes) and Lyme Regis (1¾ hours). A Day Rider ticket costs adult/child £12/6; shorter fares are available.

Other services include:
Dorchester (Bus 10; £2, 30 minutes, half-hourly)
Fortuneswell, Isle of Portland (Bus 1; £2, 20 minutes, three to four per hour)
London Victoria (National Express; £15, 4¼ hours, one direct daily)

TRAIN
Trains running at least hourly include the following direct services:
Bournemouth (£14, one hour)
Dorchester South (£5, 10 minutes)
London Waterloo (£40, three hours)
Direct services every two hours:
Bath (£20, two hours)
Bristol (£18, 2¾ hours)

Isle of Portland

The 'Isle' of Portland is a hard, high comma of rock fused to the rest of Dorset by the ridge of Chesil Beach. On its 150m central plateau, a quarrying past still holds sway, evidenced by huge craters and large slabs of limestone. Portland offers jaw-dropping views down on to 18-mile Chesil Beach and the neighbouring Fleet – Britain's biggest tidal lagoon.

Proud, and at times bleak and rough around the edges, Portland is decidedly different from the rest of Dorset, and is all the more compelling because of it. The Isle's industrial heritage, watersport facilities, rich bird life and starkly beautiful cliffs make it worth at least a day trip.

⊙ Sights

★ Tout Quarry
SCULPTURE

(near Fortuneswell; dawn-dusk; ⊙ 24hr; P) FREE
Portland's white limestone has been quarried for centuries and has been used in some of the world's finest buildings, such as the British Museum and St Paul's Cathedral. Tout Quarry's disused workings now house more than 50 sculptures that have been carved into the rock in situ, resulting in a fascinating combination of the raw material, the detritus of the quarrying process and the beauty of chiselled works.

Tout Quarry is signed off the main road, just south of Fortuneswell.

Portland Castle
CASTLE

(EH; ☐ 01305-820539; www.english-heritage.org.uk; Liberty Rd, Chiswell; adult/child £6.30/3.80; ⊙ 10am-6pm Apr-Sep, to 5pm Oct) A particularly fine product of Henry VIII's castle-building spree, with expansive views over Portland Harbour.

★ Portland Lighthouse
LIGHTHOUSE

(☐ 01305-821205; www.trinityhouse.co.uk; Portland Bill; adult/child £7/5; ⊙ 10am-5pm Sat-Thu Jun-Sep; P) For a real sense of Portland's remote nature, head to its southern tip, Portland Bill, to climb the 41m-high, candy-striped lighthouse. It offers breathtaking views of rugged cliffs and the Race, a surging vortex of conflicting tides. The interactive displays in the former lighthousekeepers' cottages include Into the Dark, a recreation of sailing into stormy seas.

The lighthouse is also open on some summer Fridays and some weekends outside the main season – call for the latest times.

☂ Activities

Andrew Simpson
Water Sports Centre
BOATING

(☐ 01305-457400; www.aswc.co.uk; Osprey Quay, Portland Harbour) Activities include Royal Yachting Association (RYA) sailing lessons (adult/child per two days £199/175). Look out for their £20 taster sessions.

OTC
WATER SPORTS

(Official Test Centre; ☐ 01305-230296; http://uk.otc-windsurf.com; Osprey Quay, Portland Harbour) Offers lessons in stand-up paddleboarding (SUP; one/two hours £25/40) and windsurfing (per two hours/one day/two days £49/99/199). It also rents out SUP boards (per hour £10) and windsurfing boards and sails (per hour £30).

⊨ Sleeping & Eating

Portland YHA
HOSTEL £

(☐ 03453 719339; www.yha.org.uk; Castle Rd, Castletown; dm £25, q £49-90; P ☎) Comfy, rambling Edwardian house with sea views from most dorms.

★ Queen Anne House
B&B ££

(☐ 01305-820028; www.queenannehouse.co.uk; 2 Fortuneswell; s/d £65/90; ☎) It's impossible to know which room to pick: White, with skylight, beams and a hobbit-esque door; Lotus, with its grand furniture; ornate Oyster with its half-tester bed; or Garden, a suite with a French bath and miniconservatory. It doesn't matter though – they're all great value and gorgeous.

★ Crab House Cafe
SEAFOOD ££

(☐ 01305-788867; www.crabhousecafe.co.uk; Ferrymans Way, Wyke Regis; mains £14-30; ⊙ noon-2.30pm & 6-9pm Wed-Sat, noon-3.30pm Sun) This is where the locals make for on hot summer days, to sit beside the Fleet Lagoon amid beach-shack-chic tucking into fresh-as-it-gets seafood. Fish is enlivened by chilli, curry, lemon and herbs; crab comes spicy Chinese-style or whole for you to crack; and the oysters come with either pesto and parmesan or bacon and cream. Book.

Cove House
PUB FOOD ££

(☐ 01305-820895; www.thecovehouseinn.co.uk; 91 Chiswell Seafront; mains £8-18; ⊙ kitchen noon-2.30pm & 6-9pm Mon-Fri, noon-9pm Sat & Sun) Extraordinary Chesil Beach views, memorable sunsets and great grub (try the Lyme Bay scallops) in a history-rich fishers' inn.

ⓘ Getting There & Away

Bus 1 runs from Weymouth to Fortuneswell (£2, 20 minutes, three to four per hour).

From late July to August the open-top 501 bus goes from Weymouth to Portland Bill (£2.40, 45 minutes, seven daily). Four buses also run on Saturday and Sunday from April to late July and in September.

Chesil Beach

One of the most breathtaking beaches in Britain, Chesil is 18 miles long, 15m high and moving inland at the rate of 5m a century. This mind-boggling, 100-million-tonne pebble ridge is the baby of the Jurassic Coast. A mere 6000 years old, its stones range from pea-sized in the west to hand-sized in the east.

⊙ Sights

Chesil Beach Centre
NATURE CENTER

(Fine Foundation; ☎01305-206191; www.dorset
wildlifetrust.org.uk; Ferrybridge; parking per hr £1;
⊙10am-5pm Easter-Sep, to 4pm Oct-Easter; 🅿)
FREE This centre at the start of the bridge to
Portland, is a great gateway to Chesil Beach.
The pebble ridge is at its highest here – 15m
compared to 7m at Abbotsbury. From the
car park an energy-sapping hike up sliding
pebbles leads to the constant surge and rattle of waves on stones and dazzling views of
the sea, with the thin pebble line and the expanse of the Fleet Lagoon behind.

★ Abbotsbury Swannery
WILDLIFE RESERVE

(☎01305-871130; www.abbotsbury-tourism.co.uk;
New Barn Rd, Abbotsbury; adult/child £12.50/9.50;
⊙10am-5pm late Mar–Oct) Every May some
600 free-flying swans choose to nest at this
swannery, which shelters in the Fleet Lagoon, protected by the ridge of Chesil Beach.
Wandering the network of trails that winds
between the swans' nests is an awe-inspiring
experience that's punctuated by occasional
territorial displays (snuffling coughs and
stand-up flapping), ensuring that even the
liveliest children are stilled.

The swannery is near the picturesque
village of Abbotsbury, 10 miles from Weymouth off the B3157.

Lyme Regis

POP 3637

Fantastically fossiliferous Lyme Regis packs
a heavyweight historical punch. Rock-hard
relics of the past pop out repeatedly from
the surrounding cliffs – exposed by the
landslides of a retreating shoreline. Lyme is
now a pivot point of the Unesco-listed Jurassic Coast: fossil fever is definitely in the
air and everyone, from proper palaeontolo-
gists to those out for a bit of fun, can engage
in a spot of coastal rummaging. Add sandy
beaches and some delightful places to sleep
and eat, and you get a charming base for
explorations.

⊙ Sights

Lyme Regis Museum
MUSEUM

(☎01297-443370; www.lymeregismuseum.co.uk;
Bridge St; adult/child £5/2.50; ⊙10am-5pm
Mon-Sat, to 4pm Sun Apr-Oct, 10am-4pm Wed-Sun
Nov-Mar) In 1814 local teenager Mary Anning
found the first full ichthyosaur skeleton near
Lyme Regis, propelling the town on to the
world stage. An incredibly famous fossilist
in her day, Miss Anning did much to pioneer the science of modern-day palaeontol-
ogy. This museum, on the site of her former
home, tells her story and exhibits spectacular fossils and other prehistoric finds.

The museum runs three to seven fossil-
hunting walks a week (adult/child £12/6),
with times dictated by the tides. It's best to
book.

Cobb
LANDMARK

First built in the 13th century, Lyme's iconic,
curling sea defences have been strengthened
and extended over the years, and so don't
present the elegant line they once did, but
it's still hard to resist wandering their length
to the tip.

Dinosaurland
MUSEUM

(☎01297-443541; www.dinosaurland.co.uk; Coombe St; adult/child £5/4; ⊙10am-4pm mid-Feb–
mid-Oct, winter hours vary) This joyful, mini, indoor Jurassic Park overflows with fossilised

---

FOSSIL HUNTING

Fossil fever is catching. Lyme Regis sits in one of the most unstable sections of Britain's
coast, and regular landslips mean nuggets of prehistory keep tumbling from the cliffs.

Joining a guided walk aids explorations. Three miles east of Lyme, the **Charmouth
Heritage Coast Centre** (☎01297-560772; www.charmouth.org; Lower Sea Lane, Charmouth; ⊙10.30am-4.30pm daily Easter-Oct, Fri-Mon Nov-Easter) FREE runs one to seven
trips a week (adult/child £8/4). Or, in Lyme itself, Lyme Regis Museum holds three to
seven walks a week (adult/child £12/6); local expert **Brandon Lennon** (☎07854 377519;
www.lymeregisfossilwalks.com; adult/child £9/7; ⊙Sat-Mon) also leads expeditions. All walks
are popular, so book early.

For the best chances of a find, visit within two hours of low water. If you do hunt by
yourself, official advice is to check tide times and collect on a falling tide, observe warning signs, keep away from cliffs, only pick up from the beach and always leave some
behind for others. Oh, and tell the experts if you find a stunner.

remains; look out for belemnites, a plesio-saurus and an impressive locally found ich-thyosaur. Lifelike dinosaur models will thrill youngsters – the rock-hard tyrannosaur eggs and 73kg dinosaur dung will have them in raptures.

Town Mill HISTORIC BUILDING
(☎01297-444042; www.townmill.org.uk; Mill Lane; requested donation £2.50; ◷11am-4pm Tue-Sun) An atmospheric, creaking, grinding, 14th-century working watermill. Cafes, art galleries, a jewellery workshop and micro-brewery sit alongside.

Winter hours vary; call to check.

🏃 Activities

★ Undercliff WALKING
This wildly undulating, 304-hectare na-ture reserve just west of Lyme was formed by massive landslides. They've left a chal-lenging hiking landscape of slipped cliffs, fissures and ridges, where paths snake be-tween dense vegetation, exposed tree roots and tangles of brambles. The Undercliff starts a mile west of central Lyme Regis; fol-low footpath signs from Holmbush Car Park.

🛏 Sleeping

Sanctuary B&B £
(☎01297-445815; www.lyme-regis.demon.co.uk; 65 Broad St; s/d £45/56) A B&B for biblio-philes: the charming, chintzy, volume-filled bedrooms here sit inside a four-floor, 18-room bookshop. Ancient tomes that just beg to be perused are everywhere – they can de-lay you en route to (the excellent) breakfast, but handily there's a wonderfully relaxed vibe. And yes – that price *is* right.

Coombe House B&B ££
(☎01297-443849; www.coombe-house.co.uk; 41 Coombe St; d £68-76; P) The airy, easygoing, stylish bedrooms in this fabulous-value guesthouse are full of bay windows, wicker and white wood. Breakfast is delivered to your room on a trolley, complete with home-made bread and a toaster – perfect for a lazy lie-in in Lyme.

★ Hix Townhouse B&B £££
(☎01297-442499; www.hixtownhouse.co.uk; 1 Pound St; s £125-135, d £135-165; 🛜) With its witty designer decor, luxury flourishes and in-town location, this 18th-century terrace is hard to resist. Each room playfully conjures a leisure theme (gardening, fishing, reading etc); the pick is Sailing with its mock port-

holes, artfully arranged ropes, mini roof ter-race and gorgeous sea views.

🍴 Eating

★ Alexandra BRITISH £
(☎01297-442010; www.hotelalexandra.co.uk; Pound St; afternoon tea £8-30; ◷3-5.30pm; P🛜) It's like the setting for an Agatha Christie mystery, minus the murder. Wicker chairs dot manicured lawns, glittering Lyme Bay sweeps out behind. The perfect spot for a proper English afternoon tea, complete with scones, jam and dainty sandwiches.

Harbour Inn PUB FOOD ££
(☎01297-442299; www.harbourinnlymeregis.co.uk; 23 Marine Pde; mains £11-19; ◷noon-2.30pm & 6-9pm, closed Sun eve Oct-Mar) A flower-framed, beachside verandah, smart but snug interi-or and some of the best bistro-pub grub in town – the bouillabaisse is suitably intense.

Millside MODERN BRITISH ££
(☎01297-445999; www.themillside.co.uk; 1 Mill Lane; mains £13-18; ◷noon-2.30pm Tue-Sun, 6.30-9pm Tue-Sat) West Country foodstuffs pack the menu in this stylish eatery, from juicy burgers topped with cheddar from Cheddar, to fish freshly caught on the local day boats. Millside's compact terrace makes a tempting spot for lunch on a sunny day.

★ Hix Oyster & Fish House SEAFOOD £££
(☎01297-446910; www.hixoysterandfishhouse.co.uk; Cobb Rd; mains £13-23; ◷noon-10pm, closed Mon & Tue Oct-Mar; 🅿) Expect sweeping views of the Cobb and dazzling food at this

superstylish, open-plan cabin. Lyme Bay shellfish soup comes with pastis liqueur; local mackerel and ling are infused with curry and piri piri heat. Perhaps start by slurping oysters: Brownsea Island or Portland molluscs come at £2.95 a pop.

ⓘ Information

Tourist Office (☏ 01297-442138; www.visit-dorset.com; Church St; ⏰ 10am-5pm Mon-Sat, 10am-4pm Sun Apr-Oct, 10am-3pm Mon-Sat Nov-Mar)

ⓘ Getting There & Away

Bus X51 (£4.80, 1¼ hours, hourly Monday to Saturday) shuttles to Dorchester.

Bus X53 (four daily to hourly, no service winter Sundays) goes east to Weymouth (£7.60) via Chesil Beach, and west to Axminster (£6), with regular connections on to Exeter from there.

Sherborne

POP 9581

Sherborne gleams with a mellow, orangey-yellow stone – it's been used to build a cluster of 15th-century buildings and the impressive abbey church at their core. This serene town exudes wealth.

◉ Sights

Sherborne Abbey CHURCH
(☏ 01935-812452; www.sherborneabbey.com; Abbey Cl; suggested donation £4; ⏰ 8am-6pm Apr-Sep, to 4pm Oct-Mar) At the height of its influence, the magnificent Abbey Church of St Mary the Virgin was the central cathedral of 26 succeeding Saxon bishops. Established early in the 8th century, it became a Benedictine abbey in 998 and functioned as a cathedral until 1075. The church has mesmerising fan vaulting that's the oldest in the country, a central tower supported by Saxon Norman piers and an 1180 Norman porch.

Sherborne Old Castle CASTLE
(EH; ☏ 01935-812730; www.english-heritage.org.uk; Castleton; adult/child £4.70/2.80; ⏰ 10am-5pm Apr-Jun, Sep & Oct, to 6pm Jul & Aug) These days the epitome of a picturesque ruin, Sherborne's Old Castle was built by Roger, Bishop of Salisbury, in 1120 – Elizabeth I gave it to her one-time favourite Sir Walter Raleigh in the late 16th century. It became a Royalist stronghold during the English Civil War, but Cromwell reduced it to rubble after a 16-day siege in 1645, leaving just the frac-

tured southwest gatehouse, great tower and north range.

Sherborne New Castle CASTLE
(☏ 01935-812072; www.sherbornecastle.com; New Rd; adult/child £12/free, gardens only £6.50/free; ⏰ 11am-5pm Tue-Thu, Sat & Sun Apr-Oct) Sir Walter Raleigh began building the impressive Sherborne New Castle in 1594, but only got as far as the central block before being imprisoned by James I. James promptly sold the castle to Sir John Digby who added the splendid wings you see today. In 1753 the grounds received a mega-makeover at the hands of landscape-gardener extraordinaire Capability Brown who added a massive lake and the 12-hectare waterside gardens.

🛌 Sleeping & Eating

★**Cumberland House** B&B ££
(☏ 01935-817554; www.bandbdorset.co.uk; Greenhill; d £80-85; ℗ 🛜) Artistry emanates from these history-rich rooms – bright scatter rugs sit on flagstone floors; lemon and oatmeal walls undulate between wonderfully wonky beams. Gourmet breakfasts include freshly squeezed orange juice, fresh fruit compote and homemade granola.

Stoneleigh Barn B&B ££
(☏ 01935-817258; www.stoneleighbarn.co.uk; North Wootton; s £80, d £90-100, f from £120; ℗ 🛜) Warm, weathered stone and extensive gardens ensure this 18th-century barn delights on the outside. Inside, exposed trusses frame spacious rooms named after their attractive colour schemes – choose from Lilac, Red or Blue.

Stoneleigh is some 2 miles southeast of Sherborne.

George PUB FOOD ££
(www.thegeorgesherborne.co.uk; 4 Higher Cheap St; mains £9-13; ⏰ noon-2.30pm & 6-9pm; 🛜) It's five centuries since Sherborne's oldest, cosiest inn pulled its first pint; today it signals its age with wooden settles polished smooth by countless behinds. The food is enduring pub grub fare: robust steaks, ham and egg, homemade puddings and a 'roast of the day'.

★**Green** MODERN BRITISH £££
(☏ 01935-813821; www.greenrestaurant.co.uk; 3 The Green; mains £16-25; ⏰ noon-2.30pm & 6.30-9.30pm Tue-Sat) In this affable, elegant eatery, the furniture is more chic than shabby and the food is pure West Country élan. Dorset goodies might include Dorset crab soup

with saffron aioli, or roast lamb made fragrant with wild garlic. For a great-value feed, plump for the cracking *menu du jour* (three courses £22).

ℹ️ Information

Tourist Office (☑ 01935-815341; www. visit-dorset.com; Digby Rd; ⊙ 9.30am-5pm Mon-Sat mid-Mar–Aug, to 4pm Sep-Nov, to 3pm Dec–mid-Mar)

ℹ️ Getting There & Away

BUS

Dorchester, via Cerne Abbas (Bus X11, £4.70, 1¼ hours, four to seven daily Monday to Saturday)

Yeovil (Bus 58, £2.50, 15 minutes, hourly Monday to Saturday)

TRAIN

Exeter (£18, 1¼ hours, hourly)
London Waterloo (£40, 2½ hours, hourly)
Salisbury (£14, 45 minutes, hourly)

Shaftesbury

Crowning a ridge of hogbacked hills and overlooking pastoral meadows, the agreeable market town of Shaftesbury circles around its medieval abbey ruins. A charismatic castle and a postcard-pretty, ancient street add to the town's appeal.

◉ Sights

Shaftesbury Abbey RUINS
(☑ 01747-852910; www.shaftesburyabbey.org.uk; Park Walk; adult/child £3/2.50; ⊙ 10am-5pm Apr-Oct) These hilltop ruins mark the site of what was England's largest and richest nunnery. It was founded in 888 by King Alfred the Great, and his daughter, Aethelgifu, was its first abbess. St Edward is thought to have been buried here, and King Knut died at the abbey in 1035. Most of the buildings were dismantled by Henry VIII, but you can wander the foundations and search out statuary and illuminated manuscripts in the museum.

Gold Hill STREET
The often-photographed, painfully steep, quaint cobbled slope, lined by chocolate-box cottages, that starred in a famous TV advert for Hovis bread.

Old Wardour Castle CASTLE
(EH; ☑ 01747-870487; www.english-heritage.org. uk; near Anstey; adult/child £5.40/3.20; ⊙ 10am-

6pm Apr-Sep, 10am-4pm Oct, 10am-4pm Sat & Sun Nov-Mar; P) Six-sided Old Wardour Castle was built around 1393 and suffered severe damage during the English Civil War, leaving these imposing remains. The views from the upper levels are fabulous while its grassy lawns make a fine spot for a picnic. It's 4 miles east of Shaftesbury.

🛏️ Sleeping & Eating

Number 5 B&B ££
(☑ 01747-228490; www.fivebimport.co.uk; 5 Bimport; d £90; P 🛜) The restoration of this Georgian town house has clearly been a labour of love: elegant fabrics and subtle colours meet bathrooms with tiled floors and slipper baths. The breakfast is rich in food from the local farmers market – walk off a bit of it on the two-minute stroll into town.

Fleur de Lys HOTEL £££
(☑ 01747-853717; www.lafleurdelys.co.uk; Bleke St; s £95-100, d £115-160 tr £170-180; P @ 🛜) In this bijou, delightfully romantic hotel soft lighting shines on satin throws and plump cushions, while minifridges, homemade biscuits and freshly ground coffee keep pamper levels high.

The **restaurant** (2/3courses £30/38; ⊙ 7-10pm Mon-Sat) is acclaimed.

Mitre PUB FOOD ££
(www.youngs.co.uk; 23 High St; mains £10-14; ⊙ 11am-3pm & 6-9pm Mon-Thu, noon-9pm Fri-Sun) It's the decked terrace that'll draw you into this old inn – its cracking views out over Blackmore Vale make for a memorable spot to tuck into salads and burgers or a duck egg with ham and chips.

ℹ️ Information

Tourist Office (☑ 01747-853514; www.shaftesburydorset.com; 8 Bell St; ⊙ 10am-4pm Mon-Sat)

ℹ️ Getting There & Away

Useful routes include bus 29 to Salisbury (£5, 1 hour, five daily Monday to Saturday).

WILTSHIRE

Wiltshire is rich in the reminders of ritual and packed with not-to-be-missed sights. Its verdant landscape is littered with more mysterious stone circles, processional avenues and ancient barrows than anywhere else in

Britain. It's a place that teases and tantalises the imagination – here you'll experience the prehistoric majesty of Stonehenge and the atmospheric stone ring at Avebury. Add the serene 800-year-old cathedral at Salisbury, the supremely stately homes at Stourhead and Longleat and the impossibly pretty village of Lacock, and you have a county crammed full of English charm waiting to be explored.

❶ Getting There & Around

BUS

Wiltshire's bus coverage can be patchy, especially in the northwest.

First (www.firstgroup.com) Serves west Wiltshire.

Salisbury Reds (www.salisburyreds.co.uk) Covers Salisbury and many rural areas; offers one-day Rover Tickets (adult/child £8.50/5.50) and seven-day passes (Salisbury area £14.50, network-wide £25).

Stagecoach (www.stagecoachbus.com) Provides services around Swindon and Salisbury.

TRAIN

Rail lines run from London Waterloo to Salisbury (£23, 1½ hours, at least hourly), and beyond to Exeter and Plymouth. Another line runs north to Bath (£11, one hour, hourly) and Bristol (£11, 1¼ hours, hourly).

Salisbury

POP 40,300

Centred on a majestic cathedral that's topped by the tallest spire in England, Salisbury makes an appealing Wiltshire base. It's been an important provincial city for more than a thousand years, and its streets form an architectural timeline ranging from medieval walls and half-timbered Tudor town houses to Georgian mansions and Victorian villas.

◎ Sights

★ **Salisbury Cathedral**　　CATHEDRAL
(☑ 01722-555120; www.salisburycathedral.org.uk; The Close; requested donation adult/child £7.50/3; ◷ 9am-5pm Mon-Sat, noon-4pm Sun) England is endowed with countless stunning churches, but few can hold a candle to the grandeur and sheer spectacle of 13th-century Salisbury Cathedral. This early English Gothic-style structure has an elaborate exterior decorated with pointed arches and flying buttresses, and a sombre, austere interior

designed to keep its congregation suitably pious. Its statuary and tombs are outstanding; don't miss the daily **tower tours** (adult/child £13.50/8.50; ◷ two to five daily, May-Sep) and the cathedral's original, 13th-century copy of the **Magna Carta** (◷ 9.30am-5pm Mon-Sat, noon-4pm Sun Apr-Oct, 9.30am-4.30pm Mon-Sat, noon-3.45pm Sun Nov-Mar).

The cathedral was built between 1220 and 1258. Beyond its highly decorative **West Front**, a small passageway leads into the 70m-long **nave**, lined with handsome pillars of Purbeck stone. In the north aisle look out for a fascinating **medieval clock** dating from 1386, probably the oldest working timepiece in the world. At the eastern end of the ambulatory the glorious **Prisoners of Conscience** stained-glass window (1980) hovers above the ornate **tomb** of Edward Seymour (1539–1621) and Lady Catherine Grey. Other monuments and tombs line the sides of the nave, including that of William Longespée, son of Henry II and half-brother of King John. When the tomb was excavated a well-preserved rat was found inside Longespée's skull.

Salisbury's 123m crowning glory, its **spire**, was added in the mid-14th century, and is the tallest in Britain. It represented an enormous technical challenge for its medieval builders; it weighs around 6500 tonnes and required an elaborate system of cross-bracing, scissor arches and supporting buttresses to keep it upright. Look closely and you'll see the additional weight has buckled the four central piers of the nave.

Sir Christopher Wren surveyed the cathedral in 1668 and calculated that the spire was leaning by 75cm. A brass plate in the floor of the nave is used to measure any shift, but no further lean was recorded in 1951 or 1970. Despite this, reinforcement of the notoriously 'wonky spire' continues to this day.

The cathedral really comes into its own during **evensong**, which takes place at 5.30pm Monday to Saturday and 4.30pm on Sunday, during term time only.

★ **Salisbury Museum**　　MUSEUM
(☑ 01722-332151; www.salisburymuseum.org.uk; 65 The Close; adult/child £8/4; ◷ 10am-5pm Mon-Sat year-round, plus noon-5pm Sun Jun-Sep) The hugely important archaeological finds here include the Stonehenge Archer, the bones of a man found in the ditch near the stone circle – one of the arrows found alongside probably killed him. With gold coins dating

Salisbury

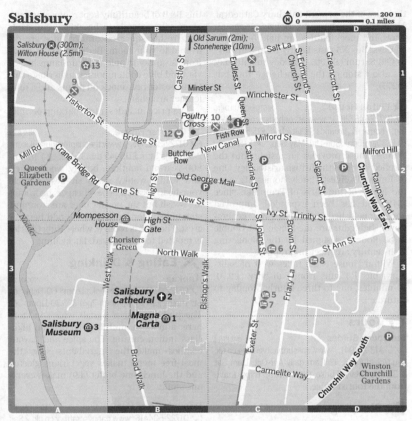

N ⬆ 0 ——— 200 m
0 ——— 0.1 miles

Salisbury

◉ Top Sights

1 Magna Carta	B4
2 Salisbury Cathedral	B3
3 Salisbury Museum	A4

✦ Activities, Courses & Tours

Salisbury Cathedral Tower Tours	(see 2)
4 Salisbury Guides	C2

🛏 Sleeping

5 Cathedral View	C3
6 Chapter House	C3
7 Spire House	C3
8 St Ann's House	D3

🍴 Eating

9 Anokaa	A1
10 Charter 1227	C2
11 Danny's Craft Bar	C1

🍷 Drinking & Nightlife

12 Haunch of Venison	B2

✪ Entertainment

13 Salisbury Playhouse	A1

from 100 BC and a Bronze Age gold necklace, it's a powerful introduction to Wiltshire's prehistory.

Old Sarum   ARCHAEOLOGICAL SITE
(EH; ☎ 01722-335398; www.english-heritage.org.uk; Castle Rd; adult/child £5.20/3.10; ⊙ 10am-6pm Mar-Sep, to 5pm Oct, to 4pm Nov-Mar; 🅿) The huge ramparts of Old Sarum sit on a grass-covered hill 2 miles north of Salisbury. You can wander the grassy ramparts, see the original cathedral's stone foundations, and look across the Wiltshire countryside to

the spire of the present Salisbury Cathedral. Medieval tournaments, jousts, open-air plays and mock battles are held on selected days. Bus X5 runs hourly from Salisbury to Old Sarum (£2.30), Monday to Saturday. It's also a stop on the Stonehenge Tour bus (p275).

★ **Wilton House** HISTORIC BUILDING
(☑ 01722-746728; www.wiltonhouse.com; Wilton; house & grounds adult/child £15.50/13.25; ⊘ 11.30am-5pm Sun-Thu May-Sep; ℗) Stately Wilton House provides an insight into the rarefied world of the British aristocracy. One of England's finest stately homes, it's been the house of the earls of Pembroke since 1542, and has been expanded, improved and embellished by successive generations. Highlights are the Single and Double Cube Rooms, designed by the pioneering 17th-century architect Inigo Jones.

Wilton House is 2.5 miles west of Salisbury; bus R3 runs from Salisbury (£2.70, 10 minutes, one to three hourly Monday to Saturday).

⏱ Tours

Salisbury Guides WALKING
(☑ 07873-212941; www.salisburycityguides.co.uk; adult/child £6/3; ⊘ 11am daily Apr-Oct, 11am Sat & Sun Nov-Mar) These 90-minute trips leave from the tourist office.

🛏 Sleeping

St Ann's House B&B ££
(☑ 01722-335657; www.stannshouse.co.uk; 32 St Ann St; s £64, d £89-110; ☞) Utter elegance reigns at 18th century St Ann's where cast iron fireplaces, mini-chandeliers and sash windows cosy up to warm colours and well-chosen antiques. Breakfast goodies include locally baked bread and homemade orange and star anise marmalade.

Cathedral View B&B ££
(☑ 01722-502254; www.cathedral-viewbandb.co.uk; 83 Exeter St; s £85-95, d £99-140; ℗☞) Admirable attention to detail defines this Georgian town house, where miniature flower displays and home-baked biscuits sit in quietly elegant rooms. Breakfasts include prime Wiltshire sausages and the B&B's own bread and jam, while homemade lemon drizzle cake will be waiting for your afternoon tea.

Spire House B&B ££
(☑ 01722-339213; www.salisbury-bedandbreakfast. com; 84 Exeter St; s/d/tr £65/80/95; ℗☞) In this B&B of beautifully kept rooms, the easy-going vibe extends to breakfast: croissants and freshly squeezed orange juice are delivered to your room. Bedroom styles range from a quirky tripple (tea cup lampshades) via vivid blue contemporary, to heritage chic (four-poster bed, mock oil paints and a mini leather armchair).

The price includes a free parking permit.

★ **Chapter House** INN £££
(☑ 01722-341277; www.thechapterhouseuk.com; 9 St Johns St; s £115-145 d £135-155; ☞) In this 800-year-old boutique beauty, wood panels and wildly wonky stairs sit beside duck-your-head beams. The cheaper bedrooms are swish but the posher ones are stunning, starring slipper baths and the odd heraldic crest. The pick is room 6, where King Charles is reputed to have stayed. Lucky him.

🍴 Eating & Drinking

Anokaa INDIAN ££
(☑ 01722-414142; www.anokaa.com; 60 Fisherton St; mains £14-19; ⊘ noon-2pm & 5.30-11pm; ☞) The pink-neon sign signals what's in store here: a modern, multilayered take on high-class Indian cuisine. The spice and flavour combos make the ingredients sing, the meat-free menu makes vegetarians gleeful, and the lunchtime buffet (£9) makes everyone smile.

Danny's Craft Bar AMERICAN ££
(☑ 01722-504416; www.dannyscraftbar.co.uk; 2 Salt Lane; burgers £7-13; ⊘ 5-9pm Mon-Thu, noon-9pm Fri, 9am-9pm Sat, 9am-5pm Sun; ☞☞) It's tempting to eat at this hip hang-out throughout the day: breakfast on chorizo and avocado tortilla, syrup-drenched pancakes or cheesy beans. Come evening, craft beer and cocktails usher in towering burgers and hand-cut fries. It's Tex-Mex, fun and cool.

Veggie options include a thick-sliced mushroom and halloumi sandwich, and there's occasional comedy and live music.

Charter 1227 BRITISH £££
(☑ 01722-333118; www.charter1227.co.uk; 6 Ox Row, Market Pl; mains £15-30; ⊘ noon-2.30pm & 6-9.30pm Tue-Sat) Ingredients that speak of classic English dishes have a firm foothold here – feast on duck confit, beef fillet or roast lamb; the cooking and presentation are assured. Canny locals eat at lunchtime or between 6pm and 7pm Tuesday to Thursday, when mains are capped at £10 to £15.

Haunch of Venison   PUB
(www.haunchpub.co.uk; 1 Minster St; ⊘11am-11pm
Mon-Sat, to 6pm Sun) Featuring wood-panelled
snugs, spiral staircases and crooked ceilings,
this 14th-century drinking den is packed
with atmosphere – and ghosts. One is a
cheating whist player whose hand was sev-
ered in a game – look out for his mummified
bones on display inside.

☆ Entertainment

Salisbury Playhouse   THEATRE
(Wiltshire Creative; ☑01722-320333; www.salis
buryplayhouse.com; Malthouse Lane) An acclaimed producing theatre that also hosts
top touring shows and musicals.

It's merged with the Salisbury Arts Centre
and International Arts Festival to form Wiltshire Creative.

❶ Information

Tourist Office (☑01722-342860; www.
visitsalisbury.co.uk; Fish Row; ⊘9am-5pm
Mon-Fri, 10am-4pm Sat, 10am-2pm Sun; ☎)

❶ Getting There & Away

BUS
National Express (www.nationalexpress.com)
services stop at Millstream Approach, near the
train station. Direct services include:
Bath (£11, 1¼ hours, one daily)
Bristol (£6, 2¼ hours, one daily)
London Victoria via Heathrow (£10, three
hours, three daily Monday to Saturday)

Local services leave from stops around the town;
they include the following:
Devizes (bus 2; £6, one hour, hourly Monday
to Saturday)
Shaftesbury (bus 29; £5, one hour, five daily
Monday to Saturday)
Stonehenge (☑01202-338420; www.
thestonehengetour.info; adult/child/family
£30/20/90) Tour buses leave Salisbury train
station regularly.

TRAIN
Salisbury's train station is half a mile northwest
of the cathedral. Half-hourly connections in-
clude the following:
Bath (£10, one hour)
Bradford-on-Avon (£14, 40 minutes)
Bristol (£16, 1¼ hours)
London Waterloo (£42, 1½ hours)
Southampton (£10, 40 minutes)
  Hourly connections:
Exeter (£20, two hours)
Portsmouth (£20, 1¼ hours)

Stonehenge

Welcome to Britain's most iconic archaeological site. This compelling ring of mono-
lithic stones has been attracting a steady
stream of pilgrims, poets and philosophers
for the last 5000 years and is still a mystical,
ethereal place – a haunting echo from Britain's forgotten past, and a reminder of those
who once walked the ceremonial avenues
across Salisbury Plain.

◉ Sights

★**Stonehenge**   ARCHAEOLOGICAL SITE
(EH; ☑0370 333 1181; www.english-heritage.org.
uk; near Amesbury; adult/child same-day tickets £19.50/11.70, advance booking £17.50/10.50;
⊘9am-8pm Jun-Aug, 9.30am-7pm Apr, May &
Sep, 9.30am-5pm Oct-Mar; ℗) An ultramodern makeover at ancient Stonehenge has
brought an impressive visitor centre and the
closure of an intrusive road (now restored
to grassland). The result is a strong sense of
historical context, with dignity and mystery
returned to an archaeological gem.

A pathway frames the ring of massive
stones. Although you can't walk in the circle, unless on a recommended Stone Circle
Access Visit (p277), you can get fairly close.
Admission is through timed tickets – secure
a place well in advance.

Stonehenge is one of Britain's great archaeological mysteries: despite countless theories
about the site's purpose, from a sacrificial
centre to a celestial timepiece, no one knows
for sure what drove prehistoric Britons to ex-
pend so much time and effort on its construction, although recent archaeological findings
show the surrounding area was sacred for
hundreds of years before work began.

The first phase of building started around
3000 BC, when the outer circular bank and
ditch were erected. A thousand years later,
an inner circle of granite stones, known

❶ TICKETS FOR STONEHENGE
Stonehenge operates by timed tickets, meaning if you want to guarantee your entry you have to book in advance – even English Heritage and National Trust members entitled to free admission. If you're planning a peak-season visit, it's best to secure your ticket well in advance.

as bluestones, was added. It's thought that these mammoth 4-tonne blocks were hauled from the Preseli Mountains in South Wales, some 250 miles away – an extraordinary feat for Stone Age people equipped with only the simplest of tools. Although no one is entirely sure how the builders transported the stones so far, it's thought they probably used a system of ropes, sledges and rollers fashioned from tree trunks – Salisbury Plain was still covered by forest during Stonehenge's construction.

Around 1500 BC, Stonehenge's main stones were dragged to the site, erected in a circle and crowned by massive lintels to make the trilithons (two vertical stones topped by a horizontal one). The sarsen (sandstone) stones were cut from an extremely hard rock found on the Marlborough Downs, 20 miles from the site. It's estimated that dragging one of these 50-tonne stones across the countryside would require about 600 people.

Also around this time, the bluestones from 500 years earlier were rearranged as an inner **bluestone horseshoe** with an **altar stone** at the centre. Outside this the **trilithon horseshoe** of five massive sets of stones was erected. Three of these are intact; the other two have just a single upright. Then came the major **sarsen circle** of 30 massive vertical stones, of which 17 uprights and six lintels remain.

Much further out, another circle was delineated by the 58 Aubrey Holes, named after John Aubrey, who discovered them in the 1600s. Just inside this circle are the **South** and **North Barrows**, each originally topped by a stone. Like many stone circles in Britain (including Avebury, 22 miles away), the inner horseshoes are aligned to coincide with sunrise at the midsummer solstice, which some claim supports the theory that the site was some kind of astronomical calendar.

Prehistoric pilgrims would have entered the site via the **Avenue**, whose entrance to

Stonehenge

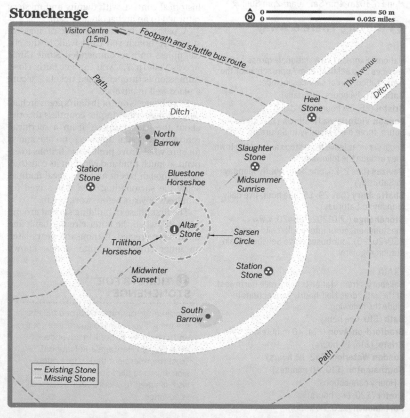

0   50 m
0   0.025 miles

Visitor Centre (1.5mi)
Footpath and shuttle bus route
Path
The Avenue
Ditch
Heel Stone
Ditch
North Barrow
Slaughter Stone
Station Stone
Bluestone Horseshoe
Midsummer Sunrise
Altar Stone
Sarsen Circle
Trilithon Horseshoe
Midwinter Sunset
Station Stone
South Barrow
Path

Existing Stone
Missing Stone

STONEHENGE'S RITUAL LANDSCAPE

Stonehenge actually forms part of a huge complex of ancient monuments.

North of Stonehenge and running roughly east–west is the Cursus, an elongated embanked oval; the smaller Lesser Cursus is nearby. Theories abound as to what these sites were used for, ranging from ancient sporting arenas to processional avenues for the dead. Two clusters of burial mounds, the Old and New Kings Barrows, sit beside the ceremonial pathway the Avenue, which originally linked Stonehenge with the River Avon, 2 miles away.

The National Trust (www.nationaltrust.org.uk) website has a downloadable 3.5-mile circular walk (search for A Kings View) that traces tracks across the chalk downland from Stonehenge, past the Cursus and Kings Barrows and along a section of the Avenue itself.

The Stonehenge visitor centre (p277) also has leaflets detailing walking routes.

the circle is marked by the Slaughter Stone and the Heel Stone, located slightly further out on one side.

Long-term plans to move the main A303 road, which runs close to the site, into a tunnel are still being debated. The proposed tunnel aims to reduce traffic around Stonehenge, although some commentators fear it could damage other, as yet undiscovered, monuments in the area.

The last admission to Stonehenge is two hours before closure. Visiting the site is free for English Heritage and National Trust members, but they still have to secure a timed ticket.

★ **Visitor Centre** MUSEUM
(EH; ☑ 0370 333 1181; www.english-heritage. org.uk; incl access to Stonehenge, adult/child same-day tickets £19.50/11.70, advance booking £17.50/10.50; ⊙ 9am-8pm Jun-Aug, 9.30am-7pm Apr, May & Sep, 9.30am-5pm Oct-Mar) The highlight here is a 360-degree projection of Stonehenge through the ages and seasons – complete with midsummer sunrise and swirling star-scape. Engaging audiovisual displays detail the transportation of the stones and the building stages, while 300 finds include flint chippings, bone pins and arrowheads. There's also a strikingly lifelike model of the face of a Neolithic man whose body was found nearby. Outside you can step into recreations of Stone Age houses and watch rope-making and flint-knapping demonstrations.

☞ Tours

★ **Stone Circle Access Visits** WALKING
(☑ 0370 333 0605; www.english-heritage.org.uk; adult/child £38.50/23.10) Visitors normally have to stay outside the stone circle itself, but on these hour-long, self-guided walks,

you get to wander around the heart of the archaeological site, getting up-close views of the iconic bluestones and trilithons. Tours take place in the evening or early morning, when the quieter atmosphere and slanting sunlight add to the effect. Each visit only takes 30 people; book at least three months in advance.

Salisbury Guided Tours HISTORY
(☑ 07775 674816; www.salisburyguidedtours.com; per person from £64) Runs a wide range of expert-led trips to Stonehenge, the wider ritual landscape and Salisbury.

❶ Getting There & Away

No regular buses go to the site.

The Stonehenge Tour (p275) leaves Salisbury's railway station half-hourly from June to August, and hourly between September and May. The ticket includes admission to Stonehenge and the Iron Age hill fort at Old Sarum (p273); it stops there on the return leg.

Longleat

★ **Longleat** ZOO
(☑ 01985-844400; www.longleat.co.uk; near Warminster; all-inclusive ticket adult/child £35/26, house & grounds £19/14; ⊙ 10am-5pm Feb–mid-Oct, to 7pm late Jul & Aug; ℗) Half ancestral mansion, half wildlife park, Longleat was transformed into Britain's first safari park in 1966, turning Capability Brown's landscaped grounds into an amazing drive-through zoo populated by a menagerie of animals more at home in the African wilderness than the fields of Wiltshire. There's a throng of attractions, too: the historic house, animatronic dinosaur exhibits, narrow-gauge railway, mazes, pets' corner, butterfly garden and bat cave.

DON'T MISS

STOURHEAD

Overflowing with vistas, temples and follies, **Stourhead** (NT; ☑ 01747-841152; www.nationaltrust.org.uk; Mere; adult/child £16.60/8.30; ⊘ 11am-4.30pm early Mar–early Nov, to 3.30pm early Nov–late-Dec; Ⓟ) is landscape gardening at its finest. The Palladian house has some fine Chippendale furniture and paintings by Claude and Gaspard Poussin, but it's a sideshow to the magnificent 18th-century gardens (open 9am to 5pm), which spread out across the valley.

A picturesque 2-mile garden circuit takes you past the most ornate follies, around the lake and to the Temple of Apollo; a 3.5-mile side trip can be made from near the Pantheon to King Alfred's Tower, a 50m-high folly with wonderful views.

Stourhead is off the B3092, 8 miles south of Frome.

Longleat was the first English stately home to open its doors to the public. That decision was prompted by finance: heavy taxes and mounting post-WWII bills meant the house had to earn its keep.

The house itself contains fine tapestries, furniture and decorated ceilings, as well as seven libraries containing around 40,000 tomes. The highlight, though, is an extraordinary series of paintings and psychedelic murals by the present-day marquess, who was an art student in the '60s and upholds the long-standing tradition of eccentricity among the English aristocracy – check out his website (www.lordbath.co.uk).

Longleat is open until 7pm on many summer weekends. It's just off the A362, 3 miles from Frome. Save around 10% by booking tickets online.

Lacock

POP 1159

With its geranium-covered cottages and higgledy-piggledy rooftops, pockets of the medieval village of Lacock seem to have been preserved in mid-19th-century aspic. The village has been in the hands of the National Trust since 1944, and in many places is remarkably free of modern development – there are no telephone poles or electric street lights and the main car park on the outskirts keeps it relatively traffic-free. Unsurprisingly, it's a popular location for costume dramas and feature films – the village and its abbey pop up in the Harry Potter films, *Downton Abbey*, *The Other Boleyn Girl* and BBC adaptations of *Wolf Hall*, *Moll Flanders* and *Pride and Prejudice*.

◉ Sights

Lacock Abbey   ABBEY

(NT; ☑ 01249-730459; www.nationaltrust.org.uk; Hither Way; adult/child £13.40/6.70; ⊘ 10.30am-5.30pm Mar-Oct, 11am-4pm Nov-Feb) Lacock Abbey is a window into a medieval world. Founded as an Augustinian nunnery in the 13th century, its deeply atmospheric rooms and stunning Gothic entrance hall are lined with bizarre terracotta figures; spot the scapegoat with a lump of sugar on its nose. Some of the original structure is evident in the cloisters and there are traces of medieval wall paintings, too.

Fox Talbot Museum   MUSEUM

(NT; ☑ 01249-730459; www.nationaltrust.org.uk; Hither Way; adult/child £13.40/6.70; ⊘ 10.30am-5.30pm Mar-Oct, 11am-4pm Nov-Feb) William Henry Fox Talbot (1800–77) pioneered the photographic negative. A prolific inventor, he began developing the system in 1834 while working at Lacock Abbey. The museum, located within the abbey (p278), details his groundbreaking work and displays a superb collection of his images.

Entry is included with admission to the abbey.

🛏 Sleeping & Eating

★ **Sign of the Angel**   INN **££**

(☑ 01249-730230; www.signoftheangel.co.uk; 6 Church St; s £110, d £110-140; Ⓟ 🛜) Every inch of this gorgeous, 15th-century restaurant-with-rooms is rich in heritage pizazz. Burnished beams, slanting floors and open fires meet duck-down duvets, upcycled furniture and neutral tones, delivering a fresh provincial rustic feel. Treats include luxury toiletries, chef-baked cookies and a free glass of prosecco (if you book one of the swisher rooms).

Pear Tree   INN **££**

(☑ 01225-704966; www.peartreewhitley.co.uk; Top Lane, Whitley; d £125-150, q £150; Ⓟ 🛜) It takes a lot of skill to make rooms look so beautifully casual and yet so smart – the bedrooms here are a mash-up of mullioned windows, worn wooden chairs, waterfall showers and framed cartoons. Rooms in the ancient inn have more heritage features, ones in the converted barn have a sleeker feel. It's 4 miles southwest of Lacock.

The restaurant (mains £14 to £18) is famous for its terrace, beamed sunroom and inventive dishes crammed with kitchen garden produce. Food is served from noon to 2.30pm and 6pm to 9pm.

Red Lion INN ££
(☎01249-730456; www.redlionlacock.co.uk; 1 High St; d £105-120; P 📶) In historic Lacock, where better to sleep than a Georgian coaching inn that oozes ambience. Step on flagstone floors past open fires, up a grand staircase to sweet rooms where padded cushions line stone window frames with picture-postcard views. The food's notable too (mains from £14, served noon to 8pm).

King John's Hunting Lodge CAFE £
(☎01249-730313; 21 Church St; snacks from £5; ⏰11am-5pm Wed-Sun Feb–mid-Dec; P) Afternoon tea is a must at Lacock's oldest building, where a cosy, beam-lined room and a peaceful garden set the scene for dainty china, light lunches and tasty cakes.

Avebury & Around

POP 530

While the tour buses head straight for Stonehenge, prehistoric purists make for the massive stone circle at Avebury. Though it lacks the dramatic trilithons of its sister site across Salisbury Plain, Avebury is just as rewarding to visit. It's bigger and older, and a large section of the village is actually inside the stones – footpaths wind around them, allowing you to really soak up the extraordinary atmosphere. Avebury also boasts an encircling landscape that's rich in prehistoric sites and a manor house where restored rooms span five completely different eras.

Sights

★**Avebury Stone Circle** ARCHAEOLOGICAL SITE
(NT; ☎01672-539250; www.nationaltrust.org.uk; ⏰24hr; P) FREE With a diameter of 348m, Avebury is the largest stone circle in the world. It's also one of the oldest, dating from 2500 to 2200 BC. Today, more than 30 stones are in place; pillars show where missing stones would have been. Wandering between them emphasises the site's sheer scale, evidenced also by the massive bank and ditch that line the circle; the quieter northwest sector is particularly atmospheric. National Trust–run guided walks (£3) are held on most days.

Avebury henge originally consisted of an outer circle of 98 standing stones of up to 6m in length, many weighing 20 tonnes. The stones were surrounded by another circle delineated by a 5m-high earth bank and a ditch up to 9m deep. Inside were smaller stone circles to the north (27 stones) and south (29 stones).

In the Middle Ages, when Britain's pagan past was an embarrassment to the Church, many of the stones were buried, removed or broken up. In 1934 wealthy businessman and archaeologist Alexander Keiller supervised the re-erection of the stones; he later bought the site for posterity using funds from his family's marmalade fortune.

Modern roads into Avebury neatly dissect the circle into four sectors. Starting at High St near the **Henge Shop** (☎01672-539229; www.hengeshop.com; High St; ⏰9.30am-5pm) and walking round the circle in an anticlockwise direction, you'll encounter 11 standing stones in the southwest sector. They include the **Barber Surgeon Stone**, named after the skeleton of a man found under it – the equipment buried with him suggests he was a barber-cum-surgeon.

The southeast sector starts with huge **portal stones** marking the entry to the circle from **West Kennet Ave**. The **southern inner circle** stood in this sector and within this ring was the **obelisk** and a group of stones known as the **Z Feature**. Just outside this smaller circle, only the base of the **Ring Stone** survives.

In the **northern inner circle** in the northeast sector, three sarsens remain of what would have been a rectangular **cove**. The northwest sector has the most complete collection of standing stones, including the massive 65-tonne **Swindon Stone**, one of the few never to have been toppled.

★**Avebury Manor** HISTORIC BUILDING
(NT; ☎01672-539250; www.nationaltrust.org.uk; adult/child £10.50/5.25; ⏰11am-5pm Apr-Oct, to 4pm mid-Feb–Mar, 11am-4pm Thu-Sun Nov & Dec) The mother of all makeovers at this 16th-century manor house used original techniques and materials to recreate interiors spanning five periods. Being hands-on is encouraged here, so now you can sit on beds, play billiards and listen to the gramophone in rooms that range from Tudor, through Georgian to the 1930s. Visits are by timed ticket only; arrive early to bag a slot.

Avebury

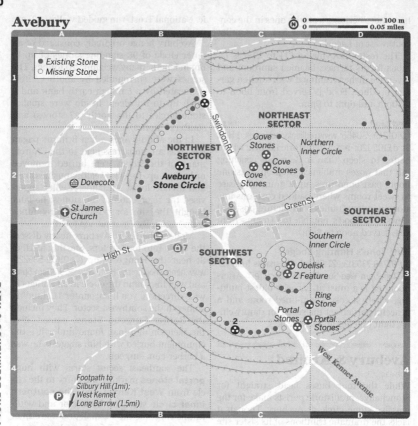

Avebury

◎ Top Sights
1 Avebury Stone Circle	B2

◎ Sights
2 Barber Surgeon Stone	C4
3 Swindon Stone	B1

🛏 Sleeping
4 Avebury Lodge	B2
5 Manor Farm	B3

🍸 Drinking & Nightlife
6 Red Lion	C2

🛍 Shopping
7 Henge Shop	B3

Silbury Hill ARCHAEOLOGICAL SITE
(EH; www.english-heritage.org.uk; near Avebury; Ⓟ) FREE Rising abruptly from the fields just south of Avebury, 40m-high Silbury Hill is the largest artificial earthwork in Europe, comparable in height and volume to the Egyptian pyramids. It was built in stages from around 2500 BC, but the precise reason for its construction remains unclear. Direct access to the hill isn't allowed, but you can view it from nearby footpaths and a layby on the A4.

West Kennet
Long Barrow ARCHAEOLOGICAL SITE
(EH; ☎ 0370 333 1181; www.english-heritage.org. uk; ⊗ dawn-dusk) FREE England's finest burial mound dates from around 3500 BC. Its entrance is guarded by huge sarsens and its roof is made out of gigantic overlapping capstones. About 50 skeletons were found when it was excavated; finds are on display at the Wiltshire Heritage Museum in Devizes. The barrow is a half-mile walk across fields from the parking layby.

A footpath also leads from Avebury Stone Circle to West Kennet (2 miles), passing the vast earthwork of Silbury Hill en route.

🛏 Sleeping & Eating

★Manor Farm   B&B **££**
(☑01672-539294; www.manorfarmavebury.com;
High St; s/d £90/100; Pဇ) A rare chance to
sleep in style inside a stone circle – this red-
brick farmhouse snuggles just inside Avebury henge. The elegant, comfy rooms blend
old woods with bright furnishings, while
the windows provide spine-tingling views of
those 4000-year-old standing stones.

Avebury Lodge   B&B **£££**
(☑01672-539023; www.aveburylodge.co.uk; High
St; s/d/tr £155/195/250; Pဇ) It's as if gentle-
manly archaeologists are still in situ: antiquarian prints of stone circles smother the
walls, pelmets and chandeliers are dotted
around. And whenever you glance from a
window, a bit of Avebury henge appears. It's
lovely, but a bit pricey – it's the location that
pushes the room rates up here.

Red Lion   PUB
(www.oldenglishinns.co.uk; High St; ⊙11am-
11pm) Having a pint here means downing a
drink at the only pub in the world inside a
stone circle. The best table is the Well Seat
where the glass tabletop covers a 26m-deep,
17th-century well – believed to be the last
resting place of at least one unfortunate vil-
lager.

ℹ Getting There & Away

Bus 49 runs hourly to Swindon (£3, 30 minutes)
and Devizes (£3, 15 minutes). There are six services on Sunday.

EXMOOR NATIONAL PARK

Exmoor is more than a little addictive,
and chances are you won't want to leave
its broad, russet views. In the middle sits
the higher moor, an empty, expansive, other-worldly landscape of tawny grasses and
huge skies. Here, picturesque Exford makes
an ideal village base. In the north, sheer,
rock-strewn river valleys cut into the plateau
and coal-black cliffs lurch towards the sea.

Amid these towering headlands, charismatic Porlock and the twin villages of Lynton and Lynmouth are atmospheric places
to stay. Relaxed Dulverton delivers a coun-
try-town vibe, while appealing Dunster
has cobbled streets and a russet-red castle.
Everywhere on Exmoor life is attuned to the
rhythms and colours of the seasons – new-
born livestock in spring, purple heather in
late summer, gold-bronze leaves in autumn,
and crisp days and log fires in winter. All
this ensures Exmoor delivers insights into
an elemental and traditional world.

🏃 Activities

★Exmoor Adventures   OUTDOORS
(☑07976 208279; www.exmooradventures.co.uk)
Runs sessions in kayaking and canoeing
(£35/70 per half/full day), mountain biking
(from £40 per half day), coasteering (£35)
and rock climbing (£65); caters to skill levels ranging from beginner to advanced. Also
rents mountain bikes (£25 per day).

Cycling

Despite (or perhaps because of) the formidable hills, cycling is hugely popular on Exmoor. Several sections of the National Cycle
Network (NCN; www.sustrans.org.uk) cross
the park, including the West Country Way
(NCN Route 3) from Bristol to Padstow, and
Devon Coast to Coast (NCN Route 27), between Ilfracombe and Plymouth, via Dartmoor and Exmoor.

Exmoor is also one of the county's most
exhilarating off-road cycling destinations,
with a wealth of bridleways and permitted
tracks. The Exmoor National Park Authority
has produced a colour-coded off-road cycle
map (£10); buy it at tourist offices.

Exmoor Adventures (p281) runs a five-
hour mountain-biking skills course (£60)
and also rents mountain bikes (£25 per day).

Pompys   CYCLING
(☑01643-704077; www.pompyscycles.co.uk; Mart
Rd, Minehead; per day £18; ⊙9am-5pm Mon-Sat)
Bike sales and hire.

Pony Trekking & Horse Riding

Exmoor is prime riding country, with stables
offering pony and horse treks from around
£30 to £46 for a two-hour ride.

Brendon Manor   HORSE RIDING
(☑01598-741246; www.brendonmanor.com) Runs
a full range of horse-riding trips, from one to
three hours, that head onto the open moor
and down into the valleys. Prices start at
£26. Based near Lynton.

Burrowhayes Farm   HORSE RIDING
(☑01643-862463; www.burrowhayes.co.uk; per hr
£25; ⊙Apr–mid-Oct) Based near Porlock, Burrowhayes runs a wide range of treks that go
into the Horner Valley and onto the moor.

Plus special half-hour pony rides for children (£14).

Outovercott Stables HORSE RIDING
(☑ 01598-753341; www.outovercott.co.uk; per hr £30) Outovercott's treks onto Exmoor's exposed moorland range from one-hour trips for novices to more-challenging excursions for intermediate and experienced riders, which take in views of the Valley of Rocks and the coastline.

Walking

The open moors and a profusion of marked bridleways make Exmoor an excellent area for hiking. The best-known routes are the Somerset & North Devon Coast Path, which is part of the South West Coast Path (www.southwestcoastpath.org.uk), and the Exmoor section of the Two Moors Way, which starts in Lynmouth and travels south to Dartmoor and beyond.

Another superb route is the Coleridge Way (www.coleridgeway.co.uk), which winds for 51 miles through Exmoor, the Brendon Hills and the Quantocks. Part of the 180-mile Tarka Trail cuts through the park: join it at Combe Martin, hike along the cliffs to Lynton and Lynmouth, then head across the moor towards Barnstaple.

Organised walks run by the national park authority (www.exmoor-nationalpark. gov.uk) are held throughout the year and include deer safaris, nightjar birdwatching walks and dark-sky strolls.

ⓘ Information

Active Exmoor (www.visit-exmoor.co.uk/active-exmoor)

Exmoor National Park (www.exmoor-national park.gov.uk)
Lonely Planet (www.lonelyplanet.com) Destination information, hotel bookings, traveller forum and more.
Visit Exmoor (www.visit-exmoor.co.uk) The official visitor website.

There are three tourist offices run by the Exmoor National Park Authority, in **Dulverton** (☑ 01398-323841; www.visit-exmoor.co.uk; 7-9 Fore St; ⏱ 10am-5pm Apr-Oct, reduced hours Oct-Apr), **Dunster** (☑ 01643-821835; www.visit-exmoor.co.uk; Dunster Steep; ⏱ 10am-5pm Apr-Oct, reduced hours Oct-Apr) and Lynmouth (p287).

The Exmoor National Park Authority (ENPA; www.exmoor-nationalpark.gov.uk) regulates the park.

ⓘ Getting Around

Exmoor isn't that easy to get around without your own vehicle. But with some planning and patience it is possible to travel between many of the moor's main towns and villages by bus.

Dulverton

POP 1500
The southern gateway to Exmoor National Park, Dulverton sits at the base of the Barle Valley near the confluence of two key rivers: the Exe and Barle. A traditional country town, it's home to a collection of gun sellers, fishing-tackle stores and gift shops, and makes an attractive edge-of-moor base.

Exmoor's most famous landmark, is the Tarr Steps, an ancient stone clapper bridge shaded by gnarled old trees. Its huge slabs are propped up on stone columns embedded in the River Barle. Local folklore aside

Exmoor National Park

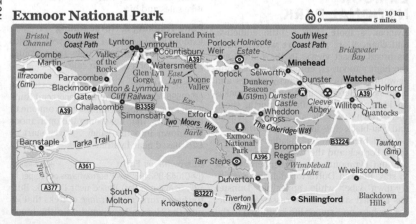

RED DEER SAFARIS

Exmoor supports one of England's largest wild red deer populations, best experienced in autumn when the annual 'rutting' season sees stags bellowing, charging at each other and clashing horns in an attempt to impress prospective mates.

The Exmoor National Park Authority (ENPA; www.exmoor-nationalpark.gov.uk) runs regular wildlife-themed guided walks (free), which include evening deer-spotting hikes. Or head out on an organised jeep safari to combine scenic sightseeing with a couple of hours of off-road wildlife-watching.

Barle Valley Safaris (☑ 07977 571494; www.exmoorwildlifesafaris.co.uk; adult/child £35/25; ⊙ tours at 9.30am & 2pm) Runs half-day 4WD wildlife-watching safaris onto the moor. Trips leave from Dulverton, Dunster, Exford and Wheddon Cross.

Discovery Safaris (☑ 01643-863444; www.discoverysafaris.com; per person £25; ⊙ tours at 10.30am & 2pm) These twice-daily jeep safaris set off from Porlock and head up onto open moorland searching for wildlife, especially Exmoor's famous red deer.

Johnny Kingdom Safaris (www.johnnykingdom.co.uk; per 4 people £100) Monthly, four-hour tours with a TV wildlife presenter and photographer. They leave from South Molton at around 8am and are popular – book well ahead.

(which declares it was used by the Devil for sunbathing), it first pops into the historical record in the 1600s, and had to be rebuilt after 21st-century floods. The steps are signed off the B3223 Dulverton–Simonsbath road, 5 miles northwest of Dulverton.

🛏 Sleeping & Eating

★**Streamcombe Farm**　　　　B&B **££**
(☑ 01398-323775; www.streamcombefarm.co.uk; Streamcombe Lane, near Dulverton; s £60-75, d £75-100; 🅿🛜) In this enchanting 18th-century farmhouse, stylish, rustic-chic bedrooms feature chimney breasts and reclaimed joists, and the only sounds are the sheep, deer and pheasants outside. Or snuggle into the bijou but beautiful two-person shepherd's hut (£85), complete with BBQ and log-burning stove.

Town Mills　　　　B&B **££**
(☑ 01398-323124; www.townmillsdulverton.co.uk; 1 High St; s/d/ste £95/105/140; 🅿🛜) The top choice in Dulverton town itself is a thoroughly contemporary riverside mill with creamy carpets, magnolia-coloured walls and bursts of floral art.

Tarr Farm　　　　HOTEL **£££**
(☑ 01643-851507; www.tarrfarm.co.uk; Tarr Steps; s/d £80/160; 🅿🛜) This is the place to really lose yourself: a charming farmhouse nestled among the woods near Tarr Steps, 7 miles from Dulverton. The nine contemporary bedrooms are spacious and luxurious, with spoil-yourself extras such as organic bath goodies and homemade biscuits. The farm is also renowned for its food.

All-comers are welcome: walkers and families arrive for cream teas (served from 11am to 5pm) and hearty lunches, while after-dark diners sample more formal country fare, such as crab rarebit and braised lamb (mains £15 to £24). Meals are served 11am to 2.30pm and 6.30pm to 9.30pm.

★**Woods**　　　　BISTRO **££**
(☑ 01398-324007; www.woodsdulverton.co.uk; 4 Bank Sq; mains £15-19; ⊙ noon-2pm & 7-9.30pm) With its deer antlers, hunting prints and big wood-burning stove, multi-award-winning Woods is Exmoor to its core. No surprise then to find menus with full-bodied flavours: expect confit leg of guinea fowl, slow-roast lamb shoulder, and asparagus and wild garlic risotto. Book ahead.

The bar menu (£7 to £13, served between 6pm and 9.30pm) is simpler stuff – think steak, omelette Arnold Bennett (a fluffy omelette with smoked haddock), lamburgers, and fish and chips.

Mortimers　　　　CAFE **£**
(☑ 01398-323850; 13 High St; mains from £9; ⊙ 9.30am-5pm Thu-Tue; 🛜) Chunky wooden tables and exposed brick defy traditional tearoom expectations; the menu is surprising, too. Expect homemade 'moo burgers' (beef sandwiched between brioche buns) and unusual rarebits – options for cheese-on-toast here include goats cheese or brie with added beer or Somerset cider.

Dunster

POP 820

Centred on a scarlet-walled castle and a medieval yarn market, Dunster is one of Exmoor's oldest villages, a tempting tangle of cobbled streets, bubbling brooks and packhorse bridges.

◉ Sights

★ **Dunster Castle** CASTLE

(NT; ☎ 01643-823004; www.nationaltrust.org. uk; Castle Hill; adult/child £11.60/5.80; ☉ 11am-5pm Mar-Oct; 🅿) Rosy-hued Dunster Castle crowns a densely wooded hill. Built by the Luttrell family, which once owned much of northern Exmoor, the oldest sections are 13th century, while the turrets and exterior walls are 19th-century additions. Look out for Tudor furnishings, 17th-century plasterwork and a ridiculously grand staircase. Leave time to explore the colourful terraced gardens, which feature riverside walks, a working watermill and views across Exmoor's shores.

Watermill HISTORIC BUILDING

(NT; ☎ 01643-821759; www.nationaltrust.org.uk; Mill Lane; ☉ 11am-5pm) Most of the original cogs, wheels and grinding stones continue to rotate in this working 18th-century mill. There's a picturesque riverside tearoom alongside and you can buy the mill's organic stoneground flour in the shop.

Admission to the mill is included in tickets to neighbouring Dunster Castle.

🛏 Sleeping & Eating

Dunster Castle Hotel HOTEL ££

(☎ 01643-823030; www.thedunstercastlehotel.co. uk; 5 High St; d £90-175; 🛜) Everything feels rich in this former coaching inn, from the ruby-red furnishings and tapestry-esque fabrics to the heraldic-style throws. The menu features quality pub-food classics and top-notch sweets, the chocolate and pistachio brownie is a treat. Food (mains £11 to £24) is served from 8am to 11am, noon to 2.30pm and 5.30pm to 8pm.

Millstream Cottage B&B ££

(☎ 01643-821966; www.millstreamcottagedunster.co.uk; 2 Mill Lane; s £65, d £79-89) In the 1600s this was Dunster's workhouse; now it's a sweet-as-pie guesthouse with country-cottage-style rooms. Enjoy a cream tea on arrival, smoked haddock for breakfast and

an oh-so-comfy guest lounge where you can snooze in front of the wood burner.

Luttrell Arms HISTORIC HOTEL £££

(☎ 01643-821555; www.luttrellarms.co.uk; High St; r £150-220; 🅿🛜) You almost need a ladder to climb up to the high four-poster bed in the feature room at this exquisite old coaching inn. In medieval times, this was the guesthouse of the Abbots of Cleeve. Even the standard rooms are gorgeous; expect a plethora of brass plates, beams and a plaster fireplace or two.

★ **Reeve's** BRITISH £££

(☎ 01643-821414; www.reevesrestaurantdunster.co.uk; 20 High St; mains £20-30; ☉ 7-9pm Tue-Sat, noon-2pm Sun) The eponymous chef at seriously stylish Reeve's is an award winner. No wonder: the complex creations here truly showcase Exmoor produce. Opt for lemon sole with a tangy lobster bisque, or meltingly tender lamb roasted with rosemary and garlic. To finish? Perhaps some toasted walnut bread with local hard and soft cheeses.

❶ Getting There & Away

Bus 198 runs north to Minehead (£2) and south to Dulverton (£4, 1¼ hours, two to three daily, Monday to Saturday), via Wheddon Cross.

The 22-mile **West Somerset Railway** (☎ 01643-704996; www.west-somerset-railway.co.uk; 24hr rover tickets adult/child £20/10) stops at Dunster during summer, with four to seven trains daily from May to October.

Porlock & Around

The coastal village of Porlock is one of the prettiest on the Exmoor coast; the huddle of thatched cottages lining its main street is framed on one side by the sea and on the other by steeply sloping hills. Winding lanes lead to the charismatic breakwater of Porlock Weir, 2 miles to the west, with an arching pebble beach and striking coastal views.

◉ Sights

★ **Porlock Weir** HARBOUR

(🅿) Porlock Weir's stout granite quay curves around a shingly beach, which is backed by pubs, fisherfolks' storehouses and a scattering of seasonal shops. The weir has been around for almost a thousand years (it's named in the Domesday Book as 'Portloc'). It makes a glorious place for a pub lunch and a stroll, with stirring views across the

Vale of Porlock and easy access to the South West Coast Path.

Holnicote Estate
ARCHITECTURE

(NT; ☎01643-862452; www.nationaltrust.org.uk; near Porlock; P) FREE The 50-sq-km Holnicote Estate sweeps southeast out of Porlock, taking in a string of impossibly pretty villages. Picturesque Bossington leads to charming Allerford and its 15th-century packhorse bridge. The biggest village, Selworthy, offers eye-catching Exmoor views, a cafe, a shop, and cob-and-thatch cottages clustering around the village green.

🛏 Sleeping & Eating

Sea View
B&B ££

(☎01643-863456; www.seaviewporlock.co.uk; High Bank; s from £37, d £70-75; 🕏) Value-for-money Sea View has tiny rooms that are pleasantly packed with painted furniture, trinkets and oil paintings. Thoughtful extras include blister plasters and muscle soak for hikers tackling Porlock's precipitous hills.

Cottage
B&B ££

(☎01643-862996; www.cottageporlock.co.uk; High St; s/d/tr £45/£75/90; P🕏) Evidence of the Cottage's 18th-century origins remains – a big fireplace in the guest lounge, duck-your-head lintels and quirkily shaped bedrooms. The decor though is stylishly modern, with candy-striped cushions in rooms of earthy or aquamarine tones.

Ship Inn
PUB FOOD ££

(Top Ship; ☎01643-862507; www.shipinnporlock. co.uk; High St; mains £10-19; ⊙noon-2.30pm & 6-8.30pm; P) Romantic poet Samuel Taylor Coleridge and pal Robert Southey both downed pints in this 13th-century thatched Porlock inn – you can even sit in a snug still dubbed 'Southey's Corner'. Substantial pub food – mainly steaks, roasts and stews – is served in the bar.

Locanda On The Weir
ITALIAN ££

(☎01643-863300; www.locandaontheweir.co.uk; Porlock Weir; mains £10-24; ⊙7-9pm Wed-Sun, 12.30-2.30pm Sat & Sun, longer summer hours; P🕏🍴) The chef-proprietor hails from Italy so the dishes here are a happy fusion of Exmoor produce and flavours of the Med. Your pizza could come with gorgonzola and pear, the pasta with local beef and Tuscan tomatoes, while the fish might be *baccala' alla Livornese* (cod with capers, potatoes and olives).

ℹ Information

Tourist Office (☎01643-863150; www. porlock.co.uk; West End, Porlock; ⊙10am-5pm Mon-Sat Easter-Oct, to 12.30pm Mon-Sat Nov-Easter)

ℹ Getting There & Away

BUS

Bus 300 heads from Porlock east along the coast to Minehead (£6, 15 minutes), and west to Lynmouth (£10, 55 minutes). It runs from mid-July to early-September, with two buses a day, Monday to Friday only.

CAR

Drivers can choose from two picturesque routes into Porlock village. The New Rd toll road sweeps through pine forests and round U-bends, while Porlock Hill (A39) is a brake-burning 1:4 descent. A further toll road, the Porlock Scenic (Worthy) Toll Rd, provides an alternative, bouncing, route up out of Porlock Weir.

Lynton & Lynmouth

Tucked in amid precipitous cliffs and steep, tree-lined slopes, these twin coastal towns are a landscape-painter's dream. Bustling Lynmouth sits beside the shore, a busy harbour lined with pubs and souvenir shops.

STARGAZING ON EXMOOR

Exmoor holds the distinction of being named Europe's first International Dark Sky Reserve, in recognition of the nighttime inky blackness overhead. But what does that mean in practice? Namely, a whole host of local organisations striving to limit light pollution, plus, for visitors, some simply spectacular star displays.

The Exmoor National Park Authority (www.exmoor-nationalpark.gov.uk) runs occasional moonlit strolls and has produced the *Dark Skies Guide*, which includes star charts and maps pinpointing the best light-free spots. Pick one up at a visitor centre or download it from the authority's website. It also runs a **Dark Skies Festival** (☎01398-322236; www.exmoor-nationalpark.gov.uk; ⊙late Oct) and hires out suitable telescopes (£25 per night).

For optimum stargazing, central, higher Exmoor is best – try Brandon Two Gates (on the B3223) or Webber's Post (just north of Dunkery Beacon).

On the clifftop, Lynton feels much more genteel and well to do. A cliffside railway links the two: it's powered by the rushing West Lyn River, which feeds numerous cascades and waterfalls nearby.

◎ Sights

★ Cliff Railway
HERITAGE RAILWAY

(☑01598-753486; www.cliffrailwaylynton.co.uk; The Esplanade, Lynmouth; one-way/return adult £2.90/3.90, child £1.80/2.40; ⊙10am-5pm Feb, Mar & Oct, to 6pm Apr, May & Sep, to 7pm Jun-Aug) This extraordinary piece of Victorian engineering sees two cars, linked by a steel cable, descend and ascend the steeply sloping cliff face according to the weight of water in the cars' tanks. All burnished wood and polished brass, it's been running since 1890 and makes for an unmissable ride.

Flood Memorial
MUSEUM

(The Esplanade, Lynmouth; ⊙9am-6pm Easter-Oct) FREE On 16 August 1952 a huge wave of water swept through Lynmouth following torrential rain. The devastation was immense: 34 people lost their lives, and four bridges and countless houses were washed away. This exhibition features photos of the aftermath and personal testimonies of those involved.

🏃 Activities

Popular hiking trails amid Lynton and Lynmouth's spectacular scenery include those to the lighthouse at Foreland Point; to Watersmeet, 2 miles east of Lynmouth (reached via the gorgeous East Lyn river glade); and along the scenic Glen Lyn Gorge. The dramatic Valley of the Rocks (p286), just a mile west of Lynton along the coast path, is a real highlight.

★ Valley of the Rocks
WALKING

The dramatic geology in this valley was described by poet Robert Southey as 'rock reeling upon rock, stone piled upon stone, a huge terrifying reeling mass'. Look out for the formations dubbed the Devil's Cheesewring and Ragged Jack – and also the feral goats that wander the tracks. It's a mile's walk west of Lynton along a coast path that hugs steep cliffs.

🛏 Sleeping

Bath Hotel
HOTEL ££

(☑01598-752238; www.bathhotellynmouth.co.uk; The Harbour, Lynmouth; d £80-130; P 🐾 🛜) A pair of third-generation hoteliers are breathing fresh life into the Bath Hotel, a feature of the town since Victorian days. To a stylish cocktail bar add revamped bedrooms teaming gorgeously nautical styling and supremely comfortable beds with expansive harbour and headland views. Standard rooms are much, much less snazzy – but they're also £50 cheaper.

Lynn Valley
B&B ££

(☑01598-753300; www.lynvalleyguesthouse.com; Riverside Rd, Lynmouth; s from £60 d £80-110 q £150; 🛜) Walkers love this smart little guesthouse thanks to a setting right on the coast path, baths to soak in and the loan of flasks. Even if you're not hiking you'll like the crisp, bright decor, harbour views and mini-decanters of sherry in the rooms.

Rising Sun
INN £££

(☑01598-753223; www.risingsunlynmouth.co.uk; Harbourside, Lynmouth; d £160-190) What was a 14th-century smugglers' haunt has been transformed into an intimate hideaway with a sleek designer feel. Elegant flourishes are all around, from the subtle lighting and local art to the soft, tasteful throws. Ask for a seaview room to watch the tide rise and fall in the harbour just outside.

★ Old Rectory
HOTEL £££

(☑01598-763368; www.oldrectoryhotel.co.uk; Martinhoe; s £135-155 d £180-230 ste £230-260; P 🛜) This romantic hotel delivers beautifully in terms of style. Boutique bedrooms are supremely plush, with elegant baths, silky fabrics and luxury toiletries; the gardens are a tranquil, flower-filled delight. The hotel's chefs cook up own-grown produce for the restaurant. It's all tucked away in the village of Martinhoe, 6 miles west of Lynton.

🍴 Eating

★ Charlie Friday's
CAFE £

(☑07544 123324; www.charliefridays.co.uk; Church Hill, Lynton; snacks from £4; ⊙10am-6pm Apr-Oct, reduced hours winter; 🛜 🍴 ♿ 🌳) A funky, friendly hang-out serving melt-in-your-mouth pastries, thick sarnies, tasty nachos and fair-trade two-shot espresso that really packs a punch. The cafe's guitar, knitting and board games help keep the atmosphere set to chilled.

★ Ancient Mariner
PUB FOOD ££

(☑01598-752238; www.bathhotellynmouth.co.uk; The Harbour, Lynmouth; mains £12-19; ⊙noon-3pm & 6-9pm; 🛜) The Mariner brings a burst of shipwreck chic to Lynmouth, thanks to a copper bar top, curved ship's decking and a figurehead that isn't entirely clothed. Drink it all in while tucking into a stacked-high Mariner Burger, complete with Exmoor ale and black-treacle-braised brisket, onion jam and blue-cheese mousse.

★ **Rising Sun**   MODERN BRITISH **££**
(☑01598-753223; www.risingsunlynmouth.co.uk; Harbourside, Lynmouth; 2/3 courses £30/39; ⊙noon-2.30pm & 6-9pm) At the harbourside Rising Sun, they delight in showcasing not only Exmoor meat and veg but also the seafood landed on this rugged shore. Seasonal treats might include succulent lobster, fresh sea bass and local mussels, all served up with confidence and more than a dash of élan. Booking advised.

ⓘ Information

Lynmouth Tourist Office (☑01598-752509; www.visit-exmoor.co.uk; The Esplanade, Lynmouth; ⊙10am-5pm) An Exmoor National Park Authority visitor centre.

Lynton Tourist Office (☑0845 458 3775; www.lynton-lynmouth-tourism.co.uk; Lynton Town Hall, Lee Rd, Lynton; ⊙10am-5pm Mon-Sat, to 2pm Sun Apr-Oct, 10am-3pm Tue-Thu Nov-Mar)

DEVON

Devon offers freedom. Its rippling, beach-fringed landscape is studded with historic homes, vibrant cities and wild, wild moors. Here you can ditch schedules and to-do lists and hike a rugged coast path, take a scenic boat trip, or get lost in hedge-lined lanes that aren't even on your map.

Discover collegiate Exeter, touristy Torquay, yachting-haven Dartmouth and alternative Totnes. Or escape to wilderness Dartmoor and the remote, surf-dashed north coast. To replenish your energy, you can sample wines made from the vines beside you and food that's fresh from field, furrow or sea. However you decide to explore Devon – surfing, cycling, kayaking, horse riding, sea swimming or barefoot beachcombing – it'll feel like coming home.

ⓘ Information

Visit Devon (www.visitdevon.co.uk) The official tourism website.

ⓘ Getting Around

BUS

Most bus services between larger towns and villages are now run by Stagecoach (www.stage coachbus.com), with a number of smaller coach companies offering infrequent services to other areas. Dartmoor is poorly served by buses; you'll need a car or bike to access its more remote areas.

There are several bus passes available: the **Devon Day Ticket** (adult/child/family £9.30/6.20/18.60) covers all companies, while the **Stagecoach South West Explorer** (adult/child/family £8.30/5.50/16.60) and **South West Megarider Gold** tickets (one week £30) only cover Stagecoach buses. Check the Stagecoach website for details.

Traveline South West (www.travelinesw.com) is a great online tool for travel planning, while the **Devon interactive bus map** (https://new.devon.gov.uk/travel) provides a useful visual map of bus routes.

TRAIN

Devon's main line skirts southern Dartmoor, running from Exeter to Plymouth and on to Cornwall. Branch lines include the 39-mile Exeter–Barnstaple Tarka Line, the 15-mile Plymouth–Gunnislake Tamar Valley Line and the scenic Exeter–Torquay Paignton line. There are also several lovely steam railways including Dartmouth Steam Railway (p296), Bodmin & Wenford Railway (p343) and South Devon Steam Railway (p299).

The **Freedom of Devon & Cornwall Rover** ticket (three days travel in seven days adult/child £49/24.50, eight days travel in 15 £79/39.50) is good value if you're using the train extensively.

Exeter

POP 117,800

Well-heeled and comfortable, Exeter exudes evidence of its centuries-old role as the spiritual and administrative heart of Devon. The city's Gothic cathedral presides over pockets of cobbled streets; medieval and Georgian buildings and fragments of the Roman city stretch out all around. A snazzy contemporary shopping centre brings bursts of the modern; thousands of university students ensure a buzzing nightlife; and the vibrant quayside acts as a launch pad for cycling or kayaking trips. Throw in some stylish places to stay and eat, and you have a relaxed but lively base for explorations.

History

Exeter's past can be read in its buildings. The Romans marched in around AD 55; their 17-hectare fortress included a 2-mile defensive wall, crumbling sections of which

Exeter

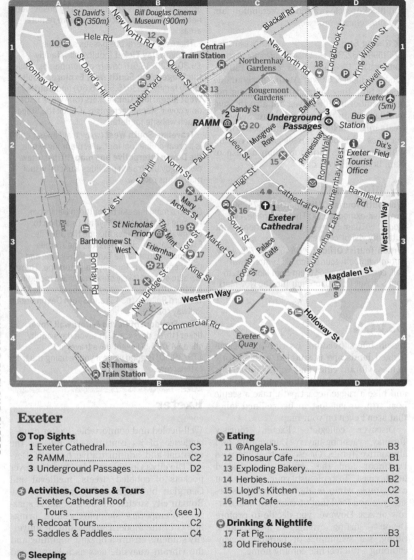

Exeter

⊙ Top Sights

⊕ Activities, Courses & Tours

⊜ Sleeping

⊗ Eating

⊜ Drinking & Nightlife

⊕ Entertainment

remain, especially in Rougemont and Northernhay Gardens. Saxon and Norman times saw growth: a castle went up in 1068, the cathedral 40 years later. The Tudor wool boom brought Exeter an export trade, riches and half-timbered houses; prosperity continued into the Georgian era, when hundreds of merchants built genteel homes. The Blitz of WWII brought devastation; in just one night in 1942, 156 people died and 12 hectares of the city were flattened. In the 21st century, the £220-million Princesshay Shopping Centre added shimmering glass and steel lines to the architectural mix. But 2016 brought a devastating fire at the Royal Clarence Hotel – a much-loved 18th-century building in the heart of Cathedral Yard. At time of writing, plans were being discussed to rebuild the hotel and restore its iconic facade.

◉ Sights

★ **Exeter Cathedral**   CATHEDRAL
(Cathedral Church of St Peter; ☑ 01392- 285983; www.exeter-cathedral.org.uk; The Close; adult/child £7.50/free; ☺ 9am-5pm Mon-Sat, 11.30am-5pm Sun) Magnificent in warm, honey-coloured stone, Exeter's cathedral is one of Devon's most impressive ecclesiastical sights. Dating largely from the 12th and 13th centuries, the **west front** is framed by extraordinary medieval statuary, while inside the ceiling soars upwards to the longest span of unbroken Gothic vaulting in the world, dotted with ornate ceiling bosses in gilt and vibrant colours. Look out for the scale Lego model that's being built beside the main entrance; for £1 you can add a brick.

The site has been a religious one since at least the 5th century, but the Normans started the current building in 1114; the towers of today's cathedral date from that period. In 1270 a 90-year remodelling process began, introducing a mix of Early English and Decorated Gothic styles.

Above the **Great West Front** scores of weather-worn figures line a once brightly painted screen that now forms England's largest collection of 14th-century sculpture. Inside, the exquisitely symmetrical ceiling soars up and along, towards the north transept and the 15th-century **Exeter Clock**: in keeping with medieval astronomy, the clock shows Earth as a golden ball at the centre of the universe with the sun, a fleur-de-lys, travelling around it. Still ticking and whirring, it chimes on the hour.

The huge oak canopy over the **Bishop's Throne** was carved in 1312. The 1350 **minstrels' gallery** is decorated with 12 angels playing musical instruments. Cathedral staff will point out the famous sculpture of the lady with two left feet and the tiny **St James Chapel**, built to repair the one destroyed in the Blitz. Look out for the chapel's unusual carvings: a cat, a mouse and, oddly, a rugby player.

There are free informative **guided tours** of the cathedral every day included in the admission price, or you can DIY with one of the free audio guides. But for the most dramatic perspective you really need to head up into one of the towers and drink in the views. Roof tours (p289) run on Tuesdays and Saturdays (you can book in advance online). There's a minimum age of eight.

Choral **evensong** services are held at 5.30pm from Monday to Friday, and 4pm on Saturday and Sunday.

★ **RAMM**   MUSEUM
(Royal Albert Memorial Museum & Art Gallery; ☑ 01392-265858; www.rammuseum.org.uk; Queen St; ☺ 10am-5pm Tue-Sun; ☎) **FREE** A fixture on the city's cultural scene since Victorian times, this hulking red-brick museum recently received a £24 million revamp. It's a treasure trove of rambling rooms, filled with glass cases of curiosities and archaeological finds – from samurai armour, African masks and Egyptian mummies in the World Cultures galleries to a truly amazing echinoderm collection of starfish and sea urchins amassed by the inveterate Victorian collector Walter Percy Sladen. Exeter's own history also figures strongly.

★ **Underground Passages**   TUNNEL
(☑ 01392-665887; www.exeter.gov.uk/passages; 2 Paris St; adult/child £6/4; ☺ 9.30am-5.30pm Mon-Sat, 10.30am-4pm Sun Jun-Sep, 10.30am-4.30pm Tue-Fri, 9.30am-5.30pm Sat, 11.30am-4pm Sun Oct-May) Prepare to crouch down, don a hard hat and possibly get spooked in what is the only publicly accessible system of its kind in England. These medieval vaulted

---

LOCAL KNOWLEDGE

CATHEDRAL ROOF TOURS

Don't miss the chance to climb up one of Exeter Cathedral's towers for panoramic views over the city's **rooftops** (☑ 01392-285983; www.exeter-cathedral. org.uk; incl Exeter Cathedral admission adult/child £13/5; ☺ 2pm Tue, 10.30am Sat Jul-Sep). Quite a lot of steps are involved (251 to be precise), and there's a minimum visitor age of eight. You can book online, which is highly recommended as places are limited.

BATH & SOUTHWEST ENGLAND EXETER

passages were built to house pipes bringing fresh water to the city. Guides lead you on a scramble through the network, relating tales of ghosts, escape routes and cholera. The last tour is an hour before closing; they're popular – book ahead.

Bill Douglas Cinema Museum MUSEUM
(☎01392-724321; www.bdcmuseum.org.uk; Old Library, Prince of Wales Rd; ⏲10am-5pm; P) FREE This eccentric museum is a must for cinephiles. It contains a hoard of film-themed memorabilia amassed by Scottish film-maker Bill Douglas, best known for his semi-autobiographical trilogy about his childhood. Douglas was also an avid collector, amassing more than 50,000 cinematic collectables: magic lanterns, peep shows, original celluloid from Disney films, Charlie Chaplin bottle stoppers, James Bond board games, vintage film posters, *Star Wars* toys and more. It's on the Exeter University campus, a mile northwest of the city centre.

Powderham Castle HISTORIC BUILDING
(☎01626-890243; www.powderham.co.uk; adult/child £12.95/10.95; ⏲11am-4.30pm Sun-Fri Apr-Jun, Sep & Oct, to 5.30pm Jul & Aug; P) The historic home of the Earl of Devon, Powderham is a stately but still friendly place built in 1391 and remodelled in the Victorian era. A visit takes in a fine wood-panelled Great Hall, parkland with 650 deer and glimpses of life 'below stairs' in the kitchen. Powderham is on the River Exe near Kenton, 8 miles south of Exeter.

Activities

Saddles & Paddles OUTDOORS
(☎01392-424241; www.sadpad.com; Exeter Quay; ⏲9am-6pm) This hire shop by the quay rents out bikes (adult per hour/day £7/18), single and double kayaks (£12/45) and Canadian canoes (£18/60), and offers advice on suggested routes.

Tours

★**Redcoat Tours** WALKING
(☎01392-265203; www.exeter.gov.uk/leisure-and-culture) FREE These informative, free 1½-hour tours explore different periods of the city's history (Roman, Tudor, Georgian), with fun options like evening ghost walks and torchlit expeditions through the catacombs. Most leave from Cathedral Green; a few in summer depart from Exeter Quay.

There are at least a couple of tours per day, even in winter; there's no need to book.

Sleeping

Globe Backpackers HOSTEL £
(☎01392-215521; www.exeterbackpackers.co.uk; 71 Holloway St; dm/d £17.50/45; ⏲reception 8.30am-noon & 3.30-11pm; P 📶) Rightly a firm favourite among budget travellers, this spotlessly clean, relaxed, rambling former town house boasts three doubles, roomy dorms and six shared wet-room showers. There's a pleasant lounge, a rather undersized kitchen, free wi-fi and lockers for storage.

★**Telstar** B&B ££
(☎01392-272466; www.telstar-hotel.co.uk; 77 St David's Hill; s £35-50, d £60-85, f £85-105; P 📶) 'Victoriana with a twist' best defines this excellent B&B, where stately fireplaces meet mock-flock wallpaper and stag heads wearing aviator goggles. Rooms team a heritage feel with modern comforts; bathrooms feature 19th-century-style tiles. If you like outdoors space, request the double with its own roomy deck.

Silversprings APARTMENT ££
(☎01392-494040; www.silversprings.co.uk; 12 Richmond Rd; 1/2 bedroom apt per night £85/100; P 📶) There are so many reasons to make these serviced apartments your Exeter pied-à-terre. Tucked away off a square a short walk from the city centre, they each come with a lounge and minikitchen, plus home comforts such as a DVD player and satellite TV. Furnishings are fabulous, with plush fabrics and sleek designs.

★**Hotel du Vin Exeter** BOUTIQUE HOTEL £££
(☎01392-790120; www.hotelduvin.com/locations/exeter; Magdalen St; r £105-195; @ 📶 🏊) This grand red-brick edifice (once Exeter's eye hospital) is now part of the plush Hotel du Vin chain. Quietly stylish rooms incorporate aspects of the building's Victorian architecture (bay windows, cornicing, wood floors) into their palette of muted colours, offbeat wallpapers and Scandi-style sofas. There's a stylish octagon-shaped restaurant, an excellent bar and a sleek spa.

Headweir Mill House B&B £££
(☎01392-210869; www.headweir-house.co.uk; Bonhay Rd; d £110-150; P 📶) Overlooking the banks of the River Exe (and busy Bonhay Rd), this house has more than two centuries of history, not that you'd guess from the 11 contemporary rooms: spacious and elegant in greys, taupes, slatted wood and stripes, all seamlessly blended with the house's period

WORTH A TRIP

RIVER COTTAGE CANTEEN

Known for his media campaigns on sustainability and organic food, TV chef Hugh Fearnley-Whittingstall broadcasts most of his TV shows from his home base at River Cottage HQ (☑ 01297-630300; www.rivercottage.net; Trinity Hill Rd, Axminster; 2-course lunch £55, 4-course dinner £70), near Axminster, 30 miles from Exeter. If you fancy seeing where the magic happens, you can book in for a sumptuous four-course meal, made with produce from Hugh's own garden, or attend one of the regular cooking courses. A cheaper option is to dine at his canteen (☑ 01297-631715; www.rivercottage.net; Trinity Sq, Axminster; mains £7-18; ⊙ 9am-5pm Sun-Tue, to 11pm Wed-Sat; ☑) in Axminster village nearby.

features. Ask for one with a bay window and river view.

Eating

⭐ Exploding Bakery   CAFE £
(☑ 01392-427900; www.explodingbakery.com; 1b Central Cres, Queen St; snacks £2.50; ⊙ 8am-4pm Mon-Fri, 9am-4pm Sat; 🛜) Excellent news: one of Exeter's hippest little bakeries has now added half-a-dozen tables, meaning there's even more room to sample superb flat whites, macchiato and inventive cakes – the lemon, polenta and pistachio is a hit.

Plant Cafe   VEGETARIAN £
(1 Cathedral Yard; mains £6-9; ⊙ 8.30am-5pm Mon-Sat; 🛜 ☑) Seats are at a premium at this casually cool wholefood cafe. That'll be down to its prime spot overlooking Cathedral Green and its imaginative frittata, pies and salads. When it's sunny you can sit outside.

Dinosaur Cafe   MIDDLE EASTERN £
(☑ 01392-490951; 5 New North Rd; mains £6-8; ⊙ 10am-9pm Mon-Sat) In this cheery Turkish mezze bar, lemon-yellow walls and chunky wooden furniture set the scene for tasty couscous, kofta and spicy *mücver* fritters. The Turkish breakfasts (eggs, pepperoni and feta) are a welcome change from the norm.

Herbies   VEGETARIAN ££
(☑ 01392-258473; 15 North St; mains £7-14; ⊙ 11am-2.30pm Mon-Sat, 6.30-9.30pm Tue-Sat; ☑) Herbies has been cheerfully feeding Exeter's vegetarians and vegans for more than 20 years. Expect the old classics here: Greek vegetable pie, mushroom and butternut-squash risotto or Moroccan tagine.

Lloyd's Kitchen   BISTRO ££
(☑ 01392-499333; www.lloydskitchen.co.uk; 16 Catherine St; mains lunch £6.95-11.95, dinner £14-22; ⊙ 9am-3pm Mon-Thu, 9am-3pm & 6.30-9.30pm Fri & Sat, 10am-3pm Sun) Squeezed in among the city-centre chains is this independent diner run by energetic owner Lloyd. With its sliding-glass frontage, bare bulbs, tiles and banquettes, it's a lovely space, and food-wise, it's classic and comforting: frittatas, open sandwiches, burgers, salads and 'British classics' by day; by night, corn-fed chicken, confit duck and steaks (Fridays and Saturdays only). Breakfasts are copious.

@Angela's   MODERN BRITISH £££
(☑ 01392-499038; www.angelasrestaurant.co.uk; 38 New Bridge St; mains £17-32; ⊙ 6-9pm Wed-Sat) One of the most well-known of Exeter's fine-dining restaurants, good for formal, French-inspired dishes served in a starchy, white-tablecloth setting. Expect rich things like roast duck, aged Aberdeen Angus beef and steamed turbot, heavy on cream, sauce or red-wine jus.

🍷 Drinking & Nightlife

⭐ Fat Pig   MICROBREWERY
(☑ 01392-437217; www.fatpig-exeter.co.uk; 2 John St; ⊙ 5-11pm Mon-Fri, noon-11pm Sat, noon-5pm Sun) There are few better spots for a pint in town than this fine craft brewery, which makes its own ales and brews its own gin, vodka and more 'experimental' spirits. It's a pleasant space, with quirky decor and fixtures, divided between a main bar and a small conservatory. Bar meals are good too, especially the Sunday roast.

Old Firehouse   PUB
(☑ 01392-277279; www.oldfirehouseexeter.co.uk; 50 New North Rd; ⊙ noon-2am Mon-Wed, to 3am Thu-Sat, to 1am Sun) Step into the snug, candlelit interior of this Exeter institution and instantly feel at home. Dried hops hang from rafters above flagstone floors and walls of exposed stone. The range of draught ciders and cask ales is truly impressive, while the pizzas, served after 9pm, have kept countless students fed.

Beer Engine   MICROBREWERY
(☎01392-851282; www.thebeerengine.co.uk; Newton St Cyres; mains £12; ⏰11am-11pm, kitchen noon-3pm & 6-9.30pm Mon-Sat, noon-6.30pm Sun) The decor in this former railway hotel is varnished floorboards, leather settles and exposed red brick, but the best bit is downstairs: the brewery's gleaming stainless-steel tubs and tubes. The building's past is the inspiration for the brews' names: fruity Rail Ale, sharp and sweet Piston Bitter and well-rounded Sleeper Heavy.

Flavoursome food includes slow-cooked shoulder of West Country lamb, a range of ploughman's platters made with local Quickes cheddar, and steak and Sleeper Ale pie. Newton St Cyres is on the A377, 5 miles north of Exeter. Train services from Exeter (return £7) chug into the village in time for supper; the return trip just after 11pm (10.30pm on Sunday) is very handy indeed.

☆ Entertainment

Bike Shed   THEATRE
(☎01392-434169; www.bikeshedtheatre.co.uk; 162 Fore St; ⏰5pm-midnight Mon-Thu, to 2am Fri & Sat, to 11pm Sun) Emerging writers are profiled in the Bike Shed's rough 'n' ready subterranean, brick-lined performance space. Its vintage cocktail bar makes a hip setting for live music and DJ sets on Friday and Saturday nights.

Exeter Phoenix   ARTS CENTRE
(☎01392-667080; www.exeterphoenix.org.uk; cnr Bradninch Pl & Gandy St; ⏰10am-11pm Mon-Sat; 🖥) Exeter's art and soul, the Phoenix is a buzzing blend of indie cinema, a performance space, galleries and a cool cafe-bar (snacks to 7pm).

Exeter Picturehouse   CINEMA
(☎0871 902 5730; www.picturehouses.co.uk; 51 Bartholomew St W) An intimate, independent cinema, screening mainstream and arthouse movies.

ℹ Information

Exeter Tourist Office (☎01392-665700; www.visitexeter.com; Dix's Field; ⏰9am-5pm Mon-Sat Apr-Sep, 9.30am-4.30pm Mon-Sat Oct-Mar)

ℹ Getting There & Away

AIR
Exeter International Airport (☎01392-367433; www.exeter-airport.co.uk) is 6 miles east of the city. Flights connect with several UK cities, including Manchester, Newcastle, Edinburgh and Glasgow, and with the Isles of Scilly and the Channel Islands.

Bus 56/56A/56B runs from Exeter St David's train station and Exeter bus station to Exeter International Airport (£3.90, 30 minutes), hourly between around 6.30am and 6.30pm.

BUS
Exeter's **bus station** (Paris St) is due a multi-million-pound revamp, during which time some services may depart from other locations. There's no set date. Check with the tourist office for the latest.

Services include the following.

Exmouth Bus 57 (£4.30, 35 minutes, two to four per hour).

Lyme Regis Bus 9A (£7.50, at least hourly, six on Sunday), via Beer. No Sunday service in winter.

Plymouth Bus X38 (£7.50, 1¼ hours, six daily Monday to Friday, four Saturday, two Sunday).

Sidmouth Bus 9/9A (£7, 35 minutes, two per hour Monday to Saturday, hourly on Sunday).

Topsham Bus 57 (£2.50, 10 minutes, two to four per hour).

Totnes Bus X64 (£6.10, 50 minutes, six or seven daily Monday to Saturday, two Sunday).

TRAIN
For main towns in Devon and Cornwall, it's generally much faster to take the train than the bus, though it's rarely cheaper. Main-line trains stopping at St David's train station include the following.

Bristol £29, 1¼ hours, half-hourly

London Paddington £71.20, 2½ hours, half-hourly

Paignton £7.70, 50 minutes, half-hourly

Penzance £21.80, three hours, half-hourly to hourly

Plymouth £9.70, one hour, half-hourly

Torquay £7.70, 45 minutes, half-hourly to hourly

Totnes £7, 35 minutes, half-hourly

Some branch-line services also go through Exeter Central train station.

ℹ Getting Around

BICYCLE
Saddles & Paddles (p290) Rents out bikes.

BUS
Bus H (two to four per hour) links St David's train station with Central train station (£1) and the High St, passing near the bus station.

TAXI
There are taxi ranks at St David's train station and on **High** and **Sidwell Sts**.

Apple Central Taxis (☑ 01392-666666; www.appletaxisexeter.co.uk)

Exeter City Cars (☑ 01392-975808; www.exetercitycars.com; ⊘ 24hr)

Z Cars (☑ 01392-595959)

Torquay & Around

POP 114,270

A seaside resort since Victorian times – and, famously, the setting for Basil Fawlty's fictional hotel in *Fawlty Towers* – Torquay remains a classic destination for the good, old-fashioned British summer getaway. Rather fancifully billing itself as the heart of the 'English Riviera', a reference to its palm-lined seafront and russet-red cliffs, it's a curious mix: as popular as ever with coach tours, sun-seeking families and stag- and hen parties, but with a fresh smattering of fine-dining restaurants and boutique B&Bs that indicate the town might be sloughing off its old image in favour of something a bit more classy. And in fact, it's the sprawling, bargain-basement resort of Paignton 3 miles south that's in more dire need of an image overhaul.

Regardless, there's plenty to see and do: a bizarre model village, a cliff railway, Agatha Christie connections and a bevy of impressive beaches.

◉ Sights & Activities

Torquay boasts no fewer than 20 beaches and an impressive 22 miles of coast. Tidal **Torre Abbey Sands** (Torbay Rd) is central, locals head for the sand-and-shingle beaches beside the 73m red-clay cliffs at **Oddicombe Beach** and sea swimmers love picturesque **Anstey's Cove**.

★ **Living Coasts**   ZOO
(☑ 01803-202470; www.livingcoasts.org.uk; Beacon Quay; adult/child £11.80/3.90, joint admission with Paignton Zoo £22.50/15.95; ⊘ 10am-5pm Apr-early Jul, Sep & Oct, to 6pm early Jul-Aug, to 4pm Nov-Mar; ℗) Clinging to the cliffs beside Torquay Harbour, the open-plan Living Coasts aviary brings you close to exotic birds. The immense enclosure features a series of underwater viewing tunnels and mocked-up microhabitats that include Penguin Beach, Auk Cliff and Fur Seal Cove. A

AGATHA CHRISTIE

Torquay is the birthplace of one-woman publishing phenomenon **Dame Agatha Mary Clarissa Christie** (1890–1976), a writer of murder mysteries who is beaten only by the Bible and William Shakespeare in terms of sales. Her characters are world famous: Hercule Poirot, the moustachioed, conceited Belgian detective; and Miss Marple, the surprisingly perceptive busybody spinster.

Born Agatha Miller in Torquay's Barton Rd, the young writer had her first piece published by the age of 11. By WWI she'd married Lieutenant Archie Christie and was working at the Red Cross Hospital in Torquay Town Hall, acquiring a knowledge of poisons that would lace countless plot lines, including that of her first novel, *The Mysterious Affair at Styles* (1920). Christie made her name with *The Murder of Roger Ackroyd* six years later with the use of what was then an innovative and cunning plot twist.

Then came 1926: in one year her mother died, Archie asked for a divorce and the writer mysteriously disappeared for 10 days, her abandoned car prompting a massive search. She was eventually discovered in a hotel in Harrogate, where she'd checked in under the name of the woman her husband wanted to marry. Christie always maintained she'd suffered amnesia; some critics saw it as a publicity stunt.

Christie later married archaeologist Sir Max Mallowan, and their trips to the Middle East provided masses of material for her work. By the time she died in 1976, Christie had written 75 novels and 33 plays.

Torquay's tourist office (p295) stocks the free *Agatha Christie Literary Trail* leaflet (also available to download from the website), which guides you around significant local sites. **Torquay Museum** (☑ 01803-293975; www.torquaymuseum.org; 529 Babbacombe Rd; adult/child £6.45/3.95; ⊘ 10am-4pm Mon-Sat) has a fine collection of photos, handwritten notes and displays devoted to Christie's famous detectives. The highlight, though, is Greenway (p295), the author's summer home near Dartmouth. Get there via the ferry from Dartmouth (p297) or take the steam train from Paignton (p296) to Greenway Halt, from where it's a half-mile walk through the woods to the house itself.

joint admission ticket with Paignton Zoo offers a 25% discount.

★ **Babbacombe Model Village** MUSEUM
(☎ 01803-315315; www.model-village.co.uk; Hampton Ave; adult/child £11.95/9.95; ◷ 10am-4pm; P) There are 413 tiny buildings, inhabited by 13,160 even tinier people, on display at this Lilliputian attraction, the epitome of English eccentricity. Settings include a small-scale Stonehenge, a football stadium, a beach (complete with nude sunbathers), an animated circus, a castle (under attack from a fire-breathing dragon) and a thatched village where firefighters are tackling a blaze. It's all brilliantly bizarre.

★ **Paignton Zoo** ZOO
(☎ 01803-697500; www.paigntonzoo.org.uk; Totnes Rd, Paignton; adult/child £16.50/12.35, joint admission with Living Coasts £22.50/15.95; ◷ 10am-6pm Apr-Oct, to 4.30pm Nov-Mar; P) This innovative, 32-hectare zoo is by far and away Paignton's top draw. Spacious enclosures recreate habitats from savannah and wetland to tropical forest and desert. Highlights include the orangutan island, a glass-walled big-cat enclosure and a lemur wood, where you walk over a plank suspension bridge as the primates leap around the trees. Then there's the crocodile swamp with pathways winding over and beside Nile, Cuban and saltwater crocs. Joint tickets also cover the Living Coasts seabird centre.

Babbacombe Cliff Railway RAIL
(☎ 01803-328750; www.babbacombecliffrailway. co.uk; Babbacombe Downs Rd; adult/child return £2.80/2; ◷ 9.30am-4.30pm Feb-Oct) A marvel of engineering in its day, Babbacombe's glorious 1920s funicular railway sees you climbing into a tiny carriage and rattling up and down rails set into the cliff. At the very least, it saves you the aching legs after walking down and back up.

🛏 **Sleeping**

Torquay Backpackers HOSTEL £
(☎ 01803-299924; www.torquaybackpackers.co. uk; 119 Abbey Rd; dm £18-20, d £38; @ 🛜) Set inside a Victorian terraced house, this budget stalwart is looking its age, but it's a reliably cheap option for budget travellers. There's a decent-sized kitchen, DVD den and a decked, al fresco pool-table terrace, but dorms can be noisy, as it's popular with stag and hen dos.

★ **The 25** B&B ££
(☎ 01803-297517; www.the25.uk; 25 Avenue Rd; r £108-168; P 🛜) 'We banished magnolia,' says the owner proudly. And how: the playful bedrooms here team zebra print with acid yellow, or burgundy with peacock blue. Pop-art flourishes, and great gadgets abound; play with the mood lighting via the iPad or watch TV in the shower. Munch on homemade brownies. Great value, great fun. There's usually a three-night minimum in summer.

Hillcroft B&B ££
(☎ 01803-297247; www.thehillcroft.co.uk; 9 St Lukes Rd; d £89-130; P 🛜) One of the better B&B options in Torquay town, with bedrooms styled after Morocco, Bali, Lombok and Tuscany. The pick is the spacious suites: Provençal, with an ormolu bed and a sitting room, or India, with Indian art and a four-poster bed.

★ **Cary Arms** BOUTIQUE HOTEL £££
(☎ 01803-327110; www.caryarms.co.uk; Babbacombe Beach; d £245-395, ste £375-450; P 🛜 ♿) In a dreamy spot beside Babbacombe's sands, this heritage hotel has more than a hint of a New England beach retreat. Bright, light-filled rooms with candy-stripe throws and white furniture shimmer with style, but for the best view book a stylish beach 'hut', complete with Smeg fridge, mezzanine bedroom and knockout beach-view patio. There's a divine spa, too.

✕ **Eating**

Me & Mrs Jones CAFE £
(☎ 01803-298745; www.meandmrsjonesdeli.com; 11 Ilsham Rd; dishes from £6; ◷ 8am-5.30pm Mon-Fri, 9am-4pm Sat) In this chilled-out cafe-deli, twinkling fairy lights are strung above a scattering of upcycled tables surrounded by gourmet goodies: organic sourdough, 'squealer' (pork) pies, flavoursome salads, quality charcuterie and oozing cheeses.

★ **Elephant** MODERN BRITISH ££
(☎ 01803-200044; www.elephantrestaurant.co. uk; 3 Beacon Tce; lunch 2-/3-course menu £18.50/21.95, dinner mains £16.50-26.50; ◷ noon-2pm & 6.30-9pm Tue-Sat) The jumbo on Torquay's fine-dining scene: Michelin-starred and critically lauded, Elephant belongs to chef Simon Hulstone, whose taste for seasonal food (much of it grown on his own farm) and delicate presentation takes centre stage. The food is modern with classical underpinnings – though expect surpris-

ing flavour combos – and every plate looks as pretty as a painting. Lunch is a steal.

Rockfish
SEAFOOD ££

(☑ 01803-212175; www.therockfish.co.uk; 20 Victoria Pde; mains £12-20; ☺ noon-9.30pm) The Torquay branch of award-winning chef Mitch Tonks' minichain of seafood restaurants showcases his taste for relaxed catch-of-the-day dining. Whitewashed wood and nautical knick-knacks give a shipshape ambience, while the food takes in everything from classic fish and chips and monkfish scampi to chargrilled seafood platters and seaweedy tartare sauce. For Devon lobster, preorder.

On the Rocks
BISTRO ££

(☑ 01803-203666; www.ontherocks-torquay.co.uk; 1 Abbey Cres; mains £13-26; ☺ 11am-midnight) Sliding doors and pavement tables make the most of the seaside view at this relaxed, informal cafe-bistro – it's just a shame the main beach road gets in the way. Still, it makes a pleasant spot to tuck into a bowl of mussels, a juicy steak or a creamy monkfish fillet, and reclaimed finds give it a rustic, semi-hipster vibe.

CoCo (www.cocotorquay.co.uk; 1 Abbey Cres; 5pm-midnight Mon-Fri, 11am-midnight Sat & Sun) cocktail bar is next door.

ℹ Information

Torquay Tourist Office (☑ 01803-211211; www.theenglishriviera.co.uk; 5 Vaughan Pde; ☺ 10am-5pm Mon-Sat) Torquay's main tourist office by the central harbour covers Torquay, Paignton and Brixham.

ℹ Getting There & Away

BUS

Services from Torquay **bus station** (Lymington Rd) are as follows.

Brixham Stagecoach Bus 12 (£4.50, 45 minutes, half-hourly) runs via Paignton.

Totnes Stagecoach Gold (£3.50, 45 minutes, half-hourly to hourly). From Totnes bus X64 goes on to Dartmouth.

FERRY

Between April and September the **Western Lady** (☑ Brixham 01803-852041, Torquay 01803-293797; www.westernladyferry.com; single/return £2/3; ☺ Apr-Sep) shuttles between the harbours of Torquay (The Harbour) and Brixham.

TRAIN

Trains run from Exeter St David's to Torquay (£7.70, 45 minutes, half-hourly to hourly) and on to Paignton (52 minutes) for the same fare.

WORTH A TRIP

BRIXHAM

An appealing, pastel-painted tumbling of fisher cottages leads down to Brixham's horseshoe harbour, where arcades and gift shops coexist with winding streets, brightly coloured boats and one of England's busiest fishing ports.

Life in Brixham revolves around the **fish market** (www.englishriviera.co.uk; The Quay; tours incl breakfast £15; ☺ Apr-Oct), which can be visited on an early-morning guided tour, starting at 6am. They're hugely popular – book well in advance. Down by Brixham's harbour, look out for a replica of the **Golden Hind** (☑ 01803-856223; www.goldenhind.co.uk; The Quay; adult/child £7/5; ☺ 10.30am-4pm Mar-Oct), Francis Drake's famous globetrotting ship.

The most enjoyable way to arrive in Brixham is aboard the venerable Western Lady (p295), which runs along the coast between Brixham Harbour and Torquay.

Dartmouth & Around

POP 10,720

Home to the nation's most prestigious naval college, the riverside town of Dartmouth is one of Devon's prettiest, awash with pastel-coloured, punch-drunk 17th- and 18th-century buildings leaning at angles, and a picturesque harbour stacked with yachts and clanking boat masts. It may be distinctly chic these days, but it's still a working port, and the triple draw of regular riverboat cruises, the art deco house of Coleton Fishacre and the former home of Agatha Christie make Dartmouth all but irresistible.

Dartmouth is on the west side of the Dart estuary. It's linked to the village of Kingswear on the east bank by fleets of car and foot ferries, also providing a key transport link to Torquay. It makes a lovely base for exploring Devon's south coast and the South Hams area.

◉ Sights

★ **Greenway**
HISTORIC BUILDING

(NT; ☑ 01803-842382; www.nationaltrust.org.uk/greenway; Greenway Rd, Galmpton; adult/child £11.60/5.80; ☺ 10.30am-5pm mid-Feb–Oct, 11am-4pm Sat & Sun Nov & Dec) High on Devon's must-see list, the captivating summer home of crime writer Agatha Christie sits beside the placid River Dart. Part-guided tours allow you to wander between rooms where the furnishings and knick-knacks are much as the author left them. The bewitching waterside gardens include features that pop up in Christie's mysteries, so you get to spot locations made notorious by fictional murders. Car parking must be prebooked; the better options are to arrive by Greenway Ferry or on foot.

★ **Coleton Fishacre**   HISTORIC BUILDING

(NT; ☑ 01803-842382; www.nationaltrust.org.uk/coleton-fishacre; Brownstone Rd, near Kingswear; adult/child £11.60/5.80; ⊘ 10.30am-5pm mid-Feb–Oct, 11am-4pm Sat & Sun Nov & Dec; P) For an evocative glimpse of jazz-age glamour, drop by the former home of the D'Oyly Carte family of theatre impresarios. Built in the 1920s, its faultless art deco embellishments include original Lalique tulip uplighters, comic bathroom tiles and a stunning saloon – complete with tinkling piano. The croquet terrace leads to deeply shelved subtropical gardens and suddenly revealed vistas of the sea. Hike the 4 miles along the cliffs from Kingswear, or drive.

Dartmouth Castle   CASTLE

(EH; ☑ 01803-833588; www.english-heritage.org.uk/visit/places/dartmouth-castle; Castle Rd; adult/child £6.80/4.10; ⊘ 10am-6pm Apr-Sep, to 5pm Oct, to 4pm Sat & Sun Nov-Mar; P) Discover maze-like passages, atmospheric guardrooms and great views from the battlements of this picturesque castle. The best way to arrive is via the tiny, open-top Castle Ferry (p297), or walk or drive along the coast road from Dartmouth (1.5 miles).

★ **Dartmouth Steam Railway**   RAIL

(☑ 01803-555872; www.dartmouthrailriver.co.uk; Torbay Rd, Paignton; adult/child return £17.50/10.50; ⊘ 4-9 trains daily mid-Feb–Oct) Chugging from seaside Paignton to the beautiful banks of the River Dart, these vintage trains roll back the years to the age of steam. The 7-mile, 30-minute journey puffs past Goodrington Sands, stopping at Greenway Halt (near Agatha Christie's former home), then the village of Kingswear, where ferries shuttle across to picturesque Dartmouth.

The service is run by the Dartmouth Steam Railway & Riverboat Company (p299). It operates a wealth of other trips, including coastal cruises and excursions on a paddle steamer; see the website for a full round-up.

🛏 Sleeping

Alf Resco   B&B ££

(☑ 01803-835880; www.cafealfresco.co.uk; Lower St; d from £90-105, apt £125; ☎) Not content with providing some of the town's yummiest food (p296), Alf's also offers a couple of cosy rooms, bunk beds in the 'Crew's Quarters' and the self-contained 'Captain's Cabin', squeezed in under the rafters with all the atmosphere of a ship's cabin (lanterns, panelled walls, watery views and all).

Dartmouth Boutique B&B   B&B ££

(☑ 01803-834553; www.thedartmouthbandb.co.uk; 7 Church Rd; d £95-155; P ☎) Although set high on one of Dartmouth's steeply sloping streets, this exquisite B&B is only a 15-minute walk into the town centre. The gradient offers extensive views across the hills and out to sea. Bedrooms are light-filled and luxurious, all with swish fabrics, baroque flourishes and subtle tones.

★ **Bayard's Cove**   B&B £££

(☑ 01803-839278; www.bayardscoveinn.co.uk; 27 Lower St; d £165-175, f £185-305; ☎) Crammed with character and bursting with beams, Bayard's Cove has you sleeping within whitewashed stone walls and among huge church candles. The lavish family suites feature grand double beds and kids' cabins, complete with bunk beds and tiny TVs; there are even estuary glimpses from the rooms.

🍴 Eating

★ **Alf Resco**   CAFE £

(☑ 01803-835880; www.cafealfresco.co.uk; Lower St; mains from £6; ⊘ 7am-2pm; ☎) This indie cafe is the preferred hang-out for a variety of discerning Dartmouthians, from yachties to families, tourists and riverboat crews. The same menu is available throughout the day: copious all-day breakfasts, toasties and chunky baguettes are the mainstays, and the coffee is great.

Crab Shell   SANDWICHES £

(1 Raleigh St; sandwiches £5; ⊘ 10.30am-2.30pm Apr-Dec) Sometimes all you want is a classic crab sarnie, and this little establishment will happily oblige: the shellfish is landed on the quay a few steps away. Salmon, lobster and mackerel butties also available.

Rockfish   SEAFOOD ££

(☑ 01803-832800; www.therockfish.co.uk; 8 South Embankment; mains £10-18; ⊘ noon-9.30pm) At the Dartmouth outpost of award-winning chef Mitch Tonks' five-strong bistro chain, seafood is firmly the speciality, and the weathered boarding and maritime decor fit right in along Dartmouth's streets. The fish and chips are delicious.

★ **Seahorse**   SEAFOOD **£££**
(☑ 01803-835147; www.seahorserestaurant.co.uk; 5 South Embankment; mains £23-34; ☺ noon-2.30pm & 6-9.30 Tue-Sat) What celebrity chef Rick Stein is to Cornwall, Mitch Tonks is to Devon – a seafood supremo, with a clutch of restaurants across the county. The Seahorse is the original, and the best: a classic fish restaurant where the just-landed produce is roasted over open charcoals. Leather banquettes, wood floors and a wine wall give it a French-bistro feel. Book ahead.

ⓘ Information

Dartmouth Visitor Centre (☑ 01803-834224; www.discoverdartmouth.com; Mayor's Ave; ☺ 10.30am-2.30pm Mon-Sat) Lots of information on Dartmouth and the South Hams is available at the town's small tourist office, in a standalone building beside Mayor's Ave car park.

ⓘ Getting There & Away

BUS

Plymouth Stagecoach bus 3 (£7.30, 2½ hours, hourly Monday to Saturday) travels via Kingsbridge. On Sunday there are only two **buses** (South Embankment) that travel as far as Kingsbridge (£7, one hour).

Totnes Stagecoach bus X64 (£3.70, 50 minutes, every two hours Monday to Saturday, two Sunday) heads to Totnes and then continues to Exeter (£6.60, two hours).

FERRY

Several ferries run from Dartmouth's waterfront.

Castle Ferry (www.dartmouthcastleferry. co.uk; adult/child return £5/3; ☺ 10am-4.45pm Easter-Oct) Runs to Dartmouth Castle.

Dartmouth–Dittisham Ferry (☑ 01803-882811; www.greenwayferry.co.uk; adult/child return £8.50/6.50; ☺ Easter-Oct) Shuttles upriver to the quaint village of Dittisham.

Dartsmouth–Kingswear Higher Ferry (☑ 07866 531687; www.dartmouthhigherferry. com; car/pedestrian one-way £5.60/60p; ☺ 6.30am-10.50pm Mon-Sat, from 8am Sun) Carries cars and pedestrians across the estuary every six minutes, enabling you to avoid the town's narrow streets.

Dartmouth–Kingswear Lower Ferry (www. southhams.gov.uk; per car/pedestrian £5/1.50; ☺ 7.10am-10.45pm) The town's oldest ferry

service, in business since the 1300s. It's a floating platform that's pulled by a tug moored alongside.

Greenway Ferry (☑ 01803-882811; www. greenwayferry.co.uk; adult/child return £8.50/6.50; ☺ 5-8 ferries daily mid–Mar-Oct) Boats to Greenway and on to Dittisham, plus scenic river cruises.

TRAIN

The Dartmouth Steam Railway (p296) links Kingswear and Paignton. The nearest mainline connections are from Totnes.

Totnes & Around
POP 8041

Totnes has such a reputation for being alternative that local jokers wrote 'twinned with Narnia' under the town sign. For decades famous as Devon's hippie haven, ecoconscious Totnes also became Britain's first 'transition town' in 2005, when it began to wean itself off a dependence on oil. Sustainability aside, Totnes boasts a tempting vineyard, a sturdy Norman castle and a mass of fine Tudor buildings, and is the springboard for a range of outdoor activities.

◉ Sights & Activities

★ **Sharpham Wine & Cheese**   WINERY
(☑ 01803-732203; www.sharpham.com; vineyard £2.50; ☺ 10am-6pm May-Sep, to 5pm Mar & Apr, to 3pm Mon-Sat Oct-Dec; ℗) Three miles south of Totnes off the A381, this renowned vineyard is chiefly known for its crisp, sparkling white wines, as well as its delicious cheeses. Perched above the meandering River Dart, it's become one of the UK's best-known winemakers. You can explore the vine-covered slopes solo (£2.50), followed by a wine and/or cheese tasting in the shop (£7 and £3 respectively), or plump for the full guided tour (£20, 3pm Saturday and Sunday, April to September).

Dartington Estate   HISTORIC SITE
(☑ 01803-847000; www.dartington.org; ☺ gardens dawn-dusk, visitor centre 9am-5pm; ℗) **FREE** Henry VIII gave this pastoral 324-hectare estate to two of his wives (Catherines Howard and Parr). For many years it was home to the town's art college; now the 14th-century manor house hosts events, including renowned classical-music and literature festivals. There's also an art-house cinema, shops, a decent pub and B&B accommodation. The grounds are also worth exploring. It's about 2 miles northwest of Totnes.

Totnes Castle

CASTLE

(EH; ☑ 01803-864406; www.english-heritage.org. uk; Castle St; adult/child £4.30/2.60; ⊘10am-6pm Apr-Sep, to 5pm Oct, to 4pm Sat & Sun Nov-Mar) High on a hilltop above town, Totnes' castle is among the best-preserved examples of a Norman 'motte and bailey' castle (a round keep sitting on a raised earthwork). The views over Totnes's rooftops and the South Hams beyond are captivating, but the interior is largely empty. Look out for the medieval toilet (but don't use it).

★ Dynamic Adventures

ADVENTURE SPORTS

(☑ 01803-862725; www.dynamicadventurescic. co.uk; Park Rd, Dartington Hall) The superb activities on offer include canoeing and kayaking (half/full day £35/70) and sea kayaking (from £75), as well as caving (half day £35), rock climbing and archery (both per hour £15). Booking is required.

It's 2 miles northwest of Totnes on the Dartington Estate.

★ Totnes Kayaks

KAYAKING

(☑ 07799 403788; www.totneskayaks.co.uk; The Quay, Stoke Gabriel; single kayak half/full day £30/40; ⊘10am-5pm Fri-Sun Apr-Jun, Sep & Oct, daily Jul & Aug) The River Dart looks pretty enough from the bank, but to see it at its best, you really need to get out on the water. Five miles southeast of Totnes in Stoke Gabriel, this friendly outdoors company rents out single and double sit-on-top kayaks for you to explore the river – but it's worth ringing ahead to check on tide times.

🛏 Sleeping

★ Dartington Hall

B&B ££

(☑ 01803-847150; www.dartington.org; Dartington Estate; s/d from £55/119; P ﹖) ✔ The wings of this idyllic ancient manor house have been carefully converted into rooms that range from heritage themed to deluxe modern. Ask for one overlooking the grassy, cobble-fringed courtyard, and settle back for a truly tranquil night's sleep. The estate is about 1.5 miles from Totnes.

★ Cott Inn

PUB ££

(☑ 01803-863777; www.cottinn.co.uk; Cott Lane, Dartington; s/d £100/125; P) The 14th-century Cott is pretty much the perfect English inn: rambling, thatched and lined with beams. Rooms blend undulating walls with artfully distressed furniture, crisp eco-linens, and lilac and olive tones. Ingredients for the classy gastro pub fare are sourced entirely locally –

lamb from Dartington, potatoes from Kingsbridge and crab from Salcombe.

✗ Eating

Pie Street

PIES £

(☑ 01803-868674; www.piestreet.co.uk; 26 High St; pies £9.95; ⊘11.30am-6pm Mon, to 8pm Tue-Thu, to 9pm Fri & Sat, noon-4pm Sun) 'British soul food', runs the slogan here – in other words, poshed-up pies, served with your choice of mash or chips, and lashings of gravy. You can go classic with steak-and-ale or chicken, ham and leek, or plump for something more unusual: an Anglo-Indian curry pie or veggie homity pie, perhaps. Sit down in the bistro-style interior, or takeaway.

Willow

VEGETARIAN £

(☑ 01803-862605; 87 High St; mains £6-10; ⊘10am-5pm Mon-Sat, plus 6.30-9pm Wed, Fri & Sat; ✔) ✔ Totnes simply wouldn't be Totnes if it didn't have its own veggie-friendly, wholefood hang-out – and Willow has occupied that slot handsomely for many a year. Inside, it's suitably hippy-chic, and the menu is full of quiches, pies, moussakas, salads and soups – many of which are vegan and/or gluten-free.

★ Riverford Field Kitchen

MODERN BRITISH ££

(☑ 01803-762074; https://fieldkitchen.riverford. co.uk; Wash Farm; 3-course lunch/dinner £23.50/27.50; ⊘sittings 12.30pm Mon-Sat, noon & 3.30pm Sun, 7pm most evenings; ✔) ✔ This ecofriendly, organic, plough-to-plate farm is where everyone wants to eat when they visit Totnes. It began as a food-box scheme, and has now branched out into a delightful barn bistro, where diners sit communally at long wooden tables and share dishes of the day. Rustic flavours rule: expect delicious salads, roast meats and imaginative veggie options. Bookings required.

Rumour

PUB FOOD ££

(☑ 01803-864682; www.rumourtotnes.com; 30 High St; mains £9-18; ⊘noon-3pm Mon-Sat, 6-10pm daily; ✔) ✔ Rumour is a local institution – a narrow, cosy pub-restaurant with low lighting, local art and newspapers for reading. It's legendary for its pizzas (£9.50), but there's plenty to choose from, such as risottos, steaks, stews and fish of the day. The bar is open from 10am to 11pm.

🍷 Drinking

★ The Totnes Brewing Co

MICROBREWERY

(☑ 01803-849290; www.thetotnesbrewingco.co. uk; 59a High St; ⊘5pm-midnight Mon-Thu, noon-midnight Fri-Sun) There are scores of craft beers to choose from at this trendy town hang-out, from Trappist-style wheat brews to imperial stouts, all with witty names (personal favourites: Hopless Romantic, Nutty Old England and Duck Medicine). It's no dark old dive – expect stripped wood and big glass windows looking out on to the high street.

Upstairs, the **Barrel House Ballroom** hosts live gigs.

Hairy Barista COFFEE
(☑ 07916-306723; coffee@thehairybarista.co.uk; 69 High St; coffee from £2; ☺ 8am-5pm Mon-Sat, 9am-5pm Sun) Aeropress, cold-brew, V60, flat white or just plain-old espresso, the aptly named hairy barista (aka Roe Yekutiel) will oblige – his little shop has become the town's go-to place for speciality coffee. There are cakes and pastries on offer too, but the space is a little cramped inside (and mind the step on the way in!).

ⓘ Getting There & Around

BOAT

Boats shuttle downriver to Dartmouth with the **Dartmouth Steam Railway & Riverboat Company** (☑ 01803-555872; www.dartmouthrailriver.co.uk; North Embankment).

BUS

Totnes is well serviced by bus.
Exeter Stagecoach Bus X64 (£6.10, 50 minutes, six or seven daily Monday to Saturday, two Sunday). Continues to Kingsbridge and Dartmouth in the opposite direction.
Plymouth Stagecoach Gold (£3.60, one hour, half-hourly Monday to Saturday, hourly Sunday).
Torquay Stagecoach Gold (£3.50, 45 minutes, half-hourly Monday to Saturday, hourly Sunday).

TRAIN

Trains run at least hourly to Exeter (£7, 35 minutes) and Plymouth (£6.50, 30 minutes).

The quaint **South Devon Steam Railway** (☑ 01364-644370; www.southdevonrailway.co.uk; adult/child return £15/9; ☺ Apr-Oct) chuffs to Buckfastleigh, on the edge of Dartmoor.

Plymouth & Around

POP 258,000
For decades, some have dismissed Plymouth as sprawling and ugly, pointing to its architectural eyesores and sometimes palpable poverty. But the arrival of high-profile chefs Hugh Fearnley-Whittingstall and Mitch Tonks and an ongoing waterfront regeneration begs a rethink. Yes the city, an important Royal Naval port, suffered heavy WWII bomb damage, and even today it can appear more gritty than pretty, but Plymouth is also packed with possibilities for visitors: swim in an art deco lido, tour a gin distillery, learn to SUP, kayak and sail, roam an aquarium, take a boat trip across the bay, then see a top-class theatre show and party till dawn. And the aces in the pack? The history-rich Barbican district and Plymouth Hoe – a cafe-dotted, wide, grassy headland offering captivating views of a boat-studded bay.

History

Plymouth's history is dominated by the sea. The first recorded cargo left in 1211, and by the late 16th century it was the port of choice for explorers and adventurers. It has waved off Sir Francis Drake, Sir Walter Raleigh, the fleet that defeated the Spanish Armada, the pilgrims who founded America, Charles Darwin, Captain Cook and countless boats carrying emigrants to Australia and New Zealand.

During WWII Plymouth suffered horrendously at the hands of the German Luftwaffe – more than 1000 civilians died in the Blitz, which reduced the city centre to rubble. The 21st century has brought regeneration to waterfront areas, the £200-million Drake Circus shopping centre, and a growing university, bringing with it a burst of new buildings and 30,000 students to the heart of town.

⊙ Sights

★ **Plymouth Hoe** LANDMARK
Francis Drake supposedly spied the Spanish fleet from this grassy headland overlooking Plymouth Sound (the city's wide bay); the bowling green on which he continued to finish his game after the sighting was probably where his **statue** (Plymouth Hoe) now stands. The wide villa-backed promenade features scores of war memorials.

Smeaton's Tower LIGHTHOUSE
(☑ 01752-304774; www.plymhearts.org; The Hoe; adult/child £4/2; ☺ 10am-5pm) The red-and-white stripes of Smeaton's Tower rise from the middle of the Plymouth Hoe headland. For an insight into past lighthouse keepers'

Plymouth

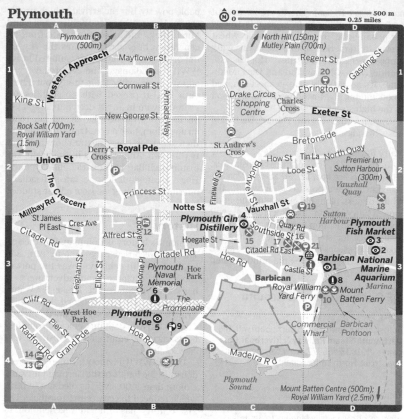

Plymouth

lives, head up 93 stone steps and through the circular rooms to emerge on to an open-air platform for stunning views of the city, Dartmoor and the sea.

The whole 21m structure previously stood on the Eddystone Reef, 14 miles offshore, and was transferred to its current site, brick by brick, in the 1880s.

★**Barbican** AREA
(www.barbicanwaterfront.com) For a glimpse of ancient Plymouth, head down to this historic harbour area, where part-cobbled streets are lined with Tudor and Jacobean buildings, and old dockside warehouses have been turned into bars, restaurants and art galleries. It's also famous as the point from which the Pilgrim Fathers set sail for the New World in 1620: the **Mayflower Steps** (Sutton Harbour) mark the approximate spot.

The original passenger list for the *Mayflower* can be seen on the side of **Island House** (Sutton Harbour) nearby. The steps also commemorate Captain James Cook's 1768 voyage of discovery and the first emigrant ships to depart for Australia and New Zealand.

These days the Barbican is one of the city's liveliest areas – not to mention one of its prettiest. Drink it all in, me hearties.

★**Plymouth Gin Distillery** DISTILLERY
(☑01752-665292; www.plymouthdistillery.com; 60 Southside St; tours £7) This heavily beamed distillery has been concocting gin since 1793, making it the oldest working producer of the spirit in England. Four to six tours per day thread past the stills and take in a tutored tasting before retiring to the beautiful Grade II–listed cocktail bar for a complimentary G&T.

★**Plymouth Fish Market** MARKET
(☑01752-204738; www.plymouthfisheries.co.uk; Sutton Harbour) Around 60,000 tonnes of fish pass through this market, making it the second biggest by volume in England after London's Billingsgate. It's an amazing sight when it's in full flow. Tours can be arranged with the harbourmaster (p.bromley@sutton-harbour.co.uk). There are also regular Fish in Sutton Harbour (FISH) guided tours with a local fisher; check www.facebook.com/suttonharbour for the latest.

★**National Marine Aquarium** AQUARIUM
(☑0844 893 7938; www.national-aquarium.co.uk; Rope Walk; year passes adult/child £16.95/12.95; ⊙10am-5pm) The UK's biggest – and perhaps best – aquarium is lodged beside the Barbican harbour. There's a huge amount to see, but the highlight is the impressive Atlantic Ocean tank, the deepest in the UK, with over 2 million litres of water and a population of sand tiger sharks, lemon sharks, barracuda and rays, as well as a replica of a WWII Walrus Seaplane. Other zones explore the Great

Barrier Reef, and local habitats including Eddystone Reef and Plymouth Sound.

Tickets are 10% cheaper if you buy in advance online, and remain valid for a year's entry.

🏃 **Activities**

★**Tinside Lido** SWIMMING
(☑01752-261915; www.everyoneactive.com/centre/tinside-lido; Hoe Rd; adult/child £4.50/3.50; ⊙noon-6pm Mon-Fri, from 10am Sat, Sun & school holidays late May–early Sep) This glorious outdoor swimming pool is one of Plymouth's best-loved sights. Nestled beneath the Hoe with views on to Plymouth Sound, it's a gem of the jazz age: built in 1935, with sleek white curves and candy-striped light- and dark-blue tiles – like something straight out of an F Scott Fitzgerald novel. Tinside's saltwater is unheated, but there are hot showers.

Mount Batten Centre WATER SPORTS
(☑01752-404567; www.mount-batten-centre.com; 70 Lawrence Rd) Set on the Mount Batten peninsula and linked to the Barbican by a **passenger ferry** (☑07930 838614; www.mountbattenferry.co.uk; Barbican Pontoon; adult/child return £3/1), this centre offers a range of water-sports tuition, including two-hour taster sessions in sit-on-top kayaks (£19), stand-up paddleboarding and sailing (£20).

★**Plymouth Boat Trips** BOATING
(☑01752-253153; www.plymouthboattrips.co.uk; Barbican Pontoon) The pick of this firm's trips is the **Cawsand Ferry**, a 30-minute blast across the bay to the quaint, pub-packed Cornish fishing villages of Kingsand and Cawsand (adult/child return £8/4, six daily) from Easter to October. Year-round, one-hour excursions head around Plymouth's dockyards and naval base (adult/child £8.50/5). There is also a combination cruise including entry to **Mount Edgcumbe** (☑01752-822236; www.mountedgcumbe.gov.uk; Cremyll; adult/child £7.20/3.75; ⊙11am-4.30pm Sun-Thu Mar-Sep).

🎊 **Festivals**

★**British Fireworks Championships** FIREWORKS
(www.britishfireworks.co.uk; ⊙mid-Aug) Over two nights in mid-August, six professional companies battle it out for the title, with three firms each staging 10-minute displays nightly. It's hugely popular, drawing tens of

ROYAL WILLIAM YARD

In the 1840s this imposing complex of waterfront warehouses supplied stores for countless Royal Navy vessels. Today it's home to sleek apartments, a clutch of galleries and shops, and a cluster of restaurants and bars, including the excellent social enterprise bakery, **Column Bakehouse** (☑ 01752-395137; www.columnbakehouse.org; Ocean Studios, Royal William Yard; dishes £4-8; ⊙ 9am-4pm Tue-Wed, to 5pm Thu-Sat, 10am-5pm Sun) and the elegant Vignoble (p303) wine bar.

It's an atmospheric spot; roaming past a former slaughterhouse, bakery, brewery and cooperage underlines just how big the supplies operation was.

The yard is 2 miles west of the city centre. Hop on bus 34 (£1.30, nine minutes, half-hourly) or, better still, catch the hourly **ferry** (☑ 07979 152008; www.royalwilliamyard. com/getting-here/by-waterbus; Barbican Pontoon; one-way adult/child £3/2; ⊙ 10am-5pm May-Sep). A 10-minute walk north of the yard, the **Cremyll Ferry** (☑ 01752-822105; www. cremyll-ferry.co.uk; Admirals Hard; adult/child return £3/1.50; ⊙ half-hourly) chugs across the Tamar to Cornwall, to the coast walks of the Mount Edgcumbe estate.

thousands of people to Plymouth's waterfront amid a carnival atmosphere.

🛏 Sleeping

Rusty Anchor
B&B £

(☑ 01752-663924; www.therustyanchor-plymouth. co.uk; 30 Grand Pde; s/d £40/50) One of a string of B&Bs along Grand Pde, this cute little town house makes a cosy Plymouth base. Decorative driftwood and shells lend this relaxed B&B a flavour of the sea; four rooms have views of Plymouth Sound's wide waters. Owner Jan will try to meet your breakfast requests – be that kippers, pancakes or homemade rolls.

★ St Elizabeth's House
BOUTIQUE HOTEL ££

(☑ 01752-344840; www.stelizabeths.co.uk; Longbrook St, Plympton St Maurice; d £129-149; P 🛜) Prepare to be pampered. In this 17th-century manor house turned boutique bolthole, free-standing slipper baths, oak furniture and Egyptian cotton grace the rooms; the suites feature palatial bathrooms and private terraces. The only drawback is its out-of-town location: it's in the suburb-village of Plympton St Maurice, 5 miles east of Plymouth.

Imperial
HOTEL ££

(☑ 01752-227311; www.imperialplymouth.co.uk; Lockyer St; s £61-91, d £91-122, f £121-141; P 🛜) The pick of the small hotels on Plymouth Hoe is in this 1840s town house that once belonged to an admiral. A few heritage features remain but it has been thoroughly updated and feels quite modern, with beige carpets, wooden furniture and the odd bit of Orla Kiely wallpaper.

Sea Breezes
B&B ££

(☑ 01752-667205; www.plymouth-bedandbreak fast.co.uk; 28 Grand Pde; s £55-65, d £85-95, f £110-125; 🛜) With its sea-themed colours and pristine rooms Sea Breezes is a supremely comfortable place to stay. Add a charming owner, cast-iron bedsteads, old-fashioned alarm clocks and sea views, and you have a winner. The two sets of interconnecting rooms are particularly good for families.

Premier Inn Sutton Harbour
HOTEL ££

(☑ 0871 527 8882; www.premierinn.com; 28 Sutton Rd; r £70-100; P ❄ 🛜 🐾) Yes, it's part of a national chain, and decor is corporate and functional, but it's still an eminently practical sleep. To the cream walls and MDF furniture you can add a prime location overlooking Sutton Harbour.

It won't be your most memorable night's sleep, but setting trumps posh sometimes.

🍴 Eating

★ Jacka Bakery
BAKERY £

(☑ 01752-264645; 38 Southside St; snacks £3-8; ⊙ 9am-4pm Wed-Mon) Quietly groovy, fantastically friendly and extremely good at baking things, Jacka is much loved by locals. It excels at immense croissants, cinnamon swirls and three type of sourdough loaves. The 'on toast' options are fabulous – the wild-mushroom, tarragon and fried-egg version is something very fine indeed.

★ Supha's Street Emporium
ASIAN £

(☑ 01752-228513; www.suphas.co.uk; Unit 1, E Quay House; dishes small £2.95-4.95, large £7.50-15.95; ⊙ noon-9pm Tue & Sun, to 10pm Wed-Sat; 🐾) An exotic addition to the up-and-coming area around Sutton Harbour, this joint specialises in spicy, flavourful Thai-style street food: classic Massaman curry, steamed sea bass, *larb* (a meat salad) and papaya salads, and much more. Whether you opt for small street plates, platters to share or mix-and-match your curries, you'll enjoy authentic, delicious flavours. It's strong on veggie options too.

Harbourside Fish & Chips   FISH & CHIPS £
(www.barbicanfishandchips.co.uk; 35 Southside St; takeaway fish & chips from £5.65; ⊘ 11am-10pm, to 11pm Fri & Sat) This top-notch chip shop is renowned across the city – there are often queues out the door at peak times. If you're planning on eating al fresco, be warned – Plymouth's dive-bombing seagulls have a nasty habit of snatching your meal, so a better plan is to accompany your meal with a pint in the Dolphin (p303) next door.

★ **Rock Salt**   MODERN BRITISH ££
(☑ 01752-225522; www.rocksaltcafe.co.uk; 31 Stonehouse St; 2-/3-course lunch menu £12/16, dinner £16.95-24.95; ⊘ 10am-3pm & 5-9.30pm; ☜) Local boy Dave Jenkins has worked wonders at his little brasserie, which has deservedly built up a loyal local following and scooped up foodie awards. It suits all times of day: tuck into fluffy American pancakes for breakfast, enjoy a light artichoke risotto for lunch and savour confit beef blade for dinner. A local diner par excellence.

Barbican Kitchen   MODERN BRITISH ££
(☑ 01752-604448; www.barbicankitchen.com; 60 Southside St; 2-/3-course lunch menu £13/16, mains £11-17.95; ⊘ noon-2.30pm & 6-9.30pm Mon-Sat) Plymouth's chef brothers Chris and James Tanner have brightened up the Barbican with their relaxed-but-refined bistro at the Plymouth Gin Distillery (p301). It's a quirky, fun place to dine – turquoise banquettes and pop-art pics of Yoda and Bruce Lee on the walls – and the food is fresh and contemporary.

🍷 Drinking & Nightlife

Like any Royal Navy city, Plymouth has a more than lively nightlife. Union St is clubland, Mutley Plain and North Hill have a studenty vibe, and the Barbican has more restaurants amid the bars. All three areas can get rowdy, especially at weekends.

★ **Dolphin**   PUB
(☑ 01752-660876; 14 The Barbican; ⊘ 10am-11pm) This gloriously unreconstructed Barbican boozer is all scuffed tables, padded bench seats and an authentic, no-nonsense atmosphere. Feeling peckish? Get a fish-and-chip takeaway from Harbourside Fish & Chips (p303) two doors down, then settle in with your pint.

Be sure to check out the cheeky paintings by much-loved local artist (and one-time regular) Beryl Cook on the walls.

★ **Annabel's**   CLUB
(www.annabelscabaret.co.uk; 88 Vauxhall St; ⊘ 9pm-2am Thu, 8.30pm-3am Fri & Sat) Saucy performances come to the Barbican at this late-night cabaret-nightclub. It's great fun: the DJ sets and lounge-bar vibe are spot on, and you never quite know what the entertainment might be – burlesque or blues, comedy or country.

Bread & Roses   PUB
(☑ 01752-659861[]; www.breadandrosesplymouth.co.uk; 62 Ebrington St; ⊘ 4pm-1am Mon-Fri, noon-1am Sat, noon-11pm Sun; ☜) Plymouth's arty crowd loves this characterful combo of hip boozer, social-enterprise visionary and cultural hub. Amid its Edwardian-meets-modern decor you'll find a good pint, occasional appearances by cool local bands, and lots of people hatching creative plans.

Vignoble   WINE BAR
(☑ 01752-222892; www.levignoble.co.uk; Royal William Yard; ⊘ noon-11.30pm, to midnight Fri & Sat) A bijou hang-out where you can sample taster-sized glasses of your chosen vintages. It's at the Royal William Yard, 2 miles west of the city centre.

ℹ Information

Tourist Office (☑ 01752-306330; www.visitplymouth.co.uk; 3 The Barbican; ⊘ 9am-5pm Mon-Sat, 10am-4pm Sun Apr-Oct, 10am-4pm Mon-Sat Nov-Mar) Local leaflets aplenty, plus free accommodation-booking service and advance tickets for many attractions.

ℹ Getting There & Away

BUS

National Express services call at Plymouth's bus station (Mayflower St). They include the following.

Bristol £13 to £24, three hours, four to six daily

Exeter £7.60 to £12.70, one to 1½ hours, four daily

London £15.50 to £28.20, five to six hours, six daily

Penzance £8, 3¼ hours, five daily

Local services include the following.

Exeter Bus X38 (£7.50, 1¼ hours, six daily Monday to Friday, four on Saturday, two on Sunday).

Totnes Stagecoach Gold (£3.60, one hour, half-hourly Monday to Saturday, hourly on Sunday).

TRAIN

Services include the following.

Bristol £41.90, two hours, two or three hourly

Exeter £9.70, one hour, half-hourly

London Paddington £79.80, 3¼ hours, half-hourly

Penzance £10.70, two hours, half-hourly

Totnes £6.50, 30 minutes, half-hourly to hourly

Dartmoor National Park

Dartmoor (☎ 01822-890414; www.visitdartmoor.co.uk) is Devon's wild heart. Covering 368 sq miles, this vast national park feels like it's tumbled straight out of a Tolkien tome, with its honey-coloured heaths, moss-smothered boulders, tinkling streams and eerie granite hills (known locally as tors).

On sunny days, Dartmoor is idyllic: ponies wander at will and sheep graze beside the road. It makes for a cinematic location, used to memorable effect in Steven Spielberg's WWI epic *War Horse*. But when sleeting rain and swirling mists arrive, you'll understand why Dartmoor is also the setting for Sir Arthur Conan Doyle's *The Hound of the Baskervilles:* the moor morphs into a bleak wilderness where tales of a phantom hound can seem very real indeed.

Dartmoor is an outdoor activities hot spot for hiking, cycling, riding, climbing and white-water kayaking, and has plenty of rustic pubs and country-house hotels where you can hunker down when the fog rolls in.

🏃 Activities

Dartmoor is a fantastic place to get out and be active, whether that means an afternoon hike or a horseback hack. For a broad-based overview, multiactivity providers such as **CRS Adventures** (☎ 01364-653444; www.crsadventures.co.uk; Holne Park; per person per day from £35) and Adventure Okehampton (p305) offer a range of ways to get your pulse racing.

Walking

Some 730 miles of public footpaths snake across Dartmoor's open heaths and rocky tors. The Ordnance Survey (OS) Pathfinder *Dartmoor Walks* (£12) guide includes 28 hikes of up to 9 miles, while its *Dartmoor Short Walks* (£8) focuses on family-friendly treks.

The 18-mile **Templer Way** is a two- to three-day stretch from Haytor to Teignmouth, while the **West Devon Way** forms a 36-mile trek linking Okehampton and Plymouth. The 95-mile **Dartmoor Way** circles from Buckfastleigh in the south, through Moretonhampstead, northwest to Okehampton and south through Lydford to Tavistock. The 117-mile **Two Moors Way** runs from Wembury on the south Devon coast, across Dartmoor and Exmoor to Lynmouth, on the north coast.

Be prepared for Dartmoor's notoriously fickle weather, and carry a map and a compass – many trails are not waymarked. The Ordnance Survey (OS) Explorer 1:25,000 map No 28, *Dartmoor* (£9), is the most comprehensive and shows park boundaries and Ministry of Defence firing-range areas.

⭐**Moorland Guides**   HIKING
(www.moorlandguides.co.uk; adult/child from £2.50/free) A wide range of walks, from one-hour rambles to strenuous all-day hikes, on themes spanning heritage, geology, wildlife, myths and navigation. The walks leave from various locations – you'll be told where at the time of booking.

Cycling

Routes include the 11-mile **Granite Way** (part of NCN Route 27), which runs entirely off-road along a former railway line between Okehampton and Lydford. The 13-mile **Princetown & Burrator Mountain Bike Route** is a challenging moorland circuit along tracks and bridleways, taking in Princetown, Sheepstor village and Burrator Reservoir.

Tourist offices sell the *Dartmoor for Cyclists* map (£13).

Devon Cycle Hire   CYCLING
(☎ 01837-861141; www.devoncyclehire.co.uk; Sourton Down, near Okehampton; per day adult/child £16/12; ⊙9am-5pm Thu-Tue Apr-Sep, plus Wed school holidays) Located on the Granite Way (part of NCN Route 27). Will deliver bikes for a small charge.

Fox Tor Cafe Cycle Hire   CYCLING
(☎ 01822-890238; www.foxtorcafe.com/cycles; Fox Tor Cafe, Two Bridges Rd; per day adult/child £18.50/10; ⊙9am-5pm) This is handy for

Dartmoor National Park

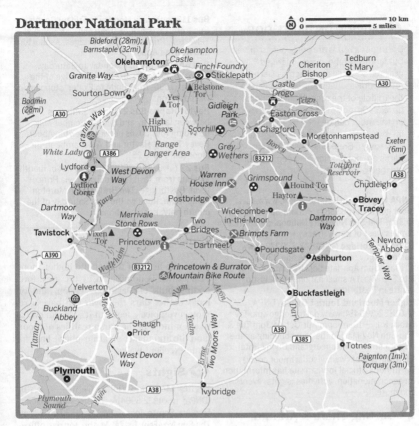

the Princetown & Burrator Mountain Bike Route.

Horse Riding

A number of local stables across the moor cater to all abilities.

Babeny Farm HORSE RIDING
(☏ 01364-631296; www.babenystables.co.uk; Poundsgate; rides per 30min/1hr £35/50; ☺ Apr-Oct) A friendly, family-run farm that offers rides, lessons and 'Horse Holidays' (ie stabling) for £15 per horse, per night. It's 8 miles northwest of Ashburton.

Cholwell HORSE RIDING
(☏ 01822-810526; www.cholwellridingstables.co.uk; near Mary Tavy; 1/2hr rides £23/42) A family-run stables that caters for novices and experts. It's near an old silver mine on the edge of the moor near the village of Mary Tavy, about halfway between Okehampton and Tavistock.

Climbing

Adventure Okehampton OUTDOORS
(☏ 01837-53916; www.adventureokehampton.com; Klondyke Rd; per half/full day £25/50; ☺ school holidays only) There are endless ways to get your pulse racing at this outdoors company, from standard activities like climbing, archery and kayaking to more unusual pastimes such as 'weasling' (squeezing through narrow gaps in Dartmoor's tors) and 'the Big Oke Abseil' (rappelling down from Meldon Viaduct to the Okement River).

ⓘ Information

Dartmoor National Park Authority (DNPA; www.dartmoor.gov.uk) The main administrative body for Dartmoor has an excellent website with lots of information on sights and activities. It has also produced a few free audio guides to popular sights, including Princetown, Postbridge, Haytor and Bellever.

ⓘ DRIVING ON DARTMOOR

Dartmoor's roads are gorgeous to drive, but large stretches have unfenced grazing, so you'll come across Dartmoor ponies, sheep and even cows in the middle of the road. Many sections have a 40mph speed limit. Car parks on the moor can be little more than lay-bys; their surface can be rough to very rough. Break-ins at isolated car parks are not unknown – keep valuables stashed out of sight.

DNPA Haytor (☑01364-661904; www.dartmoor.gov.uk; off B3387; ☉10am-5pm Apr-Oct, to 3pm Thu-Sun Nov-Mar) National-park office 3 miles west of Bovey Tracey.

DNPA Postbridge (☑01822-880272; www.dartmoor.gov.uk; car park beside B3212; ☉10am-5pm Apr–late Sep, to 3pm Thu-Sun late Sep–Mar) A small national-park visitor centre in Postbridge.

Higher Moorland Tourist Office (DNPA; ☑01822-890414; www.dartmoor.gov.uk; Tavistock Rd; ☉10am-5pm Apr-Oct, to 3pm Tue & Thu-Sun Nov-Mar) In the same building as the visitor centre – the once-grand Duchy Hotel.

Visit Dartmoor (www.visitdartmoor.co.uk) Dartmoor's official tourism site has information on accommodation, activities, sights, events and more.

ⓘ Getting There & Around

It is possible to get around Dartmoor by bus; however, services can be infrequent, and some are very seasonal.

Tourist offices stock bus timetables; Traveline South West (www.travelinesw.com) is a good online resource.

Bus 98 (one daily Monday to Saturday) Operated by Target Travel, this is the only regular bus into the centre of the moor. It runs from Tavistock to Princetown, Two Bridges and Postbridge, then circles back to Yelverton. A couple of afternoon buses only go as far as Princetown and back.

Bus 173 (five daily Monday to Saturday) Run by Dartline Coaches, this service goes from Exeter to Chagford, with two buses a day continuing to Moretonhampstead.

Bus 1 (four per hour Monday to Saturday, hourly Sunday) This Stagecoach service shuttles from Plymouth to Tavistock, via Yelverton.

Bus 178 (one daily Monday to Saturday) Travels from Newton Abbot to Okehampton, via Bovey Tracey, Moretonhampstead and Chagford. Operated by Country Bus.

Bus 113 (one daily Monday to Friday) Country Bus from Tavistock to Trago Mills, stopping at Yelverton, Princetown, Two Bridges, Ashburton and Newton Abbot.

Bus 6A (four per day Monday to Saturday, one Sunday) Skirts the northern edge of the moor en route from Bude to Exeter, stopping in Okehampton.

Haytor Hoppa Bus 271 Runs Saturdays between late-May and mid-September only, providing four buses between Newton Abbot, Bovey Tracey, Haytor and Widecombe-in-the-Moor (daily fare £5).

Bus 23 (☑07580 260683; ☉1st Sat of month) Minibus from Tavistock to Exeter, via Princetown, Postbridge, Two Bridges and Moretonhampstead. Runs on the first Saturday of the month only; book by phone.

Princetown

POP 1770

Set in the heart of the remote higher moor, Princetown is dominated by the grey, foreboding bulk of Dartmoor Prison, and on bad-weather days the town can have a remote, even bleak, feel. But it's also an evocative reminder of the harsh realities of moorland life and makes an atmospheric base for some excellent walks.

⊙ Sights

Higher Moorland Visitor Centre   MUSEUM
(DNPA; ☑01822-890414; Tavistock Rd; ☉10am-5pm Apr-Sep, to 4pm Mar & Oct, 10.30am-3.30pm Thu-Sun Nov-Feb) FREE At the tourist office–visitor centre, heritage displays include those on tin workings, gunpowder factories, ecology and legends – there's also a stunning time-lapse video.

The building used to be the Duchy Hotel; one former guest was Sir Arthur Conan Doyle, who went on to write *The Hound of the Baskervilles*. Dartmoor lore recounts that local man Henry Baskerville took the novelist on a carriage tour, and the brooding landscape he encountered, coupled with legends of huge phantom dogs, inspired the thriller.

Dartmoor Prison Museum   MUSEUM
(☑01822-322130; www.dartmoor-prison.co.uk; adult/child £3.50/2.50; ☉9.30am-4.30pm Mon-Thu & Sat, to 4pm Fri & Sun; ℗) In the early 1800s, Princetown's infamous jail was home to French and American prisoners of war. It became a convict jail in 1850, and today still houses around 640 inmates. Just up from the looming gates, this museum provides a chilling glimpse of life inside. Look out for

BATH & SOUTHWEST ENGLAND DARTMOOR NATIONAL PARK

straitjackets, manacles, escape stories and the makeshift knives made by modern-day prisoners.

In 2015, it was announced that the prison was likely to close within the next 10 years.

🛏 Sleeping & Eating

Tor Royal Farm
B&B ££

(☎01822-890189; www.torroyal.co.uk; Tor Royal Lane, near Princetown; s £60, d £80-110; 🅿🛜) An easygoing, country-cottage-styled farmhouse packed with lived-in charm. Heritage-style rooms (cream-and-white furniture, puffy bedspreads, easy chairs) are cosy, and the free afternoon tea of Victoria sponges, cupcakes and fancies galore is reason alone to stay here.

Two Bridges
HOTEL £££

(☎01822-892300; www.twobridges.co.uk; Two Bridges; r £140-240; 🅿🛜) This is perhaps the definitive historic moorland hotel: polished wood panels, huge inglenook fireplaces, and a guest list that includes Wallis Simpson, Winston Churchill and Vivien Leigh. The Premier and Historic rooms are positively museum worthy, with massive wooden four-poster beds and antique furniture aplenty; cheaper rooms are heavy on the florals. It's 1.5 miles northeast of Princetown.

⭐ Prince of Wales
PUB, HOSTEL £

(☎01822-890219; Tavistock Rd; mains £10-18; ⊙11am-11pm; 🅿🛜) Roaring fires, low ceilings, a friendly landlord – the Prince is the place where everyone pops in for a pint of home-brewed Jail Ale and a plate of something hot and filling.

B&B accommodation is also available (double rooms from £50), and there's a bargain bunkhouse, with unexpected luxuries including central heating and a drying room.

⭐ Fox Tor Cafe
CAFE £

(☎01822-890238; www.foxtorcafe.com; Two Bridges Rd; mains £5-12; ⊙9am-5pm Mon-Fri, 7.30am-6pm Sat, 7.30am-5pm Sun; 🛜) Known as FTC to locals, this friendly little cafe is a favourite for hearty breakfasts, doorstep sandwiches and massive chunks of cake, but it does more-filling fare, too, such as spicy chilli and mushroom stroganoff. On cold, wet Dartmoor days the two wood-burning stoves are particularly welcoming.

There's a basic bunkhouse (dorm beds £12) out the back, where hikers and cyclists stay. Fox Tor also hires out bikes (p304).

Postbridge & Around
POP 170

The quaint hamlet of Postbridge owes its popularity, and its name, to its medieval stone slab or clapper bridge: a 13th-century structure with four, 3m-long slabs propped up on sturdy columns of stacked stones. Walking the bridge takes you across the rushing East Dart; it's a picturesque spot to whip off your boots and plunge your feet into water that's quite possibly the coldest you've ever felt.

🛏 Sleeping & Eating

Brimpts Farm
B&B £

(☎0845 034 5968; www.brimptsfarm.co.uk; Dartmeet; sites per person £5, s/d/f £40/70/105; 🅿) A beauty of a Dartmoor farm, as traditional as afternoon tea, and all the better for it. Choose from quaint, frilly B&B rooms, basic camping fields (£5 per tent) or a timber-and-aluminium camping pod (per night £30 to £35), all with bewitching moorland views. Hearty breakfasts, packed lunches and cracking cream teas. It's on the B3357, Two Bridges–Dartmeet road.

Dartmoor YHA
HOSTEL £

(Bellever; ☎0845 371 9622; www.yha.org.uk; dm/q £25/90; 🅿🛜) A characterful former farm on the edge of a conifer plantation, with a huge kitchen, lots of rustic stone walls and cosy dorms. It also rents out bikes. It's a mile south of Postbridge.

ⓘ WARNING

The military uses three adjoining areas of Dartmoor as training ranges where live ammunition is employed. Tourist offices can outline these locations; they're also marked on Ordnance Survey (OS) maps. You're advised to check if the hiking route you're planning falls within a range; if it does, find out if firing is taking place at the time you plan to walk via the **Firing Information Service** (☎0800 458 4868; www.mod.uk/access). During the day, red flags fly at the edges of in-use ranges, while red flares burn at night. Even when there's no firing, beware of unidentified metal objects lying in the grass. Don't touch anything you find: note its position and report it to the **Commandant** (☎01837-650010).

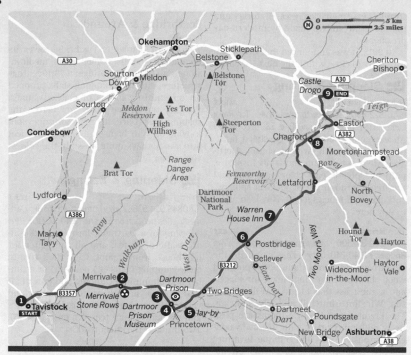

Driving Tour
A Dartmoor Road Trip

START TAVISTOCK
END CASTLE DROGO
LENGTH 20 MILES; ONE DAY

Driving on Dartmoor is like being inside a feature film: compelling 360-degree views are screened all around. This scenic, west-to-east transmoor traverse sweeps up and through this wilderness, taking in a bleak prison, prehistoric remains, a rustic pub and a unique castle. Start by strolling among the fine 19th-century architecture of ❶ **Tavistock**, perhaps dropping by its Pannier Market to rummage for antiques. Next take the B3357 towards Princetown. It climbs steeply (expect ears to pop), crosses a cattle grid (a sign you're on the moor 'proper') and crests a hill to reveal swaths of honey-coloured tors. Soon you're at ❷ **Merrivale**. Park up on the right, just after the Dartmoor Inn, and stroll over the rise (due south) to discover a snaking stone row; a tiny stone circle and

a standing stone are just 100m further on. Back in the car, after a short climb, turn right towards Princetown, glimpsing the brooding bulk of Dartmoor Prison (you can't stop here; there's a better vantage point later). Call in at the ❸ **Dartmoor Prison Museum** (p306) to explore the jail's grim story. Cut through rugged ❹ **Princetown**, before picking up the B3212 towards Two Bridges; the ❺ **lay-by** immediately after you leave Princetown provides prime Dartmoor Prison views. As you follow signs for Moretonhampstead, an expansive landscape unfurls. At ❻ **Post-bridge**, park and stroll over the 700-year-old bridge, then dangle hot feet in the cold River Dart. A few miles further on, the ❼ **Warren House Inn** (p309) makes an atmospheric spot for lunch. Around Lettaford take one of the signed, plunging lanes to ❽ **Chagford** to visit its quaint, thatch-dotted square. Scour some of its wonderfully old-fashioned shops, then head to ❾ **Castle Drogo** (p309) to explore a unique 1920s stately home.

★**Warren House Inn**   PUB FOOD **££**
(☑ 01822-880208; www.warrenhouseinn.co.uk; near Postbridge; mains £9-15; ☺ noon-8.30pm, bar 11am-11pm, shorter hours winter; **P**) Marooned amid miles of moorland, this Dartmoor institution exudes a hospitality only found in pubs in the middle of nowhere. A fire that's been burning (apparently) since 1845 warms stone floors, trestle tables and hikers munching on robust food; the Warreners Pie (local rabbit) is legendary. It's on the B3212, some 2 miles northeast of Postbridge.

Widecombe-in-the-Moor

POP 570

With its honey-grey buildings and imposing church tower, this is archetypal Dartmoor, down to the ponies grazing on the village green. The village is commemorated in the traditional English folk song 'Widecombe Fair', a reference to the traditional country pageant that takes place on the second Tuesday of September.

◉ Sights

St Pancras Church   CHURCH
(☑ 01364-621334; The Green; ☺ 8am-5pm) St Pancras' immense 40m tower has seen it dubbed the Cathedral of the Moor. Inside, search out the boards telling the fire-and-brimstone tale of the violent storm of 1638 – it knocked a pinnacle from the roof, killing several parishioners. As ever on Dartmoor, the Devil was blamed, said to be in search of souls.

⌂ Sleeping & Eating

Manor Cottage   B&B **£**
(☑ 01364-621218; www.manorcottagedartmoor. co.uk; s £45-60, d £55-70; **P**⚡) Roses climb around the doorway of this quaint, ancient, village-centre cottage. The best billet is the bedroom-bathroom suite at the top of a private spiral staircase. Breakfasts feature berry compote, local sausages and eggs freshly laid by the hens that cluck around outside.

★**Rugglestone Inn**   PUB FOOD **££**
(☑ 01364-621327; www.rugglestoneinn.co.uk; mains £11; ☺ noon-2pm & 6.30-9pm) Just one pint at this wisteria-clad pub is enough to make you want to drop everything and move to Dartmoor. It's a classic wood-beamed, low-ceilinged, old-fashioned village boozer, full of local characters and packed with history. There are lots of real ales on tap, and

the menu features filling dishes like pies, lasagne, quiches and potted crab.

ⓘ Getting There & Away

Widecombe's bus service is severely limited – bus 672 stops once a week (Wednesday) en route to Buckfastleigh, Ashburton and Newton Abbot.

On summer Saturdays Widecombe is served by the Haytor Hoppa (daily fare £5), which sees four services running to Newton Abbot, Bovey Tracey and Haytor.

Chagford & Moretonhampstead

One of the prettiest of the Dartmoor villages, Chagford's stone-walled cottages, white-washed buildings and thatched roofs are set around a quintessential village square. It's a handsome, vibrant little village, with some great places to sleep and eat, and there are views over the tors practically everywhere you look.

◉ Sights

★**Castle Drogo**   HISTORIC BUILDING
(NT; ☑ 01647-433306; www.nationaltrust.org. uk/castle-drogo; near Drewsteignton; adult/child £11.60/5.80; ☺ 11am-5pm mid-Mar–Oct; **P**) Three miles northeast of Chagford, this outlandish architectural flight of fancy was designed by Sir Edwin Lutyens for self-made food-millionaire Julius Drewe. Built between 1911 and 1931, it was intended to be a modern-day medieval castle, with all the comforts of a country house. Unfortunately, the property hasn't worn well – it's currently the focus of a massive six-year restoration project. Parts of the house remain open, though, and imaginative midrenovation displays include a scaffolding viewing tower.

⌂ Sleeping & Eating

Sparrowhawk   HOSTEL **£**
(☑ 01647-440318; www.sparrowhawkbackpackers. co.uk; 45 Ford St; dm/d/f £19/40/50; ⚡) ✿ One of only a few independent hostels on Dartmoor, Sparrowhawk is a reliable budget base. It's located in a converted house, with lots of wood and exposed stone, and a central courtyard ringed by rickety outbuildings. The accommodation is basic, but serviceable. There is a kitchen, too.

★**Gidleigh Park**   HOTEL **£££**
(☑ 01647-432367; www.gidleigh.co.uk; Gidleigh; r £315-545, ste £750-1095, 3-course lunch/dinner

£65/125; ⊘ restaurant noon-2pm & 7-9pm; P 🛜) Without doubt Devon's grandest, fanciest and priciest hotel. At the end of a long private drive, the mock-Tudor house is an unashamedly opulent pamper pad: vast suites with wet-room showers, luxurious lounges with crackling fires, and a restaurant overseen by multiple-award-winning Chris Simpson. It's 2 miles west of Chagford.

★ Horse   GASTROPUB ££
(☑ 01647-440242; www.thehorsedartmoor.co.uk; 7 George St; mains £8-20; ⊘ 12.30-2.30pm Tue-Sat, 6.30-9pm daily) You've got to love a place that bills itself as a 'pub and nosebag'. Despite the village location, this is a hip gastropub that wouldn't feel out of place in the big city: it serves simple, well-done food including tapas, mussels, home-cured tuna, chargrilled rib-eye and lots of pizzas.

Okehampton & Lydford

Okehampton huddles on the edge of an uninhabited tract of bracken-covered slopes and granite tors – the mind-expanding landscape known as the higher moor. The town has a staging-post feel, and its traditional shops and pubs are good places to prepare for a foray into the Dartmoor wilderness.

It's also near an impressive local landmark, the 46m-high Meldon Viaduct, a remnant of the old London and South Western Railway line that ran across the moor from 1874 to 1968.

The little village of Lydford is best known for the dramatic gorge that cuts through the landscape nearby en route to a beautiful waterfall. Once a strategic stronghold, its medieval castle has long since tumbled into ruins. It's 9 miles southwest of Okehampton.

◉ Sights

★ Lydford Gorge   WATERFALL
(NT; ☑ 01822-820320; www.nationaltrust.org.uk; adult/child £9.40/4.70; ⊘ 10am-5pm mid-Mar–Oct, 11am-3.30pm Nov & Dec) This plunging gorge is the deepest in the southwest, and can be reached via a 1.5-mile rugged riverside hike past a series of bubbling whirlpools (including the fearsome Devil's Cauldron) to the thundering 30m-high White Lady waterfall. Not quite Niagara, but quite an impressive sight nonetheless.

Okehampton Castle   CASTLE
(EH; ☑ 01837-52844; www.english-heritage.org. uk; Castle Lodge; adult/child £4.80/2.90; ⊘ 10am-

5pm Apr-Jun, Sep & Oct, to 6pm Jul & Aug) Okehampton's castle dates back to Norman times, and is strategically sited on top of a rocky escarpment. Later it became a sumptuous residence for Hugh Courtenay, Earl of Devon, who enlarged it into Devon's largest castle. It's now a picturesque ruin; little remains of the interior, but several of the stout exterior walls still stand, some careering off at improbable angles.

Finch Foundry   HISTORIC BUILDING
(NT; ☑ 01837-840046; www.nationaltrust.org.uk; Sticklepath; adult/child £7.10/3.55; ⊘ 11am-5pm early Mar–Oct; P) A century ago, this dramatic building would have thundered to the sound of clanging hammers and grinding metal. It was one of the busiest tool factories in the southwest, turning out hundreds of chisels, knives, shears and scythes a day. Though it's not quite the industrial powerhouse of yesteryear, it's still a working forge, powered by three working watermills. You can drive or cycle here, or follow a 4-mile (3½-hour) walk east along the Tarka Trail from Okehampton.

🛏 Sleeping & Eating

Okehampton Bracken Tor YHA   HOSTEL £
(☑ 01837-53916; www.yha.org.uk; Saxongate; dm £27; ⊘ reception 8-10am & 5-10pm; P @ 🛜) Budget-conscious outdoors types love this one: a 100-year-old country house, set in 1.6-hectare grounds on the fringe of the higher moor. It also offers climbing, canoeing and bike hire. It's a mile south of Okehampton; be aware, there's another YHA hostel in Okehampton itself.

★ Dartmoor Inn   INN ££
(☑ 01822-820221; www.dartmoorinn.com; Moorside; d £115; ⊘ restaurant noon-2.30pm & 6.45-9pm Tue-Sat; P) It looks venerable, but behind the whitewashed exterior, this coaching inn is a thoroughly modern affair: light, bright and bang up to date. Most people stop for the superb food, such as slow-cooked oxtail and butterflied lamb rump (mains £12 to £20), but it's worth spending the night: rooms sparkle with Roberts radios, sleigh beds and posh linens.

ⓘ Information

Tourist Office (☑ 01837-52295; www. everythingokehampton.co.uk; 3 West St; ⊘ 10am-3pm Mon-Fri, to 1pm Sat Apr-Oct) Based at the Museum of Dartmoor Life.

Croyde & Braunton

POP 8130

Croyde has the kind of cheerful, chilled vibe you'd expect from its role as North Devon's surf central. The old world meets a new surfing wave here: thatched roofs peep out over racks of wetsuits; crowds of hip wave-riders sip beers outside 17th-century inns; and powerful waves line up to roll in towards acres of sand.

⊙ Sights & Activities

The water's hard to resist in Croyde. **Ralph's** (☑ 01271-890147; Hobbs Hill; surfboard & wetsuit hire per 4/24hr £12/18, bodyboard & wetsuit £10/15; ⊙ 9am-dusk mid-Mar–Dec) is among those hiring out wetsuits and surfboards. Lessons are provided by **Surf South West** (☑ 01271-890400; www.surfsouthwest.com; Croyde Burrows car park; per half/full day £35/65; ⊙ late Mar–Oct) and **Surfing Croyde Bay** (☑ 01271-891200; www.surfingcroydebay.co.uk; Baggy Point; per half/full day £35/70).

★ **Museum of British Surfing**　　MUSEUM
(☑ 01271-815155; www.museumofbritishsurfing.org.uk; Caen St; adult/child £2/free; ⊙ 11am-3pm Wed-Mon Easter-Dec) Few museums are this cool. Vibrant surfboards and vintage wetsuits line the walls; sepia images catch your eye. The stories are compelling: 18th-century British sailors riding Hawaiian waves – England's 1920s homegrown surf pioneers. Here, heritage meets hanging ten.

Braunton Burrows　　WILDLIFE RESERVE
(www.explorebraunton.org; near Braunton; P) **FREE** The vast network of dunes here is the UK's largest. Paths wind past sandy hummocks, salt marshes, purple thyme, yellow hawkweed and pyramidal orchids. The burrows fringe an immense sweep of sandy beach, and were the main training area for American troops before D-Day. Mock landing craft are still hidden in the tufted dunes near the car park at its southern tip.

⌷ Sleeping & Eating

★ **Baggy**　　HOSTEL, B&B £
(☑ 01271-890078; www.baggys.co.uk; Baggy Point; dm/d from £33/110; ?) Forget your crammed-in beds and wetsuit-strewn dorms – this hostel and surf lodge is light, bright and enormously inviting. It has a fine coastal location, and rooms are lovely, with lots of wood and minimal clutter. There's also a surfy cafe with

an outside deck where you can eat breakfast while watching the waves roll in.

Ocean Pitch　　CAMPSITE £
(☑ 07581 024348; www.oceanpitch.co.uk; Moor Lane; sites per 2 adults £30; ⊙ mid-Jun–early Sep; P ?) A surfers' favourite, set at the northern end of Croyde Bay with brilliant views of the breakers. If you don't feel like pitching a tent, you can rent a luxury sleeping pod (£99 per night, two-night minimum) or even a classic VW camper (£99 per night, two-night minimum).

Thatch　　INN ££
(☑ 01271-890349; www.thethatchcroyde.com; 14 Hobbs Hill; d £60-100, f £120) A legendary venue among surfers, this cavernous, thatched pub's trendy bedrooms feature subtle creams, stripes and checks; the owners offer extra rooms above another pub and in the cottage opposite. The pick are at the nearby (quieter) Priory, where elegant beams frame exposed stone. The Thatch also serves famously hearty pub grub (mains from £10, from 8am to 10pm).

❶ Information

Braunton Tourist Office (☑ 01271-816688; www.visitbraunton.co.uk; Caen St; ⊙ 10am-3pm Mon-Fri year-round, plus to 1pm Sat Jun-Dec) Inside the town's (free) museum.

Ilfracombe & Around

POP 11,510

If there's anywhere that sums up the faded grandeur of the British seaside, it's surely Ilfracombe. Framed by precipitous cliffs, elegant town houses, golf greens and a promenade strung with twinkling lights, it's a place that might seem pickled in a bygone age. But look beneath the surface and you'll find there's another side to Ilfracombe – it's a favourite hang-out for the artist Damien Hirst, who's added a controversial statue to the seafront, and it's now home to some top-notch eateries. Ilfracombe more than deserves a look.

⊙ Sights & Activities

★ **Verity**　　LANDMARK
(The Pier) Pregnant, naked and holding aloft a huge spear, Damien Hirst's 20m statue *Verity* towers above Ilfracombe's harbour mouth. On the seaward side her skin is peeled back, revealing sinew, fat and foetus. Critics say she detracts from the scenery; the

DON'T MISS

CLOVELLY

Clovelly (☑ 01237-431781; www.clovelly.co.uk; adult/child £7.50/4.50; ⊙ 9am-6pm Jun-Sep, 9.30am-5pm Apr, May & Oct, 10am-4pm Nov-Mar; 🅿) is the quintessential picture-postcard Devon village. Its cottages cascade down cliffs to meet a curving claw of a harbour that is lined with lobster pots backed by a deep-blue sea. A clutch of impossibly picturesque inns and B&Bs makes it hard to leave.

Clovelly is privately owned, and admission is charged at the hilltop visitor centre. The village's cobbled streets are so steep that cars can't cope, so supplies are brought in by sledge; you'll see these big bread baskets on runners leaning outside homes. Charles Kingsley, author of the children's classic *The Water Babies*, spent much of his early life in Clovelly – don't miss his former house, or the highly atmospheric fisher's cottage and the village's twin chapels.

Guided tours (☑ 07974 134701; www.clovellyvillagetours.co.uk; tours £5) provide interesting context on the village's buildings and history.

If you don't feel up to the steep uphill slog – or you're carting luggage to one of the village B&Bs – you can book a space back to the car park on the Land Rover taxi (£2).

artist says she's an allegory for truth and justice. Either way, she's drawing the crowds.

Ilfracombe Aquarium   AQUARIUM
(☑ 01271-864533; www.ilfracombeaquarium.co.uk; The Pier; adult/child £4.75/3.75; ⊙ 10am-3pm early Feb–late May & Oct, to 5pm or 5.45pm late May–Sep) Recreates aquatic environments from Exmoor to the Atlantic, via estuary, rock pool and harbour.

★ Tunnelsbeaches   SWIMMING
(☑ 01271-879882; www.tunnelsbeaches.co.uk; Bath Pl; adult/child £2.50/1.95; ⊙ 10am-5pm Apr-Jun, Sep & Oct, to 7pm Jul & Aug) In 1823 hundreds of Welsh miners hacked, by hand, the four tunnels here out of solid rock. It was a remarkable feat. The tunnels lead to a strip of beach where you can plunge into the sea from Victorian tidal bathing pools.

🛏 Sleeping & Eating

Ocean Backpackers   HOSTEL £
(☑ 01271-867835; www.oceanbackpackers.co.uk; 29 St James Pl; dm £18-20, d £45-50, f from £55-80; 🅿@🤶) Brightly painted en-suite dorms, a convivial kitchen and free coffee lend this long-established indie hostel a laid-back vibe; the giant world map in the lounge has kick-started countless traveller tales. The doubles and family rooms are great value.

★ Norbury House   B&B ££
(☑ 01271-863888; www.norburyhouse.co.uk; Torrs Park; d £85-110, f £120-145; 🅿🤶) Each of the rooms in this gorgeous guesthouse is done up in a different style: choose from pop art, art deco or contemporary chic. Fabulous

soft furnishings, a light-filled sitting room (complete with baby grand piano), charming hosts and cracking sea-and-town views seal the deal.

★ Olive Branch & Room   BISTRO £££
(☑ 01271-867831; www.thomascarrchef.co.uk; 56 Fore St; mains £21-23; ⊙ 6.30-9pm Tue-Sat; 🤶) Having trained under Michelin-starred chef Nathan Outlaw, Thomas Carr has earned his own star at this Ilfracombe bistro, showcasing his skills while championing local produce and seafood. For the full experience, go for the six- or eight-course taster menu (£75 and £95). Carr has also announced plans to open a seafood grill in the town: watch this space.

Rooms are available (doubles £115 to £130), and as you'd expect, breakfast is a treat.

Quay   EUROPEAN ££
(☑ 01271-868090; www.11thequay.co.uk; 11 The Quay; mains £11-25; ⊙ noon-2.30pm & 6-9pm daily Apr-Sep, Wed-Sat Oct-Mar) Ilfracombe's hippest harbourside hang-out by far is owned by artist Damien Hirst (he of the cut-in-half cows and pickled sharks). His creations line the walls, so you get to tuck into a cognac-laced lobster bisque or pan-roasted Exmoor chicken breast while studying models of his local statue *Verity* and, with delicious irony, fish in formaldehyde.

ⓘ Information

Tourist Office (☑ 01271-863001; www.visit ilfracombe.co.uk; The Seafront; ⊙ 9.30am-4.30pm Mon-Fri, 10.30am-4.30pm Sat & Sun

Easter-Oct, closed Sun Nov-Easter) Inside the seafront Landmark Theatre building.

ⓘ Getting There & Away

Bus 21/21A Runs to Barnstaple (£2.50, 40 minutes, half-hourly) via Braunton (£1.90, 30 minutes).
Bus 300 Runs to Lynmouth in July and August only (£3, two daily Monday to Friday).

CORNWALL

You can't get further west than the ancient Celtic kingdom of Cornwall (or Kernow, as it's known to Cornish speakers). Blessed with the southwest's wildest coastline and most breathtakingly beautiful beaches, this proudly independent peninsula has always marched to its own tune.

While the staple industries of old – mining, fishing and farming – have all but disappeared, Cornwall has since reinvented itself as one of the nation's creative corners. Whether it's exploring the space-age domes of the Eden Project, sampling the culinary creations of a celebrity chef or basking on a deserted beach, you're guaranteed to feel the itch of inspiration. Time to let a little Kernow into your soul.

Since 2006, Cornwall's historic mining areas have been designated a Unesco World Heritage Site, the Cornwall and West Devon Mining Landscape (www.cornish-mining.org.uk).

ⓘ Getting There & Away

It's pretty easy to get to Cornwall these days, although its far westerly location means travel times from most locations in the UK are long.

The county's main airport (p323) is just outside Newquay, with links to London Gatwick and other major cities. First Kernow bus A5 (26 minutes, every two hours Monday to Saturday, three on Sunday) runs from Newquay's bus station to Padstow, stopping at the airport en route. Taxis cost £15 to £25 from the town centre. Various seasonal destinations around the UK and Europe are also offered during summer.

The main train line from London Paddington runs through the centre of the county before terminating at Penzance, stopping at major towns in between.

The major road into Cornwall, the A30, is very prone to traffic jams in summer. The A38 from Plymouth over the Tamar Bridge into Cornwall is another alternative, but it's a more circuitous route. You are only required to pay the bridge toll when leaving Cornwall.

ⓘ Getting Around

Bus, train and ferry timetables can be found on the **Traveline South West** (☑0871 200 2233; www.travelinesw.com) website.

The useful website of Great Scenic Railways (www.greatscenicrailways.com) features online booking and timetables for Cornwall's regional railways.

BUS

Cornwall's main bus provider, **First Kernow** (☑customer service 0845 600 1420, timetables 0871 200 2233; www.firstgroup.com/cornwall), operates the majority of services between major towns. The county's other big bus company, Western Greyhound, went into administration in 2015, and although some of its routes are now operated by smaller coach companies, many were axed, leaving some rural communities stranded without a regular bus service.

A one-day ticket covering all buses costs £12/6, but it's only slightly cheaper than the Ride Cornwall Ranger (adult/child/family £13/9.75/26), which also covers train travel.

Somewhat annoyingly, First has separate apps for timetable queries and for ticket purchases (mTickets). Currently, only one-day and multiday travel passes can be bought through its mTickets ticketing app.

TRAIN

Cornwall's main railway line follows the coast as far as Penzance, with branch lines to Gunnislake, Looe, Falmouth, St Ives and Newquay.

Most trains are provided by Great Western Railway (p221), although CrossCountry Trains (p221) also run through major stations.

Both companies have useful apps that enable timetable queries and e-ticket purchases.

TRANSPORT PASSES

Several passes cover public transport in Cornwall.

Ride Cornwall Ranger (adult/child/family £13/9.75/26) is the best all-round value covering a day's bus and train travel across Cornwall, and between Cornwall and Plymouth. The ticket can be purchased from train and bus stations, and from bus drivers, and is valid after 9am Monday to Friday and weekends.

The **Freedom of Devon & Cornwall Rover** (three days travel in seven days adult/child £49/24.50, eight days travel in 15 days £79/39.50) ticket is good value if you're using the train extensively through Devon and Cornwall.

There are also Day Ranger tickets for all of Cornwall's branch railway lines, as well as 'Two Together' and 'Groupsave' tickets for two and four adults travelling together.

If you have a permanent address in Cornwall (eg a holiday home), you can also buy a **Devon & Cornwall Railcard** (£10, www.railrover.org/railcards), which qualifies you for a 30% discount on off-peak train travel within Devon and Cornwall, including all the branch lines.

Bude

POP 9240

A scant few miles from the Devon border, Bude is a breezy seaside town with a bevy of impressive beaches, as well as a lovely seawater lido built in the 1930s. The town itself isn't much to look at, but the stunning coastline on its doorstep makes it worthy of a stop.

◉ Sights & Activities

Bude has plenty of good beaches within easy reach of the town centre, but to reach the more out-of-the-way ones, you'll need to drive or hike along the coast path. Three miles south of town is Widemouth Bay (*wid*-muth), a broad, sandy beach great for both families and surfers. Two miles further is the shingly beach of Millook, followed by the dramatic cliffs around Crackington Haven.

Three miles north of town are the National Trust–owned Northcott Mouth and Sandymouth.

A mile further on is pebbly Duckpool, often quiet even in summer.

Raven Surf School SURFING
(☑ 07860 465499; www.ravensurf.co.uk; per lesson £35) A reliable school run by Mike Raven, a former surfing champion. It also offers surf life-saving and instructor courses, and has accommodation in 'surf pods' (ecofriendly wooden cabins) and a campsite nearby.

Big Blue Surf School SURFING
(☑ 01288-331764; www.bigbluesurfschool.co.uk; per lesson £30) A recommended school that offers lessons mainly to beginner and intermediate surfers. Special lessons for surfers with disabilities, and a 'women's club' on Tuesday evenings and Saturday mornings are some of its main attractions. Look for the trailer in the Summerleaze beach car park.

⌕ Sleeping & Eating

Elements Hotel HOTEL ££
(☑ 01288-275066; www.elements-life.co.uk; Marine Dr; s £69, d £89-130, f from £130; P ⓢ ⓐ ⓢ) This hotel has a super clifftop position, but looks a bit bland and boxy from the outside. Fear not: inside it sports soothing sea colours, swirly patterned fabrics, big coastal views and thoughtful mod cons such as Bluetooth speakers, Playstations in the family rooms and a Finholme sauna. Surf packages are offered by Raven Surf School (p314).

Hebasca DESIGN HOTEL ££
(☑ 01288-352361; www.hebasca.co.uk; Downs View; r £84-235; P ⓢ) Boutique-on-a-budget best describes this hotel, a sister establishment to Tommy Jacks (☑ 01288-356013; www.tommyjacks.co.uk; Crooklets Beach; r £70-165; P ⓢ ⓐ) at Crooklets beach. It's designed for grown-ups, with pleasant rooms blending earth tones and technicolour upholstery, bright patterned cushions and plenty of Scandi-style slate and wood. They feel efficient rather than out-and-out elegant. Downstairs there's a grill restaurant and cocktail bar, with cow-print furnishings and pop-art murals of fishermen.

★ **Beach at Bude** HOTEL £££
(☑ 01288-389800; www.thebeachatbude.co.uk; Summerleaze Cres; r incl breakfast £179-254; P ⓢ ⓐ) This lovely hotel steals the show in practically every category: space, style, welcome and definitely view. It has a fine position behind Summerleaze beach, and the rooms are really attractive, with pale wood furniture, Lloyd Loom chairs and peach-and-taupe colour schemes conjuring the feel of a New England beach cabin. The restaurant (mains £14 to £24) is reliably good, too.

Life's a Beach CAFE ££
(☑ 01288-355222; www.lifesabeach.info; Summerleaze; mains lunch £5.75-9.50, 2-/3-course dinner menu £25/30; ⊙ 10.30am-3.30pm & 7-10pm Mon-Sat, 10.30am-3pm Sun) Affectionately known as LAB, this beachside bistro diner is an old favourite in Bude. It's a nice place for a baguette or a burger by day, but it's at its best as the sun goes down, when you can dine on whole salt-baked sea bream and roast halibut with the best view in town.

ⓘ Information

Bude Tourist Office (☑ 01288-354240; www.visitbude.info; The Crescent; ⊙ 10am-5pm Mon-Sat, plus to 4pm Sun summer) Beside the main car park near Bude Castle.

ⓘ Getting There & Away

First Kernow bus 95 (£3.50 to £6, six daily Monday to Saturday, four on Sunday) runs between

CORNISH VINEYARDS

Cornwall might not seem an obvious place for winemaking, but father-and-son team Bob and Sam Lindo have been producing award-winning vintages at **Camel Valley Vineyard** (☑ 01208-77959; www.camelvalley.com; ☺ shop 10am-5pm Mon-Sat, tours 2.30pm Mon-Fri plus 5pm Wed) since 1989. The range includes whites and rosés, and a bubbly that's Champagne in all but name. Aficionados say the wines have a fresh, light quality that comes from the mild climate and pure sea air. Vineyard tours run regularly and you can taste and buy the goods in the on-site shop.

Trevibban Mill (☑ 01841-541413; www.trevibbanmill.com; Dark Lane, St Issey; ☺ noon-5pm Wed-Thu & Sun, to 10pm Fri & Sat) has a fast-growing reputation in the wine world, and it's a fine place to sample vintages in a dreamy Cornish setting. In total there are some 11,000 vines and 1700 apple trees spread across the estate, producing a range of whites and rosés in both still and sparkling versions (there are even a couple of fruity reds on the roster). The ciders and juices are delicious, too.

Guided tours (£30) exploring the art of winemaking and the estate's organic ethos take place on Sundays and include a tasting. There's also a lovely restaurant, **Appleton's at the Vineyard** (☑ 01841-541413; www.trevibbanmill.com/appletons-at-the-vineyard; St Issey; mains £17-24; ☺ noon-5pm Wed-Sun, 6.30-10.30pm Fri & Sat), and a wine-tasting bar.

Bude and Boscastle (30 minutes), Tintagel (40 minutes), Camelford (one hour) and Wadebridge (1½ hours).

The 96 bus (four daily Monday to Saturday) connects Camelford with Port Isaac, Polzeath and Rock. Note that on Sunday, the 95 service stops at all the places normally served by the 96.

Boscastle

POP 640

Nestled in the crook of a steep coombe (valley) at the confluence of three rivers, Boscastle's seafaring heritage stretches back to Elizabethan times. With its quaint cottages, flower-clad cliffs, tinkling streams and a sturdy quay, it's almost impossibly photogenic. But the peaceful setting belies some turbulent history: in 2004 Boscastle was hit by one of Britain's largest-ever flash floods, which carried away cars, bridges and buildings. Happily, the village has since been rebuilt, but look closely even now and you'll be able to spot reminders of the floods dotted around the village.

◉ Sights

Museum of Witchcraft & Magic MUSEUM
(☑ 01840-250111; www.museumofwitchcraftand magic.co.uk; The Harbour; adult/child £5/4; ☺ 10.30am-6pm Mon-Sat, 11.30am-6pm Sun Mar-Nov) This oddball museum has been a fixture in Boscastle since 1960, and apparently houses the world's largest collection of witchy memorabilia, from haunted skulls to hags' bridles and voodoo dolls (known

as poppets). It's half-tacky, half-spooky, and some of the more 'controversial' exhibits might perturb kids of a sensitive disposition (and some adults, for that matter). Recent exhibitions have covered curses and ritual magic.

🛏 Sleeping & Eating

Boscastle YHA HOSTEL £
(☑ 0845 371 9006; www.yha.org.uk; Palace Stables, The Harbour; dm £19-25; ☺ Apr-Nov) Boscastle's shoebox-sized hostel was all but washed away by the 2004 floods, but it's since been completely renovated. The dorms are very small, but in return you get a historic location in one of the village's oldest buildings, and a super harbour location. There's no food available, but you can self-cater.

Boscastle House B&B ££
(☑ 01840-250654; www.boscastlehouse.co.uk; Doctors Hill; d from £128; P ☎) The best of Boscastle's B&Bs, in a Victorian house overlooking the valley. Five classy rooms have a bright, contemporary feel that mixes neutral colours with bold print wallpapers. Charlotte has bay-window views; Nine Windows has twin sinks and a free-standing bath; and Trelawney has ample space and its own sofa. Two-night minimum.

★ Boscastle Farm Shop CAFE £
(☑ 01840-250827; www.boscastlefarmshop.co.uk; cakes & teas £3-5; ☺ 10am-5pm; P) Half a mile uphill from the harbour on the B3263, this excellent farm shop sells its own produce,

including ruby-red beef and possibly the best sausages on the north coast, plus a comprehensive range of Cornish goodies. In the spacious cafe, tall windows look out on to green fields and the coast – the perfect setting for a cream tea.

ℹ️ Information

Boscastle Tourist Office (📞 01840-250010; www.visitboscastleandtintagel.com; The Harbour; ⊙ 10am-5pm Mar-Oct, 10.30am-4pm Nov-Feb) Not far from the quay, and with some useful leaflets on local history and walks.

ℹ️ Getting There & Away

Coastal bus 95 (£3.20 to £5.20, six daily Monday to Saturday, four on Sunday) stops in Boscastle on its way from Bude (30 minutes), then continues on to Tintagel (13 minutes), Camelford (30 minutes) and Wadebridge (one hour).

From Camelford, you can catch the connecting bus 96 to Port Isaac.

Tintagel

POP 1820

The spectre of legendary King Arthur looms large over Tintagel and its dramatic clifftop castle. Though the present-day ruins mostly date from the 13th century, archaeological digs have revealed the foundations of a much earlier fortress, fuelling speculation that Arthur may indeed have been born at the castle, as locals like to claim. It's a stunningly romantic sight, with its crumbling walls teetering precariously above the sheer cliffs, and well worth devoting at least half a day to exploring.

A highly controversial plan has been announced to connect the mainland and the rock tower on which the castle sits by an ambitious 72m-long footbridge. Despite much local opposition, the plan was approved by councillors in late 2017, although as yet a completion date hasn't been set.

The village itself isn't terribly exciting, but if you're looking for cheesy King Arthur souvenirs, you'll find them in ample supply.

◉ Sights

⭐ **Tintagel Castle** CASTLE
(EH; 📞 01840-770328; www.english-heritage.org. uk; adult/child £8.40/5; ⊙ 10am-6pm Apr-Sep, to 5pm Oct, to 4pm Nov-Mar) Famous as the supposed birthplace of King Arthur, Tintagel's epic clifftop castle has been occupied since Roman times and once served as a residence

for Cornwall's Celtic kings. The present castle is largely the work of Richard, Earl of Cornwall, who built a castle here during the 1230s. Though the Arthurian links may be tenuous, it's certainly a fine spot for a fortress: clinging to black granite cliffs, surrounded by booming surf and wheeling gulls, it's the classic fairy-tale castle.

Old Post Office HISTORIC BUILDING
(NT; 📞 01840-770024; www.nationaltrust.org. uk; Fore St; adult/child £4.60/2.30; ⊙ 10.30am-5.30pm mid-Mar–Sep, 11am-4pm Oct) This is one of the best-preserved examples of a traditional 16th-century Cornish longhouse, topped by pepper-pot chimneys and a higgledy-piggledy roof, and riddled with tiny rooms. As its name suggests, it was used as a post office during the 19th century.

ℹ️ Getting There & Away

First Kernow bus 95/96 (£3.50 to £6.50, six daily Monday to Saturday, four on Sunday) stops in Tintagel en route from Camelford (15 minutes) to Bude (50 minutes).

Port Isaac

POP 720

If you're looking for a classic Cornish fishing town, you've found it in Port Isaac, where a cluster of cobbled alleyways, slender opes (lanes) and cob-walled cottages collect around a medieval harbour and slipway.

Though still a working harbour, Port Isaac is best known as a filming location: the hit TV series *Doc Martin* has used the village as a ready-made backdrop. A sign near the quayside directs visitors straight to Doc Martin's cottage. A short walk along the coast path leads to the neighbouring harbour of **Port Gaverne**, while a couple of miles west is **Port Quin**, now owned by the National Trust.

Cornwall's chef *du jour* Nathan Outlaw has made the village his culinary centre of operations.

🛏️ Sleeping & Eating

Old School Hotel HOTEL ££
(📞 01208-880721; www.theoldschoolhotel.co.uk; Fore St; s £67-101, d £119-185; 🅿️🛜) A small hotel that was originally Port Isaac's schoolhouse. Eagle-eyed fans of the *Doc Martin* TV series might recognise it as the show's village school. Appropriately, rooms are named after school subjects: the best is Latin, with

its sleigh bed and cupboard bathroom; Biology, with its sofa and church-style windows; and split-level Mathematics, with a shared terrace and bunk beds.

Outlaw's Fish Kitchen
SEAFOOD **£**

(☑ 01208-881183; www.nathan-outlaw.com/outlaws-fish-kitchen; 1 Middle St; mains £6.50-17; ⊙ noon-3pm & 6-9pm Mon-Sat Jun-Sep, Tue-Sat Oct-May) Top chef Nathan Outlaw's newest venture is this tiny fish restaurant down beside the harbour. It specialises in small seafood plates, designed to share. The exact menu is dictated by whatever's brought in on the day by Port Isaac's fishers, and the restaurant is tiny – literally just a few tables – so bookings are essential.

Fresh from the Sea
SEAFOOD **££**

(☑ 01208-880849; www.freshfromthesea.co.uk; 18 New Rd; sandwiches £5.50-9.50, mains £10.50-20; ⊙ 9am-4pm Mon-Sat) Local man Callum Greenhalgh takes out his boat daily in search of crab and lobster, then brings back the catch to sell at his tiny Port Isaac shop. Seafood doesn't get any fresher; a crab salad costs £10.50, and a whole lobster is a very reasonable £20. Depending on the season, oysters from nearby Porthilly cost £1.50 each.

★ Restaurant Nathan Outlaw
SEAFOOD **£££**

(☑ 01208-862737; www.nathan-outlaw.com; 6 New Rd; tasting menu £130; ⊙ 7-9pm Wed-Sat, plus noon-2pm Thu-Sat) Port Isaac's prestige has skyrocketed since Cornwall's top chef, Nathan Outlaw, moved his main operation here from Rock. This is the place to experience Outlaw's passion for Cornish fish and seafood. His style is surprisingly classic, relying on top-notch ingredients rather than cheffy tricks. As you'd expect of a twice-Michelin-starred restaurant, you'll pay top dollar, but it's a tell-your-friends experience.

❶ Getting There & Away

First Kernow bus 95/96 stops in Port Isaac at least four times daily en route between Camelford (£4.50, 30 minutes) and St Minver (£4.50, 30 minutes).

Padstow & Rock
POP 3160

If anywhere symbolises Cornwall's increasingly chic credentials, it's Padstow. This old fishing port has become the county's most cosmopolitan corner thanks to the bevy of celebrity chefs who have set up shop here –

including Rick Stein, whose Padstow-area property portfolio encompasses several restaurants and hotels, plus a gift shop, bakery, pub, seafood school and fish-and-chip bar.

There's no doubting that Padstow has changed beyond recognition in recent years: it feels more Kensington chic than Cornish quaint these days, with restaurants and boutiques sitting alongside its pubs and pasty shops. Whether the town's held on to its soul in the gentrification process is debatable, but it's hard not to be charmed by the seaside setting.

Across the Camel Estuary from Padstow lies Rock, a small village turned uber-exclusive getaway for well-to-do holidaymakers. Nearby, the sandy sweep of Daymer Bay unfurls along the estuary, a lifelong favourite of poet John Betjeman.

⊙ Sights & Activities

Padstow is surrounded by fine beaches, including the so-called Seven Bays: Trevone, Harlyn, Mother Ivey's, Booby's, Constantine, Treyarnon and Porthcothan.

In the middle of the Camel estuary runs a treacherous sandbank known as the Doom Bar, which has claimed many ships over the years, and also gave its name to a popular local ale.

Prideaux Place
HISTORIC BUILDING

(☑ 01841-532411; www.prideauxplace.co.uk; Prideaux Pl; house & grounds adult £8.50, grounds only £3; ⊙ house 1.30-4pm, grounds & tearoom 12.30-5.30pm Sun-Thu Apr-Oct) Much favoured by directors of costume dramas and period films, this stately Grade I–listed manor was built by the Prideaux-Brune family, purportedly descendants of William the Conqueror. Guided tours last around an hour and take in staterooms, staircases and Prideaux-Brune heirlooms, as well as the house's extensive collection of teddy bears.

National Lobster Hatchery
NATURE DISPLAY

(☑ 01841-533877; www.nationallobsterhatchery.co.uk; South Quay; adult/child £3.95/1.85; ⊙ 10am-7.30pm Jul & Aug, to 4pm or 5pm Sep-Jun) In an effort to combat falling lobster stocks, this harbourside hatchery rears baby lobsters in tanks before returning them to the wild. Displays detail the crustaceans' life cycle, and there are viewing tanks where you can watch the residents in action. Booking a 30-minute 'Meet the Expert' tour (adult/child £12/6) allows you a glimpse into work behind the scenes.

1000 WORDS / SHUTTERSTOCK ©

1. Banksy's *Naked Man* (p226), Bristol
Banksy is one of the world's most famous street artists, and his artworks have become tourist attractions.

2. Fishing boats, Lyme Regis (p268)
Lyme Regis is a popular stop along the Jurassic Coast.

3. St Michael's Mount (p331)
Island abbey St Michael's Mount was built in the 12th century by Benedictine monks.

4. Salisbury Cathedral (p272)
Spectacular 13th-century Salisbury Cathedral is home to one of the four original copies of the Magna Carta.

★ **Camel Trail** CYCLING
(www.cornwall.gov.uk/cameltrail) Closed in the 1950s, the old Padstow–Bodmin railway has been turned into Cornwall's most popular bike trail. The main section starts in Padstow and runs east through Wadebridge (5.75 miles); the trail then runs on all the way to Poley Bridge on Bodmin Moor (18.3 miles).

Bikes can be hired from **Padstow Cycle Hire** (☑01841-533533; www.padstowcyclehire. com; South Quay; per day adult £16-18, child £6-11; ⊙9am-5pm, to 9pm summer) or **Trail Bike Hire** (☑01841-532594; www.trailbikehire.co.uk; Unit 6, South Quay; adult £14, child £5-8; ⊙9am-6pm) at the Padstow end, or from **Bridge Bike Hire** (☑01208-813050; www.bridgebikehire.co.uk; Camel Trail; adult £12-14, child £6-9; ⊙10am-5pm) at the Wadebridge end.

Pumps and helmets are usually included. Tandems and kids' trailers cost extra.

Most people do the route from Padstow and back, so it's often quieter (and much easier to find parking) if you start from the Wadebridge side.

Padstow Boat Trips BOATING
(www.padstowboattrips.com; South Quay) Between Easter and October, the **Jubilee Queen** (☑07836-798457; adult/child £12/7) runs scenic trips along the coastline, while **Padstow Sealife Safaris** (☑01841-521613; www.padstowsealifesafaris.co.uk; 2hr cruises adult/ child £39/25) visits local seal and seabird colonies.

For something racier, 15-minute **speedboat trips** (£7) zip past the treacherous sandbank of Doom Bar and the beaches of Daymer Bay, Polzeath, Hawkers Cove and Tregirls.

The website has listings of all the local operators.

✪ Festivals & Events

May Day CULTURAL
(⊙1 May) Also known as 'Obby 'Oss Day, Padstow's biggest party is said to have its roots in an ancient pagan fertility rite, and sees two coloured 'osses (red and blue) twirl through the streets before meeting up beneath the maypole. It attracts thousands of visitors, so plan well ahead.

🛏 Sleeping

Treyarnon Bay YHA HOSTEL £
(☑0845 371 9664; www.yha.org.uk; Treyarnon Bay; dm £15-29; ⊙reception 8-10am & 2-10pm; P🖙) A super 1930s beach hostel on the bluffs above Treyarnon Bay. Rooms are big, there's a good cafe, plus barbecues in summer, and the sunsets are spectacular. It's 4.5 miles east of Padstow: there's parking on-site, but the nearest bus stop is at Constantine, about a 20-minute walk away.

Althea Library B&B ££
(☑01841-532579; www.altheahouse-padstow. co.uk; 64 Church St; d £90-120; P🖙) If you want to stay in Padstow proper, this charming ivy-clad house is hard to better. There are two stylish self-catering suites: Rafters is accessed via a private staircase, while Driftwood has a pine four-poster bed. It's luxurious – both suites have sofas, Nespresso coffee machines, baths and small studio kitchens. There's also a nearby cottage called Inglenook for longer stays.

Woodlands B&B ££
(☑01841-532426; www.woodlands-padstow.co.uk; Treator; d £130-150; P🖙) Offering green fields and distant flashes of sea, this is a great B&B base for Padstow. Rooms are a bit heavy on the creams and frills, but cosy nonetheless, and the breakfasts are prodigious. It's a mile or so from Padstow's harbourside, on the A389.

Symply Padstow B&B ££
(☑01841-532814; www.symply-padstow.co.uk; 32 Dennis Rd; s £61-67, d £97-109; 🖙) There's no way around it – staying in Padstow is pricey, but this B&B turns the tables with rates that would be a bargain even in a less starry location. The three rooms are cute and feminine, decorated with florals and checks, and all come with stellar sea views. The business also runs a self-catering cottage (£400 to £920 per week).

🍴 Eating

★ **Chough Bakery** BAKERY £
(☑01841-533361; www.thechoughbakery.co.uk; 1-3 The Strand; pasties £3-5; ⊙9am-5pm Mon-Sat) A family-run bakery right in the heart of town, renowned for its traditionally made pasties – they're among the best in the county, and several times have scooped top honours in the World Pasty Championships.

Prawn on the Lawn BISTRO ££
(☑01841-532223; www.prawnonthelawn.com; 11 Duke St; mains £7.50-45; ⊙noon-midnight Tue-Sat Easter-Sep) An offshoot of a London original, this tiny seafood bar is a new addition to Padstow's dining line-up. It's a simple one-

room affair, with bare brick, white tiles and blackboards, and a handful of tables lined up along one wall. But frills aren't important here: the seafood is what counts, served as small plates, sharing platters or by weight.

Rojano's in the Square ITALIAN **££**
(☎ 01841-532796; www.paul-ainsworth.co.uk; 9 Mill Sq; pizza & pasta £8.50-20; ◷ 10am-10pm) Under the stewardship of Michelin-starred chef Paul Ainsworth, this excellent little Italian bistro turns out fantastic wood-fired pizza, spicy pasta and antipasti. It's a fun and laid-back place to dine, and prices are very reasonable.

Cornish Arms GASTROPUB **££**
(☎ 01841-520288; www.rickstein.com/eat-with-us/the-cornish-arms; St Merryn; mains £10.95-17.95; ◷ 11.30am-11pm) This country pub near the village of St Merryn is owned by chef Rick Stein's foodie empire, and offers pub classics such as scampi in a basket, rump steak and ham, egg and chips – all with a creative twist and firm local provenance, naturally. The Sunday roast is phenomenally popular, so arrive early. It's a 3-mile drive from Padstow.

★ **Paul Ainsworth at No 6** BRITISH **£££**
(☎ 01841-532093; www.paul-ainsworth.co.uk/number6; 6 Middle St; 2-/3-course lunch £25/29, dinner mains £31-45; ◷ noon-2.30pm & 6-10pm Tue-Sat) Rick Stein might be the household name, but Paul Ainsworth is often touted as Padstow's pretender to the throne. His food combines surprising flavours and impeccable presentation with a refreshingly unpretentious approach, and the town-house setting is a relaxed, unfussy place to dine. Now Michelin-starred, this is Padstow's most sought-after table – advance bookings essential.

★ **Seafood Restaurant** SEAFOOD **£££**
(☎ 01841-532700; www.rickstein.com; Riverside; 3-course lunch £40, mains £26-71; ◷ lunch 11.30am-4pm, dinner 6-9pm Sat, 6.30-9.30pm Sun-Fri) The restaurant that started the Stein dynasty, and still one of Cornwall's top places to dine. Stein senior rarely puts in any hours these days – Rick's son Jack runs the show. As ever, fish is the raison d'être: from fresh lobster to turbot, John Dory and *fruits de mer,* all served in an elegant, light-filled dining room.

❶ Information

Padstow Tourist Office (☎ 01841-533449; www.padstowlive.com; North Quay; ◷ 10am-5pm Mon-Sat, to 4pm Sun Apr-Sep, Mon-

BEDRUTHAN STEPS

Roughly halfway between Newquay and Padstow loom the stately rock stacks of **Bedruthan** (Carnewas, NT; www.nationaltrust.org.uk) **FREE**. These mighty granite pillars have been carved out by the relentless action of thousands of years of wind and waves, and now provide a stirring spot for a stroll. The area is owned by the National Trust (NT), which also runs the car park and cafe. Admission to the site is free, but non-NT members have to pay for parking.

Sat Oct-Mar) In a red-brick building on the quayside.

❶ Getting There & Away

There are a couple of car parks beside the harbour in Padstow, but they fill up quickly, so it's usually better to park at one of the large car parks at the top of town and walk down.

The only useful bus serving Padstow is First Kernow bus 5A to Newquay (alternate hours Monday to Saturday, three on Sunday, one hour 25 minutes), which runs along the coast via Harlyn Bay, Constantine Bay, Porthcothan, Mawgan Porth, Newquay Cornwall Airport and Porth Beach.

Newquay

POP 19,420

Newquay: naughty, and apart from its stunning beaches, not really very nice, actually. For many years, that's been the prevailing opinion of Cornwall's surfing capital, and honestly, Newquay has no one but itself to blame for the bad rap. With a notorious nightlife, and a main street lined with trashy clubs, rowdy pubs and blinking amusement arcades, it's no surprise the town has found itself struggling to transcend its party-hard, alcohol-fuelled, bargain-basement image.

But things are changing: Newquay is making a concerted effort to smarten up its act. Several of the big clubs have closed down; trendy bistros, cafes, bakeries and health-food shops have appeared in the town centre; and along the coast, a bevy of boutique hotels are attracting a more discerning clientele. There's a way to go, but at last it feels like Newquay might be growing up. About time, too.

◉ Sights

Newquay has a truly knockout location among some of North Cornwall's finest beaches. The trio close to town – Towan, Great Western and Tolcarne – are guaranteed to be packed in the middle of summer. Most surfers head for Fistral, but the very best beaches such as Crantock, Holywell Bay and Watergate Bay lie a couple of miles out of town.

Blue Reef Aquarium   AQUARIUM
(📞 01637-878134; www.bluereefaquarium.co.uk/newquay; Towan Promenade; adult/child £10.95/8.50; ⏲ 10am-6pm; ♿) A small aquarium on Towan beach, with touch pools and various deep-sea denizens, including reef sharks, loggerhead turtles and a giant Pacific octopus. There's a discount for online bookings.

Newquay Zoo   ZOO
(📞 01637-873342; www.newquayzoo.org.uk; Trenance Gardens; adult/child £13.20/9.90; ⏲ 10am-5pm; ♿) Newquay's pint-sized zoo isn't a world-beater, but its population of penguins, lemurs, parrots and snakes will keep the kids happy. The Tropical House and Toad Hall are good fun, and key events include penguin feeding at noon and lion feeding at 2.30pm.

Trerice   HISTORIC BUILDING
(NT; 📞 01637-875404; www.nationaltrust.org.uk; adult/child £10/5; ⏲ house 11am-5pm, gardens 10.30am-5pm) Built in 1751, this National Trust–owned Elizabethan manor is most famous for the elaborate barrel-roofed ceiling of the Great Chamber, and some fantastic original 16th-century stained glass among the 576 panes that make up the great window. It's 3.3 miles southeast of Newquay.

🏃 Activities

Newquay is brimming with surf schools, but quality is variable. Choose one that offers small-group sessions, and that ideally has a no-stag-party policy. Ask about teachers' accreditation and experience, and whether they travel to beaches other than Fistral – good schools follow the best waves.

Extreme Academy   ADVENTURE SPORTS
(📞 01637-860840; www.extremeacademy.co.uk; Watergate Bay) Owned by the nearby Watergate Bay Hotel (p322), this watersports provider offers the full gamut: surfing lessons, of course, as well as more unusual options such as stand-up paddleboarding and hand-planing (which involves catching a wave with a miniature surfboard attached to your wrist). A 2½-hour beginners' surf lesson costs £35, bodyboarding £25 and SUP £40.

EboAdventure   OUTDOORS
(📞 0800 781 6861; www.eboadventure.co.uk) This multiactivity centre is based at the Penhale Training Camp, at the northern end of Holywell Bay. Surfing's definitely not the only sport on offer: you can also try kite-buggying, kayaking, power-kiting, stand-up paddleboarding and coasteering (a mix of rock climbing, scrambling and wild swimming). It also runs bushcraft training sessions.

Rip Curl English Surf School   SURFING
(📞 01637-879571; www.englishsurfschool.com; lessons from £35) Based on Towan Beach, this is one of the most experienced and efficient large schools, linked with Rip Curl and staffed by English Surfing Federation–approved instructors (including the British team coach). Also offers coasteering and bodyboarding. Beginner lessons cost £35, or £42 if you're more advanced and want to hone your technique.

Kingsurf Surf School   SURFING
(📞 01637-860091; www.kingsurf.co.uk; Mawgan Porth; lessons from £35) A good option for avoiding the Fistral beach hustle, this school at Mawgan Porth has five young instructors and gets a tick for personal attention and small class sizes.

🛌 Sleeping

★ Scarlet   HOTEL £££
(📞 01637-861600; www.scarlethotel.co.uk; Mawgan Porth; r from £260; P 🅿 🛜 🏊) For out-and-out luxury, Cornwall's fabulously chic adults-only eco-hotel takes the crown. In a regal location above Mawgan Porth, 5 miles from Newquay, it screams designer style, from the huge sea-view rooms with their funky furniture and minimalist decor to the luxurious spa, complete with meditation lounge, outdoor hot tubs and wild-swimming pool. The restaurant's a beauty, too.

★ Watergate Bay Hotel   HOTEL £££
(📞 01637-860543; www.watergatebay.co.uk; Watergate Bay; d £290-440; P 🛜) This stylish, popular beach hotel combines luxury with lifestyle: guests are positively encouraged to explore the many outdoor activities on offer at the in-house Extreme Academy. With beachy rooms decked out in coastal colours and slatted wood, and a glorious indoor pool

overlooking the bay, it's posh but reassuringly unpretentious: wet feet and sandy footprints are not a problem here.

✖ Eating

★ Pavilion Bakery

BAKERY £

(www.pavilionbakery.com; 37 Fore St; breads £2-4; ⊙8am-4pm) After opening three outposts in London's hippest-of-hip corners (Victoria Park, Columbia Rd and Broadway Market), this fabulous bakery has set up its first shop outside the capital in Newquay, in an A-frame building with the requisite exposed brick, rough wood and open-plan kitchen. Come for stunning sourdoughs, artisan breads and possibly Cornwall's finest croissants and pains au chocolat.

Sprout

VEGETARIAN £

(☑01637-875845; www.sprouthealth.co.uk; Crescent Lane; mains £3.50-5.50; ⊙9am-5pm Mon-Sat; ☑) If you like your food organic and your ingredients fair trade, then this excellent wholefood shop down an uninviting backstreet is the best address in town. The one-pot veggie meals (such as vegan African peanut stew and hearty Moroccan stew) are delicious and sell out fast – almost as fast as the delectable gluten-free cakes.

★ Fish House Fistral

SEAFOOD ££

(☑01637-872085; www.thefishhousefistral.com; Fistral Beach; mains lunch £8.50-16.95, dinner £12.95-19.95) This beachside seafooderie has become a firm favourite for local diners and Fistral visitors alike, and it's thoroughly deserved. Filling fishy dishes are the catch of the day, underscored by French, Italian and Asian flavours, and the beach-shack vibe is bang-on. Chef Paul Harwood trained under Rick Stein, and it shows in his seafood skills.

Beach Hut

BISTRO ££

(☑01637-860877; Watergate Bay; mains £12.50-22; ⊙9am-9pm) After a beach walk or a quick surf at Watergate, this cafe is where everyone tends to head for a coffee, cake or something more filling. With its wood-lined interior and big picture windows, it's a lovely spot, and the blackboards are filled with easygoing dishes such as burgers, meze, mussels, pad Thai and seafood curry.

It's underneath **Fifteen Restaurant** (☑01637-861000; www.fifteencornwall.co.uk; lunch mains £16-21, dinner mains £19-28, 5-course dinner £65; ⊙8.30-10am, noon-2.30pm & 6.15-9.15pm), but is owned by the Watergate Bay Hotel. Parking can be tricky in summer.

Lewinnick Lodge

BISTRO ££

(☑01637-878117; www.lewinnicklodge.co.uk; Pentire Head; mains £12.50-20; ⊙8am-10pm) Perched on the cliffs of Pentire Head, giving a knock-out perspective on Newquay's coastline, this gastropub is hard to better for lunch with a view. The decor is modern – lots of wood and plate glass – and the food is decent: gourmet burgers, mussels and Thai-style salads.

🍸 Drinking & Nightlife

Newquay's drinking spots aren't sophisticated. Cheesy clubs and brash bars abound, and the town centre gets notoriously rowdy on Friday and Saturday nights, especially in summer.

Tom Thumb

BAR

(☑01637-498180; www.tom-thumb.co.uk; 27a East St; ⊙noon-midnight) Now then Newquay: this is much, much more like it. A proper cocktail bar with reclaimed wood furniture, a cool spiral staircase and a fine selection of home-mixed drinks (divided into fun categories like 'Something Saucy' and 'Giggle Water'). A few more like this, and the days of the beer boy really will be numbered.

☆ Entertainment

Whiskers

LIVE MUSIC

(☑01637-498100; www.whiskersnewquay.co.uk; 5-7 Gover Lane; ⊙5pm-midnight) A grungy cool hang-out with a regular line-up of live gigs, both from local bands and a few bigger names from upcountry and further afield. The rest of the time, DJs fill in the musical gaps. Occasionally Whiskers hosts oddball events such as life drawing and spoken-word slams.

ℹ Information

Newquay Tourist Office (☑01637-854020; www.visitnewquay.org; Marcus Hill; ⊙9.15am-5.30pm Mon-Fri, 10am-4pm Sat & Sun) Small but well-stocked office that can help you arrange everything from accommodation to surf lessons.

ℹ Getting There & Away

AIR

Cornwall Airport Newquay (☑01637-860600; www.cornwallairportnewquay.com) Cornwall's main airport, 5 miles from Newquay, offers direct daily flights to Manchester and London Gatwick with Flybe (www.flybe.com) and the Isles of Scilly with Isles of Scilly Travel (p343).

First Kernow bus A5 (26 minutes, every two hours Monday to Saturday, three on Sunday) runs from Newquay's bus station to Padstow, stopping at the airport en route. Taxis cost £15 to £25 from the town centre.

Various seasonal destinations around the UK and Europe are also offered during summer.

BUS

Newquay's bus station is on Manor Rd.

Padstow Bus A5 (£5.20, 90 minutes, every two hours Monday to Saturday, three on Sunday) stops at the airport and then trundles up the coast via Mawgan Porth, Porthcothan, Constantine Bay and Harlyn Bay. Note that only a few buses a day stop at Bedruthan Steps.

St Agnes Bus 87 (£5.20, 50 minutes, hourly Monday to Saturday, five on Sunday) stops at Crantock, Holywell Bay and Perranporth en route to St Agnes, and continues to Truro.

Truro Bus 90/92/93 (£5.20, 70 minutes, half-hourly Monday to Saturday, five on Sunday); the various routes travel via different villages but all terminate in Truro.

Wadebridge Bus 95 (£4.20, 50 minutes, five daily Monday to Saturday).

TRAIN

Newquay is on the branch line between Newquay and Par (Atlantic Coast Line, £6.50, 45 minutes), from where you can hop aboard the main London–Penzance line.

Perranporth to Porthtowan

Southwest of Newquay, Cornwall's craggy northern coastline dips and curves through a stunning panorama of wild, sea-smacked cliffs and golden bays, including the family-friendly beach of Perranporth, the old mining town of St Agnes and the surfy hang-out of Porthtowan.

◉ Sights & Activities

⭐ **Perranporth Beach** BEACH

(P🏊) Perranporth's huge, flat, sandy beach is a favourite for everyone: dog-walkers, bucket-and-spade families, kite-buggiers and surfers alike. Its main draw is its sheer size – more than a mile long, backed by dunes and rocky cliffs – meaning there's usually space for everyone even on the busiest days. It's home to the Watering Hole, the hub of local nightlife.

⭐ **Chapel Porth** BAY

(NT; www.nationaltrust.org.uk; P) Two miles from St Agnes is one of Cornwall's most beautiful coves, Chapel Porth, a wild, rocky beach framed by steep, gorse-covered cliffs, owned by the National Trust. Above the cove is the ruined engine stack of **Wheal Coates**, which still boasts its chimney and winding house, from where the coast path winds all the way to the blustery outcrop of **St Agnes Head**. It's a panorama that graces many a postcard – don't forget your camera.

Blue Hills Tin Streams MUSEUM
(📞 01872-553341; www.cornishtin.com; adult/child £6.50/3; ⊙10am-2pm Tue-Sat mid-Apr–mid-Oct) A mile east of St Agnes (signed to Wheal Kitty) is the rocky valley of **Trevellas Porth**, home to one of Cornwall's last tin manufacturers. You can watch the whole tinning process, from mining and smelting through to casting and finishing. Handmade jewellery is sold in the shop.

🍴 Eating & Drinking

Chapel Porth Cafe CAFE £
(Chapel Porth; sandwiches & cakes £2-5; ⊙10am-5pm) This cafe down on the edge of Chapel Porth beach is a local institution, serving hot chocolate, cheesy baguettes, sausage butties, flapjacks and the house speciality: hedgehog ice cream (vanilla ice cream topped with clotted cream and hazelnuts).

⭐ **Blue Bar** BAR
(📞 01209-890329; www.blue-bar.co.uk; mains £8-16; ⊙10am-11pm) For a seaside sundowner or a lunchtime burger by the sand, this surfy Porthtowan cafe is tough to beat. There are tables outside overlooking the sand, plus more inside (arrive early to bag the prime bay window tables). The beachy decor, decent grub and regular music nights make it one of the north coast's most popular hang-outs.

Watering Hole BAR
(📞 01872-572888; www.the-wateringhole.co.uk; Perranporth Beach; ⊙10am-11pm) Generations of Cornish youth have passed through this venerable beach bar, and it's still going strong, despite nearly being swept away during recent storms. It's a bit shabby, but good for a morning coffee or an evening beer as the sun goes down. It also has regular live music – Tom Jones and Snoop Dogg have played shows here.

❶ Getting There & Away

Bus 87 (£6, 45 minutes, hourly in summer) stops in St Agnes on its way from Newquay, via Crantock, Holywell, Perranporth and Trevellas, to Truro.

St Ives

POP 9870

If there was a prize for the prettiest of Cornish ports, then St Ives would undoubtedly be a contender for the top spot. A tightly packed cluster of slate roofs, fishers' cottages and church towers spread out around turquoise bays – it's an unfailingly dazzling sight. Once a busy pilchard harbour, St Ives later became the centre of Cornwall's arts scene in the 1920s and '30s, when luminary figures such as Barbara Hepworth, Terry Frost, Ben Nicholson and Naum Gabo migrated here in search of artistic freedom.

The town remains an artistic centre, with numerous galleries lining its cobbled streets, as well as the renowned Tate St Ives, which recently received a multimillion pound extension. Whether the town has managed to retain its artistic soul is another matter – it's one of Cornwall's holiday home hot spots, and uncomfortably packed with tourists in summer, so visit in spring or autumn if you can.

◉ Sights & Activities

The largest town beaches are **Porthmeor** and **Porthminster**, both of which have sand and space aplenty. Between them juts the grassy promontory known as the Island, topped by the tiny pre-14th-century **Chapel of St Nicholas**. On the peninsula's east side is the little cove of **Porthgwidden**, a smaller beach that's often a good place to escape the crowds.

As you'd expect, there are lots and lots of art galleries to visit dotted around town.

★ **Tate St Ives**   GALLERY
(✆01736-796226; www.tate.org.uk/stives; Porthmeor Beach; adult/child £9.50/free, joint ticket with Barbara Hepworth Museum £13/free; ◷10am-5.20pm, last admission 4pm) After an 18-month, multimillion-pound refit, St Ives' most illustrious gallery reopened its doors, complete

West Cornwall

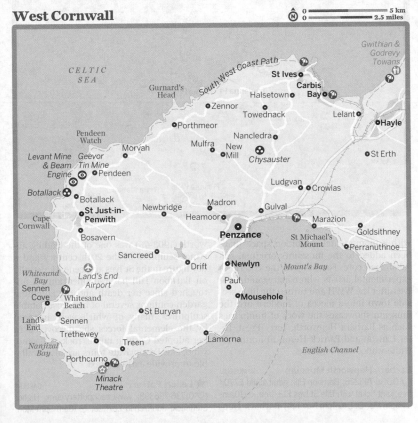

BATH & SOUTHWEST ENGLAND ST IVES

St Ives

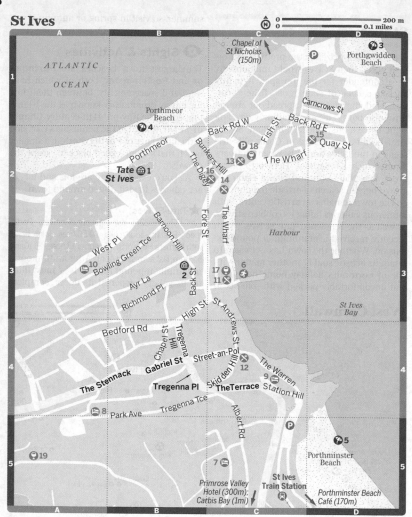

ATLANTIC
OCEAN

Chapel of
St Nicholas
(150m)

Porthgwidden
Beach

Porthmeor
Beach

Carncrows St

Back Rd E

Back Rd W

Fish St

Quay St

The Wharf

Tate
St Ives

The Digey

Bunker's Hill

Porthmeor

The Wharf

Harbour

Barnoon Hill

West Pl

Bowling Green Tce

Fore St

Back St

Ayr La

Richmond Pl

St Ives
Bay

High St

St Andrews St

Bedford Rd

Chapel St

Tregenna Hill

Gabriel St

Street-an-Pol

The Warren

Skidden Hill

The Stennack

Tregenna Pl

TheTerrace

Station Hill

Park Ave

Tregenna Tce

Albert Rd

Porthminster
Beach

Primrose Valley
Hotel (300m);
Carbis Bay (1mi)

St Ives
Train Station

Porthminster Beach
Café (170m)

with a monumental exhibition space that's been added to the museum's original, spiral-shaped core. Focusing on the coterie of experimental artists who congregated at St Ives after the WWII and turned the little seaside town into a mecca of modern art, the museum showcases the work of luminaries such as Barbara Hepworth, Terry Frost, Peter Lanyon and Patrick Heron in luminous, white-walled surroundings.

Barbara Hepworth Museum
MUSEUM
(☎01736-796226; Barnoon Hill; adult/child £7.70/ free, joint ticket with Tate St Ives £13/free; ☉10am-5.20pm Mar-Oct, to 4pm Nov-Feb) Barbara Hep-

worth (1903–75) was one of the leading abstract sculptors of the 20th century and a key figure in the St Ives art scene. Her studio on Barnoon Hill has remained almost untouched since her death and the adjoining garden contains several of her most notable sculptures, many of which were inspired by the elemental forces she discovered in her adopted Cornish home: rock, sea, sand, wind, sky. Free private tours are also available to provide extra context.

★ Leach Pottery
GALLERY
(☎01736-796398; www.leachpottery.com; Higher Stennack; adult/child £6/free; ☉10am-5pm Mon-

St Ives

Sat year-round, 11am-4pm Sun Mar-Oct) While other St Ives artists broke new ground in sculpture and abstract art, potter Bernard Leach was hard at work reinventing British ceramics in his studio in Higher Stennack. Drawing inspiration from Japanese and oriental sculpture, and using a unique hand-built 'climbing' kiln based on ones he had seen in Japan, Leach's pottery created a unique fusion of Western and Eastern ideas.

St Ives Boats BOATING
(☎0777 300 8000; www.stivesboats.co.uk; adult/child from £16/10) St Ives Boats is one of several operators along the harbour front to offer fishing trips and scenic cruises, including to the grey-seal colony on Seal Island and out to the lighthouse at Godrevy. If you're really lucky, you might even spot a porpoise or a basking shark in summer.

🛏 Sleeping

Channings B&B ££
(☎01736-799500; www.channingsstives.co.uk; 3 Talland Rd; s £50-65, d £95-115; P🅿️🛜🐾) This small terraced B&B would be pretty good value anywhere, but in St Ives it's an absolute bargain. If you can, book one of the panoramic suites, which have sitting areas and sloping skylights offering views over St Ives and Godrevy lighthouse. The standard seaview rooms don't have quite the same wow factor, but they're comfortable enough.

West by 5 B&B ££
(☎01736-794584; www.westbyfive.com; 7 Clodgy View; r £80-140; 🛜) Much recommended and reliable B&B in a stone-fronted Edwardian villa, with four rooms offering elevated views over the harbour (rooms 1 and 2 are the best of the quartet). It's simply decorated, with blue bedspreads, stripy blinds and pine bedsteads – and luxury extras including Hypnos beds and goose-down duvets add a dash of panache. The only major drawback? No parking.

Little Leaf Guest House B&B ££
(☎01736-795427; www.littleleafguesthouse.co.uk; Park Ave; r £75-125; 🛜🐾) Another top option to keep your St Ives spending nonstratospheric. It's small, with just six rooms – and while space isn't a strong point, rooms are attractively appointed in creams and pine furniture. Room 2 has the best view, followed by room 5 with its elevated position and dormer window.

★Primrose Valley Hotel HOTEL £££
(☎01736-794939; www.primroseonline.co.uk; Primrose Valley; r £180-230; P🅿️🛜🐾) Reopened after refurbishment, this chic hotel has one massive selling point – it's a one-minute walk from Porthminster's sands. But there are more pluses – such as its light, attractive rooms in taupes, greys, checks and sea blues, and quirky design touches including wicker lamps, Scandi-style dressers, wooden cladding and model ships. It feels very modern and impeccably designed throughout.

Trevose Harbour House B&B £££
(☎01736-793267; www.trevosehouse.co.uk; 22 The Warren; d £195-275; 🛜) A stylish six-room town house on the lovely backstreet known as the Warren, restored with a sea-themed combo of fresh whites and stripy blues. It's been beautifully finished – Neal's Yard bath goods, iPod docks and retro design pieces in the rooms, plus a book-lined lounge and minimalist courtyard patio. It's boutique through and through – but undeniably expensive.

✕ Eating

Moomaid of Zennor
ICE CREAM £

(www.moomaidofzennor.com; The Wharf; ice cream from £2; ⊙ 9am-5pm) This ice-cream maker is a local legend, and makes all its 30 flavours on the home farm just outside Zennor, using only its own milk and Rodda's clotted cream. Exotic concoctions include fig and mascarpone and pear-cider sorbet.

The Digey Food Room
CAFE £

(✑ 01736-799600; www.digeyfoodroom.co.uk; 6 The Digey; mains £6-8.50; ⊙ 9am-4pm) On one of St Ives' oldest – and loveliest – backstreets, this little cafe is a newcomer, but already a local favourite. It's small, cosy and friendly, with a well-stocked deli shop and a counter filled with homemade cakes and pastries – but it's the hearty lunches (fennel frittatas, smashed avo on toast, salmon-and-dill quiche) that really sell it.

★ Porthminster Beach Café
BISTRO ££

(✑ 01736-795352; www.porthminstercafe.co.uk; Porthminster Beach; mains £15-22; ⊙ 9am-10pm) This is no ordinary beach cafe: it's a full-blown bistro with a gorgeous sun-trap terrace and a superb Mediterranean-influenced menu, specialising in seafood. Tuck into rich bouillabaisse, seafood curry or Provençal fish soup, and settle back to enjoy the breezy beach vistas. It's published its own cookbook, too, if you fancy taking the recipes home.

Porthminster Kitchen
BISTRO ££

(✑ 01736-799874; www.porthminster.kitchen; The Wharf; mains lunch £7.50-16, dinner £11-19; ⊙ 9am-10pm) Run by the same team as Porthminster Beach Café (p328), this is a welcome addition to the harbour front in St Ives. It's a relaxed, bistro-style kind of place, with beachy dishes such as *moules-frites,* seafood curry and hake fillet on bubble-and-squeak. The food's reliable, and the 1st-floor dining room has a hard-to-beat view of the harbour.

SILCo Searoom
CAFE ££

(✑ 01736-794325; www.silcosearoom.com; 1 Wharf House; tapas £3.25-12; ⊙ 9am-10pm Mon-Sat) Now run by the St Ives Liquor Company (makers of the town's premium craft gin), this wharfside restaurant specialises in Cornish-tinged tapas: crab gratin, mackerel fillet, mussels and the like, alongside the usual Padrón peppers and bread-and-olives combo. Richly furnished in gentlemen's club style (leather chairs, dark wood, sombre colours), it's great for cocktails and has a cracking harbour view.

Blas Burgerworks
CAFE ££

(✑ 01736-797272; The Warren; burgers £10-12.50; ⊙ noon-9.30pm Jul & Aug, 5.30-9.30pm rest of year) 🌱 St Ives' boutique burger joint, with an ecofriendly manifesto and an imaginative menu. Go for a 6oz Classic Blasburger, or branch out with a guacamole and corn-salsa-topped Rancheros, or a Smokey with beetroot, aged cheddar and homemade piccalilli (there are plenty of veggie options, too). The owners also run the excellent Halsetown Inn (✑ 01736-795583; www.halsetowninn.co.uk; Halsetown; mains £13-22.50; ⊙ noon-2pm & 6-9pm), just outside St Ives.

★ Alba
MODERN BRITISH £££

(✑ 01736-797222; www.alba-stives.co.uk; Old Lifeboat House; 2-/3-course dinner menu £24/28, mains £16-28.95; ⊙ 6-10pm) Other restaurants come and go, but this harbourside bistro beside the old lifeboat station continues to excel. It's in a converted boathouse, with a split-level layout: dining is upstairs, with picture windows looking over the harbour; downstairs is the sleek A-Bar. Head chef Grant Nethercott has a Michelin-starred background, so standards are high: first-class fish and seafood are the mainstays.

The set dinner menu is available from 5.30pm to 7.30pm.

🍷 Drinking & Entertainment

St Ives Brewery
MICROBREWERY

(✑ 01736-793467; www.stives-brewery.co.uk; Trewidden Rd; mains £3-8; ⊙ 9am-5pm Mon-Sat, 10am-4pm Sun) Since its foundation in 2010 St Ives' own microbrewery has expanded operations and opened its own cafe and tasting room. The flagships are Boiler's, a golden session ale, and the hoppy IPA-style Knill By Mouth; you can sample both in the cafe while enjoying an absolutely cracking outlook over the town's rooftops.

Sloop Inn
PUB

(✑ 01736-796584; www.sloop-inn.co.uk; The Wharf; ⊙ 11am-11pm) This whitewashed, beam-ceilinged boozer is as comfy as an old pair of slippers, with a few tables on the harbour and lots of local ales. On a sunny day, the picnic tables on the tiny harbourside patio are just about the best spot for a pint in town.

Hub
BAR

(www.hub-stives.co.uk; The Wharf; ⊙ 9am-11pm) The open-plan Hub is the heart of St Ives' (admittedly limited) nightlife: coffee and burgers by day, cocktails after dark and a great location on the harbour.

ℹ️ Getting There & Away

BUS

Bus 17/17A/17B (£5, 30 minutes, half-hourly Monday to Saturday, hourly Sunday) The quickest route to Penzance, via Lelant and Marazion.

Bus 16/16A (£5, hourly Monday to Saturday) An alternative route to Penzance; bus 16A travels via Zennor and the Gurnard's Head pub, while bus 16 goes via Halsetown, Ludgvan and Gulval.

TRAIN

The branch train line from St Ives is worth taking just for the coastal views.

Trains shuttle between St Ives train station via Lelant to St Erth (£3, 14 minutes, half-hourly) where you can catch connections along the Penzance–London Paddington main line.

Zennor & St Just

The B3306 coast road between St Ives and Zennor ventures into a wild corner of Cornwall, a long way from the prettified harbour towns and manicured beaches. This tiny village is set around the medieval Church of St Senara. Its main claim to fame is as the home of the legend of the Mermaid of Zennor, but it has another literary connection, too: the writer DH Lawrence sojourned here between 1915 and 1917, but his liberal habits and metropolitan tastes (not to mention a wild party or two) earned short shrift from the locals, and the writer was drummed out of the village as a suspected communist spy (an episode recounted in his novel *Kangaroo*).

◎ Sights

Church of St Senara CHURCH

This little church in the hamlet of Zennor dates from at least 1150. Inside, a famous carved chair depicts the legendary Mermaid of Zennor, who is said to have fallen in love with the singing voice of local lad Matthew Trewhella. Locals say you can still sometimes hear them singing down at nearby Pendour Cove – and even if you don't, the views along the coast path are reward enough.

★ Geevor Tin Mine MINE

(📞 01736-788662; www.geevor.com; adult/child £14.60/8.50; ⏰ 9am-5pm Sun-Fri Mar-Oct, 10am-4pm Nov-Feb) Just north of St Just near Pendeen, this historic mine closed in 1990 and now provides a powerful insight into the dark, dingy and dangerous conditions in which Cornwall's miners worked. Above ground, you can view the dressing floors and the original machinery used to sort the minerals and ores, before taking a guided tour into some of the underground shafts. Claustrophobes need not apply.

★ Botallack RUINS

(NT; www.nationaltrust.org.uk/botallack) Clinging to the cliffs near Levant, this dramatic complex of mine-workings is one of the most atmospheric sights from Cornwall's industrial past. The main mine stack, properly known as the Crowns, teeters picturesquely on the cliff edge above a cauldron of boiling surf. It's famously photogenic and a frequent filming location, most recently used by the BBC's latest version of *Poldark*. It's a steep walk down, but well worth the trek; an audio guide can be downloaded from the NT website.

During its 19th-century heyday, the mine was one of the county's richest and deepest, producing 14,500 tonnes of tin and 20,000 tonnes of copper ore from shafts that snaked out nearly half a mile out to sea. You can explore the site's history at the Count House workshop, which once contained the stables that housed the mine's pit ponies.

Levant Mine & Beam Engine HISTORIC SITE

(www.nationaltrust.org.uk/levant-mine-and-beam-engine; adult/child £8.10/4.05; ⏰ 10.30am-5pm Apr-Oct) At this clifftop site, one of the world's only working beam engines is still in thunderous action. Built in 1840, these great engines were the powerhouses behind the Cornish mining boom, powering mineral trains, running lifts down into the mine shafts, and pumping water from the underground tunnels. Closed in 1930, it's since been lovingly restored by a team of enthusiasts, and is a sight to behold when it's in full steam.

Cape Cornwall LANDMARK

Jutting out from the cliffs near St Just is Cornwall's only cape, a craggy outcrop of land topped by an abandoned mine stack. Below the cape is the rocky beach of **Priest's Cove**, while nearby are the ruins of **St Helen's Oratory**, supposedly one of the first Christian chapels built in West Cornwall.

🛏️ Sleeping & Eating

Zennor Chapel Guesthouse B&B ££

(📞 01736-798307; www.zennorchapelguesthouse. com; Wayside St; r from £80; 🅿️) As its name hints, this attractive B&B (previously a

WORTH A TRIP

MINACK THEATRE & PORTHCURNO

Teetering right out on Cornwall's far-western tip, the sandy wedge of **Porthcurno** is one of the best beaches in west Cornwall for swimming and sunbathing, and around the headland, the lesser-known beach of **Pednvounder** nearby is good if you like to sunbathe *au naturel* – it's one of Cornwall's few naturist beaches.

But the area is best known for its spectacular clifftop theatre, the **Minack** (☏01736-810181; www.minack.com; tickets from £10), carved out from the granite rock with sweeping views of the Atlantic waves below. Created between the 1930s and 1970s by theatre-lover Rowena Cade, there are few finer places to watch a play than this.

Porthcurno was also once an unlikely hub for transatlantic telecommunications, and a small **museum** (☏01736-810966; www.telegraphmuseum.org; adult/child £9.50/5.50; ⊙10am-5pm) explores the story.

---

hostel) occupies a former church on the edge of the village. There are five rooms, most of which still boast original ecclesiastical features, including beautiful arched windows. There's a range of sleeping configurations – doubles, twins and family rooms with bunk beds. There's also a cafe and gift shop downstairs.

★**Gurnard's Head**　　　　　BRITISH **££**
(☏01736-796928; www.gurnardshead.co.uk; B3306, near Zennor; mains £11.50-24, r £125-190; P🛜🐾) On the wonderful coast road between Zennor and St Just, you can't possibly miss the Gurnard's – its name is emblazoned on the roof. It's earned a reputation as one of west Cornwall's top dining pubs, known for its classic, traditionally inspired British dishes, and a top Sunday roast. Wooden furniture, book-lined shelves and sepia prints conjure a cosy, lived-in feel.

Sennen & Land's End

Beyond St Ives, the coastline gets wilder and emptier as you near Cornwall's tip at Land's End, the westernmost point of mainland England, where the coal-black cliffs plunge into the pounding surf, and the views stretch all the way to the Isles of Scilly on a clear day.

Unfortunately, the decision to build the **Legendary Land's End** (☏0871 720 0044; www.landsend-landmark.co.uk; day ticket adult/child £12.60/9; ⊙10am-5pm Mar-Oct; ♿) theme park on the headland in the 1980s hasn't done much to enhance the view. Take our advice: just pay for the car park, skip the tacky multimedia shows and opt for an exhilarating clifftop stroll instead. Look for the historic Longships Lighthouse, on a reef 1.25 miles out to sea.

From Land's End, follow the coast path west to the secluded cove of **Nanjizal Bay**, or east to the old harbour of Sennen, which overlooks the glorious beach of **Whitesand Bay**, the area's most impressive stretch of sand.

Mousehole

POP 697

With a tight tangle of cottages and alleyways gathered behind the granite breakwater, Mousehole (pronounced *mowzle*) looks like something from a children's storybook (a fact not unnoticed by author Antonia Barber, who set her much-loved fairy tale *The Mousehole Cat* here). In centuries past this was Cornwall's busiest pilchard port, but the fish dried up in the late 19th century, and the village now survives mostly on tourist traffic. Packed in summer and deserted in winter (Mousehole is renowned for its high proportion of second homes), it's ripe for a wander, with a maze of slips, net lofts and courtyards.

🛏 Sleeping & Eating

★**Old Coastguard Hotel**　　　HOTEL **£££**
(☏01736-731222; www.oldcoastguardhotel.co.uk; The Parade; d£140-245; P🛜🐾) Run by the owners of the Gurnard's Head (p330), this coastal beauty on the edge of Mousehole ranks as one of Cornwall's top coastal hotels. Rooms are classic – restrained colour schemes, stately beds – and the best obviously have a sea view. Seafood takes prominence in the **restaurant** (mains £13.50 to £18.50), and there's a cliff garden for soaking up the rays.

2 Fore St　　　　　　　　FRENCH **££**
(☏01736-731164; www.2forestreet.co.uk; Fore St; dinner mains £14-18.25; ⊙noon-2pm & 7-9pm)

This laid-back bistro is squeezed into a small space along Mousehole's backstreets, and majors in French-inspired classics – unsurprising, given the head chef trained under Raymond Blanc. There's a small dining room, a sweet garden and a locally focused menu strong on seafood.

Penzance

POP 21,168

Overlooking the majestic sweep of Mount's Bay, the old harbour of Penzance has a salty, sea-blown charm that feels altogether more authentic than many of Cornwall's polished-up ports. Its streets and shopping arcades still feel real and a touch ramshackle, and there's nowhere better for a windyday walk than the town's seafront Victorian promenade.

◉ Sights & Activities

Penlee House Gallery & Museum GALLERY
(☑ 01736-363625; www.penleehouse.org.uk; Morrab Rd; adult/child £5/4; ⊗ 10am-5pm Mon-Sat Easter-Sep, 10.30am-4.30pm Mon-Sat Oct-Easter) This small museum is ideal for a primer on the artistic heritage of West Cornwall. It has a fine collection of paintings by artists of the Newlyn School (including Stanhope and Elizabeth Forbes, Walter Langley and Lamorna Birch) and hosts regular exhibitions inside a handsome 19th-century building. The nearby Penlee Gardens are well worth a stroll.

Tremenheere Sculpture Garden GARDENS
(☑ 01736-448089; www.tremenheere.co.uk; adult/child £8/4.50; ⊗ gardens 10am-5pm; 👪) This inventive garden opened just outside Penzance in 2012. The landscaped gardens sit in a sheltered valley awash with artworks and installations: look out for a 'sky-view' chamber by James Turrell; 'Black Mound', a pile of tree stumps by David Nash; and 'Camera Obscura' by Billy Wynter, offering a unique panorama of the gardens and Mount's Bay.

There's also a super cafe, Tremenheere Kitchen (lunches £8 to £14), and family events such as den-building and art workshops during school holidays.

★ Jubilee Pool SWIMMING
(☑ 01736-369224; www.jubileepool.co.uk; Western Promenade Rd; adult/child £5/3.50; ⊗ 10.30am-6pm, to 8pm Tue, early Jun–late Sep) After being battered during recent winter storms, Penzance's glorious seawater lido has reopened and regained its rightful place as the town's

---

DON'T MISS

ST MICHAEL'S MOUNT
....

Looming up in the middle of Mount's Bay and connected to the mainland at Marazion via a cobbled causeway, St Michael's Mount (NT; ☑ 01736-710507; www.stmichaelsmount.co.uk; house & gardens adult/child £15/7.50; ⊗ house 10.30am-5.30pm Sun-Fri Jul-Sep, to 5pm Mar-Jun & Oct) is an unforgettable sight, and one of Cornwall's most iconic images. Initially a Benedictine monastery, and later the seat of the St Aubyn family, it's a must-visit. You can catch the ferry (adult/child £2/1) from Marazion at high tide, but it's worth arriving at low tide so you can walk across the causeway, as pilgrims did centuries ago.

There's been a monastery here since at least the 5th century, but the present abbey was mostly built by Benedictine monks during the 12th century (the same religious order that also constructed the island's sister abbey at Mont St-Michel in France). Highlights of the main house include the rococo drawing room, the armoury and the 14th-century church, but it's the amazing clifftop gardens that really steal the show. Thanks to the local sub-climate, many exotic flowers and shrubs flourish here, and it's all a riot of colour in summer.

Recent excavations, with finds including an axe head, a dagger and a metal clasp, have proved the island has been inhabited since at least the Bronze Age, but it was almost certainly used by prehistoric people long before. According to some scholars, the island may have been a trading post for locally mined copper and tin for several thousand years.

During winter, access to the island is only possible by boat, but in summer, walking across on the causeway is a magical experience: there's a useful guide to the causeway's opening hours on the website (www.stmichaelsmount.co.uk/plan-your-visit/causeway-opening-times).

Penzance

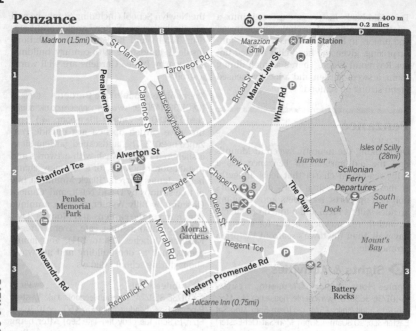

Penzance

◎ Sights
1 Penlee House Gallery & Museum B2

⊕ Activities, Courses & Tours
2 Jubilee Pool D3

⊜ Sleeping
3 Artist Residence Penzance C2
4 Chapel House Penzance C2
5 Venton Vean A3

⊗ Eating
6 Cornish Barn C2
7 Shore B2

⊕ Drinking & Nightlife
8 Admiral Benbow....................................C2
9 Turk's Head C2

pride and joy. Built in 1935, it's a bold statement of art deco styling, sleek, sharp and whitewashed – the perfect backdrop for some bracing seawater bathing.

There's discounted entry after 3.30pm (adult/child £3.15/2.50).

The pool has announced an exciting project to heat part of the pool using geothermal technology: check the website for the latest announcements.

⊨ Sleeping

Penzance YHA HOSTEL **£**
(☑0845 371 9653; www.yha.org.uk; Castle Horneck, Alverton; dm £19-25; ℗⏚) Penzance's YHA is inside an 18th-century house on the edge of town. It's a rambling place, with a cafe, a laundry and four- to 10-bed dorms. It's a 15-minute walk from the harbour front.

★Venton Vean B&B **££**
(☑01736-351294; www.ventonvean.co.uk; Trewithen Rd; r £88-100; ⏚) The picture of a modern B&B, finished in stylish greys and blues, with stripped wood floors, bay windows and a keen eye for design. Rooms 1 and 2 are the most spacious; the former overlooks Penlee Memorial Park. The sumptuous breakfast choice includes pancakes, smoked Newlyn fish, avocado on sourdough toast, and a Mexican-style feast of tortillas and refried beans.

★Artist Residence Penzance B&B **£££**
(☑01736-365664; www.artistresidence.co.uk/our-hotels/cornwall; 20 Chapel St; d £135-255, deluxe ste from £315; ⏚⏧⏨) Hands down Penzance's most entertaining hotel, this converted town house on Chapel St has been renovated with impeccable taste, marrying period architecture with modern boutique

style. It's full of detail: Robert's radios, roll-top baths, antique furniture, old tea chests and the odd wall mural or two. The Loft rooms are lovely, particularly the luxurious Lookout.

★ **Chapel House Penzance**   B&B £££
(☎ 01736-362024;   www.chapelhousepz.co.uk; Chapel St; r from £190; ☎) In one of Chapel St's most historic buildings – a sea-captain's house that was for many years an arts centre – this beautiful B&B has become a favourite of travel supplements, and it's not hard to see why. The six rooms ooze design credentials: retro furniture, waterfall baths, oak beds, sleek bathrooms, skylight windows, all carefully blended with the house's Georgian architecture.

✖ Eating

★ **Shore**   MODERN BRITISH ££
(☎ 01736-362444;   www.theshorerestaurant.uk; 13/14 Alverton St; dinner mains from £20.50, 5-/7-course tasting menu £42/60; ⊙ 6.30-9pm Wed-Sat) This brilliant seafood bistro is overseen by chef Bruce Rennie, a veteran of many a Michelin-starred kitchen. It's all about classic fish and shellfish here, sourced from the Newlyn day boats and served with a strong French-Italian influence. Odds are that this is the next address in Cornwall to bag a Michelin star; get in while you can.

★ **Ben's Cornish Kitchen**   BRITISH ££
(☎ 01736-719200;   www.benscornishkitchen.com; West End; 2-/3-course dinner £27/33; ⊙ noon-1.30pm & 7-8.30pm Tue-Sat; ☎) Blink and you'll miss Ben Prior's restaurant as you zip along Marazion's main street, but diners travel from far and wide to taste his superlative cooking, which majors in meaty Cornish flavours with a French influence. Ben's cooking has earned glowing reviews, and awards from Waitrose, the *Good Food Guide* and the *Trencherman's Guide,* so tables are scarce – book ahead.

★ **Tolcarne Inn**   PUB FOOD ££
(☎ 01736-363074; www.tolcarneinn.co.uk; Tolcarne Pl; mains £15-22; ⊙ noon-2.15pm & 7-9pm Tue-Sat, noon-2.15pm Sun) This Newlyn inn is run by chef Ben Tunnicliffe, a long-standing name on the Cornish dining scene. The ethos here is refreshingly honest – top-quality fish, seafood and locally sourced meat, served with minimal fuss. It's a snug space, full of smuggler's pub charm – blackboard menus, whitewashed walls and views of the har-bour. Bookings advisable, especially for Sunday lunch.

Cornish Barn   BISTRO ££
(☎ 01736-339414;   www.thecornishbarn.co.uk;   20 Chapel St; dishes £8-20; ⊙ 7.30am-2.30pm & 5.30-9.30pm Mon-Fri, 7.30am-3pm & 5.30-9.30pm Sat, 7.30am-3.30pm & 6-9pm Sun) With its exposed brick, scuffed timber, bare bulbs and blazing wood-burner, this bistro on the ground floor of the Artist Residence Penzance (p332) nails the hipster aesthetic, but it has sub-stance as well as style. Tuck into baked eggs or buttermilk chicken burgers for lunch, and after dark go for something from the in-house smoker (think smoked steak or beer-can chicken).

🍷 Drinking & Nightlife

Admiral Benbow   PUB
(☎ 01736-363448;   46 Chapel St; ⊙ 11am-11pm) On historic Chapel St, the salty old Benbow looks as if it's dropped from the pages of *Treasure Island,* with nautical decor mostly reclaimed from shipwrecks: anchors, lan-terns, figureheads and all.

Turk's Head   PUB
(☎ 01736-363093;   Chapel St; ⊙ 11am-11pm) Purportedly the town's oldest pub; there's been a tavern here since the 13th century. It was supposedly a favourite hang-out for Penzance's 'free traders' (aka smugglers); a subterranean tunnel once led to the harbour from the cellar (now the dining room). There are Skinner's and Sharp's ales on tap, and a seafood-dominated menu that features crab sandwiches and grilled lobster.

ℹ Getting There & Away

BUS

Buses depart from the **bus station** (Wharf Rd). Local destinations include the following.
Helston (bus U4, £6, hourly Monday to Satur-day, two hourly Sunday) Travels via Marazion and connects onward to Falmouth and Penryn.
St Ives (bus 16/16A/A17, £6, 30 minutes, hourly Monday to Saturday, five on Sunday).
Land's End (bus A1, £6, 50 minutes, every two hours Monday to Saturday, five on Sunday).

TRAIN

Penzance is the last stop on the line from Lon-don Paddington.
Truro £7, 30 minutes
St Ives £4.50, 50 minutes, change at St Erth
Exeter £40.30, three hours
London Paddington £91.10, 5½ hours

The Lizard

Cornwall's southern coastline takes a sudden wild turn around the Lizard Peninsula, where fields and heaths plunge into a melee of black cliffs, churning surf and saw-tooth rocks. Cut off from the rest of Cornwall by the River Helford, and ringed by treacherous seas, the Lizard was once an ill-famed graveyard for ships, and the peninsula still has a raw, untamed edge. Wind-lashed in winter, in summer its clifftops blaze with wildflowers, and its beaches and coves are perfect for a bracing wild swim.

It's also a stronghold for the Cornish chough, the red-billed, crow-like bird featured on the county's coat of arms. Once all but extinct, it's slowly reestablishing itself around the Lizard's rugged cliffs.

You may catch sight of slow-worms and even an adder in summer, but the peninsula's peculiar name actually has no reptilian connections; it comes from the old Celtic words *'lys ardh'*, meaning 'high court'.

◎ Sights & Activities

★ Kynance Cove
BEACH

A mile north of Lizard Point, this National Trust–owned inlet is an absolute showstopper, studded with craggy offshore islands rising out of searingly blue seas that seem almost tropical in colour. The cliffs around the cove are rich in serpentine, a red-green rock popular with Victorian trinket-makers. It's an impossibly beautiful spot and, when the seas aren't too rough, an exhilarating place for a wild swim. Drinks and snacks are available at the ecofriendly beach cafe (☑ 01326-290436; www.kynancecovecafe.co.uk; mains £5-14; ◷ 9am-5.30pm).

Lizard Lighthouse Heritage Centre
MUSEUM

(☑ 01326-290202; www.trinityhouse.co.uk/lighthouse-visitor-centres/lizard-lighthouse-visitor-centre; adult/child £3.50/2.50; ◷ 11am-5pm Sun-Thu Mar-Oct) Rising above Lizard Point, the whitewashed lighthouse was built in 1751 and has protected ships from the treacherous rocks ever since. Although it's now automated, like all UK lighthouses, you can visit the heritage centre to learn more about its mechanics and the many ships that have come to grief nearby. It's also the only lighthouse in Cornwall you can actually climb; guided tours (adult/child £8/5) ascend into the tower to see the lamp room and foghorn.

★ Cornish Seal Sanctuary
ANIMAL SANCTUARY

(☑ 0871 423 2110; www.visitsealife.com/gweek; adult/child £15.50/12.50; ◷ 10am-5pm May-Sep, 9am-4pm Oct-Apr) The 'ah' factor goes into overdrive at this sea-life centre in Gweek, about 12 miles drive from Falmouth along the Helford River. It cares for sick and orphaned seals washed up along the Cornish coastline before returning them to the wild. It's a guaranteed kids' favourite, and parents will doubtless find themselves seduced by the seals' antics, too. There are regular talks and feeding sessions. Online bookings get a hefty 30% discount.

🛌 Sleeping & Eating

Lizard YHA
HOSTEL £

(☑ 0845 371 9550; www.yha.org.uk; dm £16-25; ◷ Apr-Oct) Once a Victorian hotel next to the lighthouse, now a YHA hostel, this has to rank pretty high on the 'UK's best budget beds' list. It's in a spectacular location, overlooking miles of wild cliffs and coast, and it's typically well run: a range of dorms, a self-catering kitchen and spacious lounge, but no cafe.

★ Kota
INTERNATIONAL ££

(☑ 01326-562407; www.kotarestaurant.co.uk; 2-/3-course menu £20/25, mains £14-24; ◷ 6-9pm Tue-Sat) Porthleven's top restaurant is run by half Maori, half Chinese-Malay chef Jude Kereama. Set in an old harbourside mill, the menu is spiced with Far Eastern and fusion flavours, underpinned by classic French credentials. Presentation is a strong point – the dishes look beautiful, with edible flowers and other flourishes – but some flavour combinations work better than others. Bookings essential.

There's also a more easygoing bistro, Kota Kai (☑ 01326-574411; www.kotakai.co.uk; mains £8.95-18.95; ◷ noon-2pm Thu-Tue, 5.30-9.30pm Mon-Sat; 🐾), just along the harbour.

Halzephron Inn
PUB FOOD ££

(☑ 01326-240406; www.halzephron-inn.co.uk; mains £10-22; ◷ 11am-11pm) On the cliffs above the cove of Gunwalloe, 5 miles south of Helston, this is a historic Cornish local, whitewashed and slate-topped, with brassy trinkets above the bar, stout beams and a menu of beer-battered fish, grilled gammon steak, duck breast and the like. It's cosy and stone-walled, with lots of nooks and crannies, and a small patio outside.

Falmouth & Around

POP 20,775

Few seaside towns in Cornwall boast such an arresting location as Falmouth, overlooking the broad Fal River as it empties into the English Channel. Surrounded by green hills and blue sea, Falmouth is an appealing jumble of lanes, old pubs, slate roofs and trendy cafes. It's an ideal base for exploring Cornwall's south coast, and has a wealth of bars and bistros, a trio of beaches and Cornwall's finest maritime museum.

Though it's now mainly supported by students at Falmouth University in nearby Penryn, the town made its fortune during the 18th and 19th centuries thanks to lucrative maritime trade – Falmouth has the third-deepest natural harbour in the world, and the town grew rich when tea clippers, trading vessels and mail packets stopped here to unload their cargoes. Falmouth is still an important centre for ship repairs – you can look over the dockyard cranes as you head to Pendennis Point.

◉ Sights

Falmouth's trio of bucket-and-spade beaches – **Gyllyngvase**, **Swanpool** and **Maenporth** – aren't quite up to north coast standards, but they're nice enough for paddling and sun lounging. All the beaches have car parks, but they fill up quickly in summer; a bus service (p338) is also available.

Two of Cornwall's great subtropical gardens, **Trebah** (☑01326-252200; www.trebah garden.co.uk; adult/child £10/5; ◷10.30am-5.30pm, last entry 4.30pm) and **Glendurgan** (NT; ☑01326-250906; www.nationaltrust.org.uk/glendurgan-garden; adult/child £9.50/4.75; ◷10.30am-5.30pm Tue-Sun), sit side by side along the river's northern bank, about 4 miles south of Falmouth.

★ Potager Garden   GARDENS

(☑01326-341258; www.potagergarden.org; suggested donation £3; ◷10am-5pm Thu-Sun) It's a bit of a drive from Falmouth but this gorgeous kitchen garden near Constantine is well worth the detour. Rescued from dilapidation by its current owners, it's been renovated by volunteers into a delightful working garden modelled on the French 'potager'. Highlights include the 30m greenhouse and the super veggie **cafe**, which is very popular with lunching locals at weekends (mains £6 to £10). There's always a good selection of plants for sale, too.

National Maritime Museum   MUSEUM

(☑01326-313388; www.nmmc.co.uk; Discovery Quay; adult/child £12.95/5; ◷10am-5pm) Falmouth's most high-profile museum is located on the revamped area around Discovery Quay. It's the sister outpost of the National Maritime Museum in Greenwich, London, and focuses on Falmouth's history as a seafaring port, supplemented by regular nautically themed exhibitions – recent shows covered the history of the Royal National Lifeboat Institution (RNLI), the exploration of the Pacific and the tradition of tattooing. The centrepiece is the impressive **Flotilla Gallery**, where an array of small boats is suspended from the ceiling.

Pendennis Castle   CASTLE

(EH; ☑01326-316594; www.english-heritage.org.uk; adult/child £8.40/5; ◷10am-6pm Mar-Sep, to 5pm Oct, to 4pm Sat & Sun Nov-Feb) Designed in tandem with its sister castle in St Mawes across the estuary, this Tudor castle sits proudly on Pendennis Point, and was built as part of Henry VIII's massive castle-building program to reinforce England's coastline. You can wander around the central keep and the Tudor gun deck, as well as the governor's bedroom, a WWI guardhouse and the WWII-era Half-Moon Battery. Listen out for the Noonday Gun, which rings out at 12pm sharp every day in July and August.

☆ Activities

Fal River Boat Trips   BOATING

Falmouth's main pier is the departure point for boat trips along the Fal River and ferries to Flushing and St Mawes. There are several operators, all offering similar routes: Enterprise Boats (p338) is the best known, and runs regular trips to Truro and St Mawes via Trelissick Gardens.

AK Wildlife Cruises   WILDLIFE WATCHING

(☑01326-753389; www.akwildlifecruises.co.uk; adult/child £50/45) Run by the amiable and unfailingly enthusiastic 'Captain Keith', this specialist wildlife cruise sets out from Falmouth Harbour in search of local marine life. Depending on the season, there's a good chance of spotting dolphins, porpoises, basking sharks, puffins and seals – and it's not unheard of to spy minke whales.

Gylly Adventures   KAYAKING

(☑07341 890495; www.gyllyadventures.co.uk; kayak tour per person £40) Based on Gyllyngvase

DON'T MISS

THE EDEN PROJECT & THE LOST GARDENS OF HELIGAN

Five miles from St Austell, at the bottom of a china clay pit, the giant biomes of the **Eden Project** (☑ 01726-811911; www.edenproject.com; adult/child £27.50/14, joint ticket with Lost Gardens of Heligan £38.05/18.45; ☺ 9.30am-6pm, last admission 4.30pm) – the world's largest greenhouses – have become Cornwall's most famous landmark, and an absolutely essential visit. Looking rather like a lunar landing station, Eden's bubble-shaped biomes maintain miniature ecosystems that enable all kinds of weird and wonderful plants to flourish – from stinky rafflesia flowers and banana trees in the Rainforest Biome to cacti and soaring palms in the Mediterranean Biome. Book online for discounted admission.

The Eden Project is the brainchild of former record producer turned entrepreneur Tim Smit, who also rescued the **Lost Gardens of Heligan** (☑ 01726-845100; www.heligan.com; Pentewan; adult/child £14.50/6.50; ☺ 10am-6pm Mar-Oct, to 5pm Nov-Feb) from ruin. Formerly the family estate of the Tremaynes, Heligan's magnificent 19th-century gardens fell into disrepair following WWI, but have been splendidly restored by an army of gardeners and volunteers. It's a horticultural wonderland: you'll encounter formal lawns, working kitchen gardens, fruit-filled greenhouses, a secret grotto and a 25m-high rhododendron, plus a lost-world Jungle Valley of ferns, palms and tropical blooms. Heligan is 7 miles from St Austell.

Beach, this watersports company hires the usual kit – stand-up paddleboards, kayaks, bodyboards and the like – but it also offers some great guided kayaking trips. Options include a tour of Falmouth harbour, a trip down the Helford River, a pub paddle and (best of all) a night kayak trip illuminated by LED head torches (£45 per person).

✵✦ Festivals

Falmouth Oyster Festival FOOD & DRINK
(www.falmouthoysterfestival.co.uk; ☺ Oct) Feast on fresh oysters, mussels and other crustaceans during this festival, which also hosts cookery classes and culinary demos.

🛏 Sleeping

★**Highcliffe Contemporary B&B** B&B ££
(☑ 01326-314466; www.highcliffefalmouth.com; 22 Melvill Rd; s £55-70, d £80-160; 🛜) Vintage furniture and upcycled design pieces give each of the rooms here an individual feel. The pick of the bunch is the light-filled Attic Penthouse, with skylight windows overlooking Falmouth Bay. Room-service breakfasts are served in picnic baskets, or you can tuck into pancakes and hog's pudding in the dining room.

Bosanneth B&B ££
(☑ 01326-314649; www.bosanneth.co.uk; Gyllyngvase Hill; d from £90; 🛜) There's a mix-and-match decorative vibe running through this eight-room B&B. Some of the rooms feel

vintage, with old mirrors, reclaimed furniture and classic colours, while others go for a more up-to-date look. The 'oasis' garden is a particular delight.

★**Greenbank** HOTEL £££
(☑ 01326-312440; www.greenbank-hotel.co.uk; Harbourside; r £130-260; ℗🛜) Greenbank is the queen of Falmouth's hotels, with a knockout position overlooking the boat-filled estuary towards Flushing. It feels like the setting for an Agatha Christie novel – nautical knick-knacks and ships in cabinets dot public areas, and tall windows look out on to the water. The rooms are more modern, decorated in beige and cream. Sea views command premium prices.

🍴 Eating

★**Stone's Bakery** BAKERY £
(☑ 07791 003183; www.stonesbakery.co.uk; 28a High St; breads £1.50-3, mains £6-9; ☺ 9am-4pm Mon-Sat; 🛜) Freshly baked loaves line the window like pieces of art at this gorgeous bakery, which focuses on traditional hand-shaped rustic loaves – the tangy maltster and the organic sourdough are as delicious as you'll ever taste. It recently moved up the street to new premises, and now has space to serve great breakfasts and lunchtime pizzas and tarts.

Good Vibes Café CAFE £
(☑ 01326-211870; www.facebook.com/goodvibescafefalmouth; 28 Killigrew St; sandwiches & sal-

ads £6-8; 8.30am-5.30pm Mon-Sat;) This friendly, contemporary cafe on the Moor is popular for its copious breakfasts (veggie and nonveggie), as well as its creative sandwiches (which range from pulled spiced chicken to peanut-and-mackerel bagel), crunchy salads and irresistible cakes. There's free cucumber water on tap, plus smoothies and juices galore.

★**Oliver's**   BISTRO ££

(01326-218138; www.oliversfalmouth.com; 33 High St; mains £15-24; noon-2pm & 7-9pm Tue-Sat) Run by well-respected chef Ken Symons, this little bistro is everyone's tip in Falmouth, but the tiny dining room means you'll have to book well ahead. White walls and pine tables provide a stripped-back match for Ken's imaginative, Mediterranean-inspired food. Local foragers provide many ingredients. Bookings are essential.

★**Wheelhouse**   SEAFOOD ££

(01326-318050; Upton Slip; mains £8-15; 6-10pm Wed-Sat) Hidden down a narrow alley off Church St, this tiny, nautically themed backstreet shellfish bar is all about the hands-on seafood experience: crab, scallops, mussels and lobsters are served in their shells, complete with cracking tools. There are two sittings, but both are always sold out – you will need to book well ahead, ideally a month in advance.

★**Star & Garter**   GASTROPUB ££

(01326-316663; www.starandgarterfalmouth. com; 52 High St; dinner mains £16-23; noon-10pm) At the top of the old High St among antique shops and health-food stores, this ancient old boozer has been reincarnated as a gourmet gastropub focusing on nose-to-tail dining, locally sourced wherever possible. It's proved a great success, with a bevy of foodie awards and cracking views across the water to Flushing. The menu is meat-heavy, so veggies might struggle.

★**Ferryboat Inn**   GASTROPUB ££

(01326-250625; www.staustellbrewery.co.uk/ pub/falmouth/ferryboat-inn; Helford Passage; mains £8-20; 11am-11pm) This lovely riverside pub is a Cornish classic. Outside, there are wooden picnic tables with dreamy views over the Helford River; inside, it's all wood, slate and open plan. It's great for food – oysters, shellfish and the Sunday roast are strong points – and a big blackboard is full

of fishy specials. Bus 35 passes hourly from Falmouth.

○ **Drinking & Nightlife**

★**Beerwolf Books**   PUB

(01326-618474; www.beerwolfbooks.com; 3 Bells Ct; noon-midnight) Probably the greatest idea ever, anytime, anywhere: a prime pub and brilliant bookshop rolled into one, meaning you can browse for reading material before settling down for a pint of real ale. Beers change weekly, and you're welcome to bring in food. It feels well worn and welcoming, like a comfy pair of slippers, with old chairs and mix-and-match tables.

Chintz Symposium   BAR

(01326-617550; www.thechintzbar.com; Old Brewery Yard; 5-11.30pm;) Wine, charcuterie, cheese and cocktails take centre stage at this uber-trendy hang-out on the 1st floor above Hand Bar. Junk shop furniture and patches of reclaimed wallpaper fill the A-framed attic space, and the wine list is copious.

Hand Bar   BAR

(01326-319888; www.facebook.com/handbeerbaruk; 3 Old Brewery Yard; noon-1am) Peter Walker's craft-beer bar showcases his knowledge, gained while running Leeds' North Bar. Esoteric choices such as New York's Brooklyn Brewery and Bodmin's Harbour Brewing Co are among the regulars on tap – although esoterica equals expensiveness. It's fittingly situated in a former brewery, with a few courtyard tables outside, but space is limited inside.

Front   PUB

(01326-212168; Custom House Quay; 11am-11.30pm) The beer-buffs' choice in Falmouth: a cosy spit-and-sawdust pub, with scuffed wood floors and a copious choice of real ales chalked up above the bar, served straight from wooden casks. The entrance is down a small hill off Arwenack St.

★**Espressini**   CAFE

(01326-236582; www.espressini.co.uk; 39 Killigrew St; 8am-6pm Mon-Sat, 10am-4pm Sun;) Cornwall's best coffee house, bar none, run by committed coffee aficionado Rupert Ellis. The choice of blends, roasts and coffees is enough to fill a 2m-long blackboard (literally) and it has recently started serving a small selection of breakfast and lunch dishes, too. There's another coffee-only branch across town on Arwenack St.

ⓘ Information

The small **Fal River Information Centre**
(☑ 01326-741194; www.falriver.co.uk; 11 Market
Strand, Prince of Wales Pier; ⊘ 9.30am-5.30pm
Mon-Sat, 10am-4pm Sun) by Prince of Wales
Pier is run by the Fal River Company, and provides useful advice. It also operates most of the
ferries along the Fal River, and offers an accommodation booking service.

ⓘ Getting There & Away

Falmouth is at the end of the branch train line
from Truro (£4.20, 24 minutes), where you can
catch connections with the mainline service
from Penzance to stations including Plymouth,
Exeter and London Paddington.

Falmouth's **Moor Bus Station** (The Moor) is
central. **First Kernow** (www.firstgroup.com/
cornwall) has the following bus routes.

Helston (£5.40, hourly Monday to Saturday)
Bus 35/35A stops at Glendurgan and Trebah
Gardens en route.

Penzance (every two hours Monday to Saturday) Bus 2 via Helston.

Redruth (£5.40, hourly) Bus U2 via Penryn.

Truro (£5.40, half-hourly Monday to Saturday,
hourly Sunday) Bus U1 via Penryn.

To reach Gyllyngvase and Swanpool beaches,
bus 367 runs from the station to both (hourly
Monday to Friday, four times on Saturday).

Truro

POP 17,430

Dominated by the three mighty spires of its
19th-century cathedral, which rises above
town like a neo-Gothic supertanker, Truro
is Cornwall's capital and its only city. It's
the county's main centre for shopping and
commerce: the streets here are packed with
high-street chains and independent shops,
and there are regular weekly markets held
on the paved piazza at Lemon Quay (opposite the Hall for Cornwall).

Traces of Truro's wealthy past remain in
the smart Georgian town houses and Victorian villas dotted around the city – especially along Strangways Tce, Walsingham Pl and
Lemon St – although a rash of 60s and 70s
architecture has somewhat marred the city's
architectural appeal.

⊙ Sights & Activities

Truro Cathedral   CHURCH
(www.trurocathedral.org.uk; High Cross; suggested donation £5; ⊘ 7.30am-6pm Mon-Sat, 9am-
7pm Sun) Built on the site of a 16th-century

parish church in soaring Gothic Revival
style, Truro Cathedral was completed in
1910, making it the first cathedral built in
England since St Paul's. Inside, the vast
nave contains some fine Victorian stained
glass and the impressive Father Willis
Organ.

Royal Cornwall Museum   MUSEUM
(☑ 01872-272205; www.royalcornwallmuseum.org.
uk; River St; ⊘ 10am-5pm Mon-Sat) **FREE** Collections at the county's main museum encompass everything from geological specimens
to Celtic torques and a ceremonial carriage.
Upstairs there's an Egyptian section and a
little gallery with some surprising finds:
a Turner here, a van Dyck there, and several works by the Newlyn artist Stanhope
Forbes.

★ Enterprise Boats   BOATING
(☑ 01326-374241; www.falriver.co.uk/getting-about/
ferries/enterprise-boats; day return adult/child
£15.30/7.20) Two miles downriver from Truro's
city centre, past Boscawen Park, lies the riverside hamlet Malpas, from where ferries chug
out along the Fal River and on to Falmouth.
Depending on the tide, boats either depart
from the pontoon at Malpas, or from the
Truro harbour-master's office; double-decker
buses link the two.

The boats putter past wooded riverbanks
and hidden inlets; some stop at Trelissick en
route. It's a wonderfully scenic trip.

There's a 10% discount for online
bookings.

★ Trelissick   GARDENS
(NT; ☑ 01872-862090; www.nationaltrust.org.uk/
trelissick-garden; house & gardens adult/child
£12/6, grounds £4; ⊘ grounds 10.30am-5.30pm,
house 11am-5pm) Grandly located at the head
of the Fal estuary, 4 miles south of Truro,
Trelissick is one of Cornwall's most beautiful aristocratic estates, with a formal garden
filled with magnolias and hydrangeas, surrounded by a huge expanse of green fields
and parkland criss-crossed by trails. The
grand, 19th-century neo-Palladian house
has been reopened to the public, and hosts
exhibitions exploring the estate's history. If
you just want to explore the estate grounds,
parking costs £4.

⌂ Sleeping

Mannings Hotel   HOTEL **££**
(☑ 01872-270345;   www.manningshotels.co.uk;
Lemon St; r £115-125, apt £145; 🅿 🛜) The

best place to stay in the city centre. The part-Georgian building has been tastefully modernised, with bright colours and functional furniture, even if the general vibe feels a tad corporate. There are nine self-contained apartments for longer stays, which come with small kitchens and spiral staircases. The private gated car park is very useful.

Merchant House Hotel HOTEL **££**
(☑ 01872-272450; www.merchant-house.co.uk; 49 Falmouth Rd; s/d/f £79/99/119; P 🛜 🛗) This Victorian house is handy for town, and refurbishment has brightened up the rooms with cheery sea-blue colour schemes. Some have skylights, others overlook the garden. It's popular with business travellers and organised coach tours, however, so it's worth reserving well ahead. It's a steep walk up Lemon St past the Lander monument.

🍴 Eating & Drinking

Craftworks Street Kitchen STREET FOOD **£**
(☑ 01872-857117; www.craftworkskitchen.co.uk; Lemon Quay; mains £6-8; ⊙ 11am-6pm Mon-Thu, to 8pm Fri & Sat, to 4pm Sun) Inside an old shipping container, this rough-and-ready little diner turns out the best street food in the city. Choose from delicious tacos and burritos like peri-peri chicken and beef brisket, served with taco slaw and red-onion pickle, or go the whole hog with a fish po-boy or a Korean chicken burger.

Bustopher Jones BISTRO **££**
(☑ 01872-430000; www.bustophersbarbistro.com; 62 Lemon St; mains £12.95-24; ⊙ noon-10pm Mon-Sat) It's been open, closed and open again over recent years, but Bustopher's is back for downtown bistro dining: expect substantial dishes like pan-seared hake with a mussel-butter sauce and duck with dauphinoise potatoes, served in an attractive, wood-panelled dining room. There's a small patio at the rear.

Thomas Daniell BRITISH **££**
(☑ 01872-858110; www.tdtruro.com; 1 Infirmary Hill; mains lunch £6.95-10.95, dinner £11.95-21.50; ⊙ lunch noon-5pm daily, dinner 5-10pm Mon-Sat) Run by the owners of the Old Grammar School (☑ 01872-278559; www.theoldgrammar school.com; 19 St Mary's St; ⊙ 10am-late Mon-Sat) cocktail bar, this sophisticated gastropub is looking sleek and modern since its recent refurbishment, and it's become one of the city's new favourites. Big wooden tables, lo-

cal ales on tap and a choice of dining spaces, plus a good wine choice. Food is fairly standard gastropub stuff, like surf-and-turf and battered fish.

⭐ **108 Coffee** CAFE
(☑ 07582 339636; www.108coffee.co.uk; 109 Kenwyn St; ⊙ 7am-6pm Mon-Fri, 8am-6pm Sat) Set up by unapologetic coffee nuts Paul and Michelle, this is the premier place for a caffeine fix in Truro. The beans come courtesy of Cornish coffee roasters Origin, and the flat whites and espressos are as good as any the county has to offer (you can even text your order ahead to save waiting).

Old Ale House PUB
(☑ 01872-271122; www.old-ale-house.co.uk; 7 Quay St; ⊙ noon-11pm) A proper ale-drinker's pub, with sawdust on the floor, beer mats on the ceiling and a menu of guest ales. Ask at the bar for a handful of peanuts to snack on – they're even happy for you to chuck your shells on the floor. Most of the beers come from Skinner's Brewery.

ℹ️ Information

Tourist Office (☑ 01872-274555; www.visit truro.org.uk; Boscawen St; ⊙ 9am-5.30pm Mon-Fri, to 5pm Sat) In a small office beside the Hall for Cornwall's rear entrance.

ℹ️ Getting There & Away

BUS
Truro's **bus station** is beside Lemon Quay.
Falmouth (£5.40, half-hourly Monday to Saturday, hourly Sunday) The U1 bus runs via Penryn.
St Ives (£5.40, 1½ hours, hourly Monday to Saturday) Bus 14/14A.
Penzance (£5.40, half-hourly Monday to Saturday, hourly Sunday) Bus 18.

TRAIN
Truro is on the main London Paddington–Penzance line and the branch line to Falmouth.
Bristol £49, 3½ hours
Exeter £19.60, 2¼ hours
Falmouth £4.40, 30 minutes
London Paddington £91.10, 4½ hours
Penzance £11, 30 minutes

Fowey
POP 2275
In many ways, Fowey feels like Padstow's south-coast sister; a workaday port turned

well-heeled holiday town, with a tumble of pastel-coloured houses, portside pubs and tiered terraces overlooking the wooded banks of the Fowey River. The town's wealth was founded on the export of china clay from the St Austell pits, but it's been an important port since Elizabethan times, and later became the adopted home of the thriller writer Daphne du Maurier, who used the nearby house at Menabilly Barton as the inspiration for *Rebecca*.

Today it's an attractive and increasingly upmarket town, handy for exploring Cornwall's southeastern corner.

A few miles north along the creek, the riverside hamlet of **Golant** is also well worth a detour, with a waterfront pub for lunch and excellent kayaking opportunities.

◉ Sights & Activities

Polkerris Beach   BEACH
(www.polkerrisbeach.com) A couple of miles west of Fowey, this is the area's largest and busiest beach. Sailing lessons, windsurfing and stand-up paddleboarding are all available.

Fowey River Expeditions   KAYAKING
(☑ 01726-833627; www.foweyexpeditions.co.uk; 47 Fore St; adult/child £30/15; ⊘ Apr-Oct) Guided trips in single- and double-seater open-top canoes, which are ideal for beginners. Standard trips last about three hours and leave from Fowey.

★ Encounter Cornwall   KAYAKING
(☑ 07976 466123; www.encountercornwall.com; Golant; adult/child £30/15) Three-hour guided kayaking trips from Golant, just north of Fowey, with a choice of exploring creek or coastline. It also offers two-hour 'sundowner' expeditions and stand-up paddleboarding trips.

🛏 Sleeping

★ Coriander Cottages   B&B ££
(☑ 01726-834998; www.foweyaccommodation.co.uk; Penventinue Lane; 1-bed cottages £125-145; P � ⏷) ❂ A delightfully rural cottage complex on the outskirts of Fowey, with ecofriendly accommodation in open-plan, self-catering barns, all with quiet country views. The stone barns have been beautifully modernised, and use a combination of solar panels, ground-source heating and rainwater harvesting to reduce environmental impact. Handily, cottages are available

per night, so you're not restricted to weekly stays.

Old Quay House   HOTEL £££
(☑ 01726-833302; www.theoldquayhouse.com; 28 Fore St; d £195-300, ste from £340; ☎) The epitome of Fowey's upmarket trend, this exclusive quayside hotel is all natural fabrics, rattan chairs and tasteful monochrome tones, and the rooms are a mix of estuary-view suites and attic penthouses. It's right in the centre of town, in a handsome riverside building. The restaurant specialises in upmarket seafood.

Cormorant Hotel   HOTEL £££
(☑ 01726-833426;   www.cormoranthotel.co.uk; Golant; d £90-180; P ☎) Up the creek from Fowey in Golant (about 5 miles by road), this small hotel has a superb riverside location, and many of its rooms have water-view balconies. They're split into three comfort levels: go for a Superior overlooking the river for the premium price-to-comfort ratio. Considering the lovely view, rates are very reasonable.

✕ Eating & Drinking

Lifebuoy Cafe   CAFE £
(☑ 07715 075869; www.thelifebuoycafe.co.uk; 8 Lostwithiel St; mains £5-10; ⊘ 8am-5pm) Everyone's favourite brekkie stop in Fowey, this friendly cafe is a riot of character, from the brightly coloured furniture and polka-dot bunting to the vintage Action Men on the shelves. Wolf down a Fat Buoy brekkie or a classic fish-finger butty, washed down with a mug of good old English tea.

Dwelling House   CAFE £
(☑ 01726-833662; 6 Fore St; tea £3-6; ⊘ 10am-6.30pm May-Sep, to 5.30pm Wed-Sun Oct-Apr) There is no better spot for afternoon tea in town than this delightful cafe, which makes all its own cakes, from lemon drizzle to coffee and walnut, decorated with sprinkles and icing swirls, and served on a proper cake stand. Unapologetically English.

Sam's   BISTRO ££
(☑ 01726-832273; www.samscornwall.co.uk/fowey; 20 Fore St; mains £12-18; ⊘ noon-9pm) Sam's has been a stalwart in Fowey for years. Booth seats, Day-Glo menus and a lively local vibe keep the feel laid-back, and the menu of burgers, fish, salads and steaks proves perennially popular – although you're not getting haute cuisine here. No bookings.

POLPERRO & MEVAGISSEY

Even in a county where picturesque fishing harbours seem to fill every cove, it's hard not to fall for **Polperro** – a warren of cottages, boat stores and alleyways, all set around a stout granite harbour. Unsurprisingly, this was once a smugglers' hideout, and it's still a place with a salty, sea-dog atmosphere, despite the inevitable summer crowds. The coast path between Polperro and Looe is particularly scenic. The main car park is 750m uphill from the village, from where it's a 15-minute stroll down to the quayside.

Just along the coast, the little village of **Mevagissey** has not been gentrified to quite the same degree as other ports along the coast, and feels all the better for it. There are alleys to wander, great pubs, secondhand bookshops and galleries to browse, and the harbour is one of the best places on the south coast for crabbing. In summer, ferries run along the coast from Mevagissey Harbour to Fowey.

King of Prussia　　　　　　　　　　PUB
(☏ 01726-833694; www.kingofprussiafowey.co.uk; Town Quay; ☺ 11am-11pm) Fowey has lots of pubs, but you might as well go for the one with the best harbour view, named after notorious 'free trader' (otherwise known as smuggler) John Carter. Head up the steps into the candy-pink building, and aim to get one of the river-view tables.

ⓘ Information

Fowey Tourist Information Centre (☏ 01726-833616; www.fowey.co.uk; 5 South St; ☺ 9.30am-5pm Mon-Sat, 10am-4pm Sun) Lots of information on Fowey and southeast Cornwall.

ⓘ Getting There & Away

Bus services are limited: the only really useful service is bus 24 (hourly Monday to Saturday, six on Sunday), which runs to St Austell, Heligan and Mevagissey. It also stops at Par train station, where you can catch trains on the main London–Penzance line.

There are two ferry services from Fowey: the Bodinnick Ferry, which carries cars over the river to Bodinnick en route to Polruan, and the pedestrian-only Polruan Ferry.

Polruan Ferry (www.ctomsandson.co.uk/polruan-ferry; adult/child £2.80/80p, bicycle £1, dog 40p; ☺ 7.15am-11pm May-Sep, 7.15am-7pm Mon-Sat, 10am-5pm Sun Oct-Apr) Passenger ferry to Polruan. In winter and on summer evenings, it runs from Town Quay; during the day, it runs from Whitehouse Slipway on the Esplanade.

Bodinnick Ferry (www.ctomsandson.co.uk/bodinnick-ferry; car & 2 passengers/pedestrian/bicycle £4.80/1.80/free; ☺ 7am-7.30pm Mon-Sat, 8am-7.30pm Sun May-Sep, last ferry 7pm Oct-Apr) Car ferry crossing the river to Bodinnick.

Looe

POP 5280

Nestled in the crook of a steep-sided valley, the twin towns of East and West Looe stand on either side of a broad river estuary, connected by a multiarched Victorian bridge built in 1853. There's been a settlement here since the days of the Domesday Book, and the town thrived as a medieval port before reinventing itself as a holiday resort for well-to-do Victorians – famously, the town installed one of the county's first 'bathing machines' beside **Banjo Pier** (named for its circular shape) in around 1800, and it's been a popular beach retreat ever since.

In contrast to Fowey, Looe still feels a little behind-the-times – chip shops, souvenir sellers and chintzy B&Bs still very much rule the roost here – but if it's a classic bucket-and-spade seaside town you're looking for, you've definitely found it in Looe.

⊙ Sights

Looe Island　　　　　　　　　　ISLAND
(www.cornwallwildlifetrust.org.uk/looeisland; guided walks £25) A mile offshore from Hannafore Point is densely wooded Looe Island (officially known as St George's Island), a 9-hectare nature reserve and haven for marine wildlife. You can explore on foot, or book a guided walk with the island ranger, who can help spot local wildlife including grey seals, cormorants, shags and oystercatchers. Bookings are advised for guided walks.

Between April and September, the **Moonraker** (☏ 07814 264514; Buller Quay; return adult/child £7/5, plus landing fee £4/1) putters over from Buller Quay, but trips are dependent on weather and tides.

WORTH A TRIP

COTEHELE HOUSE

At the head of the Tamar Valley sits the Tudor manor of **Cotehele** (NT; ☎01579-351346; www.nationaltrust.org.uk/cotehele; St Dominick; adult/child £11.60/5.80; ⊙ house 11am-4pm, gardens dawn-dusk), one of the Edgcumbe dynasty's modest country retreats. The cavernous great hall is the centrepiece, and the house has an unparalleled collection of Tudor tapestries, armour and furniture.

Outside, the gardens sweep down past the 18th-century Prospect Folly to Cotehele Quay, where there's a discovery centre exploring the history of the Tamar Valley and a vintage sailing barge, the *Shamrock*.

🛌 Sleeping

Penvith Barns   B&B ££

(☎01503-240772; www.penvithbarns.co.uk; St-Martin-by-Looe; r £85-110; P🅿🛜❄) Escape the Looe crowds at this rural barn conversion in the nearby hamlet of St-Martin-by-Looe, run by friendly owners Graham and Jules. Rooms range from small to spacious: the Piggery is tiny and tucked under the eaves, while the Dairy has enough space for a spare bed and sofa. Each room has its own private entrance. Two-night minimum in summer.

Commonwood Manor   B&B ££

(☎01503-262929; www.commonwoodmanor.com; St Martins Rd; d £90-115; P🅿🛜❄) In a prime position on the East Looe hillside, this elegant manor house is a cut above the bargain-basement B&Bs you'll find around the rest of Looe. Rooms are a touch frilly and pastel heavy, but if you can bag one of the bay-window bedrooms, you'll be rewarded with the best sea views in town. There's usually a two-night minimum.

❶ Information

Looe Tourist Office (☎01503-262072; www.looeguide.co.uk; Guildhall, Fore St; ⊙10am-5pm Easter-Oct) Looe's efficient and well-staffed visitor centre is the hub for all tourist things: accommodation, activities, restaurant recommendations and so on.

❶ Getting There & Away

The branch line from Liskeard to Looe is almost a day out in itself, tracking through wooded valleys all the way out to the seaside. The Looe Valley Line Day Ranger ticket (adult/child £4.40/2.20) allows one day's unlimited travel; the journey from Liskeard to Looe takes about 40 minutes.

Bodmin Moor

It can't quite boast the wild majesty of Dartmoor, but Bodmin Moor has a bleak beauty all of its own. With its heaths and granite hills, including Rough Tor ('row-tor'; 400m) and Cornwall's highest point, Brown Willy (420m), it's a desolate place that works on the imagination, with prehistoric remains and legends of mysterious beasts.

The northern and central parts of the Moor are largely barren and treeless, while the southern section is greener. Apart from the hills, the moor's main landmark is Jamaica Inn, made famous by Daphne du Maurier's novel of the same name.

◉ Sights & Activities

⭐**Lanhydrock**   HISTORIC BUILDING

(NT; ☎01208-265950; www.nationaltrust.org.uk/lanhydrock; adult/child £14.35/7.20; ⊙ house 11am-5.30pm, grounds 10am-5.30pm) This magnificent manor, 2.5 miles southeast of Bodmin, offers a fascinating insight into *Upstairs, Downstairs* life in Victorian England. The house was rebuilt after a devastating fire in 1881 as a home for the Agar-Robartes family, complete with mod cons such as radiators, roasting ovens, warming cupboards and flushing loos. The centrepieces are the drawing room, packed with artworks and antiques, and the enormous kitchens, complete with a pioneering refrigerator room. The ornate Long Gallery is famous for its plaster ceiling.

⭐**Golitha Falls**   WATERFALL

Around 1.25 miles west of St Cleer, these crashing waterfalls are one of the most renowned beauty spots on the moor. Around the falls are the remains of the ancient oak woodland that once covered much of the moor. There is a car park half a mile's walk from the reserve, near Draynes Bridge.

Carnglaze Caverns   CAVE

(☎01579-320251; www.carnglaze.com; adult/child £7/5; ⊙10am-5pm, to 8pm Aug; 🅿❄) Slate was once an important local export on Bodmin Moor, and these deep caverns were cut out by hand by miners, leaving behind an atmospheric network of subterranean caves and a glittering underground pool. Concerts and plays are sometimes held inside the caves in summer. The site is just outside St Neot and well signed.

★ **Bodmin & Wenford Railway**   RAIL
(☑ 01208-73555; www.bodminrailway.co.uk; Rover Pass adult/child £13.50/6.50; ☺ 3-5 daily trains May-Sep, fewer at other times) Run by enthusiasts, this steam railway – the only 'standard gauge' line of its type left in Cornwall – chuffs and clatters for 6.5 miles between Bodmin and Boscarne Junction. Many trains are still decked out in original 1950s livery. At the Boscarne end, the line links up with the Camel Trail (p320); bikes can be taken on the trains if there's space.

✕ **Eating**

★ **St Tudy Inn**   MODERN BRITISH ££
(☑ 01208-850656; www.sttudyinn.com; St Tudy; mains £14-25; ☺ meals noon-2.30pm & 6.30-9pm Mon-Sat, noon-2.30pm Sun) Run by the locally lauded chef Emily Scott, this first-rate village pub has fast become one of East Cornwall's top dining destinations. The old pub has been stripped down and smartened up, and Scott's imaginative food combines traditional British flavours with a modern, season-driven style. There is also a selection of elegant rooms (doubles from £135) in attached barns.

★ **Woods Cafe**   CAFE ££
(☑ 01208-78111; www.woodscafecornwall.co.uk; Cardinham Woods; mains £6-12; ☺ 10.30am-4.30pm) In an old woodsman's cottage lost among the trees of Cardinham, this cracking cafe has become a dining destination in its own right – it's locally famous for its home-baked cakes, cockle-warming soups and sausage sarnies (sandwiches). Perfect for post-walk sustenance.

ISLES OF SCILLY

While only 28 miles west of the mainland, in many ways the Isles of Scilly feels like a different world. Life on this archipelago of around 140 tiny islands seems hardly to have changed in decades: there are no traffic jams, no supermarkets, no multinational hotels, and the only noise pollution comes from breaking waves and cawing gulls. That's not to say that Scilly is behind the

times – you'll find a mobile-phone signal and broadband internet on the main islands – but life ticks along at its own island pace. Renowned for its glorious beaches, there are few places better to escape.

Only five islands are inhabited: St Mary's is the largest, followed by Tresco, while only a few hardy souls remain on Bryher, St Martin's and St Agnes. Regular ferry boats run between all five islands.

Unsurprisingly, summer is by far the busiest time. Many businesses shut down completely in winter.

🛈 **Information**

Isles of Scilly Tourist Information Centre
(☑ 01720-424031; www.visitislesofscilly.com; Porthcressa Beach; ☺ 9am-5.30pm Mon-Sat, 9am-2pm Sun Mar-Oct, 10am-2pm Mon-Fri Nov-Feb) The islands' only tourist office.

Scilly Online (www.scillyonline.co.uk) A locally run website with lots of info on the islands.

Simply Scilly (www.simplyscilly.co.uk) The official tourist site.

🛈 **Getting There & Away**

Isles of Scilly Travel (☑ 01736-334220; www.islesofscilly-travel.co.uk) There are several flights daily from Land's End Airport, near Zennor, and from Newquay Airport. Adult fares start at £80 one way. Summer flights also run from Exeter, Bristol and Southampton. Since 2018 there has also been a helicopter service from Land's End Airport to St Mary's. The flight time is around 20 minutes.

Scillonian III (☑ 0845 710 5555; www.islesofscilly-travel.co.uk; ☺ Apr-Oct) Scilly's ferry plies the notoriously choppy waters between Penzance and St Mary's (one-way adult £49.50). There's at least one daily crossing in summer, but there are no ferries in winter. It sails in most weathers, but seasickness is a distinct possibility: be prepared.

🛈 **Getting Around**

Inter-island ferries between St Mary's and the other islands are provided by the **St Mary's Boatmen's Association** (☑ 01720-423999; www.scillyboating.co.uk; adult/child return to any island £9.50/4.75). If you're staying at one of the hotels on Tresco, there's also a separate transfer service.

The only bus and taxi services are on St Mary's. All flights are met by **Paulgers Transport** (☑ 01720-423701; adult/child return £7.50/3.50), which will run you to wherever you're staying, or straight to the quayside if you're travelling to other islands.

St Mary's

POP 2200

First stop for every visitor to Scilly (unless you're arriving aboard your own private yacht) is St Mary's, the largest and busiest of the islands, and home to the vast majority of hotels, shops, restaurants and B&Bs. Just over 3 miles at its widest point, St Mary's is shaped like a crooked circle, with a claw-shaped peninsula at its southwestern edge – home to the island's capital, Hugh Town, and the docking point for the Scillonian ferry. The main airport is a mile east near Old Town.

◉ Sights

Isles of Scilly Museum　MUSEUM
(☑ 01720-422337; www.iosmuseum.org; Church St, Hugh Town; adult/child £3.50/1; ⊙ 10am-4.30pm Mon-Fri, to noon Sat Easter-Sep, to noon Mon-Sat Oct-Easter) The small Isles of Scilly Museum explores the islands' history, with an eclectic mix of archaeological finds and artefacts from shipwrecks. Among the collection are Neolithic remains such as tools and jewellery, clay pipes left behind by generations of sailors, a couple of sailing boats and a small exhibition on Edward Heath, the British prime minister who loved Scilly so much he was buried here.

⛳ Tours

Scilly Walks　WALKING
(☑ 01720-423326; www.scillywalks.co.uk; adult/child £7/3.50) Three-hour archaeological and historical tours of St Mary's, plus regular guided walking trips to other islands, conducted by local historian and archaeologist Katherine Sawyer.

Island Wildlife Tours　WALKING
(☑ 01720-422212; www.islandwildlifetours.co.uk; half/full day £7/14) Regular birdwatching and wildlife walks with local character and resident twitcher Will Wagstaff, the undisputed authority on Scilly's natural history. Most tours start at 9.45am or 10am on St Mary's, but there are regular tours on other islands too. You need to add on the cost of the boat transfer.

Island Sea Safaris　BOATING
(☑ 01720-422732; www.islandseasafaris.co.uk) Trips to see local seabird and seal colonies (adult/child £34/25), plus one-hour 'island taster' tours (£25 per person). Also rents wetsuits and snorkelling gear.

🛏 Sleeping

Garrison Campsite　CAMPSITE £
(☑ 01720-422670; www.garrisonholidaysscilly. co.uk; Tower Cottage, Garrison; adult £10.50-12.50, child £5.25-6.25, dog £5; 🛜 🐾) St Mary's main campsite sits in a lofty spot above Hugh Town, not far from the Garrison fort. It's a big site, covering 3.5 hectares, with plenty of pitches (some with electrical hook-ups), plus wi-fi, a small shop and a laundry-shower block. It also offers a couple of cottages, including an old lookout tower (£495 to £695 per week).

Mincarlo　B&B ££
(☑ 01720-422513; www.mincarloscilly.com; s £43-51, d £77-114; 🛜 🐾) There's no better location on St Mary's than this little guesthouse in a prime spot with views all the way to Hugh Town from the western end of Town Beach. Rooms are plain and cosy (the attic's a bargain), there's a lounge with local books to browse, breakfast is great, and owners Nick and Bryony are full of local info.

Star Castle Hotel　HOTEL £££
(☑ 01720-422317; www.star-castle.co.uk; Garrison; s £157, d £248-327; 🛜 ⛱ 🐾) Shaped like an eight-pointed star, this former fort on Garrison Point is one of Scilly's star hotels, with heritage-style castle rooms and more-modern garden suites. It's stuffy and expensive, but the views are the best on the island, and at least prices include dinner. It gets a lot cheaper outside the peak months between May and September.

Atlantic Hotel　INN £££
(☑ 01720-422417; www.atlanticinnscilly.co.uk; r £175-240; 🛜 🐾) Revamped courtesy of owners St Austell Brewery, this long-standing inn is looking a lot fresher. Upstairs there are summery rooms with colourful prints, pastel colours and plush fabrics; there are three categories, but here the harbour view is definitely worth the premium. Food is similar to the brewery's other inns: mussels, lobster burgers, seafood platters and other pub-style mains.

🍴 Eating

Juliet's Garden Restaurant　BISTRO ££
(☑ 01720-422228; www.julietsgardenrestaurant. co.uk; mains lunch £7-15, dinner £14-24.95; ⊙ noon-4pm & 6-9pm) St Mary's long-standing bistro, in business for over three decades, is still the best place to eat. It's in a converted barn 15 minutes' walk from town: expect gourmet

salads and sandwiches by day, plus classier plates of pan-roasted bream, slow-roasted lamb and lobster after dark, served by candlelight. The garden is glorious on a sunny day, but it gets busy.

Dibble & Grub　　　　　　　　CAFE ££
(☑ 01720-423719; www.dibbleandgrub.com; lunch £6-12, dinner £10-16; ⊙ 10am-10pm Apr-Sep) Smart beachside cafe beside Porthcressa beach, housed in the island's old fire station. The menu dabbles in tapas and Mediterranean-style classics.

✪ Getting Around

The airport bus (£3) departs from Hugh Town 40 minutes before each flight, while the **Island Rover** (☑ 01720-422131; www.islandrover.co.uk; tickets £9) offers sightseeing trips in a vintage bus: there are usually a couple a day, with an extra one in high summer.

For taxis on St Mary's, try **Island Taxis** (☑ 01720-422126), **Scilly Cabs** (☑ 01720-422901) or **St Mary's Taxis** (☑ 01720-422142), or airport taxi **Paulgers Transport** (p343).

Tresco

POP 175

A short boat hop across the channel from St Mary's brings you to Tresco, the second-largest island, once owned by the monks of Tavistock Abbey, and now privately leased by the Dorrien-Smith family from the Duchy of Cornwall.

The main attraction here is the island's fabulous subtropical garden, but the rest of the island is a lovely place just to explore by bike – although since the whole place is privately leased, it feels a little more manicured and packaged than the other, more community-driven islands, especially since the focus here is very much on high-end visitors.

◉ Sights

★ Tresco Abbey Garden　　　　GARDENS
(☑ 01720-424105; www.tresco.co.uk/enjoying/abbey-garden; adult £15, child 5-16yr £5; ⊙ 10am-4pm) Tresco's key attraction – and one of Scilly's must-see gems – is this subtropical estate, laid out in 1834 on the site of a 12th-century Benedictine priory by the horticultural visionary Augustus Smith. The 7-hectare gardens are now home to more than 20,000 exotic species, from towering palms to desert cacti and crimson flame trees, all nurtured by the temperate Gulf Stream. Admission also covers the Valhal-

la collection, made up of figureheads and nameplates salvaged from ships wrecked off Tresco.

⊨ Sleeping & Eating

★ New Inn　　　　　　　　PUB, HOTEL £££
(☑ 01720-422849; www.tresco.co.uk; r £130-340; 🛜⌨) By Tresco standards, New Inn is a bargain. The rooms are soothingly finished in buttery yellows and pale blues, although inevitably you'll have to fork out for a view. The inn itself serves good food (mains £10 to £18), mainly standards such as pollock and chips, steaks, burgers and the like, and the low-beamed bar is full of island atmosphere.

Bryher

Only around 80 people live on Bryher, Scilly's smallest and wildest inhabited island. Covered by rough bracken and heather, and fringed by white sand, this slender chunk of rock takes a fearsome battering from the Atlantic – Hell Bay hasn't earned its name for nothing. But on a bright sunny day, it's an island idyll par excellence, ideal for exploring on foot.

The island has a strong sense of community; you'll see little stalls selling freshly cut flowers, homegrown veg, jams and packets of fudge.

⊨ Sleeping & Eating

Bryher Campsite　　　　　　CAMPSITE £
(☑ 01720-422886; www.bryhercampsite.co.uk; sites £10.75; 🚻🐾) Bare-bones but beautiful, the island's campsite sits in a secluded spot surrounded by drystone walls and is just steps from the sea.

Hot showers and tractor transport from the quay are included in the nightly rates.

★ Hell Bay Hotel　　　　　　HOTEL £££
(☑ 01720-422947; www.hellbay.co.uk; d £140-360; 🅿🛜🐾) Pretty much the poshest place to stay in Scilly, and a true island getaway blending New England–style furnishings with sunny golds, sea blues and pale wood beams. It has the feel of a luxurious beach villa, with lovingly tended gardens and an excellent restaurant (three-course menu £45). Garden-view suites are the cheapest.

Fraggle Rock　　　　　　　　CAFE ££
(☑ 01720-422222; www.bryher.co; mains £8-15; ⊙ 9am-9pm; 🛜) This relaxed cafe also doubles as Bryher's pub. The menu is mainly

quiches, salads and burgers, ideally served in the front garden, where chickens scratch around and there are views out to Hangman's Rock. It's a lively evening hang-out in season. There are a few timber-clad **cabins** (£620 to £1090 per week) if you feel like staying.

Bryher Shop DELI
(☑01720-423601; www.bryhershop.co.uk; ☺9am-5.30pm Mon-Sat, 10am-1pm Sun) Pick up all your essential supplies at the island's charming general store, which also has a post office.

St Martin's

POP 136

The third-largest and furthest north of the islands, St Martin's is the main centre for Scilly's flower-growing industry, and the island's fields are a riot of colourful blooms in season. It's also blessed with gin-clear waters and the kind of untouched sands you'd more usually associate with St Lucia than Cornwall.

The main settlement is Higher Town, where you'll find the village shop and diving operation, but there are small clusters of cottages in nearby Middle and Lower Towns.

Sights & Activities

St Martin's Vineyard WINERY
(☑01720-423418; www.stmartinsvineyard.co.uk; ☺10.45am-4pm Tue-Thu, conducted tours 11am) The UK's smallest and most southwesterly vineyard produces its own range of white wines. Tours are conducted by owners Val and Graham Thomas.

⭐ **Scilly Seal Snorkelling** SWIMMING
(☑01720-422848; www.scillysealsnorkelling.com; per person £49; ☺Mar-Sep) Now here's an experience to remember – the chance to swim with wild grey seals in the clear waters of St Martin's. the more inquisitive ones come right up close – and the boldest have even been known to nibble your fins. Trips last about three hours.

It'll collect you from your accommodation on St Martin's, but it also provides a morning transfer from Tresco or St Mary's harbour.

Sleeping

Accommodation is limited apart from a superexpensive hotel and a handful of B&Bs.

St Martin's Campsite CAMPSITE £
(☑01720-422888; www.stmartinscampsite.co.uk; sites £11-12, dogs £3; ☺Mar-Oct) The second-largest campsite in Scilly, at the western end of Lawrence's Bay, with 50 pitches (maximum 100 people) spread across three fields. There are coin-operated washing machines and showers, and eggs and veg are available for your morning fry-up.

Polreath B&B ££
(☑01720-422046; www.polreath.com; Higher Town; d £110-130; 🖤) This friendly granite cottage has small rooms and a sunny conservatory serving cream teas, homemade lemonade and evening meals. Weekly stays required May to September.

✖ Eating & Drinking

Little Arthur Farm CAFE £
(☑01720-422457; www.littlearthur.co.uk; cafe meals £5-8; ☺10.30am-4pm) 🍃 A little slice of the good life on tiny St Martin's, this small-scale farm has diversified in all kinds of imaginative directions. There's a cafe-bistro, it grows its own produce and even makes environmentally friendly shoes. There's an eco-cabin to stay in too (£280 to £380 per week).

Adam's Fish & Chips SEAFOOD £
(☑01720-422457; www.adamsfishandchips.co.uk; fish & chips takeaway £9, dine-in £10.50; ☺6-8.30pm Tue-Thu & Sat, noon-2pm Sun Jul & Aug, 6-8.30pm Tue, Thu & Sat Easter-Jun & Sep) The fish here is about as fresh as it gets – whatever's caught on the day is what ends up in your batter. It's run by Adam and Emma, who live and work on Little Arthur Farm nearby. Takeaway is available, but you'll need to book if you want one of the six tables.

Seven Stones PUB
(☑01720-423777; sevenstonesinn@gmail.com; ☺10am-11pm) A fine pub and the island's only boozer, so it's the heart of the action every night of the week. Decent grub (mains £8 to £14), Cornish ales and super views of the other islands from the terrace.

St Agnes

POP 170

Scilly's southernmost island feels really remote, with a string of empty coves and a scattering of prehistoric sites. Visitors disembark at Porth Conger, near the old lighthouse, from where you wander along the coast path around the whole island.

At low tide, a narrow sandbar appears and provides a bridge to the neighbouring island of Gugh, where many ancient burial sites and a few chamber tombs can be found.

🛏 Sleeping & Eating

★ Troytown Farm
CAMPSITE **£**

(☏ 01720-422360; www.troytown.co.uk; adult/child £10/5, tents £2-8) The journey to St Agnes' campsite is almost the best bit; you're picked up in a tractor trailer and rattle across the island down the hedge-lined lanes. The camping field is small, but wonderfully located on the island's sunset coast, surrounded by drystone walls and a sea-blue, big-sky horizon. There are his-and-hers loos, token-operated showers (60p) and lockers for device-charging.

Luggage transfer costs £3.50. The campsite also rents prepitched bell tents (from £420 per week) and three self-catering cottages (£385 to £1045 per week). Bring a torch, as the island gets very, very dark.

Covean Cottage
COTTAGE **££**

(☏ 01720-422620; www.coveancottage.com; d £88-104) Pretty much the only B&B on the island, this little stone-walled cottage has three pretty sea-view rooms. There's also a small cafe, which serves brekkies and light meals cooked up by the owner.

★ Turk's Head
PUB FOOD **££**

(☏ 01720-422434; mains £8-14; ◷ 11am-11pm Mon-Sat, noon-10.30pm Sun) You can almost smell the history at Britain's most southerly alehouse. It's covered in maritime memorabilia – model ships in glass cabinets, vintage maps of the islands, black-and-white photos of seafarers – and there are few finer places to sup a pint. You might even be treated to a sea shanty if the local lads are in the mood.

Cambridge & East Anglia

Best Places to Eat

➡ Midsummer House (p362)

➡ Roger Hickman's (p379)

➡ Great House (p372)

➡ Eric's Fish & Chips (p385)

➡ Butley Orford Oysterage (p374)

➡ Orchard Tea Garden (p365)

Best Places to Stay

➡ Varsity (p361)

➡ Swan (p376)

➡ 3 Princes (p378)

➡ Victoria (p384)

➡ Cley Windmill (p382)

➡ Deepdale Farm (p384)

Why Go?

Unfurling gently eastwards to the sea, the vast flatlands of East Anglia are a rich web of lush farmland, melancholy Fens and sparkling rivers. The area is justly famous for its sweeping sandy beaches, big skies and the bucolic landscape that once inspired Constable and Gainsborough.

It's not all rural idyll though: rising out of the Fens is the world-famous university city of Cambridge, with its stunning classical architecture and earnest attitude, while to the east is the cosmopolitan city of Norwich. Around them, magnificent cathedral cities, pretty market towns and implausibly picturesque villages are testament to the enormous wealth amassed here during medieval times, when the wool and weaving industries flourished.

The meandering coastline is peppered with charismatic fishing villages and traditional seaside resorts, while inland lie the languid, hypnotic charms of the Norfolk Broads, an ideal location for serious relaxation.

When to Go

➡ To best explore the Cambridge colleges, avoid spring (early April to mid-June), when they close to visitors as students prepare for exams.

➡ June and August show the Norfolk and Suffolk beaches and the Norfolk Broads at their best. But in school holidays (late July to August) it gets busy and accommodation prices rise.

➡ World-class classical music comes to Suffolk during the Aldeburgh Festival in June. In July, Southwold's eclectic Latitude Festival offers alternative rock, comedy and theatre.

➡ November's Ways With Words literature festival draws big-name authors to Southwold.

➡ Exquisite music fills Cambridge's King's College Chapel in December, culminating in the Festival of Nine Lessons and Carols on Christmas Eve.

History

East Anglia was a major Saxon kingdom; the dazzling treasures unearthed in the ship burial at Sutton Hoo (p371) in Suffolk have revealed how complex a society it was.

The region's heyday came during the wool boom of the Middle Ages when Flemish weavers settled in the area; many of the grand local churches date from this time – Cambridge University was founded in this period, too.

By the 17th century, much of the region's marshland and bog had been drained and converted into arable land.

It was in East Anglia's emergent, Puritan bourgeoisie that the seeds of the English Civil War were sown. Oliver Cromwell, the uncrowned king of the Parliamentarians, was a small-time merchant residing in Ely when he answered God's call to take up arms against what he saw as the fattened and corrupt monarchy of Charles I.

East Anglia's fortunes waned in the 18th century, when the Industrial Revolution flourished in northern England. During WWII the region became an ideal base for the Royal Air Force and the United States Air Force in the fight against Nazi Germany, thanks to its flat, open landscape and close proximity to mainland Europe.

🏃 Activities

East Anglia is a magnet for walkers, cyclists and kayakers. Here you can discover miles of coastline, tour vast expanses of level land and glide along snaking inland waterways – the Norfolk Broads are utterly idyllic. North Norfolk's wide, often empty beaches are ideal for land yachting and kitesurfing.

Cycling

Famously one of England's flattest regions, East Anglia offers gorgeous cycling along the Suffolk and Norfolk coastlines and in the Fens. Mountain bikers should head for Norfolk's Thetford Forest (www.forestry.gov.uk/thetfordforestpark), while much of the popular on- and off-road Peddars Way is also open to cyclists.

Walking

The Peddars Way and Norfolk Coast Path (www.nationaltrail.co.uk/peddarsway) is a seven-day, 93-mile national trail from Knettishall Heath, near Thetford, to Cromer. The first half takes in an ancient Roman road. The trail then finishes by meandering along the beaches, sea walls, salt marshes (great for birdwatching) and fishing villages of the coast.

Curving further south, the 50-mile Suffolk Coast Path links Felixstowe and Lowestoft, via Snape Maltings, Aldeburgh, Dunwich and Southwold.

Boating & Canoeing

East Anglia's coast and the Norfolk Broads are beloved by boating enthusiasts – those without their own craft can easily hire boats and arrange lessons. Alternatively, wend your way gently around the Broads in a kayak or canoe along the slow-moving rivers.

ℹ Information

Visit East of England (www.visiteastofengland.com) has more info.

ℹ Getting There & Around

Public transport links between London, the Midlands and East Anglia are excellent. Services within the region are generally good; as ever there are fewer connections to smaller towns and villages.

AIR

Key flights to Norwich International Airport (p379) include those to Amsterdam, Aberdeen, Edinburgh, Exeter and Manchester.

BUS

➡ A host of smaller firms, plus two main companies, First (www.firstgroup.com) and Stagecoach (www.stagecoachbus.com), run the region's bus networks.

➡ Traveline East Anglia (www.travelineeastanglia.org.uk) has timetables.

TRAIN

➡ Regional rail provider Greater Anglia (www.greateranglia.co.uk) offers the Anglia Plus Pass. It's valid for a week; you can pay to use it for one day (£19) or three days (£38) within that time.

CAMBRIDGESHIRE

Many visitors to Cambridgeshire never make it past the captivating university city of Cambridge, where august old buildings, student cyclists in academic gowns and glorious chapels await. But beyond this breathtaking seat of learning, the flat reclaimed Fens, lush farmland and myriad waterways make perfect walking and cycling territory, while the extraordinary cathedral at Ely and the rip-roaring Imperial War Museum at

Cambridge & East Anglia Highlights

1 **Cambridge** (p352) Punting past historic colleges before enjoying the heavenly evensong at King's College Chapel.

2 **Sandringham** (p383) Nosying around the drawing room of the Queen's country estate.

3 **Norfolk Broads** (p380) Canoeing your way through tranquil waterways.

4 **Audley End** (p368) Delighting in one of Britain's grandest stately homes.

5 **Holkham Beach** (p384) Wandering barefoot along immense, pine-backed golden sands.

6 **Lavenham** (p372) Soaking up the medieval architecture in this atmospheric market town.

7 **Norwich** (p376) Marvelling at the exquisite rib vaulting in the city's fine cathedral.

8 **Aldeburgh** (p374) Dining on sublime seafood and walking the prom in a laid-back resort.

9 **Imperial War Museum** (p364) Discovering the history of the British and American air forces.

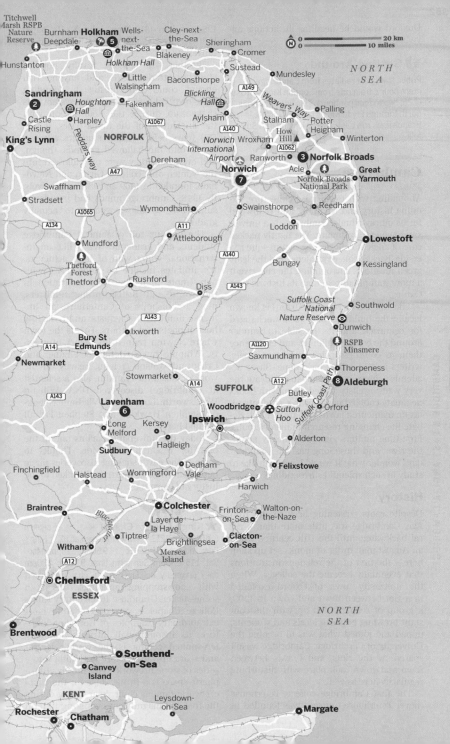

Duxford would be headline attractions anywhere else.

Getting Around

Public transport radiates from Cambridge, a mere hour's train ride from London King's Cross (£25, two to four per hour). This line continues north through Ely to King's Lynn in Norfolk. Branch lines run east to Norwich and into Suffolk.

Cambridge

📞 01223 / POP 123,900

Abounding with exquisite architecture, exuding history and tradition, and renowned for its quirky rituals, Cambridge is a university town extraordinaire. The tightly packed core of ancient colleges, the picturesque riverside 'Backs' (college gardens) and the leafy green meadows surrounding the city give it a more tranquil appeal than its historic rival Oxford.

Like 'the Other Place', as Oxford is known locally, the buildings here seem unchanged for centuries, and it's possible to wander around the college buildings and experience them as countless prime ministers, poets, writers and scientists have done. Sheer academic achievement seems to permeate the very walls: cyclists loaded down with books negotiate cobbled passageways, students relax on manicured lawns and great minds debate life-changing research in historic pubs. First-time punters zigzag erratically across the river, and those long past their student days wonder what it would have been like to study in such splendid surroundings.

History

Despite roots stretching back to the Iron Age, Cambridge was little more than a rural backwater until the 11th century, when an Augustinian order of monks set up shop here – the first of the religious institutions that eventually became the colleges. When the university town of Oxford exploded in a riot between town and gown in 1209, a group of scholars, fed up with the constant brawling between locals and students, upped and joined what was to become the University of Cambridge. Cambridge wasn't spared by the riots, and brawls between town and gown took place with disturbing regularity here as well.

The first Cambridge college, Peterhouse (never Peterhouse *College*), was founded in 1284, and in 1318 Pope John XXII's papal bull declared Cambridge to be an official university.

By the 14th century, royalty, nobility, churches, trade guilds and anyone rich enough could court prestige by founding their own colleges, though the system was shaken up during the Reformation with the dissolution of the monasteries. It was 500 years before female students were allowed into the hallowed grounds, though, and even then they were only allowed into the women-only colleges Girton and Newnham, founded in 1869 and 1871 respectively. By 1948, Cambridge minds had broadened sufficiently to allow women to actually graduate.

The honour roll of famous Cambridge students and academics reads like an international who's who of high achievers. It's affiliates include 98 Nobel Prize winners (more than any other institution in the world), 13 British prime ministers, nine archbishops of Canterbury, an immense number of scientists, and a healthy host of poets and authors. This is the town where Newton refined his theory of gravity, Whipple invented the jet engine, and Crick and Watson (relying heavily on the work of Rosalind Franklin, also a scientist at Cambridge) discovered DNA. William Wordsworth, Lord Byron, Vladimir Nabokov, Stephen Hawking and Stephen Fry all studied here too.

Today the university remains one of the best for research worldwide. Thanks to some of the earth-shaking discoveries made here, Cambridge is inextricably linked to the history of learning.

◎ Sights

★ **King's College Chapel**　　　CHURCH
(📞 01223-331212; www.kings.cam.ac.uk; King's Pde; adult/child £9/6; ◷ 9.30am-3.15pm Mon-Sat, 1.15-2.30pm Sun term time, 9.30am-4.30pm daily university holidays) In a city crammed with showstopping buildings, this is a scene-stealer. Grandiose 16th-century King's College Chapel is one of England's most extraordinary examples of Gothic architecture. Its inspirational, intricate 80m-long fan-vaulted ceiling is the world's largest and soars upwards before exploding into a series of stone fireworks. This hugely atmospheric space is a fitting stage for the chapel's world-famous choir; hear it sing during the free and magnificent **evensong** in term

time (5.30pm Monday to Saturday, 10.30am and 3.30pm Sunday).

King's steeples have long been a magnet for student night climbers (p360), and today images of the chapel adorn thousands of postcards, tea towels and choral CDs. But it was begun in 1446 as an act of piety by Henry VI and was only finished by Henry VIII around 1516.

The lofty stained-glass windows that flank the chapel's sides ensure it's remarkably light. The glass is original, a rare survivor of the excesses of the 17th-century Civil War in this region. It's said that these windows were ordered to be spared by Oliver Cromwell, who knew of their beauty from his own studies in Cambridge.

The antechapel and the choir are divided by a superbly carved wooden screen, designed and executed by Peter Stockton for Henry VIII. The screen bears his master's initials entwined with those of Anne Boleyn. Look closely and you may find an angry human face (possibly Stockton's) amid the elaborate jungle of mythical beasts and symbolic flowers. Above is the magnificent bat-wing organ, originally constructed in 1686, though much altered since.

Beyond the thickly carved dark-wood choir stalls, light suffuses the high altar, which is framed by Rubens' masterpiece *Adoration of the Magi* (1634) and the magnificent east window. To the left of the altar in the side chapels, an exhibition charts the construction stages and methods.

Note the chapel itself (but not the grounds) is open during the exam period (April to June).

Each Christmas Eve, King's College Chapel stages the Festival of Nine Lessons & Carols. It's broadcast globally by the BBC, and to around 300 US radio stations. You can also queue for a place – if you arrive early enough (often by around 9am), you could well get in.

★ Trinity College   COLLEGE
(🏛 01223-338400; www.trin.cam.ac.uk; Trinity St; adult/child £3/1; ⏰ 10am-4.30pm Jul-Oct, to 3.30pm Nov-Jun) The largest of Cambridge's colleges, Trinity offers an extraordinary Tudor gateway, an air of supreme elegance and a sweeping Great Court – the largest of its kind in the world. It also boasts the renowned and suitably musty Wren Library (⏰ noon-2pm Mon-Fri year-round, plus 10.30am-12.30pm Sat term time) FREE, containing 55,000 books published before 1820 and more than 2500 manuscripts. Works include those by Shakespeare, St Jerome, Newton and Swift – and AA Milne's original *Winnie the Pooh;* both Milne and his son, Christopher Robin, were graduates.

As you enter Trinity through the part-gilded gate, have a look at the statue of the college's founder, Henry VIII, that adorns it. His left hand holds a golden orb, while his right grips not the original sceptre but a table leg, put there by student pranksters and never replaced. It's a wonderful introduction to one of Cambridge's most venerable colleges, and a reminder of who really rules the roost.

In the Great Court beyond, scholastic humour gives way to wonderment, thanks to its imposing architecture and sheer size. To the right of the entrance is a small tree, planted in the 1950s and reputed to be a descendant of the apple tree made famous by Trinity alumnus Sir Isaac Newton. Other alumni include Francis Bacon, Lord Byron, Tennyson, HRH Prince Charles (legend has it his bodyguard scored higher in exams than he did), at least nine prime ministers (British and international) and more than 30 Nobel Prize winners.

The college's vast hall has a dramatic hammer-beam roof and lantern; beyond lie the dignified cloisters of Nevile's Court. Henry VIII would have been proud to note, too, that his college would eventually come to throw the best party in town, the lavish May Ball (p360) in early June, though you will need a fat purse, and a friend on the inside, to get an invitation.

★ Fitzwilliam Museum   MUSEUM
(www.fitzmuseum.cam.ac.uk; Trumpington St; by donation; ⏰ 10am-5pm Tue-Sat, from noon Sun)

CHARIOTS OF FIRE

Trinity College's immense Great Court (p353) has been the setting for countless attempts at a feat of impressive athleticism – a 350m-sprint around the courtyard in 43 seconds (the time it takes the clock to strike 12). It's a challenge made famous by the film *Chariots of Fire*, but although many students did try it, Harold Abrahams (the hero of the movie) never did, and the run in the film was actually shot at Eton. If you fancy your chances, remember that you'll need Olympian speed to even come close.

Cambridge

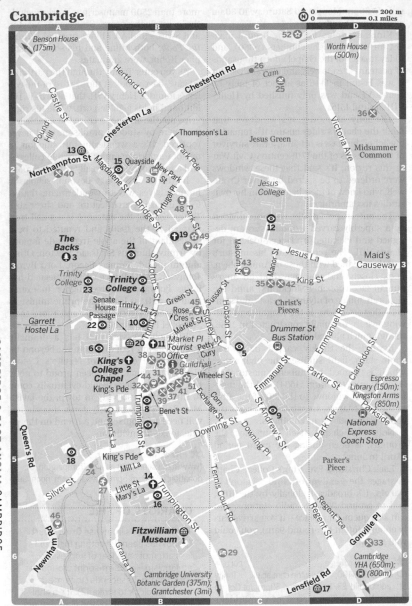

FREE Fondly dubbed 'the Fitz' by locals, this colossal neoclassical pile was one of the first public art museums in Britain, built to house the fabulous treasures that the seventh Viscount Fitzwilliam bequeathed to his old university. Expect Roman and Egyptian grave goods, artworks by many of the great masters and some quirkier collections: banknotes, literary autographs, watches and armour.

The building's unabashedly over-the-top appearance sets out to mirror its contents;

Cambridge

CAMBRIDGE & EAST ANGLIA CAMBRIDGE

this ostentatious jumble of styles mixes mosaic with marble, and Greek with Egyptian. The lower galleries are filled with priceless treasures spanning the ancient world; look out for a Roman funerary couch, an inscribed copper votive plaque from Yemen (c AD 100–200), a figurine of Egyptian cat goddess Bastet, splendid Egyptian sarcophagi and mummified animals, plus dazzling illuminated manuscripts. The upper galleries showcase works by Leonardo da Vinci, Titian, Rubens, the Impressionists, Gainsborough, Constable, Rembrandt and Picasso; standout works include the tender *Pietà* by Giovanni del Ponte and Salvator Rosa's dark and intensely personal *L'Umana Fragilita*.

The Fitz has a tragic footnote: although begun by George Basevi in 1837, he didn't live to see its completion. While working on Ely Cathedral he stepped back to admire his handiwork, slipped and fell to his death.

One-hour guided tours (£6) of the museum are held at 2.30pm on Saturdays.

★ **The Backs** PARK
Behind the Cambridge colleges' grandiose facades and stately courts, a series of gardens and parks line up beside the river. Collectively known as the Backs, the tranquil green spaces and shimmering waters offer unparalleled views of the colleges and are often the most enduring image of Cambridge for visitors. The picture-postcard snapshots of student life and graceful bridges can be seen from the riverside pathways and pedestrian bridges – or the comfort of a chauffeur-driven punt.

For the best views of the fanciful Bridge of Sighs head into St John's College (p357). Built in 1831, it's best observed from the stylish bridge designed by Wren just to the south, also on St John's grounds. The oldest river crossing is at Clare College (☏01223-333200; www.clare.cam.ac.uk; Trinity Lane; adult/

child £5/free; ⊘ dawn-dusk, closed early Apr–mid-Jun), built in 1639 and ornamented with decorative balls. Its architect was paid a grand total of 15p for his design and, feeling aggrieved at such a measly fee, it's said he cut a chunk out of one of the balls adorning the balustrade so the bridge would never be complete.

Most curious of all is the flimsy-looking wooden construction (visible from Silver St) that joins the two halves of Queens' College (p357). Known as the **Mathematical Bridge**, it was first built in 1749. Despite what unscrupulous guides may tell you, it wasn't the handiwork of Sir Isaac Newton (he died in 1727), originally built without nails, or taken apart by academics who then couldn't figure how to put it back together.

Gonville & Caius College COLLEGE

(✆ 01223-332400; www.cai.cam.ac.uk; Trinity St; ⊘ 8am-noon Mon-Fri mid-Jun–Sep, 9am-2pm daily Oct–mid-Apr) **FREE** Known locally as Caius (pronounced 'keys'), Gonville and Caius boasts three fascinating **gates**: Virtue, Humility and Honour. They symbolise the progress of the good student; the third gate (the Porta Honoris, a fabulous domed and sundial-sided confection) leads to the **Senate House** (Senate House Passage) and thus graduation. Former students include Francis Crick (of DNA-discoverers Crick and Watson) and Edward Wilson, of Scott's tragic Antarctic expedition. The megastar of astrophysics, the late Stephen Hawking, was a fellow here for more than 50 years.

The college was actually founded twice, first by a priest called Gonville, in 1348, and then again in 1557 by Dr Caius (his given name was Keys – it was common for academics to use the Latin form of their names), a brilliant physician who suppos-

edly spoiled his legacy by insisting in the statutes that the college admit no 'deaf, dumb, deformed, lame, chronic invalids, or Welshmen'.

Christ's College COLLEGE

(✆ 01223-334900; www.christs.cam.ac.uk; St Andrew's St; ⊘ 9am-4pm, closed early May–mid-Jun) **FREE** Christ's College is a venerable institution at more than 500 years old. Its gleaming **Great Gate** is emblazoned with heraldic carvings of Tudor roses, a portcullis and spotted Beaufort yale (mythical antelope-like creatures). Its founder, Lady Margaret Beaufort, hovers above like a guiding spirit. A stout oak door leads into picturesque **First Court**, Cambridge's only circular front court. Hunt out the **gardens** dedicated to alumnus Charles Darwin; they feature plant species brought back from his famous Galapagos voyage.

The Second Court has a gate to the **Fellows' Garden** (open Monday to Friday only), which contains a mulberry tree under which 17th-century poet John Milton reputedly wrote *Lycidas*. Other notable alumni include Sacha Baron Cohen (aka Ali G and Borat) and historian Simon Schama.

Magdalene College COLLEGE

(✆ 01223-332100; www.magd.cam.ac.uk; Magdalene St; ⊘ 8am-6pm, closed early Apr–mid-Jun) **FREE** Riverside Magdalene often catches people out – the college name is properly pronounced 'Maud-lyn'. This former Benedictine hostel's greatest asset is the **Pepys Library** (⊘ 2-4pm Mon-Fri, 11.30am-12.30pm & 1.30-2.30pm Sat Easter-Aug, 2-4pm Mon-Sat Oct-Easter, closed Sep) **FREE**, housing 3000 books bequeathed by the mid-17th-century diarist to his old college. This idiosyncratic collection of beautifully bound tomes is ordered by height. Treasures include vivid medieval manuscripts and the *Anthony Roll,* a 1540s depiction of the Royal Navy's ships.

Magdalene was the last college to let women study there; when they were finally admitted in 1988, some male students wore black armbands and flew the college flag at half mast.

Emmanuel College COLLEGE

(✆ 01223-334200; www.emma.cam.ac.uk; St Andrew's St; ⊘ 9am-6pm, closed early Apr–mid-Jun) **FREE** The 16th-century Emmanuel College ('Emma' to students) is famous for its exquisite **chapel** designed by Sir Christopher Wren. Seek out the plaque commemorating John Harvard (who graduated with a BA in

ⓘ VISITING CAMBRIDGE'S COLLEGES

Cambridge University comprises 31 colleges, though not all are open to the public. Colleges close to visitors over the two-week Christmas break, and while students are preparing for and sitting exams – between early April and mid-June. Be aware, too, that opening hours can vary from day to day, so if you have your heart set on visiting a particular college, contact it in advance to avoid disappointment.

1632), a scholar here who later settled in New England and left his money to a certain Cambridge College in Massachusetts – now Harvard University.

Queens' College   COLLEGE

(☑ 01223-335511; www.queens.cam.ac.uk; Silver St; £3.50; ☺ 10am-3pm, closed early Apr–mid-Jun) Gorgeous 15th-century Queens' College sits elegantly astride the river, connected by the unscientific-looking Mathematical Bridge (p355). Highlights include two enchanting medieval courtyards, Old Court and Cloister Court, the beautiful half-timbered President's Lodge, and the tower in which Dutch scholar and reformer Desiderius Erasmus lodged from 1510 to 1514.

Corpus Christi College   COLLEGE

(☑ 01223-338000; www.corpus.cam.ac.uk; King's Pde; £3; ☺ 10.30am-4.30pm mid-Jun–Sep, 2-4pm Oct-early Apr) Corpus Christi was founded in 1352, a heritage reflected in its exquisite buildings and a monastic atmosphere that radiates from the medieval Old Court. Look out for the fascinating sundial and plaque to playwright and past student Christopher Marlowe (1564–93), who penned *Doctor Faustus* and *Tamburlaine*. New Court (a mere 200 years old) leads to the Parker Library, which holds the world's finest collection of Anglo-Saxon manuscripts (open Monday and Thursday afternoons to tourist office–run tours only).

Note the college was closed to visitors in 2018 for building work, reopening in 2019.

Trinity Hall College   COLLEGE

(☑ 01223-332500; www.trinhall.cam.ac.uk; Trinity Lane; admission by donation; ☺ 10am-noon & 2pm-5pm Tue & Thu, 9am-noon Sun, closed Apr-Jun) Wedged cosily among the great and famous colleges (but unconnected to better-known Trinity), diminutive Trinity Hall was founded in 1350 as a refuge for lawyers and clerics escaping the ravages of the Black Death. The college's chapel is one of the most beautiful in Cambridge; you can visit for evensong during some terms; check with the college for details.

Jesus College   COLLEGE

(☑ 01223-339339; www.jesus.cam.ac.uk; Jesus Lane; ☺ 9am-5pm, closed early Apr–mid-Jun) FREE This tranquil 15th-century college was once a nunnery of St Radegund before the Bishop of Ely, John Alcock, expelled the nuns for 'improvidence, extravagance and incontinence'. Highlights include a Norman arched gallery, a 13th-century chancel and art-nouveau features by Pugin, Ford Madox Brown, William Morris (ceilings) and Burne-Jones (stained glass). Illustrious alumni include Thomas Cranmer, burnt in Oxford for his faith during the Reformation, and long-running BBC and PBS radio journalist and presenter Alistair Cooke.

St John's College   COLLEGE

(☑ 01223-33860; www.joh.cam.ac.uk; St John's St; adult/child £10/5; ☺ 10am-5pm Mar-Oct, to 3.30pm Nov-Feb, closed mid-Jun) Alma mater of six prime ministers, three saints and Douglas Adams (author of *The Hitchhiker's Guide to the Galaxy*), St John's is superbly photogenic. Founded in 1511 by Henry VII's mother, Margaret Beaufort, it sprawls along both riverbanks, joined by the Bridge of Sighs, a masterpiece of stone tracery and a focus for student pranks. Going into the college or taking a punting tour are the only ways to get a clear view of the structure.

Cambridge University
Botanic Garden   GARDENS

(☑ 01223-336265; www.botanic.cam.ac.uk; 1 Brookside; adult/child £6/free; ☺ 10am-6pm Apr-Sep, to 5pm Feb, Mar & Oct, to 4pm Nov-Jan) Founded by Charles Darwin's mentor, Professor John Henslow, the beautiful Botanic Garden is home to 8000 plant species, a wonderful arboretum, glasshouses (containing both fierce carnivorous pitcher plants and the delicate slipper orchid), a winter garden and flamboyant herbaceous borders. Hour-long guided tours (free) are held at 2.30pm every Sunday from May through to September.

Free tours are also held on the first Sunday of the month from February to April and October to December. The gardens are 1200m south of the city centre via Trumpington St.

Kettle's Yard   MUSEUM

(☑ 01223-748100; www.kettlesyard.co.uk; Castle St; ☺ noon-5pm Tue-Sun) FREE An £11 million revamp has added high-tech contemporary-art galleries to much-loved Kettle's Yard. The big draw for many though will be the original collection still set in the home of HS 'Jim' Ede, a former curator at the Tate Gallery in London. Ede knocked three houses into one to create a quirky, intimate space in which to display a wealth of top-notch painting and sculpture, including works by Miró and Henry Moore, in a country-cottage atmosphere.

Round Church CHURCH

(☑ 01223-311602; www.christianheritage.org.uk; Bridge St; £3.50; ☺ 10am-5pm Tue-Sat, from 1.30pm Sun) Cambridge's intensely atmospheric Round Church is one of only four such structures in England. It was built by the mysterious Knights Templar in 1130 and shelters an unusual circular nave ringed by chunky Norman pillars. The carved stone faces crowning the pillars bring the 12th century vividly to life.

Polar Museum MUSEUM

(☑ 01223-336540; www.spri.cam.ac.uk/museum; Lensfield Rd; ☺ 10am-4pm Tue-Sat) FREE Tales of hostile environments, dogged determination and, sometimes, life-claiming mistakes are evoked powerfully at this compelling museum. Its focus on polar exploration charts the feats of the likes of Roald Amundsen, Fridtjof Nansen, Ernest Shackleton and Captain Robert Falcon Scott. The affecting collections include paintings, photographs, clothing, equipment, maps, journals and last messages left for loved ones by Scott's polar crew.

Corpus Clock LANDMARK

(Bene't St) Made from 24-carat gold, the Corpus Clock displays the time through a series of concentric LED lights. A hideous-looking insect 'time-eater' crawls across the top. The clock is only accurate once every five minutes. At other times it slows or stops and then speeds up, which, according to its creator, JC Taylor, reflects life's irregularity.

Great St Mary's Church CHURCH

(www.gsm.cam.ac.uk; Senate House Hill; ☺ 10am-4pm Mon-Sat, from 1pm Sun) FREE The foundations of Cambridge's sublime university church date from 1010. It was burnt to the ground in the 1290s and rebuilt in 1351. The major expansion of 1478–1519 resulted in the late-Gothic Perpendicular style you see today. Striking features include the mid-Victorian stained-glass windows, seating galleries and two organs – unusual in a church. The tower (adult/child £4/2.50) was added in 1690; climb it for superb vistas of Cambridge's dreamy spires.

Little St Mary's Church CHURCH

(☑ 01223-366202; www.lsm.org.uk; Trumpington St; ☺ 7.30am-6.30pm) FREE The church's unwieldy original name was St Peter's-without-Trumpington-Gate, which gave St Peter's College (latterly Peterhouse) its name. Inside is a memorial to student Godfrey Washing-

ton, great-uncle of George. His family coat of arms was the stars and stripes, the inspiration for the US flag.

Peterhouse COLLEGE

(☑ 01223-338200; www.pet.cam.ac.uk; Trumpington St; ☺ 9am-5pm, closed early Apr–mid-Jun) FREE The oldest and smallest college, charming Peterhouse was founded in 1284. Much of the college was rebuilt or added to over the years, including the exceptional little chapel built in 1632, but the beautifully restored main hall is bona-fide 13th century.

Rumours abound among students – vigorously denied by college authorities – of hauntings and spectral happenings on the site. Three Nobel Prize winners count themselves among Peterhouse's alumni.

🏃 Activities

Scudamore's Punting BOATING

(☑ 01223-359750; www.scudamores.com; Mill Lane; chauffeured punts per 45 min adult/child £20/10, 6-person self-punt per hr £30; ☺ 9am-dusk) Rents punts, rowing boats, kayaks and canoes. Offers discounts if you book online.

Jesus Green Pool SWIMMING

(☑ 01223-302579; www.cambridge.gov.uk/jesus-green-outdoor-pool; Jesus Green; adult/child £4.60/2.45; ☺ 7.30am-7.30pm Mon, Tue & Fri, noon-7.30pm Wed, Thu, Sat & Sun May-Sep) A slender, 91m, 1920s open-air swim spot; popular with poolside sunbathers too.

🕝 Tours

★ Walking Tours WALKING

(☑ 01223-791501; www.visitcambridge.org; Peas Hill; ☺ 1-5 tours daily) The best guided tours of the city take in one of the colleges and the city's main sights. Options include the two-hour Kings College & The Backs tour (adult/child £20/10), and a 90-minute Highlights tour (adult/child £15/8), which often includes Pembroke College – the price covers college admission in both cases. They're popular – book ahead.

There's also a one-hour Essential Cambridge (adult/child £12.50/6) tour. The walks leave from the tourist office. Colourful one-hour Ghost Tours (adult/child £7/5) take place two evenings a week.

Cambridge Chauffeur Punts BOATING

(☑ 01223-354164; www.punting-in-cambridge.co.uk; Silver St Bridge; chauffeured punts per hr adult/child £16/7, 6-person self-punt per hr £24; ☺ 9am-8pm

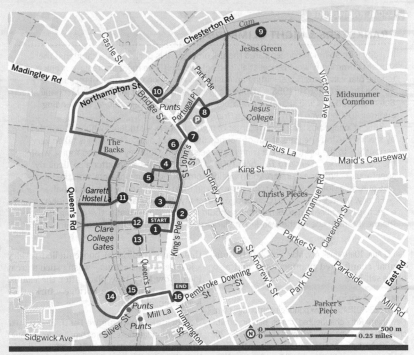

🏃 City Walk
The Colleges and the Backs

START KING'S COLLEGE CHAPEL
END FITZBILLIES
LENGTH 3 MILES; FOUR HOURS

From divine **1** **King's** (p352), stroll north, diverting into **2** **Great St Mary's** (p358) and climbing the tower for fine Cambridge views. Next, dodge the cyclists and tour guides before ducking into atmospheric **3** **Gonville & Caius** (p356) to marvel at its ornate gates. **4** **Trinity's** (p353) elaborate entranceway towers up on the left; head through it into the college's (genuinely) Great Court; marvel at the architecture, then make for the absorbing **5** **Wren Library** (p353), with its extraordinary historic books. Next, pause to admire the front of gorgeous **6** **St John's** (p357) before dropping into the captivating 12th-century **7** **Round Church** (p358). Cut right between the sweet terraces of narrow Portugal Pl – at the end, the **8** **Maypole** (p363) pub is a friendly place to eat or drink.

Next, head diagonally across Jesus Green, past lounging picnickers and tennis players, to consider a dip in the bijou open-air **9** **pool**

(p358). Then stroll southwest beside the river, passing locks and houseboats before a water-side boardwalk leads to a punt launching pad. Cross at the bridge beside **10** **Magdalene College** (p356), where the unique Pepys Library is well worth a detour.

Northampton St reminds you that the 21st century does exist, then it's on to the path through the Backs, where the stately sweep of St John's College shelters amid the trees, while Trinity sits next door. Next play zigzag with college paths and the river: nip up **11** **Garret Hostel Lane** for a closer view of punts, bridges and college facades. Then it's back to the path, before another detour left leads to the often-open gates of **12** **Clare College** (p355), where the Fellow's Garden is a real must-see.

Back on the Backs, next comes the impressive west end of King's; the Palladian **13** **Fellows' Building** is just to the right. After curving beside **14** **Queens'** (p357), cut left. On Silver St's bridge spy the chunky **15** **Mathematical Bridge** on the left, and fleets of about-to-embark punts on the right. Time to rest. Where better than **16** **Fitzbillies** (p362) for a Chelsea bun and a steaming cup of tea?

PRANKSTERS & NIGHT CLIMBERS

In a city with so much concentrated mental prowess, it is perhaps inevitable that the student community would excel at all kinds of mischief. The most impressive prank ever to take place in Cambridge – lifting an Austin Seven van on to the roof of the landmark Senate House (p356) in 1958 – involved a great deal of planning from four Mechanical Sciences students and spawned a number of copycat pranks, including suspending another Austin Seven from the ornate Bridge of Sighs (p357).

King's College has long been a target of night climbers – students who get their thrills by scaling the lofty heights of out-of-bounds buildings at night. The sport is taken very seriously – to the point where a Trinity College student, Geoffrey Winthrop Young, wrote the *Roof Climber's Guide to Trinity* in 1900. If you're in Cambridge after a particularly spectacular climber excursion, you may find some out-of-place objects atop the pinnacles of King's College Chapel (p352) – anything from a traffic cone to a Santa hat.

Finally, there's the Cubes (Cambridge University Breaking and Entering Society): its objective is to access places members shouldn't be and leave distinctive calling cards – the most famous being the wooden mallard in the rafters of Trinity's Great Hall.

Jun & Aug, 10am-dusk Apr, May, Sept & Oct) Runs regular chauffeured punting tours and also offers self-hire.

Granta Moorings   BOATING
([✆] 01223-301845; www.puntingincambridge.com; Newnham Rd; chauffeured punts per hr adult/child £14/8, 6-person self-punt per hr £22-26; ⊙9.30am-dusk Apr-Oct) ☛ Conveniently situated punt-rental company if you're heading towards Grantchester (p365).

Riverboat Georgina   BOATING
([✆] 01223-929124; www.riverboatgeorginacambridge.co.uk; Jesus Lock; 1/2hr cruises £10/20; ⊙Apr-Sep) Boat cruises along the Cam. Optional extras include lunch, fish and chips, wine or a cream tea.

★ Festivals & Events

Bumps   SPORTS
(www.cucbc.org/bumps; ⊙Feb & Jun) Traditional rowing races along the Cam (or the Granta, as the Cambridge stretch is called), in which college boat clubs compete to 'bump' the crew in front.

Beer Festival   BEER
(www.cambridgebeerfestival.com; ⊙May) Hugely popular five-day beer and cider extravaganza on Jesus Green, featuring brews from all over the country as well as a great range of British cheeses.

May Balls   CULTURAL
(⊙early Jun) The biggest student events of the year, the name of these formal balls doesn't match the month they're held in (June) because college authorities decided

that May's traditional booze-fuelled revelry – just before the exams – wasn't such a great idea. Now they take place after the exams, but in a typically Cambridge quirk, they keep their old name.

Cambridge Shakespeare Festival   THEATRE
(www.cambridgeshakespeare.com; ⊙Jul & Aug) The bard's best-loved works performed in a handful of college gardens.

Folk Festival   MUSIC
(www.cambridgefolkfestival.co.uk; ⊙late Jul–early Aug) Acclaimed four-day music fest in Cherry Hinton Hall, 4 miles southeast of the city centre. It has hosted the likes of Van Morrison, Ladysmith Black Mambazo, Christy Moore, Imelda May, Paul Simon and KT Tunstall.

🛏 Sleeping

Cambridge YHA   HOSTEL £
([✆] 0345-371 9728; www.yha.org.uk; 97 Tenison Rd; dm/d £25/60; @🛜) A smart, friendly and deservedly popular hostel with compact dorms and good facilities. Handily, it's very near the railway station.

Tudor Cottage   B&B ££
([✆] 01223-565212; www.tudorcottageguesthouse.co.uk; 292 Histon Rd; s/d £55/90; 🅿🛜; 🚌8) Sweet features help make this neat-as-a-pin guesthouse feel like a home from home, from the tiny patio garden to the ranks of speciality teas, cereals, cakes and muffins at the breakfast table. It's just under 2 miles north of the city centre; bus 8 stops just outside.

Rosa's
B&B **££**

(📞 01223-512596; www.rosasbedandbreakfast. co.uk; 53 Roseford Rd; s £45-60; P 🎧; 🖥 8) One for solo travellers: a friendly, family-run B&B where the three bright, snug singles are decked out in neutral tones. It's 2 miles north of the city centre; there's free on-road parking outside and bus 8 runs nearby.

Worth House
B&B **££**

(📞 01223-316074; www.worth-house.co.uk; 152 Chesterton Rd; s £75-95, d £100-140, tr £165, q £192; P @ 🎧) The welcome is wonderfully warm and the great-value rooms are delightful. Soft grey and cream meets candy-stripe reds, fancy bathrooms boast claw-foot baths and tea trays are full of treats. The choice of rooms for families is particularly good.

University Rooms Cambridge
B&B **££**

(www.universityrooms.com/en/city/cambridge; s/d from £50/80) For an authentic taste of university life, check into a student room in one of the colleges. Accommodation varies from functional singles (with shared bathroom) overlooking college courts to more modern, en-suite rooms in nearby annexes. Breakfast is often in hall (the students' dining room).

You'll find a bigger selection of available rooms during university holidays (June to August, Christmas, and March to April).

Benson House
B&B **££**

(📞 01223-311594; www.bensonhouse.co.uk; 24 Huntingdon Rd; s £80-120, d £120; P 🎧) Lots of little things lift Benson a cut above – sleep on feather pillows and beds made with Egyptian-cotton linen, sip tea from Royal Doulton bone china, then tuck into award-winning breakfasts featuring ground coffee, croissants and fresh fruit.

⭐ Hotel du Vin
BOUTIQUE HOTEL **£££**

(📞 01223-928991; www.hotelduvin.com; 15 Trumpington St; d £190-270, ste £290-430; @ 🎧) One of the country's swishest, coolest chains delivers again here. Achingly beautiful rooms sport roll-top baths, monsoon showers and custom-made beds, the cosy cellar bar is vaulted, the bistro (two/three courses £18/21) is chic, and the luxuriously appointed suites (expect rotating TVs, mini-cinemas and surround sound) are simply divine.

⭐ Varsity
BOUTIQUE HOTEL **£££**

(📞 01223-306030; www.thevarsityhotel.co.uk; Thompson's Lane; d £195-360; ❋ @ 🎧) In the 44 individually styled rooms of riverside Varsity, wondrous fixtures and furnishings (such as roll-top baths and travellers' trunks) sit beside floor-to-ceiling glass windows, espresso machines and smartphone docks. The views out over the colleges from the roof terrace are utterly sublime.

Valet parking costs £20 a night.

Felix
BOUTIQUE HOTEL **£££**

(📞 01223-277977; www.hotelfelix.co.uk; Whitehouse Lane, Huntingdon Rd; s £220, d £165-280, ste £315-335; P @ 🎧 ❋) It's the bold modern art and imaginative design that nudge Felix into the boutique sleep spots. You'll find vividly coloured chairs set beside polished wood panels in the lounge, and silk curtains, duckdown duvets and underfloor heating in the bathrooms. Felix is 1.5 miles northwest of the city.

🍴 Eating

⭐ Urban Shed
SANDWICHES **£**

(📞 01223-324888; www.theurbanshed.com; 62 King St; sandwiches from £5; ⏱ 8.30am-5pm Mon-Fri, 9am-5.30pm Sat, 10am-5pm Sun; 🖉) Unorthodox, retro Urban Shed has a personal-service ethos so strong that regular customers have a locker for their own mug. Old aeroplane seats perch beside cable-drum tables, their own-blend coffee is mellow and the choice of sandwiches is superb, with fillings including BBQ aubergine and Swiss cheese, coconut satay chicken, and grilled courgette with sunflower seeds.

Steak & Honour
BURGERS **£**

(www.steakandhonour.co.uk; 4 Wheeler St; burgers £6-9; ⏱ 11.30am-3pm & 5-9.30pm Mon-Fri, 11.30am-10pm Sat, to 5pm Sun) 'Don't try eating these with one hand', warns a joint that started out as a couple of burger vans. These beef patties come squished between brioche buns and dripping with cheese. You can take them away, but they're easier to manage in the bare-bones cafe (plastic trays, no cushions, Formica tables). Grab a stack of napkins and enjoy.

Aromi
ITALIAN **£**

(📞 01223-300117; www.aromi.co.uk; 1 Bene't St; mains from £5; ⏱ 9am-7pm Sun-Thu, to 10pm Fri & Sat; 🖉) Sometimes you should yield to temptation. So be drawn in by a window full of stunning Sicilian pizza, and feast on light, crisp bases piled high with fresh spinach and Parma ham. Then succumb to the indecently thick hot chocolate: may as well make it a large.

Aromi also has another cafe a few doors down on Peas Hill and a *gelateria* on Fitzroy St.

Fitzbillies
CAFE **£**

(☑01223-352500; www.fitzbillies.com; 52 Trumpington St; mains £9-12; ⊙8am-6pm Mon-Fri, from 9am Sat, from 9.30am Sun) Cambridge's oldest bakery has a soft, doughy place in the hearts of generations of students, thanks to its ultrasticky Chelsea buns and other sweet treats. Pick up a bagful to take away or munch in comfort in the quaint cafe.

Locker
CAFE **£**

(☑07566 216042; www.thelockercafe.co.uk; 54 King St; snacks from £5; ⊙8.30am-5.30pm Mon-Fri, from 9.30am Sat, 10am-4pm Sun; 🖥🖉) 🍃 Ethical coffee, homemade soup, and flavoursome bread, cakes and pies from a wealth of Cambridge producers lift this artsy cafe above the crowd.

Espresso Library
CAFE **£**

(☑01223-367333; www.espressolibrary.com; 210 East Rd; mains £7.50-11; ⊙7am-6pm Mon-Sat, from 8am Sun; 🖥🖉) A chilled soundtrack and customers with laptops at almost every table signal that this industrial-chic cafe is a student favourite. That'll be partly down to the wholesome food – dishes might include frittata with sweet potatoes and spinach, or juicy portobello mushrooms in brioche buns – and partly down to some cracking coffee.

Rainbow
VEGETARIAN **££**

(☑01223-321551; www.rainbowcafe.co.uk; 9a King's Pde; mains £10-13; ⊙10am-10pm Tue-Sat, to 3pm Sun; 🖉) Quite a treat for non-meat eaters: a cheery basement bistro, tucked away at the end of an alley off King's Parade. In this warren of cosy rooms, rickety tables set the scene for an eclectic range of veg that's been transformed into a variety of bakes, roasts, pasta dishes and pies.

Kingston Arms
PUB FOOD **££**

(☑01223-319414; www.facebook.com/pg/Kingston Arms; 33 Kingston St; mains £8-14; ⊙5-11pm Mon-Thu, noon-midnight Fri & Sat, to 11pm Sun; 🖥) Great gastropub grub – from roasts to homemade risotto and gourmet sausages – keeps stomachs satisfied at the award-winning Kingston. More than 10 real ales, stacked board games and a students-meet-locals clientele deliver a contemporary Cambridge vibe. It's located 1 mile southeast of the centre.

Pint Shop
MODERN BRITISH **££**

(☑01223-352293; www.pintshop.co.uk; 10 Peas Hill; snacks from £5, mains £12-22; ⊙noon-10pm Mon-Fri, 11am-10.30pm Sat, 11am-10pm Sun) Popular Pint Shop's vision is to embrace eating and drinking equally. To this end, it's both a busy bar specialising in draught craft beer and a stylish dining room serving classy versions of traditional grub (dry-aged steaks, gin-cured sea trout, coal-baked fish and meat kebabs). All in all, hard to resist.

Smokeworks
BARBECUE **££**

(www.smokeworks.co.uk; 2 Free School Lane; mains £11-20; ⊙11.30am-10pm Mon-Thu, to 10.30pm Fri & Sat, to 9.30pm Sun; 🖥) This dark, industrial-themed dining spot draws discerning carnivores with its melt-in-your-mouth ribs, wings and wonderfully smoky pulled pork. The service is friendly and prompt, and the salted-caramel milkshakes come in a glass the size of your head.

Cambridge Chop House
BRITISH **££**

(☑01223-359506; www.cambscuisine.com/cam bridge-chop-house; 1 King's Pde; mains £17-26; ⊙9am-11.30pm, noon-10.30pm Mon-Sat, to 9.30pm Sun) The window seats here deliver some of the best views in town – onto King's College's hallowed walls. The food is pure English establishment too: hearty steaks and chops and chips, plus fish dishes and suet puddings. It's also open for breakfast (9-11.15am) and coffee and pastries (10-11.30am).

Sister restaurant **St John's Chop House** (☑01223-353110; www.cambscuisine.com/st-johns-chop-house; 21 Northampton St; mains £14-26; ⊙noon-3pm & 6-9.30pm Mon-Fri, noon-10.30pm Sat, to 9pm Sun) sits near the rear entrance to St John's College.

★ Midsummer House
MODERN BRITISH **£££**

(☑01223-369299; www.midsummerhouse.co.uk; Midsummer Common; 5/8 courses £69/145; ⊙noon-1.30pm Wed-Sat, 7-9pm Tue-Sat; 🖉) At the region's top table, chef Daniel Clifford's double-Michelin-starred creations are distinguished by depth of flavour and immense technical skill. Savour transformations of pumpkin (into velouté), mackerel (with Jack Daniels), quail, sea scallops and grouse, before a coriander white-chocolate dome, served with coconut, mango and jasmine rice.

Unusually, there are vegetarian, vegan and pescatarian versions of the eight-course menu.

Cotto   INTERNATIONAL **£££**
(☑ 01223-302010; www.cottocambridge.co.uk;
Gonville Pl; 3 courses £70-75; ⏱ 6.30-9pm Tue-Sat;
🅿) 🏁 Now set inside the swish Gonville
Hotel, Cotto delivers an irresistible blend
of artistry and precision. Delights might include seafood velouté or the signature dish
Cotto venison Wellington, perhaps followed
by roasted apple with omega-3 crumble and
mascarpone mousse.

🍷 Drinking & Nightlife

⭐**Cambridge Brew House**   MICROBREWERY
(☑ 01223-855185; www.thecambridgebrewhouse.
com; 1 King St; ⏱ 11am-11pm Sun-Thu, to midnight
Fri & Sat) Pick a pint from the array on offer
here and there's a fair chance it'll have been
brewed in the gleaming vats beside the bar.
Add a buzzy vibe, eclectic upcycled decor,
dirty burgers and British tapas (mains £10
to £15) and you have the kind of pub you
heartily wish was just down your road.

Hidden Rooms   COCKTAIL BAR
(☑ 01223-514777; www.facebook.com/pg/hidden
rooms; Jesus Lane; ⏱ 7-11pm Wed & Thu, to midnight Fri & Sat) A cocktail bar for aficionados
of the craft. At Hidden Rooms (if you can
find it), booths and table service add an
edge of exclusivity, while twice-monthly jazz
and mixology lessons add another layer of
class.

It's a little tricky to locate: head for the
Pizza Express and drop down a floor.

Maypole   PUB
(☑ 01223-352999; www.maypolefreehouse.co.uk;
20a Portugal Pl; ⏱ 11.30am-midnight Sun-Thu,
to 1am Fri & Sat) A dozen pumps dispensing
real ale, 50 gins, a roomy beer garden and
a friendly, unreconstructed vibe make this
red-brick pub popular with the locals. That
and hearty, homemade Italian food, plus
festivals championing regional and microbrewery beers.

Fez   CLUB
(www.cambridgefez.com; 15 Market Passage;
⏱ 10pm-3am Tue-Sun) Hip hop, dancehall,
R&B, techno, funk, indie, house and garage;
top-name DJs and club nights – you'll find
it all at Cambridge's most popular club, the
Moroccan-themed Fez.

Eagle   PUB
(☑ 01223-505020; www.eagle-cambridge.co.uk;
Bene't St; ⏱ 11am-11pm Sun-Thu, to midnight Fri
& Sat; 🛜🍴) Cambridge's most famous pub
has loosened the tongues and pickled the

grey cells of many an illustrious academic;
among them Nobel Prize–winning scientists
Crick and Watson, who discussed their research into DNA here (note the blue plaque
by the door). Fifteenth-century, wood-panelled and rambling, the Eagle's cosy rooms
include one with WWII airmen's signatures
on the ceiling.

The food (mains £10-15), served all day,
is good too; it includes some thoughtful options for children.

Granta   PUB
(☑ 01223-505016; www.granta-cambridge.co.uk;
14 Newnham Rd; ⏱ 11am-11pm) If the exterior
of this picturesque waterside pub, overhanging a pretty mill pond, looks strangely
familiar, it could be because it is the darling
of many a TV director. No wonder: with
its snug deck, riverside terrace and punts
moored up alongside, it's a highly atmospheric spot to sit, sup and watch the world
drift by.

☆ Entertainment

ADC   THEATRE
(☑ 01223-300085; www.adctheatre.com; Park
St) This famous student-run theatre is
home to the university's Footlights comedy
troupe whose past members include Emma
Thompson, Hugh Laurie and Stephen Fry.

Cambridge Arts Theatre   THEATRE
(☑ 01223-503333;   www.cambridgeartstheatre.
com; 6 St Edward's Passage) Cambridge's biggest bona-fide theatre puts on everything
from highbrow drama and dance, to panto
and shows fresh from London's West End.

Corn Exchange   PERFORMING ARTS
(☑ 01223-357851; www.cornex.co.uk; Wheeler St)
Venue attracting the top names, from pop
and rock to comedy.

Junction   PERFORMING ARTS
(☑ 01223-511511; www.junction.co.uk; Clifton Way)
Theatre, dance, comedy, live bands and club
nights at a contemporary performance venue near the railway station.

It's 1.5 miles southeast of the city centre,
down Regent St (later Hills Rd).

Portland Arms   LIVE MUSIC
(☑ 01223-357268; www.theportlandarms.co.uk;
129 Chesterton Rd; ⏱ noon-11.30pm Mon-Thu, to
12.30am Fri & Sat, to 11pm Sun) A popular student haunt, the 200-capacity Portland is
the best spot in town to catch a gig and see
the pick of up-and-coming bands. It has a

WORTH A TRIP

IMPERIAL WAR MUSEUM

At Europe's biggest **aviation museum** (01223-835000; www.iwm.org.uk; Duxford; adult/child £19/9.50; ⊙10am-6pm; P 🚻), 200 lovingly preserved vintage aircraft are housed in several enormous hangars. The vast airfield showcases everything from dive bombers to biplanes, Spitfire and Concorde. The awe-inspiring American Air Museum hangar pays homage to US WWII servicemen, hosting the largest collection of American civil and military aircraft outside the USA.

Duxford is 9 miles south of Cambridge at Junction 10 of the M11. Buses only run to the museum on Sunday (bus 132; £3.90, 50 minutes).

wood-panelled saloon bar, a spacious terrace and monthly comedy nights too.

ℹ Information

Tourist Office (☑ 01223-791500; www.visitcambridge.org; The Guildhall, Peas Hill; ⊙9.30am-5pm Mon-Sat Nov-Mar, plus 11am-3pm Sun Apr-Oct) Offers information plus a booking service for accommodation, walking and punting tours, events and tickets for King's College Chapel. Also sells maps, guides and souvenirs.

ℹ Getting There & Away

BUS

Buses run by **National Express** (☑ 0871 781 8181; www.nationalexpress.com; Parkside; 🛜) leave from Parkside. Direct services include:

Gatwick £41, four hours, seven daily

Heathrow £31, 2¾ hours, hourly

London Victoria £11, 2½ hours, every two hours

Oxford £14, 3½ hours, hourly

Stansted Airport £10, 45 minutes, every two hours

CAR

Cambridge's centre is largely pedestrianised. The city's multistorey car parks charge between £2.40 and £4 for two hours.

Five Park & Ride car parks (parking per day/week £1/5) circle the city on the major routes, with buses (return tickets £3) shuttling into the city centre every 10 to 15 minutes between around 7am and 8pm Monday to Saturday, 9am to 5.45pm Sunday – check for specific times.

TRAIN

The train station is 1.5 miles southeast of the centre. Direct services include:

Birmingham New Street £35, three hours, hourly

Bury St Edmunds £11, 40 minutes, hourly

Ely £5,15 minutes, three per hour

King's Lynn £7, 50 minutes, hourly

London King's Cross £25, one hour, two to four per hour

Stansted Airport £11, 35 minutes, every 30 minutes

ℹ Getting Around

BICYCLE

Cambridge is incredibly bike-friendly, with two wheels providing an ideal, and atmospheric, way to get around town.

Recommended bicycle-hire outfits:

City Cycle Hire (☑ 01223-365629; www.citycyclehire.com; 61 Newnham Rd; per half-day/day/week £9/12/25; ⊙9am-5.30pm Mon-Fri, plus 9am-5pm Sat Easter-Oct) A mile southwest of the city centre.

Rutland Cycling (☑ 01223-307655; www.rutlandcycling.com; Corn Exchange St; per 4hr/day £7/10; ⊙9am-6pm Mon-Fri, 10am-5pm Sun) In the heart of town at the Grand Arcade shopping centre. There's another branch just off Station Rd at the train station.

BUS

➜ Bus routes run around town from the **main bus station** (Drummer St).

➜ Many operate from 6am until around 11pm.

➜ C1, C3 and C7 stop at the train station.

➜ A city Dayrider ticket (£4.30) provides 24 hours of unlimited bus travel around Cambridge.

Ely

☑ 01353 / POP 20,256

A small but charming city dominated by a jaw-dropping cathedral, Ely makes an excellent day trip from Cambridge. It takes its name (*ee*-lee) from the eels that once inhabited the surrounding undrained Fens. From the Middle Ages onward, Ely was one of the biggest opium-producing centres in Britain, with high-class ladies holding 'poppy parties' and local mothers sedating their children with 'poppy tea'. Today, beyond the dizzying heights of its cathedral towers, Ely is a cluster of medieval streets lined with traditional tearooms and pretty Georgian houses; a quaint quayside adds extra appeal.

Sights

★ Ely Cathedral   CATHEDRAL

(☑ 01353-667735; www.elycathedral.org; The Gallery; adult/child £9/free, incl tower tour £16.50/free; ☉ 7am-6.30pm) Ely Cathedral's stunning silhouette dominates the whole area; it's dubbed the 'Ship of the Fens' because it's so visible across the vast, flat sweeps of land. The early-12th-century **nave** dazzles with clean, uncluttered lines and a lofty sense of space. Look out for the entrancing ceiling, the masterly 14th-century **Octagon**, and **towers** that soar upwards in shimmering colours. Standard admission includes a ground-floor **guided tour**. The **tower tours** (four to five daily) deliver behind-the-scenes glimpses, 165 steps and remarkable views.

Ely has been a place of worship and pilgrimage since at least 673, when Etheldreda, daughter of the king of East Anglia, founded a nunnery here (shrugging off the fact that she had been twice married, in her determination to become a nun). She was canonised shortly after her death. The nunnery was sacked by the Danes, rebuilt as a monastery, demolished and then resurrected as a church after the Norman Conquest. In 1109, Ely became a cathedral. Gothic arches were added later to support the weight of the mighty walls.

The vast 14th-century **Lady Chapel** is filled with eerily empty niches that once held statues of saints and martyrs. They were hacked out unceremoniously by iconoclasts during the English Civil War. But the delicate tracery remains, overseen by a rather controversial statue of *Holy Mary* by David Wynne, unveiled in 2000 to mixed reviews. The cathedral's beauty has made it a popular film location: you may recognise some of its fine details from scenes in *Elizabeth: The Golden Age* and *The Other Boleyn Girl*. For optimum atmosphere, visit during evensong (5.30pm Monday to Saturday, 4pm Sunday) or a choral service (10.30am Sunday).

Oliver Cromwell's House   MUSEUM

(☑ 01353-662062; www.olivercromwellshouse.co.uk; 29 St Mary's St; adult/child £5/3; ☉ 10am-5pm Apr-Oct, 11am-4pm Nov-Mar) England's premier Puritan (p636) lived in this attractive, half-timbered house with his family from 1636 to 1647, when he was the local tithe collector. The interior has been restored to reflect the fixtures and fittings of their daily lives – expect flickering candles, floppy hats and writing quills.

It's engaging and entertaining, and also challenges you to answer one question: was this complex character a hero or a villain?

Ely Museum   MUSEUM

(☑ 01353-666655; www.elymuseum.org.uk; Market St; adult/child £4.50/1; ☉ 10.30am-5pm Mon-Sat, from 1pm Sun Apr-Oct, 10.30am-4pm Mon & Wed-Sat, from 1pm Sun Nov-Mar) Housed in the Old Gaol House, this quirky little museum appropriately features gruesome tableaux inside prisoners' cells, plus displays on the Romans, the Anglo-Saxons, the Long Barrow burial ground at nearby Haddlington, and the formation of the Fens. You are also initiated into the mysteries of old Ely trades such as leatherwork and eel-catching.

🛏 Sleeping

Many visitors treat Ely as a day trip from Cambridge, so it's not overrun with places to sleep, but some charming B&Bs can put you up if you do decide to stay.

OFF THE BEATEN TRACK

GRANTCHESTER

Old thatched cottages with flower-filled gardens, breezy meadows and classic cream teas aren't the only reason to make the pilgrimage along the Cam to the picture-postcard village of Grantchester. You'll also be following in the footsteps of some of the world's greatest minds on a 3-mile walk, cycle or punt from Cambridge that has changed little since Edwardian times.

After the trip, flop into a deckchair under a leafy apple tree and wolf down cakes or light lunches at the lovely **Orchard Tea Garden** (☑ 01223-840230; www.theorchard-teagarden.co.uk; 47 Mill Way; lunch mains £5-10, cakes £3; ☉ 9am-6pm Apr-Oct, to 4pm Nov-Mar), the favourite haunt of the Bloomsbury Group who came to camp, picnic, swim and discuss their work.

Bus 18 runs from Cambridge to Grantchester (£2.60, 15 minutes, hourly Monday to Saturday).

★ **Peacocks**   B&B **£££**
(📞 07900 666161; www.peacockstearoom.co.uk;
65 Waterside; s £110-135, d £135-160; 🛜) Walk
into the roomy suites here and feel instantly at home. In 'Cottage', floral Laura Ashley
wallpaper graces a sweet sitting area and
bedroom; in 'Brewery', the vintage books,
gilt mirrors and burnished antiques are
reminiscent of a grand gentlemen's club.

Riverside   B&B **£££**
(📞 01353-661677; www.riversideinn-ely.co.uk; 8
Annesdale; s £72, d £129-139; 🅿🛜) In this Georgian guesthouse on Ely's quay, rooms are
enriched by dull golds, deep reds, brocade
bedspreads, dark furniture and sparkling
bathrooms. Just the place to gaze at the
houseboats and rowers bobbing about on
the River Great Ouse.

✖ Eating

★ **Peacocks**   CAFE **£**
(📞 01353-661100; www.peacockstearoom.co.uk;
65 Waterside; snacks from £8, cream teas £9-19;
🕙 10.30am-4.30pm Wed-Sun, plus Tue Jun-Sep)
An award-winning cafe serving a vast selection of cream teas – some include chocolate
scones and sparkling rose wine. Or opt for
luscious homemade soups, salads and cakes.
Eat inside surrounded by fun knick-knacks
and bone china, or in the bijou garden
framed by drooping wisteria.

Old Fire Engine House   BRITISH **££**
(📞 01353-662582; www.theoldfireenginehouse.
co.uk; 25 St Mary's St; lunch 2/3 courses £17/22,
mains £17; 🕙 noon-2pm & 7-9pm Mon-Sat, noon-
2pm Sun; ✏) 🥢 Eating here is like sampling
food from a classic East Anglian farmhouse
kitchen. Seasonal and local produce rule, so
dishes might include Denham Estate venison, Norfolk samphire, and – fittingly for
Ely – locally smoked eels. Puddings include
nursery favourites such as tangy apple and
blackberry crumble with cream.

ℹ Information

The **Tourist Office** (📞 01353-662062; www.
visitely.org.uk; 29 St Mary's St; 🕙 10am-5pm
Apr-Oct, 11am-4pm Nov-Mar) stocks leaflets on
the picturesque 'Eel Trail' (50p) and Fen Rivers
Way circular walks (£2).

ℹ Getting There & Away

You can walk to Ely from Cambridge along the 17-
mile riverside Fen Rivers Way. Rail connections
include the following:

Cambridge £3, 20 minutes, one to three per
hour
King's Lynn £7, 30 minutes, one to two per
hour
Norwich £17, one hour, every 30 minutes

ESSEX

The county's inhabitants have been the butt
of snobbery and some of England's cruellest
jokes for years, thanks to pop-culture stere-
otypes. But beyond the fake tans and slots
'n' bumper-car resorts, Essex's still-idyllic
medieval villages and rolling countryside
provided inspiration for Constable, one of
England's best-loved painters. Here, too, is
the historic town of Colchester, while even
Southend-on-Sea, the area's most popular
resort, has a softer side in the traditional cockle-sellers and cobbled lanes of the
sleepy suburb Old Leigh.

ℹ Getting There & Around

➡ Essex is well served by public transport.

➡ Trains shuttle between Colchester and
London Liverpool St (£25, one hour, every 15
minutes), and between Southend-on-Sea and
London's Liverpool St and Fenchurch St stations (£12-15, 1¼ hours, three per hour).

➡ Regular buses head for Dedham Vale and
Saffron Walden; **Traveline East Anglia** (www.
travelineeastanglia.org.uk) provides timetables.

Colchester

📞 01206 / POP 180,420

Dominated by its sturdy castle and extensive
Roman walls, Colchester is Britain's oldest
recorded city, dating from the 5th century
BC. In AD 43 the Romans came, saw, conquered and constructed their northern capital Camulodunum. It was razed by Boudica
just 17 years later. In the 11th century, the invading Normans built a mighty castle; today
it's set amid narrow streets that are home to
a striking new arts space and some beautiful
half-timbered houses.

◉ Sights

★ **Colchester Castle**   CASTLE
(www.cimuseums.org.uk; Castle Park; adult/child
£7.75/4.80; 🕙 10am-5pm Mon-Sat, from 11am Sun)
Built in 1076 on the foundations of the Roman Temple of Claudius, England's largest
surviving Norman keep is bigger than that
of the Tower of London. Over the centuries

it's been a royal residence, a prison and home to the Witchfinder General. An imaginative £4-million restoration has added a cracking *son et lumière* which recreates lost internal structures.

Other highlights include the 'Fenwick Hoard' of Roman gold and silver jewellery, and guided tours onto the castle roof (adult/child £3/1.50, booking required).

firstsite ARTS CENTRE
(☑ 01206-713700; www.firstsite.uk.net; Lewis Gardens; ☻ 10am-5pm; ♿) **FREE** Colchester's shiny, curved, glass-and-copper arts centre is as striking inside as out: installations flow seamlessly into one another amid a wealth of space and light. Temporary art displays are cunningly juxtaposed with historical works; the one permanent exhibition is the magnificent **Berryfield Mosaic** – a Roman artefact found here in 1923, and now under glass in the centre of the gallery space.

Hollytrees Museum MUSEUM
(www.cimuseums.org.uk; Castle Park; ☻ 10am-5pm Mon-Sat) **FREE** In this Georgian town house, toys, costumes, watches and clocks form reminders of the domestic life of the wealthy owners and their servants. Quirky exhibits include a shipwright's baby carriage in the shape of a boat, a make-your-own Victorian silhouette feature and an intricate, envy-inducing doll's house.

Dutch Quarter AREA
The best of the city's half-timbered houses and rickety roof lines are clustered together in this Tudor enclave just a short stroll north of High St. The area remains as a testament to the 16th-century Protestant weavers who fled here from Holland.

🛏 Sleeping & Eating

Four Sevens B&B ££
(☑ 01206-546093; www.foursevens.co.uk; 28 Inglis Rd; s £55-65, d £65-80, f £90-95; ℗ 🖤) The far-from-frilly furnishings here include stand-alone bowl sinks, wicker chairs and platform beds. Impressive breakfasts feature eight cereal options, and guests are often welcomed with homemade cake. It's a mile southwest of the centre, off the B1022 to Maldon.

North Hill HOTEL ££
(☑ 01206-574001; www.northhillhotel.com; 51 North Hill; s £65-87, d £85-107, ste £127; 🖤) Ask for a room in the characterful, cottage-style back building of this sleek sleep spot and you'll be rewarded with wonky beams, ex-posed red brick and plush modern furnishings. Stylish, more contemporary rooms sit in the former solicitor's chambers next door – complete with ranks of law books on the shelves.

★ Company Shed SEAFOOD ££
(☑ 01206-382700; http://thecompanyshed.co; 129 Coast Rd, West Mersea; mains £6-18; ☻ 9am-4pm Tue-Sat, from 10am Sun) Bring your own bread and wine to this seaside shack to tuck into mussels, oysters, prawns, lobster, jellied eels, smoked fish or their signature seafood platter. It's all courtesy of the Howard family, eighth-generation oyster-harvesters. The shed is on Mersea Island, 9 miles south of Colchester. Check the times of high water – it's not accessible on particularly high tides.

Green Room MODERN BRITISH ££
(☑ 01206-574001; www.northhillhotel.com; 51 North Hill; mains £8.50-26; ☻ 7am-10am daily, noon-2pm & 6-9pm Mon-Sat, noon-5pm Sun) Local and seasonal comfort-food classics are given a contemporary twist at this smart, friendly restaurant, where dishes range from fish and chips or slow-roast belly pork, to creamy crab, rocket and Parmesan risotto.

ℹ Information

The **Tourist Office** (☑ 01206-282920; www.visitcolchester.com; Castle Park; ☻ 10am-5pm Mon-Sat) is inside the Hollytrees Museum.

ℹ Getting There & Away

➡ Direct National Express buses go to and from London Victoria roughly every three hours (£15, three hours).

➡ Trains run to London Liverpool St (£25, one hour, every 15 minutes).

Dedham Vale

John Constable's romantic visions of country lanes, springtime fields and babbling creeks were inspired by and painted in this serene vale. The artist was born and bred in East Bergholt in 1776 and, although you may not see the rickety old cart depicted in his renowned painting *The Hay Wain*, the picturesque cottages, rolling countryside and languid charm remain.

Now known as Constable Country, Dedham Vale centres on the villages of Dedham, East Bergholt and Flatford. With leafy lanes, arresting pastoral views and graceful old churches, it's a glorious area to explore on foot or by bike.

◎ Sights

Flatford
HISTORIC BUILDING

(NT; ☑ 01206-298260; www.nationaltrust.org. uk; Bridge Cottage, near East Bergholt; parking £4; ☉ 10am-5pm Apr-Oct, to 3.30pm Sat & Sun Nov-Mar; P) FREE Set right beside Flatford Mill, thatched Bridge Cottage has an exhibition that provides a fine introduction to the artist's life and works. Between April and October, daily guided tours (£3.50, noon Monday to Friday, 11.30am and 1.30pm Saturday and Sunday) take in views of Flatford Mill, Willy Lott's House (which features in *The Hay Wain*) and other sites that pop up in Constable's paintings. There are also self-guided routes.

Flatford Mill
HISTORIC BUILDING

(Flatford, near East Bergholt; P) Constable fans will recognise red-brick Flatford Mill immediately, as it appears in many of his canvases and still looks idyllic today. It was once owned by the artist's family and is now used as an education centre, so although you can take in picture-perfect views from front and back, you can't go in.

⊨ Sleeping & Eating

★ Dedham Hall
B&B ££

(☑ 01206-323027; www.dedhamhall.co.uk; Brook St, Dedham; s/d £75/120; P) An air of authentic old England infuses Dedham Hall, a delightfully relaxed 15th-century farmhouse where overstuffed armchairs sit beside ancient beams, candlesticks perch above red-brick fireplaces and plump pillows rest on cosy beds. Add a dappled garden dotted with chairs and it's really rather hard to leave.

Residents can also tuck into elegant, imaginative dinners (dinner and B&B for two costs £180).

Sun
INN £££

(☑ 01206-323351; www.thesuninndedham.com; High St, Dedham; s/d £90/145; P ☎) The centuries-old Sun is the epitome of heritage-chic: creaking floors and wonky walls surround upcycled mirrors, brass bedsteads and subtle colour schemes that team terracotta with a gentle yellow and olive with green.

Milsoms
HOTEL £££

(☑ 01206-322795; www.milsomhotels.com; Stratford Rd, Dedham; d £145-190; P ✳ ☎) Sure-footed design gives the rooms here a real sense of fun: red-leather armchairs, anglepoise lamps and retro phones meet vibrant candy stripes and jazzy modern art. Their bicycle and canoe hire service enables tranquil explorations of Dedham Vale.

Drop by the buzzy restaurant (open noon to 9.30pm, mains £9 to £23) for local steaks, smoked salmon and blinis, duck tacos and lush ice cream.

❶ Getting There & Away

Flatford Mill is a lovely 2-mile walk from Manningtree train station.

Bus links from Colchester:

Dedham Buses 80, 81 and 102 (£2.60, 30 minutes, two to seven daily)

East Bergholt Buses 93 and 94 (£8.50, 40 minutes, hourly Monday to Saturday)

Saffron Walden

☑ 01799 / POP 15,210

The 12th-century market town of Saffron Walden is a delightful knot of half-timbered houses, narrow lanes, crooked roofs and ancient buildings. It gets its name from the purple saffron crocus (the source of the world's most expensive spice), which was cultivated in the surrounding fields between the 15th and 18th centuries. If you can, visit on a Tuesday or a Saturday morning when markets stalls fill the centre of town.

◎ Sights

★ Audley End
House & Gardens
HISTORIC BUILDING

(EH; ☑ 01799-522842; www.english-heritage.org. uk; off London Rd; adult/child £18/11; ☉ house noon-5pm Apr-Sep, to 4pm Oct, gardens 10am-6pm Apr-Sep, to 5pm Oct) Positively palatial in its scale, style and the all-too-apparent ambition of its creator, the first Earl of Suffolk, the fabulous early-Jacobean Audley End House eventually did become a royal palace when it was bought by Charles II in 1668. Lavishly decorated rooms glitter with silverware, priceless furniture and paintings, making it one of England's grandest country homes. The fine landscaped park was designed by Lancelot 'Capability' Brown. Audley End House is 1 mile west of Saffron Walden off the B1383.

Saffron Walden Museum
MUSEUM

(☑ 01799-510333; www.saffronwaldenmuseum. org; Museum St; adult/child £2.50/free; ☉ 10am-4.30pm Tue-Sat, from 2pm Sun; ⛾) In this excellent museum dating back to 1835, you'll find eclectic collections covering everything from local history and 18th-century costumes to geology, Victorian toys and ancient Egyptian artefacts. The bramble-covered ruins of Walden Castle Keep, built around 1125, lie in the grounds.

Bridge End Gardens
GARDENS

(Bridge End; ⊘ gardens 24hr, maze & kitchen garden 9am-3.30pm Mon-Fri, plus 10am-5pm Sat & Sun Easter-Oct) FREE Careful restoration of these seven interlinked gardens has brought them back to their former Victorian glory. For extra atmosphere, try to visit when the maze and produce-packed kitchen garden are open too.

Old Sun Inn
HISTORIC BUILDING

(Church St) Saffron Walden's most famous landmark sits at a crossroads surrounded by timber-framed buildings. An ornate, 14th-century structure, it was once used as Cromwell's HQ and its exterior walls still bear intricate 17th-century pargeting (decorative plasterwork).

✗ Eating

Cafe Coucou
CAFE £

(☑ 01799-513863; www.cafecoucou.co.uk; 17 George St; mains £6-10; ⊘ 9am-5pm Mon-Sat) Delicious homemade quiches, huge scones, chunky doorstep sandwiches and imaginative salads sell like hot cakes at this cheerful family-run cafe.

Eight Bells
PUB FOOD ££

(☑ 01799-522790; www.8bells-pub.co.uk; 18 Bridge St; mains £12-19; ⊘ noon-3pm & 6-9.30pm; ♪) You'll find a warm mix of medieval character and contemporary style in this 16th-century pub. Local lamb, venison and game is teamed with southern European flavours, so expect antipasti and mezze boards as well as burgers, prime sausages, and fish and chips.

ℹ Information

Tourist Office (☑ 01799-524002; www.visitsaffronwalden.gov.uk; 1 Market Pl; ⊘ 9.30am-5pm Mon-Sat) Stocks a good (free) leaflet outlining a trail around the town's historic buildings.

ℹ Getting There & Away

Bus 7 runs between Saffron Walden and Cambridge (£4.60, 1¼ hours), hourly between Monday and Saturday. Bus 132 makes the same journey once a day on Sunday.

The nearest train station is 2 miles west of Saffron Walden at Audley End. Bus 301 links Audley End train station with Saffron Walden (£2, 15 minutes, hourly Monday to Saturday). Train services from there include the following:

Cambridge £7, 15 minutes, every 20 minutes

London Liverpool St £10, 1¼ hours, every 30 minutes

Southend-On-Sea

☑ 01702 / POP 177,900

Full of flashing lights and fairground rides, Southend is London's weekend playground, replete with gaudy amusements and packed-out nightclubs. But as well as all that, there's a glorious stretch of sandy beach, an absurdly long pier and, in the suburb of Old Leigh, echoes of a traditional fishing village.

◉ Sights

Southend Pier
LANDMARK

(www.southend.gov.uk/pier; Western Esplanade; adult/child £2/1; ⊘ 8am-8pm late-May-Aug, to 6pm Apr–late-May & Sep-Oct, 9am-5pm Wed-Sun Nov-Mar) Welcome to the world's longest pier – a staggering 1.341 miles long, to be precise – built in 1830 and a magnet for boat crashes, storms and fires, the last of which ravaged its tip in 2005. Today, a peaceful if windy stroll to the restored Pier Head reveals a cafe, a sun deck, a gift shop, an exhibition space and an active lifeboat station. Hopping on the **Pier Railway** (one-way adult/child £4.50/2.25) saves the long slog back.

Pier Museum
MUSEUM

(☑ 01702-611214; www.southendpiermuseum.co.uk; Western Esplanade; adult/child £1.50/50p; ⊘ 11am-5pm Sat, Sun, Tue & Wed May-Oct) Southend's seaside heyday springs to life in this charming museum, where a Victorian toast-rack pier tram sits beside sepia photos and a functioning signal box. The best bits are the still-working antique penny slot machines. The museum is volunteer-run so hours can vary – call to check.

Old Leigh
AREA

Cobbled streets, cockle sheds, art galleries and craft shops define atmospheric Old Leigh. It's a long stroll west along Southend's seafront, or a short hop on the local train.

⌫ Sleeping

Hamiltons
BOUTIQUE HOTEL ££

(☑ 01702-332350; www.hamiltonsboutiquehotel.co.uk; 6 Royal Terrace; d £70-140; ☎) With its wrought-iron mini-balconies and views of the pier, there's a sense of Southend's glamorous heyday at this Georgian retreat. The neutral tones of the pristine rooms have accents of subtle aquamarine, while the occasional French settee and crystal chandelier add to its period charm.

Roslin Beach HOTEL ££
(☎ 01702-586375; www.roslinhotel.com; Thorpe Esplanade; s £80-170, d £118-209, ste £160-325; ⊙ food noon-9pm; P ❖ 🐾 🖢 🐕) Seafront Roslin is all coastal chic – sand drifts up to the front steps, bedrooms have swirling seashell designs and suites feature glitzy, glass-fronted balconies. De-knot in the sauna, soak in the spa and then sample locally caught whitebait (mains £10 to £26) on the water-view terrace, framed by swaying palms.

Beaches B&B ££
(☎ 01702-585858; www.beachesguesthouse.co.uk; 192 Eastern Esplanade; s £60-70, d £95-110; 🖢) At Beaches you'll find gentle candy stripes, tasteful tones and zingy citrus-coloured cushions. Bag a bedroom with a balcony to look out over a beach dotted with boats and the slender silhouette of Southend's pier.

✗ Eating

Osborne Bros SEAFOOD £
(☎ 01702-477233; High St, Leigh-on-Sea; snacks/mains £3/9; ⊙ 8am-5pm) Part fish stall, part bare-bones cafe, Osborne's is set right on Old Leigh's waterfront. It serves up expansive Thames Estuary views, best observed while tucking into crab, jellied eels or a seafood platter (cockles, mussels, prawns and crayfish; £9) and downing a pint from the pub next door.

★ Simply Seafood SEAFOOD £££
(☎ 01702-716645; www.simply-seafood.com; 1 The Cockle Sheds, Leigh-on-Sea; mains £16-37; ⊙ noon-3.30pm & 5-9.30pm Tue-Sat, to 4.30pm Sun) Tucked away under the flyover just west of Old Leigh, this light, bright little eatery lets locally sourced seafood shine. The oysters are from Essex, the crab is from Cromer and the fish is from the boats just outside. Scallops come perfectly seared and the *fruits de mer* platter is superb.

❶ Information

Tourist Office (☎ 01702-215620; www.visitsouthend.co.uk; Southend Pier, Western Esplanade; ⊙ 8am-8pm late-May–Aug, to 6pm

Apr–late-May & Sep-Oct, 9am-5pm Wed-Sun Nov-Mar) At the entrance to the pier.

❶ Getting There & Away

Southend's most useful train stations are Central and Victoria (10 and 15 minutes walk from the shore, respectively). Direct services include:
Leigh-on-Sea (from Central) £3, seven minutes, every 15 minutes
London Fenchurch St (from Central) £12, 1¼ hours, three per hour
London Liverpool St (from Central) £15, 1¼ hours, two per hour

SUFFOLK

Suffolk is dotted with picturesque villages seemingly lost in time. The county made its money on the back of the medieval wool trade, and magnificent churches and lavish Tudor homes attest to its wealthy past. To the west are the picture-postcard villages of Lavenham and Long Melford. Further north, Bury St Edmunds ushers in historic buildings and a market-town vibe, while the appealing seaside resorts of Aldeburgh and Southwold overflow with genteel charm.

❶ Getting There & Around

Ipswich is the county's main transport hub. Traveline (www.travelineeastanglia.org.uk) details bus routes.

Train connections from Ipswich include the following:
Bury St Edmunds £9, 30 minutes, one to two per hour
London Liverpool St £17, 1¼ hours, two to three per hour
Norwich £16, 40 minutes, two per hour

Long Melford

☎ 01787 / POP 2800
Two Elizabethan manors and some good restaurants make Long Melford deserving of a detour. Its expansive village green, antiques shops and string of independent stores provide other fine reasons to meander through.

⊙ Sights

Kentwell Hall HISTORIC BUILDING
(☎ 01787-310207; www.kentwell.co.uk; adult/child £11.25/8.55; ⊙ hours vary; P) Gorgeous, turreted Kentwell Hall may date from the 1500s and be full of Tudor grandeur, but it's still used as a private home, lending it a

SUTTON HOO

Located 11 miles northeast of Ipswich off the B1083, the site of **Sutton Hoo** (NT; ☑ 01394-389700; www.nationaltrust.org.uk; near Woodbridge; adult/child £8.90/4.50; ⊙ 10.30am-5pm Feb-Sep, to 4pm Sat & Sun Jan; P ⊞) revealed one of England's greatest Anglo-Saxon treasure hoards when it was discovered in 1939. Excavations unearthed the hull of an enormous Anglo-Saxon ship belonging to the grave of Raedwald, an East-Anglian king, stuffed with Saxon riches.

A full-scale reconstruction of his ship and burial chamber can be seen in the visitor centre. The finest treasures, including the king's exquisitely crafted helmet, shields, gold ornaments and Byzantine silver, are displayed in the British Museum, but replicas are on show here, along with an original prince's sword.

Paths encircle the 18 burial mounds that make up the 'royal cemetery'. You can only walk along them as part of one-hour guided tours (adult/child £2.50/1.25). There's normally at least one tour a day; call to check for times.

The site was undergoing a dramatic £4-million redevelopment in winter 2018, closing to visitors until Spring 2019.

---

wonderfully lived-in feel. Kentwell is framed by a rectangular moat, lush gardens and an irresistible rare-breeds farm. During Tudor re-enactment events, the whole estate bristles with bodices, codpieces and hose. Opening hours are erratic: it tends to be open from 11am to 5pm during school summer holidays, plus other weekends; call to check.

Melford Hall   HISTORIC BUILDING
(NT; ☑ 01787-379228; www.nationaltrust.org.uk; Hall St; adult/child £8.20/4.10; ⊙ noon-5pm Wed-Sun Easter-Oct; P) From outside, the romantic Elizabethan mansion of Melford Hall seems little changed since it entertained Queen Elizabeth I in 1578. Inside, there's a panelled banqueting hall, masses of Regency and Victorian finery, and a display on Beatrix Potter, a cousin of the Hyde Parkers, who owned the house from 1786 to 1960.

Holy Trinity   CHURCH
(☑ 01787-310845; www.longmelfordchurch.com; Church Walk; donation requested; ⊙ 10am-6pm Easter-Sept, to 4pm Oct-Easter) FREE Magnificent Holy Trinity is more cathedral- than church-sized, a spectacular example of a 15th-century wool church. The stained-glass windows and flint-and-stone flushwork are outstanding.

🛏 Sleeping & Eating

Black Lion   HOTEL ££
(☑ 01787-312356; www.blacklionhotel.net; The Green; s £80, d £85-95, ste £145, f £150; P 🛜) At the Black Lion, there's a heritage-meets-modern mash-up of oil paintings, antlers and log fires combined with elegant sofas, cute win-

dow seats and rich throws. Colour schemes range from soothing oatmeal to vivid lime; choose to look out over the churchyard or village green.

The food (mains £10 to £18), served noon to 2.30pm and 6.30pm to 9pm, includes stone-baked pizzas, pub-food classics and classy restaurant mains.

Bull   INN ££
(☑ 0845 6086040; www.oldenglishinns.co.uk; Hall St; s/d £72/82-125; P 🛜) Built, probably, for a wool merchant in 1450, this cavernous pub has been pulling pints since around 1580. The carved ceilings and heraldic crests in its bars attest to its grand age. Check into a front-facing bedroom for maximum atmosphere enhanced by aged beams and dark wood.

Decent pub grub (such as slow-cooked belly pork, and stacked burgers) is served between noon and 9.30pm (mains £10 to £14).

★ Scutcher's   MODERN BRITISH £££
(☑ 01787-310200; www.scutchers.com; Westgate St; mains £22-28; ⊙ noon-2pm & 7-9.30pm Thu-Sat) Beautiful reinventions of traditional ingredients ensure this unpretentious place is renowned throughout the Stour Valley. Pea soup comes with a hint of curry, Parma ham has a drizzle of pomegranate molasses and local beef is given an Asian twist. It's modern, classy and assured.

ℹ Getting There & Away

Bus links include the following:
Bury St Edmunds Bus 753 (£4.30, one hour, hourly Monday to Saturday)

Sudbury Bus 753 (£1.60, 10 minutes, hourly Monday to Saturday)

Lavenham

📞 01787 / POP 1413

One of East Anglia's most beautiful and rewarding towns, the former wool-trade centre of Lavenham is home to a collection of exquisitely preserved medieval buildings that lean and lurch to dramatic effect. Lavenham's 300 half-timbered, pargeted and thatched houses have been left virtually untouched since the 15th century; many are now superb places to eat and stay.

👁 Sights

Lavenham Guildhall   HISTORIC BUILDING
(NT; 📞 01787-247646; www.nationaltrust.org.uk; Market Pl; adult/child £6.80/3.40; ⊘ 11am-5pm Mar-Oct, to 4pm Fri-Sun Nov-Feb) Lavenham's most enchanting buildings are clustered along High St, Water St and around the unusually triangular Market Pl. They're dominated by this early-16th-century white-washed guildhall – a superb example of a close-studded, timber-framed building. It is now a local-history museum with displays on the wool trade and medieval guilds; in its tranquil garden you can see dye plants that produced the typical medieval colours.

Little Hall   HISTORIC BUILDING
(📞 01787-249078; www.littlehall.org.uk; Market Pl; adult/child £4/free; ⊘ 10am-1pm Mon, 1-4pm Tue-Sun Easter-Oct) Caramel-coloured, 14th-century Little Hall museum was once home to a successful wool merchant. Inside, you'll see how the rooms of this medieval mini-manor have been restored to period splendour through the efforts of the Gayer-Anderson twins who made it their home in the 1920s and 1930s.

St Peter & St Paul   CHURCH
(www.lavenhamchurch.onesuffolk.net; Church St; ⊘ 8.30am-5.30pm) This late-Perpendicular structure seems to lift into the sky, with its beautifully proportioned windows, soaring flint tower and gargoyle waterspouts. Built between 1485 and 1530, it was one of Suffolk's last great wool churches, completed on the eve of the Reformation, and is now a lofty testament to Lavenham's past prosperity.

🛏 Sleeping & Eating

Angel   HOTEL ££
(📞 01787-247388; www.cozypubs.co.uk; Market Pl; s £90-109, d £100-120; ⊘ food noon-3pm & 6-10pm Mon-Fri, noon-10pm Sat, to 8pm Sun; P 🅿) In Lavenham's oldest building, dark-green corridors lead to gorgeously renovated, large, bright and beam-scored rooms. The eclectic decor in the bar (including theatrical spotlights and battered travelling trunks) echoes a menu that ranges confidently from pizza and English inn standards to gourmet salads and à la carte dishes (mains £12 to £26).

★**Swan**   HOTEL £££
(📞 01787-247477; www.theswanatlavenham.co.uk; High St; s £180-310, d £195-375, ste £385-435; P 🅿) Marvellously medieval and utterly indulgent, the Swan might just spoil you in terms of other places to stay. Tasteful furnishings team oatmeal with olive and gentle reds; latticework of ancient wood climbs all around. The service is smooth, while the suites are simply stunning: soaring arched ceilings are criss-crossed with beams.

★**Great House**   MODERN BRITISH £££
(📞 01787-247431; www.greathouse.co.uk; Market Pl; 3-course lunch/dinner £26/37; ⊘ noon-2.30pm Wed-Sun, 7-9.30pm Tue-Sat) Contrasting cultures combine so well at this restaurant: traditional meets modern, East Anglian ingredients meet French cuisine. Dining here could see you eating roasted Norfolk (Gressingham) duck or braised Suffolk pork, then dispatching coffee and praline *millefeuille* or tangy morsels of French and Suffolk cheese.

❶ Getting There & Away

Bus 753 runs to and from Bury St Edmunds (£4.20, 30 minutes, hourly Monday to Saturday).

Bury St Edmunds

📞 01284 / POP 41,113

In Bury, the past is ever present. A centre of pilgrimage for centuries, its history-rich features include an atmospheric ruined abbey, handsome Georgian architecture and tranquil gardens. The chance to visit two breweries is tempting too.

👁 Sights

Abbey Gardens   RUINS
(Mustow St; ⊘ dawn-dusk) FREE Now a picturesque ruin in parkland behind the cathedral, Bury's once-mighty abbey still impresses despite the townspeople having made off with much of the stone after the dissolution

of the monasteries. The walls are striking (especially on the west side), having crumbled and eroded into a series of fantastical shapes. Other highlights are the decorative Great Gate, the diminutive dovecote and the flower-filled gardens.

St Edmundsbury Cathedral   CATHEDRAL

(✆ 01284-748720;   www.stedscathedral.co.uk; Angel Hill; requested donation adult/child £3/50p; ⏰ 7am-6pm Sun-Fri, from 8am Sat) The 45m-high tower of this cathedral was only completed in 2005 and is a vision in Lincolnshire limestone – its traditional Gothic-style construction conveys how many English cathedrals must have looked fresh from the stonemason's chisel. Most of the building is early 16th century, though the eastern end is post-1945. The overall effect is light and lofty, with a gorgeous hammer-beam roof and a striking sculpture of the crucified Christ by Dame Elisabeth Frink in the north transept.

Moyse's Hall   MUSEUM

(✆ 01284-706183; www.moyseshall.org; Cornhill; adult/child £4/2; ⏰ 10am-5pm Mon-Sat, noon-4pm Sun; ☝) Set in an impressive 12th-century undercroft, Moyse's Hall's rarities include a locket containing some of Mary Tudor's hair, finds from the town's ruined abbey and displays on the chilling Bury witch trials. They also run excellent talks and activities.

Theatre Royal   HISTORIC BUILDING

(NT; ✆ 01284-769505; www.theatreroyal.org; Westgate St) A rare treat – Britain's only working Regency playhouse features ornate gilding, sweeps of boxes and a *trompe l'oeil* ceiling, all revealed on self-led (free) and guided (£7.50) front-of-house and backstage **tours**. These guided tours tend to be held at 11am on Wednesday, Thursday and Saturday, between February and November, but times vary – call to check.

St Mary's Church   CHURCH

(✆ 01284-754680; www.wearechurch.net; Honey Hill; donation requested; ⏰ 10am-4pm Mon-Sat, to 3pm Oct-Easter) St Mary's is one of the largest parish churches in England, and it contains the tomb of Mary Tudor – Henry VIII's sister and a one-time queen of France. Built around 1430, it's famous for its hammer-beam roof, which features a host of vampire-like angels swooping from the ceiling. A bell is still rung to mark curfew, as it was in the Middle Ages.

🛏 Sleeping

★ Chantry   HOTEL ££

(✆ 01284-767427; www.chantryhotel.com; 8 Sparhawk St; s/ste £90/175, d £109-149; ⓟ@🛜) Pretty much everything feels right about the Chantry – a family-run town house that's somewhere between a hotel and a B&B. Sash windows and cast-iron fireplaces signal its Georgian origins; French beds and walk-in showers add contemporary comfort; the convivial lounge and tiny bar help you to feel at home.

Fox   INN ££

(✆ 0845 6086040; www.oldenglishinns.co.uk; 1 Eastgate St; d £107-122; ⓟ🛜) Slumber in these converted animal barns and be surrounded by carefully kept original features: bleached beams, weathered brick walls and even the livestock tethering rings. Painted wicker chairs and the odd chandelier add another layer of class.

Old Cannon   B&B ££

(✆ 01284-768769; www.oldcannonbrewery.co.uk; 86 Cannon St; s/d £105/120) In these rooms run by a hip microbrewery, converted outhouses feature smart bedrooms with subtle check patterns and terracotta walls. Each room is named after one of their beers – you get a free bottle on arrival. If you like it, have some more in the pub next door.

🍴 Eating & Drinking

★ Pea Porridge   MODERN BRITISH ££

(✆ 01284-700200; www.peaporridge.co.uk; 29 Cannon St; mains £13-18; ⏰ noon-1.45pm Thu-Sat, 6.30-9pm Tue-Sat) Warmth, happy chatter and great aromas greet you at an intimate neighbourhood restaurant where local, seasonal produce meets ingredients from the Med – ingredients might include prosciutto, *piquillo* pepper and pomegranate. Many dishes are cooked in a charcoal oven giving the quail, veal and venison heart a smoky tang.

Maison Bleue   FRENCH £££

(✆ 01284-760623; www.maisonbleue.co.uk; 31 Churchgate St; mains £22-29; ⏰ noon-2pm & 7-9.30pm, closed Mon) Settle into this elegant restaurant for modern French cuisine that's supremely stylish and bursting with flavour. Creative combinations might include beef with gnocchi, rabbit with snails or halibut with clams. The set menus (three-course lunch/dinner £26/36) are excellent value.

ORFORD NESS

Wind-whipped, remote **Orford Ness** (NT; ☑01728-648024; www.nationaltrust.org.uk; adult/child incl ferry crossing £4/2; ⊙10am-5pm Tue-Sat late Jun-Sep, 10am-5pm Sat Easter–late Jun & Oct) is the largest vegetated shingle spit in Europe and was once used as a secret military testing ground; now it's a nature reserve that's home to rare wading birds, animals and plants. Ferries run from Orford Quay: the last ferry from Orford (11 miles north-east of Aldeburgh) leaves at 2pm, the last ferry back from the island returns at 5pm. Spaces are limited – arrive early to reserve a seat.

The town's 12th-century **castle** (EH; www.english-heritage.org.uk; adult/child £7.30/4.40; ⊙10am-6pm Easter-Sep, to 5pm Oct, to 4pm Sat & Sun Nov-Easter; P) is also worth a look for its innovative 18-sided drum design. For dinner, don't miss the fresh Butley oysters, garlic-laced griddled prawns and superb seafood from **Butley Orford Oysterage** (☑01394-450277; www.pinneysoforford.co.uk; Market Hill; mains £9-20; ⊙noon-2.15pm daily, plus 6.30-9pm daily Aug, Wed-Sat Apr-Jul, Sep & Oct, Fri & Sat Nov-Mar).

★**Old Cannon** PUB
(☑01284-768769; www.oldcannonbrewery.co.uk; 86 Cannon St; ⊙11am-11pm; 🔊) 🍴 In this microbrewery, gleaming mash tuns (vats in which malt is mashed) sit alongside the funky bar – try the feisty Gunner's Daughter (ABV 5.5%) or St Edmund's Head (5%).

A fair bit of the ale goes into the food (served noon to 9pm Monday to Saturday, to 2.45pm Sunday); perhaps sample some sausages and bacon cured in stout.

Nutshell PUB
(☑01284-764867; www.thenutshellpub.co.uk; The Traverse; ⊙11am-11pm Mon-Thu, to midnight Fri & Sat, noon-10.30pm Sun) Tiny benches and tables, a ceiling smothered in international banknotes and a suspended pufferfish: it's amazing what they've squeezed into this thimble-sized, memorabilia-packed, timber-framed pub, recognised by the *Guinness Book of Records* as one of Britain's smallest.

If you're not squeamish, look out for the almost-mummified 400-year-old cat.

ℹ️ Information

Tourist Office (☑01284-764667; www.visit-burystedmunds.co.uk; The Apex, Charter Sq; ⊙10am-5pm Mon-Sat) Set within the Arc shopping centre on the west side of town.

ℹ️ Getting There & Away

BUS
The main bus station is on St Andrew's St North. Direct services include:
Cambridge Stagecoach bus 11 (£5.50, one hour, hourly Monday to Saturday)
London Victoria National Express (£10, 3½ hours, one daily)

TRAIN
The train station is a 10-minute walk north of the centre of town. Services include:
Cambridge £10, 40 minutes, hourly
Ely £10, 30 minutes, every two hours

Aldeburgh

☑01728 / POP 3225

The time-warped coastal town of Aldeburgh (pronounced *orld*-bruh) is one of the region's most charming. Pastel-coloured houses, independent shops, art galleries and ramshackle fresh-fish kiosks line its picturesque streets and sweeping shingle beach. Its two festivals and connections with composer Benjamin Britten are also a big draw.

👁 Sights

Minsmere NATURE RESERVE
(RSPB; www.rspb.org.uk; near Westleton; adult/child £9/5; ⊙reserve dawn-dusk, visitor centre 9am-5pm, to 4pm Nov-Jan; P) The coast near Dunwich draws ranks of birdwatchers, thanks to RSPB Minsmere. The reserve is home to one of England's rarest birds, the bittern, with hundreds of migrant birds dropping by in the autumn. Year-round, binoculars are available for rent from the visitor centre, while the hides along the reserve's trails are prime species-spotting sites.

Minsmere is 8 miles north of Aldeburgh by car. With public transport lacking you'll need to drive, cycle or walk.

Scallop PUBLIC ART
(near Thorpe Rd car park) Maggi Hambling's sculpture commemorates Aldeburgh's links with the 20th-century composer Benjamin Britten, who spent much of his life in the

town. It manifests as two 4m-high, scallop-shell-shaped steel structures inscribed with quotes from Britten's opera *Peter Grimes*. The beachside setting of *Scallop* has proved controversial locally. It's a short stroll north of town along the seafront.

🎊 Festivals & Events

Aldeburgh Festival   MUSIC
(www.snapemaltings.co.uk/season/aldeburgh-festival; ⊘ Jun) Founded by Benjamin Britten in 1948, this exploration of classical music is one of East Anglia's biggest, taking in new, reinterpreted and rediscovered pieces, as well as the visual arts.

**Aldeburgh Food
& Drink Festival**   FOOD & DRINK
(www.aldeburghfoodanddrink.co.uk; ⊘ late Sep) A two-day celebration of Suffolk produce and top-class cooking.

🛏 Sleeping & Eating

⭐ **Ocean House**   B&B ££
(☑ 01728-452094; www.oceanhousealdeburgh.co.uk; 25 Crag Path; s £80, d £100-120, apt per week £1400) You're just seven paces (count them) from the beach at Ocean House, and many of the rustic-chic bedrooms directly overlook the surging sea. The five-person self-catering apartment comes with a homely kitchen and a pint-sized balcony, while the top-floor double is a true delight with water views on three sides and a sitting room with a baby grand piano.

Fish & Chip Shop   FISH & CHIPS £
(☑ 01728-452250; www.aldeburghfishandchips.co.uk; 226 High St; mains £5-7; ⊘ noon-2pm daily, 5-8pm Thu-Mon) Aldeburgh has a reputation for the finest fish and chips in the area; this is the best place to find out why.

⭐ **Lighthouse**   MODERN BRITISH ££
(☑ 01728-453377; www.lighthouserestaurant.co.uk; 77 High St; mains £11-19; ⊘ noon-2pm & 6.30-10pm; 🛊) The owner of this bright bistro was a waiter here for years and a sense of enthusiastic friendliness pervades the place. Local fish (baked, battered or pan fried) and veg are its real strengths, although juicy steaks with peppercorn, blue cheese or garlic and herb butter sauce are also pretty hard to beat.

ℹ Getting There & Away

Bus 64/65 runs hourly from Monday to Saturday, linking Aldeburgh with Ipswich (£6.50, 1½

hours). From there you can connect to the rest of the region.

Southwold

📋 01502 / POP 1090

Southwold's reputation as a well-heeled holiday getaway has earned it the nickname 'Kensington-on-Sea', after the upmarket London borough, and its lovely sandy beach, pebble-walled cottages, cannon-dotted clifftop and rows of beachfront bathing huts are undeniably picturesque. It has attracted many artists, including JMW Turner, Charles Rennie Mackintosh, Lucian Freud and Damien Hirst.

👁 Sights

Adnams   BREWERY
(☑ 01502-727225; www.adnams.co.uk; Adnams Pl; tours £20; ⊘ 2-4 tours daily Mar-Sep) Spend an hour touring the high-tech kit inside this Victorian brewery, indulge in a 30-minute tutored tasting, then select a free bottle of beer to take home. Book ahead.

It's now possible to tour the Adnams gin distillery (£20) too. Under-18s can't go on the tours.

Seafront & Pier   AREA
(☑ 01502-722105; www.southwoldpier.co.uk; North Pde; ⊘ pier 9am-5pm, to 8pm Fri-Sun) FREE Southwold's shore-front is its main attraction. Amble along the promenade, admire the squat 19th-century lighthouse, then drop by the 190m-long pier, first built in 1899 and recently reconstructed. Its Under the Pier Show (open 10am to 5pm, to 7pm Friday and Saturday) sports a kooky collection of vintage amusement machines combining daft fun with political satire.

Coastal Voyager   BOATING
(☑ 07887 525082; www.coastalvoyager.co.uk; Blackshore, Southwold Harbour; ⊘ hourly trips, year-round) Trips include a 30-minute high-speed blast around the bay (adult/child £29/14), a leisurely 3½-hour cruise up the Blyth Estuary (£34/16) and a three-hour voyage to Scroby Sands (£44/22) to see a seal colony and wind farm.

🎊 Festivals & Events

Latitude Festival   ART
(www.latitudefestival.co.uk; Henham Park; ⊘ Jul) An eclectic mix of music, literature, dance, drama and comedy set in a country estate.

Ways with Words LITERATURE
(www.wayswithwords.co.uk; ⊘Nov) Talks and readings by big-name authors in venues around town.

🛏 Sleeping & Eating

⭐**Sutherland House** HOTEL **£££**
(📞01502-724544; www.sutherlandhouse.co.uk; 56 High St; r £100-169; [P][🖥]) Past guests at this former mayor's residence include the prince who later became James II, and the Earl of Sandwich. They'd probably approve of its present appearance: gorgeous rooms with pargeted ceilings, exposed beams and free-standing baths – it's top-quality, luxurious and dramatic heritage-chic.

Meals (mains £12 to £23; noon to 2pm and 7pm to 9pm, closed Monday) see prime local ingredients transformed into tapas, bisque, aioli and soufflé.

Swan HOTEL **£££**
(📞01502-722186; www.adnams.co.uk; Market Sq; s £160-325, d £200-350; [P][🖥][🏊]) It's a boon for beer lovers – a super-stylish hotel owned by Southwold brewery giant Adnams. A bold and brilliant refurb has brought bright-pink chairs, minimalist four-poster beds and industrial-chic lights into this 17th-century building to great effect. In the Tap Room bar, staff are just itching to serve you a beer brewed right next door.

Modern British dishes (£12 to £16, served noon to 10pm) might include truffle-infused

---

THOMAS GAINSBOROUGH'S HOUSE

Thomas Gainsborough's atmospheric **birthplace** (📞01787-372958; www.gainsborough.org; 46 Gainsborough St; adult/child £7/2; ⊘10am-5pm Mon-Sat, from 11am Sun) is now home to the world's largest collection of his work. The 16th-century house and gardens feature a Georgian facade built by the artist's father. Inside, look out for *Pitminster Boy* in the entrance hall; the exquisite *Portrait of Harriett, Viscountess Tracy*, celebrated for its delicate portrayal of drapery; and the landscapes that were his passion.

Regular buses from Sudbury run to Ipswich (one hour), Long Melford (13 minutes), Lavenham (30 minutes), Bury St Edmunds (1½ hours) and Colchester (50 minutes).

---

baked cauliflower, ham, egg and chips, or chicken-liver parfait.

❶ Getting There & Away

Bus 146 links Southwold with Norwich (£4.40, 1½ hours, hourly Monday to Saturday).

For services south, including those to and from Aldeburgh, catch bus 88A to Halesworth (£2.80, 30 minutes, hourly Monday to Saturday) and continue on the 521 (£4.80, one hour, four daily).

NORFOLK

Big skies, sweeping beaches, windswept marshes, meandering inland waterways and pretty flint houses combine to great effect in Norfolk. They say the locals have 'one foot on the land, and one in the sea', and you're never far from water here, whether it's beside the windmill-framed rivers of the tranquil Norfolk Broads or the wide, birdlife-rich sands of the shore. Inland, the bustling city of Norwich offers a fine castle and a cathedral, a lively market and some truly excellent places to sleep and eat.

❶ Getting There & Around

Norwich is the county's transport hub. Train connections include a direct line to London Liverpool St (£18, two hours, two per hour).

Traveline (www.travelineeastanglia.org.uk) details bus routes. One of the most useful is the frequent Coasthopper Bus (www.sanderscoaches.com), which hugs the shore on its route between Cromer and King's Lynn.

Norwich

📞01603 / POP 132,512
The affluent and easy-going city of Norwich (*norr*-ich) is a rich tapestry of meandering alleys liberally sprinkled with architectural jewels – spoils of the city's medieval wool boom. A magnificent cathedral and impressive Norman castle bookend the city centre; in-between, crooked half-timbered buildings line quiet lanes. Thriving markets and a large student population enhance the city's relaxed vibe. Add quick access to the Broads and Norfolk's beaches, and you have an excellent base from which to explore.

👁 Sights

⭐**Norwich Cathedral** CATHEDRAL
(📞01603-218300; www.cathedral.org.uk; 65 The Close; donations requested; ⊘7.30am-6pm) Nor-

Norwich

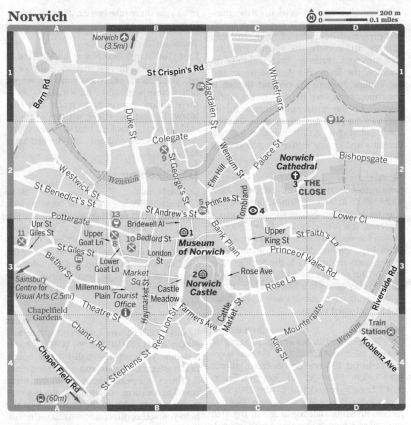

N 0 — 200 m
0 — 0.1 miles

Norwich

◎ Top Sights
1 Museum of Norwich B3
2 Norwich Castle..................................... B3
3 Norwich Cathedral................................ C2

◎ Sights
4 Tombland & Elm Hill C2

⬤ Sleeping
5 3 Princes... B2
6 38 St Giles A3
7 Gothic House.. B1

✸ Eating
8 Grosvenor Fish Bar B3
9 Last Wine Bar & Restaurant B2
10 Library B3
   Mustard... (see 1)
11 Roger Hickman's A3

⬤ Drinking & Nightlife
12 Adam & Eve.. D1
13 Birdcage... B3

wich's most impressive landmark is a magnificent Anglican cathedral. Its barbed spire soars higher than any in England except Salisbury's, while the size of its cloisters is second to none. Highlights include the mesmerising ceiling, the ornate roof bosses, and the striking modern features of the Hostry. The 50-minute guided tours (donation requested, hourly Monday to Saturday, 11am to 3pm) are an engaging way to find out more.

★ Norwich Castle   MUSEUM
(☎ 01603-495897; www.museums.norfolk.gov.uk;
Castle Hill; adult/child £9.15/7.30; ⊙ 10am-4.30pm
Mon-Sat, from 1pm Sun) Crowning a hilltop

overlooking central Norwich, this massive 12th-century castle is one of England's best-preserved examples of Anglo-Norman military architecture. Its superb **interactive museum** crams in lively exhibits on Boudica, the Iceni, the Anglo-Saxons and the Vikings. Perhaps the best bit though is the atmospheric keep itself with its graphic displays on the grisly punishments meted out in its days as a medieval prison. **Guided tours** (adult/child £3.70/3) around the battlements and creepy dungeons run at least twice daily.

★ **Museum of Norwich**   MUSEUM
(www.museums.norfolk.gov.uk; Bridewell Alley; adult/child £5.70/4.55; ⊘10am-4.30pm Tue-Sat) Stay on your best behaviour: 14th-century Bridewell is a former house of correction, a 'prison for women, beggars and tramps'. Displays here explore Norwich's prominence as England's second city in the Middle Ages and its 19th-century industrial heritage. You can also play games in a 1950s parlour, listen to shoe-workers' memories, and watch films in a pocket-sized cinema.

Blickling Hall   HISTORIC BUILDING
(NT; ☑01263-738030; www.nationaltrust.org.uk; Blickling; adult/child £14.35/7.20; ⊘house noon-5pm Easter-Oct, 10.30am-3pm Nov-Easter, grounds 10am-5.30pm Easter-Oct, to 3pm Nov-Easter; P🐾) Largely remodelled in the 17th century for Sir Henry Hobart, James I's chief justice, Blickling Hall began life in the 11th century as a manor house and bishop's palace. The grand Jacobean state rooms are stuffed with fine Georgian furniture, pictures and tapestries; the plaster ceiling in the Long Gallery is spectacular. The estate's vast parklands are criss-crossed with cycling and walking routes.

Blickling Hall is 15 miles north of Norwich off the A140.

Sainsbury Centre for Visual Arts GALLERY
(☑01603-593199; www.scva.ac.uk; University of East Anglia (UEA); ⊘10am-6pm Tue-Fri, to 5pm Sat & Sun; 🚌22, 25, 26) **FREE** The region's most important centre for the arts is housed in the first major public building by renowned architect Norman Foster. Its eclectic collections include works by Picasso, Moore, Degas and Bacon, which are displayed beside curios from Africa, the Pacific and the Americas.

The gallery is in the University of East Anglia's grounds, 2 miles west of the city cen-

tre. To get there take bus 22, 25 or 26 (£2.20, 15 minutes).

Tombland & Elm Hill   AREA
Leafy Tombland, near Norwich Cathedral, is where the city's market was originally located ('tomb' is an old Norse word for empty, hence there being space for a market). From there, follow Princes St to reach Elm Hill, Norwich's prettiest street, with its medieval cobblestones, crooked timber beams and doors, intriguing shops and tucked-away cafes.

🛏 Sleeping

Gothic House   B&B ££
(☑01603-631879; www.gothic-house-norwich. com; King's Head Yard, Magdalen St; s/d £75/105; P🛜) Step through the door to be whisked straight back to the Regency era. Original panelling, columns and cornices border the swirling stairs; fresh fruit and mini-decanters of sherry await in floral bedrooms that are studies in olive green, lemon yellow and duck-egg blue.

★ **3 Princes**   B&B £££
(☑01603-622699; www.3princes-norwich.co.uk; 3 Princes St; s/d £85/140-160; 🛜) With its warm welcome, cosy yet minimalist decor, homemade afternoon treats and spacious rooms, 3 Princes is a perfect spot for an overnight stay. The location, on a quiet, pretty but very central street, adds to the charm, as do the help-yourself continental breakfasts (including fresh croissants and granola) and the wonderfully comfortable beds.

38 St Giles   B&B £££
(☑01603-662944; www.38stgiles.co.uk; 38 St Giles St; s/ste £95/240, d £120-150; P🛜) At boutique 38 St Giles it seems everything gleams – from the highly polished floorboards to the aged cherry-red sofas. Mustard-yellow walls and rich rugs add another layer of charm. Breakfast includes local and organic meat and eggs, plus treats such as crème-fraiche pancakes with Norfolk bacon and maple syrup.

🍴 Eating

★ **Grosvenor Fish Bar**   FISH & CHIPS £
(www.fshshop.com; 28 Lower Goat Lane; mains from £5; ⊘11am-7.30pm Mon-Sat) At this groovy chippy-with-a-difference, chips come with fresh cod goujons, a 'Big Mack' is a crispy mackerel fillet in a bread roll, and the 'Five Quid Squid' (squid rings with garlic aioli)

really is £5. Either eat in the basement or they'll deliver to the Birdcage (p379) pub opposite, so you can have a pint with your meal.

Mustard
CAFE £

(www.mustardcoffeebar.co.uk; 3 Bridewell Alley; snacks/mains £2/7; ⊘ 8am-5pm Mon-Sat; 🛜) You'll find a suitably bright-yellow colour scheme at this cool cafe set on the site of the original Colman's Mustard shop. Quality dishes might include breakfast bagels with halloumi and maple syrup, and chorizo Scotch eggs.

Library
BRASSERIE ££

(☑ 01603-616606; www.thelibraryrestaurant.co.uk; 4a Guildhall Hill; mains £12-25; ⊘ noon-2.30pm & 6-10pm Mon-Sat, noon-4pm Sun; 🚸) The chef here has a penchant for grilling over woodsmoke; smoky flavours infuse everything from chicken, lamb and beef to fennel seeds. It's a hit, as is the setting – with Victorian bookcases lining the walls of what was once a library; dining here has a club-like feel.

Last Wine Bar & Restaurant
BRITISH ££

(☑ 01603-626626; www.lastwinebar.co.uk; 70 St George's St; mains £14-24; ⊘ noon-2.30pm & 6-9.30pm Mon-Sat) The decor in the bar is fabulous and reflects the building's past life as a shoe factory, with lasts (wooden shoe moulds) as light fittings and Singer sewing machines as tables. The food lives up to the setting – top-notch burgers, steaks, gnocchi and fish pie in the bar, and creative twists on British classics in the à la carte restaurant.

★ Roger Hickman's
MODERN BRITISH £££

(☑ 01603-633522; www.rogerhickmansrestaurant. com; 79 Upper St Giles St; dinner 2/3/7 courses £38/47/63; ⊘ noon-2.30pm & 7-10pm Tue-Sat) Understated elegance is everywhere here: pale floorboards, white linen and unobtrusive service. Dishes might include confit salmon and rabbit or blow-torched mackerel – flair, imagination and a simple dedication to quality run right through. The lunches (two/three courses £20/25) are a cracking deal.

🍷 Drinking & Nightlife

★ Birdcage
PUB

(www.thebirdcagenorwich.co.uk; 23 Pottergate; ⊘ 11am-midnight; 🛜) Formica tables, chilled tunes, cupcakes and cocktails make this beatnik drinking den a one-of-a-kind delight. Book for a Bums life-drawing session (yes, really; £4, Tuesday 7pm) or ferry in fish and chips from the Grosvenor Fish Bar (p378) over the lane.

Adam & Eve
PUB

(Bishopsgate; ⊘ 11am-11pm Mon-Sat, noon-10.30pm Sun) Norwich's oldest-surviving pub has been slaking thirst since 1249, when the cathedral builders used to drop by. Tiny, with a sunken floor and part-panelled walls, it attracts a mixed band of regulars, choristers and ghost hunters, drawn by the fine malt whiskies and real ales.

ⓘ Information

Tourist Office (☑ 01603-213999; www.visit-norwich.co.uk; Millennium Plain; ⊘ 9.30am-5.30pm Mon-Sat, plus 10.30am-3.30pm Sun mid-Jul–mid-Sep) Inside the Forum.

ⓘ Getting There & Away

AIR

Norwich International Airport (☑ 01603-411923; www.norwichairport.co.uk; Holt Rd) is 4 miles north of town. Connections go to Amsterdam, Aberdeen, Edinburgh, Exeter and Manchester year-round; there are also summer flights to Spain and the Channel Islands.

BUS

The **bus station** (Queen's Rd) is 400m south of the castle. National Express (www.nationalexpress.com) and First (www.firstgroup.com) are among the operators:

Cromer Bus X44; £3.70, one hour, hourly Monday to Saturday

King's Lynn Excel (XL); £6.40, 1½ hours, hourly

London Victoria £12, three hours, every two hours

TRAIN

The train station is off Thorpe Rd, 600m east of Norwich Castle. Destinations include:

Cambridge £20, 1¼ hours, hourly

Ely £17, one hour, every 30 minutes

London Liverpool St £20, two hours, every 30 minutes

Cromer

☑ 01263 / POP 7949

The once-fashionable Victorian resort of Cromer is a relaxed mix of an old-school English seaside holiday hotspot and an appealing fishing port. Brightly painted houses line narrow lanes dotted with independent shops. Its main attractions remain sweet-tasting Cromer crab, the atmospheric pier and an appealing stretch of pebbly shore.

THE NORFOLK BROADS

Why should I visit a swamp?

These vast wetlands were formed when the rivers Wensum, Bure, Waveney and Yare flooded the big gaping holes inland, which had been dug by 12th-century crofters looking for peat. They comprise fragile ecosystems and are protected as a **national park** (www.visit-thebroads.co.uk). They're also home to some of the UK's rarest plants and birds – the appeal to birdwatchers and naturalists is obvious. Apart from that, if you've ever envisioned yourself captaining your own boat and living afloat, there are 125 miles of lock-free waterways to explore. Or if paddling a canoe and losing yourself in lapping water away from the rest of humanity appeals, there's plenty of scope for that, too.

Exploring by boat

Launches range from large cabin cruisers to little craft with outboards; they can be hired for anything from a couple of hours' gentle messing about on the water to week-long trips. Tuition is given. Depending on boat size, facilities and the season, a four-person boat costs from around £25 per hour, from £80 for four hours and from £110 for one day. Week-long rental ranges from around £550 to £1400, including fuel and insurance.

Broadland Day Boats (☑01692-581653; www.dayboathire.com; Sutton Staithe Boatyard, Sutton Staithe; boat hire per day £95-110, canoe hire per half-/full day £25/40) hires boats and canoes. **Barnes Brinkcraft** (☑01603-782625; www.barnesbrinkcraft.co.uk; Riverside Rd, Wroxham; canoe hire per half day £30, boat hire per hr/day £18/152, 4-berth boat per week from £470; ◎ Apr-Oct) offers short- and long-term rental, while **Broads Tours** (☑01603-782207; www.broads.co.uk; The Bridge, Wroxham; boat hire per hr/day/week from £20/175/1400; ◎8am-5.30pm Mar-Oct) lets out boats by the day and week, and runs boat trips. **Blakes** (☑0345 498 6184; www.blakes.co.uk; 4-berth boat per week £550-1000) arranges all manner of boating holidays.

Exploring by canoe

Paddlers can find canoes for hire for around £35 to £40 per day; **Whispering Reeds** (☑01692-598314; www.whisperingreeds.net; Staithe Rd, Hickling; canoe hire per 3/6hr £25/35; ◎Easter-Oct) and **Waveney River Centre** (☑01502-677343; www.waveneyrivercentre.co.uk; Burgh St Peter; kayak/canoe hire per day £28/36; ◎Easter-Oct) are recommended. **Mark the Canoe Man** (☑01603-783777; www.thecanoeman.com; half-day trips adult/child £25/15; ◎Apr-Oct) knows the secrets of the Broads and arranges guided trips to areas the cruisers can't reach (from £25), as well as offering canoe and kayak hire, weekend camping canoe trails, and two-day canoe and bushcraft trips (adult/child £175/125).

Exploring on foot & by bike

A web of walking trails stretches across the region, including the 61-mile **Weavers' Way**, which stretches from Cromer to Great Yarmouth, taking in some choice landscapes along

◉ Sights

Felbrigg Hall HISTORIC BUILDING
(NT; ☑01263-837444; www.nationaltrust.org.uk; Felbrigg; adult/child £11/5.25; ◎noon-5pm late Mar-Oct, to 3pm early Feb-late Mar; P) An elegant Jacobean mansion boasting a fine Georgian interior, a splendid facade, an orangery and gorgeous walled gardens. It's 2 miles southwest of Cromer, off the B1436.

Henry Blogg Museum MUSEUM
(RNLI Lifeboat Museum; ☑01263-511294; www.rnli.org; The Gangway; ◎10am-5pm Tue-Sun Apr-Sep, to 4pm Oct, Nov, Feb & Mar) FREE Tap out a message in Morse and spell your name in semaphore flags – hands-on gizmos add to the appeal of this excellent museum, as do the well-told tales of brave sea rescues and the WWII lifeboat sitting proudly inside.

The museum is named after one of the Royal National Lifeboat Institution's most decorated coxswains, and features accounts of his extraordinary rescues.

🛏 Sleeping & Eating

★**Red Lion** INN ££
(☑01263-514964; www.redlioncromer.co.uk; Brook St; s £65-95, d £115-160, ste £160-180; P🖥) Coloured floor tiles, wooden banisters and stained glass signal this seafront inn's

the way. The Broads' highest point, How Hill, is just 12m above sea level, so superhero levels of fitness are not required. The section between Aylsham and Stalham is open to bicycles.

Broadland Cycle Hire (☑07887 480331; www.norfolkbroadscycling.co.uk; Bewilderwood, Hoveton; bike hire per day adult/child £18/7, per week £70/45; ☺10am-5pm Jul-early Sept) and Mark the Canoe Man are among those hiring out bikes. Expect to pay between £18 and £20 per day; child seats and tandems are also available.

What is there to see & do that doesn't involve water?

Museum of the Broads (☑01692-581681; www.museumofthebroads.org.uk; The Staithe, Stalham; adult/child £5.50/2.50; ☺10am-4.30pm Sun-Fri Easter-Oct) Five miles north of Potter Heigham off the A149, this museum features fine boats and colourful displays on the local marshmen, their traditional lifestyles, peat extraction and modern conservation. You can ride on a steam launch too.

Toad Hole Cottage (☑01692-678555; www.howhilltrust.org.uk; How Hill; ☺10.30am-5pm Apr-Oct) **FREE** The life of Fen dwellers is revealed at this tiny cottage, which shows how an eel-catcher's family lived and the tools they used to work the surrounding marshes.

Bewilderwood (☑01692-633033; www.bewilderwood.co.uk; Horning Rd, Hoveton; adult/child £16.50/14.50; ☺10am-5.30pm Easter-Oct; ☐5B) A forest playground for children and adults alike, with zip wires, jungle bridges, tree houses and old-fashioned outdoor adventure involving plenty of mud, mazes and marsh walks.

St Helen's Church (☑01603-270340; Ranworth; ☺9am-5pm) The Broads' most impressive ecclesiastical attraction is this 14th-century church, known locally as the 'Cathedral of the Broads'. It features a magnificent painted medieval rood screen and a 15th-century *antiphoner* – a rare illustrated book of prayers.

Bure Valley Steam Railway (☑01263-733858; www.bvrw.co.uk; Aylsham; adult/child return £13.50/6.50; ☺2-9 trains daily Apr-Oct; ℗) Steam buffs will love this train, which puffs along 9 miles of narrow-gauge tracks between Aylsham and Wroxham. You can make the return trip by boat.

How do I get around?

Driving around the Broads is missing the point and pretty useless. The key centres of Wroxham, on the A1151 from Norwich, and Potter Heigham, on the A1062 from Wroxham, are reachable by bus from Norwich and Great Yarmouth, respectively. From there, you can either take to the water or to the trails.

18th-century heritage; stylish, sea-themed rooms bring it right up to date. All bedrooms come with baths, cafetière coffee and fresh milk – the pick is the suite (room 7), where you can see the sea from both the balcony and the roll-top tub.

★**Davies** SEAFOOD **£**
(☑01263-512727; 7 Garden St; crab £3.50-6; ☺8.30am-5pm Mon-Sat, 10am-4pm Sun Apr-Oct, 8.30am-4pm Tue-Sat Nov-Mar) Less a fish shop, more a local institution – at Davies the crab is caught by its own day boat (the *Richard William*) and then boiled, cracked and dressed on-site. Other treats include cockles,

mussels and homemade pâté; the mackerel and horseradish pâté has quite a kick.

Rocket House CAFE **£**
(☑01263-519126; www.rockethousecafe.co.uk; The Gangway; mains £6.50-11; ☺9am-5pm Mon-Fri, from 10am Sat & Sun; ⊕) Rocket House delivers an airy interior and widescreen sea views, thanks to a balcony that almost overhangs the waves. Light dishes include ploughman's with Norfolk Dapple and Binham Blue cheese, locally smoked mackerel salad, and their renowned Cromer crab platter.

ℹ️ Getting There & Away

➡ Trains link Cromer with Norwich (£8, 45 minutes, hourly).

➡ Cromer is on the Coasthopper (www.sanders coaches.com) bus route, with regular services to Cley-next-the-Sea, Blakeney and Wells. From Wells there are frequent connections through to King's Lynn.

Cley-next-the-Sea

📞 01263 / POP 450

As the name suggests, the sleepy village of Cley (pronounced 'cly') huddles beside the shore. Here, a cluster of pretty cottages surrounds a photogenic windmill, and bird-rich marshes fan out all around.

👁️ Sights

Cley Marshes   NATURE RESERVE
(📞 01263-740008.; www.norfolkwildlifetrust.org. uk; near Cley-next-the-Sea; adult/child £4.50/free; ☺ dawn-dusk; 🅿️) 🏃 One of England's premier birdwatching sites, Cley Marshes has more than 300 resident bird species, plentiful migrants and a network of walking trails and bird hides amid its golden reeds.

Even if you're not into birdwatching, don't miss the views from the (free) visitor centre (p382) and cafe. This is birdwatching for softies; sip a latte while enjoying zoomed-in images of marsh harriers.

🛏️ Sleeping & Eating

⭐ Cley Windmill   B&B £££
(📞 01263-740209; www.cleymill.co.uk; High St; d £190-205, apt per week from £560; 🅿️) With the kind of wonky walls you'd expect from a circular 18th-century agricultural building, Cley Windmill is packed with character. Rooms are named after their former functions (the crazy-shaped Barley Bin is gorgeous), and many look out directly over reed-filled salt marshes. A sweet four-person self-catering cottage sits just next door.

George   INN £££
(📞 01263-740652; www.thegeorgehotelatcley.co. uk; High St; d £120-335) The George may be an age-old English inn, but the style is all contemporary north-Norfolk chic. Sure-footed design sees bare floorboards and feature fireplaces meet upcycled armchairs and quirky chests of drawers. Opt for a room overlooking the marshes for mesmerising views of wind-ruffled reeds.

⭐ Picnic Fayre   DELI £
(📞 01263-740587; www.picnic-fayre.co.uk; High St; snacks from £3; ☺ 9am-5pm Mon-Sat, 10am-4pm Sun) A deli to ditch the diet for, crammed full of imaginative versions of English picnic classics – pork pies with chorizo, sausages smothered with sweet-chilli sauce, and home-baked lavender bread. Plus gooey homemade fudge and Portuguese custard tarts. Yum.

ℹ️ Information

Visitor Centre (📞 01263-740008; www. norfolkwildlifetrust.org.uk; Cley Marshes; ☺ 10am-5pm Mar-Oct, to 4pm Nov-Feb) Seats and telescopes line up beside vast picture windows with panoramic views of the bird reserve. There's a cafe too.

ℹ️ Getting There & Away

Cley is on the Coasthopper (www.sanderscoach es.com) bus route, with regular services to Cromer, Blakeney and Wells. From Wells there are frequent connections through to King's Lynn.

Blakeney

📞 01263 / POP 801

The pretty village of Blakeney was once a busy fishing and trading port before its harbour silted up. These days it offers an inviting seafront walk lined with yachts, and boat trips out to a 500-strong colony of common and grey seals that live, bask and breed on nearby Blakeney Point.

👉 Tours

Bishop's Boats   BOATING
(📞 01263-740753; www.bishopsboats.com; Blakeney Quay; adult/child £12/6; ☺ 1-4 daily Apr-Oct) Hour-long trips to see the seals at Blakeney Point; the best time to come is between June and August when the common seals pup.

Beans Seal Trips   BOATING
(📞 01263-740505; www.beansboattrips.co.uk; Morston Quay; adult/child £12/6; ☺ 1-3 daily Apr-Oct) Boat journeys out to the hundreds-strong Blakeney Point seal colony. The departure point is Morston Quay, 1.5 miles east of Blakeney.

🛏️ Sleeping & Eating

Kings Arms   INN ££
(📞 01263-740341; www.blakeneykingsarms.co.uk; Westgate St; s/d £65/85; 🅿️ 🐕) Sweet, simple, old-style rooms (expect bright colours and pine) in a pub that's so welcoming you might

not want to leave. Order some substantial pub grub (their fish and chips are famous; mains from £9 to £18; meals served noon to 9pm), then, for great theatre gossip, ask landlady Marjorie about her career on the stage.

Moorings
MODERN BRITISH ££

(☑ 01263-740054; www.blakeney-moorings.co.uk; High St; mains £7-19; ☺ 10.30am-8pm Tue-Sat, to 5pm Sun) Perfectly pitched fish dishes have won this bistro a loyal following – try the spicy Norfolk crab cake or herb-crusted local mackerel. Mustn't-miss puddings include ripe Norfolk cheese, and a rhubarb, honey and saffron tart.

❶ Getting There & Away

Blakeney is on the Coasthopper (www.sanders coaches.com) bus route, with regular services to Cromer, Cley-next-the-Sea and Wells. From Wells there are frequent connections through to King's Lynn.

Wells-next-the-Sea
☑ 01328 / POP 2165

Charming Wells excels at both land and sea. Rows of attractive Georgian houses and flint cottages snake down to a boat-lined quay; to the north sits a vast golden beach, backed by pine-covered dunes.

◉ Sights

Wells Beach
BEACH

(Ⓟ) Fringed by dense pine forests and undulating dunes, Wells' sandy shore stretches for miles to the west, with brightly coloured beach huts clustering beside the water and wooden steps leading up into the woods. It's all tucked away at the end of a mile-long road; you can walk, drive or hop on a miniature train. Parking is available.

Wells & Walsingham Railway
HERITAGE RAILWAY

(☑ 01328-711630; www.wellswalsinghamrailway.co.uk; Stiffkey Rd; adult/child return £9.50/7.50; ☺ 4-5 trains daily late Mar-Oct; Ⓟ) The longest 10.25in narrow-gauge railway in the world puffs for 5 picturesque miles from Wells to the village of Little Walsingham, the site of religious shrines and the ruined but still impressive Walsingham Abbey.

🛏 Sleeping & Eating

Wells YHA
HOSTEL £

(☑ 0345 371 9544; www.yha.org.uk; Church Plain; dm/d/f £25/70/80; Ⓟ🛜) Set in the heart of town in an ornately gabled early-20th-century church hall. Modern furnishings and a friendly vibe make it hard to beat.

★ Old Customs House
B&B ££

(☑ 01328-711463; www.eastquay.co.uk; East Quay; s £85-95, d £105-115; Ⓟ🛜) The stately but comfy feel here comes courtesy of worn-wood panels, alcoves full of books and gorgeous creek views. Choose from the snug 'Captain's Quarters' or a grand four-poster room. Discuss what you'd like for breakfast with the owner – perhaps locally baked bread with homemade jam or smoked haddock?

Wells Beach Cafe
CAFE £

(www.holkham.co.uk; Wells Beach; mains from £5; ☺ 10am-5pm Easter-Oct, to 4pm Nov-Easter; 🛜) This locals' favourite rustles up bacon baps, homemade chilli and decadent hot chocolates. Outside there's a corral of picnic tables; inside there's a wood-burning stove for when the wind whips in.

CAMBRIDGE & EAST ANGLIA WELLS-NEXT-THE-SEA

THE QUEEN'S COUNTRY ESTATE

Both monarchists and those bemused by the English system will have plenty to mull over here at Sandringham (☑ 01485-545400; www.sandringhamestate.co.uk; adult/child £16.50/8; ☺ 11am-4.30pm Easter-Sep, to 3.30pm Oct; Ⓟ; 🚌 35), the Queen's country estate.

Sandringham was built in 1870 by the then Prince and Princess of Wales (who later became King Edward VII and Queen Alexandra), and the house's features and furnishings remain much as they were in Edwardian days. The stables, meanwhile, now house a flag-waving museum filled with diverse royal memorabilia. The superb vintage-car collection includes the very first royal motor, from 1900, and the buggy in which the Queen Mother would bounce around race tracks. It's set in 25 hectares of beautifully landscaped gardens.

There are guided tours of the gardens (£3.50, 11am and 2pm Wednesday and Saturday). The shop stocks organic goodies produced on the vast estate.

Sandringham is 6 miles northeast of King's Lynn off the A149. Bus 35 runs from King's Lynn (£2.50, 20 minutes, hourly).

Information

Tourist Office (☎ 01328-710885; www.visit-northnorfolk.com; Freeman's St; ☺ 10am-4pm Mon-Sat, to 1pm Sun Apr-Oct)

Getting There & Away

Wells is a pivot point on coastal bus services. From here regular services include:

Coasthopper (www.sanderscoaches.com) Provides links with Cromer, via Blakeney and Cley-next-the-Sea.

Coastliner (www.lynxbus.co.uk) Heads to King's Lynn, via Holkham, Burnham Deepdale, Brancaster Staithe and Titchwell.

Holkham

☑ 01328 / POP 200

Little Holkham may only have two big assets, but both are highly impressive: a grand country-house estate and a spectacular stretch of sandy shore.

Sights

★ **Holkham National Nature Reserve**   WILDLIFE RESERVE
(www.holkham.co.uk; parking per 2hr/day £3/7; ☺ car park: 6am-9pm Apr-Sep, to 6pm Oct-Mar) Beach, dunes, salt marsh, grazing marsh, pinewoods and scrub – a high number of habitats pack into 37-sq-km Holkham Reserve. It's easily accessed from the car park at Lady Anne's Dr in Holkham village. From there, ribboning pathways lead through forests via bird hides and on to an expansive, pristine shore.

Holkham Hall & Estate   HISTORIC BUILDING
(☎ 01328-713111; www.holkham.co.uk; adult/child £16/8, parking £3; ☺ noon-4pm Sun, Mon & Thu Easter-Oct; ℗) Holkham Hall is the ancestral seat of the original Earl of Leicester and still belongs to his descendants. A severe Palladian mansion, it's largely unadorned on the outside but the interior is sumptuous, with a red-velvet-lined saloon, copies of Greek and Roman statues, the luxurious Green State Bedroom, and fluted columns in the Marble Hall. It's set in a vast deer park (open 10am to 5pm daily), which was designed by William Kent.

Sleeping

★ **Victoria**   INN £££
(☎ 01328-711008; www.holkham.co.uk; Park Rd; s £135-160, d £160-250, f £260-290; ☺ food: 8-10am & noon-9pm; ℗ ☎ ☀) A pint at the Victoria after a walk along sweeping Holkham Beach is pretty much a tradition. Extending your drink to an overnight stay is richly rewarding. Bathrooms gleam while sea tones and crisp modern styling are complemented by the odd antique. The food (mains £7 to £20), often sourced from Holkham Estate, is stylish country cooking at its best.

Getting There & Away

Holkham is on the Coastliner (www.lynxbus. co.uk) route, with regular buses linking King's Lynn and Wells. From Wells, frequent services shuttle to Cromer.

Burnham Deepdale

☑ 01485 / POP 800

Walkers flock to this lovely coastal spot, with the tiny village of Burnham Deepdale (which merges seamlessly into Brancaster Staithe) strung along a rural road. Edged by the beautiful Norfolk Coast Path, surrounded by beaches and reedy marshes, alive with birdlife and criss-crossed by cycling routes, Burnham Deepdale is also the base for a whole host of water sports.

Sights

Titchwell Marsh   NATURE RESERVE
(RSPB; ☎ 01485-210779; www.rspb.org.uk; Titchwell; parking £6; ☺ dawn-dusk; ℗) The marshland, sandbars and lagoons of Titchwell Marsh Nature Reserve attract vast numbers of birds. In the spring, listen out for the booming call of the bittern; summer brings marsh harriers, avocets, terns and nesting bearded tits. In winter you'll see more than 20 species of wading birds and countless ducks and geese.

Titchwell Marsh is 3 miles west of Burnham Deepdale.

Sleeping & Eating

★ **Deepdale Farm**   HOSTEL £
(☎ 01485-210256; www.deepdalefarm.co.uk; Burnham Deepdale; dm/d/f/q £18/60/70/80, camping sites from £26; ℗ @ ☎) ✔ For backpackers it really doesn't get much better than Deepdale Farm: spick-and-span en-suite dorms and doubles in converted stables, a homely well-equipped kitchen, a barbecue area, and a cosy lounge warmed by a wood-burning stove. Campers can go glam in a safari-style, fully equipped tent, or bring their own – you'll find a heated shower block either way.

The hostel also operates a **tourist office** (✆01485-210256; www.deepdalefarm.co.uk; Burnham Deepdale; ⊗9am-5pm Mon-Sat, 10am-4pm Sun), the best place to go to organise kitesurfing or windsurfing on nearby beaches.

★**Titchwell Manor** HOTEL **£££**
(✆01485-210221; www.titchwellmanor.com; Titchwell, nr Brancaster; r £170-220; P@🐾) Dreamy Titchwell Manor is a swish, oh-so-contemporary hotel set in a grand Victorian house. You'll find lovingly upcycled furniture and bold colours in chic rooms ranging from those beside the herb-garden courtyard to ones with corking sea views.

The stylish restaurant and terrace set the scene for modern tapas and acclaimed à la carte dishes (mains £14 to £35; food served from noon to 2pm and 6pm to 9pm).

★**White Horse** MODERN BRITISH **££**
(✆01485-210262; www.whitehorsebrancaster.co.uk; Main Rd, Brancaster Staithe; mains £14-24; ⊗9am-9pm; P🐾) The White Horse gastropub's imaginative menu more than sets it apart from its competitors. Seasonal Norfolk ingredients pepper the menu – you might see foraged wild garlic, local duck *rillettes*, tempura Brancaster oysters and salt-marsh lamb. The bedrooms (doubles £160 to £250) evoke the shoreline with subtle colour schemes.

Eric's Fish & Chips FISH & CHIPS **££**
(✆01485-525886; www.ericsfishandchips.com; Drove Orchards; mains £9-15; ⊗noon-9pm) Eric's reimagines the classic British chippy in fine north Norfolk trendy style. It has retro menus, bright tiles, bar stools and dishes that breathe fresh life into a well-established formula: Gruyère and spinach *arancini*, haddock with black garlic aioli, scallops with lime. Eat in or take away.

ⓘ Getting There & Away

Burnham Deepdale is on the Coastliner bus route (www.lynxbus.co.uk), which stops here frequently en route between King's Lynn and Wells.

From Wells, there are regular connections through to Cromer.

King's Lynn

✆01553 / POP 12,200

Once one of England's most important ports, King's Lynn was long known as 'the Warehouse on the Wash' (the Wash being the neighbouring bay). In its heyday, it was

---

HOUGHTON HALL

Built for Britain's first de-facto prime minister, Sir Robert Walpole, in 1730, Palladian-style **Houghton Hall** (✆01485-528569; www.houghtonhall.com; near King's Lynn; adult/child £15/5; ⊗11am-5pm Wed, Thu & Sun May–late Sep; P) is worth seeing for the ornate staterooms alone, where stunning interiors overflow with gilt, tapestries, velvets and period furniture. The surrounding grounds, home to 600 deer, and the 2-hectare walled garden are dotted with contemporary sculptures, making for grand but pleasant rambling. Houghton Hall is just off the A148, 13 miles east of King's Lynn.

---

said you could cross from one side of the River Great Ouse to the other by simply stepping from boat to boat. Something of the salty port-town tang can still be sensed in old King's Lynn, with its cobbled lanes, vibrant weekly markets, and narrow streets flanked by old merchants' houses.

⦿ Sights

Stories of Lynn MUSEUM
(✆01553-777775; www.kingslynntownhall.com; Saturday Market Pl; adult/child £4/2; ⊗10am-4.30pm) A £2-million revamp has seen archive sources converted into multimedia exhibits, so you'll experience the stories of local seafarers, explorers, mayors and ne'er-do-wells. It's all set in the 15th-century Guildhall and parts of the town's Georgian jail, where you get to roam around the cells.

Lynn Museum MUSEUM
(www.museums.norfolk.gov.uk; Market St; adult/child £4.50/3.80; ⊗10am-5pm Tue-Sat, plus noon-4pm Sun Apr-Sep) High points here include a large hoard of Iceni gold coins and the **Seahenge Gallery**, which tells the story behind the construction and preservation of the early Bronze Age timber circle, which survived for 4000 years, despite being submerged on the Norfolk shoreline – it was only discovered in 1998. The exhibits include a life-size replica of the monument, which you can stand inside.

True's Yard MUSEUM
(✆01553-770479; www.truesyard.co.uk; North St; adult/child £3/1.50; ⊗10am-4pm Tue-Sat) Housed in two restored fishers' cottages –

the only legacy of the district's once bustling, fiercely independent fishing community – this museum explores the lives and traditions of the fisherfolk, who were packed like sardines into cottages such as these.

King's Lynn Minster   CHURCH
(St Margaret's Church; ☑01553-767090; www. stmargaretskingslynn.org.uk; St Margaret's Pl; ◎8am-6pm) The patchwork of styles here includes Flemish brasses and a remarkable 17th-century moon dial, which tells the tide, not the time. You'll find historic flood-level markings by the west door.

✵ Festivals & Events

King's Lynn Festival   CULTURAL
(www.kingslynnfestival.org.uk; ◎Jul) East Anglia's most important cultural gathering, with a diverse mix of music, from medieval ballads to opera, as well as literary talks.

⌂ Sleeping & Eating

★ Bank House   BOUTIQUE HOTEL ££
(☑01553-660492; www.thebankhouse.co.uk; King's Staithe Sq; s £85-120, d £115-220; ℗ 🛜) 🍴 There's so much to love here: a quayside setting, gently funky decor and luxury bathrooms all make this stylish Georgian town house pretty hard to turn down. The best bedroom (the expansive Captain's Room) is gorgeous; but even cheaper, river-view 'Cosy' is still charming.

Downstairs, the hip brasserie (dishes £7 to £18; open noon to 8.30pm) serves seriously good modern British food.

Market Bistro   MODERN BRITISH ££
(☑01553-771483; www.marketbistro.co.uk; 11 Saturday Market Pl; mains £14-22; ◎noon-2pm Wed-Sat, 6-8.30pm Tue-Sat) 🍴 A commitment to Norfolk ingredients has won this friendly, family-run bistro heaps of fans. Seasonal specials might include halibut with smoked cauliflower, or roast venison with beetroot relish. Their set menus (two/three/five courses £16/20/35) are creative and reveal a wide range of culinary skills.

ⓘ Information

Tourist Office (☑01553-763044; www.visit-westnorfolk.com; Purfleet Quay; ◎10am-5pm Mon-Sat, from noon Sun Apr-Sep, to 4pm Oct-Mar) Arranges guided heritage walks (adult/child £5/1) at 2pm on Tuesdays, Fridays and Saturdays between May and October.

ⓘ Getting There & Away

Bus Both Coasthopper (www.sanderscoaches.com) and Coastliner (www.lynxbus.co.uk) buses run regularly from King's Lynn along the shore all the way to Cromer (£10, 2½ hours).

Train There are hourly trains from Cambridge (£10, 50 minutes) via Ely, and also from London King's Cross (£37, 1¾ hours).

Birmingham & the Midlands

Best Places to Eat

→ The Cross (p401)

→ Hammer & Pincers (p449)

→ Chatsworth Estate Farm Shop Cafe (p467)

→ Fischer's Baslow Hall (p468)

→ Salt (p407)

Best Places to Stay

→ The Cow (p452)

→ Coombe Abbey Hotel (p399)

→ St Pauls House (p394)

→ George Hotel (p444)

→ Brownsover Hall (p400)

Why Go?

If you're searching for quintessentially English countryside – green valleys, chocolate-box villages of wonky black-and-white timbered houses, woodlands steeped in legend such as Nottinghamshire's Sherwood Forest, and stately homes that look like the last lord of the manor just clip-clopped out of the stables – you'll find it here in the country's heart.

You'll also find the relics of centuries of industrial history, exemplified by the World Heritage–listed mills of Ironbridge and the Derwent Valley, and by today's dynamic cities, including Britain's second-largest, Birmingham: a canal-woven industrial crucible reinvented as a cultural and creative hub, with striking 21st-century architecture and vibrant nightlife. Beyond them are tumbling hills where the air is so clean you can taste it. Walkers and cyclists flock to these pristine areas, particularly the Peak District National Park and the Shropshire Hills in the Marches, along the English–Welsh border, to vanish into the vastness of the landscape.

When to Go

→ February or March (depending when Lent falls) sees the wonderful chaos of Shrovetide football in Ashbourne.

→ Shakespeare takes a back seat to contemporary wordsmiths at Stratford's Literary Festival in April/May.

→ From May to September, on weekends and bank holidays, Shropshire Hills Shuttles run from the Carding Mill Valley near Church Stretton to the villages atop the Long Mynd heath and moorland plateau in the glorious Shropshire Hills.

→ June to September is the best season for walking and cycling in the Peak District.

→ Foodies will want to head to Ludlow's famous Food Festival in September.

Birmingham & the Midlands Highlights

1 Library of Birmingham (p390) Surveying the buzzing city of Birmingham from its library's rooftop 'secret garden'.

2 Peak District (p456) Hiking, cycling or driving through England's inaugural national park.

3 Lincoln (p439) Strolling the William the Conqueror–built castle walls overlooking the cathedral in this history-steeped city.

4 Ironbridge Gorge (p421) Museum-hopping in the birthplace of the Industrial Revolution.

5 King Richard III: Dynasty, Death & Discovery (p446) Learning about King Richard III's life and death and the extraordinary discovery of his remains in Leicester.

6 Stratford-upon-Avon (p403) Visiting the Bard's schoolroom and reimagined town house before catching a Royal Shakespeare Company performance in his Tudor hometown.

7 Morgan Motor Company (p413) Touring Great Malvern's venerable car factory and taking a car for a spin through the surrounding hills.

8 Burghley House (p444) Wandering the opulent halls and grand gardens of this stately Stamford home.

BIRMINGHAM & THE MIDLANDS BIRMINGHAM

🏃 Activities

Famous walking trails such as the Pennine Way and Limestone Way wind across the Peak District's hills, while challenging cycling routes include the Pennine Cycleway. The Marches, tracing the English–Welsh border, are also wonderful walking territory.

Watersports abound at Rutland Water; Hereford and Ironbridge Gorge offer canoeing and kayaking.

❶ Getting There & Around

Birmingham Airport (p397) and East Midlands Airport (p454), near Derby, are the main air hubs.

There are excellent rail connections to towns across the Midlands. **National Express** (☑ 08717 818181; www.nationalexpress.com), at Birmingham Coach Station, and local bus companies connect larger towns and villages to each other and to destinations further afield, though services are reduced in the low season. For general route information, consult Traveline for the **East Midlands** (☑ 0871 200 2233; www.travelineeastmidlands.co.uk) or the **West Midlands** (☑ 0871 200 2233; www.traveline midlands.co.uk). Ask locally about discounted all-day tickets.

BIRMINGHAM

☑ 0121 / POP 1,128,100

Regeneration, renewal and grand-scale construction continue apace in Britain's second-largest city. A state-of-the-art library, gleaming shopping centre atop revitalised New St station and beautifully restored Victorian buildings are just some of the successful initiatives of its Big City Plan, following on from the striking Mailbox and Bullring shopping malls and the iconic Selfridges building's 'bubblewrapped' facade. Work is underway on extensions to the Metro (light rail/tram) network, and on the centrepiece Paradise development's new hotels, public spaces, and glitzy residential and commercial buildings, with final completion due in 2025.

Alongside Birmingham's picturesque canals, waterside attractions, outstanding museums and galleries is an explosion of gastronomic restaurants, cool and/or secret cocktail bars and craft breweries. Thriving legacies of the city's industrial heritage include its Jewellery Quarter, Cadbury manufacturing plant and former custard factory turned cutting-edge creative hub.

And in 2022, Birmingham will host the Commonwealth Games. 'Brum', as it's locally dubbed, is buzzing.

◉ Sights

◉ City Centre

Birmingham's grandest civic buildings are clustered around pedestrianised Victoria Square, at the western end of New St, dominated by the stately facade of Council House (Victoria Sq), built between 1874 and 1879. Public art here includes modernist sphinxes and a fountain (Victoria Sq) topped by a naked female figure, dubbed 'the floozy in the Jacuzzi', overlooked by a disapproving statue of Queen Victoria (Victoria Sq).

To the west, Centenary Square is bookended by the art deco Hall of Memory War Memorial, the International Convention Centre (ICC; ☑ 0121-644 5025; www.the-icc.co.uk; 8 Centenary Sq) and the Symphony Hall (☑ 0121-780 3333; www.thsh.co.uk; 8 Centenary Sq). There's a gleaming golden statue (Centenary Sq) of the leading lights from Birmingham's Industrial Revolution: Matthew Boulton, James Watt and William Murdoch. Centenary Sq's showpiece is the spiffing Library of Birmingham (p390).

⭐ **Library of Birmingham**   LIBRARY
(☑ 0121-242 4242; www.birmingham.gov.uk/librar ies; Centenary Sq; ◷ ground fl 9am-9pm Mon & Tue, from 11am Wed-Fri, 11am-5pm Sat, rest of bldg 11am-7pm Mon & Tue, to 5pm Wed-Sat) Resembling a glittering stack of gift-wrapped presents, the Francine Houben–designed Library of Birmingham is an architectural triumph. The 2013-opened building features a subterranean amphitheatre, spiralling interior, viewing decks and glass elevator to the 7th-floor 'secret garden' with panoramic views over the city. In addition to its archives, and photography and rare-book collections (including Britain's most important Shakespeare collection), there are gallery spaces, 160-plus computers and a cafe. The British Film Institute Mediatheque provides free access to the National Film Archive.

Birmingham Back to Backs   HISTORIC BUILDING
(NT; ☑ 0121-666 7671; www.nationaltrust.org.uk; 55-63 Hurst St; 75min tour adult/child £8.65/5.25; ◷ tours by reservation Tue-Sun) Quirky tours of this cluster of restored back-to-back terraced houses take you through four working-class homes, telling the stories of those who lived

here between the 1840s and the 1970s. Book ahead by phone for the compulsory guided tour.

For an even more vivid impression of what life was like here, you can book to stay in basic three-storey period cottages at 52 and 54 Inge St (doubles with wi-fi from £130). Guests receive a free Back to Backs tour.

Birmingham Museum & Art Gallery
MUSEUM, GALLERY

(☑0121-348 8038; www.birminghammuseums. org.uk; Chamberlain Sq; ⊙10am-5pm Sat-Thu, from 10.30am Fri) **FREE** Major Pre-Raphaelite works by Rossetti, Edward Burne-Jones and others are among the highlights of the delightful Birmingham Museum & Art Gallery's impressive collection of ancient treasures and Victorian art. Excellent temporary exhibitions range from historical collections to emerging contemporary artists.

Its Edwardian Tearooms are an elegant spot for afternoon tea and have 'champagne buzzers' installed in its booths to order bubble at the touch of a button. There's also a casual cafe.

Birmingham Cathedral
CATHEDRAL

(☑0121-262 1840; www.birminghamcathedral. com; Colmore Row; by donation; ⊙7.30am-6.30pm Mon-Fri, to 5pm Sat & Sun) Dedicated to St Philip, this small but perfectly formed cathedral was constructed in a neoclassical style between 1709 and 1715. Pre-Raphaelite artist Edward Burne-Jones was responsible for the magnificent stained-glass windows.

Thinktank
MUSEUM

(☑0121-348 0000; www.birminghammuseums. org.uk; Millennium Point, Curzon St; adult/child £13.50/9.75, planetarium show £1.50; ⊙10am-5pm) Surrounded by the footprints of vanished factories, the Millennium Point development incorporates this entertaining and ambitious attempt to make science accessible to children. Highlights include galleries on the past (Birmingham's industrial breakthroughs), present (how stuff works) and future, as well as an outdoor science garden and a planetarium.

◉ Birmingham Canals

During the industrial age, Birmingham was a major hub on the English canal network and today the city has more miles of canals than Venice. Narrow boats still float through the heart of the city, passing a string of glitzy wharfside developments.

Ikon Gallery
GALLERY

(☑0121-248 0708; www.ikon-gallery.org; 1 Oozells Sq; ⊙11am-5pm Tue-Sun) **FREE** Within the glitzy Brindley Pl development of banking offices and designer restaurants, a converted Gothic schoolhouse contains the cutting-edge Ikon Gallery. Prepare to be thrilled, bemused or outraged, depending on your take on conceptual art.

National Sea Life Centre
AQUARIUM

(☑0121-643 6777; www.visitsealife.com; 3a Brindley Pl; £20, incl behind-the-scenes tour €23.50; ⊙10am-5pm Mon-Fri, to 6pm Sat & Sun) Exotic marine creatures including otters, jellyfish, piranhas and razor-jawed hammerhead sharks swim in the Sir Norman Foster–designed National Sea Life Centre. Prepurchase tickets online for fast-track entry and significant discounts off walk-in rates. Talks and feedings take place regularly. Book online too for 30-minute behind-the-scenes tours offering access to otherwise out-of-bounds areas, and for one-hour tours feeding turtles, penguins or (if you're game) sharks (£65 to £105; minimum age 12 to 14).

◉ Jewellery Quarter

Birmingham has been a major jewellery player since Charles II acquired a taste for it in 17th-century France. The gentrifying Jewellery Quarter, three-quarters of a mile northwest of the city centre, still produces 40% of UK-manufactured jewellery. Dozens of workshops open to the public are listed online at www.jewelleryquarter.net.

Take the Metro from Snow Hill or the train from Moor St to the Jewellery Quarter station.

Museum of the Jewellery Quarter
MUSEUM

(☑0121-348 8140; www.birminghammuseums.org. uk; 75 Vyse St; adult/child £7/3; ⊙10.30am-4pm Tue-Sat) The Smith & Pepper jewellery factory is preserved as it was on its closing day in 1981 after 80 years of operation. Guided tours lasting around one hour explain the long history of the trade in Birmingham and let you watch master jewellers at work. Entry to the temporary exhibition space and shop is free.

◉ Outlying Areas

★ **Barber Institute of Fine Arts**
GALLERY

(☑0121-414 7333; www.barber.org.uk; University of Birmingham, Edgbaston; ⊙10am-5pm Mon-Fri, from 11am Sat & Sun) **FREE** At the University of Birmingham, 3 miles south of the city

Birmingham

Jewellery Quarter (0.75mi)

15 Caroline St
18
Shadwell St
St Chads Queensway
James St 23
Brook St
St Paul's Sq
Mary Ann St
34
Weaman St
St Paul's Church
Frederick St
Vittoria St
Graham St
Ludgate Hill
Livery St
George St
Charlotte St
Newhall Hill
Snow Hill Station
Great Western Arcade (covered arcade)
Sandpits Parade
Summer Row
Great Charles St Queensway
Fleet St
Newhall St
Lionel St
Cornwall St
Edmund St
16
38 Bull St
19
Colmore Row
Birmingham & Fazeley Canal
Temple Row W
Newhall St
Temple Row
3
Cambridge St
22
32
Dalton St
4 5
24 25
Waterloo St
Temple St
Corporation St
Corporation Union St
8
1
Library of Birmingham
Chamberlain Sq
Town Hall
Victoria Sq
10 11
20
31
21
Cannon St
New St
Corporation St Bus Stand
13
36
Centenary Sq
9
Ethel St
Pinfold St
28
New Street Train Station
7
29
Gas St Basin
Bridge St
Holliday St
Navigation St
John Bright St
Hill St
Station St
33
St Martin's Circus
Broad St
26
Berkley St
Gas St
Granville St
Suffolk St Queensway
35
Pershore St
Simpsons (1mi)
39
17
Commercial St
Gough St
Blucher St
Thorp St
CHINATOWN
Worcester & Birmingham Canal
Holloway Head
Bristol St
Horsefair
Inge St
Hurst St
2
Arcadian Centre
27
GAY VILLAGE

centre, the Barber Institute of Fine Arts has an astonishing collection of Renaissance masterpieces; European masters, such as Rubens and Van Dyck; British greats, including Gainsborough, Reynolds and Turner; and classics from modern titans Picasso, Magritte and others. Trains run from Birmingham New St to University station (£2.50, seven minutes, every 10 minutes), from where it's a 10-minute walk.

Custard Factory   ARTS CENTRE
(☎0121-224 7777; www.custardfactory.co.uk; Gibb St; ⊗shops 10am-6pm Tue-Sat, event times vary) Just over a mile southeast of the city centre,

Digbeth's creative quarter centres on the Custard Factory, a hip art-and-design enclave set in the converted buildings of the factory that once churned out British favourite Bird's Custard. The open-plan space is now full of artists' galleries, quirky design boutiques, vintage-clothing outlets, one-off shops such as a skateboard specialist, and affordable, offbeat cafes and pop-up street-food stalls. Regular events include cinema screenings.

Cadbury World   MUSEUM
(☎0844 880 7667; www.cadburyworld.co.uk; Linden Rd, Bournville; adult/child £17/12.50; ⊗11am-4.30pm, hours vary) The next best thing to

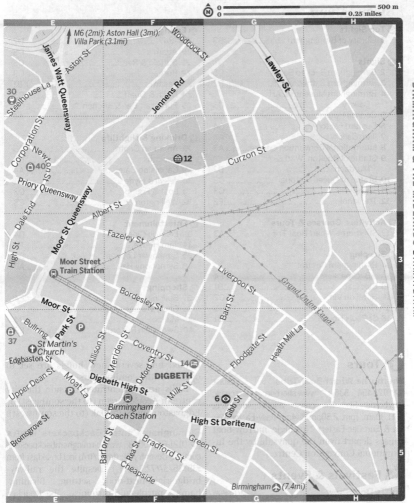

Willy Wonka's chocolate factory is Cadbury World, 4 miles south of Birmingham. It educates visitors about the history of cocoa and the Cadbury family, sweetening the deal with free samples, displays of chocolate-making machines and chocolate-themed attractions, including a 4D cinema with motion-sensor seats. Opening hours vary substantially; bookings are essential at peak times. Trains run from Birmingham New St to Bournville (£2.70, seven minutes, every 10 minutes), from where it's a signposted 10-minute walk.

Surrounding the aromatic chocolate works, pretty Bournville Village was built by the philanthropic Cadbury family to accommodate early-20th-century factory workers.

Aston Hall HISTORIC BUILDING
(☏ 0121-348 8100; www.birminghammuseums.
org.uk; Trinity Rd, Aston; house adult/child £8/3,
grounds free; ⊘ 11am-4pm Tue-Sun Easter-Oct)
Set in lush grounds 3 miles north of the city centre, this well-preserved hall was built in extravagant Jacobean style between 1618 and 1635. The sumptuous interiors are full of friezes, moulded ceilings and tapestries. Trains run from Birmingham New St to Aston station (£2.40, seven minutes, every 10 minutes), from where it's a 10-minute walk.

Birmingham

◎ **Top Sights**
1 Library of Birmingham B3

◎ **Sights**
2 Birmingham Back to Backs D5
3 Birmingham Cathedral........................ D2
4 Birmingham Museum & Art
   Gallery... C3
5 Council House...................................... C3
6 Custard Factory.................................... G4
7 Ikon Gallery A4
8 International Convention Centre.......... A3
9 Statue of Boulton, Watt &
   Murdoch B3
10 Statue of Queen Victoria...................... C3
11 The River C3
12 Thinktank... F2

◉ **Activities, Courses & Tours**
13 Sherborne Wharf Boat Trips................. A3

◉ **Sleeping**
14 Birmingham Central
   Backpackers F4
15 Bloc..B1
16 Hotel du Vin..C2
17 Hotel Indigo B5
18 St Pauls House......................................B1

◉ **Eating**
19 1847 .... D2
20 Adam's C3
21 Buffalo & Rye C3
22 Bureau C3
23 Lasan B1
24 Nosh & Quaff C3
25 Purecraft Bar & Kitchen....................... C3
26 Pushkar A4

◉ **Drinking & Nightlife**
27 Arcadian Centre D5
28 Bacchus D3
29 Canalside Cafe....................................... A4
30 Jekyll & Hyde E1
31 Lost & Found... C3
32 Wellington C3

◉ **Entertainment**
33 Electric Cinema D4
34 Jam House B1
35 Sunflower Lounge D4
36 Symphony Hall A3

◉ **Shopping**
37 Bullring...E4
38 Great Western Arcade D2
39 Mailbox... B4
40 Swordfish Records.................................E2

☞ Tours

Sherborne Wharf Boat Trips   CRUISE
(📞0121-454 5367; www.sherbornewharf.co.uk;
Sherborne St; 1hr cruise adult/child £8/6;
⊙11.30am, 1pm, 2.30pm & 4pm daily Easter-Nov,
Sat & Sun Dec-Easter) Nostalgic narrow-boat
cruises depart from the quayside by the International Convention Centre.

✯ Festivals & Events

Crufts Dog Show   ANIMAL SHOW
(www.crufts.org.uk; ⊙early Mar) The world's
greatest collection of pooches on parade at
the National Exhibition Centre over four
days in early March.

Birmingham Pride   LGBT
(www.birminghampride.com; ⊙late May) One of
the biggest and most colourful celebrations
of LGBTIQ culture in the country takes
place over a weekend in late May.

🛏 Sleeping

Chains dominate Birmingham's hotel scene,
which is aimed at business travellers, ensuring high weekday prices. Look out for cheap
deals at weekends. Accommodation is often

limited but several new hotels are set to
open over the coming years.

B&Bs are concentrated outside the city
centre in Acocks Green (to the southeast) or
Edgbaston and Selly Oak (to the southwest).

Birmingham Central Backpackers HOSTEL **£**
(📞0121-643 0033; www.birminghambackpackers.
com; 58 Coventry St; dm/d/tr/q incl breakfast from
£15/36/57/72; @🛈) Despite the railway-
bridge-right-next-door setting, Birmingham's purple-and-turquoise backpacker
hostel is recommended for its convenience
to the bus station and for its choice of clean,
multicoloured dorms or capsule-style pods.
Excellent facilities include a lounge with
DVDs and regular movie nights, a bar (note
you can't BYO alcohol) and a self-catering
kitchen.

★**St Pauls House**   BOUTIQUE HOTEL **££**
(📞0121-272 0999; www.saintpaulshouse.com;
15-20 St Paul's Sq; d from £119; 🅿✳🛈) Overlooking a park in the Jewellery Quarter,
this 2016-opened independent hotel has 34
fresh, contemporary rooms with welcoming
touches, such as hot-water bottles in woollen
covers. Upcycled decor in its hip bar (with

live music Friday to Sunday) and restaurant includes industrial-style ropes (as wall hangings and in furnishings) referencing the building's original use as a rope factory.

Hotel Indigo
BOUTIQUE HOTEL ££

(☑0121-643 2010; www.ihg.com; The Cube, Wharfside St; d from £119; 🛜🏊) A stylish operation on the 23rd and 24th floors of the Mailbox's annexe, The Cube, Birmingham's branch of the high-end Hotel Indigo chain marries a handy location with snazzy amenities, including a small swimming pool and great views from its 52 rooms (some with balconies).

Bloc
HOTEL ££

(☑0121-212 1223; www.blochotels.com; 77 Caroline St; d from £89; ✳🛜) Located in the Jewellery Quarter, Bloc excels in sharp, contemporary pod design. Rooms are tiny but space is cleverly stretched: flatscreen TVs are built into walls; there's under-bed storage; and bathrooms are compact but with luxe shower heads. Book carefully: rooms come with window or without.

Hotel du Vin
BOUTIQUE HOTEL £££

(☑0121-794 3005; www.hotelduvin.com; 25 Church St; d/ste from £129/191; ✳@🛜) Housed in the Victorian red-brick former Birmingham Eye Hospital, this branch of the upmarket Hotel du Vin chain has real class, with wrought-iron balustrades and classical murals. Its 66 rooms have spectacular bathrooms; there's a spa and a gym, a bistro with worn floorboards and a stellar wine list, plus a pub and lounge bar with comfy, duffed-up leather furniture.

✖ Eating

Buffalo & Rye
GRILL £

(www.buffaloandrye.co.uk; 11 Bennetts Hill; dishes £7.50-17; ⊙kitchen noon-11pm Mon-Thu, to midnight Fri & Sat, to 10pm Sun, bar to midnight Sun-Thu, to 2am Fri & Sat; 🛜) Aromatic Buffalo & Rye specialises in smoky slow-cooked ribs, jerk-marinated poussin and Cajun-spiced buffalo wings. Beneath upturned glass jars, cocktails such as its Moonshine Margarita with peach moonshine, peach syrup and lime juice are also infused with smoke. Dozens of craft beers are sourced from small US breweries.

Pushkar
INDIAN ££

(☑0121-643 7978; www.pushkardining.com; 245 Broad St; 2-/3-course lunch menus £11/14, mains £8.25-19; ⊙noon-2.30pm & 5-11.30pm Mon-Fri, 5-11.30pm Sat, to 11pm Sun) Classy north Indi-

an and Punjabi cuisine takes centre stage in this glass-fronted, white tableclothed, gold-trimmed dining room. The elegant presentation extends to boxed menus and serviette-wrapped naan bread as well as stunning cocktails. Lunch menus are an excellent deal. Its swanky spin-off, Praza (☑0121-456 4500; www.praza.co.uk; 94-96 Hagley Rd, Edgbaston; mains £7-18, banquet menus £29-39, Sun Indian afternoon tea adult/child £19/10; ⊙5-11.30pm Mon-Sat, 1-6pm Sun), in Edgbaston, is also superb.

Purecraft Bar & Kitchen
GASTROPUB ££

(☑0121-237 5666; www.purecraftbars.com; 30 Waterloo St; mains £13.50-19; ⊙kitchen noon-10pm Mon-Fri, from 9am Sat, noon-5pm Sun, bar 11am-11pm Mon-Thu, to midnight Fri & Sat, noon-10pm Sun) Fabulous dishes created in the open kitchen of this craft-beer-lover's paradise come with suggested beer pairings. The menu changes monthly but might include Lawless Lager–battered fish and chips (with Veltins Pilsener); Brewer's Grain asparagus and broad-bean risotto (with Odell St Lupulin American Pale Ale); or grilled plaice with beer-and-parsley butter and Jersey Royal new potatoes (with Purity Mad Goose).

Bureau
GASTROPUB ££

(☑0121-236 1110; www.thebureaubar.co.uk; 110 Colmore Row; mains £7-15.50, platters £16; ⊙noon-10pm Mon & Tue, to 11pm Wed & Thu, to midnight Fri, to 1am Sat) While this gleaming marble ex-office building dating from 1902 serves stupendous cocktails (like hickory-smoked Bloody Marys), it's worth visiting for its food. Winning deli-style dishes include a duck Scotch egg (soft-boiled duck egg encased in confit of duck and a deep-fried breadcrumb shell, served in a nest of watercress with red-onion jam). Its roof terrace is a suntrap.

Nosh & Quaff
AMERICAN ££

(☑0121-236 4246; www.noshandquaff.co.uk; 130 Colmore Row; mains £8-23, whole lobster £29.50; ⊙noon-10pm Sun-Thu, to 11pm Fri & Sat) North American fare at this cavernous venue spans gourmet burgers, hot dogs and slow-cooked, hickory-glazed ribs, plus sides such as charred corn on the cob and sweet-potato wedges with sour cream, but the star is the whole lobster flown in live from Canada and dressed with garlic and lemon-butter sauce. The rockin' bar serves great craft beers.

Lasan
INDIAN ££

(☑0121-212 3664; www.lasan.co.uk; 3-4 Dakota Bldgs, James St; mains £14.50-22; ⊙noon-2.30pm

& 6-11pm Mon-Fri, 6-11pm Sat, noon-9pm Sun) Expletive-loving chef Gordon Ramsay famously proclaimed elegant, upmarket Lasan, in Birmingham's Jewellery Quarter, Britain's 'Best Local Restaurant'. Its changing menu of elevated Indian dishes are served in an intimate dining room, accompanied by cocktails (and mocktails).

1847
VEGETARIAN, VEGAN ££

(⏱ 0121-236 2313; www.by1847.com; 26 Great Western Arcade, Colmore Row; 2-/3-course menu £22/29; ⏲ noon-2.30pm & 4.30-9pm Mon-Thu, noon-2.30pm & 4.30-9.30pm Fri, noon-9.30pm Sat, to 8pm Sun; ☑) ✐ Occupying two levels in a gorgeous, heritage-listed Victorian shopping arcade, this chic spot proves that vegetarian and vegan food can be cutting-edge, from starters such as goats-cheese bonbons with kohlrabi, chilli jam and chard to mains including buttermilk-battered halloumi, and lush desserts like rhubarb with soya custard, puffed rice and coconut snow.

★ Simpsons
BRITISH £££

(⏱ 0121-454 3434; www.simpsonsrestaurant.co.uk; 20 Highfield Rd, Edgbaston; menus lunch £45-75, dinner £75-110; ⏲ noon-2pm & 7-9pm Mon-Thu, noon-2pm & 7-9.30pm Fri & Sat, noon-4.30pm Sun; ☑🅿) It's worth the 2.5-mile journey southwest of the centre to this gorgeous Georgian mansion in leafy Edgbaston for sensational Michelin-starred menus (kids and vegetarians catered for) in its contemporary dining rooms. You can also stay in one of three luxurious bedrooms upstairs (£110) or take an all-day Saturday cookery class (£150 including three-course lunch) at its Eureka Kitchen. Book ahead.

Adam's
BRITISH £££

(⏱ 0121-643 3745; www.adamsrestaurant.co.uk; New Oxford House, 16 Waterloo St; 3-course midweek lunch menu £39.50, 3-course/tasting dinner menu £65/90; ⏲ noon-2pm & 7-9pm Tue-Sat) Michelin-starred Adam's wows with intricately prepared and presented flavour combinations, such as lamb sweetbreads with goats curd, mint and radish, monkfish with wild mussels, champagne and caviar, and pear, toasted hay, caramel and praline. English vintages are represented on its excellent wine list, which has extensive by-the-glass options. Book well ahead.

🍸 Drinking & Nightlife

Independent pubs and bars proliferate throughout the city.

Nightlife hubs in Birmingham include Broad St (aka the 'golden mile' – some say for the prevalence of fake tan here) and Chinatown's **Arcadian Centre** (www.thearcadian.co.uk; Hurst St; ⏲ individual venue hours vary).

Postindustrial Digbeth has alternative clubs and club events in and around the Custard Factory (p392).

★ Jekyll & Hyde
PUB

(⏱ 0121-236 0345; www.thejekyllandhyde.co.uk; 28 Steelhouse Lane; ⏲ noon-11pm Mon-Thu, to midnight Fri, to 1am Sat; 📶) Potent cocktails (or rather 'elixirs, concoctions and potions') at this trippy spot are served in sweets jars, watering cans, teapots and miniature bathtubs – even a top hat. Downstairs, Mr Hyde's emporium has a cosy drawing room and an *Alice in Wonderland*–themed courtyard; upstairs is Dr Jekyll's Gin Parlour with more than 90 different gins.

Lost & Found
BAR

(www.the-lostandfound.co.uk; 8 Bennett's Hill; ⏲ 11am-11pm Sun-Wed, to midnight Thu, to 1am Fri & Sat; 📶) Fictitious Victorian-era explorer/professor Hettie G Watson is the inspiration for the botanical-library theme of this bar in an 1869-built former bank. Inside the domed entrance, amid soaring columns and timber panelling, its elevated seating is surrounded by plants, books, globes and maps. Hettie's 'secret emporium' bar-within-a-bar has antique mirrors, brass and steel fixtures, and more plants.

Wellington
PUB

(www.thewellingtonrealale.co.uk; 37 Bennett's Hill; ⏲ 10am-midnight) The pastel wallpaper, timber bar and polished brass give the impression the Welly is frozen in time, but this spruced-up pub sheltering a timber-decked roof terrace is the best in the city for real ale. Its 27 hand-pulled beers and ciders include favourites from Black Country and Wye Valley as well as rare brews.

Bacchus
BAR

(⏱ 0121-632 5445; www.nicholsonspubs.co.uk; Burlington Arcade, New St; ⏲ 11am-11pm Mon-Thu, to 1am Fri & Sat, noon-10.30pm Sun; 📶) Buried beneath the Burlington Arcade, this darkened drinking den has the ambience of a decadent underworld. Down a faux-marble-encased staircase, crumbling pillars and giant Grecian murals give way to soaring medieval-style stone arches, swords, suits of armour and candelabras. There's a great range of cask ales, gins and whiskies.

Canalside Cafe CAFE
(☏ 0121-643 3170; 35 Worcester Bar, Gas St; ☺ 9am-11pm Mon-Sat, to 10.30pm Sun) Narrow boats glide past the terrace of this 18th-century lock-keeper's cottage, where the low-ceilinged interior is strung with nautical paraphernalia and warmed by an open fire. Drop by for a cuppa, a real ale, or a steaming mulled cider in winter.

☆ Entertainment

Sunflower Lounge LIVE MUSIC
(☏ 0121-632 6756; www.thesunflowerlounge.com; 76 Smallbrook Queensway; ☺ bar noon-11.30pm Sun-Tue, to 1am Wed & Thu, to 2am Fri & Sat) This quirky little indie bar pairs a magnificent alternative soundtrack with a packed program of live gigs and DJ nights.

Electric Cinema CINEMA
(www.theelectric.co.uk; 47-49 Station St; standard/sofa seats £10.50/12, sofa seats with waiter service £14.80) Topped by its art deco sign, this is the UK's oldest working cinema, operating since 1909. It screens mainly art-house films. Be waited upon in plush two-seater sofas, or have a drink in the small bar, which has a traditional absinthe fountain, cocktails themed around films currently showing and 'poptails' (popcorn-flavoured cocktails, in lieu of popcorn being available).

Jam House LIVE MUSIC
(☏ 0121-200 3030; www.thejamhouse.com; 3-5 St Paul's Sq; ☺ 6pm-midnight Tue & Wed, to 1am Thu, to 2am Fri & Sat) Pianist Jools Holland was the brains behind this moody, smart-casual music venue (dress accordingly). Acts range from jazz big bands to famous soul crooners. Over 21s only.

🔒 Shopping

Great Western Arcade SHOPPING CENTRE
(www.greatwesternarcade.co.uk; btwn Colmore Row & Temple Row; ☺ individual shop hours vary) Topped with a glass roof, this tile-floored Victorian-era arcade is a jewel filled with mostly independent shops.

Swordfish Records MUSIC
(www.swordfishrecords.co.uk; 66 Dalton St; ☺ 10am-5.30pm Mon-Sat) A Birmingham institution, this independent record shop down a tiny backstreet brims with new and secondhand vinyl (and some CDs), including its own label releases. Robert Plant, Duran Duran's John Taylor, Dave Grohl and Neil Diamond are among its past customers. It's a great place to find out about under-the-radar gigs and festivals.

Mailbox MALL
(www.mailboxlife.com; 7 Commercial St; ☺ mall 10am-7pm Mon-Sat, 11am-5pm Sun, individual shop hours vary) Birmingham's stylish canal-side shopping experience, the redevelopment of the former Royal Mail sorting office, comes complete with designer hotels, a fleet of up-market restaurants, the luxury department store Harvey Nichols and designer boutiques. Its super-snazzy metallic extension, the Cube (www.thecube.co.uk), houses Marco Pierre White's panoramic Steakhouse Bar & Grill on the 25th floor.

Bullring MALL
(www.bullring.co.uk; St Martin's Circus; ☺ 10am-8pm Mon-Fri, from 9am Sat, 11am-5pm Sun, individual shop hours vary) Split into two vast retail spaces – the East Mall and West Mall – the Bullring has all the international brands and chain cafes you could ask for, plus the standout architectural wonder of Selfridges, which looks out over the city like the compound eye of a giant robot insect.

ℹ Information

Comprehensive tourist information is available at www.visitbirmingham.com.

The ground-floor reception of the Library of Birmingham (p390) can also provide information for tourists.

➜ The city centre, especially south of the Bullring and on and around Broad St, can get very rowdy with revellers on weekend nights.

➜ Digbeth bus station and its surrounds can be quite rough after dark.

ℹ Getting There & Away

AIR

Birmingham Airport (BHX; ☏ 0800 655 6470; www.birminghamairport.co.uk), 8 miles east of the city centre, has direct flights to destinations around the UK and Europe, as well as direct long-haul routes to Dubai, India and the USA.

Fast and convenient trains run regularly between Birmingham New St and Birmingham International stations (£3.80, 15 minutes, every 10 minutes). Birmingham International is linked to the terminal by the Air-Rail Link monorail (free, two minutes, frequent), which runs from 3.30am to 12.30am.

Alternatively, take bus X1 (£2.40, 35 minutes, up to two hourly) from Moor St Queensway, which run 24 hours.

A taxi from the airport to the city centre costs about £45.

BUS

Most intercity buses run from **Birmingham Coach Station** (☏ 0871 781 8181; Mill Lane, Digbeth), but the X20 to Stratford-upon-Avon (£5.50, 1½ hours, hourly) also leaves from a more convenient stop on Carr's Lane, opposite Moor St station.

National Express (p390) coaches link Birmingham with major cities across the country, including the following:

London Victoria £4.70 to £13.80, 3¼ hours, hourly or better

Manchester £3 to £15, three hours, hourly

Oxford £6 to £25, 2¼ hours, eight daily

TRAIN

Most long-distance trains leave from Birmingham New St station, but Chiltern Railways runs to London Marylebone (£54, two hours, hourly) from Birmingham Snow Hill, and London Midland runs to Stratford-upon-Avon (£8.30, 50 minutes, half-hourly) from Birmingham Snow Hill and Birmingham Moor St stations.

Construction on the High Speed Rail (HS2) line – connecting London with Birmingham in just 40 minutes – is set to commence in 2019 and to be completed by 2026.

Useful services from New St:

Derby £19.30, 40 minutes, four per hour

Leicester £14.50, one hour, two per hour

London Euston £54, 1½ hours, up to six per hour

Manchester £37.40, 1¾ hours, half-hourly

Nottingham £33.10, 1¼ hours, two per hour

Shrewsbury £15.30, one hour, two per hour

❶ Getting Around

CAR

During central Birmingham's ongoing construction, traffic into and around the city is severely disrupted and parking is limited. Check with your accommodation about access (don't rely on your satnav, or assume hotels' car parks are operational). Updated details of road closures are posted at www.visitbirmingham.com/travel/latest-travel-updates.

PUBLIC TRANSPORT

Local buses run from a convenient hub on Corporation St, just north of where it connects with New St. For routes, pick up a free copy of the *Network Birmingham Map and Guide* from the tourist office. Single-trip tickets start from £1.50.

Be aware that bus stops may change during construction works in the city centre and journey times may be extended.

Birmingham's single tram line, the Metro (www.nxbus.co.uk), links New St station with Wolverhampton via the Jewellery Quarter, West Bromwich and Dudley. Tickets start from £1.

An extension from New St to Birmingham Town Hall and Centenary Sq is due to open in 2021.

Various saver tickets covering buses and trains are available from the **Network West Midlands Travel Centre** (www.networkwestmidlands.com; New St station; ◷8.30am-5.30pm Mon-Sat) at New St station.

WARWICKSHIRE

Warwickshire could have been just another picturesque county of rolling hills and market towns were it not for the English language's most famous wordsmith. William Shakespeare was born and died in Stratford-upon-Avon, and the sights linked to his life draw tourists from around the globe. Famous Warwick Castle attracts similar crowds. Elsewhere visitor numbers dwindle but Kenilworth has atmospheric castle ruins, Rugby celebrates the sport that takes its name at its World Rugby Hall of Fame, and Coventry, which will be in the spotlight in 2021 as the UK City of Culture, claims two extraordinary cathedrals and an unmissable motoring museum.

❶ Getting There & Around

Coventry is the main transport hub, with frequent rail connections to London Euston and Birmingham New St.

Coventry

☏ 024 / POP 352,900

Coventry was once a bustling hub for the production of cloth, clocks, bicycles, automobiles and munitions. It was this last industry that drew the German Luftwaffe in WWII: on the night of 14 November 1940, the city was so badly blitzed that the Nazis coined a new verb, *coventrieren,* meaning 'to flatten'. A handful of medieval streets that escaped the bombers offer a glimpse of old Coventry.

The city faced a further setback with the collapse of the British motor industry in the 1980s, but is undergoing a resurgence today thanks to its redeveloped and expanded university, and its vibrant cultural scene, which has seen it awarded the UK City of Culture 2021, bringing renewed investment and new openings during the run-up, and events and celebrations throughout the year.

◉ Sights

★ **Coventry Transport Museum** MUSEUM
(☎024-7623 4270; www.transport-museum.com; Hales St; museum free, speed simulator adult/child £5/3.50; ⊙10am-5pm) This stupendous museum has hundreds of vehicles, from horseless carriages to jet-powered, land-speed-record breakers. There's a brushed-stainless-steel DeLorean DMC-12 (of *Back to the Future* fame) with gull-wing doors, alongside a gorgeous Jaguar E-type, a Daimler armoured car and, for 1970s British-design-oddity enthusiasts, a Triumph TR7 and an Austin Allegro 'Special'. View the Thrust SCC, the current holder of the World Land Speed Record and the Thrust 2, the previous record holder. Kids will love the 4D Thrust speed simulator.

★ **Coventry Cathedral** CATHEDRAL
(☎024-7652 1210; www.coventrycathedral.org.uk; Priory Row; cathedral & ruins by donation, tower climb £4, Blitz Experience Museum £2; ⊙cathedral & tower 10am-4pm Mon-Sat, noon-3pm Sun, ruins 9am-5pm daily, museum closed Nov–mid-Feb, hours can vary) The evocative ruins of St Michael's Cathedral, built around 1300 but destroyed by Nazi incendiary bombs in the Blitz, stand as a memorial to Coventry's darkest hour and as a symbol of peace and reconciliation. Climb the 180 steps of the Gothic spire for panoramic views.

Symbolically adjoining St Michael's Cathedral's sandstone walls is the Sir Basil Spence–designed modernist architectural masterpiece Coventry Cathedral, with a futuristic organ, stained glass, and Jacob Epstein statue of the devil and St Michael.

Fargo Village CULTURAL CENTRE
(www.fargovillage.co.uk; Far Gosford St; ⊙hours vary) Markets, live-music gigs, moonlight cinema screenings and workshops (eg gardening or blacksmithing) are just some of the events that take place at this post-industrial cultural hub spread over a former car-radiator plant. Shops here sell everything from secondhand books to upcycled furniture; there are also art-and-craft studios, a hairdresser in a vintage Freedom Jetstream caravan, and a brilliant microbrewery, the Twisted Barrel, along with cafes, bakeries and street-food stalls.

St Mary's Guildhall HISTORIC BUILDING
(☎024-7683 3328; www.stmarysguildhall.co.uk; Bayley Lane; ⊙10am-4pm Sun-Thu mid-Mar–Sep) FREE One of the most evocative insights into pre-WWII Coventry is this half-timbered and brick hall where the town's trades came together in the Middle Ages to discuss town affairs. As one of England's finest guildhalls, it was chosen to be a jail for Mary Queen of Scots. Stained-glass windows glorify the kings of England; further down the hall stands WC Marshall's statue of Lady Godiva. Look out for the Coventry Tapestry, dating from 1500, depicting the Virgin Mary's assumption.

The vaulted stone undercroft houses an atmospheric cafe.

Herbert Art Gallery & Museum GALLERY, MUSEUM
(☎024-7623 7521; www.theherbert.org; Jordan Well; ⊙10am-4pm Mon-Sat, from noon Sun) FREE Behind Coventry's twin cathedrals, the Herbert has an eclectic collection of paintings and sculptures (including work by TS Lowry, Stanley Spencer and David Hockney), and thought-provoking history galleries spanning natural history and archaeology to Coventry's social and industrial history. Poignant and uplifting exhibits focus on conflict, peace and reconciliation. There are lots of activities aimed at kids, creative workshops for adults (calligraphy, silversmithing etc) and a light-filled cafe.

⌸ Sleeping & Eating

★ **Coombe Abbey Hotel** HISTORIC HOTEL ££
(☎024-7645 0450; www.coombeabbey.com; Brinklow Rd, Binley; d incl breakfast from £105; P🅿🛜) Queen Elizabeth I lived as a child at this 200-hectare estate, 5.5 miles east of Coventry. The 12th-century abbey was converted into a stately manor in 1581, with parkland, formal gardens and a lake. Many of its 119 uniquely decorated rooms have ornate four-poster beds; some have bathrooms hidden behind bookcases. There's a glass-paned conservatory restaurant and regular themed banquets.

Golden Cross PUB FOOD ££
(☎024-7655 1855; www.thegoldencrosscoventry. co.uk; 8 Hay Lane; mains £9-18; ⊙kitchen noon-9pm Mon-Sat, to 5pm Sun, bar 11am-11pm Mon-Thu, to 1am Fri & Sat, noon-8pm Sun; 🛜🐕) Constructed in 1583, this beautiful Tudor building with beamed ceilings, original stained glass and a toasty wood-burning stove is an inviting place for a pint, but the food (much of it gluten-free), such as ale-battered scampi with mushy peas or sirloin with Stilton

WORTH A TRIP

RUGBY

Warwickshire's second-largest hub, Rugby is an attractive market town whose history dates back to the Iron Age. But it's most famous for the sport that was invented here and now takes its name, and is a place of pilgrimage for fans.

The game was invented at prestigious Rugby School in 1823 when William Webb Ellis is said to have caught the ball during a football match and broken the rules by running with it. Situated just across from the **Webb Ellis Rugby Football Museum** (☑01788-567777; 5-6 Matthews St; ⊙9.30am-5pm Mon-Sat) FREE, the school itself is closed to the public, but you can peek at the hallowed ground through the gates on Barby Rd. A **statue of William Webb Ellis** (cnr Lawrence Sheriff St & Dunchurch Rd) stands outside the main Rugby School gates.

The whizz-bang interactive World Rugby Hall of Fame is inside the **Rugby Art Gallery & Museum** (☑01788-533201; www.ragm.co.uk; Little Elborow St; gallery & museum free, World Rugby Hall of Fame adult/child £6/3; ⊙gallery & museum 10am-5pm Tue-Fri, to 4pm Sat, World Rugby Hall of Fame 10am-5pm Mon-Sat, to 4pm Sun) complex.

The top place to stay is **Brownsover Hall** (☑01788-546100; www.brownsoverhall.co.uk; Brownsover Lane, Old Brownsover; d from £90; P🔊), a Grade II–listed Gothic Revival manor (where Frank Whittle designed the turbo jet engine). Set in 2.8 hectares of woodland and manicured gardens, it's 2.7 miles north of Rugby.

Rugby is 13 miles east of Coventry, served by regular trains (£6, 10 minutes, up to four per hour). Trains also link Rugby with Birmingham (£9.90, 40 minutes, up to four per hour) and Leicester (£14.70, 1¼ hours, hourly).

---

sauce, merits a visit in its own right. Mellow live music plays upstairs on weekends.

ℹ Information

Tourist Office (☑024-7623 4284; www.visitcoventryandwarwickshire.co.uk; Herbert Art Gallery & Museum, Jordan Well; ⊙10am-4pm Mon-Sat, from noon Sun) Located in the reception area of the Herbert Art Gallery & Museum (p399).

ℹ Getting There & Away

BUS

Buses X17 and X18 (every 20 minutes) go to Kenilworth (£3, 35 minutes) and Warwick (£3.20, 40 minutes).

TRAIN

Regular services include the following:
Birmingham (£4.70, 30 minutes, every 10 minutes)
London Euston (£49, 1¼ hours, every 10 to 20 minutes)
Rugby (£6, 10 minutes, up to four per hour)

Kenilworth

☑01926 / POP 22,413

An easy deviation off the A46 between Warwick and Coventry, the atmospheric ruin of Kenilworth Castle was the inspiration for Walter Scott's 1821 novel *Kenilworth,* and it still feels pretty inspiring today. The town is essentially split into two by Finham Brook: the historic village-like area, of most interest to visitors, is on the northern side, while the southern side is the commercial centre.

⊙ Sights

Kenilworth Castle CASTLE, RUINS
(EH; ☑01926-852078; www.english-heritage.org.uk; Castle Green; adult/child £11.30/6.80; ⊙10am-6pm Apr-Sep, to 5pm Oct, to 4pm Sat & Sun Nov–mid-Feb, to 4pm Wed-Sun mid-Feb–Mar) This spine-tingling ruin sprawls among fields and hedges on Kenilworth's outskirts. Built in the 1120s, the castle survived the longest siege in English history in 1266, when the forces of Lord Edward (later Edward I) threw themselves at the moat and battlements for six solid months. The fortress was dramatically extended in Tudor times, but it fell in the English Civil War and its walls were breached and water defences drained. Don't miss the magnificent restored Elizabethan gardens.

Stoneleigh Abbey HISTORIC BUILDING
(☑01926-858535; www.stoneleighabbey.org; B4115; adult/child grounds & tour £11/4.50, grounds only £5/1; ⊙tours 11.30am, 1pm & 2.30pm Sun-Thu Easter-Oct, grounds 11am-5pm Sun-Thu Easter-Oct; P) The kind of stately home that makes

film directors go weak at the knees, Stoneleigh name-drops Charles I and Jane Austen among its past visitors. Completed in 1726 and only viewable on tours (included in admission), the splendid Palladian west wing contains richly detailed plasterwork ceilings and wood-panelled rooms. A 'reflecting lake' effect is created by the widened stretch of the River Avon, which runs through the grounds. It's 2 miles east of Kenilworth.

🛏 Sleeping & Eating

The Old Bakery B&B ££
(☑ 01926-864111; www.theoldbakery.eu; 12 High St; s/d/tr from £75/95/115; P🛜) East of the castle, with restaurants nearby, this appealing B&B has attractively attired modern rooms and a cosy, welcoming bar (open 5.30pm to 11pm Monday to Thursday, 5pm to 11pm Friday and Saturday, and 5pm to 10.30pm Sunday) serving well-kept real ales on the ground floor.

★ The Cross GASTROPUB £££
(☑ 01926-853840; www.thecrosskenilworth.co.uk; 16 New St; 2-/3-course lunch menus £30/32.50, 5-course dinner tasting menu £75, mains £28-42; ⊗ noon-2pm & 6.30-9.30pm Tue-Thu, noon-2pm & 6-9.30pm Fri, noon-2.30pm & 6-9.30pm Sat, noon-3.30pm Sun; ☑🚼) One of England's culinary jewels, this Michelin-starred gastropub occupies a romantic 19th-century inn. Prepare to be dazzled by exquisite creations like seared scallops with seaweed butter, duck breast with smoked beetroot and raspberry vinegar, and brioche pudding with apple-and-blackberry compote and bay leaf ice cream.

Vegetarian menus are available; junior gourmands have their own three-course children's menu (£12).

❶ Getting There & Away

From Monday to Saturday, buses X17 and X18 run every 20 minutes between Coventry (£3, 25 minutes) and Kenilworth and on to Warwick (£4.20, 30 minutes). There are no buses on Sunday.

Warwick

☑ 01926 / POP 31,345
Regularly name-checked by Shakespeare, Warwick was the ancestral seat of the earls of Warwick, who played a pivotal role in the Wars of the Roses. Despite a devastating fire in 1694, Warwick remains a treasure house of medieval architecture, with rich veins of history and charming streets, dominated by the soaring turrets of Warwick Castle.

◉ Sights

★ Warwick Castle CASTLE
(☑ 01926-495421; www.warwick-castle.com; Castle Lane; castle adult/child £27/24, castle & dungeon £32/28; ⊗ 10am-5pm Apr-Sep, to 4pm Oct-Mar; P) Founded in 1068 by William the Conqueror, stunningly preserved Warwick Castle is the biggest show in town. The ancestral home of the earls of Warwick remains impressively intact, and the Tussauds Group has filled the interior with flamboyant, family-friendly attractions that bring the castle's rich history to life. Waxworks populate the private apartments; there are also jousting tournaments, daily trebuchet firings, themed evenings and a dungeon. Discounted online tickets provide fast-track entry. Great accommodation options (p402) are available on-site.

Collegiate Church of St Mary CHURCH
(☑ 01926-403940; www.stmaryswarwick.org.uk; Old Sq; church by donation, tower adult/child £3/1.50; ⊗ 10am-4.30pm Mon-Sat, from 12.30pm Sun) This magnificent 1123-founded Norman church was badly damaged in the Great Fire of Warwick in 1694, but is packed with 16th- and 17th-century tombs. Highlights include the Norman crypt with a 14th-century extension; the impressive Beauchamp Chapel, built between 1442 and 1464 to enshrine the mortal remains of the earls of Warwick; and, up 134 steps, the tower, which provides supreme views over town (kids must be aged over eight).

Lord Leycester Hospital HISTORIC BUILDING
(☑ 01926-491422; www.lordleycester.com; 60 High St; adult/child £8.50/5, garden only £2; ⊗ 10am-5pm Tue-Sun Apr-Sep, to 4pm Oct-Mar) A survivor of the 1694 fire, the wonderfully wonky Lord Leycester Hospital has been used as a retirement home for soldiers (but never as a hospital) since 1571. Visitors can wander around the chapel, guildhall, regimental museum and restored walled garden, which includes a knot garden and a Norman arch.

🛏 Sleeping & Eating

Tilted Wig PUB ££
(☑ 01926-400110; www.tiltedwigwarwick.co.uk; 11 Market Pl; d £85; 🛜) Bang on the central Market Pl, this brilliantly named 17th-century

Warwick

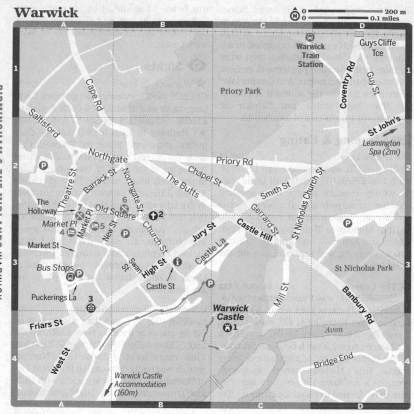

Warwick

◎ Top Sights
1 Warwick Castle	C4

◎ Sights
2 Collegiate Church of St Mary	B3
3 Lord Leycester Hospital	A3

🛏 Sleeping
4 Rose & Crown	A3
5 Tilted Wig	A3

✖ Eating
6 Old Coffee Tavern	B2
7 Tailors	A3

Georgian inn has four snug but comfortable rooms overlooking the square and some of the better pub food in town, such as Warwickshire rare-breed sausages with garlic mash (mains £9 to £18).

Rose & Crown   PUB ££
(📞01926-411117; www.roseandcrownwarwick. co.uk; 30 Market Pl; s/d/f incl breakfast from £90/100/110; 🛜) Dating from the 17th century, this family-run inn on the town square has five lovely, spacious and tastefully decorated rooms upstairs from the pub and another eight in the building across the lane, as well as great ales and bottled beers, and an excellent Modern British menu (mains £13 to £27.50). Four of its rooms are set up for families.

★ Warwick Castle Accommodation   RESORT £££
(📞0871 097 1228; www.warwick-castle.com; Warwick Castle; tower ste/lodge/glamping per night from £550/242/212; ⊙ tower ste & lodge year-round, glamping Jul–early Sep; P🛜) Atmospheric accommodation at Warwick Castle (p401) includes two days' castle admission. The castle itself contains two four-poster-bed Tower

Suites (including a private tour, champagne and breakfast). The riverside Knight's Village has woodland and knight-themed lodges (all with terraces and some with kitchenettes) and medieval entertainment. Themed tents (with shared bathrooms) make up the glamping ground. All sleep up to five people.

Old Coffee Tavern
BRITISH ££

(📞 01926-679737; www.theoldcoffeetavern.co.uk; 16 Old Sq; mains £9.50-12.50; ⊙ kitchen 7am-10pm Mon-Fri, from noon Sat, noon-8pm Sun, bar 7am-11pm Mon-Thu, to 12.30am Fri, 8am-12.30am Sat, to 10pm Sun; 🐾) An 1880-built beauty with many of its Victorian features intact, this tavern was originally established as a teetotal alternative to Warwick's pubs. Today you can order real ales, craft ciders, cocktails and wines, along with elevated versions of British classics like toad-in-the-hole and chicken-and-ham-hock pie. Upstairs are 10 stylish oyster-toned guest rooms (doubles including breakfast from £92.50).

Tailors
MODERN BRITISH £££

(📞 01926-410590; www.tailorsrestaurant.co.uk; 22 Market Pl; 2-/3-course lunch menus £17/21, 2-/3-/6-course dinner menus £29.50/39.50/60; ⊙ noon-2pm & 6.30-9pm Tue-Sat) Set in a former tailor's shop, this elegant restaurant, owned and run by two hot-shot chefs, serves prime ingredients – guinea fowl, pork belly and lamb from named farms – complemented by intricate creations like brown butter crumb, powdered coleslaw, and black truffle and fennel candy.

ℹ️ Information

Tourist Office (📞 01926-492212; www.visitwarwick.co.uk; Court House, Jury St; ⊙ 9.30am-4.30pm Mon-Fri, from 10am Sat year-round, plus 10am-4pm Sun Apr–mid-Dec) Within the flagstone-floored Court House (1725).

ℹ️ Getting There & Away

BUS

Buses depart from outside **Westgate House** (Market St).

National Express coaches serve London Victoria (£20.50, four hours, up to four daily).

Stagecoach X17 and X18 run to Coventry (£5.80, 1¼ hours, every 20 minutes Monday to Saturday) via Kenilworth (£4.20, 30 minutes). Bus X18 also runs to Stratford-upon-Avon (£5.40, 40 minutes, two per hour Monday to Saturday, hourly Sunday).

TRAIN

The train station is half a mile northeast of the town centre on Station Rd.

Trains run to Birmingham (£7.10, 30 minutes, hourly), Stratford-upon-Avon (£6.90, 30 minutes, every two hours) and London Marylebone (£34, 1½ hours, every 30 minutes; some require a change in Leamington Spa).

Stratford-upon-Avon

📞 01789 / POP 27,455

The author of some of the most quoted lines ever written in the English language, William Shakespeare was born in Stratford in 1564 and died here in 1616. Experiences linked to his life in this unmistakably Tudor town range from the touristy (medieval recreations and Bard-themed tearooms) to the humbling (Shakespeare's modest grave in Holy Trinity Church) and the sublime (taking in a play by the world-famous Royal Shakespeare Company).

👁️ Sights

⭐ Shakespeare's New Place
HISTORIC SITE

(📞 01789-338536; www.shakespeare.org.uk; cnr Chapel St & Chapel Lane; adult/child £12.50/8; ⊙ 10am-5pm Apr-Aug, to 4.30pm Sep & Oct, to 3.30pm Nov-Feb) When Shakespeare retired, he swapped the bright lights of London for a comfortable town house at New Place, where he died of unknown causes in April 1616. The house was demolished in 1759, but an attractive Elizabethan knot garden occupies part of the grounds. A major restoration project has uncovered Shakespeare's kitchen and incorporated new exhibits in a reimagining of the house as it would have been. You can also explore the adjacent Nash's House, where Shakespeare's granddaughter Elizabeth lived.

⭐ Shakespeare's Birthplace
HISTORIC BUILDING

(📞 01789-204016; www.shakespeare.org.uk; Henley St; adult/child £17.50/11.50; ⊙ 9am-5pm Apr-Aug, to 4.30pm Sep & Oct, 10am-3.30pm Nov-Mar) Start your Shakespeare quest at the house where the renowned playwright was born in 1564 and spent his childhood days. John Shakespeare owned the house for a period of 50 years. William, as the eldest surviving son, inherited it upon his father's death in 1601 and spent his first five years of marriage here. Behind a modern facade, the house has restored Tudor rooms, live presentations from famous Shakespearean

Stratford-upon-Avon

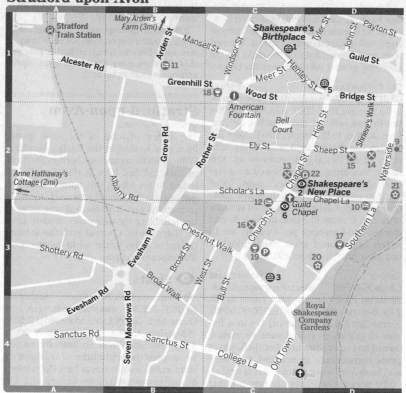

characters and an engaging exhibition on Stratford's favourite son.

Holy Trinity Church
CHURCH

(☎ 01789-266316; www.stratford-upon-avon.org; Old Town; Shakespeare's grave adult/child £3/2; ⏰ 9am-6pm Mon-Sat, 12.30-5pm Sun Apr-Sep, 9am-5pm Mon-Sat, 12.30-5pm Sun Mar & Oct, 9am-4pm Mon-Sat, 12.30-5pm Sun Nov-Feb) The final resting place of the Bard, where he was also baptised and where he worshipped, is said to be the most visited parish church in England. Inside are handsome 16th- and 17th-century tombs (particularly in the Clopton Chapel), some fabulous carvings on the choir stalls and, of course, the grave of William Shakespeare, with its ominous epitaph: 'cvrst be he yt moves my bones'.

MAD Museum
MUSEUM

(☎ 01789-269356; www.themadmuseum.co.uk; 4-5 Henley St; adult/child £7.60/5.20; ⏰ 10am-5.30pm) Fun, hands-on exhibits at Stratford's Mechanical Art & Design Museum (aka MAD) make physics accessible for kids, who can build their own gravity-propelled marble run, use their energy to light up electric panels, and pull levers and turn cranks to animate displays. Tickets are valid all day, so you can come and go as you please.

Mary Arden's Farm
HISTORIC SITE, FARM

(☎ 01789-338535; www.shakespeare.org.uk; Station Rd, Wilmcote; adult/child £15/10; ⏰ 10am-5pm Apr-Aug, to 4.30pm Sep & Oct; ⊞) Shakespeare genealogists can trace the family tree to the childhood home of the Bard's mother at Wilmcote, 3 miles west of Stratford. Aimed squarely at families, the working farm traces country life over the centuries, with nature trails, falconry displays and a collection of rare-breed farm animals. You can get here on the City Sightseeing bus (☎ 01789-299123; www.city-sightseeing.com; adult/child 24hr £16.82/8.41, 48hr £25.52/13; ⏰ 9.30am-5pm Apr-Sep, to 4pm Oct-Mar), or cycle via Anne

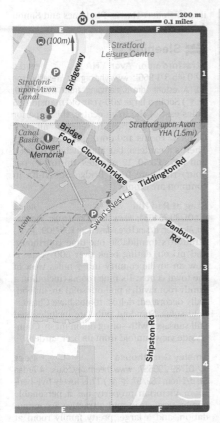

Hathaway's Cottage, following the Stratford-upon-Avon Canal towpath. Note that, unlike the other Shakespeare properties, it's closed from November to March.

Shakespeare's School Room HISTORIC SITE
(☏ 01789-203170; www.shakespearesschoolroom. org; King Edward VI School, Church St; adult/child £8/5; ⊗ 11am-5pm) Shakespeare's alma mater, King Edward VI School (still a prestigious grammar school today), incorporates a vast black-and-white timbered building, dating from 1420, that was once the town's guildhall, where Shakespeare's father John served as bailiff (mayor). In the Bard's former classroom, you can sit in on mock-Tudor lessons, watch a short film and test yourself on Tudor-style homework.

Anne Hathaway's Cottage HISTORIC BUILDING
(☏ 01789-338532; www.shakespeare.org.uk; Cottage Lane, Shottery; adult/child £12.50/8; ⊗ 9am-5pm Apr-Aug, to 4.30pm Sep & Oct, 10am-3.30pm Nov-Mar) Before tying the knot with Shakespeare, Anne Hathaway lived in Shottery, 1 mile west of the centre of Stratford, in this delightful thatched farmhouse. As well as period furniture, it has gorgeous gardens and an orchard and arboretum, with examples of all the trees mentioned in Shakespeare's plays. A footpath (no bikes allowed) leads to Shottery from Evesham Pl. The City Sightseeing (p404) bus stops here.

Hall's Croft HISTORIC BUILDING
(☏ 01789-338533; www.shakespeare.org.uk; Old Town; adult/child £8.50/5.50; ⊗ 10am-5pm Apr-Aug, to 4.30pm Sep & Oct, 11am-3.30pm Nov-Feb) The handsome Jacobean town house belonging to Shakespeare's daughter Susanna and her husband, respected doctor John

Hall, stands south of Stratford's centre. The exhibition offers fascinating insights into medicine in the 16th and 17th centuries, and the lovely walled garden sprouts with aromatic herbs employed in medicinal preparations.

👉 Tours

Avon Boating
BOATING

(📞01789-267073; www.avon-boating.co.uk; The Boathouse, Swan's Nest Lane; river cruises adult/child £6/4; ⊙9am-dusk Easter-Oct) Avon Boating runs 40-minute river cruises that depart every 20 minutes from either side of the main bridge. It also hires rowboats, canoes and punts (per hour £6) and motorboats (per hour £40).

Stratford Town Walk
WALKING

(📞07855 760377; www.stratfordtownwalk.co.uk; town walk adult/child £6/3, ghost walk £7/5; ⊙town walk 11am Mon-Fri, 11am & 2pm Sat & Sun, ghost walk by reservation 7.30pm Sat) Popular two-hour guided town walks depart from Waterside, opposite Sheep St (prebooking not necessary). Chilling ghost walks lasting 90 minutes leave from the same location but must be booked ahead.

✨ Festivals & Events

Stratford Literary Festival
LITERATURE

(📞01789-207100; www.stratfordliteraryfestival.co.uk; ⊙late Apr/early May) A highlight of Stratford's cultural calendar is the week-long annual Stratford Literary Festival, which has attracted literary big-hitters of the cal-

---

ℹ️ SHAKEPEARE HISTORIC HOMES

Five of the most important buildings associated with Shakespeare – Shakespeare's Birthplace (p403), Shakespeare's New Place (p403), Hall's Croft (p405), Anne Hathaway's Cottage (p405) and Mary Arden's Farm (p404) – contain museums that form the core of the visitor experience at Stratford. All are run by the Shakespeare Birthplace Trust (www.shakespeare.org.uk).

A Full Story ticket (adult/child £22/14.50) covering all five properties is available online or at the sites and provides up to a 60% discount off individual admission prices.

---

ibre of Robert Harris, PD James and Simon Armitage.

🛏️ Sleeping

Stratford-upon-Avon YHA
HOSTEL £

(📞0345 371 9661; www.yha.org.uk; Wellesbourne Rd, Alveston; dm/d/glamping from £13/58/49; 🅿️🛜) Set in a large 200-year-old mansion 1.5 miles east of the town centre, this superior 134-bed hostel attracts travellers of all ages. Of its 32 rooms and dorms, 16 are en suite. There's a canteen, bar and kitchen. Buses 6 and X17 (£3.50, 12 minutes, up to two per hour) run here from Bridge St. Wi-fi's in common areas only.

Stag at Red Hill
INN ££

(📞01789-764634; www.stagredhill.co.uk; Alcester Rd, Alcester; d/f incl breakfast from £99/109; 🅿️🛜) Stratford's formidable one-time courthouse and prison, dating back over 500 years, is now an idyllic country inn 4 miles west of the town centre. Its nine rooms (including a family room with a pull-out sofa) are individually decorated; deluxe rooms have Chesterfield sofas. Standout pub fare includes Red Hill sausages with spring onion mash. Countryside views unfold from its beer garden.

Emsley Guesthouse
B&B ££

(📞01789-299557; www.theemsley.co.uk; 4 Arden St; d/f from £82/97; 🅿️🛜) This lovely five-bedroom Victorian property has a personable owner, very clean and attractive accommodation, and a large, pretty family room at the top with an exposed-beam ceiling. Two rooms are set up for families. There's a two-night minimum stay.

Townhouse
BOUTIQUE HOTEL £££

(📞01789-262222; www.stratfordtownhouse.co.uk; 16 Church St; d incl breakfast from £130; 🛜) Some of the dozen rooms at this exquisite hotel have free-standing claw-foot bathtubs, and all have luxurious bedding and Temple Spa toiletries. The building is a centrally located 400-year-old gem with a first-rate restaurant (mains £9.50-24; ⊙kitchen noon-3pm & 5-10pm Mon-Fri, noon-10pm Sat, to 8pm Sun, bar 8am-midnight Mon-Sat, to 10.30pm Sun; 🛜) Light sleepers should avoid room 1, nearest the bar. There's a minimum two-night stay on weekends.

Arden Hotel
HOTEL £££

(📞01789-298682; www.theardenhotelstratford.com; Waterside; s/d incl breakfast from £115/130; 🅿️🛜) Facing the Swan Theatre, this elegant property has a sleek brasserie and champagne bar. Its 45 rooms feature designer fabrics and its bathrooms are full of polished marble. Interconnecting rooms are ideal for families. Kids receive welcome bags with games.

✗ Eating

Fourteas CAFE £
(☑ 01789-293908; www.thefourteas.co.uk; 24 Sheep St; dishes £4.60-7.55, afternoon tea with/without Prosecco £20/15; ⊙ 9.30am-5pm Mon-Sat, 11am-4.30pm Sun) Breaking with Stratford's Shakespearean theme, this tearoom takes the 1940s as its inspiration with beautiful old teapots, framed posters and staff in period costume. As well as premium loose-leaf teas and homemade cakes, there are all-day breakfasts, soups, sandwiches (including a chicken and bacon 'Churchill club') and lavish afternoon teas.

Lambs MODERN EUROPEAN ££
(☑ 01789-292554; www.lambsrestaurant.co.uk; 12 Sheep St; mains £14.50-23.50; ⊙5-9pm Mon, noon-2pm & 5-9pm Tue-Sat, noon-2pm & 6-9pm Sun) Lambs swaps Shakespeare chintz in favour of modern elegance but throws in authentic 16th-century ceiling beams for good measure. The menu embraces Gressingham duck, Hereford steaks and, yes, lamb (a herb-crusted rack with dauphinoise potatoes, mustard green beans and rosemary jus), backed up by a strong wine list.

Edward Moon's BRITISH ££
(☑ 01789-267069; www.edwardmoon.com; 9 Chapel St; mains £12.25-17; ⊙noon-2.30pm & 5-9.30pm Mon-Fri, noon-3pm & 5-10pm Sat, noon-3pm & 5-9pm Sun; 🖐) Named after a famous travelling chef who cooked up the flavours of home for the British colonial service, this snug independent restaurant serves hearty English dishes, such as steak-and-ale pie and meltingly tender lamb shank with redcurrant gravy. Kids get a two-course menu for £6.95.

Rooftop Restaurant INTERNATIONAL ££
(☑ 01789-403449; www.rsc.org.uk; 3rd fl, Royal Shakespeare Theatre, Waterside; mains £12.50-25.50; ⊙10.30am-9.30pm Mon-Thu, to 9.45pm Sat, to 3.30pm Sun; 🔊🖐) Glorious views of the River Avon extend from the dining room and outdoor terrace of this restaurant atop the Royal Shakespeare Theatre (p408). Global flavours range from crab linguine to Sri Lankan cauliflower, squash and cashew

---

WORTH A TRIP

CHARLECOTE PARK

A youthful Shakespeare allegedly poached deer in the grounds of Charlecote (NT; ☑ 01789-470277; www.nationaltrust.org.uk; Loxley Lane, Charlecote; house & garden adult/child £11.45/5.70, garden only £7.60/3.80; ⊙ house 11am-4.30pm Thu-Tue mid-Mar–Oct, noon-3.30pm Thu-Tue mid-Feb–mid-Mar, noon-3.30pm Sat & Sun Nov & Dec, garden 10.30am-5.30pm Mar-Oct, to 4.30pm Nov-Feb), a lavish Elizabethan pile on the River Avon, 5 miles east of Stratford-upon-Avon. Fallow deer still roam the grounds today. The interiors were restored from Georgian chintz to Tudor splendour in 1823. Highlights include Victorian kitchens, filled with culinary moulds, and an original 1551 Tudor gatehouse.

Bus X17 runs to Charlecote hourly from Stratford (£4.40, 30 minutes, two per hour Monday to Friday, hourly Saturday and Sunday).

---

curry; there are various set menus, including for vegans and gluten-free diners, and for kids. Its bar mixes the best cocktails in town.

★ Salt BRITISH £££
(☑ 01789-263566; www.salt-restaurant.co.uk; 8 Church St; 2-/3-course menus lunch £33.50/37, dinner £37/45; ⊙noon-2pm & 6.30-10pm Wed-Sat, noon-2pm Sun) Stratford's gastronomic star is this intimate, beam-ceilinged bistro. In the semi-open kitchen, owner-chef Paul Foster produces stunning creations influenced by the seasons: spring might see glazed parsley root with chicory and black-truffle shavings, onglet of beef with malted artichoke, cured halibut with oyster and apple emulsion, and sea-buckthorn mille-feuille with fig and goats-milk ice cream.

🍺 Drinking & Nightlife

★ Old Thatch Tavern PUB
(www.oldthatchtavernstratford.co.uk; Greenhill St; ⊙11.30am-11pm Mon-Sat, from noon Sun; 🔊) To truly appreciate Stratford's olde-worlde atmosphere, join the locals for a pint at the town's oldest pub. Built in 1470, this thatch-roofed treasure has great real ales and a gorgeous summertime courtyard.

BIRMINGHAM & THE MIDLANDS STRATFORD-UPON-AVON

NATIONAL BREWERY CENTRE

Burton-upon-Trent grew up around its 7th-century abbey, which was famed for its healing spring waters. Brewing began here around 1700, and in the early 18th century the River Trent was opened for navigation, allowing Burton to become a major brewing centre. Its fascinating history is brought to life through two-hour guided tours of the **National Brewery Centre** (☑ 01283-532880; www.nationalbrewerycentre.co.uk; Horninglow St, Burton-upon-Trent; adult/child £11.95/6.95; ☺10am-5pm, guided tours 11am & 2pm Apr-Sep; 10am-4pm, guided tours 11am & 1.30pm Oct-Mar), which contains a museum and still has a microbrewery today. Staff can point you to Burton's other breweries and traditional ale houses.

During tours, you'll learn, for example, that Burton developed pale ale to export to colonial-era India: the origins of IPA (Indian Pale Ale) today. You'll also get to taste samples (there are soft drinks for kids).

Trains run from Derby (£7.60, 15 minutes, three per hour) and Birmingham (£16.90, 30 minutes, three per hour) to Burton's train station, a half-mile walk southwest of the National Brewery Centre.

Dirty Duck   PUB
(Black Swan; www.oldenglishinns.co.uk; Waterside; ☺11am-11pm Mon-Sat, to 10.30pm Sun) Also called the 'Black Swan', this enchanting riverside alehouse is the only pub in England to be licensed under two names. It's a favourite thespian watering hole, with a roll call of former regulars (Olivier, Attenborough et al) that reads like a who's who of actors.

Windmill Inn   PUB
(www.greeneking-pubs.co.uk; Church St; ☺11am-11pm Sun-Thu, to midnight Fri & Sat; 🛜) Ale was already flowing at this low-ceilinged pub when rhyming couplets gushed from Shakespeare's quill. Flowers frame the whitewashed facade; there's a shaded rear beer garden.

☆ Entertainment

★ Royal Shakespeare Company   THEATRE
(RSC; ☑ box office 01789-403493; www.rsc.org.uk; Waterside; tours adult £7-9, child £4.50-5, tower adult/child £2.50/1.25; ☺tour times vary, tower 10am-5pm Sun-Fri, 10am-12.15 & 2-5pm Sat mid-Mar–mid-Oct, 10am-4.30pm Sun-Fri, to 12.15pm Sat mid-Oct–mid-Mar) Stratford has two grand stages run by the world-renowned Royal Shakespeare Company – the **Royal Shakespeare Theatre** and the Swan Theatre on Waterside – as well as the smaller Other Place. The theatres have witnessed performances by such legends as Lawrence Olivier, Richard Burton, Judi Dench, Helen Mirren, Ian McKellan and Patrick Stewart. Various one-hour **guided tours** take you behind the scenes.

Zipping up the lift/elevator of the Royal Shakespeare Theatre's **tower** rewards with panoramic views over the town and River Avon. Spectacular views also unfold from its 3rd-floor Rooftop Restaurant (p407), which opens to a terrace.

Contact the RSC for performance times, and book well ahead. There are often special deals for under-25-year-olds, students and seniors. A few tickets are held back for sale on the day of the performance but get snapped up fast.

Other Place   THEATRE
(☑ box office 01789-403493; www.rsc.org.uk; 22 Southern Lane) The smallest stage of the Royal Shakespeare Company has 200 seats. New work is presented here; it also hosts regular free live music and spoken word nights.

Swan Theatre   THEATRE
(☑ 01789-403493; www.rsc.org.uk; Waterside) Hosting productions by the Royal Shakespeare Company, this grand stage has a capacity of 426 people.

Shopping

Chaucer Head   BOOKS
(www.chaucerhead.com; 21 Chapel St; ☺11am-5.30pm Mon-Thu, 10am-5pm Fri & Sat) Bargain-priced paperbacks through to rare antiquarian books worth thousands of pounds are stocked at the Chaucer Head, which was originally founded in Birmingham in 1830 and relocated to literary-famed Stratford in 1960.

ⓘ Information

Tourist Office (☑ 01789-264293; www.shakespeares-england.co.uk; Bridge Foot; ☺9am-

5.30pm Mon-Sat, 10am-4pm Sun) Just west of Clopton Bridge.

🛈 Getting There & Away

BUS

National Express coaches and other bus companies run from Stratford's Riverside bus station (behind the Stratford Leisure Centre on Bridgeway). National Express services include the following:

Birmingham £9, one hour, two per day

London Victoria £13.10, three hours, two direct services per day

Oxford £10.10, 1¼ hours, one per day

CAR

If you're driving, be warned that town car parks charge high fees, 24 hours a day.

TRAIN

From Stratford-upon-Avon train station, London Midland runs to Birmingham (£8, 50 minutes, two per hour), Chiltern Railways serves London Marylebone (£30.40, 2¾ hours, up to two per hour) with a change in Leamington Spa, and East Midlands runs to Warwick (£6.90, 30 minutes, every two hours).

The nostalgic **Shakespeare Express Steam Train** (☑ 0121-708 4960; www.vintagetrains. co.uk; one way/return £17.50/27.50; ⊙ Sun Jul–mid-Sep) chugs twice every Sunday in summer between Stratford and Birmingham Moor St; the one-way journey time is one hour.

STAFFORDSHIRE

Wedged between the ever-expanding conurbations of Birmingham and Manchester, Staffordshire is surprisingly green, with the northern half of the county rising to meet the rugged hills of the Peak District.

Regular trains and buses serve Lichfield, Stafford and other major towns.

Lichfield

☑ 01543 / POP 32,219

Even without its magnificent Gothic cathedral – one of the most spectacular in the country – this charming cobbled market town would be worth a visit to tread in the footsteps of lexicographer and wit Samuel Johnson, and natural philosopher Erasmus Darwin, grandfather of Charles. Johnson once described Lichfield folk as 'the most sober, decent people in England', which was rather generous considering that this was the last place in the country to stop burning people at the stake.

⊙ Sights

★**Lichfield Cathedral**   CATHEDRAL
(☑ 01543-306100; www.lichfield-cathedral.org; 19 Cathedral Close; cathedral by donation, tower tours adult/child £6/4; ⊙ cathedral 9.30am-6.15pm Mon-Sat, 12.30-5pm Sun, tower tours vary) Crowned by three dramatic towers, Lichfield Cathedral is a Gothic fantasy, constructed in stages from 1200 to 1350. The enormous vaulted nave is set slightly off line from the choir, creating a bizarre perspective when viewed from the west door, and carvings inside the cathedral still bear signs of damage caused by Civil War soldiers sharpening their swords.

Check schedules online for 45-minute tower tours climbing 160 steps for sweeping views from the central spire.

Erasmus Darwin House   HISTORIC BUILDING
(☑ 01543-306260; www.erasmusdarwin.org; Beacon St; ⊙ 11am-5pm Apr-Oct, to 4pm Thu-Sun Nov-Mar) FREE After turning down the job of royal physician to King George III, Erasmus Darwin became a leading light in the Lunar Society, debating the origins of life with luminaries including Wedgwood, Boulton and

---

ALTON TOWERS

Phenomenally popular **Alton Towers** (☑ 0871 222 3330; www.altontowers.com; Farley Lane, Alton; adult/child amusement park £55/48, water park £18/14; ⊙ hours vary), 4 miles east of Cheadle off the B5032, offers maximum G-force for your buck. Wild rides include the Th13teen, Nemesis, Oblivion, Galactica and Wickerman roller coasters. Gentler thrills span carousels and stage shows to a pirate-themed aquarium and splashtastic water park.

Check seasonal schedules online and pre-purchase tickets to skip ticket queues and take advantage of discounted entry deals. Five on-site hotels with themed rooms offer perks such as an hour's early park entry.

Your own transport is best (a monorail loops between the car park and the main entrance). In summer, one daily bus links Alton Towers with Stoke-on-Trent, Nottingham and Derby; schedules are available from Traveline (p390).

Watt decades before his grandson Charles came up with the theory of evolution. The former house of the 'Grandfather of Evolution' contains intriguing exhibits, including his notebook containing drawings of his inventions. At the back, a fragrant culinary and medicinal herb garden leads to Cathedral Close.

Samuel Johnson Birthplace Museum
MUSEUM

(☎01543-264972; www.samueljohnsonbirthplace. org.uk; Breadmarket St; ⊙10.30am-4.30pm Mar-Oct, 11am-3.30pm Nov-Feb) FREE This absorbing museum charts the life of the pioneering lexicographer, wit, poet and critic Samuel Johnson, who moved to London from his native Lichfield and devoted nine years to producing the first major dictionary of the English language. Johnson's dictionary helped define the word 'dull' with this example: 'to make dictionaries is dull work'. On the 1st floor, a short dramatised film narrates Johnson's life story. It's a lovely property to explore.

Lichfield Museum
MUSEUM

(☎01543-256611; www.stmaryslichfield.co.uk; Market Sq) FREE Exhibits cover 1300 years of Lichfield history at this museum inside the revamped St Mary's Church, which also contains the town's library and art gallery. Climb the tower's 120 steps for sweeping city views.

🛏 Sleeping & Eating

George Hotel
HOTEL ££

(☎01543-414822; www.thegeorgelichfield.co.uk; 12-14 Bird St; s/d from £90/120; P🞄) An old Georgian pub has been upgraded into a comfortable, midrange hotel with 45 rooms that scores points for location rather than atmosphere. Family rooms sleep up to four.

Swinfen Hall Hotel
HISTORIC HOTEL £££

(☎01543-481494; https://swinfenhallhotel.co.uk; Swinfen; s/d/ste incl breakfast from £151/165/331; P🞄) Georgian manor house Swinfen Hall, built in 1757, sits 3 miles southeast of Lichfield amid 40 wooded hectares with formal gardens, wild hay meadows and a deer park. Parkland views extend from its 17 rooms, which have either traditional or contemporary styling. Its fine-dining restaurant has multicourse tasting menus accompanied by wine flights.

THE POTTERIES – STOKE-ON-TRENT

Situated at the heart of the Potteries (the famous pottery-producing region of Staffordshire), Stoke-on-Trent is famed for its ceramics. Don't expect cute little artisanal producers: this was where pottery shifted to mass production during the Industrial Revolution, and Stoke today is a sprawl of industrial townships tied together by flyovers and bypasses. There are dozens of active potteries that you can visit in the greater area, including the famous Wedgwood factory.

The **tourist office** (☎01782-236000; www.visitstoke.co.uk; Bethesda St, Hanley; ⊙10am-5pm Mon-Sat, 11am-4pm Sun) has information on all the potteries that are open to the public.

Potteries Museum & Art Gallery (☎01782-236000; www.stokemuseums.org.uk; Bethesda St, Hanley; ⊙10am-5pm Mon-Sat, 11am-4pm Sun) For a thorough overview of the Potteries area's history, this museum and gallery houses an extensive ceramics display, from Toby jugs and jasperware to outrageous ornamental pieces. Other highlights include treasures from the 2009-discovered Staffordshire Hoard (the largest hoard of Anglo-Saxon gold and silver metalwork ever found, incorporating 5.1kg of gold, 1.4kg of silver and some 3500 pieces of jewellery); displays on the WWII Spitfire, created by the Stoke-born aviator Reginald Mitchell; and artworks by TS Lowry and Sir Henry Moore.

World of Wedgwood (☎01782-282986; www.worldofwedgwood.com; Wedgwood Dr, Barlaston; factory tour & museum adult/child £10/8, museum only free; ⊙factory 10am-4pm Mon-Fri, museum 10am-5pm Mon-Fri, to 4pm Sat & Sun) Set in attractive parkland 8 miles south of Hanley, the modern production centre for Josiah Wedgwood's porcelain empire displays an extensive collection of historic pieces, including plenty of Wedgwood's delicate, neoclassical blue-and-white jasperware at its museum. On weekdays, there are self-guided factory tours and first-come, first-served guided factory tours lasting one hour. Pot throwing and design workshops take place at its Master Craft and Decorating studios.

Damn Fine Cafe
CAFE **£**

(www.damnfinecafelichfield.co.uk; 16 Bird St; dishes £4.50-10; ⊗9am-3.30pm Tue-Sat, 10am-3pm Sun) Teeming with locals, this cafe is a handy spot for all-day bacon-and-sausage or vegetarian toad-in-the-hole breakfasts, soup (with a free taster of the day's special), mozzarella melts and sandwiches on a variety of breads.

Trooper
GASTROPUB **££**

(☑01543-480413; www.thetrooperwall.co.uk; Watling St, Wall; mains £12-26; ⊗kitchen noon-9.15pm Mon-Wed, to 9.45pm Thu-Sat, to 8pm Sun, bar noon-midnight Mon-Sat, to 10pm Sun; ⊛) ⊘ Idyllically situated 3 miles southwest of Lichfield in the tiny village of Wall, this gastropub prides itself on ingredients sourced from local suppliers and herbs from its gardens. Steaks are the house speciality, alongside contemporary twists on pub classics, such as ham-and-cider pie. In fine weather, enjoy its fabulous real ales in the sunny beer garden.

Its kids' menu includes a mini 4oz steak with fries.

Wine House
BRITISH **££**

(☑01543-419999; www.thewinehouselichfield. co.uk; 27 Bird St; mains £12.50-27; ⊗noon-10pm Mon-Sat, to 6pm Sun) Well-chosen wines complement the upmarket pub fare at these smart, red-brick premises. Choices range from slow-cooked pork belly with apple sauce to steaks and seafood, such as line-caught sea bass with white wine, shallots and clams.

🍷 Drinking & Nightlife

Beerbohm
BAR

(www.beerbohm.co.uk; 19 Tamworth St; ⊗11am-11pm Tue-Sat; ⊜) Behind a peppermint-painted traditional shopfront, Beerbohm's richly coloured lounge-style interior is filled with handmade furniture. Its discerning drinks list includes its own brew, Dandy Bitter, along with local ales and small-batch gins, English wines and artisan malt whiskies plus imported craft beers (some gluten-free). It doesn't serve food but provides plates and cutlery for you to bring your own.

Whippet Inn
PUB

(www.whippetinnmicro.co.uk; 21 Tamworth St; ⊗noon-2.30pm & 4.30-10pm Wed & Thu, noon-10pm Fri & Sat, noon-5pm Sun) Ales and craft keg beers from independent British breweries are the hallmark of this adorable little one-room micropub, along with a wonderful

---

WORTH A TRIP

LORD LICHFIELD'S SHUGBOROUGH

The regal, neoclassical mansion of **Shugborough** (NT; ☑01889-880160; www.nationaltrust.org.uk; Great Haywood; adult/child £13/6.50; ⊗house 11am-4.30pm Mar-Oct, 10am-3pm Dec, grounds 9am-6pm Mar-Oct, 9am-4pm Nov & Dec) is the ancestral home of royal photographer Lord Lichfield. A good proportion of the wall space is devoted to his work; the highlight is the staterooms' collection of exquisite Louis XV and XVI furniture. One-hour guided tours (included in admission) run between 11am and 1pm. Shugborough is 6 miles east of Stafford on the A513; bus 825 linking Stafford and Lichfield stops 1 mile from the manor (£4.20, 30 minutes, two per hour Monday to Saturday).

---

selection of ciders and wines, but it resolutely doesn't serve lager or spirits. Artisan bar snacks include pork pies, Scotch eggs and sausage rolls.

ℹ️ Information

Tourist Office (☑01543-256611; www.stmaryslichfield.co.uk; Market Sq) In the revamped St Mary's Church.

ℹ️ Getting There & Away

The bus station is opposite the main Lichfield City train station on Birmingham Rd. Bus 825 serves Stafford (£4.20, 1¼ hours, two per hour Monday to Saturday).

Lichfield has two train stations:

Lichfield City Trains to Birmingham (£5.30, 35 minutes, up to four per hour) leave from Lichfield City station in the town centre.

Lichfield Trent Valley Trains to London Euston (£49.40, 1¾ hours, up to two per hour) run from Lichfield Trent Valley station on the eastern side of town, 1.5 miles east of the centre.

WORCESTERSHIRE

Famed for its eponymous condiment, invented by two Worcester chemists in 1837, Worcestershire marks the transition from the industrial heart of the Midlands to the peaceful countryside of the Marches along the English–Welsh border. The southern

THE FIRS – ELGAR'S BIRTHPLACE

England's most popular classical composer, Edward Elgar, is celebrated at the humble country cottage (NT; www.nationaltrust.org.uk/the-firs; Crown East Lane, Lower Broadheath) where he was born in 1857. The National Trust was set to run the museum from mid-2018; check the website for prices and opening times, and details of concerts here. In the flower-filled garden there's a sculpture of Elgar, sitting on a bench looking out over the Malvern Hills; it was created by artist Jemma Pearson.

The cottage is 4 miles west of Worcester; you'll need your own transport.

and western fringes of the county burst with lush countryside and sleepy market towns, while the capital is a classic English county town, whose magnificent cathedral inspired the composer Edward Elgar to write some of his greatest works.

🏃 Activities

The 210-mile riverside Severn Way winds through Worcestershire en route from Plynlimon in Wales to the sea at Bristol. A shorter challenge is the 100-mile Three Choirs Way, linking Worcester to Hereford and Gloucester. The Malvern Hills are also prime country for walking and cycling; information is available at www.malvernhillsaonb.org.uk.

ℹ Getting There & Around

Worcester is a convenient rail hub. Kidderminster is the southern railhead of the quaint Severn Valley Railway (p428).

Buses and trains connect larger towns, but bus services to rural areas can be frustratingly infrequent. Search the transport pages at www.worcestershire.gov.uk or Traveline (p390) for bus companies and timetables.

Worcester

☎ 01905 / POP 101,328

Worcester (*woos*-ter) has enough historic treasures to forgive the architectural eyesores from the postwar love affair with all things concrete. The home of the famous Worcestershire sauce (an unlikely combination of fermented tamarinds and anchovies), this ancient cathedral city was the site of the last battle of the Civil War, the Battle of Worcester, which took place on 3 September 1651. The defeated Charles II only narrowly escaped the pursuing Roundheads by hiding in an oak tree, an event still celebrated in Worcester every 29 May, when government buildings are decked out with oak sprigs.

◉ Sights

★ Worcester Cathedral   CATHEDRAL
(☎ 01905-732900; www.worcestercathedral.co.uk; 8 College Yard; cathedral by donation, tower adult/child £5/free, tours £5/free; ☉ cathedral 7.30am-6pm Mon-Sat, from noon Sun, tower hours vary, tours 11am & 2.30pm Mon-Sat Mar-Nov, Sat Dec-Feb) Rising above the River Severn, Worcester's majestic cathedral is the final resting place of Magna Carta signatory King John. The strong-legged can scale 235 steps to the top of the tower (confirm times ahead), from where Charles II surveyed his troops during the disastrous Battle of Worcester. Hour-long tours run from the gift shop. Several works by local composer Edward Elgar had their first public outings here – to appreciate the acoustics, come for evensong (5.30pm Monday to Saturday, 4pm Sunday).

Royal Worcester Porcelain Works   MUSEUM
(☎ 01905-21247; www.museumofroyalworcester.org; Severn St; adult/child incl audio guide £6.50/free; ☉ 10am-5pm Mon-Sat, 11am-4pm Sun) Up there with the country's most famous potteries, the Royal Worcester porcelain factory gained an edge over its rivals by picking up the contract to provide fine crockery to the British monarchy. An entertaining audio tour reveals some quirkier sides to the Royal Worcester story, including its brief foray into porcelain dentures and 'portable fonts' designed for use during cholera outbreaks. The shop has some splendid pieces, from monk-shaped candle snuffers to decorated thimbles and pill boxes.

Greyfriars   HISTORIC BUILDING
(NT; ☎ 01905-23571; www.nationaltrust.org.uk; Friar St; adult/child £5.45/2.70; ☉ 11am-5pm Tue-Sat Mar-Oct, to 4pm Nov–mid-Dec) Friar St was largely chock-a-block with historic architecture until the iconoclastic 1960s when much was demolished, including the lovely medieval Lich Gate. Some creaky old almshouses survive and Greyfriars was saved in the nick of time by the National Trust, offering

the chance to poke around a timber-framed merchant's house from 1480. It's full of atmospheric wood-panelled rooms and is backed by a pretty walled garden.

🛏 Sleeping & Eating

Diglis House Hotel HOTEL **££**
(🖉 01905-353518; www.diglishousehotel.co.uk; Severn St; s/d/ste incl breakfast from £90/115/145; P🛜) Next to the boathouse in a gorgeous waterside setting, this rambling yet cosy 28-room Georgian house is a short stroll from the cathedral. The best rooms have four-poster beds, luxe bathrooms and river views. Its elegant restaurant (mains £13 to £19) opens to a terrace overlooking the river. Guests can work out at the nearby gym for free.

Mac & Jac's DELI, CAFE **£**
(www.macandjacs.co.uk; 44 Friar St; dishes £4.50-18; ⊙9am-5pm Tue-Sat) This Friar St outfit has a lovely deli downstairs and a relaxing cafe upstairs for caffeine, sandwiches with fillings like Brie and grape, and hot dishes such as crispy pork belly with toasted almonds and coriander. Look out for gourmet supper evenings.

★Cardinal's Hat PUB
(🖉 01905-724006; www.the-cardinals-hat.co.uk; 31 Friar St; ⊙4-11pm Mon, from noon Tue-Sat, noon-10.30pm Sun; 🛜) Dating from the 14th century, and claiming a resident ghost, Worcester's oldest and grandest pub retains original features, including timber panelling and log-burning stoves. English craft beers and ciders dominate the taps; its menu concentrates on locally sourced British classics (Scotch eggs, pies, kippers, artisan cheese platters). Upstairs are six Georgian-style boutique guest rooms (doubles £82.50 to £125).

★Old Rectifying House BRITISH **££**
(🖉 01905-619622; www.theoldrec.co.uk; North Parade; mains £9.50-18; ⊙kitchen noon-3pm & 6-9pm Tue-Thu, noon-4pm & 6-9.30pm Fri & Sat, noon-4pm Sun, bar noon-11pm Tue-Thu & Sun, to 12.30am Fri & Sat; 🖉🛜) Worcester's hippest dining space has a candlelit, painted-brick interior and umbrella-shaded terrace tables. Its switched-on menu features dishes such as braised pork cheek with a crispy ham bonbon. DJs often hit the decks in the lounge bar, which mixes craft cocktails including a 'Hedgerow Shire' with local gin and birch liqueur.

Kids, vegetarians and vegans are catered for; vegan dishes include a Sunday nut roast (advance orders essential).

ℹ Information

Tourist Office (🖉 01905-726311; www.visit worcestershire.org/worcester; Guildhall, High St; ⊙9.30am-5pm Mon-Fri, 10am-4pm Sat) Inside the Grade I–listed Guildhall, dating from 1721.

ℹ Getting There & Away

BUS

The **bus station** (Crowngate Centre, Friary Walk) is inside the Crowngate Centre on Friary Walk. National Express has services to London Victoria (£16.90, four hours, two daily).

TRAIN

Worcester Foregate is the main rail hub, but services also run from Worcester Shrub Hill. Regular trains:

Birmingham £8.50, one hour, every 20 minutes

Great Malvern £5.50, 15 minutes, up to three per hour

Hereford £9.90, 50 minutes, hourly

Ledbury £7.10, 25 minutes, hourly

London Paddington £35, 2½ hours, up to three per hour

Great Malvern

🖉 01684 / POP 29,626

Tumbling down the side of a forested ridge about 7 miles southwest of Worcester, the picturesque spa town of Great Malvern is the gateway to the Malverns, a soaring 9-mile-long range of volcanic hills that rise unexpectedly from the surrounding meadows. In Victorian times, the medicinal waters were prescribed as a panacea for everything from gout to sore eyes – you can test the theory by sampling Malvern water straight from the ground at public wells dotted around the town.

◉ Sights

★Morgan Motor Company FACTORY, MUSEUM
(🖉 01684-573104; www.morgan-motor.co.uk; Pickersleigh Rd; museum free, tours adult/child £22.50/11.25; ⊙museum 8.30am-5pm Mon-Thu, to 2pm Fri, tours by reservation) Morgan has been handcrafting elegant sports cars since 1909. You can see the mechanics at work on two-hour guided tours of the unassuming shedlike buildings comprising the

factory (prebooking essential), and view a fleet of vintage classics adjacent to the museum. If buying one of these beautiful machines is beyond your budget, it's possible to hire one (per day/weekend/week from £220/595/1050, including insurance) for a spin through the Malvern Hills.

Great Malvern Priory
MONASTERY

(☑ 01684-561020; www.greatmalvernpriory.org.uk; Church St; ⊙ 9am-5pm) **FREE** The 11th-century Great Malvern Priory is packed with remarkable features, from original Norman pillars to surreal modernist stained glass. The choir is enclosed by a screen of 15th-century tiles and the monks' stalls are decorated with delightfully irreverent 14th-century misericords, depicting everything from three rats hanging a cat to the mythological reptile, the basilisk. Charles Darwin's daughter Annie is buried here.

🛏 Sleeping & Eating

Abbey Hotel
HOTEL £££

(☑ 01684-892332; www.sarova-abbeyhotel.com; Abbey Rd; d/f from £160/180; 🅿 🐾 🛜 🐕) Tangled in vines like a Brothers Grimm fairy-tale castle, this stately property has 103 elegant rooms in a prime location by the local-history museum and priory.

WALKING IN THE MALVERN HILLS

The jack-in-the-box Malvern Hills, which dramatically pop up out of the Severn plains on the boundary between Worcestershire and Herefordshire, rise to the lofty peak of the Worcester Beacon (419m), reached by a steep 3-mile climb above Great Malvern. More than 100 miles of trails traipse over the various summits, which are mostly capped by exposed grassland, offering the kind of views that inspire orchestral movements.

Great Malvern's tourist office (p414) has racks of pamphlets covering popular hikes, including a map of the mineral-water springs, wells and fountains of the town and surrounding hills. The enthusiast-run website www.malverntrail.co.uk is also a goldmine of useful walking information.

A single £4 parking ticket per day is valid at locations throughout the hills.

Mac & Jac's
CAFE £

(www.macandjacs.co.uk; 23 Abbey Rd; dishes £4.50-18; ⊙ 9am-6pm Tue-Sat, 10am-3.30pm Sun) Creative salads, flatbreads, sharing plates, spelt risotto and a savoury tart of the day are served at this light, bright cafe set in a chic white-painted shopfront near the priory.

St Ann's Well Cafe
CAFE, VEGETARIAN £

(☑ 01684-560285; www.stannswell.co.uk; St Ann's Rd; dishes £2-4.50; ⊙ 11.30am-3.30pm Tue-Fri, 10am-4pm Sat & Sun Easter-Sep; 🖉) A s-t-e-e-p climb above St Ann's Rd (so best to check opening times beforehand), this quaint cafe is set in an early-19th-century villa, with mountain-fresh spring water bubbling into a carved basin by the door. All-vegetarian food (including vegan options) spans soups to pies, filled baguettes, cakes, pastries and puddings.

Fig Tree
MEDITERRANEAN ££

(☑ 01684-569909; www.thefigtreemalvern. co.uk; 99b Church St; mains lunch £8.50-13, dinner £14-19; ⊙ noon-2pm & 5.30-9.30pm Tue-Sat) Tucked down an alleyway off Church St, this 19th-century former stable serves Mediterranean-inspired fare at lunch (eg focaccia, pastas and salads) and dinner (chorizo-stuffed squid, lamb souvlaki with tzatziki and saffron rice). Day or night, don't miss its signature almond-and-lemon polenta cake with fig ice cream.

❶ Information

Tourist Office (☑ 01684-892289; www. visitthemalverns.org; 21 Church St; ⊙ 10am-5pm Apr-Oct, 10am-5pm Mon-Sat, to 4pm Sun Nov-Mar) The tourist office is a mine of walking and cycling information.

❶ Getting There & Away

Buses are limited, making trains your best bet. The train station is east of the town centre, off Avenue Rd.

Services include the following:

Hereford £8.20, 30 minutes, hourly

Ledbury £5.20, 10 minutes, hourly

Worcester £5.50, 15 minutes, up to three per hour

HEREFORDSHIRE

Adjoining the Welsh border, Herefordshire is a patchwork of fields, hills and cute little black-and-white villages, many dating back to the Tudor era and beyond.

🏃 Activities

As well as the famous Offa's Dyke Path, which follows the English–Welsh border for 177 miles alongside the 8th-century Offa's Dyke, walkers can follow the Herefordshire Trail (www.herefordshiretrail.com) on a 150-mile circular loop through Leominster, Ledbury, Ross-on-Wye and Kington.

Only slightly less ambitious is the 136-mile Wye Valley Walk (www.wyevalleywalk.org), which runs from Chepstow in Wales through Herefordshire and back out again to Plynlimon.

The Three Choirs Way is a 100-mile route connecting the cathedrals of Hereford, Worcester and Gloucester.

Cyclists can trace the Six Castles Cycleway (NCN Route 44) from Hereford to Leominster and Shrewsbury, or NCN Route 68 to Great Malvern and Worcester.

ℹ️ Getting Around

Trains run frequently to destinations including Hereford and Ledbury, with bus connections on to the rest of the county. For bus timetables, contact Traveline (p390).

Hereford

📞 01432 / POP 58,896

Surrounded by apple orchards and rolling pastures at the heart of the Marches, Hereford straddles the River Wye. This lively city's key draw for visitors is its magnificent cathedral.

⊙ Sights

⭐ **Hereford Cathedral**   CATHEDRAL
(📞 01432-374200; www.herefordcathedral.org; 5 College Cloisters, Cathedral Close; cathedral entry by donation, Mappa Mundi £6; ⊙ cathedral 9.15am-5.30pm Mon-Sat, to 3.30pm Sun, Mappa Mundi 10am-5pm Mon-Sat mid-Mar–Oct, to 4pm Mon-Sat Nov–mid-Mar) After Welsh marauders torched the original Saxon cathedral, the Norman rulers of Hereford erected a larger, grander cathedral on the same site. The building was subsequently remodelled in a succession of medieval architectural styles.

The signature highlight is the magnificent Mappa Mundi, a single piece of calf-skin vellum intricately painted with some rather fantastical assumptions about the layout of the globe in around 1290. The same wing contains the world's largest surviving chained library of rare manuscripts manacled to the shelves.

HEREFORDSHIRE CIDER

The Herefordshire Cider Route (www.ciderroute.co.uk) drops in on numerous local cider producers, where you can try before you buy, and then totter off to the next cidery. Mindful of road safety, tourist offices have maps and guide booklets to help you explore by bus or bicycle.

If you only have time to visit one Herefordshire cider-maker, make it Westons Cider Mills (📞 01531-660108; www.westons-cider.co.uk; The Bounds, Much Marcle; tours adult/child £10/4; ⊙ 9am-5pm Mon-Fri, from 10am Sat & Sun), whose house brew is even served in the Houses of Parliament. Informative tours (1½ hours) start at 11am, 12.30pm, 2pm and 3.30pm, with free cider and perry tastings for the grown-ups. There's also a fascinating bottle museum. Its just under a mile west of the tiny village of Much Marcle.

Cider Museum Hereford   MUSEUM
(📞 01432-354207; www.cidermuseum.co.uk; Pomona Pl; adult/child £5.50/3; ⊙ 10.30am-4.30pm Mon-Sat) Mills and presses, glassware, watercolours, photographs and films are among the displays at this former cider-making factory (Bulmer's original premises), along with costrels (minibarrels) used by agricultural workers to carry their wages, which were partially paid in cider. Download brochures outlining walks through Herefordshire's orchards from its website. It's half a mile west of the city centre; follow Eign St and turn south along Ryelands St.

🛏️ Sleeping

Charades   B&B £
(📞 01432-269444; www.charadeshereford.co.uk; 32 Southbank Rd; s/d from £55/61; 🅿️ @ 🛜) Handy for the bus station, this imposing Victorian house dating from 1877 has six inviting rooms with high ceilings, big and bright windows, and some with soothing countryside views. The house itself has character in spades – look for old service bells in the hall and the plentiful *Titanic* memorabilia. Traditional or vegetarian breakfasts are available.

⭐ **Castle House**   BOUTIQUE HOTEL £££
(📞 01432-356321; www.castlehse.co.uk; Castle St; s/d/ste from £140/155/190; 🅿️ 🛜) In a regal

Georgian town house where the Bishop of Hereford once resided, this tranquil 16-room hotel has two sophisticated restaurants using ingredients sourced from its own nearby farm, a sunny garden spilling down to Hereford's former castle moat, and magnificent rooms and suites. Another eight newer rooms (some wheelchair accessible) are a short walk away at 25 Castle St.

✗ Eating & Drinking

★ A Rule of Tum
BURGERS £

(☑ 01432-351764; www.aruleoftum.com; 32 Aubrey St; burgers £7.50-11.50; ☺ noon-10pm Mon-Sat, to 8pm Sun; ☎ 🖶) Exposed brick, elongated wooden benches and a courtyard garden are the backdrop for brilliant brioche-bun burgers such as the Hereford Hop (pulled beef shin, Hereford Hop cheese, dill pickles and mustard mayo). Veggie burgers are cooked on a separate grill; you can order gluten-free buns made from quinoa flour. Alongside local ciders, kickin' cocktails include a vodka-fuelled Marmalade Mule.

Hereford Deli
DELI £

(www.thehereforddeli.com; 4 The Mews, St Owen St; sandwiches £2-3; ☺ 8am-6pm Mon-Fri, 9am-4pm Sat) At this gourmet emporium with a clutch of tables, fantastic sandwiches are a steal. Combinations include curried free-range chicken with mango chutney, Scottish smoked salmon with lemon-and-dill butter, or local roast beef with Cropwell Bishop Stilton and rosehip jelly. It's hidden down

---

BLACK & WHITE VILLAGES

A triangle of Tudor England survives almost untouched in northwest Herefordshire, where higgledy-piggledy black-and-white houses cluster around idyllic village greens, seemingly oblivious to the modern world. A delightful 40-mile circular drive follows the **Black and White Village Trail** (www.black andwhitetrail.org), meandering past the most handsome timber-framed buildings. It starts at Leominster and loops round through Eardisland and Kington, the southern terminus of the 30-mile way-marked Mortimer Trail footpath from Ludlow.

Pick up guides to exploring the villages by car, bus or bicycle at tourist offices.

---

a narrow laneway near a large public car park.

★ Beer in Hand
PUB

(www.beerinhand.co.uk; 136 Eign St; ☺ 5-10.30pm Mon, to 11pm Tue-Thu, noon-11pm Fri & Sat, 3-9pm Sun) Ciders at this independent pub are sublime and most are locally sourced. It's also the tap room for its own Odyssey beers (such as Black Out, a dark-malt, full-bodied American black ale brewed with fresh oranges, which it brews on the nearby National Trust Brockhampton Estate). There are board games but no TVs.

❶ Information

Tourist Office (☑ 01432-370514; www.rural-concierge.co.uk; Hereford Butter Market; ☺ 10am-4pm Mon-Sat) Information centre run by bespoke tour company Rural Concierge.

❶ Getting There & Away

BUS

The bus station is on Commercial Rd, 500m northeast of the city centre. Stagecoach runs to Gloucester (£4.20, 1½ hours, hourly Monday to Saturday).

Local services to destinations including Ross-on-Wye (bus 33; £3.70, 50 minutes, hourly Monday to Saturday) depart from St Owen St in the city centre.

TRAIN

The train station is 950m northeast of the city centre.

Regular services:

Birmingham £23.60, 1½ hours, hourly

Ledbury £6.50, 15 minutes, hourly

London Paddington £57.70, three hours, up to two per hour – either direct or with a change in Newport, South Wales

Ludlow £10.40, 25 minutes, up to two per hour

Worcester £13, 45 minutes, hourly

Ledbury

☑ 01531 / POP 9290

Creaking with history and dotted with antique shops, Ledbury's crooked black-and-white streets zero in on a delightfully leggy medieval Market House. The timber-framed structure is precariously balanced atop a series of wooden posts supposedly taken from the wrecked ships of the Spanish Armada.

Almost impossibly cute Church Lane, crowded with tilting timber-framed buildings, runs its cobbled way from High St to the town church.

🛏 Sleeping & Eating

Feathers Hotel
HOTEL **££**

(☑ 01531-635266; www.feathers-ledbury.co.uk; 25 High St; d incl breakfast from £89; P🅿🛜🏊) A Ledbury landmark, this black-and-white Tudor hotel built in 1564 looms over the main street. Of its 22 rooms, those in the oldest part of the building come with sloping floorboards, painted beams and much more character than rooms in the modern extension. There's an atmospheric wood-panelled restaurant, Quills (mains £13.50 to £28), and an indoor swimming pool.

Verzon House Hotel
HOTEL **£££**

(☑ 01531-670381; www.verzonhouse.com; Hereford Rd, Trumpet; s/d/ste from £80/110/180; P🛜) 🐾 The ultimate country-chic retreat, this lovely Georgian farmhouse 3.8 miles northwest of Ledbury on the A438 has eight luxuriously appointed rooms with free-standing baths, goose-down pillows and deep-pile carpets. Locally sourced produce underpins the Modern British menu at its restaurant (mains £14 to £30).

Malthouse Cafe & Gallery
CAFE **£**

(☑ 01531-634443; Church Lane; mains lunch £4.50-8, dinner £12-16; ⊘9am-5pm Tue-Thu, 9am-5pm & 6-11pm Fri & Sat, 10am-4pm Sun & Mon; 🖉) Set back from the street in a cobbled courtyard, this ivy-draped building is a delightful spot for breakfast (such as poached eggs with a thyme, leek and parsnip cake) or lunch (black-pudding sausage rolls, goats cheese and rosemary filo parcels). On Friday and Saturday evenings, mains might include mustard-glazed pork belly or slow-cooked Herefordshire beef ribs.

🛍 Shopping

★ Malvern Hills Vintage
ANTIQUES

(☑ 01531-633608; www.malvernhillsvintage.com; Lower Mitchell Barns, Eastnor; ⊙shop & cafe 10am-4pm Wed-Sat, from 11am Sun) A vast timber barn 1.5 miles northeast of Ledbury is packed to the rafters with retro, antique and industrial treasures – everything from Victorian lamps and brass cash registers to mahogany dressers, oak-framed mirrors, leather Chesterfield and even classic cars, such as a 1956 Porche 356 Speedster. On the mezzanine, its tearoom serves scones, cakes and slices.

ℹ Getting There & Away

Buses are limited, but regular train services include the following:

Great Malvern £5.20, 10 minutes, hourly
Hereford £6.50, 15 minutes, hourly
Worcester £7.10, 25 minutes, hourly

Ross-on-Wye
☑ 01989 / POP 10,582

Set on a red sandstone bluff over a kink in the River Wye, hilly Ross-on-Wye was propelled to fame in the 18th century by Alexander Pope and Samuel Taylor Coleridge, who penned tributes to philanthropist John Kyrle, 'Man of Ross', who dedicated his life and fortune to the poor of the parish.

◉ Sights

Market House
GALLERY

(☑ 01989-769398; www.madeinross.co.uk; Market Pl; ⊙10am-5pm Mon-Sat, 10.30am-4pm Sun Apr-Oct, 10.30am-4pm Mon-Sat Nov-Mar) 🐾 FREE The 17th-century Market House sits atop weathered sandstone columns in Market Pl. The salmon-pink building is now home to artist collective Made in Ross, whose members live and work in a 20-mile radius, and exhibit and sell their arts and crafts here. Regular markets take place on the square at the front.

🛏 Sleeping & Eating

King's Head
INN **££**

(☑ 01989-763174; www.kingshead.co.uk; 8 High St; d/f from £77/95; P🛜🏨) Dating from the 14th century, this half-timbered inn is a charmer. Some of its 15 sage- and oyster-toned rooms have four-poster beds, and there's a timber bar serving local ales and ciders, and a candlelit, book-lined library, as well as a conservatory restaurant. Limited parking is available for guests.

Pots & Pieces
CAFE **£**

(www.potsandpieces.com; 40 High St; dishes £3-7.50; ⊙9am-4.45pm Mon-Fri, 10am-4.45pm Sat year-round, plus 11am-3.45pm Sun Jun-Sep) Browse ceramics and crafts at this tearoom by the marketplace, and choosing from cakes such as lemon drizzle, coffee, and walnut and carrot. Savoury options include quiches, sandwiches and a soup of the day.

Truffles Delicatessen
DELI **£**

(www.trufflesdeli.co.uk; 46 High St; dishes £2.50-5.50; ⊙8am-5pm Mon-Sat, from 11am Sun) Packed to the rafters with local artisan products (cheeses, breads, chutneys et al), Truffles also has stellar sandwiches, soups and salad boxes to take away for a riverside picnic.

ⓘ Getting There & Away

The bus stand is on Cantilupe Rd. Bus 33 runs to Hereford (£3.70, 50 minutes, hourly Monday to Saturday). Bus 32 serves Gloucester (£4.20, one hour, hourly Monday to Saturday, every two hours Sunday).

SHROPSHIRE

Sleepy Shropshire is a glorious scattering of hills, castles and timber-framed villages tucked against the Welsh border. Highlights include castle-crowned Ludlow, industrial Ironbridge and the beautiful Shropshire Hills, which offer the best walking and cycling in the Marches.

🏃 Activities

The rolling Shropshire Hills call out to walkers like a siren. Between Shrewsbury and Ludlow, the landscape rucks up into dramatic folds, with spectacular trails climbing the flanks of **Wenlock Edge** and the **Long Mynd** near Church Stretton. The county is also crossed by long-distance trails, including the famous **Offa's Dyke Path** and the popular **Shropshire Way**, which meanders around Ludlow and Church Stretton.

Mountain bikers head for the muddy tracks that scramble over the **Long Mynd** near Church Stretton, while road riders aim for the **Six Castles Cycleway** (NCN 44), which runs for 58 miles from Shrewsbury to Leominster.

Tourist offices sell copies of *Cycling for Pleasure in the Marches,* a pack of five maps and guides covering the entire county.

ⓘ Getting There & Away

Shrewsbury is the local transport hub, with good bus and rail connections. Church Stretton and Ludlow also have handy rail services.

From May to September, **Shropshire Hills Shuttles** (www.shropshirehillsaonb.co.uk; Day Rover ticket adult/child £10/4; ⏱ hourly Sat, Sun & bank holidays May-Sep) runs an hourly bus service along popular hiking routes on weekends and bank holidays.

Shrewsbury

☏ 01743 / POP 71,715

A delightful jumble of winding medieval streets and timbered Tudor houses leaning at precarious angles, Shrewsbury was a crucial front in the conflict between the English and the Welsh in medieval days. Even today, the road bridge running east towards London is known as the English Bridge to mark it out from the Welsh Bridge leading northwest towards Holyhead. Shrewsbury is also the birthplace of Charles Darwin (1809–82).

The pronunciation of the town's name has long been a hot topic. A charity debate hosted by University Centre Shrewsbury in 2015 declared '*shroos*-bree' (rhyming with 'grew') the winner over the posher '*shrows*-bree' (rhyming with 'grow'), as did a survey by the *Shropshire Star,* though you'll still hear both pronunciations in the town and across British media.

◉ Sights

Shrewsbury Castle　　　CASTLE, MUSEUM
(☏ 01743-358516; www.shropshireregimentalmuseum.co.uk; Castle St; adult/child £4/1; ⏱ 10.30am-5pm Mon-Wed, Fri & Sat, to 4pm Sun Jun–mid-Sep, to 4pm Mon-Wed, Fri & Sat mid-Feb–May & mid-Sep–mid-Dec) Hewn from flaking red Shropshire sandstone, the town castle contains the **Shropshire Regimental Museum**. There are fine views from **Laura's Tower** and the battlements. The lower level of the **Great Hall** dates from 1150.

Shrewsbury Abbey　　　CHURCH
(☏ 01743-232723; www.shrewsburyabbey.com; Abbey Foregate; by donation; ⏱ 10am-4pm Apr-Oct, 10.30am-3pm Nov-Mar) All that remains of a vast, cruciform Benedictine monastery founded in 1083 is the lovely red-sandstone Shrewsbury Abbey. Twice used for meetings of the English Parliament, the abbey church lost its spire and two wings when the monastery was dissolved in 1540. It sustained further damage in 1826 when engineer Thomas Telford ran the London–Holyhead road right through the grounds. Nevertheless, you can still see some impressive Norman, Early English and Victorian features, including an exceptional 14th-century west window.

St Mary's Church　　　CHURCH
(www.visitchurches.org.uk; St Mary's St; by donation; ⏱ 10am-4pm Mon-Sat) The fabulous interior of this tall-spired medieval church contains an impressive collection of stained glass, including a 1340 window depicting the Tree of Jesse (a biblical representation of the lineage of Jesus) and a magnificent oak ceiling in the nave, which largely collapsed in a huge gale in 1894 when the top

Shrewsbury

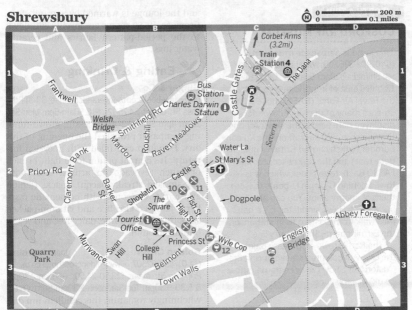

Shrewsbury

of the spire blew off. Much of the glass in the church is sourced from Europe, including some outstanding Dutch glass from 1500.

Shrewsbury Prison HISTORIC BUILDING
(☑ 01743-343100; www.shrewsburyprison.com; The Dana; prison adult/child £15/9.50, ghost tour £20; ⊙ prison tours 10am-5pm, ghost tours 7pm & 9pm) Built in 1793, this was a working prison as recently as 2013. Today tours are led by former prison guards: when you arrive, you're 'processed' as a prisoner and escorted into the general population wing, before having the opportunity to enter a cell, which is ominously locked behind you. Alternatively, you can take a self-guided tour. Chilling evening ghost tours (not recommended for kids) include the prison's execution room where 11 inmates were hanged.

**Shrewsbury Museum
& Art Gallery** MUSEUM
(☑ 01743-258885; www.shrewsburymuseum.org.uk; The Square; adult/child £4.50/2; ⊙ 10am-5pm Mon-Sat, 11am-4pm Sun) Diverse exhibits at Shrewsbury's town museum cover everything from Roman treasures to Shropshire gold, including the Bronze Age Perry Bracelet. Its Prehistory and Roman Gallery is free of charge.

⌂ Sleeping

Corbet Arms PUB ££
(☑ 01743-709232; www.thecorbetarms.com; Church Rd, Uffington; d/f incl breakfast from

WORTH A TRIP

COSFORD RAF MUSEUM

This famous aerospace **museum** (☑ 01902-376200; www.rafmuseum.org.uk; Shifnal; ☺ 10am-5pm Mar-Oct) **FREE** 13 miles east of Ironbridge is run by the Royal Air Force (RAF), whose pilots steered many of the winged wonders displayed here across the skies. Among the museum's 70 aircraft are the Vulcan bomber (which carried Britain's nuclear deterrent) and the tiny helicopter-like FA330 Bachstelze glider, which was towed behind German U-boats to warn them of enemy ships. You can also try out a Black Hawk simulator. It's a half-mile walk from Cosford train station, on the Birmingham–Shrewsbury line.

The Red Arrows stunt team paint the sky with coloured smoke during the Cosford Air Show (www.cosfordairshow.co.uk) in early June.

£90/105; ☐ ⛆) Peacefully situated 4 miles east of Shrewsbury in the pint-sized village of Uffington on the banks of the River Severn, this family-friendly pub has nine stylish en-suite rooms reached by a staircase. Try for top-floor room 10, which has exposed beams, a spacious sitting area and panoramic views of the surrounding countryside. High-quality pub food includes outstanding Sunday roasts.

Lion & Pheasant
BOUTIQUE HOTEL ££
(☑ 01743-770345; www.lionandpheasant.co.uk; 50 Wyle Cop; s/d incl breakfast from £80/109; ☐ ⛆) This former coaching inn is now a stylish town house offering 22 individually styled rooms with comfy goose- and duck-down pillows, and some with Severn views. Original features throughout the property include magnificent exposed timber beams. Classy Modern British fare is served in the whitewashed restaurant (mains £18.50 to £25). Parking for overnight guests is first come, first served.

Lion Hotel
HOTEL ££
(☑ 01743-353107; www.thelionhotelshrewsbury.com; Wyle Cop; s/d/ste incl breakfast from £74/109/135; ☐ ⛆) A gilded wooden lion crowns the doorway of this famous 16th-century coaching inn, decked out inside with portraits of lords and ladies in powdered wigs. Charles Dickens was a former guest,

and the lounge is warmed by a grand stone fireplace. Its 59 rooms are lovely, right down to the period-pattern fabrics and ceramic water jugs.

✕ Eating & Drinking

Ginger & Co
CAFE £
(www.facebook.com/gingerandcocoffee; 30-31 Princess St; dishes £4.75-12; ☺ 8.30am-5pm Mon-Sat, 10am-4pm Sun; ☑) A successful crowd-funding campaign propelled the opening of this airy, L-shaped cafe filled with upcycled furniture. It's a great option for a light brunch or lunch (avocado on artisan toast with oak-smoked streaky bacon), snacks (lemon and Earl Grey scones with homemade raspberry jam), good coffee and vitamin-packed smoothies. Gluten-free, dairy-free and vegan options abound.

Golden Cross
MODERN BRITISH ££
(☑ 01743-362507; www.goldencrosshotel.co.uk; 14 Princess St; mains £13.50-24.50; ☺ noon-2.30pm & 5.30-9.30pm Tue-Sat, noon-2.30pm Sun) Overwhelmingly romantic, this candlelit inn dating from 1428 has an upmarket pub menu (port- and clementine-glazed baked ham, pot-roast ox cheek) and five exquisite guest rooms (doubles £75 to £150) with luxurious touches like freestanding bathtubs and chaises longues.

Number Four Butcher Row
CAFE ££
(☑ 01743-366691; www.number-four.com; 4 Butcher Row; mains breakfast £3.25-11, lunch £7-12, 2-/3-course dinner menus £16/20; ☺ 9am-4pm Mon, to 9pm Tue-Thu, to 9.30pm Fri & Sat; ☑) Tucked away near St Alkmund's Church, this bare-boards split-level cafe is best known for its fantastic breakfasts, from eggs Benedict to bacon baguettes or a full English with freshly squeezed juices. Light lunches include burgers and gourmet salads (eg black pudding with mustard vinaigrette); dinner is a more upmarket affair (slow-roast pork belly with apple and potato gratin).

Harvey's of Fish St
BISTRO ££
(☑ 01743-344789; www.harveysfishstreet.com; 11 Fish St; mains £13-28, 5-course tasting menu £38; ☺ 11am-10.30pm Tue-Thu, to 11pm Fri & Sat, noon-4pm Sun) Foraged herbs and flowers feature in dishes such as pigeon breast with wild-garlic risotto or nettle-crusted lamb shoulder with mint and blackberry sauce at this classy bistro on charming Fish St. The sofa-strewn lounge bar is a cosy spot for cocktails.

Henry Tudor House   PUB
(www.henrytudorhouse.com; Barracks Passage; ⊙noon-11pm Mon-Thu, 11am-1am Fri & Sat, noon-10pm Sun) Tucked off Wyle Cop, this seriously overhanging black-and-white beauty was built in the early 15th century and is where Henry VII stayed before the Battle of Bosworth. Today it melds old and new with a zinc bar, a light-filled conservatory and birdcage-encased chandeliers. Live gigs regularly take to the stage. Food (mackerel with cucumber purée; Shropshire beef Wellington) is superb, too.

ⓘ Information

The **tourist office** (☑01743-258888; www.originalshrewsbury.co.uk; The Square; ⊙10am-4.30pm Tue-Sat, 11am-4pm Sun) shares space with the Shrewsbury Museum and Art Gallery.

ⓘ Getting There & Away

BUS

The **bus station** (Smithfield Rd) is beside the river.
   Direct services include the following:
Church Stretton Bus 435; £3.70, one hour, hourly Monday to Friday, every two hours Saturday
Ironbridge Bus 96; £4.50, 35 minutes, every two hours
Ludlow Bus 435; £4.10, 1¼ hours, hourly Monday to Saturday

TRAIN

The train station is on the northeastern edge of the town centre at the bottom of Castle Foregate.
   Destinations include the following:
Birmingham £15.30, one hour, two per hour
Holyhead £48.50, three hours, hourly
London Euston £74.30, 2¾ hours, every 20 minutes; change in Crewe or Wolverhampton
Ludlow £13.50, 30 minutes, up to two per hour

Ironbridge Gorge

☑01952 / POP 2582

Strolling or cycling through the woods, hills and villages of this leafy river gorge, it's hard to believe such a peaceful enclave could really have been the birthplace of the Industrial Revolution. Nevertheless, it was here that Abraham Darby perfected the art of smelting iron ore with coke in 1709, making it possible to mass-produce cast iron for the first time.

Abraham Darby's son, Abraham Darby II, invented a new forging process for producing single beams of iron, allowing Abraham Darby III to astound the world with the first-ever iron bridge, constructed in 1779. The bridge remains the focal point of this World Heritage Site, and 10 very different museums tell the story of the Industrial Revolution in the buildings where it took place.

◉ Sights

★Iron Bridge   BRIDGE
(www.ironbridge.org.uk; ⊙bridge 24hr, tollhouse 10am-4pm mid-Mar–Sep, closed Mon Oct–mid-Mar) **FREE** The arching Iron Bridge, which gives the area its name, was built to flaunt the new technology invented by the pioneering Darby family. At the time of its construction in 1779, nobody could believe that anything so large – it weighs 384 tonnes – could be built from cast iron without collapsing under its own weight. There's a small exhibition on the bridge's history at the former **toll house**. Following restoration work completed in 2018, the bridge is illuminated at night.

★ Museum of the Gorge   MUSEUM
(www.ironbridge.org.uk; The Wharfage; adult/child £4.50/3.15; ⊙10am-4pm mid-Mar–Sep, closed Mon Oct–mid-Mar) An ideal place to kick off your Ironbridge Gorge visit is the Museum of the Gorge. Occupying a Gothic riverside warehouse, it offers an overview of the World Heritage Sites using film, photos and exhibits, including a 12m-long 3D model of the town in 1796.

Enginuity   MUSEUM
(www.ironbridge.org.uk; Wellington Rd; adult/child £9/6.95; ⊙10am-4pm mid-Mar–Sep, closed Mon Oct–mid-Mar) Kids will love this levers-and-pulleys science centre where they can control robots, move a steam locomotive with their bare hands (and a little engineer-

---

ⓘ IRONBRIDGE GORGE PASSPORT

The 10 Ironbridge museums are administered by the Ironbridge Gorge Museum Trust (www.ironbridge.org.uk). You'll save considerably by buying a Passport ticket (adult/child £26.50/16.50) at any of the museums or from the tourist office. Valid for 12 months, it allows unlimited entry to all of Ironbridge Gorge's sites.

Ironbridge Gorge

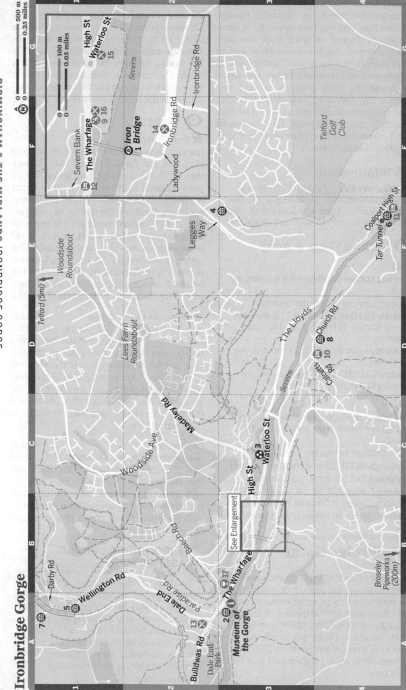

Ironbridge Gorge

ing know-how) and power up a vacuum cleaner with self-generated electricity.

Blists Hill Victorian Town MUSEUM
(☏ 01952-433424; www.ironbridge.org.uk; Legges Way; adult/child £17.95/10.90; ⊙10am-4.30pm daily mid-Mar–Sep, to 4pm Tue-Sun Oct–mid-Mar) Set at the top of the Hay Inclined Plane (a cable lift that once transported coal barges uphill from the Shropshire Canal), Blists Hill is a lovingly restored Victorian village repopulated with townsfolk in period costume, busy with day-to-day chores. There's even a bank, where you can exchange your modern pounds for shillings to use at the village shops. In summer, a Victorian fair is an added attraction for young ones.

Darby Houses MUSEUM
(☏ 01952-433424; www.ironbridge.org.uk; Darby Rd; adult/child £5.65/3.75, incl Museum of Iron £10.45/6.55; ⊙11am-3pm mid-Mar–Sep) Just uphill from the Museum of Iron (p423), these beautifully restored 18th-century homes housed generations of the Darby family in gracious but modest Quaker comfort. In the Rosehill house, kids and adults can try on Victorian dress and view china displays. The highlight of the Darby family house is the study where Abraham Darby III designed the Iron Bridge.

Coalport China Museum MUSEUM
(www.ironbridge.org.uk; Coalport High St; adult/child £9/5.50; ⊙10am-4pm daily mid-Mar–Sep, closed Mon Oct–mid-Mar) As ironmaking fell into decline, Ironbridge diversified into manufacturing china pots, using the fine clay mined around Blists Hill. Dominated by a pair of towering bottle kilns, the atmospheric old china-works now contains an absorbing museum tracing the history of the industry, with demonstrations of traditional pottery techniques.

Jackfield Tile Museum MUSEUM
(www.ironbridge.org.uk; Salthouse Rd; adult/child £9/5.90; ⊙10am-4pm mid-Mar–Sep, closed Mon Oct–mid-Mar) Once the largest tile factory in the world, Jackfield was famous for its encaustic tiles, with ornate designs produced using layers of different coloured clay. Tiles are still produced here today for period restorations. Gas-lit galleries recreate ornately tiled rooms from past centuries, including Victorian public conveniences. The museum is on the south bank of the Severn – cross the footbridge at the bottom of the Hay Inclined Plane.

Coalbrookdale Museum of Iron MUSEUM
(www.ironbridge.org.uk; Wellington Rd; adult/child, £9/5.90, incl Darby Houses £10.45/6.55; ⊙10am-4pm mid-Mar–Sep, closed Mon Oct–mid-Mar) Set in the brooding buildings of Abraham Darby's original iron foundry, the Coalbrookdale Museum of Iron contains some excellent interactive exhibits. As well as producing the girders for the Iron Bridge, the factory became famous for heavy machinery and extravagant ornamental castings, including the gates for London's Hyde Park.

🏃 Activities

Ironbridge Canoe & Kayak Hire CANOEING, KAYAKING
(☏ 07594 486356; www.facebook.com/ironbridge canoeandkayakhire; 31 High St; canoe/kayak rental per hour from £20; ⊙by appointment Mon-Fri, 9am-8pm Sat & Sun Easter-Oct) In summer,

when the river is at a safe level, you can rent canoes and kayaks to explore the gorge and surrounding areas.

Shropshire Raft Tours RAFTING
(☑ 01952-427150; www.shropshirerafttours.co.uk; The Wharfage; rafting trips adult/child £14.95/6.95, canoe & kayak hire per hour/day £15/45, bike hire per half-/full day from £19/29; ☉ equipment hire 9am-5pm Easter-Oct, tours by reservation 11.30am, 2pm & 4.30pm Easter-Oct, plus 7pm Jul & Aug) 🖋 Ironbridge Gorge might not have any rapids but you can take a gentle, highly enjoyable 90-minute trip along a 1.2-mile stretch of the River Severn floating past stunning gorge scenery with this eco-conscious outfit. Life jackets are provided. It also hires canoes, kayaks and bikes, including electric bikes.

🛏 Sleeping

Coalport YHA HOSTEL £
(☑ 0845 371 9325; www.yha.org.uk; Coalport High St; dm/d from £13/50; P 🛜) In a converted china factory in the quietest, prettiest corner of Ironbridge, this YHA hostel has 82 beds in 21 modern, functional rooms, but the biggest drawcard is the facilities, which include a laundry, a kitchen and a licensed cafe, with wi-fi in common areas.

★**Library House** B&B ££
(☑ 01952-432299; www.libraryhouse.com; 11 Severn Bank; s/d from £75/110; P 🛜) Up an alley off the main street, this lovingly restored Georgian library building built in 1730 is hugged by vines, backed by a beautiful garden and decked out with stacks of vintage books, curios, prints and lithographs. There are three charmingly well-preserved, individually decorated rooms, named Milton, Chaucer and Eliot. The affable dog whipping around is Millie.

Calcutts House B&B ££
(☑ 01952-882631; www.calcuttshouse.co.uk; Calcutts Rd; d from £91; P 🛜) This former ironmaster's pad dates from the 18th century. Traditionally decorated rooms have heaps of character, and one is furnished with an outsized 200-year-old four-poster bed. It's tucked away on the south bank around the corner from the Jackfield Tile Museum (p423), a mile east of the bridge.

🍴 Eating & Drinking

Dale End Café DELI £
(☑ 01952-872650; http://dale-end-cafe.business. site; Dale End, Coalbrookdale; dishes £3.50-12.50;

☉ 8.30am-4.30pm Mon, Tue & Thu-Sat, 10am-4pm Sun; 🛜 👫) This wonderful cafe is far and away the best place in the area for a light meal. Steaming soups, salads, sandwiches and pizzas are all freshly made; take them away or else dine in the cosy shop or at umbrella-shaded picnic tables in the courtyard. Kids are warmly welcomed.

Pondicherry INDIAN ££
(☑ 01952-433055; www.pondicherryrestaurant. co.uk; 57 Waterloo St; mains £10-16; ☉ 5.30-11pm Tue-Sat, 5-9pm Sun) Original features of this 1862-built former police station and courtroom include four lock-up cells (one's now the takeaway waiting area), the magistrate's bench and blue-painted bars on the windows. Above-average contemporary Indian cuisine includes crowd-pleasers like tandoori platters and chicken tikka masala along with chef specialities, such as lamb *saag mamyam* (braised Staffordshire lamb with spinach and spices).

D'arcys at the Station MEDITERRANEAN ££
(☑ 01952-884499; www.darcysironbridge.co.uk; Ladywood; mains £12-15, 2-course menu £13.95; ☉ 6-9.30pm Wed-Sat) Just over the bridge by the river, the handsome old station building is the backdrop for flavoursome Mediterranean dishes, from Moroccan chicken to Cypriot kebabs and Tuscan bean casserole. Kids aged over 10 are welcome.

Restaurant Severn EUROPEAN £££
(☑ 01952-432233; www.restaurantsevern.co.uk; 33 High St; lunch mains £8.50-12.50, 2-/3-course dinner menus from £23/27, 2-/3-course Sunday lunch menus £20/25; ☉ lunch Wed-Sat by reservation, 6-11pm Wed-Sat, noon-6pm Sun) The menu at this highly praised fine-dining restaurant changes frequently but might feature dishes such as Shropshire venison medallions with cognac and sundried cranberry sauce. The setting is intimate, food is artistically presented and the riverside location beautiful.

Malthouse PUB
(☑ 01952-433712; www.themalthouseironbridge. co.uk; The Wharfage; ☉ 11.30am-11pm Sun-Thu, to 1am Fri & Sat) Renovated in 2018, this inn on the Severn's riverbanks makes a great place to drink, eat and/or sleep. Local ales, craft gins and cocktails feature on the drinks list, the street-food-inspired menu spans fish tacos to southern fried chicken and ultra-contemporary rooms (doubles including breakfast from £75) are splashed

with vibrant colours. Live music plays on weekends.

ℹ Information

Tourist Office (☎01952-433424; www.discovertelford.co.uk/visitironbridge; Museum of the Gorge, The Wharfage; ⊙10am-4pm mid-Mar–Sep, closed Mon Oct–mid-Mar) Located at the Museum of the Gorge (p421).

ℹ Getting There & Away

The nearest train station is 6 miles away at Telford, from where you can travel to Ironbridge on bus 18 (£4.50, 15 minutes, every two hours Monday to Saturday). The same bus continues to Much Wenlock (£4.50, 30 minutes).

Bus 9 runs from Bridgnorth to Ironbridge (£4.50, 30 minutes, every two hours Monday to Saturday).

Bus 96 links Ironbridge with Shrewsbury (£4.50, 35 minutes, every two hours).

Much Wenlock

📞 01952 / POP 2877

With one of those quirky names that abound in the English countryside, Much Wenlock is as charming as it sounds. Surrounding the time-worn ruins of Wenlock Priory, the streets are studded with Tudor, Jacobean and Georgian houses, and locals say hello to everyone. This storybook English village also claims to have jump-started the modern Olympics.

◉ Sights

Wenlock Priory   RUINS
(EH; ☎01952-727466; www.english-heritage.org.uk; 5 Sheinton St; adult/child incl audio guide £6.30/3.80; ⊙10am-6pm Apr-Sep, to 5pm Oct, to 4pm Sat & Sun Nov-Mar) The maudlin Cluniac ruins of Wenlock Priory rise up from vivid green lawns, sprinkled with animal-shaped topiary. The priory was raised by Norman monks over the ruins of a Saxon monastery from AD 680, and its hallowed remains include a finely decorated chapterhouse and an unusual carved lavabo, where monks came to ceremonially wash before eating.

Guildhall   HISTORIC BUILDING
(☎01952-727509; www.muchwenlock-tc.gov.uk; Wilmore St; ⊙11am-4pm Fri-Mon Apr-Oct) FREE Built in classic Tudor style in 1540, the wonky Guildhall features some splendidly ornate woodcarving. One of the pillars sup-

porting it was used for public floggings in medieval times.

🛏 Sleeping & Eating

Wilderhope Manor YHA   HOSTEL £
(☎0845 371 9149; www.yha.org.uk; Longville-in-the-Dale; dm/d/f from £13/50/116, camping per person £12; ⊙hostel year-round, camping Apr-Oct; 🅿@🛜) A gloriously atmospheric gabled greystone Elizabethan manor, with spiral staircases, wood-panelled walls, an impressive stone-floored dining hall and spacious, oak-beamed rooms – this is hostelling for royalty. Wi-fi's available in public areas. In the warmer months, the camping field has space for a handful of tents. It's 7.5 miles southwest of Much Wenlock, best reached by your own wheels.

Raven Hotel   INN ££
(☎01952-727251; https://ravenhotel.com; 30 Barrow St; d/ste incl breakfast from £120/150; 🅿🛜) Much Wenlock's finest place to stay is this 17th-century coaching inn and converted stables with oodles of charm and country-chic styling in its spacious guest rooms. Overlooking a flower-filled courtyard, the excellent restaurant (lunch mains £12 to £22, two-/three-course dinner menus £29/39) serves Mediterranean and British fare.

Fox   PUB FOOD ££
(☎01952-727292; www.foxinnmuchwenlock.co.uk; 46 High St; mains £8.50-20; ⊙kitchen 5-9pm Mon-Fri, from noon Sat, noon-8pm Sun, bar to 11pm; 🛜) Warm yourself by the massive fireplace, then settle down in the dining room to savour locally sourced venison, pheasant and beef, swished down with a pint of Shropshire ale, in this 16th-century inn. Candlelit dinners here are lovely. It also has five contemporary rooms (single/double/family from £50/75/115).

ℹ Information

Tourist Office (☎01952-727679; www.visitmuchwenlock.co.uk; The Square; ⊙10.30am-1pm & 1.30-4pm daily Apr-Oct, Fri-Sun Nov-Mar) Has a modest museum of local history (admission free).

ℹ Getting There & Away

Bus 436 links Shrewsbury with Much Wenlock (£4.50, 35 minutes, hourly Monday to Saturday) and continues on to Bridgnorth (£4.20, 20 minutes). Bus 18 runs to Ironbridge (£4.50, 30 minutes, every two hours Monday to Saturday).

DIANA MILLER / GETTY IMAGES ©

Flavours of England

England has shaken off its reputation for bland food. Today, wherever you go in the country it's possible to find good quality dishes, which focus on locally sourced or seasonally grown ingredients. There's still no English equivalent of 'bon appetit' but at least the term can be used genuinely these days – instead of with a dash of irony.

Breakfast

For many visitors to England, the culinary day begins in a hotel or B&B with the phenomenon known as the 'Full English' – a large plateful of mainly fried food that may be a shock if you usually have just a bowl of cereal. But perseverance is recommended, as there's enough fuel here to see you through hours of sightseeing.

Lunch & Dinner

For lunch or an evening meal, England has a good range of local and international options to suit all budgets, but you should definitely sample two quintessentially English eateries: the cafe and the pub. In cities, cafes are a good cheaper option, while in country areas they're often called teashops – perfect for a traditional afternoon tea with scones, jam and cream. Pubs are the obvious place to sample English beer, as well as being a reliable option for good-value meals.

1. Full English breakfast 2. Fish and chip shop
3. Roast beef and Yorkshire puddling

3

ENGLISH CLASSICS

Fish & chips Long-standing favourite, best sampled in coastal towns.

Sandwich Global snack today, but an English 'invention' from the 18th century.

Ploughman's lunch Bread and cheese, a pub menu regular, perfect with a pint.

Roast beef & Yorkshire pudding Traditional English Sunday lunch.

Cumberland sausage Northern speciality, so big it's coiled to fit on your plate.

Cornish pasty Once restricted to the southwest, now available country-wide.

Bridgnorth

📞 01746 / POP 12,079

Cleaved into two by a dramatic sandstone bluff that tumbles down to the River Severn, Bridgnorth is one of Shropshire's finest-looking historic towns, with a wealth of architectural charm despite much of the High Town succumbing to fire in 1646 during the Civil War.

Around its namesake church, the High Town's adorable St Leonard's Close contains some of the most attractive buildings and almshouses in town, including a splendid six-gabled house, once part of the grammar school.

A 19th-century cliff railway – Britain's steepest – and several narrow lanes drop down from the High Town to the Low Town, including the vertiginous pedestrian Cartway, at the bottom of which is Bishop Percy's House, dating from 1580.

👁 Sights

★ Severn Valley Railway RAIL

(📞 01299-403816; www.svr.co.uk; Hollybush Rd; adult/child one way £14.50/9.50, day ticket £21/14; ⊘ daily May-Sep, Sat & Sun Oct-Apr) Bridgnorth is the northern terminus of the Severn Valley Railway; its historic steam or diesel locomotives chug down the valley to Kidderminster (one hour), starting from the station on Hollybush Rd. Check the calendar for additional event dates, such as afternoon teas, gin and whisky tastings, 1940s re-enactments and evening ghost trains.

Cyclists can follow a beautiful 20-mile section of the Mercian Way (NCN Route 45) beside the railway line towards the Wyre Forest; bikes are free to bring on board the trains.

'Driving experiences', during which you can learn how to drive the steam or diesel trains, start from £160.

Bridgnorth Cliff Railway RAIL

(📞 01746-762052; www.bridgnorthcliffrailway.co.uk; entrances 6a Castle Tce & Underhill St; return £1.60; ⊘ 8am-8pm Mon-Sat, from noon Sun May-Sep, to 6.30pm Oct-Apr) Britain's steepest inland railway has trundled 50m up the cliff since 1892. At the top, a pedestrian walkway (affording astonishing night-time panoramas) curves around the bluff to a pretty park dotted with scattered masonry, some leaning at an incredible angle (all that remains of Bridgnorth Castle), and passes the grand and imposing Thomas Telford–designed and cupola-topped St Mary's Church.

Daniels Mill HISTORIC BUILDING

(📞 01746-769793; www.danielsmill.co.uk; The Cankhorn, Eardington; adult/child £5/4; ⊘ 11am-4pm Thu-Sun Apr-Oct) England's largest working water-powered mill still produces flour for local bakers. Visitors get a personal tour of the machinery in action from the resident miller. It's located 1 mile south of the town centre, reached on foot or with your own wheels.

🛏 Sleeping & Eating

Severn Arms B&B £

(📞 01746-764616; www.thesevernarms.co.uk; 3 Underhill St; s/d/f from £50/60/80, s/d without bathroom from £36/60; 📶) At the bottom of the bluff, conveniently positioned right next to the cliff railway, this riverside Georgian property has nine comfortable rooms, many with bridge views. The helpful owners can direct you to nearby parking. Family rooms can sleep up to two adults and two children.

Fish SEAFOOD, TAPAS £

(📞 01746-768292; www.fishbridgnorth.co.uk; 54 High St; tapas £7-10; ⊘ noon-5pm Wed, Thu & Sat, to 8pm Fri Easter-Oct, 11am-3pm Wed-Fri, to 5pm Sat Nov-Easter) Upturned wine barrels are used as tables at this stylish spot where tapas incorporates premium British seafood (Brixham oysters, dressed Whitby crab, Arbroath smokies, Dover sole, Cornish cockles, smoked North Sea mackerel and Stornoway mussels) from its adjoining fishmonger. By-the-glass wines span the globe.

ℹ Information

Tourist Office (📞 01746-763257; www.visit bridgnorth.co.uk; Listley St; ⊘ 9.30am-6pm Mon, to 5pm Tue, Wed & Fri, to 3pm Sat) Inside the town library.

ℹ Getting There & Away

Bus 436 runs from Shrewsbury to Bridgnorth (£4.20, one hour, hourly Monday to Saturday), via Much Wenlock (£4.20, 20 minutes). Bus 9 runs to Ironbridge (£4.50, 30 minutes, every two hours Monday to Saturday).

Church Stretton

📞 01694 / POP 2789

Tucked in a deep valley formed by the Long Mynd and the Caradoc Hills, Church Stretton is an ideal base for walks or cycle tours through the Shropshire Hills. Although black-and-white timbers are heavily in evidence, most of the buildings in town are 19th-century fakes, built by the Victorians who flocked here to take the country air.

◉ Sights

Walking is the big draw here. The tourist office has maps and details of local mountain-biking circuits and horse-riding stables. Information on activities is also available at www.shropshiresgreatoutdoors.co.uk.

Snailbeach MINE
(☑ 07850 492036; www.shropshiremines.org.uk; tours £7.50/3; ⊙ site 24hr, tours by reservation Sun & Mon Apr-Oct) The former lead- and silver-mining village of Snailbeach is littered with intriguing, rusting machinery relics. You can download a self-guided trail from the website of the **Bog Centre tourist office** (☑ 01743-792484; www.bogcentre.co.uk; The Bog, Stiperstones; ⊙ noon-5pm Mon, from 10am Tue-Sun Easter-Sep, noon-4pm Mon, from 10am Tue-Sun Oct; ☜) to explore the site, or reserve ahead for guided tours (waterproof footwear required) that take you into the mine.

Acton Scott Estate FARM
(☑ 01694-781307; www.actonscott.com; Marshbrook; adult/child £9/5; ⊙ farm 10am-4.30pm Sat-Wed, courses Apr-Dec) On the sprawling Acton Scott Estate, 4 miles south of Church Stretton, this historic working farm has traditional breeds of poultry and livestock, and daily demonstrations of Victorian farming techniques, such as barrel making, horseshoeing and cartwheel construction. Book ahead for courses including blacksmithing, beekeeping, plant identification and 19th-century cookery.

🛏 Sleeping

Bridges Long Mynd YHA HOSTEL £
(☑ 01588-650656; www.yha.org.uk; Bridges; dm from £22, camping per person from £10; ℗) ⵏ On the Long Mynd's western side, this wonderfully isolated hiker favourite, with 38 beds (plus garden tent sites), is housed in a former school in the tiny hamlet of Bridges. No wi-fi, no mobile-phone reception, no credit cards. Cross the Mynd to Ratlinghope, from where it's 1.1 miles southwest, or take buses run by Shropshire Hills Shuttles (p418) in season.

Mynd Guest House B&B ££
(☑ 01694-722212; www.myndhouse.co.uk; Ludlow Rd, Little Stretton; s/d from £60/80; ℗☜) Just under 2 miles south of Church Stretton, this inviting guesthouse has splendid views across the valley and backs directly onto the Mynd. Its eight rooms are named after local landmarks. There's a small bar and lounge stocked with local books, as well as bike storage and a room for drying your boots.

✖ Eating

Van Doesburg's DELI £
(☑ 01694-722867; www.vandoesburgs.co.uk; 3 High St; dishes £1.85-5; ⊙ 9am-5pm Mon-Sat; ☑) A fantastic place to pick up picnic ingredients, Van Doesburg's has over 80 British cheeses and other deli items, such as chutneys. Ready-to-eat dishes to take away include chicken-and-mushroom pies, salads, quiches, soups and outstanding sandwiches (eg roast beef with pickles and mustard or farmhouse cheddar with plum-and-apple relish). Phone ahead to order customised hampers.

Bridges PUB FOOD ££
(☑ 01588-650260; www.thebridgespub.co.uk; Ratlinghope; mains lunch £6-11, dinner £10.50-16; ⊙ kitchen 11.30am-9pm Mon-Sat, 12.30-8.30pm Sun, bar 9.30am-11pm; ☜🐾🐕) Some 5 miles northeast of Church Stretton, at the base of Long Mynd by the river, this is one of those secret country pubs revered for its Three Tuns ale, live music, riverside terrace, relaxed accommodation (dorm/double/family from £30/60/120) and impressive food (lamb shank and mint sauce, beef lasagne...). Mini burgers are among the choices on the kids' menu.

❶ Information

Tourist Office (☑ 01694-723133; www.church stretton.co.uk; Church St; ⊙ 9.30am-1pm & 1.30-5pm Mon-Sat Apr-Sep, 9.30am-1pm & 1.30-3pm Mon-Sat Oct-Mar) Adjoining the library, Church Stretton's tourist office has abundant walking information.

❶ Getting There & Away

BUS

Bus 435 runs from Church Stretton north to Shrewsbury (£3.80, 40 minutes, hourly Monday to Friday, every two hours Saturday) and south to Ludlow (£3.80, 40 minutes, hourly Monday to Friday, every two hours Saturday).

On summer weekends, Shropshire Hills Shuttles (p418) runs an hourly service from the Carding Mill Valley near Church Stretton to the villages atop the Long Mynd, passing the YHA at

Bridges, and Stiperstones near the Snailbeach mine.

TRAIN

Trains between Ludlow (£7.60) and Shrewsbury (£6.60) stop in Church Stretton hourly, taking 15 minutes from either end.

Bishop's Castle

☑ 01588 / POP 1630

Set amid blissfully peaceful Shropshire countryside, Bishop's Castle is a higgledy-piggledy tangle of timbered town houses and Old Mother Hubbard cottages. The High St climbs from the town church to the Georgian town hall.

⊙ Sights

⭐ **Kerry Vale Vineyard**   WINERY
(☑ 01588-620627; www.kerryvalevineyard.co.uk; Pentreheyling; tours £16-35; ⊙ tours noon Thu, Sat, Sun mid-Mar–Nov, shop & cafe 10am-4pm Tue-Sun mid-Mar–Oct, to 3pm Nov & Dec) More than 6000 vines are now planted over 2.4 hectares of the former Pentreheyling Roman Fort, where pottery and metalwork have been uncovered and are displayed at the winery shop. Tours range from an hour-long guided walk through the vines, with a talk on the site's Roman history and tastings, to two-hour guided visits with tastings, a tutorial and an afternoon tea including the vineyard's own sparkling wine. Or pop by the cafe for a wine tasting flight.

House on Crutches   MUSEUM
(☑ 01588-630556; www.hocmuseum.org.uk; High St; ⊙ 2-5pm Sat & Sun Apr-Sep) FREE The crooked 16th-century House on Crutches is home to the small town museum covering Shropshire life over the past two centuries.

🛏 Sleeping

Castle Hotel   HOTEL ££
(☑ 01588-638403; www.thecastlehotelbishopscastle.co.uk; Market Sq; s/d/f incl breakfast from £115/125/180; ▣ 🛜 🐾) This solid-looking 18th-century coaching inn was built with stones from the now-vanished Bishop's Castle, which also contributed the gorgeous wood panelling in the dining room (mains £11 to £22). All 12 en-suite rooms are lovely, with modern fabrics meeting antique furniture; three-bed family rooms and cots are available. Its bar is decidedly cosy and the garden delightful.

Poppy House   B&B ££
(☑ 01588-638443; www.poppyhouse.co.uk; 20 Market Sq; s/d/f from £50/70/90; 🛜) This sweet guesthouse has lovely individual rooms with latch doors and loads of old beams. Children are warmly welcomed; under fives stay free. Breakfast is served at the attached cafe, which opens to the public from 10am to 4pm Wednesday to Monday (dishes £4 to £8.50).

✕ Eating & Drinking

New Deli   DELI £
(32 High St; dishes £2.50-8.50; ⊙ 9am-4pm Tue-Sat) Locally made English and Welsh cheeses and breads, along with hams, salamis and sausages, premade salads, preserves, chutneys and pickles, cakes and biscuits, and ales, wines and liqueurs at this enticing deli mean you're spoiled for choice for picnic fare to take into the surrounding hills.

Three Tuns   PUB
(www.thethreetunsinn.co.uk; Salop St; ⊙ noon-11pm Mon-Sat, to 10.30pm Sun; 🛜) Bishop's Castle's finest watering hole is attached to the tiny Three Tuns Brewery, which has been rolling barrels of nut-brown ale across the courtyard since 1642. It's a lively local, and the ales are delicious. Jazz, blues and brass bands perform regularly in summer.

❶ Information

Tourist Office (☑ 01588-630023; www.bishopscastletownhall.co.uk; High St; ⊙ 10am-4pm Mon-Sat) In the restored town hall (1765), Bishop's Castle's tourist office has details of walking and cycling trails in the surrounding hills. Local artists' work is exhibited in the gallery upstairs.

❶ Getting There & Away

Bus 553 runs to and from Shrewsbury (£3.80, one hour, five per day Monday to Saturday).

Ludlow

☑ 01584 / POP 11,003

On the northern bank of the swirling River Teme, this genteel market town fans out from the rambling ruins of its fine Norman castle, with some magnificent black-and-white Tudor buildings lining its cobbled streets. Premium produce from the lush surrounding countryside has helped the town become a gastronomic beacon, with superb markets, delis, restaurants and food festivals.

◉ Sights

Ludlow Castle
CASTLE

(☑ 01584-873355; www.ludlowcastle.com; Castle Sq; adult/child £6/3; ☉ 10am-5pm mid-Mar–Oct, to 4pm Nov-early Jan & early Feb–mid-Mar, to 4pm Sat & Sun early Jan-early Feb) Perched in an ideal defensive location atop a cliff above a crook in the river, the town castle was built to ward off the marauding Welsh – or to enforce the English expansion into Wales, perspective depending. Founded after the Norman conquest, the castle was dramatically expanded in the 14th century.

The Norman chapel in the inner bailey is one of the few surviving round chapels in England, and the sturdy keep (built around 1090) offers wonderful views over the hills.

Ludlow Brewing Company
BREWERY

(☑ 01584-873291; www.theludlowbrewingcompany. co.uk; The Railway Shed, Station Dr; tours £7; ☉ tours by reservation 3pm Mon-Fri, 2pm Sat, visitor centre & tap room 10am-5pm Mon-Thu & Sat, to 6pm Fri, 11am-4pm Sun) ⏀ Up an inconspicuous laneway, the Ludlow Brewing Company produces award-winning all-natural brews and sells directly from the brewery and its airy, post-industrial-style bar. Hour-long tours include one pint and six samples.

Church of St Laurence
CHURCH

(www.stlaurences.org.uk; 2 College St; admission by £3 donation; ☉ 10am-5pm) One of Britain's largest parish churches, the church of St Laurence contains grand Elizabethan alabaster tombs and delightfully cheeky medieval misericords carved into its medieval choir stalls, including a beer-swilling chap raiding his barrel. The Lady Chapel contains a marvellous Jesse Window, originally dating from 1330 (although the glass is mostly Victorian). Four windows in St John's Chapel date from the mid-15th century, including the honey-coloured Golden Window. Climb 200 steps up the tower (included in donation) for stunning views.

✹✹ Festivals & Events

Ludlow Spring Festival
CULTURAL

(www.ludlowspringestival.co.uk; ☉ mid-May) The two-day Ludlow Spring Festival uses the castle (p431) as its dramatic backdrop for beer, cider and food stalls, a vintage car show and live concerts.

Ludlow Food Festival
FOOD & DRINK

(www.ludlowfoodfestival.co.uk; ☉ early Sep) At Ludlow Castle (p431), the Ludlow Food Fes-

tival spans three days in early September, with over 180 exhibitors from the town and the Welsh Marches.

🛏 Sleeping

Clive
BOUTIQUE HOTEL ££

(☑ 01584-856565; www.theclive.co.uk; Bromfield Rd, Bromfield; d/f incl breakfast from £115/140; 🅿 ❋ 🛜) For foodies, this is Ludlow's ultimate place to stay. Located 4 miles northwest of town adjoining the Ludlow Food Centre (p432), it has its own top-end restaurant; breakfast is served at the Ludlow Kitchen (p431). Many of its 15 spacious rooms are on ground level; family rooms have two sleeping areas separated by a bathroom, giving parents and kids their own space.

Charlton Arms
INN ££

(☑ 01584-872813; www.thecharltonarms.co.uk; Ludford Bridge; d incl breakfast £100-160; 🅿 🛜) The pick of the rooms at this landmark inn overlook the River Teme, and the pick of those have terraces (one with an outdoor hot tub as well as a four-poster bed). Its pub, also opening to a terrace, serves top-quality Modern British cuisine. Service is superb. There's a large free car park on-site.

Feathers Hotel
HISTORIC HOTEL £££

(☑ 01584-875261; www.feathersatludlow.co.uk; 21 Bull Ring; s/d from £95/140; 🅿 🛜) Behind its impossibly ornate timbered Jacobean facade, this 1619-built treasure is all tapestries, creaky furniture, timber beams and stained glass: you can almost hear the cavaliers toasting the health of King Charles. The best rooms are in the old building; rooms in the newer wing lack character and romance. Dinner, bed and breakfast packages are available at its restaurant.

✗ Eating

Ludlow Kitchen
CAFE £

(☑ 01584-856020; www.ludlowkitchen.co.uk; Bromfield Rd, Bromfield; breakfast £3.50-9, lunch mains £7-13; ☉ 8am-5pm Mon-Sat, to 4pm Sun; 🖈) ⏀ Produce from the Ludlow Food Centre (p432) artisanal farm shop is served at its sunlit cafe. Fantastic breakfasts (granola with homemade yoghurt; full English fry-ups with farmhouse eggs, artisan bacon and black pudding; eggs royale) are the precursor to lunch dishes such as Ludlow Brewing Company beer-battered fish with zingy tartar.

Fish House
SEAFOOD ££

(📞01584-879790; www.thefishhouseludlow.co.uk; 51 Bull Ring; dishes £8-15, sharing platters £25-60; ⊙noon-3pm Wed-Sat) Except on Saturdays when it's first-come, first-served, bookings are recommended for the barrel tables at this stylish fish and oyster bar. It sources Britain's best seafood – Whitby crab and lobster, Arbroath smokies, Bigbury Bay oysters – and serves it with organic bread, lemon and mayo, along with wines, local ales, ciders and champagne.

Bistro 7
BISTRO ££

(📞01584-877412; www.bistro7ofludlow.co.uk; 7 Corve St; mains £15.50-21.50; ⊙noon-2.30pm & 6.30-9.30pm Tue-Sat) Ludlow's red-brick former post office is the setting for creative bistro cooking. Knowledgeable staff can guide you through the regularly changing menu, which might feature dishes like wood pigeon salad, black-pudding-stuffed pork loin and red-wine-poached plums with rosemary meringue. Or finish with a platter of local cheeses served with nettle and spiced-apple chutney.

Mortimers
BRITISH £££

(📞01584-872325; www.mortimersludlow.co.uk; 17 Corve St; 2-/3-course lunch menu £22.50/26, 3-course dinner menu £47.50, 7-course tasting menu £62.50, with paired wines £100; ⊙noon-2pm

& 6.30-9pm Tue-Sat; 📋) For fine dining, this is Ludlow's top table. Dark timber panelling and cosy nooks and crannies create a romantic backdrop for intricate dishes such as scallops with truffled pumpkin purée or lacquered Ludlow duck with pastrami-wrapped celeriac. Vegetarians can prebook a meat-free version of the seven-course tasting menu, featuring creations like asparagus with roast baby beetroot and sorrel panna cotta.

🛍 Shopping

⭐ **Ludlow Food Centre**
FOOD & DRINKS

(📞01584-856000; www.ludlowfoodcentre.co.uk; Bromfield Rd, Bromfield; ⊙9am-5.30pm Mon-Sat, 10am-5pm Sun) 🍴 More than 80% of the cheeses, meats, breads, fruit and vegetables are sourced from the surrounding region and tantalisingly displayed at this enormous farm shop, including many produced on the estate. Watch through viewing windows to see traditional preserves, pies, ice cream and more being made. It's signposted 2.8 miles northwest of Ludlow off Bromfield Rd (the A49).

Look out for regular events including tastings. There's a kids' playground and a picnic area. Produce is used by the adjoining cafe-restaurant, the Ludlow Kitchen (p431).

Ludlow Market
MARKET

(www.ludlowmarket.co.uk; Castle Sq; ⊙9.30am-2pm Mon, Wed, Fri & Sat) Ludlow Market's stalls sell fresh produce, artisan food and drink, flowers, books, gifts and more. Various spin-off markets (farmers markets, flea markets, book markets and craft markets) take place on Thursdays and Sundays.

ℹ Information

Tourist Office (📞01584-875053; www.visitshropshirehills.co.uk; 1 Mill St; ⊙10am-4pm Mon-Sat Mar-Dec, to 2pm Mon-Sat Jan & Feb) On the 3rd floor of the Ludlow Assembly Rooms.

ℹ Getting There & Away

BUS

Bus 435 runs to Shrewsbury (£4.10, 1¼ hours, hourly Monday to Saturday) via Church Stretton (£3.10, 35 minutes).

TRAIN

Trains run frequently from the station on the north edge of town to Hereford (£10.40, 25 minutes, up to two per hour) and Shrewsbury

---

BYRON'S NEWSTEAD ABBEY

Founded as an Augustinian priory in around 1170, lakeside **Newstead Abbey** (📞01623-455900; www.newstead abbey.org.uk; Newstead; house & gardens adult/child £10/6, park free; ⊙house & gardens noon-4pm Sat & Sun, park 10am-5pm daily) was converted into a residence in 1539. It's inextricably associated with the original tortured romantic, Lord Byron (1788–1824), who inherited the house in 1798, selling it in 1818.

Byron's old living quarters are full of suitably eccentric memorabilia, and the landscaped grounds include a monument to his yappy dog, Boatswain.

Newstead Abbey is 12 miles north of Nottingham, off the A60. Pronto buses (£3.50, 25 minutes, every 10 minutes Monday to Saturday, half-hourly Sunday) from Nottingham's Victoria bus station stop at the gates, a mile from the house and gardens.

(£13.50, 30 minutes, up to two per hour), via Church Stretton (£7.60, 15 minutes).

NOTTINGHAMSHIRE

Say Nottinghamshire and people think of one thing – Robin Hood. Whether the hero woodsman existed is hotly debated, but the county plays up its connections to the outlaw. Storytelling seems to be in Nottinghamshire's blood – local wordsmiths include provocative writer DH Lawrence, of *Lady Chatterley's Lover* fame, and hedonistic poet Lord Byron. The city of Nottingham is the bustling hub; venture into the surrounding countryside and you'll discover historic towns and stately homes surrounding the green bower of Sherwood Forest.

❶ Getting There & Away

National Express and **Trent Barton** (✐ 01773-712265; www.trentbarton.co.uk) buses provide the majority of bus services. See Traveline (p390) for timetables. Trains run frequently to most large towns, and to many smaller villages in the Peak District.

Nottingham

✐ 0115 / POP 321,550

Forever associated with men in tights and a sheriff with anger-management issues (aka the Robin Hood legend), Nottingham is a dynamic county capital with big-city aspirations, evocative historical sights, and a buzzing music and club scene thanks to its spirited student population.

◎ Sights

Nottingham Castle CASTLE, GALLERY
(www.nottinghamcity.gov.uk; Lenton Rd) Nottingham's castle crowns a sandstone outcrop worm-holed with caves and tunnels. Founded by William the Conqueror, the original castle was held by a succession of English kings before falling in the English Civil War.

Its 17th-century manor-house-like replacement is undergoing major renovations, and is closed until spring 2020. When it reopens, it will feature a new Robin Hood Gallery, a Rebellion Gallery, covering social unrest from medieval times, and displays on art and manufacturing, including salt-glazed stoneware and lacemaking.

Access to the cave system will be extended, parts of the castle grounds will be remodelled to reveal more of the medieval site, and a new visitor centre and cafe will open here. The 17th-century cottages comprising the **Museum of Nottingham Life at Brewhouse Yard** will also reopen in mid-2020.

The much-photographed **statue of Robin Hood** stands in the former moat and remains accessible while works take place.

Wollaton Hall HISTORIC BUILDING
(✐ 0115-876 3100; www.wollatonhall.org.uk; Wollaton Park, Derby Rd; tours adult/child £5/free, grounds free; ◎ tours noon & 2pm, grounds 8am-dusk Mon-Fri, from 9am Sat & Sun) Built in 1588 for coal mogul Sir Francis Willoughby by avant-garde architect Robert Smythson, Wollaton Hall sits within 200 hectares of grounds roamed by fallow and red deer. Tours lasting 45 minutes lead you through extravagant rooms from the Tudor, Regency and Victorian periods. There's also a natural-history museum here.

Wollaton Hall is 2.5 miles west of Nottingham city centre; take bus L2, 30 or 'The 2' from Victoria bus station (£4, 15 minutes, every 15 minutes Monday to Saturday, half-hourly Sunday).

The hall starred as Wayne Manor in 2012's Batman film *The Dark Knight Rises*.

City of Caves CAVE
(✐ 0115-952 0555; www.cityofcaves.com; Drury Walk, Upper Level, Broadmarsh shopping centre; adult/child £7.95/6.95, incl National Justice Museum £16/11.95; ◎ tours 10.30am-4pm) Over the centuries, the sandstone underneath Nottingham has been carved into a honeycomb of caverns and passageways. Tours lead you from the top level of the Broadmarsh shopping centre through a WWII air-raid shelter, a medieval underground tannery, several pub cellars and a mock-up of a Victorian slum dwelling. Book ahead.

National Justice Museum MUSEUM
(✐ 0115-952 0555; www.nationaljusticemuseum. org.uk; High Pavement; adult/child £9.95/7.95, incl City of Caves £16/11.95; ◎ 9am-5.30pm Mon-Fri, from 10am Sat & Sun) In the grand Georgian Shire Hall, the National Justice Museum offers a ghoulish stroll through centuries of British justice, including medieval trials by fire and water. There are costumed characters representing historical figures, and activities, exhibitions and re-enacted courtroom performances regularly take place. Tickets are valid all day.

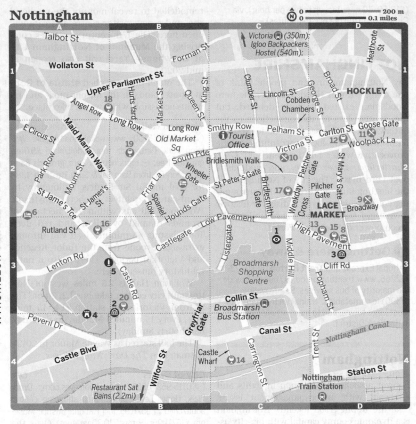

Nottingham

◉ Sights

1	City of Caves	C3
2	Museum of Nottingham Life at Brewhouse Yard	B3
3	National Justice Museum	D3
4	Nottingham Castle	A4
5	Statue of Robin Hood	A3

🛏 Sleeping

6	Hart's	A2
7	Igloo Hybrid Hostel	B2
8	Lace Market Hotel	D3

✦ Eating

9	Annie's Burger Shack	D2
10	Delilah Fine Foods	C2
	Hart's Restaurant	(see 6)
11	Larder on Goosegate	D2
	Merchants	(see 8)

🍷 Drinking & Nightlife

12	Boilermaker	D2
13	Brass Monkey	D3
14	Canal House	C4
15	Cock & Hoop	D3
16	Crafty Crow	A3
17	Cross Keys	C2
18	Dragon	A1
19	Malt Cross	B2
20	Ye Olde Trip to Jerusalem	B3

👉 Tours

★ **Ezekial Bone Tours** WALKING
(☏ 07941 210986; www.ezekialbone.com; adult/child Robin Hood Town Tour £14.50/8, Nottingham

in a Nutshell Tour £12/6; ⊙ Robin Hood Town Tour 2pm Sat Mar-Oct, Nottingham in a Nutshell Tour 11am Sat Mar-Oct) Hugely entertaining, history-focused tours led by multi-award-winning 'modern-day Robin Hood' Ezekial Bone (aka historian/actor/writer/local legend Ade Andrews) are a highlight of visiting Nottingham. **Robin Hood Town Tours** lasting 2½ hours depart from the **Cross Keys pub** (www.crosskeysnottingham.co.uk; 15 Byard Lane; ◉9am-11pm Sun-Wed, to midnight Thu & Fri, to 1am Sat); whistle-stop 90-minute **Nottingham in a Nutshell** tours depart from the tourist office (p437). Tours run most Saturdays in season; confirm departures ahead.

Lace Market tours and **Robin Hood Sherwood Forest tours** are also available by request.

✦ Festivals & Events

Goose Fair FAIR
(◉early Oct) The five-day Goose Fair has evolved from a medieval travelling market to a modern funfair with over 500 attractions and rides.

Robin Hood Beer & Cider Festival DRINK
(www.beerfestival.nottinghamcamra.org; ◉mid-Oct) This four-day tasting festival features more than 1000 beers and 250 ciders and perries.

Robin Hood Pageant CULTURAL
(www.visit-nottinghamshire.co.uk; ◉late Oct) The family-friendly Robin Hood Pageant takes place over two days in late October. Check with the tourist office (p437) for details of 2019's event; from 2020 the pageant is expected to return to the grounds of Nottingham Castle following its reopening after renovations.

🛏 Sleeping

Igloo Hybrid Hostel HOSTEL £
(☑0115-948 3822; www.igloohostel.co.uk; 4-6 Eldon Chambers, Wheeler Gate; dm from £19, s/d sleep box from £32/64, s with/without en suite from £39/34, d with/without en suite £84/72; ☎) The sister property of the much-loved **Igloo Backpackers Hostel** (☑0115-947 5250; www.igloohostel.co.uk; 110 Mansfield Rd; dm/s/d/tr from £20/29/64/78; ☎) has a central location footsteps from the Old Market Sq. Cabin-style 'sleep boxes' incorporate USB ports and reading lights; there's a well-equipped self-catering kitchen and a sociable courtyard garden.

★ Lace Market Hotel BOUTIQUE HOTEL ££
(☑0115-948 4414; www.lacemarkethotel.co.uk; 29-31 High Pavement; s/d/ste incl breakfast from £76/122/184; P✳☎) In the heart of the gentrified Lace Market, this elegant Georgian town house's 42 sleek rooms have state-of-the-art furnishings and amenities; some come with air-conditioning. Its fine-dining restaurant, Merchants (p436), and adjoining pub, the **Cock & Hoop** (www.lacemarkethotel.co.uk; 25 High Pavement; ◉noon-11pm Mon-Thu, to midnight Fri, to 1am Sat, to 10.30pm Sun, hours can vary), are both superb.

Hart's BOUTIQUE HOTEL £££
(☑0115-988 1900; www.hartsnottingham.co.uk; Standard Hill, Park Row; d/ste incl breakfast from £139/279; P☎) Within the former Nottingham General Hospital compound, this swish hotel has ultra-contemporary rooms (some with small terraces) in a striking modernist building. Its renowned **restaurant** (mains £17.50-32.50; ◉7am-2.30pm & 6-10pm Mon-Fri, 7.30am-2.30pm & 6-10.30pm Sat, 7.30am-2.30pm & 6-9pm Sun; ✎) is housed in a historic red-brick wing. Work out in the small gym or unwind in the private garden.

🍴 Eating

★ Delilah Fine Foods DELI, CAFE £
(☑0115-948 4461; www.delilahfinefoods.co.uk; 12 Victoria St; dishes £4-10, platters £17-20; ◉8am-7pm Mon-Fri, from 9am Sat, 11am-5pm Sun; ✎) ✿ Impeccably selected cheeses (more than 150 varieties), pâtés, meats and more from artisan producers are available to take away or eat on-site at this foodie's fantasy land, housed in a grand former bank with mezzanine seating. It doesn't take reservations but you can preorder customised hampers for a gourmet picnic.

Annie's Burger Shack BURGERS, AMERICAN £
(☑0115-684 9920; www.anniesburgershack.com; 5 Broadway; burgers £8.90-13.20, breakfast £6-10; ◉8-10.30am & noon-11pm Sun-Thu, 8-10.30am & noon-midnight Fri & Sat; ☎✎) More than 30 different burgers (available in vegan, veggie or meat versions) are on the menu at Annie's, a wildly popular joint in the Lace Market that stays true to its owner's US roots (and adds real ales to its offerings). Midweek breakfast menus feature American classics (blueberry pancakes with maple syrup and bacon; Boston franks 'n' beans). Book ahead.

Larder on Goosegate BRITISH ££
(☑0115-950 0111; www.thelarderongoosegate.co.uk; 16-22 Goosegate; mains £13.50-22, afternoon tea from £16.50; ◉5.30-10pm Tue-Thu, noon-2.30 & 5.30-11pm Fri & Sat) Floor-to-ceiling windows fill this 1st-floor restaurant with light and provide bird's-eye views of busy Goosegate

below. Blue goats cheese and beetroot cheesecake, Shetland Queen scallops with wild-garlic butter and roast spring lamb with smoked aubergine are among its superbly executed British dishes. On Fridays and Saturdays, afternoon tea is served on antique bone china. Book ahead.

Merchants
EUROPEAN £££

(☑ 0115-948 4414; www.lacemarkethotel.co.uk; 29-31 High Pavement; mains £16-30; ⊗ 7am-10pm Mon-Fri, 8-10.30am & noon-5pm Sat, 7-10.30am & noon-2pm Sun) A stunning, coffered-ceilinged dining room sets the stage for some of Nottingham's finest dining. Knock-out combinations on its changing menu might include Texel lamb with pistachio and courgette; Irish sea trout with samphire and radish; or morrels, broad beans and goats curd. Follow up with desserts such as poached-rhubarb panna cotta with black-pepper crumble and basil ice cream.

Restaurant Sat Bains
GASTRONOMY £££

(☑ 0115-986 6566; www.restaurantsatbains.com; Lenton Lane; 7-/10-course tasting menus £95/110; ⊗ 6-9pm Wed & Thu, to 9.45pm Fri & Sat; ☑) Boundary-pushing chef Sat Bains has been awarded two Michelin stars for his wildly inventive tasting menus (no à la carte; dietary restrictions can be catered for with advance notice). Book *well* ahead and beware of hefty cancellation charges. It also has chic guest rooms (double £140 to £190, suite £285). It's 2 miles southwest of the city centre off the A52.

🍷 Drinking & Nightlife

★ Ye Olde Trip to Jerusalem
PUB

(☑ 0115-947 3171; www.triptojerusalem.com; Brewhouse Yard, Castle Rd; ⊗ 11am-11pm Sun-Thu, to midnight Fri & Sat) Carved into the cliff below the castle, this atmospheric alehouse claims to be England's oldest pub. Founded in 1189, it supposedly slaked the thirst of departing crusaders, and its warren of rooms and cobbled courtyards make it the most ambient place in Nottingham for a pint.

Call ahead to ask about tours of its cellars and caves.

★ Crafty Crow
PUB

(www.craftycrownotts.co.uk; 102 Friar Lane; ⊗ noon-11pm Sun-Thu, 11am-midnight Fri & Sat; ☑) ♪ Rotating brews at this beer specialist include several from its own Nottingham-based Magpie Brewery, made from British hops and malts, plus hand-pulls

from local microbreweries and craft beers and ciders on tap. Timber-planked walls line the TV-free split-level space; don't miss the bathrooms with sinks and taps made out of kegs. Gastropub food is locally sourced.

Dragon
PUB

(☑ 0115-941 7080; www.the-dragon.co.uk; 67 Long Row; ⊗ noon-11.30pm Sun-Wed, to midnight Thu, to 1am Fri & Sat; ☑) The Dragon has a fabulous atmosphere at any time, thanks to homemade food, a good beer garden and vinyl played on weekends. But it peaks from 7.30pm on Tuesdays when it hosts Race Night (race entry £5) in the Racing Room (www.theracingroom.co.uk), with an awesome Scalextric slot-car race around a scale model of Nottingham along 180ft of track.

Boilermaker
COCKTAIL BAR

(www.boilermakerbar.co.uk; 36b Carlton St; ⊗ 5pm-1am Mon-Fri, from 2pm Sat, from 7pm Sun) Entering what appears to be an industrial boilermaker's shop and navigating your way through two secret doors brings you into this cavernous, low-lit speakeasy spinning chilled lounge music. Out-there cocktail combinations (eg Figgy Stardust, with tequila, artichoke-based Cynar liqueur, figs, pomegranate shrub and black walnuts) add to the unique-and-then-some experience.

Malt Cross
PUB

(www.maltcross.com; 16 St James's St; ⊗ 11am-11pm Mon-Thu, to 1am Fri, 10am-1am Sat, 10am-9pm Sun) A fine place for a pint, the Malt Cross occupies a stately old Victorian music hall, where past performers included Charlie Chaplin. It's now a community space run by the Christian Charity Trust hosting art exhibitions and live music. Top-notch bar food includes towering burgers.

Brass Monkey
COCKTAIL BAR

(www.brassmonkeybar.co.uk; 11 High Pavement; ⊗ 5pm-3am Mon-Sat) Nottingham's original cocktail bar rocks the Lace Market with DJ sets and quirky takes on favourites such as elderflower mojitos. The roof terrace gets packed on summer evenings.

Canal House
PUB

(☑ 0115-955 5060; www.castlerockbrewery.co.uk/pubs/the-canalhouse; 48-52 Canal St; ⊗ 11am-11pm Mon-Wed, to midnight Thu, to 1am Fri & Sat, to 10.30pm Sun) Split in two by a watery inlet, the Canal House is the best of the city's canal-front pubs, with plenty of waterside seating and beers by Nottingham-based

DON'T MISS

SHERWOOD FOREST NATIONAL NATURE RESERVE

If Robin Hood wanted to hide out in Sherwood Forest today, he'd have to disguise himself as day trippers on mountain bikes. Now covering just 182 hectares of old-growth forest, it's nevertheless a major destination for Nottingham city dwellers. The week-long **Robin Hood Festival** (www.nottinghamshire.gov.uk; ⊘ Aug) is a massive medieval reenactment that takes place in the forest in August.

The reserve's curved-timber **visitor centre** (www.visitsherwood.co.uk; Forest Corner, Edwinstowe; forest & visitor centre free, parking £4; ⊘ 10am-6pm Mar-Sep, to 4pm Oct-Feb) 🖉 , reopened in 2018, provides information about the forest's wildlife, walking trails and Robin Hood legends – including the 800-year-old **Major Oak**, a broad-boughed oak tree (propped up by supporting rods) alleged to have sheltered Robin of Locksley.

Located 2 miles south of Sherwood Forest on the B6030, **Sherwood Pines Cycles** (☑ 01623-822855; www.sherwoodpinescycles.co.uk; Sherwood Pines Forest Park, Old Clipstone; bike hire adult/child per hour £9/8, per day £28/20; ⊘ 9am-5pm Thu-Tue, to 7pm Wed) rents mountain bikes for exploring the area's trails.

Castle Rock Brewery on tap. Regular events range from comedy to craft beer festivals.

ℹ Information

Nottingham's **tourist office** (☑ 0844 477 5678; www.experiencenottinghamshire.com; The Exchange, 1-4 Smithy Row; ⊘ 9.30am-5.30pm Mon-Sat year-round, plus 11am-5pm Sun Jul, Aug & early Dec-Christmas) has racks of information along with Robin Hood merchandise.

ℹ Getting There & Away

AIR

East Midlands Airport (p454) is 13.5 miles southwest of central Nottingham. Skylink buses pass the airport (one way/return £5.20/10.40, one hour, at least hourly, 24 hours).

BUS

Local services run from the Victoria bus station, behind the Victoria shopping centre on Milton St. Bus 100 runs to Southwell (£4.30, one hour, hourly) and bus 90 to Newark (£5.50, 50 minutes, hourly Monday to Saturday, every two hours Sunday).

Long-distance buses operate from the **Broadmarsh bus station** (Collin St).

Frequent National Express services:

Birmingham £11.10, 2¼ hours, nine daily
Derby £9, 40 minutes, seven daily
Leicester £4.60, 55 minutes, hourly or better
London Victoria £9.30, 3½ hours, every two hours

TRAIN

The train station is on the southern edge of the city centre.

Derby £7.60, 30 minutes, four hourly
Lincoln £11.80, 55 minutes, hourly

London King's Cross/St Pancras £47, 1¾ hours, two per hour
Manchester £27.50, 1¾ hours, up to two per hour

Newark-on-Trent

☑ 01636 / POP 27,700

Newark-on-Trent paid the price for backing the wrong side in the English Civil War. After surviving four sieges by Oliver Cromwell's men, the town was ransacked by Roundheads when Charles I surrendered in 1646. Today, the riverside town is a peaceful place worth a stop to wander its castle ruins.

⊙ Sights

Newark Castle   CASTLE
(www.newark-sherwooddc.gov.uk/newarkcastle; Castle Gate; grounds free, tours adult/child £5.50/2.75; ⊘ grounds dawn-dusk, tours by reservation Wed & Fri-Sun) In a pretty park overlooking the River Trent, the ruins of Newark Castle include an impressive Norman gate and a series of underground passages and chambers. The real King John, portrayed as a villain in the Robin Hood legend, died here in 1216. Book tour tickets online at www.palacenewarktickets. com. Concerts, festivals and various cultural events regularly take place in the grounds.

Newark Air Museum   MUSEUM
(☑ 01636-707170; www.newarkairmuseum.org; Drove Lane, Winthorpe; adult/child £9/4.50; ⊘ 10am-5pm Mar-Oct, to 4pm Nov-Feb) Situated 2 miles east of Newark by the Winthorpe Showground, this aviation museum has over 100 aircraft, including a fearsome Vulcan bomber, a Vampire T11, a Gloster Meteor and a de

Havilland Tiger Moth, along with a small exhibition on the Royal Air Force.

✕ Eating & Drinking

Old Bakery Tea Rooms
CAFE £

(☑ 01636-611501; www.oldbakerytearooms.co.uk; 4 Queens Head Ct; mains £6-12; ⊙ 9.30am-5pm Mon-Sat; ✔) Everything, including heavenly sweet and savoury scones, is baked fresh on the premises at the Old Bakery Tea Rooms, housed in an enchanting 15th-century Tudor building. Lunch specials include soups, frittata, bruschetta and smoked-salmon brioche. Cash only.

Castle Barge
BAR

(www.castlebarge.com; The Wharf; ⊙ 10.30am-midnight) Moored on the River Trent overlooking Newark Castle, this former grain barge, which once plied the waters between Hull and Gainsborough, is an idyllic spot for a local ale inside or up on deck, with additional picnic seating on the riverbanks. Its menu includes stone-baked pizzas.

ℹ Information

Tourist Office (☑ 01636-655765; www.newark-sherwooddc.gov.uk; 14 Appleton Gate; ⊙ 10am-4pm) On the northeastern edge of the historic centre.

ℹ Getting There & Away

Buses 28 and 29 serve Southwell (£6.70, 45 minutes, two per hour).

Newark has two train stations:

Newark Castle East Midlands trains serve Leicester (£18.30, 1¼ hours, hourly), Nottingham (£6.40, 30 minutes, two per hour) and Lincoln (£5.40, 25 minutes, two per hour).

Newark North Gate Trains on the East Coast Main Line serve London King's Cross (£34.50, 1½ hours, two per hour); destinations to the north require a change in Doncaster (£24.80, 25 minutes, hourly).

Southwell

☑ 01636 / POP 7297

A graceful scattering of grand, wisteria-draped country houses, pretty little Southwell is straight out of the pages of a novel from the English Romantic period.

◉ Sights

★ Southwell Minster
CHURCH

(www.southwellminster.org; Church St; suggested donation £5; ⊙ 8am-7pm Mar-Oct, to 6.30pm Nov-Feb) Rising from the village centre, the awe-inspiring Southwell Minster, built over Saxon and Roman foundations, blends 12th-and 13th-century features, including zigzag door frames and curved arches. Its chapter-house features some unusual stained glass and detailed carvings of faces, animals and leaves of forest trees.

Southwell Workhouse
MUSEUM

(NT; ☑ 01636-817260; www.nationaltrust.org.uk; Upton Rd; adult/child £9.10/4.55; ⊙ guided exteriors tours 11am, Workhouse noon-5pm Mar-early Nov) On the road to Newark, 1 mile east of the village centre, the Southwell Workhouse is a sobering reminder of the tough life faced by paupers in the 19th century. You can explore the factory floors and workers' chambers accompanied by an audio guide narrated by 'inmates' and 'officials'. One-hour guided tours of the exteriors take place at 11am.

🛏 Sleeping & Eating

Saracen's Head Hotel
HISTORIC HOTEL ££

(☑ 01636-812701; www.saracensheadhotel.com; Market Pl; s/d/f/ste incl breakfast from £90/100/130/150; P🐾🌐😮) Set around a flower-filled courtyard in the village heart, this rambling, black-and-white timbered coaching inn has 27 beautifully refurbished rooms (some with four-poster beds and claw-foot baths) across its old and new wings. Illustrious past guests included Charles I, Lord Byron and Dickens. Its oak-panelled restaurant serves traditional British fare (two-/three-course menus £19.50/23.50).

Family rooms sleep up to four; baby cots are available.

Old Theatre Deli
CAFE, DELI £

(www.theoldtheatredeli.co.uk; 4 Market Pl; dishes £6-12; ⊙ 8.30am-6pm) Artisan breads from the Midlands' renowned Hambleton Bakery, gourmet sandwiches, quiches, pies, salads and hot specials, such as corn-and-bacon fritters, are among the treats to take away or eat inside or out on the pavement terrace. You can also order picnic hampers complete with blankets. It's housed inside a Georgian former theatre.

ℹ Getting There & Away

Bus 100 runs from Nottingham (£4.30, one hour, hourly). For Newark-on-Trent, take bus 28 or 29 (£6.70, 45 minutes, two per hour).

LINCOLNSHIRE

Lincolnshire unfolds over low hills and the sparsely populated, pancake-flat Fens where the farmland is strewn with windmills and, more recently, wind turbines. Surrounding the history-steeped county town of Lincoln you'll find seaside resorts, scenic waterways, serene nature reserves and stone-built towns tailor-made for English period dramas.

Two of the county's most famous 'yellowbellies' (as Lincolnshire locals call themselves) were Sir Isaac Newton, whose home, Woolsthorpe Manor, can be visited, and the late former prime minister Margaret Thatcher, the daughter of a humble greengrocer from the market town of Grantham.

🏃 Activities

Traversing the area occupied by Norse invaders in the 9th century, the 147-mile **Viking Way** walking trail snakes across the gentle hills of the Lincolnshire Wolds from the banks of the River Humber to Oakham in Rutland.

Cyclists can find information on routes across the county in any of the local tourist offices. The 33-mile **Water Rail Way** is a flat, sculpture-lined on-road cycling route that follows the River Witham through classic Fens countryside along the former railway line between Lincoln and Boston.

ℹ Getting There & Away

East Midlands trains connect Lincoln, Newark Castle and Nottingham. Newark North Gate and Grantham lie on the East Coast Main Line between London King's Cross and Edinburgh.

Local buses link Lincolnshire's towns, but services are slow and infrequent. Check the transport pages at www.lincolnshire.gov.uk.

Comprehensive transport information is available from Traveline (p390).

Lincoln

📞 01522 / POP 97,541

Ringed by historic city gates – including the Newport Arch on Bailgate, a relic from the original Roman settlement – this beautiful city's old centre is a tangle of cobbled medieval streets surrounding its 11th-century castle and colossal 12th-century cathedral. The lanes that topple over the edge of Lincoln Cliff are lined with Tudor town houses, ancient pubs and independent shops.

BELTON HOUSE

Amid 14.2 hectares of elegant formal gardens, **Belton House** (NT; 📞 01476-566116; www.nationaltrust.org.uk; Belton; house & grounds adult/child £15.70/10, grounds only £12/8.20; ⏰ house 12.30-5pm Wed-Sun Mar-Oct, closed Nov-Feb, grounds 9.30am-5.30pm Mar-Oct, to 4pm Nov-Feb) is a dream filming location for English period dramas, *Jane Eyre*, *Tom Jones* and the Colin Firth version of *Pride and Prejudice* among them. Built in 1688 in classic Restoration style, the house retains stunning original features, including ornate woodcarvings by master Dutch carver Grinling Gibbons. It's off the A607, 2.5 miles northeast of Grantham, and is served by Stagecoach bus 1 (£2.50, 15 minutes, hourly Monday to Saturday, every two hours Sunday).

The surrounding 526-hectare grounds have been home to a fallow deer herd for more than 300 years. Also on the site are a farm shop, a restaurant, a cafe and an adventure playground.

Flanking the River Witham at the base of the hill, the new town is less absorbing, but the revitalised Brayford Waterfront development by the university is a popular spot to watch the boats go by.

⊙ Sights

⭐**Lincoln Cathedral**　　　　　　CATHEDRAL
(📞 01522-561600; www.lincolncathedral.com; Minster Yard; adult/child joint ticket with castle £17.20/9.60, cathedral £8/4.80 Mon-Sat, by donation before 9am, after 4.30pm & all day Sun; ⏰ 7.15am-8pm Mon-Fri, to 6pm Sat & Sun Jul & Aug, 7.15am-6pm Mon-Sat, to 5pm Sun Sep-Jun) Towering over the city like a medieval skyscraper, Lincoln's magnificent cathedral is a breathtaking representation of divine power on earth. The great tower rising above the crossing is the third-highest in England at 83m, but in medieval times, a lead-encased wooden spire added a further 79m, topping even the great pyramids of Giza. One-hour **guided tours** (included in admission) take place at least twice Monday to Saturday; there are also tours of the roof and tower (£4; book in advance).

The vast interior of the church is too large for modern congregations – services

Lincoln

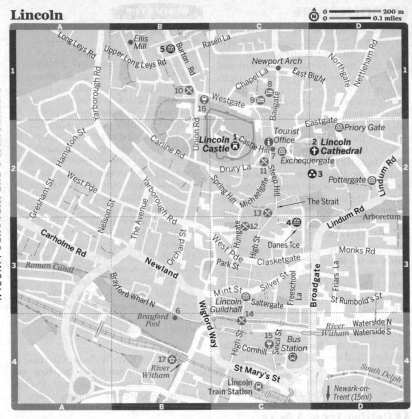

Lincoln

take place instead in **St Hugh's Choir**, a church within a church running east from the crossing. The choir stalls are accessed through a magnificent carved stone screen;

look north to see the stunning rose window known as the Dean's Eye (c 1192), mirrored to the south by the floral flourishes of the Bishop's Eye (1330). There's more stained glass in the three Services Chapels in the north transept.

Beyond St Hugh's Choir, the **Angel Choir** is supported by 28 columns topped by carvings of angels and foliate scrollwork. Other interesting details include the 10-sided **chapterhouse** – where Edward I held his parliament and where the climax of the *Da Vinci Code* was filmed in 2005.

The best time to hear the organ resounding through the cathedral is during **evensong**; check times online.

★ **Lincoln Castle**   CASTLE
(☑ 01522-554559; www.lincolncastle.com; Castle Hill; adult/child joint ticket with cathedral £17.20/9.60, castle day ticket £13.50/7.20, walls only £7.50/5, grounds free; ◷ 10am-5pm Apr-Sep, to 4pm Oct-Mar) One of the first castles erected by the victorious William the Conqueror, in 1068, to keep his new kingdom in line, Lincoln Castle offers awesome views over the city and miles of surrounding countryside. A major 2015-completed restoration program opened up the entire castle walls and gave the 1215 **Magna Carta** (one of only four copies) a swanky, subterranean new home. One-hour guided tours, included in the castle admission, depart from the eastern gate; check the blackboard for times.

Bishops' Palace   RUINS
(EH; ☑ 01522-527468; www.english-heritage.org.uk; Minster Yard; adult/child £5.90/3.50; ◷ 10am-6pm Wed-Sun Apr-Sep, to 5pm Wed-Sun Oct, to 4pm Sat & Sun Nov-Mar) Beside Lincoln Cathedral lie the time-ravaged but still imposing ruins of the 12th-century Bishops' Palace, gutted by parliamentary forces during the Civil War. From here, the local bishops once controlled a diocese stretching from the Humber to the Thames. Entertaining audio guides are included in admission. Grapevines are planted in its hillside terraced garden.

Museum of Lincolnshire Life   MUSEUM
(☑ 01522-782040; www.lincolnshire.gov.uk; Old Barracks, Burton Rd; ◷ 10am-4pm) **FREE** Displays at this charming community museum housed in an old Victorian barracks span everything from Victorian farm implements to the tin-can tank built in Lincoln for WWI.

Collection   MUSEUM
(☑ 01522-782040; www.thecollectionmuseum.com; Danes Tce; ◷ 10am-4pm, from 10.45am 1st Mon of month) **FREE** Archaeology bursts into life at this museum, with loads of hands-on

displays. Kids can handle artefacts and dress up in period costume. Check out the crushed skull of a 4000-year-old 'yellowbelly' (as locals are dubbed), pulled from a Neolithic burial site near Sleaford. Free one-hour tours run at 2pm on Saturdays. Look out for various evening events.

Exchequergate   HISTORIC BUILDING
Located between the castle and the cathedral, the triple-arched, battlement-topped Exchequergate, where the church's tenants paid their rent, dates from the 14th century. A black-and-white chequered cloth was used to help count the payments, giving rise to the term exchequer.

ⓖ Tours

Ghost Walks   WALKING
(☑ 01673-857574; www.lincolnghostwalks.co.uk; adult/child £5/3; ◷ 7pm Wed-Sat) Genuinely spooky 75-minute ghost walks depart adjacent to the tourist office year-round. Bookings aren't required; turn up 10 minutes before tours begin.

Brayford Belle   CRUISE
(☑ 01522-881200; www.lincolnboattrips.co.uk; Brayford Wharf North; adult/child £7/4; ◷ tours 11am, 12.15pm, 1.30pm, 2.45pm & 3.45pm daily Easter-Sep, hours vary Oct) Boat trips lasting around 50 minutes aboard the *Brayford Belle* travel along the River Witham and Fossdyke Navigation, a canal system dating back to Roman times. No credit cards.

🛏 Sleeping

Castle Hotel   BOUTIQUE HOTEL ££
(☑ 01522-538801; www.castlehotel.net; Westgate; s/d/coach house incl breakfast from £90/120/220; 🅿 🛜) Each of the Castle Hotel's 18 rooms have been exquisitely refurbished in olive, truffle and oyster tones, as has its family-friendly four-person coach house. Built on the site of Lincoln's Roman forum in 1852, the red-brick building's incarnations variously included a school and a WWII lookout station. Take advantage of great-value dinner, bed and breakfast deals with its award-winning restaurant **Reform** (www.reformrestaurant.co.uk; mains £15-22; ◷ noon-2.30pm & 7-9pm Wed-Sat, noon-3pm Sun).

Bail House   B&B ££
(☑ 01522-541000; www.bailhouse.co.uk; 34 Bailgate; d/f from £84/134; 🅿 🛜 🏊) Stone walls, worn flagstones, secluded gardens and one room with an extraordinary timber-vaulted

ceiling are just some of the charms of this lovingly restored Georgian town house in central Lincoln. There's limited on-site parking, a garden and a children's playground, and even a seasonal heated outdoor swimming pool. Family rooms sleep four.

Eating

Stokes High Bridge Café
CAFE £

(www.stokes-coffee.co.uk; 207 High St; dishes £5-9; ⊗8am-5pm Mon-Sat, 11.30am-4pm Sun; 🛜🅿️♿) A Lincoln landmark, this soaring 1540-built black-and-white Tudor building is England's only one atop a medieval bridge (1160). Within its preserved half-timbered interior, 1892-established, family-run roastery Stokes brews superb coffees made from speciality beans. Classic fare includes English breakfasts, traditional roasts and afternoon teas.

Cheese Society
CHEESE £

(www.thecheesesociety.co.uk; 1 St Martin's Lane; dishes £5-9, cheese boards £9-18; ⊗kitchen 11am-3.30pm Mon-Fri, to 4pm Sat, shop 10am-4.30pm Mon-Fri, to 5pm Sat) Not only does this light, bright place stock over 90 mostly British cheeses, it also serves them at its 12-seat cafe. Try its elaborate cheese boards or dishes such as twice-baked Dorset Blue Vinney soufflé or Wensleydale and herb scones with smoked salmon.

Brown's Pie Shop
PIES, BRITISH ££

(☏01522-527330; www.brownspieshop.co.uk; 33 Steep Hill; mains £9.75-26.50; ⊗noon-2.30pm & 5-9.30pm Mon-Fri, noon-9.30pm Sat, to 8pm Sun) Hearty 'pot pies' (no pastry bottoms) at this long-established, quintessentially British restaurant are stuffed with locally sourced beef, rabbit and game. Pies aside, traditional dishes include Lincolnshire sausages with caramelised onion gravy and slow-roasted pork belly.

★ Bronze Pig
BRITISH £££

(☏01522-524817; www.thebronzepig.co.uk; 4 Burton Rd; mains £16-27; ⊗by reservation 6.30-10pm Wed-Sat, 11.30am-2pm Sun) BBC *MasterChef* finalist Irishman Eamonn Hunt and Sicilian chef Pompeo Siracusa have taken Lincoln's dining scene by storm since opening the Bronze Pig. Their exceptional Modern British cooking has an Italian accent and ingredients are locally sourced. Reserve well ahead and prepare to be wowed. It also has four deluxe guest rooms (doubles from £105).

Jews House
EUROPEAN £££

(☏01522-524851; www.jewshouserestaurant. co.uk; 15 The Strait (Steep Hill); mains £16.50-25.50; ⊗7-9.30pm Tue, noon-2pm & 7-9.30pm Wed-Sat) This local favourite serves gourmet fare (roast wood pigeon, truffle custard and bacon foam; baked lemon sole with scallop mousse) in one of England's oldest houses, the 1160-built Romanesque Jews House.

Drinking & Nightlife

Cosy Club
BAR

(www.cosyclub.co.uk; Sincil St; ⊗9am-11pm Sun-Wed, to midnight Thu, to 1am Fri & Sat; 🛜) Spectacularly converted with soaring skylit ceilings, this 1848-built corn exchange now contains one of Lincoln's liveliest bars. Along with cocktails like English Rose (gin, rosewater, strawberries and sparkling wine) and the Earl's Breakfast (vodka, Earl Grey tea and lime juice), it serves breakfast, brunch, tapas and international dishes.

Strugglers Inn
PUB

(www.strugglers-lincoln.co.uk; 83 Westgate; ⊗noon-midnight Tue & Wed, to 1am Thu-Sat, to 11pm Sun & Mon) A sunny walled-courtyard beer garden out the back, an interior warmed by an open fire and a superb selection of real ales on tap make this the pick of Lincoln's independent pubs.

Engine Shed
LIVE MUSIC

(☏0871 220 0260; www.engineshed.co.uk; Brayford Pool) Lincoln's largest live-music venue occupies a former railway-container storage facility. Past acts have included Kings of Leon, Fat Boy Slim and Manic Street Preachers. Music aside, it also hosts sports events, comedy and pop-up markets.

ⓘ Information

Tourist Office (☏01522-545458; www. visitlincoln.com; 9 Castle Hill; ⊗10am-5pm Mon-Sat, 10.30am-4pm Sun) In a half-timbered, 16th-century building.

ⓘ Getting There & Away

BUS
The **bus station** (Melville St) is just northeast of the train station in the new town.

Stagecoach buses include bus 1 to Grantham (£5.60, 1½ hours, hourly Monday to Saturday, five on Sunday).

TRAIN
The train station is 250m east of the Brayford Waterfront development in the new town.

Boston £14.40, 1¼ hours, hourly, change at Sleaford

London King's Cross £79.50, 2¼ hours, up to three per hour; change in Newark or Peterborough

Newark-on-Trent Newark Castle; £5.40, 25 minutes, up to two per hour

Nottingham £11.90, one hour, hourly

Sheffield £15.30, 1¼ hours, hourly

Boston

01205 / POP 35,124

It's hard to believe that sleepy Boston was the inspiration for its larger and more famous American cousin. Although no Boston citizens sailed on the *Mayflower*, the port became a conduit for persecuted Puritans fleeing Nottinghamshire for religious freedom in the Netherlands and America. In the 1630s the fiery sermons of Boston vicar John Cotton inspired many locals to follow their lead, among them the ancestors of John Quincy Adams, the sixth American president. These pioneers founded a namesake town in the new colony of Massachusetts and the rest, as they say, is history.

Sights

Maud Foster Windmill HISTORIC BUILDING

(01205-352188; www.maudfoster.co.uk; 16 Willoughby Rd; adult/child £4/2; 10am-5pm Wed & Sat) About 800m northeast of Market Pl, England's tallest working windmill, with five sails rather than the usual four, has seven creaking, trembling floors reached by steep, ladder-like staircases; it sells bags of flour milled on-site. Self-caterers can stay in the granary next door (double from £430 for three nights including a windmill tour and parking; children not permitted).

Guildhall MUSEUM

(01205-365954; www.bostonguildhall.co.uk; South St; 10.30am-3.30pm Wed-Sat) FREE Before escaping to the New World, the Pilgrim Fathers were briefly imprisoned in the 14th-century Guildhall. It's one of Lincolnshire's oldest brick buildings, dating from the 1390s and situated close to the River

---

LINCOLNSHIRE: BOMBER COUNTY

The Royal Air Force (RAF) was formed in 1918 following WWI and two years later its college was established in Lincolnshire. During WWII, England's 'Bomber County' was home to numerous squadrons and by 1945 had more airfields (49) than any other in the country. US Navy flying boats flew antisubmarine patrols from here and B-29 bombers were also based here.

Just south of Lincoln, the 2018-opened International Bomber Command Centre (p443) has a moving memorial and an attached museum. Lincoln's tourist office (p442) has details of other aviation legacies throughout the county.

International Bomber Command Centre (01522-514755; www.internationalbcc. co.uk; Kanwick Hill; memorial free, museum adult/child £7.20/4.50; memorial 24hr, museum 9.30am-5pm Tue-Sun) Opened in 2018, this 4.5-hectare site 1.5 miles south of Lincoln centres on a 31m-high metallic spire (at 102ft, the exact length of the wingspan of a Lancaster Bomber) surrounded by rusted-metal walls inscribed with the names of the 57,861 men and women who served and supported Britain's Bomber Command. Next to the memorial, a state-of-the-art museum has high-tech interactive displays covering the history of Bomber Command, including poignant stories from those who witnessed WWII's bombings first-hand.

Battle of Britain Memorial Flight Visitor Centre (01522-552222; www.lincolnshire. gov.uk; Dogdyke Rd, Coningsby; museum free, hangar tours adult/child £8.50/4.60; hangar tours by reservation 10am-5pm Mon-Fri) See Spitfires and the four-engined *Lancaster City of Lincoln* at the Battle of Britain Memorial Flight Visitor Centre on 90-minute hangar tours. Bus IC5 (£4.60, one hour, hourly Monday to Saturday) runs here from Lincoln.

Lincolnshire Aviation Heritage Centre (01790-763207; www.lincsaviation.co.uk; East Kirkby, near Spilsby; adult/child £8.50/3; 9.30am-5pm Mon-Sat Easter-Oct, 10am-4pm Mon-Sat Nov-Easter) An original WWII Bomber Command airfield complete with its original wartime control tower is now home to the Lincolnshire Aviation Heritage Centre, with wartime planes and automobiles on display. It's 30 miles southeast of Lincoln via the A153; there's no public transport.

Witham. Inside are fun interactive exhibits, as well as a restored 16th-century courtroom and a recreated Georgian kitchen. Regular temporary exhibitions are also free.

St Botolph's Church
CHURCH

(www.parish-of-boston.org.uk; Church St; tower adult/child £5/free; ⊙ church visiting hours 8.30am-4pm Mon-Sat, from 7.30am Sun, tower 10am-3.30pm Mon-Sat, from 1pm Sun, last climb 3pm) Built in the early 14th century, St Botolph's Church (the name Boston is a corruption of 'St Botolph's Stone') is known locally as the Stump, in reference to the truncated appearance of its 88m-high tower. Puff your way up the 209 steps on a clear day and you'll see out to Lincoln, 32 miles away.

ⓘ Getting There & Away

Trains connect Boston with Lincoln (£14.40, 1¼ hours, hourly) via a change at Sleaford, and with Nottingham (£18.20, 1½ hours, hourly).

Stamford

☏ 01780 / POP 19,704

One of England's prettiest towns, Stamford seems frozen in time, with elegant streets lined with honey-coloured limestone buildings and hidden alleyways dotted with alehouses, interesting restaurants and small independent boutiques. A forest of historic church spires rises overhead and the gently gurgling River Welland meanders through the town centre. It's a favourite with filmmakers seeking the postcard vision of England, and has appeared in everything from *Pride and Prejudice* to the *Da Vinci Code*.

◉ Sights

★ Burghley House
HISTORIC BUILDING

(www.burghley.co.uk; house & garden adult/child £19/10, garden only £13/9; ⊙ house 11am-5pm Sat-Thu mid-Mar–Oct, garden 11am-5pm daily mid-Mar–Oct, park 8am-6pm or dusk if earlier daily year-round) Set in more than 810 hectares of grounds, landscaped by Lancelot 'Capability' Brown, opulent Burghley House (bur-lee) was built by Queen Elizabeth's chief adviser William Cecil, whose descendants still live here. It bristles with cupolas, pavilions, belvederes and chimneys; the lavish staterooms are a particular highlight. In early September, the renowned Burghley Horse Trials take place here. The estate is 1.3 miles southeast of Stamford; follow the marked path for 15 minutes through the park by Stamford's train station.

St Mary's Church
CHURCH

(www.stamfordbenefice.com; St Mary's St; ⊙ 8am-6pm, hours can vary) An endearingly wonky 13th-century broach spire tops the 12th-century St Mary's Church. Classical concerts are held here in summer; tickets (from £14) are sold at Stamford's tourist office.

⌂ Sleeping

William Cecil at Stamford   HISTORIC HOTEL ££
(☏ 01780-750070; www.hillbrookehotels.co.uk; High St, St Martin's; s/d/f incl breakfast from £100/110/175; 🅿🛜) Within the Burghley Estate, this stunningly renovated hotel has 27 rooms inspired by Burghley House, with period furnishings and luxuries such as Egyptian cotton linens and complimentary organic vodka. Family rooms sleep two adults and two kids; interconnecting rooms are also available. The smart restaurant turns out stylish British classics and opens to a wicker-chair-furnished patio.

★ George Hotel
HISTORIC HOTEL £££

(☏ 01780-750750; www.georgehotelofstamford. com; 71 High St, St Martin's; s/d/ste/4-poster incl breakfast from £130/215/290/320; 🅿🛜🐾) Stamford's luxurious landmark inn opened its doors in 1597. Today its 45 individually sized and decorated rooms impeccably blend period charm and modern elegance. Superior Modern British cuisine is served at its oak-panelled restaurant, while its more informal garden-room restaurant hosts af-

---

THE HOME OF SIR ISAAC NEWTON

Sir Isaac Newton fans may feel the gravitational pull of the great man's birthplace, **Woolsthorpe Manor** (NT; ☏ 01476-862823; www.nationaltrust.org. uk; Water Lane; house & grounds adult/child £7.70/3.85, grounds only £3.86/2.68; ⊙ 11am-5pm Wed-Mon mid-Mar–Oct, Fri-Sun Nov–mid-Mar), about 8 miles south of Grantham. The humble 17th-century house contains reconstructions of Newton's rooms; the apple that inspired his theory of gravity allegedly fell from the tree in the garden. There's a nifty kids' science room and a cafe. Take Centrebus 9 from Grantham (£2.80, 20 minutes, four per day Monday to Saturday).

ternoon teas in its courtyard. Its two bars include a champagne bar.

Drinking

Paten & Co   PUB
(www.kneadpubs.co.uk; 7 All Saints' Pl; ⊙ 11am-midnight Mon-Sat, noon-6pm Sun; 🛜) When the current owners stripped back this 18th-century building during renovations, they uncovered Paten & Co wine and spirits merchants' painted sign and got permission to use the original name. Twists on old-fashioned cocktails (eg raspberry and thyme Collins) are its speciality, along with charcoal-smoked street food. The top floor has breathtaking views of All Saints' church spires.

All Saints Brewery   BREWERY
(www.allsaintsbrewery.co.uk; 22 All Saints' St; ⊙ noon-11pm Mon-Sat, to 10.30pm Sun; 🛜) 🌿 Victorian-era steam-brewing equipment is used to make organic fruit beers at this operation, which has revived the site's original 1825 brewery after it was shuttered for several decades. Try its cherry, strawberry, raspberry and apricot brews at the attached pub or in the umbrella-shaded courtyard. Bar staff can advise on informal brewery tours.

Tobie Norris   PUB
(www.kneadpubs.co.uk; 12 St Paul's St; ⊙ 10am-11pm Mon-Thu, to midnight Fri & Sat, noon-10.30pm Sun) A wonderful stone-walled, flagstone-floored pub, the Tobie Norris has a warren of rooms with open fireplaces, a sunny, flower-filled courtyard and local ales. Wood-fired pizzas are a highlight of its wide-ranging menu.

❶ Information

Tourist Office (📞 01780-755611; www.south westlincs.com; 27 St Mary's St; ⊙ 9.30am-5pm Mon-Sat; 🛜) Inside the Stamford Arts Centre.

❶ Getting There & Away

BUS
Centrebus 4 runs to Grantham (£4.60, 1¼ hours, three per day Monday to Saturday) and Centrebus 9 serves Oakham (£3.50, 45 minutes, hourly Monday to Saturday).

TRAIN
Trains run to Birmingham (£32.80, 1½ hours, hourly), Nottingham (£25.30, 1¾ hours, hourly) with a change in Leicester (£19.10, 40 minutes), and Stansted Airport (£38.40, 1¾ hours, hourly) via Peterborough (£8.30, 15 minutes).

> **WORTH A TRIP**
>
> ### ALTHORP HOUSE
>
> The ancestral home of the Spencer family, **Althorp House** (📞 01604-770107; www.spencerofalthorp.com; adult/child £18.50/11; ⊙ noon-5pm mid-Jul–early Sep) – pronounced 'altrup' – is the final resting place of Diana, Princess of Wales, commemorated by a memorial. The outstanding art collection features works by Rubens, Gainsborough and Van Dyck. Profits go to charities supported by the Princess Diana Memorial Fund.
>
> Althorp is off the A428, 5.5 miles northwest of Northampton, and is not served by public transport; a taxi costs around £20.

LEICESTERSHIRE

Leicestershire was a vital creative hub during the Industrial Revolution, but its factories were a major target for German air raids in WWII and most towns in the county still bear the scars of war-time bombing. Nevertheless, there are some impressive remains, from Elizabethan castles to Roman ruins. The busy, multicultural capital Leicester is enjoying fame arising from the 2012 discovery and 2015 reburial of King Richard III's remains.

❶ Getting There & Around

Leicester is well served by buses and trains. For bus routes and timetables, visit the 'Roads and Transport' pages at www.leicestershire.gov.uk.

Regular buses connect Rutland to Leicester, Stamford and other surrounding towns.

Leicester

📞 0116 / POP 348,300

Built over the buried ruins of two millennia of history, Leicester (*les*-ter) suffered at the hands of the Luftwaffe and postwar planners but an influx of textile workers from India and Pakistan from the 1960s transformed the city into a bustling multicultural hub.

The astonishing 2012 discovery and 2013 identification of the remains of King Richard III in a Leicester car park sparked a flurry of developments, including a spiffing visitor centre on the site, and the restoration

WORTH A TRIP

GEORGE WASHINGTON'S ANCESTRAL HOME

Sulgrave Manor ([☎ 01295-760205; www.sulgravemanor.org.uk; Manor Rd, Sulgrave; adult/child £7.20/3.60; ⏰ 11am-5pm Thu, Fri & Sun Apr-Sep) was built by Lawrence Washington in 1539. The Washington family lived here for almost 120 years before Colonel John Washington, the great-grandfather of America's first president George Washington, sailed to Virginia in 1656.

Sulgrave Manor is 20 miles southwest of Northampton, just off the B4525 near Banbury; you'll need your own wheels to get here.

of the cathedral, where the king was reburied in 2015.

◉ Sights

★ **King Richard III:**
Dynasty, Death & Discovery   MUSEUM
(www.kriii.com; 4a St Martin's Pl; adult/child £8.95/4.75; ⏰ 10am-4pm Sun-Fri, to 5pm Sat) Built following the incredible 2012 discovery of King Richard III's remains, Leicester's high-tech King Richard III visitor centre encompasses three fascinating sections. Dynasty explores his rise to become the final Plantagenet king. Death delves into the Battle of Bosworth, when Richard became the last English king to be killed in battle. Discovery details the University of Leicester's archaeological dig and identification, and lets you view the site of the grave in which he was found.

Its Murder, Mystery and Mayhem exhibition covers the key players, battles and milestones of the Wars of the Roses between the House of York (symbolised by a white rose) and House of Lancaster (red rose).

★ **Leicester Cathedral**   CATHEDRAL
(☎ 0116-261 5357; www.leicestercathedral.org; Peacock Lane; by donation; ⏰ 10am-5pm Mon-Sat, 12.30-2.30pm Sun) Pride of place at this substantial medieval cathedral goes to the contemporary limestone tomb atop the vault where the remains of King Richard III were reburied in 2015. Look too for the striking carvings on the cathedral's roof supports.

One-hour guided tours (adult/child £5/free) take place at 11.30am and 2.30pm from Monday to Friday. On Saturday, 30-minute

King Richard III tours (adult/child £3/free) depart on the hour from 11am to 4pm.

National Space Centre   MUSEUM
(www.spacecentre.co.uk; Exploration Drive; adult/child £14/11; ⏰ 10am-4pm Mon-Fri, to 5pm Sat & Sun) Although British space missions usually launch from French Guiana or Kazakhstan, Leicester's space museum is a fascinating introduction to the mysteries of the spheres. The ill-fated 2003 *Beagle 2* mission to Mars was controlled from here. Fun, kid-friendly displays cover everything from astronomy to the status of current space missions. It's 1.5 miles north of the city centre. Take bus 54 or 54A (£1.60, 15 minutes, every 10 minutes Monday to Saturday, every 20 minutes Sunday) from **Haymarket bus station** (Charles St).

Leicester Castle   RUINS
(Castle View) Scattered around the **Newarke Houses Museum** (☎ 0116-225 4980; www.leicester.gov.uk/leisure-and-culture; The Newarke; ⏰ 10am-4pm Mon-Sat, from 11am Sun) **FREE** are the ruins of Leicester's medieval castle, where Richard III spent his final days before the Battle of Bosworth. The monumental gateway known as the **Magazine** (Newarke St) was once a storehouse for cannonballs and gunpowder. Dating from the 12th century and clad in Georgian brickwork, the **Great Hall** (www.dmu.ac.uk; Castle Yard) stands behind a 15th-century gate near the church of **St Mary de Castro** (www.stmarydecastro.co.uk; 15 Castle View; ⏰ noon-2pm Mon-Fri, 2-4pm Sat), where Geoffrey Chaucer was married in 1366.

New Walk Museum
& Art Gallery   MUSEUM, GALLERY
(☎ 0116-225 4900; www.leicester.gov.uk/leisure-and-culture; 53 New Walk; ⏰ 11am-4.30pm Mon-Fri, to 5pm Sat & Sun) **FREE** Highlights of this grand Victorian museum include the dinosaur galleries, the painting collection (with works by Turner and Degas), ceramics by Picasso, and the Egyptian gallery, where real mummies rub shoulders with displays about Boris Karloff's 1932 film *The Mummy*.

Jewry Wall Museum   MUSEUM
(www.visitleicester.info; St Nicholas Circle; ⏰ 11am-4.30pm Feb-Oct) **FREE** This museum exploring the history of Leicester from Roman times to the modern day was undergoing renovations at the time of writing, and was expected to reopen to the public in spring 2019. In front of the museum is the **Jewry**

Leicester

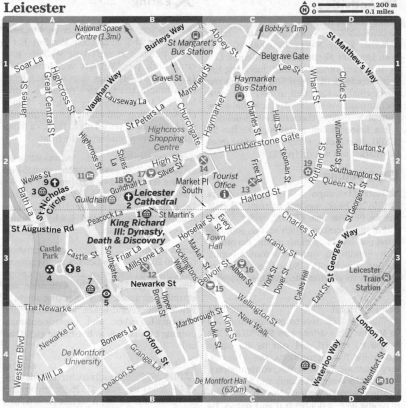

Leicester

◉ Top Sights
1 King Richard III: Dynasty, Death & Discovery	B3
2 Leicester Cathedral	B2

◉ Sights
Great Hall	(see 4)
3 Jewry Wall Museum	A2
4 Leicester Castle	A3
5 Magazine	B3
6 New Walk Museum & Art Gallery	D4
7 Newarke Houses Museum	A3
8 St Mary de Castro	A3
9 St Nicholas Church	A2

⊨ Sleeping
10 Belmont Hotel	D4
11 Hotel Maiyango	A2

⊗ Eating
12 Boot Room	B3
13 Good Earth	C2
14 Walkers	C2

⊙ Drinking & Nightlife
15 Bread & Honey	C3
16 Gate 38	C3
17 Globe	B2

✿ Entertainment
18 Cookie	B2
19 Curve Theatre	D2

Wall, part of Leicester's Roman baths. Tiles and masonry from the baths were incorporated in the walls of neighbouring **St Nich-** **olas Church** (www.stnicholasleicester.com; St Nicholas Circle; admission by donation; ⊙ 2-4pm Sat, 6.30-8.30pm Sun).

BIRMINGHAM & THE MIDLANDS LEICESTER

🏃 Activities

Great Central Railway RAIL
(☑ 01509-632323; www.gcrailway.co.uk; return adult/child £17/9) Steam locomotives chug from Leicester North station on Redhill Circle to Loughborough Central, following the 8-mile route along which Thomas Cook ran the original package tour in 1841. The locos operate most weekends year-round and some summer weekdays; check timetables online.

For Leicester North station, take bus 25 (£1.60, 20 minutes, every 10 minutes) from Haymarket bus station (p446).

🛏 Sleeping

★ Hotel Maiyango BOUTIQUE HOTEL ££
(☑ 0116-251 8898; www.maiyango.com; 13-21 St Nicholas Pl; d/ste from £79/109; ❄ 🛜) At the end of the pedestrian High St, this sophisticated pad has 14 spacious rooms, decorated with handmade furniture, contemporary art and massive TVs. Superb cocktails are served at its rooftop bar (guests only) with city-skyline views.

Belmont Hotel HOTEL ££
(☑ 0116-254 4773; www.belmonthotel.co.uk; 20 De Montfort St; s/d/f/ste from £62/81/105/139; P ❄ @ 🛜) Owned and run by the same family for four generations, the 19th-century Belmont has 74 stylish, contemporary, individually designed rooms and a fantastic location overlooking leafy New Walk. Family rooms have a double bed and bunks. Its restaurant is highly regarded; the two bars, Jamie's and Bowie's, open to a terrace and a conservatory respectively.

🍴 Eating

Walkers PIES £
(Walker & Son; www.walkerspies.co.uk; 4-6 Cheapside; dishes £1-5; ⊙ 8am-5pm Mon-Sat) For a quick lunch, you can't beat Walkers' towering pork pies. Walkers was founded in Leicester in 1824; it has since sold its famous crisp brand, but the pies remain a family business today. Other pie varieties include chicken, bacon and mushroom, farmhouse steak, game and pulled pork. There's a handful of pavement tables out the front.

Bobby's INDIAN, VEGETARIAN £
(☑ 0116-266 0106; www.eatatbobbys.com; 154-156 Belgrave Rd; dishes £4-8; ⊙ 11am-10pm Mon-Fri, from 10am Sat & Sun; 🥄) The top pick along Leicester's Indian restaurant-lined Golden Mile is 1970s-established Bobby's, serving all-vegetarian classics.

Good Earth VEGETARIAN £
(☑ 0116-262 6260; www.facebook.com/veggiegoodearth; 19 Free Lane; mains £3.50-7; ⊙ noon-3pm Mon-Fri, to 4pm Sat; 🥄) This venerable vegetarian cafe has a daily changing menu of wholesome veggie bakes, huge salads and homemade cakes, and hosts occasional evening events such as live-music gigs. Cash only.

Boot Room BISTRO ££
(☑ 0116-262 2555; www.thebootroomeaterie.co.uk; 29 Millstone Lane; mains £13.25-25; ⊙ noon-2pm & 6-9.30pm Tue-Sat; 🛜) A former shoe factory now houses this contemporary independent bistro. Premium ingredients are used in dishes spanning sea bass with fondant pota-

---

THE BATTLE OF BOSWORTH

Given a few hundred years, every battlefield ends up simply a field, but the site of the **Battle of Bosworth** (☑ 01455-290429; www.bosworthbattlefield.org.uk; Ambion Lane, Sutton Cheney; adult/child £8.95/5.75, guided walk £4.50/3; ⊙ heritage centre 10am-5pm, last admission 4pm, grounds 7am-dusk) – where Richard III met his maker in 1485 – is enlivened by an entertaining heritage centre full of skeletons and musket balls; guided walks around the site last 90 minutes. Enthusiasts in period costume reenact the battle each August.

Although it lasted just a few hours, the Battle of Bosworth marked the end of the Plantagenet dynasty and the start of the Tudor era. This was where the mortally wounded Richard III famously proclaimed: 'A horse, a horse, my kingdom for a horse'. (Actually, he didn't: the quote was invented by that great Tudor propagandist William Shakespeare.)

After visiting the battlefield, head for lunch at the 17th-century coaching inn, **Hercules Revived** (☑ 01455-699336; www.herculesrevived.co.uk; Sutton Cheney; mains £11.50-20; ⊙ kitchen noon-2.30pm & 6-9pm Mon-Sat, noon-4pm, bar to 11.30pm daily), which serves top-tier gastropub food.

The battlefield is 16 miles southwest of Leicester at Sutton Cheney, off the A447.

toes, king prawns, squid and prawn bisque to duck leg with Puy lentils and tamarind sauce. Save room for the soufflé of the day for dessert.

★ **John's House** BRITISH £££
(📞 01509-415569; www.johnshouse.co.uk; Stonehurst Farm, 139-141 Loughborough Rd, Mountsorrel; 2-/3-course lunch menus £26/30, 2-/3-/7-course dinner menus £48/55/124; ⏰ noon-2pm & 7-9pm Tue-Sat) Chef John Duffin was born here on 16th-century Stonehurst Farm, 8 miles north of Leicester. After working in Michelin-starred restaurants, he returned in 2014 to open his restaurant, and has since gained a Michelin star of his own. Multicourse menus (no à la carte) showcase his imagination in dishes like creamed Porthilly oysters with smoked Mountsorrel eels and foraged loveage.

Still a working farm today, Stonehurst (www.stonehurstfarm.co.uk) also has a fabulous farm shop, a tearoom, a petting farm and a motor museum housing vintage vehicles.

🍷 Drinking & Nightlife

Gate 38 COCKTAIL BAR
(38b Belvoir St; ⏰ 9pm-3.30am Fri & Sat; 🛜) Look for the tiny yellow airport-gate sign on Albion St to find this super-cool speakeasy with aeroplane-cabin seats and plane windows with pictures of Leicester's lights mimicking flying in at night. Its 'departure board' lists destinations for which cocktails are named, eg Kyoto, with sake, tomato juice and smoked pepper, or Buenos Aires, with Pisco, lime, ginger beer and cucumber.

Bread & Honey COFFEE
(www.breadnhoneycoffee.com; 15 King St; ⏰ 7.45am-3pm Mon-Fri; 🛜) Beans from single farm estates and co-ops sourced and roasted by London-based Monmouth are brewed at this little bare-boards hole in the wall; the flat whites are the best for miles around. Steaming soups, preservative-free bread, made-from-scratch hot dishes and fantastic cakes (chocolate fudge cake with white-chocolate icing; honey-glazed banana loaf) are all available, too.

Globe PUB
(www.eversosensible.com/globe; 43 Silver St; ⏰ 11am-11pm Sun-Thu, to 1am Fri & Sat) In the atmospheric Lanes – a tangle of alleys south of the High St – this old-fashioned pub has fine draught ales and a crowd that rates its drinks by quality rather than quantity.

HAMMER & PINCERS

For a mind-blowing meal, head to this idyllic **gastropub** (📞 01509-880735; www.hammerandpincers.co.uk; 5 East Rd, Wymeswold; mains £19-27.50, 7-/10-course menu £45/60, with wine £75/100; ⏰ noon-2pm & 6-9.30pm Tue-Sat, to 4pm Sun; 🖋) set in bucolic gardens at the edge of the cute village of Wymeswold. Everything is homemade, down to the breads and condiments; seasonal specialities might include cider-cured sea trout, gin-marinated pheasant and rosemary rhubarb sorbet. Don't miss its signature twice-baked cheese soufflé. It's 16 miles north of Leicester via the A46.

☆ Entertainment

Cookie LIVE MUSIC
(📞 0116-253 1212; www.thecookieleicester.co.uk; 68 High St; ⏰ bar 3-11pm Tue & Wed, from noon Thu, noon-1am Fri & Sat, noon-5pm Sun, concert hours vary) With a capacity of 350 in its brick cellar, this indie venue is a brilliant place to catch live bands and comedy nights in an intimate setting.

Curve Theatre THEATRE
(📞 0116-242 3595; www.curveonline.co.uk; 60 Rutland St; backstage tours adult/child £5/4) This sleek artistic space hosts big-name shows and some innovative modern theatre, and has good accessibility for theatregoers who are aurally or visually impaired. Call the ticket office to book backstage tours.

De Montfort Hall LIVE MUSIC
(📞 0116-233 3111; www.demontforthall.co.uk; Granville Rd) Orchestras, ballets, musicals and other big song-and-dance performances are on the bill at this huge venue.

❶ Information

Tourist Office (📞 0116-299 4444; www.visitleicester.info; 51 Gallowtree Gate; ⏰ 10.30am-4.30pm Mon-Fri, from 9.30am Sat, 11am-4pm Sun) Helpful office with reams of city and county info.

❶ Getting There & Away

BUS

Intercity buses operate from **St Margaret's bus station** (Gravel St), north of the city centre. The useful Skylink bus runs to East Midlands Airport

OFF THE BEATEN TRACK

STOKE BRUERNE & THE GRAND UNION CANAL

Brightly painted barges frequent this charming little village 8.2 miles south of Northampton on the Grand Union Canal, the main thoroughfare of England's canal network. From here, you can follow the waterways all the way to Leicester, Birmingham or London.

A converted corn mill houses the entertaining **Canal Museum** (www.canalrivertrust. org.uk/thecanalmuseum; 3 Bridge Rd; adult/child £4.75/3.10; ⊙10am-5pm Apr-Oct, shorter hours Nov-Mar), which charts the history of the canal network and its bargemen, lock-keepers and pit workers. Scale models abound; outside you can see the historic narrowboat *Sculptor*, listed on the National Historic Boat Register.

The **Boat Inn** (☑01604-862428; www.boatinn.co.uk; mains restaurant £15-25, bistro £7-13; ⊙restaurant noon-2pm & 7-9pm Tue-Sat, noon-2.30pm Sun, bar 9am-11pm Mon-Sat, to 10.30pm Sun) is a canalside landmark; with picnic tables on the quay, this sociable local pub has a relaxed bistro serving pub classics until 9pm, a more formal restaurant with refined dishes such as steaks, and a great range of ales.

(£7.30, one hour, at least hourly, 24 hours) and continues on to Derby.

National Express services:

Coventry £5.50, 45 minutes, three daily
London Victoria £11.60, 2¾ hours, hourly
Nottingham £4.60, 45 minutes, up to two per hour

TRAIN

East Midlands trains:

Birmingham £19.20, one hour, up to two per hour
London St Pancras £86.50, 1¼ hours, up to four per hour

Rutland

Tiny Rutland was merged with Leicestershire in 1974, but in 1997 regained its 'independence' as England's smallest county.

Rutland centres on Rutland Water, a vast artificial reservoir created by the damming of the Gwash Valley in 1976. Covering 4.19 sq miles, the reservoir attracts some 20,000 birds, including ospreys.

◉ Sights & Activities

Rutland Water
Nature Reserve   NATURE RESERVE
(www.rutlandwater.org.uk; Egleton; adult/child incl parking £6/3.50, binocular hire per day £5; ⊙9am-5pm Mar-Oct, to 4pm Nov-Feb) Near Oakham, the Rutland Water Nature Reserve has 31 hides throughout the reserve and a viewing section upstairs in the **Anglian Water Birdwatching Centre**, which has an exhibition on the area's abundant birdlife, including ospreys, long-tailed tits, lesser whitethroats, bullfinches, garden warblers and jays.

Look out too for water voles, which thrive here. The reserve's **Lyndon Visitor Centre** (☑01572-737378; www.rutlandwater.org.uk; Manton; adult/child incl parking £6/3.50; ⊙9am-5pm mid-Mar–early Sep), for which tickets are valid, opens during the warmer months.

Rutland Watersports   WATER SPORTS
(☑01780-460154; www.anglianwater.co.uk; Whitwell Leisure Park, Bull Brigg Lane, Whitwell; windsurf/kayak/SUP rental per hr from £20/8.50/10; ⊙9am-7pm Fri-Tue, to 8pm Wed & Thu Apr-Oct, shorter hours Nov-Mar) Aquatic activities offered by Rutland Watersports include windsurfing, kayaking and stand-up paddleboarding (SUP). You can hire gear or take lessons.

Rutland Belle   CRUISE
(☑01572-787630; www.rutlandwatercruises.com; Whitwell; adult/child £9.50/6.50; ⊙hourly noon-3pm Mon-Sat, from 11am Sun mid-Jul–Aug, shorter hours Apr–mid-Jul, Sep & Oct) Take a 45-minute round-trip cruise from Whitwell to Normanton on the southern shore of the Rutland reservoir. On some afternoons, it also runs later birdwatching cruises lasting 90 minutes (adult/child £22/13).

🛏 Sleeping & Eating

Hambleton Hall   HISTORIC HOTEL £££
(☑01572-756991; www.hambletonhall.com; Hambleton; s/d/ste incl breakfast from £225/310/625; P🅿🛜🐾🏊) One of England's finest country hotels, rambling former hunting lodge Hambleton Hall, built in 1881, sits on a peninsula jutting out into Rutland Water, 3 miles east of Oakham. Its luxuriant floral rooms and Michelin-starred restaurant (two-course lunch menu £31.50, three-/four-

course dinner menus £75/95) are surrounded by gorgeous gardens, which also shelter an outdoor heated swimming pool (May to September).

Otters Fine Foods
DELI, CAFE £

(☑01572-756481; www.ottersfinefoods.co.uk; 19 Mill St, Oakham; dishes £5-8.50; ☺9am-5.30pm Mon-Sat) A storybook-pretty whitewashed cottage with a thatched roof houses this Oakham deli. Pick up sandwiches, quiches, soups, salads, cheeses, meats, charcuterie and more for a lakeside picnic, or preorder a hamper. If it's not picnic weather, dine at its in-store cafe.

Mill Street Pub & Kitchen
GASTROPUB ££

(☑01572-729600; www.millstreetoakham.com; 6 Mill St, Oakham; mains £12.50-26.50; ☺kitchen 7.30am-9pm Mon-Thu, to 9.45pm Fri & Sat, to 8pm Sun, bar 7.30am-11pm Mon-Thu, to midnight Fri & Sat, to 10.30pm Sun; ☺☑☑☺) On Oakham's main shopping street, this handsome pub's dining spaces span a vaulted brick cellar, a glass conservatory and a sun-drenched terrace. Menu highlights include ham-hock and tarragon terrine with house-made piccalilli and toasted sourdough; there are vegan and kids' menus, and ales from Oakham's Grainstone brewery. Upstairs, seven contemporary rooms (doubles including breakfast from £90) are painted in beautiful countryside hues.

❶ Getting There & Away
Bus 9 links Oakham with Stamford (£3.50, 45 minutes, hourly Monday to Saturday) via Rutland Water's north shore.

Trains link Oakham with Leicester (£15.70, 30 minutes, hourly).

DERBYSHIRE

The Derbyshire countryside is painted in two distinct tones: the lush green of rolling valleys criss-crossed by dry-stone walls, and the barren mottled-brown hilltops of the high, wild moorlands. The biggest draw here is the Peak District National Park, which preserves some of England's most evocative scenery, attracting legions of hikers, climbers, cyclists and cave enthusiasts.

❶ Getting There & Away
East Midlands Airport (p454) is the nearest air hub, and Derby is well served by trains, but connecting services to smaller towns are few. In the Peak District, the Derwent Valley Line runs from Derby to Matlock. Edale and Hope lie on the Hope Valley Line from Sheffield to Manchester.

For a comprehensive list of Derbyshire bus routes, visit the 'Transport and Roads' pages at www.derbyshire.gov.uk.

Derby
☑01332 / POP 248,752

Gloriously sited at the southeastern edge of the Derbyshire hills that roll towards the Peak District, Derby is one of the Midlands' most energetic, creative cities. This was one of the crucibles of the Industrial Revolution: almost overnight, a sleepy market town was transformed into a major manufacturing

---

OFF THE BEATEN TRACK

CONKERS & THE NATIONAL FOREST

The National Forest (www.nationalforest.org) is an ambitious project to generate new areas of sustainable woodland by planting 30 million trees in Leicestershire, Derbyshire and Staffordshire, covering a total area of 51,800 hectares or 200 sq miles. More than 8.5 million saplings have already taken root. Visitor attractions here include the kid-friendly nature centre, **Conkers** (☑01283-216633; www.visitconkers.com; Rawdon Rd, Moira; adult/child £9.05/8.14; ☺10am-6pm Easter-Sep, to 5pm Oct-Easter). There are also several bike trails; bikes can be hired from **Hicks Lodge** (☑01530-274533; Willesley Wood Side, Moira; bike hire per 3hr/day adult/child £16/30; ☺trails 8am-dusk, bike hire & cafe 9am-5pm Fri-Wed, to 9pm Thu mid-Feb–Oct, 10am-4pm Mon-Wed & Fri, 9am-9pm Thu, to 5pm Sat & Sun Nov–mid-Feb).

If you fancy overnighting, the **National Forest YHA** (☑0845 371 9672; www.yha.org. uk; 48 Bath Lane, Moira; dm/d/f from £13/50/70; ℗☺) ☻ has impressive eco features (such as rainwater harvesting and solar biomass boiler usage), 23 spotless en-suite rooms, bike storage, and a restaurant serving local produce and organic wines. It's 300m west of Conkers along Bath Lane.

centre, producing everything from silk to bone china and, later, locomotives and Rolls-Royce aircraft engines. The city suffered the ravages of industrial decline in the 1980s, but bounced back with impressive cultural developments and a rejuvenated riverfront.

◉ Sights

Royal Crown Derby Factory   MUSEUM, FACTORY
(☏ 01332-712800;   www.royalcrownderby.co.uk; Osmaston Rd; museum & factory tour adult/child £5/2.50, museum only £2/1; ⊙ museum 10am-4pm Mon-Sat, factory tours 11am & 1.30pm Mon-Thu, 11am Fri) Derby's historic potteries still turn out some of the finest bone china in England, from edgy Asian-inspired designs to the kind of stuff your grandma collects. Reservations are essential for factory tours, which last 90 minutes and include a visit to the museum. Royal Crown Derby's china (including seconds and discontinued items) is sold at its on-site shop, and is used as tableware at its elegant tearoom.

Derby Cathedral   CATHEDRAL
(☏ 01332-341201; www.derbycathedral.org; 18 Irongate; cathedral by donation, tower tours adult/child £5/4; ⊙ cathedral 8.30am-5.30pm, tower tours vary) Founded in AD 943 and reconstructed in the 18th century, Derby Cathedral's vaulted ceiling towers above a fine collection of medieval tombs, including the opulent grave of the oft-married Bess of Hardwick, who at various times held court at Hardwick Hall, Chatsworth House and Bolsover Castle. Check the website for dates when historians lead tours up 189 steps into the Tudor tower, the second-highest bell tower in the UK.

Peregrine falcons nest in the tower; follow their progress at www.derbyperegrines.blogspot.com.

Derby Museum & Art Gallery   MUSEUM
(www.derbymuseums.org; The Strand; ⊙ 10am-5pm Tue-Sat, noon-4pm Sun) FREE Local history and industry displays include fine ceramics produced by Royal Crown Derby and an archaeology gallery, along with paintings by renowned artist Joseph Wright of Derby (1734–97).

Quad   GALLERY, CINEMA
(☏ 01332-290606; www.derbyquad.co.uk; Market Pl; gallery free, cinema tickets adult/child £9/7; ⊙ gallery 11am-5pm Mon-Sat, from noon Sun) A striking modernist cube on Market Pl, Quad contains a futuristic art gallery and an arthouse cinema.

🛏 Sleeping

Coach House   B&B £
(☏ 01332-554423;   www.coachhousederby.com; 185a Duffield Rd; s/d from £47/60; P 🐾 ☎ 🖥) Surrounded by a rambling cottage garden, this red-brick 1860-built property 1.7 miles north of Derby has four countrified rooms with richly patterned wallpapers in the main house, and three contemporary loft-style rooms in the superbly converted stables. Personalised touches include free homemade brownies. Vegan and gluten-free breakfasts are possible (reserve ahead). Off-street parking is first come, first served.

Farmhouse at Mackworth   INN ££
(☏ 01332-824324;   www.thwfarmhouseatmackworth.com; 60 Ashbourne Rd; d/f incl breakfast from £85/110; P ☎) The Farmhouse at Mackworth is just 2.5 miles northwest of Derby in undulating countryside, with the bonus of plentiful free parking. The designer inn's 10 boutique rooms have checked fabrics, rustic timber cladding and chrome fittings, plus amenities including Nespresso machines and fluffy robes. There's a fabulous bar and a restaurant with a Josper charcoal oven.

Cathedral Quarter Hotel   HOTEL ££
(☏ 01332-546080;   www.cathedralquarterhotel.com; 16 St Mary's Gate; d/ste incl breakfast from £95/145; 🖥 ☎) A bell's peal from the cathedral, this grand Georgian edifice houses a 38-room hotel. The service is as polished as the grand marble staircase, and there's an on-site spa and a fine-dining restaurant.

★ The Cow   INN £££
(☏ 01332-824297;   www.cowdalbury.com; The Green, Dalbury Lees; d incl breakfast from £145; P ☎) Stunningly restored in 2017, this whitewashed 19th-century inn 6.5 miles west of Derby has solid oak floors, stone walls and timber-lined ceilings. Its 12 individually styled rooms range from Victorian and art deco to retro vintage, and feature locally handcrafted mattresses and Egyptian cotton sheets. The bar-restaurant's stools are fashioned from milk cans and food is sourced within a 30-mile radius.

✕ Eating

Jack Rabbits   CAFE £
(☏ 01332-206322;   www.jackrabbitskitchen.com; 53-55 Queen St; dishes £4.85-9; ⊙ 8.30am-5pm Mon-Sat, 10am-4pm Sun; ✐ 🖥) Jack Rabbits' sunlit cafe is perfect for lazy grazing on in-

KEDLESTON HALL

Sitting pretty in vast landscaped grounds, neoclassical **Kedleston Hall** (NT; 01332-842191; www.nationaltrust.org.uk; Kedleston Rd, Quarndon; house & gardens adult/child £13.60/6.80, garden only £6.80/3.40; house noon-5pm Sat-Thu Feb-Oct, garden 10am-6pm Feb-Oct, to 4pm Nov-Jan) is a must for fans of stately homes. Entering the house through a grand portico, you'll reach the breathtaking Marble Hall with massive alabaster columns and statues of Greek deities.

The Curzon family has lived here since the 12th century, but the current wonder was built by Sir Nathaniel Curzon in 1758. Meanwhile, the poor old peasants in Kedleston village had their humble dwellings moved a mile down the road, as they interfered with the view. Ah, the good old days...

Highlights include Indian treasures amassed by Viceroy George Curzon and a domed, circular saloon modelled on the Pantheon in Rome, as well as 18th-century-style pleasure gardens.

Kedleston Hall is 5 miles northwest of Derby, off the A52. Bus 114 between Derby and Ashbourne (£3.60, 25 minutes, up to six daily Monday to Saturday) stops at the gates when the hall is open.

ternationally inspired dishes, from breakfast (Mexican huevos rancheros, French/American hybrid croque monsieur Benedict) through to lunch (Swedish potato pancake with a poached egg, pickled cucumber and sour cream). Breads, cakes and slices are baked in-house; coffee is from Nottingham roastery Outpost. 'Little bunnies' has a top-quality kids' menu.

Wonky Table　　　　　　　BISTRO ££
(01332-295000; www.wonkytable.co.uk; 32 Sadler Gate; mains lunch £8-10, dinner £13-19; 5-10pm Mon, noon-3pm & 5-10pm Tue-Fri, noon-3.30pm & 5-10pm Sat;) Inside an inviting retro-vintage dining room with exposed-brick walls, Wonky Table features a slimmed-down daytime menu alongside salads and sandwiches, but it really comes into its own at dinner with dishes such as apricot-stuffed slow-roasted pork loin. Vegetarian options abound.

Darleys　　　　MODERN BRITISH £££
(01332-364987; www.darleys.com; Waterfront, Darley Abbey Mill; mains £23-26.30, 2-/3-course lunch menus £20/25; noon-2pm & 7-8.30pm Tue-Thu, noon-2pm & 7-9pm Fri & Sat, noon-2.30pm Sun;) Two miles north of the city centre, this upmarket restaurant has a gorgeous setting in a bright converted mill overlooking the river, with a beautiful waterside terrace. It serves classy fare such as sea trout with cockle cream, curry oil and a samphire pakora. Vegetarian and vegan menus are available at all times.

 Drinking & Nightlife

⭐**Old Bell Hotel**　　　　　　　　PUB
(www.bellhotelderby.co.uk; 51 Sadler Gate; 11.30am-11.30pm Sun-Thu, to 1.30am Fri & Sat) Dating from 1650 and hosting Bonnie Prince Charlie's soldiers in 1745, this history-steeped black-and-white inn was valiantly restored by local entrepreneur Paul Hurst in 2013, retaining original features, antiques and photographs. There's a central courtyard and, allegedly, several ghosts. Real-ale tasting flights, snacks and lunches are served in its Tavern and Tudor bars; the Belfry Bar has an upmarket steakhouse.

The Tap　　　　　　　　　　　PUB
(www.brewerytap-dbc.co.uk; 1 Derwent St; noon-11pm Mon-Thu, to 1am Fri, 11am-1am Sat, 11am-11pm Sun) The Tap serves its own brews, guest ales and over 80 craft beers from around the world in elegant Victorian surrounds.

🔒 **Shopping**

Bennetts　　　　　DEPARTMENT STORE
(www.facebook.com/bennettsirongate; 8 Irongate; 9am-5pm Mon-Sat, 11am-4pm Sun) Founded as an ironmongers in 1734 and still retaining an ironmongery today, Derby's historic department store has evolved over the centuries to sell beautiful clothes, homewares, gifts and more.

On the 1st-floor interior balcony, **Lisa Jean at Bennetts Brasserie** (01332-344621; www.lisajean-bennetts.co.uk; mains £10-13, champagne breakfast £25; 9am-3.30pm

Mon-Sat, 11am-2pm Sun) specialises in champagne breakfasts.

ℹ️ Information

Tourist Office (☑ 01332-643411; www.visit derby.co.uk; Market Pl; ⊙ 9.30am-8pm Mon-Sat) Under the Assembly Rooms in the main square.

ℹ️ Getting There & Away

AIR

East Midlands Airport (EMA; ☑ 0808 169 7032; www.eastmidlandsairport.com), 11.5 miles southeast of Derby, is served by regular Skylink buses (£4.70, 40 minutes, at least hourly). Buses operate 24 hours.

BUS

Local and long-distance buses run from Derby's bus station, immediately east of the Westfield shopping mall. High Peak has hourly buses between Derby and Buxton (£8, 1¾ hours), via Matlock (£4.50, 45 minutes) and Bakewell (£6.50, 1¼ hours). One bus continues to Manchester (£8, 2¼ hours).

Other services:

Leicester Skylink; £7.30, 1¾ hours, one to two hourly

Nottingham Red Arrow; £5.20, 35 minutes, every 10 minutes Monday to Saturday, three per hour Sunday

TRAIN

The train station is about half a mile southeast of the city centre on Railway Tce.

Birmingham £19.30, 40 minutes, four hourly

Leeds £35.40, 1½ hours, two hourly

London St Pancras £65.50, 1¾ hours, up to two hourly

Ashbourne

☑ 01335 / POP 8377

Perched at the southern edge of the Peak District National Park, Ashbourne is a pretty patchwork of steeply slanting stone streets lined with cafes, pubs and antique shops.

🏃 Activities

Ashbourne Cycle Hire Centre   CYCLING
(☑ 01335-343156; www.peakdistrict.org; Mapleton Rd; per half-day/day standard bike from £14/17, electric bike £23/27; ⊙ 9.30am-5.30pm Mar-Oct, shorter hours Nov-Feb) Situated 1km northwest of town, the Cycle Hire Centre is right on the Tissington Trail, at the end of a huge and atmospheric old railway tunnel leading under Ashbourne. Helmets, puncture repair kits and maps are included. You can also rent mountain bikes as well as children's bikes, bikes with baby seats, trailers for buggies and tandems.

🛏️ Sleeping & Eating

Compton House   B&B ££
(☑ 01335-343100; www.comptonhouse.co.uk; 27-31 Compton St; s/d from £55/75; P 🅿) Fresh, clean, frilly rooms, a warm welcome and a central location make this the pick of Ashbourne's B&Bs. There's a minimum two-night stay on weekends.

Flower Cafe   CAFE £
(www.theflowercafe.co.uk; 5 Market Pl; mains £5-12.50; ⊙ 8.30am-5pm Sun-Fri, to 8pm Sat; 🍴) Soups such as parsnip, chorizo and chestnut, broccoli and Stilton, and spicy bean and lentil are a year-round speciality at this cute-as-a-button cafe where everything is homemade. In summer it also cooks delicious quiches (cheesy leek and mushroom; bacon, brie and cranberry...). Gluten-free and dairy-free dishes are plentiful.

ℹ️ Information

Tourist Office (☑ 01335-343666; www.ashbournetowncouncil.gov.uk; Market Pl; ⊙ 10am-5pm Mon-Sat Jun-Oct, shorter hours Nov-May) Inside the town hall.

ℹ️ Getting There & Away

Bus services include the following:

Buxton High Peak routes 441 and 442; £4.50, 1¼ hours, 10 daily Monday to Friday, eight Saturday, five Sunday

Derby Trent Barton Swift; £4.30, 40 minutes, hourly Monday to Saturday, five Sunday

Matlock Bath

☑ 01629 / POP 753

Matlock Bath (not to be confused with the larger, workaday town of Matlock, 2 miles north) looks like a British seaside resort that somehow lost its way and ended up at the foot of the Peak District National Park. Following the River Derwent through a sheer-walled gorge, the main promenade is lined with amusement arcades, tearooms, fish-and-chip shops, pubs and shops catering to the motorcyclists who congregate here on summer weekends. Outside summer, the town is considerably quieter.

◉ Sights

Peak District Lead Mining Museum
MUSEUM

(☑ 01629-583834; www.peakdistrictleadmining museum.co.uk; The Grand Pavilion, South Pde; museum adult/child £4/3, mine £4.50/3.50, combined ticket £7/5; ⊙ 10am-5pm Apr-Apr, 11am-4pm Sep & Oct, 11am-4pm Sat & Sun Nov-Mar) An educational introduction to the mining history of Matlock is provided by this enthusiast-run museum set in an old Victorian dance hall. Kids can wriggle through its maze of tunnels and shafts while adults browse historical displays. At 1pm daily from April to October (at weekends only from November to March) you can go into the workings of the Temple Mine and pan for 'gold' (well, shiny minerals). Reservations for mine tours are recommended.

Cromford Mill
MUSEUM

(☑ 01629-823256; www.cromfordmills.org.uk; Mill Lane, Cromford; audio guide or guided tour adult/child £5/free; ⊙ 9am-5pm, guided tours by reservation 11am Fri) Founded in the 1770s by Richard Arkwright, the Cromford Mill was the first modern factory, producing cotton on automated machines powered by a series of waterwheels along the River Derwent. This prototype inspired a succession of mills, ushering in the industrial age. In addition to 90-minute audio-guide tours, there are weekly one-hour guided tours. It's 1 mile south of Matlock Bath (a 20-minute walk), or you can take the train one stop to Cromford (£2.50, five minutes, hourly).

Caudwell's Mill
MUSEUM

(☑ 01629-734374; www.caudwellsmill.co.uk; Rowsley; mill tours adult/child £4.50/2; ⊙ mill tours 9.30am-4.15pm, shop 9am-5pm) FREE This chugging, grinding, water-powered mill still produces flour the old-fashioned way – 20 different types are for sale, along with six different oat products, and yeast and biscuits. The mill has various craft workshops and a tearoom. You can get to Rowsley direct from Matlock Bath by bus (£3.40, 20 minutes, hourly) on the route to Bakewell, or take the Peak Rail (p455) steam train and follow the riverside path from the station.

Masson Mills
MUSEUM

(☑ 01629-581001; www.massonmills.co.uk; Derby Rd; adult/child £3/2; ⊙ 10am-4pm Mon-Sat, from 11am Sun, closed Dec) A museum tells the story of the valley's textile mills at this large complex 1 mile south of Matlock Bath. The attached shopping village is full of outlet stores for big clothing brands.

🏃 Activities

Peak Rail
RAIL

(☑ 01629-580381; www.peakrail.co.uk; Station Yard, Matlock; adult/child return £9.50/4.50, one-way £5/2.75; ⊙ Mar-Nov, hours vary) From a tiny platform by Sainsbury's supermarket on the outskirts of the town of Matlock (not Matlock Bath), nostalgic steam trains trundle along a 4-mile length of track to the nearby village of Rowsley, home to Caudwell's Mill.

Heights of Abraham
AMUSEMENT PARK

(☑ 01629-582365; www.heightsofabraham.com; Dale Rd; adult/child £17/11.50; ⊙ 10am-4.30pm daily mid-Mar–early Nov) A spectacular cable-car ride (accessible with admission ticket only) from the bottom of the gorge brings you to this hilltop leisure park – its cave and mine tours and fossil exhibitions are a winner with kids. The cave is a constant 10ºC, so bring a jacket.

🛏 Sleeping

Grouse & Claret
INN ££

(☑ 01629-733233; www.grouseclaretpub.co.uk; Station Rd, Rowsley; d incl breakfast from £90; P 🛜) In the village of Rowsley, 6.2 miles northwest of Matlock Bath, this 18th-century stone inn has eight comfy, country-style wallpapered rooms, a restaurant specialising in spit-roasted chicken, and a huge, sunny beer garden with umbrella-shaded tables.

Hodgkinson's Hotel & Restaurant
HOTEL ££

(☑ 01629-582170; www.hodgkinsons-hotel.co.uk; 150 South Pde; s/d/f incl breakfast from £60/110/155; P 🛜) The eight rooms at this central Grade II–listed Victorian beauty conjure up Matlock's golden age with antique furnishings, cast-iron fireplaces, flowery wallpaper, handmade soaps and goose-down duvets. The restaurant (open Monday to Saturday evenings; two-/three-course menus £27/30) has just 18 seats, so bookings are advised. From April to September, there's a minimum two-night stay on weekends.

🔒 Shopping

Scarthin Books
BOOKS

(www.scarthinbooks.com; The Promenade, Cromford; ⊙ 9am-6pm Mon-Sat, from 10am Sun) More than 100,000 new and secondhand books cram 12 rooms in this biblio-paradise, which hosts regular literary events and has a vegetarian cafe (dishes £3.50 to £6.50) serving organic pizza, soups, wraps, pies and burritos.

❶ Information

Tourist Office (✆ 01629-583834; www.visit-peakdistrict.com; The Grand Pavilion, South Pde; ☉ 10am-5pm Apr-Aug, 11am-4pm Sep & Oct, 11am-4pm Sat & Sun Nov-Mar) At the Peak District Lead Mining Museum (p455).

❶ Getting There & Away

Matlock is a hub for buses around the Peak District.

Bakewell High Peak; £3.80, 35 minutes, hourly
Derby High Peak; £4.60, 40 minutes, hourly

Trains run hourly between Matlock Bath and Derby (£6.30, 35 minutes, hourly).

Chesterfield

✆ 01246 / POP 103,800

The eastern gateway to the Peaks, Chesterfield is a busy service centre that's famed for the twisted spire atop its church.

Nearby is the magnificent Elizabethan mansion Hardwick Hall.

◉ Sights

Hardwick Hall   HISTORIC BUILDING
(NT; ✆ 01246-850430; www.nationaltrust.org.uk; Doe Lea; house & garden adult/child £13.95/7, garden only £7/3.54, incl Hardwick Old Hall £20.75/11.10; ☉ house 11am-5pm Wed-Sun mid-Feb–Oct, to 3pm Wed-Sun Nov–mid-Feb, garden 10am-6pm daily year-round) One of the most complete Elizabethan mansions in the country, Hardwick Hall was designed by eminent architect Robert Smythson. The hall featured all the latest mod-cons of the time, including fully glazed windows. The atmospheric interiors are decked out with magnificent tapestries and oil paintings of forgotten dignitaries.

Hardwick Hall is 10 miles southeast of Chesterfield, just off the M1; it's best reached by your own wheels.

The hall was home to the 16th-century's second-most powerful woman, Elizabeth, Countess of Shrewsbury (known to all as Bess of Hardwick), who amassed a staggering fortune by marrying wealthy noblemen with one foot in the grave. Hardwick Hall was constructed using her inheritance from husband number four, who shuffled off this mortal coil in 1590.

Set aside time to explore the formal gardens or the longer walking trails of Hardwick Park.

Next door to the manor are the ruins of Bess' first house, **Hardwick Old Hall** (EH; www.english-heritage.org.uk; Doe Lea; adult/child £7.50/4.60, incl Hardwick Hall £20.75/11.10; ☉ 10am-6pm Wed-Sun Easter-Sep, to 5pm Oct, shorter hours Nov-Easter).

St Mary & All Saints Church   CHURCH
(✆ 01246-206860; www.crookedspire.org; Church Way; spire tours adult/child £6/4; ☉ church 9am-5pm Mon-Sat, 8am-6.30pm Sun, spire tours Mon-Sat) **FREE** Chesterfield is worth a visit to see the astonishing crooked spire that rises atop St Mary and All Saints Church. Dating from 1360, the 68m-high spire is twisted in a right-handed corkscrew that leans several metres southwest. It's the result of the lead casing on the south-facing side having buckled in the sun. Spire tours lasting 45 minutes take you up into the tower. Tour times are posted inside the front door from Monday to Saturday, or phone ahead to check.

❶ Information

Tourist Office (✆ 01246-345777; www.visitchesterfield.info; Rykneld Sq; ☉ 9.30am-6pm Mon-Sat) Directly opposite St Mary and All Saints Church.

❶ Getting There & Away

BUS

From Chesterfield coach station on Beetwell St, bus 170 serves Bakewell (£3.60, 45 minutes, hourly).

TRAIN

Chesterfield lies on the main rail line between Nottingham (£13.20, 45 minutes, up to three hourly) and Derby (£11.70, 20 minutes, up to three hourly), which continues to Sheffield (£5.50, 15 minutes). The station is just east of the centre.

PEAK DISTRICT

Rolling across the Pennines' southernmost hills is the glorious Peak District National Park. Ancient stone villages are folded into creases in the landscape, and the hillsides are littered with stately homes and rocky outcrops. The Dark Peak is dominated by exposed moorland and gritstone 'edges', while to the south, the White Peak is made up of the limestone dales.

Peak District National Park

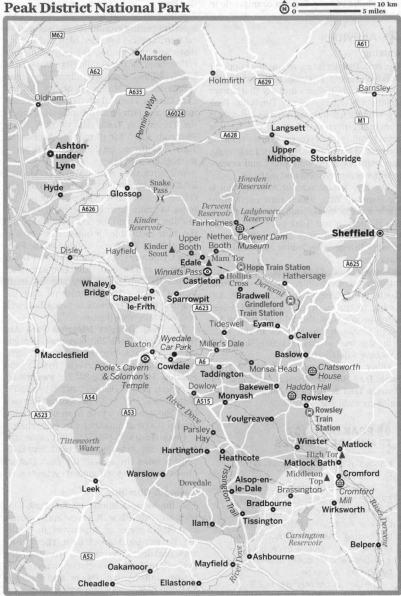

No one knows how the Peak District got its name – certainly not from the landscape, which has hills and valleys, gorges and lakes, wild moorland and gritstone escarpments, but no peaks. The most popular theory is that the region was named for the Pecsae-

tan, the Anglo-Saxon tribe who once populated this part of England.

Founded in 1951, the Peak District was England's first national park and is Europe's busiest. But even at peak times, there are

555 sq miles of open English countryside in which to find solitude.

🏃 Activities

Walking

The Peak District is one of the most popular walking areas in England, with awe-inspiring vistas of hills, dales and sky that attract legions of hikers in summer. The White Peak is perfect for leisurely strolls, which can start from pretty much anywhere. Be sure to close gates behind you as you go. When exploring the rugged territory of the Dark Peak, make sure your boots are waterproof and beware of slipping into rivulets and marshes.

The Peak's most famous walking trail is the **Pennine Way**, which runs north from Edale for 268 miles, finishing in the Scottish Borders. If you don't have three weeks to spare, you can reach the pretty town of Hebden Bridge in Yorkshire comfortably in three days.

The 46-mile **Limestone Way** winds through the Derbyshire countryside from Castleton to Rocester in Staffordshire, following footpaths, tracks and quiet lanes. Many people walk the 26-mile section between Castleton and Matlock in one long, tiring day, but two days is better. Tourist offices have a detailed leaflet.

Other popular routes include the **High Peak Trail**, the **Tissington Trail** and the **Monsal Trail & Tunnels**. Numerous short walks are available.

ⓘ PEAK DISTRICT TRANSPORT PASSES

Handy bus passes cover travel in the Peak District.

The Peaks Plus ticket (adult/child £7.50/5) offers all-day travel on High Peak buses, including the Transpeak between Ashbourne, Matlock Bath and Buxton. The Peaks Plus Xtra ticket (£12.50/8) includes all transport on Transpeak and TM buses between Derby, Sheffield and Buxton.

The Derbyshire Wayfarer ticket (adult/child £12.40/6.20) covers buses and trains throughout the county and as far afield as Sheffield.

The Greater Manchester Wayfarer ticket (adult/child £12/6) covers trains and buses in the Peak District, along with Greater Manchester and parts of Cheshire and Staffordshire.

Cycling

Plunging dales and soaring scarps provide a perfect testing ground for cyclists, and local tourist offices are piled high with cycling maps and trail guides. For easy traffic-free riding, head for the 17-mile **High Peak Trail**, which follows the old railway line from Cromford, near Matlock Bath, to Dowlow near Buxton. The trail winds through beautiful hills and farmland to Parsley Hay, where the **Tissington Trail**, part of NCN Route 68, heads south for 13 miles to Ashbourne. Trails are off-road on dedicated cycle paths, suitable for road bikes.

Mirroring the Pennine Way, the **Pennine Bridleway** is another top spot to put your calves through their paces. Around 120 miles of trails have been created between Middleton Top and the South Pennines, and the route is suitable for horse riders, cyclists and walkers. You could also follow the **Pennine Cycleway** (NCN Route 68) from Derby to Buxton and beyond. Other popular routes include the **Limestone Way**, running south from Castleton to Staffordshire, and the **Monsal Trail & Tunnels** between Bakewall and Wyedale, near Buxton.

The **Peak District National Park Authority** (☑01629-816200; www.peakdistrict.gov.uk) operates cycle-hire centres at Ashbourne (p454), Derwent Reservoirs (p464) and **Parsley Hay** (☑01298-84493; www.peakdistrict.gov.uk; per half-/full day standard bike £14/17, electric bike £23/27; ☉9.30am-5pm mid-Feb–early Nov). You can hire a bike from one location and drop it off at another for no extra charge.

Peak Tours (☑01457-851462; www.peaktours.com; self-guided tour per 2 nights from £140) delivers bikes throughout the Peak District for seven different self-guided cycling tours.

Caving & Climbing

The limestone sections of the Peak District are riddled with caves and caverns, including a series of 'showcaves' in Castleton, Buxton and Matlock Bath. The website www.peakdistrictcaving.info, run by the Derbyshire Caving Association, has comprehensive information. **Peaks and Paddles** (☑07896 912871; www.peaksandpaddles.org; canoeing & caving from £55, abseiling from £25; ☉by reservation) runs caving trips, along with canoeing and abseiling expeditions.

England's top mountaineers train in this area, which offers rigorous technical climbing on a series of limestone gorges, exposed tors (crags) and gritstone 'edges' that extend south into the Staffordshire Moorlands. Gritstone climbing in the Peak District is predominantly on old-school trad routes, requiring a decent rack of friends, nuts and hexes. Bolted sport routes are found on several limestone crags in the Peak District, but many use ancient pieces of gear and most require additional protection. Contact the British Mountaineering Council (www.thebmc.co.uk) for advice and details of local resources.

❶ Getting There & Away

Buses run from regional centres such as Sheffield and Derby to destinations across the Peak District. Be aware that buses are much more frequent at weekends, and many services close down completely in winter. Bakewell and Matlock (not Matlock Bath) are the two main hubs – from these you can get anywhere in the Peak District. Timetables are available from all tourist offices as well as Traveline (p390). Trains run to Matlock Bath, Buxton, Edale and several other towns and villages.

Buxton

📞 01298 / POP 22,115

The 'capital' of the Peak District National Park, albeit just outside the park boundary, Buxton is a confection of Georgian terraces, Victorian amusements and parks in the rolling hills of the Derbyshire dales. The town built its fortunes on its natural warm-water springs, which attracted health tourists in Buxton's turn-of-the-century heyday.

Today, visitors are drawn here by the flamboyant Regency architecture and the natural wonders of the surrounding countryside. Tuesdays and Saturdays are market days, bringing colour to the grey limestone marketplace.

◉ Sights & Activities

★ **Pavilion Gardens** GARDENS
(www.paviliongardens.co.uk; ⊙10am-5pm Jul & Aug, 10am-5pm Mon-Fri, from 10.30am Sat & Sun Apr-Jun, 10.30am-5pm Sep, to 4pm Oct & Nov, 11am-4pm Dec, Feb & Mar) FREE Adjoining Buxton's opulent opera house are the equally flamboyant Pavilion Gardens. These 9.3 hectares are dotted with domed pavilions; concerts take place in the bandstand throughout the year. The main building contains a tropical greenhouse, an arts and crafts gallery, a nostalgic cafe and the tourist office (p461).

Poole's Cavern CAVE
(📞01298-26978; www.poolescavern.co.uk; Green Lane; adult/child £9.95/5.50; ⊙9.30am-5pm,

tours every 20min Mar-Oct; 10am-4pm, tours 10.30am, 12.30pm & 2.30pm Mon-Fri, every 20min Sat & Sun Nov-Feb) A pleasant mile-long stroll southwest from the town centre brings you to Poole's Cavern. This magnificent natural limestone cavern is reached by descending 28 steps; the temperature is a cool 7°C. Tours last 50 minutes.

From the cavern's car park, a 20-minute walk leads up through Grin Low Wood to **Solomon's Temple**, a ruined tower with fine views over the town. Built in 1896 to replace an earlier structure, it sits atop a burial mound where Bronze Age skeletons were discovered.

Buxton Crescent & Thermal Spa HISTORIC BUILDING
(https://buxtoncrescent.com; The Crescent) In Victorian times, spa activities centred on Buxton's extravagant baths, built in Regency style in 1854 and fronted by the Crescent, a grand, curving facade inspired by the Royal Crescent in Bath. The complex was due to reopen in 2019 following extensive works. Alongside a five-star hotel and spa, its pump room, which dispensed the town's spring water for nearly a century, will be the centrepiece of a new visitor attraction, the Pump Room and Crescent Heritage Experience, covering Buxton's spa-town heritage.

Buxton Museum & Art Gallery MUSEUM, GALLERY
(www.derbyshire.gov.uk/leisure/buxton_museum; Terrace Rd; ⊙10am-5pm Tue-Sat year-round, plus noon-4pm Sun Easter-Sep) FREE In a handsome Victorian building, the town museum has records of fossils found in the Peak District, photographs, fine arts, bric-a-brac covering the town's social history, and curiosities from Castleton's Victorian-era 'House of Wonders', including Harry Houdini's handcuffs.

Devonshire Dome HISTORIC BUILDING
(www.devonshiredome.co.uk; 1 Devonshire Rd) A glorious piece of Victoriana, the glass Devonshire Dome, built in 1779, is the largest unsupported dome in Europe. It's home to a training restaurant run by students from the University of Derby and Buxton & Leek College, as well as the **Devonshire Spa** (📞01298-330334; spa treatments from £40; ⊙9am-7pm Tue, Wed, Sat & Sun, to 9pm Thu & Fri, 10am-6pm Sun).

★ **Buxton Tram** BUS
(📞01298-79648; https://discoverbuxton.co.uk; adult/child £7.50/5; ⊙by reservation late Mar-

Buxton

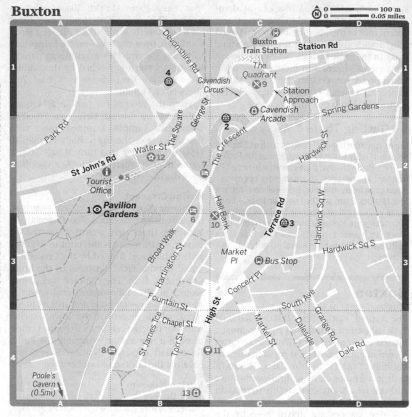

Buxton

◎ Top Sights
1 Pavilion Gardens.................................. A2

◎ Sights
2 Buxton Crescent & Thermal
   Spa... C2
3 Buxton Museum & Art
   Gallery... C3
4 Devonshire Dome.............................. B1

◈ Activities, Courses & Tours
5 Buxton Tram...................................... B2
   Devonshire Spa..........................(see 4)

◉ Sleeping
6 Grosvenor House.............................. B2

7 Old Hall Hotel................................... B2
8 Roseleigh Hotel................................ B4

◉ Eating
9 Barbarella's...................................... C1
10 Columbine Restaurant...................... C3

◉ Drinking & Nightlife
11 Old Sun Inn....................................... B4

◉ Entertainment
12 Opera House...................................... B2

◉ Shopping
13 Scrivener's Books &
   Bookbinding..................................... B4

Oct) From the Pavilion Gardens (p459), this eight-seat vintage milk float takes you on a 12mph, hour-or-so circuit of the town centre on its entertaining 'Wonder of the Peak' tour.

The same company also offers several hour-long walking tours (from £7), such as Victorian Buxton, from the same departure point.

✦ Festivals & Events

Buxton Festival ARTS
(www.buxtonfestival.co.uk; ⊙ Jul) One of the largest cultural festivals in the country, the 17-day Buxton Festival attracts top names in literature, music and opera at venues including the opera house.

🛏 Sleeping

Old Hall Hotel HISTORIC HOTEL ££
(☎ 01298-22841; www.oldhallhotelbuxton.co.uk; The Square; s/d incl breakfast from £69/79; 🛜🖥) There's a tale to go with every creak of the floorboards at this history-soaked establishment, supposedly the oldest hotel in England. Among other esteemed residents, Mary, Queen of Scots stayed here from 1576 to 1578, albeit against her will. The rooms still retain their grandeur (some have four-poster beds), and there are several bars, lounges and dining options.

Roseleigh Hotel B&B ££
(☎ 01298-24904; www.roseleighhotel.co.uk; 19 Broad Walk; s/d from £51/86; 🅿@🛜) This gorgeous family-run B&B in a roomy old Victorian house has lovingly decorated rooms, many with fine views over the Pavilion Gardens. The owners are a welcoming couple, both seasoned travellers, with plenty of interesting stories. There's a minimum two-night stay on summer weekends.

Grosvenor House B&B ££
(☎ 01298-72439; www.grosvenorbuxton.co.uk; 1 Broad Walk; s/d/f from £55/70/100; 🅿🛜) Overlooking the Pavilion Gardens, the Grosvenor is an old-school Victorian guesthouse with a huge parlour overlooking the park. Its eight rooms (including one family room sleeping three people plus space for a cot) have antique furniture and patterned wallpaper and drapes. At peak times, there's a minimum two-night stay and singles aren't available.

🍴 Eating & Drinking

Barbarella's INTERNATIONAL ££
(☎ 01298-71392; www.barbarellaswinebar.co.uk; 7 The Quadrant; mains £10-20; ⊙ noon-11pm Sun-Thu, to midnight Fri & Sat; 🛜🖥) Black-and-white paisley wallpaper, chandeliers and glossy timber tables make this sleek retro wine bar the hottest drinking den in Buxton, but it's an equally stellar place to dine on sharing boards and deli platters, or more substantial seafood dishes (including a creamy chowder) and chargrilled steaks.

Columbine Restaurant MODERN BRITISH ££
(☎ 01298-78752; www.columbinerestaurant.co.uk; 7 Hall Bank; mains £14-23.50; ⊙ 7-10pm Mon & Wed-Sat, noon-2pm Sun) 🍴 On the lane leading down beside the town hall, this understated restaurant is the top choice among discerning Buxtonites. The chef conjures up imaginative dishes primarily made from local produce, such as High Peak lamb with mint butter. Two of its three dining areas are in the atmospheric stone cellar. Bookings are recommended.

Old Sun Inn PUB
(www.theoldsuninnbuxton.co.uk; 33 High St; ⊙ noon-11pm Sun-Wed, to midnight Thu-Sat) The cosiest of Buxton's pubs, this 17th-century coaching inn has a warren of rooms full of original features, proper cask ales and a lively crowd that spans the generations.

☆ Entertainment

Opera House OPERA
(☎ 01298-72190; https://buxtonoperahouse.org.uk; Water St; tours £10; ⊙ tours by reservation) Designed by theatre architect Frank Matcham in 1903 and restored in 2001, Buxton's gorgeous opera house hosts a full program of drama, dance, concerts and comedy. Guided backstage tours lasting 90 minutes can be booked via the website. Its neighbouring **Pavilion Arts Centre** also hosts performances and has a 360-seat cinema.

🛍 Shopping

Scrivener's Books & Bookbinding BOOKS
(☎ 01298-73100; www.scrivenersbooks.co.uk; 42 High St; ⊙ 9.30am-5pm Mon-Sat, noon-4pm Sun) At this delightfully chaotic bookshop, sprawling over five floors, books are filed in piles and the Dewey system has yet to be discovered.

Cavendish Arcade SHOPPING CENTRE
(www.cavendisharcade.co.uk; Cavendish Circus; ⊙ 9am-6pm Mon-Sat, 10am-5pm Sun, individual shop hours vary) Covered by a barrel-vaulted, stained-glass canopy, Cavendish Arcade houses boutiques selling upmarket gifts.

ℹ Information

Tourist Office (☎ 01298-25106; www.visitpeakdistrict.com; Pavilion Gardens; ⊙ 10am-5pm Jul & Aug, 10am-5pm Mon-Fri, from 10.30am Sat & Sun Apr-Jun, 10.30am-5pm Sep, to 4pm Oct & Nov, 11am-4pm Dec, Feb & Mar; 🛜) Well-organised office with details of walks in the area.

THE CATHEDRAL OF THE PEAK

Dominating the former lead-mining village of Tideswell, the massive parish church of **St John the Baptist** (☑ 01298-871317; https://tideswellchurch.org; Commercial Rd, Tideswell; ⊙ 9am-6pm) – aka the Cathedral of the Peak – has stood here virtually unchanged since the 14th century. Look out for the wooden panels inscribed with the Ten Commandments and the grand 14th-century tomb of local landowner Thurston de Bower, depicted in full medieval armour. It's 8 miles east of Buxton, linked by bus 66 (£4, 25 minutes, every two hours Monday to Saturday).

Bus 173 links Tideswell with Bakewell (£3.10, 30 minutes, every two hours daily).

❶ Getting There & Away

Buses stop on both sides of the road at **Market Pl**. The hourly High Peak service runs to Derby (£8, 1¾ hours), via Bakewell (£5, 30 minutes) and Matlock Bath (£5.20, one hour); five services daily continue to Manchester (£6, 1¼ hours).

Bus 66 serves Chesterfield (£5.90, 1¼ hours, every two hours Monday to Saturday) via Tideswell (£4, 25 minutes) and Eyam (£4.60, 40 minutes).

To reach Sheffield, take bus 65 (£6.40, 1¼ hours, every two hours Monday to Saturday, three services Sunday).

Northern Rail has trains to/from Manchester (£10.60, one hour, hourly).

Castleton

☑ 01433 / POP 742

Guarding the entrance to the forbidding Winnats Pass gorge, charming Castleton is a magnet for Midlands visitors on summer weekends – come midweek if you want to enjoy the sights in relative peace and quiet. Castleton village's streets are lined with leaning stone houses, with walking trails criss-crossing the surrounding hills. The atmospheric ruins of Peveril Castle crown the ridge above, while the bedrock below is riddled with fascinating caves.

◉ Sights

Situated at the base of 517m-high Mam Tor, Castleton is the northern terminus of the Limestone Way, which follows narrow, rocky Cave Dale, far below the east wall of the castle. The tourist office (p463) has maps and leaflets, including details of numerous easier walks.

Peveril Castle   CASTLE, RUINS
(EH; ☑ 01433-620613; www.english-heritage.org.uk; adult/child £5.90/3.50; ⊙ 10am-6pm Easter-Sep, to 5pm Oct, to 4pm Sat & Sun Nov-Easter) Topping the ridge to the south of Castleton, a 350m walk from the town centre, this evocative castle has been so ravaged by the centuries that it almost looks like a crag itself. Constructed by William Peveril, William the Conqueror's son, the castle was used as a hunting lodge by Henry II, King John and Henry III, and the crumbling ruins offer swooping views over the Hope Valley. Before heading up here, check ahead to avoid closures for maintenance.

Castleton Museum   MUSEUM
(☑ 01433-620679; www.peakdistrict.gov.uk; Buxton Rd; ⊙ 9.30am-5pm Apr-Oct, to 4.30pm Nov-Mar) **FREE** Attached to the tourist office (p463), the cute town museum has displays on everything from mining and geology to rock climbing, hang-gliding and the curious Garland Festival (p463).

Treak Cliff Cavern   CAVE
(☑ 01433-620571; www.bluejohnstone.com; Buxton Rd; adult/child £9.95/5.30; ⊙ 10am-4.15pm Mar-Oct, to 3.15pm Nov-Feb) Captivating Treak Cliff has a forest of stalactites and exposed seams of colourful Blue John stone, which is still mined to supply the jewellery trade. Tours lasting 40 minutes depart every half-hour and focus on the history of mining; kids can polish their own Blue John stone during school holidays. It's just under a mile west of Castleton's village centre.

Blue John Cavern   CAVE
(☑ 01433-620638; www.bluejohn-cavern.co.uk; adult/child £12/6; ⊙ 9.30am-4pm Mon-Fri, to 5pm Sat & Sun Apr-Oct, 9.30am-dusk Nov-Mar) Up the southeastern side of Mam Tor, 2 miles west of Castleton, Blue John is a maze of natural caverns with rich seams of Blue John stone that are still mined every winter. Access is via a one-hour guided tour that departs every 20 minutes. You can get here on foot up the closed section of the Mam Tor road.

Speedwell Cavern   CAVE
(☑ 01433-623018; www.speedwellcavern.co.uk; Winnats Pass; adult/child £12/10, incl Peak Cavern

£19/15.50; ⏰10am-5pm daily Apr-Oct, Sat & Sun Nov-Mar) Just over half a mile west of Castleton at the mouth of Winnats Pass, this claustrophobe's nightmare is reached by descending 106 steps for an eerie boat ride through flooded tunnels, emerging by a huge subterranean lake called the Bottomless Pit. New chambers are discovered here all the time by potholing expeditions.

Peak Cavern CAVE
(☑01433-620285; www.peakcavern.co.uk; Peak Cavern Rd; adult/child £11.25/9.25, incl Speedwell Cavern £19/15.50; ⏰10am-5pm daily Apr-Oct, Sat & Sun Nov-Mar) Castleton's most convenient cave is easily reached by a pretty streamside 250m walk south of the village centre. It has the largest natural cave entrance in England, known (not so prettily) as the Devil's Arse. Dramatic limestone formations are lit with fibre-optic cables. Buy tickets ahead online in the high season.

✦✦ Festivals & Events

Garland Festival CULTURAL
(www.peakdistrict.gov.uk; ⏰29 May) Castleton celebrates Oak Apple Day on 29 May (28 May if the 29th is a Sunday) as it has for centuries, with the Garland King (buried under an enormous floral headdress) and Queen parading through the village on horseback.

🛏 Sleeping & Eating

Ye Olde Nag's Head Hotel PUB ££
(☑01433-620248; www.yeoldenagshead.co.uk; Cross St; d £50-105; 🛜🐾) The cosiest of the 'residential' pubs along the main road has nine comfortable, well-appointed rooms; top-category rooms have four-poster beds and spas. Ale tasting trays are available in its bar, which has regular live music and a popular restaurant serving pub classics.

Three Roofs Cafe CAFE £
(www.threeroofscafe.com; The Island; dishes £5-11; ⏰9.30am-4pm Mon-Fri, to 5pm Sat & Sun; 🛜) Castleton's most popular purveyor of cream teas, opposite the turn-off to the tourist office, also has filling sandwiches, pies, fish and chips, burgers and jacket potatoes.

★ Samuel Fox BRITISH £££
(☑01433-621562; www.samuelfox.co.uk; Stretfield Rd, Bradwell; 2-/3-/7-course menus £28/35/55; ⏰6-9pm Wed-Sat, 1-4pm Sun Feb-Dec; 🅿🛜) In the Hope Valley village of Bradwell, 2.5 miles southeast of Castleton, this enchanting inn owned by pedigreed chef James Duckett

serves exceptional British cuisine: venison with pickled red cabbage, and roast pheasant with braised sprouts, bacon and parsnips. Guests staying in its four pastel-shaded guest rooms upstairs (doubles including breakfast from £130) can dine on Monday and Tuesday evenings.

Look out for dinner, bed and breakfast deals.

ℹ Information

Tourist Office (☑01433-620679; www.peakdistrict.gov.uk; Buxton Rd; ⏰9.30am-5pm Apr-Oct, 10am-4.30pm Nov-Mar) In the Castleton Museum (p462).

ℹ Getting There & Away

BUS
Bus services include the following:
Bakewell Bus 173; £3.30, 50 minutes, every two hours via Hope (£2.20, five minutes) and Tideswell (£5.30, 30 minutes)
Sheffield Buses 271 and 272; £5.90, 1¼ hours, four per day Monday to Friday, three Saturday

TRAIN
The nearest train station is at Hope, an easy 2-mile walk east of Castleton, on the line between Sheffield (£5.80, 30 minutes, hourly) and Manchester (£11.80, 55 minutes, hourly).

Derwent Reservoirs

North of the Hope Valley, the upper reaches of the Derwent Valley were flooded between 1916 and 1935 to create three huge reservoirs – the Ladybower, Derwent and Howden Reservoirs – to supply Sheffield, Leicester, Nottingham and Derby with water. These constructed lakes soon proved their worth – the Dambusters (Royal Air Force Squadron No 617) carried out practice runs over Derwent Reservoir before unleashing their 'bouncing bombs' on the Ruhr Valley in Germany in WWII.

These days, the reservoirs are popular destinations for walkers, cyclists and mountain bikers – and lots of ducks, so drive slowly!

◎ Sights & Activities

Derwent Dam Museum MUSEUM
(www.dambusters.org.uk; Fairholmes; ⏰10am-4pm Sun) FREE The exploits of the Royal Air Force Squadron No 617, aka the Dambusters, are detailed in the Derwent Dam Museum

in the western tower atop the dam where they tested their 'bouncing bombs'.

Derwent Cycle Hire Centre CYCLING
(☎01433-651261; www.peakdistrict.gov.uk; Fairholmes; per half-/full day standard bike £14/17, electric bike £23/27; ☺9.30am-5pm early Feb-early Nov) Fairholmes' cycle-hire centre rents wheels including mountain bikes, kids' bikes and electric bikes.

❶ Information

Tourist Office (☎01433-650953; www.peak-district.gov.uk; Fairholmes; ☺9.30am-5pm early Feb-early Nov, 10am-3.30pm Mon-Fri, to 4.30pm Sat & Sun early Nov-early Feb) Provides walking and cycling advice.

Edale

☎01433 / POP 353

Surrounded by majestic Peak District countryside, this cluster of stone houses centred on a pretty parish church is an enchanting place to pass the time. Edale lies between the White and Dark Peak areas, and is the southern terminus of the Pennine Way. Despite the remote location, the Manchester–Sheffield train line passes through the village, bringing throngs of weekend visitors.

⌖ Sleeping & Eating

Fieldhead Campsite CAMPSITE £
(☎01433-670386; www.fieldhead-campsite.co.uk; Fieldhead; site per person/car £7/3.50; ☺Feb-Dec; ℗☎) Next to the Moorland Tourist Office (p464), this pretty and well-equipped campsite spreads over six fields, with some pitches right by the river. Showers cost 20p. No campervans are allowed; fires and barbecues are not permitted.

Edale YHA HOSTEL £
(☎0845 371 9514; www.yha.org.uk; Rowland Cote, Nether Booth; dm/d/f from £13/50/70; ℗☎) Spectacular views across to Back Tor unfold from this country-house hostel 1.5 miles east of Edale, signposted from the Hope road. All 157 beds are bunks; wi-fi in public areas only. Check availability ahead as it's often busy with school groups.

Stonecroft B&B ££
(☎01433-670262; https://stonecroftguesthouse.co.uk; Grindsbrook; s/d from £60/105; ℗☎) ✿ This handsomely fitted-out stone house, built in the 1900s, has three comfortable guest rooms (two doubles, one single). Host

Julia's organic breakfasts are gluten-free, with vegetarian and vegan options; packed lunches (£7.50) are available by request when booking. Bike rental costs £25 per half-day. Pick-up from the train station can be arranged. Kids aren't permitted.

Cooper's Cafe CAFE £
(☎01433-670401; Grindsbrook; dishes £2-11; ☺9am-4pm Mon, Tue, Thu & Fri, 8am-5pm Sat & Sun; ☎) Fuel up on soups, burgers, jacket potatoes, house-speciality vegetarian chilli and cakes at this cheerful cafe close to the village school.

Rambler Inn PUB FOOD ££
(☎01433-670268; www.dorbiere.co.uk; Grindsbrook; mains £7.50-11; ☺kitchen noon-9.30pm Mon-Sat, to 8pm Sun, bar noon-11pm Mon-Sat, to 10.30pm Sun; ☎⬛) Opposite the train station, this stone pub warmed by open fires serves real ales and pub standards, such as stews and sausages and mash. There's a kids' menu, nine basic B&B rooms (double/triple/family from £90/110/155) and occasional live music.

❶ Information

Moorland Tourist Office (☎01433-670207; www.peakdistrict.gov.uk; Fieldhead; ☺9.30am-5pm Apr-Sep, reduced hours Oct-Dec & Feb-Mar) Topped by a sedum-turf 'living roof', with a waterfall splashing across its glass panels, this eco-conscious visitor centre has maps, displays on the moors and an adjacent campsite (p464).

❶ Getting There & Away

Trains run from Edale to Manchester (£11.60, 45 minutes, hourly) and Sheffield (£7.40, 30 minutes, hourly).

Eyam

☎01433 / POP 969

Quaint little Eyam (ee-em), a former lead-mining village, has a poignant history. In 1665 the town was infected by the dreaded Black Death plague, carried here by fleas on a consignment of cloth from London, and the village rector, William Mompesson, convinced villagers to quarantine themselves. Some 270 of Eyam's 800 inhabitants succumbed, while surrounding villages remained relatively unscathed. Today, Eyam's sloping streets of old cottages backed by rows of green hills are delightful to wander.

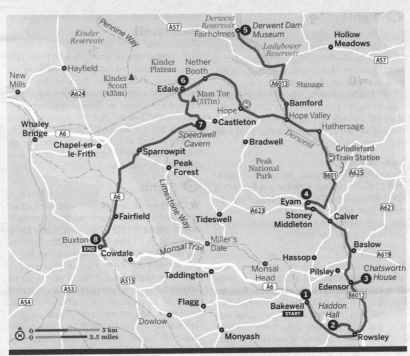

Driving Tour
Peak District

START BAKEWELL
END BUXTON
LENGTH 52 MILES; ONE TO TWO DAYS

Although you can drive this route in just a few hours, there's a lot to see and even more to do, so pack your hiking boots and consider breaking your journey overnight.

Fuel up at the pretty town of ❶ **Bakewell** (p466), famed for its distinctive Bakewell pudding. Head south on the A6 for 3.5 miles to Rowsley and turn left on winding Church Lane for 2 miles to visit the atmospheric medieval manor, ❷ **Haddon Hall** (p466).

Return to Rowsley, turn left on the A6 and left on the B6012 – follow it for 2.9 miles before turning right to reach the 'Palace of the Peak', ❸ **Chatsworth House** (p466).

Back on the B6012, turn right to join the A619. At Baslow, home to the country hotel and Michelin-starred restaurant Fischer's Baslow Hall, turn left at the roundabout and travel along the A623 for 3.4 miles to the turn-off for ❹ **Eyam**. Drive up the hill to reach its quaint museum, where you can learn about the town's poignant plague history. There's fantastic walking here.

Continue up the hill and turn right on Edge Rd, then right on Sir William Hill Rd and left on the B601 at Grindleford. Continue to Hathersage and turn left on the A6187 to Hope Valley. From here, turn right on the A6013, passing Ladybower Reservoir, to reach the ❺ **Derwent Dam Museum** (p463). Pop in to learn about the Dambusters squadron's 'bouncing bombs' tests here during WWII.

It's 5.8 miles back to the Hope Valley turn-off. Then turn right onto Hathersage Rd, right again on Edale Rd and follow the valley to stretch your legs at another prime walking destination, ❻ **Edale**.

Scenery peaks when you travel towards Castleton, climbing the steep hill near 517m-high Mam Tor to Winnats Rd, then following the spectacular former coral-reef canyon Winnats Pass to explore ❼ **Speedwell Cavern** (p462).

From Speedwell Cavern, head west along Arthurs Way on to Winnats Rd. Turning right on the A623 brings you to the riot of Victoriana in the former spa town of ❽ **Buxton** (p459).

◎ Sights

Eyam Parish Church
CHURCH

(St Lawrence's Church; www.eyam-church.org; Church St; by donation; ⊙9am-6pm Easter-Sep, to 4pm Oct-Easter) Many victims of the village's 1665 Black Death plague outbreak were buried at Eyam's church, whose history dates back to Saxon times. You can view stained-glass panels and moving displays telling the story of the outbreak. The churchyard contains a cross carved in the 8th century.

Eyam Museum
MUSEUM

(www.eyam.museum.org.uk; Hawkhill Rd; adult/child £2.50/2; ⊙10am-4pm Tue-Sun Easter-Oct) Vivid displays on the Eyam plague are the centrepiece of the engaging town museum, alongside exhibits on the village's history of lead mining and silk weaving.

Eyam Hall
HISTORIC BUILDING

(https://eyamhall.net; Main Rd; craft centre free, house & garden adult/child £12/6; ⊙craft centre 10am-4.30pm Wed-Sun year-round, house & garden 11am-3pm Wed, Thu & Sun mid-Feb–late Apr) Surrounded by a traditional English walled garden, this solid-looking 17th-century manor house with stone windows and door frames has a craft centre, a cheese shop, a craft-beer shop and a cafe in its grounds.

🛏 Sleeping & Eating

Miner's Arms
PUB ££

(☑01433-630853; www.theminersarmseyam.co. uk; Water Lane; s/d from £45/70; 🛜) Although its age isn't immediately obvious, this traditional village inn was built shortly before the Black Death hit Eyam in 1665. Inside you'll find beamed ceilings, affable staff, a blazing open fire, comfy en-suite rooms and good-value pub food (mains £9 to £14.50).

Village Green
CAFE £

(www.cafevillagegreen.com; The Square; dishes £2-7; ⊙9.15am-4.15pm Thu-Mon; 🛜) On the village square, with tables on the cobblestones outside, this sweet cafe has homemade soups, a mouthwatering array of cakes and slices (some gluten-free), and decent coffee.

❶ Getting There & Away

Bus services include the following:

Bakewell Bus 275; £3.90, 20 minutes, three per day Monday to Saturday

Buxton Buses 65 and 66; £4.60, 40 minutes, every two hours Monday to Saturday

Sheffield Bus 65; £5.90, 50 minutes, every two hours Monday to Saturday

Bakewell

☑01629 / POP 3950

The second-largest town in the Peak District, charming Bakewell is a great base for exploring the limestone dales of the White Peak. Filled with storybook stone buildings, the town is ringed by famous walking trails and stately homes, but it's probably best known for its famous Bakewell pudding, a pastry shell filled with jam and a custard-like mixture of eggs, butter, sugar and almonds, invented here in 1820.

◎ Sights

★Chatsworth House
HISTORIC BUILDING

(☑01246-565300; www.chatsworth.org; house & gardens adult/child £21/12.50, gardens only £14/7, playground £6.50, park free; ⊙10.30am-5pm late May-early Sep, shorter hours mid-Mar–late May & early Sep-early Jan) Known as the 'Palace of the Peak', this vast edifice 3 miles northeast of Bakewell has been occupied by the earls and dukes of Devonshire for centuries. Inside, the lavish apartments and mural-painted staterooms are packed with priceless paintings and period furniture. The house sits in 25 sq miles of grounds and ornamental gardens, some landscaped by Lancelot 'Capability' Brown. Kids will love the farmyard adventure playground.

From Bakewell, take bus 218 (£2.70, 15 minutes, half-hourly).

The manor was founded in 1552 by the formidable Bess of Hardwick and her second husband, William Cavendish, who earned grace and favour by helping Henry VIII dissolve the English monasteries. Mary, Queen of Scots was imprisoned at Chatsworth on the orders of Elizabeth I in 1569.

Look out for the portraits of the current generation of Devonshires by Lucian Freud.

Also on the estate is one of the country's premier farm shops (p467) and an attached cafe.

Walkers can take footpaths through Chatsworth park via the mock-Venetian village of Edensor (en-sor), while cyclists can pedal via Pilsley.

Haddon Hall
HISTORIC BUILDING

(☑01629-812855; www.haddonhall.co.uk; Haddon Rd; adult/child £15.75/free; ⊙10.30am-5pm daily late Mar-Sep, 10.30am-5pm Fri-Mon Oct, 10.30am-4pm Dec) With stone turrets, time-worn timbers and walled gardens, Haddon Hall, 2 miles south of Bakewell on the A6, looks exactly like a medieval manor house should. Founded in the 12th century, it was expanded and remodelled throughout medieval times but lay dormant from 1700 until its restoration in the 1920s. Take the High Peak bus from Bakewell (£2.50, 10 minutes, hourly) or walk along the footpath through the fields, mostly on the east side of the river.

Spared from the more florid excesses of the Victorian period, Haddon Hall has been used as the location for numerous period blockbusters (such as 2005's *Pride and Prejudice* and 1998's *Elizabeth*).

Thornbridge Brewery BREWERY
(☑ 01629-815999; www.thornbridgebrewery.com; Buxton Rd; tours adult/child £10/3; ☺ tours by reservation 3pm Wed, Thu & Fri, shop 9am-4.30pm Mon-Fri) Brews by this riverside brewery include bottled varieties (such as a fruity strawberry-blonde ale, I Love You Will You Marry Me), keg beers (eg its Vienna-style lager Kill Your Darlings) and cask ales (including its hoppy Brother Rabbit). Tours lasting 1½ hours take you behind the scenes and include tastings in Thornbridge glasses, which you get to keep afterwards. Under-five-year-olds aren't permitted on tours. It's half a mile from the centre of Bakewell on the northwestern edge of town.

Old House Museum MUSEUM
(☑ 01629-813642; www.oldhousemuseum.org.uk; Cunningham Pl; adult/child £5/2.50; ☺ 11am-4pm late Mar-early Nov) Bakewell's local-history museum occupies a time-worn stone house that was built as a tax collector's premises during Henry VIII's rule and was expanded in the Elizabethan era, before being split into tiny mill workers' cottages during the Industrial Revolution. Check out the Tudor toilet and the displays on wattle and daub, a traditional technique for building walls using woven twigs and cow dung.

🏃 Activities

The scenic **Monsal Trail** follows the path of a disused railway line from Combs Viaduct on the outskirts of Bakewell to Topley Pike in Wye Dale (3 miles east of Buxton), including a number of reopened old railway tunnels, covering 8.5 miles in all.

For a rewarding shorter walk, follow the Monsal Trail for 3 miles to the dramatic viewpoint at Monsal Head, where you can pause for refreshment at the Monsal Head Hotel (p468), which serves real ales and excellent Modern British cuisine. With more

time, continue to **Miller's Dale**, where viaducts give a spectacular vista across the steep-sided valley. The tourist offices at Bakewell and Buxton have full details.

Other walking routes go to the stately homes of Haddon Hall and Chatsworth House.

🛏 Sleeping

Hassop Hall Hotel HISTORIC HOTEL ££
(☑ 01629-640488; www.hassophallhotel.co.uk; Hassop Rd, Hassop; d from £110; ℗ 🛜) Built in the 14th century and extensively remodelled in the 17th century, this magnificent property 3 miles north of Bakewell amid formal gardens and woodland is entered via a grand driveway with a gatehouse. Some of its 13 rooms have four-poster beds, decorative fireplaces and freestanding baths. Its restaurant serves refined dishes, such as salt-crusted English duckling.

Rutland Arms Hotel HOTEL ££
(☑ 01629-338051; https://rutlandarmsbakewell.co.uk; The Square; s/d incl breakfast from £64/116; ℗ 🛜 🐕) Jane Austen is said to have stayed in room 2 of this aristocratic, 1804-built stone coaching inn while working on *Pride and Prejudice*. Its 33 rooms are located in the main house and adjacent courtyard building; higher-priced rooms have lots of Victorian flourishes.

🍴 Eating

⭐**Chatsworth Estate
Farm Shop Cafe** CAFE, DELI £
(www.chatsworth.org; Pilsley; dishes £6-14.50; ☺ cafe & shop 9am-5pm Mon-Sat, from 10am Sun; 🚻) 🌱 One of the finest places to eat in the Peak District, this bucolic cafe serves hearty breakfasts (eggs Benedict with Chatsworth-cured bacon or salmon; strawberry-and-honey Chatsworth yoghurt with muesli) until 11.30am, segueing to lunches (steak-and-kidney suet pudding; traditional roasts) until 3pm, and an afternoon menu. Over half the products at its adjacent farm shop are produced on the estate.

**Old Original Bakewell
Pudding Shop** BAKERY, CAFE £
(www.bakewellpuddingshop.co.uk; The Square; dishes £7-12.50; ☺ 8.30am-6pm Mon-Sat, from 9am Sun) One of those that claims to have invented the Bakewell Pudding, this place has a lovely 1st-floor tearoom with exposed beams. It serves light meals and afternoon teas on tiered trays.

Monsal Head Hotel BRITISH ££

(☎01629-640250; www.monsalhead.com; Monsal Trail; mains £11.50-16; ⊙kitchen noon-9.30pm Mon-Sat, to 9pm Sun; P☎🐾) At the dramatic viewpoint of Monsal Head, its namesake hotel serves real ales and brilliant British cuisine, such as Cheshire cheese and horseradish soufflé, braised Derbyshire beef with smoked-garlic mash, and blackberry crumble with spiced vanilla custard and crystallised stinging nettle leaves. Book ahead to stay in its seven simple but comfortable rooms (doubles including breakfast from £110).

Juniper PIZZA ££

(☎01629-815629; www.juniperbakewell.co.uk; Rutland Sq; pizza £8-13.75; ⊙3-10pm Sun-Thu, 11am-11pm Fri & Sat; ☎🖊) Done out with juniper-berry-coloured walls and tartan-upholstered chairs, this chic little spot combines a gin bar stocking 40-plus varieties (and Bakewell-brewed Thornbridge beers) with a contemporary pizza kitchen. Steaming pizzas include Let's Meat (salami, bacon, sausage, spiced beef and pepperoni), Billy Goat (goats cheese, caramelised red onion and mozzarella) and Mighty Brunch (black pudding, mushrooms and eggs).

Piedaniel's FRENCH ££

(☎01629-812687; www.piedaniels-restaurant.com; Bath St; mains lunch £13, dinner £16-25; ⊙noon-2pm & 7-9pm Tue-Sat) Chefs Eric and Christiana Piedaniel's Modern French cuisine is the toast of the in-town restaurants. A whitewashed dining room is the exquisite setting for the likes of Normandy onion soup with cider and Gruyère cheese, followed by pork roulade with braised red cabbage and grain-mustard sauce, and flaming crêpes Suzette.

★**Fischer's Baslow Hall** GASTRONOMY £££

(☎01246-583259; www.fischers-baslowhall.co.uk; 259 Calver Rd, Baslow; 2-/3-/6-course lunch menus £25/33.50/68, 2-/3-/8-course dinner menus £64.50/78.50/88; ⊙noon-2pm & 7-9pm; ☎🖊) This 1907-built manor house, 4 miles northeast of Bakewell, has a magnificent Michelin-starred dining room showcasing British produce (Derbyshire lamb, Yorkshire game, Cornish crab...) along with vegetables from its kitchen garden. Six sumptuous floral bedrooms are in the main house, with another five in the adjacent garden house (doubles including breakfast from £260, including a three-course dinner menu from £367).

Drinking & Nightlife

Pointing Dog & Duck PUB

(www.pointingdog.co.uk; Coombs Rd; ⊙11am-11pm; 🐾) A restored saw mill once powered by the river on which it sits now houses this pub with soaring beamed ceilings, exposed stone walls and views of the river's ducks from its waterside terrace. It's an idyllic spot for a pint or pub food, such as ale-battered fish and chips or chargrilled steaks.

Shopping

Bakewell Deli FOOD & DRINKS

(www.facebook.com/bakewelldeli; Rutland Sq; ⊙9am-5pm) Peak District–roasted Full Moon coffee, Matlock Bath honey, Bakewell puddings, and locally cured meats, chutneys, jams and pies fill the shelves of this enticing deli, along with over 50 British cheeses, including artisan varieties made nearby at the Hope Valley's Cow Close Farm. You can also pick up sandwiches, wraps and soups for a riverside picnic.

Bakewell Market MARKET

(Granby Rd; ⊙9am-4pm Mon) Local producers including Hope Valley Ice Cream, Peak Ales, Bittersweet Chocolates, Brock & Morten (cold-pressed oils) and Caudwell Mill (flour) are among the 160-plus regular stalls at Bakewell's lively Monday market.

❶ Information

Tourist Office (☎01629-816558; www.visitpeakdistrict.com; Bridge St; ⊙9.30am-5pm Apr-Oct, 10.30am-4.30pm Nov-Mar) In the old Market Hall, with a photography gallery on the mezzanine.

❶ Getting There & Away

Bakewell lies on the High Peak bus route. Buses run hourly to Buxton (£5, 30 minutes), Derby (£6.50, 1¼ hours) and Matlock Bath (£2.70, 35 minutes). Five services a day continue to Manchester (£8, 1¾ hours).

Other services:

Castleton Bus 173; £3.30, 50 minutes, four per day, via Tideswell (£3.10, 30 minutes)

Chesterfield Bus 170; £4.80, 50 minutes, hourly Monday to Saturday, every two hours Sunday

Yorkshire

Best Places to Eat

➡ Pipe and Glass Inn (p522)

➡ Norse (p484)

➡ Bridge Cottage Bistro (p496)

➡ Talbot Yard (p491)

➡ Ox Club (p508)

➡ Cochon Aveugle (p480)

Best Places to Stay

➡ La Rosa Hotel (p495)

➡ Talbot Hotel (p491)

➡ Grays Court (p479)

➡ Art Hostel (p507)

➡ Lister Barn (p502)

Why Go?

With a population as big as Scotland's and an area half the size of Belgium, Yorkshire is almost a country in itself. It has its own flag, its own dialect and its own celebration, Yorkshire Day (1 August).

People have long been drawn to this region for walking and cycling, framed by some of Britain's finest scenery – brooding moors and green dales rolling down to a dramatic coastline. Then there's the sheer breadth of history, from Roman times to the 21st century. Medieval York is the heartthrob of the north, but there are countless other atmospheric towns and villages to explore, via abbey ruins, craggy castles and classical gardens.

But Yorkshire refuses to fade into the past and one of its greatest charms lies in the ways innovative locals are driving its cities and towns forward. Once-derelict urban areas are seeing regeneration, and modern Britishness is being fused with Yorkshire heritage in cafes, pubs and restaurants.

When to Go

➡ The weeklong Jorvik Festival in February sees York taken over by a Viking invasion.

➡ Spring brings drifts of yellow daffodils to brighten the roadsides in the Dales and North York Moors; the Three Peaks Race takes place in Horton-in-Ribblesdale; thousands descend for Malton's annual food festival.

➡ Agriculture is celebrated at the Great Yorkshire Show in Harrogate in July. At the same time of year, Yorkshire's coastal sea cliffs become a frenzy of nesting seabirds.

➡ September is the ideal time for hiking in the Yorkshire Dales; the Walking Festival in Richmond also takes place in this month. Harrogate gets green-fingered during its Autumn Flower Show; and Whitby celebrates its biggest Goth Weekend around Halloween.

Yorkshire Highlights

① York (p473)
Exploring the medieval streets of the city and its awe-inspiring cathedral.

② Yorkshire Dales National Park (p497)
Getting off the beaten track and exploring lesser-known corners.

③ Fountains Abbey (p485)
Wandering among the atmospheric medieval ruins.

④ North Yorkshire Moors Railway (p492) Riding on one of England's most scenic train lines.

⑤ Whitby (p492)
Sitting on the pier and tucking into the world's best fish and chips.

⑥ Castle Howard (p482) Reliving the story of *Brideshead Revisited* amid the aristocratic splendour.

⑦ Malham Cove (p501) Pulling on your hiking boots and tackling the steep paths around this scenic cove.

⑧ Leeds (p504)
Getting stuck into Yorkshire's craft-beer scene, hopping around innovative brewery taprooms.

⑨ Hull (p518)
Exploring maritime heritage and the regenerated marina area of Yorkshire's biggest east-coast town.

⑩ Malton (p491)
Touring artisan food and drink producers in a revitalised Georgian market town.

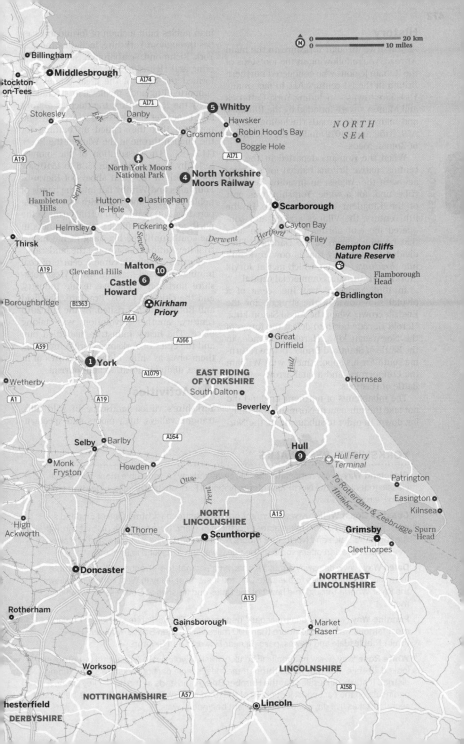

History

As you drive through Yorkshire on the main A1 road, you're following in the footsteps of the Roman legions who conquered northern Britain in the 1st century AD. In fact, many Yorkshire towns – including York, Catterick and Malton – were founded by the Romans, and many modern roads (including the A1, A59, A166 and A1079) follow the alignment of Roman roads.

When the Romans departed in the 5th century, native Britons battled for supremacy with the Angles, an invading Teutonic tribe, and, for a while, Yorkshire was part of the Kingdom of Northumbria. In the 9th century, the Vikings arrived and conquered most of northern Britain, an area that became known as the Danelaw. They divided the territory that is now Yorkshire into *thridings* (thirds), which met at Jorvik (York), their thriving commercial capital.

In 1066 Yorkshire was the scene of a pivotal showdown in the struggle for the English crown, when the Anglo-Saxon king, Harold II, rode north to defeat the forces of the Norwegian king, Harold Hardrada, in the Battle of Stamford Bridge, before returning south for his appointment with William the Conqueror – and a fatal arrow – in the Battle of Hastings.

The inhabitants of northern England did not take the subsequent Norman invasion lying down. In order to subdue them, the Norman nobles built a chain of formidable castles throughout Yorkshire, including those at York, Richmond, Scarborough, Skipton, Pickering and Helmsley. The Norman land grab formed the basis of the great estates that supported England's medieval aristocrats.

By the 15th century, the duchies of York and Lancaster had become so wealthy and powerful that they ended up battling for the English throne in the Wars of the Roses (1455–87). The dissolution of the monasteries by Henry VIII from 1536 to 1540 saw the wealth of the great abbeys of Rievaulx, Fountains and Whitby fall into the hands of noble families, and Yorkshire quietly prospered for 200 years, with fertile farms in the north and the Sheffield cutlery business in the south, until the big bang of the Industrial Revolution transformed the landscape.

South Yorkshire became a centre of coal mining and steel-making, while West Yorkshire nurtured a massive textile industry, and the cities of Leeds, Bradford, Sheffield and Rotherham flourished. By the late 20th century, another revolution was taking place. The heavy industries had died out, and the cities of Yorkshire were reinventing themselves as shiny, high-tech centres of finance, digital innovation and tourism.

 Activities

Yorkshire's varied landscape of wild hills, tranquil valleys, high moors and spectacu-

---

YORKSHIRE'S BEST WALKS

Cleveland Way (www.nationaltrail.co.uk/clevelandway) A venerable moor-and-coast classic that circles the North York Moors National Park on its 109-mile, nine-day route from Helmsley to Filey.

Coast to Coast Walk (www.wainwright.org.uk/coasttocoast.html) One of England's most popular walks: 190 miles across northern England from the Lake District through the Yorkshire Dales and North York Moors National Parks. The Yorkshire section takes a week to 10 days and offers some of the finest walking of its kind in England.

Dales Way (www.dalesway.org.uk) A charming and not-too-strenuous 80-mile amble from the Yorkshire Dales to the Lake District. It starts at Ilkley in West Yorkshire, follows the River Wharfe through the heart of the Dales and finishes at Bowness-on-Windermere.

Pennine Way (www.nationaltrail.co.uk/pennineway) The Yorkshire section of England's most famous walk runs for more than 100 miles via Hebden Bridge, Malham, Horton-in-Ribblesdale and Hawes, passing near Haworth and Skipton.

White Rose Way (www.nationaltrail.co.uk/yorkshirewoldsway) A beautiful but oft-overlooked 79-mile walk that winds through the most scenic part of Yorkshire's East Riding district. It starts at Hessle near the Humber Bridge and ends at the tip of Filey Brigg, a peninsula on the east coast just north of the town of Filey. Billed as 'Yorkshire's best-kept secret', it takes five days and is an excellent beginners' walk.

lar coastline offers plenty of opportunities for outdoor activities. See www.outdoor yorkshire.com for more details.

Cycling

Yorkshire's hosting of the start of the 2014 Tour de France saw a huge upsurge in interest in cycling, and resulted in the establishment of the Tour de Yorkshire (www.letour.york shire.com) annual cycle race from 2015. The county has a vast network of country lanes that are perfect for road cyclists, although the national parks also attract lots of motorists so even minor roads can be busy at weekends.

Mountain bikers can avail themselves of the network of bridleways, former railways and disused mining tracks now converted for two-wheel use. Dalby Forest (www. forestry.gov.uk/dalbyforest), near Pickering, sports purpose-built mountain-biking trails of all grades from green to black, and there are newly waymarked trails at the Sutton Bank National Park Centre (p489).

Walking

For shorter walks and rambles, the best area is the Yorkshire Dales, with a great selection of walks through scenic valleys or over wild hilltops, plus a few higher summits thrown in for good measure. The East Riding's Yorkshire Wolds hold hidden delights, while the quiet valleys and dramatic coast of the North York Moors are also home to some excellent trails.

ⓘ Information

The Yorkshire Tourist Board (www.yorkshire. com) has plenty of general leaflets and brochures. For more detailed information, try the excellent network of local tourist offices.

ⓘ Getting There & Around

BUS

Long-distance coaches operated by National Express (☑ 0871 781 8181; www.national express.com) serve most cities and large towns in Yorkshire from London, the south of England, the Midlands and Scotland.

Bus transport around Yorkshire is frequent and efficient, especially between major towns. Services are more sporadic in the national parks, but are still adequate for reaching most places if you're not in a rush, particularly in summer months (June to September).

CAR

The major north–south road transport routes – the M1 and A1 motorways – run through the middle of Yorkshire, serving the key cities of

Sheffield, Leeds and York. If you're arriving by sea from northern Europe, Hull in the East Riding district is the region's main port.

Traveline Yorkshire (☑ 0871 200 2233; www. yorkshiretravel.net) provides public-transport information for all of Yorkshire.

TRAIN

The main rail line between London and Edinburgh runs through Yorkshire, with at least 10 trains calling each day at York and Doncaster, where you can change trains for other Yorkshire destinations. There are also direct links to northern cities such as Manchester and Newcastle. For timetable information, contact National Rail Enquiries (☑ 03457 48 49 50; www.nationalrail. co.uk).

NORTH YORKSHIRE

This, the largest of Yorkshire's four counties – and the largest county in England – is also the most beautiful. Unlike the rest of northern England, it has survived almost unscathed by the Industrial Revolution. Since the Middle Ages, North Yorkshire has been almost exclusively about sheep and the woolly wealth they produce.

Rather than closed-down factories, mills and mines, the human-made monuments dotting the landscape in these parts are of the stately variety – the great houses and wealthy abbeys that sit, ruined or restored, as a reminder that there was plenty of money to be made off the sheep's back.

All the same, North Yorkshire's biggest attraction is an urban one. While the genteel spa town of Harrogate and the storied seaside resort of Whitby have many fans, nothing compares to the unparalleled splendour of medieval York, England's most-visited city outside London.

York

☑ 01904 / POP 152,841

No other city in northern England says 'medieval' quite like York, a city of extraordinary cultural and historical wealth that has lost little of its pre-industrial lustre. A magnificent circuit of 13th-century walls encloses a medieval spider's web of narrow streets. At its heart lies the immense, awe-inspiring York Minster, one of the most beautiful Gothic cathedrals in the world. York's long history and rich heritage is woven into virtually every brick and beam, and the modern, tourist-oriented city – with its myriad museums,

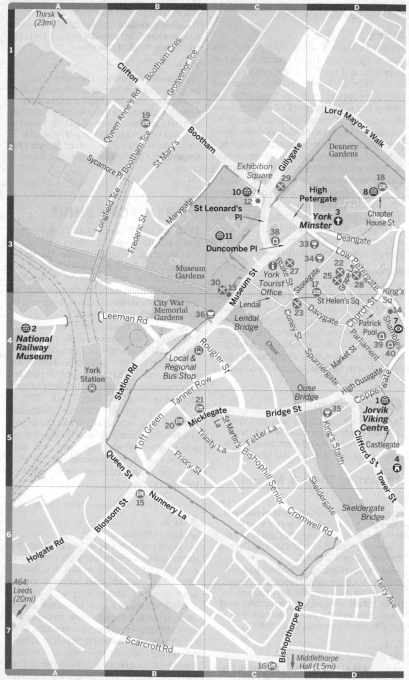

Thirsk
(23mi)

Clifton

Bootham Cres

Grosvenor Tce

Queen Anne's Rd

19

Bootham Tce

Bootham

St Mary's

Lord Mayor's Walk

Deanery
Gardens

Gillygate

Sycamore Pl

Longfield Tce

Marygate

Exhibition
Square

29

High
Petergate

18

8

Chapter
House St

Frederic St

10

St Leonard's
Pl

12

York
Minster 3

Deangate

38

11

Duncombe Pl

33

34

Low Petergate

22

Museum
Gardens

30

13

Museum St

York
Tourist
Office

Blake St

27

Stonegate

25

17

28

Grape La

King's
Sq

14

7

Shambles

City War
Memorial
Gardens

36

Lendal

Lendal
Bridge

Coney St

23

St Helen's Sq

Davygate

Church St

Patrick
Pool

39

40

National
Railway
Museum

2

Leeman Rd

Ouse

Spurriergate

Market St

Parliament St

York
Station

Station Rd

Local &
Regional
Bus Stop

Rougier St

Tanner Row

Ouse
Bridge

High Ousegate

Coppergate

1

Jorvik
Viking
Centre

Toft Green

21

20

Micklegate

Trinity La

St Martin's

Fetter La

Bridge St

35

King's Staith

Castlegate

4

Clifford St

Tower St

Queen St

Priory St

Bishophill Senior

Skeldergate

Skeldergate
Bridge

Blossom St

15

Nunnery La

Cromwell Rd

Holgate Rd

A64:
Leeds
(20mi)

Terry Ave

Scarcroft Rd

Bishopthorpe Rd

16

Middlethorpe
Hall (1.5mi)

restaurants, cafes and traditional pubs – is a carefully maintained heir to that heritage.

Try to avoid the inevitable confusion by remembering that around these parts, *gate* means street and *bar* means gate.

◉ Sights

★ York Minster CATHEDRAL

(☎ 01904-557200; www.yorkminster.org; Deangate; adult/child £10/free, incl tower £15/5; ⊙ 9am-6pm Mon-Sat, 12.30-6pm Sun, last admission 4.30pm Mon-Sat, 3pm Sun) York Minster is the largest medieval cathedral in northern Europe, and one of the world's most beautiful Gothic buildings. Seat of the archbishop of York, primate of England, it is second in importance only to Canterbury, seat of the primate of *all* England – the separate titles were created to settle a debate over the true centre of the English Church. Note that the quire, east end and undercroft close in preparation for evening service around the time of last admission.

The first church on this site was a wooden chapel built for the baptism of King Edwin of Northumbria on Easter Day 627; its location is marked in the crypt. This was replaced with a stone church built on the site of a Roman basilica, parts of which can be seen in the foundations. The first Norman minster was built in the 11th century and, again, you can see surviving fragments in the foundations and crypt.

The present minster, built mainly between 1220 and 1480, manages to encompass all the major stages of Gothic architectural development. The transepts (1220–55) were built in Early English style; the octagonal chapter house (1260–90) and nave (1291–1340) in the Decorated style; and the west towers, west front and central (or lantern) tower (1470–72) in Perpendicular style.

Don't miss the **undercroft** (open 10am to 4.15pm Monday to Saturday, 1pm to 3pm Sunday), which houses an excellent interactive exhibition – York Minster Revealed – buried within the foundations, leading visitors through 2,000 years of history on the site of the cathedral, amid Roman and Norman remains. At the heart of York's cathedral is the massive **tower**, which is well worth climbing for the unparalleled views of York; it's £5 extra for a ticket and a fairly claustrophobic climb of 275 steps.

★ National Railway Museum MUSEUM

(www.nrm.org.uk; Leeman Rd; ⊙ 10am-6pm Apr-Oct, to 5pm Nov-Mar; P ⟨⟩) FREE York's

York

National Railway Museum – the biggest in the world, with more than 100 locomotives – is well-presented and crammed with fascinating stuff. It is laid out on a vast scale and is housed in a series of giant railway sheds – allow at least two hours to do it justice. The museum also now includes a high-tech simulator experience of riding on the Mallard (£4), which set the world speed record for a steam locomotive in 1938 (126mph).

Highlights for trainspotters include a replica of George Stephenson's Rocket (1829), the world's first 'modern' steam locomotive; a 1960s Japanese Shinkansen bullet train; and an exhibition dedicated to the world-famous Flying Scotsman, the first steam engine to break the 100mph barrier (now restored to full working order and touring the UK). There's also a massive 4-6-2 loco from 1949, which has been cut in half to demonstrate how it works (daily talk at 4pm).

Even if you're not a rail nerd, you'll enjoy looking through the gleaming, silk-lined carriages of the royal trains used by Queens Mary, Adelaide and Victoria, and King Edward VII.

The museum is about 400m west of the train station. A road train (adult/child £3/2) runs between the minster and museum every 30 minutes from 11am to 4pm, weather permitting.

★ **Jorvik Viking Centre** MUSEUM
(⌨ ticket reservations 01904-615505; www.jorvik-viking-centre.co.uk; Coppergate; adult/child £11/8; ⊙ 10am-5pm Apr-Oct, to 4pm Nov-Mar) Interactive multimedia exhibits aimed at bringing history to life often achieve exactly the opposite, but the much-hyped Jorvik manages to pull it off with aplomb. It's a smells-and-all reconstruction of the Viking settlement unearthed here during excavations in the late 1970s, experienced via a 'time-car' monorail that transports you through 9th-century Jorvik (the Viking name for York). You can reduce time waiting in line by booking timed-entry tickets online; there is almost always a queue to get in.

While some of the 'you will now travel back in time' malarkey might seem a bit annoying, it's all done with a sense of humour tied to historical authenticity that will give you a pretty good idea of what life must have been like in Viking-era York. The museum exhibition at the end of the monorail includes items on loan from the British Museum. Look out for the Lloyds Bank coprolite, a fossilised human stool that measures an eye-watering 9in long and half a pound in weight, and might be the only turd in the world to have its own Wikipedia entry.

Dig   MUSEUM
(☎ 01904-615505; www.digyork.com; St Saviour's Church, St Saviourgate; adult/child £6.50/6; ⊙ 10am-5pm, last admission 4pm; 🖼) Under the same management as Jorvik (p476) and housed in an atmospheric old church, Dig gives you the chance to be an 'archaeological detective', unearthing the secrets of York's distant past as well as learning something of the archaeologist's world – what they do, how they do it and so on. Aimed mainly at kids, it's much more hands-on than Jorvik and a lot of its merit depends on how good – and entertaining – your guide is.

The Shambles   STREET
The Shambles takes its name from the Saxon word *shamel*, meaning 'slaughterhouse' – in 1862 there were 26 butcher shops on this street. Today the butchers are long gone, but this narrow cobbled lane, lined with 15th-century Tudor buildings that overhang so much they seem to meet above your head, is the most picturesque in Britain, and one of the most visited in Europe, often filled with visitors wielding cameras.

Yorkshire Museum   MUSEUM
(www.yorkshiremuseum.org.uk; Museum St; adult/child £7.50/free; ⊙ 10am-5pm) Most of York's Roman archaeology is hidden beneath the medieval city, so the superb displays in the Yorkshire Museum are invaluable if you want to get an idea of what Eboracum was like. There are maps and models of Roman York, funerary monuments, mosaic floors and wall paintings, and a 4th-century bust of Emperor Constantine. Kids will enjoy the dinosaur exhibit, centred around giant ichthyosaur fossils from Yorkshire's Jurassic coast.

There are excellent galleries dedicated to Viking and medieval York as well, including priceless artefacts such as the beautifully decorated 9th-century York helmet.

York Castle Museum   MUSEUM
(www.yorkcastlemuseum.org.uk; Tower St; adult/child £10/free; ⊙ 9.30am-5pm) This excellent museum has displays of everyday life through the centuries, with reconstructed domestic interiors, a Victorian street and a prison cell where you can try out a condemned man's bed – and it could be that of highwayman Dick Turpin (imprisoned here before being hanged in 1739). There's a bewildering array of evocative objects from the past 400 years, gathered together by a certain Dr Kirk from the 1920s onwards for fear the items would become obsolete and disappear completely.

York City Art Gallery   GALLERY
(☎ 01904-687687; www.yorkartgallery.org.uk; Exhibition Sq; adult/child £7.50/free; ⊙ 10am-5pm; 🖼) As well as an impressive collection of Old Masters, York Art Gallery possesses works by LS Lowry, Pablo Picasso, Grayson Perry, David Hockney, and the controversial York artist William Etty who, in the 1820s, was the first major British painter to specialise in nudes. A unique feature is the gallery's hands-on sculpture sessions (where you can handle the works), and its brilliant interactive ceramics centre (www.centreofceramicart.org.uk), housing more than 1,000 pieces dating from Roman times to the present day.

Clifford's Tower   CASTLE
(EH; www.english-heritage.org.uk; Tower St; adult/child £5/3; ⊙ 10am-6pm Apr-Sep, to 5pm Oct, to 4pm Nov-Mar) There's precious little left of York Castle except for this evocative stone tower, a highly unusual four-lobed design built into the castle's keep after the original one was destroyed in 1190 during anti-Jewish riots. An angry mob forced 150 Jews to be locked inside the tower and the hapless victims took their own lives rather than be killed. There's not much to see inside, but the views over the city are excellent.

Richard III Experience   MUSEUM
(www.richardiiiexperience.com; Monk Bar; adult/child incl Henry VII Experience £5/3; ⊙ 10am-5pm Apr-Oct, to 4pm Nov-Mar) The best-preserved of York's medieval city gates houses this museum which explores the life and reign of Richard III (r 1483–85) and his impact on York, and sets out the case of the 'Princes in

---

❶ YORK PASS

If you plan on visiting a number of sights, you can save yourself some money by using a YorkPass (https://yorkpass.com). It gives you free access to many of the best pay-to-visit sights in and around York, including York Minster, Jorvik and Castle Howard (p482). You can buy it at the York Tourist Office or online; prices for one/two/three days are adult £42/60/70, child £26/30/35.

the Tower', inviting visitors to judge whether they were murdered by Richard, who was their uncle.

Treasurer's House
HISTORIC BUILDING

(NT; www.nationaltrust.org.uk; Chapter House St; adult/child £8.10/4; ⊙11am-4.30pm Mar-Oct; 🐾) This historic home, which once housed York Minster's medieval treasures, is an anomaly: in the 19th century it was bought by Yorkshire industrialist Frank Green as a collection of rundown interconnected properties. At great expense and using historical archives, Green spent years remodelling the house to what it might once have looked like, but refused to pick just one period, resulting in a collection of authentic-looking rooms that span from medieval times to the 18th century.

The house is also the setting for one of York's most enduring ghost stories: during the 1950s a plumber working in the basement swore he saw a band of Roman soldiers marching through the walls. Regular tours (£4), including one of the haunted cellar, run every day but Wednesday.

🏃 Activities

★ Brewtown
BEER TOUR

(📞01904-636666; www.brewtowntours.co.uk; £60; ⊙11.30am-5pm) These craft-brewery minivan tours are a fuss-free way to get behind the scenes at Yorkshire's smaller breweries, some of which only open to the public for these tours. Owner Mark runs different routes (around York, Malton or Leeds) depending on the day of the week; each tour visits three breweries with tastings along the way, and sometimes even beer-pairing nibbles.

👉 Tours

Association of Voluntary Guides
WALKING

(www.avgyork.co.uk; ⊙tours 10.15am & 1.15pm year-round, 6.15pm Jun-Aug) FREE Free two-hour walking tours of the city, setting out from Exhibition Sq in front of York Art Gallery.

City Cruises York
BOATING

(www.citycruisesyork.com; Lendal Bridge; adult/child from £9.50/5.50; ⊙tours 10.30am, noon, 1.30pm & 3pm; 🐾) These hour-long cruises on the River Ouse depart from King's Staith and, 10 minutes later, Lendal Bridge. Special lunch, afternoon tea and evening cruises are also offered. You can buy tickets on board or book at the office by Lendal Bridge.

Ghost Hunt of York
WALKING

(📞01904-608700; www.ghosthunt.co.uk; adult/child £6/4; ⊙tours 7.30pm) The kids will just love this award-winning and highly entertaining 75-minute tour laced with authentic ghost stories. It begins at the top end of the Shambles, whatever the weather (it's never cancelled), and there's no need to book – just turn up and wait till you hear the handbell ringing...

🎪 Festivals & Events

Jorvik Viking Festival
CULTURAL

(www.jorvik-viking-festival.co.uk) For a week in mid-February, York is invaded by Vikings as part of this festival, which features battle re-enactments, themed walks, markets and other bits of Viking-related fun.

York Food Festival
FOOD & DRINK

(www.yorkfoodfestival.com; ⊙late Sep) A 10-day celebration of all that's good to eat and drink in Yorkshire, with food stalls, tastings, a beer tent, cookery demonstrations and more. The main event is in late September, but there's a small taster festival in June and a chocolate festival on Easter weekend.

🛏 Sleeping

★ Safestay York
HOSTEL £

(📞01904-627720; www.safestay.com; 88-90 Micklegate; dm/tw/f from £15/60/75; @ 🛜) Housed in a Grade I Georgian townhouse, this is a large boutique hostel with colourful decor and good facilities including a bar with pool table. Rooms are mostly en suite and have a bit more character than you'd usually find in hostels, with the added intrigue of plaques outside doors describing the history of different rooms in the house.

It's popular with school groups and stag and hen parties – don't come here looking for peace and quiet. Family rooms are strategically positioned right at the top of the house.

York YHA
HOSTEL £

(📞0345 371 9051; www.yha.org.uk; 42 Water End, Clifton; dm/tw from £15/39; 🅿🛜) Originally the Rowntree (Quaker confectioners) mansion, this handsome Victorian house makes a spacious and child-friendly youth hostel, with more than 250 beds, a broad garden and on-site restaurant. It's often busy, so book early. It's about a mile northwest of the city centre; there's a riverside footpath from Lendal Bridge (poorly lit, so avoid after dark).

Alternatively, take bus 2 from the train station or Museum St, though be aware it doesn't run in the evenings.

Fort
HOSTEL £

(☑ 01904-620222; www.thefortyork.co.uk; 1 Little Stonegate; dm/d from £22/85; ☜) This boutique hostel showcases the interior design of young British talents, creating affordable accommodation with a dash of character and flair. There are six- and eight-bed dorms, along with five doubles, but don't expect a peaceful retreat – it's central and there's a lively club downstairs (earplugs are provided!). Towels are included, as well as free tea, coffee and laundry.

★ The Lawrance
APARTMENT ££

(☑ 01904-239988; www.thelawrance.com/york/; 74 Micklegate; 1-bed/2-bed from £75/160; ✳☜) Set back from the road in a huddle of old red-brick buildings that once formed a factory, the Lawrance is an excellent find: super-swish serviced apartments with all mod cons on the inside and heritage character on the outside. Some apartments are split-level, all are comfy and spacious, with leather sofas, flatscreen TVs and luxurious fixtures and fittings.

Dairy Guesthouse
B&B ££

(☑ 01904-639367; www.dairyguesthouse.co.uk; 3 Scarcroft Rd; s/d/f from £70/80/100; P☜) This Victorian home offers tasteful rooms that mesh fresh decor and five-star bathrooms with original features like cast-iron fireplaces. The flower- and plant-filled courtyard is a lovely place to pause for a rest after a day of sightseeing. It leads to a pair of cottage-style rooms, which are not as nice as those inside but are more private.

Bar Convent
B&B ££

(☑ 01904-643238; www.bar-convent.org.uk; 17 Blossom St; s w/without bath from £64/39, d w/without bath from £74/90, f w/without bath £102/116; ☜) This mansion just outside Micklegate Bar is less than 10 minutes' walk from the train station. It houses a working convent, a cafe, meeting rooms and an exhibition, and also offers good B&B accommodation. Open to visitors of all faiths and none. Charming bedrooms are modern and well-equipped, breakfasts are superb, and there's a garden and hidden chapel to enjoy.

Hedley House Hotel
HOTEL ££

(☑ 01904-637404; www.hedleyhouse.com; 3 Bootham Tce; d/f from £105/130; P☜) ⊘ This large red-brick terrace-house hotel sports a variety of options including family-friendly rooms sleeping up to five and self-catering apartments. The designer lounge has the feel of a much bigger hotel, plus there's a yoga studio and Jacuzzi on the outdoor terrace at the back. It's also barely five minutes' walk from the city centre through the Museum Gardens.

★ Grays Court
HISTORIC HOTEL £££

(☑ 01904-612613; www.grayscourtyork.com; Chapter House St; d £190-235, ste £270-290; P☜) This medieval mansion with just 11 rooms feels like a country-house hotel. It's set in lovely gardens with direct access to the city walls, and bedrooms combine antique furniture with modern comfort and design. The oldest part of the building was built in the 11th century, and King James I once dined in the Long Gallery.

✖ Eating

★ Mannion & Co
CAFE, BISTRO £

(☑ 01904-631030; www.mannionandco.co.uk; 1 Blake St; mains £7-12; ☺9am-5pm Mon-Sat, 10am-4.30pm Sun) Expect to queue for a table at this busy bistro (no reservations), with its convivial atmosphere and selection of delicious daily specials. Regulars on the menu include eggs Benedict for breakfast, a chunky Yorkshire rarebit (cheese on toast) made with home-baked bread, and lunch platters of cheese and charcuterie. Oh, and pavlova for pudding.

Hairy Fig
CAFE £

(☑ 01904-677074; www.thehairyfig.co.uk; 39 Fossgate; mains £5-12; ☺9am-4.30pm Mon-Sat) This cafe-deli is a standout in York. On the one side you've got the best of Yorkshire tripping over the best of Europe, with Italian white anchovies and truffle-infused olive oil stacked alongside York honey mead and baked pies; on the other you've got a Dickensian-style sweet store and backroom cafe serving dishes crafted from the deli.

★ No 8 Bistro
BISTRO ££

(☑ 01904-653074; www.no8york.co.uk/bistro; 8 Gillygate; dinner mains £17-19; ☺noon-10pm Mon-Fri, 9am-10pm Sat & Sun; ☜⊕) ⊘ A cool little place with modern artwork mimicking the Edwardian stained glass at the front, No 8 offers a day-long menu of top-notch bistro dishes using fresh local produce, such as Jerusalem artichoke risotto with fresh herbs, and Yorkshire lamb slow-cooked in hay and lavender.

It also does breakfast (mains £6 to £9) and Sunday lunch. Booking recommended.

Mr P's Curious Tavern
BRITISH ££

(01904-521177; www.mrpscurioustavern.co.uk; 71 Low Petergate; dishes £5-14; noon-10pm Mon-Fri, 11am-11pm Sat, noon-6pm Sun) Mr P's specialises in imaginative small plates, deli meats and cheeses, with a quality wine list – not what you'd expect from its touristy location. It's housed inside a creaky (allegedly haunted) old house, and is part of the mini-empire from Michelin-starred Yorkshire chef Andrew Pern, of Star Inn (p491) fame.

Star Inn The City
BRITISH ££

(01904-619208; www.starinnthecity.co.uk; Lendal Engine House, Museum St; mains £14-28; 9.30-11.30am, noon-9.30pm Mon-Sat, to 7.30pm Sun;) Its riverside setting in a Grade II–listed engine house and quirky British menu make Andrew Pern's York outpost of the Star Inn (p491) an exceedingly pleasant place to while away the hours. Expect country-themed cosiness in winter, and dining out on the broad terrace in summer.

El Piano
VEGAN ££

(01904-610676; www.el-piano.com; 15 Grape Lane; lunch £12, 2-course dinner £15; noon-10pm Mon-Sat, noon-9pm Sun;) With a menu that's 100% vegan, as well as being nut-, gluten-, palm oil- and refined sugar-free, this Hispanic-style spot is a vegetarian haven. Downstairs there's a lovely cafe and suntrap patio, and upstairs, three themed rooms. The menu offers dishes such as falafel, onion bhaji, corn fritters and mushroom-and-basil salad, either in tapas-sized portions or as mixed platters. There's also a takeaway counter.

Bettys
CAFE ££

(01904-659142; www.bettys.co.uk; 6-8 St Helen's Sq; mains £6-14, afternoon tea £19.95; 9am-9pm Sun-Fri, 8.30am-9pm Sat;) Old-school afternoon tea, with white-aproned waiters, linen tablecloths and a teapot collection ranged along the walls. The house speciality is the Yorkshire Fat Rascal, a huge fruit scone smothered in melted butter, while breakfast and lunch dishes, like bacon and raclette rösti, and Yorkshire rarebit, show off Betty's Swiss–Yorkshire heritage. No bookings, but be prepared to queue.

1331
BRITISH ££

(01904-661130; www.1331-york.co.uk; 13 Grape Lane; mains £11-20; 8am-10pm;) This

courtyard complex houses a bar, a cocktail lounge and even a private cinema, along with an appealing 1st-floor restaurant serving a menu of crowd-pleasing classics like sausage and mash, Sunday roasts and beef Wellington. Vegetarians are catered for, too, with a good selection of dishes such as chickpea and coriander burgers. There's a two-course set menu for £14.95.

★ Cochon Aveugle
FRENCH £££

(01904-640222; www.lecochonaveugle.uk; 37 Walmgate; 4-course lunch £40, 8-course tasting menu £60; 6-9pm Wed-Sat, noon-1.30pm Sat) Black-pudding macaroon? Strawberry and elderflower sandwich? Blowtorched mackerel with melon gazpacho? Fussy eaters beware – this small restaurant with huge ambition serves an ever-changing tasting menu (no à la carte) of infinite imagination and invention. You never know what will come next, except that it will be delicious. Bookings are essential.

Drinking & Nightlife

★ Blue Bell
PUB

(01904-654904; 53 Fossgate; 11am-11pm Mon-Thu, to midnight Fri & Sat, noon-10.30pm Sun;) This is what a proper English pub looks like – a tiny, 200-year-old wood-panelled room with a smouldering fireplace, decor untouched since 1903, a pile of ancient board games in the corner, friendly and efficient bar staff, and weekly cask-ale specials chalked on a board. Bliss, with froth on top – if you can get in (it's often full). Cash only.

House of Trembling Madness
BAR

(01904-640009; www.tremblingmadness.co.uk; 48 Stonegate; 10am-midnight Mon-Sat, from 11am Sun) When a place describes itself as a 'medieval drinking hall', it clearly deserves investigation. The ground floor and basement host an impressive shop stacked with craft beers, gins, vodkas and even absinthes; but head upstairs to the first floor and you'll find the secret drinking den – an ancient timber-framed room with high ceilings, a bar and happy drinkers.

Guy Fawkes Inn
PUB

(01904-466674; www.guyfawkesinnyork.com; 25 High Petergate; 11am-11pm Mon-Thu & Sun, to midnight Fri & Sat) The man who famously plotted to blow up the Houses of Parliament and inspired Bonfire Night in the UK was born on this site in 1570. Walk through the lovely Georgian wood-panelled pub to find

Guy Fawkes' grandmother's cottage at the far end of the back patio, watched over by a giant wall mural.

Brew York   MICROBREWERY
(☑ 01904-848448; www.brewyork.co.uk; Enterprise Complex, Walmgate; ⊕ 6-11pm Wed & Thu, from 4pm Fri, noon-11pm Sat, to 10pm Sun) Housed in a cavernous old warehouse, half the floor space in this craft brewery is occupied by giant brewing tanks while the rest is given over to simple wooden drinking benches and a bar with rotating keg and cask beers. At the far end of the brewery there's a small riverside terrace overlooking Rowntree Wharf.

Perky Peacock   CAFE
(www.perkypeacockcoffee.co.uk; Lendal Bridge; ⊕ 7am-5pm Mon-Fri, from 9am Sat, to 4pm Sun) One of York's charms is finding teeny places like this cafe, shoe-horned into historic buildings. In this case the host is a 14th-century, rotund watchtower crouched by the riverbank. Sup an excellent coffee under the ancient wood beams, or grab a street-side table for a tasty pastry.

King's Arms   PUB
(☑ 01904-659435; King's Staith; ⊕ noon-11pm Mon-Sat, to 10.30pm Sun) York's best-known pub enjoys a fabulous riverside location, with tables spilling out onto the quayside. It's the perfect spot on a summer evening, but be prepared to share it with a few hundred other people.

🔒 Shopping

Fossgate Books   BOOKS
(☑ 01904-641389; fossgatebooks@hotmail.co.uk; 36 Fossgate; ⊕ 10am-5.30pm Mon-Sat) A classic, old-school secondhand bookshop, with towers of books on the floor and a maze of floor-to-ceiling shelves crammed with titles covering every subject under the sun, from crime fiction and popular paperbacks to arcane academic tomes and 1st editions.

Red House   ANTIQUES
(www.redhouseyork.co.uk; Duncombe Pl; ⊕ 9.30am-5.30pm Mon-Fri, to 6pm Sat, 10.30am-5pm Sun) The goods of about 60 antiques dealers are displayed in 10 showrooms spread over two floors, with items ranging from jewellery and porcelain to clocks and furniture.

**The Shop That
Must Not Be Named**   GIFTS & SOUVENIRS
(30 The Shambles; ⊕ 10am-6pm) Casting a spell over Harry Potter fans, this shop opened on the Shambles – the street said to be the inspiration for Diagon Alley – in 2017. Wands? Tick. Quidditch fan gear? Tick. Potions? Tick. Pure magic for muggles. There's now no less than three Potter shops on the Shambles, but this is the original and still the most convincing.

Shambles Market   FOOD
(www.shamblesmarket.com; The Shambles; ⊕ 9am-5pm) Yorkshire cheeses, Whitby fish and local meat make good fodder for self-caterers at this anything-goes market behind the Shambles, which also touts arts, crafts and Yorkshire flat caps. The food-court section near where the Shambles joins Pavement is a good spot for cheap eats, coffee and ice-cream at picnic tables.

ⓘ Information

York Tourist Office (☑ 01904-550099; www.visityork.org; 1 Museum St; ⊕ 9am-5pm Mon-Sat, 10am-4pm Sun) Visitor and transport info for all of Yorkshire, plus accommodation bookings (for a small fee) and ticket sales.

ⓘ Getting There & Away

BUS

York does not have a bus station; intercity buses stop outside the train station, while local and regional buses stop here and also on **Rougier St** (Rougier St), about 200m northeast of the train station.

For timetable information, call **Traveline Yorkshire** (☑ 0871 200 2233; www.yorkshiretravel. net) or check the computerised 24-hour information points at the train station and Rougier St. There's a bus information point (8am to 4pm Monday to Saturday) in the train station's Travel Centre.

Birmingham £20, 3½ hours, one daily
Edinburgh £40, 5½ hours, two daily
London from £36, 5½ hours, three daily
Newcastle £12, 2¼ hours, two daily

CAR

A car is more hindrance than help in the city centre, so use one of the Park & Ride (www.itravelyork.info/park-and-ride) car parks at the edge of the city. If you want to explore the surrounding area, rental options include **Europcar** (☑ 0371 384 3458; www.europcar.co.uk; Queen St; ⊕ 8am-6pm Mon-Fri, to 4pm Sat), located next to the long-stay car park at the train station.

TRAIN

York is a major railway hub, with frequent direct services to many British cities.

Birmingham £45, 2¼ hours, two per hour

Edinburgh £70, 2½ hours, two to three per hour

Leeds £7, 25 minutes, at least every 15 minutes

London King's Cross £80, two hours, every 30 minutes

Manchester £21, 1½ hours, four per hour

Newcastle £20, one hour, four to five per hour

Scarborough £11.50, 50 minutes, hourly

❶ Getting Around

Central York is easy to get around on foot – you're never more than 20 minutes' walk from any of the major sights.

BICYCLE

The tourist office has a useful free map showing York's cycle routes, or visit iTravel-York (www. itravelyork.info/cycling). Castle Howard (15 miles northeast of York via Haxby and Strensall) is an interesting destination, and there's also a section of the **Trans-Pennine Trail cycle path** (www. transpenninetrail.org.uk) from Bishopthorpe in York to Selby (15 miles) along the old railway line.

You can rent bikes from **Cycle Heaven** (☑ 01904-622701; www.cycle-heaven.co.uk; York Railway Station, Station Rd; 2/24hr £10/20; ⊘ 8.30am-5.30pm Mon-Fri, 9am-5pm Sat year-round, 11am-4pm Sun May-Sep) at the train station.

BUS

Local bus services are operated by First York (www.firstgroup.com/york). Single fares range from £1 to £3, and a day pass valid for all local buses is £4.50 (available on the bus or at Park & Ride car parks).

Castle Howard

Stately homes may be two a penny in England, but you'll have to try pretty damn hard to find one as breathtakingly stately as Castle Howard (☑ 01653-648333; www.castlehoward.co.uk; adult/child house & grounds £18.95/9.95, grounds only £11.95/7.95; ⊘ house 10am-4pm, grounds 10am-5pm, last admission 4pm; ℙ), a work of theatrical grandeur and audacity set in the rolling Howardian Hills. This is one of the world's most beautiful buildings, instantly recognisable from its starring role in the 1980s TV series *Brideshead Revisited* and in the 2008 film of the same name (both based on Evelyn Waugh's 1945 novel of nostalgia for the English aristocracy).

When the Earl of Carlisle hired his pal Sir John Vanbrugh to design his new home in 1699, he was hiring a man who had no formal training and was best known as a playwright. Luckily, Vanbrugh hired Nicholas Hawksmoor, who had worked as Christopher Wren's clerk of works on St Paul's Cathedral. Not only did Hawksmoor have a big part to play in the design, bestowing on the house a baroque cupola modelled after St Paul's – the first on a domestic building in England – but he and Vanbrugh would later work wonders with Blenheim Palace. Today the house is still home to the Hon Nicholas Howard and his family, and he can often be seen around the place.

If you can, try to visit on a weekday when it's easier to find the space to appreciate this hedonistic marriage of art, architecture, landscaping and natural beauty. As you wander about the peacock-haunted grounds, views open up over Vanbrugh's playful Temple of the Four Winds, Hawksmoor's stately mausoleum and the distant hills. Inside, you'll find the house split into two distinct styles; the east wing, which includes the Great Hall, was built in the 1700s and is extravagantly baroque in style, whereas the west wing wasn't completed until the 1800s, by which time the fashion was for much more classical Palladian. The house is full of treasures – the breathtaking Great Hall with its soaring Corinthian pilasters, Pre-Raphaelite stained glass in the chapel, and corridors lined with classical antiquities.

Keep an eye out for talks and tours of the house and gardens, which run on an ad-hoc basis depending on what staff are available. There are also boat tours down at the lake, and the entrance courtyard has a good cafe, a gift shop and a farm shop filled with foodie delights from local producers – you could quite easily spend an entire day at the site.

Castle Howard is 15 miles northeast of York, off the A64. There are several organised tours from York; check with the tourist office for up-to-date schedules. Bus 181 from York goes to Malton via Castle Howard (£10 return, one hour, four times daily Monday to Saturday year-round).

Harrogate

☑ 01423 / POP 73,576

The quintessential Victorian spa town, prim and pretty Harrogate has long been associated with a certain kind of old-fashioned Englishness – the kind that seems the preserve of retired army majors and formidable dowagers who take the *Daily Telegraph* and always vote Tory. They come to Harrogate to enjoy the flower shows and gardens that fill the town with magnificent displays of colour, especially in spring and autumn. It is fitting that the town's most famous visitor was Agatha Christie, who fled here incognito in 1926 to escape her broken marriage.

And yet, this picture of Victoriana redux is not quite complete. While it's undoubtedly true that Harrogate remains a firm favourite of visitors in their golden years, the town has plenty of smart hotels and trendy eateries catering to the boom in Harrogate's newest trade – conferences. All those dynamic young sales-and-marketing guns have to eat and sleep somewhere.

◉ Sights & Activities

Royal Pump Room Museum　　　MUSEUM
(www.harrogate.gov.uk; Crown Pl; adult/child £4/2.50; ⊘10.30am-5pm Mon-Sat, 2-5pm Sun Apr-Oct, to 4pm Nov-Mar) You can learn all about Harrogate's history as a spa town in the ornate Royal Pump Room, built in 1842 over the most famous of the town's sulphurous springs. It gives an insight into how the phenomenon of visiting spas to 'take the waters' shaped the town, and records the illustrious visitors it attracted. Beside the stained-glass counter where tonics would have once been dispensed, you can sit down and watch old black-and-white film of patients taking treatments such as peat baths.

The ritual of visiting spa towns as a health cure became fashionable in the 19th century and peaked during the Edwardian era in the years before WWI. Charles Dickens visited Harrogate in 1858 and described it as 'the queerest place, with the strangest people in it, leading the oddest lives of dancing, newspaper-reading and dining' – sounds quite pleasant, really.

Montpellier Quarter　　　AREA
(www.montpellierharrogate.com) The most attractive part of town is the Montpellier Quarter, overlooking Prospect Gardens between Crescent Rd and Montpellier Hill. It's an area of pedestrianised streets lined with restored 19th-century buildings that are now home to art galleries, antique shops, fashion boutiques, cafes and restaurants – an upmarket annex to the main shopping area around Oxford and Cambridge Sts.

★ Turkish Baths　　　SPA
(☑01423-556746; www.turkishbathsharrogate. co.uk; Parliament St; Mon-Thu £18, Fri £21.50, Sat & Sun £29.50, guided tour per person £3.75; ⊘guided tours 9-10am Wed) Plunge into Harrogate's past at the town's fabulously tiled Turkish Baths. This mock-Moorish facility is gloriously Victorian and offers a range of watery delights: hot rooms, steam rooms, a plunge pool and so on, plus use of the original wooden changing cubicles and historic Crapper toilets. There's a complicated schedule of opening hours that are by turns single sex or mixed, so call or check online for details. The weekly guided tour of the building is fascinating and cheap – book ahead.

★★ Festivals & Events

Spring Flower Show　　　HORTICULTURE
(www.flowershow.org.uk; £17.50; ⊘late Apr) The year's main event, held at the Great Yorkshire Show Ground. A colourful three-day extravaganza of blooms and blossoms, flower competitions, gardening demonstrations, market stalls, crafts and gardening shops.

Great Yorkshire Show　　　AGRICULTURE
(www.greatyorkshireshow.co.uk; adult/child £25/ 12.50; ⊘mid-Jul) Staged over three days by the Yorkshire Agricultural Society. Expect all manner of primped and prettified farm animals competing for prizes, and entertainment ranging from showjumping and falconry to cookery demonstrations and hot-air-balloon rides. Plus a Black Sheep bar.

⌸ Sleeping

Hotel du Vin　　　BOUTIQUE HOTEL **££**
(☑01423-856800; www.hotelduvin.com/locations/ harrogate; Prospect Pl; r/ste from £124/244, parking per night £10; ℗☎) An extremely stylish boutique hotel with dapper lounge – the loft suites with exposed oak beams, hardwood floors and extravagant bathrooms featuring two claw-footed baths and dual showers are among the nicest rooms in town, but even the standard bedrooms are spacious and very comfortable (though they can be noisy). Rates can plummet at quiet times, so keep an eye online.

Bijou　　　B&B **££**
(☑01423-567974; www.thebijou.co.uk; 17 Ripon Rd; s/d from £59/74; ℗☎) Bijou by name, bijou by nature – this jewel of a Victorian villa sits firmly at the boutique end of the B&B spectrum, with a grand piano to tinkle on in the lounge and bottles of Prosecco for £10 a pop in the honesty bar. It's just a bit of a schlep up the hill from the conference centre.

Acorn Lodge　　　B&B **££**
(☑01423-525630; www.acornlodgeharrogate. co.uk; 1 Studley Rd; s/d from £49/89; ℗☎)

Attention to detail is spot on at Acorn Lodge: stylish decor, crisp cotton sheets, powerful showers and perfect poached eggs for breakfast. Rooms 5, 6 and 7 in the eaves at the top of the house are particularly lovely. The location is good too, just 10 minutes' walk from the town centre.

★ **Harrogate Brasserie Hotel**   BOUTIQUE HOTEL **£££**
(☑ 01423-505041; www.harrogatebrasserie.co.uk; 26-30 Cheltenham Pde; s/d £95/135, apt from £155; P 🖥) The incredibly central location makes this one of Harrogate's most appealing places to stay. Rooms are all individual, with subtle colour combinations and the occasional leather armchair; number 5 has a huge bathroom, and there's a pair of sweet studios with little balconies tucked at the top of the house; behind the main building, there's also two larger apartments that would suit families.

✕ Eating

Baltzersen's   CAFE **£**
(☑ 01423-202363; www.baltzersens.co.uk; 22 Oxford St; lunch £5.50-9; ⊗ 8am-5pm Mon-Sat, 10am-4pm Sun; 🖥🛗) Norse's little brother is a simple Scandi-style cafe with good coffee (from North Star in Leeds), Nordic waffles and pastries, plus Norwegian stew and open-sided sandwiches such as curried herring with potato salad on the lunch menu.

Bettys   CAFE **££**
(☑ 01423-814070; www.bettys.co.uk; 1 Parliament St; mains £6-14, afternoon tea £19.95; ⊗ 9am-9pm; 🛗) A classic tearoom in a classic location with views across the park, Bettys is a local institution. It was established in 1919 by a Swiss immigrant confectioner who took the wrong train, ended up in Yorkshire and decided to stay. Everything's made in-house, and there is almost always a queue for a table for speciality tea and cake; come early or late.

Tannin Level   BISTRO **££**
(☑ 01423-560595; www.tanninlevel.co.uk; 5 Raglan St; mains £13-29; ⊗ noon-2pm & 5.30-9pm Tue-Fri, to 9.30pm Sat, noon-5pm Sun) 🍴 Old terracotta floor tiles, polished mahogany tables and gilt-framed mirrors and paintings create a relaxed yet elegant atmosphere at this popular bistro. A competitively priced menu based on seasonal British produce – think Yorkshire lamb rump or heirloom courgette and Yorkshire Fettle cheese tart – means you'd best book a table on weekends.

★ **Norse**   SCANDINAVIAN **£££**
(☑ 01423-313400; www.norserestaurant.co.uk; 28a Swan Rd; mains £16-23, 9-course tasting menu £59; ⊗ 6-9pm Tue-Sat, noon-2pm Sat) 🍴 Norse injects some fun into fine dining, with a choice of tasting menus that blend the best of British produce with Scandinavian inspiration to produce unusual flavour combinations such as beetroot, cocoa and horseradish; pork, oyster and peas; and yoghurt, gooseberry and orange blossom. The drinks list includes carefully chosen craft beers and cocktails as well as wine. Bookings essential.

🍷 Drinking & Nightlife

★ **Bean & Bud**   COFFEE
(☑ 01423-508200; www.beanandbud.co.uk; 14 Commercial St; ⊗ 8am-5pm Mon-Sat, 10am-4pm Sun; 🖥) Small and bohemian, this cafe takes its drinks seriously, with names of coffee growers and altitudes of their plantations displayed proudly on the walls. It's also the sort of place that serves single-origin hot chocolates and puts fairtrade unrefined sugar on the tables. There's a choice of two or three freshly ground blends every day, plus top-quality white, green, oolong and black teas.

★ **Major Tom's Social**   CRAFT BEER
(☑ 01423-566984; www.majortomssocial.co.uk; The Ginnel, off Montpellier Gardens; ⊗ noon-11.30pm Sun-Thu, to 1am Fri & Sat) Grungy and effortlessly cool, this 1st-floor drinking den is the type of place where locals cram onto sociable wooden bench tables and talk rubbish all night, sampling far more of the interesting draft beers than they meant to. Mismatched retro sofas and walls lined with vintage film and music posters complete the picture. There's also a cheap pizza menu (£6.50 to £8.50).

Harrogate Tap   CRAFT BEER
(☑ 01423-501644; www.harrogatetap.co.uk; Station Pde; ⊗ 11am-11pm Sun-Thu, 11am-midnight Fri, 10am-midnight Sat; 🖥) Set in a restored redbrick railway-station building dating from 1862, the Tap does a grand job of conjuring up the ambience of a bustling Victorian pub, but with the added attractions of a dozen rotating hand-pulled cask ales, another dozen keg taps, and a menu of around 120 bottled craft beers from all over the world.

ℹ Information

Harrogate Tourist Office (☑ 01423-537300; www.visitharrogate.co.uk; Crescent Rd; ⊗ 9am-

FOUNTAINS ABBEY

The alluring and strangely obsessive water gardens of the Studley Royal estate were built in the 18th century to enhance the picturesque ruins of 12th-century **Fountains Abbey** (NT; www.fountainsabbey.org.uk; adult/child £15/7.50; ⏱10am-5pm Mar-Oct, to 4pm Sat-Thu Nov-Jan, 10am-4pm Feb; Ⓟ). Together, they present a breathtaking picture of pastoral elegance and tranquillity that have made them a Unesco World Heritage site and the most visited of all the National Trust's pay-to-enter properties.

After falling out with the Benedictines of York in 1132, a band of rebel monks came here to establish their own monastery. Struggling to make it alone, they were formally adopted by the Cistercians in 1135. By the middle of the 13th century, the new abbey had grown wealthy from trading wool and had become the most successful Cistercian venture in the country. After the Dissolution, when Henry VIII confiscated Church property, the abbey's estate was sold into private hands, and between 1598 and 1611 Fountains Hall was partly built using stone from the abbey ruins. The hall and ruins were united with the Studley Royal estate in 1768.

Studley Royal was owned by John Aislabie, once Chancellor of the Exchequer, who dedicated his life to creating the park after a financial scandal saw him expelled from Parliament. The main house of Studley Royal burnt down in 1946, but the superb landscaping, with its serene artificial lakes, survives almost unchanged from the 18th century.

The remains of the abbey are impressively grandiose, gathered around the sunny Romanesque cloister, with a huge vaulted cellarium leading off the west end of the church. Here, the abbey's 200 lay brothers lived, and food and wool from the abbey's farms were stored. At the east end is the soaring Chapel of Nine Altars, and on the outside of its northeast window is a green man carving (a pre-Christian fertility symbol).

A choice of scenic walking trails leads for a mile from the abbey ruins to the famous water gardens, designed to enhance the romantic views of the ruined abbey. Don't miss **St Mary's Church** (Studley Royal; ⏱noon-4pm Easter-Sep) FREE above the gardens.

Fountains Abbey is 4 miles west of Ripon off the B6265. Bus 139 travels from Ripon to Fountains Abbey visitor centre year-round (£4.40 return, 15 minutes, four times daily on Monday, Thursday and Saturday).

5.30pm Mon-Sat, 10am-1pm Sun Apr-Oct, 9.30am-5pm Mon-Sat Nov-Mar)

ⓘ Getting There & Away

Bus Harrogate & District (www.harrogatebus.co.uk) bus 36 connects Harrogate with Leeds (£6.30, 45 minutes, two to four hourly) and Ripon (£6.30, 30 minutes).

Train There are trains to Harrogate from Leeds (£8.30, 35 minutes, every 30 minutes) and York (£8.90, 35 minutes, hourly).

Scarborough

📋 01723 / POP 61,750

Surveying Scarborough today, it's hard to imagine the busy medieval fishing village that flourished beneath its impressive headland castle. Much of that history has been blasted away with the salt-sea air, its castle now a toothsome ruin, but what remains is the holiday-resort atmosphere that ran away with the town in the 18th and 19th centuries, capitalising on Scarborough's natural

spa waters. These days, its two attractive beaches are the main draw for loyal local holidaymakers.

Cliff-scaling tramways ferry visitors down to the South Bay promenade (where you'll find free wi-fi), lined with arcades and fish-and-chip shops. There's much to recommend a visit to Scarborough – including a redeveloped Victorian spa, grand water park, Edwardian pleasure gardens and interesting geology museum – yet the downbeat city centre still feels like it's stuck in the past, and not in a fashionably retro sort of way.

◉ Sights & Activities

Scarborough Castle CASTLE
(EH; www.english-heritage.org.uk; Castle Rd; adult/child £6.50/3.90; ⏱10am-6pm Apr-Sep, to 5pm Oct, to 4pm Sat & Sun Nov–mid-Feb, Wed-Sun mid-Feb–Mar) The massive medieval keep of Scarborough Castle occupies a commanding position atop its headland. Legend has it that Richard I loved the views from here so much that his ghost just keeps coming back. Take

YORKSHIRE SCARBOROUGH

Scarborough

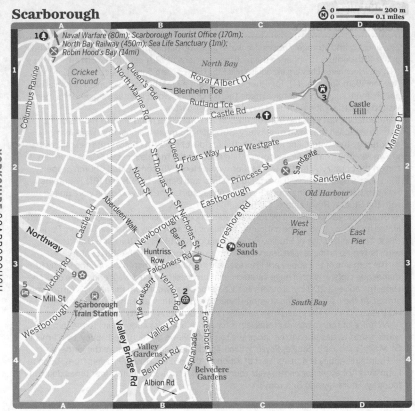

Naval Warfare (80m); Scarborough Tourist Office (170m);
North Bay Railway (450m); Sea Life Sanctuary (1mi);
Robin Hood's Bay (14mi)

Scarborough

◎ Sights
1 Peasholm Park	A1
2 Rotunda Museum	B3
3 Scarborough Castle	D1
4 St Mary's Church	C1

🛏 Sleeping
5 Windmill	A3

✕ Eating
6 Golden Grid	C2
7 Jeremy's	A1

🍸 Drinking & Nightlife
8 Cat's Pyjamas	B3

✪ Entertainment
9 Stephen Joseph Theatre	A3

a walk out to the edge of the cliffs, where you can see the 2000-year-old remains of a **Roman signal station**. There's also a cafe and picnic tables.

Peasholm Park PARK
(www.peasholmpark.com; Columbus Ravine; ⊘ 24hr) FREE Set back from North Bay, Scarborough's beautiful Edwardian pleasure gardens, complete with hilltop pagoda, are famous for their summer sessions of **Naval**

Warfare (adult/child £4.50/2.50; ⊘ 3pm Mon, Thu & Sat Jul & Aug), when large model ships reenact famous naval battles on the boating lake (check the website for dates).

Rotunda Museum MUSEUM
(www.rotundamuseum.co.uk; Vernon Rd; adult/child £3/free; ⊘ 10am-5pm Tue-Sun; 🚼) The Rotunda Museum is dedicated to the coastal geology of northeast Yorkshire, which has yielded many of Britain's most important

dinosaur fossils. The strata in the local cliffs were also important in deciphering England's geological history. Founded by William Smith, 'the father of English geology', who lived in Scarborough in the 1820s, the museum has original Georgian exhibits as well as a hands-on gallery for kids.

Sea Life Sanctuary   AQUARIUM

(www.sealife.co.uk; Scalby Mills; adult/child under 3 £19/free; ⏰ 10am-4pm Mon-Fri, to 5pm Sat & Sun, last admission 1hr before closing; P☝) At this family-oriented attraction you can see coral reefs, turtles, octopuses, seahorses, otters and many other fascinating creatures. The biggest draws are the talks and feeding times at the seal pool and penguin enclosure. The centre is at the far north end of North Beach; the miniature North Bay Railway (p488) runs the 0.75-mile route. Note tickets are 50% cheaper if you buy online, but you'll still have to queue to enter; at weekends and during school holidays it's swamped by kids.

Scarborough Surf School   SURFING

(☎ 01723-585585; www.scarboroughsurfschool. co.uk; Killerby Cliff, Cayton Bay; ⏰ 9am-5pm) Scarborough Surf School offers full-day surfing lessons from £33 per person, wetsuit and surfboard hire for £25 per day, and stand-up paddleboarding from £50 per person for a two-hour lesson. Beach parking by the school costs £3 per vehicle for the day.

🛏 Sleeping

YHA Scarborough   HOSTEL £

(☎ 01723-361176; www.yha.org.uk; Burniston Rd; dm/q from £15/55; P) An idyllic hostel set in a converted 17th-century water mill, with bike storage and a piano in the lounge, 2 miles north of town along the A166 to Whitby. Take bus 12 from York Place to the Ivanhoe pub; it's a five-minute walk from there.

★ Windmill   B&B ££

(☎ 01723-372735; www.scarborough-windmill.co. uk; Mill St; d/f from £85/120, apt £100-130; P☝) Quirky doesn't begin to describe this place, a beautifully converted 18th-century windmill in the middle of town. There are two self-catering apartments in the windmill itself, along with cottages, a family room and four-poster doubles around a cobbled courtyard. Try to secure the upper apartment (from £100 a night) in the windmill, which has great views from its wraparound balcony.

Waves   B&B ££

(☎ 01723-373658; www.scarboroughwaves.co.uk; 39 Esplanade Rd, South Cliff; s/d from £54/73; P☝) Crisp cotton sheets and powerful showers make for comfortable accommodation at this Australian-owned, retro-styled B&B, but it's the second B that's the real star – the breakfasts range from vegan-friendly kedgeree and smoothies to fry-ups and kippers. A unique selling point is the jukebox in the lounge, loaded with 1960s and '70s hits. It's 0.75 miles south of the centre, off the A165 (Ramshill Rd).

🍴 Eating & Drinking

★ Jeremy's   BRITISH, FRENCH ££

(☎ 01723-363871; www.jeremys.co; 33 Victoria Park Ave; mains £18-27, 3-course lunch Sun £27.50; ⏰ 6-9.30pm Wed-Sat, noon-3pm Sun, plus 6-9.30pm Tue Aug; ☝) 🍴 A fantastic bistro run by a chef who won Michelin credentials as a head chef for Marco Pierre White, this off-the-beaten-track gem sports an art-deco ambience and a menu that blends the best of Yorkshire and British produce with French inventiveness and flair. Best to book at weekends.

Golden Grid   FISH & CHIPS ££

(☎ 01723-360922; www.goldengrid.co.uk; 4 Sandside; mains £10-20; ⏰ 11am-8.45pm Mon-Thu, 10.30am-9.30pm Fri-Sun; ☝) The Golden Grid is a sit-down fish restaurant that has been serving the best cod in Scarborough since 1883. Its starched white tablecloths and starched white aprons are staunchly traditional, as is the menu: as well as cod and chips, oysters, and freshly landed crab and lobster, there's sausage and mash, roast beef and Yorkshire pudding, and steak and chips.

Cat's Pyjamas   CAFE

(☎ 01723-331721; www.thecatspyjamascafebars. co.uk; 2 St Nicholas Cliff; ⏰ 8am-5pm Sun-Thu, 9am-10pm Fri & Sat; ☝) Tucked inside the heritage Central Tramway shed and with sea views from its upstairs seating area, this 1920s-themed cafe and gin bar is a breath of fresh air in staid Scarborough. It serves simple brunches and lunches such as posh fish butties, plus coffee, cakes and G&Ts accompanied by jazz and swing music.

ℹ Information

Scarborough Tourist Office (☎ 01723-383636; www.discoveryorkshirecoast.com; Burniston Rd; ⏰ 10am-6pm Jul & Aug, to 5pm Sep-Jun) Scarborough's staffed tourist office is part of the Open Air Theatre box office, opposite the entrance to Peasholm Park. Useful leaflets can also be found in the lobby of the **Stephen Joseph Theatre** (☑ 01723-370541; www.sjt.uk.com; Westborough).

ⓘ Getting There & Away

BUS
Bus 128 (www.eyms.co.uk) travels along the A170 from Helmsley to Scarborough via Pickering, while Arriva (www.arrivabus.co.uk) buses 93 and X93 come from Middlesborough and Whitby via Robin Hood's Bay. Coastliner (www.coastliner.co.uk) bus 843 runs to Scarborough from Leeds and York.

Helmsley £8, 1¾ hours, hourly Monday to Saturday, at least four daily on Sunday

Leeds £12, 2¾ hours, hourly

Whitby £6.20, one hour, once or twice hourly

York £12, 1¾ hours, hourly

TRAIN
Book in advance for cheaper tickets to York and Leeds.

Hull £16, 1½ hours, nine daily Monday to Saturday, six on Sunday

Leeds £29.80, 1¼ hours, hourly

Malton £8.90, 25 minutes, hourly

York £17.30, 45 minutes, hourly

ⓘ Getting Around

Tiny Victorian-era funicular railways rattle up and down Scarborough's steep cliffs between town and beach. The **Central Tramway** (www.centraltramway.co.uk; Marine Pde; per person £1; ☺ 9.30am-5.45pm mid-Feb–Jun, Sep & Oct, to 9.45pm Jul & Aug) connects the Grand Hotel with the promenade, while the **Spa Cliff Lift** (www.scarboroughspa.co.uk/cliff_lift; Esplanade; per person £1; ☺ at least 10am-5pm, hours vary) runs between Scarborough Spa and the Esplanade.

Open-top bus 109 shuttles back and forth along the seafront between Scarborough Spa and the Sands complex on North Bay (£2, every 20 minutes 9.30am to 3pm). The service runs daily from Easter to September, weekends only in October. An all-day, hop on-hop off ticket costs £3.

The miniature **North Bay Railway** (☑ 01723-368791; www.nbr.org.uk; return adult/child 3yr & over £4/3; ☺ 10.30am-3pm daily Apr-May & Sep, to 5.30pm Jul & Aug, Sat & Sun year-round) also runs to North Beach.

For a taxi, call **Station Taxis** (☑ 01723-361009, 01723-366366; www.taxisinscarborough.co.uk); £5 should get you to most places in town.

NORTH YORK MOORS NATIONAL PARK

Inland from the North Yorkshire coast, the wild and windswept North York Moors rise in desolate splendour. Three-quarters of all the world's heather moorland is found in Britain, and this is the largest expanse in England. Ridge-top roads climb up from lush green valleys to the bleak open moors, where weather-beaten stone crosses mark the lines of ancient roadways. In summer, heather blooms in billowing drifts of purple haze.

This is classic walking country. The moors are criss-crossed with footpaths old and new, and dotted with pretty, flower-bedecked villages. The national park is also home to one of England's most picturesque steam railways, and at its eastern edge lies historic Whitby – one of England's dreamiest and most haunting coastal towns.

The park produces the useful *Out & About* visitor guide, available from tourist offices and hotels, with information on things to see and do. See also www.northyorkmoors.org.uk.

🏃 Activities

Yorkshire Cycle Hub CYCLING
(☑ 01287-669098; www.yorkshirecyclehub.co.uk; Fryup; 🖫) Wedged in the middle of the North York Moors National Park, this new centre is hell bent on making itself an indispensable aid for local and visiting cycling enthusiasts. There's cycle hire (mountain bikes and e-bikes), a repairs shop, a simple bunkhouse (£25 per night), bike wash and storage, and an excellent cafe with a log-burner and fabulous rural views.

North York Moors Guided Walks WALKING
(☑ 01439-772738; http://northyorkmoors.eventbrite.com) **FREE** Each year the national park publishes a schedule of mostly-free guided walks led by volunteers and specialists. Some skirt high moors along ancient paths to seek out medieval sites or ruined castles; others pass through bluebell woods, track birds, or delve into the myths and mysteries of the coastal villages. Places must be booked online or by phone.

ⓘ Information

There are two national park visitor centres, providing information on walking, cycling, wildlife and public transport.

North York Moors National Park

Moors National Park Centre (☑01439-772737; www.northyorkmoors.org.uk; Lodge Lane, Danby; parking 2/24hr £2.50/4.50; ⏱10am-5pm Apr-Oct, 10.30am-4pm Nov–mid-Feb, Sat & Sun only Jan & mid-Feb; 🖶)

Sutton Bank National Park Centre (☑01845-597426; www.northyorkmoors.org.uk; Sutton Bank, by Thirsk; ⏱10am-5pm Apr-Oct, 10.30am-4pm Nov–mid-Feb, Sat & Sun only Jan & mid-Feb; 🛜)

❶ Getting Around

On Sundays and bank holiday Mondays from late May to September, a number of minibus services aimed at hikers shuttle around various locations within the national park; all are detailed on the Moorsbus (www.moorsbus.org) website.

For example, the **Moors Explorer** (☑8am-6pm Mon-Sat 01482-592929; www.eyms.co.uk; all-day hop-on, hop-off ticket £12.50.) service runs from Hull to the Moors National Park Centre in Danby with stops along the way, but only runs six or so times a year. An all-day hop-on, hop-off ticket costs £12.50. Download the EYMS app with timetables and track bus arrival times live.

The North Yorkshire Moors Railway (p492), running between Pickering and Whitby, is an excellent way of exploring the central moors in summer.

If you're planning to drive on the minor roads over the moors, beware of wandering sheep and

lambs – hundreds are killed by careless drivers every year.

Helmsley

☑01439 / POP 1515

Helmsley is a classic North Yorkshire market town, a handsome huddle of old stone houses, historic coaching inns and – inevitably – a cobbled market square (market day is Friday), which marks the start of the long-distance Cleveland Way (p472). It basks under the watchful gaze of a sturdy Norman castle ruin and stately home surrounded by rolling fields. Nearby are the romantic ruins of Rievaulx Abbey, several excellent restaurants and a fistful of country walks.

◉ Sights

★ **Rievaulx Abbey**   RUINS
(EH; www.english-heritage.org.uk; adult/child £8.90/5.30; ⏱10am-6pm Apr-Sep, to 5pm Oct, to 4pm Sat & Sun Nov–mid-Feb, daily Mar; 🅿) In the secluded valley of the River Rye about 3 miles west of Helmsley, amid fields and woods loud with birdsong, stand the magnificent ruins of Rievaulx Abbey (*ree*-voh). The extensive remains give a wonderful sense of the size and complexity of the community that once lived here, and their story

WORTH A TRIP

HUTTON-LE-HOLE

With a scatter of gorgeous stone cottages, a gurgling brook and a flock of sheep grazing contentedly on the village green, Hutton-le-Hole must be a contender for the best-looking village in Yorkshire. The dips and hollows on the green may have given the place its name – it was once called simply Hutton Hole; the Frenchified 'le' was added in Victorian times. The village is home to a couple of tearooms, a pub, ice-cream shops, and the fascinating **Ryedale Folk Museum** (www.ryedalefolkmuseum.co.uk; Hutton-le-Hole; adult/child £7.95/6.95; ☉10am-5pm Apr-Sep, to 4pm Mar & Oct-Nov).

The tourist office (in the folk museum) has leaflets (£1) about walks in the area, including a 4-mile (2½-hour) circuit to the nearby village of Lastingham. The Daffodil Walk is a 3.5-mile circular walk following the banks of the River Dove. As the name suggests, the main drawcard is the daffs, usually at their best in March or April.

is fleshed out in a series of fascinating exhibits in a new museum. There's also a cafe with floor-to-ceiling windows and outdoor terrace from which to gawp at the ruins.

This idyllic spot was chosen by Cistercian monks in 1132 as a base for their missionary activity in northern Britain. St Aelred, the third abbot, famously described the abbey's setting as 'everywhere peace, everywhere serenity, and a marvellous freedom from the tumult of the world'. But the monks of Rievaulx were far from unworldly and soon created a network of commercial interests ranging from sheep farms to lead mines.

There's an excellent 3.5-mile **walking trail** from Helmsley to Rievaulx Abbey; Helmsley tourist information point can provide route leaflets and advise on buses if you don't want to walk both ways. This route is also the opening section of the Cleveland Way.

On the hillside above the abbey is **Rievaulx Terrace** (NT; www.nationaltrust.org.uk; adult/child £5.95/3; ☉10am-5pm May-Sep, to 4pm Mar-Apr & Oct; P ⚑), built in the 18th century by Thomas Duncombe II as a place to admire views of the abbey. Note that there's no direct access between the abbey and the terrace, and the two sites have separate admission fees. Their entrance gates are about a mile apart along a narrow road (a 20-minute walk steeply uphill if you're heading from the abbey to the terrace).

Helmsley Castle CASTLE
(EH; www.english-heritage.org.uk; Castlegate; adult/child £6.40/3.80; ☉10am-6pm Apr-Sep, to 5pm Oct, to 4pm Fri-Sun Nov-Mar; P) The impressive ruins of 12th-century Helmsley Castle are defended by a striking series of deep ditches and banks, to which later rulers added the thick stone walls and defen-

sive towers. Only one tooth-shaped tower survives, following the dismantling of the fortress after the Civil War. The castle's tumultuous history is well explained in the 14-century West Range at the back of the site.

Duncombe Park Gardens GARDENS
(www.duncombepark.com; adult/child £5/3; ☉gardens 10.30am-5pm Sun-Fri Apr-Aug; P ⚑) On the outskirts of Helmsley lies the superb ornamental landscape of Duncombe Park estate, laid out in 1718 for Thomas Duncombe (whose son would later build Rievaulx Terrace), with the stately Georgian mansion of Duncombe Park House at its heart. From the house (not open to the public) and formal gardens, wide grassy walkways and terraces lead through woodland to mock-classical temples, while longer walking trails are set out in the landscaped parkland, now protected as a nature reserve.

🛏 Sleeping

Feathers Hotel INN ££
(☎01439-770275; www.feathershotelhelmsley. co.uk; Market Pl; s/d from £80/100; P ⚑ ⚑) One of a number of old coaching inns on the market square that offer B&B, decent grub and a pint of hand-pumped real ale. Many of the bedrooms have been refurbished recently, and there are historical trimmings throughout.

Canadian Fields GLAMPING ££
(☎01439-772409; www.canadianfields.co.uk; Gale Lane; safari tents £65-100; ☉Feb–mid-Nov; P ⚑) This luxury campsite 3 miles east of Helmsley offers comfortable and unusual accommodation in spacious 'safari tent' cabins with kitchens, electricity and wood-burning stoves under canvas, alongside private out-

door showers. There are also sites where you can pitch your own tent (from £15 a night), and a bar-restaurant housed in a giant tepee provides a convivial social hub.

Feversham Arms HOTEL £££
(☏01439-772935; www.fevershamarms.com; High St; d/ste from £120/190; P🗲🛋) Just behind Helmsley's church, the Feversham Arms has a snug and sophisticated atmosphere where country charm meets boutique chic. Service is excellent and rooms are comfy (the luxury pool suites with balconies are especially light and spacious), but it's the spa and lovely heated outdoor pool that guests come from far and wide for; the on-site restaurant is not worth the money.

 Eating

Vine Cafe CAFE £
(☏01439-771194; www.vinehousecafehelmsley.co.uk; Helmsley Walled Garden, Cleveland Way; 10am-5pm; ☉Apr-Oct; 🗲🖐) Goodies plucked from the gardens take centre stage at this whimsical cafe housed in vine-draped Victorian greenhouses within creepers distance of **Helmsley Walled Garden** (www.helmsleywalledgarden.org.uk; adult/child £7.50/free; ☉10am-5pm Apr-Oct). Everything on the menu is fresh and simple, like the homemade hummus and chickpea curry, organic frittata and Helmsley butcher's ham sandwich. It's licensed, too, so you can take a Yorkshire G&T with lunch in the sun.

★ Star Inn MODERN BRITISH £££
(☏01439-770397; www.thestaratharome.co.uk; Harome; mains £20-32; ☉11.30am-2pm Tue-Sat, 6-9.30pm Mon-Sat, noon-6pm Sun; P🖐) This thatch-roofed country pub is home to a Michelin-starred restaurant, with a menu specialising in top-quality produce from the surrounding countryside: Whitby crab with pickled cockles and avocado 'ice', or roast English quail with braised salsify and bergamot preserve. There's also a set three-course menu for £25 (Monday to Saturday). Harome is about 2 miles southeast of Helmsley off the A170.

The Star is the sort of place you won't want to leave, and the good news is you don't have to – the adjacent lodge has nine magnificent bedrooms (£150 to £240), each decorated in classic but luxurious country style.

★ Hare Inn MODERN BRITISH £££
(☏01845-597769; www.thehare-inn.com; Scawton; 6-course lunch £55, 10-course dinner £70; ☉noon-2.30pm & 6-9pm Wed-Sat; P) 🌱 The phrase 'hidden gem' is overused, but here it is entirely appropriate – drowsing in a secluded hamlet 4 miles west of Helmsley, the Hare is a 21st-century restaurant in a 13th-century inn, where gourmet dining is relaxed, informal and even fun. There's no à la carte, just a seasonal tasting menu – and only seven tables; bookings must be made in advance.

YORKSHIRE HELMSLEY

YORKSHIRE'S FOOD CAPITAL

It was the legendary late Italian chef Antonio Carluccio who first gave Malton the moniker of 'Yorkshire's food capital', and this sweet market town has worked hard to make the title stick – even to the extent of splashing it across road signs on the way in to town and commissioning a street mural to that effect.

The food scene is certainly extraordinary for a town of its size. The best place to start is **Talbot Yard** (www.visitmalton.com/talbot-yard-food-court; Yorkersgate; ☉hours vary), an extraordinary food court offering gourmet goodies from gelato, posh pork pies, award-winning ales and freshly ground coffee to Chelsea buns and macarons. Guided tours are offered by **Malton Artisan Food Tour** (www.maltoncookeryschool.co.uk; pick-up Talbot Hotel; per person £45; ☉Thu & Sat).

While you're here, it's worth seeking out Malton's own Shambles, where butchers would have once slaughtered the lambs brought in for the town's sheep markets. It's now crammed with vintage shops. Afterwards, head for **Brass Castle** (☏01653-698683; https://brasscastle.co.uk; 10 Yorkersgate; ☉4-9pm Tue-Thu, noon-10pm Fri & Sat, to 8pm Sun) for fantastic craft ales, and overnight at the lovely **Talbot Hotel** (☏01653-639096; www.talbotmalton.co.uk; Yorkersgate; d/ste from £110/300; P🛜).

Malton is easily accessible by train from York (£10, 25 minutes, hourly), and the train station is less than a 10-minute walk south from Market Pl.

At the time of writing the owners were also adding a pair of guest rooms, due to be completed in early 2019.

❶ Getting There & Away

Buses stop in the main square. From Scarborough, bus 128 (£8, 1¾ hours, hourly Monday to Saturday) runs to Helmsley via Pickering, with an additional Sunday service April to October (six daily).

Pickering

📞 01751 / POP 6830

Pickering is a lively market town with an imposing Norman castle that advertises itself as the 'gateway to the North York Moors'. That gateway is also the terminus of the wonderful North Yorkshire Moors Railway, a picturesque survivor from the great days of steam.

Two scenic drives head north across the moors: the A169 to Whitby leads past the Hole of Horcum beauty spot and the hiking trails of Goathland (p494); and the Blakey Ridge road (beginning 6 miles west of town) passes the pretty village of Hutton-le-Hole (p490) and the famous Lion Inn on the way to Danby.

◎ Sights

★North Yorkshire
Moors Railway   HERITAGE RAILWAY
(NYMR; www.nymr.co.uk; Park St; Pickering–Whitby day-rover ticket adult/child £30/15; ⊙ Easter-Oct, reduced service Nov-Easter) This privately owned railway runs for 18 miles through beautiful countryside from Pickering to Whitby. Lovingly restored steam locos pull period carriages with wooden booths, appealing to railway buffs and day trippers alike. For visitors without wheels, it's excellent for reaching out-of-the-way spots and devising walks between stations. Book online the day before travel for a 10% discount and to sidestep ticket office queues.

Pickering Castle   CASTLE
(EH; www.english-heritage.org.uk; Castlegate; adult/child £5.40/3.20; ⊙10am-6pm Apr-Sep, to 5pm Oct) Pickering Castle is a lot like the castles we drew as kids: thick stone outer walls circle the keep, and the whole lot is perched atop a high motte (mound) with great views of the surrounding countryside. Founded by William the Conqueror around 1070, it was added to and altered by later kings, but there's not much of it left.

🛏 Sleeping & Eating

★White Swan Hotel   HOTEL £££
(📞01751-472288; www.white-swan.co.uk; Market Pl; s from £129, d £150-210; P🐾🅰) 🐾 The top spot in town successfully combines a smart pub, a superb restaurant serving a daily changing menu of local produce (mains £14 to £22), and a luxurious boutique hotel. Nine rooms lie within the converted coach house itself, but the best are in a quiet, hidden block out back, where guests get the added perks of underfloor heating and free robes.

Black Swan   PUB
(📞01751-798209; www.blackswan-pickering.co.uk; 18 Birdgate; ⊙11.30am-11pm Mon-Thu, to 11.30pm Fri & Sat, to 10.30pm Sun; 🅰) This 18th-century coaching inn has had an ambitious makeover to return it to its former glory. The food is recommended, the beers are brewed in-house (ask behind the bar and you might get a mini guided tour of the microbrewery), and there's also a 1920s-themed cocktail den that you enter around the back of the pub. Fresh, modern B&B rooms upstairs cost from £95.

Pickering Station Tearoom   CAFE £
(Station platform, North Yorkshire Moors Railway; mains £4-6; ⊙8.30am-4pm) The vintage 1930s tearoom on platform 1 at Pickering station serves locally sourced treats such as Brymor ice cream from Masham, and simple lunches like cheese and Yorkshire ham panini; or come for a mug of Yorkshire tea to watch the train come in. Food service stops at 2.30pm.

❶ Getting There & Away

Bus 128 between Helmsley (£5, 40 minutes) and Scarborough (£6.20, one hour) runs hourly via Pickering. Bus 840 between Leeds and Whitby also travels via Pickering (hourly).

Whitby

📞 01947 / POP 13,213

Whitby is a town of two parts, with the River Esk carving a path between a huddle of 18th-century fishermen's cottages along its East Cliff and a genteel Victorian suburb atop the West Cliff. It's also a town with two personalities – on the one hand, a busy commercial and fishing port (it was here that 18th-century explorer Captain James Cook gained his seafaring legs) with a bustling quayside awash with fish; on the other, an

Whitby

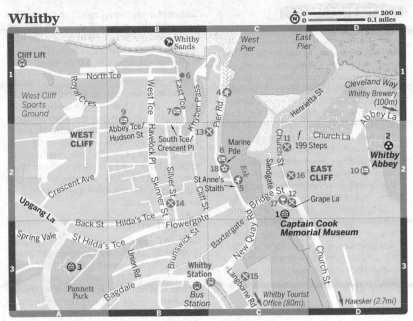

Whitby

◉ Top Sights
1 Captain Cook Memorial Museum	C2
2 Whitby Abbey	D2

◉ Sights
3 Whitby Museum	A3

➕ Activities, Courses & Tours
4 Captain Cook Experience	C1
5 Whitby Coastal Cruises	C2
6 Whitby Ghost Walks	B1

⊟ Sleeping
7 La Rosa Hotel	B1
8 Marine Hotel	C2
9 Rosslyn House	B1

10 YHA Whitby	D2

⊗ Eating
11 Blitz	C2
12 Humble Pie 'n' Mash	C2
13 Quayside	C2
14 Rusty Shears	B2
15 Star Inn the Harbour	C3
16 White Horse & Griffin	C2

⊙ Drinking & Nightlife
17 Green Dragon	C2

✦ Entertainment
18 Dracula Experience	C2

oh-so-pretty, traditional seaside resort complete with sandy beach, amusement arcades and promenading holidaymakers.

Keeping a watchful eye over the town is an atmospheric ruined abbey, the inspiration and setting for part of Bram Stoker's Gothic horror story *Dracula*. But tales of witchery and ghostly legends have haunted Whitby ever since Anglo-Saxon St Hilda landed here to found a monastic community in AD 657. The town embraces its reputation for the weird and wonderful, which culminates in two hugely successful Goth Weekends each year.

◉ Sights

★ Whitby Abbey   RUINS
(EH; www.english-heritage.org.uk; East Cliff; adult/child £8.70/5.20; ☺10am-6pm Apr-Sep, to 5pm Oct, to 4pm Tue-Sat Nov, to 4pm Sat & Sun Dec-Mar; ℗) There are ruined abbeys, and there are picturesque ruined abbeys. And then there's Whitby Abbey, dominating the skyline above the East Cliff like a great Gothic tombstone

GOATHLAND

This picture-postcard halt on the North Yorkshire Moors Railway stars as Hogsmeade train station in the Harry Potter films, while the village appeared as Aidensfield in the British TV series *Heartbeat*. It's also the starting point for lots of easy and enjoyable walks, often with the chuff-chuff-chuff of passing steam engines in the background.

The nearby hamlet of Beck Hole is home to the wonderfully atmospheric Birch Hall Inn (www.beckhole.info; Beck Hole; ⏰ 11am-11pm May-Sep, 11am-3pm & 7.30-11pm Wed-Mon Oct-Apr; 🚻 🎁), where it's like stepping into the past. The 'bar' is a tiny sitting room, with a hole in the wall where drinks are served; or you can sit outside by the beck. Order a pork pie and pint of ale brewed in the village. Cash only.

silhouetted against the sky. Looking as though it was built as an atmospheric film set rather than a monastic establishment, it is hardly surprising that this medieval hulk inspired the Victorian novelist Bram Stoker (who holidayed in Whitby) to make it the setting for Count Dracula's dramatic landfall.

The stately mansion beside the abbey ruins was built by the Cholmley family, who leased the Whitby estate from Henry VIII after the dissolution of England's monasteries in the 1530s. An excellent free audio guide is included with the entrance fee, and at the time of writing the visitor centre displays inside the mansion were being revamped with updated interpretations of the site's history.

From the end of Church St, the 199 steps of Church Stairs will lead you steeply up to Whitby Abbey. By car, you have to approach from the A171 Scarborough road to the east side of the bridge over the River Esk.

★ Captain Cook Memorial Museum
MUSEUM

(www.cookmuseumwhitby.co.uk; Grape Lane; adult/child £5.90/3.50; ⏰ 9.45am-5pm Apr-Oct, 11am-3pm mid-Feb–Mar) This fascinating museum occupies the house of the ship owner with whom Cook began his seafaring career. Highlights include the attic where Cook lodged as a young apprentice, Cook's own maps and letters, etchings from the South

Seas, and a wonderful model of the *Resolution,* with the crew and stores all laid out for inspection. Cook lived in Whitby for nine years and later returned to have all three of his voyage ships built in Whitby's dockyards.

Whitby Museum
MUSEUM

(www.whitbymuseum.org.uk; Pannett Park; adult/child £5/free; ⏰ 9.30am-4.30pm Tue-Sun; 🚻) Set in a park to the west of the town centre is the wonderfully eclectic Whitby Museum, with displays of fossil plesiosaurs and dinosaur footprints, Captain Cook memorabilia, ships in bottles, jet jewellery and the gruesome 'Hand of Glory', a preserved human hand reputedly cut from the corpse of an executed criminal.

🏃 Activities

Captain Cook Experience
BOATING

(📞 01723-364100; www.endeavourwhitby.com; Fish Quay, Pier Rd; 25min trip £3.50) Take a spin out beyond Whitby harbour on this authentic replica of the *HM Bark Endeavour,* which at 40% of the size of the original still has the feel of an atmospheric large voyaging ship. The skipper will regale you with tales of Captain Cook's ordeals at sea and his long-standing associations with Whitby. Good fun for young and old.

Whitby Coastal Cruises
BOATING

(📞 07981 712419; www.whitbycoastalcruises.co.uk; Brewery Steps; 3½hr trip £15) Spot birds, seals, dolphins or even steam trains on a coastal or River Esk boat trip with this long-running family business. September is whale-watching season, during which time you can join its sister business Whitby Whale Watching (www.whitbywhalewatching.net; trips £40) on a trip where the chances of seeing Minke whales (and more rarely humpbacks) are high.

👉 Tours

★ Whitby Ghost Walks
WALKING

(📞 01947-880485; www.whitbywalks.com; Whale Bone Arch, West Cliff; adult/child £5/3; ⏰ 7.30pm) Whitby wouldn't be Whitby without ghoulish tales and strange happenings, and nobody knows them better than Dr Crank, who manages to confidently keep to the right side of naff with his fascinating 75-minute tour around West Cliff's most haunted and storied alleyways. You'll learn of legends like the screaming tunnel, the hand of glory and the headless horseman, plus tidbits of local history.

Hidden Horizons OUTDOORS

(☑ 01723-817017; www.hiddenhorizons.co.uk; adult/child from £8/5) You can get down on the beaches around Whitby to hunt for fossils (and there's plenty to find), take a dinosaur footprint walk, go rock-pooling, or join a star-gazing session with this local tour company. Sessions are entertaining but also educational. Check the online calendar for upcoming events, and book ahead.

✦ Festivals & Events

Whitby Goth Weekends CULTURAL

(www.whitbygothweekend.co.uk; tickets 1/2 days £34/65) Goth heaven attracting more than 8000 visitors biannually, with live-music gigs, events and the Bizarre Bazaar – dozens of traders selling Goth gear, jewellery, art and music. Held twice yearly in late April or early May and late October or early November (around Halloween).

Whitby Steampunk Weekend CULTURAL

(www.wswofficial.com; Whitby Pavilion; ⊘ late Jul) Science fiction meets Victoriana fantasy in Whitby on the last weekend in July, when fans of the steampunk genre descend for balls, costumed promenading, entertainment and shopping at the Steampunk Emporium. A little bit Gothic, a little bit geeky; very Whitby. Events are anchored on the Whitby Pavilion on West Cliff.

⌂ Sleeping

YHA Whitby HOSTEL £

(☑ 0845 371 9049; www.yha.org.uk; Church Lane; dm/tw/f from £13/29/25; ℙ 🖘) With an unbeatable setting in an old mansion next to the abbey, this hostel is incredibly popular – you'll have to book well in advance to get your body into one of the bunks here. Hike up the 199 steps from the town, or take bus 97 from the train station to Whitby Abbey (twice hourly Monday to Saturday).

★ La Rosa Hotel HOTEL ££

(☑ 01947-606981; www.larosa.co.uk/hotel; 5 East Tce; d £86-135; ℙ 🖘) Weird, but wonderful. Lewis Carroll, author of *Alice in Wonderland*, once stayed in this house while holidaying in Whitby. Entering today is like stepping through the looking glass into a world of love-it-or-hate-it Victorian bric-a-brac and kitsch, peppered with vintage film props. Eight quirky and atmospheric bedrooms, great sea views, no TVs, an in-house bar and breakfast served in a basket in your room.

Rosslyn House B&B ££

(☑ 01947-604086; www.rosslynhousewhitby.co.uk; 11 Abbey Tce; s/d/f from £65/90/100; 🖘) Lovely Victorian terrace house that stands out amid the sea of B&Bs on West Cliff, with a friendly welcome and bright, modern decor. The single room is snug; the family room large (though the hotel does not admit children under 12). There's a convenient drying room for walkers.

★ Marine Hotel INN £££

(☑ 01947-605022; www.the-marine-hotel.co.uk; 13 Marine Pde; r £150-195; 🖘) Feeling more like minisuites than ordinary hotel accommodation, the four bedrooms at the Marine are quirky, stylish and comfortable; it's the sort of place that makes you want to stay in rather than go out. Ask for one of the two rooms with a balcony – they have great views across the harbour.

✗ Eating

★ Rusty Shears BRITISH £

(☑ 01947-605383; 3 Silver St; brunch £3.50-6.50; ⊘ 9.30am-5pm; 🖘) This vintage cafe covers many bases. There's an astounding drinks menu with more than 100 gins (despite the fact it's closed evenings) and gin flights, a walled courtyard for al-fresco light lunches, and a cluster of retro-styled rooms for cosy chats over excellent coffee and cakes like treacle tart or Yorkshire tea loaf. The brunches with Fortune's smoked bacon and creamy scrambled eggs deserve a medal.

Humble Pie 'n' Mash BRITISH £

(☑ 01947-606444; www.humblepie.tccdev.com; 163 Church St; pie meal £6.99; ⊘ noon-8pm) Superb homemade gravy-laden pies with fillings ranging from lamb, leek and rosemary to roast veg and goats cheese, served in a cosy timber-framed cottage with a 1940s nostalgia vibe. No bookings, cash only.

Blitz CAFE £

(☑ 01947-606935; www.theblitzwhitby.co.uk; 97-98 Church St; lunch £3-9, evening tapas plates £4-9; ⊘ 10am-11pm) War nostalgia is the theme of this 1940s-style cafe serving coffees, G&Ts and food on Whitby's East Cliff. London's war-ravaged night skyline is writ large on a mural, and the trenches are reimagined as walls. During the day the food menu focuses on basics like the 'Blitz Bomber' chip butty; at night there's a decent world-food tapas menu.

WORTH A TRIP

ROBIN HOOD'S BAY

Picturesque Robin Hood's Bay has nothing to do with the hero of Sherwood Forest – the origin of its name is a mystery, and the locals call it Bay Town or just Bay. But there's no denying that this fishing village is one of the prettiest spots on the Yorkshire coast.

Leave your car at the parking area in the upper village (£4 for four hours), where 19th-century ships' captains built comfortable Victorian villas, and walk downhill to Old Bay, the oldest part of the village (don't even think about driving down). This maze of narrow lanes and passages is dotted with tearooms, pubs, craft shops and artists' studios (there's even a tiny cinema), and at low tide you can go down onto the beach and fossick around in the rock pools.

Robin Hood's Bay is 6 miles southeast of Whitby. Bus 93 runs hourly between Whitby and Scarborough via Robin Hood's Bay.

★ **Bridge Cottage Bistro** BRITISH ££
(📞 01947-893438; www.bridgecottagebistro.com; East Row, Sandsend; mains £12-28; ⊙10am-4pm Tue-Sun, 6.30-9pm Thu & Sat, 7-9pm Fri) This outstanding Modern British restaurant, in the pretty coastal village of Sandsend 3 miles north of Whitby, may well be the east coast's best eating experience. Its no-nonsense setting in a bare old coastal cottage lets the food sing, and the spotlight is always on Yorkshire, with delights like hay-baked lamb, Whitby sea trout with cured beetroot, and Eccles cakes with Wensleydale ice cream.

★ **White Horse & Griffin** BRITISH ££
(📞 01947-604857; www.whitehorseandgriffin.com; 87 Church St; mains £15-24; ⊙noon-9pm Mon-Sat, 12.30-4pm & 5.30-9pm Sun; 🐾🍴) This splendid old coaching inn is as old as Captain Cook, and indeed the man himself used it as a meeting place to fix his crews in the 17th century. Squeeze into the narrow bar and the restaurant behind it is barely noticeable, but what a find: expect elegantly presented, top-quality British cooking that celebrates both local seafood and Yorkshire meat.

Quayside FISH & CHIPS ££
(📞 01947-825346; www.quaysidewhitby.co.uk; 7 Pier Rd; mains £9-15; ⊙11am-8pm; 🐾) 🎣 Top-notch fish and chips minus the 'world's best' tag line used by nearby competitor the Magpie Cafe – this place is your best bet if you want to avoid the queues there. Takeaway fish and chips are £4.60.

Star Inn the Harbour BRITISH ££
(📞 01947-821900; www.starinntheharbour.co.uk; Langborne Rd; mains £12-24; ⊙11.30am-9pm Mon-Fri, from noon Sat, noon-7pm Sun) Yorkshire food hero Andrew Pern, of Michelin-starred Star Inn (p491) fame, gutted the former tourist office to create this spin-off restaurant on the harbour front in his home town of Whitby. It's no surprise that the theme is nautical and the menu leans heavily on its fishy environs, though there are also playful dishes such as Yorkshire pudding and foie gras.

🍷 Drinking & Nightlife

★ **Whitby Brewery** MICROBREWERY
(📞 01947-228871; www.whitby-brewery.com; Abbey Lane, East Cliff; ⊙11am-5pm; 🍺) Walkers are pleased as punch when they find this place on the clifftop behind Whitby Abbey. There's just enough room inside the modern brew plant for three tables – half the space is taken up by a gloriously incongruous Edwardian bar counter, behind which the bartender is well and truly trapped. There's a short selection of craft ales, and extra seating out front.

Green Dragon CRAFT BEER
(www.thegreendragonwhitby.co.uk; Grape Lane; ⊙noon-7.30pm Mon-Sat, to 6pm Sun) In a quaint old house on Whitby's most crooked lane, Green Dragon has grabbed the bull by the horns and dragged Britain's progressive craft-beer scene into this traditional real-ale town. It's part bottle shop, part teeny-weeny beer bar with five rotating taps running Yorkshire breweries like Northern Monk, Abbeydale and Vocation. Or buy any bottle (at shop price) to drink in.

☆ Entertainment

Dracula Experience THEATRE
(📞 01947-601923; 9 Marine Pde; adult/child £3/2.50; ⊙9.45am-5pm Easter-Oct, Sat & Sun Nov-Easter) There's definitely an element of Gothic geekdom about this theatrical walk-

through of *Dracula*'s tale, with special effects, an occasional live actor appearing out of thin air and many a thing that goes bump in the night designed to spook you in the darkness. Wonderfully weird and very Whitby; not suitable for under eights.

Information

Whitby Tourist Office (☎01723-383636; www.visitwhitby.com; Harbour Master's Office, Langborne Rd; ⊙9.30am-5pm May-Oct, 10.30am-4pm Thu-Sun Nov-Apr)

Getting There & Away

BUS

Two buses, 93 and X93, run south to Scarborough (£6.20, one hour, every 30 minutes), with every second bus going via Robin Hood's Bay (£4.30, 15 minutes, hourly); and north to Middlesborough (£6.20, one hour, hourly), with fewer services on Sunday. The **bus station** is next to Whitby's train station.

The Coastliner service 840 runs from Leeds to Whitby (£14, 3¼ hours, four times daily Monday to Saturday, twice on Sundays, though you'll need to change at Malton) via York and Pickering.

TRAIN

Coming from the north, you can get to Whitby by train along the Esk Valley Railway from Middlesbrough (£7.10, 1½ hours, four daily), with connections from Durham and Newcastle. From the south, it's easier to get a train from York to Scarborough, and then a bus from Scarborough to Whitby.

YORKSHIRE DALES NATIONAL PARK

The Yorkshire Dales – named from the old Norse word *dalr*, meaning 'valleys', and protected as a national park since the 1950s – are beloved as one of England's best hiking and cycling areas. The park's glacial valleys are characterised by a distinctive landscape of high heather moorland, stepped skylines and flat-topped hills, punctuated by delightful country pubs and windswept trails.

Down in the green valleys, patchworked with drystone dykes and little barns, are picture-postcard villages where sheep still graze on village greens. And in the limestone country of the southern Dales you'll find England's best examples of karst scenery (created by rainwater dissolving the underlying limestone bedrock).

The whole area is seriously scenic and easy to explore. Consequently it's popular with holidaying Britons – book accommodation ahead as there are no big hotels here. Beds get particularly scarce on public holiday weekends and during events such as the annual Tour de Yorkshire.

Getting There & Away

About 90% of visitors to the park arrive by car, and the narrow roads can become extremely crowded in summer. Parking can also be a serious problem. If you can, try to use public transport as much as possible.

Bus services are limited, and many run in summer only, some on Sundays and bank holidays only; pick up a DalesBus timetable from tourist offices, or consult the DalesBus (www.dalesbus.org) website.

By train, the best and most interesting access to the Dales is via the famous **Settle–Carlisle Line** (SCL; ☎01768-353200; www.settle-carlisle.co.uk). Trains run between Leeds and Carlisle, stopping at Skipton, Settle and numerous small villages, offering unrivalled access to the hills straight from the station platform.

Skipton

☎01756 / POP 14,625

Home to one of England's best-preserved medieval castles and gateway to the southern Dales, this busy market town takes its name from the Anglo-Saxon *sceape ton* (sheep town). There are no prizes for

OFF THE BEATEN TRACK

FORBIDDEN CORNER

There can surely be no other place like **Forbidden Corner** (☎01969-640638; www.theforbiddencorner.co.uk; Tupgill Park Estate, near Leyburn; adult/child £12.50/10.50; ⊙noon-dusk Mon-Sat Easter-Oct, Sun only Nov & Dec; P 👪) in the world: a modern walled garden furnished with Victorian-style follies, some veering into Gothic horror, others merely surreal fantasy. There's no map, so it's a case of diving in to explore the many tunnels, twisted turns and dead-ends – an experience that may make you feel like you've fallen into David Bowie's *Labyrinth*. Small children are guaranteed to feel scared witless at some turns; adults may leave feeling a little rattled, too. Tickets must be pre-booked.

guessing how it made its money. Monday, Wednesday, Friday and Saturday are market days, bringing crowds from all over and giving the town something of a festive atmosphere.

The Leeds–Liverpool Canal carves right through central Skipton, making the town a good jumping-off point for canal-boat trips.

◉ Sights & Activities

★Skipton Castle   CASTLE
(www.skiptoncastle.co.uk; High St; adult/child £8.30/5.20; ⊙10am-6pm Mon-Sat, noon-6pm Sun Apr-Sep, to 5pm Oct-Mar) What makes Skipton Castle so fascinating is its splendid state of preservation, providing a striking contrast to the ruins you'll see elsewhere. Although it is lauded as one of the best-preserved medieval castles in England, many of its most memorable features date to Tudor times. Entrance is through the original Norman archway, which leads to a Tudor courtyard

with a yew tree planted by Lady Anne Clifford in 1659, and beyond that a warren of rooms to explore. Grab the informative free illustrated guide to the castle from the ticket office, available in several languages.

Timber foundations were laid here in 1090 by a Norman baron, then soon replaced by a tougher stone castle after relentless attacks by marauding Scots. It was given to the Clifford family in 1310 by King Edward II and the same family ruled it for more than 350 years. During the English Civil War, the castle was the last Royalist stronghold in the North of England and was heavily damaged by a three-year siege that led to defeat in 1645. Much of what exists today is the result of restoration efforts by Lady Anne Clifford in the 17th century.

Pennine Cruisers   BOATING
(☑01756-795478; www.penninecruisers.com; The Wharf, Coach St; per person £4; ⊙10.30am-dusk Mar-Oct) No trip to Skipton is complete with-

Yorkshire Dales National Park

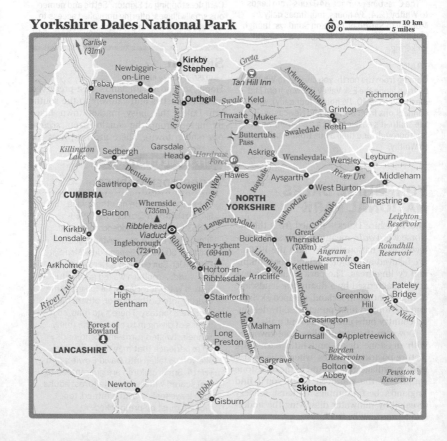

out a cruise along the Leeds–Liverpool Canal, which runs through the middle of town. Pennine Cruisers runs half-hour trips along the canal and back, as well as canal-boat day hire, skippered trips and longer holiday rentals.

🛏 Sleeping

★ The Pinfold
GUESTHOUSE ££

(📞 07510 175270; http://thepinfoldskipton.wixsite.com/pinfold; Chapel Hill; r £60-80; 🅿🛜) This petite, room-only guesthouse has three light and airy, oak-beamed rooms with a lovely fresh country feel. Forgive the tiny shower rooms, because the excellent location around the corner from Skipton Castle and the High St more than compensates. The largest room has its own sitting area, but the best deal is the Littondale room with its own entrance, parking and small grassy patio.

Park Hill
B&B ££

(📞 01756-792772; www.parkhillskipton.co.uk; 17 Grassington Rd; d £90; 🅿🛜) From the complimentary glass of sherry on arrival to the hearty breakfasts based on local produce, such as farm-fresh eggs and home-grown tomatoes, this B&B provides a real Yorkshire welcome. It enjoys an attractive semi-rural location half a mile north of the town centre, on the B6265 road towards Grassington. No children under 12.

🍴 Eating & Drinking

Bizzie Lizzies
FISH & CHIPS £

(📞 01756-701131; www.bizzielizzies.co.uk; 36 Swadford St; mains £9-12; ⊗11am-9pm; 🍴) An award-winning, old-fashioned fish-and-chip restaurant overlooking the canal, with a busy takeaway counter offering fish and chips for £5.80 (counter open to 11.30pm). Gluten-intolerant? No problem – Bizzie Lizzies also dishes up gluten-free chips accredited by Coeliac UK.

★ Le Caveau
BRITISH ££

(📞 01756-794274; www.lecaveau.co.uk; 86 High St; mains £17-20; ⊗noon-2.30pm & 7-9pm Tue-Fri, 5-9pm Sat) 🌿 Thanks to the stylish decoration there's no hint that this 16th-century cellar was once a prison for sheep rustlers. It's now one of Skipton's best bistros, offering a seasonal menu built lovingly around fresh local produce, with tempting dishes such as twice-baked smoked Ribblesdale goats cheese soufflé and slow-roasted Nidderdale lamb shoulder. On weekdays you can get a two-course lunch for £12.95.

WORTH A TRIP

BRITAIN'S HIGHEST PUB

At an elevation of 328m (1732ft) **Tan Hill Inn** (📞 01833-628246; www.tanhillinn.com; Tan Hill, Swaledale; ⊗8am-11.30pm Jul & Aug, 9am-9.30pm Sep-Jun; 🛜🍴🐾) is Britain's highest pub. Built to cater for 19th-century miners, it perches in the middle of nowhere about 11 miles northwest of Reeth. At times the howling wind can make it feel a bit wild up here, but inside it's unexpectedly comfortable and welcoming, with an ancient fireplace in the atmospheric, stone-flagged public bar and leather sofas in the lounge.

Narrow Boat
PUB

(www.markettowntaverns.co.uk; 38 Victoria St; ⊗noon-11pm; 🛜🍴🐾) Down a back alley beside Skipton's canal basin, this friendly pub is essentially a modern craft beer bar but still manages to cultivate a traditional feel with wooden beams and old bar furniture. The beer selection is great; soak it up with interesting bar food such as halloumi chips, southern fried chicken burgers and a rotating range of flatbread pizzas.

ℹ Information

Tourist Office (📞 01756-792809; www.welcometoskipton.com; Town Hall, High St; ⊗9.30am-4pm Mon-Sat)

ℹ Getting There & Away

Skipton is the last stop on the Metro rail network from Leeds (from £5.80, 45 minutes, frequent departures). Buses 580 to 582 link Skipton with Settle Monday to Saturday (£5.50, 40 minutes, hourly during the day), with many departures continuing on to Ingleton. There are also twice daily buses from Skipton to Malham (£4, 40 minutes) Monday to Saturday, and frequent departures from Skipton to Grassington.

Grassington

📞 01756 / POP 1611

A good base for jaunts around the south Dales, Grassington's handsome Georgian centre teems with walkers and visitors throughout the summer months, soaking up an atmosphere that – despite the odd touch of faux rusticity – is as attractive and traditional as you'll find in these parts.

RIBBLESDALE & THE THREE PEAKS

Scenic Ribblesdale cuts through the southwestern corner of the Yorkshire Dales National Park, where the skyline is dominated by a trio of distinctive hills known as the Three Peaks: Whernside (735m), Ingleborough (724m) and Pen-y-ghent (694m). Easily accessible via the Settle–Carlisle railway line (p497), this is one of England's most popular areas for outdoor activities, attracting thousands of hikers, cyclists and cavers each weekend.

At the head of the valley, 5 miles north of Horton, is the spectacular 30m-high Ribblehead Viaduct, built in 1874 and, at 400m, the longest on the Settle–Carlisle Line. You can hike there along the Pennine Way and travel back by train from Ribblehead station.

A traditional cafe run by the same family since 1965, the **Pen-y-Ghent Cafe** (☑ 01729-860333; mains £3-6; ☺ 9am-5.30pm Mon & Wed-Fri, 8am-5.30pm Sat, from 8.30am Sun; P ☑ ♿) in Horton-in-Ribblesdale fills walkers' fuel tanks with fried eggs and chips, homemade scones and pint-sized mugs of tea, and can cater for vegans and those on gluten-free diets. It also sells maps, walking guidebooks and hiking gear.

✨ Festivals & Events

Grassington Festival　　　ART
(www.grassington-festival.org.uk; ☺ Jun) Highlight of the cultural year in the Yorkshire Dales is the Grassington Festival, a two-week arts extravaganza that attracts many big names in music, theatre and comedy, and also includes offbeat events like drystone-walling workshops.

🛏 Sleeping & Eating

Ashfield House　　　B&B ££
(☑ 01756-752584; www.ashfieldhouse.co.uk; Summers Fold; d £80-127, ste £155-215; P 🛜) A secluded 17th-century country house with a walled garden, open fireplaces, honesty bar, and all-round cosy feel. It's just off the main square.

★ Devonshire Fell　　　HOTEL £££
(☑ 01756-718111; www.devonshirefell.co.uk; Burnsall; r from £129; P 🛜🐾) This former gentleman's club for mill owners in the scenic village of Burnsall has a very contemporary feel and spacious rooms, many with beautiful valley views. The conservatory (used as a restaurant, breakfast room and for afternoon tea) has a stunning outlook. It's 3 miles southeast of Grassington, which can be reached via a walking path by the river.

Corner House Cafe　　　CAFE £
(☑ 01756-752414; www.cornerhousegrassington. co.uk; 1 Garr's Lane; mains £6-10; ☺ 10am-4pm; 🛜🐾🐾) This cute little white cottage, just uphill from the village square, serves good coffee and unusual homemade cakes (citrus and lavender syrup sponge is unexpectedly delicious), as well as tasty made-to-order

sandwiches and lunch specials such as Dales lamb hotpot or chicken and chorizo gratin. Breakfast, served till 11.30am, ranges from cinnamon toast to the full-English fry-up.

ℹ️ Information

Grassington National Park Centre (☑ 01756-751690; Hebden Rd; 2/24hr parking £2.50/5; ☺ 10am-5pm Apr-Oct, to 4pm Sat & Sun Nov, Dec, Feb & Mar)

ℹ️ Getting There & Away

Grassington is 6 miles north of Skipton; take bus 72 from Skipton bus or train station (£4.20, 30 minutes, hourly Monday to Saturday), or X43 (hourly, Sunday and public holidays) from the bus station only. For onward travel, bus 72 continues up the valley to the villages of Kettlewell and Buckden.

Hawes

POP 1137

Hawes is the beating heart of Wensleydale, a thriving and picturesque market town (market day is Tuesday) surrounded by rolling hills and hiking trails. It has several antique, art and craft shops, and the added attraction of its own waterfall in the village centre. On busy summer weekends, however, Hawes' narrow arteries can get seriously clogged with traffic. Leave the car in the parking area beside the national park centre at the eastern entrance to the village.

A mile northwest of Hawes, the pretty village of Hardraw has an even more impressive waterfall, a country church and an excellent old pub offering accommodation for those who prefer a quieter rural base.

◉ Sights

Hardraw Force WATERFALL
(www.hardrawforce.com; Hardraw; adult/child £2.50/1.50; P) About 1.5 miles north of Hawes is 30m-high Hardraw Force, the highest unbroken waterfall in England, but by international standards not that impressive (except after heavy rain). Access is via a lovely landscaped walk (400m) from the car park behind the Green Dragon Inn. There's an admission fee (cash only) to access the walk, and a cafe selling local ice cream.

Wensleydale Creamery MUSEUM
(www.wensleydale.co.uk; Gayle Lane; adult/child £3.95/2.45; ◎10am-5pm; P🍴) Wensleydale Creamery is devoted to the production of a crumbly white cheese that's the favourite of animation characters Wallace and Gromit. You can visit the cheese museum, watch cheesemakers in action in the viewing gallery (Monday to Friday), and then try-before-you-buy in the shop (which is free to enter). An interactive exhibit for kids explains the process from grass to cow to cheese.

There's also a cafe on-site serving giant scones, Wensleydale cheese on toast and grilled-cheese sandwiches.

Dales Countryside Museum MUSEUM
(🖉01969-666210; www.dalescountrysidemuseum.org.uk; Station Yard; adult/child £4.80/free; ◎10am-5pm, closed Jan; P🍴) Sharing a building with the national park centre, the Dales Countryside Museum is a beautifully presented social history of the area that explains the forces shaping the landscape, from geology to lead mining to land enclosure and the railways.

🛏️ Sleeping & Eating

★**Green Dragon Inn** INN ££
(🖉01969-667392; www.greendragonhardraw.co.uk; Hardraw; dm/d/ste £18/97/120; P🛜🐾) A lovely old pub with flagstone floors, low timber beams, ancient oak furniture and Theakston's on draught. The Dragon serves up a tasty steak-and-ale pie and offers bunkhouse accommodation or B&B in pleasant, simple rooms behind the pub, as well as a pair of fancy suites above the bar. One mile northwest of Hawes.

Herriot's Guest House B&B ££
(🖉01969-667536; www.herriotsinhawes.co.uk; Main St; s/d from £50/82; 🛜) This petite guesthouse in an old stone building is in a great location close to the town waterfall, with six comfy en-suite bedrooms set above a coffee shop, free homemade biscuits and walkers' packages. Top-floor rooms have lovely Dales views.

ℹ️ Information

Hawes National Park Centre (🖉01969-666210; Station Yard; parking 2/24hr £2.50/5; ◎10am-5pm Apr-Oct, early closing Nov, Dec, Feb & Mar, closed Jan)

Malham

POP 238

Even in the Dales, where competition is fierce, Malham stands out as a strikingly attractive village. Stone cottages and inns huddle around a river that meanders through its centre and there is always a buzz about the place because of its famed hiking paths, which draw walking enthusiasts from all over the world. If you have time for only one stop in the Dales, make it here.

The village sits within the largest area of limestone country in England, stretching west from Grassington to Ingleton – a distinctive landscape pockmarked with potholes, dry valleys, limestone pavements and gorges. Two of the most spectacular features – Malham Cove and Gordale Scar – are within walking distance of Malham's centre.

◉ Sights & Activities

★**Malham Cove** NATURAL FEATURE
North of Malham village, a 0.75-mile field walk beside a lovely babbling stream leads to Malham Cove, a huge rock amphitheatre lined with 80m-high vertical cliffs. A large glacial waterfall once tumbled over this cliff, but it dried up hundreds of years ago. You can hike up the steep steps on the left-hand side of the cove (follow Pennine Way signs) to see the extensive limestone pavement above the cliffs – a filming location in *Harry Potter and the Deathly Hallows*.

Peregrine falcons nest at the top in spring, when the Royal Society for the Protection of Birds (RSPB) sets up a birdwatching lookout with telescopes near the base of the cliff – call the national park centre (p502) for the schedule as it changes every year.

Malham Landscape Trail WALKING
(www.malhamdale.com) This 5-mile circular trail is one of the best day hikes in Yorkshire, linking three impressive natural features:

Malham Cove (p501); spectacular **Gordale Scar**, a deep limestone canyon with scenic cascades; and the remains of an Iron Age settlement, and **Janet's Foss** waterfall. A leaflet describing the trail in detail can be downloaded from the website or picked up at pubs and hotels in the village.

Malham Tarn   LAKE
A glacial lake and nature reserve 3.5 miles north of Malham village, accessible via a 1.5-mile walk north from Malham Cove, or by car. There are two car parks: the one at the southern edge is bigger and picks up a trail that skirts the eastern side of the lake; the one to the north (follow signs to Arncliffe/Grassington) allows easy access to an extensive bog-skimming boardwalk that wends through fen and woodland scrub. Roe deer, heron and water voles can sometimes be spotted here.

🛏 Sleeping & Eating

Malham YHA   HOSTEL £
(☑ 0845 371 9529; www.yha.org.uk; Finkle St; dm/tw from £13/49; 🅿 🛜) This purpose-built hostel has a central village location across the bridge from the main road, with a pretty garden out front and useful facilities such as bike storage, a drying room, and a shop selling beer and wine. A handful of private rooms have quite luxurious en-suite bathrooms; rates vary wildly depending on day of the week and demand.

⭐ **Lister Barn**   B&B £££
(☑ 01729-830444; www.thwaites.co.uk; Cove Rd; d £140-180; 🅿 🛜 🐾) The Lister Arms pub in Malham runs this chic barn conversion

on the main road through the village, with eight modern rooms centred on a lovely open-plan communal area with free herbal teas and a log burner to huddle around after long walks. One room is suitable for wheelchair users and there are two family rooms with bunks and a separate bedroom.

Lister Arms   PUB FOOD ££
(☑ 01729-830444; www.thwaites.co.uk; Cove Rd; mains £10-18; ⊙ 8am-11pm Mon-Sat, to 10.30pm Sun; 🅿 🛜 🐾 🐾) This comfy coaching inn is the best spot in Malham to kick back after a walk, with open fires for chilly days, a beer garden out back and classic pub meals plus chalkboard specials. In the busy summer months drinkers lounge out on the grass in front of the pub.

ℹ Information

Malham National Park Centre (☑ 01729-833200; www.yorkshiredales.org.uk; parking 2/24hr £2.50/5; ⊙ 10am-5pm Apr-Oct, to 4pm Sat & Sun Nov, Dec, Feb & Mar) In the car park at the southern edge of Malham village; the walking leaflets it sells (£1.50) include more detail than the free leaflet given out around the village.

ℹ Getting There & Away

There are at least two buses a day Monday to Saturday year-round from Skipton to Malham (£4.10, 35 minutes). The scenic Malham Tarn Shuttle bus route links Settle with Malham (£4, 30 minutes), Malham Tarn and Ingleton six times daily on Sundays and bank holidays only, Easter to October. Check the DalesBus website (www.dalesbus.org) or ask at Malham National Park Centre for details.

MASHAM

Located 9 miles northwest of Ripon, the little village of Masham is famous for producing some of Yorkshire's best beers. Yorkshire's best-known brewery, **Theakston's** (☑ 01765-680000; www.theakstons.co.uk; The Brewery, Masham; tour adult/child £8.50/4.95; ⊙ 10.30am-4.30pm Sep-Jul, to 5pm Aug), was founded way back in 1827, then taken over by global brewer Scottish & Newcastle in 1987, but since 2004 has been back in family hands. Old Peculier, its most famous ale, takes its name from the Peculier of Masham, a medieval parish court established to deal with offences such as drunkenness and brawling. There's a visitor centre that doubles as a bar, and four tours a day (five in August).

Across the village, **Black Sheep Brewery** (☑ 01765-680101; www.blacksheepbrewery.com; Wellgarth, Masham; tours adult/child £9.50/4.95; ⊙ 10am-5pm Sun-Wed, to 11pm Thu-Sat; 🅿 🐾) was founded in 1992 by the 'black sheep' of the Theakston family, Paul Theakston, who left to start his own brewery after the controversial Scottish & Newcastle takeover. It's now almost as famous as its near neighbour, with four entertaining tours a day, an excellent casual bistro, and a bar where you can sample most of the brewery's ales and craft beers.

Note that Malham is reached via narrow roads that can get very congested in summer, so leave your car at the national park centre and walk into the village.

Richmond

☎ 01748 / POP 8415

The handsome market town of Richmond perches on a rocky outcrop overlooking the River Swale and is guarded by the ruins of a massive castle, beneath which a small, frothy waterfall flows. It has been a garrison town for centuries and home to one of England's most prized regiments, which now resides nearby at modern-day Catterick Garrison.

Elegant Georgian buildings and photogenic stone cottages line the streets that radiate from the broad cobbled market square (market day is Saturday), with glimpses of the surrounding hills and dales peeking through the gaps. There are plenty of local walks, and the town makes a pleasant base for exploring the northern Dales, though it is sorely lacking decent eating and drinking options; you'll find no cute old inns here.

◉ Sights

★ **Georgian Theatre Royal**　HISTORIC BUILDING
(www.georgiantheatreroyal.co.uk; Victoria Rd; adult/child £5/2; ⊙ tours hourly 10am-4pm Mon-Sat mid-Feb–mid-Nov) Built in 1788, this is the most complete Georgian playhouse in Britain. It closed in 1848 and was used as an auction house into the early 20th century, reopening as a working theatre again in 1963 after a period of restoration. Fascinating tours (starting on the hour) include a look at the country's oldest surviving stage scenery, painted between 1818 and 1836.

Richmond Castle　CASTLE
(EH; www.english-heritage.org.uk; Tower St; adult/child £6.20/3.70; ⊙ 10am-6pm Easter-Sep, to 5pm Oct, to 4pm Sat & Sun Nov-Easter) The impressive heap that is Richmond Castle, founded in 1070, has had many uses through the years, including a stint as a prison for conscientious objectors during WWI (there's a small and fascinating exhibition about their part in the castle's history – enter through the shop). The best part of a visit is the view from the top of the remarkably well-preserved 30m-high keep, which dates to the late 12th century and towers over the town.

BIKING IN THE DALES

The centre of mountain biking in the Yorkshire Dales, the **Dales Bike Centre** (☎ 01748-884908; www.dalesbike centre.co.uk; Fremington; mountain bike/e-bike per day from £30/50; ⊙ 9am-5pm), 12 miles west of Richmond, provides quality rentals (mountain and road bikes, as well as e-bikes), a bike shop and repair service, advice and trail maps, guided rides (£199 per day for up to seven people), a cosy cafe with decent coffee and comfortable bunkhouse accommodation (two-bunk room £58 a night).

🛏 Sleeping

Old Dairy　B&B ££
(☎ 01748-886057; www.olddairylowrow.wordpress. com; Low Row, Swaledale; s/d £65/80; 🅿 🐕 📶) Guests will feel right at home in this 200-year-old village house in the heart of the Dales, where the owners have converted two rooms into comfortable, modern guest bedrooms with lovely views across the dale. There's cake in the afternoons, and the owners are a fount of knowledge on local walking, biking, stargazing and astrophotography. It's near Reeth, 15 miles west of Richmond.

Frenchgate Hotel　BOUTIQUE HOTEL ££
(☎ 01748-822087; www.thefrenchgate.co.uk; 59-61 Frenchgate; s/d from £88/118; 🅿 📶) Nine elegant bedrooms occupy the upper floors of this converted Georgian town house, with flash touches such as memory-foam mattresses and heated marble floors in luxurious bathrooms. Parts of the house date to 1650, so we can forgive a crack here or peeling paint there. Downstairs there's an excellent restaurant (three-course dinner £39), an oasis of a garden and a private car park at the rear.

🍴 Eating

★ **George & Dragon**　PUB FOOD £
(☎ 01748-518373; www.georgeanddragonhudswell. co.uk; Hudswell; mains £8-10; ⊙ food served noon-2pm & 6-9pm Mon-Sat, noon-4pm Sun; 📶 ♿) A mile and a half west of Richmond, the George & Dragon is a genuine local pub, owned and managed by the community. It serves a small menu of freshly prepared pub grub, including roast beef and Yorkshire pudding on Sundays, and has won awards

for its excellent rotating beer selection. The backyard terrace has gorgeous Dales views.

The Station
BRITISH £

(🗹 01748-850123; www.thestation.co.uk; Station Yard) Richmond's defunct Victorian railway station has been converted into a bold multipurpose space housing exhibition galleries, an independent cinema, craft brewery (offering tastings and sales) and ice-cream parlour. Locals come for takeaway lunch at Angel's Share Bakery, which bakes fresh breads, quiches and local specialities such as Yorkshire curd tart on-site. Take your goodies to a grassy picnic table outside.

Rustique
FRENCH ££

(🗹 01748-821565; www.rustiquerichmond.co.uk; Chantry Wynd, Finkle St; mains £11-23; ⊘ noon-9pm) 🖉 Tucked away in a quirky vaulted arcade space, this bistro has consistently impressed with its mastery of French country cooking, from *confit de canard* (duck slow roasted in its own fat) to *moules marinière* (mussels with white wine, garlic and cream). Booking is recommended.

❶ Information

Richmond Tourist Office (🗹 01609-532980; www.richmond.org; Richmond Library, Queens Rd; ⊘ 10am-5pm Mon & Thu-Fri, to 7pm Tue, to noon Wed, to 1pm Sat, from 10.30am Jan & Feb) A tiny tourist office with less information than can be found at other outlets across Yorkshire.

❶ Getting There & Away

From Darlington (on the railway between London and Edinburgh) it's easy to reach Richmond on bus X26 or X27 (£5.30, 30 minutes, every half-hour, hourly on Sunday). All buses stop in Trinity Church Sq.

On Sundays and bank-holiday Mondays only, from May to September, the Northern Dalesman bus 830 runs from Richmond to Hawes (£4, 1½ hours, twice daily) via Reeth, and the afternoon bus continues to Ribblehead.

WEST YORKSHIRE

It was the tough and unforgiving textile industry that drove West Yorkshire's economy from the 18th century onward. The woollen mills, factories and canals built to transport raw materials and finished products defined much of the county's landscape. But that's all in the past, and recent years have seen the transformation of this once hard-bitten area into quite the picture postcard.

Leeds and Bradford, two adjoining cities so big they've virtually become one, are undergoing radical redevelopment and reinvention, prettifying their centres and tempting more adventurous tourists with new museums, galleries and restaurants. Beyond the cities lies a landscape of wild moorland dissected by deep valleys dotted with old mill towns and villages, scenes that were so vividly described by the Brontë sisters, West Yorkshire's most renowned literary export and biggest tourist draw.

❶ Getting There & Around

The Metro is West Yorkshire's highly efficient train and bus network, centred on Leeds and Bradford, which are also the main gateways to the county. For transport information, contact **West Yorkshire Metro** (🗹 0113-245 7676; www. wymetro.com).

Day Rover tickets (£8.40) are good for one day's unlimited travel on Metro buses and trains from 9.30am to 4pm and after 6.30pm on weekdays, and all day at weekends. A range of additional Rover tickets covering buses and/ or trains, plus heaps of useful Metro maps and timetables, are available from bus and train stations and most tourist offices in West Yorkshire.

Leeds
🗹 0113 / POP 474,632

Just an hour south of the southern Dales and one of the fastest-growing cities in the UK, Leeds is the glitzy embodiment of rediscovered northern self-confidence. A decade and a half of redevelopment has transformed the city centre from a near-derelict mill town into a vision of 21st-century urban chic, with architecturally daring malls woven into the fabric of the city centre, a revitalised Victorian mill district and an innovative independent dining and drinking scene.

People come from all over the north to indulge in shopping weekends, concert trips and the lively nightlife, giving the town a decidedly confident Yorkshire swagger. There's not much in the way of tourist sights except for the national Royal Armouries museum, but excellent transport links to the Dales, York, Harrogate, Manchester and Haworth (of Brontë literary fame) can make it a good base, without the touristy veneer of neighbouring York.

Leeds

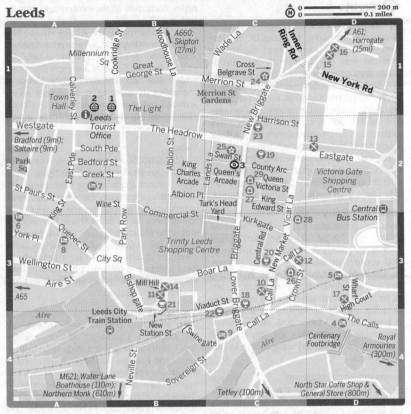

Leeds

◉ Sights
1 Henry Moore Institute	B1
2 Leeds Art Gallery	A1
3 Thornton's Arcade	C2

🛏 Sleeping
4 42 The Calls	D4
5 Art Hostel	D3
6 Chambers	A3
7 Dakota	A2
8 Quebecs	A3
9 Roomzzz Leeds City	C4

🍴 Eating
10 Art's Cafe Bar & Restaurant	C3
Belgrave Music Hall & Canteen	(see 24)
11 Bundobust	B3
12 Caravanserai	C3
13 Cat's Pyjamas	D2
14 Friends of Ham	B3
15 Hansa's Gujarati	D1

Ox Club	(see 19)
16 Reliance	D1
17 Shears Yard	D3

🍷 Drinking & Nightlife
18 Bar Fibre	C3
19 Headrow House	C2
20 HiFi Club	C3
21 Laynes Espresso	B3
22 Mission	C4
23 North Bar	C2

✪ Entertainment
24 Belgrave Music Hall & Canteen	C1
25 City Varieties	C2

🛍 Shopping
26 Corn Exchange	C3
27 Harvey Nichols	C2
28 Kirkgate Market	C3
29 Victoria Quarter	C2

◉ Sights

★ Royal Armouries
MUSEUM

(www.royalarmouries.org; Armouries Dr; ⊙10am-5pm; P🚼) FREE Leeds' most interesting museum was originally built in 1996 to house armour and weapons from the Tower of London, but subsequently expanded to cover 3000 years of combat and self-defence, becoming home to the national collections. The exhibits are as varied as they are fascinating, covering subjects such as jousting, fencing and Indian elephant armour. To get here, walk east along the river from Centenary Footbridge (approx 10 minutes), or take the free boat from Granary Wharf outside Leeds train station's southern entrance.

Leeds Art Gallery
GALLERY

(www.leeds.gov.uk/artgallery; The Headrow; ⊙10am-5pm Tue-Sat, 11am-3pm Sun) FREE This major gallery is packed with 19th- and 20th-century British heavyweights – Turner, Constable, Stanley Spencer, Wyndham Lewis et al – along with contemporary pieces by more recent arrivals such as Antony Gormley, sculptor of the *Angel of the North*. It reopened in October 2017 after a major restoration program that uncovered a lost Victorian barrel-vaulted glass ceiling in one of its rooms.

Leeds Industrial Museum
MUSEUM

(Armley Mills; ☎0113-3783173; www.leeds.gov.uk/ museumsandgalleries/armleymills; Canal Rd, Armley; adult/child £4/2; ⊙10am-5pm Tue-Sat, 1-5pm Sun; P🚼) One of the world's largest textile mills has been transformed into a museum telling the story of Leeds' industrial past, both glorious and ignominious. The city grew rich from the textile industry, but at some cost in human terms – working conditions were Dickensian. As well as a selection of mill machinery, there's an informative display about how cloth is made. The museum is 2 miles west of the city centre; take bus 15 from Vicar Lane near Kirkgate Market.

Kirkstall Abbey
CHURCH

(www.leeds.gov.uk/kirkstallabbey; Abbey Rd, Kirkstall; ⊙10am-4.30pm Tue-Sun Apr-Sep, to 4pm Oct-Mar) FREE Leeds' most impressive medieval structure is beautiful Kirkstall Abbey, founded in 1152 by Cistercian monks from Fountains Abbey in North Yorkshire. These days the city makes good use of it as an atmospheric backdrop for pop-up events and a monthly weekend food market (April to November; check online for dates). It's 3

miles northwest of the centre; take bus 33, 33A or 757.

Across the road is the **Abbey House Museum** (www.leeds.gov.uk/museumsandgalleries; Abbey Walk, Kirkstall; adult/child £4.95/2.50; ⊙10am-5pm Tue-Fri & Sun, noon-5pm Sat; P🚼), which was once the Great Gate House to the abbey. It contains meticulously reconstructed shops and houses that evoke Victorian Leeds, plus rotating exhibitions mostly aimed at kids.

Tetley
GALLERY

(☎0113-3202423; www.thetetley.org; Hunslet Rd; ⊙10am-5pm Thu-Tue, to 8pm Wed) Tetley Brewery's defunct 1930s offices have been converted into a contemporary-arts venue with a restaurant and pub on the ground floor, spilling out onto an outdoor terrace. Upstairs the old meeting rooms have been put to good use as quirky gallery spaces, housing rotating exhibitions from international and local artists and photographers. An immaculately preserved 1930s lift dominates the central stairwell shaft.

Thornton's Arcade
NOTABLE BUILDING

(enter off Briggate or Lands Lane) Though not the grandest, Thornton's Arcade was the first Victorian shopping arcade to be built in Leeds and remains one of the most interesting. Its sky-coloured, neo-Gothic arches rise up to a glass ceiling and its cupboard-sized shops host some of the city's best independent retailers and cafes. At the western end of the arcade, a giant automaton clock manned by life-sized figures of Robin Hood and Friar Tuck rings in the time on the hour.

Henry Moore Institute
GALLERY

(www.henry-moore.org/hmi; The Headrow; ⊙11am-5.30pm Tue & Thu-Sun, to 8pm Wed) FREE Housed in a converted Victorian warehouse in the city centre, this gallery showcases the work of 20th-century sculptors, but not, despite the name, anything by Henry Moore (1898–1986), who graduated from the Leeds School of Art. To see works by Moore, head to the Yorkshire Sculpture Park (p509) and Hepworth Wakefield (p509).

★☆ Festivals & Events

Leeds Indie Food
FOOD & DRINK

(www.leedsindiefood.co.uk; ⊙mid-May; 🚼) This home-grown festival, launched in 2015, takes over Leeds' food scene for two weeks each May and has become one of the UK's most inventive celebrations of independent local producers, restaurants, cafes and boozers. There are dozens of quirky events around town, such as kitchen takeovers, wine- and beer-pairing dinners, film nights, food photography workshops, foraging walks and brewery crawls.

Leeds Festival MUSIC
(www.leedsfestival.com; ⊘ end Aug) The August bank holiday weekend (the weekend preceding the last Monday in August) sees 50,000-plus music fans converge on Bramham Park, 10 miles outside the city centre, for the Leeds Festival. Spread across several stages, it's one of England's biggest rock-music extravaganzas. There are various camping/glamping options on-site, or you can buy day tickets.

🛏 Sleeping

★ Art Hostel HOSTEL £
(🗷 0113-345 3363; www.arthostel.org.uk; 83 Kirkgate; dm/tw/tr £22.50/55/70; 🛜) Set in an appealingly grungy 200-year-old brick building near to Leeds' nightlife zone, this hostel is a great advert for the revitalisation of the city centre. Each room has been individually designed by a local artist, and the hostel is full of recycled furniture and innovative ideas.

Roomzzz Leeds City APARTMENT ££
(🗷 0203-504 5555; www.roomzzz.com/leeds-city; 10 Swinegate; studio/2-person apt from £69/89; @🛜) This outfit offers bright and modern luxury apartments complete with fitted kitchens, with the added advantage of 24-hour hotel reception, and a great city-centre location; there are two other branches, both on Burley Rd, but this is by far the most central.

42 The Calls BOUTIQUE HOTEL ££
(🗷 0113-244 0099; www.42thecalls.co.uk; 42 The Calls; r £85-160, ste from £180; @🛜) This pioneer of the boutique-hotel scene (it opened in 1991), set in a 19th-century grain mill, has been somewhat overshadowed by Leeds' clutch of new modern hotels, but its riverside setting and quirky original mill features in rooms still make it one of the city's most interesting places to stay. Breakfast costs extra and is pricey, but there are plenty of places to eat nearby.

★ Chambers APARTMENT £££
(🗷 0113-386 3300; www.morethanjustabed.com; 30 Park Pl; 2-person apt £145-190, parking per night £12; P🛜) This grand Edwardian office

building has been converted into 63 luxury serviced apartments, ranging from two-person studios to a two-bedroom penthouse (£342 a night) that will sleep up to four adults. Simple, fresh and spotlessly clean, there's also a 24-hour reception with great service, a gym, honesty bar and pretty little patio for aperitifs or night caps.

★ Dakota HOTEL £££
(🗷 0113-322 6261; http://leeds.dakotahotels.co.uk; 8 Russell St; d from £112, ste from £250; ❋🛜) Raising the bar for luxury sleeps in Leeds, this gleaming new hotel has quickly become popular thanks to its central location close to shops and bars, swanky yet muted designer interior and five-star service. Rooms are plush, modern and classic, and the suites are like mini-apartments, with open-plan lounge areas and dressing rooms with robes. Rates are room only.

Quebecs BOUTIQUE HOTEL £££
(🗷 0113-244 8989; www.quebecshotel.co.uk; 9 Quebec St; d £85-165, ste £165-285; P🛜) Victorian grace at its opulent best is the theme of Quebecs, a conversion of the former Leeds & County Liberal Club. The elaborate wood panelling and heraldic stained-glass windows in the public areas are mirrored by the grand design flourishes in the bedrooms, but it's a listed building (which means no double glazing) so expect some street noise.

🍴 Eating

Caravanserai NORTH AFRICAN £
(🗷 0113-234 1999; www.caravanseraileeds.co.uk; 1 Crown St; dishes £3-8; ⊘ 10.30am-11pm Mon-Thu, to 3am or later Fri & Sat; 🛜) Emulating the traditional *caravansersai* (roadside inn) with cart wheels out front and carpets thickly draped over every inch of wall in the teeny upstairs 'banquet' room, this excellent street-food joint serves freshly prepared mezze, falafel and Ottoman barbecue from a hole in the wall. Don't miss the date-and-honey milkshake, served in a cinnamon-dusted jar. Cash only.

Belgrave Music Hall & Canteen STREET FOOD £
(www.belgravemusichall.com; 1 Cross Belgrave St; mains £2.50-8; ⊘ food served 11am-10pm; 🛜🍴) This bar and music venue has two great kitchens. One serves artisan pizza (watch out for the napalm chilli sauce); the other offers brunch and probably the best burgers in Yorkshire, all at great-value prices. Every

second Saturday of the month the place hosts the **Belgrave Feast** (11am to 8pm), an art market and street-food festival.

Hansa's Gujarati INDIAN £

(☑ 0113-244 4408; www.hansasrestaurant.com; 72-74 North St; mains £6.50-8; ⊙ 5-10pm Mon-Fri, to 11pm Sat, buffet noon-2pm Sun; 🖋 🗱) A Leeds institution, Hansa's has been dishing up wholesome Gujarati vegetarian cuisine for almost 20 years. The restaurant is plain and unassuming (save for a Hindu shrine), but the food is exquisite – specialities of the house include *khasta kachori* (fried pastries stuffed with chickpeas and potato laced with tamarind and mint), garnished with pomegranate.

Cat's Pyjamas INDIAN £

(☑ 0113-234 0454; www.thecatspjs.co.uk; 9 Eastgate; mains £7-10; ⊙ 5-11pm Mon-Fri, from noon Sat, noon-10pm Sun) This popular suburban Indian street-food hall opened in Leeds city centre in mid-2017. Loud Bollywood wall murals offset a northern industrial aesthetic in the dining hall. The menu plays with an eclectic mash-up of subcontinent dishes (Goan chicken cafreal, tandoori grills and street-food bites like paneer tacos) and craft beers.

Bundobust INDIAN £

(☑ 0113-243 1248; www.bundobust.com; 6 Mill Hill; dishes £3.75-6.50; ⊙ kitchen noon-9.30pm Mon-Thu, to 10pm Fri & Sat, to 8pm Sun; 🖋) What could be more Yorkshire than craft beer and Indian street food rolled into one no-frills, brick-walled bar? The beers come from both local and international breweries, and food inspiration comes from vegetarian street-hawker offerings across India. The okra fries are a favourite with drinkers; more substantial bites include paneer and mushroom tikka, and biryani bhaji balls.

⭐ Friends of Ham DELI ££

(☑ 0113-242 0275; www.friendsofham.co.uk; 4-8 New Station St; dishes £6-17; ⊙ 11am-11pm Mon-Wed, to midnight Thu-Sat, to 10pm Sun; 🖈) This stylish bar serves the finest charcuterie and cheeses – Spanish, French, British – accompanied by fine wines and craft beers. The food is carefully selected and prepared, and utterly delicious; you can order individual tapas-like portions, or huge sharing platters with olive-oil-drizzled bread. Brunch served 11am till 2pm.

⭐ Ox Club GRILL ££

(☑ 07470 359961; www.oxclub.co.uk; Bramleys Yard, The Headrow; mains £16-30; ⊙ 5-10pm Tue-Sat, brunch 11am-3pm Sat & Sun) Arguably the best restaurant in Leeds (or at least, the best without a Michelin star), Ox Club occupies an intimate, minimalist space and champions local produce with a deceptively simple menu. Though it bills itself as a grill restaurant, the Modern British dishes are far more inventive than what you'll find in your average BBQ joint – venison tartare with smoked fat, for example.

Reliance BRITISH ££

(☑ 0113-295 6060; www.the-reliance.co.uk; 76-78 North St; mains £5-16; ⊙ noon-10pm Mon-Wed, to 10.30pm Thu-Sat, to 8.30pm Sun; 🖈) The Reliance is a comfortable-as-old-slippers bar where you can happily while away an afternoon reading or chatting with a Yorkshire beer or good glass of natural wine in hand. Yet it's also one of Leeds' best gastropubs, serving Sunday roasts, seasonal Modern British dishes like pig cheeks with beetroot and smoked apple, and platters of homemade charcuterie (yes, they make it themselves).

Shears Yard MODERN BRITISH ££

(☑ 0113-244 4144; www.shearsyard.com; 11-15 Wharf St; mains £14-25; ⊙ 5.30-10pm Tue-Sat, 11am-3pm Sat, noon-4pm Sun; 🖈) 🖋 Acres of exposed brick, concrete floors and a soaring roof provide an industrial-chic setting (it's a former rope-making yard) for painterly presentations of imaginative dishes such as ox-cheek fritter with roast-onion consommé, or squid with puffed potato and coriander emulsion. A two-/three-course dinner menu is available for £17.50/21.50 Tuesday to Thursday evenings, and before 7pm on Friday.

🍷 Drinking & Nightlife

⭐ Laynes Espresso COFFEE

(☑ 07828 823189; www.laynesespresso.co.uk; 16 New Station St; ⊙ 7am-7pm Mon-Fri, 9am-6pm Sat & Sun; 🖈) 🖋 Locals have Laynes to thank for the complete reinvention of the Leeds coffee scene; when it opened in 2011 there was nothing else like it in the city. Now expanded and serving excellent all-day brunch – buckwheat pancakes and smashed avocado on toast, naturally – and Yorkshire rarebit alongside strong coffee, it's still the best indie cafe in town for an espresso or flat white.

⭐ Northern Monk BREWERY

(☑ 0113-243 0003; www.northernmonkbrewco.com; The Old Flax Store, Marshall St; ⊙ 11.45am-11pm Tue-Thu, to 1am Fri & Sat, 11.45am-9pm Sun)

So successful has this craft brewery become that its beers are now stocked in UK supermarkets. But it's best drunk at the source, in the brewery's Grade II–listed taproom just south of Leeds city centre in the regeneration 'hood of Holbeck. Draft options run the gamut from hoppy IPAs or rich porters to small-batch collaborations and guest beers; brewery tours also available.

★ **North Star Coffee Shop & General Store** COFFEE
(www.northstarroast.com; Unit 33, The Boulevard, Leeds Dock; ⊙7.30am-5.30pm Mon-Fri, 9am-5pm

Sat, 10am-4pm Sun) This minimalist cafe and coffee emporium is attached to the production facility of Leeds' first independent roastery, near the Royal Armouries. Watch the daily grind through giant glass doors and inhale the aromas while sampling a flat white and cake (baked fresh on-site each day), or indulge in brunch – the slow-cooked scrambled eggs on a buttery four-cheese rye scone is small yet deliciously decadent.

★ **Headrow House** BAR
(☏0113-245 9370; www.headrowhouse.com; Bramleys Yard, The Headrow; ⊙noon-11pm Sun &

ART IN YORKSHIRE
....

Yorkshire Sculpture Park (☏01924-832631; www.ysp.co.uk; Bretton Park, near Wakefield; parking 2hr/all day £6/10; ⊙10am-6pm; P ♿ 🅿) One of England's most impressive collections of sculpture is scattered across the formidable 18th-century estate of Bretton Park, 200-odd hectares of lawns, fields and trees. A bit like the art world's equivalent of a safari park, the Yorkshire Sculpture Park showcases the work of dozens of sculptors both national and international. The park is partly a homage to local heroes Barbara Hepworth (1903–75), who was born in Wakefield, and Henry Moore (1898–1986), though more of their works are on display at the Hepworth Wakefield.

The rural setting is especially fitting for Moore's work, as the artist was hugely influenced by the outdoors and preferred his art to be sited in the landscape rather than indoors. Other highlights include pieces by Andy Goldsworthy and Eduardo Paolozzi, and Roger Hiorns' famous work *Seizure 2008/2013*, an apartment coated in blue copper sulphate crystals (open weekends only). There's also a program of temporary exhibitions and installations by visiting artists, plus a bookshop and cafe.

The park is 12 miles south of Leeds and 18 miles north of Sheffield, just off Junction 38 on the M1 motorway. If you're on public transport, take a train from Leeds to Wakefield (£3.90, 15 to 30 minutes, frequent departures), or from Sheffield to Barnsley (£4.30, 25 minutes, four hourly), and then take bus 96, which runs between Wakefield and Barnsley via Bretton Park (£3 to £3.40, 30 minutes, hourly Monday to Saturday).

Hepworth Wakefield (☏01924-247360; www.hepworthwakefield.org; Gallery Walk, Wakefield; parking £5; ⊙10am-5pm; P) West Yorkshire's standing in the international arts scene got a boost in 2011 when the Yorkshire Sculpture Park was joined by this award-winning gallery of modern art, housed in a stunningly angular building on the banks of the River Calder. The gallery has been built around the works of Wakefield-born sculptor Barbara Hepworth, perhaps best known for her work *Single Form*, which graces the UN Headquarters in New York.

The gallery is smaller than it looks from the outside, but showcases more than a dozen Hepworth originals, as well as works by other 20th-century British artists including Ivon Hitchens, Paul Nash, Victor Pasmore, John Piper and Henry Moore.

The gallery is near the centre of Wakefield, a 10-minute walk south of Wakefield Kirkgate train station, easily reached from Leeds by train (£3.90, 15 to 30 minutes, three to four hourly).

Salts Mill (☏01274-531163; www.saltsmill.org.uk; Victoria Rd; ⊙9.30am-5pm Mon-Fri, to 5.30pm Sat & Sun; P) Saltaire, a Victorian-era landmark and Unesco World Heritage Site, was an industrial village purpose-built in 1851 by philanthropic wool baron and teetotaller Titus Salt. The village's huge factory was once the largest in the world. It is now Salts Mill, a splendidly bright and airy cathedral-like building where the main draw is a permanent exhibition of works by Bradford-born artist David Hockney.

Saltaire is easily reached by train from Leeds (£4.10, 15 minutes, every 30 minutes).

Mon, to 11.30pm Tue, to midnight Wed, to 12.30am Thu, to 2am Fri, to 3am Sat) A former textile mill and one-time grotty dive pub, the historic building that now houses Headrow House was given a hefty makeover to transform it into the four-floor nightlife venue it is today. The ground-floor beer hall sells its own pilsner straight from tanks lining one wall. Upstairs there's a cocktail bar and Leeds' best roof-terrace drinking spot. It's also home to Ox Club (p508) restaurant.

North Bar
CRAFT BEER
(www.northbar.com; 24 New Briggate; ⊙11am-1am Mon & Tue, to 2am Wed-Sat, noon-midnight Sun; 🛜) This narrow bar has long been an institution in Leeds as a haven of international craft beers. It now brews its own under the banner North Brewing Co, and they're rather good. Drink them here, or visit the brewery taproom (Sheepscar Grove), which is BYO food and open Fridays 4pm to 10pm and Saturdays noon to 10pm, a 10-minute walk north of North Bar.

Water Lane Boathouse
CRAFT BEER
(✆0113-246 0985; www.waterlaneboathouse.com; Water Lane; ⊙11am-11pm Sun-Thu, to 12.30am Fri & Sat) Watch canal boats chug into Granary Wharf from the floor-to-ceiling windows or generous outside seating area at this beer bar, occupying a prime historic spot on the water close enough to clink glasses with boaters. The top-quality global craft beers are pricey, but the setting is hard to beat. There's also tasty pizza available from £5.

Bar Fibre
CLUB
(www.barfibre.com; 168 Lower Briggate; ⊙noon-1am Sun-Thu, to 3am Fri, to 4am Sat) In the heart of Leeds' LGBTIQ area, spilling out onto the cheekily named Queen's Court, this is the city's most popular gay bar although it's not just the gay crowd that loves its party atmosphere. This is where the beautiful people congregate; the dress code is...dressy, so look your best or you won't get in. Download the bar's app for deals such as buy one, get one free.

Mission
CLUB
(www.clubmission.com; Viaduct St; from £4; ⊙10.30pm-3.30am Thu, 11pm-5am Fri, 11pm-8am Sat) Describing itself as 'the home of house', this massive club redefines the term 'up for it'. Friday night Teatro hosts visiting talent from around the world, while Saturday is a feast of cutting-edge music from the resident DJs and special guests, and an af-

ter-party that keeps the beat going until the sun comes up on Sunday morning.

HiFi Club
CLUB
(✆0113-242 7353; www.thehificlub.co.uk; 2 Central Rd; ⊙11pm-4am Tue-Sun) If it's Tamla Motown or the percussive beats of dancefloor jazz that shake your booty, this is the spot for you. Also has stand-up comedy sessions (£14) on Saturdays from 7pm, which can be combined with dinner at **Art's Cafe** (✆0113-243 8243; www.artscafebar.com; 42 Call Lane; mains £13-18; ⊙noon-11pm Mon-Sat, to 9pm Sun; 🛜🍴) for £26.95 (book online).

☆ Entertainment

★Belgrave Music Hall & Canteen
LIVE MUSIC
(✆0113-234 6160; www.belgravemusichall.com; 1 Cross Belgrave St; ⊙11am-midnight Sun-Thu, to 3am Fri & Sat) Belgrave is the city's best live-music venue, with a diverse roll call of acts from burlesque to comedy and folk to hip-hop. Its three floors also encompass a huge bar bristling with craft-beer taps, two kitchens (p507), loads of shared tables and sofa space, and a fantastic roof terrace with views across the city. Why would you ever leave?

City Varieties
LIVE MUSIC, COMEDY
(✆0113-243 0808; www.cityvarieties.co.uk; Swan St) Founded in 1865, City Varieties is the world's longest-running music hall, where the likes of Harry Houdini, Charlie Chaplin and Lily Langtry once trod the boards. Its programme features stand-up comedy, live music, pantomime and old-fashioned variety shows.

🛍 Shopping

Corn Exchange
SHOPPING CENTRE
(www.leedscornexchange.co.uk; Call Lane; ⊙10am-6pm Mon-Wed, Fri & Sat, to 9pm Thu, 10.30am-4.30pm Sun; 🛜) The dramatic Corn Exchange, built in 1863 to house grain-trade merchants, has a wonderful wrought-iron roof that today shelters a fine collection of independent shops and boutiques. They sell everything from vinyl and craft beer to fashion, jewellery and Yorkshire design.

Kirkgate Market
MARKET
(www.leeds.gov.uk/leedsmarkets; Kirkgate; ⊙8am-5.30pm Mon-Sat) Britain's largest covered market sells fresh meat, fish, and fruit and vegetables, as well as household goods, and now boasts a popular new street-food hall. The best section is at the top near Vicar

Lane, where the original Victorian stalls are still inhabited by traders – this was where UK retailing giant Marks & Spencer started out in 1884.

Victoria Quarter
SHOPPING CENTRE

(www.victorialeeds.co.uk; Vicar Lane; ☎) The mosaic-paved, stained-glass-roofed Victoria Quarter shopping arcade, between Briggate and Vicar Lane, is well worth visiting for aesthetic reasons alone, as is County Arcade, which runs parallel. Dedicated shoppers can join the footballers' wives browsing boutiques such as Louis Vuitton and Vivienne Westwood. The flagship store here is Harvey Nichols (www.harveynichols. com; 107-111 Briggate; ⊙10am-7pm Mon-Sat, 11am-5pm Sun).

ⓘ Information

Leeds Tourist Office (☎ 0113-378 6977; www. visitleeds.co.uk; Leeds Art Gallery, Headrow; ⊙10am-5pm Mon-Sat, 11am-3pm Sun; ☎) In the basement of the city art gallery, next to the gallery shop.

ⓘ Getting There & Away

AIR
Leeds Bradford International Airport (www. leedsbradfordairport.co.uk) is 11 miles north-west of the city via the A65, and has flights to a range of domestic and international destinations. The Flying Tiger 757 bus (£3.80, 40 minutes, every 20 to 30 minutes) runs between Leeds bus and train stations and the airport. A taxi costs about £20.

BUS
National Express (www.nationalexpress.com) serves most major cities, while Yorkshire Coastliner (www.coastliner.co.uk) buses run to York, Pickering, Malton, Scarborough and Whitby. A Daytripper Plus ticket (£16) gives unlimited travel on all Coastliner buses for a day. The **Central Bus Station** is near Victoria Gate Shopping Centre.

London £7.50 to £20, 4½ hours, hourly
Manchester £3 to £6, 1¼ hours, at least hourly
Scarborough £12, three hours, hourly
Whitby £13, 3½ hours, four daily Monday to Saturday, twice daily Sundays
York £6, 1¼ hours, at least hourly

TRAIN
Leeds train station has good rail connections with the rest of the country and Manchester's international airport. It's also the starting point for trains on the scenic Settle–Carlisle line (p497). Tickets for Manchester and York can be had for a song if you book ahead and can be flexible on times.

London King's Cross £65, 2¼ hours, at least hourly
Manchester £10, 1 to 1½ hours, every 10 to 20 minutes
Manchester Airport £24, 1½ hours, three hourly
Sheffield £11, one hour, six hourly
York £7, 25 minutes, at least every 15 minutes

ⓘ Getting Around

Leeds has a compact city centre and it's quicker to walk everywhere than attempt to take a bus. CityBus 70 South Bank (50p flat fare) links the train station with Leeds Dock (for the Royal Armouries), but a nicer way to travel between the two is the free taxi ferry that runs from Granary Wharf, at the train station's southern entrance.

Various WY Metro (www.wymetro.com) Day Rover passes covering trains and/or buses are good for reaching Bradford, Haworth and Hebden Bridge.

Bradford
☎ 01274 / POP 349,561

Their suburbs may have merged into one sprawling urban conurbation, but Bradford remains far removed from its much more glamorous neighbour, Leeds. Thanks to its role as a major player in the wool trade, Bradford attracted large numbers of immigrants from Bangladesh and Pakistan during the 20th century.

Despite occasional racial tensions, these new arrivals have helped reinvigorate the city and give it new energy, plus a reputation for superb curry restaurants – Bradford has been crowned Curry Capital of Britain six times in recent years. But the main reason to visit is still the National Science & Media Museum.

⊙ Sights

National Science & Media Museum
MUSEUM

(www.nationalmediamuseum.org.uk; off Little Horton Lane; ⊙10am-6pm) FREE Bradford's top attraction is housed in an impressive glass-fronted building and chronicles the story of photography, film, TV, radio and the web from 19th-century cameras and early animation to digital technology and the psychology of advertising. International visitors may find themselves a little lost with the British-focused TV exhibits, but there is lots of other hands-on stuff, including a trippy interactive image-and-sound tech gallery and a room crammed with 1980s video games (Pacman! Street Fighter!). There's also an IMAX cinema (www.picturehouses. com; adult/child from £8.50/6).

The museum looks out over City Park, Bradford's award-winning central square, which is home to the Mirror Pool, the country's largest urban water feature.

✖ Eating

Bradford is famous for its curries, so don't miss out on trying one of the city's hundred or so restaurants. A great help is the Bradford Curry Guide (www.visitbradford. com/explore/Bradford_Curry_Guide.aspx), which helps sort the rogan josh from the rubbish nosh.

Kashmir   INDIAN £
(☎ 01274-726513; 27 Morley St; mains £4.50-7; ⓧ 11am-2am Sun-Thu, to 4am Fri & Sat; 🅿) Don't be put off by the dodgy-looking facade: Bradford's oldest curry house has top tucker, served with no frills and no booze (although it is BYO). At quieter times you'll be seated in the windowless basement, with all the character of a 1950s factory canteen, but the food is still excellent. It's just around the corner from the National Science & Media Museum.

Zouk Tea Bar   INDIAN, PAKISTANI ££
(☎ 01274-258025; www.zoukteabar.co.uk; 1312 Leeds Rd; mains £8.50-13; ⓧ noon-midnight; 🛜🅿🕸) This modern and stylish cafe-restaurant staffed by chefs from Lahore offers an upmarket menu and some unusual twists on traditional Indian and Pakistani food, such as delicious schwarma wraps and curried lamb shank slow-cooked in aromatic spices. It's in a Bradford suburb; the 72 bus that runs between Bradford Interchange and Leeds bus station will drop you outside.

❶ Getting There & Away

Bradford is on the Metro train line from Leeds (£4.20, 20 minutes, three to five per hour) and also a stop on the line that links Leeds with Hebden Bridge.

Hebden Bridge
☏ 01422 / POP 4235

Tucked tightly into a fold of a steep-sided valley, Yorkshire's funkiest small town is a former mill centre that refused to go gently with the dying of industry's light. Instead, it

raged a bit and then morphed into an attractive outdoorsy tourist trap with a distinctly bohemian atmosphere. The town is home to university academics, artists, diehard hippies and a substantial gay community. All of this explains the abundance of vintage shops, organic and vegan cafes, and secondhand bookstores. Walking trails leading from the centre of town and up into the hills are another attraction.

◉ Sights & Activities

Gibson Mill   HISTORIC BUILDING
(NT; ☎ 01422-846236; www.nationaltrust.org.uk; parking £5; ⓧ 11am-4pm mid-Mar–Oct, to 3pm Sat & Sun Nov–mid-Mar; 🅿) 🐾 This renovated, sustainably powered 19th-century cotton mill houses a cafe and visitor centre with exhibitions covering the industrial and social history of the mill and its former workers. It is set amid the woods and waterfalls of local beauty spot Hardcastle Crags (open dawn to dusk, admission free), 1.5 miles north of town, reachable via a 45-minute walk from St George's Sq, partly following the river. The route is difficult to find alone; visit www.hbwalkersaction. org.uk for directions.

Hebden Bridge Mill   HISTORIC BUILDING
(www.innovationhebdenbridge.co.uk; St George's Sq; ⓧ hours vary) The spindly chimney of Hebden Bridge's old red-brick mill is a central landmark that predates the town itself, and was saved from demolition in 1974. It is now a home for vintage stores and small studios, anchored by the Innovation Shop & Cafe-Bar on the ground floor, where the mill's working water wheel and Archimedes' screw (water pump) are located. Heritage panels explain the history of the site, which is now run on sustainable water power. Shop opening hours vary; weekends are most reliable.

Heptonstall   VILLAGE
(www.heptonstall.org) Above Hebden Bridge lies the much older village of Heptonstall, its narrow cobbled street lined with 500-year-old cottages and the ruins of a beautiful 13th-century church. But it's the churchyard of the newer St Thomas' Church (1854) that draws literary pilgrims, for here is buried the poet Sylvia Plath (1932–63), whose husband, poet Ted Hughes (1930–98), was born in nearby Mytholmroyd. You'll have to hunt hard to find her grave, in the new cemetery beyond the church's far wall.

YORKSHIRE'S BLACK GOLD

For close to three centuries, West and South Yorkshire were synonymous with coal production. The collieries shaped and scarred the landscape, and entire villages grew up around the pits. The industry came to a shuddering halt in the 1980s, but the imprint of coal is still very much in evidence, even if there's only a handful of collieries left. One of these, the former Caphouse Colliery, is now the **National Coal Mining Museum for England** (www.ncm.org.uk; Overton, near Wakefield; parking £2, tour £4, miniature train return £1.50; ⊙10am-5pm, last tour 3.15pm; P 🚼) FREE.

The highlight of a visit is the underground tour (departing every 10 to 15 minutes): equipped with helmet and head-torch, you descend almost 140m in the 'cage', then follow subterranean passages to the coal seam, where massive drilling machines now stand idle. Former miners work as guides and explain the detail – sometimes with a suitably authentic and almost impenetrable mix of local dialect (known in Yorkshire as 'Tyke') and technical terminology.

The museum is 10 miles south of Leeds on the A642 between Wakefield and Huddersfield, reached via Junction 40 on the M1. By public transport, take a train from Leeds to Wakefield (£3.90, 15 to 30 minutes, three to four hourly), and then bus 232 or 128 towards Huddersfield (£3.10, 25 minutes, hourly).

Hebden Bridge Cruises CRUISE
(☑07966 808717; http://hebdenbridgecruises.com; Stubbing Wharf, King St; per person from £15; ⊙1pm & 2.15pm Sat) Join a colourful canal boat for a guided cruise along the Rochdale Canal with tea and scones or a two-course Sunday roast. Departs from the Stubbing Wharf Pub, half a mile west of the town centre.

🛏 Sleeping

Hebden Bridge Hostel HOSTEL £
(☑07786 987376, 01422-843183; www.hebdenbridgehostel.co.uk; Birchcliffe Centre, Birchcliffe Rd; dm/tw/q £20/55/75; ⊙Easter-early Nov; P🛜) Just 10 minutes' walk uphill from the town centre, this eco-hostel is set in a peaceful stone building, complete with sunny patio, tucked behind a former Baptist chapel. There's a cosy library, comfy and clean en-suite rooms, and a vegetarian-food-only kitchen. A minor inconvenience is that the hostel locks guests out of their rooms from 10.30am to 5pm daily.

★**Thorncliffe B&B** B&B ££
(☑07949 729433, 01422-842163; www.thorncliffe.uk.net; Alexandra Rd; s/d £55/75; 🛜) This delightful Victorian house is perched on the hill above town, and the guest accommodation is perched at the top of the house – a spacious and peaceful attic double with private bathroom and lovely views across the valley, and a 1st-floor en-suite double room, but without the views. A healthy vegetarian continental breakfast is served in your room.

🍴 Eating & Drinking

Mooch CAFE £
(☑01422-846954; https://moochcafebar.wordpress.com; 24 Market St; mains £8-12; ⊙9am-8pm; 🛜) This chilled-out little cafe-bar exemplifies Hebden's alternative atmosphere, with a menu that includes a full-vegan breakfast, brie-and-grape ciabatta, and Mediterranean lunch platters of olives, hummus, stuffed vine leaves, tabouli and more. There's also bottled beers, wine, excellent espresso, and a petite enclosed outdoor terrace through the back.

★**Green's Vegetarian Café** VEGETARIAN ££
(☑01422-843587; www.greensvegetariancafe.co.uk; Old Oxford House, Albert St; mains lunch £5-9, dinner £11.95; ⊙11am-3pm Wed-Sun, 6.30-10pm Fri & Sat; 🍴) One of Yorkshire's best vegetarian restaurants, Green's adopts a gourmet attitude towards veggie and vegan world cuisine, serving dishes such as Sicilian *caponata* (aubergines, red pepper, celery, olives and capers) with spaghetti, and Thai green curry with chickpeas, squash and tofu. Breakfast (11am to noon) includes superb scrambled organic eggs on toasted focaccia. Reservations recommended for dinner.

★**Vocation & Co** CRAFT BEER
(☑01422-844838; www.vocationbrewery.com; 10 New Rd; ⊙4-11pm Mon, noon-11pm Tue-Sun; 🛜) A goldmine for hopheads, the first taproom from local craft brewer Vocation Brewery is housed in an imposing Victorian building

overlooking Hebden Bridge's marina. Inside it's quite a contrast: an ultramodern, minimalist set-up with 20 draft lines including beers from other top northern breweries such as Magic Rock and Cloudwater, plus a delicious taco menu (Tuesday to Sunday).

☆ Entertainment

Trades Club　　　　　　　　LIVE MUSIC
(☎01422-845265; www.thetradesclub.com; Holme St) Built in 1923 as a social club by the local trade unions, this place was revived in the 1980s and has since gone on to become one of the UK's coolest live-music venues, hosting names as big and diverse as the Buzzcocks, Patti Smith, the Fall and George Ezra in recent years, as well as a host of up-and-coming indie talent.

❶ Information

Hebden Bridge Visitor Centre (☎01422-843831; www.hebdenbridge.co.uk; Butlers Wharf, New Rd; ⊙10am-5pm) Has a good stock of maps and leaflets on local walks and bicycle routes.

❶ Getting There & Away

There's only one main road through town and it can become horribly congested on sunny days, so try to arrive by train. Hebden Bridge is on the line from Leeds (£5.80, 50 minutes, every 20 minutes Monday to Saturday, twice hourly on Sunday) to Manchester (£10, 35 minutes, three or four per hour).

Haworth

☑01535 / POP 6380
It seems that only Shakespeare himself is held in higher esteem than the beloved Brontë sisters – Emily, Anne and Charlotte – judging by the thousands of visitors a year who come to pay their respects at Haworth's handsome parsonage where the literary classics *Jane Eyre* and *Wuthering Heights* were penned.

Not surprisingly, the village is the beating heart of a cottage industry that has grown up around Brontë-linked tourism, but even without the literary associations Haworth is worth a visit. Its cobbled heritage high street has become a home for interesting independent vintage, craft and art shops selling work by local Yorkshire artisans, and it's possible to strike out onto the famed Brontë moors right from the parsonage's back door.

◉ Sights

Haworth Parish Church　　　　CHURCH
(www.haworthchurch.co.uk; Church St; ⊙9am-5.30pm Mon-Sat) Your first stop in Haworth should be the parish church, a lovely old place of worship built in the late 19th century on the site of the older church that the Brontë sisters knew, which was demolished in 1879. The Brontë family vault lies beneath a pillar in the southeast corner, and a polished brass plaque on the floor commemorates Charlotte and Emily; Anne is buried at **St Mary's Church** (Castle Rd; ⊙10am-4pm Mon-Fri, 1-4pm Sun May-Sep) FREE in Scarborough.

Brontë Parsonage Museum　　　MUSEUM
(☑01535-642323; www.bronte.org.uk; Church St; adult/child £8.50/4; ⊙10am-5.30pm Apr-Oct, to 5pm Nov-Mar) Set in a pretty garden overlooking Haworth parish church and graveyard, the house where the Brontë family lived from 1820 to 1861 is now a museum. The rooms are meticulously furnished and decorated exactly as they were in the Brontë era, including Charlotte's bedroom, her clothes and her writing paraphernalia. There's also an informative exhibition, which includes the fascinating miniature books the Brontës wrote as children.

**Keighley & Worth
Valley Railway**　　　　HERITAGE RAILWAY
(www.kwvr.co.uk; Station Rd; adult/child return £12/6, Day Rover £18/9) This vintage railway runs steam and classic diesel engines between Keighley and Oxenhope via Haworth. The classic 1970 movie *The Railway Children* was shot along this line: Mr Perks was stationmaster at Oakworth, where the Edwardian look has been meticulously maintained. Trains operate about hourly every day June to August but the timetable is sporadic in other months; check the website. Tickets to view the Haworth platform and incoming trains cost 50p, but you can get a good look from the nearby pedestrian bridge.

🛏 Sleeping

YHA Haworth　　　　　　　HOSTEL £
(☑0845 371 9520; www.yha.org.uk; Longlands Dr; dm/tw £13/29; P🐾📶) In keeping with Haworth's Brontë heritage, the YHA hostel is set in a brooding Victorian Gothic mansion, complete with pool table, lounge, cycle store, laundry and Black Sheep ale for sale. It's on the northeastern edge of town, off Lees Lane, and has a large garden out back.

Apothecary Guest House B&B **£**
(📞 01535-643642; www.theapothecaryguesthouse.
co.uk; 86 Main St; s/d £40/60; 🛜) A quaint and
ancient building at the top end of Main St,
with narrow, slanted passageways that lead
to simple rooms with cheerful modern decor; excellent value.

★ **Old Registry** B&B **££**
(📞 01535-646503; www.theoldregistryhaworth.co.
uk; 2-4 Main St; d £80-135; 🅿 🛜) This place is
a bit special. It's an elegantly rustic guesthouse where each of the carefully themed
rooms has either a four-poster bed, whirl-
pool bath or valley views. The Secret Garden
room has a glorious view across parkland
to the lower village with, if you're lucky, a
steam train chuffing sedately by. Parking is
£3 per night, at nearby Haworth Old Hall.

✗ Eating & Drinking

Cobbles & Clay CAFE **£**
(www.cobblesandclay.co.uk; 60 Main St; mains
£5-8; ⊗ 9am-5pm; 🛜 🖊 🖴) This buzzy,
child-friendly cafe not only offers fair-trade
coffee and healthy salads and snacks – Tuscan bean stew, or hummus with pita bread
and raw veggie sticks – but also provides the
opportunity to indulge in a bit of pottery
painting. Its ploughman's lunch comes with
local Haworth cheese.

Hawthorn BRITISH **££**
(📞 01535-644477; www.thehawthornhaworth.
co.uk; 103-109 Main St; lunch £5.50-11, dinner £13-
20; ⊗ 11am-11pm Wed-Sun) A famed Georgian
clockmaker used to inhabit this building,
which has been given new life as a classy,
candlelit restaurant-bar serving Modern
British dishes such as pea-and-ham soup
with quails egg, Yorkshire Dales lamb, and
North Sea hake with foraged garlic. The
lunch menu is a simpler affair, or come for a
filter coffee and cake, or refreshing glass off
dandelion and burdock.

Haworth Steam Brewery MICROBREWERY
(📞 01535-646059; www.haworthsteambrewery.
co.uk; 98 Main St; ⊗ 11am-11pm Thu-Sat, to 6pm
Sun-Wed) This cosy bar must surely be one
of Britain's smallest microbreweries, serving its own award-winning real ales and
Haworth's Lamplighter gin, plus specials
such as an IPA and gin created for Haworth's
annual steampunk weekend in November.
There's also a good pub grub menu featuring
brewhouse lamb shank, Whitby scampi and
beef brisket sandwiches.

🛍 Shopping

Cabinet of
Curiosities COSMETICS, GIFTS & SOUVENIRS
(https://the-curiosity-society.myshopify.com; 84
Main St; ⊗ 10am-5pm) It was to this apothecary that Branwell Brontë staggered for his
laudanum drug hits in the 1840s, contributing to his untimely death in September
1848. The current owners have restored it to
its Victorian glory and it's now a fancy shop
selling Gothic curios and beautiful bath
products. Well worth a look inside.

ℹ Information

Haworth Tourist Office (📞 01535-642329;
www.visitbradford.com/discover/Haworth.
aspx; 2-4 West Lane; ⊗ 10am-5pm Apr-Sep, to
4pm Oct-Mar) The tourist office has an excellent supply of information on the village, the
surrounding area and, of course, the Brontës.
At the time of writing it was expected to be
taken over by the Brontë Parsonage Museum
and opening hours were in flux; call ahead to
check if you plan to visit.

ℹ Getting There & Away

From Leeds, the easiest approach is via Keighley, which is on the Metro rail network. The B1,
B2 and B3 buses (www.keighleybus.co.uk) run
from Keighley bus station to Haworth (£2.70, 20
minutes, every 20 minutes) and the hourly B3
continues to Hebden Bridge. However, the most
interesting way to get from Keighley to Haworth is
via the Keighley & Worth Valley Railway (p514).

SOUTH YORKSHIRE

What wool was to West Yorkshire, so steel
was to South Yorkshire. A confluence of natural resources – coal, iron ore and ample water – made this part of the country a crucible
of the British iron and steel industries. From
the 18th to the 20th centuries, the region
was the industrial powerhouse of northern
England.

Sheffield's and Rotherham's blast furnaces and the coal pits of Barnsley and
Doncaster may have closed long ago, but
the hulking reminders of that irrepressible
Victorian dynamism remain, not only in the
old steelworks and pit heads (some of which
have been converted into museums and exhibition spaces), but also in the grand civic
buildings that grace Sheffield's city centre,
fitting testaments to the untrammelled am-
bitions of their 19th-century patrons.

WORTH A TRIP

THE AGE OF STEEL

At its peak, the Templeborough steelworks was the world's most productive steel smelter, with six 3000°C furnaces producing 1.8 million tonnes of metal a year, and a 10,000-strong workforce. It has now been reborn as **Magna** (☑ 01709-720002; www.visit magna.co.uk; Sheffield Rd, Templeborough, Rotherham; adult/child £11.95/9.95; ⊘ 10am-5pm, last entry 4pm; ℗ ♿), an unashamed celebration of heavy industry, and a hands-on paradise for kids of all ages. Displays are based on the themes of earth, air, water and fire. The latter section is especially impressive, with a towering tornado of flame as a centrepiece and the chance to use a real electric arc to create your own tiny puddle of molten steel (if only for a moment or two). The hourly 'Big Melt' – a massive sound, light and fireworks show – memorably reenacts the firing up of one of the original arc furnaces.

Magna is 4 miles northeast of Sheffield, just off the M1 near Rotherham; phone before visiting as it closes at 2pm some days.

Sheffield

☑ 0114 / POP 518,090

The steel industry that made Sheffield famous is long gone, but after many years of decline this industrious city is on the up again – like many of northern England's cities, it has grabbed the opportunities presented by urban renewal with both hands and, shored up by a thriving student population, is working hard to reinvent itself.

Some of its old foundries, mills and forges are now interesting museums celebrating South Yorkshire's industrial heyday, and Kelham Island in particular is in the throes of a fascinating redevelopment. Sheffield isn't likely to win any prizes for its looks anytime soon, but its history is interesting enough to warrant a day or two's exploration.

⊙ Sights

★ **Kelham Island Museum**   MUSEUM
(www.simt.co.uk; Alma St; adult/child £6/free; ⊘ 10am-4pm Mon-Thu, 11am-4.45pm Sun; ℗ ♿) Sheffield's prodigious industrial heritage is the subject of this excellent museum, set on a human-made island in the city's oldest industrial district. Exhibits cover all aspects of industry, from steel-making to knife-sharpening. The most impressive display is the thundering 12,000-horsepower River Don steam engine (the size of a house), which gets powered up twice a day, at noon and 2pm. The museum is 800m north of the city centre; take the tram (£1.70) from Sheffield train station to the Shalesmoor stop.

Winter Gardens   GARDENS
(Surrey St; ⊘ 8am-8pm Mon-Sat, to 6pm Sun) Pride of place in Sheffield's city centre goes to this wonderfully ambitious public space with a soaring glass roof supported by graceful arches of laminated timber. The 21st-century architecture contrasts sharply with the nearby Victorian **town hall** and the **Peace Gardens** – complete with fountains, sculptures, and lawns full of lunching office workers.

Millennium Gallery   GALLERY
(www.museums-sheffield.org.uk; Arundel Gate; ⊘ 10am-5pm Mon-Sat, 11am-4pm Sun) FREE Sheffield's cultural revival is embodied in this collection of four galleries under one roof. Inside, the **Ruskin Collection** houses an eclectic display of paintings, manuscripts and interesting objects established and inspired by Victorian artist, writer, critic and philosopher John Ruskin, who saw Sheffield as the embodiment of Britain's industrial age. The **Sykes Gallery Metalwork Collection** charts the transformation of Sheffield's steel industry into craft and design, with 13,000 glinting objects – the 'Sheffield steel' stamp now has the cachet of designer chic.

Graves Gallery   GALLERY
(www.museums-sheffield.org.uk; Surrey St; ⊘ 11am-4pm Tue-Sat) FREE This gallery has a neat and accessible display of British and European art from the 16th century to the present day, plus touring exhibitions; the big names represented include Turner, Sisley, Cézanne, Gaugin, Miró, Klee, LS Lowry and Damien Hirst.

Abbeydale Industrial Hamlet   MUSEUM
(www.simt.co.uk; Abbeydale Rd S; adult/child £4/free; ⊘ 10am-4pm Mon-Thu & Sat, 11am-4.45pm Sun; ℗ ♿) In the days before steel mills, metalworking was carried out in hamlet communities like Abbeydale, situated by riv-

ers and dams that were harnessed for water power. This industrial museum, now swallowed up by Sheffield's suburban sprawl, gives an excellent run-down of that innocent era, with restored 18th-century forges, workshops and machinery including the original, working water wheel. It's 4 miles southwest of the centre on the A621 (towards the Peak District).

🛏 Sleeping

Leopold Hotel   BOUTIQUE HOTEL ££
(☎0114-252 4000; www.leopoldhotels.com; 2 Leopold St; r £70-160, ste £90-200; 🖰) Housed in a Grade II–listed former grammar-school building, Sheffield's first boutique hotel offers style and sophistication at a reasonable rate. Rooms can suffer late-night noise from the bars on Leopold Sq – ask for a quiet room at the back.

Houseboat Hotels   HOUSEBOAT ££
(☎07776   144693;   www.houseboathotels. com; Victoria Quays, Wharfe St; s/d/tr/q £85/110/145/170; 🅿) Here's something a bit different: kick off your shoes and relax on board your very own permanently moored houseboat, complete with self-catering kitchen and patio area.

✕ Eating

Street Food Chef   MEXICAN £
(☎0114-275 2390; www.streetfoodchef.co.uk; 90 Arundel St; mains £3-6; ⊙8am-10pm Mon-Sat, 10am-9pm Sun) Local students flock to this down-to-earth, healthy Mexican canteen, which started life as a street-food truck and now has several outlets in Sheffield. It focuses on freshly prepared, great-value burritos, tacos and quesadillas, available to sit in or take away. Look for its brekky and lunch deals, and gluten- or dairy-free options.

Blue Moon Cafe   VEGETARIAN £
(www.bluemooncafesheffield.com; 2 St James St; mains £7.70; ⊙8am-8pm Mon-Sat; 🖉) A Sheffield institution offering tasty veggie and vegan creations, breakfasts till 11am and a rotation of single-price mains with a side of rice. It's famed for the magnificent heritage room within which it sits, with high blue ceilings and an atrium glass roof – perfect for a spot of Saturday afternoon lounging.

Marmaduke's   CAFE £
(www.marmaduke scafedeli.co.uk; 22a Norfolk Row; mains £6-12; ⊙9am-5pm Mon-Sat, 10am-4pm Sun; 🖰🖉) 🖉 This appealingly cramped and chaotic cafe, crammed with recycled furniture and fittings, and run by a young and enthusiastic crew, serves an all-day breakfast menu that highlights local and organic produce, and lunch dishes that range from deli sandwiches and quiches to vegetarian specials such as the halloumi and herb burger.

Vero Gusto   ITALIAN ££
(☎0114-276 0004; www.verogusto.com; 12 Norfolk Row; lunch mains £9-26, dinner £15-30; ⊙11am-11pm Tue-Sat; 🖰) Gusto is a *real* Italian restaurant, from the Italian waistcoated servers dishing out homemade Italian food to the genuine Italian coffee enjoyed by Italian customers reading Italian newspapers...you get the idea. Pizza is on the menu at lunchtimes, coffee and home-baked Italian cakes and pastries are served in the afternoon, and the dinner menu focuses on exquisite Italian cuisine. Book for dinner.

🍷 Drinking & Nightlife

Fat Cat   PUB
(☎0114-249 4801; www.thefatcat.co.uk; 23 Alma St; ⊙noon-11pm Sun-Thu, to midnight Fri & Sat) This old-fashioned independent boozer is in a handy spot around the corner from Kelham Island Museum and serves Kelham Island Brewery beers and ales made in the building next door, along with pork pies (£1.50) and pub grub. Its fans are an eclectic mix of students and local fixtures.

Sheffield Tap   CRAFT BEER
(☎0114-273 7558; www.sheffieldtap.com; Sheffield Train Station; ⊙11am-11pm Sun-Thu, 10am-midnight Fri & Sat; 🖰) This lovingly restored Edwardian railway bar is a reliable stalwart for Sheffield beer drinkers. It has several bar areas, and the aroma of hops and malts gets stronger as you approach the far room where the bar produces its own Two Tapped Brew Co beers, with working brewery kit towering above drinking tables. Dozens of other local and international beers are sold here, too.

☆ Entertainment

Showroom   CINEMA
(☎0114-275 7727; www.showroomworkstation.org. uk; 15 Paternoster Row) This is the largest independent cinema in England, set in a grand art-deco complex and screening a great mix of art-house, offbeat and not-quite-mainstream films.

Leadmill LIVE MUSIC
(☑0114-272 7040; www.leadmill.co.uk; 6 Leadmill Rd) Every touring band has played the dark and dingy Leadmill on the way up (or on the way down), and it remains the best place in town to hear live rock and alternative music. There are club nights too, but they tend to play cheesy 1970s and '80s disco classics.

ⓘ Information

Sheffield's tourist information office closed in 2017, but www.welcometosheffield.co.uk is a good source of information on the city.

ⓘ Getting There & Away

For all travel-related info for Sheffield and South Yorkshire, contact **Travel South Yorkshire** (☑01709-515151; www.travelsouthyorkshire. com).

BUS

The bus station, called the Interchange, is just east of the centre, about 250m north of the train station. National Express coaches run from here to London (from £5, 4½ hours, eight daily).

TRAIN

Prices can double on the day of travel; book ahead.
Leeds From £6, one hour, two to five hourly
London St Pancras From £62, 2¼ hours, at least hourly
Manchester From £8, one hour, twice hourly
York From £11, 1¼ hours, twice hourly

EAST RIDING OF YORKSHIRE

The rolling farmland of the East Riding of Yorkshire meets the sea at Hull, a no-nonsense port that looks to the broad horizons of the Humber estuary and the North Sea for its livelihood. Just to its north, and in complete contrast to Hull's salt and grit, is Beverley, the East Riding's most attractive town, with lots of Georgian character and one of England's finest churches.

Hull

☑01482 / POP 284,321
Properly known as Kingston-upon-Hull (the ancient harbour on the River Hull was granted a royal charter in 1299 and became King's Town), Hull has long been the principal port of England's east coast, with an economy that grew up around wool, wine trading, whaling and fishing.

Its designation as UK City of Culture in 2017 has given the town a massive confidence boost, and redevelopment of its waterfront and Old Town has sparked a minor cultural flowering, particularly in the Fruit Market district around Humber St, where derelict buildings have been reclaimed as artists' studios and cool cafes and bars have flourished. Watch out: Hull is getting hip.

Though its modern centre isn't going to win prizes for prettiness, Hull's old cobbled Georgian enclave is an under-the-radar delight. Other attractions include fascinating museums, Philip Larkin heritage (the poet lived here) and an excellent aquarium – finally, the city is emerging as a great-value tourist destination.

◉ Sights

★**The Deep** AQUARIUM
(☑01482-381000; www.thedeep.co.uk; Tower St; adult/child £13.50/11.50; ⊙10am-6pm, last entry 5pm; Ⓟ♿) Hull's biggest tourist attraction is The Deep, Britain's most spectacular aquarium, housed in a colossal angular building that appears to lunge above the muddy waters of the Humber like a giant shark's head. Inside, it's just as dramatic, with echoing commentaries and computer-generated interactive displays that guide you through the formation of the oceans, the evolution of sea life, and global conservation issues.

The largest aquarium tank is 10m deep, filled with sharks, stingrays and colourful coral fishes, with moray eels draped over rocks like scarves of iridescent slime. A glass elevator plies up and down inside the tank, though you'll get a better view by taking the stairs. Don't miss the cafe on the top floor, which has a great view of the Humber estuary.

★**Old Town** AREA
Hull's Old Town is where a grand minster and cobbled streets flush with Georgian town houses give a flashback to the prosperity the town once knew. It occupies the thumb of land between the River Hull to the east and Princes Quay to the west. Recent regeneration efforts have brought back to life the dockside **Fruit Market**, where vintage shops, art studios and independent bars and cafes are flourishing along Humber St; and the Old Town's indoor **Trinity Market**, now

housing street-food vendors like Shoot the Bull.

⭐ **Wilberforce House** MUSEUM
(www.hullcc.gov.uk/museums; High St; ⊙10am-5pm Mon-Sat, 11am-4.30pm Sun) FREE The wealth that Britain amassed as the world's first industrial nation was directly aided by the transatlantic slave trade, and this important museum ensures that the facts are told, detailing the part that Britain played in bringing millions of Africans to Europe between the 17th and 19th centuries. Wilberforce House (1639) was the birthplace in 1759 of politician and antislavery crusader William Wilberforce, whose campaigning efforts eventually led to the abolition of slavery in England in 1833.

Humber St Gallery GALLERY
(www.humberstreetgallery.co.uk; 64 Humber St; ⊙10am-6pm Tue-Sun, to 8pm 1st Thu of month) FREE This slick three-storey contemporary gallery in a former banana-ripening warehouse anchors Hull's revamped Fruit Market. Rotating exhibitions celebrate international and local visual art, design, photography and film, but a permanent feature is a beloved piece of 1960s graffiti by Len 'Pongo' Rood saved from demolition by local campaigners. Behold *Dead Bod* – a rusty shed wall from Hull's docks that would have once signified home for returning sailors. The site was demolished in 2015, but *Dead Bod* lives on in Humber St Gallery's cafe.

Ferens Art Gallery GALLERY
(☑01482-300300; www.hullcc.gov.uk/ferens; Queen Victoria Sq; ⊙10am-5pm Mon-Sat, 1.30-4.30pm Sun; ♿) FREE Following extensive renovations, the Ferens Art Gallery reopened in 2017 as part of Hull's City of Culture celebrations. The permanent art collection ranges from old masters like Frans Hals to modern works by Lucian Freud, Peter Nash, Peter Blake, David Hockney and Gillian Wearing.

Humber Bridge BRIDGE
(www.humberbridge.co.uk; P) Opened in 1981, the Humber Bridge swoops gracefully across the broad estuary of the River Humber. Its 1410m span made it the world's longest single-span suspension bridge – until 1998 when it lost the title to Japan's Akashi Kaikyo bridge, but it is still a Grade I–listed structure. The best way to appreciate the scale of the bridge, and the vastness of the estuary, is to walk or cycle out along the footway from the Humber Bridge tourist office at its north end on Ferriby Rd.

The bridge is a mile west of the small riverside town of Hessle, about 4 miles west of Hull. It links Yorkshire to Lincolnshire along the A15, opening up what was once an often-overlooked corner of the country.

Bus 350 runs from Hull Paragon Interchange to Ferriby Rd in Hessle (25 minutes, every 30 minutes), from where it's a 300m walk to the tourist office.

Maritime Museum MUSEUM
(☑01482-300300; www.hcandl.co.uk; Queen Victoria Sq; ⊙10am-5pm Mon-Sat, 11am-4.30pm Sun; ♿) FREE In the early 19th century Hull had the largest whaling fleet in Britain, providing the whale oil that greased the wheels of the country's industrial revolution. This interesting museum is stuffed to the gills with seafaring artefacts from that period, including harpoons, replica boats, a whale skeleton and crow's nest (invented in Yorkshire), as well as an extensive scrimshaw collection.

Hull Pier Toilets HISTORIC BUILDING
(Nelson St) There are not too many places where a public toilet counts as a tourist attraction, but coach parties regularly stop to take photos of these Edwardian lavatories. The building is interesting but inside they're not very special. Serviceable, but no tourist attraction, that's for sure.

🛏 Sleeping

Hull Trinity Backpackers HOSTEL £
(☑01482-223229; www.hulltrinitybackpackers.com; 51-52 Market Pl; dm/s/tw from £19/30/39; 🛜) This centrally located hostel with simple rooms is just the ticket for a cheap sleep in Hull. It's clean and friendly, and the owner is passionate about showing off the city's best sides. There's a lovingly designed common area, free laundry, fluffy bedding and bike storage. Plus handy USB and plug sockets by each bed.

Garden Mews B&B £
(☑01482-215574; http://the-garden-mews-gb.book.direct; 13-14 John St; s/d/f £40/65/90, with shared bath £30/55/80; 🛜) This cheap and homely B&B is on the edge of leafy Kingston Sq, close to the New Theatre yet a bit of a hike from Hull's charming Old Town and Fruit Market. The rooms are comfortable but nothing fancy; breakfast costs an extra £5 per person.

★**Hideout** APARTMENT ££

(☑ 01482-212222; www.hideouthotel.co.uk; North Church Side; d from £90, 1-bed apt £110-130, 2-bed apt from £130; P 🛜) These luxury serviced apartments show just how far Hull has come since its City of Culture year. Slick and contemporary, it's the type of place where staff put retro radio on for you before check-in, and leave an easel in the living room for spontaneous creative scribbles. It's also incredibly central, in the shadow of the Old Town's minster.

✗ Eating

★**Thieving Harry's** CAFE £

(www.thievingharrys.co.uk; 73 Humber St; mains £6-8.50; ⊙ kitchen 10am-4pm Mon-Fri, 9am-4pm Sat, 9am-6pm Sun; 🗷) Thieving Harry's has all the trappings of a favourite local cafe: friendly faces, a breezy casual vibe, strong coffee and generous brunches, all wrapped up in a comfy warehouse conversion with mismatched retro furniture and lovely marina views of bobbing boats. The menu is interesting, with excellent dishes like fried eggs with chorizo, sourdough and coriander sourcream, plus good veggie options.

Hull Pie PIES £

(☑ 01482-345735; www.thehullpie.co.uk; 202 Newland Ave; mains £3.50-6.50; ⊙ 11am-9pm) 🍴 This famous takeaway offers award-winning freshly baked pies with a range of delicious fillings, from caramelised beer and beef brisket, to chicken, ham and mushroom with white wine and thyme, served with gravy and a choice of sides that include mushy peas, glazed carrots and chips. Look out for pop-up stalls in the city centre and at farmers markets.

★**The Old House** BRITISH ££

(☑ 01482-210253; www.shootthebull.co.uk/the-old-house; 5 Scale Lane; mains £13-24; ⊙ 4.30-9.30pm Mon, noon-9.30pm Tue-Sun) Once an old pub, now the base of Hull street-food brand Shoot the Bull, this lovely restaurant does refined comfort food exceptionally well. Locally sourced meat and fish might translate into blow-torched mackerel followed by a rare-breed beef pie with smoked eel mash and parsley sauce. Its signature dish is on the street-food menu: a butter-lathered, rare-breed flat-iron steak sandwich in a posh bun.

A second outlet focusing solely on street food is inside Trinity Market in the Old Town.

Hitchcock's Vegetarian Restaurant VEGETARIAN ££

(☑ 01482-320233; www.hitchcocksrestaurant.co. uk; 1 Bishop Lane, High St; per person £20; ⊙ 8-10.30pm Tue-Sat; 🗷🦽) The word 'quirky' could have been invented to describe this place. It's an atmospheric maze of small rooms, with an all-you-can-eat vegetarian buffet whose theme – Mexican, Indian, Caribbean, whatever – is chosen by the first person to book that evening. But the food is excellent and the welcome is warm. Bookings necessary. There's one sitting; arrive between 8pm and 9pm.

Bait SEAFOOD ££

(☑ 01482-343088; www.baithull.co.uk; 13-15 Princes Ave; mains £12-21; ⊙ noon-2.30pm & 5-9pm Tue-Thu, noon-9pm Fri & Sat, to 9.30pm Sun) 🍴 Hull's seafaring tradition is reflected in a menu dominated by the best of British seafood, including Lindisfarne oysters au naturel and Whitby lobster bisque, but also an unexpected array of Asian-influenced dishes such as fresh sushi and nigiri. There are meat and vegetarian dishes too, and a three-course £34 midweek menu Tuesday to Thursday and on Sunday.

🍷 Drinking & Entertainment

★**Olde Black Boy** PUB

(☑ 01482-215040; 150 High St; ⊙ 5-11.30pm Mon & Tue, noon-11.30pm Wed-Sun) A favourite watering hole of poet Philip Larkin, Hull's oldest pub has been serving ale since 1729. Oak floors and roof beams, dark-wood panelling and a snug log fire in winter make for a great atmosphere, and there's live folk music on Wednesday afternoons.

Humber St Distillery COCKTAIL BAR

(☑ 01482-219886; www.hsdc.co.uk; 18 Humber St; ⊙ noon-11pm Tue-Sun) This ambitious, gin-obsessed cocktail bar in the heart of Hull's Fruit Market area has dark-wood bar panelling offset by exposed-brick walls. The gin menu is a tome of around 150 world gins, including many local and limited-edition releases; you can take a gin flight (weeknights only); and the bar has even started producing its own gin.

Minerva PUB

(www.minerva-hull.co.uk; Nelson St; ⊙ 11.30am-11pm Mon-Sat, noon-11pm Sun; 🦽) If you're more into pubbing than clubbing, try a pint of Black Sheep at this lovely 200-year-old pub down by the waterfront. On a sunny day you can sit outdoors and watch the ships go by, while tucking into a plate of fish and chips (£9.50). A unique feature is its real-ale and gin flights.

Früit LIVE MUSIC, COMEDY
(☑ 01482-221113; www.fruitspace.co.uk; 62-63 Humber St; ☎) A focus for the cultural revival of Hull's Fruit Market district, this former industrial space is now a multipurpose venue incorporating a bar, cinema and stage. There are regular live gigs by local bands (and occasional big names), a monthly comedy club and, on the third Sunday of the month, the Humber Street Market.

ℹ Information

Hull Tourist Office (☑ 01482-300306; www.visithullandeastyorkshire.com; Paragon Interchange, Ferensway; ⊘8am-6.30pm Mon-Fri, from 9am Sat, 10am-5pm Sun) Inside Hull's Paragon Interchange, at the train station.

ℹ Getting There & Away

BOAT

The ferry port is 3 miles east of the centre at King George Dock; a bus connects the train station with the ferries. There are ferry services to Zeebrugge (Belgium) and Rotterdam (Netherlands).

BUS

Intercity buses depart from Hull Paragon Interchange. Mega Bus (https://uk.megabus.com) runs cheap buses to London. The X62 is a direct link to Leeds. During the summer months the X21 runs direct to Scarborough, but at other times of year you'll need to change at Bridlington. The X46/47 to York runs via Beverley.

London £10, 4½ hours, four daily
Leeds £8, two hours, three daily
York £7.70, 1¾ hours, hourly

TRAIN

The train station is part of Hull Paragon Interchange, an integrated rail and bus station.

Leeds £13, one hour, hourly
London King's Cross £85, 2¾ hours, every two hours
York £20, 1¼ hours, hourly

Beverley

☑ 01482 / POP 10,109

Handsome Beverley is one of the most attractive towns in Yorkshire, largely due to its magnificent minster – a rival to any cathedral in England – and the tangle of streets that lie beneath it, each brimming with Georgian and Victorian buildings.

All the sights are a short walk from either the train or bus station. There's a large market on Saturdays in the square called Saturday Market, and a smaller one on Wednesdays in the square called…Wednesday Market.

◉ Sights

Beverley Minster CHURCH
(www.beverleyminster.org; St John St; 1hr roof tour adult/child £10/5; ⊘9am-5.30pm Mon-Sat, noon-5pm Sun Apr-Oct, to 4pm Nov-Mar) **FREE** One of the great glories of English religious architecture, Beverley Minster is the most impressive church in the country that is not a cathedral. The soaring lines of the exterior are imposing, but it is inside that the charm and beauty lie. The 14th-century north aisle is lined with original stone carvings, mostly of musicians; much of our knowledge of early musical instruments comes from these images. You'll also see goblins, devils and grotesque figures. Look out for the bagpipe player.

Construction began in 1220 – this was the third church to be built on this site, with the first dating from the 7th century – and continued for two centuries, spanning the Early English, Decorated and Perpendicular periods of the Gothic style.

Close to the altar, the elaborate and intricate **Percy Canopy** (1340), a decorative frill above the tomb of local aristocrat Lady Eleanor Percy, is a testament to the skill of the sculptor and the finest example of Gothic stone carving in England. In complete contrast, in the nearby chancel is the 10th-century Saxon **frith stool**, a plain and polished stone chair that once gave sanctuary to anyone escaping the law.

In the roof of the tower is a restored treadwheel crane, where workers ground around like hapless hamsters to lift the huge loads necessary to build a medieval church. Access to the roof is by guided tours held on Saturdays at 11am.

Beverley Westwood PARK
(Walkington Rd) The western edge of Beverley is bounded by this large area of common pasture studded with mature trees, which has been used as grazing for local livestock for centuries. The land, owned 'in common' by the community since 1380, is overseen by the Pasture Masters, a group of men elected from the Freemen of Beverley each March. Contented cows amble across the unfenced

road, while walkers stroll and enjoy the gorgeous views of Beverley Minster.

🛏 Sleeping & Eating

★ YHA Beverley Friary   HOSTEL £

(☎ 0345 371 9004; www.yha.org.uk; Friar's Lane; dm/d from £15/49; ⊘ May-Dec; P 🛜) In Beverley, the cheapest accommodation also has the best setting and location. This hostel is housed in a beautifully restored 14th-century Dominican friary mentioned in Chaucer's *The Canterbury Tales,* and is only 100m from the minster and a short walk from the train station. Rooms sleep two to eight and some are en suite.

Kings Head   INN ££

(☎ 01482-868103; www.kingsheadpubbeverley. com; 38 Saturday Market; r from £90; P 🛜) A Georgian coaching inn given a modern makeover, the Kings Head is a lively pub with 10 bright and stylish rooms above the bar. The pub opens late on weekend nights, but earplugs are supplied for those who don't want to join the revelry!

Vanessa Delicafe   CAFE £

(☎ 01482-868190; www.vanessadelicafe.co.uk; 21-22 Saturday Market; mains £4.50-10; ⊘ 9am-4.30pm Mon-Sat, 10am-3.30pm Sun; 🛜 👪) This popular cafe sits above a delicatessen, with sofas and bookshelves scattered among the tables, and window seats overlooking the market square. Settle down for cappuccino and cake with the Sunday papers, or tuck into hearty lunch specials such as venison burger or a Yorkshire platter of pork pie, roast ham, cheese and chutney.

★ Pipe and Glass Inn   GASTROPUB £££

(☎ 01430-810246; www.pipeandglass.co.uk; West End, South Dalton; mains £11-30; ⊘ noon-2pm & 6-9.30pm Tue-Sat, noon-4pm Sun; P 🛜 👪) 🍴 Set in a picturesque hamlet 4 miles northwest of Beverley, this charming Michelin-starred country pub has a delightfully

informal setting, with weathered timber tables, stone hearths and leather sofas. Yet a great deal of care is lavished on the food – even seemingly simple dishes such as fish pie are unforgettable. After your meal, you can tour its herb gardens.

If you want to stay the night, there are five luxurious bedrooms to choose from (£200 to £245 per night, including breakfast), but the waiting list for a weekend night is several months long; weeknights can be booked about two months in advance.

🍷 Drinking & Nightlife

Cockpit Cafe   CAFE

(☎ 07421 225900; www.thecockpitcafe.com; 8 Wednesday Market; ⊘ 10am-4.30pm Tue-Thu & Sun, 10am-midnight Fri & Sat; 🛜 👪) What fun: preening itself on one of Beverley's Georgian market squares, this glamorous retro cafe is a throwback to the golden age of air travel with servers dressed in 1940s airline uniforms, furniture fashioned from old suitcases and nostalgic wartime ditties as background music. The drinks list includes Fentimans tonics, dandelion and burdock, coffees and cocktails, and there's a small food menu.

ℹ Information

Beverley Tourist Office (☎ 01482-391672; www.visithullandeastyorkshire.com/beverley; Treasure House, Champney Rd; ⊘ 9.30am-5pm Mon, Wed & Fri, to 8pm Tue & Thu, 9am-4pm Sat) Beverley Tourist Office lives inside Treasure House, also home to the town's art gallery, next to the library.

ℹ Getting There & Away

There are frequent bus services from Hull, including numbers 121, 122, 246 and X46/X47 (£4.60, 30 minutes, hourly). Bus X46/X47 links Beverley with York (£7.20, 1¼ hours, hourly).

Trains run regularly to Scarborough (£14, 1¼ hours, every one to two hours) and Hull (£7, 15 minutes, twice hourly).

Manchester, Liverpool & Northwest England

Best Places to Eat

➡ 20 Stories (p534)

➡ Freemasons at Wiswell (p553)

➡ Northcote Hotel (p554)

➡ Mackie Mayor (p534)

➡ Restaurant Fraiche (p548)

Best Places to Stay

➡ Inn at Whitewell (p554)

➡ 2 Blackburne Terrace (p547)

➡ King Street Townhouse (p533)

➡ Edgar House (p539)

➡ Saba's Glen Yurt (p556)

Why Go?

Two cities brimming with history, a Tudor delight, an island that marches to the beat of its own drum and some of the most pleasant countryside in Britain...welcome to the northwest of England. Dominating the region is mighty Manchester, a city built on innovation and bursting with creativity. Just across the Pennines is perennial rival Liverpool, fiercely proud of its own heritage and well able to hold its own against its neighbour in all matters, from food to football. Between them is Chester, a Tudor gift enveloped by Roman walls. But the northwest is more than just mankind's concrete footprint: you don't have to go far to find yourself surrounded by the bucolic charms of northern Lancashire, while offshore is the Isle of Man, so pretty that Unesco gave the whole place Biosphere Reserve status.

When to Go

➡ The world's most famous steeplechase – the Aintree Grand National – is run just outside Liverpool over the first weekend in April.

➡ May and June are Tourist Trophy (TT) Festival season on the Isle of Man – beloved of motor enthusiasts the world over.

➡ In the arts, the highlight is the Manchester International Festival, a biennial showstopper held in July.

➡ Music buffs should visit Liverpool in the last week of August for madness at Creamfields dance-fest and for the Mathew St Festival, an ode to all things Beatles.

➡ The football (soccer) season runs from late August until May.

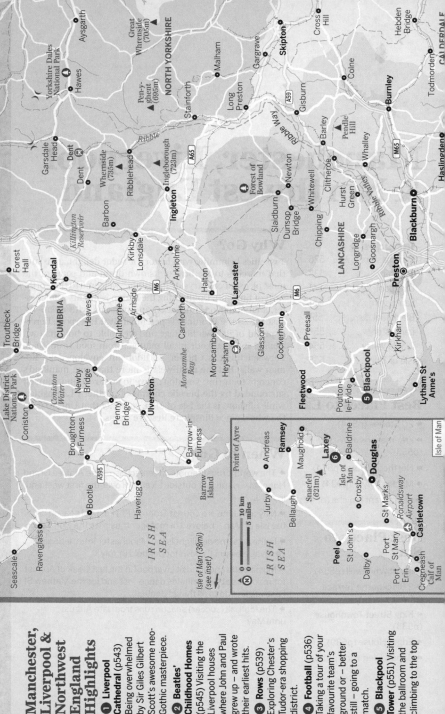

Manchester, Liverpool & Northwest England Highlights

❶ Liverpool Cathedral (p543) Being overwhelmed by Sir Giles Gilbert Scott's awesome neo-Gothic masterpiece.

❷ Beatles' Childhood Homes (p545) Visiting the Liverpool houses where John and Paul grew up – and wrote their earliest hits.

❸ Rows (p539) Exploring Chester's Tudor-era shopping district.

❹ Football (p536) Taking a tour of your favourite team's ground or – better still – going to a match.

❺ Blackpool Tower (p551) Visiting the ballroom and climbing to the top of Blackpool's iconic structure.

❻ Great Laxey Wheel (p557) Visiting the world's largest working waterwheel.

❼ People's History Museum (p527) Learning about social justice in Manchester.

❽ Philharmonic (p549) Enjoying a drink in this Liverpool pub, one of Britain's most beautiful.

ℹ Information

Visit North West (www.visitnorthwest.com) is the centralised tourist authority, but all cities and most towns have their own dedicated tourist authorities; for the Isle of Man check out **Isle of Man** (www.visitisleofman.com).

ℹ Getting There & Away

Both Manchester and Liverpool have international airports and are well served by trains from all over the UK, including London, only two hours away. The West Coast Line serves Preston, Lancaster and Blackpool. For Lancashire's smaller towns, there's an extensive bus service. The Isle of Man is accessible by ferry from Liverpool and Heysham, and there are regular flights from throughout the UK.

ℹ Getting Around

The towns and cities covered are all within easy reach of each other, and are well linked by public transport. The two main cities, Manchester and Liverpool, are only 34 miles apart and are linked by hourly bus and train services. Chester is 18 miles south of Liverpool, but is also easily accessible from Manchester by train or via the M56. Blackpool is 50 miles to the north of Manchester and Liverpool, and is also well connected on the M6.

MANCHESTER

☑ 0161 / POP 535,475

'This is Manchester, we do things differently here', declared culture catalyst and Factory Records founder Tony Wilson in 1977. It was a ballsy statement, given that Manchester's musical renaissance hadn't yet happened, the football teams were mediocre and the city was mired in economic depression.

But bold statements and ironclad self-confidence have long been a thing in Manchester, the one-time engine room of the Industrial Revolution and a city that incubated communism, suffragism, vegetarianism and a bunch of other 'isms' aimed at improving humanity's lot. In the 21st century, invention, discovery and progress remain the driving forces of this remarkable place, which responded to a terrible act of terrorism in 2017 by doubling down on the tolerant and inclusive attitudes toward all those who've made it home.

For Mancunians born or based here, it is the best home in the world; for everyone else, it's a brilliant place to visit.

History

Canals and steam-powered cotton mills were what transformed Manchester from a small, disease-infested provincial town into a big, disease-infested industrial city. It all happened in the 1760s, with the opening of the Bridgewater Canal between Manchester and the coal mines at Worsley in 1763, and with Richard Arkwright patenting his super cotton mill in 1769. Thereafter Manchester and the world would never be the same again. When the canal was extended to Liverpool and the open sea in 1776, Manchester – dubbed 'Cottonopolis' – kicked into high gear and took off on the coal-fuelled, steam-powered gravy train.

MANCHESTER IN ONE DAY

Start your exploration in the light-filled galleries of the **Manchester Art Gallery**, home to one of the most important collections in the north. The **Museum of Science & Industry** will take up at least a couple of hours – more if you've got kids or you're a science geek. Alternatively, the **People's History Museum** is a fascinating exploration of social history. Lunch on Chinese food at **Tattu** (☑ 0161-819 2060; www.tattu.co.uk; Gartside St, 3 Hardman Sq, Spinningfields; mains £14-27; ⊙ noon-3pm & 5-10.45pm Mon-Thu, noon-10.45pm Fri-Sun; ☑ all city centre) or take your pick at **Mackie Mayor** (p534).

Hop on the tram to Salford Quays, where you can explore the **Imperial War Museum North** (p530) or take a guided tour of the northern headquarters of the **BBC** (p531); fans of Manchester United should take the tour of **Old Trafford** (p536), where they'll get to stand in the tunnel and pretend they're players. Make dinner reservations (well in advance) for **20 Stories** (p534).

After dinner, there's drinks at the **Refuge** (p535), a choice of bars in the Northern Quarter, or even a concert at the **Bridgewater Hall** (☑ 0161-907 9000; www.bridgewater-hall.co.uk; Lower Mosley St; ☑ Deansgate-Castlefield). Alternatively, you can always head south towards Castlefield and take in a film or a play at the superb **HOME** (p536) arts centre.

There was plenty of gravy to go around, but the good burghers of 19th-century Manchester made sure that the vast majority of the city's swollen citizenry (with a population of 90,000 in 1801, and two million 100 years later) never got their hands on any of it despite producing most of it. Their reward was life in a new kind of urban settlement: the industrial slum. Working conditions were dire, with impossibly long hours, child labour, work-related accidents and fatalities all commonplace. Mark Twain commented that he would like to live here because the 'transition between Manchester and Death would be unnoticeable'. So much for Victorian values.

The wheels started to come off towards the end of the 19th century. The USA had begun to flex its own industrial muscles and was taking over a sizeable chunk of the textile trade; production in Manchester's mills began to slow, and then it stopped altogether. By WWII there was hardly enough cotton produced in the city to make a tablecloth. The postwar years weren't much better: 150,000 manufacturing jobs were lost between 1961 and 1983, and the port – still the UK's third largest in 1963 – finally closed in 1982 due to declining traffic.

Things got worse for Manchester on 15 June 1996, when an IRA bomb wrecked a chunk of the city centre, but the subsequent reconstruction proved to be the beginning of the glass-and-chrome revolution so much in evidence today.

◉ Sights

◉ City Centre

★**People's History Museum** MUSEUM
(☑0161-838 9190; www.phm.org.uk; Left Bank, Bridge St; ⊙10am-5pm) FREE The story of Britain's 200-year march to democracy is told in all its pain and pathos at this superb museum, housed in a refurbished Edwardian pumping station. You clock in on the 1st floor (literally: punch your card in an old mill clock, which managers would infamously fiddle with so as to make employees work longer) and plunge into the heart of Britain's struggle for basic democratic rights, labour reform and fair pay.

Amid displays like the (tiny) desk at which Thomas Paine (1737–1809) wrote *Rights of Man* (1791), and an array of beautifully made and colourful union banners, are

compelling interactive displays, including a screen where you can trace the effects of all the events covered in the museum on five generations of the same family. The 2nd floor takes up the struggle for equal rights from WWII to the current day, touching on gay rights, anti-racism initiatives and the defining British sociopolitical landmarks of the last 50 years, including the founding of the National Health Service (NHS), the Miners' Strike and the widespread protests against the Poll Tax.

★**Museum of Science & Industry** MUSEUM
(MOSI; ☑0161-832 2244; www.msimanchester.org.uk; Liverpool Rd; suggested donation £3, special exhibits £6-8; ⊙10am-5pm; ☐1 or 3, ☐Deansgate-Castlefield) FREE Manchester's rich industrial legacy is explored in this excellent museum set within the enormous grounds of the old Liverpool St station, the oldest rail terminus in the world. The large collection of steam engines, locomotives and original factory machinery tell the story of the city from the sewers up, while a host of new technology looks to the future.

It's an all-ages kind of museum, but the emphasis is on making sure the young 'uns don't get bored – they could easily spend a whole day poking about, testing an early electric-shock machine here and trying out a printing press there. You can get up close and personal with fighter jets and get to grips with all kinds of space-age technology; the museum now includes an astronaut virtual-reality experience called Space Descent VR with Tim Peake. A unifying theme is that Manchester and Mancunians had a key role to play: this is the place to discover that Manchester was home to the world's first stored-program computer (a giant contraption nicknamed 'baby') in 1948 and that the world's first steam-powered submarine was built to the designs of local curate Reverend George Garrett in 1879.

★**Manchester Art Gallery** GALLERY
(☑0161-235 8888; www.manchesterartgallery.org; Mosley St; ⊙10am-5pm Fri-Wed, to 9pm Thu; ☐St Peter's Square) FREE A superb collection of British art and a hefty number of European masters are the highlights at the city's top art gallery. It's home to the best assemblage of Pre-Raphaelite art as well as a permanent collection of pre-17th-century art, mostly by Dutch and early Renaissance masters. It also hosts exciting exhibitions of modern and contemporary art. The gallery runs a free

Manchester

Chetham's 1
Library &
School of Music

Blackfriars St

Chapel St

Blackfriars St

River Irwell

Victoria St

Marks &
Spencer

Cross St

Chapel St

Dearman's Pl

Salford Train Station

Stanley St

People's History Museum

4 Left Bank

Irwell St

St Anne's Sq

St Anne St

Back Bridge St

Bridge St

29

King St

South King St

John Dalton St

Tib Ln

26

Wood St

Crown Sq

Gartside St

SPINNINGFIELDS

Brazennose St

Albert Sq

Princess St

Albert Sq

Town Hall

30

Hardman St

21

Lloyd St

Water St

Quay St

Bootle St

St Peter's Sq

Granada Studios

Great John St

11

Lower Byrom St

Byrom St

Quay St

18

Longworth St

Deansgate

Peter St

Watson St

Windmill St

Central Library

7

24

19

Museum of Science & Industry

3

Liverpool Rd

Manchester YHA (200m)

CASTLEFIELD

Great Northern

G-Mex Exhibition Centre

Medlock St

Lower Mosley St

Bridgewater Hall

42

38

Great Bridgewater St

G-Mex

32

Rochdale Canal

Castle St

Chester Rd

Deansgate Train Station

Hewitt St

Whitworth St West

Cambridge St

DEANSGATE LOCKS

43

HOME

Chester St

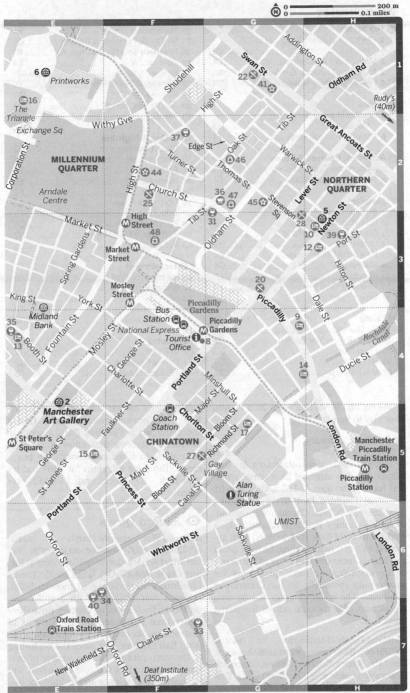

Manchester

hour-long highlights tour from 2pm to 3pm Thursday to Sunday.

★ **Chetham's Library & School of Music**   LIBRARY
(📞0161-834 7861; www.chethams.org.uk; Long Millgate; donation suggested £3; ⊘timed admission hourly 10am-noon & 1.30-3.30pm Mon-Fri; 🚇Victoria) Founded in 1653 in a building that dates from 1421, Chetham's is the oldest public library in the English-speaking world, a trove of dark shelves lined with ancient books and manuscripts. In 1845, Marx and Engels spent time studying in the alcove of the main reading room, prep work for what would eventually be the Communist Manifesto. The wider complex has its own life as part of a national school for young musicians.

National Football Museum   MUSEUM
(📞0161-605 8200; www.nationalfootballmuseum. com; Urbis Building, Cathedral Gardens, Corporation St; donations welcome; ⊘10am-5pm) **FREE** This museum charts the evolution of British football from its earliest days to the multi-billion-pound phenomenon it is today. One of the highlights is **Football Plus**, a series of interactive stations that allow you to test your skills in simulated conditions; buy a credit (three for £6, eight for £10) and try your luck – it's recommended for kids over seven.

◉ Salford Quays

Imperial War Museum North   MUSEUM
(📞0161-836 4000; www.iwm.org.uk/north; Trafford Wharf Rd, The Quays; ⊘10am-5pm; 🚇Harbour City or MediaCityUK) **FREE** Inside Daniel Libeskind's aluminium-clad modern building is a war museum with a difference, exploring the effects of conflict on society rather than fetishising the instruments of destruction. Six mini exhibitions within the main hall examine war since the beginning of the 20th century from a variety of perspectives, including the role of women and the influence of science and technology.

MediaCityUK
ARTS CENTRE

(☑0161-886 5300; www.mediacityuk.co.uk; Salford Quays; adult/child £11/7.25; ⊙tours 10.30am, 12.30pm & 3pm Mon-Wed, Sat & Sun; ⑤Harbour City or MediaCityUK) The BBC's northern home is but one significant element of this vast 81-hectare site. Besides hosting six departments of the national broadcaster (BBC Breakfast, Children's, Sport, Radio 5 Live, Learning, and Future Media & Technology), it is also home to the set of the world's longest-running soap opera, ITV's perennially popular *Coronation Street*.

There are no plans as yet to offer tours of the Corrie set, but you can visit the BBC's impressive set-up and see the sets of some of TV's most iconic programs on a guided 90-minute tour that also includes a chance for kids to 'make' a program in an interactive studio; see www.bbc.co.uk/showsandtours. For refuelling, there are plenty of cafes and restaurants in the area.

Lowry
ARTS CENTRE

(☑box office 0843-208 6000; www.thelowry.com; Pier 8, Salford Quays; ⊙gallery 11am-5pm Sun-Fri, from 10am Sat; ⑤Harbour City or MediaCityUK) With multiple performance spaces, bars, restaurants and shops, this contemporary arts centre attracts more than a million visitors a year to its myriad functions, which include everything from big-name theatrical productions to comedy, kids' theatre and even weddings. The centre is also home to 300 beautifully humanistic depictions of urban landscapes by LS Lowry (1887–1976), who was born in nearby Stretford, and after whom the complex is named.

🏃 Activities

Three Rivers Gin
GUIDED TOUR

(☑0161-839 2667; www.manchesterthreerivers. com; 21 Red Bank Parade; £95; ⊙7.30pm Thu-Sat, 1pm Sat & Sun) This award-winning Manchester micro-distillery cranks back the shutters a few times a week to let visitors behind the scenes with the master distiller. Its three-hour 'Gin Experience' starts with a potted history of Manchester and the city's relationship with gin, throws in several gin cocktails and culminates in mixing botanicals to cook up your own 1L batch to take home.

The distillery lives under the railway arches north of Manchester Victoria station. If you don't want to pay for the tour but still want to taste the booze you'll find it stocked in bars around town, including Impossible's gin palace.

WORTH A TRIP

WHITWORTH ART GALLERY

Manchester's second most important art gallery (☑0161-275 7450; www.whitworth.manchester.ac.uk; University of Manchester, Oxford Rd; ⊙10am-5pm Fri-Wed, to 9pm Thu; ☐15, 41, 42, 43, 140, 143 or 147 from Piccadilly Gardens) **FREE** is arguably its most beautiful, following a restoration that saw the doubling of its exhibition space through the opening of its sides and back, and the construction of glass-screened promenades. Inside is a fine collection of British watercolours, the best selection of historic textiles outside London and galleries devoted to the work of artists from Dürer and Rembrandt to Lucian Freud and David Hockney.

All this high art aside, you may find that the most interesting part of the gallery is the group of rooms dedicated to wallpaper – proof that bland pastels and horrible flowery patterns are not the final word in home decoration. There's also a lovely cafe on the grounds.

👉 Tours

Manchester Guided Tours
WALKING

(☑07505 685942; www.manchesterguidedtours. com; £10; ⊙11am) A daily walking tour of the city's highlights (departing from the Central Library at 11am), including Manchester Cathedral and the Royal Exchange. There's also a huge range of other themed tours such as Cottonopolis (looking at Manchester's industrial legacy), a John Ryland Library tour and tours of outlying suburbs like Didsbury and Chorlton.

New Manchester Walks
WALKING

(☑07769 298068; www.newmanchesterwalks. com; £8-10) The complete menu of tours includes explorations of every aspect of Manchester's personality, from music to history and politics to pubs. There are a handful of football-related walks and an extensive list of 'weird and wonderful' walks, from Victorian eating habits to the history of Strangeways prison. Starting points differ.

⭐ Festivals & Events

Manchester Day
ARTS, PARADE

(http://manchesterday.co.uk; ⊙mid-Jun) A day to celebrate all things Manchester inspired by New York's Thanksgiving Day parade:

OFF THE BEATEN TRACK

MANCHESTER POLICE MUSEUM

One of the city's best-kept secrets is this superb **museum** (☏0161-856 4500; www.gmpmuseum.co.uk; 57a Newton St; ⊙10.30am-3.30pm Tue) **FREE** housed within a former Victorian police station. The original building has been magnificently – if a little creepily – brought back to life, and you can wander in and out of 19th-century cells where prisoners rested their heads on wooden pillows; visit a restored magistrates' court from 1895 and examine the case histories (complete with mugshots and photos of weapons) of some of the more notorious names to have passed through its doors.

50 performances across three city centre squares culminate in a colourful parade.

Manchester International Festival ART (☏0161-238 7300; www.mif.co.uk) A three-week-long biennial arts festival of artist-led new work across visual arts, performance and popular culture. Recent performers included Damon Albarn, Marina Abramović, Björk and Steve McQueen. The next festival is scheduled for July 2019; 2020 will see the opening of The Factory, a new multimedia arts venue that will be a flagship host of the festival.

★**Manchester Pride Festival** LGBT (☏0161-831 7700; www.manchesterpride.com; ⊙late Aug; ☐Piccadilly Gardens) One of England's biggest celebrations of gay, lesbian, bisexual and transgender life, held over three days of the August bank holiday weekend at the end of the month. There's music and dance (the Big Weekend); debate, films, lectures and community projects (the Superbia Weekend); a huge parade; and, on the last night, a moving candlelit vigil for all victims of HIV.

Manchester Food & Drink Festival FOOD & DRINK (www.foodanddrinkfestival.com; Albert Sq; ⊙Oct) Manchester's superb foodie scene shows off its wares over 10 days at the beginning of October. Farmers markets, pop-up restaurants and gourmet events are just part of the UK's biggest urban food fest. Much of the action takes place on Albert Square, in front of the town hall.

🛌 Sleeping

Hatters HOSTEL £ (☏0161-236 9500; http://hattershostels.com; 50 Newton St; dm/s/d from £20/40/56; 🅿@🛜; ☐all city centre) The old-style lift and porcelain sinks are the only leftovers of this former millinery factory, now one of the best hostels in town. The location is a boon: smack in the heart of the Northern Quarter, you won't have to go far to get the best of alternative Manchester.

Manchester YHA HOSTEL £ (☏0345 371 9647; www.yha.org.uk; Potato Wharf; dm/d from £15/65; 🅿@🛜; ☐Deansgate-Castlefield) This purpose-built canalside hostel in the Castlefield area is one of the best in the country. It's a top-class option, with four- and six-bed dorms, all with bathroom, as well as three doubles and a host of good facilities. Potato Wharf is just left off Liverpool Rd.

Roomzzz APARTMENT ££ (☏0161-236 2121; www.roomzzz.co.uk; 36 Princess St; r from £100; ❄@🛜; ☐all city centre) The inelegant name belies the designer digs inside this beautifully restored Grade II–listed building, which features serviced apartments equipped with a kitchen and the latest connectivity gadgetry, including sleek iMac computers and free wi-fi throughout. There's a small pantry, with food for sale downstairs. Highly recommended if you're planning a longer stay. There's a new **branch** (Exchange Sq; r from £119; ☐Exchange Square) in the Corn Exchange.

Malmaison HOTEL ££ (☏0161-278 1000; www.malmaison.com; Piccadilly St; r from £110; ❄@🛜; ☐all city centre, ☐Piccadilly Gardens) Drop-dead trendy and full of red crushed velvet, deep purples, art-deco ironwork and signature black-and-white tiles, Malmaison Manchester follows the chain's quirky design style and passion for cool, although rarely at the expense of comfort: the rooms are terrific.

ABode HOTEL ££ (☏0161-247 7744; www.abodemanchester.co.uk; 107 Piccadilly; r from £100; ❄@🛜; ☐all city centre, ☐Piccadilly Gardens) The original fittings at this converted textile factory have been combined successfully with 61 bedrooms divided into four categories of ever-increasing luxury: Comfortable, Desirable, Enviable and Fabulous on Fifth, the latter being five seriously swanky top-floor suites.

Cow Hollow
BOUTIQUE HOTEL ££

(☎07727 159727; www.cowhollow.co.uk; 57 Newton St; r/ste from £120/140; ☎; 🖥all city centre) Set in a stick-thin 19th-century weavers' mill, Cow Hollow offers a lot of charm in a compact space. Sixteen snug rooms are graced with original beams, brick walls and flashy bathrooms; some have original machinery incorporated into the decor. Little luxury touches include Hypnos beds, goose-down duvets, and free Prosecco and tapas each evening. Reception is in the ground-floor bar.

★ King Street Townhouse
BOUTIQUE HOTEL £££

(☎0161-667 0707; www.eclectichotels.co.uk; 10 Booth St; r/ste from £225/£335; ✷@☎✷; 🖥all city centre) This beautiful 1872 Italian Renaissance–style former bank is now an exquisite boutique hotel with 40 bedrooms ranging from snug to suite. Furnishings are the perfect combination of period elegance and contemporary style. On the top floor is a small spa with an infinity pool overlooking the town hall; downstairs is a nice bar and restaurant.

Velvet Hotel
BOUTIQUE HOTEL £££

(☎0161-236 9003; www.velvetmanchester.com; 2 Canal St; r from £140; ☎; 🖥all city centre) Nineteen beautiful bespoke rooms each oozing style: there's the sleigh bed in room 24, the double bath of room 34, the saucy framed photographs of a stripped-down David Beckham (this is Gay Village, after all!). Despite the tantalising decor and location, this is not an exclusive hotel and is as popular with straight visitors as it is with the same-sex crowd.

Great John Street Hotel
HOTEL £££

(☎0161-831 3211; www.eclectichotels.co.uk; Great John St; r from £160; P✷@☎; 🖥2 & 3 to Museum of Science & Industry) Elegant designer luxury? Present. Fabulous rooms with all the usual delights (Egyptian cotton sheets, quality toiletries, free-standing baths and lots of high-tech electronics)? Present. This former schoolhouse (ah, now you get it) is small but sumptuous – beyond the art-deco lobby are the fabulous bedrooms, each an example of style and luxury. If only school left such comfortable memories.

✕ Eating

Rudy's
PIZZA £

(www.rudyspizza.co.uk; 9 Cotton St, Ancoats; pizzas £4.90-8.90; ☉noon-3pm & 5-10pm Mon-Fri, noon-10pm Sat, to 9pm Sun; 🖥Piccadilly Gardens) Mak-

ers of the best pizza in town, Rudy's can be a tough table to get (put your name down and wait) but it is oh so worth it. It makes its own dough, and uses proper San Marzano tomatoes and *fior di latte* mozzarella to create pies that a Neapolitan would approve of. There's another branch on Peter St.

Northern Soul Grilled Cheese
SANDWICHES £

(www.northernsoulmcr.com; 10 Church St; mains £4-7; ☉11am-6pm Sun, to 8pm Mon-Wed, to 9pm Thu-Sat) Carving out a niche for artery-clogging, gooey grilled-cheese delights in Manchester's grungy Northern Quarter, Northern Soul is a great spot for a budget meal. It bills itself as 'gourmet' but there's nothing fancy about the makeshift shack it occupies, or its prices. The menu features cheese sandwiches in various guises, plus deliciously tangy mac 'n' cheese, and milkshakes.

Richmond Tea Rooms
CAFE £

(☎0161-237 9667; www.richmondtearooms.com; Richmond St; mains £5-8, afternoon teas £10.50-24.95; 🖥all city centre) If the Mad Hatter were to have a tea party in Manchester, it would be in this wonderfully haphazard tearoom with a potpourri of period furniture and a counter painted to look like the icing on a cake. Sandwiches and light meals are the mainstay, but the real treat is the selection of afternoon teas, complete with finger sandwiches, scones and cakes.

Bundobust
INDIAN £

(☎0161-359 6757; www.bundobust.com; 61 Piccadilly; dishes £3.75-6.50; ☉noon-9.30pm Mon-Thu,

---

DON'T MISS

VICTORIA BATHS

The **Victoria Baths** (☎0161-224 2020; www.victoriabaths.org.uk; Hathersage Rd, Chorlton-on-Medlock; adult/child £6/5; ☉guided tour 2pm Wed Apr-Oct; 🖥50 or 147 from city centre) were designed to be the grandest in Britain when they opened in 1906; this Grade II–listed Edwardian classic retains much of its former grandeur despite being left virtually derelict for more than 30 years. A laborious restoration of its three pools, Turkish bath and the stunning art nouveau decor is underway, and the governing trust runs excellent hour-long guided tours of the building every Wednesday.

to 10pm Fri & Sat, to 8pm Sun; 🚲; 🚇 all city centre, 🚇 Piccadilly Gardens) Indian veggie street food and craft beer are the order of the day at this export from Leeds. The format's the same in Manchester, right down to the pallet wall-panelling at the entrance, but this basement venue is much bigger than the original. Come for the two-dish express lunch (noon to 4pm, Monday to Friday; £7).

★**Rosylee**   CAFE ££
(www.rosylee.com; 11 Stevenson Sq; mains £10-18, 2-/3-course menu £11.95/14.95; ⊙10am-9pm Mon-Thu, to 10pm Fri-Sat, to 8pm Sun; 🚇 all city centre) A touch of Edwardian and Georgian elegance in the heart of the Northern Quarter, this gorgeous tearoom has expanded its menu to offer a range of British classics like beer-battered haddock and chips, and steak suet pudding. The afternoon tea (£18.25, or £25.25 if you want a glass of bubbles) is superb.

★**Refuge by Volta**   INTERNATIONAL ££
(📞0161-233 5151; www.refugemcr.co.uk; Oxford St; ⊙noon-2.45pm & 5pm-9pm Mon-Thu, to 9.30pm Fri, noon-9.30pm Sat, noon-9pm Sun; 🚇all city centre) Manchester's snazziest dining room occupies one half of The Refuge, one of the city's best bars. The menu is made up of *voltini*, sharing plates with global influences from the Middle East to Korea (think lamb schwarma and kimchi), inspired by the travels of restaurateurs and DJs Luke Cowdrey and Justin Crawford (aka the Unabombers). Superb.

★**Mackie Mayor**   FOOD HALL ££
(www.mackiemayor.co.uk; 1 Eagle St; mains £9-15; ⊙10am-10pm Tue-Thu, to 11pm Fri, 9am-11pm Sat, 9am-8pm Sun; 🚇all city centre) This restored former meat market is now home to a superb food hall with a fine selection of 10 individual traders. The pizzas from Honest Crust are divine; the pork-belly bao from Baohouse is done just right; Nationale 7 does wonders with a basic sandwich; and Tender Cow serves really tasty steaks. Dining is communal, across two floors.

Oast House   INTERNATIONAL ££
(📞0161-829   3830;   www.theoasthouse.uk.com; Crown Sq, Spinningfields; mains £11-18; ⊙noon-midnight Mon-Wed & Sun, to 1am Thu, to 2am Fri-Sat; 🚇all city centre) Modelled on a Kentish oast house (a medieval kiln used to dry out hops), this Spinningfields staple was completely refurbished in 2018, including a remodelled courtyard for outdoor dining. The broad-ranging menu has burgers, kebabs, steaks and rotisserie chickens cooked in the BBQ oven, but you can also get a delicious fondue and a fine selection of homemade pies.

**Mr Cooper's
House & Garden**   MODERN BRITISH ££
(https://mrcoopers.co.uk; Midland Hotel, 16 Peter St; mains £9.50-23; ⊙noon-10pm Mon-Sat, 1pm-10pm Sun; 🚇St Peter's Square) Rob Taylor's beautifully presented cuisine is Modern British at its tasty, unpretentious best. Interesting options include dishes like swordfish steak with edamame beans and miso butter, or slow-roasted pork belly with cavolo nero. The name comes from a local coach maker, whose house was on the land before the Midland was built.

San Carlo Cicchetti   ITALIAN ££
(www.sancarlocicchetti.co.uk; King St W, House of Fraser; small plates £6.95-8.95; ⊙8am-11pm Mon-Fri, from 9am Sat, 9am-10pm Sun; 🚇all city centre) Celebrity chef Aldo Zilli has designed the superlative menu at this ornate Italian restaurant on the ground floor of House of Fraser. Instead of big plates of carb overload, though, you get smaller dishes known as *cicchetti*. The truffle and pecorino ravioli are divine. It also serves standard egg dishes for breakfast.

★**20 Stories**   BRITISH £££
(📞0161-204 3333; https://20stories.co.uk; 1 Spinningfields, Hardman Sq; mains £15-27; ⊙noon-2.45pm & 5.30-10.15pm Mon-Thu, noon-3.45pm & 5.30-10.30pm Fri-Sat, noon-3.15pm & 5.30-8.45pm Sun; 🚇all city centre) The most anticipated opening of 2018 was this rooftop restaurant atop a 20-storey tower, marshalled by local star Aiden Byrne (formerly of Manchester House). Great views and great food, courtesy of Byrne's signature style of supremely elegant, unpretentious cuisine. There's an outdoor terrace with a firepit and a grill that serves up good burgers and fish and chips.

Adam Reid at The French MODERN BRITISH £££
(📞0161-932 4198; www.the-french.co.uk; Midland Hotel, 16 Peter St; 4-/6-/9-course menu £45/65/85; ⊙noon-1.30pm & 6.30-9.30pm; 🚇St Peter's Square) 🌱 Adam Reid's exquisite Modern British cuisine is considered one of Manchester's culinary highlights, especially if you opt for one of the three tasting menus. The room is dark and moody, the soundtrack indie rock, but the food is wonderfully subtle and beautifully presented. Reservations are very much recommended.

Hawksmoor

STEAK £££

(☑ 0161-836 6980; www.thehawksmoor.com; 184-186 Deansgate; steaks £19-36; 🚇 St Peter's Square) The steakhouse that has had London's carnivores salivating landed in Manchester in 2017 and hasn't disappointed. The setting, inside a Grade II–listed courthouse, is stunning, with everything carefully put together to create an authentic 1930s-style atmosphere. The steaks – also available by weight – are prepared perfectly and the sides are just divine.

Manchester House

MODERN BRITISH £££

(www.manchesterhouse.uk.com; Tower 12, 18-22 Bridge St; mains £37, 10-/14-course tasting menu £70/95; 🖉) How would Manchester's most celebrated restaurant survive the departure of its head chef Aiden Byrne? Seamlessly, it seems, judging by the superb cooking of Nathan Tofan, who was senior sous to Byrne when he designed his menu of molecular cuisine with a Manchester twist. Tofan has made the simplified version of Blumenthal and Adriá very much his own. Reservations essential.

🍷 Drinking & Nightlife

★ Refuge

BAR

(☑ 0161-233 5151; www.refugemcr.co.uk; Oxford Rd; ⊙ 8am-midnight Mon-Wed, to 1am Thu, to 2am Fri-Sat, to 11.30pm Sun; 🚇 all city centre) Occupying what was once the Victorian Gothic ground floor of the Refuge Assurance Building, this is not just Manchester's most beautiful bar, but arguably its coolest too – all thanks to the rep and aesthetic sensibilities of its creative director duo, DJs and restaurateurs Luke Cowdrey and Justin Crawford, aka the Unabombers, who run Homoelectric, the best club nights in the northwest.

★ Homoelectric

CLUB

(www.twitter.com/homoelectric; The Refuge, Oxford Rd; ⊙ 10pm-4am on periodic Sat; 🚇 all city centre) The year 2018 saw the revival of one of Manchester's legendary club nights, advertised as 'a non-stop exotic disco for homos, heteros, lesbos and don't knows'. Fronted by legendary DJs, the Unabombers (Luke Cowdrey and Justin Crawford), the (roughly) monthly night takes place in the basement of The Refuge, where Cowdrey and Crawford run the bar and restaurant. Check Twitter for details.

Cloudwater Barrel Store Tap Room

BREWERY

(www.cloudwaterbrew.co; Arch 13, Sheffield St; ⊙ 4-9pm Thu, 2-10pm Fri, noon-10pm Sat, noon-8pm Sun; 🚇 Piccadilly) Take a warehouse space under the arches behind Manchester Piccadilly Station, roll in a double deck of beer barrels and set out simple seating, and you've got the perfect brew for an atmospheric tap room. Cloudwater is one of England's most raved about microbreweries and this drinking den serving draft and selling cans is the bee's knees for its fans.

Fac251

CLUB

(☑ 0161-272 7251; www.factorymanchester.com; 112-118 Princess St; £1-6; ⊙ 11pm-4am Mon-Sat; 🚇 all city centre) Located in Tony Wilson's former Factory Records HQ, Fac251 is one of the most popular venues in town. There are three rooms, all with a broad musical appeal, from drum and bass to Motown and indie rock. Something for everybody, from Monday's Quids In (for students) to the Big Weekender on Saturday (commercial R&B).

Peveril of the Peak

PUB

(☑ 0161-236 6364; 127 Great Bridgewater St; ⊙ 11am-11pm; 🚇 Deansgate-Castlefield) The best of Manchester's collection of beautiful Victorian pubs. Check out the gorgeous glazed tilework outside.

Britons Protection

PUB

(☑ 0161-236 5895; 50 Great Bridgewater St; ⊙ noon-midnight Mon-Thu, to 1am Fri & Sat, to 11pm Sun; 🚇 Castlefield-Deansgate) Whisky – over 300 different kinds of it (the Cu Dhub 'black whisky' is a particular treat with its touch of coffee and honey) – is the beverage of choice at this liver-threatening, proper English pub that also does home-style meals (gammon, pies etc). An old-fashioned boozer with open fires in the back rooms and a cosy atmosphere...perfect on a cold evening.

Odd

BAR

(☑ 0161-833 0070; www.oddbar.co.uk; 30-32 Thomas St; ⊙ 11am-midnight Sun-Wed, to 1am Thu, to 2am Fri & Sat; 🚇 Piccadilly Gardens) This eclectic little bar – with its oddball furnishings, wacky tunes and anti-establishment crew of customers – is a Northern Quarter stalwart and the perfect antidote to the increasingly similar look of so many modern bars. A slice of Mancuniana to be treasured.

Lily's Bar

COCKTAIL BAR

(☑ 0161-714 0414; www.1761mcr.co.uk; 2 Booth St; ⊙ noon-midnight; 🎤; 🚇 all city centre) This basement champagne bar inside the 1761 restaurant is named after Madame

Bollinger, whose nickname was 'Aunt Lily', though the bar itself has little association beyond selling the French champagne. It's done out like a prohibition den with chesterfield chairs, a sepia film projector screen and a giant fish tank (yes, you heard us right).

North Tea Power
CAFE

(📞 0161-833 3073; www.northteapower.co.uk; 36 Tib St; ⏰ 8am-7pm Mon-Fri, from 9am Sat, 10am-6pm Sun; 📶) The name may say tea but the interior of this cafe screams coffee shop. North Tea Power is one of Manchester's early adopters on the artisanal coffee scene, with the requisite communal tables, industrial pillars and Macbook-wielding tribe. As well as flat whites, AeroPress and pour-overs, the menu features a load of loose-leaf teas, cakes and all-day breakfast options.

Port Street Beer House
CRAFT BEER

(www.portstreetbeerhouse.co.uk; 39-41 Port St; ⏰ noon-midnight Sun-Fri, to 1am Sat; 🚇 Piccadilly Gardens) Fans of real ale love this Northern Quarter boozer, with its seven hand pulls, 18 draught lines and more than 100 beers from around the world, including gluten-free ales and some heavy hitters: Brewdog's Tactical Nuclear Penguin is a 32% stout but at £45 a bottle you won't need more than one. It hosts regular tastings and tap takeovers.

Black Dog Ballroom
BAR

(📞 0161-839 0664; www.blackdogballroom.co.uk; 52 Church St; ⏰ noon-4am Mon-Fri & Sun, to 5am Sat; 📶; 🚇 all city centre) A basement bar with a speakeasy vibe, but there's nothing illicit about drinking here: the cocktails are terrific (it runs occasional mixology sessions), the atmosphere is always buzzing and the music always good and loud – the resident DJs spin some great tunes Thursday through Saturday nights.

☆ Entertainment

★ HOME
ARTS CENTRE

(📞 0161-200 1500; www.homemcr.org; 2 Tony Wilson Pl, First St; tickets £5-20; ⏰ box office noon-8pm, bar 10am-11pm Mon-Thu, to midnight Fri-Sat, 11am-10.30pm Sun; 🚇 all city centre) One of Britain's best arts centres, HOME has two theatre spaces that host provocative new work in a variety of contexts, from proscenium sets to promenade pieces. The five cinema screens show the latest indie releases as well as classics. There's also a ground-floor bar and a cafe that serves good food on the first floor.

Band on the Wall
LIVE MUSIC

(📞 0161-834 1786; www.bandonthewall.org; 25 Swan St; ⏰ 5pm-late; 🚇 all city centre) A top-notch venue that hosts everything from rock to world music, with splashes of jazz, blues and folk thrown in.

FOOTBALL TOURS

Manchester United Museum & Tour (📞 0161-826 1326; www.manutd.com; Sir Matt Busby Way; tours adult/child £18/12; ⏰ museum 9.30am-5pm Mon-Sat, 10am-4pm Sun, tours every 10min 9.40am-4.30pm Mon-Sat, to 3.30pm Sun, closed match days; 🚇 Old Trafford or Exchange Quay) You don't have to be a fan of the world's most famous football club to enjoy a visit to their impressive 75,000-plus capacity Old Trafford stadium, but it helps. The museum tour includes a walk down the tunnel onto the edge of the playing surface, where Manchester United's superstar footballers ply their lucrative trade.

Other highlights of the excellent tour include a seat in the stands, a stop in the changing rooms and a peek at the players' lounge (from which the manager is banned unless invited by the players) – all ecstatic experiences for a Man United devotee. The museum has a comprehensive history of the club and a state-of-the-art call-up system that means you can view your favourite goals.

Manchester City Stadium Tour (📞 0161-444 1894; www.mcfc.co.uk; Etihad Campus; tours adult/child £17.50/12; ⏰ 9am-5pm Mon-Sat, 10am-4pm Sun except match days; 🚇 Etihad Campus) On this 90-minute tour of Manchester City's stadium you'll visit both the home and away dressing rooms (note the huge difference between the two); the pitchside dugouts; the press room; and the Tunnel Club, where VIP guests get to see the players walk through on match days. Other tours combine the stadium with the nearby academy. Online bookings are cheaper.

The tour also includes a visit to the trophy room, which has seen the addition of another Premier League title in 2018, their third since 2012 and their first under the world's most celebrated manager, the Catalan Josep 'Pep' Guardiola.

Ruby Lounge   LIVE MUSIC
(☑ 0161-834 1392; www.therubylounge.com; 28-34 High St; tickets around £8-10; ☺ noon-midnight, clubs 11pm-3am; ⊠ Exchange Square) Terrific live-music venue in the Northern Quarter that features mostly rock bands. It gets very loud. After the bands there's usually a club night that runs until late.

Deaf Institute   LIVE MUSIC
(www.thedeafinstitute.co.uk; 135 Grosvenor St; ☺ 10am-midnight; ⊠ all city centre) Excellent midsized venue in a former institute for deaf people; also includes a smaller venue in the basement and a cafe on the ground floor. It's where you'll hear alt rock and pop by dozens of local bands we guarantee you've never heard of (as well as some visiting bands you may have).

Soup Kitchen   LIVE MUSIC
(http://soup-kitchen.co.uk; 31-33 Spear St; £3-5; ☺ noon-11pm Mon-Wed & Sun, to 1am Thu, to 4am Fri & Sat; ⊠ Market Street) By day a typical Northern Quarter canteen-style cafe, but at night this is one of the city's best places to catch live music, with a full schedule of gigs by all kinds of indie acts passing through town. When the bands are done, the excellent DJs kick in and it often goes until 6am.

🛍 Shopping

Oi Polloi   CLOTHING
(www.oipolloi.com; 63 Thomas St; ☺ 10am-6pm Mon-Sat; ⊠ all city centre) Besides the impressive range of casual footwear, this hip boutique also stocks a huge range of designers including A Kind of Guise, LA Panoplie, Nudie Jeans Co and Maison Kitsuné.

Tib Street Market   MARKET
(☑ 0161-234 7357; Tib St; ☺ 10am-5pm Sat; ⊠ all city centre) Up-and-coming local designers get a chance to display their wares at this weekly market where you can pick up everything from purses to lingerie and hats to jewellery.

Oxfam Originals   VINTAGE
(Unit 8, Smithfield Bldg, Oldham St; ☺ 10am-6pm Mon-Sat, noon-5pm Sun; ⊠ all city centre) If you're into retro, this terrific store has high-quality gear from the 1960s and '70s. Shop in the knowledge that it's for a good cause.

ℹ Information

Tourist Office (www.visitmanchester.com; 1 Piccadilly Gardens; ☺ 9.30am-5pm Mon-Sat, 10.30am-4.30pm Sun; ⊠ Piccadilly Gardens) This is mostly a self-service tourist office, with brochures and interactive maps to help guide visitors.

ℹ Getting There & Away

AIR

Manchester Airport (☑ 0808-169 7030; www. manchesterairport.co.uk) The airport is 12 miles south of the city.

Bus £4.20, 30 minutes, every 20 minutes to Piccadilly Gardens

Metrolink £4.20, 40 minutes, every 12 minutes; change at Cornbrook or Firswood for city centre

Taxi £20 to £30, 25 to 40 minutes

Train £5, 20 minutes, every 10 minutes to Piccadilly Station

BUS

National Express (☑ 08717 81 81 81; www. nationalexpress.com) serves most major cities from the **coach station** (Chorlton St), including the following:

Leeds £5.20, one hour, hourly

Liverpool £7.10, 1½ hours, hourly

London £14.10, 4¼ hours, hourly

TRAIN

Manchester Piccadilly (east of Piccadilly Gardens) is the main station for most mainline train services across Britain; Victoria Station (north of the National Football Museum) serves destinations in the northwest including Blackburn, Halifax and Huddersfield but also Leeds and Liverpool. The two stations are linked by Metrolink. Off-peak fares are considerably cheaper. Destinations include the following:

Blackpool £17.70, 1¼ hours, half-hourly

Liverpool Lime St £11.40, 45 minutes, half-hourly

London Euston £85.90, three hours, seven daily

Newcastle £69.50, three hours, six daily

ℹ Getting Around

BUS

The Metroshuttle is a free service with three separate routes around the heart of Manchester every 10 minutes. Pick up a map from the tourist office. Most local buses start from Piccadilly Gardens.

METROLINK

The Metrolink (www.metrolink.co.uk) light-rail network is the best way to get between Victoria and Piccadilly train stations, as well as further afield to Salford Quays, Didsbury and other suburbs. It also serves the airport, but you need to change at either Cornbrook or Firswood. Trams run every few minutes throughout the day from

6am to 11pm. Buy your tickets from the platform machine.

TRAIN

Castlefield is served by Deansgate station with suburban rail links to Piccadilly, Oxford Rd and Salford stations.

CHESTER

☎ 01244 / POP 118,200

Chester's Tudor-and-Victorian heart is justifiably famous as one of Britain's prettiest town centres. This collection of black-and-white timber-framed beauties and red-sandstone buildings surrounded by an original set of Roman-era walls is one of the north-west's biggest tourist attractions.

Beyond the cruciform-shaped historic centre, Chester is an ordinary, residential town; it's hard to believe today, but throughout the Middle Ages Chester made its money as the most important port in the northwest. However, the River Dee silted up over time and Chester fell behind Liverpool in importance.

⊙ Sights & Activities

★ City Walls   LANDMARK

A good way to get a sense of Chester's unique character is to walk the 2-mile circuit along the walls that surround the historic centre. Originally built by the Romans around AD 70, the walls were altered substantially over the following centuries but have retained their current position since around 1200. The tourist office's *Walk Around Chester Walls* leaflet is an excellent guide and you can also take a 90-minute guided walk.

Of the many features along the walls, the most eye-catching is the prominent Eastgate, where you can see the most famous clock in England after London's Big Ben, built for Queen Victoria's Diamond Jubilee in 1897.

At the southeastern corner of the walls are the wishing steps, added in 1785. Local legend claims that if you can run up and down these uneven steps while holding your breath your wish will come true.

Just inside Southgate, known here as Bridgegate (as it's located at the northern end of the Old Dee Bridge), is the Bear & Billet (www.bearandbillet.com; 94 Lower Bridge St; ⊙ noon-11.30pm) pub, Chester's oldest timber-framed building, built in 1664, and once a toll gate into the city.

Chester Cathedral   CATHEDRAL

(☎ 01244-324756; www.chestercathedral.com; 12 Abbey Sq; ⊙ 9am-6pm Mon-Sat, 1-4pm Sun) FREE Chester Cathedral was originally a Benedictine abbey built on the remains of an earlier Saxon church dedicated to St Werburgh (the city's patron saint); it was shut down in 1540 as part of Henry VIII's Dissolution frenzy, but reconsecrated as a cathedral the following year. Despite a substantial Victorian facelift, the cathedral retains much of its original 12th-century structure. You can amble about freely, but the tours (adult/child full tour £8/6, short tour £6; ⊙ full tour 11am & 3pm daily, short tour 12.30pm & 1.15pm Mon-Tue, also 2pm & 4pm Wed-Sat) are excellent, as they take you up to the top of the panoramic bell tower.

Roman Amphitheatre   ARCHAEOLOGICAL SITE

(Little St John St) FREE Just outside the city walls is what was once an arena that seated 7000 spectators (making it the country's largest); some historians have suggested that it may have also been the site of King Arthur's Camelot and that his knights' 'round table' was really just this circular construction. Excavations continue; during summer months there are occasional shows held here.

Blue Planet Aquarium   AQUARIUM

(www.blueplanetaquarium.com; adult/child £17/12.25; ⊙ 10am-5pm Mon-Fri, to 6pm Sat & Sun; ⊒ 1 & 4 from Bus Exchange) Things aren't done by halves around Chester, where you'll find Blue Planet, which was the country's largest aquarium when it opened in 1998. It's home to 10 different kinds of shark, which can be viewed from a 70m-long moving walkway that lets you eye them up close. The aquarium is 9 miles north of Chester at Junction 10 of the M53 to Liverpool. Book online for a 10% discount.

Grosvenor Museum   MUSEUM

(☎ 01244-972197; www.grosvenormuseum.co.uk; 27 Grosvenor St; ⊙ 10.30am-5pm Mon-Sat, 1-4pm Sun) FREE Excellent museum with the country's most comprehensive collection of Roman tombstones. At the back of the museum is a preserved Georgian house, complete with kitchen, drawing room, bedroom and bathroom.

Chester Boat   BOATING

(☎ 01244-325394; www.chesterboat.co.uk; Boating Station, Souters La, The Groves; tours £7-20; ⊙ 11am-5pm) Runs hourly 30-minute and two-hour-long cruises (the latter at noon and 2.30pm Saturday and Sunday) up and down the Dee, including a foray into the gorgeous Eaton Estate, home of the Duke and Duchess of Westminster. All departures are from the riverside along the promenade known as the Groves.

🛏 Sleeping

Chester Backpackers · HOSTEL £
(☑01244-400185; www.chesterbackpackers.co.uk; 67 Boughton; dm/s/d from £16/22/34; ⊙ reception 8am-11am & 4-7.30pm only; ⏉) Comfortable dorm and private rooms with nice pine beds in a typically Tudor white-and-black building. They're small but comfortable. It's just a short walk from the city walls and there's also a pleasant garden. Reception is only open at certain times during the day.

★ Edgar House · BOUTIQUE HOTEL ££
(☑01244-347007; www.edgarhouse.co.uk; 22 City Walls; ⊙r from £105) This award-winning digs is the ultimate in boutique luxury. A Georgian house with seven rooms, each decorated in its own individual style – some have free-standing claw-foot tubs and French doors that lead onto an elegant terrace. There's beautiful art on the walls and fabulous touches of the owners' gorgeous aesthetic throughout. The superb Twenty2 (www.restauranttwenty2.co.uk; tasting menu £59; ⊙6-9pm Wed-Sat, afternoon tea noon-4pm Fri-Sun) restaurant is open to nonguests.

Stone Villa · B&B ££
(☑01244-345014; www.stonevillachester.co.uk; 3 Stone Pl, Hoole Rd; s/d from £60/85; ℗⏉; 🚍9 from city centre) This award-winning, beautiful 1850 villa has everything you need for a memorable stay. Elegant bedrooms, a fabulous breakfast and welcoming, friendly owners all add up to excellent lodgings. The property is about a mile from the city centre. You can even rent the whole house – which sleeps 22 – for £900 a night.

ABode Chester · HOTEL ££
(☑01244-347000; www.abodechester.co.uk; Grosvenor Rd; r/ste from £89/289; ℗✳⏉) Contemporary hotel with 84 rooms all equipped with handcrafted Vispring beds and handsome bathrooms complete with monsoon showers. Good toiletries, flat-screen TVs and cashmere throws on the bed give it a touch of elegance. Rooms come in categories: Comfortable, Desirable, Enviable, Most Enviable and Fabulous suites. South-facing

---

DON'T MISS

THE ROWS

Besides the City Walls, Chester's other great draw is the **Rows**, a series of two-level galleried arcades along the four streets that fan out in each direction from the Central Cross. The architecture is a handsome mix of Victorian and Tudor (original and mock) buildings that house a fantastic collection of independently owned shops.

The origin of the Rows is a little unclear, but it is believed that as the Roman walls slowly crumbled, medieval traders built their shops against the resulting rubble banks, while later arrivals built theirs on top.

---

rooms have great views of the Roodee racecourse.

★ Chester Grosvenor Hotel & Spa · HOTEL £££
(☑01244-324024; www.chestergrosvenor.com; 58 Eastgate St; r from £200; ℗@⏉) The black-and-white timbered Grosvenor is the city's top hotel by location – right next to the Eastgate Clock – and quality, offering a five-star experience throughout. The lobby's main feature is the chandelier, with 28,000 pieces of crystal; move on from there to the huge rooms with exquisite period furniture. There's also a top spa (open to nonguests) and a Michelin-starred restaurant (p540).

🍴 Eating

The Kitchen · LEBANESE £
(www.thekitchenstoryhouse.co.uk; Storyhouse, Hunter St; mains £8-9; ⊙8am-9.30pm Mon-Sat, 9.30am-9pm Sun) Delicious mezze and other small plates from the Levant are the mainstay at the ground-floor restaurant in Storyhouse (p541), Chester's exciting new arts centre. The Express Lunch (£7.50) is served between noon and 3pm, and gives you the option of chicken with spices or squash and halloumi.

Joseph Benjamin · MODERN BRITISH ££
(☑01244-344295; www.josephbenjamin.co.uk; 134-140 Northgate St; mains £11-18; ⊙noon-3pm Tue-Sat, also 6-9.30pm Thu-Sat & noon-4pm Sun) A bright star in Chester's culinary firmament is this combo restaurant, bar and deli that delivers carefully prepared local produce to take out or eat in. Excellent sandwiches

Chester

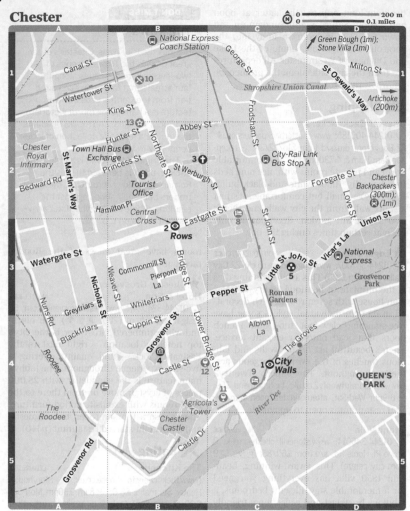

and gorgeous salads are the mainstay of the takeaway menu, while the more formal dinner menu features fine examples of Modern British cuisine.

Artichoke
MODERN BRITISH ££

(www.artichokechester.co.uk; The Steam Mill, Steam Mill St; mains £14-17; ⏱10am-3.30pm & 5-10pm Mon-Sat, 10am-8pm Sun) One of a number of warehouse conversions along the Shropshire Union Canal (now known as the Canal Quarter), this cafe-bar serves sandwiches and smaller bites as well as tasty main courses such as sea trout in a sweet

pea wasabi velvet cream, and confit of duck legs with Jersey potatoes, pancetta and red cabbage. It's a popular drinking spot too.

★ Simon Radley at the Grosvenor
MODERN BRITISH £££

(☏01244-324024; www.chestergrosvenor.com; 58 Eastgate St, Chester Grosvenor Hotel; tasting menu £99, à la carte menu £75; ⏱6.30-9pm Tue-Sat) Simon Radley's formal restaurant (you're instructed to arrive 30 minutes early for drinks and canapés) has served near-perfect Modern British cuisine since 1990, when it was first awarded the Michelin star that it has kept

Chester

ever since. The food is divine and the wine list extensive. One of Britain's best, but why no second star? Note that attire must be smart and no children under 12 are permitted.

☕ Drinking & Entertainment

Brewery Tap PUB
(www.the-tap.co.uk; 52-54 Lower Bridge St; ⊙noon-11pm, to 10.30pm Sun) If you're looking for the best pint in the city, the aficionados at the Campaign for Real Ale (Camra) reckon you'll get it at this boozer in a Grade II–listed Jacobean banqueting hall; its seven taps offer a rotating range of quality brews from all over England.

★ Storyhouse ARTS CENTRE
(☏01244-409113; www.storyhouse.com; Hunter St) The 1930s art deco Odeon has been converted into an award-winning modern arts centre with two theatre spaces – a larger 800-seater arena and a 150-seat studio theatre – plus a cinema that screens indie and art movies. The Lebanese-inspired Kitchen (p539) restaurant on the ground floor is excellent.

ⓘ Information

Tourist Office (☏01244-402111; www. visitchester.com; Town Hall, Northgate St; ⊙9am-5.30pm Mon-Sat, 10am-5pm Sun Mar-Oct, 9am-5pm Mon-Sat, 10am-4pm Sun Nov-Feb) Tourist information, accommodation booking service and brochures.

ⓘ Getting There & Away

BUS
Local buses leave from the **Town Hall Bus Exchange** (Princess St). **National Express** (☏08717 81 81 81; www.nationalexpress.com)

coaches stop on Vicar's Lane, just opposite the tourist office by the Roman amphitheatre. Destinations include the following:

Birmingham £15.30, two hours, four daily
Liverpool £9.20, 45 minutes, four daily
London £33, 5½ hours, three daily
Manchester £7.60, 1¼ hours, three daily

TRAIN
The train station is about a mile from the city centre via Foregate St and City Rd, or Brook St. City-Rail Link buses are free for people with rail tickets, and operate between the station and **Bus Stop A** (Frodsham St). Destinations include the following:

Liverpool £7.30, 45 minutes, hourly
London Euston £85.90, 2½ hours, hourly
Manchester £17.60, one hour, hourly

ⓘ Getting Around

Much of the city centre is closed to traffic from 10.30am to 4.30pm, so a car is likely to be a hindrance. The city is easy to walk around anyway, and most places of interest are close to the wall. There are regular buses to both the zoo and the aquarium.

LIVERPOOL

☏0151 / POP 467,500
It's hard not to be infected by a Liverpudlian's love for their own city. For decades this was a hardscrabble town beset by all manner of social ills, but still the love endured, finding its expression in a renowned gallows wit and an obsession with football.

With the worst of times now firmly behind them, it's much easier to feel the love. The city's impressive cultural heritage,

Liverpool

0 0 200 m
0 0.1 miles

G1
Daulby St
Pembroke Pl
London Rd
National Express Coach Station
Hotham St
Lord Nelson St
Russell St
Brownlow Hill
Mt Pleasant
Oxford St
Metropolitan Cathedral of Christ the King
Clarence St
Hope St
Myrtle St
Catherine St
Blackburne St
Blackburne Tce
Canning St
Blackburne Pl
Falkner St
Rice St
Upper Duke St
Hardman St
Hope Pl
Rodney St
Leece St
Roscoe Street
Berry St
Great George St
CHINATOWN
Nelson St
Tabley St
BALTIC TRIANGLE
Wapping
Park La
Liver St
Strand St
Wapping Basin
Wapping Dock
Monarch's Quay
King's Pde
ALBERT DOCK
Salthouse Dock
Canning Dock
Canning Half Tide Bus
PIER HEAD
International Slavery Museum
The Beatles Story
Strand St
Liverpool ONE Bus Station
Hanover St
ROPEWALKS
Duke St
Slater St
Seel St
Parr St
Campbell Sq
Concert Sq
Bold St
Wood St
Renshaw St
Ranelagh St
Church St
School La
Paradise St
Williamson Sq
Queen Sq
Victoria St
Mathew St
Harrington St
Lord St
Temple La
Cavern Quarter
Dale St
Hatton Gdn
Moorfields
Tithebarn St
Old Hall St
Town Hall
Castle St
Water St
Chapel St
New Quay
Goree Piazza
James St
Rumford St
Brunswick St
Port of Manm
Liverpool Building Island
Mersey Ferry
Cunard Building
Royal Liver Building
William Jessop Way
Bath St
King Edward St
Princes Dock
Mersey Tunnel
The Wirral (2km)
Mersey
Mersey Tunnel
Lime St
Lime St Train Station
St George's Hall
William Brown St
World Museum
Walker Art Gallery
Tourist Office
Arriva Express Bus 500
Coppera Hill
Brownlow Hill
Clayton Sq
Central
Renshaw St
Liverpool Cathedral
District (200m); Constellations (350m)

5 World Museum
4 Walker Art Gallery
2 Liverpool Cathedral
1 International Slavery Museum
6 Museum
8 ALBERT DOCK
3 The Beatles Story
7
9
10
11
12
13
14
15
16
17
18
19
20
21
22
23
24
25
26
27
28
29
30
31
32
33
34
35

Liverpool

dating back to when Liverpool was Britain's second-most important city, is a source of justifiable pride to Scousers – as the locals are named, after Scouse, a fish-and-biscuit stew popular with sailors – but what really excites them is the ongoing program of urban regeneration that is transforming a once dilapidated city centre into one of the most pleasant cities in northern England.

History

Liverpool grew wealthy on the back of the triangular trading of slaves, raw materials and finished goods. From 1700 ships carried cotton goods and hardware from Liverpool to West Africa, where they were exchanged for slaves, who in turn were carried to the West Indies and Virginia, where they were exchanged for sugar, rum, tobacco and raw cotton.

As a great port, the city drew thousands of Irish and Scottish immigrants, and its Celtic influences are still apparent. Between 1830 and 1930, however, nine million emigrants – mainly English, Scots and Irish, but also Swedes, Norwegians and Russian Jews – sailed from here to the New World.

The start of WWII led to a resurgence of Liverpool's importance. More than one million American GIs disembarked here before D-Day and the port was, once again, hugely important as the western gateway for transatlantic supplies. The GIs brought with them the latest American records, and Liverpool was thus the first European port of call for the new rhythm and blues that would eventually become rock and roll. Within 20 years, the Mersey Beat was *the* sound of British pop, and four mop-topped Scousers had formed a skiffle band...

◉ Sights

The main attractions are Albert Dock (west of the city centre) and the trendy Ropewalks area (south of Hanover St and west of the two cathedrals). Lime St station, the bus station and the Cavern Quarter – a mecca for Beatles fans – lie just to the north.

◉ City Centre

★**Liverpool Cathedral**   CHURCH
(☎0151-709 6271; www.liverpoolcathedral.org.uk; Upper Duke St; Tower Experience adult/student £5.50/4.50; ⊙8am-6pm, Tower Experience 10am-4.30pm; ⎚82 & 86 from city centre) Britain's largest church, this magnificent neo-Gothic building is also the world's largest Anglican cathedral. It was designed by Sir Giles Gilbert Scott (creator of the red telephone box) and is a stunning bit of architecture, managing at once to provoke awe at its size as well

as a profound feeling of intimacy. You can climb the tower for an unparalleled view of the city and beyond: on a clear day you can see Blackpool Tower 55 miles away.

The Tower Experience also features *Great Space*, a 10-minute, panoramic high-definition movie about the history of the cathedral, which was begun in 1904 but not completed until 1978; and a view of Great George, the world's heaviest set of bells. The vast interior is marked by a studied emptiness, but worth noting is the organ, split between two chambers on opposite sides of the Choir and comprising 10,268 pipes and 200 stops, making it most likely the world's largest operational model. The cathedral is also home to a collection of artworks, including a piece over the West Doors called *For You* by Tracey Emin: a pink neon sign that says 'I felt you and I knew you loved me'. Guides are on hand to offer tours; a donation of £3 is suggested.

★ **Walker Art Gallery** GALLERY
(☎0151-478 4199; www.liverpoolmuseums.org.uk/walker; William Brown St; ☺10am-5pm; ▣all city centre) **FREE** The city's foremost art gallery is the national gallery for northern England, housing an outstanding collection of art from the 14th to the 21st centuries. Its strong suits are Pre-Raphaelite art, modern British art and sculpture – not to mention the rotating exhibits of contemporary expression. It's a family-friendly place too: the ground-floor Big Art for Little Artists gallery is designed for under-eights and features interactive exhibits and games that will (hopefully) result in a lifelong love affair with art.

★ **World Museum** MUSEUM
(☎0151-478 4399; www.liverpoolmuseums.org.uk/wml; William Brown St; ☺10am-5pm; ▣all city centre) **FREE** Natural history, science and technology are the themes of the oldest museum in town, which opened in 1853. Its exhibits range from live bugs to human anthropology. This vastly entertaining and educational museum is spread across five themed floors, from the aquarium on the 1st floor to the planetarium on the 5th, where you'll also find exhibits dedicated to space (moon rocks, telescopes etc) and time (clocks and timepieces from the 1500s to 1960). Highly recommended.

Western Approaches Museum MUSEUM
(www.liverpoolwarmuseum.co.uk; 1-3 Rumford St; adult/child £10.50/9; ☺10am-4.15pm Mon-Tue & Thu-Sun; ▣all city centre) Between 7 February 1941 and 15 August 1945 the secret command centre for the Battle of the Atlantic was in the basement rooms of Derby House. Known as Western Approaches because its main task was to monitor enemy approaches in the Atlantic west of the British Isles, the labyrinthine nerve centre of Allied operations is pretty much as it was at war's end. Highlights include the all-important map room, where you can imagine playing a real-life, full-scale version of Risk.

◉ Albert Dock

Liverpool's biggest tourist attraction is Albert Dock, 2.75 hectares of water ringed by enormous cast-iron columns and impressive five-storey warehouses that make up the country's largest collection of protected

---

LIVERPOOL IN ONE DAY

Start your day at the **Beatles Story** on the Albert Dock: it's an excellent intro to the Fab Four, but fans should make sure to have booked a morning **tour** to **Mendips** and **20 Forthlin Road**, the childhood homes of John Lennon and Paul McCartney respectively; the tour leaves from Albert Dock. If you're not a die-hard Beatles fan, then visit the **International Slavery Museum** and then head into town for a visit to the stunning **cathedral** (p543). For lunch, try either the **Salt House** (p548) or **HOST** (p548).

If you've still got a cultural hunger, you can explore the **Walker Art Gallery** or the wonderful natural science exhibits of the **World Museum**. Football fans should make the trip to Anfield and take the tour of **Liverpool Football Club** (p550). For dinner, if you've planned it long enough in advance, go to **Restaurant Fraiche** (p548); otherwise try **Wreckfish** (p548).

After dinner, be sure to get a drink at the **Philharmonic** (p549), after which you can take in a gig across the street at the **Philharmonic Hall** (p550). If you're into something a little more adrenalised, the clubs of the Baltic Triangle are worth a punt: our favourite is **Constellations** (p550), which always has something interesting going on.

DON'T MISS

(NEVER) LET IT BE

They broke up nearly 50 years ago and two of their members are dead, but the Beatles are bigger business than ever in Liverpool.

Most of it centres around tiny Mathew St, site of the original Cavern Club, which is now the main thoroughfare of the 'Cavern Quarter', an unashamedly commercial effort to cash in on the legacy of the Fab Four. Here you can shuck oysters in the Rubber Soul Oyster Bar, buy a George pillowcase in the From Me to You shop and put it on the pillows of the Hard Days Night Hotel (p547). **The Beatles Story** (☑0151-709 1963; www. beatlesstory.com; Albert Dock; adult/child/student £15.95/9.50/12; ⊗9am-7pm, last admission 5pm; ▣all city centre) in Albert Dock is the city's most visited museum, but if you really want to dig deep into Beatles lore, we strongly recommend a visit to the National Trust–owned **Mendips**, the home where John lived with his aunt from 1945 to 1963, and **20 Forthlin Road**, the plain terraced home where Paul grew up, available only by prebooking a place on the **Beatles' Childhood Homes Tour** (☑0151-427 7231; www. nationaltrust.org.uk; Jury's Inn, 31 Keel Wharf, Wapping Dock; adult/child £23/7.25; ⊗10am, 11am, 2.10pm & 3pm Wed-Sun Mar-Nov).

If you'd rather do it yourself, the tourist offices stock the *Discover Lennon's Liverpool* guide and map, and Ron Jones' *The Beatles' Liverpool*.

buildings and are a World Heritage Site. A fabulous redevelopment program has really brought the dock to life – here you'll find several outstanding museums and an extension of the Tate Gallery, as well as some good restaurants and bars.

⭐**International Slavery Museum**   MUSEUM
(☑0151-478 4499; www.liverpoolmuseums.org.uk/ism; Albert Dock; ⊗10am-5pm) FREE Museums are, by their very nature, like a still of the past, but the extraordinary International Slavery Museum resonates very much in the present. It reveals slavery's unimaginable horrors – including Liverpool's own role in the triangular slave trade – in a clear and uncompromising manner. It does this through a remarkable series of multimedia and other displays, and it doesn't baulk at confronting racism, slavery's shadowy ideological justification for this inhumane practice.

The history of slavery is made real through a series of personal experiences, including a carefully kept ship's log and captain's diary. These tell the story of one slaver's experience on a typical trip, departing Liverpool for West Africa. The ship then purchased or captured as many slaves as it could carry before embarking on the gruesome 'middle passage' across the Atlantic to the West Indies. The slaves that survived the torturous journey were sold for sugar, rum, tobacco and raw cotton, which were then brought back to England for profit. Exhibits include original shackles, chains and instruments used to punish rebellious slaves

– each piece of metal is more horrendous than the next.

Tate Liverpool   GALLERY
(☑0151-702 7400; www.tate.org.uk/liverpool; Albert Dock; special exhibitions adult/child from £6/5; ⊗10am-5pm; ▣all city centre) FREE Touted as the home of modern art in the north, this gallery features a substantial checklist of 20th-century artists across its four floors, as well as touring exhibitions from the ancient ship on London's Bankside. But it's all a little sparse, with none of the energy we'd expect from the world-famous Tate.

Merseyside Maritime Museum   MUSEUM
(☑0151-478 4499; www.liverpoolmuseums.org.uk/maritime; Albert Dock; ⊗10am-5pm; ▣all city centre) FREE The story of one of the world's great ports is the theme of this excellent museum and, believe us, it's a graphic and compelling page-turner. One of the many great exhibits is Emigration to a New World (in the basement), which tells the story of nine million emigrants and their efforts to get to North America and Australia; the walk-through model of a typical ship shows just how tough conditions on board really were.

Museum of Liverpool   MUSEUM
(☑0151-478 4545; www.liverpoolmuseums.org.uk/mol; Pier Head; ⊗10am-5pm; ▣all city centre) FREE Liverpool's storied past is explored through an interactive exploration of the city's cultural and historical milestones: the railroad, poverty, wealth, *Brookside* (a popular '80s and '90s TV soap opera set in

THE THREE GRACES

The area to the north of Albert Dock is known as **Pier Head**, after a stone pier built in the 1760s. This is still the departure point for ferries across the River Mersey, and was for millions of migrants their final contact with European soil.

The Museum of Liverpool is an impressive architectural interloper, but pride of place in this part of the dock still goes to the trio of Edwardian buildings known as the 'Three Graces', dating from the days when Liverpool's star was still ascending: the Port of Liverpool Building, the Cunard Building and the Royal Liver Building, which is topped by Liverpool's symbol, the famous 5.5m copper Liver Bird.

the city), the Beatles and football (the film on the meaning of the game to the city is worth the 15 minutes). The desire to tell all of the city's rich story means there isn't a huge amount of depth, but the kids will love it.

The museum is constantly introducing new elements and temporary exhibitions, with a view towards ensuring that all visits are connected with a contemporary experience of the city. Recent exhibits include Liverpool and War (the collection of photographs taken during the Blitz in WWII is especially poignant) and Pride and Prejudice, an exploration of the city's LGBT identity.

🕮 Tours

⭐ **Anfield Stadium Tour**   TOUR
(www.liverpoolfc.com; Anfield Stadium; stadium tour adult/child £20/15; ⏲9am-5pm except match days; 🚌26 & 27 from Liverpool ONE Bus Station, 17 from Queens St Bus Station) For fans of Liverpool FC, Anfield is a special place, and this is reflected in the reverential tone of the hour-long self-guided audio tour that starts at the top of the new Main Stand and continues down to pitchside. Stops along the way include the home and away dressing rooms and the luxurious players' lounge.

You'll also see the press room and the home dugout, accessed via the new 'walk of champions' tunnel, where you can touch the iconic 'This is Anfield' sign. Staff positioned at various points throughout the tour are on hand to answer questions, generally with a touch of humour that makes the whole experience a memorable one for fans and especially kids. The ground is 2.5 miles northeast of the city centre.

Old Docks Tour   TOURS
(☎0151-478 4499; www.liverpoolmuseums.org.uk/maritime; Merseyside Maritime Museum, Albert Dock; ⏲10.30am, noon & 2.30pm Mon-Wed; 🚌all city centre) FREE Free and a lot of fun, the guided tours of the Old Dock – the world's first commercial enclosed wet dock – offer an insight into the history of Liverpool as a powerful port city (and the source of all its wealth). You'll also get to see the bed of the Pool, the creek that gave the city its name.

Magical Mystery Tour   CULTURAL
(☎0151-703 9100; www.cavernclub.org; per person £18.95; ⏲tours hourly 11am-4pm; 🚌all city centre) Two-hour tour that takes in all Beatles-related landmarks – their birthplaces, childhood homes, schools and places such as Penny Lane and Strawberry Field – before finishing up in the Cavern Club (which isn't the original). Departs from opposite the tourist office on Albert Dock.

✴️ Festivals & Events

⭐ **Grand National**   HORSE RACING
(☎0151-523 2600; http://aintree.thejockeyclub.co.uk; Aintree Racecourse, Ormskirk Rd; ⏲Apr; 🚌300, 311, 345, 350 & 351 from Liverpool ONE Bus Station, 🚉Aintree from Liverpool Central) The world's most famous steeplechase – and one of England's most cherished events – takes place on the first Saturday in April and is run across 4.5 miles and over the most difficult fences in world racing. Its protagonists are 40-odd veteran stalwarts of the jumps, ageing bruisers full of the oh-so-English qualities of grit and derring-do. Book tickets well in advance. Aintree is 6 miles north of the city centre.

Liverpool Sound City   MUSIC
(www.soundcity.uk.com; Baltic Triangle; ⏲May; 🚌all cross city buses) The first weekend in May sees one of the biggest alternative music festivals in town take over the Baltic Triangle and Cains Brewery.

Liverpool International Music Festival   MUSIC
(☎0151-239 9091; www.limfestival.com; Sefton Park; ⏲late Jul; 🚌75 from Lime St Station) A festival showcasing local bands and international acts during the last weekend of July. There's even a VIP experience that gives you access to private bars.

International Beatleweek
MUSIC
(www.internationalbeatleweek.com; ⊙late Aug; 🚍all main bus station services) Sing along to your favourite Beatles song with 70 tribute acts from 20 countries over four days in late August. Organised by the Cavern Club, there are some serious and talented acts on display; some are so good you'll wonder if they're even better than the real thing. They're not.

🛏 Sleeping

Liverpool YHA
HOSTEL £
(☑0345-371 9527; www.yha.org.uk; 25 Tabley St; dm from £13; P �; 🚍all city centre) It may have the look of an Eastern European apartment complex, but this award-winning hostel, adorned with plenty of Beatles memorabilia, is one of the most comfortable you'll find anywhere in the country – and it's recently gotten a spruce up. The dorms with en-suite bathrooms even have heated towel rails.

Tune Hotel
HOTEL £
(☑0151-239 5070; www.tunehotels.com; 3-19 Queen Bldgs, Castle St; r from £35; ✳@索; 🚍all city centre) A slightly upscale version of a pod hotel, Tune offers a comfortable night's sleep (courtesy of a superb mattress and good-quality linen) in a range of en-suite rooms. The cheapest of them have no windows and are quite small, but at this price and in this location, it's an easy sacrifice to make. Bathrooms have power showers.

Titanic Liverpool
HOTEL ££
(☑0151-559 1444; www.titanichotelliverpool.com; Stanley Dock, Regent Road; r/ste from £100/250; 🚍135 & 235 from Liverpool ONE Bus Station) The preferred choice of visiting football teams is this fabulous warehouse conversion on Stanley Dock, now a huge hotel with massive rooms decorated in Scandi-minimalist style – lots of space, leather and earth-tones. Downstairs is the Rum Bar – a tribute to the primary stock of the 19th-century warehouse – and the basement is home to a nice spa.

Hard Days Night Hotel
HOTEL ££
(☑0151-236 1964; www.harddaysnighthotel.com; Central Bldgs, North John St; r £90-140, ste from £350; @索; 🚍all city centre) You don't have to be a fan to stay here, but it helps: unquestionably luxurious, the 110 ultramodern rooms are decorated with specially commissioned drawings of the Beatles. And if you opt for one of the suites, named after Lennon and McCartney, you'll get a white baby grand piano in the style of 'Imagine' and a bottle of fancy bubbly.

Hope Street Hotel
BOUTIQUE HOTEL ££
(☑0151-709 3000; www.hopestreethotel.co.uk; 40 Hope St; r/ste from £100/165; @索; 🚍all city centre) One of the classiest digs in town is this handsome boutique hotel on the city's most elegant street. King-sized beds draped in Egyptian cotton, oak floors with underfloor heating, LCD TVs and sleek modern bathrooms are but the most obvious touches of sophistication at this supremely cool address. Breakfast, taken in the marvellous London Carriage Works (p549), is £18.50.

62 Castle St
BOUTIQUE HOTEL ££
(☑0151-702 7898; www.62castlest.com; 62 Castle St; r from £60; P @索) This elegant property successfully blends the traditional Victorian features of the neoclassical building with a sleek, contemporary style. The 20 fabulously different suites come with high-definition plasma-screen TVs, drench showers and luxe toiletries as standard.

Malmaison
HOTEL ££
(☑0151-229 5000; www.malmaison.com; 7 William Jessop Way, Princes Dock; r/ste from £75/125; P @索; 🚍135 or 235 from Liverpool ONE Bus Station) Malmaison's preferred colour scheme of plum and black is everywhere in this purpose-built hotel, which gives it an air of contemporary sophistication. Everything about the Liverpool Mal is plush, from the huge beds and the deep baths to the heavy velvet curtains and the excellent buffet breakfast. After a while, you'll ignore the constantly piped music of the Beatles.

★2 Blackburne Terrace
B&B £££
(www.2blackburneterrace.com; 2 Blackburne Tce; r £160-180; ✳@索; 🚍all city centre) This exquisite B&B, in a converted Grade II-listed Georgian townhouse from 1826, might just be the most elegant option in town. It only has four rooms, but each is impeccably appointed with a mix of period furniture and modern touches. Breakfast is fabulous and the lounge an absolute delight. Only Room 1 has a shower; all have free-standing baths.

🍴 Eating

Mowgli Street Food
INDIAN £
(www.mowglistreetfood.com; 69 Bold St; mains £3.95-6.95; ⊙noon-9.30pm Sun-Wed, to 10.30pm Thu-Sat; 🚍all city centre) Nisha Katona's ambition to serve authentic Indian street food has been so successful that this is just the first of a handful of restaurants spread throughout the northwest and south as far as Oxford. You'll find no stodgy curries or bland kormas

SPEKE HALL

A marvellous example of an Elizabethan half-timbered hall, **Speke Hall** (NT; www.national trust.org.uk; house & gardens adult/child £11.70/5.85, gardens only adult/child £8.10/4.05; ⏰12.30am-5pm Wed-Sun, also Tue Aug; 🚌500 from Liverpool ONE Bus Station) is filled with gorgeously timbered and plastered rooms. The house contains several 'priest's holes', where the hall's sympathetic owners hid Roman Catholic priests during the anti-Catholic 16th and 17th centuries.

This diagonally patterned Tudor house dates from 1490–1612 and was once surrounded by thousands of acres of land, but these days all that remains is the drive and an oasis of meticulously maintained gardens; the hall's Chapel Farm became the nucleus of nearby Liverpool Airport.

Speke Hall is about 7.5 miles from central Liverpool; the bus will drop you about half a miles from the entrance. The afternoon tours to Paul McCartney's and John Lennon's childhood homes (p545) leave from here.

here, just flavoursome dishes that would pass muster with a resident of Delhi. No bookings.

⭐**Wreckfish** MODERN BRITISH ££
(www.wreckfish.co; 60 Seel St; mains £17-25; 🚇all city centre) Restaurateur Gary Usher's crowd-funded restaurant is a marvellous example of Modern British cuisine at its best: nothing overly fussy, but everything done just right. From the open kitchen come fine dishes such as a roast wing of skate in a brown butter dressing and a near-perfect ribeye with truffle and parmesan chips.

HOST ASIAN, FUSION ££
(www.ho-st.co.uk; 31 Hope St; mains £10-14, Chop Chop £7; ⏰11am-11pm Mon-Sat, noon-10pm Sun; 🍴🚇; 🚇all city centre) A bright, airy room with the look of a chic, contemporary New York brasserie serves up superb pan-Asian dishes such as Indonesian braised lamb with fried rice, and red duck coconut curry with lychees. The starter nibbles are pretty delicious too. The Chop Chop single dish afternoon menu (noon to 5pm) is exceptional.

Monro GASTROPUB ££
(☎0151-707 9933; www.themonro.com; 92 Duke St; 2-course lunch £12.50, dinner mains £12-18; ⏰11am-11pm; 🚇all city centre) 🍴 The Monro is one of the city's favourite spots for lunch, dinner and, especially, weekend brunch. The constantly changing menu of classic British dishes made with ingredients sourced as locally as possible has transformed this handsome old pub into a superb dining experience. It's tough to find pub grub this good elsewhere.

Etsu JAPANESE ££
(☎0151-236 7530; www.etsu-restaurant.co.uk; 25 The Strand, off Brunswick St; mains £13-17, 15-piece

sashimi £15; ⏰noon-2.30pm & 5-9pm Tue, Thu & Fri, 5-9pm Wed & Sat, 4-9pm Sun; 🚇all city centre) The best Japanese food in town is in this contemporary spot on the ground floor of an office building. The speciality of the house is its fresh sushi and sashimi, but you'll find the usual selection of Japanese classics, from chicken *kara-age* (crispy fried chicken pieces marinated in soy, ginger and garlic) to *unagi don* (grilled eel over rice).

Salt House SPANISH ££
(www.salthousetapas.co.uk; Hanover Sq; tapas £5-8; ⏰noon-10.30pm; 🚇all city centre) Liverpool has grown fond of its Spanish tapas bars, and this gorgeous spot – half deli, half restaurant – is the best of them. The cooking is authentic, varied and delicious, from the choice of charcuterie to the wonderful fish dishes. The takeaway counter at the deli does fab sandwiches too.

The Art School MODERN BRITISH ££
(☎0151-230 8600; www.theartschoolrestaurant. co.uk; 1 Sugnall St; 2-/3-course prix fixe £25/32, tasting menu £89; 🍴; 🚇all city centre) The old lantern room of a Victorian 'home for destitute children' is now one of the top spots in town for contemporary British cuisine, courtesy of chef Paul Askew (ex–London Carriage Works). Take your pick of expertly presented British classics from a series of menus, including two vegetarian and one vegan. The wine list is superb.

⭐**Restaurant Fraiche** BRITISH £££
(www.restaurantfraiche.com; 11 Rose Mount, Oxton, Wirral; 6-course menu £88, with wine £133; 🚉Birkenhead Park) Five tables, one solitary chef and a gleaming Michelin star: Marc Wilkinson's tiny restaurant in Oxton on the Wirral is

worth the effort precisely because he goes to great lengths to provide one of the best culinary experiences in Britain. There's no menu and tables are like gold dust – try your luck up to three months in advance.

London Carriage Works MODERN BRITISH £££
(☏0151-705 2222; www.thelondoncarriageworks.co.uk; 40 Hope St; 2-/3-course meal £22/27.50, mains £17-29; ⊗7-10am, noon-3pm & 5-10pm Mon-Fri, 8-11am & noon-10pm Sat, to 9pm Sun; 🖳all city centre) This award-winning restaurant successfully blends ethnic influences from around the globe with staunch British favourites and serves up the result in a beautiful dining room – actually more of a bright glass box divided only by a series of sculpted glass shards. Reservations are recommended.

🍷 Drinking & Nightlife

Ropewalks is Liverpool's busiest bar district – with a lot of late-night spots that keep them drinking and dancing until the wee hours – but there's a fine selection of great bars spread throughout the city. If you're looking to hang with the city's creative crowd, you'll most likely find them in the Baltic Triangle.

★**Botanical Garden** BAR
(www.baltictriangle.co.uk/botanical-garden; 49 New Bird St; ⊗noon-11pm Mar-Sep; 🖳all city centre) A seasonal pop-up bar that specialises in gin cocktails, this is one of the city's coolest summer bars. There's a fine selection of beers if you prefer, and a kitchen that serves excellent Mexican food; in rainy weather you can retreat to the indoor greenhouse, which has a bar made from a converted VW campervan. Weekends feature top-class DJs.

★**Grapes** PUB
(www.thegrapesliverpool.co.uk; 60 Roscoe St; ⊗3.30pm-1am Sun-Wed, to 2am Thu-Sat; 🖳all city centre) One of the friendliest boozers in town is this superb old pub that serves a fine range of local ales (Bier Head, from the Liverpool Organic Brewery, is our favourite). The Beatles would stop in here during their Cavern days, but that's well down the list of reasons to stop in to this wonderful, higgledy-piggledy classic.

Roscoe Head PUB
(☏0151-709 4365; www.roscoehead.co.uk; 24 Roscoe St; ⊗11.30am-midnight Tue-Sat, noon-midnight Sun, 11.30am-11pm Mon; 🖳all city centre) An institution amongst Liverpool boozers is this venerable old pub, which serves a good

selection of ales to its ever-loyal clientele. It gets pretty crowded at weekends, but that just makes for an even better atmosphere.

24 Kitchen Street CLUB
(☏0780 1982583; www.facebook.com/24kitchen street; 24 Kitchen St; tickets £8-12; ⊗9pm-4am Fri & Sat; 🖳all city centre) This multipurpose venue splits its focus between the arts and electronic music. The converted Victorian building is one of the best places in town to dance.

Philharmonic PUB
(36 Hope St; ⊗10am-midnight; 🖳all city centre) This extraordinary bar, designed by the shipwrights who built the *Lusitania,* is one of the most beautiful bars in all of England. The interior is resplendent with etched and stained glass, wrought iron, mosaics and ceramic tiling – and if you think that's good, just wait until you see inside the marble men's toilets, the only heritage-listed lav in the country.

Arts Club CLUB
(☏0151-707 6171; www.academymusicgroup.com/artsclubliverpool; 90 Seel St; £5-13; ⊗7pm-3am Mon-Sat; 🖳all city centre) This converted theatre is home to one of Liverpool's most beloved clubs, despite going through several name and management changes. It still hosts some fabulous nights, with a mix of live music and DJs keeping everyone entertained with some of the best music in town.

Merchant BAR
(40 Slater St; ⊗noon-midnight Mon-Thu & Sun, to 2am Fri, to 3am Sat; 🖳all city centre) First opening in 2016, this bar is in a converted merchant's house and has something of a Scandi feel to it – stripped-back walls, wooden bar tables – which made it the 'in' spot at the time of writing. The bar serves 50

THE BALTIC TRIANGLE

Forget Ropewalks – most of Liverpool's best nightlife is in the Baltic Triangle, a once-run-down area of warehouses roughly between the city centre and the docks just north of Toxteth that is now the city's self-styled creative hub. Best spots to check out include 24 Kitchen Street, pop-up gin bar Botanical Garden, the-recycling-yard-turned-multipurpose-venue Constellations (p550) and District (p550), the first venue to open in the area.

different craft beers, gin by the goblet and – wait for it – Prosecco on tap. Good DJs provide the soundtrack.

☆ Entertainment

★ Liverpool Football Club FOOTBALL

(☑ 0151-263 9199, ticket office 0151-220 2345; www.liverpoolfc.com; Anfield Rd; ☐ 26 from Liverpool ONE Bus Station, 17 from Queen Square Bus Station or 917 from St Johns La) A dominant footballing force for most of the 1970s and 1980s, Liverpool FC remains one of the world's most famous and best-supported clubs, despite not winning a league championship since 1991. Its current crop of stars, led by the magnetic German Jürgen Klopp, play their home games at the wonderful Anfield stadium, north of the city centre.

The experience of a live match – and especially the sound of the fans singing the club's anthem, 'You'll Never Walk Alone', is one of England's sporting highlights. If you can't get a ticket for a game, you can still visit the stadium as part of the Anfield Stadium Tour (p546), which brings fans to the home dressing room and down the tunnel into the pitchside dugout. On match days, the **Soccerbus** (www.merseyrail.org; Sandhills Station; adult single/return £2/3.50, child £1/1.50; ⊙ From 2hr before kick-off) runs from Sandhills Station on the Merseyrail Northern Line.

★ Constellations LIVE PERFORMANCE

(☑ 0151-345 6302; www.constellations-liv.com; 35-39 Greenland St; ⊙ 9am-midnight Mon-Thu, to 2am Fri & Sat, 10am-midnight Sun; ☐ all city centre) Whether you're looking to join a drumming circle, take part in a martial-arts workshop or lose yourself at a rave, this terrific venue in a former recycling yard will have something worth checking out. In good weather DJs play in the garden – one of the best spots in town. It does Sunday meals in summer.

Philharmonic Hall CLASSICAL MUSIC

(☑ 0151-709 3789; www.liverpoolphil.com; Hope St; ☐ 75, 80, 86 from city centre) One of Liverpool's most beautiful buildings, the art deco Phil is home to the city's main orchestras and is the place to go for classical concerts and opera – as well as a broad range of other genres, from synth pop to avant-garde.

District LIVE MUSIC

(☑ 07812 141936; www.facebook.com/District-473 098799400626; 61 Jordan St; ⊙ 7pm-4am Fri-Sat) The first venue to open in the Baltic Triangle, District is an old-school club in a warehouse, which hosts live music and cinema screenings as well as fabulous dance-floor nights. The sound system is reputed to be the best in Liverpool.

Cavern Club LIVE MUSIC

(☑ 0151-236 1965; www.cavernclub.org; 8-10 Mathew St; admission before/after 2pm free/£5; ⊙ 10am-midnight Mon-Wed & Sun, to 1.30am Thu, to 2am Fri & Sat; ☐ all city centre) It's a faithful reconstruction of the club where the Beatles played their early gigs, and not even on the same spot (the original club was a few doors away), but the 'world's most famous club' is still a great spot to see local bands, including (invariably) Beatles cover bands.

ℹ Information

Tourist Office (www.visitliverpool.com; Liverpool Central Library, William Brown St; ⊙ 9.30am-5pm; ☐ all city centre) Leaflets, maps and information are provided in the small tourist office.

ℹ Getting There & Away

AIR

Liverpool John Lennon Airport (☑ 0870 750 8484; www.liverpoolairport.com; Speke Hall Ave; ☐ 86 or 500 from city centre) serves a variety of international destinations as well as destinations in the UK (Belfast, London and the Isle of Man).

The airport is 8 miles south of the centre.
Arriva Express Bus 500 (www.arriva.co.uk; £5; ⊙ 4.30am-7pm) runs every 30 minutes to Liverpool ONE bus station. The journey is about 30 minutes. A taxi to the city centre should cost no more than £20.

BUS

The **National Express Coach Station** (www.nationalexpress.com; Norton St) is 300m north of Lime St train station. There are services to/from most major towns including the following:
Birmingham £14, 2½ hours, five daily
London £30.10, five to six hours, six daily
Manchester £6.10, one hour, hourly
Newcastle £16, 5½ hours, three daily

TRAIN

Liverpool's main station is Lime St. It has hourly services to almost everywhere, including the following:
Chester £7.30, 45 minutes
London Euston £44, 3¼ hours
Manchester £5.90, 45 minutes

ℹ Getting Around

If you plan on using a lot of public transport you should invest in a Walrus card, a contactless fare card available throughout the city for an initial cost of £1. You can then load up the following fare-saver passes on it:

Saveaway (adult/child £5.30/2.70) Single-day pass valid for off-peak travel on buses, trains and Mersey ferries.

Solo Ticket (1/3/5 days £4.80/13.50/21) For unlimited bus travel throughout Merseyside.

BOAT

The famous **Mersey ferry** (www.merseyferries. co.uk; one-way/return £2.70/3.50) crossing for Woodside and Seacombe departs from Pier Head Ferry Terminal, next to the Royal Liver Building (to the north of Albert Dock).

BUS

Liverpool ONE Bus Station (www.mersey travel.gov.uk; Canning Pl) is in the city centre. Local public transport is coordinated by **Merseytravel** (www.merseytravel.gov.uk).

CAR

You won't really have much use for a car in Liverpool, but if you have a car the good news is that parking in most sheltered and open car parks is relatively cheap – usually between £3 and £6 *per day*. The only exception is the huge car park at Liverpool ONE, which costs £2.50 an hour and £17 for a day. Car break-ins are a significant problem, so leave absolutely nothing of value in the car.

TRAIN

Merseyrail (www.merseyrail.org) is an extensive suburban rail service linking Liverpool with the Greater Merseyside area. There are four stops in the city centre: Lime St, Central (handy for Ropewalks), James St (close to Albert Dock) and Moorfields (for the Liverpool War Museum).

LANCASHIRE

As you travel north, past the concrete blanket that covers much of the southern half of the county, Lancashire's undulating landscape begins to reveal itself in all its bucolic glory. East of Blackpool – the faded queen of beachside holidays – the Ribble Valley is a gentle and beautiful appetiser for the Lake District that lies beyond the county's northern border. Lancaster is the county's handsome Georgian capital.

Blackpool

☑ 01253 / POP 150,331

Blackpool's enduring appeal – in the face of low-cost airlines transporting its natural constituents to sunnier coasts – is down to its defiant embrace of a more traditional kind of holiday, coupled with the high-tech adrenaline hit of its famed Pleasure Beach amusement park.

The town is also famous for its tower and its three piers. A successful ploy to extend the brief summer holiday season is the Illuminations, when, from early September to early November, 5 miles of the Promenade are illuminated with thousands of electric and neon lights.

◉ Sights

★ **Blackpool Tower**　　　　　AMUSEMENT PARK
(☑ 0844 856 1000; www.theblackpooltower.com; Tower Pass door price adult/child £56.45/44; ☺ from 10am, closing hours vary) Built in 1894, this 154m-high tower is Blackpool's most recognisable landmark. Watch a 4D film on the town's history in the **Blackpool Tower Eye** before taking the elevator up to the observation deck, which has splendid views and only a (thick) glass floor between you and the ant-sized people below. Visitors are *strongly* urged to buy their tickets online as buying them at the door can be up to 50% more expensive.

Down at ground level, the **dungeon** exhibit sits alongside the old Moorish circus and the magnificent rococo **ballroom**, with its extraordinary sculptured and gilded plasterwork, murals, chandeliers and couples gliding across the beautifully polished wooden floor to the melodramatic tones of a huge Wurlitzer organ. There's also **Jungle Jim's** adventure playground for kids and **Dino Golf** on level 7 – a 9-hole mini-golf course.

Blackpool Pleasure Beach　　AMUSEMENT PARK
(☑ box office 0871 222 9090, enquiries 0871 222 1234; www.blackpoolpleasurebeach.com; Ocean Beach; Pleasure Beach Pass £6, 1-day Unlimited Ride wristband adult/child £39/33; ☺ hours vary, usually 10am-8pm in summer) The lifeblood of Blackpool's commercial life is the Pleasure Beach, a 16-hectare collection of more than 145 rides that attracts some seven million visitors annually. As amusement parks go, it's Britain's most popular by far.

Rides are divided into categories, and once you've gained entry to the park with your Pleasure Beach Pass you can buy tickets for individual categories or for a mixture of them all. Alternatively, an Unlimited Ride wristband includes the £6 entrance fee; there are great discounts if you book your tickets online in advance. There's also the option of a Speedy Pass (£15), which saves you the hassle of queuing for rides by allocating

MANCHESTER, LIVERPOOL & NORTHWEST ENGLAND BLACKPOOL

you a specific ride time – rent it and add as many people to it as you want. You can go one better with the VIP Speedy Pass (£25), which cuts queuing time by 50%; or with the VIP Plus Speedy Pass (£50), which reduces wait time to almost nothing. There are no set times for closing; it depends how busy it is.

North Pier LANDMARK
(Promenade) FREE Built in 1862 and opening a year later, the most famous of Blackpool's three Victorian piers once charged a penny for admission; its plethora of unexciting rides are now free.

🛏 Sleeping

Number One BOUTIQUE HOTEL ££
(☑ 01253-343901; www.numberoneblackpool.com; 1 St Lukes Rd; s/d from £80/110; P ⌂) Far fancier than anything else around, this stunning boutique guesthouse is all luxury and contemporary style. Everything exudes a discreet elegance, from the dark-wood furniture and high-end mod cons to the top-notch breakfast. It's on a quiet road just set back from the South Promenade near the Pleasure Beach amusement park.

Big Blue Hotel HOTEL ££
(☑ 01253-400045; www.bigbluehotel.com; Blackpool Pleasure Beach; r from £70; P @ ⌂) A handsome family hotel with smartly kitted-out rooms. Kids are looked after with DVD players and computer games, while its location at the southern entrance to Blackpool Pleasure Beach should ensure that everyone has something to do.

ℹ Information

Tourist Office (☑ 01253-478222; www.visit blackpool.com; Festival House, Promenade; ⊙9am-6pm Mon-Tue, to 5pm Wed-Sat, 10am-4pm Sun) The tourist office is just south of the North Pier on the Promenade.

ℹ Getting There & Away

BUS
The central coach station is on Talbot Rd, near the town centre. Services include the following:
London £39.70, seven hours, four daily
Manchester £8, 1¾ hours, four daily

TRAIN
The main train station is Blackpool North, about five blocks east of the North Pier on Talbot Rd. Most arrivals change in Preston, but there's a direct service from the following:
Liverpool £16.20, 1½ hours, seven daily

Manchester £17.70, 1¼ hours, half-hourly
Preston £7.50, 30 minutes, half-hourly

ℹ Getting Around

With more than 14,000 car-parking spaces in Blackpool, you'll have no problem parking. A host of travel-card options for trams and buses ranging from one day to a week are available at the tourist office and most newsagents. The **tramway** (one stop £1.70, up to 16 stops £2.70; ⊙ from 10.30am Apr-Oct) shuttles funsters for 11 miles, including along the pier and as far as the Fylde Coast (also serving the central-corridor car parks), every eight minutes or so throughout the day.

Lancaster
☑ 01524 / POP 143,500

Lancashire's handsome Georgian county town is a quiet enough burg these days, but its imposing castle and beautiful, honey-coloured architecture are evidence of its former power and wealth accrued in its 18th-century heyday, when it was an important trading port and a key player in the slave trade.

◉ Sights

★**Lancaster Castle** CASTLE
(☑ 01524-64998; www.lancastercastle.com; Castle Park; adult/child £8/6.50; ⊙9.30am-5pm, guided tours hourly 10am-3pm Mon-Fri, every 30min Sat & Sun) Lancaster's most imposing building is the castle, built in 1150 but added to over the centuries: the Well Tower dates from 1325 and is also known as the Witches' Tower because its basement dungeon was used to imprison the accused in the infamous Pendle Witches Trial of 1612. Also dating from the early 14th century is the impressive twin-towered gatehouse. Visits are by guided tour only as the castle is used as a Crown Court.

Also imprisoned here was George Fox (1624–91), founder of the Quaker movement. The castle was heavily restored in the 18th and 19th centuries to suit a new function as a prison, and it continued to house Category C prisoners until 2011 – the A wing of the prison is part of the guided tour.

Williamson Park &
Tropical Butterfly House GARDENS
(Tropical Butterfly House adult/child £4/3; ⊙9am-5pm Apr-Sep, to 4pm Oct-Mar; ☑18 from bus station) Lancaster's highest point is the 22-hectare spread of this gorgeous park, the highlights of which are (besides the views)

GREAT LANCASHIRE GASTROPUBS

Freemasons at Wiswell (☑ 01254-822218; www.freemasonsatwiswell.com; 8 Vicarage Fold, Wiswell; mains £24-32, 2-/3-course menu £22.50/27.50; ☺ noon-2.30pm & 6-9pm Wed-Sat, noon-6pm Sun) Steven Smith's multi-award-winning restaurant in the lovely village of Wiswell serves a proper feast of the best of New British cuisine. The room is classic English pub, with plain wooden tables and a roaring fire, in contrast to the sophisticated menu. We recommend the suckling pig, slow cooked and served with black pudding, baked sweet potato and fermented-rhubarb sauce.

The White Swan (www.whiteswanatfence.co.uk; 300 Wheatley Ln Rd, Fence, Burnley; mains £19-28; ☺ noon-2pm & 5.30-8.30pm Tue-Thu, to 9.30pm Fri-Sat, noon-4pm Sun) It mightn't look like much from the outside, but this pub in the working village of Fence serves simply outstanding Modern British cuisine. It's all courtesy of chef Tom Parker, who cut his chops in the kitchen of Michelin-starred Nigel Haworth at Northcote (p554). The menu is deliberately small – only three mains – but oh so good.

the **Tropical Butterfly House**, full of exotic and stunning species, and the **Ashton Memorial**, a 67m-high baroque folly built by Lord Ashton (the son of the park's founder, James Williamson) for his wife. The memorial stands on what was once Lancaster Moor, the spot where until 1800 those sentenced to death at the castle were brought to meet the hangman.

Take the bus from the station, or else it's a steep, short walk up Moor Lane.

Lancaster Priory CHURCH
(☑ 01524-65338; www.lancasterpriory.org; Priory Cl; ☺ 9.30am-5pm) Immediately next to Lancaster Castle is the equally fine priory church, founded in 1094 but extensively remodelled in the Middle Ages.

🛏 Sleeping

Sun Hotel & Bar HOTEL ££
(☑ 01524-66006; www.thesunhotelandbar.co.uk; 63-65 Church St; r from £80; 🅿 🛜) A fine hotel in a 300-year-old building with a rustic, old-world look that stops at the bedroom doors – beyond them are 16 stylish and contemporary rooms. The pub downstairs is one of the best in town and a top spot for a bit of grub; mains cost between £10 and £12.

The Borough BOUTIQUE HOTEL ££
(☑ 01524-64170; www.theboroughlancaster.co.uk; 3 Dalton Sq; r from £120; 🅿 @ 🛜) The Borough has nine beautifully appointed rooms – each with an Italian-marble wet-room bathroom for added luxury – spread over two floors of this elegant Georgian building. The downstairs bar has a microbrewery attached, so you don't have to go far to get your fill of locally made cask ales.

🍴 Eating & Drinking

⭐ **Bay Horse Inn** GASTROPUB ££
(☑ 01524-791204; www.bayhorseinn.com; Bay Horse La, Ellel; mains £18-29; ☺ noon-2pm & 6.30-9pm Wed-Sat, noon-3pm & 6-8pm Sun; 🚍 40, 41 & 42 from Lancaster Bus Station) One of Lancashire's best spots for exquisite local dishes is this handsome pub 6 miles south of Lancaster. Chef Craig Wilkinson displays his locavore links with a sign outside showing distances to the farms that supply his produce, which he then transforms into fabulous dishes like slow-cooked, maize-fed duck legs with grilled figs or a perfectly grilled hake fillet.

⭐ **The Hall** CAFE
(☑ 01524-65470; https://thecoffeehopper.com; 10 China St; ☺ 8am-6pm Mon-Sat, 10am-5pm Sun) Nitro, Chemex, batch brew, siphon...whatever way you want it, this superb cafe in the old parish hall can satisfy even the most demanding coffee connoisseur with the perfect brew. It's part of Atkinsons Coffee Roasters, which has been roasting beans since 1840. It also does excellent sandwiches and cakes.

🛍 Shopping

⭐ **Charter Market** MARKET
(www.lancaster.gov.uk; Market Sq; ☺ 9am-4.30pm Wed & Sat Apr-Oct, to 4pm Nov-Mar) Lancaster's historic market is one of the best in the northwest, a gathering place for local producers to sell their goodies. You'll find potted shrimp from Morecambe Bay, locally made hotpots and pies, as well as a range of more exotic dishes from around the world. It extends from Market Sq onto Market St and Cheapside.

ℹ️ Information

Tourist Office (☑ 01524-582394; www.visit lancaster.org.uk; The Storey, Meeting House Lane; ⊙10am-4pm Mon-Sat) Books, maps, brochures and tickets for a variety of events and tours.

ℹ️ Getting There & Away

Lancaster Bus Station is the main hub for transport throughout Lancashire, with regular buses to all the main towns and villages.

Lancaster is on the main west-coast railway line and on the Cumbrian coast line. Destinations include the following:

Carlisle £22.20, one hour, hourly

Manchester £18.20, one hour, hourly

Ribble Valley

Known locally as 'Little Switzerland', Lancashire's most attractive landscapes lie east of brash Blackpool and north of the sprawling urban areas of Preston and Blackburn.

Clitheroe, the Ribble Valley's largest market town is best known for its impressive Norman keep, built in the 12th century and now, sadly, standing empty; from it there are great views of the river valley below.

The northern half of the valley is dominated by the sparsely populated moorland of the Forest of Bowland, an Area of Outstanding Natural Beauty since 1964 and a fantastic place for walks. The southern half features rolling hills, attractive market towns and ruins, with the River Ribble flowing between them.

👁️ Sights & Activities

Norman Keep &
Castle Museum   HISTORIC BUILDING
(www.lancashire.gov.uk; Castle Hill; museum adult/child £4.40/3.30; ⊙keep dawn-dusk, museum 11am-4pm Mar-Oct, noon-4pm Mon-Tue & Fri-Sun Nov-Feb) Dominating the skyline for the last 800 years is this Norman keep, England's smallest and the only remaining castle in the country to have kept a royal garrison during the Civil War. It was built in 1186 and captured by Royalist troops in 1644, but managed to avoid destruction afterwards. The extensive grounds are home to a museum that explores 350 million years of local history.

⭐ Cycle Adventure   CYCLING
(☑ 07518 373007; www.cycle-adventure.co.uk) A bike-hire service that will deliver and collect a bike almost anywhere in the northwest of England. Day rates range from £25 for a mountain bike to £34 for a road bike. A child's mountain bike costs from £19 a day. Helmets and other gear are also available, and it has lots of information, trail maps and other guides.

Ribble Way   WALKING
One of the most popular long-distance paths in northern England is the Ribble Way, a 70-mile footpath that follows the River Ribble from its source at Ribblehead (in the Yorkshire Dales), passing through Clitheroe to the estuary at Preston.

Lancashire Cycle Way   CYCLING
(www.visitlancashire.com) The Ribble Valley is well covered by the northern loop of the Lancashire Cycle Way; for more information about routes, safety and so on, check out Cycle Adventure.

🛏️ Sleeping & Eating

⭐ Inn at Whitewell   INN £££
(☑ 01200-448222; www.innatwhitewell.com; Forest of Bowland; s/d from £99/137) Once the home of Bowland's forest keeper, this superb guesthouse with antique furniture, peat fires and Victorian claw-foot baths is one of the finest accommodations in northern England. Everything is top-notch, including the views: it's like being in the French countryside. Its **restaurant** (mains £15-27) is excellent too.

⭐ Parkers Arms   GASTROPUB ££
(☑ 01200-446236; www.parkersarms.co.uk; Newton-in-Bowland; mains £15-20; ⊙12.30-2.30pm & 6.30-8.30pm Wed-Fri, 12.30-9pm Sat, 12.30-6pm Sun) This unspoilt village pub is where you'll find the simply exceptional cooking of *terroir* chef Stosie Madi. She's best known for her superb pies, but her menus – which change up to twice daily depending on what's available – explore the very best of Lancashire cuisine, from Newton venison with local bramble and unpasteurised cheese to a superb Lancashire hotpot.

⭐ Northcote Hotel   MODERN BRITISH £££
(☑ 01254-240555; www.northcote.com; Northcote Rd, Langho; mains £23-48; ⊙noon-2pm & 7-9.30pm) One of the finest restaurants in northern England, Northcote's Michelin-starred menu is the unpretentious, delicious creation of chef Lisa Goodwin-Allen and sommelier Craig Bancroft. Duck, lamb, beef and chicken are given Modern British treat-

ment and the result is fantastic. Upstairs are 26 beautifully styled bedrooms (£240 to £380), making this one of the northwest's top gourmet getaways. Bookings strongly recommended.

ISLE OF MAN

Forget what you may have heard on the mainland: there's nothing odd about the Isle of Man (Ellan Vannin in the local lingo, Manx). The island's reputation for oddity is entirely down to its persistent insistence that it do its own thing, rejecting England's warm embrace in favour of a semiautonomous status (it is home to the world's oldest continuous parliament, the Tynwald).

What you'll find here is beautiful scenery in the lush valleys, barren hills and rugged coastlines. In 2016 Unesco designated the Isle of Man a biosphere reserve (one of five in the UK), marking it out as one of the most beautiful spots in Britain to enjoy nature. That bucolic charm is shattered during the world-famous Tourist Trophy (TT) motorbike racing season, which attracts 50,000 punters every May and June. Needless to say, if you want a slice of silence, avoid the high-rev bike fest.

❶ Getting There & Away

AIR

Ronaldsway Airport (www.iom-airport.com) is 10 miles south of Douglas near Castletown. The following airlines have services to the island:

Aer Lingus Regional (www.aerlingus.com; from £25)

British Airways (www.britishairways.com; from £82)

Easyjet (www.easyjet.com; from £20)

Flybe (www.flybe.com; from £25)

Loganair (www.loganair.co.uk; from £60)

BOAT

Isle of Man Steam Packet (www.steam-packet.com; foot passenger single/return from £25/42, car & 2 passengers return from £170) offers a car ferry and high-speed catamaran service from Liverpool and Heysham to Douglas. From mid-April to mid-September there's also a service to Dublin and Belfast.

❶ Getting Around

Buses link the airport with Douglas every 30 minutes between 7am and 11pm. Taxis have fixed fares to destinations throughout the island; a cab to Douglas costs £20, to Peel £25.

---

❶ MANX HERITAGE HOLIDAY PASS

The island's 11 major sights are managed by Manx Heritage (MH; www.manxnationalheritage.im), the island's version of the British National Trust. They include castles, historic homes, museums and the world's largest working waterwheel. Unless otherwise indicated, Manx Heritage sites are open 10am to 5pm daily, from Easter to October. The Manx Heritage Holiday Pass (www.manxheritageshop.com; adult/child £25/12) grants entry to all of the island's heritage attractions; it's available at tourist offices or online.

The island has a comprehensive bus service (www.gov.im); the tourist office in Douglas has timetables and sells tickets. It also sells the Go Explore ticket (one day adult/child £16/8, three day £32/16), which gives you unlimited public-transport use, including the tram to Snaefell and Douglas' horse-trams.

Bikes can be hired from **Simpsons Ltd** (☑ 01624-842472; www.simpsons.im; 15-17 Michael St, Peel; per day/week £20/100; ⊙ 9am-5pm Mon-Sat) in Peel.

Petrolheads will love the scenic, sweeping bends that make for some exciting driving – and the fact that outside of Douglas town there's no speed limit. Naturally, the most popular drive is along the Tourist Trophy route. Car-hire operators have desks at the airport, and charge from £35 per day.

The 19th-century electric and steam **rail services** (☑ 01624-663366; www.iombusandrail. info; ⊙ Mar-Oct) are a thoroughly satisfying way of getting from A to B:

Douglas–Castletown–Port Erin Steam Train Return £12.40

Douglas–Laxey–Ramsey Electric Tramway Return £12.40

Laxey–Summit Snaefell Mountain Railway Return £12

Douglas

☑ 01624 / POP 26,218

The island's largest town and most important commercial centre is a little faded around the edges and a far cry from its Victorian heyday when it was, like Blackpool across the water, a favourite with British holidaymakers. The bulk of the island's hotels and restaurants are still here – as well as most of the finance houses that are frequented so regularly by tax-allergic Brits.

◉ Sights

Manx Museum & National Art Gallery MUSEUM
(MH; www.manxnationalheritage.im; Kingswood Grove; ◷10am-5pm Mon-Sat) FREE This modern museum begins with an introductory film to the island's 10,000-year history and then races through it, making various stops including Viking gold and silver, the history of the Tynwald, the island's internment camps during WWII and the famous TT races. Also part of the museum is the National Art Gallery, which has works by the island's best-known artists including Archibald Knox and John Miller Nicholson. Overall a fine introduction to the island.

⌂ Sleeping

★ Saba's Glen Yurt YURT ££
(www.sabasglenyurt.com; Close Ny Howin, Main Rd, Union Mills; 2-person yurt £110) ∥ In the conservation area of Union Mills you can bed down in a solar-powered eco-yurt that comes equipped with a king-sized bed and a wood burner. Outside are hot tubs filled with steaming water that you can sink into up to your shoulders.

There's a two-night minimum weekend stay between April and September. It's 2.5 miles northeast of town on the road to Peel.

Inglewood BOUTIQUE HOTEL ££
(☎01624-674734; www.inglewoodhotel-isleofman.com; 26 Palace Tce, Queens Promenade; s/d incl breakfast from £42.50/85; 🅿@🛜) Sea-view suites in this beautifully refurbished, friendly hotel have big wooden beds and leather sofas. The homemade breakfasts are superb,

---

PEEL

Peel is the west coast's most appealing town, with a fine sandy beach. Its big attraction is the ruin of the 11th-century Peel Castle (MH; www.manxnational heritage.im; adult/child £6/3; ◷10am-5pm Jun-Aug, to 4pm Mar-May & Sep-Oct), stunningly positioned atop St Patrick's Island and joined to Peel by a causeway. There's an audio guide available to help you make sense of the ruins, and you're also advised to keep your eyes open for the castle's ghost – a black dog called Moddey Dhoo.

---

and the residents' bar specialises in whisky from all over the world.

Claremont Hotel HOTEL £££
(☎01624-617068; www.claremonthoteldouglas. com; 18-22 Loch Promenade; r from £150; 🅿❄@🛜) The island's fanciest hotel is this classic on the promenade, with huge rooms kitted out with handsome wooden floors, seaside colours and comfortable beds with crisp linen.

✗ Eating

★ Little Fish Cafe SEAFOOD ££
(www.littlefishcafe.com; 31 North Quay; mains £11.50-14.50; ◷11am-9pm) Superb seafood presented in a variety of ways, from hake with mustard and lemon butter to a Kerala-style fish curry. For brunch, the Queenie Po'Boy – battered Manx queenies (queen scallops), paprika mayo and avocado on sourdough brioche – is divine. It also does meat dishes, but the real focus is on the sea.

Tanroagan SEAFOOD ££
(☎01624-472411; www.tanroagan.co.uk; 9 Ridgeway St; mains £15-21; ◷noon-2pm & 6-9.30pm Tue-Sat) The place for all things from the sea, this elegant restaurant serves fresh fish straight off the boats, giving them the merest of continental twists or just a spell on the hot grill. Reservations are recommended.

14North MODERN BRITISH ££
(☎01624-664414; www.14north.im; 14 North Quay; mains £16-25; ◷noon-2.30pm & 6-9.30pm Mon-Sat) An old timber merchant's house is home to this smart restaurant specialising in local dishes including pickled herring, lamb rump and, of course, queenies – all sourced locally, of course.

❶ Information

Tourist Office (☎01624-686766; www.visit isleofman.com; Sea Terminal Bldg, Douglas; ◷9.15am-7pm, closed Sun Oct-Apr)

Northern Isle of Man

North of the capital, the dominant feature is Snaefell (621m), the island's tallest mountain. You can follow the Tourist Trophy circuit up and over the mountain towards Ramsey, or take the alternate route along the coast, going through Laxey, where you can also take the electric tram to near the top of Snaefell, from which it's an easy walk to the summit.

◎ Sights

★ Great Laxey Wheel
HISTORIC SITE

(MH; https://manxnationalheritage.im/our-sites/laxey-wheel/; Mines Rd, Laxey; adult/child £8/4; ⊙9.30am-5pm Apr-Oct) It's no exaggeration to describe the Lady Isabella Laxey Wheel, built in 1854 to pump water from a mine, as a 'great' wheel: it measures 22m across and can draw 1140L of water per minute from a depth of 550m. The largest wheel of its kind in the world, it's named after the wife of the then lieutenant-governor.

Grove Museum of Victorian Life
MUSEUM

(MH; www.manxnationalheritage.im; Andreas Rd, Ramsey; adult/child £6/3; ⊙10am-5pm Jun-Aug, to 4pm Sep, 11am-3pm Sat & Sun Mar) This imposing house was built in the mid-19th century by Liverpool shipping merchant Duncan Gibb as a summer retreat for himself and his family. It has been maintained pretty much as it was in its Victorian heyday, and you can wander through its period rooms – and even learn what it was like to be a scullery maid! The house was occupied by the Gibb family until the 1970s. It's on the edge of Ramsey.

❶ Getting There & Away

Bus Vannin services travel the 15 miles between Ramsey and Douglas either via Laxey and the coast (bus 3, 3A) or more directly inland past Snaefell (bus X3). Alternatively, there's the electric tram, which trundles up the coast to Ramsey. Another tram serves Snaefell from Laxey.

Southern Isle of Man

The quiet harbour town of Castletown, at the southern end of the island, was the Isle of Man's original capital. It is home to a fabulous castle and the old parliament.

Port Erin is a smallish Victorian seaside resort that plays host to the small **Railway Museum** (Station Rd; adult/child £2/1; ⊙9.30am-4.30pm Apr-Oct, guided tours also 7.30pm & 9.30pm Thu, 11am-1pm Sun mid-Jul–mid-Sep). Port St Mary lies across the headland and is linked to by steam train. The Calf of Man bird sanctuary is accessed from Port St Mary.

◎ Sights

★ Castle Rushen
CASTLE

(MH; www.manxnationalheritage.im; Castletown Sq, Castletown; adult/child £8/4; ⊙10am-5pm May-Aug) Castletown is dominated by the impressive 13th-century Castle Rushen, one of the most complete medieval structures in Europe. You can visit the gatehouse, medieval kitchens, dungeons and the Great Hall. The flag tower affords fine views of the town and coast.

Cregneash Village Folk Museum
MUSEUM

(MH; www.manxnationalheritage.im; adult/child £6/3; ⊙10am-5pm Jun-Aug, to 4pm Apr-May & Sep-Oct) Until the early part of the 20th century, most farmers on the island engaged in a practice known as crofting – a social system defined by small-scale communal food production. This folk museum on a raised plateau on the island's southern tip includes a traditional Manx cottage where you can see how crofters lived, while out in the fields you can see four-horned sheep and Manx cats, which you're encouraged to pat.

Old House of Keys
MUSEUM

(MH; www.manxnationalheritage.im; Parliament Sq; debate adult/child £6/3, other times free; ⊙10am-4pm Apr-Oct) The former home of the Manx Parliament (lower house of the Tynwald) has been restored to its 1866 appearance – a key date in island history as it was then that the parliament voted to have its members elected by popular mandate. At 11am and 2.45pm visitors can participate in a debate on the hot topics of the day – gaining an insight into how this parliamentary democracy went about its business. You can also learn about the island's struggle for self-determination.

Calf of Man
BIRD SANCTUARY

(www.manxnationalheritage.im; ⊙Apr-Sep) This small island just off Cregneash is on one of western Britain's major bird migration routes, and 33 species breed annually here, including Manx shearwaters, kittiwakes, razorbills and shags. Other species normally observed on the island include peregrines, hen harriers, choughs and ravens. It's been an official bird sanctuary since 1939. **Gemini Charter** (☏01624-832761; www.geminicharter.co.uk; trips 1-4hr per person £15-30) runs birdwatching trips to the island from Port St Mary.

❶ Getting There & Away

There is a regular Bus Vannin service between Castletown and Douglas (and the airport en route), and between Castletown, Port Erin and Port St Mary (£5.70 return). There's also the Douglas to Port Erin Steam Train (£12.40 return) which stops in Castletown. A taxi from the airport to Castletown costs around £8.

The Lake District & Cumbria

POP 499,800

Best Places to Eat

➡ L'Enclume (p589)

➡ Old Stamp House (p569)

➡ Jumble Room (p572)

➡ Punch Bowl Inn (p588)

➡ Drunken Duck (p573)

➡ Fellpack (p580)

Best Places to Stay

➡ Forest Side (p571)

➡ Brimstone Hotel (p577)

➡ Daffodil Hotel (p571)

➡ Wasdale Head Inn (p578)

➡ Cottage in the Wood (p580)

➡ Eltermere Inn (p577)

Why Go?

'No part of the country is more distinguished by its sublimity', mused the grand old bard of the lakes, William Wordsworth, and a couple of centuries on, his words still ring true. For natural splendour, nowhere in England can compare to the Lake District. For centuries, poets, painters and perambulators alike have been flocking here in search of inspiration and escape, and it's still the nation's favourite place to revel in the majesty of the English landscape.

The main draw in the region is undoubtedly the Lake District – England's largest national park (885 sq miles) and, since 2017, a Unesco World Heritage Site. Every bend in the road reveals more eye-popping views: deep valleys, plunging passes, glittering lakes, whitewashed inns, barren hills. But it's worth exploring beyond the national park's boundaries, too: the old towns of Carlisle, Kendal and Penrith are full of historical interest and Cumbria's coast has a windswept charm all of its own.

When to Go

➡ The Lake District is the UK's most popular national park; visit in early spring and late autumn for the smallest crowds.

➡ The weather is notoriously fickle – showers can strike at any time of year, so bring wet-weather gear just in case.

➡ Cumbria's largest mountain festival is held in Keswick in mid-May, while the Beer Festival in June welcomes ale aficionados from across the globe.

➡ Ambleside's traditional sports day on the last Saturday in July features events such as hound trailing and Cumbrian wrestling; Grasmere's annual sports day takes place on the August bank holiday.

➡ In November the world's greatest liars congregate on Santon Bridge for their annual fibbing contest.

History

Neolithic settlers arrived in the Lake District around 5000 BC. The region was subsequently occupied by Celts, Angles, Vikings and Romans. During the Dark Ages it was the centre of the ancient kingdom of Rheged.

During the Middle Ages, Cumbria marked the start of the 'Debatable Lands', the wild frontier between England and Scotland. Bands of raiders known as Border Reivers regularly plundered the area, prompting the construction of defensive pele towers and castles at Carlisle, Penrith and Kendal.

The area became a centre for the Romantic movement during the 19th century, largely thanks to the Cumbrian-born poet William Wordsworth, who also championed the need to protect the Lake District's landscape from overdevelopment – a dream that was achieved in 1951 when the Lake District National Park was formed.

The present-day county of Cumbria was formed from the neighbouring districts of Cumberland and Westmorland in 1974.

🏃 Activities

Cycling

Cycling is a great way to explore the Lake District and Cumbria, as long as you don't mind the hills. For short mountain-bike rides, the trails of Grizedale Forest (www.forestry.gov.uk/grizedale) and Whinlatter Forest Park (p579) are very popular.

Long-distance touring routes include the 70-mile Cumbria Way between Ulverston, Keswick and Carlisle; the 140-mile Sea To Sea Cycle Route (C2C, NCN 7; www.c2c-guide.co.uk), which begins in Whitehaven and cuts east across the northern Pennines to Newcastle; and the 173-mile Reivers Route (NCN 10; www.reivers-route.co.uk) from the River Tyne to Whitehaven.

Walking

For many people, hiking is the main reason for a visit to the Lake District. All tourist offices and bookshops sell maps and guidebooks, such as Collins' *Lakeland Fellranger* and Ordnance Survey's *Pathfinder Guides*. Purists prefer Alfred Wainwright's seven-en-volume *Pictorial Guides to the Lakeland Fells* (1955–66) – part walking guides, part illustrated artworks, part philosophical memoirs – with painstakingly hand-penned maps and text.

Maps are essential: the Ordnance Survey's 1:25,000 *Landranger* maps are used by most official bodies, while some hikers prefer the Harvey *Superwalker* 1:25,000 maps.

Long-distance trails that pass through Cumbria include the 54-mile Allerdale Ramble from Seathwaite to the Solway Firth, the 70-mile Cumbria Way from Ulverston to Carlisle, and the 191-mile Coast to Coast from St Bees to Robin Hood's Bay in Yorkshire. Door-to-door baggage services such as Coast to Coast Packhorse (✓ 017683-71777; www.c2cpackhorse.co.uk) or Sherpa Van (✓ 0871-520 0124; www.sherpavan.com) transport luggage from one destination to the next.

Other Activities

Cumbria is a haven for outdoor activities, including rock climbing, orienteering, horse riding, archery, fell (mountain) running and *ghyll* (waterfall) scrambling. Contact the Outdoor Adventure Company (✓ 01539-722147; www.theoutdooradventurecompany.co.uk; Old Hutton), Rookin House (✓ 017684-83561; www.rookinhouse.co.uk) or Keswick Adventure Centre (✓ 017687-75687; www.keswickadventurecentre.co.uk; Newlands).

ℹ Getting There & Away

The nearest major airport is in Manchester, but Carlisle's minuscule airport also now has direct flights to/from London Southend, Belfast and Dublin.

Carlisle is on the main West Coast train line from London Euston to Manchester and Glasgow. To get to the Lake District, you need to change at Oxenholme for Kendal and Windermere. The lines around the Cumbrian coast and between Settle and Carlisle are particularly scenic.

National Express coaches run direct from London Victoria and Glasgow to Windermere, Carlisle and Kendal.

ℹ Getting Around

BOAT

There are round-the-lake ferry services on Windermere, Coniston Water, Ullswater and Derwentwater. Windermere also has cruises and a cross-lake ferry service.

BUS

The main bus operator is **Stagecoach** (www.stagecoachbus.com). Services on most routes are reduced in winter. You can download timetables from the Stagecoach website or the Cumbria County Council website (www.cumbria.gov.uk). Bus timetables are also available from tourist offices.

Lake District & Cumbria Highlights

1 Scafell Pike (p577) Climbing to the summit of England's highest mountain.

2 Hill Top (p572) Spotting the inspirations for Beatrix Potter's tales.

3 Steam Yacht Gondola (p574) Cruising Coniston Water in stately 19th-century style.

4 Grizedale Forest (p559) Cycling woodland trails surrounded by outdoor art.

5 Honister Slate Mine (p583) Delving into the depths of the Lake District's last slate mine.

6 La'al Ratty (p588) Catching the miniature steam trains into Eskdale.

7 Dove Cottage (p570) Exploring Wordsworth's much-loved Lakeland cottage.

8 Carlisle Castle (p590) Patrolling the battlements of Carlisle's mighty medieval fortress.

9 Borrowdale and Buttermere (p584) Taking a road trip through the loveliest Lakeland valleys.

10 Lowther Estate (p592) Visiting a great Cumbrian estate that's slowly being brought back to life.

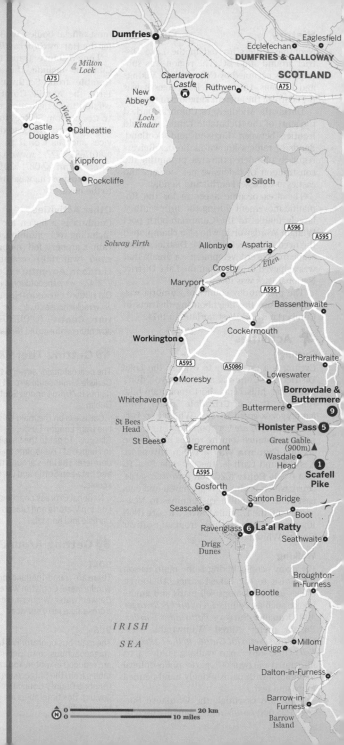

Useful services:

Bus 555 (Lakeslink) Lancaster to Keswick, stopping at all the main towns, including Windermere and Ambleside.

Bus 505 (Coniston Rambler) Kendal, Windermere, Ambleside and Coniston.

Bus X4/X5 Penrith to Workington via Troutbeck, Keswick and Cockermouth.

CAR

Traffic can be heavy during peak season and holiday weekends. Many Cumbrian towns use timed parking permits for on-street parking, which you can pick up free from local shops and tourist offices.

If you're driving to the Lake District, National Trust membership is a good idea, as it means you can park for free at all of the National Trust's car parks (which otherwise charge extortionately high rates).

TRAVEL PASSES

Several travel passes are available in Cumbria.

Lakes Day Ranger (adult/child/family £23/11.50/45) The best-value one-day ticket, allowing a day's unlimited travel on trains and buses in the Lake District. It also includes a boat cruise on Windermere, 10% discount on the steam railways and 20% discount on the Coniston Launch, Keswick Launch and Ullswater Steamers.

Cumbria Day Ranger (adult/child £43/21.50) This pass provides one day's train travel in Cumbria and parts of Lancashire, North Yorkshire, Northumberland and Dumfries and Galloway.

Central Lakes Dayrider (adult/child/family £8.30/6.20/23) This pass covers Stagecoach buses around Bowness, Ambleside, Grasmere, Langdale and Coniston; it includes buses 599, 505 and 516. For an extra £4/2 per adult/child you can add a boat cruise on Windermere or Coniston.

Keswick & Honister Dayrider (adult/child/family £8.30/6.20/23) Covers buses from Keswick through Borrowdale, Buttermere, Lorton and the Whinlatter Forest Park.

North West Megarider Gold (per week £28) Covers seven days' travel on all Stagecoach buses operating in Lancashire, Merseyside, Cumbria, West Cheshire and Newcastle.

THE LAKE DISTRICT

POP 40,800

The Lake District (or Lakeland, as it's commonly known round these parts) is by far the UK's most popular national park. Every year, some 15 million people pitch up to explore the region's fells and countryside, and it's not hard to see why. Ever since the Romantic po-

ets arrived in the 19th century, its postcard panorama of craggy hilltops, mountain tarns and glittering lakes has been stirring the imaginations of visitors. Since 2017 it has also been a Unesco World Heritage Site, in recognition of its unique hill-farming culture.

ℹ️ Information

The national park's main visitor centre is at Brockhole (p567), just outside Windermere, and there are tourist offices in Windermere (p567), Bowness (p567), Ambleside (p570), Keswick (p581), Coniston (p576) and Carlisle (p592).

Windermere & Around

☏ 015395 / POP 5423

Stretching for 10.5 miles between Ambleside and Newby Bridge, Windermere isn't just the queen of Lake District lakes – it's also the largest body of water anywhere in England, closer in stature to a Scottish loch. It's been a centre for tourism since the first trains chugged into town in 1847 and it's still one of the national park's busiest spots.

Confusingly, the town of Windermere is split in two: Windermere Town is actually 1.5 miles from the lake, at the top of a steep hill, while touristy, overdeveloped Bowness-on-Windermere (usually shortened just to Bowness) sits on the lake's eastern shore.

Accommodation (and parking) can be hard to come by during holidays and busy periods, so plan accordingly.

◎ Sights & Activities

★**Wray Castle**　　　　　HISTORIC SITE

(NT; www.nationaltrust.org.uk/wray-castle; adult/child £9.60/4.80; ⊙10am-5pm) An impressive sight with its turrets and battlements, this mock-Gothic castle was built in 1840 for James Dawson, a retired doctor from Liverpool, but it has been owned by the National Trust since 1929. Though the interior is largely empty, the lakeside grounds are glorious. It was once used as a holiday home by Beatrix Potter's family. The best way to arrive is by boat from Bowness; there's limited parking and preference is given to non-driving visitors on busy days.

Blackwell House　　　　HISTORIC BUILDING

(☏01539-722464; www.blackwell.org.uk; adult/child under 16yr £8/free; ⊙10.30am-5pm Apr-Oct, to 4pm Feb, Mar, Nov & Dec) Two miles south of Bowness on the B5360, Blackwell House is a glorious example of the 19th-century Arts

Lake District

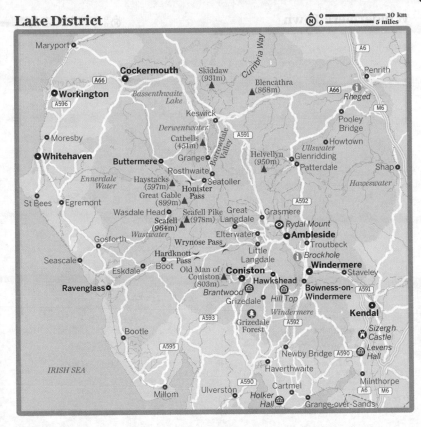

and Crafts Movement, which championed handmade goods and craftsmanship over the mass-produced mentality of the Industrial Revolution. Designed by Mackay Hugh Baillie Scott for Sir Edward Holt, a wealthy brewer, the house shimmers with Arts and Crafts details: light, airy rooms, bespoke craftwork, wood panelling, stained glass and delft tiles. The mock-medieval Great Hall and serene White Drawing Room are particularly fine.

The cafe has brilliant views over Windermere.

Fell Foot Park GARDENS

(NT; www.nationaltrust.org.uk/fell-foot-park; ⊙8am-8pm Apr-Sep, 9am-5pm Oct-Mar, cafe 10am-5pm) **FREE** Located at the southern end of Windermere, 7 miles south of Bowness, this 7-hectare lakeside estate originally belonged to a manor house. It's now owned by the National Trust and its shoreline paths and grassy lawns are ideal for a sunny-day picnic. There's a small cafe and rowing boats are available for hire.

Lakeland Motor Museum MUSEUM

(☑015395-30400; www.lakelandmotormuseum.co.uk; Backbarrow; adult/child £8.75/5.25; ⊙9.30am-5.30pm Apr-Sep, to 4.30pm Oct-Mar) Two miles south of Newby Bridge on the A590, this museum houses a wonderful collection of antique cars: classic (Minis, Austin Healeys, MGs), sporty (DeLoreans, Audi Quattros, Aston Martins) and downright odd (Scootacars, Amphicars). There are also quirky exhibits on the history of caravans and vintage bicycles. A separate building explores Donald and Malcolm Campbell's record attempts on Coniston Water, with replicas of the 1935 Bluebird car and 1967 *Bluebird K7* boat. Online bookings get a 10% discount.

Lakes Aquarium AQUARIUM

(☑015395-30153; www.lakesaquarium.co.uk; Lakeside; adult/child £7.45/5.45; ⊙10am-6pm) At the southern end of the lake near Newby Bridge, this aquarium explores a range

Windermere Town

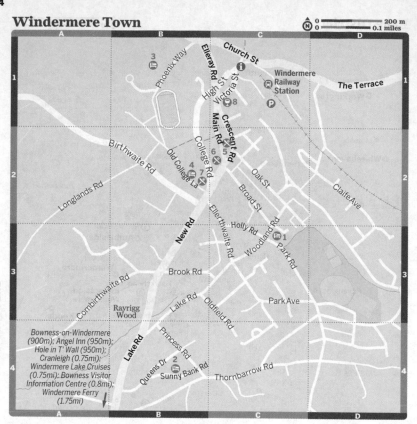

Windermere Town

🛏 Sleeping
1 1 Park Road	C3
2 Rum Doodle	B4
3 The Hideaway	B1
4 Wheatlands Lodge	B2

✕ Eating
5 Francine's	C2
6 Homeground	C2
7 Hooked	B2

🍷 Drinking & Nightlife
8 Crafty Baa	C1

of underwater habitats from tropical Africa through to Morecambe Bay. Windermere Lake Cruises (p566) and the Lakeside & Haverthwaite Railway (p564) stop right beside the aquarium, or you could catch bus 6/X6 from Bowness. There's a £1 discount per ticket for online bookings.

Lakeside & Haverthwaite Railway   RAIL
(📞 015395-31594; www.lakesiderailway.co.uk; adult/child/family return from Haverthwaite to Lakeside £6.90/3.45/19, 1-day rover ticket adult/child £10/5; ⏰ mid-Mar–Oct) Built to carry ore and timber to the ports at Ulverston and Barrow, these vintage steam trains puff their way between Haverthwaite, near Ulverston, and Newby Bridge and Lakeside. There are five to seven trains a day, timed to correspond with the Windermere cruise boats – you can buy combo tickets that include an onward lake cruise to Bowness or Ambleside.

🛏 Sleeping

Windermere YHA   HOSTEL £
(📞 0845-371 9352; www.yha.org.uk; Bridge Lane; dm £13-35; ⏰ reception 7.30-11.30am & 3-10pm; 🅿 @) Slightly misleadingly, the closest YHA to Windermere is actually about 1.5 miles from the lake, halfway between Troutbeck Bridge and Troutbeck village. Once a

mansion, the imposing building has been modernised with the usual YHA set-up: bunk-bed dorms, canteen, self-catering kitchen, lounge and gear-drying room. There are fine Windermere views from the front rooms, and space to camp outside, too.

Inconveniently, buses from Windermere stop about a mile downhill at Troutbeck Bridge.

★ Rum Doodle B&B ££

(☎015394-45967; www.rumdoodlewindermere.com; Sunny Bank Rd, Windermere Town; d £95-139; P 📶) Named after a classic travel novel about a fictional mountain in the Himalayas, this B&B zings with imagination. Its rooms are themed after places and characters in the book, with details such as book-effect wallpaper, vintage maps and old suitcases. Top of the heap is the Summit, snug under the eaves with a separate sitting room. Two-night minimum in summer.

The Hideaway B&B ££

(☎015394-43070; www.thehideawayatwindermere.co.uk; Phoenix Way; d £90-170; P 📶) There's a fine range of rooms available at this much-recommended B&B in a former schoolmaster's house. There's a choice for all budgets, from Standard Comfy (simple decor, not much space) all the way to Ultimate Comfy (claw-foot tub, split-level mezzanine, space galore). Regardless which you choose, you'll be treated to spoils such as homemade cakes and afternoon tea every day.

Wheatlands Lodge B&B ££

(☎015394-43789; www.wheatlandslodge-windermere.co.uk; Old College Lane; d £105-140; P 📶) There's nary a whiff of pretension about this B&B, halfway between Windermere and Bowness – it just does its job with elegance and efficiency. The house is Victorian, and rooms range from Club (a tad cramped) to Master (space and then some). Breakfast is a high point, with homemade muesli, local bacon and sausages, plus smoked salmon from Loch Ewe.

1 Park Road B&B ££

(☎015394-42107; www.1parkroad.co.uk; 1 Park Rd, Windermere Town; d £80-112; P 📶 🐾) A reliable choice in Windermere Town, with six pleasant, spacious rooms (including a couple of dog-friendly ones). Thoughtful touches such as in-room DVD players, fresh (not UHT) milk for tea and welcome treats such as made-in-Cumbria fudge and marshmallow elevate it above the competition – and rates aren't bad for Windermere, especially during the week.

Gilpin Hotel HOTEL £££

(☎015394-88818; www.gilpinlodge.co.uk; Crook Rd; r £275-465; P) Windermere's B&Bs might be pushing up their rates to silly levels, but this famously posh country-house retreat shows them how it should be done. The fabulously fancy rooms are named after fells, garden suites have their own decks and outdoor hot tubs, and the exclusive Lake House nearby comes with its own chauffeur.

A superb Michelin-starred restaurant, a lovely spa and hectares of grounds complete the high-class package.

Cranleigh HOTEL £££

(☎015394-43293; www.thecranleigh.com; Kendal Rd, Bowness-on-Windermere; d £110-190, ste £305-525; P 📶) This super-snazzy B&B takes the prize for most-over-the-top decor in Windermere: from sleigh beds to jaguar-print throws and backlit bathroom mirrors, it's had every trick in the design book thrown at it (with varying degrees of success). Still, it's not a dull place to stay – and for extra luxury, you can book one of its boutique church suites.

Eating

Homeground CAFE £

(☎015394-44863; www.homegroundcafe.co.uk; 56 Main Rd, Windermere Town; coffee £2-4, mains £7-10; ⏰9am-5pm) Windermere gets its own boutique coffee house, serving excellent flat whites, pourovers and ristrettos, accompanied by a fine display of milk art. It's super for brunch too, with bang-on-trend options such as a lavish eggs Benedict and maple-bacon waffles. All in all, a thoroughly welcome new addition to town.

★ Mason's Arms PUB FOOD ££

(☎015395-68486; www.masonsarmsstrawberrybank.co.uk; Winster; mains £12.95-18.95) Three miles east, near Bowlands Bridge, the marvellous Mason's Arms is a local secret. The rafters, flagstones and cast-iron range haven't changed in centuries, and the patio has to-die-for views across fields and fells. The food is hearty – Cumbrian stewpot, slow-roasted Cartmel lamb – and there are lovely rooms and cottages for rent (£175 to £350). In short, a cracker.

Brown Horse Inn PUB FOOD ££

(☎015394-43443; www.thebrownhorseinn.co.uk; Winster; mains £12.95-16.95; ⏰lunch noon-2pm,

WINDERMERE & THE ISLANDS

Windermere gets its name from the old Norse, Vinandr mere (Vinandr's lake; so Lake Windermere is actually tautologous). Encompassing 5.7 sq miles between Ambleside and Newby Bridge, the lake is a mile wide at its broadest point, with a maximum depth of about 220m.

The lake's shoreline is owned by a combination of private landholders, the National Park Authority and the National Trust, but the lakebed itself (and thus the lake itself) officially belongs to the people of Windermere (local philanthropist Henry Leigh Groves purchased it on their behalf in 1938).

There are 18 islands on Windermere: the largest is Belle Isle, encompassing 16 hectares and an 18th-century Italianate mansion, while the smallest is Maiden Holme, little more than a patch of soil and a solitary tree.

Windermere Lake Cruises (☑ 015394-43360; www.windermere-lakecruises.co.uk; tickets from £2.70) offers sightseeing cruises, departing from Bowness Pier.

---

dinner 6-9pm) Three miles from Windermere in Winster, the Brown Horse is a popular dining pub. Produce is sourced from the Brown Horse Estate, furnishing the chefs with meat and game such as venison, spring lamb and pigeon. Beams and fireplaces conjure rustic atmosphere, and there are several ales on tap from the in-house Winster Brewery.

Angel Inn PUB FOOD ££
(☑ 015394-44080; www.the-angelinn.com; Helm Rd, Bowness-on-Windermere; mains £10.95-16.50; ⏲11.30am-4pm & 5-9pm) This smart gastropub sits atop a grassy knoll near the Bowness shoreline and offers superior pub grub: think focaccia pizzas, sea bass with pak choi and trio of Lakeland sausage. Arrive early if you want to bag a table on the lawn – the lake views are great, so they go fast.

Upstairs are 13 bright, reasonably good-value rooms (£106 to £186).

Francine's BISTRO ££
(☑ 015394-44088; www.francinesrestaurantwindermere.co.uk; 27 Main Rd, Windermere Town; 2-/3-course dinner menu £16.95/19.95; ⏲10am-2.30pm & 6.30-11pm Tue-Sat) The definition of a neighbourhood bistro: it's a locals' favourite and if you come more than once you'll probably be greeted by name. It's a tiny space with crammed-in tables, so watch your elbows with your neighbours. Food is solid if not stellar, with tastes tending toward the hearty, such as roast guinea fowl, confit pork belly and chicken supreme.

Hooked SEAFOOD £££
(☑ 015394-48443; www.hookedwindermere.co.uk; Ellerthwaite Sq, Windermere Town; mains £19.95-21.95; ⏲5.30-10.30pm Tue-Sun) Seafood might not be something you immediately think of when deciding what to eat in Windermere, but Paul White's first-class fish restaurant is well worth considering. He likes to keep things classic: hake with Mediterranean veg and pesto, sea trout with peas and pancetta, or lemon sole with capers and parsley butter. It's small, so bookings are essential.

🍷 Drinking & Nightlife

⭐ **Crafty Baa** CRAFT BEER
(☑ 015394-88002; 21 Victoria St, Windermere Town; ⏲11am-11pm) The clue's in the name – the craft-beer revolution comes to Windermere, with a vast selection of brews: Czech pilsners, weissbiers, smoked lagers, even mango, gooseberry and coconut beers, chalked up on a wall of slates and served (if you wish) with snack platters. The space (a former house) is tiny, but plans are afoot to expand next door.

Hawkshead Brewery BREWERY
(☑ 01539-822644; www.hawksheadbrewery.co.uk; Mill Yard, Staveley) This renowned craft brewery has its own beer hall in Staveley, 3 miles east of Windermere. Core beers include Hawkshead Bitter, dark Brodie's Prime and fruity Red. Guided tours can be arranged in advance.

Hole in T' Wall PUB
(☑ 015394-43488; Fallbarrow Rd, Bowness-on-Windermere; ⏲11am-11pm) Bowness' oldest boozer, dating back to 1612 and offering lashings of rough-beamed, low-ceilinged atmosphere.

ℹ Information

There are several visitor information centres in and around Windermere.

Brockhole National Park Visitor Centre
(☑ 015394-46601; www.brockhole.co.uk;
⊙ 10am-5pm) The lakes' main information
centre in a former country house 3 miles from
Windermere along the A591.

Windermere Information Centre (☑ 015394-
46499; www.windermereinfo.co.uk; Victoria St,
Windermere Town; ⊙ 8.30am-5.30pm) A small
information point in Windermere Town, near
the railway station, run by Mountain Goat.

Bowness Visitor Information Centre (☑ 0845
901 0845; bownesstic@lake-district.gov.uk;
Glebe Rd, Bowness-on-Windermere; ⊙ 9.30am-
5.30pm) Basic information point near the
Bowness jetty, with a shop and cafe.

❶ Getting There & Away

BOAT

To cross Windermere by car, bike or on foot,
head south of Bowness to the **Windermere
Ferry** (www.cumbria.gov.uk/roads-transport/
highways-pavements/windermereferry.asp;
car/bicycle/pedestrian £4.40/1/50p; ⊙ every
20 min 6.50am-9.50pm Mon-Fri, 9.10am-
9.50pm Sat & Sun Mar-Oct, to 8.50pm Nov-Feb),
which shuttles between Ferry Nab on the east
bank to Ferry House on the west bank.

Expect car queues in summer.

BUS

There's one daily National Express coach from
London (£46, eight hours) via Lancaster and
Kendal.

Note that if you're travelling any further than
Grasmere – or if you're planning on returning
from anywhere – you're better off buying a **Central Lakes Dayrider** (p562) ticket.

Bus 555/556 Lakeslink (£4.70 to £9.80,
at least hourly every day) Starts at the train
station, stopping at Troutbeck Bridge (five
minutes), Brockhole Visitor Centre (seven minutes), Ambleside (£4.70, 15 minutes), Grasmere
(£7.20, 30 minutes) and Keswick (£9.80, one
hour). In the opposite direction it continues to
Kendal (£6.50, 25 minutes).

Bus 505 Coniston Rambler (hourly every day)
Travels from Bowness to Coniston (£9.80, 50
minutes) via Troutbeck, Brockhole, Ambleside,
Skelwith Fold, Hawkshead and Hawkshead Hill.
Two buses a day serve Kendal.

Bus 599 Lakes Rider (£4.20 to £7.20, three
times hourly every day) Open-top bus between
Bowness, Troutbeck, Brockhole, Rydal Church
(for Rydal Mount), Dove Cottage and Grasmere.
Some buses stop at Windermere train station.

TRAIN

Windermere is the only town inside the national
park accessible by train. It's on the branch
line to Kendal and Oxenholme, with onward

connections to Edinburgh, Manchester and
London Piccadilly.

DESTINATION	ONE-WAY FARE (£)	DURATION
Edinburgh	67	2½hr
Glasgow	68.60	2¼-2¾hr
Kendal	5.90	15min
Lancaster	14.70	45min
London Euston	108.10	3½hr
Manchester Piccadilly	37	1½hr

Ambleside

☑ 015394 / POP 2529

Once a busy mill and textile centre at Windermere's northern tip, Ambleside is an attractive little town, built from the same slate
and stern grey stone that's so characteristic
of the rest of Lakeland. Ringed by fells, it's
a favourite base for hikers, with a cluster of
outdoors shops and plenty of cosy pubs and
cafes providing fuel for adventures.

◉ Sights & Activities

★ Rydal Mount   HISTORIC BUILDING
(☑ 015394-33002; www.rydalmount.co.uk; adult/
child £7.50/4, grounds only £5; ⊙ 9.30am-5pm Mar-
Oct, 11am-4pm Nov, Dec & Feb) The poet William
Wordsworth's most famous residence in the
Lake District is undoubtedly Dove Cottage
(p570), but he actually spent a great deal
more time at Rydal Mount, 1.5 miles northwest of Ambleside, off the A591. This was the
Wordsworth family's home from 1813 until
the poet's death in 1850 and the house contains a treasure trove of Wordsworth memorabilia. Bus 555 (and bus 599 from April to
October) stops at the end of the drive.

Downstairs you can wander around the
library, dining room and drawing room (look
out for William's pen, inkstand and picnic box
in the cabinets, as well as a famous portrait
of the poet by the American painter Henry
Inman hanging above the fireplace). Upstairs
are the family bedrooms and Wordsworth's
attic study, containing his encyclopedia and
a sword belonging to his brother John, who
was lost in a shipwreck in 1805.

The gardens are lovely, too; Wordsworth
fancied himself as a landscape gardener
and much of the grounds were laid out according to his designs. Below the house is
Dora's Field, a peaceful meadow in which

Wordsworth planted daffodils in memory of his eldest daughter, who died from tuberculosis in 1847.

Armitt Museum
MUSEUM

(☑ 015394-31212; www.armitt.com; Rydal Rd; adult/child £5/free; ☺ 10am-5pm) Despite some damage incurred during the 2015 floods, Ambleside's excellent little museum is now back up and running. It hosts some intriguing seasonal exhibitions alongside its core collection, populated with artefacts relating to important Lakeland characters such as National Trust founder Canon Hardwicke Rawnsley, pioneering Lakeland photographers Herbert Bell and the Abraham Brothers and a certain Beatrix Potter, who bequeathed a number of botanical watercolours to the museum, along with several first editions of her books.

There are also original canvases by the modernist artist Kurt Schwitters, a German refugee who settled in Ambleside after WWII.

Stock Ghyll Force
WALKING

Ambleside's most popular walk is the half-hour stroll up to the 18m-high waterfall of Stock Ghyll Force; the trail is signposted behind the old Market Hall at the bottom of Stock Ghyll Lane. If you feel energetic, you can follow the trail beyond the falls up **Wansfell Pike** (482m), a reasonably steep walk of about two hours.

Low Wood Watersports
BOATING

(☑ 015394-39441; www.englishlakes.co.uk/low-wood-bay/watersports; Low Bay Marina) This watersports centre offers waterskiing, sailing and kayaking and has row boats and motor boats for hire. Kayaks cost from £15 per hour, canoes from £18 per hour.

🛏 Sleeping

★ Ambleside YHA
HOSTEL £

(☑ 0345 371 9620; www.yha.org.uk; Lake Rd; dm £18-32; P 🛜) One of the YHA's flagship Lake District hostels, this huge lakeside house is a fave for activity holidays (everything from kayaking to ghyll scrambling). Great facilities (kitchen, bike rental, boat jetty, bar) mean it's heavily subscribed, so book well ahead. Families can book out dorms as private rooms. It's halfway between Ambleside and Windermere on Lake Rd (A591).

Low Wray
CAMPSITE £

(NT; ☑ bookings 015394-63862; www.nationaltrust.org.uk/features/lake-district-camping; campsites for 2 adults £16-43, ecopods £45-80; ☺ campsite arrivals 3-7pm Sat-Thu, to 9pm Fri Mar-Oct) One of the most popular of the National Trust's four Lakeland campsites, in a fine spot along Windermere's shores, 3 miles from Ambleside along the B5286. There are 120 tent pitches and nine hard pitches for caravans, plus a handful of camping pods and safari tents. Choose from lake view, woodland, field or water's edge. Bus 505 stops nearby.

Waterwheel
B&B ££

(☑ 015394-33286; www.waterwheelambleside.co.uk; 3 Bridge St; d £90-110; 🛜) You'll be lulled to sleep by the sound of the river at this tiny B&B, tucked off the main street. The three rooms are small but sweet: Rattleghyll is cosily Victorian, Loughrigg squeezes under the rafters and Stockghyll features a brass bed and claw-foot bath. The drawback? The only parking is in a public car park 250m away. Two-night minimum.

Gables
B&B ££

(☑ 015394-33272; www.thegables-ambleside.co.uk; Church Walk; s £52-60, d £104-140; P 🛜) One of Ambleside's best-value B&Bs, in a double-gabled house (hence the name) in a quiet spot overlooking the recreation ground. Spotty cushions and colourful prints keep things cheery, but room sizes are variable (in this instance, bigger is definitely better). Guests receive discounts at the owner's restaurant, **Sheila's Cottage** (☑ 015394-33079; The Slack; mains £12.50-18; ☺ noon-2.30pm & 6.30-10pm). There's a tiny first-come, first-served car park.

★ Nanny Brow
B&B £££

(☑ 015394-33232; www.nannybrow.co.uk; Nanny Brow, Clappersgate; d £145-280; P 🛜) There's a compelling reason to choose this premium B&B – and that's the knockout view. The whitewashed house sits on a crag with a top-drawer view down the Brathay valley, with generously sized rooms (all named after local fells) full of handsome wooden beds, gilded mirrors and antique pieces to match the house's Arts and Crafts, turn-of-the-century heritage.

Lakes Lodge
B&B £££

(☑ 015394-33240; www.lakeslodge.co.uk; Lake Rd; r £132-162; P 🛜) Halfway between a posh B&B and a midrange mini-hotel, this place makes a good Ambleside base. The rooms are all about clean lines, stark walls and zero clutter and most have a full-size wall mural featuring a local beauty spot. Some are in the main building, while others are

TOP 5 CLASSIC LAKELAND HIKES

The Lake District's most famous fell-walker, the accountant-turned-author Alfred Wainwright, recorded 214 official fells in his seven-volume *Pictorial Guides* (as if that weren't enough, he usually outlined at least two possible routes to the top or, in the case of Scafell Pike, five). If you only have limited time, here are five hikes that offer a flavour of what makes fell-walking in the Lake District so special.

Scafell Pike (978m) The daddy of Lakeland hikes, a six- to seven-hour slog to the top of England's highest peak. The classic route is from Wasdale Head.

Helvellyn (950m) Not for the faint hearted; a vertiginous scramble along the knife-edge ridge of Striding Edge. It takes at least six hours starting from Glenridding or Patterdale.

Blencathra (868m) A mountain on its own, Blencathra offers a panoramic outlook on Keswick and the northern fells. Count on four hours from Threlkeld.

Haystacks (597m) Wainwright's favourite mountain and the place where his ashes were scattered. It's a steep, three-hour return hike from Buttermere village.

Catbells (451m) The fell for everyone, accessible to six-year-olds and septuagenarians. It's on the west side of Derwentwater and takes a couple of hours to climb.

in an attached annexe. Breakfast is served buffet-style.

Waterhead Hotel HOTEL £££
(☏ 08458 504503; www.englishlakes.co.uk; Lake Rd; r £142-350; [P][⊜][❄]) For a proper hotel stay in Ambleside (complete with the all-essential Windermere view, of course), the Waterhead is definitely the choice. Outside, it's clad in traditional Lakeland stone; inside, there are 40-something rooms that, while perfectly comfortable, feel a tad corporate in style. Lake views command a premium, but there are often good online deals.

✖ Eating

★ Great North Pie PIES £
(☏ 01625 522112; www.greatnorthpie.co; Unit 2 The Courtyard, Rothay Rd; pies £4-8; ⊗ 9am-5pm) Based in Wilmslow, this much-garlanded pie maker has opened an Ambleside outlet, and it's rightly become a town favourite. Go for a classic such as Swaledale beef mince or Lancashire cheese and onion, or opt for something on the seasonal pie menu: they're all delicious, and served with lashings of mash and gravy (veggie, should you wish).

Stockghyll Fine Food DELI £
(☏ 015394-31865; www.stockghyllfinefood.co.uk; Rydal Rd; sandwiches £3-4; ⊗ 9am-5pm Wed-Sun) For premium Cumbrian cheeses, chutneys, cold cuts, beers and breadsticks, this fine food emporium is impossible to top in Ambleside – and it also does a nice line in pork pies, sausage rolls and takeaway sandwiches.

Apple Pie CAFE £
(☏ 015394-33679; www.applepieambleside.co.uk; Rydal Rd; lunches £4-10; ⊗ 9am-5.30pm) For a quick lunch stop, you won't go far wrong at this friendly little caff, which serves stuffed sandwiches, hot pies, baked spuds and yummy cakes (the apple pie is a local legend). Everything is available either eat in or takeaway.

It also runs an excellent-value **B&B** (☏ 015394-33679; www.applepieambleside.co.uk; Rydal Rd; d £52-85; [P][⊜]).

Zeffirelli's ITALIAN £
(☏ 015394-33845; www.zeffirellis.com; Compston Rd; pizzas & mains £8-15; ⊗ 11am-10pm) A beloved local landmark, Zeff's is often packed out for its quality pizza and pasta. The £21.75 Double Feature deal includes two courses and a ticket to the cinema (☏ 015394-33100; Compston Rd) next door.

Fellini's VEGETARIAN ££
(☏ 015394-32487; www.felliniSambleside.com; Church St; mains £12-15; ⊗ 5.30-10pm; ☏) Fear not, veggies: even in the land of the Cumberland sausage and the tattie hotpot (lamb, vegetable and potato stew), you won't go hungry thanks to Fellini's sophisticated 'vegeterranean' food. The dishes are creative and beautifully presented – think delicate Moroccan filo parcels, stuffed portobello mushrooms and radicchio provolne ravioli.

★ Old Stamp House BISTRO £££
(☏ 015394-32775; www.oldstamphouse.com; Church St; dinner mains £24-28; ⊗ 12.30-2pm

Wed-Sat, 6.30-10pm Tue-Sat) In the cellar of the building where Wordsworth worked as distributor of stamps, this fine-dining bistro champions Cumbrian produce, much of it raised, caught, shot or cured within a few miles' radius. You'll find ingredients like Arctic char, Herdwick hogget and roe deer on the menu, partnered with foraged ingredients, surprising flavour combinations and delicate sauces, all impeccably presented. Outstanding.

★ **Lake Road Kitchen**　　　BISTRO £££
(📞 015394-22012;　www.lakeroadkitchen.co.uk; Lake Rd; 5-/8-course tasting menu £65/90; ⏱ 6-9.30pm Wed-Sun) This much-lauded bistro has brought some dazzle to Ambleside's dining scene. Its Noma-trained head chef, James Cross, explores the 'food of the north', and his multicourse tasting menus are chock-full of locally sourced, seasonal and foraged ingredients, from shore-sourced seaweed to forest-picked mushrooms. Presentation is impeccable, flavours are experimental and the Scandi-inspired decor is just so.

ℹ Information

Hub (📞 015394-32582; tic@thehubofambleside.com; Central Bldgs, Market Cross; ⏱ 9am-5pm) Central information centre that's also home to the post office. Also has a good shop selling maps, books and souvenirs.

ℹ Getting There & Away

Bus 555 Runs at least hourly (including Sundays) to Grasmere (£4.70) and Keswick (£8.80), and to Bowness, Windermere (£4.70) and Kendal (£7.60) in the opposite direction.

Bus 599 Open-top service that leaves at least hourly (including weekends) to Grasmere, Bowness, Windermere and Brockhole Visitor Centre; four buses daily continue to Kendal. Prices as for bus 555.

Bus 505 To Hawkshead and Coniston (£5.90, hourly each day).

Bus 516 To Elterwater and Langdale (£4.40, six daily).

Grasmere

📞 015394 / POP 1458

If it's Romantic connections you're looking for, the little village of Grasmere is the place to be. Huddled at the edge of an island-studded lake surrounded by woods, pastures and slate-coloured hills, it's most famous as the former home of the grand old daddy of the Romantics himself, poet William Wordsworth, who set up home at nearby Dove Cottage in 1799, and spent much of the rest of his life here. Three of the poet's former houses can be visited nearby, as well as an excellent museum – and, poignantly, his family's plot in the village churchyard.

Grasmere's literary cachet has its drawbacks, though: the village's streets are crammed to bursting throughout summer, and the modern-day rash of gift shops, tearooms and coach-tour hotels has done little to preserve the quiet country charm that drew Wordsworth here in the first place.

◉ Sights

★ **Dove Cottage & The Wordsworth Museum**　　HISTORIC BUILDING
(📞 015394-35544; www.wordsworth.org.uk; adult/child £8.95/free; ⏱ 9.30am-5.30pm Mar-Oct, 10am-4.30pm Nov, Dec & Feb) On the edge of Grasmere, this tiny, creeper-clad cottage (formerly a pub called the Dove & Olive Bough) was famously inhabited by William Wordsworth between 1799 and 1808. The cottage's cramped rooms are full of artefacts – try to spot the poet's passport, a pair of his spectacles and a portrait (given to him by Sir Walter Scott) of his favourite dog, Pepper. Entry is by timed ticket to avoid overcrowding and includes an informative guided tour.

Wordsworth lived here happily with his sister Dorothy, wife Mary and three children, John, Dora and Thomas, until 1808 when the family moved to a nearby house at Allen Bank. The cottage was subsequently rented by Thomas de Quincey (author of *Confessions of an English Opium Eater*).

Tickets also include admission to the excellent **Wordsworth Museum & Art Gallery** next door, which houses one of the nation's main collections relating to the Romantic movement, including many original manuscripts and some creepy death masks of famous Romantic figures.

Grasmere Lake & Rydal Water　　LAKE
Quiet paths lead along the shores of Grasmere's twin-set lakes. Rowing boats can be hired at the northern end of Grasmere Lake from the **Grasmere Tea Gardens** (📞 015394-35590; Stock Lane; ⏱ 9.30am-5pm), which is a five-minute walk from the village centre.

St Oswald's Church　　CHURCH
(Church Stile) Named after a Viking saint, Grasmere's medieval chapel is where Wordsworth and his family attended church service every Sunday for many years. It's also their final

TROUTBECK

This out-of-the-way hamlet on the way to Kirkstone Pass is worth visiting for its National Trust-owned farmhouse of **Townend** (NT; ☎ 01539-432628; www.nationaltrust.org.uk/townend; adult/child £6.50/3.25; ☺1-5pm Wed-Sun Mar-Oct, daily school holidays), which offers an insight into Lakeland life c 1700. It once belonged to farmer Ben Browne and his family, who owned the house until 1943. Now restored, the whitewashed house contains a collection of vintage farming tools, possessions and furniture. Hourly guided tours run from 11am to 1pm.

The **Mortal Man** (☎ 015394-33193; www.themortalman.co.uk; Troutbeck; mains £12.50-18.95; P 🐾) makes a fine spot for a pint of ale and some grub – the views from the beer garden are epic.

Bus 508 from Windermere (£4.80, 25 minutes, five daily) stops in Troutbeck, then continues over Kirkstone Pass to Ullswater and Penrith.

resting place – under the spreading bows of a great yew tree, the Wordsworth's family graves are tucked into a quiet corner of the churchyard. A peaceful memorial garden to fund the church's restoration has recently been established next door – planted, of course, with swathes of daffodils.

Among the tombstones are those belonging to William, his wife Mary, his sister Dorothy and his children Dora, William, Thomas and Catherine. Samuel Taylor Coleridge's son Hartley is also buried here, along with several Quillinans; Edward Quillinan became Wordsworth's son-in-law in 1841, having married his beloved daughter Dora.

The church itself is worth a look. Inside you'll find Wordsworth's own prayer book and his favourite pew, marked by a plaque. The church is one of the oldest in the Lake District, mostly dating from the 13th century, but thought to have been founded sometime in the 7th century. It was restored and re-rendered in 2017.

🛏 Sleeping

Butharlyp How YHA HOSTEL £
(☎ 0845 371 9319; www.yha.org.uk; Easedale Rd; dm £18-30; ☺reception 7am-11pm; P 🛜) Grasmere's YHA is in a large Victorian house set among grassy grounds, all in easy walking distance of the village. There's a good range of different-sized dorms, a licensed bar and the cafe serves breakfast and the three-course 'Supper Club' menu.

Grasmere Hostel HOSTEL £
(☎ 015394-35055; www.grasmerehostel.co.uk; Broadrayne Farm; dm £20-24; P @ 🛜) This stylish indie hostel has a vaguely Scandi feel, with unexpected luxuries such as a Nordic sauna, skylights, two kitchens and en suite

bathrooms for each (mixed sex) dorm. Porthole windows provide impressive views over the fells. It's in a converted farmhouse on the A591 about 1.5 miles north of the village, near the Traveller's Rest pub.

Heidi's Grasmere Lodge B&B ££
(☎ 0774 382 7252; www.heidisgrasmerelodge.co.uk; Red Lion Sq; d £99-130; 🛜) This plush B&B in the centre of the village offers six super-feminine rooms full of frilly cushions and Cath Kidston–style patterns. They're quite small but very comfy: room 6 has its own sun patio, reached via a spiral staircase.

How Foot Lodge B&B ££
(☎ 015394-35366; www.howfootlodge.co.uk; Town End; d £78-85; P) Just a stroll from Dove Cottage, this stone house has six rooms finished in fawns and beiges. The nicest are the deluxe doubles, one with a sun terrace and the other with a private sitting room. Rates are an absolute bargain considering the location.

★ **Forest Side** BOUTIQUE HOTEL £££
(☎ 015394-35250; www.theforestside.com; Keswick Rd; r incl full board £230-400; P 🛜) For out-and-out-luxury, plump for this boutique beauty. Run by renowned hotelier Andrew Wildsmith, it's a design palace: chic interiors decorated with crushed-velvet sofas, bird-of-paradise wallpaper, stag heads and 20 swish rooms from 'Cosy' to 'Jolly Good', 'Superb', 'Grand' and 'Master'. Chef Kevin Tickle previously worked at L'Enclume (p589), and now runs the stellar restaurant here using produce from its kitchen garden.

★ **Daffodil Hotel** BOUTIQUE HOTEL £££
(☎ 015394-63550; www.daffodilhotel.co.uk; d £145-260, ste £180-340; P 🛜) Opened in 2012 this upscale hotel occupies a Victorian building,

but the 78 rooms zing with modern style: swirly carpets, art prints and bold shades of lime, purple and turquoise. There's a choice of lake or valley views and lovely bathrooms with pan-head showers and Molton Brown bath products. A fine restaurant and luxurious spa complete the package. Rather good.

✗ Eating

Brew CAFE £
(☑ 015394-35248; www.heidisgrasmerelodge.co.uk; Red Lion Sq; mains £4-8; ⊙ 9am-5.30pm) This cheery village cafe is the place for a quick lunch of homemade soup and a thick-cut sandwich. The house-special flapjacks and savoury cheese smokeys are sinfully good.

★ Jumble Room MODERN BRITISH ££
(☑ 015394-35188; www.thejumbleroom.co.uk; Langdale Rd; dinner mains £14.50-23; ⊙ 5.30-9.30pm Wed-Mon) Husband-and-wife team Andy and Crissy Hill have turned this village bistro into a much-loved dining landmark. It's a really fun and friendly place to eat. Spotty crockery, cow murals and primary colours set the boho tone, matched by a magpie menu that borrows flavours and ingredients from a global cookbook – Malaysian seafood curry one week, Persian lamb the next.

Lewis's BISTRO ££
(☑ 015394-35266; Broadgate; mains £14.95-24.95; ⊙ 6-9pm Tue-Sat) A reliable village bistro, Lewis's eponymous restaurant turns out hearty, classic British bistro dishes – steak, roast lamb, belly pork, sea bass and the like. It's solid rather than sensational, but a good bet for dinner all the same.

🛍 Shopping

★ Sarah Nelson's Gingerbread Shop FOOD
(☑ 015394-35428; www.grasmeregingerbread.co. uk; Church Cottage; ⊙ 9.15am-5.30pm Mon-Sat, 12.30-5pm Sun) In business since 1854, this famous sweet shop next to the village church makes Grasmere's essential souvenir: traditional gingerbread with a half-biscuity, half-cakey texture (six/12 pieces for £3.50/6.70), cooked using the original top-secret recipe. Friendly service is provided by ladies dressed in frilly pinafores and starched bonnets.

❶ Getting There & Away

The regular 555 bus (at least hourly, including Sundays) runs from Windermere to Grasmere (15 minutes) via Ambleside, Rydal Church and Dove Cottage, then travels onwards to Keswick.

The open-top 599 (two or three per hour in summer) runs from Grasmere via Ambleside, Troutbeck Bridge, Windermere and Bowness.

Both buses charge the same fares: Grasmere to Ambleside is £4.70, to Bowness and Windermere is £7.20.

Hawkshead

☑ 015394 / POP 1640

Lakeland villages don't come much more perfect than pint-sized Hawkshead, a jumble of whitewashed cottages, cobbled lanes and old pubs lost among bottle-green countryside between Ambleside and Coniston. The village has literary cachet, too – Wordsworth went to school here and Beatrix Potter's husband, William Heelis, worked here as a solicitor for many years (his old office is now an art gallery).

Cars are banned in the village centre.

◉ Sights

★ Hill Top HISTORIC BUILDING
(NT; ☑ 015394-36269; www.nationaltrust.org.uk/ hill-top; adult/child £10.90/5.45, admission to garden & shop free; ⊙ 10am-5.30pm Jun-Aug, to 4.30pm Sat-Thu Apr, May, Sep & Oct, weekends only Nov-Mar) Two miles south of Hawkshead, in the tiny village of Near Sawrey, this idyllic farmhouse was purchased in 1905 by Beatrix Potter and was used as inspiration for many of her tales: the house features directly in *Samuel Whiskers, Tom Kitten, Pigling Bland* and *Jemima Puddleduck*, among others, and you might recognise the kitchen garden from *Peter Rabbit*. Entry is by timed ticket in order to manage demand, but you can't prebook, and it's very popular, so prepare to queue.

Clad in climbing ivy and stocked with memorabilia, the house looks like something out of a storybook, but Beatrix only actually lived here until her marriage to William Heelis. In 1913 the newlywed couple moved to a larger farm at nearby Castle Cottage, where the author wrote many more tales until her death in 1943.

She bequeathed Hill Top (along with Castle Cottage and more than 1600 hectares of land) to the National Trust with the proviso that the house should be left with her belongings and decor in situ. Perhaps the most fascinating insight into the author's private life is provided by the many antiques, collectibles and objets d'art – from antique fans, delicate chinaware and butterfly collections to her own well-used paint tin. For Beatrix scholars, it's an absolute treasure trove. The house formed the centrepiece for celebrations to mark the author's 150th birthday in 2016.

The only drawback is the house's huge – and seemingly boundless – popularity. It's simply one of the must-see places for every visitor to the Lakes. Try visiting in the late afternoon or on weekdays to avoid the worst crowds.

★ Tarn Hows   LAKE

(NT; www.nationaltrust.org.uk/coniston-and-tarn -hows) Two miles off the B5285 from Hawkshead, a winding country lane leads to this famously photogenic artificial lake, now owned by the National Trust. Trails wind their way around the lakeshore and surrounding woodland – keep your eyes peeled for red squirrels in the treetops.

There's a small National Trust car park, but it fills quickly. Several buses, including the 505, stop nearby.

Beatrix Potter Gallery   GALLERY

(NT; www.nationaltrust.org.uk/beatrix-potter-gallery; Red Lion Sq; adult/child £6.50/3.25; ⊙10.30am-5pm Sat-Thu mid-Mar–Oct) As well as being a children's author, Beatrix Potter was also a talented botanical painter and amateur naturalist. This small gallery, housed in what were once the offices of Potter's husband, solicitor William Heelis, contains a collection of her watercolours depicting local flora and fauna. She was particularly fascinated by mushrooms.

Hawkshead Grammar School   HISTORIC BUILDING

(www.hawksheadgrammar.org.uk; admission £2.50; ⊙10.30am-1pm & 1.30-5pm Mon-Sat Apr-Oct) In centuries past, promising young gentlemen were sent to Hawkshead's village school for their educational foundation. Among the former pupils was a certain William Wordsworth, who attended the school from 1779 to 1787 – you can still see a desk where the naughty young poet carved his name. The curriculum was punishing: 10 hours' study a day, covering weighty subjects such as Latin, Greek, geometry, science and rhetoric. Upstairs is a small exhibition exploring the history of the school.

🛏 Sleeping & Eating

Hawkshead YHA   HOSTEL £

(☑0845 371 9321; www.yha.org.uk; dm £13-30; 🅿@🛜) This impressive YHA is lodged in a Grade II–listed Regency house overlooking Esthwaite Water, a mile from Hawkshead along the Newby Bridge road. It's a fancy spot considering the bargain prices: the dorms and kitchen are large and there are camping pods outside as well as bike rentals. The 505 bus stops at the end of the lane.

Yewfield   B&B ££

(☑015394-36765; www.yewfield.co.uk; Hawkshead Hill; s £85-120, d £90-140; 🅿🛜) 🍴 This rambling Victorian mansion is one of the best options around Hawkshead, although it's out of the way on the road to Coniston, near Tarn Hows. It's run by the owners of Zeffirelli's in Ambleside and offers a range of comfortable rooms and antique-stocked lounges, plus ecofriendly touches such as a wood-mass boiler and all-veggie breakfasts. Discounts available for three nights.

★ Drunken Duck   PUB FOOD £££

(☑015394-36347; www.drunkenduckinn.co.uk; Barngates; lunch/dinner mains £10/22; ⊙noon-2pm

---

GRIZEDALE FOREST

Stretching for 2428 hectares across the hilltops between Coniston Water and Esthwaite Water is Grizedale Forest, a dense conifer forest whose name derives from the Old Norse 'griss-dale', meaning 'valley of the pigs'. Though it looks lush and unspoilt today, the forest has been largely replanted over the last 100 years – by the late 19th century the original woodland had practically disappeared thanks to the demands of the local logging, mining and charcoal industries.

The forest has nine walking trails and seven cycling trails to explore – some are easy and designed for families, while others are geared towards hardcore hikers and cyclists. Along the way you'll spot more than 40 outdoor sculptures hidden in the undergrowth, created by artists since 1977 (there's a useful online guide at www.grizedalesculpture.org).

Trail maps are sold at the **visitors centre** (☑0300 067 4495; www.forestry.gov.uk/ grizedale; ⊙10am-5pm summer, to 4pm winter), while bikes can be hired from **Grizedale Mountain Bikes** (☑01229-860335; www.grizedalemountainbikes.co.uk; adult/child per half-day from £25/15; ⊙9am-5pm).

& 6-10pm; P 🛜) Long one of the Lakes' premier dining destinations, the Drunken Duck blends historic pub and fine-dining restaurant. On a wooded crossroads on the top of Hawkshead Hill, it's renowned for its luxurious food and home-brewed ales, and the flagstones and sporting prints conjure a convincing country atmosphere. Book well ahead for dinner or take your chances at lunchtime.

If you fancy staying, you'll find the rooms (£125 to £250) are just as fancy as the food. The pub's tricky to find: drive along the B5286 from Hawkshead towards Ambleside and look out for the brown signs.

ℹ Getting There & Away

Bus 505 (£4.70 to £5.90, hourly every day) links Hawkshead with Windermere, Ambleside and Coniston.

Coniston

📞 015394 / POP 641

Hunkered beneath the pockmarked peak known as the **Old Man of Coniston** (803m), this lakeside village was originally established to support the local mining industry, and the surrounding hilltops are littered with the remains of old copper workings. These days most people visit with two things in mind: to cruise on the lovely old Coniston Launch, or to tramp to the top of the Old Man, a steep but rewarding return hike of around 6 miles.

Coniston's other claim to fame is as the location for a string of world-record speed attempts made by Sir Malcolm Campbell and his son, Donald, between the 1930s and 1960s. Tragically, after beating the record several times, Donald was killed during an attempt in 1967 when his futuristic jetboat *Bluebird* flipped at around 320mph. The boat and its pilot were recovered in 2001, and Campbell was buried in the cemetery of St Andrew's church.

◉ Sights

Coniston Water   LAKE

Coniston's gleaming 5-mile-long lake – the third largest in the Lake District after Windermere and Ullswater – is a half-mile walk from town along Lake Rd. The best way to explore the lake is on one of the two cruise services or, better still, by paddling it yourself. Dinghies, rowing boats, canoes, kayaks and motor boats can be hired from the Coniston Boating Centre.

Along with its connections to the speed attempts made here by Malcolm and Donald Campbell, the lake is famous for inspiring Arthur Ransome's classic children's tale *Swallows and Amazons*. Peel Island, towards the southern end of Coniston Water, supposedly provided the model for Wild Cat Island in the book.

Brantwood   HISTORIC BUILDING

(📞 015394-41396; www.brantwood.org.uk; adult/child £7.70/free, gardens only £5.35/free; ⊙ 10.30am-5pm mid-Mar–mid-Nov, to 4pm Wed-Sun mid-Nov–mid-Mar) John Ruskin (1819–1900) was one of the great thinkers of 19th-century society. A polymath, philosopher, painter and critic, he expounded views on everything from Venetian architecture to lace making. In 1871 Ruskin purchased this lakeside house and spent the next 20 years modifying it, championing handmade crafts (he even designed the wallpaper). Look out for his vast shell collection. Boats run regularly to Brantwood from Coniston. Alternatively, look out for signs on the B5285.

Highlights include the grand but surprisingly cosy drawing room, the tome-filled study and the tiny upstairs bedroom decorated with some of his favourite watercolours (mostly by JMW Turner, and mostly copies of the originals). In the corner of the room is the little circular turret where Ruskin whiled away hours looking out across the lake and pondering the great issues of the day. Later in life he was afflicted by bouts of deep depression, and suffered some kind of mental collapse in the room. He never slept in there again.

Outside the house, 100 hectares of gardens and terraces stretch up the fellside ('Brant' derives from a Norse word meaning steep). Of particular note are the Hortus Inclusus, a herb garden modelled along medieval designs, and the Zig-Zaggy, inspired by the purgatorial mount in Dante's Inferno. The best views are from the High Walk, designed by Ruskin's cousin Joan Severn.

Afterwards, you can have lunch at the cafe in the house's former stables.

🏃 Activities

⭐ **Steam Yacht Gondola**   BOATING

(NT; 📞 015394-63850; www.nationaltrust.org.uk/steam-yacht-gondola; Coniston Jetty; half lake adult/child/family £11/6/25, full lake adult/child/family £21/10/48) 🚢 Built in 1859 and restored in the 1980s by the National Trust, this wonderful steam yacht looks like a cross between a Venetian *vaporetto* and an English houseboat, complete with cushioned saloons and polished wood seats. It's a stately way to see the lake, especially if you're visiting Brantwood, and it's ecofriendly – since 2008 it's been powered by waste wood.

Coniston Launch
BOATING

(☑ 015394-36216; www.conistonlaunch.co.uk; Coniston Jetty; Red Route adult/child return £11.50/5.75, Yellow Route £12.75/6.40, Green Route £17.25/8.65) *✎* Coniston's two modern launches have been solar-powered since 2005. The regular 45-minute **Northern Service (Red Route)** calls at the Waterhead Hotel, Torver and Brantwood. The 60-minute **Wild Cat Island Cruise (Yellow Route)** tours the lake's islands.

The 105-minute **Southern Service (Green Route)** is themed: it's Swallows and Amazons on Monday and Wednesday, and the Campbell story on Tuesday and Thursday.

Coniston Boating Centre
BOATING

(☑ 015394-41366; www.conistonboatingcentre.co.uk; Coniston Jetty) Hires out rowing boats (£15 per hour), kayaks and stand-up paddleboards (£20 for two hours), Canadian canoes (£25 for two hours) and motor boats (£30 per hour). It also rents out bikes (adult/child £15/5 for two hours).

Sleeping

Hoathwaite Campsite
CAMPSITE £

(NT; ☑ bookings 015394-63862; www.nationaltrust.org.uk/holidays/hoathwaite-campsite-lake-district; adult, tent & car £8-14, extra adult/child £6/3; ☺ Easter-Nov) This back-to-basics National Trust–owned campsite is on the A5394 between Coniston and Torver. There's a toilet block, water taps and not much else – but the views over Coniston Water are super.

Lakeland House
B&B ££

(☑ 015394-41303; www.lakelandhouse.co.uk; Tilberthwaite Ave; s £50-70, d £70-99, ste £130-190) You're smack bang in the centre of Coniston at this good-value, basic B&B above Hollands cafe. The rooms have been recently renovated with fresh colours and updated bathrooms; some have dormer windows, others have views of the Old Man. The Lookout Suite has its own sitting room and in-room bathtub.

Bank Ground Farm
B&B ££

(☑ 015394-41264; www.bankground.com; East of the Lake; d from £90; ℗) This lakeside farmhouse has literary cachet: Arthur Ransome used it as the model for Holly Howe Farm in *Swallows and Amazons*. Parts of the house date back to the 15th century, so the rooms are snug. Some have sleigh beds, others exposed beams. The tearoom is a beauty, and there are cottages for longer stays. Two-night minimum.

Eating

Herdwicks
CAFE £

(☑ 015394-41141; Yewdale Rd; mains £4-10; ☺ 10am-4pm) Run by a local family, this bright and cheery cafe makes the perfect stop for lunch – whether you're in the mood for homemade soup, a big chunky sandwich, or a slice of sinful cake. Everything is locally sourced where possible, and the light-filled, large-windowed space is inviting.

Bluebird Cafe
CAFE £

(☑ 015394-41649; Lake Rd; mains £4-8; ☺ 9.30am-5.30pm) This lakeside cafe does a brisk trade from people waiting for the Coniston launches. The usual salads, jacket spuds and sandwiches are on offer and there are lots of tables outside where you can look out on the lake.

Steam Bistro
BISTRO ££

(☑ 015394-41928; www.steambistro.co.uk; Tilberthwaite Ave; 2-/3-course menu £22.95/26.95; ☺ 6-11pm Wed-Sun) This swish new bistro has become the go-to address for Coniston dining. Its magpie menu borrows lots of global flavours – you'll find everything from Japanese dumplings to Cajun pulled pork and Greek-style *kleftiko* (slow-cooked lamb) on the specials board. Even better, everything is *prix fixe* (fixed price).

Drinking & Nightlife

Sun Hotel
PUB

(☑ 015394-41248; www.thesunconiston.com; ☺ 10am-11pm) Famously used as a headquarters by Donald Campbell during his fateful campaign, this trad boozer is a good place for a pint, with a fell-view beer garden and cosy crannies to hunker down in – look out for Campbell memorabilia. Food (mains £12 to £21) is hit-and-miss at busy times. It's up a small hill beside the bridge over Church Beck.

Black Bull
PUB

(☑ 015394-41335; www.conistonbrewery.com/black-bull-coniston.htm; Yewdale Rd; ☺ 10am-11pm) Coniston's main meeting spot, the old

WORTH A TRIP

THE STEEPEST ROAD IN ENGLAND

Zigzagging over the fells between the valleys of Little Langdale and Eskdale, an infamous mountain road traverses England's two highest road passes: **Wrynose** and **Hardknott**. In use since ancient times, the old packhorse route was substantially improved by the Romans: at the top of Hardknott Pass, there's a ruined **Roman fort** – you can still see the remains of the walls, parade ground and commandant's house. The views from here to the coast are stunning.

A favourite of TV motoring shows and weekend bikers, the road is perfectly drivable if you take things slow and steady, but probably best avoided if you're a hesitant reverser or don't like driving next to steep drops. This is not a road to rush; you'll need to be prepared for plenty of reversing when you meet vehicles going the opposite way.

To get to the passes from Ambleside, follow road signs on the A593 to Skelwith Bridge, then turn off to Little Langdale. When you reach the Three Shires Inn, the road gets really steep. Alternatively, you can approach from the west: drive along the A595 coast road and turn off towards Eskdale, then follow the road past Boot to the passes.

Black Bull offers a warren of rooms and a popular outside terrace. The pub grub's good (mains £8 to £18), but it's mainly known for its home-brewed ales: Bluebird Bitter and Old Man Ale are always on tap and there are seasonal ones, too.

ℹ Information

Coniston Tourist Office (☎ 015394-41533; www.conistontic.org; Ruskin Ave; ⏰ 9.30am-4.30pm Mon-Sat, 10am-2pm Sun)

ℹ Getting There & Away

Bus 505 runs to Windermere (£9.80, hourly every day) via Hawkshead and Ambleside. A couple of buses a day go on to Kendal. Note that for most bus journeys, it's better value to buy a 24-hour Central Lakes Dayrider (p562) ticket instead.

The Coniston Bus-and-Boat ticket (adult/child £19/8.30) includes return bus travel on the 505, plus a trip on the launch and entry to Brantwood (p574).

Elterwater & Great Langdale

☎ 015394

Travelling north from Coniston, the road passes into the wild, empty landscape of Great Langdale, one of Lakeland's iconic hiking valleys. As you pass the pretty village of Elterwater, imposing fells stack up like dominoes along the horizon, looming over a pastoral patchwork of tumbledown barns and lime-green fields.

The circuit around the line-up of fells known as the **Langdale Pikes** – Pike O' Stick-le (709m), Loft Crag (682m), Harrison Stickle (736m) and Pavey Ark (700m) – is the valley's most popular hike, allowing you to tick off between three and five Wainwrights depending on your route, and covering around six steep, hard-going miles. Allow a good six hours.

🛏 Sleeping

Langdale YHA HOSTEL £
(☎ 0845 371 9748; www.yha.org.uk; High Close, Loughrigg; dm £13-32; ⏰ Mar-Oct, reception 7-10am & 3-11pm; P @ ☎) If you didn't know this was a hostel, you'd think it was a grand country hotel: vast, Victorian and set in private grounds with its own arboretum. Big dorms with sash windows overlook the fells and there's a cavernous kitchen and lounge (with original ornate fireplace). The cafe serves breakfast, packed lunches and a two-course 'supper club'.

Note that it's a couple of miles from Great Langdale, but the 516 bus runs right past.

Great Langdale Campsite CAMPSITE £
(NT; ☎ 015394-63862; www.nationaltrust.org.uk/features/great-langdale-campsite; Great Langdale; sites £12-25, extra adult £6, pods £35-70; ⏰ arrivals 3-7pm Sat-Thu, to 9pm Fri; P) Quite possibly the most spectacularly positioned campsite in the Lake District, spread over grassy meadows overlooked by Langdale's fells. It gets crowded in high season, but 120 sites can be booked in advance; another 50 or so are on a first-come, first-served basis. Camping pods and yurts are also available.

Elterwater Hostel HOSTEL £
(☎ 015394-37245; www.elterwaterhostel.co.uk; Elterwater; dm/d/f £25/58/124; @) Formerly

owned by the YHA, this indie hostel is in a lovely spot just a short walk from Elterwater's grassy green. It was once a farmhouse but now has 40 beds split across several (mostly six-bed) dorms, some of which can be taken as private family rooms. Breakfast and dinner is available in the cafe, or there's a self-caterers' kitchen.

★**Old Dungeon Ghyll**   HOTEL **££**
(☑ 015394-37272; www.odg.co.uk; Great Langdale; s £58, d £116-132; P ⛱ 🐾) Affectionately known as the ODG, this inn is awash with Lakeland heritage: many famous walkers have stayed here, including Prince Charles and mountaineer Chris Bonington. It's endearingly olde worlde (well-worn furniture, four-poster beds) and even if you're not staying, the slate-floored, fire-warmed Hiker's Bar is a must for a posthike pint – it's been the hub of Langdale's social life for decades.

★**Brimstone Hotel**   HOTEL **£££**
(☑ 015394-38062; www.brimstonehotel.co.uk; Langdale Estate, Great Langdale; r £340-520; P) This lavish complex on the Langdale Estate offers next-level luxury. The huge suites are more London-chic than Lakeland-cosy – mezzanine floors, sleek tiles, private patios and futuristic log burners are standard, and there's a reading room, Arc'teryx-stocked kit room, private woodland and the superb Stove restaurant. The new Brimstone Spa adds even more spoils: outdoor pool, chill-out rooms, private spa for two.

★**Eltermere Inn**   HOTEL **£££**
(☑ 015394-37207; www.eltermere.co.uk; Elterwater; r £149-295; P 🛜) This charming inn is one of Lakeland's loveliest backwater boltholes. Rooms are simple and classic, tastefully decorated in fawns and taupes with quirky features such as window seats and free-standing baths. The food's excellent, too, served in the inn's snug bar; afternoon tea is served on the lawn on sunny days.

✖ Eating

Sticklebarn   PUB FOOD **£**
(☑ 015394-37356; Great Langdale; lunch mains £5-8, dinner mains £11-13.50; ⊘ 11am-9pm) Now run by the National Trust, this converted barn is a walkers' favourite: it's packed with people nursing pints and aching fell-sore legs at the end of the day. Food is wholesome and hearty: herdwick and ale stew, venison ragu and ropa vieja chilli, washed down with a good ale selection.

Chesters by the River   CAFE **££**
(☑ 015394-32553; www.chestersbytheriver.co.uk; Skelwith Bridge; lunch mains £8-15; ⊘ 9am-5pm) Beside a rattling brook at Skelwith Bridge, halfway between Ambleside and Elterwater, this smart cafe is definitely more gourmet than greasy spoon: delicious salads, specials and cakes make it well worth a stop. There's a chic gift shop, too – items include slate souvenirs from the workshop around the corner.

❶ Getting There & Away

Bus 516 (six daily) is the only bus, with stops at Ambleside, Skelwith Bridge, Elterwater and the Old Dungeon Ghyll hotel in Great Langdale. The fare from Ambleside all the way into Great Langdale is £5.90.

Wasdale
☑ 019467

Carving its way for 5 miles from the Cumbrian coast, the craggy, wind-lashed valley of Wasdale is where the Lake District scenery takes a turn for the wild. Ground out by a long-extinct glacier, the valley is home to the Lake District's highest and wildest peaks, as well as the steely grey expanse of Wastwater, England's deepest and coldest lake.

Wasdale's fells are an irresistible draw for hikers, especially those looking to conquer England's tallest mountain, **Scafell Pike** (978m).

✖ Activities

★**Scafell Pike**   HIKING
At 978m, England's highest mountain features on every self-respecting hiker's bucket list. The classic route starts from Wasdale Head; it's hard going but within the reach of most moderately fit walkers, although it's steep and hard to navigate in bad weather. It's a return trip of around six to seven hours.

Proper gear is essential: raincoat, rucksack (backpack), map, food, water and hiking boots. A favourable weather forecast is preferable to make the most of the views.

▨ Sleeping

★**Wasdale Hall YHA**   HOSTEL **£**
(☑ 0845-371 9350; www.yha.org.uk; Wasdale Hall, Nether Wasdale; dm £13-30; ⊘ reception 8-10am & 5-10.30pm; P) This hostel on the shores of Wastwater has the kind of location you'd normally pay through the nose for. It's in a

19th-century mock-Tudor mansion that still has most of its period architecture, including original roof trusses and latticed windows. It has the usual self-catering facilities, plus a very decent restaurant.

Wasdale Head Campsite
CAMPSITE £

(NT; ✔bookings 015394-63862; www.national trust.org.uk/features/lake-district-camping; sites £12-25, extra adult £6, pods £35-80) This National Trust campsite is in a fantastically wild spot, nestled beneath the Scafell range. Facilities are basic (laundry room, showers), but the views are out of this world. Camping pods (some with electric hook-ups) and tepees provide a bit more shelter in case Wasdale's notorious weather decides to make an appearance.

★ Wasdale Head Inn
B&B ££

(✔019467-26229; www.wasdale.com; s £59, d £118-130, tr £177; ☐❖) A slice of hill-walking heritage here. Hunkering beneath the brooding bulk of Scafell Pike, this 19th-century hostelry is gloriously old-fashioned and covered in vintage photos and climbing memorabilia. The rooms are cosy, with roomier suites in a converted stable. The wood-panelled dining room serves fine food, with pub grub and ales from the Great Gable Brewing Co in Ritson's Bar.

Camping is also available for £5 a night.

Cockermouth

✔01900 / POP 9146

Set at the confluence of the River Cocker and River Derwent, the Georgian town of Cockermouth is best known as the birthplace of William Wordsworth and the home base of the renowned Jennings Brewery. Unfortunately, its position beside two major rivers means it has suffered frequent episodes of flooding – most recently in 2009 and 2015, when much of the town centre was swamped.

◉ Sights

★ Wordsworth House
HISTORIC BUILDING

(NT; ✔01900-824805; www.nationaltrust.org.uk/wordsworth-house; Main St; adult/child £7.90/3.95; ◷11am-5pm Sat-Thu Mar-Oct) The poet William Wordsworth was born on 7 April 1770 at this handsome Georgian house at the end of Main St. Built around 1745, the house has been meticulously restored based on accounts from the Wordsworth archive: the kitchen, drawing room, study and bedrooms all look much as they would have to a young

William. Costumed guides wander around the house for added period authenticity. Outside, the walled kitchen garden was mentioned in Wordsworth's autobiographical epic *The Prelude*.

The house also has some interesting hands-on experiences: you can try using a quill pen in the former clerk's office, play some chords on a harpsichord and (if the maid is in residence on the day you visit) watch meals being prepared over the kitchen's blazing fire. Exhibitions document the Wordsworth family's story and William's poetic legacy.

Jennings Brewery
BREWERY

(✔01900-821011; www.jenningsbrewery.co.uk; adult/child £9/4.50; ◷guided tours 1.30pm Wed-Sat) Real-ale aficionados will be familiar with the Jennings name – it has been brewing beers since 1874 and its pints are pulled at pubs all over the Lake District. Guided tours trace the brewing process, followed by a tasting session of Cocker Hoop and Sneck Lifter in the Old Cooperage Bar. Children must be over 12.

⌷ Sleeping

Old Homestead
B&B ££

(✔01900-822223; www.byresteads.co.uk; Byresteads Farm; s £40-50, d £60-80; ☐) Byre is an old English dialect word meaning 'cowshed', but you certainly won't be roughing it with the animals at this lovely farm conversion. The rooms are sweet and traditional, blending classic pine, flagstones and rendered walls with modern luxuries like power showers and underfloor heating. The Cruck Rooms and Master's Loft are the pick of the bunch.

It's 2 miles from Cockermouth.

Croft House
B&B ££

(✔01900-827533; www.croft-guesthouse.com; 6/8 Challoner St; s £68-88, d £78-98; ❖) A pleasant little base in a lemon-yellow terraced house along a side road off the town's main street. All the rooms are decorated with great care: from tasteful tartan bedsteads and contemporary wallpapers to little posable bedside lights. Homemade granola and orange pancakes make breakfast a treat.

✖ Eating

★ Merienda
CAFE £

(✔017687-72024; www.merienda.co.uk; 7a Station St; mains £4-8; ◷8am-9pm Mon-Thu, to 10pm Fri & Sat, 9am-9pm Sun) This Cockermouth fave is open daily and has a second branch in

Keswick. The interior is light and airy and the Med-tinged food is packed with flavour. There's a good balance between meat and veggie-friendly dishes. Carnivores might enjoy a generous slow-cooked BBQ brisket burger, while herbivores should try the excellent baked eggs with feta and aubergine.

Quince & Medlar   VEGETARIAN ££
(☑ 01900-823579; www.quinceandmedlar.co.uk; 13 Castlegate; mains £15.50; ⏱ 7-10pm Tue-Sat; ♪) ✿ Even if you're a committed carnivore, it's well worth dining here to see that vegetarian food isn't just nut roast and baked mushrooms – here, you could find yourself feasting on courgette-wrapped cheese soufflé, root veg and puy lentil 'haggis' or French onion tartlet. The location in a Georgian house is very handsome.

Bitter End   PUB
(☑ 01900-828993; www.bitterend.co.uk; 15 Kirkgate; ⏱ noon-2.30pm & 6-10pm) This brewpub produces its own award-winning beers such as Cockermouth Pride, Lakeland Honey Beer and Cuddy Lugs. You can watch the vats at work through a glass partition in the bar.

ℹ Information

Cockermouth Tourist Office (☑ 01900-822634; www.cockermouth.org.uk; 88 Main St; ⊙ 10am-4pm Mon-Fri, to 2pm Sat)

ℹ Getting There & Away

Bus X4/X5 (half-hourly Monday to Saturday, hourly Sunday) travels from Cockermouth to Keswick (£6.10) and Penrith (£7.40).

Keswick

☑ 017687 / POP 4821

The most northerly of the Lake District's major towns, Keswick has perhaps the most beautiful location of all: encircled by cloud-capped fells and nestled alongside the idyllic, island-studded lake of Derwentwater, a silvery curve criss-crossed by puttering cruise boats. It's also brilliantly positioned for further adventures into the nearby valleys of Borrowdale and Buttermere, and a great base for walking – the hefty fells of Skiddaw and Blencathra rise nearby.

◉ Sights

★ Keswick Museum   MUSEUM
(☑ 017687-73263; www.keswickmuseum.org.uk; Station Rd; adult/child £4.50/3; ⊙ 10am-4pm)

Keswick's quirky town museum explores the area's history, from ancient archaeology through to the arrival of industry in the Lakes. It's a diverse collection, taking in everything from neolithic axe heads mined in the Langdale valley to a huge collection of taxidermied butterflies. Its best-known exhibits are a 700-year-old mummified cat and the Musical Stones of Skiddaw, a weird instrument made from hornsfel rock that was once played for Queen Victoria.

Castlerigg Stone Circle   MONUMENT
FREE Set on a hilltop a mile east of town, this jaw-dropping stone circle consists of 48 stones that are between 3000 and 4000 years old, surrounded by a dramatic ring of mountain peaks.

Lakes Distillery   DISTILLERY
(☑ 017687-88850; www.lakesdistillery.com; tours £12.50; ⊙ 11am-6pm) The first craft distillery in the Lake District has made a big splash since opening in 2014. It's located on a 'model farm' built during the 1850s and was founded by a team of master distillers. So far its range includes a gin, a vodka and a flagship whisky, plus liqueurs flavoured with damson plum, elderflower, rhubarb and rosehip, and salted caramel. Guided tours take you through the process and include a tasting of the three spirits.

You can also take a specialist whisky tour, and meet the distillery's resident herd of alpacas. The **Bistro at the Distillery** is worth a look for lunch, too.

Whinlatter Forest Park   FOREST
(www.forestry.gov.uk/whinlatter) **FREE** Encompassing 4.6 sq miles of pine, larch and spruce, Whinlatter is England's only true mountain forest, rising sharply to 790m about 5 miles from Keswick. The forest is a designated red squirrel reserve; you can check out live video feeds from squirrel cams at the **visitor centre** (☑ 017687-78469; ⊙ 10am-4pm). It's also home to two exciting mountain-bike trails and the **Go Ape** (www.goape.co.uk/days-out/whinlatter; adult/child £33/25; ⊙ 9am-5pm mid-Mar–Oct) treetop assault course. You can hire bikes from **Cyclewise** (☑ 017687-78711; www.cyclewise.co.uk; 3hr hire adult/child from £19.50/15; ⊙ 10am-5pm), next to the visitor centre.

Entry to the forest is free, but you have to pay for parking (£2 for one hour, £8 all day).

Bus 77 (four daily) runs from Keswick or, if you're driving, head west on the A66 and look out for the brown signs near Braithwaite.

Derwent Pencil Museum   MUSEUM

(☑ 017687-73626; www.pencilmuseum.co.uk; Southy Works; adult/child £4.95/3.95; ⊙ 9.30am-5pm) Reopened after being badly damaged in the 2015 floods, Keswick's oddest museum is devoted to the charms of the humble pencil – with exhibits including a pencil made for the Queen's Diamond Jubilee, wartime spy pencils that were hollowed out for secret maps, and the world's largest pencil (a mighty 8m long). It all stems from the discovery of graphite in the Borrowdale valley during the 17th century, after which Keswick became a major pencil manufacturer.

🏃 Activities

Keswick Launch   BOATING

(☑ 017687-72263; www.keswick-launch.co.uk; round-the-lake pass adult/child/family £10.75/5.65/25.50) Shimmering to the south of Keswick, studded with islands and ringed by craggy fells, Derwentwater is undoubtedly one of the prettiest of the Lakeland lakes. As always, getting out on the water is the best way to explore. The Keswick Launch runs regular cross-lake excursions, and rowboats and motor boats (£12/27 per hour) can be hired next to the jetties.

🎉 Festivals & Events

Keswick Mountain Festival   OUTDOORS

(www.keswickmountainfestival.co.uk; ⊙ May) This May festival celebrates all things mountainous.

Keswick Beer Festival   BEER

(www.keswickbeerfestival.co.uk; ⊙ Jun) Lots and lots of beer is drunk during Keswick's real-ale fest in June.

🛏 Sleeping

Keswick YHA   HOSTEL £

(☑ 0845 371 9746; www.yha.org.uk; Station Rd; dm £15-35; ⊙ reception 7am-11pm; 🛜) Refurbished after flooding in 2015, Keswick's handsome YHA looks as good as new – its premium facilities include an open-plan ground-floor cafe, a seriously smart kitchen and cracking views over Fitz Park and the rushing River Greta. The dorm decor is standard YHA, but some rooms have private riverside balconies. What a treat!

★ Howe Keld   B&B ££

(☑ 017687-72417; www.howekeld.co.uk; 5-7 The Heads; s £65-90, d £110-140; P🛜) This gold-standard B&B pulls out all the stops: goose-down duvets, slate-floored bathrooms, chic colours and locally made furniture. The best rooms have views across Crow Park and the golf course, and the breakfast is a pick-and-mix delight. Free parking is available on The Heads if there's space.

Lookout   B&B ££

(☑ 017687-80407; www.thelookoutkeswick.co.uk; Chestnut Hill; d £90-120; P🛜) The clue's in the name: this three-room B&B is all about the views – there's a panorama of fells filling every window. It's in a gabled 1920s house, but feels modern with cappuccino-and-cream colour schemes, wooden beds and minimalist glass showers. There's a pleasant garden, too. Take Penrith Rd west and turn right onto Chestnut Hill; the B&B is on the left.

Linnett Hill   B&B ££

(☑ 017687-44518; www.linnetthillkeswick.co.uk; 4 Penrith Rd; s £50, d £88-98; 🛜) Much recommended by travellers, this lovingly run B&B has lots going for it: crisp white rooms, a great location near Fitz Park and keen prices that stay the same year-round. Breakfast is good, too: there's a blackboard of specials to choose from and the dining room has gingham-check tablecloths and a crackling wood burner.

★ Cottage in the Wood   HOTEL £££

(☑ 017687-78409; www.thecottageinthewood.co.uk; Braithwaite; d £130-220; ⊙ restaurant 6.30-9pm Tue-Sat; P🛜) For a secluded spoil, head for this out-of-the-way bolthole, on the road to Whinlatter Forest, in a completely modernised coaching inn. Elegant rooms survey woods and countryside: the Mountain View rooms overlook the Skiddaw Range, but we liked the super-private Attic Suite and the Garden Room, with its wood floors and wetroom. The restaurant's fantastic, too (set dinner menu £45).

🍴 Eating

★ Fellpack   CAFE £

(☑ 017687-71177; www.fellpack.co.uk; 19 Lake Rd; lunches £4-8; ⊙ 10am-4pm Wed-Mon, 6-9pm Thu-Sat) This on-trend cafe specialises in 'fell pots' – a Lakeland-style Buddha bowl, incorporating an all-in-one meal such as sweet potato and curry, smoked macaroni and peas, or braised chilli beef, all freshly made and flavour-packed. Flatbreads and baguettes are offered for lunch to go. The owners are full of enthusiasm and the food is zingy and imaginative. We like it. It's also open three nights a week for dinner.

★ **Lingholm Kitchen** CAFE £
(☑017687-71206; www.thelingholmkitchen.co.uk; mains £7-9; ☺9am-5pm) What a setting this splendid cafe has: in a delightful walled garden on the Lingholme Estate, with a 30m glass wall that presents cinematic views of Skiddaw, plus a dainty old greenhouse. For lunch, expect modern brunch dishes such as chickpea fritters, baked eggs, pork croquettes and (of course) avocado on toast.

Jasper's Coffee House CAFE £
(☑017687-73366; 20 Station St; sandwiches from £4, dishes £6-8; ☺10am-4pm Mon-Thu, 9am-5pm Fri-Sun; ☻) Dog fans rejoice: this popular Keswick cafe is nuts about canines. Dishes here are named after dogs of legend (The Muttley, The Old Yeller, The Huckleberry Hound), there are doggie prints on the walls, and naturally, canine companions are welcome. Food-wise, it's standard brunch-lunch fare: pittas, sausage rolls, wraps and sandwiches and cooked breakfasts.

Pheasant Inn PUB FOOD ££
(☑017687-76234; www.the-pheasant.co.uk; Bassenthwaite Lake; mains £13.50-21, restaurant dinner menu £45; ☺restaurant 7-9pm Wed-Sat, noon-2.30pm Sun, bistro noon-2.30pm & 6-9pm) A short drive along Bassenthwaite Lake is this fine-dining pub. Hunting prints and pewter tankards cover the old bar, stocked with vintage whiskies and Lakeland ales, and the two restaurants (informal bistro and very formal restaurant) serve superior country food. The afternoon tea's done in the proper English fashion too, served on a tiered cake stand with scones and cucumber sandwiches.

Square Orange CAFE ££
(☑017687-73888; www.thesquareorange.co.uk; 20 St John's St; ☺10am-11pm Sun-Thu, to midnight Fri & Sat) This lively cafe-bar seems to have become everyone's favourite hangout in Keswick – thanks no doubt to its superb thin-based pizzas, excellent wine and craft beer selection and a regular programme of live gigs. With its big wooden bar and packed-in tables, it feels rather continental – and the coffee is hands-down the best in Keswick.

Morrel's BRITISH ££
(☑017687-72666; www.morrels.co.uk; Lake Rd; 3-course menu £21.95, mains £12.50-22.50; ☺5.30-9pm Tue-Sun) Probably the best option in Keswick for a sit-down dinner, Morrel's is

an attractive restaurant majoring in British bistro-style food. Glossy wood, spotlights and glass give it a refined feel.

🍷 Drinking & Nightlife

Dog & Gun PUB
(☑017687-73463; 2 Lake Rd; ☺11am-11pm) Benches, beams, hearths, rugs: the old Dog is the picture of a Lakeland pub. Look out for Thirst Rescue ale, which donates part of its proceeds to the Keswick Mountain Rescue Team.

Cafe-Bar 26 BAR
(☑017687-80863; 26 Lake Rd; ☺9am-11pm Mon-Sat, 10am-10pm Sun) A cosy corner wine bar that also serves good lunches and evening tapas (£4 to £10).

🛍 Shopping

★ **George Fisher** SPORTS & OUTDOORS
(☑017687-72178; www.georgefisher.co.uk; 2 Borrowdale Rd; ☺9am-5.30pm Mon-Sat, 10am-4pm Sun) Quite possibly the most famous outdoors shop in the Lake District, founded in 1967 and still the place where discerning hikers go to buy their gear (even if it is a bit more expensive than the chains). There are three floors of boots, tents and gear, and the boot-fitting service is legendarily thorough.

ℹ Information

Keswick Tourist Office (☑017687-72645; www.keswick.org; Moot Hall, Market Pl; ☺9.30am-4.30pm; ☻) The town's tourist office is well run and the staff are very informed. It also sells discounted tickets for the Keswick Launch, and has free wi-fi.

ℹ Getting There & Away

The Keswick & Honister Dayrider (p562) buys unlimited travel on buses in the Keswick area, including on the 77 and 78 buses to Borrowdale and Buttermere (if you're returning the same day, it's also bizarrely cheaper than buying a return). All buses leave from and arrive at the **bus station**.

Useful buses from Keswick:

555/556 Lakeslink Hourly to Grasmere (£8.30, 40 minutes), Ambleside (£8.80, 45 minutes), Windermere (£9.80, one hour) and Kendal (£10.60, 1½ hours).

77/77A Circular route (five to seven daily) from Keswick via Portinscale, Catbells, Grange, Seatoller, Honister Pass, Buttermere, Lorton and Whinlatter.

78 (at least hourly Monday to Friday, half-hourly weekends) The main Borrowdale bus, with stops at Lodore, Grange, Rosthwaite and Seatoller.

Borrowdale

☑ 017687 / POP 417

With their patchwork of craggy hills, broad fields, tinkling streams and drystone walls, the side-by-side valleys of Borrowdale and Buttermere are many people's idea of the quintessential Lakeland landscape. Once a centre for mineral mining (especially slate, coal and graphite), this is walkers' country these days and, apart from the odd rickety barn or puttering tractor, there's precious little to spoil the view.

South of Keswick, the B5289 tracks Derwentwater into the heart of Borrowdale, winding past the small farming villages of Grange-in-Borrowdale, Rosthwaite and Stonethwaite.

◉ Sights & Activities

Watendlath Tarn LAKE
This National Trust–owned tarn is reached via a turn-off on the B5285 south of Keswick. On the way the road passes over one of the Lake District's most photographed packhorse crossings at **Ashness Bridge**. Parking at the tarn is free for NT members, but the road is narrow and has few passing places, so it's more pleasant to walk up in summer.

Lodore Falls WATERFALL
At the southern end of Derwentwater, this famous waterfall featured in a poem by Robert Southey, but it's only worth visiting after a good spell of rain. It's in the grounds of the Lodore Hotel; there's an honesty box for donations.

Bowder Stone NATURAL FEATURE
A mile south from Grange, a turn-off leads up to the geological curiosity known as the Bowder Stone, a 1700-tonnes lump of rock left behind by a retreating glacier. A small stepladder leads to the top of the rock.

Platty+ BOATING
(☑ 017687-76572; www.plattyplus.co.uk; kayaks & canoes per hour £8-15) Based at the Lodore Boat Landings at the southern end of Derwentwater, this company hires out kayaks, canoes, rowing boats and sailing dinghies. It also runs instruction courses.

🛏 Sleeping

Seatoller Farm CAMPSITE £
(☑ 017687-77232; www.seatollerfarm.co.uk; adult/child £7/3; ⊙ Easter-Oct) A lovely, tucked-away site on a 500-year-old farm near Seatoller

with a choice of riverside or woodland pitches. B&B rooms (double £75 to £90) are offered in the farmhouse.

Borrowdale YHA HOSTEL £
(☑ 0845 371 9624; www.yha.org.uk; Longthwaite; dm £15-30; ⊙ Feb-Dec; P 🛜) This friendly hostel makes a super, outdoorsy base for forays around Borrowdale. It's in a lovely spot next to a babbling brook, surrounded by gardens and fells. Part timber-clad, it has the feel of a ski chalet with convivial dorms, a big kitchen and lounge, table tennis and snooker tables as well as a wildlife area outside.

Derwentwater Independent Hostel HOSTEL £
(☑ 017687-77246; www.derwentwater.org; Barrow House; dm £24, s & d £60, tr £66-75, q £83-96; P @) Built as a 19th-century mansion, this grand Grade II–listed house is one of Britain's most architecturally ostentatious hostels. Previously YHA-owned, now private, it's a thing of beauty: many rooms have original features such as plasterwork and fireplaces. The 7-hectare grounds encompass an artificial waterfall.

★ Langstrath Inn B&B ££
(☑ 017687-77239; www.thelangstrath.com; Stonethwaite; d £114-140; ⊙ restaurant noon-2.30pm & 6-8.30pm Tue-Sun; P 🛜) This simple country inn makes one of the best little bases in Borrowdale. Its eight rooms are snug and simple, with crimson throws and the occasional roof beam to add character – but it's the views that really sell the place. Hearty, unpretentious food (dinner mains £13.25) and ales from Hawkshead Brewery are served in the restaurant.

Glaramara Hotel HOTEL ££
(☑ 017687-77222; www.glaramarahouse.co.uk; Seatoller; s £59, d £74-118; P 🛜 ❄) If your budget won't stretch to one of Borrowdale's plush country hotels, this great-value, activity-focused place makes a good alternative. The decor is corporate (pine-effect furniture, no-frills furnishings), but the location can't be faulted: on the doorstep of Honister Pass, surrounded by fells and greenery. The hotel has its own outdoor activities centre for ghyll scrambling, rock climbing, mine exploring and more.

ℹ Getting There & Away

Bus 77/77A (from £3.10, seven daily Monday to Saturday, five on Sunday) makes a circular route from Keswick via Portinscale, the trailhead for Catbells and all the Borrowdale villages, then heads over Honister Pass, through Buttermere and Lorton, over the Whinlatter Pass and back to Keswick.

Bus 78 (£6.20 to £8.30, at least hourly, half-hourly on weekends from July to August) shuttles through Borrowdale as far as Seatoller, then heads back the same way to Keswick.

If you're planning on making a return journey the same day, it's nearly always cheaper to buy the Keswick & Honister Dayrider (p562) than a return fare.

Buttermere

🎵 017687 / POP 121

Stretching 1.5 miles northwest of Honister Pass, the deep bowl of Buttermere was gouged out by a steamroller glacier and backed by a string of impressive peaks and emerald-green hills. The valley's twin lakes, Buttermere and Crummock Water, were once joined but became separated by glacial silt and rockfall.

The little village of Buttermere sits halfway between the two and provides a wonderfully cosy base for exploring the rest of the valley and the many nearby fells, including Haystacks (597m), the favourite mountain and the last resting place of the patron saint of Lakeland walkers, the author Alfred Wainwright.

🛏 Sleeping & Eating

⭐ **Buttermere YHA**   HOSTEL £
(🎵 0845 371 9508; www.yha.org.uk; dm £13-32; ☺ mid-Mar–Oct, reception 8.30-10am & 5-10.30pm; 🅿 🛜) Perched in a perfect position on the Honister–Buttermere road, this excellent slate-fronted hostel (once a hotel) has rooms looking out across the lake. The decor is smart, colourful and surprisingly modern, and there's a great cafe-kitchen and plenty of four- and six-bed dorms. There's also space to pitch a tent during summer holidays.

Syke Farm   CAMPSITE £
(🎵 017687-70222; www.sykefarmcampsite.com; adult/child £8/4; ☺ Easter-Oct) Set on a bumpy riverside site, Syke Farm is back-to-basics camping, but you'll wake up to views of Red Pike, High Stile and Haystacks. Check in at the farm shop in the village first and don't forget to sample some of its homemade ice cream.

⭐ **Kirkstile Inn**   PUB FOOD ££
(🎵 01900-85219; www.kirkstile.com; mains £11.50-15.95) A finer country pub you could not

HONISTER PASS

From Borrowdale, a narrow, perilously steep road snakes up the fellside to Honister Pass, home to the last working slate mine in the UK. Though you can still pick up slate souvenirs in the on-site shop, these days the **Honister Slate Mine** (🎵 017687-77230; www.honister. com; mine tour adult/child £14.50/8.50, all-day pass incl mine tour & classic/extreme via ferrata £56.50/64; ☺ tours 10.30am, 12.30pm & 3.30pm Mar-Oct) has diversified with a range of adventure activities, ranging from subterranean tours to thrilling **via ferrata** (classic route £40, extreme incl Infinity Bridge £45, all day pass incl mine tour & classic/extreme via ferrata £56.50/64) walks. An all-day pass covering all activities costs £56.50/43.50 per adult/child.

hope to find. Hidden away near the little lake of Loweswater, a mile or so north of Buttermere, the Kirkstile is a joy: crackling fires, oak beams, worn carpets, wooden bar and all. It's particularly known for its award-winning ales (try the Loweswater Gold).

Rooms (singles £85 to £105, doubles £117 to £137) are quaint; some have views across Lorton Vale.

Bridge Hotel   PUB FOOD ££
(🎵 017687-70252; www.bridge-hotel.com; mains £10-16; 🅿 🛜) As the name suggests, this venerable hostelry is right beside Buttermere's village bridge. There's standard pub food in the bar, or more upmarket fare in the smart-casual restaurant. Frilly rooms (singles from £84.50, doubles £169 to £189) and an antique ambience define the old Bridge.

Fish Inn   PUB FOOD ££
(🎵 017687-70253; www.fishinnbuttermere.co.uk; mains £8-16; 🅿) This whitewashed inn (doubles £90 to £125) once employed the 18th-century beauty known as the 'Maid of Buttermere', but these days it's just a welcoming locals' pub serving basic staples such as lasagne and battered haddock, washed down with ales from several local breweries.

ⓘ Getting There & Away

Bus 77/77A (£6.20, five to seven daily) serves Buttermere and Honister Pass from Keswick. For return journeys the same day, save a bit of

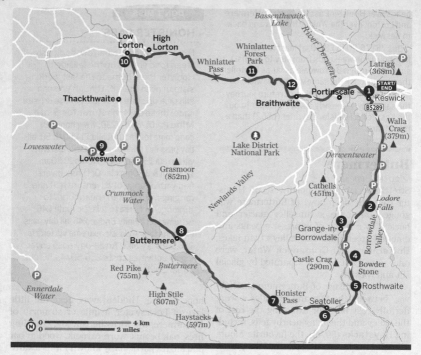

Driving Tour
Borrowdale & Buttermere

START KESWICK
END KESWICK
LENGTH 28 MILES; THREE TO FOUR HOURS

This is one of the Lakes' most beautiful road trips, a perfect day trip out of Keswick.

Begin with breakfast in ❶ **Keswick**, then head along the B5289 into Borrowdale. First stop is ❷ **Lodore Falls** (p582), a pretty cascade at the southern end of Derwentwater. Next, detour to the little hamlet of ❸ **Grange-in-Borrowdale**, where a trail leads up the slate-strewn sides of Castle Crag, a small fell with great views over Borrowdale.

From Grange carry on to the huge boulder known as the ❹ **Bowder Stone** (p582), shifted into position by the long-gone glacier that carved out the Borrowdale Valley. Pootle on to ❺ **Rosthwaite** for tea and cake at the Flock In Tea-Room, or continue to ❻ **Seatoller** for lunch.

In the afternoon tackle the steep crawl up to ❼ **Honister Pass** (p583), where you can

pick up some slate souvenirs, take a tour into the depths of the old slate mine or venture out onto the hair-raising *via ferrata*.

From here the road drops down into the beautiful valley of ❽ **Buttermere** (p583). Spot the zigzag peaks of High Stile, Haystacks and Red Pike looming on your left-hand side over the lake, stop off for a drink at the Fish Inn and remember to pay your respects to hiker and author Alfred Wainwright inside St James' Church.

Continue along the shore of Crummock Water past ❾ **Loweswater**, where you could make an optional but very worthwhile detour via the excellent Kirkstile Inn. When you reach ❿ **Low Lorton**, a right-hand turn carries you over Whinlatter Pass to ⓫ **Whinlatter Forest Park** (p579).

There are a couple of great options for dinner on your way back to Keswick, such as the ⓬ **Cottage in the Wood** (p580) just before Braithwaite, or the traditional Pheasant Inn on the shores of Bassenthwaite Lake.

cash by buying the Keswick & Honister Dayrider (p562).

Ullswater & Around

☑ 017684

After Windermere, the second-largest lake in the Lake District is Ullswater, stretching for 7.5 miles between Pooley Bridge at the northern end and Glenridding and Patterdale at the southern end. Carved out by a long-extinct glacier, the deep valley in which the lake sits is flanked by an impressive string of fells, most notably the razor ridge of Helvellyn, Cumbria's third-highest mountain at 950m.

The lake's eastern shore is where the three main villages are located. The remote west side is well off the beaten track, and great for crowd-free hiking around the village of Howtown and the picturesque valley of Martindale.

The villages around Ullswater were badly hit in the 2015 floods. You'll see major flood defence works in Glenridding, while the eponymous bridge in Pooley Bridge was swept away – there's a temporary one in place for now, with plans ongoing to replace it with a permanent flood-resistant structure.

◎ Sights & Activities

★ Helvellyn   HIKING
Along with Scafell Pike (p577), this challenging hike is the one everyone wants to do. The classic ascent takes in the twin ridges of Striding and Swirral Edge, which are spectacular but very exposed and involve some scrambling and dizzyingly steep drops on either side – if you're at all nervous of heights, Helvellyn is not the fell for you.

The usual routes climb up through Glenridding or Patterdale. Always check the weather forecast and take all the necessary supplies.

Ullswater 'Steamers'   BOATING
(☑ 017684-82229; www.ullswater-steamers.co.uk; cruise all piers pass adult/child £15.95/6.95) Ullswater's historic steamers are a memorable way to explore the lake. The various vessels include the stately *Lady of the Lake*, launched in 1877 and supposedly the world's oldest working passenger boat. The boats run east–west from Pooley Bridge to Glenridding via Howtown; there are nine daily sailings in summer, three in winter.

Gowbarrow Park
& Aira Force   PARK, WATERFALL
(NT) **FREE** This rolling park stretches out across the lakeshore between Pooley Bridge and Glenridding. Well-marked paths lead up to the impressive 20m waterfall of Aira Force. Another waterfall, High Force, is further up the hillside. South of Gowbarrow Park is Glencoyne Bay, where the springtime daffodils inspired William Wordsworth to pen one of his most famous poems.

🛏 Sleeping

Quiet Site   CAMPSITE £
(☑ 07768-727016; www.thequietsite.co.uk; campsites £25-44, pods £35-65, hobbit holes £65-100; ⊙ year-round; ℗ 🛜) Ecofriendly campsite on the fells above Ullswater, with pre-erected tents and ecopods available as well as 'hobbit holes' (timber-lined cabins built into the hillside). Camping is very pricey in summer, but there's plenty of space, and the views are outstanding.

Helvellyn YHA   HOSTEL £
(☑ 0845 371 9742; www.yha.org.uk; Greenside; dm £13-30; ⊙ Easter-Oct) This back-of-beyond hostel is a favourite of hikers looking to get an early start on Helvellyn. It's in an old miner's cottage about a 900m hike up from the valley. Dorms are small and facilities are basic, but meals are provided by hostel staff. There's even a bar.

Patterdale YHA   HOSTEL £
(☑ 0845 371 9337; www.yha.org.uk; Patterdale; dm £13-30; ⊙ Easter-Oct, reception 7.30-10am & 3-11pm) This 1970s hostel lacks the heritage of some of the Lakeland YHAs, but it has a great location by the lake and all the usual YHA trappings (kitchen, cafe, TV lounge) – as long as you don't mind the rather institutional architecture.

Old Water View   B&B ££
(☑ 017684-82175; www.oldwaterview.co.uk; Patterdale; d £98; ℗ 🛜) Patterdale has several B&Bs, but this one's the pick. It's a simple place focusing on the essentials: friendly service, comfy rooms and good value. The split-level Bothy room is ideal for families, with attic beds for the kids, while Little Gem overlooks a stream and Place Fell was a favourite of Alfred Wainwright (his signature is on the wall).

★ Another Place,
The Lake   BOUTIQUE HOTEL £££
(☑ 017684-86442; www.another.place; Watermillock; r £230-290, f £345-385; ℗ 🛜 🚲 🐾)

Acquired by the owners of Cornwall's Watergate Bay Hotel, the former Rampsbeck Hotel has been reinvented as one of the Lakes' most luxurious, family-friendly, activity-focused getaways. A striking new wing has added an infinity pool and contemporary rooms – rooms in the old house feel more traditional. There's a restaurant, bar, well-stocked library and lakefront lawns, and activities including SUP, kayaking and wild swimming.

✗ Eating

Granny Dowbekin's   CAFE £
(📞017684-86453; www.grannydowbekins.co.uk; Pooley Bridge; mains £6-12; ⊗9am-5pm) For a filling all-day brekkie, a ploughman's lunch, chunky sandwich or a slice of something naughty and cake-shaped, this attractive cafe in Pooley Bridge is a favourite option. The homemade 'gingerbridge' makes a yummy souvenir.

Fellbites   CAFE ££
(📞017684-82781; Glenridding; lunch mains £3.95-9.95, dinner mains £12.50-18; ⊗9am-8.30pm Thu-Tue, to 5.30pm Wed) This cafe beside the main car park in Glenridding has something to fill you up at any time of day: generous fry-ups for breakfast; soups, pulled-pork burgers and rarebits for lunch; lamb shanks and duck breast for dinner. It's honest, no-fuss grub.

1863   BISTRO ££
(📞017684-86334; www.1863ullswater.co.uk; High St, Pooley Bridge; mains £13.50-22.50; ⊗dinner 6-9pm, bar 2-10pm) A classy new addition to Pooley Bridge's dining scene, overseen by head chef Phil Corrie, who has a fondness for the classics but is abreast of modern tastes, too – so you get dishes like Goosnargh Chicken with morels and truffled potato, or mead-glazed duck with sweet damson jam.

There are rooms upstairs, too (doubles £95 to £150), showcasing some adventurous wallpaper choices.

❶ Information

Lake District National Park Ullswater Information Centre (📞017684-82414; ullswatertic@lake-district.gov.uk; Glenridding; ⊗9.30am-5.30pm Apr-Oct, to 3.30pm weekends Nov-Mar)

❶ Getting There & Away

Bus 508 travels from Penrith to Glenridding and Patterdale (£5.50, nine buses daily). Five buses continue over Kirkstone Pass to Windermere.

The Ullswater Bus-and-Boat Combo ticket (adult/child/family £16/9/34) includes a day's travel on bus 508 with a return trip on an Ullswater Steamer; buy the ticket on the bus.

Kendal

📍 015395 / POP 28,586

Technically Kendal isn't in the Lake District, but it's a major gateway town. Often known as the 'Auld Grey Town' thanks to the sombre grey stone used for many of its buildings, Kendal is a bustling shopping centre with some good restaurants, a funky arts centre and intriguing museums. But it'll forever be synonymous in many people's minds with its famous mint cake, a staple item in the nation's hiking packs ever since Edmund Hillary and Tenzing Norgay munched it during their ascent of Everest in 1953.

◉ Sights

Abbot Hall Art Gallery   GALLERY
(📞01539-722464; www.abbothall.org.uk; adult/child £7/free, joint ticket with Museum of Lakeland Life & Industry £9; ⊗10.30am-5pm Mon-Sat Apr-Oct, to 4pm Nov-Mar) Kendal's fine-art gallery houses one of the northwest's best collections of 18th- and 19th-century art. It's especially strong on portraiture and Lakeland landscapes: look out for works by Constable, John Ruskin and local boy George Romney, who was born in Dalton-in-Furness in 1734 and became a sought-after portraitist, as well as a key figure in the 'Kendal School'.

Kendal Museum   MUSEUM
(📞01539-815597; www.kendalmuseum.org.uk; Station Rd; £2; ⊗10am-4pm Tue-Sat) Founded in 1796 by the inveterate Victorian collector William Todhunter, this mixed-bag museum features everything from stuffed beasts and transfixed butterflies to medieval coin hoards. There's also a reconstruction of the office of Alfred Wainwright, who served as honorary curator at the museum from 1945 to 1974: look out for his well-chewed pipe and knapsack.

Museum of Lakeland
Life & Industry   MUSEUM
(📞01539-722464; www.lakelandmuseum.org.uk; adult/child £5/free, joint ticket with Abbot Hall Art Gallery £9; ⊗10.30am-5pm Mon-Sat Mar-Oct, to 4pm Nov-Feb) Directly opposite Abbot Hall, this museum recreates various scenes from Lakeland life during the 18th and 19th centuries, including a farmhouse parlour,

ENNERDALE

If you really want to leave the outside world behind, the remote valley of Ennerdale is definitely the place. Just to the north of Wasdale, this valley and its namesake lake were once home to slate mines and large timber plantations, but these are slowly being removed and the valley is being returned to nature as part of the Wild Ennerdale (www. wildennerdale.co.uk) project.

Needless to say, the valley is paradise if you prefer your trails quiet. Several popular routes head over the fells to Wasdale, while walking towards Buttermere takes you past the **Black Sail YHA** (🖉0845-371 9680; www.yha.org.uk; dm £35; ⊘mid-Mar–Oct, check-in 5-9pm) 🍴, a marvellously remote hostel inside a shepherd's bothy. Much loved by mountaineers and hikers, it's become a YHA landmark. Space is very limited, so make sure you book ahead.

a Lakeland kitchen, an apothecary and the study of Arthur Ransome, author of *Swallows and Amazons* – look out for some of his original sketchbooks.

Levens Hall   HISTORIC BUILDING
(🖉015395-60321; www.levenshall.co.uk; house & gardens adult/child £13.90/5, gardens only £9.90/4; ⊘house noon-4pm, gardens 10am-5pm Sun-Thu Mar-Oct) This Elizabethan manor is built around a mid-13th-century fortified pele tower, and fine Jacobean furniture litters its interior, although the real draw is the 17th-century topiary garden – a surreal riot of pyramids, swirls, curls, pompoms and peacocks straight out of *Alice in Wonderland*.

Sizergh Castle   CASTLE
(NT; 🖉015395-60070; www.nationaltrust.org. uk/sizergh; adult/child £11.50/5.75, gardens only £7.50/3.75; ⊘house noon-4pm Apr-Oct, gardens 10am-5pm) Three-and-a-half miles south of Kendal along the A591, this castle is the feudal seat of the Strickland family. Set around a pele tower, its finest asset is the lavish wood panelling on display in the Inlaid Chamber, as well as a huge 650-hectare estate encompassing lakes, orchards, woods and pastureland.

🛏 Sleeping

Kendal Hostel   HOSTEL £
(🖉01539-724066; www.kendalhostel.com; 118-120 Highgate; dm/d £20/40; ⊘reception open 5-8pm; @🛜) An ex-YHA, this basic hostel has 14 rooms variously sleeping two to 14 people in mixed and single-sex dorms. Spread over four floors, it's a friendly place. There's a shared kitchen, lounge and a free pool table on the ground floor, plus lockers for storage (you might need your own padlock). It's next door to the Brewery Arts Centre (p588).

Sonata Guest House   B&B ££
(🖉01539-732290; www.sonataguesthouse.co.uk; 19 Burneside Rd; d £85-90; 🛜) Nothing too swish at this B&B in a Kendal-typical greystone terraced house, but it's cosy enough with feminine rooms, floral wallpapers and nice little touches such as goose-down pillows and well-stocked tea trays. Parking is a pain.

Lyth Valley Country Inn   HOTEL £££
(🖉015395-68295; www.lythvalley.com; Lyth; d £150-200, ste £240-300; P🛜) It's seven miles west of Kendal, but there's a reason to head out so far – this hotel sits in a gorgeous spot overlooking the little-visited Lyth Valley, famous locally for its damson plums. Rooms are really attractive, with solid wooden furniture and patches of exposed brickwork (we liked the quirky names too, such as Hopping Hare and Quacking Duck).

The oak-panelled restaurant (mains £13.95 to £18.95) is high quality.

🍴 Eating

Brew Brothers   CAFE £
(🖉01539-722237; www.brew-brothers.co.uk; 69 Highgate; mains £8.50-10; ⊘8.30am-5.30pm Mon-Sat) The hipster cafe comes to Kendal at this new number on Highgate. With its scruffy wood furniture and black-aproned baristas, it's got the aesthetic down, but its owners are Lakeland through and through – they previously ran a cafe in Windermere. Go for smashed avocado and poached eggs for brekkie, then for lunch wolf down a hot-smoked-salmon sandwich. Yum.

Yard 46   CAFE £
(🖉07585-320522; www.yard46.co.uk; Branthwaite Brow; lunches £3-8; ⊘10am-4pm Mon-Fri, to 5pm Sat) Kendal is well stocked with cafes, but

this gem is well worth seeking out. It's down a blink-and-you'll-miss-it alleyway, with a little courtyard and an old whitewashed building with cruck-framed attic dining room. Delicious soups, imaginative salads and yummy cakes, plus unusual options such as *pan con tomate* (tomato bruschetta) and veggie brunch baps with a fried duck's egg.

Baba Ganoush DELI £
(☑ 01539-738210; www.baba-ganoush.co.uk; Finkle St; mains £5-9; ⊙10.30am-3pm Tue-Sat) Down a side alley, this Mediterranean-inspired cafe serves up delicious lunches of falafels, lamb stews, veggie meze and Moroccan tagines, plus a big range of salads. It's recently moved a little way down the street to give more space for diners.

★**Punch Bowl Inn** PUB FOOD ££
(☑ 015395-68237; www.the-punchbowl.co.uk; Crosthwaite; mains £15.95-24.50; ⊙noon-4pm & 5.30-8.30pm; ℗) If you don't mind a drive, this renowned gastropub in the village of Crosthwaite has long been known for its top-notch food. Whitewashed outside, carefully modernised inside, it's a cosy, inviting space to dine. Chef Scott Fairweather's superb food blends classic dishes with cheffy ingredients (oyster mousse, potato croquettes, pea fricassée, salsify).

The rooms (£135 to £320) are lovely, too: they're all different, but the nicest ones have reclaimed beams, sloping eaves, slate-floored bathrooms and his-and-hers claw-foot tubs.

★**The Moon Highgate** BISTRO ££
(☑ 01539-729254; www.themoonhighgate. com; 129 Highgate; lunch £6-12, dinner £17-21; ⊙11.30am-2.15pm Tue-Sat & 5.30-9.15pm Tue-Fri, 6-9.30pm Sat) Now run by prodigiously talented chef Leon Whitehead, this smart bistro takes its cue from the seasons and the pick of Cumbrian produce. Classic flavours sit alongside surprises: watercress panna cotta, or hen's egg with onion broth. Dishes are beautifully plated, veggie choice is good and the uncluttered space is a winner. The town's top table, no question.

☆ Entertainment

Brewery Arts Centre THEATRE, CINEMA
(☑ 01539-725133; www.breweryarts.co.uk; Highgate) A cracking arts centre with a gallery, cafe, theatre and two cinemas, hosting the latest films as well as music, theatre, dance and much more.

🛍 Shopping

★**Low Sizergh Barn** FOOD
(☑ 015395-60426; www.lowsizerghbarn.co.uk; ⊙9am-5.30pm) A prodigious selection of Lakeland goodies are available at this farm shop, just outside Kendal on the A590. There's also a farm trail and woodland walk to follow if the weather's nice, and you can watch the cows being milked – look out for the raw-milk vending machine beside the shop entrance. Only in Cumbria!

❶ Getting There & Away

The train line from Windermere runs to Kendal (£5.90, 15 minutes, hourly) en route to Oxenholme.

Bus 555/556 Regular bus (half-hourly Monday to Friday, hourly at weekends) to Windermere (£6.50, 30 minutes), Ambleside (£7.60, 40 minutes) and Grasmere (£8.80, 1¼ hours).

Bus 106 To Penrith (£11.30, 80 minutes, one or two daily Monday to Friday).

CUMBRIAN COAST

☑ 01229
While the central lakes and fells pull in a never-ending stream of visitors, surprisingly few ever make the trek west to explore Cumbria's coastline. And that's a shame. While it might not compare to the wild grandeur of Northumberland, or the rugged splendour of Scotland's shores, Cumbria's coast is well worth exploring – a bleakly beautiful landscape of long sandy bays, grassy headlands, salt marshes and seaside villages stretching all the way from Morecambe Bay to the shores of the Solway Coast. There's an important seabird reserve at St Bees Head and the majestic grounds of Holker Hall are well worth a wander.

Historically, Cumbria's coast served the local mining, quarrying and shipping industries and Barrow-in-Furness remains a major shipbuilding centre. More controversial is the nuclear plant of Sellafield, a major employer but still dividing opinion half a century on from its inception.

◉ Sights & Activities

★**Ravenglass & Eskdale Railway** RAIL
(☑ 01229-717171; www.ravenglass-railway.co.uk; adult/child/family 24hr pass £15/9/44.95; 🚃) Affectionately known as La'al Ratty, this pocket-sized railway was built to ferry iron ore from the Eskdale mines to the coast. These

DON'T MISS

CARTMEL

Tiny Cartmel is known for three things: its 12th-century **priory** (⊙ 9am-5.30pm May-Oct, to 3.30pm Nov-Apr) **FREE**, its small **racecourse** and its world-famous sticky toffee pudding, sold at the **Cartmel Village Shop** (☑ 015395-36280; www.cartmelvillageshop.co.uk; 1 The Square; ⊙ 9am-5pm Mon-Sat, 10am-4.30pm Sun).

More recently it's become known as the home of chef Simon Rogan (dubbed Cumbria's answer to Heston Blumenthal). His flagship restaurant, **L'Enclume** (☑ 015395-36362; www.lenclume.co.uk; Cavendish St; set lunch £59, lunch & dinner menu £155; ⊙ noon-1.30pm & 6.30-8.30pm Tue-Sun), showcases his boundary-pushing cuisine and madcap presentation as well as his passion for foraged ingredients.

He also runs a less formal bistro, **Rogan & Company** (☑ 015395-35917; www.roganandcompany.co.uk; The Square; 2-/3-course set lunch £20/26, mains £18-25; ⊙ noon-2pm & 6-9pm Mon & Wed-Sat, 12.15-3.15pm Sun), across the village. Bookings are essential for both.

days it's one of Cumbria's most beloved family attractions, with miniature steam trains that chug for 7 miles through the Eskdale valley between the coastal town of Ravenglass and the village of Dalegarth, and several stations in between.

There are seven to 14 trains a day depending on the season; fares are cheaper outside summer. Dogs (£1.50) are welcome on board, and you can take bikes (£4), but they have to be booked in advance. You also get a 50% discount on trips on Ullswater Steamers (p585).

★ **Holker Hall**   HISTORIC BUILDING
(☑ 015395-58328; www.holker.co.uk; adult/child £12.50/free; ⊙ house 11am-4pm, grounds 10.30am-5pm Wed-Sun Mar-Oct) Three miles east of Cartmel on the B5278, Holker Hall has been the family seat of the Cavendish family for nigh on four centuries. Though parts of it date from the 16th century, the house was almost entirely rebuilt following a devastating fire in 1871. It's a typically ostentatious Victorian affair, covered with mullioned windows, gables and copper-topped turrets outside and filled with a warren of lavishly over-the-top rooms inside.

Among the highlights are the **drawing room**, packed with Chippendale furniture and historic oil paintings, and the **library**, containing an antique microscope belonging to Henry Cavendish (discoverer of nitric acid) and more than 3500 antique books (some of which are fakes, designed to conceal light switches when the house was converted to electric power in 1911). The showstopper is the **Long Gallery**, notable for its plasterwork ceiling and fine English furniture – look for the 19th-century sphinx-

legged table and a wonderful walnut cabinet inlaid with ivory and rosewood.

Outside, Holker's grounds sprawl for more than 10 hectares, encompassing a rose garden, a woodland, ornamental fountains and a 22m-high lime tree.

There's also a food hall that stocks produce from the estate, including two renowned products: venison and salt marsh lamb.

St Bees Head   WILDLIFE RESERVE
(RSPB; stbees.head@rspb.org.uk) Five-and-a-half miles south of Whitehaven and 1½ miles north of the tiny town of St Bees, this wind-battered headland is one of Cumbria's most important reserves for nesting seabirds. Depending on the season, species nesting here include fulmars, kittiwakes and razorbills, as well as Britain's only population of resident black guillemots. There are more than 2 miles of cliff paths to explore.

Muncaster Castle   CASTLE
(☑ 01229-717614; www.muncaster.co.uk; adult/child £14.50/7.30; ⊙ gardens & owl centre 10.30am-5pm, castle noon-4pm Sun-Fri) This crenellated castle, 1.5 miles east of Ravenglass, was originally built around a 14th-century pele tower, constructed to resist Reiver raids. Home to the Pennington family for seven centuries, the castle's architectural highlights are its great hall and octagonal library, and outside you'll find an ornamental maze and splendid grounds. The castle is also home to a hawk and owl centre, which stages several flying displays a day. There's a 15% discount for booking online.

Muncaster is also known for its numerous ghosts: keep your eyes peeled for the

THE LAKE DISTRICT & CUMBRIA CUMBRIAN COAST

Muncaster Boggle and a malevolent jester known as Tom Fool (hence 'tomfoolery').

Laurel & Hardy Museum · MUSEUM

(☑ 01229-582292; www.laurel-and-hardy.co.uk; Brogden St, Ulverston; adult/child £5/2.50; ☉ 10am-5pm Easter-Oct, closed Mon & Wed rest of year) Founded by avid Laurel and Hardy collector Bill Cubin back in 1983, this mad-cap museum in Ulverston (the birthplace of Stan Laurel) has new premises inside the town's old Roxy cinema. It's crammed floor-to-ceiling with cinematic memorabilia, from original posters to film props, and there's a shoebox-sized cinema showing back-to-back Laurel and Hardy classics. Now run by Bill's grandson, it's a must for movie buffs.

ⓘ Getting There & Away

The Furness and Cumbrian Coast railway lines loop 120 miles from Lancaster to Carlisle, stopping at the coastal resorts of Grange, Ulverston, Ravenglass, Whitehaven and Workington. The **Cumbria Coast Day Ranger** (adult/child £20.20/10.10) covers a day's unlimited travel on the line and works out cheaper than a return journey from Carlisle or Lancaster.

NORTHERN & EASTERN CUMBRIA

Many visitors speed through the northern and eastern reaches of Cumbria in a headlong dash for the Lake District, but it's worth taking the time to venture inland from the national park. It might not have the big-name fells and chocolate-box villages, but it's full of interest, with traditional towns, crumbling castles, abandoned abbeys and sweeping moors set alongside the magnificent Roman engineering project of Hadrian's Wall.

Carlisle

☑ 01228 / POP 75,306

Carlisle isn't Britain's prettiest city, but it has history and heritage aplenty. Precariously perched on the frontier between England and Scotland, in the area once ominously dubbed the 'Debatable Lands', Cumbria's capital is a city with a notoriously stormy past: sacked by the Vikings, pillaged by the Scots and plundered by the Border Reivers, the city has been on the front line of England's defences for more than 1000 years.

Reminders of the past are evident in its great crimson castle and cathedral, built from the same rosy-red sandstone as most of the city's houses. On English St, you can also see two massive circular towers that once flanked the city's gateway.

The closest section of Hadrian's Wall begins at nearby Brampton.

ⓞ Sights

★ Carlisle Castle · CASTLE

(EH; ☑ 01228-591922; www.english-heritage.org.uk/visit/places/carlisle-castle; Castle Way; adult/child £8/4.80, combined ticket with Cumbria's Museum of Military Life £9.20/5.15; ☉ 10am-6pm Apr-Sep, to 5pm Oct-Mar) Carlisle's brooding, rust-red castle lurks on the north side of the city. Founded around a Celtic and Roman stronghold, the castle's Norman keep was added in 1092 by William Rufus, and later refortified by Henry II, Edward I and Henry VIII (who added the supposedly cannon-proof towers). From the battlements, the stirring views stretch as far as the Scottish borders. The castle also houses **Cumbria's Museum of Military Life** (☑ 01228-532774; adult/child £4.50/2.50, combined ticket with Carlisle Castle £9.20/5.15; ☉ 10am-6pm Apr-Oct, to 5pm Sat-Thu Nov-Mar), which has collections of military memorabilia associated with the region's regiments.

The castle has witnessed some dramatic events over the centuries: Mary, Queen of Scots, was imprisoned here in 1568, and it was the site of a notorious eight-month siege during the English Civil War, when the Royalist garrison survived by eating rats, mice and the castle dogs before finally surrendering in 1645. Look out for some medieval graffiti and the 'licking stones' in the dungeon, which Jacobite prisoners supposedly lapped for moisture.

Carlisle Cathedral · CHURCH

(☑ 01228-548151; www.carlislecathedral.org.uk; 7 The Abbey; suggested donation £5, photography £1; ☉ 7.30am-6.15pm Mon-Sat, to 5pm Sun) Built from the same red sandstone as Carlisle Castle, Carlisle's cathedral began life as a priory church in 1122 and became a cathedral when its first abbot, Athelwold, became the first bishop of Carlisle. Among its notable features are the 15th-century choir stalls, the barrel-vaulted roof and the 14th-century East Window, one of the largest Gothic windows in England. Surrounding the cathedral are other priory relics, including the 16th-century fratry and the prior's tower.

Tullie House Museum
MUSEUM

(📞01228-618718; www.tulliehouse.co.uk; Castle St; adult/child £6.50/free; ⊙10am-5pm Mon-Sat, 11am-5pm Sun) Carlisle's flagship museum covers 2000 years of the city's past. The Roman Frontier Gallery explores Carlisle's Roman foundations, while the Border Galleries cover the Bronze Age through to the Industrial Revolution. Two galleries flesh out the story: the Border Reivers covers the marauding bandits who once terrorised the area, while the Vikings Revealed exhibition displays finds from the Cumwhitton Viking cemetery, including helmets, swords and grave goods. The top-floor Lookout has cracking views of the castle.

🛏 Sleeping

⭐ Halston Aparthotel
HOTEL ££

(📞01228-210240; www.thehalston.com; 20-34 Warwick Rd; 1-bed apt £120-140, 2-bed apt £240-280; 🅿🛜) For a city-centre base, this complex of self-catering apartments really has to be the pick of places to stay in Carlisle. While not huge, the apartments are well appointed with small studio kitchens, modern decor, parquet-style flooring, sash windows and zero clutter, and the setting in the Edwardian-era building (formerly Carlisle's General Post Office) is a real stunner.

⭐ Willowbeck Lodge
B&B ££

(📞01228-513607; www.willowbeck-lodge.com; Lambley Bank, Scotby; d £100-140; 🅿🛜) If staying in the city centre isn't important, then this palatial B&B is the top choice in the city. The four rooms are huge, contemporary and plush, with luxuries such as underfloor heating, Egyptian-cotton bedding and tasteful shades of beige and taupe. Some rooms have balconies overlooking the gardens and pond.

Warwick Hall
B&B £££

(📞01228-561546; www.warwickhall.org; Warwick-on-Eden; s £85-150, d £90-220) This fine country house, 2 miles from the centre along Warwick Rd, is a real country retreat. With its huge rooms, high ceilings and old-fashioned decor, it feels a bit like staying on an aristocratic friend's estate. There are hectares of grounds and it even has its own stretch of river for fishing.

🍴 Eating

Foxes Cafe Lounge
CAFE £

(📞01228-491836; www.foxescafelounge.co.uk; 18 Abbey St; mains £4-8; ⊙9am-4pm Mon-Fri, 10am-4.30pm Sat) Swing by this cool cafe for a pastry and cappuccino or an Apple Refresher smoothie – or better still, settle in for a hearty brunch (available in Full Fox carnivorous and Herbivore veggie versions).

David's
BRITISH ££

(📞01228-523578; www.davidsrestaurant.co.uk; 62 Warwick Rd; 2-course lunch £17.95, dinner mains £16.95-25.95; ⊙noon-3.30pm & 6.30-11pm Tue-Sat) For many years this town house restaurant has been the address for formal dining in Carlisle and there's no sign that's going to change. It majors in rich, traditional dishes with a strong French flavour: lamb with a pistachio crust and port gravy, roast chicken with leek and tarragon mash. The house is full of period architecture, too.

Thin White Duke
BISTRO ££

(📞01228-402334; www.thinwhiteduke.info; 1 Devonshire St; mains £9.95-14.95; ⊙11.45am-11pm) This place scores points for the name alone (at least for Bowie fans), although the Duke himself would have been most unlikely to tuck into the burgers, tandoori chicken and flat-iron steak on the menu. He might have liked the cocktails, though, and the location – in a former monastery, with plenty of exposed brick and ramshackle-chic decor.

Foxborough Smokehouse
BARBECUE ££

(📞01228-317925; www.foxboroughrestaurant.com; 52 Cecil St; lunch mains £10, dinner mains £12-16; ⊙noon-2pm & 5-9pm Wed & Thu, noon-2pm & 5-10pm Fri, 10am-10pm Sat, noon-2pm & 5-8.30pm Sun) Low and slow; pig, chicken and cow. That pretty much sums up this cellar smokehouse, where everything is spiced, full-on-flavoured and unashamedly meaty. The house special is the Jacob's Ladder – dry-aged beef short rib cooked for aeons in a 'green egg' cooker. Veggies have options – salads, chilli – but this is one for meat eaters, really.

🍷 Drinking & Nightlife

Hell Below
BAR

(📞01228-548481; 14-16 Devonshire St; ⊙noon-midnight Mon-Fri, to 2am Sat, to 6pm Sun) This brick-walled bar is a popular haunt for Carlisle's hipster drinkers, with craft beers and a bargain cocktail menu (with fun concoctions to try such as bubblegum sours and starburst cosmos). Snacky food – burgers, nachos, pizzas and the like – will fill a hole if you're hungry.

Shabby Scholar
CAFE

(📞01228-402813; 11-13 Carlyle Court; tapas £3-7, lunch mains £7-9.50; ⊙10am-midnight Mon-Sat) As its name suggests, this popular place is stylishly shabby, with scruffy furniture, a bar made out of old crates and a determinedly chilled vibe. It's fine for tapas, light bites and burgers, but many people just come for cocktails.

☆ Entertainment

Brickyard CONCERT VENUE
(📌 01228-512220; www.thebrickyardonline.com; 14 Fisher St) Carlisle's grungy gig venue, housed in the former Memorial Hall.

ⓘ Information

Carlisle Tourist Office (📌 01228-598596; www.discovercarlisle.co.uk; Greenmarket; ⊙ 9.30am-5pm Mon-Sat, 10.30am-4pm Sun)

ⓘ Getting There & Away

AIR
From Carlisle's tiny **airport** (www.carlisleairport. co.uk), 8 miles northeast of the city centre, **Loganair** (www.loganair.co.uk) operates direct flights to/from London Southend, Dublin and Belfast.

BUS
National Express coaches depart from the bus station on Lonsdale St for destinations including London (£25.50 to £39.10, 7½ hours, two or three direct daily), Manchester (£17 to £24.40, three to 3½ hours, three daily) and Glasgow (£12 to £17.10, two hours, four to six daily).

Bus 554 goes to Keswick (£14.60, 70 minutes, four daily Monday to Saturday, three on Sunday) and bus 104 goes to Penrith (£6.30, 40 minutes, half-hourly Monday to Saturday, nine on Sunday).

TRAIN
Carlisle is on the west-coast line from London to Glasgow. It's also the terminus for the scenic Cumbrian Coast and Tyne Valley lines, as well as the historic **Settle to Carlisle Railway** (www. settle-carlisle.co.uk; adult return £28) across the Yorkshire Dales. The following are the main destinations:

Glasgow £28.50, 1¼ hours
Lancaster £32.40, 45 minutes
London Euston £119.70, 3½ hours
Manchester £56, two hours 10 minutes
Newcastle-upon-Tyne £16.70, 1½ hours

Penrith

📌 01768 / POP 15,181

Just outside the borders of the national park, red-brick Penrith perhaps has more in common with the stout market towns of the Yorkshire Dales. It's a solid, traditional place with plenty of cosy pubs and quaint teashops and a lively market on Tuesdays. It's also the main gateway for exploring the picturesque Eden Valley.

◉ Sights

★ Lowther Estate HISTORIC SITE
(📌 01931-712192; www.lowthercastle.org; adult/child £9/7; ⊙ 10am-5pm) This sprawling country estate once belonged to one of the Lake District's most venerable families and is currently undergoing a huge, multimillion-pound restoration project. The 400-year-old crenellated castle and the estate's grounds are now open to the public again. Though the castle itself is to remain a ruin, restoration work is gradually breathing life back into the gardens, which have been largely forgotten since the estate fell into disrepair following WWII.

Among the areas to visit are the Iris Garden, the Great Yew Walk, a restored parterre and a wealth of hidden follies, lakes and woodland areas.

Rheged VISITOR CENTRE
(📌 01768-868000; www.rheged.com; ⊙ 10am-6pm) Cunningly disguised as a Lakeland hill 2 miles west of Penrith, this visitor centre houses an IMAX cinema and temporary exhibitions. There's also a large retail hall selling Cumbrian foodstuffs and souvenirs. Local chef Peter Sidwell runs cooking classes and is also responsible for the cafe menu.

🛏 Sleeping

Lounge HOTEL ££
(📌 01768-866395; www.theloungehotelandbar. co.uk; King St; d/f from £80/110; 🛰) For a town-centre hotel at reasonable prices, you can't do any better than this chic little number. Pine furniture, laminate floors and tasteful tints of pistachio, cream and taupe feel a tad generic, but it's chintz-free and central. The three-bed apartment (£160) has its own mini-kitchen. Breakfast and dinner is served in the ground-floor bistro.

★ Augill Castle HOTEL £££
(📌 01768-341967; www.stayinacastle.com; Kirkby Stephen; r/ste from £180/240; 🅿🛰) If you've always dreamed of staying in a bona fide British castle, this stately pile near Kirkby Stephen is definitely the place. All the trappings are here – crenellated turrets, stained-glass windows, cavernous rooms – and the design vibe inside is rather groovy, with a mix of antique furniture and contemporary

furnishings. There's even a mini-cinema. It's 25 miles southeast of Penrith.

George Hotel
HOTEL **£££**

(☑ 01768-862696; www.lakedistricthotels.net/georgehotel; Devonshire St; d £125-165; P) Penrith's venerable red-brick coaching inn offers classically decorated rooms in prim stripes and country patterns, plus a quaint bar and restaurant. It's not quite the heritage beauty it might appear to be at first glance – rooms are comfortable but disappointingly free of original features. The free parking's a boon.

✗ Eating

★ Four & Twenty
BISTRO **££**

(☑ 01768-210231; www.fourandtwentypenrith.co.uk; 14 King St; lunch mains £14-16, dinner mains £16.50-19.50; ⊘ noon-2.30pm & 6-9.30pm Tue-Sat) Proper fine dining with a reasonable price tag is the modus operandi at this bistro, which blends sleek decor with rustic wood, banquette seats and mix-and-match furniture. Expect sophisticated dishes such as pork tenderloin with garlic, sage and Parma ham, or sea bass 'bouillabaisse-style'. If you're going to eat out in Penrith town, this is the place to do it.

George & Dragon
PUB FOOD **££**

(☑ 01768-865381; www.georgeanddragonclifton.co.uk; Clifton; mains £13.95-21.95; ⊘ noon-2.30pm & 6-9pm) If you don't mind a drive, this pretty pub in the village of Clifton makes a good lunch or dinner stop. It's situated on the Lowther Estate and sources much of its produce (including game) from there. Fires, benches and rafters make for a cosy setting and the food is generally good, if not quite gastropub standard.

★ Allium at Askham Hall
GASTRONOMY **£££**

(☑ 01931-712350; www.askhamhall.co.uk; Askham; dinner menu £50; ⊘ 7-9.30pm Tue-Sat) Regal setting, royally good dining. Chef Richard Swale's passion for Cumbrian produce was learned from a childhood spent shooting, fishing and foraging (he keeps his own chickens). His food combines richness and delicacy – such as chicken, cauliflower cheese and truffles – and everything looks like a work of art. The setting inside the hall is quite formal; dress nicely.

🛍 Shopping

JJ Graham
FOOD & DRINKS

(☑ 01768-862281; www.jjgraham.co.uk; 6-7 Market Sq; ⊘ 8.30am-5.30pm Mon-Sat) There's been a grocer here since 1793 and this endearingly old-fashioned deli is still the place to pick up treats such as local cheeses, homemade chutneys and loose-leaf teas.

❶ Information

Penrith Tourist Office (☑ 01768-867466; pen.tic@eden.gov.uk; Middlegate; ⊘ 9.30am-5pm Mon-Sat, 1-4.45pm Sun) Also houses the town's small museum.

❶ Getting There & Away

There are frequent train connections north to Carlisle (£5.90, 15 minutes) and south to Oxenholme (£7, 25 minutes), where you can change for branch trains to Windermere.

The bus station is northeast of the centre, off Sandgate. Bus 104 goes to Carlisle (£6.30, 40 minutes, half-hourly Monday to Saturday, nine on Sunday), and bus X4/X5 goes to the Cumbrian coast (£6.80 to £11.20, half-hourly Monday to Saturday, hourly Sunday) via Rheged, Keswick and Cockermouth.

1. Cyclists in the Peak District National Park (p456)
2. Surfing Croyde Bay (p311)
3. View of the Cotswolds near Painswick (p202)

England's Great Outdoors

The English love the great outdoors, and every weekend sees a mass exodus from the towns and cities to the hills, moors and coastline. Hiking and biking are the most popular pursuits but there's a huge range of activities available – and getting wet and muddy can actually be a highlight of your trip!

Walking

England can seem crowded, but away from the cities there are many beautiful areas, perfect for walking. You can go for a short riverside stroll or a major hike over mountain ranges – or anything in between. The best places include the Cotswolds, the Lake District and the Yorkshire Dales.

Cycling

A bike is ideal for getting to know England's countryside. Areas such as Suffolk, Yorkshire and Wiltshire offer a vast network of quiet country roads ideal for cycle touring. For off-road fun, mountain bikers can go further into the wilds in places such as the Peak District, the North Yorkshire Moors and the South Downs.

Horse Riding

If you want to explore the hills and moors at a more leisurely place, seeing the wilder parts of England from horseback is the way to go. In rural areas and national parks such as Dartmoor and Northumberland there are riding centres catering to all levels of proficiency.

Surfing

England may not be an obvious destination for surfers, but conditions can be surprisingly good at key locations. Top of the list are the west-facing coasts of Cornwall and Devon, while there are smaller scenes on the east coast, notably in Norfolk and Yorkshire.

Newcastle & Northeast England

Best Places to Eat

➜ Riley's Fish Shack (p607)

➜ House of Tides (p604)

➜ Raby Hunt (p612)

➜ Knitsley Farm Shop & Cafe (p611)

➜ Bay Horse (p612)

Best Places to Stay

➜ Lumley Castle (p609)

➜ Lord Crewe Arms (p616)

➜ Langley Castle Hotel (p617)

➜ Otterburn Castle Country House Hotel (p619)

➜ Jesmond Dene House (p602)

Why Go?

The irrepressible city of Newcastle-upon-Tyne anchors England's northeast. Set on the mighty River Tyne, this former industrial powerhouse's steep hills are lined with handsome Victorian buildings, and many of its one-time factories and warehouses have been transformed into galleries, museums, bars and entertainment venues. Newcastle's nightlife is legendary, and an evening out on the tiles is a quintessential experience.

Newcastle is also an ideal gateway for escaping into the northeast's utterly wild, starkly beautiful countryside – from the rounded Cheviot Hills to brooding Northumberland National Park and the remote North Pennines. Spectacular Hadrian's Wall cuts a lonely path through the landscape, dotted with dramatic fortress ruins that are haunting reminders of the bloody struggle with the Scots to the north, while the region's unspoilt coastline takes in long, desolate beaches, wind-worn castles and tiny, magical islands offshore.

When to Go

➜ Costumed re-enactments and Roman celebrations take place throughout the year at Hadrian's Wall.

➜ The best time to discover the region's miles of wide sandy beaches is during the summer season (June to August), although for surfers, Tynemouth's world-class waves are best (if chilliest) in winter and spring.

➜ September and October are great for losing yourself in the autumnal landscapes of Northumberland National Park.

➜ September is also the month to grab a Newkie Brown ale, or your running shoes, and join the party along the route of Tyneside's Great North Run, one of the world's biggest half-marathons.

History

Violent history has shaped this region more than any other in England, primarily because of its frontier position. Although Hadrian's Wall didn't serve as a defensive barrier, it marked the northern limit of Roman Britain and was the Empire's most heavily fortified line. Following the Romans' departure, the region became part of the Anglian kingdom of Bernicia, which united with the kingdom of Deira (encompassing much of modern-day Yorkshire) to form Northumbria in 604.

The kingdom changed hands and borders shifted several times over the next 500 years as Anglo-Saxons and Danes struggled to seize it. The land north of the River Tweed was finally ceded to Scotland in 1018, while the nascent kingdom of England kept everything below it.

The arrival of the Normans in 1066 saw William I eager to secure his northern borders against the Scots. He commissioned most of the castles you see along the coast, and cut deals with the prince bishops of Durham to ensure their loyalty. The new lords of Northumberland became very powerful because, as Marcher Lords (from the use of 'march' as a synonym of 'border'), they kept the Scots at bay.

Northumberland's reputation as a hotbed of rebellion intensified during the Tudor years, when the largely Catholic north, led by the seventh duke of Northumberland, Thomas Percy, rose up against Elizabeth I in the defeated Rising of the North in 1569. The Border Reivers, raiders from both sides of the border in the 16th century, kept the region in a perpetual state of lawlessness that only subsided after the Act of Union between England and Scotland in 1707.

Coal mines were the key to the 19th-century industrialisation of the northeast, powering steelworks, shipyards and armament works that grew up along the Tyne and Tees. In 1825 the mines also spawned the world's first steam railway, the Stockton & Darlington, built by local engineer George Stephenson. Social strife emerged in the 20th century, with mines, shipbuilding, steel production and the railway industry all winding down during the Great Depression and postwar years. Reinventing the northeast has been a mammoth task but regeneration continues apace.

🏃 Activities

Cycling

The northeast has some of England's most inspiring cycle routes.

Part of the National Cycle Network (NCN), a long-time favourite is the 200-mile Coast & Castles Cycle Route (www.coast-and-castles.co.uk), which runs south–north along the glorious Northumberland coast between Newcastle-upon-Tyne and Berwick-upon-Tweed and Edinburgh, Scotland.

The 140-mile Sea to Sea Cycle Route (www.c2c-guide.co.uk) runs across northern England between the Cumbrian coast (St Bees, Whitehaven or Workington) and Tynemouth or Sunderland via the northern Lake District and wild North Pennines' hills.

Another coast-to-coast option is the Hadrian's Cycleway (www.hadrian-guide.co.uk), a 174-mile route between South Shields or Tynemouth and Ravenglass in Cumbria along Hadrian's Wall.

Also running coast to coast is the 173-mile Reivers Route (http://reivers-route.co.uk) from Whitehaven to Tynemouth via Kielder Forest, the Scottish Borders and the Lake District.

Hiking

The North Pennines – along with the Cheviots further north – are considered 'England's last wilderness'. Long routes through the hills include the famous Pennine Way (www.nationaltrail.co.uk), Britain's first national trail, established in 1965, which keeps mainly to the high ground between the Yorkshire Dales and the Scottish border, but also crosses sections of river valley and some tedious patches of plantation. The whole route is 268 miles, but the 70-mile section between Bowes and Hadrian's Wall is a fine four-day taster.

Hadrian's Wall has a huge range of easy loop walks taking in forts and other historical highlights.

One of the finest walks along the windswept Northumberland coast, between the villages of Craster and Bamburgh via Dunstanburgh, includes two of the region's most spectacular castles. Another superb coastal trail is the 30-mile Berwickshire Coastal Path (www.walkhighlands.co.uk/borders/berwickshire-coastal-path.shtml) from Berwick-upon-Tweed to the village of Cockburnspath in Scotland.

ⓘ Getting There & Around

BUS

Bus transport around the region can be sporadic, particularly around the more remote reaches of western Northumberland. Contact **Traveline**

Newcastle & Northeast England Highlights

1 Holy Island, Lindisfarne (p624) Negotiating the tidal causeway to reach this other-worldly pilgrimage site.

2 Victoria Tunnel (p601) Exploring a coal-wagon tunnel and WWII air-raid shelter beneath Newcastle's streets.

3 Kielder Observatory (p618) Stargazing from this observatory in the Northumberland International Dark Sky Park.

4 Barnard Castle (p611) Viewing extraordinary objets d'art in the chateau-housed Bowes Museum.

5 Berwick Walls (p625) Circumnavigating

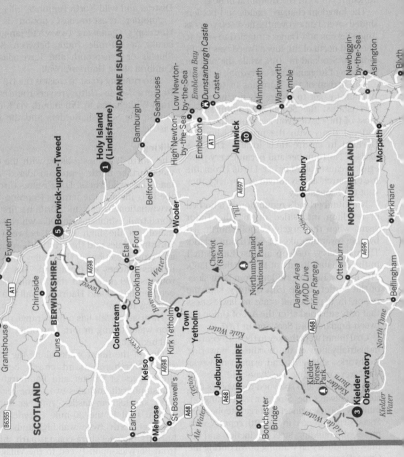

NORTH SEA

EAST LOTHIAN

SCOTLAND

Cockburnspath

Grantshouse

Coldingham

St Abbs

Eymouth

Duns

Chirnside

B6355

A1

BERWICKSHIRE

Coldstream

Kelso

ROXBURGHSHIRE

Melrose

Earlston

St Boswell's

A68

Jedburgh

A698

A68

Bonchester Bridge

Kirk Yetholm

Town Yetholm

Kielder Observatory

Kielder Forest Park

Kielder Water

NORTHUMBERLAND

Bellingham

Otterburn

A68

A696

North Tyne

Northumberland National Park

Danger Area (MOD Live Firing Range)

Cheviot (815m)

Kirkharle

Morpeth

Rothbury

A697

Berwick-upon-Tweed

Holy Island (Lindisfarne)

FARNE ISLANDS

Bamburgh

Seahouses

Belford

Wooler

Ford

Etal

Crookham

High Newton-by-the-Sea

Low Newton-by-the-Sea

Embleton Bay

Dunstanburgh Castle

Craster

Embleton

A1

Alnwick

Alnmouth

Warkworth

Amble

Newbiggin-by-the-Sea

Ashington

Blyth

Till

Coquet

Kale Water

Teviot

Tweed

Bowmont Water

Ale Water

Kielder Water

Lewder Burn

0 ——— 20 km
0 ——— 10 miles

N

the Elizabethan walls of England's northernmost city, Berwick-upon-Tweed.

6 Durham River Cruises (p609) Cruising on the tranquil River Wear, taking in Durham's city, castle and wondrous cathedral.

7 Hadrian's Wall (p612) Hiking along the remains of Britain's mightiest Roman legacy.

8 Hartlepool (p622) Learning about the fascinating maritime and wartime history of this coastal town.

9 Beamish Open-Air Museum (p610) Reliving the northeast's industrial age at this working museum.

10 Alnwick Castle (p619) Wandering the halls of Harry Potter's Hogwarts, aka Alnwick Castle.

Whitley Bay
Tynemouth
South Shields
Sunderland
Seaham
Peterlee
Hartlepool
Saltburn-by-the-Sea
Loftus
Danby
Redcar
Guisborough
Castleton
North York Moors National Park
Billingham
Middlesbrough
Stokesley
Eaglescliffe
Stockton-on-Tees
Sedgefield
Darlington
Huworth-on-Tees
Northallerton
Catterick
Bedale
Croxdale
Durham
Bishop Auckland
Shildon
Summerhouse
Pierce Bridge
Crook
West Auckland
Raby Castle
Richmond
NORTH YORKSHIRE
Newcastle-upon-Tyne
Beamish Open-Air Museum
Angel of the North
Stanley
Consett
Knitsley
Wolsingham
Frosterley
Hamsterley Forest
Middleton-in-Teesdale
Teesdale
Barnard Castle
Bowes Castle
The Pennines
Reeth
Ponteland
Newcastle
Newcastle International Airport
Wallsend
Corbridge
Hedley on the Hill
Edmundbyers
Stanhope
North Pennines
Pennine Way
Yorkshire Dales National Park
Hawes
Belsay
Hexham
Allendale Town
Blanchland
Weardale
Langdon Beck
Newbiggin
Buttertubs Pass
Haltwhistle
Hadrian's Wall
Allenheads
Killhope
Ireshopeburn
Brough
Kirkby Stephen
Alston
Nenthead
CUMBRIA
South Tyne
Coupland
Newbiggin-on-Line
Appleby
Tebay
Carlisle (20mi)
Eden
Ais Gill
Derwent Reservoir
Wear
Tyne
Derwent
Tees
Greta

(📞0871-200 2233; www.travelinenortheast.info) for information on connections, timetables and prices.

TRAIN

The East Coast Main Line runs north from London King's Cross to Edinburgh via Durham, Newcastle and Berwick; Northern Rail operates local and interurban services in the north, including west to Carlisle.

There are numerous Rover tickets for single-day travel and longer periods; check http://networkonetickets.co.uk.

Newcastle-upon-Tyne

📞0191 / POP 293,204

Against its dramatic backdrop of Victorian elegance and industrial grit, this fiercely independent city harbours a spirited mix of heritage and urban sophistication, with excellent art galleries and a magnificent concert hall, along with boutique hotels, some exceptional restaurants and, of course, interesting bars: Newcastle is renowned throughout Britain for its thumping nightlife, bolstered by an energetic, 42,000-strong student population. The city retains deep-rooted traditions, embodied by the no-nonsense, likeable locals.

Allow at least a couple of days to explore the Victorian city centre and quayside areas along the Tyne and across the river in Gateshead, as well as the rejuvenated Ouseburn Valley to the east, gentrified Jesmond to the north, and, on the coast, the surf beaches of Tynemouth.

⊙ Sights

⊙ City Centre

Newcastle's grand Victorian centre, a compact area bordered roughly by Grainger St to the west and Pilgrim St to the east, is one of the most compelling examples of urban rejuvenation in England. Down by the quays are the city's most recognisable attractions – the iconic bridges that span the Tyne and the striking buildings that flank it.

★ Great North Museum   MUSEUM

(📞0191-208 6765; https://greatnorthmuseum.org.uk; Barras Bridge; general admission free, planetarium adult/child £3/2; ⊙10am-5pm Mon-Fri, to 4pm Sat, 11am-4pm Sun) **FREE** The contents of Newcastle University's museums and the prestigious Hancock Museum's natural-history exhibits come together in the latter's neoclassical building. The result is a fascinating jumble of dinosaurs, Roman altar stones, Egyptian mummies, Samurai warriors and impressive taxidermy. Standout exhibits include a life-size *Tyrannosaurus rex* recreation and an interactive model of Hadrian's Wall showing every milecastle and fortress. There's also lots of hands-on stuff for kids and a planetarium with screenings throughout the day.

★ Life Science Centre   MUSEUM

(📞0191-243 8210; www.life.org.uk; Times Sq; adult/child £15/8; ⊙10am-6pm Mon-Sat, 11am-6pm Sun) Part of a sober-minded institute devoted to the study of genetic science, this centre lets you discover the secrets of life through a fascinating series of hands-on exhibits. The highlight is the Motion Ride, a simulator that lets you 'experience' bungee jumping and the like (the 4D film changes every year). There are lots of thought-provoking arcade-style games, and if the information sometimes gets lost on the way, never mind, kids will love it. Book ahead at busy times.

★ Discovery Museum   MUSEUM

(📞0191-232 6789; https://discoverymuseum.org.uk; Blandford Sq; ⊙10am-4pm) **FREE** Tyneside's rich history is explored at this unmissable museum. Exhibitions spread across three floors of the former Co-operative Wholesale Society building around the mightily impressive 30m-long *Turbinia,* the fastest ship in the world in 1897 and the first to be powered by steam turbine. Other highlights are a section on shipbuilding on the Tyne, with a scale model of the river in 1929, and the 'Story of Newcastle', spanning the city's history from Pons Aelius (Roman Newcastle) to Cheryl Cole.

Newcastle Castle   CASTLE

(📞0191-230 6300; www.newcastlecastle.co.uk; Castle Garth; adult/child £6.50/3.90; ⊙10am-5pm) The stronghold that put both the 'new' and 'castle' into Newcastle has been largely swallowed up by the train station, leaving only a few remaining fragments including the square Norman keep and the Black Gate. Exhibits inside the two restored buildings cover the history of the city, its castle and its residents from Roman times onwards. The 360-degree city views from the keep's rooftop are the best in town.

Laing Art Gallery   GALLERY

(📞0191-278 1611; www.laingartgallery.org.uk; New Bridge St; ⊙10am-5pm Tue-Sat, 2-5pm Sun) **FREE**

The exceptional collection at the Laing includes works by Gainsborough, Gauguin and Henry Moore, and an important collection of paintings by Northumberland-born artist John Martin (1789–1854). Check the 'What's On' section of the website for events including talks and tours. Temporary exhibitions may incur an extra charge.

Biscuit Factory GALLERY
(www.thebiscuitfactory.com; 16 Stoddart St; ☉10am-5pm Mon-Fri, to 6pm Sat, 11am-5pm Sun) FREE No prizes for guessing what this commercial art gallery used to be. These days, it's the UK's biggest contemporary art, craft and design gallery/shop, where you can browse and/or buy works by more than 200 artists each season in a variety of mediums, including painting, sculpture, glassware and furniture, many with a northeast theme. There's an on-site cafe, the Factory Kitchen, and fine-dining restaurant, Artisan.

◉ Ouseburn Valley

Now semi-regenerated, Newcastle's 19th-century industrial heartland, Ouseburn Valley, 1 mile east of the city centre, has potteries, glass-blowing studios and other creative workspaces, along with pubs, bars and entertainment venues.

★Victoria Tunnel HISTORIC SITE
(☑9am-5pm Mon-Fri 0191-230 4210; www.ouseburntrust.org.uk; Victoria Tunnel Visitor Centre, 55 Lime St; tours adult/child £7/4; ☉by reservation) Walking Newcastle's streets, you'd never know this extraordinary tunnel runs for 2.5 miles beneath your feet. Built between 1839 and 1842 as a coal-wagon thoroughfare, it was used as an air-raid shelter during WWII. Volunteer-led, two-hour tours take you through an atmospheric 700m-long level section of the tunnel. Book ahead as numbers are limited, and wear good shoes and a washable jacket for the limewashed walls; it's not suitable for kids under seven. Tours finish back at the Victoria Visitor Centre.

Seven Stories – The Centre for Children's Books MUSEUM
(www.sevenstories.org.uk; 30 Lime St; adult/child £7.70/6.60; ☉10am-5pm Tue-Sat, to 4pm Sun) A marvellous conversion of a handsome Victorian mill has resulted in Seven Stories, a very hands-on museum dedicated to the wondrous world of children's literature. Across the seven floors you'll find original

manuscripts and artwork from the 1930s onwards, and a constantly changing program of kid-oriented exhibitions, activities and events designed to encourage the AA Milnes of the new millennium. There's a bookshop, coffee shop and cafe.

◉ Gateshead

The area of Newcastle south of the Tyne is the 'town' (neighbourhood, really) of Gateshead. Local authorities are now promoting the whole kit-and-caboodle–on-Tyne as 'NewcastleGateshead'.

★BALTIC – Centre for Contemporary Art GALLERY
(☑0191-478 1810; http://baltic.art; Gateshead Quays; ☉10am-6pm Wed-Mon, 10.30am-6pm Tue) FREE Once a huge mustard-coloured grain store, BALTIC is now a huge mustard-coloured art gallery rivalling London's Tate Modern. There are no permanent exhibitions; instead, rotating shows feature the work and installations of some of contemporary art's biggest show-stoppers. The complex has artists in residence, a performance space, a cinema, a bar, a spectacular rooftop restaurant (bookings essential) and a ground-floor restaurant with riverside tables. A 4th-floor outdoor platform and 5th-floor viewing box offer fabulous panoramas of the Tyne.

✷✷ Festivals & Events

Great North Run SPORTS
(www.greatrun.org; ☉mid-Sep) Newcastle's 13.1-mile half-marathon takes place in mid-September. Entry is by ballot, with 57,000 places available. Otherwise join the locals cheering on the entrants along the route, which goes from the city centre across the Tyne Bridge and through Gateshead to South Shields.

🛏 Sleeping

Grey Street Hotel BOUTIQUE HOTEL ££
(☑0191-230 6777; www.greystreethotel.co.uk; 2-12 Grey St; d from £89; ✷🛜🛎) On the city centre's most elegant street, this beautiful Grade II–listed former bank has been adapted for contemporary needs, including triple glazing on the sash windows. Its 49 individually designed rooms have big beds and stylish colour combinations; some have giant black-and-white photographs covering one wall.

Malmaison BOUTIQUE HOTEL ££
(☑0191-389 8627; www.malmaison.com; 104 Quayside; d/ste from £115/190; P✷🛜) The affectedly

Newcastle-upon-Tyne

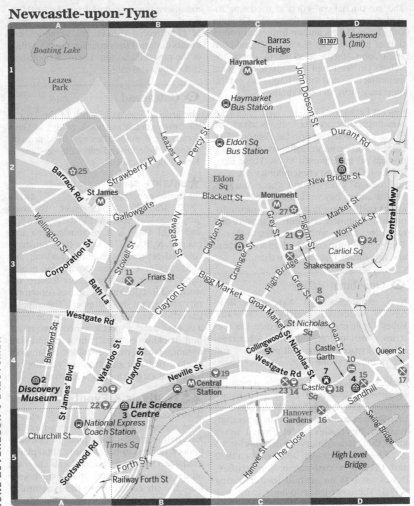

stylish Malmaison touch has been applied to this former warehouse with considerable success, even down to the French-speaking lifts. Big beds, sleek lighting and designer furniture embellish the 122 plush rooms. The best rooms have views of the Millennium Bridge. There's a spa, gym and on-site brasserie.

Newcastle Jesmond Hotel HOTEL **££**
(☎0191-239 9943; www.newcastlejesmondhotel. co.uk; 105 Osborne Rd; s/d/tr from £60/77/95; P🖘) Rooms aren't huge at this refurbished red-brick property footsteps from the bars and restaurants of Osborne Rd, but they're cosy, comfy and spotlessly clean, and come with the bonus of free parking (though spaces are limited, so get in quick). Wi-fi can be patchy.

★ **Jesmond Dene House** BOUTIQUE HOTEL **£££**
(☎0191-212 3000; https://jesmonddenehouse.co.uk; Jesmond Dene Rd; d from £140; P🅿🌐🖘) Large bedrooms at this exquisite 40-room property are furnished in a modern interpretation of the Arts and Crafts style and have stunning bathrooms complete with underfloor heating, as well as the latest tech; some have private terraces. The fine-dining restaurant (☎0191-

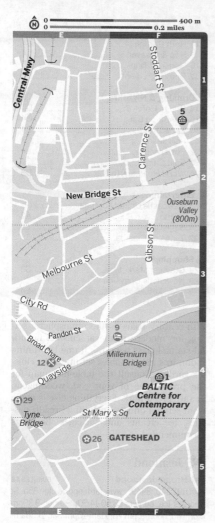

rooms and glossy timber (including interconnecting rooms for families and sumptuous suites), two bars and a smart-casual restaurant. Limited on-site parking is first-come, first-served but free. Its 11 luxury self-catering apartments are located nearby.

Eating

City Centre

Quay Ingredient CAFE £
(📞0191-447 2327; http://quayingredient.co.uk; 4 Queen St; dishes £2-8; ⊘8am-5pm; 🛜) Beneath the Tyne Bridge's soaring steel girders, this chic hole-in-the-wall has a devoted following for cooked breakfasts (scrambled eggs with white truffle oil and toasted brioche, Craster kippers with lemon parsley) served until 11.30am on weekdays and all day on weekends. At lunch there are soups and spectacular sandwiches (eg hoisin confit duck wrap or Toulouse sausage with fried onions).

★ **Broad Chare** GASTROPUB ££
(📞0191-211 2144; www.thebroadchare.co.uk; 25 Broad Chare; mains £10-24, bar snacks £2.25-3.85; ⊘kitchen noon-2.30pm & 5.30-10pm Mon-Sat, noon-5pm Sun, bar 11am-11pm Mon-Sat, to 10pm Sun) Spiffing English classics and splendid cask ales are served in the dark-wood bar and mezzanine of this perfect gastropub. Starters such as crispy pig ears, pork pies and venison terrine are followed by mains that might include a divine grilled pork chop with black pudding and cider sauce, and desserts like treacle tart with walnut brittle to finish.

Hop & Cleaver GASTROPUB ££
(📞0191-261 1037; www.hopandcleaver.com; 44 Sandhill; mains £9.50-14; ⊘kitchen 5-9pm Mon-Thu, noon-10pm Fri & Sat, noon-9pm Sun, bar 5pm-midnight Mon-Thu, 11am-1am Fri-Sun) Inside the magnificent Jacobean **Bessie Surtees House** (📞0191-269 1255; https://historiceng land.org.uk; ⊘10am-4pm Mon-Fri) `FREE`, this hip spot is great for a drink (it brews its own small-batch craft beers) but the food is equally outstanding: smoky brisket with apple-and-onion fritters; 12-hour cooked pulled pork with homemade slaw and BBQ sauce; charred, Bourbon-marinated ribs; beer-steamed roasted chicken. Meats are smoked in-house; veggie options exist but are limited.

Herb Garden PIZZA ££
(📞0191-222 0491; www.theherbgardenuk. com; Arch 8, Westgate Rd; pizzas £8.50-16.50;

212 5555; mains £17.50-32, 2-/3-course menus £20/25, afternoon tea £25; ⊘7-10am, noon-5pm & 7-9pm Mon-Thu, 7-10am, noon-5pm & 7-9.30pm Fri, 7.30-10.30am, noon-5pm & 7-9.30pm Sat, 7.30-10.30am & noon-9pm Sun) 🍃 is sublime; dinner, bed and breakfast packages are available.

Vermont Hotel HERITAGE HOTEL £££
(📞0191-233 1010; www.vermont-hotel.com; Castle Garth; d from £132, 2-/4-person apt from £169/189; 🅿🛜) Early 20th-century elegance reigns at this magnificent stone building (the former County Hall), which has an art deco ballroom, 101 rooms with marble bath-

Newcastle-upon-Tyne

⊙ 11.30am-11.30pm; 🛜🍴) 🅿 The Herb Garden lives up to its name with a wall of barrel-like cylinders where herbs and salad greens grow under glowing lights. Its 17 different pizza varieties include two calzoni; on weekends it serves breakfast pizzas, such as the Twisted English (sausages, black pudding, tomato, mushrooms and eggs) and Breakfast in Bed (chocolate, hazelnuts, banana and honey). No reservations.

★**House of Tides** GASTRONOMY £££
(☏0191-230 3720; http://houseoftides.co.uk; 28-30 The Close; tasting menus lunch £70, with paired wines £130, dinner £85, with paired wines £150; ⊙6-8.30pm Tue-Thu, noon-1.15pm & 6-8.30pm Fri, noon-1.15pm & 5-9pm Sat) A 16th-century merchant's house is now the home of Newcastle's most celebrated restaurant, the Michelin-starred House of Tides. Established by acclaimed Newcastle-born chef Kenny Atkinson, it incorporates premium ingredients – Orkney scallops, Norfolk quail, wild blackberries, black truffles and nasturtiums – in regularly changing multicourse tasting menus. Diners with dietary requirements including vegetarians (though not vegans) can be catered for by prior arrangement.

Blackfriars BRITISH £££
(☏0191-261 5945; www.blackfriarsrestaurant. co.uk; Friars St; mains £16-34; ⊙noon-2.30pm & 5.30-11pm Mon-Sat, noon-4pm Sun; 🪑) 🅿 A

13th-century friary is the atmospheric setting for 'modern medieval' cuisine. Beautiful stained-glass windows frame the dining room; in summer tables set up in the cloister garden. Consult the table-mat map for the provenance of your cod, woodpigeon or rare-breed pork. Everything else is made from scratch on site, including breads, pastries, ice creams and sausages. Bookings recommended.

✖ Jesmond

Fat Hippo Jesmond BURGERS ££
(☏0191-340 8949; www.fat-hippo.co.uk; 35a St Georges Tce; burgers £8.50-14.50; ⊙noon-9.30pm Mon-Thu, noon-10pm Fri, 11am-10pm Sat, 11.30am-9.30pm Sun) Humongous burgers arrive on wooden planks with stainless-steel buckets of triple-fried, hand-cut chips at this local success story. Stinky Pete comes with blue cheese, jalapeño peppers and red-onion jam; 4x4 has a whopping four patties. Veggie burgers include spicy bean; sides span deep-fried gherkins to mac 'n cheese balls and house-made slaw. There are craft beers, ciders and boozy shakes.

Its city-centre sibling, the **Fat Hippo Underground** (☏0191-447 1161; www.fathippo. co.uk; 2-6 Shakespeare St; burgers £8-14; ⊙noon-10pm Mon-Thu, 11am-10.30pm Fri & Sat, 11.30am-10pm Sun), occupies a vaulted cellar.

Patricia
BISTRO **££**

(☑ 0191-281 4443; www.the-patricia.com; 139 Jesmond Rd; mains £16-24, sharing plates £3-10, 2-/3-course dinner menus £20/25; ⊘ 5-10pm Wed-Fri, noon-2.30pm & 6-10pm Sat, noon-4pm Sun; ☑) Named for owner-chef Nick Grieves' grandmother, the Patricia is perpetually busy; book ahead to feast on dishes like raw Orkney scallops with fermented red pepper, and roast quail with chocolate and fennel prepared in the semi-open kitchen. Excellent vegetarian choices might include roast leeks with aged feta foam. Many of its old- and new-world wines are available by the glass.

Peace & Loaf
BISTRO **£££**

(☑ 0191-281 5222; www.peaceandloaf.co.uk; 217 Jesmond Rd, Jesmond; mains £18-29, 3-course lunch/dinner menu £25/30; ⊘ noon-2pm & 5.30-9pm Mon-Wed, noon-2pm & 5.30-9.30pm Thu-Sat, noon-3.30pm Sun) A double-height space with mezzanine seating is the stage for creations by *MasterChef: The Professionals* finalist David Coulson, who subsequently worked for two-Michelin-starred chef Michel Roux Jr. Coulson's refined Modern British flavours include black pudding–stuffed guinea fowl with pear cider–braised red cabbage. Many ingredients are foraged in the Jesmond Dene woodland or grown by Coulson in his garden.

Drinking & Nightlife

City Centre

Lola Jeans
COCKTAIL BAR

(☑ 0191-230 1921; www.lolajeans.co.uk; 1-3 Market St; ⊘ noon-midnight Mon-Thu, to 1am Fri-Sun) At this Jazz Age–styled bar with chandeliers, velveteen chairs and dazzling murals, cocktails served in vintage glassware include locally inspired concoctions such as Fog on the Tyne (Bols Genever, Newcastle Brown Ale reduction, rose lemonade and nettle cordial) and Coal Faced Flip (Fernet Branca, coffee-infused Jagermeister, egg, stout-and-vanilla reduction and chocolate bitters).

World Headquarters
CLUB

(☑ 0191-281 3445; www.welovewhq.com; Curtis Mayfield House, Carliol Sq; ⊘ 11pm-5am Fri & Sat, weekday hours vary) Dedicated to the genius of black music – funk, rare groove, dance-floor jazz, northern soul, genuine R&B, lush disco, proper house, reggae and more – this brilliant club is a world away from commercial blandness.

Bridge Hotel
PUB

(http://sjf.co.uk/our-pubs/bridge-hotel; Castle Sq; ⊘ 11.30am-11pm Mon-Thu, to midnight Fri & Sat, noon-10.30pm Sun) Dating from 1901, this traditional pub retains original features including Victorian snugs, carved woodwork, stained-glass windows and mosaic tiles. At least 10 hand-pulled ales are on tap; there's also a great whisky selection. Its panoramic beer garden overlooking the High Level and Tyne Bridges incorporates part of Newcastle's medieval city walls.

Centurion Bar
BAR

(www.centurion-newcastle.com; Central Station; ⊘ 10am-11pm Mon-Thu, to midnight Fri & Sat, to 10.30pm Sun) With magnificent floor-to-ceiling ornate Victorian tiling, Central Station's former 1st-class waiting room – a Grade I–listed treasure dating from 1893 – is ideal for a pre-club drink in style.

Split Chimp
PUB

(www.splitchimp.pub; Arch 7, Westgate Rd; ⊘ 3-10pm Mon-Thu, noon-11pm Fri & Sat) Covered in retro chimp montages but actually named for the wood that's wedged behind ale casks to tip them, this tiny, two-level micropub inside a railway viaduct has a 31ft-long skittle alley and hosts occasional live music. Hand-pulled local ales rotate on the taps; it also has bottled craft beers, ciders and wine.

LGBT NEWCASTLE

Newcastle's vibrant gay scene centres on the 'Pink Triangle', formed by Waterloo, Neville and Collingwood Sts, though venues stretch south to Scotswood Rd.

Eazy Street (☑ 0191-222 0606; 8-10 Westmorland Rd; ⊘ noon-3am) Gay and all-welcoming Eazy Street draws a crowd for its nightly feast of cabaret drag shows, karaoke and DJs.

Powerhouse (www.facebook.com/PowerhouseClub; 9-19 Westmorland Rd; ⊘ 11pm-4am Mon, 11.30pm-4am Thu & Fri, 11.30pm-5am Sat) Mixed but mainly gay, this massive four-floor club has flashing lights, a pumping sound system and lots of suggestive posing.

Quilliam Brothers' Tea House TEAHOUSE
(☑0191-261 4861; www.quilliambrothers.com; Claremont Bldgs, 1 Eldon Pl; ☉10am-midnight Mon-Fri, 9am-midnight Sat, 10am-4pm Sun) Set up by a trio of brothers as 'an alternative to Newcastle's boozy scene', this hip Hungarian-style teahouse with postindustrial decor has over 100 types of tea as well as a tiny cinema screening cult films, plus various gigs and art events.

🍷 Ouseburn Valley

⭐**Tyne Bar** PUB
(☑0191-265 2550; www.thetyne.com; 1 Maling St; ☉noon-11pm Mon-Thu, to midnight Fri & Sat, to 10.30pm Sun; 🎧) An outdoor stage hosting free gigs, a free jukebox, beer-garden-style seating under one of the brick arches of the Glasshouse Bridge and a sprawling expanse of grass with knockout river views make this tucked-away waterfront pub a magnet for locals. Free bar food is laid on between 7pm and 9pm on Tuesdays (you'll still need to pay for drinks).

Ship Inn PUB
(☑0191-222 0878; www.facebook.com/ship ouseburn; Stepney Bank; ☉noon-11pm Sun-Thu, to midnight Fri & Sat) Spilling onto a small green out front, this red-brick charmer in the Ouseburn Valley has been pouring pints since the early 1800s. Its current owners have breathed new life into its interior, with art on the walls and an excellent vegan kitchen turning out dishes from tacos to tofu pot-sticker dumplings.

☆ Entertainment

Sage Gateshead LIVE MUSIC
(☑0191-443 4661; www.sagegateshead.com; St Mary's Square, Gateshead Quays) Norman Foster's magnificent chrome-and-glass horizontal bottle is a stunner in itself but, as the home of the Northern Sinfonia and Folkworks, also presents outstanding live music.

Tyneside Cinema CINEMA
(☑0191-227 5500; www.tynesidecinema.co.uk; 10 Pilgrim St; adult/child from £8.75/5.25, newsreels free) Opened in 1937 as Newcastle's first newsreel cinema, this art deco picture house with plush red-velvet seats still screens newsreels (11.15am daily) as well as mainstream and offbeat movies, and archive British Pathé films. Free one-hour guided tours of the building run at 11am on Monday, Tuesday, Friday and Saturday.

Newcastle United Football Club FOOTBALL
(NUFC; ☑0844 372 1892; www.nufc.co.uk; St James Park, Strawberry Pl; ☉box office 10am-5pm Mon-Fri, 9am-4pm Sat, 9am until half-time on match days) NUFC is more than just a football team – it's the collective expression of Geordie hope and pride. Buy match tickets online, by phone or at the box office in the Milburn Stand of the club's hallowed ground, St James Park. Various **stadium tours** (stadium tours adult/child £15/8, rooftop tours £20/15; ☉tours by reservation) include rooftop tours.

Cluny LIVE MUSIC
(☑0191-230 4474; https://thecluny.com; 36 Lime St; ☉noon-11pm Mon-Thu, to midnight Fri & Sat, to 10.30pm Sun) In the Ouseburn Valley touring acts and local talent – from experimental prog-rock heads to up-and-coming pop goddesses – fill the bill every night of the week at this beloved venue, which has been independently owned since 2017. There's a great restaurant on site.

🛍 Shopping

Grainger Market MARKET
(www.graingermarket.org; btwn Grainger & Clayton Sts; ☉9am-5.30pm Mon-Sat) Trading since 1835, Newcastle's gorgeous covered market has over 110 stalls selling everything from fish, farm produce, meat and vegetables to clothes, accessories and homewares. Between alleys 1 and 2, look out for the historic Weigh House, where goods were once weighed. There are some fantastic food stalls to pick up lunch on the run.

Newcastle Quayside Market MARKET
(under the Tyne Bridge; ☉9am-4pm Sun) Stalls displaying jewellery, photographic prints, art, clothing, homewares and more set up along the quays around the Tyne Bridge every Sunday (except in adverse weather). Buskers and food stalls add to the street-party atmosphere.

ℹ Information

Newcastle doesn't have a physical tourist office, but information is available at www.newcastlegateshead.com.

ℹ Getting There & Away

AIR

Newcastle International Airport (NCL; ☑0871 882 1121; www.newcastleairport.com; Woolsington), 7 miles north of the city off the A696, has direct services to many UK and European cities as well as long-haul flights to

Dubai. Tour operators fly charters to the USA, Middle East and Africa.

The airport is linked to town by the Metro (£3.10, 25 minutes, every 12 minutes).

A taxi to central Newcastle costs around £25.

BUS

Local and regional buses leave from **Haymarket** (Percy St) or **Eldon Sq** bus stations. National Express buses arrive and depart from the **coach station** (Churchill St). For local buses around the northeast, the excellent-value Explorer North East ticket (adult/child £10.50/5.50) is valid on most services.

Bus X15 runs north along the A1 to Berwick-upon-Tweed (£6.60, 2½ hours, hourly Monday to Saturday, every two hours Sunday). Bus X18 travels along the coast to Berwick (£6.60, four hours, three daily).

National Express operates services to Edinburgh (£11.50, 2¾ hours, three daily), London (£18.60, eight hours, three daily) and Manchester (£22.30, 4½ hours, four daily).

CAR

Two tollway vehicle tunnels (www.tt2.co.uk, one-way £1.70) travel beneath the Tyne.

TRAIN

Newcastle is on the main rail line between London and Edinburgh and is the starting point of the scenic Tyne Valley Line west to Carlisle.

Alnmouth (for bus connections to Alnwick) £10.60, 35 minutes, hourly

Berwick-upon-Tweed £10.50, 50 minutes, up to two per hour

Carlisle £8.10, 1½ hours, hourly

Durham £5.50, 20 minutes, up to five hourly

Edinburgh £33, 1½ hours, up to two hourly

Hartlepool £9.50, 50 minutes, hourly

London King's Cross £153, 3¼ hours, up to four hourly

York £21.50, 1¼ hours, up to four hourly

🛈 Getting Around

There's a large bus network, but the best means of getting around is the excellent Metro (www.nexus.org.uk).

Single fares for public transport start from £1.50.

The DaySaver pass (£3 to £5.10) gives unlimited Metro travel for one day for travel after 9am, and the DayRover (adult/child £10.50/5.50) gives unlimited travel on all modes of transport in the Tyne and Wear county for one day for travel any time.

On weekend nights taxis can be rare; try **Noda Taxis** (☑ 0191-222 1888; www.noda-taxis. co.uk), which has a kiosk outside the entrance to Central Station.

> **DON'T MISS**
>
> ### THE ANGEL OF THE NORTH
>
> Nicknamed the Gateshead Flasher, this extraordinary 200-tonne, rust-coloured, **winged human frame** (www.gateshead. gov.uk; Durham Rd, Low Eighton) has loomed over the A1 motorway some 6 miles south of Newcastle since 1998. Sir Antony Gormley's iconic work (which saw him knighted in 2014) stands 20m high, with a wingspan wider than a Boeing 767. Bus 21 from Newcastle's Eldon Sq (£2.20, 20 minutes) stops here. There's a free car park by the base.

Tynemouth

☑ 0191 / POP 67,520

The mouth of the Tyne, 9 miles east of Newcastle, is one of the best surf spots in England, with great all-year breaks off the immense, crescent-shaped Blue Flag beach, which occasionally hosts major surf competitions.

👁 Sights & Activities

Tynemouth Priory   RUINS

(EH; www.english-heritage.org.uk; Pier Rd; adult/child £5.90/3.50; ⊙10am-6pm Apr-Sep, to 5pm Oct, 10am-4pm Sat & Sun Nov-Mar) Built by Benedictine monks on a strategic bluff above the mouth of the Tyne in the 11th-century ruins, Tynemouth Priory was ransacked during the Dissolution in 1539. The military took over for four centuries, only leaving in 1960, and today the ruined remains of the priory church sit alongside old military installations, their guns aimed out to sea at an enemy that never came.

🛏 Sleeping & Eating

Grand Hotel   HERITAGE HOTEL ££

(☑0191-293 6666; www.grandhoteltynemouth.co. uk; Grand Pde; d/f incl breakfast from £98/118; P@🖘) Built in 1872, the one-time summer residence of the Duke and Duchess of Northumberland is a local landmark. Many of the 46 rooms in the main building and neighbouring town house overlook the beach; some have four-poster beds and spa baths. Its Victorian-style real-ale pub, drawing room serving high tea, and brasserie are excellent. Book well ahead at peak times.

★ Riley's Fish Shack   SEAFOOD ££

(☑0191-257 1371; http://rileysfishshack.com; King Edward's Bay; dishes £6-18.50, mains £18.50-26.50;

9.30am-10pm Mon-Sat, to 5.30pm Sun, hours can vary) Steep timber stairs lead from East St to the beach and this rustic, tucked-away shack. Phenomenal local seafood underpins wood-fired dishes from wraps to empanadas and mains like cod on puy lentils with pancetta and parmesan crumb, served in environmentally friendly wooden boxes. Indoor seating is limited; there's also a handful of stools outside and deckchairs spread on the sand.

Staith House   GASTROPUB ££

(☑ 01912-708441; www.thestaithhouse.co.uk; 57 Low Lights; mains £15-26; ☺kitchen noon-3pm & 6-9pm Mon-Thu, noon-3.30pm & 6-9.30pm Fri & Sat, bar 11am-1am Mon-Sat, noon-10.30pm Sun; ☎) Opposite the fishing quay where catches are landed daily, gastropub Staith House has a sunny beer garden, bar made from recycled timbers and an outstanding menu drawing on local, sustainable produce including seaweed foraged from Tynemouth's beaches. Seafood is the star (South Shields crab, Lindisfarne oysters, North Sea hake...) but there are also meat dishes such as Northumberland lamb rump.

❶ Getting There & Away

From Newcastle, the easiest way to reach Tynemouth is by Metro (£3.10, 25 minutes, every 12 minutes).

Durham

☑ 0191 / POP 48,069

England's most beautiful Romanesque cathedral, a huge castle, and, surrounding them both, a cobweb of hilly, cobbled streets – filled with upper-crust students attending England's third university of choice (after Oxford and Cambridge) during term time – make Durham an ideal day trip from Newcastle or overnight stop.

◉ Sights

★**Durham Cathedral**   CATHEDRAL

(☑ 0191-386 4266; www.durhamcathedral.co.uk; Palace Green; cathedral by donation, guided tours adult/child £5/4.50; ☺cathedral 9.30am-6pm Mon-Sat, 12.30-5.30pm Sun, cathedral tours 10.30am, 11am & 2pm Mon-Sat) Monumental Durham Cathedral is the definitive structure of the Anglo-Norman Romanesque style, a resplendent monument to the country's ecclesiastical history and, since 1986, a Unesco World Heritage Site. Beyond the main door – and the famous **Sanctuary Knocker**,

which medieval felons would strike to gain 37 days asylum within the cathedral before standing trial or leaving the country – the interior is spectacular. Highly worthwhile guided tours last one hour. At the time of writing, the tower, reached by 325 steps, was closed for renovations until 2019.

Durham was the first European cathedral to be roofed with stone-ribbed vaulting, which upheld the heavy stone roof and made it possible to build pointed transverse arches – a great architectural achievement. The central tower dates from 1262, but was damaged in a fire caused by lightning in 1429 and unsatisfactorily patched up until it was entirely rebuilt in 1470. The western towers were added in 1217–26.

The northern side of the beautiful, 1175-built **Galilee Chapel** features rare surviving examples of 12th-century wall painting (thought to feature portraits of Sts Cuthbert and Oswald). Galilee Chapel also contains the **tomb of the Venerable Bede**, the 8th-century Northumbrian monk turned historian: his *Ecclesiastical History of the English People* is still the prime source of information on the development of early Christian Britain. Among other things, Bede introduced the AD system for the numbering of years from the birth of Jesus. He was first buried at Jarrow, but in 1022 a miscreant monk stole his remains and brought them here.

Other highlights include the 14th-century **Bishop's Throne**; the beautiful stone **Neville Screen** (1372–80), which separates the high altar from **St Cuthbert's tomb**; and the mostly 19th-century **Cloisters** where you'll find the **Monk's Dormitory**, now a library of 30,000 books, with Anglo-Saxon carved stones. There are audiovisual displays on the building of the cathedral and the life of St Cuthbert, and a rolling program of exhibitions.

★**Durham Castle**   CASTLE

(☑ 0191-334 2932; www.dur.ac.uk/durham.castle; Palace Green; admission by guided tour only, adult/child £5/4; ☺by reservation) Built as a standard motte-and-bailey fort in 1072, Durham Castle was the prince bishops' home until 1837, when it became the University of Durham's first college. It remains a university hall today. Highlights of the 50-minute tour include the 17th-century Black Staircase and the beautifully preserved Norman chapel (1080). Book ahead by phone, or at the Palace Green Library or the World Heritage

Durham

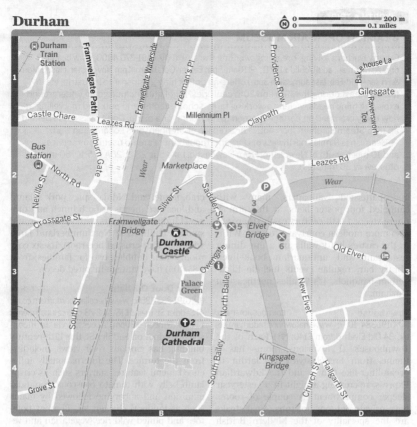

Site Visitor Centre (p610); tours run most days, with additional tours during university holidays.

🏃 Activities

Browns Boathouse BOATING
(📞 0191-386 3779; www.brownsboats.co.uk; Elvet Bridge; adult/child per hour £7/4.50; ⏱ 10am-6pm mid-Mar–late Sep) Hire a traditional, hand-built row boat for a romantic river excursion.

Prince Bishop River Cruiser CRUISE
(📞 0191-386 9525; www.princebishoprc.co.uk; Browns Boathouse, Elvet Bridge; adult/child £8/5; ⏱ cruises 12.30pm, 2pm & 3pm Mar-Oct) Wonderfully scenic one-hour cruises take you out on the Wear.

🛏 Sleeping

⭐ **Lumley Castle** CASTLE £££
(📞 0191-389 1111; www.lumleycastle.com; Ropery Lane, Chester-le-Street; d courtyard/castle from

£170/190, ste from £230; P 🛜) Spiralling stone tower steps and creaking corridors lead to richly decorated rooms with heavy drapes

BEAMISH OPEN-AIR MUSEUM

County Durham's living, breathing, working **museum** (☑ 0191-370 4000; www.beamish. org.uk; Beamish; adult/child £19/11; ⊘ 10am-5pm Easter-Oct, 10am-4pm Nov-Easter, closed Mon & Fri Jan–mid-Feb, last admission 3pm) offers an unflinching glimpse into industrial life in the northeast during the 19th and 20th centuries. Highlights include going underground, exploring mine heads, visiting a working farm, school, dentist and pub, and marvelling at how every cramped pit cottage seemed to find room for a piano. Don't miss a ride behind an 1815 Steam Elephant locomotive or a replica of Stephenson's Locomotion No 1.

Beamish is 9 miles northwest of Durham (though there are no useful bus services), and 10 miles south of Newcastle. From Newcastle, take bus 28 or 28A (£5.10, 50 minutes, every 30 minutes).

and patterned wallpapers, many with canopied four-poster beds, at this atmosphere-steeped 14th-century castle (there are also more modern courtyard rooms). Within the castle's hefty walls are a fine-dining restaurant and antiquarian book–lined library bar; regular events include Elizabethan banquets. It's 7 miles northeast of Durham.

Townhouse　　　　BOUTIQUE HOTEL **£££**
(☑ 0191-384 1037; www.thetownhousedurham.co. uk; 34 Old Elvet; d from £140; ☎) Each of the Townhouse's 11 luxurious rooms has a theme, from French-styled Le Jardin to ocean-liner-like Cruise and the Edwardian Express, re-creating a night in a yesteryear sleeper compartment. A couple of rooms have private outdoor hot tubs. Aged steaks are the speciality of the Modern British restaurant.

🍴 Eating

Tealicious　　　　CAFE **£**
(☑ 0191-340 1393; www.tealicioustearoom.co.uk; 88 Elvet Bridge; dishes £2.60-6.25, high tea adult/ child £13.50/8.50; ⊘ 10am-4pm Tue-Sat, noon-4pm Sun; 🚴) Inside this quaint pastel-blue and white building, homemade cakes (such as white-chocolate cheesecake or ginger and lime), soups and sandwiches are complemented by 24 blends of tea served from individual pots in fine bone china. High tea here is a treat for both adults and kids. It's tiny so book ahead.

Garden House Inn　　　　BRITISH **££**
(☑ 0191-386 3395; www.gardenhouseinn.com; Framwellgate; sandwiches £5-12, mains £12-18; ⊘ noon-3pm & 5-9.30pm Mon-Sat, noon-6pm Sun; 🚴🚴) Dating from the 18th century, rustic country-style inn Garden House does great lunchtime sandwiches, such as lobster or

crab, fennel and 'Nduja (spicy pork salami) and locavore menus at both lunch and dinner (Lindisfarne oysters with wild garlic and smoked chilli, roast Northumberland lamb with hazelnut-crusted beetroot). Its six cosy rooms (four doubles, two for families; from £85/105) have vintage-inspired decor.

Cellar Door Durham　　　　BRITISH **££**
(☑ 0191-383 1856; www.thecellardoordurham.co.uk; 41 Saddler St; mains £16-24, 2-/3-course lunch menus £14/16; ⊘ noon-9.30pm) Accessed via an inconspicuous door on Saddler St, this 12th-century building has glorious river views, including from the terrace. The internationally influenced menu features starters such as crispy lamb belly with tomato couscous, coriander emulsion and aubergine followed by mains such as tandoori chicken leg, Bombay potatoes and puffed wild rice (vegetarian and vegan options available). Service is spot on.

🍷 Drinking & Nightlife

Shakespeare Tavern　　　　PUB
(63 Saddler St; ⊘ 11am-11.30pm) Built in 1190, this authentic-as-it-gets locals' boozer is complete with dartboard, cosy snugs, a terrific selection of beers and spirits, and wise-cracking characters propping up the bar – as well as, allegedly, a resident ghost. Look out for folk-music jam sessions.

ℹ Information

Durham's **World Heritage Site Visitor Centre** (World Heritage Site Visitor Centre; ☑ 0191-334 3805; www.durhamworldheritagesite. com/visit/whs-visitor-centre; 7 Owengate; ⊘ 9.30am-5pm Feb-Dec, to 4.30pm Jan) is in the shadow of the castle.

Comprehensive information on the city and county is available online at www.thisisdurham. com.

ℹ Getting There & Away

BUS

The East Coast Main Line provides speedy connections to destinations including the following:

Edinburgh £44.90, 1¾ hours, hourly

London King's Cross £68.20, three hours, hourly

Newcastle £5.50, 18 minutes, five hourly

York £25, 55 minutes, four hourly

TRAIN

The **bus station** (North Rd) is on North Rd, on the western side of the river.

Destinations include the following:

Hartlepool Bus 57A; £7, one hour, two hourly

London National Express; £30, 6¾ hours, two daily

Newcastle Bus 21, X12 and X21; £4.40, 1¼ hours, at least four hourly

Barnard Castle

📞 01833 / POP 5495

The charming market town of Barnard Castle, better known as 'Barney', is a traditionalist's dream, full of antique and craft shops, and atmospheric old pubs. It's a wonderful setting for the town's twin draws: a daunting ruined castle and an extraordinary French chateau.

◉ Sights

★ **Bowes Museum**   MUSEUM
(📞 01833-690606; www.thebowesmuseum.org.uk; Newgate; adult/child £14/5; ⊙10am-5pm) A monumental chateau half a mile east of the centre contains the lavishly furnished Bowes Museum. Funded by 19th-century industrialist John Bowes, and opened in 1892, this brainchild of his Parisian actress wife, Josephine, was built by French architect Jules Pellechet to display a collection the Bowes had travelled the world to assemble. The star attraction is the marvellous 18th-century mechanical silver swan, which performs every day at 2pm. If you miss it, a film shows it in action.

Barnard Castle   RUINS
(EH; 📞 01833-638212; www.english-heritage.org.uk; Scar Top; adult/child £5.60/3.40; ⊙10am-6pm Easter-Sep, to 5pm Oct, 10am-4pm Sat & Sun Nov-Easter) Built on a cliff above the River Tees by Guy de Bailleul and rebuilt around 1150, Barnard Castle was partly dismantled some four centuries later, but its ruins still manage to cover two very impressive hec-

tares with wonderful river views. A sensory garden is also here.

Raby Castle   CASTLE
(📞 01833-660202; www.rabycastle.com; Staindrop; castle, gardens & park adult/child £12/6, gardens & park only £7/3; ⊙11am-4.30pm Tue-Sun Jul & Aug, 11am-4.30pm Wed-Sun late Mar-Jun & Sep) Sprawling Raby Castle was a stronghold of the Catholic Neville family until it engaged in ill-judged plotting (the 'Rising of the North') against the Protestant Queen Elizabeth in 1569. Most of the interior dates from the 18th and 19th centuries, but the exterior remains true to the original design, built around a courtyard and surrounded by a moat. It's 6.8 miles northeast of Barnard Castle; take bus 85A (£3.10, 15 minutes, eight daily Monday to Friday, six Saturday and Sunday).

🛏 Sleeping & Eating

Old Well Inn   INN ££
(📞 01833-690130; http://theoldwellinn.co.uk; 21 The Bank; s/d incl breakfast from £65/85; 🛜) Built over a huge well (not visible), this old coaching inn has 10 enormous rooms. No 9 is the most impressive with its own private entrance, flagstone floors and a bath. The pub has regional ales on tap that you can sip in the leafy beer garden in fine weather.

**Cross Lanes
Organic Farm Shop**   DELI, CAFE £
(📞 01833-630619; www.crosslanesorganics.co.uk; Cross Lanes, Barnard Castle; dishes £4-13; ⊙8.30am-5pm Mon-Sat, 10am-5pm Sun; 🛜🚼) 🌿 Sheep graze on the grass-covered roof of

KNITSLEY FARM SHOP

It's worth stopping off 12 miles northwest of Durham en route to Northumberland National Park and Hadrian's Wall to stock up on incredible cheeses, meats, fruits, veggies, homemade sweets, biscuits, cakes and breads at **Knitsley Farm Shop** (📞 01207-592059; www.knitsleyfarmshop.co.uk; East Knitsley Grange Farm, Knitsley; dishes £5-12.50; ⊙shop 10am-5pm Tue-Sat, to 4pm Sun, cafe 10am-5pm Tue-Fri, 9.30am-5pm Sat, 9.30am-4pm Sun) 🌿. Make time to dine at its wonderful cafe on fresh-as-it-gets soups, farmyard sausages, and pulled-pork and crackling baps.

this award-winning farm shop and cafe 1.5 miles south of Barnard Castle. The cavernous interior brims with all-organic produce; breakfasts (home-cured bacon, homemade sausages and eggs from the farm's chickens) segue into lunches including gourmet sandwiches, steak or veggie burgers and wood-fired pizzas, and 'rustic afternoon tea' with organic cream and wild-fruit jams.

★ **Raby Hunt**   GASTRONOMY £££

(☑ 01325-374237; www.rabyhuntrestaurant.co.uk; Summerhouse, Darlington; tasting menu £115, chef's table £150; ◷ 6-9.30pm Wed-Sat, noon-2pm Sun; ⛶) A two-century-old, ivy-clad drovers' inn 11 miles east of Barnard Castle is now the staging post for gastronomic expeditions by self-taught chef James Close, who received his first Michelin star in 2012 and second in 2017. Tasting menus (no à la carte) typically feature 12 to 15 intricate courses, such as in-the-shell razor clams with brown shrimp. Reserve weeks ahead.

In the former stables are three luxurious guest rooms (doubles including breakfast from £180).

★ **Bay Horse**   GASTROPUB £££

(☑ 01325-720663; www.thebayhorsehurworth. com; The Green, Hurworth-on-Tees; mains lunch £8-22, dinner £20-25; ◷ kitchen noon-2.30pm & 6-9.30pm Mon-Sat, noon-4pm Sun, bar 11am-11pm Mon-Sat, noon-10.30pm Sun; ☑) It's well worth the 19-mile trip east of Barnard Castle to this 15th-century coaching inn in the pretty riverside village of Hurworth-on-Tees, but book ahead so you don't miss out on exceptional locally sourced dishes such as pan-fried hake with smoked apple and eel croquettes or rabbit loin with rabbit-leg pie. Wild garlic, leeks, nettles and herbs are foraged nearby.

❶ Getting There & Away

Barnard Castle is poorly served by public transport and several of its key draws are outside the town so you really need your own wheels.

Hadrian's Wall

Named in honour of the emperor who ordered it built, Hadrian's Wall was one of Rome's greatest engineering projects. This enormous 73-mile-long wall was built between AD 122 and 128 to separate Romans and Scottish Picts. Today, the awe-inspiring sections that remain are testament to Roman ambition and tenacity.

When completed, the mammoth structure ran across the island's narrow neck, from the Solway Firth in the west almost to the mouth of the Tyne in the east. Every Roman mile (0.95 miles) there was a gateway guarded by a small fort (milecastle) and between each milecastle were two observation turrets. Milecastles are numbered right across the country, starting with Milecastle 0 at Wallsend – where you can visit the wall's last stronghold, Segedunum (p616) – and ending with Milecastle 80 at Bowness-on-Solway.

A series of forts was developed as bases some distance south (and may predate the wall), and 16 lie astride it.

⚐ Activities

The **Hadrian's Wall Path** (www.national trail.co.uk/hadrians-wall-path) is an 84-mile national trail that runs the length of the wall from Wallsend in the east to Bowness-on-Solway in the west. The entire route should take about seven days on foot, giving plenty of time to explore the rich archaeological heritage along the way.

❶ Information

There are tourist offices in **Hexham** (☑ 01670-620450; www.visitnorthumberland.com; Queen's Hall, Beaumont St; ◷ 9am-5pm Mon-Fri, 9.30am-5pm Sat), Haltwhistle (p618) and Corbridge (p616). The Walltown Visitor Centre (p619), aka the Northumberland National Park Visitor Centre, is located at Greenhead, and will reopen in summer 2019 following renovations. Tourist information is also available from **The Sill** (National Landscape Discovery Centre; ☑ 01434-341200; www.thesill.org.uk; Military Rd, Once Brewed; ◷ 9.30am-6pm Apr-early Nov), aka the National Landscape Discovery Centre, at Once Brewed.

Hadrian's Wall Country (http://hadrians wallcountry.co.uk) is the official portal for the entire area.

❶ Getting There & Around

BUS

The AD122 Hadrian's Wall bus (five daily, Easter to September) is a hail-and-ride service that runs between Hexham and Carlisle, with one bus a day starting and ending at Newcastle's Central Station; not all services cover the entire route. Bikes can be taken aboard AD122 buses, but space is limited. Bus 185 zips between Birdoswald Roman Fort and Carlisle via Haltwhistle the rest of the year (three daily, Monday to Saturday only).

Bus 10 links Newcastle with Hexham (1½ hours, every 30 minutes Monday to Saturday, hourly on Sunday).

West of Hexham the wall runs parallel to the A69, which connects Carlisle and Newcastle. Buses X84 and X85 run along the A69 every 30 minutes, passing 2 to 3 miles south of the main sites.

All these services except the X84 and X85 can be used with the **Hadrian's Wall Rover Ticket** (one day adult/child £12.50/6.50, three day £25/13). Show your Rover Ticket to get 10% off admission to all museums and attractions.

The **Hadrian's Frontier Ticket** (adult/child one day £16/8 three day £32/16) provides unlimited transport on all buses throughout Northumberland.

Both tickets are available from bus drivers and tourist offices, where you can also get timetables.

CAR & MOTORCYCLE

Your own wheels are the easiest way to get around, with one fort or garrison usually just a short hop from the next. Parking costs £5/15 per day/week; tickets are valid at all sites along the wall.

The B6318 follows the course of the wall from the outskirts of Newcastle to Birdoswald. The main A69 road and the railway line follow 3 or 4 miles to the south.

TRAIN

The railway line between Newcastle and Carlisle (Tyne Valley Line; £16.60, 1½ hours, hourly) has stations at Corbridge, Hexham, Haydon Bridge, Bardon Mill, Haltwhistle and Brampton. Not all services stop at all stations.

Corbridge

☎ 01434 / POP 3011

Above a green-banked curve in the Tyne, Corbridge's shady, cobbled streets are lined with old-fashioned shops and pubs. Inhabited since Saxon times when there was a substantial monastery, many of the village's

Hadrian's Wall & Northumberland National Park

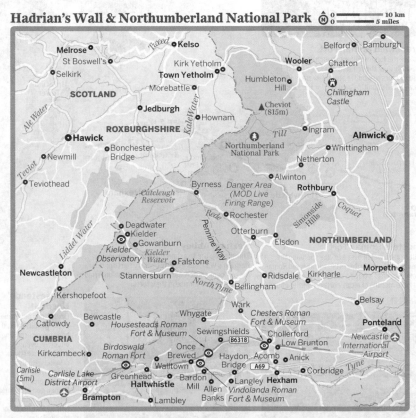

Hadrian's Wall

ROME'S FINAL FRONTIER

Of all Britain's Roman ruins, Emperor Hadrian's 2nd-century wall, cutting across northern England from the Irish Sea to the North Sea, is by far the most spectacular; Unesco awarded it World Heritage status in 1987.

We've picked out the highlights, one of which is the prime remaining Roman fort on the wall, Housesteads, which we've reconstructed here.

Housesteads' Granaries
Nothing like the clever underground ventilation system, which kept vital supplies of grain dry in Northumberland's damp and drizzly climate, would be seen again in these parts for 1500 years.

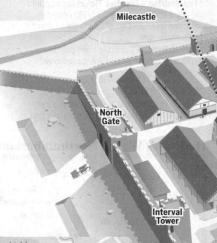

Milecastle

North Gate

Interval Tower

Birdoswald Roman Fort
Explore the longest intact stretch of the wall, scramble over the remains of a large fort then head indoors to wonder at a full-scale model of the wall at its zenith. Great fun for the kids.

Map:
- Birdoswald Roman Fort
- Harrow Scar Milecastle
- Greenhead
- Haltwhistle
- Brampton
- Irthing
- Roman Army Museum
- Once Brewed
- Bardon Mill
- South Tyne
- Sewingshields
- Housesteads Roman Fort & Museum
- Vindolanda Roman Fort & Museum
- Haydon Bridge
- **Hadrian's Wall**
- Chesters Roman Fort & Museum
- Chollerford
- Low Brunton
- Acomb
- Hexham
- B6318
- A69

Chesters Roman Fort
Built to keep watch over a bridge spanning the River North Tyne, Britain's best-preserved Roman cavalry fort has a terrific bathhouse, essential if you have months of nippy northern winter ahead.

Hexham Abbey
This may be the finest non-Roman sight near Hadrian's Wall, but the 7th-century parts of this magnificent church were built with stone quarried by the Romans for use in their forts.

Housesteads' Hospital
Operations performed at the hospital would have been surprisingly effective, even without anaesthetics; religious rituals and prayers to Aesculapius, the Roman god of healing, were possibly less helpful for a hernia or appendicitis.

Housesteads' Latrines
Communal toilets were the norm in Roman times and Housesteads' are remarkably well preserved – fortunately no traces remain of the vinegar-soaked sponges that were used instead of toilet paper.

QUICK WALL FACTS & FIGURES

Latin name Vallum Aelium

Length 73.5 miles (80 Roman miles)

Construction date AD 122–128

Manpower for construction
Three legions (around 16,000 men)

Features At least 16 forts, 80 milecastles, 160 turrets

Did you know Hadrian's wasn't the only Roman wall in Britain – the Antonine Wall was built across what is now central Scotland in the AD 140s, but it was abandoned soon after.

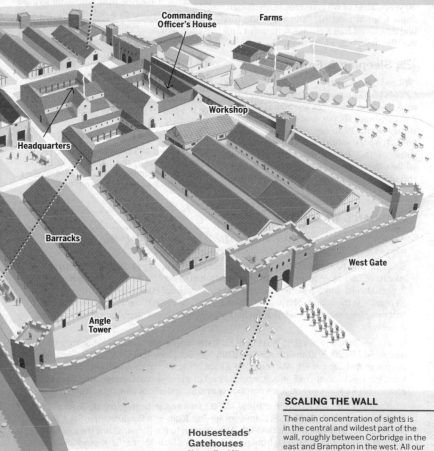

Commanding Officer's House

Farms

Workshop

Headquarters

Barracks

West Gate

Angle Tower

Housesteads' Gatehouses
Unusually at Housesteads neither of the gates faces the enemy, as was the norm at Roman forts; builders aligned them east–west. Ruts worn by cart wheels are still visible in the stone.

FREE GUIDES

At some sites, knowledgeable volunteer heritage guides are on hand to answer questions and put meat on the wall's stony bones.

SCALING THE WALL

The main concentration of sights is in the central and wildest part of the wall, roughly between Corbridge in the east and Brampton in the west. All our suggested stops are within this area and follow an east–west route. The easiest way to travel is by car, scooting along the B6318, but special bus AD122 will also get you there. Hiking along the designated Hadrian's Wall Path (84 miles) allows you to appreciate the achievement up close.

charming buildings feature stones nicked from nearby Corstopitum.

◉ Sights

Corbridge Roman Site & Museum
HISTORIC SITE

(EH; www.english-heritage.org.uk; Corchester Lane; adult/child £7.60/4.60; ⊙10am-6pm Apr-Sep, to 5pm Oct, 10am-4pm Sat & Sun Nov-Mar) What's left of the Roman garrison town of Corstopitum lies about half a mile west of Market Pl on Dere St, once the main road from York to Scotland. It's the oldest fortified site in the area, predating the wall itself by some 40 years. Most of what you see here, though, dates from around AD 200, when the fort had developed into a civilian settlement and was the main base along the wall.

🛏 Sleeping & Eating

★Lord Crewe Arms
INN £££

(☑01434-677100; www.lordcrewearmsblanchland. co.uk; The Square, Blanchland; d from £184; P🐾) An 1165-built abbot's house in the honey-stone North Pennines village of Blanchland, 11 miles south of Corbridge, shelters some of this entrancing inn's 21 rooms, while others are located in former miners' cottages. Rates almost halve outside high

season. Non-guests can dine on outstanding Modern British fare and drink in its vaulted bar, the Crypt, with a monumental medieval fireplace.

★Corbridge Larder
DELI, CAFE £

(☑01434-632948; www.corbridgelarder.co.uk; 18 Hill St; dishes £3.50-10; ⊙9am-5pm Mon-Sat, 10am-4pm Sun) Gourmet picnic fare at this fabulous deli includes bread, over 100 varieties of cheese, chutneys, cakes, chocolates and wine (you can get hampers made up) as well as made-to-order sandwiches, pies, quiches, tarts, and antipasti and mezze delicacies. Upstairs from the wonderland of provisions there's a small sit-down cafe serving dishes such as Moroccan spiced chicken.

ℹ Information

Corbridge's **tourist office** (☑01434-632815; www.visitnorthumberland.com; Hill St; ⊙10am-4.30pm Mon-Sat Apr-Oct, 11am-4pm Wed, Fri & Sat Nov-Mar) occupies a corner of the library.

ℹ Getting There & Away

Buses X84 and X85 between Newcastle (£5.10, 45 minutes, hourly) and Carlisle (£7.40, 2¼ hours, hourly) come through Corbridge, as does bus 10 from Newcastle (£5.10, one hour, every

---

HADRIAN'S WALL SITES

Along with key sites such as Housesteads (p617) and Vindolanda (p617), there are numerous other Roman remains stationed along Hadrian's Wall.

Segedunum (☑0191-278 4217; https://segedunumromanfort.org.uk; Buddle St, Wallsend; adult/child £6/free; ⊙10am-5pm Jun–mid-Sep, to 4pm Easter-May & mid-Sep–early Nov, to 2.30pm Mon-Fri early Nov–Easter) was the last strong post of Hadrian's Wall, 5 miles east of Newcastle in the suburb of Wallsend. Beneath the 35m-high tower is an absorbing site that includes a reconstructed Roman bathhouse (with steaming pools and frescos) and a museum.

Chesters Roman Fort (EH; ☑01434-681379; www.english-heritage.org.uk; Chollerford; adult/child £7/4.20; ⊙10am-6pm Apr-Sep, 10am-5pm Oct, 10am-4pm Sat & Sun Nov–mid-Feb, 10am-4pm Wed-Sun mid-Feb–Mar) near the village of Chollerford housed up to 500 troops from Asturias in northern Spain. It includes part of a bridge (best appreciated from the eastern bank), four gatehouses, a bathhouse and an underfloor heating system.

Birdoswald Roman Fort (EH; ☑01697-747602; www.english-heritage.org.uk; Gilsland, Greenhead; adult/child £8.30/5; ⊙10am-6pm Apr-Sep, 10am-5pm Oct, 10am-4pm Sat & Sun Nov–mid-Feb, 10am-4pm Wed-Sun mid-Feb–Mar) (Banna to the Romans) has the longest intact stretch of wall, extending from here to Harrow's Scar Milecastle. It overlooks Irthing Gorge, 4 miles west of Greenhead in Cumbria.

Binchester Roman Fort (www.durham.gov.uk/binchester; adult/child £5/3.50; ⊙10am-5pm Jul & Aug, 11am-5pm Easter-Jun & Sep), or Vinovia, lies 9.6 miles southwest of Durham. First built in wood around AD 80 and refashioned in stone early in the 2nd century, the fort was the largest in County Durham.

30 minutes Monday to Saturday, hourly Sunday) to Hexham (£2.20, 12 minutes, every 30 minutes Monday to Saturday, hourly Sunday). At Hexham you can connect with the Hadrian's Wall bus AD122 in summer or bus 185 year-round.

Corbridge is also on the railway line between Newcastle (£6.20, 45 minutes, hourly) and Carlisle (£14.90, 1½ hours, hourly).

Haltwhistle & Around

☑ 01434 / POP 3811

The village of Haltwhistle, little more than two intersecting streets, has more key Hadrian's Wall sights in its surrounds than anywhere else along the wall, but tourist infrastructure here is surprisingly underdeveloped.

Haltwhistle claims to be the geographic centre of the British mainland, although the jury is still out.

⊙ Sights

★ Housesteads Roman Fort & Museum   HISTORIC SITE

(EH; ☑ 01434-344363; www.english-heritage.org. uk; Haydon Bridge; adult/child £7.80/4.70; ⊙ 10am-6pm Apr-Sep, to 5pm Oct, to 4pm Nov-Mar) The most dramatic site of Hadrian's Wall – and the best-preserved Roman fort in the whole country – is at Housesteads, 4 miles north of Bardon Mill on the B6318, and 6.5 miles northeast of Haltwhistle. From here, high on a ridge and covering 2 hectares, you can survey the moors of Northumberland National Park, and the snaking wall, with a sense of awe at the landscape and the aura of the Roman lookouts.

★ Vindolanda Roman Fort & Museum   HISTORIC SITE

(☑ 01434-344277; www.vindolanda.com; Bardon Mill; adult/child £7.90/4.75, with Roman Army Museum £11.60/6.80; ⊙ 10am-6pm Apr-Sep, to 5pm early Feb-Mar & Oct, to 4pm Nov-early Feb) The extensive site of Vindolanda offers a fascinating glimpse into the daily life of a Roman garrison town. The time-capsule museum is just one part of this large, extensively excavated site, which includes impressive parts of the fort and town (excavations continue) and reconstructed turrets and temple. Extraordinary finds unearthed in 2017 include the only known pair of Roman boxing gloves.

It's 1.5 miles north of Bardon Mill between the A69 and B6318, and 5.8 miles northeast of Haltwhistle.

Roman Army Museum   MUSEUM

(☑ 01697-747485; www.vindolanda.com/roman-army-museum; Greenhead; adult/child £6.60/3.75 with Vindolanda £11.60/6.80; ⊙ 10am-6pm Apr-Sep, to 5pm mid-Feb–Mar & Oct) On the site of the Carvoran Roman Fort a mile northeast of Greenhead, near Walltown Crags, this revamped museum has three galleries covering the Roman army and the expanding and contracting Empire; the wall (with a 3D film illustrating what the wall was like nearly 2000 years ago and today); and colourful background detail to Hadrian's Wall life (such as how the soldiers spent their R&R time in this lonely outpost of the Empire).

🛏 Sleeping

★ Ashcroft   B&B ££

(☑ 01434-320213; www.ashcroftguesthouse.co. uk; Lanty's Lonnen, Haltwhistle; s/d/f/apt from £80/94/124/140; ℗ 🖨) British B&Bs don't get better than this elegant Edwardian vicarage surrounded by nearly a hectare of beautifully manicured, terraced lawns and gardens. Some rooms open to private balconies and terraces and all have soaring ceilings and 21st-century gadgets. Breakfast (included) is cooked on a cast-iron Aga and served in a grand dining room.

Holmhead Guest House   B&B ££

(☑ 01697-747402; http://bandb-hadrianswall.co. uk; Greenhead; campsites per 1/2 people £7/10, dm/s/d from £15.50/72/82; ⊙ guesthouse year-round, camping & bunk barn May-Sep; ℗ 🖨) Built using recycled bits of the wall on whose foundations it stands, this superb farmhouse half a mile north of Greenhead offers comfy rooms, a basic bunk barn and five unpowered campsites. The Pennine Way and the Hadrian's Wall Path pass through the grounds and Thirlwall Castle's jagged ruins loom above. Ask to see the 3rd-century Roman graffiti.

★ Langley Castle Hotel   CASTLE £££

(☑ 01434-688888; www.langleycastle.com; Langley; d castle view/castle from £167/255; ℗ 🖨 🐾) Soaring above 12 acres of gardens, this 1350-built castle is a beauty, with creaking hallways lined by suits of armour and an alleged resident ghost. Its nine castle rooms are appointed with antique furnishings (many have four-poster beds); there are another 18 'castle view' rooms in the grounds with access to castle facilities. Check for dinner, bed and breakfast packages.

HEXHAM ABBEY

Bustling Hexham is a handsome if somewhat scuffed market town centred on its grand Augustinian abbey (☑01434-602031; www.hexhamabbey.org.uk; Beaumont St; by donation; ⊙9.30am-5pm), a marvellous example of Early English architecture. It cleverly escaped the Dissolution of 1537 by rebranding as Hexham's parish church, a role it still has today. The highlight is the 7th-century Saxon crypt, the only surviving element of St Wilfrid's Church, built with inscribed stones from Corstopitum in 674.

❶ Information

Tourist Office (☑01434-321863; www.visitnorthumberland.com; Mechanics Institute, Westgate; ⊙10am-4.30pm Mon-Fri, to 1pm Sat) On Haltwhistle's main street.

❶ Getting There & Away

Bus 185 runs to the Roman Army Museum (£2.60, 10 minutes, three daily) and Birdoswald Roman Fort (£3.10, 25 minutes, three daily).

Haltwhistle is also linked by train to Hexham (£6.70, 20 minutes, hourly) and Newcastle (£13.10, one hour, hourly).

Northumberland National Park

England's last great wilderness is the 405 sq miles of natural wonderland that make up the country's least populated national park. The finest sections of Hadrian's Wall run along its southern edge and the landscape is dotted with prehistoric remains and fortified houses – the thick-walled peles were the only solid buildings built here until the mid-18th century.

Adjacent to the national park, the Kielder Water & Forest Park is home to the vast artificial lake Kielder Water, holding 200,000 million litres. Surrounding its 27-mile-long shoreline is England's largest plantation forest, with 150 million spruce and pine trees.

The lack of population helped see the area awarded dark-sky status by the International Dark Skies Association in 2013 (the largest such designation in Europe), with controls to prevent light pollution.

◉ Sights & Activities

The most spectacular stretch of the **Hadrian's Wall Path** is between Sewingshields and Greenhead in the south of the park.

There are many fine walks through the Cheviots (including a clamber to the top of the 815m-high Cheviot, the highest peak in the range), frequently passing by prehistoric remnants; local tourist offices can provide maps, guides and route information.

★ **Kielder Observatory** OBSERVATORY
(☑0191-265 5510; https://kielderobservatory.org; Black Fell, off Shilling Pot; adult/child from £22/20.50; ⊙by reservation) For the best views of the Northumberland International Dark Sky Park, attend a stargazing session at this state-of-the-art, 2008-built observatory. Its program spans night-time safari observing sessions to family events and astrophotography. Book well ahead for all events, which sell out quickly, and dress as you would for the ski slopes (it's seriously chilly here at night). At the signs towards Kielder Observatory and Skyspace, turn left; it's a 2-mile drive up the track.

Chillingham Castle CASTLE
(☑01668-215359; www.chillingham-castle.com; Chillingham; castle adult/child £9.50/5.50, Chillingham Wild Cattle £8/3, castle & Chillingham Wild Cattle £16/6; ⊙castle noon-5pm Apr-Oct, Chillingham Wild Cattle tours 10am, 11am, noon, 2pm, 3pm & 4pm Mon-Fri, 10am, 11am & noon Sun Apr-Oct) Steeped in history, warfare, torture and ghosts, 13th-century Chillingham is said to be one of the country's most haunted places, with spectres from a phantom funeral to Lady Mary Berkeley seeking her errant husband. Owner Sir Humphry Wakefield has passionately restored the castle's extravagant medieval staterooms, stone-flagged banquet halls and grisly torture chambers. Chillingham is 6 miles southeast of Wooler. Bus 470 (four daily Monday to Saturday) between Alnwick (£3, 25 minutes) and Wooler (£3, 20 minutes) stops at Chillingham.

**Cragside House,
Garden & Woodland** HISTORIC BUILDING, GARDENS
(NT; ☑01669-620333; www.nationaltrust.org.uk; adult/child £18/9, gardens & woodland only £13/6.50; ⊙house 11am-5pm, gardens & woodland

10am-6pm mid-Mar–Oct, hours can vary) Situated 1 mile northeast of Rothbury just off the B6341 is the astonishing country retreat of the first Lord Armstrong. In the 1880s the house had hot and cold running water, a telephone and alarm system, and was the world's first to be lit by electricity, generated through hydropower. The sprawling Victorian gardens feature lakes, moors and one of Europe's largest rock gardens. Visit late May to mid-June to see Cragside's famous rhododendrons in bloom.

🛏 Sleeping

Wooler YHA HOSTEL **£**
(📞 01668-281365; www.yha.org.uk; 30 Cheviot St, Wooler; dm/d/hut from £18/37/50; ⊘ Apr-Oct; 🅿🛜) In a low, red-brick building above Wooler, this handy hostel contains 57 beds in a variety of rooms (including handcrafted 'shepherds' huts' sleeping two to three people warmed by electric heating), a modern lounge and a small restaurant, as well as a self-catering kitchen, drying room and bike storage.

★**Otterburn Castle Country House Hotel** CASTLE **££**
(📞 01830-520620; www.otterburncastle.com; Main St, Otterburn; d/ste incl breakfast from £130/210; 🅿🛜🐾) Founded by William the Conqueror's cousin Robert de Umfraville in 1086 and set in almost 13 hectares of grounds, this story-book castle has 17 classically furnished rooms; some of its suites have four-poster beds and fireplaces. Modern British fare is served in its wood-panelled Oak Room Restaurant (2-/3-course menus £25/30); open fires blaze in its bar.

❶ Information

For information, contact the **Northumberland National Park** (📞 01434-605555; www.northumberlandnationalpark.org.uk).

As well as tourist offices in towns including **Wooler** (📞 01668-282123; www.wooler.org.uk; Cheviot Centre, 12 Padgepool Pl, Wooler; ⊘10am-4.30pm Mon-Fri, to 1pm Sat) and **Rothbury** (📞 01669-621979; www.visitkielder.com; Coquetdale Centre, Church St, Rothbury; ⊘10am-4.30pm Mon-Fri, 10.30am-4pm Sat Apr-Oct, reduced hours Nov-Mar), there's a national park office, the **Walltown Visitor Centre** (Northumberland National Park Visitor Centre; 📞 01434-344196; www.northumberlandnationalpark.org.uk; Greenhead; ⊘10am-6pm Apr-Sep, to 5pm Oct, 10am-4pm Sat & Sun Nov-

Mar), near Haltwhistle, reopening in summer 2019. Inside Kielder Castle, a hunting lodge built in 1775, the **Forest Park Centre** (📞 01434-250209; www.visitkielder.com; Forest Dr, Kielder; ⊘10am-4pm) has tourist information on the Northumberland National Park, including hiking, mountain biking and watersports in the Kielder area.

All offices can help find accommodation.

❶ Getting There & Away

Public transport options are limited at best – to explore properly you really need your own wheels.

Otterburn Bus 808 (£3.60, one hour, one daily Monday to Saturday) runs between Otterburn and Newcastle.

Wooler Buses 470 and 473 link Wooler and Alnwick (£3, 40 minutes, four daily Monday to Saturday). Buses 267 and 464 run between Wooler and Berwick-upon-Tweed (£4.50, one hour, every two hours Monday to Saturday).

Northumberland Coast

Northumberland's coast, like its wild and remote interior, is sparsely populated. You won't find any hurdy-gurdy seaside resorts, but instead charming, castle-crowned villages strung along miles of wide, sandy beaches that you might just have to yourself.

Alnwick

📞01665 / POP 8116

Northumberland's historic ducal town, Alnwick (pronounced 'annick') is an elegant maze of narrow cobbled streets around its colossal medieval castle. Alnwick is also home to an enchanting bookshop and the spectacular Alnwick Garden.

◎ Sights

★**Alnwick Castle** CASTLE
(📞 01665-511178; www.alnwickcastle.com; The Peth; adult/child £16/8.50, with Alnwick Garden £28/12.20; ⊘10am-5.30pm Apr-Oct) Set in parklands designed by Lancelot 'Capability' Brown, the imposing ancestral home of the Duke of Northumberland has changed little since the 14th century. It's a favourite set for film-makers and starred as Hogwarts for the first couple of Harry Potter films. The interior is sumptuous and extravagant; the six rooms open to the public – staterooms, dining room, guard chamber and library – have an incredible display of Italian paintings,

including Titian's *Ecce Homo* and many Canalettos.

Alnwick Garden
GARDENS

(www.alnwickgarden.com; Denwick Lane; adult/child £13.20/4.95, with Alnwick Castle £28/12.20; ⊙10am-6pm Apr-Oct, to 4pm Feb-Mar) This 4.8-hectare walled garden incorporates a series of magnificent green spaces surrounding the breathtaking Grand Cascade – 120 separate jets spurting some 30,000L of water down 21 weirs. Half a dozen other gardens include a Franco-Italian-influenced Ornamental Garden (with over 15,000 plants), Rose Garden and fascinating Poison Garden, home to some of the deadliest – and most illegal – plants in the world, including cannabis, magic mushrooms, belladonna and tobacco.

Enveloped by – but not in – the treetops, the timber-lined Treehouse (⊉01665-511852; mains £10.50-16.50; ⊙noon-2.30pm Mon & Tue, noon-2.30pm & 6-8.30pm Wed-Sat, noon-4pm Sun) restaurant serves Modern British cuisine.

🛏 Sleeping & Eating

★ Alnwick Lodge
B&B, CAMPGROUND ££

(⊉01665-604363; www.alnwicklodge.com; West Cawledge Park, A1; tent sites from £15, glamping incl linen from £58, B&B s/d/f from £55/75/100; P 🛜 🐾) Situated 3 miles south of Alnwick's centre, this gorgeous Victorian farmstead has 15 antique-filled rooms with quirky touches like free-standing, lidded baths. Cooked breakfasts are served around a huge circular banqueting table. You can also go 'glamping' in restored gypsy caravans, wagons and shepherds' huts (with shared bathrooms), or pitch up on the sheltered meadow.

White Swan Hotel
HOTEL ££

(⊉01665-602109; www.classiclodges.co.uk; Bondgate Within; d/f from £119/142; P 🛜 🐾) In the heart of town, this 300-year-old coaching inn has 56 superbly appointed rooms, including family rooms that sleep up to four. Its architectural showpiece is the fine-dining Olympic restaurant (⊉01665-602109; www.classiclodges.co.uk; Bondgate Within; mains £12.50-21, 2-/3-course lunch menus £14/18, 3-course dinner menu £35.50; ⊙noon-3pm & 5-9pm).

Plough Inn
GASTROPUB ££

(⊉01665-602395; www.theploughalnwick.co.uk; 24 Bondgate Without; mains lunch £5.50-11.50, dinner £13-22; ⊙kitchen noon-2.30pm & 5.30-9pm Mon-Thu, noon-2.30pm & 5.30-10pm Fri & Sat, noon-8pm Sun, bar to 11pm Sun-Thu, to 1am Fri & Sat) An 1896 coaching inn now contains this excellent gastropub styled like a contemporary hunting lodge. Evening dining is inspired: hot water crust mixed game pie, potted rabbit with gooseberry chutney, and whole grilled Amble lemon sole. Crab soups and sandwiches are the mainstays at lunch. Upstairs are seven spacious countrified rooms (doubles including breakfast from £145).

🛍 Shopping

★ Barter Books
BOOKS

(⊉01665-604888; www.barterbooks.co.uk; Alnwick Station, Wagon Way Rd; ⊙9am-7pm) Coal fires, velvet ottomans, reading rooms and a cafe make this secondhand bookshop in Alnwick's Victorian former railway station wonderfully atmospheric. It's responsible for the renaissance of the WWII 'Keep Calm and Carry On' slogan: while converting the station, the owner unearthed a set of posters – the framed original is above the till – and turned it into a successful industry.

ℹ Information

Alnwick's **tourist office** (⊉01670-622152; www.visitalnwick.org.uk; 2 The Shambles; ⊙9.30am-5pm Mon-Sat, 10am-4pm Sun Easter-Oct, 10am-4pm Mon-Sat Nov-Easter) is by Market Pl.

ℹ Getting There & Away

Bus X15 zips along the A1 to Berwick-upon-Tweed (£6.60, one hour, hourly Monday to Saturday, every two hours Sunday) and Newcastle (£6.60, 1½ hours, hourly Monday to Saturday, every two hours Sunday). Bus X18 follows the coast to Berwick-upon-Tweed (£6.60, two hours, three daily) and Newcastle (£6.30, two hours, hourly).

Alnwick's nearest train station is at Alnmouth, connected to Alnwick by bus X18 (£2.70, 10 minutes, hourly Monday to Saturday, every two hours Sunday). Alnmouth's train services include Berwick-upon-Tweed (£7, 20 minutes, up to two per hour), Edinburgh (£20.30, one hour, up to two per hour) and Newcastle (£10.60, 40 minutes, up to two per hour).

Craster

⊉01665 / POP 305

Sandy, salty Craster is a small, sheltered fishing village about 6 miles northeast of Alnwick, and is famous for its kippers. In the early 20th century, 2500 herring were

Driving Tour
Northumberland Coast

START NEWBIGGIN-BY-THE-SEA
END BERWICK-UPON-TWEED
LENGTH 78 MILES; ONE DAY

It's possible to shadow the coast to the Scottish border from Tynemouth, but the scenery really picks up at ❶ **Newbiggin-by-the-Sea**. Newbiggin's beach was restored in 2007, when over 500,000 tonnes of Skegness' sand was relocated here to counteract erosion, and Sean Henry's gigantic bronze sculpture *The Couple* was installed offshore.

Continuing north along the A1068 coast road for 13 miles brings you to the fishing port of ❷ **Amble**, with a boardwalk along the seafront and puffin cruises (p624). Less than 2 miles north, biscuit-coloured ❸ **Warkworth** is a cluster of houses around a loop in the River Coquet, dominated by the craggy ruin of 14th-century Warkworth Castle. The castle features in Shakespeare's *Henry IV* Parts I and II, and the 1998 film *Elizabeth* was shot here.

Some 5 miles north of Warkworth is ❹ **Alnmouth**, with brightly painted houses and pretty beaches. It's another 5 miles inland to the bustling town of ❺ **Alnwick** (p619) to see its imposing castle (p619) – which starred as Harry Potter's Hogwarts – and glorious Alnwick Garden. Turn back towards the coast and follow the B1339 for 4.7 miles before turning east on Windside Hill to ❻ **Craster** (p620), famed for its smoked kippers. From Craster, there are spectacular views of brooding Dunstanburgh Castle. Around 5 miles north at ❼ **Low Newton-by-the-Sea**, in Embleton Bay, pause for a pint brewed at the Ship Inn (p623).

Past the village of Seahouses (the jumping-off point for the Farne Islands), quaint ❽ **Bamburgh** (p623) is home to the most dramatic castle (p623) yet. Another 17 miles on, via a tidal causeway (check tide times!), the sacred priory ruins (p624) of isolated, otherworldly ❾ **Holy Island (Lindisfarne)** (p624) still attract spiritual pilgrims. Return to the mainland where, 14 miles north, you can walk almost the entire length of the Elizabethan walls (p625) encircling England's northernmost city, beautiful ❿ **Berwick-upon-Tweed** (p625).

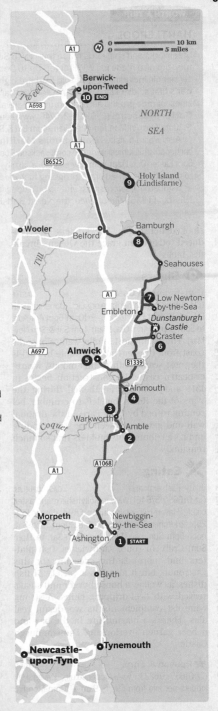

WORTH A TRIP

HARTLEPOOL

Steelworks and shipyards made this North Sea coastal town's fortunes in the 19th century, but also made it a WWI target. On 16 December 1914 it was hit by 1150 shells, killing 117 people including 29-year-old Durham Light Infantry Private Theophilus Jones, the war's first soldier killed on British soil. You can still see the town's underground magazines, parade ground and panoramic observation tower at the 19th-century **Heugh Gun Battery Museum** (☑ 01429-270746; www.heughbattery.com; Moor Tce; adult/child £6/4; ☺ 10am-5pm Fri-Mon Jun-Aug, 10am-4pm Sat & Sun Feb-May & Sep-Nov).

Also worth a visit is **Hartlepool's Maritime Experience** (☑ 01429-860077; www.hartlepoolsmaritimeexperience.com; Jackson Dock, Maritime Ave; adult/child £10/8; ☺ 10am-5pm Easter-Oct, 11am-4pm Nov-Easter), a family-friendly attraction that brings local history to life with costumed staff, intriguing historical exhibits and recreated businesses (such as a gunsmith, swordsmith and so on) along its historic quayside. It's also home to the 1817-built HMS *Trincomalee*, the oldest British warship still afloat.

smoked here daily. The kippers still produced today often grace the Queen's breakfast table.

☉ Sights

Dunstanburgh Castle CASTLE
(EH; www.english-heritage.org.uk; Dunstanburgh Rd; adult/child £5.40/3.20; ☺ 10am-6pm Apr-Aug, to 5pm Sep, to 4pm Oct, 10am-4pm Sat & Sun Nov-Mar) The dramatic 1.5-mile walk along the coast from Craster (not accessible by car) is the most scenic path to this moody, weather-beaten castle. Its construction began in 1314 and it was strengthened during the Wars of the Roses, but left to crumble, becoming ruined by 1550. Parts of the original wall and gatehouse keep are still standing and it's a tribute to its builders that so much remains.

✕ Eating

Jolly Fisherman GASTROPUB ££
(☑ 016650-576461; www.thejollyfishermancraster. co.uk; Haven Hill; mains lunch £8-14, dinner £12-25; ☺ kitchen 11am-3pm & 5-8.30pm Mon-Sat, noon-5pm Sun, bar 11am-11pm Mon-Sat, to 11pm Sun) Crab (in soup, sandwiches, fish platters and more) is the speciality of this gastropub, but it also has a variety of fish dishes, as well as a house burger and steaks served with beef-dripping chips. A strong wine list complements its wonderful real ales. There's a blazing fire in the bar and a beer garden overlooking Dunstanburgh Castle.

★ **Robson & Sons** FOOD
(☑ 01665-576223; www.kipper.co.uk; Haven Hill; kippers per kilo from £9; ☺ 9am-4.30pm Mon-Fri,

9am-3.30pm Sat, 11am-3.30pm Sun) Four generations have operated this traditional fish smokers; loyal customers include the Royal Family. It's best known for its kippers, but also smokes salmon and other fish.

ⓘ Getting There & Away

Bus X18 runs to Alnwick (£5.40, 55 minutes, three daily), Berwick-upon-Tweed (£6.60, 1½ hours, three daily) and Newcastle (£6.60, 2½ hours, three daily). From Monday to Saturday, bus 418 also links Craster to Alnwick (£5.10, 30 minutes, four daily).

Embleton Bay

Beautiful Embleton Bay, a pale wide arc of sand, stretches from Dunstanburgh past the endearing, sloping village of Embleton and curves in a broad vanilla-coloured strand around to end at Low Newton-by-the-Sea, a tiny whitewashed, National Trust–preserved village.

☉ Sights

Behind the bay is a path leading to the **Newton Pool Nature Reserve**, an important spot for breeding and migrating birds such as black-headed gulls and grasshopper warblers. There are a couple of hides where you can peer out at them. You can continue walking along the headland beyond Low Newton, where you'll find **Football Hole**, a delightful hidden beach between headlands.

The easiest access to Dunstanburgh Castle (p622) is from Craster; the walk to the castle from Embleton Bay can be cut off at high tide.

Sleeping & Eating

Joiners Arms PUB £££
(01665-576112; http://joiners-arms.com; High Newton-by-the-Sea; d from £160; P ☎ 🐾) Locals love this gastropub and for good reason: ingredients are sourced nearby, the seafood and steaks are excellent and families are warmly welcomed. But for visitors, it's also a fantastic place to stay: five contemporary guest rooms are individually and exquisitely decorated with details like exposed brick, free-standing baths and four-poster beds.

Ship Inn PUB FOOD ££
(01665-576262; www.shipinnnewton.co.uk; Low Newton-by-the-Sea; mains lunch £5.50-9, dinner £9-22.50; ⊙kitchen noon-2.30pm & 6.45-8pm Wed-Sat, noon-2.30pm Sun-Tue, bar 11am-11pm Mon-Sat, 11am-10pm Sun Apr-Oct, reduced hours Nov-Mar) Set around a village green, this idyllic pub brews over two dozen different beers – blond, wheat, rye, bitter, stout and seasonal – using local River Coquet water. The food is first-rate, too, from crab and lobster to regional farm-sourced meat. No credit cards or lunchtime reservations (arrive early); book ahead for dinner. Live music often plays at weekends.

❶ Getting There & Away

Bus X18 to Newcastle (£6.60, 2¾ hours, three daily), Berwick-upon-Tweed (£5.60, 1¼ hours, three daily) and Alnwick (£5.40, 45 minutes, three daily) stops outside the Joiners Arms. From Monday to Saturday, bus 418 (£5.10, 35 minutes, four daily) links the village of Embleton with Alnwick.

Bamburgh

01668 / POP 414
High up on a basalt crag, Bamburgh's mighty castle looms over the quaint village – a clutch of houses around a pleasant green – which continues to commemorate the valiant achievements of local heroine Grace Darling.

◉ Sights

Bamburgh Castle CASTLE
(01668-214515; www.bamburghcastle.com; Links Rd; adult/child £11/5; ⊙10am-5pm early Feb-early Nov, 11am-4.30pm Sat & Sun early Nov-early Feb) Northumberland's most dramatic castle was built around a powerful 11th-century Norman keep by Henry II. The castle played a key role in the border wars of the 13th and 14th centuries, and in 1464 was the first English castle to fall during the Wars of the Roses. It was restored in the 19th century by the great industrialist Lord Armstrong, and is still home to the Armstrong family.

RNLI Grace Darling Museum MUSEUM
(01668-214910; www.rnli.org; 1 Radcliffe Rd; ⊙10am-5pm Easter-Sep, 10am-4pm Tue-Sun Oct-Easter) FREE Born in Bamburgh, Grace Darling was the lighthouse keeper's daughter on Outer Farne who rowed out to the grounded, flailing SS *Forfarshire* in 1838 and saved its crew in the middle of a dreadful storm. This refurbished museum even has her actual coble (row boat) as well as a film on the events of that stormy night. Grace was born just three houses down from the museum and is buried in the churchyard opposite.

✖ Eating

★Mizen Head SEAFOOD ££
(01668-214254; www.mizen-head.co.uk; Lucker Rd; mains £13-27; ⊙6-9pm Mon-Wed, noon-1.45pm & 6-9pm Thu-Sun; P ☎) Bamburgh's best place to eat and/or stay is this stunning restaurant with rooms. Local seafood – lobster, mussels, crab, salmon, squid and more – is the kitchen's speciality, along with chargrilled steaks. Its 11 rooms with chequered fabrics and black-and-white coastal prints are light, bright and spacious (doubles from £98). Switched-on staff know their stuff.

Potted Lobster SEAFOOD ££
(01668-214088; www.thepottedlobsterbamburgh.co.uk; 3 Lucker Rd; mains £12-21, half-/full lobster £18/33, seafood platter £70; ⊙noon-9pm Jul & Aug, noon-3pm & 6-9pm Sep-Jun) Bamburgh lobster – served as a creamy egg and brandy thermidor stuffed in the shell; grilled with garlic and parsley butter; or poached and served cold with wild garlic mayo – is the star of this nautical-styled gem. Seafood platters for two, piled high with lobster, Lindisfarne oysters, Craster crab, pickled herring and more, come with hand-cut chips and crusty home-baked bread.

❶ Getting There & Away

Take bus X18 north to Berwick-upon-Tweed (£6.60, 50 minutes, three daily) or south to Newcastle (£6.60, 3¼ hours, three daily).

Holy Island (Lindisfarne)

There's something almost other-worldly about this tiny, 2-sq-mile island. Connected to the mainland by a narrow causeway that only appears at low tide, cutting the island off from the mainland for about five hours each day, it's fiercely desolate and isolated, scarcely different from when St Aidan arrived to found a monastery in 635.

As you cross the empty flats, it's easy to imagine the marauding Vikings who repeatedly sacked the settlement between 793 and 875, when the monks finally took the hint and left. They carried with them the illuminated *Lindisfarne Gospels* (now in the British Library in London) and the miraculously preserved body of St Cuthbert, who lived here for a couple of years but preferred the hermit's life on Inner Farne. A priory was re-established in the 11th century, but didn't survive the Dissolution in 1537.

⊙ Sights

Lindisfarne Priory RUINS, MUSEUM
(EH; www.english-heritage.org.uk; adult/child £7.50/4.60; ⊙10am-6pm Apr-Sep, to 5pm Oct, 10am-4pm Wed-Sun Nov-Dec & mid-Feb–Mar, 10am-4pm Sat & Sun Jan–mid-Feb) The skeletal, red and grey ruins of the priory are an eerie sight and give a glimpse into the isolated life of the Lindisfarne monks. The later 13th-century St Mary the Virgin Church is built on the site of the first church between the Tees and the Firth of Forth, and the adjacent museum displays the remains of the first monastery and tells the story of the

monastic community before and after the Dissolution. Hours vary according to tides.

Lindisfarne Castle CASTLE
(NT; www.nationaltrust.org.uk; adult/child £7.30/3.60; ⊙11am-5pm Tue-Sun late May-Sep, 10am-4pm Easter-late May & Oct) Built atop a rocky bluff in 1550, this tiny, storybook castle was extended and converted by Sir Edwin Lutyens from 1902 to 1910 for Mr Edward Hudson, the owner of *Country Life* magazine – you can imagine some of the glamorous parties to have graced its alluring rooms. It's half a mile east of the village. Opening times can vary due to tide times.

🛏 Sleeping & Eating

Lindisfarne Inn INN ££
(☑01289-381223; www.lindisfarneinn.co.uk; Beal Rd, Beal; s/d/f incl breakfast from £81/115/135; 🅿🛜😺) This mainland inn on the A1 next to the turn-off to the causeway is a handy alternative to island accommodation and/ or dining if you're cutting it fine with crossing times. Its 23 spotless, modern rooms are set far back enough that road noise isn't a problem. Well-above-average pub food (such as suet pudding with Northumbrian game) changes seasonally.

Crown & Anchor INN ££
(☑01289-389215; http://holyislandcrown.co.uk; Market Pl; s/d from £60/70; 🅿😺) A cornerstone of the island's social life, this venerable pub has brightly coloured guest rooms and solid pub grub, but the biggest winner is the beer garden with a postcard panorama of the castle, priory and harbour.

Barn @ Beal PUB FOOD ££
(☑01289-540044; http://barnatbeal.com; Beal Farm, Beal; mains lunch £9-11, dinner £14-20; ⊙cafe 9am-5pm, lunch & dinner by reservation, bar hours vary seasonally; 🛜♿) You can watch the causeway tides on webcam at this sociable mainland pub 1 mile northeast of the A1 turn-off (2 miles west of the island). Lindisfarne seafood, including lobster, is a menu highlight, as are house-speciality burgers utilising farm produce. There's a kids' play area. It also has 12 tent pitches (from £7) and nine caravan sites (from £25).

🔒 Shopping

St Aidan's Winery FOOD, DRINK
(Lindisfarne Mead; ☑01289-389230; www.lindisfarne-mead.co.uk; Prior Lane; ⊙9am-5pm depend-

---

THE PUFFINS OF COQUET ISLAND

For three days in late May to early June, the **Amble Puffin Festival** (http://amblepuffinfest.co.uk; ⊙late May) celebrates the hatching of puffin chicks on Coquet Island, near Amble, with events including local history talks, guided birdwatching walks, exhibitions, watersports, a craft fair, a food festival and live music.

During the breeding season, you can take a boat trip to see the birds on the island with **Dave Gray's Puffin Cruises** (☑01665-711975; www.puffincruises.co.uk; Amble Harbour, Amble; adult/child £10/5; ⊙by reservation Apr-Oct).

ing on tides) 🍷 Mead made on Lindisfarne by St Aidan's Winery to a traditional Roman recipe using locally drawn water and honey. Free tastings let you try its three varieties – original, blood orange and spiced – as well as its fortified wines, such as ginger, wild strawberry, elderberry, blackberry and cherry. Other products include mead-based chocolate truffles and jams. Check ahead for opening hours.

❶ Getting There & Away

Drivers need to pay close attention to crossing-time information, posted at tourist offices and on notice boards throughout the area, and at www.holy-island.info. Every year drivers are caught midway by the incoming tide and have to abandon their cars.

When tides permit, the Holy Island Hopper (www.berwickupontweedtaxis.co.uk; £3, 15 minutes) links the island with the mainland on the corner of Beal Rd and the A1 to connect with buses X15 and X18, serving Berwick-upon-Tweed, Alnwick and Newcastle.

Park in the signposted car park (£4.60 per day). A shuttle bus (£2 return) runs from the car park to the castle every 20 minutes from Easter to September; alternatively it's a level 300m walk to the village centre and 1 mile to the castle.

Berwick-upon-Tweed

📞 01289 / POP 12,043

England's northernmost city is a picturesque fortress town, cleaved by the River Tweed, which is spanned by the Grade I-listed Berwick Bridge (aka Old Bridge), built from sandstone between 1611 and 1624, and the Royal Tweed (1925–28).

Berwick is the stubborn holder of two unique honours: it is the most fought-over settlement in European history (between 1174 and 1482 it changed hands 14 times between the Scots and the English); and its football team, Berwick Rangers, is the only English team to play in the Scottish League (albeit in lowly Scottish League Two). Although firmly English since the 15th century, Berwick retains its own identity, with locals south of the border speaking with a noticeable Scottish burr.

◎ Sights & Activities

★ **Berwick Walls**   HISTORIC SITE
(EH; www.english-heritage.org.uk; ⊙ dawn-dusk) **FREE** You can walk almost the entire length of Berwick's hefty Elizabethan walls, begun

---

OFF THE BEATEN TRACK

THE FARNE ISLANDS
••

During breeding season (roughly May to July), you can see feeding chicks of 20 seabird species (including puffin, kittiwake, Arctic tern, eider duck, cormorant and gull), and some 6000 grey seals, on the **Farne Islands** (NT; 📞01289-389244; www.nationaltrust. org.uk; adult/child excl boat transport £27.30/13.60, cheaper outside breeding season; ⊙ by reservation, season & conditions permitting Mar-Oct), a rocky archipelago 3 miles offshore from the fishing village of Seahouses. Boat operators, contactable through Seahouses' **tourist office** (📞01670-625593; http:// visitnorthumberland.com; Seafield car park, Seahouses; ⊙9.30am-4pm Thu-Tue Apr, 9.30am-4pm daily May-Oct), depart from Seahouses' dock, including **Billy Shiel** (📞01665-720308; www.farne-islands.com; Harbour Rd, Seahouses; adult/child excl island landing fees 2½hr tour £18/12, 6hr tour £40/25; ⊙ by reservation Apr-Oct).

Crossings can be rough (impossible in bad weather); wear warm, waterproof clothing and an old hat to guard against the birds!

---

in 1558 to reinforce an earlier set built during the reign of Edward II. The mile-long walk is a must, with wonderful, wide-open views. Only a small fragment remains of the once-mighty border castle, most of the building having been replaced by the train station.

Berwick Barracks   MUSEUM, GALLERY
(EH; www.english-heritage.org.uk; The Parade; adult/child £4.90/2.90; ⊙10am-6pm Apr-Sep, to 4pm Wed-Sun Oct) Designed by Nicholas Hawksmoor, Britain's oldest purpose-built barracks (1717) now house an assortment of museums and art galleries, covering a history of the town and British soldiery since the 17th century. The Gymnasium Gallery hosts big-name contemporary art exhibitions.

Berwick Boat Trips   CRUISE
(📞07713 170845; www.berwickboattrips.co.uk; Berwick-upon-Tweed Quayside; 2hr North Sea wildlife tour adult/child £15/7, 1hr river tour £8/4, 2hr sunset estuary tour £15/7; ⊙ by reservation) Choose from a North Sea cruise spotting

seals, dolphins and sea birds, a river cruise along the Tweed, or a scenic trip along the estuary at sunset. Schedules are posted online.

🛏 Sleeping & Eating

Berwick YHA
HOSTEL £

(☎ 01629-592700; www.yha.org.uk; Dewars Lane; dm/d/f from £15/59/79; P @ 🛜) A mid-18th-century granary has been converted into a state-of-the-art hostel with 55 beds in dorms and private rooms (all with en suite bathrooms). Contemporary facilities include a TV room, a laundry and wi-fi in common areas. Staff are terrifically helpful.

★ Marshall Meadows Country House Hotel
HERITAGE HOTEL ££

(☎ 01289-331133; http://marshallmeadowshotel.co.uk; Marshall Meadows; d/f incl breakfast from £109/129; P 🛜 🐕) England's most northerly hotel, just 600m from the Scottish border, sits amid 6 hectares of woodland and ornamental gardens. The Georgian manor's 19 rooms (including a ground-floor family room) have countrified checked and floral fabrics. There are two cosy bars with open fireplaces, a conservatory, and an oak-panelled restaurant serving breakfast (including kippers), and evening meals by candlelight.

Audela
BRITISH ££

(☎ 01289-308827; www.audela.co.uk; 64 Bridge St; mains £12.50-23; ☉ noon-2.30pm & 5.30-9pm Thu-Mon) Named for the last vessel to be built at Berwick Shipyard (in 1979) and set in a former cockle shop, Audela is the town's top table. Local suppliers provide the ingredients for dishes like Berwick crab with pickled carrot and oysters with sea buckthorn, roast pheasant with artichoke and haggis purée, and caraway-crusted Northumberland lamb with wild garlic–wrapped potatoes.

❶ Getting There & Away

On the East Coast Main Line linking London and Edinburgh, Berwick-upon-Tweed is almost exactly halfway between Edinburgh (£13.40, one hour, up to two per hour) and Newcastle (£8, 45 minutes, up to two per hour).

Buses stop on Golden Sq (where it meets Marygate). National Express coaches between Edinburgh (£15.70, 1¼ hours, twice daily) and London (£38.10, eight hours, twice daily) stop here.

Newcastle is served by the X15 (via Alnwick; £6.60, 2½ hours, hourly Monday to Saturday, every two hours Sunday) and X18 (£6.60, four hours, three daily).

Understand England

England Today

It's a time of uncertainty in England: the fallout from Brexit, a sputtering economy, political wrangling and a series of public scandals have combined to cause a sense of unease in the English public. There's change in the air and no-one seems sure of what the future has in store. So what to do? Keep calm and carry on, of course.

Best on Film

Brief Encounter (1945) Classic tale of a buttoned-up English love affair.

Withnail and I (1987) Cult comedy about two out-of-work actors on a disastrous Lake District holiday.

Hope and Glory (1987) Moving tale of life in London during the Blitz, based on director John Boorman's own experiences.

War Horse (2011) Rite-of-passage story of a young man surviving WWI.

Pride (2014) Comic, compassionate depiction of lesbian and gay activists raising money for families hit by the UK Miners' Strike (1984–85).

Suffragette (2015) Compelling account of the pre-WWI fight to secure votes for women.

Best in Print

Notes from a Small Island (Bill Bryson; 1995) An American's fond and astute take on Britain.

The English (Jeremy Paxman; 1998) A perceptive take on the national character.

The Rotters Club (Jonathan Coe; 2001) Growing up in the 1970s, amid strikes, IRA bombings and punk rock.

Watching the English (Kate Fox; 2004) A fascinating field guide to the nation's peculiar habits.

A Week in December (Sebastian Faulks; 2009) A state-of-the-nation satire on 2007 London life.

The Brexit Conundrum

The fallout from the seismic decision to withdraw from the EU rumbles on across the UK. Decided by a narrow 52% to 48% vote in favour during the 2016 referendum, Britain's exit from the EU (colloquially known as Brexit) looms large wherever you care to look or listen: on every news bulletin, talk show and phone-in, and the prevailing topic of conversation in pubs, parks and workplaces up and down the land. With negotiations ongoing, so much remains up in the air: heavyweight questions over immigration, trade, investment and the hot-button topic of the Northern Irish border have yet, at the time of writing, to be decided. After the March 2019 deadline for leaving the EU, a two-year transition period has been agreed that will smooth the separation, at least for a while – but politicians can only dodge the difficult questions for so long. In the meantime, supporters of Brexit maintain that the nation can look forward to a bright new global future, while opponents (Remainers, or Remoaners, depending on your point of view) point out a swathe of negative economic forecasts. In truth, no one can say with certainty how the long-term story will play out.

What's most surprising about the Brexit issue is that no one has addressed the fact that of Britain's four constituent nations, the vote was split precisely down the middle, with 54% of English voters and 53% of Welsh voters returning a vote to leave, and 62% of Scots and 56% of Northern Irish voting to remain. The split raises a tricky question: can it really be democratically legitimate for the will of English and Welsh voters to supersede that of their neighbours in Scotland and Northern Ireland? So far, it's a question that remains unanswered – and, if nothing else, paints an unhappy picture of a nation more divided than ever. It also underlines the peculiar truth that England and Britain, and notions of Englishness and Britishness, are two very different (and not necessarily compatible) things.

English Affairs

Brexit ties in with England's shifting political scene. Following her misguided decision to call a snap general election in 2017, which resulted in a hung parliament, Theresa May and her Conservative Party continue to wobble in the House of Commons, in power only thanks to the support of MPs from Northern Ireland's Democratic Unionist Party (DUP). On the opposite side, support for Jeremy Corbyn's Labour still seems on the rise, although divisions within his own party have meant he has failed to pull away conclusively in the polls – his opponents remain sceptical over his old-school socialist policy agenda, which includes the renationalisation of rail, mail and water industries, the abolition of student tuition fees, and increased taxes on the wealthy and big business. It's an old English argument that's been had countless times before – socialism versus conservatism, state versus society, left versus right – and, true to form, neither side seems any closer to winning the argument.

And that's without factoring in the complications of devolution, which gave the national parliaments of Scotland, Wales and Northern Ireland the power to make decisions over matters such as health spending, education, local government and welfare – leaving England to decide its own affairs, often with strikingly different outcomes. Throw in the age-old division between England's south and north (so far, the Conservatives' 'northern powerhouse' project to address the north–south divide hasn't amounted to much), and newly elected mayors in London (Sadiq Khan) and Greater Manchester (Andy Burnham, the city's first directly elected mayor), both from the opposite side of the political divide to the prime minister, and it all adds up to a very uncertain political landscape indeed.

A Series of Scandals

The winds of change are blowing through other corners of England, too. A slew of scandals have hit the headlines – most notably the gender pay gap, which has revealed that many businesses and organisations are still paying male employees substantially more than their female colleagues.

Several high-profile charities have also come under fire – such as Oxfam, whose aid workers were revealed to have used the services of prostitutes during the earthquake relief effort in Haiti in 2011. Then there's the Skripal affair, in which an ex-Russian spy and his daughter were poisoned in broad daylight in Salisbury, allegedly by a Russian-made nerve agent, and the controversy over Cambridge Analytica, the London-based IT firm that used the data of Facebook users to influence the outcomes of both the Brexit and US election votes.

Most affecting of all, however, was the Grenfell Tower disaster, in which 71 residents of a London high-rise were killed in a fire fuelled by faulty cladding. It's all meant a field day for the tabloid red-tops, reminding us that if there's one thing England knows how to do, it's create a good old-fashioned scandal.

POPULATION: **53 MILLION**

AREA: **50,345 SQ MILES**

GDP GROWTH (UK): **0.2%**

INFLATION (UK): **2.3%**

UNEMPLOYMENT (UK): **4.2%**

if England were 100 people

85 would be British
4 would be South Asian
2 would be African & Afro Caribbean
9 would be Other

belief systems
(% of population)

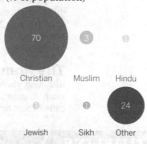

70 Christian
3 Muslim
1 Hindu
Jewish
Sikh
24 Other

population per sq km

England   UK   London

🚶 ≈ 250 people

History

Tiny geographically, England is immensely complex historically. And the extent to which its past shapes its present is profound. To really understand England you need to delve into its history, packed with drama and intrigue, with characters including incomers and invaders all leaving their mark. The result? The rich mix of culture, landscape and language that shaped the nation. For many, this vibrant heritage – whether seen in Stonehenge, Hadrian's Wall, Canterbury Cathedral or the Tower of London – is England's big draw.

Stone Age & Iron Age

Stone tools discovered on a beach in Norfolk suggest human habitation in England stretches back at least 840,000 years. These early peoples were nomadic hunter-gatherers, but by around 4000 BC, most had settled down, notably in open areas such as Salisbury Plain in southern England. Alongside fields they built burial mounds (today called barrows), but their most enduring legacies are the great stone circles of Avebury and Stonehenge, still clearly visible today.

Move on a millennium or two and it's the Iron Age. Better tools meant trees could be felled and more land turned over to farming. As landscapes altered, this was also a time of cultural change: a new wave of migrants – the Celts – arrived in Britain from the European mainland. It's not clear if the new arrivals absorbed the indigenous people, or vice versa, but the end result was the widespread adoption of Celtic language and culture, and the creation of a Celtic-British population – today often known as the Britons (or Ancient Britons to distinguish them from today's natives).

By around 100 BC, the Ancient Britons had separated into about 20 different tribes, including the Cantiaci (in today's county of Kent), the Iceni (today's Norfolk) and the Brigantes (northern England). Did you notice the Latin-sounding names? That's because the tribal tags were handed out by the next arrivals on England's shores...

> Probably constructed from around 3000 BC, Stonehenge has stood on Salisbury Plain for more than 5000 years, making it older than the pyramids of Egypt.

The Romans

Although there had been some earlier expeditionary campaigns, the main Roman invasion of what is now England began in AD 43. They called their newly won province Britannia, and within a decade most

TIMELINE	4000 BC	55 BC	AD 43
	Neolithic peoples migrate from continental Europe. Differing significantly from previous arrivals, instead of hunting and moving on, they eventually settle in one place and start farming.	Relatively small groups of Roman invaders under the command of General Julius Caesar make forays into southern England from the northern coast of Gaul (today's France).	Emperor Claudius leads the first proper Roman invasion of Britain. His army wages a ruthless campaign, and the Romans control most of southern England by AD 50.

of southern England was under Roman control. It wasn't a walkover though: some locals fought back, most famously the warrior-queen Boudica, who led a rebel army against Londinium, the Roman port on the present site of London.

Opposition was mostly sporadic, however, and no real threat to Roman military might. By around AD 80 Britannia comprised much of today's England and Wales. Though it's tempting to imagine noble natives battling courageously against occupying forces, Roman control and stability was possibly welcomed by the general population, tired of feuding chiefs and insecure tribal territories.

Roman settlement in Britain continued for almost four centuries, and intermarriage was common between locals and incomers (many from other parts of the Empire – including modern-day Belgium, Spain and Syria – rather than Rome itself). A Romano-British population thus evolved, particularly in the towns, while indigenous Celtic-British culture remained in rural areas.

Along with stability and wealth, the Romans paved the way for another cultural facet: a new religion called Christianity, after it was recognised by Emperor Constantine in the 4th century. Recent research also suggests Celtic Christians may have brought the religion to Britain even earlier. But by this time, although Romano-British culture was thriving in Britannia, back in its Mediterranean heartland the Empire was already in decline.

It was an untidy finale. The Romans were not driven out by the Ancient Britons (after more than 300 years, Romano-British culture was so established there was nowhere for many to go 'home' to). In reality, Britannia was simply dumped by the rulers in Rome, and the colony slowly fizzled out. But some historians are tidy folk, and the end of Roman power in England is often dated at AD 410.

Boudica was queen of the Iceni, a Celtic-British tribe whose territory was invaded by the Romans around AD 60. A year later, she led an army against the Roman settlements of Camulodunum (now Colchester) and Londinium (London), but was eventually defeated at the Battle of Watling Street (in today's Shropshire).

HISTORY THE ROMANS

LEGACY OF THE LEGIONS

To control their new territory, the Romans built garrisons across England. Many developed into towns, which can be recognised by names ending in 'chester' or 'caster' (from the Latin *castrum*, meaning military camp) – Lancaster, Winchester, Manchester and, of course, Chester, to name but a few. The Romans also built roads, initially so soldiers could march quickly from place to place, and later so that trade could develop. Wherever possible the roads were straight lines (because it was efficient, not – as the old joke goes – to stop Ancient Britons hiding round corners) and included Ermine St between London and York, Watling St between Kent and Wales, and the Fosse Way between Exeter and Lincoln. As you travel around England, you'll notice many modern highways still follow Roman roads. In a country better known for old lanes and turnpike routes winding through the landscape, these ruler-straight highways stand out on the map.

c 60	c 200	c 410	5th century
The Iceni warrior queen Boudica (also known as Boadicea) leads a rebel army against the Romans, destroys the Roman town of Colchester and gets as far as their port at Londinium (now London).	The Romans build a defensive wall around the city of London with four main entrance gates, still reflected today by the districts of Aldgate, Ludgate, Newgate and Bishopsgate.	As the classical world's greatest empire declines after centuries of relative peace and prosperity, Roman rule ends in Britain with more of a whimper than a bang.	Germanic tribes – known today as the Anglo-Saxons – from the area now called Germany migrate to England, and quickly spread across much of the country.

The Anglo-Saxons

When Roman power faded, the province of Britannia went downhill. Romano-British towns were abandoned and rural areas became no-go zones as local warlords fought over fiefdoms. The vacuum didn't go unnoticed, and once again migrants crossed from the European mainland – this time Germanic tribes called Angles and Saxons.

Historians disagree on what happened next; either the Anglo-Saxons largely overcame or absorbed the Romano-British and Celts, or the indigenous tribes simply adopted Anglo-Saxon language and culture. Either way, by the late 6th century much of England was predominantly Anglo-Saxon, divided into separate kingdoms dominated by Wessex (in southern England), Mercia (today's Midlands) and Northumbria (northern England).

Some areas remained unaffected by the incomers, but the overall impact was immense – the name England means 'land of the Angles', and today the core of the English language is Anglo-Saxon, many place names have Anglo-Saxon roots, and the very term 'Anglo-Saxon' has become a (much abused and factually incorrect) byword for 'pure English'.

Visitors often get confused about the various names. The country of England is part of the island of Great Britain (along with Wales and Scotland), and part of the United Kingdom of Great Britain and Northern Ireland. Hence 'English' and 'British' mean quite different things.

The Vikings & Alfred the Great

In the 9th century England was yet again invaded by a bunch of pesky Continentals. This time it was the Vikings, from today's Scandinavia. They quickly conquered the eastern and northeastern areas of England, then started to expand into central England. Blocking their route were the Anglo-Saxon armies heading north, led by Alfred the Great, the king of Wessex and one of English history's best-known characters.

Thus England was divided in two: north and east was the Viking land, known as 'Danelaw', while south and west was Anglo-Saxon territory. Alfred was hailed as king of the English – the first time the Anglo-Saxons regarded themselves as a truly united people. His capital was Winchester; if you come to visit the famous cathedral, look out for the nearby statue of Alfred.

Alfred's son and successor was Edward, known as Edward the Elder. After more battles, he gained control of Danelaw, and thus became the first king to rule the whole country – a major milestone in English history.

But it was hardly cause for celebration. Later in the 10th century, more raids from Scandinavia threatened the fledgling English unity, and as England came to the end of the 1st millennium AD, the future was anything but certain.

Despite Anglo-Saxon dominance from around AD 500, the Celtic language was still being spoken in parts of southern England when the Normans invaded in the 11th century. Irish and Scottish Gaelic, Welsh and Cornish all have their origins in the Celtic tongue.

1066 & All That

In 1066 when King Edward the Confessor died, the crown passed to Harold II, his brother-in-law. That should've settled things, but Edward had a cousin in Normandy (in northern France) called William, who thought *he* should have succeeded to the throne of England.

9th century	927	1066	1085–86
Vikings arrive and conquer east and northeast England. They establish their capital at Jorvik, today's city of York.	Athelstan, grandson of Alfred the Great and son of Edward the Elder, is the first monarch to be crowned king of England, building on his ancestors' success in regaining Viking territory.	Incumbent King Harold II is defeated by an invading Norman army at the Battle of Hastings, and England finds itself with a new monarch: William the Conqueror.	The Norman invaders compile the Domesday Book – a thorough census of England's stock and future potential; it's still a vital historical document today.

The end result was the Battle of Hastings of 1066, the most memorable of dates for anyone who has studied English history. William sailed from Normandy with an army, the English were defeated, and King Harold II was killed – by an arrow in the eye, according to legend. William became king of England, earning himself the prestigious epithet Conqueror.

In the years after the invasion, the French-speaking Normans and the English-speaking Anglo-Saxons kept pretty much to themselves. At the top of the feudal system came the monarch, and below that came the landowning nobles: barons and baronesses, dukes and duchesses, plus the bishops. Then came earls, knights and lords – and their ladies. At the bottom were landless peasants or 'serfs', and this strict hierarchy became the basis of a class system that to a certain extent still exists in England today.

Royal & Holy Squabbling

William's successor, William II, was assassinated during a hunting trip and was succeeded by Henry I, then Stephen of Blois, then Henry II who established the House of Plantagenet. This period also established the long-standing English tradition of competition for the throne, and introduced an equally enduring tendency of bickering between royalty and the Church. Things came to a head in 1170 when Henry II had the 'turbulent priest' Thomas Becket murdered in Canterbury Cathedral.

Perhaps the next king, Richard I, wanted to make amends for his forebears' unholy sentiments by fighting against what were then seen as Muslim 'infidels' in the Holy Land (today's Israel and the Palestinian Territories, plus parts of Syria, Jordan and Lebanon). Unfortunately, Richard was too busy crusading to govern England – although his battles earned him the sobriquet Lionheart – and in his absence the country fell into disarray.

Richard was succeeded by his brother John. According to legend, it was during this time that a nobleman named Robert of Loxley, better known as Robin Hood, hid in Sherwood Forest and engaged in a spot of wealth redistribution.

Plantagenet Progress

By the early 13th century King John's erratic rule was too much for the powerful barons, and they forced him to affirm a document called the Magna Carta (Great Charter), which set limits on the power of the monarch. It was signed at Runnymede, near Windsor; you can still visit the site today.

The next king was Henry III, followed in 1272 by Edward I – a skilled ruler and ambitious general. During a busy 35-year reign, he was unashamedly expansionist, leading campaigns into Wales and Scotland, where his ruthless activities earned him the title 'Hammer of the Scots'.

Myths and Legends of the British Isles by Richard Barber is an ideal read if you want a break from firm historical facts. Learn about King Arthur and the Knights of the Round Table, plus much more from the mists of time.

The Year 1000 by Robert Lacey and Danny Danziger looks long and hard at English life a millennium ago. Apparently it was cold and damp then, too.

1096	12th century	1215	1337–1453
The official start of the First Crusade – a campaign of Christian European armies against the Muslim occupation of Jerusalem and the 'Holy Land'. A series of crusades continues until 1272.	Oxford University founded. There's evidence of teaching in the area since 1096, but King Henry II's 1167 ban on students attending the University of Paris solidifies Oxford's importance.	King John signs the Magna Carta, limiting the monarch's power for the first time in English history: an early step on the path towards constitutional rule.	England battles France in a long conflict known as the Hundred Years' War. It was actually a series of small conflicts. And it lasted for more than a century too…

WHO'D WANT TO BE A KING?

The gallop through the story of England's ruling dynasties clearly shows that life is never dull for the person at the top. Despite immense power and privilege, the position of monarch (or, perhaps worse, *potential* monarch) probably ranks as one of history's least safe occupations. English kings to meet an untimely end include Harold II (killed in battle), William II (assassinated), Charles I (beheaded by Republicans), Edward V (allegedly murdered by an uncle), Richard II (probably starved to death), James II (deposed), Edward II (dispatched by his queen and her lover) and William III (died after his horse tripped over a molehill). As you visit the castles and battlefields of England, you may feel a touch of sympathy – but only a touch – for those all-powerful figures continually looking over their shoulders.

Edward I was succeeded by Edward II, who lacked his forebear's military success. He failed in the marriage department too, and came to a grisly end when, it's thought, his wife Isabella and her lover Roger Mortimer had him murdered in Berkeley Castle. Today, fans of ghoulish ends can visit the very spot where it happened.

Houses of Lancaster & York

In 1399 Richard II was ousted by a powerful baron called Henry Bolingbroke, who became Henry IV – the first monarch of the House of Lancaster. He was followed, neatly, by Henry V, who decided it was time to end the Hundred Years' War, a long-standing conflict between England and France. Henry's victory at the Battle of Agincourt and the patriotic speech he was given by Shakespeare in his namesake play ('cry God for Harry, England and St George!') ensured his position among the most famous of English monarchs.

Still keeping things neat, Henry V was followed by Henry VI. His main claims to fame were overseeing the building of great places of worship – King's College Chapel, in Cambridge; Eton Chapel, near Windsor – and suffering from great bouts of insanity.

The Hundred Years' War finally ground to a halt in 1453, but just a few years later, England was plunged into a civil conflict dubbed the Wars of the Roses. Briefly it went like this: Henry VI of the House of Lancaster (emblem: a red rose) was challenged by Richard, Duke of York (emblem: a white rose). Henry was weak and it was almost a walkover for Richard, but Henry's wife, Margaret of Anjou, was made of sterner stuff and her forces defeated the challenger. Then Richard's son Edward entered with an army, turned the tables, drove out Henry and became King Edward IV – the first monarch of the House of York.

The Isles: A History by Norman Davies provides much-acclaimed and highly readable coverage of the past 10,000 years in England, within the broader history of the British Isles.

1348	1415	1455–85	1485
The arrival of the Black Death. Commonly attributed to bubonic plague, the pandemic kills more than 1.5 million people, over a third of the country's population.	The invading English army under Henry V defeats the French army at the Battle of Agincourt – a crucial battle in the Hundred Years' War. (The war itself continues for almost another 40 years.)	The Wars of the Roses: a conflict between two competing dynasties – the Houses of Lancaster and York. The Yorkists are successful, and King Edward IV gains the throne.	Henry Tudor defeats Richard III at the Battle of Bosworth to become King Henry VII, establishing the Tudor dynasty and ending York–Lancaster rivalry for the throne.

Dark Deeds in the Tower

Edward IV hardly had time to catch his breath before facing a challenge from the Earl of Warwick, who teamed up with the energetic Margaret of Anjou to shuttle Edward into exile and bring Henry VI back to the throne. A year later Edward IV came bouncing back, killed Warwick, captured Margaret and had Henry executed in the Tower of London.

Edward IV was succeeded by his 12-year-old son, Edward V. But in 1483 the boy-king was mysteriously murdered, along with his brother, and once again the Tower of London was the scene of the crime.

With the 'little princes' dispatched, the throne was open for their uncle Richard. Whether he was the princes' killer remains the subject of debate, but his rule as Richard III was short-lived: in 1485 he was tumbled from the top job by a Welsh nobleman (from the rival Lancastrian line) named Henry Tudor, who became King Henry VII.

Peace & Dissolution

With the Wars of the Roses only recently ended, Henry VII married Elizabeth of York, so uniting the House of Lancaster and the House of York. He adopted the 'Tudor rose' symbol, which features the flower in both colours. Henry also married off his daughter to James IV of Scotland, linking the Tudor and Stuart lines. The result? A much-welcomed period of peace for England.

The next king, Henry VIII, is one of England's best-known monarchs, mainly thanks to his six wives – the result of a desperate quest for a male heir. He also had a profound impact on England's religious history; his rift with the Pope and the Roman Catholic Church led to the separation of the Church of England from papal rule, and to the 'Dissolution' – the infamous closure of many monasteries, the ruins of which can still be seen today at places such as Fountains Abbey and Rievaulx Abbey in Yorkshire.

The Elizabethan Age

Henry VIII was succeeded by his son Edward VI, and his daughter Mary I, but their reigns were short. And so Elizabeth, third in line, unexpectedly came to the throne.

Elizabeth I inherited a nasty mess of religious strife and divided loyalties, but after an uncertain start she gained confidence and turned the country around. Refusing marriage, she borrowed biblical motifs and became known as the Virgin Queen – perhaps the first English monarch to create a cult image.

The big moments in her 45-year reign included the naval defeat of the Spanish Armada, the far-flung explorations of English seafarers Walter Raleigh and Francis Drake, and the expansion of England's trading

Today, more than 500 years after the Wars of the Roses, Yorkshire's symbol is still a white rose, while Lancashire's is still a red rose, and rivalry between these two counties is still very strong – especially when it comes to cricket and football.

Hilary Mantel's Booker Prize–winning *Wolf Hall*, and its sequel *Bring Up the Bodies*, explore the rise to power of Thomas Cromwell and the wider machinations of Henry VIII's court. The third and final instalment, *The Mirror and the Light*, was due to be published in 2019.

1509–47	1558–1603	1605	1644–49
Reign of King Henry VIII. The Pope's disapproval of Henry's serial marriages and divorces partly prompts the English Reformation – the founding of the Church of England.	Reign of Queen Elizabeth I, a period of boundless English optimism. Enter stage right playwright William Shakespeare. Exit due west navigators Walter Raleigh and Francis Drake.	King James' attempts to smooth religious relations are set back by an anti-Catholic outcry following the infamous Gunpowder Plot, a terrorist attempt to blow up parliament led by Guy Fawkes.	Civil War. Royalist forces supporting the king are pitted against Oliver Cromwell's army of 'Parliamentarians'. Cromwell is victorious, and England becomes a republic.

network, including newly established colonies on the east coast of America – not to mention a cultural flourishing, thanks to writers such as William Shakespeare and Christopher Marlowe.

Meanwhile, Elizabeth's Catholic cousin Mary Stuart (daughter of Scottish king James V) had become queen of Scotland. She'd spent her childhood in France, marrying the French dauphin (crown prince), thereby becoming queen of France as well. After her husband's death (so no longer France's queen), Mary returned to Scotland to rule but was eventually forced to abdicate amid claims of infidelity and murder.

She escaped to England and appealed to Elizabeth for help. But Mary had a strong claim to the English throne. That made her a security risk and she was imprisoned by Elizabeth. Historians dispute whether the former Scottish queen then instigated or was simply the focus of numerous Catholic plots to assassinate Protestant Elizabeth and put Mary on the throne. Either way, Elizabeth held Mary under arrest for nearly 19 years, moving her frequently from house to house. As you travel around England today, you can visit many stately homes (and even a few pubs) that proudly claim, 'Mary Queen of Scots slept here'. Elizabeth eventually ordered Mary's execution in 1587.

The movie *Elizabeth*, directed by Shekhar Kapur (1998) and starring Cate Blanchett, covers the early years of the Virgin Queen's rule, as she graduates from princess to commanding monarch – a time of forbidden love, unwanted suitors, intrigue and death.

United & Disunited Britain

Elizabeth died in 1603, but despite a bountiful reign, the Virgin Queen had failed to provide an heir. She was succeeded by her closest relative, the Scottish king James, the safely Protestant son of the executed Mary. Thus, he became James I of England and VI of Scotland, the first English monarch of the House of Stuart. James did his best to soothe Catholic–Protestant tensions and united England, Wales and Scotland into one kingdom for the first time – another step towards British unity, at least on paper.

But the divide between king and parliament continued to smoulder, and the power struggle worsened during the reign of Charles I, eventually degenerating into the English Civil War. The antiroyalist (or 'Parliamentarian') forces were led by Oliver Cromwell, a Puritan who preached against the excesses of the monarchy and established Church. His army (known as the Roundheads) was pitched against the king's forces (the Cavaliers) in a conflict that tore England apart. It ended with victory for the Roundheads – the king was executed and England declared a republic, with Cromwell hailed as 'Protector'.

The Return of the King

By 1653 Cromwell was finding parliament too restricting and assumed dictatorial powers, much to his supporters' dismay. On his death in 1658, he was followed half-heartedly by his son, but in 1660 parliament decid-

1660	1749	1775–83	1799–1815
After Cromwell's death, conflicting interests beset the republic. The eldest son of Charles I is invited back to take the throne. Charles II is crowned, and the monarchy is restored (the Restoration).	Author and magistrate Henry Fielding founds the Bow Street Runners, London's first professional police force. A 1792 Act of Parliament allowed the Bow Street model to spread across England.	The American War of Independence is the British Empire's first major reversal. William Pitt the Younger becomes the country's youngest-ever prime minister at the age of 24.	The Napoleonic Wars see a weakened Britain threatened with invasion by Napoleon, whose ambitions are curtailed at the famous battles of Trafalgar (1805) and Waterloo (1815).

ed to re-establish the monarchy, as republican alternatives were proving far worse.

Charles II (the exiled son of Charles I) came to the throne, and his rule – known as 'the Restoration' – saw scientific and cultural activity bursting forth after the strait-laced ethics of Cromwell's time. Exploration and expansion were also on the agenda. Backed by the army and navy (which had been modernised by Cromwell), colonies stretched down the American coast, while the East India Company set up headquarters in Bombay, laying foundations for what was to become the British Empire.

The next king, James II, had a harder time. Attempts to ease restrictive laws on Catholics ended with his overthrow and defeat at the Battle of the Boyne by William III, the Protestant king of Holland, aka William of Orange. William was married to James' daughter Mary. William and Mary had equal rights to the throne, and their joint accession in 1689 was known as the Glorious Revolution.

Empire Building

By 1702, both Mary and William had died. They were succeeded by William's sister-in-law, Anne. During her reign, in 1707, the Act of Union was passed, uniting England, Wales and Scotland under one parliament – based in London – for the first time.

Queen Anne died without an heir in 1714, marking the end of the Stuart line. The throne passed to distant (but still safely Protestant) German relatives – the House of Hanover, commonly known as the Georgians.

Meanwhile, the British Empire continued to grow in the Americas as well as in Asia, while claims were made to Australia after James Cook's epic voyage of 1769.

The Industrial Era

While the Empire expanded abroad, at home Britain had become the crucible of the Industrial Revolution. Steam power (pioneered by James Watt in the 1760s and 1770s) and steam trains (developed by George Stephenson in the 1820s) transformed methods of production and transport, and the towns of the English Midlands became the first industrial cities.

Industrial growth led to Britain's first major period of internal migration, as vast numbers of people from the countryside came to the cities in search of work. At the same time, medical advances improved life expectancy, creating a sharp population increase. For many ordinary people the effects of Britain's economic blossoming were dislocation and poverty.

But despite the social turmoil of the early 19th century, by the time Queen Victoria took the throne in 1837 Britain's factories and fleets

---

At its height, the British Empire covered 20% of the land area of the earth and contained a quarter of the world's population.

Captain James Cook's voyage to the southern hemisphere was primarily a scientific expedition. His objectives included monitoring the transit of Venus, an astronomical event that happens only twice every 180 years or so (most recently in 2004 and 2012). 'Discovering' Australia was just a sideline.

1837–1901	1914	1939–45	1945
Reign of Queen Victoria. The British Empire – 'the Empire where the sun never sets' – expands from Canada through Africa and India to Australia and New Zealand.	Archduke Franz Ferdinand of Austria is assassinated in the Balkan city of Sarajevo – the final spark in a decade-long crisis that starts the Great War, now called WWI.	WWII rages across Europe, and much of Africa and Asia. Britain and Allies, including America, Russia, Australia, India and New Zealand, eventually defeat the armies of Germany, Japan and Italy.	WWII ends, and in the immediate postwar election the Labour Party under Clement Attlee defeats the Conservatives under Winston Churchill, despite the latter's pivotal role in Britain's WWII victory.

dominated world trade. The rest of the 19th century was seen as Britain's Golden Age – a period of patriotic confidence not seen since the days of the last great queen, Elizabeth I.

The times were optimistic, but it wasn't all tub-thumping jingoism. Prime Minister Disraeli and his successor, William Gladstone, also introduced social reforms to address the exploitative excesses of the Industrial Revolution. Education became universal, trade unions were legalised and the right to vote was extended in a series of reform acts, finally being granted to all men over the age of 21 in 1918, and to all women in 1928.

World War I

When Queen Victoria died in 1901 the country entered a period of decline. Meanwhile, in continental Europe, the military powers of Russia, Austria-Hungary, Turkey and Germany were sabre-rattling in the Balkan states, a dispute that eventually started the 'Great War' (now known as WWI). By the war's weary end in 1918, millions had died, with hardly a street or village untouched, as the sobering lists of names on war memorials all over England still show.

For the soldiers that did return from WWI, disillusion with the old social order helped strengthen the Labour Party – which represented the working class – as a political force, upsetting the balance long enjoyed by the Liberal and Conservative parties.

Labour came to power for the first time, in coalition with the Liberals, in the 1923 election, but by the mid-1920s the Conservatives were back. The world economy was now in decline and industrial unrest had become widespread.

The situation worsened in the 1930s as the Great Depression meant another decade of misery and political upheaval, and even the royal family took a knock when Edward VIII abdicated in 1936 so he could marry Wallis Simpson, a woman who was twice divorced and – horror of horrors – American.

World War II

The next monarch was Edward's less charismatic brother, George VI. Britain dithered through the rest of the decade, with mediocre governments failing to confront the country's deep-set problems.

Meanwhile, Adolf Hitler came to power in Germany and in 1939 invaded Poland. Two days later Britain was once again at war. The German army swept through Europe and pushed back British forces to the beaches of Dunkirk, in northern France. In June 1940 an extraordinary flotilla of tiny, private vessels (the 'Little Ships') turned total disaster into a brave defeat – and Dunkirk Day is still remembered with pride and sadness in Britain every year.

A History of England in a Nutshell by John Mathew provides exactly what it says on the cover: a quick overview of the nation's key events in less than 200 pages.

One of the finest novels about WWI is *Birdsong* by Sebastian Faulks. Understated, perfectly paced and intensely moving, it tells of passion, fear, waste, incompetent generals and the poor bloody infantry.

1948	1952	1960–66	1971
Aneurin Bevan, the health minister in the Labour government, launches the National Health Service: free medical care for all – the core of Britain as a 'welfare state'.	Princess Elizabeth becomes Queen Elizabeth II when her father, George VI, dies. Her coronation takes place in Westminster Abbey in June 1953.	The era of African and Caribbean independence brings the freedom of Nigeria, Tanzania, Jamaica, Trinidad and Tobago, Kenya, Malawi, Gambia and Barbados.	Britain adopts the 'decimal' currency (one pound equals 100 pence) and drops the ancient system of 20 shillings or 240 pennies per pound, the centuries-old bane of school maths lessons.

By mid-1940, most of Europe was controlled by Germany. Russia had negotiated a peace agreement and the USA was neutral, leaving Britain virtually isolated. Into this arena came a new prime minister called Winston Churchill.

Between September 1940 and May 1941, the German air force launched 'the Blitz', a series of (mainly night-time) bombing raids on London and other cities. But morale in Britain remained strong, thanks partly to Churchill's regular radio broadcasts. The USA entered the war after the Japanese bombing of Pearl Harbor, and in late 1941 the tide began to turn.

By 1944 Germany was in retreat. Russia pushed back from the east, and Britain, the USA and other Allies were again on the beaches of

WINSTON CHURCHILL

More than a century after becoming part of the British government, Winston Churchill is still one of the country's best-known political figures. He was born in 1874 and, although from an aristocratic family, his early years were not auspicious; he was famously a 'dunce' at school, an image he actively cultivated in later life.

As a young man, Churchill joined the British Army and also acted as a newspaper war correspondent, writing several books about his exploits. In 1900 he was elected to parliament as a Conservative MP. In 1904 he defected to the Liberals, the main opposition party. A year later, after a Liberal election victory, he became a government minister. Churchill rejoined the Conservatives in 1924, and held various ministerial positions through the rest of the 1920s. Notable statements during this period included calling Mussolini a 'genius' and Gandhi 'a half-naked fakir'.

Churchill criticised Prime Minister Neville Chamberlain's 1938 'appeasement' of Hitler and called for British rearmament to face a growing German threat, but his political life was generally quiet – so he concentrated on writing. His multi-volume *A History of the English-Speaking Peoples* was drafted during this period; although biased and flawed, it remains his best-known work.

In 1939 Britain entered WWII, and by 1940 Churchill was prime minister, taking additional responsibility as minister of defence. Hitler might have expected an easy victory in the war, but Churchill's extraordinary dedication (not to mention his radio speeches – most famously saying he had 'nothing to offer but blood, toil, tears and sweat' and promising to 'fight on the beaches…') inspired the British people to resist.

Between July and October 1940 the Royal Air Force withstood Germany's aerial raids to win what became known as the Battle of Britain – a major turning point in the war, and a chance for land forces to rebuild their strength. Britain's refusal to negotiate terms with Germany and the decision to stand alone against Hitler's forces was an audacious strategy, but it paid off and Churchill was lauded as a national hero – praise that continued beyond his death in 1965 and which continues today (in any survey or poll to find the greatest Englishman or Briton, Churchill inevitably tends to come out on top).

1979	1990	1992	1997
A Conservative government led by Margaret Thatcher wins the general election, a major milestone in Britain's 20th-century history, ushering in a decade of dramatic political and social change.	Thatcher ousted as leader, and the Conservative Party enters a period of decline, but remains in power, partly due to ineffective Labour opposition.	Labour remains divided between 'traditionalists' and 'modernists'. The Conservatives, under new leader John Major, confound the pundits and unexpectedly win the general election.	The general election sees Tony Blair lead 'New' Labour to victory in the polls, with a record-breaking parliamentary majority, ending 18 years of Conservative rule.

France. The Normandy landings (D-Day, as it's remembered) marked the start of the liberation of Europe's western side. By 1945 Hitler was dead and the war was over.

Swinging & Sliding

The aftermath of WWII saw an unexpected swing on the political front. An electorate tired of war tumbled Churchill's Conservatives from power in favour of the Labour Party. There was change abroad too, as parts of the British Empire became independent, including India and Pakistan in 1947 and Malaya in 1957, followed by much of Africa and the Caribbean.

But while the Empire's sun may have been setting, Britain's royal family was still going strong. In 1952 George VI was succeeded by his daughter, Elizabeth II.

By the late 1950s, postwar recovery was strong enough for Prime Minister Harold Macmillan to famously remind the British people they had 'never had it so good'. Some saw this as a boast for a confident future, others as a warning about difficult times ahead. But many people didn't care either way, as the 1960s had arrived and grey old England was suddenly more fun and lively than it had been for generations.

The '60s may have been swinging, but by the 1970s decline had set in, thanks to a combination of inflation, an oil crisis and international competition revealing the weaknesses of Britain's economy. Britain joined the European Economic Community in 1973, with the country voting in a referendum to remain two years later; 67% were in favour of remaining.

The rest of the '70s were marked by strikes, disputes and general all-round gloom, but neither the Conservatives (also known as the Tories) under Prime Minister Edward Heath, nor Labour, under Prime Ministers Harold Wilson and Jim Callaghan, proved capable of controlling the strife. The British public had had enough, and the elections of May 1979 saw the arrival of a new prime minister: a previously little-known politician named Margaret Thatcher.

The Thatcher Years

Soon everyone had heard of Margaret Thatcher. Love her or hate her, no one could argue that her methods weren't dramatic, and many policies had a lasting impact, one of the most prominent being the privatisation of state-run industries that had been nationalised in the late 1940s.

Some commentators argue that in economic terms the Thatcher government's policies were largely successful. Others claim in social terms they were a failure and created a polarised Britain: on one side were the people who gained from the prosperous wave of opportunities in the 'new' industries, while on the other were those who became unemployed

In 2017's *Dunkirk*, British director Christopher Nolan delivered a haunting depiction of the evacuation of British troops from northern France in May 1940. Its stars included Kenneth Branagh, Mark Rylance, Tom Hardy, and pop singer Harry Styles in his first film role.

History Websites

www.royal.gov.uk

www.bbc.co.uk/history

www.victorianweb.org

2003	2007	2010	2014
Britain joins the USA in the invasion of Iraq, initially with some support from parliament and the public – despite large antiwar demonstrations held in London and other cities.	Tony Blair, Britain's longest-serving Labour prime minister, resigns and Gordon Brown, Chancellor of the Exchequer, takes over as Labour leader and prime minister.	Labour is narrowly defeated in the general election as the minority Liberal Democrats align with the Conservatives to form the first coalition government in Britain's postwar history.	Scotland votes in a referendum not to become an independent country (by 55% to 45%), so remaining within the UK. It sparks a debate on the possibility of a separate English parliament.

and dispossessed as the 'old' industries, such as coal mining and steel production, became an increasingly small part of the country's economy.

Despite policies that were frequently described as uncompromising, by 1988 Margaret Thatcher was the longest-serving British prime minister of the 20th century, although her repeated electoral victories were helped considerably by the Labour Party's ineffective campaigns and destructive internal struggles.

From New Labour to Brexit

The pendulum started to swing again in the early 1990s. Margaret Thatcher was replaced as leader by John Major, but the voters still regarded Labour with suspicion, allowing the Conservatives to unexpectedly win the 1992 election. It all came to a head in the 1997 election, when 'New' Labour swept to power under a fresh-faced leader called Tony Blair.

Blair and the Labour Party enjoyed an extended honeymoon period, and the next election (in 2001) was another walkover. The Conservative Party continued to struggle, allowing Labour to win a historic third term in 2005, and a year later Blair became the longest-serving Labour prime minister in British history.

In May 2010 a record 13 years of Labour rule came to an end, and a coalition government (the first in the UK since WWII) was formed between the Conservatives and the Liberal Democrats. It was an experiment that ended disastrously for the Lib Dems at the 2015 general election: they lost 49 seats, and were left with just eight MPs. The same vote left the defeated Labour Party searching for a new identity, and the Conservatives back in sole charge under David Cameron.

But just over a year later, a referendum saw the people of the UK vote, by 52% to 48%, to leave the EU – in defiance of the main parties, which had wanted the country to stay in. Cameron resigned almost immediately after the vote, and was succeeded by former home secretary Theresa May, whose premiership has been marred by wrangling over the Brexit issue – as well as a misjudged decision to hold a snap general election in 2017, which resulted in her losing her majority in a hung parliament in the House of Commons.

May's plan had been to exploit the apparent unpopularity of the Labour leader, Jeremy Corbyn, whose strongly socialist policies had caused division in his own party. But unexpectedly, Corbyn's leftist agenda proved popular with the public – particularly disillusioned younger voters. Whether he'll ever be able to take the final step to power still remains to be seen.

Stalin's Englishman is a fascinating biography of the 'Cambridge Spy', diplomat Guy Burgess, who passed on state secrets to the Russian secret services between the 1930s and 1950s, and ultimately defected to Russia in 1951.

For detail on the 1980s, read *No Such Thing as Society* by Andy McSmith. Drawing on Margaret Thatcher's famous proclamation, this book studies the era dominated by the Iron Lady.

2015	2016	2017	2018
The Conservatives win a surprising 12-seat election majority. Their former coalition partners, the Liberal Democrats, lose 49 seats. Labour is almost wiped out in Scotland. The UK Independence Party secures one seat.	In a referendum on whether to remain within the EU, the UK votes to leave by 52% to 48%. England and Wales vote to leave the EU, but Scotland and Northern Ireland vote to stay in.	Conservatives call a snap general election which results in a hung parliament. Northern Ireland's Democratic Unionist Party (DUP) agrees to support the Conservatives in forming a minority government.	Prince Harry marries American actress Meghan Markle, the first member of the royal family to wed a person of mixed race.

Food & Drink

Wherever you travel in England, for every greasy spoon or fast-food joint, there's a local pub or speciality restaurant serving enticing homemade meals. For decades most towns have boasted Italian, Chinese and Indian restaurants, so spaghetti carbonara, chow mein and vindaloo are no longer considered exotic. London is now regarded as a global gastronomic capital, and it's increasingly easy to find decent food options in other cities, towns and villages across the country.

Meals

For the locals, the English culinary day is punctuated by the three traditional main meals of breakfast, lunch and dinner.

Many towns and cities in England hold regular farmers markets – a good chance for food producers large and small to sell direct to the public. For more info and a searchable database, see www.localfoods.org.uk.

Breakfast

Many people in England make do with toast or a bowl of cereal before dashing to work, but visitors staying in hotels and B&Bs will undoubtedly encounter a phenomenon called the 'Full English Breakfast'. This usually consists of fried bacon, sausages, eggs, tomatoes, mushrooms, baked beans and fried bread. If you don't feel like eating half a farmyard first thing in the morning, it's OK to ask for just the eggs and tomatoes, for example. Some B&Bs offer other alternatives such as kippers (smoked fish) or a 'continental breakfast', which completely omits the cooked stuff and may even add something exotic like croissants.

Lunch

One of the many great inventions that England gave the world is the sandwich, often eaten as a midday meal. Slapping a slice of cheese or ham between two bits of bread may seem a simple concept, but no one apparently thought of it until the 18th century: the Earl of Sandwich (his title comes from a town in southeast England that originally got its name from the Viking word for 'sandy beach') ordered his servants to bring cold meat between bread so he could keep working at his desk or, as some historians claim, keep playing cards late at night.

Another English classic is the ploughman's lunch. Basically it's bread, cheese and pickles, and although hearty yokels probably did carry such food to the fields in the days of yore, the meal was actually invented in the 1960s by the national cheesemakers' organisation to boost consumption, neatly cashing in on public nostalgia and fondness for tradition.

You can still find a basic ploughman's lunch offered in some pubs – and it undeniably goes well with a pint or two of local ale at lunchtime – but these days the meal has usually been smartened up to include butter, salad and dressings. At some pubs you get a selection of cheeses. You'll also find other variations, such as a farmer's lunch (bread and chicken), stockman's lunch (bread and ham), Frenchman's lunch (Brie and baguette) and fisherman's lunch (you guessed it, with fish).

Dinner

Depending on where you are in England, the evening meal is variously described as dinner, supper or often (and rather confusingly) – tea, but regardless it's generally the main meal of the day. While the traditional idea of 'meat and two veg' was an evening staple for many decades, the English have embraced global cuisine with gusto, and you're just as likely to find a curry, a pizza or a bowl of pasta on the dinner table as you are a serving of chops, chips and peas. The popularity of TV cooking shows and the profusion of celebrity chef cookbooks has helped expand England's culinary repertoire exponentially in recent years, and these days most English people are pretty cosmopolitan in their tastes.

One tradition that hasn't changed all that much is the roast dinner, customarily eaten for Sunday lunch. The classic is roast beef (always 'roast', never 'roasted') accompanied by Yorkshire pudding (portions of crispy baked batter). Another classic English dish brings Yorkshire pudding and sausages together, with the delightful name of 'toad-in-the-hole'.

Yorkshire pudding also turns up in another guise, especially in pubs and cafes in northern England, where a big bowl-shaped pudding is filled with stew, gravy or vegetables. You can even find multicultural crossover Yorkshire puddings filled with curry.

Perhaps the best-known classic English meal is fish and chips, often bought from the 'chippie' as a takeaway wrapped in paper to eat on the spot or enjoy at home. For visitors, English fish and chips can be an acquired taste. Sometimes the chips can be limp and the fish tasteless, especially once you get away from the sea, but in towns with salt in the air this classic deep-fried delight is always worth trying.

In Yorkshire, the eponymous pudding is traditionally a *starter*, a reminder of days when food was scarce and the pudding was a pre-meal stomach filler.

Dessert

After the main course – usually at an evening meal, or if you're enjoying a hearty lunch – comes dessert or 'pudding'. A classic English pudding is apple or rhubarb crumble, in which the baked fruit is topped with a crunchy 'crumble' made with flour, butter and sugar. It's usually served with custard or ice cream. Other favourites include treacle sponge (sponge cake in a sweet, sticky, caramel-like sauce), sticky toffee (made with dates and a toffee sauce), bread-and-butter pudding (slices of buttered bread cooked with raisins and custard – nicer than it sounds) and plum pudding (a dome-shaped cake with fruit, nuts and brandy or rum, traditionally eaten at Christmas).

Regional Specialities

With the country's large coastline, it's no surprise that seafood is a speciality in many English regions. Yorkshire's seaside resorts are particularly famous for huge servings of cod – certified as sustainable after years of decline – while restaurants in Devon and Cornwall conjure up prawns, oysters, mussels, crab, lobster and scallops. Other local seafood you may

THE CORNISH PASTY

A favourite speciality in southwest England is the Cornish pasty: a mix of beef, potato, onion and swede, baked in a pastry casing that's been crimped on the side. Invented long before Tupperware, the pasty was an all-in-one-lunch pack that tin miners carried underground and left on a ledge ready for mealtime. So pasties weren't mixed up, they were marked with their owners' initials – always at one end, so the miner could eat half and safely leave the rest to snack on later without it mistakenly disappearing into the mouth of a workmate. Before going back to the surface, the miners traditionally left the last few crumbs of the pasty as a gift for the spirits of the mine, known as 'knockers', to ensure a safe shift the next day.

In 2011, the pasty was awarded 'protected geographical indication' (PGI) status by the EU, meaning that by law, only pasties made in Cornwall can be called Cornish pasties – the same accolade enjoyed by Champagne and Parma ham.

encounter elsewhere on your travels include Norfolk crab and Northumberland kippers.

In northern and central England you'll find the Cumberland sausage – a tasty mix of minced pork and herbs, so large it has to be spiralled to fit on your plate. Look out too for Melton Mowbray pork pies – cooked ham in a casing of pastry, eaten cold. A legal victory in 2005 ensured that only pies from the eponymous Midlands town could carry the Melton Mowbray moniker, in the same way that only fizzy wine from the Champagne region of France can carry that name. Another English speciality that enjoys the same protection is Stilton – a strong white cheese, either plain or in a blue-vein variety. Only five dairies in all of England are allowed to produce cheese with this name.

Perhaps less appealing is black pudding, a large sausage made with pig's blood and oatmeal, and traditionally served for breakfast in northern England.

The experimental chef Heston Blumenthal made his name by taking a 'mad professor' approach to cooking, known as 'molecular cuisine' – resulting in such outlandish dishes as bacon-and-eggs ice cream, snail porridge, lickable wallpaper and edible tableware.

Eating Out

In England, 'eating out' means simply going to a restaurant or cafe – anywhere away from home. There's a huge choice across the country.

Picnics & Self-Catering

When shopping for food, as well as the more obvious chain stores and corner shops, markets can be a great place for bargains – everything from dented tins of tomatoes to home-baked cakes and organic goats cheese. Farmers markets are always worth a visit; they're a great way for producers to sell good food direct to consumers, with both sides avoiding the grip of the supermarkets.

Cafes & Teashops

The traditional English cafe is nothing like its continental European namesake. Most are basic, no-frills establishments serving simple meals, such as pies, beans on toast, baked potato or omelette with chips (costing around £3 to £6), and stuff like sandwiches, cakes and other snacks (£2 to £3). Quality varies enormously: some cafes definitely earn their 'greasy spoon' handle, while others are neat and clean.

In London and some other cities, a rearguard of classic cafes – with Formica tables, seats in booths and decor unchanged from their 1950s glory days – stand against the onslaught of the international chains. In rural areas, many market towns and villages have cafes catering to tourists, walkers, cyclists and other outdoor types, and in summer they're open every day. Whether you're in town or country, good English cafes are a wonderful institution and always worth a stop during your travels.

Smarter cafes are called teashops or tearooms (generally found in rural areas), where you pay a bit more for extras such as neat decor and table service.

In the 16th century Queen Elizabeth I decreed that mutton could only be served with bitter herbs – intended to stop people eating sheep in order to help the wool trade – but her subjects discovered mint sauce, and it's been a favourite condiment ever since.

As well as the traditional establishments, in most cities and towns you'll also find a growing number of specialist coffee shops (both chain and independent), serving cappuccinos, lattes and espressos, and offering bagels or ciabattas rather than beans on toast.

Restaurants

We've taken great pleasure in seeking out some of the best and best-value restaurants in England. Prices vary considerably across the country, with a main course in a straightforward restaurant costing around £10 or less, and anywhere between £10 and £20 at midrange places. Excellent food, service and surroundings can be enjoyed for £20 to £50 – although in London you can, if you want, pay double this.

NO SMOKING, PLEASE

All restaurants and cafes in England are nonsmoking throughout. Pubs have the same rule, which is why there's often a small crowd of smokers standing on the pavement outside. Some pubs provide specific outdoor smoking areas, ranging from a simple yard to elaborate gazebos with canvas walls and the full complement of lighting, heating, piped music and TV screens – you'd never need to know you were 'outside' at all, apart from the pungent clouds of burning tobacco.

For vegetarians, England is not too bad. Many restaurants and pubs have at least one token vegetarian dish, while better places offer much more imaginative choices. Vegans will find the going trickier, except of course at dedicated veggie/vegan restaurants.

Pubs & Gastropubs

Not so many years ago, a pub was the place to go for a drink. And that was it. If you felt peckish, your choice might be a ham or cheese sandwich, with pickled onions if you were lucky. Today many pubs serve a wide range of food, and it's usually a good-value option, whether you want a toasted sandwich between museum visits in London, or a three-course meal in the evening after touring castles and stately homes in Yorkshire.

While the food in many pubs is good quality and good value, some places raised the bar to such a degree that a whole new genre of eatery – the gastropub – was born. The finest gastropubs are effectively restaurants (with smart decor, neat menus and uniformed table service; a few have won Michelin stars). For visitors relaxing after a hard day's sightseeing, nothing beats the luxury of a wholesome shepherd's pie washed down with a decent ale without the worry of guessing which fork to use.

Drinking

The two beverages most associated with England are probably tea and beer. Both are unlike drinks of the same name found elsewhere in the world, and well worth trying on your travels around the country.

The Campaign for Real Ale (Camra) promotes the understanding of traditional British beer. Look for endorsement stickers on pub windows, and for more info see www.camra.org.uk.

What To Drink

Tea & Coffee

In England, if a local asks 'Would you like a drink?' don't automatically expect a gin and tonic. They may well mean a 'cuppa' (cup of tea), England's best-known beverage. It's usually made with dark tea leaves to produce a strong brown drink, more bitter in taste than tea served in some other Western countries, which is partly why it's usually served with a dash of milk.

Although tea is often billed as the national drink, tea consumption fell by around 20% in the five years to 2015 and coffee is becoming ever more popular. The British coffee-shop market is worth almost £8 billion a year, but with the prices some coffee shops charge, maybe that's not surprising. A final word of warning: when you're ordering a coffee and the server says 'white or black', don't panic. It simply means 'do you want milk in it?'

Beer, Wine & Cider

Among alcoholic drinks, England is probably best known for its beer. As you travel around the country you should definitely try some local brews. English beer typically ranges from dark brown to bright amber

FOOD & DRINK GLOSSARY

aubergine – large purple-skinned vegetable; 'eggplant' in the USA and Australia

bangers – sausages (colloquial)

bap – a large, wide, flat, soft bread roll

bevvy – drink (slang; originally from northern England)

bill – the total you need to pay after eating in a restaurant ('check' to Americans)

bitter – ale; a type of beer

black pudding – a type of sausage made from dried blood and other ingredients

bun – bread roll, usually sweet, eg currant bun, cream bun

BYO – bring your own (usually in the context of bringing your own drink to a restaurant)

caff – abbreviated form of cafe

candy floss – light sugar-based confectionery; called 'cotton candy' in the USA, 'fairy floss' in Australia

chips – sliced, deep-fried potatoes, eaten hot (what Americans call 'fries')

cider – beer made from apples

clotted cream – cream so heavy or rich that it's become almost solid (but not sour)

corkage – a small charge levied by the restaurant when you BYO

courgette – green vegetable ('zucchini' to Americans and Australians)

cream cracker – white, unsalted savoury biscuit

cream tea – cup of tea and a scone loaded with jam and cream

crisps – thin slices of fried potato bought in a packet, eaten cold; called 'chips' or 'potato chips' in the USA and Australia

crumpet – circular piece of doughy bread, toasted before eating, usually covered with butter

double cream – heavy or thick cream

dram – whisky measure

in colour, and is usually served at room temperature. Technically it's ale, but it's often called 'bitter'. This is to distinguish it from lager (the drink that most of the rest of the word calls 'beer'), which is generally yellow and served cold.

Beer that's brewed and served traditionally is called 'real ale' to distinguish it from mass-produced brands, and there are many regional varieties. But be ready! If you're used to the 'amber nectar' or 'king of beers', a traditional British brew may come as a shock – a warm, flat and expensive shock. This is partly to do with Britain's climate, and partly to do with the beer being served by hand pump rather than gas pressure. Most important, though, is the integral flavour: traditional British beer doesn't need to be chilled or fizzed to make it palatable.

A new breed of microbreweries has sprung up over the last decade, producing their own varieties of traditional and innovative brews, usually referred to as 'craft beers'. Outside of the microbrewery's own bar, these are usually only available in bottles.

On hot summer days, you could go for shandy – beer and lemonade mixed in equal quantities. You'll usually need to specify 'lager shandy' or 'bitter shandy'. It may seem an astonishing combination for outsiders, but it's very refreshing and of course not very strong.

fish fingers – strips of fish pieces covered in breadcrumbs, usually bought frozen and cooked by frying or grilling

greasy spoon – cheap cafe (colloquial)

ice lolly – flavoured ice on a stick; called 'popsicle' in the USA, 'icy pole' in Australia

icing – thick, sweet and solid covering on a cake

jam – fruit conserve often spread on bread

jelly – sweet dessert of flavoured gelatine; called 'jello' in the USA

joint – cut of meat used for roasting

kippers – salted and smoked fish, traditionally herring

pickle – food, usually vegetables (eg onions or beetroot), preserved in vinegar

Pimm's – popular English spirit mixed with lemonade, mint and fresh fruit

pint – beer (as in 'let me buy you a pint')

pop – fizzy drink

salad cream – creamy, vinegary salad dressing, much sharper than mayonnaise

scrumpy – a type of strong dry cider

shandy – beer and lemonade mixed together in equal quantities

shepherd's pie – two-layered dish with a ground beef and onion mixture on the bottom and mashed potato on the top, cooked in an oven

shout – to buy a group of people drinks, usually reciprocated (colloquial)

single cream – light cream (to distinguish from *double cream* and *clotted cream*)

snug – a small room in a pub, usually just inside the door

squash – fruit-drink concentrate mixed with water

stout – dark, full-bodied beer made from malt; Guinness is the most famous variety

swede – large root vegetable; sometimes called 'yellow turnip' or 'rutabaga' in the USA

sweets – what Americans call 'candy' and Australians call 'lollies'

treacle – dark treacle is molasses, but in England treacle often means golden syrup

Another option is cider, available in sweet and dry varieties and, increasingly, as 'craft cider', often with various fruit or herbal flavours added. In western and southwestern counties, you could try 'scrumpy', a very strong dry cider traditionally made from local apples.

Many visitors are surprised to learn that wine is produced in England, and has been since the time of the Romans. Today more than 400 vineyards and wineries produce around two million bottles a year, many winning major awards. English white sparkling wines have been a particular success story, especially those produced in the southeast, where the growing conditions are similar to those of the Champagne region in France.

Where to Drink

In England, the difference between a bar and a pub is sometimes vague, but generally bars are smarter and louder than pubs, possibly with a younger crowd. Drinks are more expensive too, unless there's a gallon-of-vodka-and-Red-Bull-for-a-fiver promotion – which there often is.

As well as beer and wine, pubs and bars offer the usual choice of spirits, often served with a 'mixer', producing English favourites such as gin and tonic, rum and coke or vodka and lime. These drinks are served in

THE OLDEST PUB IN ENGLAND?

Many drinkers are often surprised to learn that the word 'pub' (short for 'public house'), although apparently steeped in history, dates only from the 19th century. But places selling beer have been around for much longer, and 'the oldest pub in England' is a hotly contested title.

One of the country's oldest pubs, with the paperwork to prove it, is Ye Olde Trip to Jerusalem (p436) in Nottingham, which was serving ale to departing crusaders in the 12th century.

Other contenders dismiss Ye Olde Trip as a mere newcomer. A fine old inn called the Royalist Hotel in Stow-on-the-Wold, Gloucestershire, claims to have been selling beer since AD 947, while another pub called Ye Olde Fighting Cocks in St Albans (Hertford-shire) apparently dates back to the 8th century – although the 13th is more likely.

But then back comes Ye Olde Trip with a counterclaim: one of its bars is a cave hollowed out of living rock, and that's more than a million years old.

measures called 'singles' and 'doubles'. A single is usually 35ml – just over one US fluid ounce.

And finally, two tips: first, if you see a pub called a 'free house', it means it doesn't belong to a brewery or pub company, and thus is 'free' to sell any brand of beer. Unfortunately, it doesn't mean the booze is free of charge. Second, remember that drinks in English pubs are ordered and paid for at the bar. You can always spot the freshly arrived tourists – they're the ones sitting forlornly at an empty table hoping to spot a server.

When it comes to gratuities, it's not usual to tip pub and bar staff. However, if you're ordering a large round, or the service has been good all evening, you can say to the person behind the bar '…and one for yourself'. They may not have a drink, but they'll add the monetary equivalent to the total you pay and keep it as a tip.

English Architecture

England's architecture spans some five millennia, ranging from the mysterious stone circle of Stonehenge to London's glittering skyscrapers. If you know what to look for, a veritable design timeline can be traced through any of England's villages, towns and cities, and getting to grips with styles from different eras will greatly enhance your stay. Prepare for Roman baths, parish churches, mighty castles, magnificent cathedrals, humble cottages and grand stately homes.

Early Foundations

The oldest surviving structures in England are the grass-covered mounds of earth, called 'tumuli' or 'barrows', used as burial sites by England's prehistoric residents. These mounds – measuring anything from a rough semisphere just 2m high to much larger, elongated semiovoids 5m high and 10m long – are dotted across the countryside from Cornwall to Cumbria, and are especially common in chalk areas such as Salisbury Plain and the Wiltshire Downs in southern England.

Perhaps the most famous chalk mound – and certainly the largest and most mysterious – is Silbury Hill, near Marlborough. Archaeologists are not sure exactly why this 40m-high conical mound was built – there's no evidence of it actually being used for burial. Theories suggest it was used in cultural ceremonies or as part of the worship of deities in the style of South American pyramids. Whatever its original purpose, it still remains impressive, more than four millennia after it was built.

Even more impressive than giant tumuli are another legacy of the Neolithic era: menhirs (standing stones), especially when they're set out in rings. These include the iconic stone circle of Stonehenge and the even larger Avebury Stone Circle, both in Wiltshire. Again, their original purpose is a mystery, providing fertile ground for hypothesis and speculation. The most recent theories suggest Stonehenge may have been a place of pilgrimage for the sick, like modern-day Lourdes, though it was also used as a burial ground and as a place of ancestor worship.

The construction of Stonehenge pushed the limits of technology in the Neolithic era. Some giant menhirs were transported a great distance, and many were shaped slightly wider at the top to take account of perspective – a trick used by the Greeks many centuries later.

Bronze Age & Iron Age

Compared with the large stone circles of the Neolithic era, the surviving architecture of the Bronze Age is on a more domestic scale. Hut circles from this period can still be seen in several parts of England, most notably on Dartmoor.

By the time we reach the Iron Age, the early peoples of England were organising themselves into clans or tribes. Their legacy includes the remains of the forts they built to defend territory and protect themselves from rival tribes or other invaders. Most forts consisted of a large circular or oval ditch, with a steep mound of earth behind. A famous example is Maiden Castle in Dorset.

There are more than a thousand Iron Age hill forts in England. Impressive examples include Danebury Ring, Hampshire; Barbury Castle, Wiltshire; Uffington Castle, Oxfordshire; Carl Wark, Derbyshire; Cadbury Castle, Somerset; and the immense Maiden Castle, Dorset.

The Roman Era

Roman remains are found in many English towns and cities, including Chester, Exeter and St Albans – as well as the lavish Roman spa and bathing complex in Bath. But England's largest and most impressive Roman relic is the 73-mile sweep of Hadrian's Wall, built in the 2nd century AD as a defensive line stretching coast to coast across the neck of northern England, in a line from modern-day Newcastle to Carlisle. Originally built to separate marauding Pictish warriors to the north of the wall (in modern Scotland) from the Empire's territories to the south, it later became as much a symbol of Roman power as a necessary defence mechanism.

Medieval Masterpieces

In the centuries following the Norman Conquest of 1066, the perfection of the mason's art saw an explosion of architecture in stone, inspired by the two most pressing concerns of the day: religion and defence. Early structures of timber and rubble were replaced with churches, abbeys and monasteries built in dressed stone. The round arches, squat towers and chevron decoration of the Norman or Romanesque style (11th to 12th centuries) slowly evolved into the tall pointed arches, ribbed vaults and soaring spires of the Gothic (13th to 16th centuries), a history that can often be seen all in the one church – construction usually took a couple of hundred years to complete. Many cathedrals remain significant landmarks, such as Salisbury, Winchester, Canterbury and York.

Stone was also put to good use in the building of elaborate defensive structures. Castles range from the atmospheric ruins of Tintagel and Dunstanburgh, and the feudal keeps of Lancaster and Bamburgh, to the sturdy fortresses of Warwick and Windsor. And there's the most impressive of them all: the Tower of London, guarding the capital for more than 900 years.

Stately Homes of England

The medieval period was tumultuous, but by around 1600 life became more settled, and the nobility started to have less need for their castles. While they were excellent for keeping out rivals or the common riff-raff, they were often too dark, cold and draughty to be comfortable. So many castles saw the home improvements of the day – the installation of larger windows, wider staircases and better drainage. Others were simply abandoned for a brand-new dwelling next door; an example of this is Hardwick Hall in Derbyshire.

Following the Civil War, the trend away from castles gathered pace, as through the 17th century the landed gentry developed a taste for fine 'country houses' designed by the most famous architects of the day. Many became the 'stately homes' that are a major feature of the English landscape, celebrated by Noël Coward's famous song 'The Stately Homes of England', and a major attraction for visitors. Among the most extravagant are Holkham Hall in Norfolk, Chatsworth House in Derbyshire and Blenheim Palace in Oxfordshire.

The great stately homes all display the proportion, symmetry and architectural harmony so in vogue during the 17th and 18th centuries, styles later reflected in the fashionable town houses of the Georgian era

England's Top Castles

Berkeley Castle (Gloucestershire)

Carlisle Castle (Cumbria)

Corfe Castle (Dorset)

Leeds Castle (Kent)

Skipton Castle (Yorkshire)

Tintagel Castle (Cornwall)

Tower of London (London)

Windsor Castle (Berkshire)

HOUSE & HOME

It's not all about big houses. Alongside the stately homes, ordinary domestic architecture from the 16th century onwards can also still be seen in rural areas: black-and-white 'half-timbered' houses still characterise counties such as Worcestershire, while brick-and-flint cottages pepper Norfolk and Suffolk, and hardy centuries-old farms built with slate or local gritstone are a feature of areas such as Derbyshire and the Lake District.

Danebury Ring, Hampshire

England's Finest Stately Homes

Audley End House
(Essex)

Blickling Hall
(Norfolk)

Burghley House
(Lincolnshire)

Blenheim Palace
(Oxfordshire)

Castle Howard
(Yorkshire)

Chatsworth House
(Derbyshire)

Cotehele (Corn-
wall)

Kingston Lacy
(Dorset)

– most notably in the city of Bath, where the stunning Royal Crescent is the epitome of the genre.

Victoriana

The Victorian era was a time of great building. A style called Victorian-Gothic developed, echoing the towers and spires that were such a feature of the original Gothic cathedrals. The most famous example of this style is the Palace of Westminster (better known as the Houses of Parliament) and Elizabeth Tower (home to Big Ben), in London. Other highlights include London's Natural History Museum and London's St Pancras station.

Through the early 20th century, as England's cities grew in size and stature, the newly moneyed middle classes built streets and squares of smart town houses. Meanwhile, in other suburbs the first town planners oversaw the construction of endless terraces of red-brick two-up-two-down houses to accommodate the massive influx of workers required to fuel the country's factories – an enduring architectural legacy of the great migration from countryside to town that changed the landscape of England forever.

The Postwar Rebuild

During WWII many of England's cities were damaged by bombing, and the rebuilding that followed showed scant regard for the overall aesthetic of the cities, or for the lives of the people who lived in them. The rows of terraces were swept away in favour of high-rise tower blocks, while the 'brutalist' architects of the 1950s and '60s employed the modern and efficient materials of steel and concrete, leaving legacies such as London's South Bank Centre.

Top: Audley End House & Gardens (p368), Saffron Walden

Bottom: Sage Gateshead (p606), Newcastle-upon-Tyne

THE STIRLING PRIZE

The highlight of the year for aficionados of modern architecture is the announcement of the shortlist for the Stirling Prize for the best new building, an annual award for excellence in architecture organised by the Royal Institute of British Architects (RIBA). Established in 1996, this prestigious award is for 'the building that has made the greatest contribution to the evolution of architecture in the past year'. Famous winners include the Millennium Bridge in Gateshead (2002), 30 St Mary Axe (better known as the Gherkin) in London (2004), the Scottish Parliament Building in Edinburgh (2005), the Everyman Theatre in Liverpool (2014), the Burntwood School in London (2015) and the redevelopment of Hastings Pier (2017).

Perhaps this is why, on the whole, the English are conservative in their architectural tastes, and often resent ambitious or experimental designs, especially when they're applied to public buildings, or when form appears more important than function. But a familiar pattern often unfolds: after a few years of resentment, first comes a nickname, then grudging acceptance, and finally – once the locals have got used to it – comes pride and affection for the new building. The English just don't like to be rushed, that's all.

With this attitude in mind, over the last few decades, English architecture has started to redeem itself, and many big cities now have contemporary buildings their residents can be proud of and enjoy. Highlights in London's financial district include the bulging cone with the official address of 30 St Mary Axe (but widely known by its nickname, the Gherkin), and the former Millennium Dome (now rebranded as simply the O2), which has been transformed from a source of national embarrassment into one of the capital's leading live-music venues.

Twenty-First Century

Through the first decade of the 21st century, many areas of England placed a new importance on progressive, popular architecture as a part of wider regeneration. Top examples include Manchester's Imperial War Museum North, The Deep aquarium in Hull, Cornwall's futuristic Eden Project, and the Sage concert hall in Gateshead, near Newcastle.

From around 2010, development slowed and some plans were shelved, thanks to the global slowdown, but several significant projects continued, including the Turner Contemporary Gallery in Margate (opened 2011) and the futuristic Library of Birmingham (2013).

But England's largest and most high-profile architectural project of recent times was of course the Olympic Park, the centrepiece of the 2012 Games, in the London suburb of Stratford. As well as the main Olympic Stadium, other arenas include the Velodrome and the Aquatics Centre – all dramatic structures in their own right, using cutting-edge construction techniques. The Velodrome also won the construction industry's 2011 Better Public Buildings Award.

Meanwhile, in the centre of the capital, the tall, jagged Shard was officially opened in July 2012; at 306m, it's one of Europe's tallest buildings. On the other side of the River Thames, two more giant skyscrapers were completed in 2014: 20 Fenchurch St (nickname: the Walkie-Talkie) and the Leadenhall Building (the Cheesegrater). While in 2015 the Tate Modern unveiled a dramatic new 64.5m pyramid-like extension.

So London continues to grow upwards, and English architecture continues to push new boundaries of style and technology. The buildings may look a little different, but it's great to see the spirit of Stonehenge alive and well after all these years.

GLOSSARY OF ENGLISH ARCHITECTURE

BAILEY	OUTERMOST WALL OF A CASTLE
bar	fortified gate (York, and some other northern cities)
barrel vault	semicircular arched roof
brass	memorial consisting of a brass plate set into the side or lid of a tomb, or into the floor of a church to indicate a burial place below
buttress	vertical support for a wall; see also *flying buttress*
campanile	freestanding belfry or bell tower
chancel	eastern end of the church, usually reserved for choir and clergy
choir	area in the church where the choir is seated
cloister	covered walkway linking the church with adjacent monastic buildings
close	buildings grouped around a cathedral
cob	mixture of mud and straw for building
corbel	stone or wooden projection from a wall supporting a beam or arch
flying buttress	supporting *buttress* in the form of one side of an open arch
lancet	pointed window in Early English style
lierne vault	*vault* containing many tertiary ribs
Martello tower	small, circular tower used for coastal defence
minster	traditionally a church connected to a monastery; now a title signalling a church's importance
nave	main body of the church at the western end, where the congregation gathers
oast house	building containing a kiln for drying hops
pargeting	decorative stucco plasterwork
pele	fortified house
precincts	see *close*
priory	religious house governed by a prior
quire	medieval term for *choir*
rood	archaic word for cross (in churches)
transepts	north–south projections from a church's *nave*, giving church a cruciform (cross-shaped) plan
undercroft	vaulted underground room or cellar
vault	roof with arched ribs, usually in a decorative pattern

The English Landscape

When it comes to landscapes, England is not a place of extremes; there are no Alps or Himalayas here, no Amazon or Sahara. But there are still very diverse environments, and understanding those differences can keep you enthralled. The country may be small, but even a relatively short journey takes you through a surprising mix of scenery. Seeing the change – subtle in some areas, dramatic in others – as you travel is one of this country's great joys.

National Parks

Back in 1810, English poet and outdoor fan William Wordsworth suggested that the wild landscape of the Lake District in Cumbria should be 'a sort of national property, in which every man has a right'. More than a century later, the Lake District had indeed become a national park, along with the Peak District, Dartmoor, Exmoor, the North York Moors, the Yorkshire Dales and Northumberland. Other national parks (or equivalent status) followed, including the Norfolk and Suffolk Broads, the New Forest and the South Downs.

But the term 'national park' can cause confusion. First, in England the parks are not state-owned: nearly all land is private, belonging to farmers, private estates and conservation organisations. Second, they are *not* areas of wilderness, as in many other countries – most of the national parks have been managed by humans in some way for hundreds of years, whether for agriculture, forestry or other purposes.

In England's national parks you'll see crop fields in lower areas and grazing sheep on the uplands, as well as roads, railways and villages, and even towns, quarries and factories in some parks. It's a reminder of the balance that is struck in this crowded country between protecting the natural environment and catering for the people who live in it.

Despite these apparent anomalies, England's national parks still contain mountains, hills, downs, moors, lakes, woods, river valleys and other areas of quiet countryside, all ideal for enjoying nature however you like to experience it.

In 2017 England's most popular national park, the Lake District, was granted World Heritage status by Unesco.

Protected Areas

As well as national parks, other parts of the English countryside are designated as Areas of Outstanding Natural Beauty (AONBs), the second tier of protected landscape after national parks. Some of the finest AONBs in England include the Chilterns, Cornwall, the Cotswolds, the Isles of Scilly, the North Pennines, the Northumberland Coast, the Suffolk Coast and the Wye Valley.

There are also Conservation Areas, Sites of Special Scientific Interest (SSSIs) and many other types of protected landscape that you can enjoy as you travel around.

Flora & Fauna

For a small country, England has a diverse range of plants and animals. Many native species are hidden away, but there are some undoubted gems, from lowland woods carpeted in shimmering bluebells to stately herds of deer on the high moors. Having a closer look will enhance your trip enormously.

Animals

Farmland

In rural areas, rabbits are everywhere, but if you're hiking through the countryside be on the lookout for the much larger brown hares, an increasingly rare species. Males who battle for territory by boxing on their hind legs in early spring are, of course, as 'mad as a March hare'.

Common birds of farmland areas (and urban gardens) include the robin, with its instantly recognisable red breast and cheerful whistle; the wren, whose loud trilling song belies its tiny size; and the yellowhammer, with a song that sounds like (if you use your imagination) 'a-little-bit-of-bread-and-no-cheese'. In open fields, the warbling cry of a skylark is another classic, but now threatened, sound of the English outdoors. You're more likely to see a pheasant, a large bird originally introduced from Russia to the nobility's shooting estates, but now considered naturalised. Barn and tawny owls can sometimes be spotted, especially at dawn and dusk.

Alongside rivers, the once-rare otter is making a comeback. While in some areas, the black-and-white-striped badger has been the subject of trial culls – some believe it transmits bovine tuberculosis to cattle, others argue the case is far from proven. Also at the centre of controversy is the fox – amid much national debate, hunting foxes with dogs was banned in 2005. The animal is widespread in the countryside and well adapted to a scavenging life in rural towns, and even city suburbs.

Woodland

In woodland areas, mammals include the small white-spotted fallow deer and the even smaller roe deer. Woodland is full of birds too, but you'll hear them more than see them. Listen out for willow warblers (which have a warbling song with a descending cadence), chiffchaffs (which make a repetitive 'chiff chaff' noise) and the rat-a-tat-tat of woodpeckers.

If you hear rustling among the fallen leaves it might be a hedgehog – a spiny-backed insect-eating mammal – but it's an increasingly rare sound these days; conservationists say they'll be extinct in Britain by 2025, thanks to farming insecticides, decreased habitat and their inability to safely cross roads.

England's native red squirrels are severely endangered thanks to their more aggressive grey cousins, which were originally introduced from North America. As well as being more aggressive and competitive for food, the greys also carry a virus called squirrel pox that is particularly lethal to the reds. Attempts have been made in some areas to limit grey squirrel numbers in order to give the reds a fighting chance: Cumbria is an important stronghold.

Perhaps unexpectedly, England is home to herds of 'wild' ponies, notably in the New Forest, Exmoor and Dartmoor, but although these animals roam free they are privately owned and regularly managed. There's even a pocket of wild goats near Lynmouth in Devon, where they've apparently gambolled merrily for almost 1000 years.

Another recent arrival – or perhaps more accurately returnee – is the beaver, once a native resident of England, but trapped out of existence long ago. The animals have been reintroduced to several locations

---

Perhaps surprisingly, England's most wooded county is Surrey, despite its proximity to London. The soil is too poor for agriculture, so while woodland areas elsewhere in England were cleared, Surrey's trees got a stay of execution.

Online Resources

www.nationalparks.gov.uk

www.landscapesforlife.org.uk

www.rspb.org.uk

www.countryfile.com

www.environment-agency.gov.uk

around England, although the exact sites have been kept secret to ensure their safety.

Mountains & Moors

On some mountains and high moors the most visible mammal is the red deer. Males of the species grow their famous large antlers between April and July, and shed them again in February. Also on the high ground, well-known and easily recognised birds include the red grouse, which often hides in the heather until almost stepped on, then flies away with a loud warning call; and the curlew, with its stately long legs and elegant curved bill. Look hard, and you may see beautifully camouflaged golden plovers, while the spectacular aerial displays of lapwings are impossible to miss.

Birds of prey are also a fairly common sight on the open moors, particularly kestrels and buzzards.

Coastal Areas

By the sea, two seal species frequent English coasts: the larger grey seal, which is more often seen, and the misnamed common seal. In areas such

ENGLAND'S NATIONAL PARKS

NATIONAL PARK	FEATURES	ACTIVITIES	BEST TIME TO VISIT
Dartmoor (p304)	rolling hills, rocky outcrops, serene valleys; Bronze Age relics; wild ponies, deer, peregrine falcons	walking, mountain biking, horse riding, climbing, winter kayaking	May-Jun (wildflowers bloom)
Exmoor (p281)	sweeping moors, craggy sea cliffs; red deer, wild ponies, horned sheep	horse riding, walking, mountain biking	Aug-Sep (heather flowering)
Lake District (p562)	majestic fells, rugged mountains, shimmering lakes; literary heritage; red squirrels, ospreys	watersports, walking, mountaineering, rock climbing	Sep-Oct (summer crowds departed, autumn colours abound)
New Forest (p249)	woodlands, heath; wild ponies, otters, Dartford warblers, southern damselflies	walking, cycling, horse riding	Apr-Sep (lush vegetation)
Norfolk & Suffolk Broads (p380)	expansive shallow lakes, rivers, marshlands; windmills; water lilies, wildfowl, otters	walking, cycling, boating	Apr-May (birds most active)
North York Moors (p488)	heather-clad hills, deep-green valleys, isolated villages; merlins, curlews, golden plovers	walking, mountain biking	Aug-Sep (heather flowering)
Northumberland (p618)	wild rolling moors, heather, gorse; Hadrian's Wall; black grouse, red squirrels	walking, cycling, mountain biking, climbing	Apr-May (lambs) & Sep (heather flowering)
Peak District (p456)	high moors, tranquil dales, limestone caves; kestrels, badgers, grouse	walking, cycling, mountain biking, hang-gliding, climbing	Apr-May (even more lambs)
South Downs (p161)	rolling grassy chalky hills, chalky sea-cliffs, gorse, heather; Adonis blue butterflies	walking, mountain biking	Aug (heather flowering)
Yorkshire Dales (p497)	rugged hills, lush valleys, limestone pavements; red squirrels, hares, curlews, lapwings, buzzards	walking, cycling, mountain biking, climbing	Apr-May (visitors outnumbered by, you guessed it, lambs)

as Norfolk and Northumberland, boat trips to see seal colonies are a popular attraction. Dolphins, porpoises, minke whales and basking sharks can sometimes be seen off the western coasts, especially from about May to September when viewing conditions are better – although you may need to go with someone who knows where to look. Boat trips are available from many coastal resorts.

England's estuaries and mudflats are feeding grounds for numerous migrant wading birds; easily spotted are black-and-white oystercatchers with their long red bills, while flocks of ringed plovers skitter along the sand. On the coastal cliffs in early summer, particularly in Cornwall and Yorkshire, countless thousands of guillemots, razorbills, kittiwakes and other breeding seabirds fight for space on crowded rock ledges, and the air is thick with their sound – as well as the cries of various types of seagull, now so numerous they've managed to colonise many English cities as well as its coastline.

Plants

In the rolling hills of southern England and the limestone areas further north (such as the Peak District and Yorkshire Dales), the best places to see wildflowers are the areas that evade large-scale farming – many erupt with great profusions of cowslips and primroses in April and May.

For woodland flowers, the best time is also April and May, before the leaf canopy is fully developed and sunlight can still reach plants such as bluebells – a beautiful and internationally rare species. Another classic English plant is gorse: you can't miss this spiky bush in heath areas like Dartmoor, Exmoor and the New Forest. Its vivid yellow flowers show year-round and have a distinctive coconut-like scent.

In contrast, the blooming season for heather is quite short, but no less dramatic; through August and September areas such as the North York Moors and Dartmoor are covered in a riot of purple.

Environmental Issues

With England's long history of human occupation, it's not surprising that the country's appearance is heavily the result of human interaction with the environment. Since the earliest times, trees have been chopped down and fields created for crops or animals, but the really significant changes to rural areas came after WWII in the late 1940s, continuing into the '50s and '60s, when a drive to be self-reliant in food meant new – intensive and large-scale – farming methods. The result was dramatic: in some

Although hedgerows around fields have been reduced, new 'hedgerows' have appeared: the long strips of grass and bushes alongside motorways and major roads. These areas support thousands of insect species, plus mice, shrews and other small mammals, so kestrels are often seen hovering nearby, unconcerned by traffic.

WILDLIFE GUIDEBOOKS

Is it a rabbit or a hare? A gull or a tern? Buttercup or cowslip? If you need to know a bit more about England's plant and animal kingdoms, the following field guides are ideal for entry-level naturalists:

➡ *Collins Complete Guide to British Wildlife* by Paul Sterry is portable and highly recommended, covering mammals, birds, fish, plants, snakes, insects and even fungi, with brief descriptions and excellent photos.

➡ If feathered friends are enough, the *Collins Complete Guide to British Birds* by Paul Sterry has clear photos and descriptions, plus when and where each species may be seen.

➡ *Wildlife of the North Atlantic* by world-famous film-maker Tony Soper beautifully covers the animals seen from beach, boat and cliff top in the British Isles and beyond.

➡ The Collins Gem series includes handy little books on wildlife topics such as *Birds, Trees, Fish* and *Wild Flowers*.

FOX HUNTING

The red fox, a doglike animal with a characteristic bushy tail and an anthropomorphic reputation for cunning, is a divisive creature in England. The controversy focuses on hunting, and specifically fox hunting with hounds (a type of dog). Supporters say it's been a traditional English rural activity for centuries, and helps control the fox population; opponents say it's a savage blood sport that has little impact on overall numbers. Distaste for this type of hunting is not a new phenomenon; the activity was famously described as 'the unspeakable in pursuit of the inedible' by Oscar Wilde more than a century ago. Fox hunting has been immortalised in thousands of paintings depicting English country life, and in countless rural pub names. Today, some observers believe the hunting debate has come to represent much bigger issues: town versus country, or the relative limits of privilege, state control and individual freedom. Either way, fox hunting with dogs was banned in 2005 by law – and opinion is still very strongly divided.

areas ancient patchworks of small meadows became landscapes of vast prairie-like fields, as walls were demolished, woodlands felled, ponds filled, wetlands drained and, most notably, hedgerows ripped out.

In most cases the hedgerows were lines of dense bushes, shrubs and trees forming a network that stretched across the countryside, protecting fields from erosion, supporting a varied range of flowers, and providing shelter for numerous insects, birds and small mammals. But in the rush to improve farm yields, thousands of miles of hedgerows were destroyed in the postwar decades, and between the mid-1980s and the early 2000s another 25% disappeared.

Hedgerows have come to symbolise many other environmental issues in rural areas, and in recent years the destruction has abated, partly because farmers recognise their anti-erosion qualities, and partly because they've been encouraged – with financial incentives from UK or European agencies – to 'set aside' such areas as wildlife havens.

In addition to hedgerow clearance, other farming techniques remain hot environmental issues. Studies suggest the use of pesticides and intensive irrigation results in rivers being contaminated or simply running dry. Meanwhile, monocropping means the fields have one type of grass and not another plant to be seen. These 'green deserts' support no insects, so in turn wild bird populations have plummeted. This picture is not a case of wizened old peasants recalling the idyllic days of their forbears; you only have to be aged about 40 in England to remember a countryside where birds such as skylarks or lapwings were visibly much more numerous.

But all is not lost. In the face of apparently overwhelming odds, England still boasts great biodiversity, and some of the best wildlife habitats are protected (to a greater or lesser extent) by the creation of national parks and similar areas, or private reserves owned by conservation campaign groups such as the Wildlife Trusts (www.wildlifetrusts.org), National Trust (www.nationaltrust.org.uk), Woodland Trust (www.woodlandtrust.org.uk) and the Royal Society for the Protection of Birds (www.rspb.org.uk). Many of these areas are open to the public – ideal spots for walking, birdwatching or simply enjoying the peace and beauty of the countryside – and are well worth a visit as you travel around.

Arts

England's contributions to literature, drama, cinema and pop are celebrated around the world. As you travel around England today you'll encounter landscapes made famous as movie sets and literary locations, and places mentioned in songs. Here we've picked some major creative milestones and focused on works with connections to real locations – so your physical journey through England will be one that connects culture with place.

Literature

For extra insight, the *Oxford Guide to Literary Britain and Ireland*, edited by Daniel Hahn and Nicholas Robins, gives details of towns, villages and countryside immortalised by writers, from Geoffrey Chaucer's Canterbury to Jane Austen's Bath.

The roots of England's poetic and story-telling heritage stretch back to Nordic sagas and Early English epics such as *Beowulf,* but modern English literature starts around 1387 (yes, that is 'modern' in history-soaked England) when Geoffrey Chaucer produced *The Canterbury Tales*. This mammoth poem is a collection of fables, stories and morality tales using travelling pilgrims – the Knight, the Wife of Bath and so on – as a narrative hook.

William Shakespeare

The next significant development in English literature came in the 16th century, when John Milton penned *Paradise Lost,* charting the tale of Adam and Eve within the framework of epic poetry. But it was a young playwright by the name of William Shakespeare who left an even greater mark. Best known for his plays, penned in an astonishing burst of creativity between 1590 and 1610, he was also a remarkably prolific and influential poet, writing a series of sonnets that are still quoted to this day ('Shall I compare thee to a summer's day?' is one of Shakespeare's).

His birthplace, Stratford-upon-Avon, is stacked with Shakespearean sights, including the home of the celebrated Royal Shakespeare Company (RSC) – although the debate rages on about precisely how Shakespeare penned his plays. Some academics maintain he was the sole author, while others (including the well-known actor and former director of the RSC, Mark Rylance) maintain that the plays were much more likely to have been written as a collaborative effort. The truth will probably never be known, but the plays will endure.

The Romantics

During the late 18th and early 19th centuries, a new generation of writers drew inspiration from human imagination and the natural world (in some cases helped along by a healthy dose of laudanum). Leading lights of the movement were William Blake, John Keats, Percy Bysshe Shelley, Lord Byron and Samuel Taylor Coleridge, and perhaps the best-known English poet of all, William Wordsworth. His famous line from 'Daffodils' – 'I wandered lonely as a cloud' – was inspired by a waterside walk in the Lake District in northern England.

Victorian Writers

As industrialisation expanded during the reign of Queen Victoria, so key novels of the time explored social themes. Charles Dickens tackled many prevailing issues of his day: in *Oliver Twist,* he captures the lives of young pickpockets in the London slums; *Bleak House* is a critique of the English legal system; and *Hard Times* criticises the excesses of capitalism. At around the same time, but choosing a rural setting, George Eliot (the pen name of Mary Ann Evans) wrote *The Mill on the Floss,* where the central character struggles against society's expectations.

Thomas Hardy's classic *Tess of the D'Urbervilles* deals with the peasantry's decline, and *The Trumpet Major* paints a picture of idyllic English country life interrupted by war and encroaching modernity. Many of Hardy's works are based in the fictionalised county of Wessex, largely based on today's Dorset and surrounding counties, where towns such as Dorchester are dotted with literary links.

20th Century

The end of WWI and the ensuing social disruption fed into the modernist movement, with DH Lawrence perhaps its finest exponent; *Sons and Lovers* follows the lives and loves of generations in the English Midlands as the country changes from rural idyll to an increasingly industrial landscape, while his controversial exploration of sexuality in *Lady Chatterley's Lover* was originally banned as 'obscene'. Other highlights of this period included Daphne du Maurier's romantic suspense novel *Rebecca,* set on the Cornish coast, and Evelyn Waugh's *Brideshead Revisited,* an exploration of moral and social disintegration among the English aristocracy, set partly in Oxford.

The 1970s saw the arrival of two novelists who became prolific for the remainder of the century and beyond. Martin Amis published *The Rachel Papers,* then went on to produce a string of novels where common themes included the absurdity and unappealing nature of modern life, such as *London Fields* (1989) and *Lionel Asbo: State of England* (2012). Meanwhile, Ian McEwan debuted with *The Cement Garden,* and earned critical acclaim for finely observed studies of the English character such as *The Child in Time* (1987), *Atonement* (2001) and *On Chesil Beach* (2007), which is set on the eponymous 18-mile stretch of Dorset shore.

Recent Writers

As the 20th century came to a close, the nation's multicultural landscape proved a rich inspiration for novelists: Hanif Kureishi sowed the seeds with his groundbreaking *The Buddha of Suburbia,* about a group of British-Asians in suburban London; Zadie Smith published her acclaimed debut *White Teeth* in 2000, followed by a string of bestsellers including *The Autograph Man* and 2012's *NW;* Andrea Levy published *Small Island,*

ARTS LITERATURE

For other worlds and otherworldly humour, try two of England's funniest – and most successful – writers: Douglas Adams (*The Hitchhiker's Guide to the Galaxy* and several sequels) and Terry Pratchett (the Discworld series).

JANE AUSTEN & THE BRONTËS

The beginning of the 19th century saw the emergence of some of English literature's best-known and beloved writers: Jane Austen and the Brontë sisters.

Austen's fame stems from her exquisite observations of love, friendship, intrigues and passions boiling beneath the strait-laced surface of middle-class social convention, and from the endless stream of movies and TV costume dramas based on her works, such as *Pride and Prejudice* and *Sense and Sensibility.* For visitors today, the location most associated with Jane Austen is the city of Bath – a beautiful place even without the literary link. As one of her heroines asked, 'Who can ever be tired of Bath?'.

Of the Brontë sisters' prodigious output, Emily Brontë's *Wuthering Heights* is the best known – an epic tale of obsession and revenge, where the dark and moody landscape plays a role as great as any human character. Charlotte Brontë's *Jane Eyre* and Anne Brontë's *The Tenant of Wildfell Hall* are classics of passion and mystery. Fans still flock to their former home in the Yorkshire town of Haworth, perched on the edge of the wild Pennine moors that inspired so many of their books.

about a Jamaican couple settled in postwar London; and Monica Ali's *Brick Lane* was shortlisted for the high-profile Man Booker Prize in 2003.

Other contemporary writers include Will Self, known for his surreal, satirical novels including *The Book of Dave,* and Nick Hornby, best known for novels like *Fever Pitch,* a study of the insecurities of English blokishness. There's also Julian Barnes, whose books include *England, England,* a darkly ironic study of nationalism and tourism among other themes, and *The Sense of An Ending,* winner of the 2011 Man Booker Prize. Not to mention Hilary Mantel, author of many novels on an astoundingly wide range of subjects, and winner of the Man Booker Prize twice, first in 2009 for historical blockbuster *Wolf Hall* (about Henry VIII and his ruthless advisor Thomas Cromwell), and then in 2012 for its sequel *Bring Up the Bodies.* At the time of writing, the third and final instalment, *The Mirror and the Light,* was still a work in progress.

England's greatest literary phenomenon of the 21st century is JK Rowling's *Harry Potter* books, a series of otherworldly adventures that have entertained millions of children (and many grown-ups too) since the first book was published in 1996. The magical tales are the latest in a long line of British children's classics enjoyed by adults, stretching back to the works of Lewis Carroll *(Alice's Adventures in Wonderland),* AA Milne *(Winnie-the-Pooh)* and CS Lewis (The Chronicles of Narnia).

Helen Fielding's book *Bridget Jones's Diary,* originally a series of newspaper articles, is a fond look at the heartache of a modern single woman's blundering search for love, and the epitome of the late-1990s 'chicklit' genre. It's also (very loosely) based on *Pride and Prejudice* by Jane Austen.

Music

The British Invasion

England has been putting the world through its musical paces ever since some mop-haired lads from Liverpool created The Beatles. Elvis may have invented rock and roll, but it was the Fab Four who transformed it into a global phenomenon, backed by the other bands of the 1960s 'British Invasion': The Rolling Stones, The Who, Cream and The Kinks. And the big names have kept coming ever since.

From Glam to Punk

Glam rock arrived in the 1970s, fronted by artists such as the anthemic Queen and the chameleon-like David Bowie (whose passing in 2016 triggered a palpable sense of loss worldwide). Also in the '70s Led Zeppelin laid down the blueprint for heavy metal, and the psychedelia of the previous decade morphed into the prog rock of Pink Floyd and Yes.

At the end of the decade, it was all swept aside as punk exploded onto the scene, most famously with the Sex Pistols, The Clash, The Damned,

---

ROCK & ROLL LOCATIONS

Fans buy the single, then the T-shirt. But true fans visit the location featured on the album cover. The following are a few favourites:

➡ Abbey Rd, St John's Wood, London – *Abbey Road,* The Beatles

➡ Battersea Power Station, London – *Animals,* Pink Floyd (the inflatable pig has gone)

➡ Berwick St, Soho, London – *(What's the Story) Morning Glory,* Oasis

➡ Big Ben plus a corner of plinth under Boudica's statue, London – *My Generation* (US version), The Who

➡ Durdle Door, Dorset – *North Atlantic Drift,* Ocean Colour Scene

➡ Salford Boys Club, Manchester – *The Queen is Dead,* The Smiths

➡ Thor's Cave, Manifold Valley, near Ashbourne, Peak District National Park – *A Storm In Heaven,* The Verve

➡ Yes Tor, Dartmoor, Devon – *Tomato,* Yes

the Buzzcocks and The Stranglers. Then punk begat New Wave, with acts including The Jam and Elvis Costello blending spiky tunes and sharp lyrics into a more radio-friendly sound.

The '80s

The conspicuous consumption of the early 1980s influenced the era's pop scene. Big hair and shoulder pads became the uniform of the day, with big names including Wham! (a boyish duo headed by an up-and-coming popster called George Michael) and New Romantic bands such as Spandau Ballet and Duran Duran. Away from the glitz, fans enjoyed the doom-laden lyrics of The Cure, the heavy metal of Iron Maiden and the 'miserabilism' of The Smiths.

Dance Music & Britpop

The late 1980s and early 1990s saw the rise of ecstasy-fuelled rave culture, centred on famous clubs like Manchester's Haçienda and London's Ministry of Sound. Manchester was also a focus for the burgeoning British 'indie' scene, driven by guitar-based bands such as The Stone Roses, James and the Happy Mondays. Then indie morphed into Britpop, with Oasis, Pulp, Supergrass and Blur, whose distinctively British music chimed with the country's reborn sense of optimism after the landslide election of New Labour in 1997.

Recent Artists

The new millennium saw no let up in the music scene's continual shifting and reinventing. R&B, hip-hop and drum and bass fused into grime and dubstep, producing acts like Dizzee Rascal, Tinie Tempah and Stormzy. Initially centred on London, both scenes continue to wield an increasing global influence. Dance acts like Calvin Harris and Disclosure have also enjoyed massive international success. Meanwhile the spirit of British indie stays alive thanks to the likes of Arctic Monkeys, Coldplay, Muse, Kasabian and Radiohead.

Pop shows no sign of losing popularity either: boy bands continue to come and go, most notably One Direction, who clocked up the sales before going the way of all boy bands and splitting up in acrimonious fashion. Singer-songwriters are also a strong point – Adele's 2015 album, *25*, won critical acclaim and proved another international blockbuster, while Ed Sheeran has taken the world by storm; his third album, ÷, was released in 2017, and notched up 10 Top 10 hit singles (a British record) as well as two singles in the US Top 10, becoming the first artist in history to do so. To date, Sheeran has sold more than 26 million albums and 100 million singles worldwide, putting him in the top tier of the world's most successful (and richest) artists.

Some of Henry Moore's work can be seen at the Yorkshire Sculpture Park. Barbara Hepworth is celebrated at the eponymous gallery in Wakefield; her former home and garden are also open to visitors in St Ives, Cornwall.

Painting & Sculpture

For many centuries, continental Europe – especially the Netherlands, Spain, France and Italy – set the artistic agenda. The first artist with a truly British style and sensibility was arguably William Hogarth, whose riotous canvases exposed the vice and corruption of 18th-century London. His most celebrated work is *A Rake's Progress,* which kick-started a long tradition of British caricatures that can be traced right through to the work of modern-day cartoonists such as Gerald Scarfe and Steve Bell. You can see it at the Sir John Soane's Museum in London.

Portraits

While Hogarth was busy satirising society, other artists were hard at work showing it in its best light. The leading figures of 18th-century English portraiture were Sir Joshua Reynolds, Thomas Gainsborough (you can visit his house in Sudbury, Suffolk) and George Romney, while George Stubbs is best known for his intricate studies of animals (particularly horses). Most of these artists are represented at Tate Britain or the National Gallery in London.

Landscapes & Legends

In the 19th century leading painters favoured the English landscape. John Constable's best-known works include *Salisbury Cathedral* and *The Hay Wain*. The latter is in the National Gallery; you can also visit the setting, a mill at Flatford in Suffolk. JMW Turner, meanwhile, was fascinated by the effects of light and colour on English scenes, with his works becoming almost entirely abstract by the 1840s.

In contrast, the Pre-Raphaelite painters of the late 19th century preferred a figurative style reflecting the Victorian taste for English fables and fairy tales. Key members of the movement included Dante Gabriel Rossetti, John Everett Millais and William Holman Hunt, all represented at London's Tate Britain or the Victoria & Albert Museum.

Sticks & Stones

In the tumultuous 20th century, English art became increasingly experimental. Francis Bacon placed Freudian psychoanalysis on the canvas in his portraits, while pioneering sculptors such as Henry Moore and Barbara Hepworth experimented with natural forms in stone and new materials. At about the same time, the painter LS Lowry was setting his 'matchstick men' among the smokestacks of northern England, and is today remembered by the major art centre that bears his name in Manchester.

Pop Art

The mid-1950s and early '60s saw an explosion of English 'pop art', as artists plundered popular culture for inspiration. Leaders of this new movement included David Hockney. His bold colours and simple lines were groundbreaking at the time, and are still used to great effect half a century later. A contemporary, Peter Blake, codesigned the cut-up collage cover for The Beatles' landmark album *Sgt. Pepper's Lonely Hearts Club Band*. The '60s also saw the rise of sculptor Anthony Caro; creating large abstract works in steel and bronze, he was one of England's most influential sculptors.

Britart & Beyond

Thanks partly to the support (and money) of advertising tycoon Charles Saatchi, a new wave of British artists came to the fore in the 1990s. The movement was dubbed, inevitably, 'Britart'; its leading members included Damien Hirst, famous (or infamous) for works involving pickled sharks, a cow and calf cut into sections *(Mother and Child Divided)* and a diamond-encrusted skull entitled *For the Love of God*. His pregnant, naked and half-flayed *Verity* towers 20m high beside the harbour mouth at Ilfracombe in north Devon.

ANISH KAPOOR

The sculptor Anish Kapoor has been working in London since the 1970s. He is best known for his large outdoor installations, which often feature curved shapes and reflective materials, such as highly polished steel. You can find one of his major works, *ArcelorMittal Orbit*, in London's 2012 Queen Elizabeth Olympic Park. At over 110m high, it is the largest piece of public art in Britain, and one you can actually slide down, in a hair-raising 40-second glide.

> ### THE TURNER PRIZE
> Named after the enduringly popular landscape painter JMW Turner, the Turner Prize is a high-profile and frequently controversial annual award for British visual artists. As well as Damien Hirst, other winners have included Martin Creed (his work was a room with lights going on and off), Mark Wallinger (a collection of anti-war objects), Simon Starling (a shed converted to a boat and back again), Rachel Whiteread (a plaster cast of a house) and Antony Gormley (best known in England for his gigantic *Angel of the North*).

A contemporary is Tracey Emin. Once considered an enfant terrible, she incurred the wrath of the tabloids for works such as *My Bed* (a messed-up bedroom scene that sold for £2.5 million in 2014), but is now a respected figure and patron of the new Turner Gallery in Margate, named for the famous English artist JMW Turner. One of her recent works, a 20m light sculpture reading *I Want My Time With You*, was installed at London's St Pancras station in 2018 (the terminus for the Eurostar), and has been interpreted by some critics as Emin's response to the Brexit issue.

Cinema

English cinema has a long history, with many early directors cutting their teeth in the silent-film industry. Perhaps the best known of these was Alfred Hitchcock, who directed *Blackmail*, one of the first English 'talkies' in 1929, and who went on to direct a string of films during the 1930s before emigrating to Hollywood in the early 1940s.

War & Postwar

During WWII, films such as *In Which We Serve* (1942) and *We Dive at Dawn* (1943) were designed to raise public morale, while a young director called David Lean produced *Brief Encounter* (1945), the classic tale of buttoned-up English passion, before graduating to Hollywood epics including *Lawrence of Arabia* and *Doctor Zhivago*.

Following the hardships of war, British audiences were in the mood for escape and entertainment. During the late 1940s and early '50s, the domestic film industry specialised in eccentric British comedies epitomised by the output of Ealing Studios: notable titles include *Passport to Pimlico* (1949), *Kind Hearts and Coronets* (1949) and *The Titfield Thunderbolt* (1953).

The Ladykillers (1955) is a classic Ealing comedy about a band of hapless bank robbers holed up in a London guesthouse, and features Alec Guinness sporting the most outrageous set of false teeth ever committed to celluloid.

The '60s

'British New Wave' and 'Free Cinema' explored the gritty realities of British life in semidocumentary style, with directors Lindsay Anderson and Tony Richardson crystallising the movement in films such as *This Sporting Life* (1961) and *A Taste of Honey* (1961). At the other end of the spectrum were the *Carry On* films, the cinematic equivalent of the smutty seaside postcard, packed with bawdy gags and double entendres. The 1960s also saw the birth of another classic English genre: the James Bond films, starring Sean Connery (who is actually Scottish).

The '70s, '80s & '90s

The 1970s was a tough decade for the British film industry, but the 1980s saw a recovery, thanks partly to David Puttnam's Oscar success with *Chariots of Fire* (1981), and the newly established Channel Four investing in edgy films such as *My Beautiful Laundrette* (1985).

Another minor renaissance occurred in the 1990s, ushered in by the massively successful *Four Weddings and a Funeral* (1994), featuring

WALLACE & GROMIT

One of the great success stories of English TV and cinema has been Bristol-based animator Nick Park and the production company Aardman Animations, best known for the award-winning man-and-dog duo Wallace and Gromit. This lovable pair first appeared in Park's graduation film *A Grand Day Out* (1989) and went on to star in *The Wrong Trousers* (1993), *A Close Shave* (1995) and the full-length feature *The Curse of the Were-Rabbit* (2005). Known for their intricate plots, film homages and amazingly realistic stop-motion animation – as well as their very British sense of humour – the Wallace and Gromit films scooped Nick Park four Oscars. Other Aardman works include *Chicken Run* (2000), *Flushed Away* (2006) and *The Pirates!* (2012).

Hugh Grant in his trademark role as a floppy-haired, self-deprecating Englishman, a character type he reprised in subsequent hits, including *Notting Hill*, *About a Boy* and *Love Actually*.

The 'Brit Flick' genre – characterised by themes such as irony, social realism and humour in the face of adversity – went on to include *Brassed Off* (1996), about a struggling brass band from a mining colliery; *The Full Monty* (1997), following a troupe of laid-off steelworkers turned male strippers; and *Billy Elliott* (2000), the story of an aspiring young ballet dancer striving to escape the slagheaps and boarded-up factories of the industrial north.

Meanwhile, films such as *East Is East* (1999) and *Bend it like Beckham* (2002) explored the tensions of modern multicultural Britain, while veteran director Mike Leigh, known for his heavily improvised style, found success with *Life Is Sweet* (1991), *Naked* (1993) and the Palme d'Or–winning *Secrets and Lies* (1996).

English music-scene movies include: *Backbeat* (1994), The Beatles' early days; *Sid & Nancy* (1986), Sex Pistols' bassist and his girlfriend; *Quadrophenia* (1979), mods and rockers; *Velvet Goldmine* (1998), glam rock; *24 Hour Party People* (2002), Manchester scene; *Control* (2007), biopic of Joy Division singer Ian Curtis; and *Nowhere Boy* (2009), John Lennon pre-Beatles.

Recent Cinema

In the early part of the 21st century, literary adaptations have continued to provide the richest seam of success in the English film industry, including 2012's *Anna Karenina*, directed by Joe Wright and staring Keira Knightley, and of course the blockbuster *Harry Potter* franchise. Biopics are also a perennial favourite: recent big-screen subjects include Elizabeth I (*Elizabeth: The Golden Age*, 2007), Margaret Thatcher (*The Iron Lady*, 2011) and the 19th-century artist JMW Turner (*Mr Turner*, 2014).

Meanwhile, the oldest of English film franchises trundles on: a tough, toned, 21st-century James Bond appeared in 2006 courtesy of Daniel Craig and the blockbuster *Casino Royale* (2006), followed by *Quantum of Solace* (2008), *Skyfall* (2012) and *Spectre* (2015). Craig is set to return as Bond a final time for the 25th instalment, but there is much speculation about who will play the spy next; some critics have suggested that the role should go to a black or ethnic minority actor, while others claim it's high time that Bond changed gender. Watch this space.

Theatre

English theatre can trace its roots back to medieval morality plays, court jesters and travelling storytellers, and possibly even to dramas during Roman times in amphitheatres – a few of which still remain, such as at Chester and Cirencester. But most scholars agree that the key milestone in the story is the opening of England's first theatre – called simply The Theatre – in London in 1576. Within 25 years, the Rose and the Globe theatres appeared, and the stage was set for the entrance of England's best-known playwright.

Shakespeare & Co

For most visitors to England (and for most locals), English drama means just one name: William Shakespeare. Born in 1564, in the Midlands town of Stratford-upon-Avon (still rich in Shakespearean sights), Shakespeare made his mark in London between around 1590 and 1610, where most of his plays were performed at the Globe Theatre. His brilliant plots and spectacular use of language, plus the sheer size of his canon of work (including classics such as *Hamlet, Romeo and Juliet, Henry V* and *A Midsummer Night's Dream*), have turned him into a national – and international – icon, so that today, over 400 years after shuffling off this mortal coil, the Bard's plays still pull in big crowds.

Recent Theatre

However you budget your time and money during your visit to England, be sure to see some English theatre. It easily lives up to its reputation as the finest in the world, especially in London, while other big cities also boast their own top-class venues, such as the Birmingham Repertory Theatre, the Bristol Old Vic, Chichester Festival Theatre and the Nottingham Playhouse.

Many accomplished British actors, including Judi Dench, Mark Rylance, Ralph Fiennes, Brenda Blethyn, Toby Stephens and Simon Callow, juggle high-paying Hollywood roles with appearances on the British stage, while over the last decade or so several American stars have taken hefty pay cuts to tread the London boards, including Glenn Close, Kevin Spacey, Gwyneth Paltrow, Gillian Anderson, Christian Slater and Danny DeVito.

Venues in London include the Donmar Warehouse and the Royal Court Theatre, best known for new and experimental works. For big names, most people head for the West End, where famous spots include the Shaftesbury, the Adelphi Theatre and the Theatre Royal at Drury Lane, or the National Theatre on the South Bank. And then there's *The Mousetrap* – Agatha Christie's legendary whodunit is the world's longest-running play, showing continuously in the West End since 1952.

West End Musicals

As well as drama, London's West End means big musicals, with a long history of crowd-pullers such as *Cats, The Wizard of Oz, Les Misérables, Sweeney Todd, The Phantom of the Opera* and *The Lion King*, with many of today's shows raiding the pop world for material, such as *We Will Rock You,* inspired by the music of Queen, and Abba-based *Mamma Mia!*

The British Film Institute (BFI; www.bfi.org.uk) is dedicated to promoting film and cinema in Britain, and publishes the monthly magazine *Sight & Sound.*

ARTS THEATRE

You can enjoy Shakespeare plays at the rebuilt Globe Theatre in London or at the Royal Shakespeare Company's own theatre in Stratford-upon-Avon.

Sporting England

If you want a shortcut to the heart of English culture, watch its people at play. In this sports-mad nation thousands turn out each weekend to cheer on their favourite football team. Events such as Wimbledon (tennis), the Six Nations (rugby) and test matches (cricket) keep millions enthralled. And then there are the efforts of enthusiastic amateurs – be it in pub football leagues or village cricket matches, the English reveal a penchant for rules, hierarchies and playing the game.

Football (Soccer)

The English Premier League (www.premierleague.com) has some of the finest teams in the world, dominated in recent years by four top teams (Arsenal, Liverpool, Chelsea and Manchester United), joined in 2012 by a fifth big player in the shape of Manchester City. Their big pockets weren't enough in 2016, however, when unfancied Leicester City stunned the pundits and delighted neutrals by winning the title – although Man City returned to take back-to-back titles in 2017 and 2018.

Down in quality from the Premiership, 72 other teams play in the English divisions called the Championship, League One and League Two.

The football season is the same for all divisions (August to May), so seeing a match can easily be tied into most visitors' itineraries, but tickets for the biggest games are like gold dust – your chances of bagging one are low unless you're a club member, or know someone who is. You're better off buying a ticket to see the less fashionable teams – they're cheaper and more easily available. You can often buy tickets on the spot, or at online agencies like www.ticketmaster.co.uk and www.myticketmarket.com.

Cricket

Along with Big Ben, The Beatles and a nice cup of tea, cricket is quintessentially English. Dating from the 18th century (although its roots are much older), the sport spread throughout the Commonwealth during Britain's colonial era. Australia, the Caribbean and the Indian subconti-

---

THE FA CUP

The Football Association held its first interclub knockout tournament in 1871–72: 15 clubs took part, playing for a nice piece of silverware called the FA Cup – then worth about £20.

Nowadays, around 600 clubs compete for this legendary and priceless trophy. It differs from many other competitions in that every team – from the lowest-ranking part-timers to the stars of the Premier League – is in with a chance. The preliminary rounds begin in August, and the world-famous Cup Final is held in May at the iconic Wembley Stadium in London.

Manchester United and Arsenal have the most FA Cups, but public attention – and affection – is invariably focused on the 'giant-killers': minor clubs that claw their way up through the rounds, unexpectedly beating higher-ranking competitors. One of the best-known giant-killing events occurred in 1992, when Wrexham, then ranked 24th in Division 3, famously came from a goal down to beat league champions Arsenal in the third round.

THE ASHES

The historic test-cricket series between England and Australia known as the Ashes has been played every other year since 1882 (bar a few interruptions during the world wars). It is played alternately in England and Australia, with each of the five matches in the series held at a different cricket ground, always in the summer in the host location.

The contest's name dates back to the landmark test match of 1882, won (for the very first time) by the Australians. Defeat of the mother country by the colonial upstarts was a source of profound national shock: a mock obituary in the *Sporting Times* lamented the death of English cricket and referred to the sport's ashes being taken to Australia.

Later the name was given to a terracotta urn presented the following year to the English captain Ivo Bligh (later Lord Darnley), purportedly containing the cremated ashes of a stump or bail used in this landmark match. Since 1953 this hallowed relic has resided at the Marylebone Cricket Club (MCC) Museum at Lord's. Despite the vast importance given to winning the series, the urn itself is a diminutive 6in (150mm) high.

The recent history of the Ashes is not without drama. In the 2010–11 series England thrashed Australia, winning on Australian turf for the first time since the 1986–87 series. Then in 2013 Australia thrashed England 5-0, repeating the humiliating clean sweep they had inflicted in 2006–07. But the 2015 Ashes saw England – to national delight – defeat Australia 3-2, only to fail to win a single test in the 2017–18 series. *Plus ça change.*

nent took to the game with gusto, and today the former colonies delight in giving the old country a good spanking on the cricket pitch.

While many English people follow cricket like a religion, to the uninitiated it can be an impenetrable enigma. Spread over one-day games or five-day 'test matches', progress seems so *slow*, and dominated by arcane terminology like 'innings', 'cover drives', 'googlies', 'outswingers', 'leg-byes' and 'silly mid-off'. Nonetheless, at least one cricket match should be a feature of your travels around England. If you're patient and learn the intricacies, you could find cricket as absorbing as it is for all the Brits who remain glued to their radio or computer all summer long, 'just to see how England's getting on'.

Causing ructions is Twenty20 cricket, a relatively new format that limits the number of balls each team has to score off, putting the emphasis on fast, big-batting scores. Traditionalists see it as changing the character of the game, though there's no doubting its popularity – most Twenty20 matches sell out.

Grounds include Lord's in London, Edgbaston in Birmingham and Headingley in Leeds. Tickets cost from £30 to well over £200. The County Championship pits the best teams from around the country against each other; tickets cost £5 to £25, and only the most crucial games tend to sell out. Details are on the website of the English Cricket Board (www.ecb.co.uk).

The easiest way to watch cricket – and often the most enjoyable – is stumbling across a local game on a village green as you travel around the country. There's no charge for spectators, and no one will mind if you nip into the pub during a quiet spell.

Rugby

A wit once said that football was a gentlemen's game played by hooligans, while rugby was a hooligans' game played by gentlemen. That may be true, but rugby is very popular, especially since England became world champions in 2003, and then hosted the Rugby Union World Cup in 2015. It's worth catching a game for the display of skill (OK, and brawn), and the fun atmosphere in the grounds. Tickets for games cost around £15 to £50 depending on the club's status and fortunes.

A highlight of the international rugby calendar is the annual Six Nations Championship (www.rbs6nations.com), held in February and March, in which England battles against teams from Wales, Scotland, Ireland, France and Italy.

SPORTING HISTORY

England's intriguing sports have equally fascinating histories. No one can say when football was invented, but the word 'soccer' (the favoured term in countries where 'football' means another game) is held by some to derive from 'sock'. In medieval times this was a tough leather foot-cover worn by peasants – ideal for kicking around a pig's bladder in the park on a Saturday afternoon.

In contrast, rugby can trace its roots to a football match in 1823 at Rugby School in Warwickshire. A player called William Webb Ellis, frustrated at the limitations of mere kicking, reputedly picked up the ball and ran with it towards the goal. True to the sense of English fair play, rather than Ellis being dismissed from the game, a whole new sport was developed around his tactic, and the Rugby Football Union was formally inaugurated in 1871. The Rugby World Cup is named the Webb Ellis Trophy after this enterprising young tearaway.

There are two versions of the game: rugby union (www.rfu.com) is played more in southern England, Wales and Scotland, and is traditionally thought of as the game of the middle and upper classes. Rugby league (www.therfl.co.uk) is played predominantly in northern England, stereotypically by the 'working classes'. Today, leading rugby union clubs include Leicester, Bath, Exeter and Gloucester, while London has a host of good-quality teams (including Wasps and Saracens). In rugby league, teams to watch include the Wigan Warriors, Bradford Bulls and Leeds Rhinos.

> Around 140,000 punnets of strawberries and 10,000L of cream are consumed each year at Wimbledon during the two-week tennis championships.

Tennis

Tennis is widely played at club and regional level, but the best-known tournament is the All England Championships – known to all as Wimbledon (www.wimbledon.com) – when tennis fever sweeps through the country in the last week of June and first week of July. There's something quintessentially English about the combination of grass courts, polite applause and spectators in straw hats, with strawberries and cream devoured by the truckload.

Demand for seats at Wimbledon always outstrips supply, but to give everyone an equal chance tickets are sold through a public ballot. You can also take your chance on the spot; about 5000 tickets are sold at the gate each day, including those – at the earlier stages of the championships – for the show courts. But you'll need to be an early riser: dedicated fans start queuing (how English) the night before. See the website for more information.

> Queen Elizabeth II is a great horse-racing fan, and the royal stables have produced many winners. The 2005 Grand National famously clashed with the marriage of Prince Charles; rumours abound that the start was delayed so the Queen could attend the nuptials *and* see the race.

Horse Racing

The tradition of horse racing in Britain stretches back centuries, and there's a 'meeting' somewhere pretty much every day. For all but the major events you should be able to get a ticket on the day, or buy in advance from the sport's marketing body Great British Racing (www.greatbritishracing.com).

The top event in the calendar is Royal Ascot (www.ascot.co.uk) at Ascot Racecourse in mid-June, where the rich and famous come to see and be seen, and the fashion is almost as important as the horses. Even the Queen turns up to put a fiver each way on Lucky Boy in the 3.15.

Other big events include the Grand National steeplechase at Aintree (www.aintree.co.uk) in early April; and the Derby at Epsom (www.epsomdowns.co.uk) on the first Saturday in June. The latter is especially popular with the masses so, unlike at Ascot, you won't see so many morning suits or outrageous hats.

Survival Guide

Directory A–Z

Accessible Travel

All new buildings have wheelchair access, and even hotels in grand old country houses often have lifts, ramps and other facilities. Hotels and B&Bs in historic buildings are often harder to adapt, so you'll have less choice here.

Modern city buses and trams have low floors for easy access, but few have conductors who can lend a hand when you're getting on or off. Many taxis take wheelchairs, or just have more room in the back.

For long-distance travel, coaches may present problems if you can't walk, but the main operator, National Express (www.nationalexpress.com), has wheelchair-friendly coaches on many routes. For details, ring its dedicated Disabled Passenger Travel Helpline (0371 781 8181).

On intercity trains there's more room and better facilities, and usually station staff around; just have a word and they'll be happy to help out. A Disabled Person's Railcard (www.disabledpersons-railcard.co.uk) costs £20 and gets you 33% off most train fares.

Download Lonely Planet's free Accessible Travel guides from http://lptravel.to/AccessibleTravel.

Useful organisations:

Disability Rights UK (www.disabilityrightsuk.org) Published titles include a *Holiday Guide*. Other services include a key for 7000 public disabled toilets across the UK.

Good Access Guide (www.goodaccessguide.co.uk)

Tourism For All (www.tourismforall.org.uk)

Accommodation

Booking your accommodation in advance is recommended, especially in summer, at weekends and on islands (where options are often limited). Book at least two months ahead for July and August.

B&Bs These small, family-run houses generally provide good value. More luxurious versions are similar to a boutique hotel.

Hostels There's a good choice of both institutional and independent hostels, many housed in rustic and/or historic buildings.

Hotels English hotels range from half a dozen rooms above a pub to restored country houses and castles, with a commensurate range of rates.

B&Bs

The (bed and breakfast) B&B is a great English institution. At smaller places it's pretty much a room in somebody's house; larger places may be called a 'guesthouse' (halfway between a B&B and a full hotel). Prices start from around £40 per person for a simple bedroom and shared bathroom; for around £45 to £55 per person you get a private bathroom, either down the hall or en suite.

In cities, some B&Bs are for long-term residents or people on welfare; they don't take passing tourists. In country areas, most B&Bs cater for walkers and cyclists, but some don't, so let them know if you'll be turning up with dirty boots or wheels.

When booking, check where your B&B actually is. In country areas, postal addresses include the nearest town, which may be 20 miles away – important if you're walking! Some B&B owners will pick you up by car for a small charge.

Prices Usually quoted per person, based on two people sharing a room. Single rooms for solo travellers are harder to

---

BOOK YOUR STAY ONLINE

For more accommodation reviews by Lonely Planet authors, check out http://lonelyplanet.com/hotels. You'll find independent reviews, as well as recommendations on the best places to stay. Best of all, you can book online.

find, and attract a 20% to 50% premium. Some B&Bs simply won't take single people (unless you pay the full double-room price), especially in summer.

Booking Advance reservations are preferred at B&Bs and are essential during popular periods. You can book many B&Bs via online agencies but rates may be cheaper if you book directly. If you haven't booked in advance, most towns have a main drag of B&Bs; those with spare rooms hang up a 'Vacancies' sign. Many B&Bs require a minimum two-night stay on weekends. Some places reduce rates for longer stays (two or three nights) midweek. If a B&B is full, owners may recommend another place nearby (possibly a private house taking occasional guests, not in tourist listings).

Food Most B&Bs serve enormous breakfasts; some offer packed lunches (around £6) and evening meals (around £15 to £20).

Camping & Bunkhouses

Campsites range from farmers' fields with a tap and basic toilet, costing from £5 per person per night, to smarter affairs with hot showers and many other facilities, charging up to £15. You usually need all your own kit.

A few campsites also offer self-catering accommodation in chalets, caravans, tepees, yurts and stylish wooden camping 'pods', often dubbed 'glamping'.

If you're touring Britain with a tent or campervan (motorhome), consider joining the Camping & Caravanning Club (www.campingandcaravanningclub.co.uk), which provides up to 30% discount on its sites for an annual membership fee of £37. The club owns almost 100 campsites and lists thousands more in the invaluable *Big Sites Book* (free to members).

Another option in rural areas is a bunkhouse: usually a simple place with a communal sleeping area and a

bathroom, plus stoves for self-catering. You provide a sleeping bag and possibly cooking gear. Most charge around £12 to £15 per person per night.

Camping barns are even more basic: usually converted farm buildings. Take everything you'd need to camp except the tent. Charges are from around £6 to £10 per person.

Hostels

There are two types of hostel in England: those run by the Youth Hostel Association (YHA; www.yha.org.uk), and independent hostels. Most are listed in the Independent Hostel Guide (www.independenthostelguide.co.uk).

Hostels can be found in rural areas, towns and cities, and are aimed at all types of traveller, young and old. Some hostels are converted cottages, country houses and even castles – often in wonderful locations. Sleeping is usually in dormitories; some hostels also have twin or four-bed rooms.

YHA HOSTELS

The simplest YHA hostels cost around £13 to £17 per person per night. Larger hostels with more facilities are £18 to £30. London's YHA hostels cost from £32. Advance bookings and payments with credit card are usually possible.

You don't have to be a member of the YHA (or another Hostelling International organisation) to stay, but most hostels charge extra if you're not a member (£3 at YHA hostels), so it's usually worth joining. Annual YHA membership costs £20; people aged under 26 and families get discounts.

Most hostel prices vary according to demand and season. Book early for a Tuesday night in May and you'll get the best rate. Book late for a weekend in August and you'll pay top price – if there's space at all. We have generally quoted the cheaper rates (in line with those listed on the YHA's website); you may find yourself paying more.

YHA hostels tend to have complicated opening times and days, especially in remote locations or out of tourist season, so check before turning up.

INDEPENDENT HOSTELS

In rural areas some independent hostels are little more than simple bunkhouses (charging around £13), or almost up to B&B standard (£20 or more). In cities, independent backpacker hostels are usually aimed at young budget travellers. Most are open 24 hours, with a lively atmosphere, a range of rooms (doubles or dorms), a bar, a cafe, a laundry and wi-fi. Prices go from around £20 for a dorm bed to £40 for a bed in a private room.

Hotels

There's a massive choice of hotels in England, from small town houses to grand country mansions, from no-frills locations to boutique hideaways. At the bargain end, single/double rooms cost from £45/60. Move up the scale and you'll pay £100/150 or beyond.

If all you want is a place to put your head down, budget chain hotels can be a good option. Most are lacking in ambience, but who cares? You'll only be there for 12 hours, and for eight of them you'll be asleep. Prices vary on demand: at quiet times twin-bed rooms start from £40; at the height of the tourist season you'll pay £60 or more. Options include Ibis Hotels, Premier Inn and Travelodge.

Pubs & Inns

As well as selling drinks, many pubs and inns offer lodging, particularly in country areas. For bed and breakfast, you'll pay from £30 per person for a basic room, around £45 for something better. An advantage for solo tourists: pubs often have single rooms.

Rental Accommodation

If you want to stay in one place, renting for a week can be ideal. Choose from neat apartments in cities or quaint old houses (always called 'cottages', whatever the size) in country areas. Cottages for four people cost upwards of about £300 in high season. Rates fall at quieter times and you may be able to rent for a long weekend.

Booking Services

ABC Boat Hire (www.abc boathire.com) Canal boat rentals.

Bed & Breakfast Nationwide (www.bedandbreakfastnation wide.com) B&B listings.

Cottages & Castles (www.cot tages-and-castles.co.uk) Holiday rentals in country cottages and historic buildings.

cottages.com (www.cottages. com) Holiday cottage rentals.

National Trust (www.national trust.org.uk/holidays) Holiday rentals in historic National Trust properties.

Stilwell's (www.stilwell.co.uk) Holiday cottage rentals.

University Rooms (www. universityrooms.co.uk) Summer accommodation in university student halls.

Lonely Planet (www.lonely planet.com/england/hotels) Recommendations and bookings.

Customs Regulations

Entering or leaving the UK is usually straightforward and hassle-free, save for the occasional inconvenience of long queues at passport control and security.

A referendum result in the UK in June 2016 that favoured withdrawal from the EU renders information in this section highly liable to change; it's important to check the current regulations before travel.

Customs Rules & Charges

Britain has a two-tier customs system: one for goods bought duty-free outside the EU; the other for goods bought in another EU country where tax and duty is paid. The UK's 2016 decision to leave the EU (widely known as 'Brexit') may eventually lead to a change in these arrangements.

Following is a summary of the current rules; for more details go to www.gov.uk and search for 'Bringing goods into the UK'.

Duty-free The duty-free limit for goods from outside the EU includes 200 cigarettes or equivalent in cigars, 4L of wine, 1L of spirits and other goods worth up to £390.

Tax and duty paid There is no limit on goods from within the EU (if taxes have been paid), but customs officials use the following guidelines to distinguish personal use from commercial imports: 800 cigarettes, 200 cigars, 10L of spirits, 90L of wine and 110L of beer. Still enough to have one hell of a party.

Electricity

230V/50Hz

Climate

London

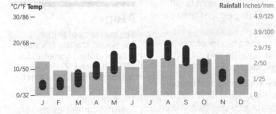

°C/°F **Temp**
Rainfall Inches/mm

J F M A M J J A S O N D

Bath

°C/°F **Temp**
Rainfall Inches/mm

J F M A M J J A S O N D

York

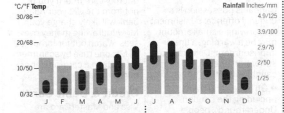

°C/°F **Temp**
Rainfall Inches/mm

J F M A M J J A S O N D

Emergency & Important Numbers

England (and UK) country code	☎44
International access code	☎00
Emergency (police, fire, ambulance, mountain rescue or coastguard)	☎112 or ☎999

Health

No vaccinations are required to travel to Britain. For more information, check with your medical provider in your own country before you travel.

➡ Quality medical treatment is widely available at National Health Service (NHS) hospitals throughout the country, and (much more expensively) through private medical practices.

➡ Chemists (pharmacies) can advise on minor ailments such as sore throats and earaches. In large cities, there's always at least one 24-hour chemist.

➡ For medical advice that is not an emergency you can call the NHS 111 service (phone 111).

Insurance

Although everyone in England receives free emergency medical treatment,

regardless of nationality, travel insurance is still highly recommended. It will usually cover medical and dental consultation and treatment at private clinics, which can be quicker than NHS places – as well as the cost of any emergency flights – plus all the usual stuff like loss of baggage.

EU citizens are entitled to reciprocal healthcare (including for the two-year transition period after Brexit in 2019), but we recommend most travellers of any nationality take out travel insurance including comprehensive medical cover and emergency repatriation. Worldwide travel insurance is available at www.lonelyplanet.com/travel-insurance. You can buy, extend and claim online anytime – even if you're already on the road.

Internet Access

➡ 3G and 4G mobile broadband coverage is good in large population centres, but limited or nonexistent in rural areas.

➡ Since 2016, EU citizens have been able to use their home data allowances across the EU zone (including the UK, at least for now), but data roaming charges can be very high for other overseas travellers – check with your mobile/cell phone provider before travelling.

EATING PRICE RANGES

••••••••••••••••••••••

The following price ranges refer to a main dish.

£ less than £10 (London £12)

££ £10 to £20 (London £12 to £25)

£££ more than £20 (London £25)

PRACTICALITIES

Newspapers Tabloids include the *Sun, Daily Mail* and *Mirror;* quality 'broadsheets' include (from right to left, politically) the *Telegraph, Times, Independent* and *Guardian.*

TV All TV in England is digital. Leading broadcasters include BBC, ITV and Channel 4. Satellite and cable-TV providers include Sky and Virgin Media.

Radio Main BBC stations and wavelengths are Radio 1 (98–99.6 FM), Radio 2 (88–92 FM), Radio 3 (90–92.2 FM), Radio 4 (92–94.4 FM) and Radio 5 Live (909 AM or 693 AM). National commercial stations include nonhighbrow classical specialist Classic FM (100–102 FM) and Virgin Radio UK (digital only). All are available on digital.

DVD PAL format (incompatible with NTSC and Secam).

Smoking Forbidden in all enclosed public places in England. Most pubs have a smoking area outside.

Weights & Measures England uses a mix of metric and imperial measures (eg petrol is sold by the litre but beer by the pint; mountain heights are in metres but road distances in miles).

➡ Most hotels, B&Bs, hostels, stations and coffee shops (even some trains and buses) have wi-fi access, charging anything from nothing to £6 per hour.

➡ Thanks to the prevalence of 3G and public wi-fi zones, internet cafes are becoming increasingly rare in England, especially away from big cities and tourist spots.

➡ Public libraries often have computers with free internet access, but only for 30-minute slots, and demand is high. All the usual warnings apply about keystroke-capturing software and other security risks.

Legal Matters

➡ Police have the power to detain, for up to six hours, anyone suspected of having committed an offence punishable by imprisonment (including drugs offences). Police have the right to search anyone they suspect of possessing drugs.

➡ Illegal drugs are widely available, especially in clubs.

Cannabis possession is a criminal offence; punishment for carrying a small amount may be a warning, a fine or imprisonment. Dealers face stiffer penalties, as do people caught with other drugs.

➡ On buses and trains (including the London Underground), people without a valid ticket are fined on the spot (£80, reduced to £40 if you pay within 21 days).

LGBTIQ+ Travellers

England is generally a tolerant place for gay and lesbian people. London, Manchester and Brighton have flourishing gay scenes, and in other sizeable cities you'll find communities not entirely in the closet. That said, you'll still find pockets of homophobic hostility in some areas. Resources include the following:

Diva (www.divamag.co.uk)

Gay Times (www.gaytimes.co.uk)

Switchboard LGBT+ Helpline (www.switchboard.lgbt; 0300 330 0630)

Money

The currency of Britain is the pound sterling (£). Paper money (notes) comes in £5, £10, £20 and £50 denominations. Some shops don't accept £50 notes because fakes circulate.

Other currencies are very rarely accepted, except at some gift shops in London, which may take euros, US dollars, yen and other major currencies.

ATMs

ATMs (usually called 'cash machines' in England) are common in cities and even small towns. Cash withdrawals from some ATMs may be subject to a small charge, but most are free. If you're not from the UK, your home bank will likely charge you for withdrawing money overseas. Watch out for tampered ATMs; one ruse by scammers is to attach a card-reader or minicamera.

Credit & Debit Cards

Visa and MasterCard are widely accepted in England, except at some smaller B&Bs, which take cash or cheque only. Other credit cards, including Amex, are not so widely accepted. Most businesses will assume your card is 'Chip and PIN' enabled (using a PIN instead of signing). If it isn't, you should be able to sign instead, but some places may not accept your card.

Changing Money

Cities and larger towns have banks and exchange bureaux for changing your money into pounds. Check rates first; some bureaux offer poor rates or levy outrageous commissions. You can also change money at many post offices – very handy in country areas, and exchange rates are fair.

Tipping

Restaurants Around 10% in restaurants and teahouses with table service, 15% at smarter restaurants. Tips may be added to your bill as a 'service charge'. Not compulsory.

Pubs & Bars Not expected if you order drinks (or food) and pay at the bar; usually 10% if you order at the table and your meal is brought to you.

Taxis Usually 10%, or rounded up to the nearest pound, especially in London.

Opening Hours

Banks

➡ 9.30am–4pm or 5pm Monday to Friday; some open 9.30am–1pm Saturday

Cafes & Restaurants

Most restaurants and cafes are open for lunch or dinner or both.

➡ Standard hours for cafes are 9am to 5pm. Most cafes open daily.

➡ In cities, some cafes open at 7am for breakfast, and shut at 6pm or later.

➡ In country areas, some cafes open until 7pm or later in the summer. In winter months hours are reduced; some cafes close completely from October to Easter.

➡ Standard hours for restaurants: lunch is noon to 3pm, dinner 6pm to 9pm or 10pm (to midnight or later in cities). Most restaurants open daily; some close Sunday evening or all day Monday.

➡ A few restaurants open for breakfast (usually 9am), but mainly cafes do this.

Museums & Sights

➡ Large museums and sights usually open daily.

➡ Some smaller places open Saturday and Sunday but close Monday and/or Tuesday.

➡ Smaller places open daily in high season but operate weekends only or completely close in low season.

Post Offices

➡ 9am to 5pm (5.30pm or 6pm in cities) Monday to Friday.

➡ 9am to 12.30pm Saturday; main branches to 5pm.

Shops

➡ 9am to 5.30pm (or 6pm in cities) Monday to Saturday, and often 11am to 5pm Sunday. London and other cities have convenience stores open 24/7.

➡ In smaller towns and country areas shops often shut for lunch (normally 1pm to 2pm) and on Wednesday or Thursday afternoon.

Post

The British postal service is generally efficient and reliable. Information on post-office locations and postage rates can be found at www.postoffice.co.uk.

Public Holidays

Holidays for the whole of Britain:

New Year's Day 1 January

Easter March/April (Good Friday to Easter Monday inclusive)

May Day First Monday in May

Spring Bank Holiday Last Monday in May

Summer Bank Holiday Last Monday in August

Christmas Day 25 December

Boxing Day 26 December

If a public holiday falls on a weekend, the nearest Monday is usually taken instead. Most businesses and banks close on official public holidays (hence the quaint term 'bank holiday').

On public holidays, some small museums and places of interest close, but larger attractions have their busiest times. If a place closes on Sunday, it'll probably be shut on bank holidays as well.

Virtually everything – attractions, shops, banks, offices – closes on Christmas Day, although pubs are open at lunchtime. There's usually no public transport on Christmas Day, and a very minimal service on Boxing Day.

Safe Travel

England is a remarkably safe country, but crime is not unknown in London and other cities.

➡ Watch out for pickpockets and hustlers in crowded areas popular with tourists, such as around Westminster Bridge in London.

➡ When travelling by tube, tram or urban train services at night, choose a carriage containing other people.

SCHOOL HOLIDAYS

Roads get busy and hotel prices go up during school holidays. Exact dates vary from year to year and region to region, but are roughly as follows:

Easter Holiday Week before and week after Easter.

Summer Holiday Third week of July to first week of September.

Christmas Holiday Mid-December to first week of January.

There are also three, week-long 'half-term' school holidays – usually late February (or early March), late May and late October. These are staggered, so the whole country is not on holiday during the same week.

➡ Many town centres can be rowdy on Friday and Saturday nights when the pubs and clubs are emptying.

➡ Unlicensed minicabs – someone with a car earning money on the side – operate in large cities, and are worth avoiding unless you know what you're doing.

Telephone
Mobile Phones

The UK uses the GSM 900/1800 network, which covers the rest of Europe, Australia and New Zealand, but isn't compatible with the North American GSM 1900. Most modern mobiles can function on both networks, but check before you leave home.

ROAMING CHARGES

The UK's decision to leave the EU (aka 'Brexit') means that British networks will eventually be able to charge whatever they want for roaming on the Continent, and EU network subscribers will have to pay roaming fees when visiting the UK. However, the UK will remain subject to EU laws for two years after the official Brexit date in March 2019, so the EU roaming agreement should remain in force until at least 2021.

Other international roaming charges can be prohibitively high, and you'll probably find it cheaper to get a UK number. This is easily done by buying a SIM card (from £5 including calling credit) and sticking it in your phone. Your phone may be locked to your home network, however, so you'll have to either get it unlocked, or buy a cheap pay-as-you-go phone along with your SIM card (from £10 including calling credit).

Pay-as-you-go phones can be recharged by buying vouchers from shops.

Phone Codes

Dialling to the UK Dial your country's international access code then 44 (the UK country code), then the area code (dropping the first 0) followed by the telephone number.

Dialling from the UK The international access code is 00; dial this, then add the code of the country you wish to dial.

Reverse-charge (Collect) International Call Dial 155 for the operator. It's an expensive option, but not for the caller.

Area Codes in the UK No standard format or length, eg Edinburgh 0131, London 020, Ambleside 015394.

Directory Assistance A host of agencies offer this service – numbers include 118 118, 118 500 and 118 811 – but fees are extortionate (around £6 for a 45-second call); search online for free at www.thephonebook.bt.com.

Mobile Phones Codes usually begin with 07.

Free Calls Numbers starting with 0800 or 0808 are free.

Call Charges Details here: www.gov.uk/call-charges

National Operator 100

International Operator 155

Time

Britain is on GMT/UTC. The clocks go forward one hour for 'summer time' at the end of March, and go back at the end of October. The 24-hour clock is used for transport timetables.

CITY	TIME DIFFERENCE WITH BRITAIN
Los Angeles	8hr behind
Mumbai	5½hr ahead Nov-Feb, 4½hr Mar-Oct
New York	5hr behind
Paris, Berlin, Rome	1hr ahead
Sydney	9hr ahead Apr-Sep, 10hr Oct, 11hr Nov-Mar
Tokyo	9hr ahead Nov-Feb, 8hr Mar-Oct

Toilets

Public toilets in England are generally clean and modern, but cutbacks in public spending mean that many facilities have been closed down. Your best bet is to use the toilets in free-to-enter museums; those in train and bus stations often charge a fee (from 20p to 50p), and most pubs and restaurants stipulate that their toilets are for customers only.

Tourist Information

Most English cities and towns have a tourist information centre or visitor information centre – for ease we've called all these places 'tourist offices'.

Tourist offices have helpful staff, books and maps for sale, leaflets to give away, and advice on things to see or do. Some can also assist with booking accommodation. Some are run by national parks and often have small exhibits about the area.

Most tourist offices keep regular business hours; in quiet areas they close from October to March, while in popular areas they open daily year-round. In recent years cost-cutting has seen many smaller tourist offices close down; some have been replaced with 'tourist information points' – racks of leaflets and maps in locations such as public libraries and town halls.

Before leaving home, check the comprehensive website of England's official tourist board, Visit England (www.visitengland.com), covering all the angles of national tourism, with links to numerous other sites.

Visas

➡ If you're a citizen of the European Economic Area (EEA) nations or Switzerland, you don't need a visa to enter or work in the UK – you can enter using your national identity card.

➡ Visa regulations are always subject to change,

and immigration restriction is big news in the UK, so it's essential to check with your local British embassy, high commission or consulate before leaving home.

➡ At the time of research, if you're a citizen of Australia, Canada, New Zealand, Japan, Israel, the USA and several other countries, you can stay for up to six months (no visa required), but are not allowed to work.

➡ Nationals of many countries, including South Africa, will need to obtain a visa: for more info, see www.gov.uk/check-uk-visa.

➡ The Youth Mobility Scheme (www.gov.uk/tier-5-youth-mobility), for Australian, Canadian, Japanese, Hong Kong, Monégasque, New Zealand,

South Korean and Taiwanese citizens aged 18 to 30, allows working visits of up to two years, but must be applied for in advance.

➡ Commonwealth citizens with a UK-born parent may be eligible for a Certificate of Entitlement to the Right of Abode, which entitles them to live and work in the UK.

➡ Commonwealth citizens with a UK-born grandparent could qualify for a UK Ancestry Employment Certificate, allowing them to work full time for up to five years in the UK.

➡ British immigration authorities have always been tough; dress neatly and carry proof that you have sufficient funds with which to support yourself. A credit card and/or an onward ticket will help.

Transport

GETTING THERE & AWAY

Most overseas visitors reach England by air. As London is a global transport hub, it's easy to fly to England from just about anywhere. The massive growth of budget ('no-frills') airlines has increased the number of routes – and reduced the fares – between England and other countries in Europe.

The other main option for travel between England and mainland Europe is ferry, either port-to-port or combined with a long-distance bus trip, although journeys can be long and financial savings not huge compared with budget airfares.

International trains are much more comfortable and a 'green' option, too; the Channel Tunnel allows direct rail services between England, France and Belgium, with onward connections to many other European destinations.

Flights, cars and rail tickets can be booked online at lonelyplanet.com/bookings.

Air

London Airports

Heathrow (www.heathrow.com) The UK's main airport for international flights; often chaotic and crowded. About 15 miles west of central London.

Gatwick (www.gatwickairport. com) Britain's number-two airport, mainly for international flights, 30 miles south of central London.

Stansted (www.stanstedairport. com) About 35 miles northeast of central London, mainly handling charter and budget European flights.

Luton (www.london-luton.co.uk) Some 35 miles north of central London, well known as a holiday-flight airport.

London City (www.londoncity airport.com) Just under nine miles east of central London, specialising in flights to/from European and other UK airports.

The national carrier is British Airways (www.britishairways. com).

Regional Airports

Some planes on European and long-haul routes avoid London and use major regional airports including Manchester and Newcastle. Smaller regional airports such as Southampton and Birmingham are served by flights to and from Continental Europe and Ireland.

Land

Bus/Coach

You can easily get between England and other European countries via long-distance bus (called 'coach' in England). The international network Eurolines (www.euro

---

CLIMATE CHANGE & TRAVEL

Every form of transport that relies on carbon-based fuel generates CO_2, the main cause of human-induced climate change. Modern travel is dependent on aeroplanes, which might use less fuel per kilometre per person than most cars but travel much greater distances. The altitude at which aircraft emit gases (including CO_2) and particles also contributes to their climate change impact. Many websites offer 'carbon calculators' that allow people to estimate the carbon emissions generated by their journey and, for those who wish to do so, to offset the impact of the greenhouse gases emitted with contributions to portfolios of climate-friendly initiatives throughout the world. Lonely Planet offsets the carbon footprint of all staff and author travel.

lines.com) connects a huge number of destinations; you can buy tickets online via one of the national operators.

Services to/from England are also operated by National Express (www.nationalex-press.com). Sample journey times to/from London include Amsterdam (12 hours), Barcelona (24 hours), Dublin (12 hours) and Paris (eight hours).

If you book early, and can be flexible with timings (ie travel when few other people want to), you can get some very good deals. For example, between London and Paris or Amsterdam from about £25 one way (although paying £35 to £45 is more usual).

Train

CHANNEL TUNNEL PASSENGER SERVICE

High-speed Eurostar (www. eurostar.com) passenger services shuttle at least 10 times daily between London and Paris (2½ hours) or Brussels (two hours). Buy tickets from travel agencies, major train stations or the Eurostar website.

The normal one-way fare between London and Paris/ Brussels costs around £154; advance booking and off-peak travel gets cheaper fares as low as £29 one way.

CHANNEL TUNNEL CAR SERVICE

Drivers use Eurotunnel (www. eurotunnel.com). At Folkestone in England or Calais in France, you drive onto a train, get carried through the tunnel and drive off at the other end.

Trains run about four times an hour from 6am to 10pm, then hourly through the night. Loading and un-loading takes an hour; the journey lasts 35 minutes.

Book in advance online or pay on the spot. The stand-ard one-way fare for a car and up to nine passengers is £75 to £100 depending on time of day; promotional

TRAIN & FERRY CONNECTIONS

As well as Eurostar, many 'normal' trains run between England and mainland Europe. You buy one ticket, but get off the train at the port, walk onto a ferry, then get another train on the other side.

Routes include Amsterdam–London (via Hook of Holland and Harwich). Travelling between Ireland and England, the main train-ferry-train route is Dublin to London, via Dun Laoghaire and Holyhead (Wales). Ferries also run between Rosslare and Fishguard or Pembroke (Wales), with train connections on either side.

fares often bring it down to £59 or less.

Sea

FERRY ROUTES

The main ferry routes between England and other countries include the following:

➜ Dover to Calais (France)

➜ Dover to Dunkirk (France)

➜ Harwich to Hook of Holland (Netherlands)

➜ Hull to Rotterdam (Netherlands)

➜ Hull to Zeebrugge (Belgium)

➜ Liverpool to Belfast (Northern Ireland)

➜ Newcastle to Amsterdam (Netherlands)

➜ Newhaven to Dieppe (France)

➜ Plymouth to Roscoff (France)

➜ Poole to Cherbourg (France)

➜ Portsmouth to Bilbao (Spain)

➜ Portsmouth to St Malo (France)

➜ Portsmouth to Santander (Spain)

FERRY FARES

Most ferry operators offer flexible fares, meaning great bargains at quiet times of day or year. For example, short cross-channel routes such as Dover to Calais or Boulogne can be as low as £45 for a car plus two passengers,

although around £75 to £105 is more likely. If you're a foot passenger, or cycling, there's less need to book ahead; fares on short crossings cost about £30 to £50 each way.

FERRY BOOKING

You can book directly with one of the ferry operators listed here, or use the very handy www.directferries. co.uk, a single site covering all sea-ferry routes, plus Eurotunnel.

Brittany Ferries (www.brittany-ferries.com)

DFDS Seaways (www.dfdsseaways.co.uk)

P&O Ferries (www.poferries. com)

Stena Line (www.stenaline.com)

GETTING AROUND

Air

England's domestic airline companies include British Airways, FlyBe/Loganair, easyJet and Ryanair. If you're really pushed for time, flights on longer routes across England (eg Exeter or South-ampton to Newcastle) are handy, and often very competitive in price – although on shorter routes (eg London to Newcastle, or Manchester to Newquay) trains compare favourably with planes on time, once airport downtime is factored in.

Bicycle

London

London is famous for its **Santander Cycles** (📞0343 222 6666; www.tfl.gov.uk/modes/cycling/santander-cycles), known as 'Boris bikes' after Boris Johnson, the then-mayor who introduced them to the city. Bikes can be hired on the spot from automatic docking stations. For more information visit the website. Other rental options in the capital are listed at www.lcc.org.uk (under Advice/Bike Shops).

Around the Country

The nextbike (www.nextbike.co.uk) bike-sharing scheme has stations in Bath, Exeter, Oxford and Coventry, while York and Cambridge also have plentiful bike-rental options. Bikes can also be hired in national parks or forestry sites now primarily used for leisure activities, such as Kielder Water in Northumberland and Grizedale Forest in the Lake District. In some areas, disused railway lines are now bike routes, notably the Peak District in Derbyshire. Rental rates start at about £12 per day, or £20 and up for a quality machine.

Bikes on Trains

Bicycles can be taken free of charge on most local urban trains (although they may not be allowed at peak times when the trains are crowded with commuters), and on shorter trips in rural areas on a first-come, first-served basis – there may be space limits.

Bikes can be carried on long-distance train journeys free of charge, but advance booking is required for most conventional bikes. (Folding bikes can be carried on pretty much any train at any time.) In theory, this shouldn't be too much trouble as most long-distance rail trips are best bought in advance anyway, but you have to go a long way down the path of booking your seat before you start booking your bike – only to find space isn't available. A better course of action is to buy in advance at a major rail station, where the booking clerk can help you through the options.

A final warning: when railways are undergoing repair work, cancelled trains are replaced by buses – and they won't take bikes.

The PlusBike scheme provides all the information you need for travelling by train with a bike. Leaflets are available at major stations, or downloadable from www.nationalrail.co.uk/118390.aspx.

Bus

If you're on a tight budget, long-distance buses (coaches) are nearly always the cheapest way to get around, although they're also the slowest – sometimes by a considerable margin. Many towns have separate stations for local buses and long-distance coaches; make sure you go to the right one!

National Express (www.nationalexpress.com) The main coach operator, with a wide network and frequent services between main centres. Fares vary: they're cheaper if you book in advance and travel at quieter times, and more expensive if you buy your ticket on the spot and it's Friday afternoon. As a guide, a 200-mile trip (eg London to York) will cost £15 to £25 if you book a few days in advance.

Megabus (www.megabus.com) Operates a budget coach service serving more than 100 destinations around the country. Go at a quiet time, book early and your ticket will be very cheap. Book later, for a busy time and… You get the picture.

Passes & Discounts

National Express offers discount passes to full-time students and under-26s, called Young Persons Coach-cards. They cost £12.50 and give you 30% off standard adult fares. Also available are coachcards for people aged over 60, families and disabled travellers.

For non-UK citizens, National Express offers Skimmer passes, allowing unlimited travel for seven/14/28 days (£69/119/199). You don't need to book journeys in advance: if the coach has a spare seat, you can take it.

Car & Motorcycle

Travelling by car or motorbike around England means you can be independent and flexible, and reach remote places. Downsides for drivers include traffic jams, the high price of fuel and high parking costs in cities.

Car Rental

Compared with many countries (especially the USA), hire rates are expensive in Britain; the smallest cars start from about £130 per week, and it's around £190 and upwards per week for a medium car with unlimited mileage.

Some main players:

Avis (www.avis.co.uk)

Budget (www.budget.co.uk)

Europcar (www.europcar.co.uk)

Sixt (www.sixt.co.uk)

Thrifty (www.thrifty.co.uk)

Another option is to look online for small, local car-hire companies in Britain that can undercut the international franchises. Generally those in cities are cheaper than in rural areas. Using a rental-broker or comparison site such as UK Car Hire (www.ukcarhire.net) or Kayak (www.kayak.com) can also help find bargains.

Motorhome Rental

Hiring a motorhome or campervan (£650 to £1100 a week) is more expensive than hiring a car, but saves on accommodation costs and gives almost unlimited freedom. Sites to check include the following:

Just Go (www.justgo.uk.com)
Wild Horizon (www.wildhorizon. co.uk)

Insurance

It's illegal to drive a car or ride a motorbike in England without (at least) third-party insurance. This will be included with all hire cars as standard, but you will usually be liable for an excess for any damage to the vehicle (sometimes up to £1500).

You can pay an extra fee to the hire company to waive the excess, but it is often quite expensive at around £5 per day; a cheaper (if more convoluted) option is to arrange your own excess insurance through a comparison site, such as Money Maxim (www.moneymaxim. co.uk). If you damage the car, you will pay the excess and reclaim it later from the insurance provider; make sure you document any damage and, in the case of an accident, receive a copy of the police report.

Parking

Many cities have short-stay and long-stay car parks; the latter are cheaper though may be less convenient. 'Park & Ride' systems allow you to park on the edge of the city then ride to the centre on frequent nonstop buses for an all-in-one price.

Yellow lines (single or double) along the edge of the road indicate restrictions. Nearby signs spell out when you can and can't park. In London and other big cities, traffic wardens operate with efficiency; if you park on the yellow lines at the wrong time, your car will be clamped or towed away, and it'll cost you £130 or more to get driving again. In some cities there are also red lines, which mean no stopping at all. Ever.

Roads

Motorways and main A-roads deliver you quickly from one end of the country to another. Lesser A-roads, B-roads and minor roads are much more scenic – ideal for car or motorcycle touring. You can't travel fast, but you won't care.

Speed limits are usually 30mph (48km/h) in built-up areas, 60mph (96km/h) on main roads and 70mph (112km/h) on motorways and most (but not all) dual carriageways.

Road Rules

A foreign driving licence is valid in Britain for up to 12 months after entering the country.

Drink-driving is taken very seriously; you're allowed a maximum blood-alcohol level of 80mg/100mL (0.08%) – campaigners want it reduced to 50mg/100mL (0.05%), in line with most European countries (including Scotland).

Some other important rules:

➡ Drive on the left (!).

➡ Wear seatbelts in cars.

➡ Wear helmets on motorcycles.

➡ Give way to your right at junctions and roundabouts.

➡ Always use the left lane on motorways and dual carriageways unless overtaking (although so many people ignore this rule, you'd think it didn't exist).

➡ Don't use a mobile phone while driving unless it's fully hands-free (another rule frequently flouted).

Local Transport

English cities usually have good public-transport systems – a combination of bus, train and tram – often run by a confusing number of separate companies. Tourist offices can provide maps and information.

Bus

There are good local bus networks year-round in cities and towns. Buses also run in some rural areas year-round, although timetables are designed to serve schools and businesses, so there aren't many noon and weekend services (and they may stop running during school holidays), or buses may link local villages to a market town on only one day each week.

In tourist areas (especially national parks) there are frequent services from Easter to September. However, it's always worth double-checking at a tourist office before planning your day's activities around a bus that may not actually be running.

If you're taking a few local bus rides in one area, day passes (with names like Day Rover, Wayfarer or Explorer) are cheaper than buying several single tickets. Often they can be bought on your first bus, and may include local rail services. It's always worth asking ticket clerks or bus drivers about your options.

Taxi

There are two sorts of taxi in England: those with meters that can be hailed in the street; and minicabs, which are cheaper but can only be called by phone. Unlicensed minicabs operate in some cities.

In London, most taxis are the famous 'black cabs' (some with advertising livery in other colours), which charge by distance and time. Depending on the time of day, a 1-mile journey takes five to 10 minutes and costs £6 to £9. Longer journeys are proportionally cheaper.

Ridesharing apps such as Uber (www.uber.com) are an option in most towns and cities, while similar apps like Kabbee (www.kabbee.com) allow you to book a minicab in double-quick time.

In rural areas, taxis need to be called by phone; the best place to find the local taxi's phone number is the local pub. Fares are £3 to £5 per mile.

Traintaxi (www.traintaxi.co.uk) is a portal site that helps 'bridge the final gap' between the train station and your hotel or other final destination.

Train

For long-distance travel around England, trains are generally faster and more comfortable than coaches but are nearly always much more expensive. The English like to moan about their trains, but around 85% run on time. The other 15% that get delayed or cancelled mostly impact commuter services rather than long-distance journeys. The main headache these days is the cost – if you leave booking your ticket to the last minute, fares can be extremely high, so it's always worth booking as far in advance as you can.

Train Operators

About 20 different companies operate train services in England, while Network Rail operates tracks and stations. For some passengers this system can be confusing at first, but information and ticket-buying services are mostly centralised. If you have to change trains, or use two or more train operators, you still buy one ticket – valid for the whole journey. The main railcards and passes are also accepted by all train operators.

Where more than one train operator services the same route, eg York to Newcastle, a ticket purchased from one company may not be valid on trains run by another. So if you miss the train you originally booked, it's worth checking which later services your ticket will be valid for.

Information

Your first stop should be National Rail Enquiries (www.nationalrail.co.uk), the nationwide timetable and fare information service. Its website advertises special offers and has real-time links to station departure boards and downloadable maps of the rail network.

Tickets & Reservations
BUYING TICKETS

Once you've found the journey you need on the National Rail Enquiries website, links take you to the relevant train operator to buy the ticket. This can be mailed to you (UK addresses only) or collected at the station on the day of travel from automatic machines. There's usually no booking fee on top of the ticket price.

You can also use a centralised ticketing service to buy your train ticket. These cover all train services in a single site, and add a small booking fee on top of every ticket price. The main players include the following:

QJump (www.qjump.co.uk)

Rail Easy (www.raileasy.co.uk)

Train Line (www.thetrainline.com)

To use operator or centralised ticketing websites, you always have to state a preferred time and day of travel, even if you don't mind when you go, but you can change it as you go through the process, and with a little delving around you can find some real bargains.

You can also buy train tickets on the spot at stations, which is fine for short journeys (under about 50 miles), but discount tickets for longer trips are usually not available and these must be bought in advance by phone or online.

Mobile train tickets are gradually becoming more common across the network, but it's a slow process – for now printed tickets are still the norm.

FARES

For longer journeys, on-the-spot fares are usually available, but for long-distance travel, tickets are much, much cheaper if bought in advance. You can also save if you travel off-peak. Advance purchase usually gets a reserved seat, too.

Whichever operator you travel with and wherever you buy tickets, these are the three main fare types:

Anytime Buy any time, travel any time – always the most expensive option.

Off-peak Travel at off-peak times (what constitutes off-peak depends on the journey). Can be bought at any time up to the point of travel.

Advance These tickets can only be purchased in advance, and travel is only permitted on specific trains. This is usually the cheapest option, as long as you're happy with the restrictions. Note that the cheapest fares are nonrefundable, so if you miss your train you'll have to buy a new ticket.

For an idea of the price difference, an Anytime single ticket from London to York will cost £127 or more, an Off-peak around £56 to £62, with an Advance around £44 to £55, and possibly less if you book early enough or don't mind arriving at midnight.

ONWARD TRAVEL

If the train doesn't get you all the way to your destination, you can add a PlusBus (www.plusbus.info) supplement when making your reservation to validate your train ticket for onward travel by bus. This is more convenient, and usually cheaper, than buying a separate bus ticket.

Classes

There are two classes of rail travel: first and standard. First class costs around 50% more than standard fare (up to double at busy periods) and gets you bigger seats, more legroom, and usually a more peaceful businesslike atmosphere, plus extras such as complimentary drinks and newspapers. At weekends some train operators offer 'upgrades' to 1st class for an extra £5 to £25 on top of your standard-class fare, payable on the spot.

Train Passes

DISCOUNT PASSES

If you're staying in England for a while, passes known as Railcards (www.railcard. co.uk) are available:

16-25 Railcard For those aged 16 to 25, or a full-time UK student.

Family & Friends Railcard Covers up to four adults and four children travelling together.

Two Together Railcard For two specified people travelling together.

Senior Railcard For anyone aged over 60.

Disabled Persons Railcard For people with registered disabilities.

Railcards cost £30 (valid for one year, available from major stations or online) and get a 33% discount on most train fares, except those already heavily discounted. With the Family card, adults get 33% and children get 60% discounts, so the fee is easily repaid in a couple of journeys.

A digital-only 25-30 Railcard was being trialled at the time of research; find out the latest at www.26-30railcard. co.uk.

LOCAL & REGIONAL PASSES

Local train passes usually cover rail networks around a city (many include bus travel, too).

If you're concentrating your travels on southeast England (eg London to Dover, Weymouth, Cambridge or Oxford), a Network Railcard (www.network-railcard.co.uk) covers up to four adults and up to four children travelling together outside peak times (£30 per year).

NATIONAL PASSES

For countrywide travel, BritRail (www.britrail.net) passes are available for visitors from overseas. They must be bought in your country of origin (not in England) from a specialist travel agency. Available in different versions (eg England only; all Britain; UK and the Republic of Ireland) for periods from four to 30 days.

TRANSPORT TRAIN

Behind the Scenes

SEND US YOUR FEEDBACK

We love to hear from travellers – your comments keep us on our toes and help make our books better. Our well-travelled team reads every word on what you loved or loathed about this book. Although we cannot reply individually to your submissions, we always guarantee that your feedback goes straight to the appropriate authors, in time for the next edition. Each person who sends us information is thanked in the next edition – the most useful submissions are rewarded with a selection of digital PDF chapters.

Visit **lonelyplanet.com/contact** to submit your updates and suggestions or to ask for help. Our award-winning website also features inspirational travel stories, news and discussions.

Note: We may edit, reproduce and incorporate your comments in Lonely Planet products such as guidebooks, websites and digital products, so let us know if you don't want your comments reproduced or your name acknowledged. For a copy of our privacy policy visit lonelyplanet.com/privacy.

WRITER THANKS

Oliver Berry

As always I've thoroughly enjoyed exploring my homeland for this update, and I'd like to extend a big thanks to everyone who's helped me along the way (you know who you are). I'd particularly like to thank all my co-authors for their hard work and help, and Cliff Wilkinson for sage advice, feedback and generally keeping the England ship on course. A special thanks also to Rosie Hillier for supporting me, putting up with long days and nights spent at the computer and providing emergency cups of tea when they were most needed.

Marc Di Duca

Huge thanks to Tanya at home in the Czech Republic for holding the fort, to Emy and David in Sandwich, to Gemma and Dave in Amesbury and to all the many employees at the various tourist offices across Kent and Sussex who helped me along the way

Belinda Dixon

Researching and writing for Lonely Planet is a real joint effort – so huge thanks to the locals who share their time, knowledge and recommendations and to the random strangers who offer countless kindnesses. And thank you to Cliff for the gig, LP's behind the scenes teams (so much work!), and fellow writers for humour, wisdom and travellers' tales.

Damian Harper

Many thanks to Ann Harper, Jasmin Tonge, Kevin and Maki Fallows, Rosemary Hadow, Lily Greensmith, Antonia Mavromatidou, Arabella Sneddon, Bill Moran, Jim Peake, my ever-helpful co-authors and a big debt of gratitude again to Daisy, Tim and Emma.

Catherine Le Nevez

Cheers first and foremost to Julian, and to all of the locals, fellow travellers and tourism professionals throughout Northeast England, the Midlands and the Marches for insights, information and good times. Huge thanks too to Destination Editor Cliff Wilkinson and the Great Britain team, and everyone at LP. As ever, merci encore to my parents, brother, belle-sœur, neveu and nièce.

Lorna Parkes

Thanks to the many friendly folk of Yorkshire for their chats, advice and excellent beer-making. And to Rob, Austin and Lily for letting me drag them all over the Dales and east coast, come rain or shine (but mostly rain).

Greg Ward

Thanks to the many people who helped me as I pounded the streets of Oxford and criss-crossed the Cotswolds, and thanks especially to Adrian, Michael and Donald Ward for their Oxford memories and expertise. Thanks too to my editor Clifton Wilkinson for giving me this opportunity, and to my dear wife, Sam, for sharing so many adventures and late nights.

ACKNOWLEDGEMENTS

Climate map data adapted from Peel MC, Finlayson BL & McMahon TA (2007) 'Updated World Map of the Köppen-Geiger Climate Classification', Hydrology and Earth System Sciences, 11, 1633–44.

Cover photograph: Stonehenge, Wiltshire, Maurizio Rellini/4Corners ©.

Illustrations: pp80–1 & pp614–5 by Javier Zarracina, pp60–1 by Javier Zarracina and Michael Weldon.

BEHIND THE SCENES

THIS BOOK

This 10th edition of Lonely Planet's *England* guide was curated by Oliver Berry, who researched and wrote it along with Fionn Davenport, Marc Di Duca, Belinda Dixon, Damian Harper, Catherine Le Nevez, Lorna Parkes and Greg Ward. This guidebook was produced by the following:

Destination Editors James Smart, Clifton Wilkinson

Senior Product Editor Genna Patterson

Product Editor Kathryn Rowan

Senior Cartographer Mark Griffiths

Cartographers Anita Banh, Laura Bailey

Book Designer Michael Weldon

Assisting Editors Sarah Bailey, Andrew Bain, Judith Bamber, Michelle Bennett, Nigel Chin, Katie Connolly, Lucy Cowie, Michelle Coxall, Jacqueline Danam, Andrea Dobbin, Alexander Knights, Kellie Langdon, Lou McGregor, Kristin Odijk, Monique Perrin

Cover Researcher Naomi Parker

Thanks to Martin Baker, Fabio Baldi, John Boon, Hannah Cartmel, Kate Chapman, David Curtis, Shona Gray, Rachel Imeson, Kate Kiely, Kate Mathews, Kirsten Rawlings, Gabrielle Stefanos

Index

Map Pages **000**
Photo Pages **000**

NOTES

Map Legend

Sights

- Beach
- Bird Sanctuary
- Buddhist
- Castle/Palace
- Christian
- Confucian
- Hindu
- Islamic
- Jain
- Jewish
- Monument
- Museum/Gallery/Historic Building
- Ruin
- Shinto
- Sikh
- Taoist
- Winery/Vineyard
- Zoo/Wildlife Sanctuary
- Other Sight

Activities, Courses & Tours

- Bodysurfing
- Diving
- Canoeing/Kayaking
- Course/Tour
- Sento Hot Baths/Onsen
- Skiing
- Snorkelling
- Surfing
- Swimming/Pool
- Walking
- Windsurfing
- Other Activity

Sleeping

- Sleeping
- Camping
- Hut/Shelter

Eating

- Eating

Drinking & Nightlife

- Drinking & Nightlife
- Cafe

Entertainment

- Entertainment

Shopping

- Shopping

Information

- Bank
- Embassy/Consulate
- Hospital/Medical
- Internet
- Police
- Post Office
- Telephone
- Toilet
- Tourist Information
- Other Information

Geographic

- Beach
- Gate
- Hut/Shelter
- Lighthouse
- Lookout
- Mountain/Volcano
- Oasis
- Park
- Pass
- Picnic Area
- Waterfall

Population

- Capital (National)
- Capital (State/Province)
- City/Large Town
- Town/Village

Transport

- Airport
- Border crossing
- Bus
- Cable car/Funicular
- Cycling
- Ferry
- Metro station
- Monorail
- Parking
- Petrol station
- S-Bahn/Subway station
- Taxi
- T-bane/Tunnelbana station
- Train station/Railway
- Tram
- Tube station
- U-Bahn/Underground station
- Other Transport

Routes

- Tollway
- Freeway
- Primary
- Secondary
- Tertiary
- Lane
- Unsealed road
- Road under construction
- Plaza/Mall
- Steps
- Tunnel
- Pedestrian overpass
- Walking Tour
- Walking Tour detour
- Path/Walking Trail

Boundaries

- International
- State/Province
- Disputed
- Regional/Suburb
- Marine Park
- Cliff
- Wall

Hydrography

- River, Creek
- Intermittent River
- Canal
- Water
- Dry/Salt/Intermittent Lake
- Reef

Areas

- Airport/Runway
- Beach/Desert
- Cemetery (Christian)
- Cemetery (Other)
- Glacier
- Mudflat
- Park/Forest
- Sight (Building)
- Sportsground
- Swamp/Mangrove

Note: Not all symbols displayed above appear on the maps in this book

Damian Harper
London With two degrees (one in modern and classical Chinese from SOAS), Damian has been writing for Lonely Planet for over two decades, contributing to titles as diverse as *China, Beijing, Shanghai, Vietnam, Thailand, Ireland, London, Mallorca, Malaysia, Singapore & Brunei, Hong Kong* and *Great Britain*. A seasoned guidebook writer, Damian has penned articles for numerous newspapers and magazines, including the *Guardian* and the *Daily Telegraph,* and currently makes Surrey, England, his home. He has other hobbies including playing the trumpet, collecting modern first editions, photography and Taekwondo. Follow Damian on Instagram (damian.harper).

Catherine Le Nevez
Newcastle & the Northeast, Birmingham & the Midlands Catherine's wanderlust kicked in when she roadtripped across Europe from her Parisian base aged four, and she's been hitting the road at every opportunity since, travelling to around 60 countries and completing her Doctorate of Creative Arts in Writing, Masters in Professional Writing, and postgrad qualifications in Editing and Publishing along the way. Over the past dozen-plus years she's written scores of Lonely Planet guides and articles covering Paris, France, Europe and far beyond. Her work has also appeared in numerous online and print publications. Topping Catherine's list of travel tips is to travel without any expectations.

Lorna Parkes
Yorkshire Londoner by birth, Melburnian by palate and ex-Lonely Planet staffer in both cities, Lorna has contributed to numerous Lonely Planet books and magazines. She's discovered she writes best on planes, and is most content when researching food and booze. Wineries and the tropics (not at the same time!) are her go-to happy places, but Yorkshire will always be special to her. Follow her @ Lorna_Explorer.

Greg Ward
Oxford & the Cotswolds Since whetting his appetite for travel by following the hippy trail to India, and later living in northern Spain, Greg Ward has written guides to destinations all over the world. As well as covering the USA from the Southwest to Hawaii, he has ranged on recent assignments from Corsica to the Cotswolds, and Japan to Corfu. See his website, www.gregward.info, for his favourite photos and memories.

Contributing writers: Emilie Filou, Steve Fallon and Peter Dragicevich.

OUR STORY

A beat-up old car, a few dollars in the pocket and a sense of adventure. In 1972 that's all Tony and Maureen Wheeler needed for the trip of a lifetime – across Europe and Asia overland to Australia. It took several months, and at the end – broke but inspired – they sat at their kitchen table writing and stapling together their first travel guide, *Across Asia on the Cheap*. Within a week they'd sold 1500 copies. Lonely Planet was born.

Today, Lonely Planet has offices in Franklin, London, Melbourne, Oakland, Dublin, Beijing and Delhi, with more than 600 staff and writers. We share Tony's belief that 'a great guidebook should do three things: inform, educate and amuse'.

OUR WRITERS

Oliver Berry
Curator, Southwest England, the Lake District & Cumbria Oliver Berry is a writer and photographer from Cornwall. He has worked for Lonely Planet for more than a decade, covering destinations from Cornwall to the Cook Islands, and has worked on more than 30 guidebooks. He is also a regular contributor to many newspapers and magazines, including Lonely Planet Traveller. His writing has won several awards, including the Guardian Young Travel Writer of the Year and the TNT Magazine People's Choice Award. His latest work is published at www.oliverberry.com.

Fionn Davenport
Manchester, Liverpool & the Northwest Irish by birth and conviction, Fionn has spent the last two decades focusing on the country of his birth and his nearest neighbour, England, which he has written about extensively for Lonely Planet and others. In between writing gigs he's lived in Paris and New York, where he was an editor, actor, bartender and whatever else paid the rent; for the last 15 years or so he's also presented a series of radio programmes on Irish radio, most recently as host of Inside Culture on RTE Radio 1. Three years ago he moved to the northwest of England where he lives (and commutes from) with his partner Laura and their car Trevor.

Marc Di Duca
Canterbury & Southeast England A travel author for over a decade, Marc has worked for Lonely Planet in Siberia, Slovakia, Bavaria, England, Ukraine, Austria, Poland, Croatia, Portugal, Madeira and on the Trans-Siberian Railway, as well as writing and updating tens of other guides for other publishers. When not on the road, Marc lives near Mariánské Lázně in the Czech Republic with his wife and two sons.

Belinda Dixon
Bath & Southwest England, Cambridge & East Anglia Only happy when her feet are suitably sandy, Belinda has been (gleefully) researching and writing for Lonely Planet since 2006. It's seen her marvelling at Stonehenge at sunrise, camping in Iceland, scrambling up Italian mountain paths, horse riding across Donegal's golden sands, kayaking down Devon rivers, gazing at Verona's frescoes and fossil hunting on Dorset's Jurassic Coast. Belinda is also an adventure writer and expedition media leader – which has seen her scale snowy Scottish mountains, paddle the Yukon, surf and swim in England's winter seas and sleep out under the stars. See her posts at https://belindadixon.com.

OVER PAGE MORE WRITERS

Published by Lonely Planet Global Limited
CRN 554153
10th edition – Apr 2019
ISBN 978 1 78657 804 4
© Lonely Planet 2019   Photographs © as indicated 2019
10 9 8 7 6 5 4 3 2 1
Printed in China